D0160510

BREWER'S POLITICS

BREWER'S POLITICS

A PHRASE AND FABLE DICTIONARY

Nicholas Comfort

CASSELL

Cassell Publishers Limited
Villiers House, 41/47 Strand
London WC2N 5JE, England

First published 1993

British Library Cataloguing in Publication Data
A catalogue entry for this book is
available from the British Library.

ISBN 0-304-34085 5

Printed and bound in Great Britain by
Mackays of Chatham Ltd

10 DOWNING STREET
LONDON SW1A 2AA

THE PRIME MINISTER

Political life has produced a rich treasury of words and phrases and it continues to do so. Every politician draws on this heritage from time to time. Many politicians add to the political lexicon - intentionally or otherwise. Until now no-one has tried to bring together in a single volume the entire folk-memory of political language, from brilliant epigrams that have made reputations, from gaffes that have made headlines, from technical Parliamentary phrases. I congratulate Brewer's for attempting so daunting a task, and for having distilled so much into one volume.

John Major

November 1993

ABBREVIATIONS

Afrik.	Afrikaans
Arab.	Arabic
attr.	attributed
Dut.	Dutch
Fr.	French
Ger.	German
Gr.	Greek
Heb.	Hebrew
Ir.	Irish
Ital.	Italian
Lat.	Latin
O.E.	Old English
Pers.	Persian
Port.	Portuguese
Russ.	Russian
Sp.	Spanish
Swed.	Swedish

CROSS-REFERENCES

These are indicated in the text by the use of SMALL CAPITALS.

INTRODUCTION

Argument is the lifeblood of politics, and persuasive argument relies on the effective marshalling of words. Consequently, politicians have always exploited the richness of language to the full. Participation in politics as a head of government, as a candidate, as a party activist or as a political journalist, in which capacity I have been lucky to work both at Westminster and in Washington, involves deploying as much of that vocabulary as one's abilities permit. There are many useful works of political reference, yet none that I am aware of lays out the broad sweep of political language, from technical and procedural terms through well-worn clichés to the most devastating of insults. This volume is intended to fill the gap; I hope readers and browsers will feel that it does. More to the point, I hope they will both find it a useful source of reference and derive as much enjoyment from delving into it as I have from compiling it.

Politics impinges on every aspect of daily life, and setting limits to it is thus an arbitrary business. This dictionary overlaps the worlds of the British aristocracy, community action, defence, economics, environmentalism, industrial relations, the law, local government, the conduct of meetings and the like. I have had to set out a cut-off point, and hope I have found one that has kept in all phrases relevant to politics and excluded those of a purely specialist nature.

This is a dictionary, not an encyclopaedia. It also perpetuates the mildly whimsical approach to the selection of entries adopted by Brewer's *Dictionary of Phrase and Fable* since Dr. Ebenezer Cobham Brewer produced the first edition in 1870. Yet there will be unmerited omissions, which I hope readers will bring to my attention. The odd error will also, inevitably, have crept in; I rely on the reader who finds any such mistake to point it out to me.

Because politics reflects life, many of the phrases used in its practice are highly emotive and even offensive. A few that I have quoted may well offend some readers; I myself find some of them objectionable, but I stand by their inclusion as showing political life "warts and all". Nor have I attempted to be "politically correct", but I have tried to avoid giving needless offence to anyone on grounds of their political or religious beliefs, race, gender, disability or sexual orientation.

I could not have completed a project of this size without help. For assistance with US political terms, I am particularly grateful to Richard A. Lidinsky Jr., Vice-President of Sea Containers America Inc. and a mine of political information, and Robert C. Gray, Professor of Government at Franklin and Marshall College, Lancaster, Pennsylvania. Each responded to frequent faxes with a promptness and thoroughness above and beyond the call of a lengthy friendship. I am also indebted to the Hon. Helen Delich Bentley, Member of Congress (Republican) for the 2nd District of Maryland; to the Parliamentarian of the House of Representatives; to Louis L. Goldstein, Comptroller of the Treasury for the State of Maryland; to KAL, the inimitable cartoonist of the *Baltimore Sun*; to Kara Hoff; and to the late Henry Brandon. For Australian material, I acknowledge assistance from Leigh Jackson and Patricia Hewitt. My coverage of Westminster matters has been aided by Jeffrey (now Lord) Archer, Gordon Brown MP, Gus O'Donnell, press secretary to the Prime Minister, Mike Ambrose of the *Morning Star*, Caroline Rathbone, Charles Reiss of the *Evening Standard*, and Alan Watkins of the *Observer*; many other MPs, peers and colleagues have unwittingly had their brains picked. I must also thank Fred Dellar of the *New Musical Express*, and my daughter Caroline for her help with the research. Above all, though, I must thank my wife, Corinne Reed Comfort, for tolerating a project that took up all my spare time for over two years, offering immense practical assistance, and above all giving me inspiration when I needed it. I cannot do better than echo Disraeli's dedication of *Sybil* to his wife Mary Ann:

> To one whose sweet voice has often encouraged, and whose taste and judgment have ever guided, its pages; the most severe of critics, but – a perfect Wife!

THE DICTIONARY

A

A. A-bomb Shorthand for the ATOMIC BOMB, the original NUCLEAR WEAPON as dropped at HIROSHIMA, and in comparison with the later and more powerful hydrogen bomb (H-BOMB).

à la lanterne! (Fr. to the lamp-post) One of the deadliest cries of the mob during the early days of the FRENCH REVOLUTION and the Reign of TERROR, meaning: "String them up!" It was at first directed against ARISTOCRATS or persons suspected of being so. *See* ÇA IRA.

ABs The sociological and marketing term for the upper, professional and managerial classes, on the scale A, B, C1, C2, D, E. It is used in OPINION POLLS to categorize those questioned and ensure a representative sample. *See* C2s for full explanation.

ABC trial The last prosecution authorized by a British Labour government under the unreformed OFFICIAL SECRETS ACT. The 21-month proceedings against Crispin Aubrey, John Berry and Duncan Campbell (their initials provide the name) for actions that allegedly endangered national security ended in 1978 in withdrawal of the most serious charges, with only Berry receiving a (suspended) prison sentence. Berry was a former corporal in Signals Intelligence; Aubrey and Campbell journalists to whom he passed information.

abdication Renunciation of the THRONE by a reigning monarch. In 1990 King Baudouin of Belgium abdicated temporarily, resuming his throne after one day, so as to avoid signing legislation permitting abortion. In Britain's **abdication crisis** of 1936, the as yet uncrowned Edward VIII determined to marry the twice-divorced American Mrs. Wallis Simpson. This required legislation both by Westminster and the Parliaments of the DOMINIONs; political leaders were opposed, as was the Church of England, whose **"Supreme Head"** the sovereign is; but when the story broke on 3 December the public was on the King's side. The confrontation between a determined King and an equally determined ESTABLISHMENT put the British constitution to one of its severest tests and endangered Stanley BALDWIN's government. Edward VIII decided he could not put his throne first; in his abdication broadcast on 11 December he told the nation and Empire:

> I have found it impossible to carry the heavy burden of responsibility, and to discharge my duties as King as I would wish to do, without the help and support of the woman I love.
>
> His mind was made up, and those who know him will know what that means.
>
> STANLEY BALDWIN to the House of Commons.

ABM Treaty The US–Soviet treaty of 1972 banning land-based anti-ballistic missile systems, except at one site each. ABMs had been deployed by each SUPERPOWER in the 1960s to give them the ability to retaliate even after a FIRST STRIKE by the other. An important breakthrough in ARMS CONTROL, it was largely but not totally complied with by both parties. But it had an important bearing on the subsequent debate over STAR WARS.

abolitionist A campaigner for the termination of a practice seen as undesirable, *e.g.* the death penalty or slavery. Applied to slavery, the abolitionist movement originated in 1831 when William Lloyd Garrison founded the LIBERATOR.

Aboriginal rights amendment An amendment to Australia's constitution, made by REFERENDUM in 1967, to remove discriminatory wording and enable the COMMONWEALTH Parliament to pass laws specifically benefiting Aborigines.

Abraham, Martin and John A tribute in song to three slain giants of American politics – Abraham LINCOLN, Martin Luther KING and John F. KENNEDY – written by Dick Holler the day after Robert F. Kennedy's assassination in June 1968. It created a new career for the former rock singer Dion who, as Dion DiMucci, recorded it late that summer; the record reached second place in the US charts and had sold a million copies by the following February. It has been widely recorded since by other artists.

Abscam (short for Arab-scam) The FBI "sting" operation which all but destroyed the reputation of the US CONGRESS in 1980. During a 23-month undercover operation, a phony Arab sheikh named Kambir Abdul Rahman (actually an ex-convict) set out to buy influence in Congress, with 100 agents in various disguises offering $1 million in public money. The scandal broke in February 1980 when the FBI released videotapes showing several Congressmen gleefully taking money. Only one of those chosen as potentially on the take, Sen. Larry Pressler, told the "sheikh" he was suggesting something illegal. Rep. Richard Kelly stuffed $25,000 into his pockets, asking: "Does it show?". Rep. John Jenrette boasted: "I've got larceny in my blood," and Rep. Michael "Ozzie" Myers rhymed:

Bullshit walks, money talks.

One Senator and one Congressman resigned as a result of Abscam, and 19 people (including six Congressmen) were sentenced to jail.

abseil In mountaineering (originally from the German), letting oneself down a rock face with a double rope. In Britain, adopted as a form of protest by militant lesbians who abseiled into the HOUSE OF LORDS from the public gallery in 1989 to highlight their opposition to CLAUSE 27. The word is also used figuratively, for political contortions, as when Ken Livingstone (see RED KEN) was accused by a fellow Labour MP of having "abseiled across the face of British politics".

absolutism Insistence on total fulfilment of a political creed or platform. Also the state of mind behind absolute MONARCHY. Ernst Friedrich Hubert Munster, Hanoverian ambassador to Russia 1801–04, characterized TSARIST Russia's political system as "absolutism tempered by ASSASSINATION".

abstain To take a deliberate decision not to vote, out of dislike for the alternatives available. The act of abstaining is **abstention**.

abstentionism A policy of refusing to participate in the political process as a protest against the system, practised at times by SINN FEIN (whose MPs have refused to take their seats at Westminster) and some far-left groups.

positive abstention The explanation by Frank Maguire, Independent Irish Republican MP, of his (rare) attendance and accompanying failure to vote in the 1979 Confidence debate (see VOTE OF CONFIDENCE) which brought down James Callaghan's Labour government.

Abu Nidal One of the most militant and deadly Palestinian groups, linked to terrorists around the world and named after its founder. Abu Nidal is one of the *noms de guerre* of Sabri Khalil al-Banna (1939–), the son of a wealthy Palestinian fruit merchant, who left school at 13 and drifted into a political extremism in which he felt outgunned by intellectuals. His Revolutionary Council of Fatah was founded in 1973 as a populist breakaway from AL-FATAH, which it regarded until a partial reconciliation in the mid-1980s as traitors under sentence of death; Abu Nidal promoted himself as "the answer to all Arab suffering and misfortune". The group first seized the Saudi embassy in Paris to force the release of the BLACK SEPTEMBER leader Abu Daoud. In 1975 it killed the Secretary-General of the Afro-Asian People's Organization in Cyprus, and in 1978 the PLO representative in Paris and several Iraqi diplomats abroad. On 3 June 1982 the group seriously wounded the Israeli ambassador in London – provoking the Israeli invasion of Lebanon three days later. In 1983 it assassinated Dr. Issam Sartawi, a close adviser of Yassir Arafat who advocated reconciliation between Palestinians and Jews. In 1986 Abu Nidal's "Che Guevara Brigade" killed the Arab mayor of Nablus in the OCCUPIED TERRITORIES. And on 8 November 1987 its guerrillas seized a yacht off the Israeli coast; the five passengers were French and Belgian tourists, but it was April 1990 before all were released. Abu Nidal has also been accused of involvement with the LOCKERBIE bombing.

By 1988 Abu Nidal was blamed by the PLO for over 100 terrorist actions, 56 against Palestinians. The group was initially based in Iraq, though from the late 1970s Syrian influence grew. In 1983 al-Banna was expelled from Baghdad to Damascus, but returned the next year for cardiac treatment. In November 1984 he was erroneously said to have died of a heart attack; on 12 February 1988 an Italian court sentenced him to life imprisonment *in absentia* for a massacre at Rome airport in 1985; the group struck at Vienna the same month. Meanwhile Syria had expelled the group and dismissed Abu Nidal's close ally General al-Khouli, head of Air Force Intelligence. And in 1989 Libya, facing SANCTIONS over Abu Nidal's presence, shut down his office in Tripoli and put him under house arrest.

All contact with the Jewish state will be punishable by death. ABU NIDAL.

abuse The deployment of insult rather than argument against one's opponents.

When political ammunition runs low, the rusty artillery of abuse is wheeled into action. ADLAI STEVENSON.

ACAS Advisory Conciliation and Arbitration Service. The body set up under the auspices of Britain's Department of Employment by the 1975 Employment Protection Act to help parties in industrial disputes resolve their differences.

acceptance speech The speech delivered by a newly-selected candidate for office, agreeing to take up the challenge and setting supporters' sights on victory. The term is especially used of the speech made by a Presidential NOMINEE to the party CONVENTION that has nominated him.

access In Washington, the decisive element – according to Hedrick Smith the "trump card" – in the power battle for the President's ear, especially between White House STAFFERS (*see* STAFF). Mike Deaver, after leaving the White House to work – illegally – as a lobbyist, boasted:

> There's no question that I've got as good access as anybody.

The word also denotes the purchase of access to an elected official in order to gain influence.

accession (1) The commencement of a MONARCH's reign on the death or ABDICATION of his or her predecessor. (2) The act of a nation in joining a grouping of states. Each country joining the EUROPEAN COMMUNITY does so by a Treaty of Accession.

accountability The requirement that a Minister or elected representative should explain his or her actions to the voters, or that an official should be answerable for his or her actions to the legislature.

Achille Lauro The TERRORIST incident in October 1985 when PALESTINIAN guerrillas HIJACKed the Italian cruise ship *Achille Lauro* in the eastern Mediterranean, shooting dead and throwing overboard a wheelchair-bound American Jewish passenger. The terrorists surrendered after the Egyptian government offered to fly them to safety in Tunisia, but US navy jets intercepted their plans and forced them to land in Sicily. The Italian government imprisoned the terrorists, but allowed their leader to escape. America's response to the incident demonstrated President Reagan's (*see* GREAT COMMUNICATOR) increasingly tough response to terrorist attacks on Americans.

ACLU American Civil Liberties Union. An essentially liberal organization which defends the civil rights of all, including its opponents.

> A criminals' lobby.
>
> Former Attorney-General ED MEESE (1931–).

ACP countries African, Caribbean and Pacific. The European Community's term for THIRD WORLD states qualifying for aid under the LOMÉ CONVENTION. Nations in Asia and the Indian subcontinent were not mentioned because the countries originally aided were primarily former French colonies.

Act A legislative measure that has passed through all its stages in a legislature as a BILL, and been assented to by the HEAD OF STATE. In the US CONGRESS, a Bill becomes an Act when one House has debated the measure, considered all amendments and had it ENGROSSED before it is passed to the other.

> There is no reference to fun in any Act of Parliament.
>
> Sir A. P. HERBERT (1890–1971).

Act of Union (1) The measure under which the kingdoms of England and Scotland were formally united on 1 May 1707, and a lingering cause for discontent among Scots. A Treaty of Union, guaranteeing Scotland 45 places in the House of Commons and 16 in the House of Lords in return for acknowledging that on Queen Anne's death the Crown would pass to the House of Hanover, was drawn up during 1706 by Commissioners from the two countries. The Scots accepted common taxation, coinage and weights and measures and a common flag (*see* UNION JACK), but retained their own legal system, based on Roman rather than Common law. The Scots Parliament voted itself out of existence by approving the Treaty in January 1707, but only after its members had been heavily bribed by England; at Westminster it also had a rough ride, largely through City of London pressure to prevent goods imported into Scotland before the Union being exported to England duty-free after it. Legislation to this effect, which would have severely strained the new Union, was only averted by Queen Anne PROROGUING Parliament.

> Now there's an end to ane old song.
>
> Lord SEAFIELD, Scotland's last LORD CHANCELLOR, sealing the Act.

(2) The Act passed by both the Westminster and the Irish Parliaments on 28 March 1800 which, from the start of the following year, abolished the Dublin assembly and put Ireland entirely under the control of Westminster. Ireland was granted 100 MPs, four spiritual peers and 28 temporal. The Act was repudiated in January 1922 by the Provisional Government of the IRISH FREE STATE under Michael Collins.

Act print In the US SENATE, the reprint of a Bill that has arrived from the HOUSE, been engrossed and has been referred by the PRESIDING OFFICER of the Senate to the relevant STANDING COMMITTEE.

action. action, and action now Franklin D. Roosevelt's (*see* FDR) promise – and demand – when he took office to implement the NEW DEAL.

action, not words! The slogan on which Edward Heath's Conservatives (*see* GROCER) fought Britain's 1966 general election. Harold WILSON's Labour government was re-elected with a greatly increased majority.

Action Directe An extreme left-wing TERRORIST group active in France during the 1980s.

Action Française An extreme right-wing group in France, most active between the wars and during the German occupation; also the name of its newspaper. Strongly nationalist and ANTI-SEMITIC, it was founded by the poet and political journalist Charles Maurras with the aim of overthrowing the Republic and restoring the monarchy. France's various Pretenders, and the Catholic church, were at times embarrassed by its support, and it lost what credibility it had through its COLLABORATION during the VICHY regime of 1940–44.

action this day CHURCHILL's annotation of documents brought to him during WORLD WAR II to which he gave the highest priority.

day of action The protests called by Britain's Trades Union Congress (TUC) against the industrial legislation of the Thatcher government. They could not be termed STRIKES, because purely political strikes have always been illegal. The response was patchy to thin, weakening further the TUC's already weak bargaining hand after the WINTER OF DISCONTENT.

direct action A general term for various forms of CIVIL DISOBEDIENCE in support of political aims. The **direct actionists** were a faction headed by Bill HAYWOOD, leader of the International Workers of the World (*see* WOBBLIES), who were expelled from the US Socialist Party in 1913 for advocating a political strategy based on violence, sabotage and general strikes.

industrial action A collective term for strikes, overtime bans, work-to-rules, sickouts, *etc.* – any action by workers designed to gain concessions from their employers.

> The continuation of negotiations by other means.
>
> DENIS McSHANE.

sympathetic action Action taken by workers in support of an industrial dispute involving others, against an employer who is in no way connected with it.

active service unit The Provisional IRA's term for one of its GUERRILLA groups, especially those operating on the British mainland or in continental Europe.

activist An eager and hard-working member of a political group. A 20th-century term, the word first being used in 1907 in connection with the philosophical theory of activism.

ADA rating The regular assessment by the ultra-liberal Americans for Democratic Action, co-founded by Eleanor Roosevelt (*see* FIRST LADY OF THE WORLD), of how Senators and Congressmen have voted on key items of legislation. Among conservative legislators a low ADA rating is a matter of pride.

Adams. Adams Chronicles The mid-1970s PBS television series, and accompanying book by Jack Shepherd, telling the story of four generations of the Adams family, at the heart of America's governing élite from the Revolution into the 20th century. Like the KENNEDYs, the Adams family were afflicted by tragedy: manic depression, alcoholism and self-destruction. The suicide of John Quincy Adams's eldest son George in 1829 made a deep impression on the nation. The family's outstanding members were **John** Adams (1735–1826), 2nd President of the United States, his wife **Abigail** (1744–1818) and their eldest son **John Quincy** Adams, the 6th President. John Adams set the tone of service and of high hopes for the future of the nation, writing to Abigail:

> I must study Politicks and War that my sons may have liberty to study Mathematicks and Philosophy. My sons ought to study Mathematicks and Philosophy, Geography, Natural History, Naval Architecture, navigation, Commerce and Agriculture, in order to give their Children a right to study Painting, Poetry, Musick, Architecture, Statuary, Tapestry and Porcelaine.

John Adams was a Massachusetts delegate to the CONTINENTAL CONGRESS, envoy to France, Holland and Britain, and the nation's first Vice-President. A FEDERALIST, he defeated Thomas JEFFERSON for the Presidency in 1797, but was unseated by him in the REVOLUTION OF 1800. He was the first President to occupy the White House, and died, aged 90, the same day as Jefferson. Of himself he said: "I do not know when I became a politician, for that I never was," and his most frequent diary entry was "at home, thinking". His chosen epitaph was: "Here lies John Adams, who took upon himself responsibility for peace with France in the year 1800." Sen. William Maclay was more critical, describing him as "self-conceited, like a monkey just put into breeches". Jefferson saw both good and bad points in John Adams: "He is vain, irritable and a bad calculator of the force and probable effect of the motives which govern men. This is all the ill which can be said of him. He is as disinterested as the Being who made him." John Adams was not a critical man, but shared with many fellow-revolutionaries an intense anger with Thomas Paine: "Such a mongrel between pig and puppy, begotten by a mongrel boar on a bitch wolf, never before in any age of the world was suffered by the poltroonery of mankind to run through such a career of mischief. Call it then the Age of Paine."

John Quincy Adams was described by Alfred Steinberg as "a short, stout, bald, brilliant and puritanical twig off a short, stout, bald, brilliant and puritanical tree". He worked as aide to his father, followed in his footsteps as a lawyer and diplomat, served as a US Senator, and as Monroe's Secretary of State devised the MONROE DOCTRINE. Elected President in 1824 by the House despite finishing second to Andrew Jackson (*see* CORRUPT BARGAIN), Adams served one term before Jackson took his revenge. Uniquely, he went back to Congress, serving in the House for 18 years before dying at his desk. He said of himself: "I am a man of cold, reserved and forbidding manners." And this view was widely shared. His son Charles Francis Adams wrote: "Quiet is not his sphere. And when a legitimate sphere of action does present itself, it is much to be feared that he will embrace an illegitimate one." W. H. Lyttleton reminisced: "Of all the men whom it was ever my lot to accost and to waste civilities upon, he was the most doggedly and systematically repulsive. With a vinegar aspect, cotton in his leathern ears and hatred in his heart, he sat . . . like a bulldog among spaniels." And Ralph Waldo Emerson wrote: "He is an old roué who cannot live on slops and must have sulphuric acid in his tea." John Quincy Adams's wife Louisa had a word for the entire clan:

> As it regards women, the Adams family are one and all particularly harsh and severe in their characters. There seems to exist no sympathy, no tenderness for the weakness of the sex.

The dynasty lasted until 1927, when the historian Brooks Adams, youngest grandson of John Quincy, died. He had written:

> It is now full four generations since John Adams wrote the constitution of Massachusetts. It is time that we perished. The world is tired of us.

Adams. Sherman Adams affair The Eisenhower administration's one notable INFLUENCE-PEDDLING scandal, arising from resentment in Washington at the power wielded by Sherman Adams, former Governor of New Hampshire, as assistant to the President. Hard-working and efficient, Adams was accused by the House of Representatives of manipulating regulatory agencies in return for a $700 vicuna coat and a $2400 oriental rug from his friend Bernard Goldfine, a Boston industrialist who was under investigation by the government. He was forced to resign in September 1958, despite Eisenhower's insistence that "I need him"; the scandal was a factor in the Democrats' LANDSLIDE victory in Congressional elections that November.

additional member A form of PROPORTIONAL REPRESENTATION in which some seats are filled by the FIRST PAST THE POST system and others are then allocated according to the parties' share of the poll.

adjournment The termination of a day's proceedings, generally at a time agreed between the parties and approved by the CHAIR. In the House of Commons, an **adjournment debate** is a half-hour debate immediately before the RISE of the House when a BACKBENCHER raises a constituency matter with a Minister; generally only the two of them and a WHIP are present. A debate **on the adjournment** is one where any vote would be on a technical motion, and consequently the views of individuals, rather than the opinion of the House, are gauged.

administration (1) The art or practice of carrying on the business of government and implementing its decisions. (2) In America, the structure and personnel of government installed by a particular President, and the period of time they serve. For example the Ford administration was the government responsible to Gerald Ford during his period as President.

> While the people retain their virtue and vigilance, no administration, by an extreme of wickedness or folly, can very seriously injure the government in the short space of four years. ABRAHAM LINCOLN.

administrative assistant A STAFFER who ensures the smooth running of the office of a US SENATOR or CONGRESSman, or of one of the committees of either House. An experienced administrative assistant can exert considerable influence, hopefully on behalf of his or her employer.

Admiralty House The building used by British Prime Ministers as offices and even a residence when NUMBER TEN Downing Street is unavailable through rebuilding. Built by S. P. Cockrell in 1786–88 as the residence of the First Lord of the Admiralty, it stands a little back from WHITEHALL just above the Horse Guards. Harold Macmillan lived there for a considerable time while Number 10 was being completely rebuilt, and John MAJOR used it for everything except CABINET meetings in 1992 during security work at Downing Street. It is used for hospitality and other purposes by the Ministry of Defence, and there are government flats there.

adoption meeting In Britain, the meeting at the start of an election campaign at which a prospective CANDIDATE is formally adopted to fight a seat. Once the candidate has been adopted, any spending on his or her behalf has to be within the legal ceiling.

Adullamites A group of right-wing Liberal MPs and peers who in 1865–67 opposed any significant extension of the FRANCHISE and reaffirmed the role of Liberals as enlightened defenders of property. The group gained its name from a Biblical reference (1 *Samuel* xxii. 1,2) by their critic John Bright, who said of the opposition of Robert Lowe and others to Gladstone's 1866 REFORM Bill:

> The Rt. Hon. Gentleman is the first of the new Party who has retired into what may be called his political cave of Adullam – and he has called about him everyone that was in distress and everyone that was discontented.

adultery An activity much practised by legislators in many of the world's great capitals, and a staple of political sex scandals. Gary Hart's Presidential hopes for 1988 were destroyed when Paul Taylor of the *Washington Post* asked him: "Have you ever committed adultery?" and Hart replied: "Follow me." The media took him at his word, and found Miss Donna Rice.

I don't see why we can't get along just as well with a polygamist who doesn't polyg as with a monogamist who doesn't monog The attributed comment of Sen. Boies Penrose (1860–1921) in support of seating the first Mormon Senator, Reed Smoot, in 1903. The sentence has also been attributed to Theodore Roosevelt in a campaign speech the previous year.

I would rather commit adultery than drink a pint of beer The statement in support of temperance delivered in the House of Commons in the 1920s by Nancy, Lady Astor (1879–1964). It produced from the veteran Labour MP Jack Jones the classic intervention: "Who wouldn't?" It was some time before order was restored.

> I was told as a young man that the two occupational hazards of the Palace of Westminster were alcohol and adultery. The huroosh that follows the intermittent revelations of the sexual goings-on of an unlucky MP has convinced us that the only safe pleasure for a parliamentarian is a bag of boiled sweets.
>
> JULIAN CRITCHLEY, MP (Con.).

advance. Advance Australia Fair The patriotic song written *c.* 1878 by Peter Dodds McCormick (d. 1916) which was declared the national anthem on 19 April 1984. The original anthem from 1788 was GOD SAVE THE KING (or QUEEN); repeated efforts to replace it produced a deadlock between *Advance Australia Fair* and *Waltzing Matilda*. In 1974 Gough WHITLAM announced, after an opinion poll and an abortive competition that produced 1400 entries, that *Advance Australia Fair* would be the national tune, though the original words were not adopted as an anthem. In a REFERENDUM in 1977 *Advance Australia Fair* beat *Waltzing Matilda* by 65.2% to 34.8% after *God Save the Queen* and *Song of Australia* had been eliminated. With the proclamation of *Advance Australia Fair* as national anthem in 1984, the playing of *God Save the Queen* was limited to occasions when a member of the Royal family was present; an authorized set of words was also adopted, the first verse being:

> Australians all let us rejoice, for we are young and free;
> We've golden soil and wealth for toil, our home is girt by sea;
> Our land abounds in nature's gifts of beauty rich and rare;
> In history's page at every stage Advance Australia Fair.
> In joyful strains then let us sing
> Advance Australia Fair.

advance man A staff member who travels ahead of a politician or candidate to make sure that everything necessary to ensure the success of the trip has been arranged, that all facilities are in place and that welcoming crowds will be on hand.

adversary A political opponent, by inference on an institutionalized basis and thus in the opposite party to oneself. Traditionally a new MP arriving at Westminster pointed to the benches opposite and said: "I see that is where the enemy sit." An elderly colleague corrected him: "Those are your adversaries. Your enemies are behind you."

> Nothing perplexes an adversary so much as an appeal to his honour. DISRAELI.

adversarial politics The system of politics, fundamental at Westminster, which depends on permanent and gladiatorial contest between two parties who in turn form the Government and a loyal OPPOSITION. The opposite of CONSENSUS politics, it is regarded as obsolete and harmful by third and minor parties.

advice and consent The phrase in the US CONSTITUTION which enshrines the prerogative of the SENATE in ratifying (*see* RATIFICATION) treaties (with a two-thirds majority required) and confirming (*see* CONFIRMATION) appointees put to it by the President. The phrase originated in the Westminster legislative process (*see* BE IT ENACTED). As *Advise and Consent*, it became the title of a Pulitzer Prize-winning 1959 novel by Allen Drury about a President's efforts to push through the appointment of a questionably liberal SECRETARY OF STATE. The procedure was thrashed out between George WASHINGTON and the first Senate in the summer of 1789, after initial disagreements. *See* Clarence THOMAS CASE.

affiliation (Lat. *filius*, son) The process by which an organization associates itself with a political party, paying a fee and gaining some say in the programme and conduct of that party. In Britain the best example is the affiliation of individual TRADE UNIONS to the LABOUR PARTY. Since the purge of the MILITANT TENDENCY in the mid-1980s Labour has published a list of affiliated organizations, most of them political societies or pressure groups, membership of which is not incompatible with membership of the party.

affirmation The process by which someone with no religious belief, or strong objections to the taking of OATHS, swears allegiance to the State on taking office or adds weight to his or her testimony.

affirmative action The policy, particularly in America since the mid-1970s, of giving preferential treatment to members of a disadvantaged group in order to make up for under-representation or past DISCRIMINATION. Also known as **reverse discrimination**, it has been used in particular to promote women and members of ethnic minorities even if they do not meet the rigid qualifications previously demanded of all candidates. As such it has provoked a BACKLASH from qualified White males and others who feel they are being unfairly excluded, but efforts by President Reagan to restrict it were thwarted by a 1986 Supreme Court ruling upholding the practice. *See* BAKKE CASE; QUOTA.

Afghan Ron The nickname given to **Ron Brown** (1940–) the left-wing Labour MP for Edinburgh Leith 1979–92, because of his close links with, and visits to, the Soviet-backed Najibullah regime in Afghanistan; he was also a guest in Tripoli, interceding with Colonel Gaddafi for the release of detained Britons. He was DESELECTED by his party after reportedly frolicking in a Commons shower with his female research assistant and subsequently appearing in court for allegedly stealing items of underwear from her flat. It was not the inferences of adultery or theft that offended Leith's Labour activists, but the bottle of champagne he opened in front of television cameras after being freed.

AFL-CIO American Federation of Labour-Congress of Industrial Organizations. The body representing most of America's labour unions, with a degree of influence on a Democratic White House and on the party in Congress. The **AFL** was founded in 1886 by Samuel Gompers (1850–1924) and rapidly became White male skilled labour's representative body. It split in 1935 when the United Mine Workers' leader John L. Lewis pulled out and formed the **CIO**; Lewis, a strong supporter of industrial unionism which the craft-orientated AFL opposed, made the break dramatically, landing a right cross on the jaw of the Carpenters' president William Hutcheson. In 1937 the AFL expelled the CIO unions, who broke with traditional AFL policy and started recruiting Black workers and women on a large scale. The AFL and CIO unions' rival recruitment campaigns initially resulted in violence and death. The CIO as it developed under the United Auto Workers' Walter Reuther was more liberal than the trenchantly anti-Communist AFL, but did not merit Rep. Clarence Brown's tag of "a conduit of communism." In 1955 the organizations merged again with 15 million members and George Meany (1894–1979) as president; Meany, who headed the AFL-CIO for 24 years, was a fierce opponent of union rackets – in 1957 the organization expelled the TEAMSTERS.

> Everything outside the AFL-CIO is Hoboken.
>
> AFL-CIO President LANE KIRKLAND (1922–).

Africa. scramble for Africa The rush by the European powers in the closing years of the 19th century to satisfy their IMPERIALIST ambitions by grabbing as yet unclaimed (by the White man) parts of Africa.

> These same powers must be told in a clear, firm and definite voice: "Scram from Africa."
>
> TOM MBOYA, Kenyan nationalist leader, 1958.

African American The favoured term in the 1990s for Americans originally of African extraction; *Negro*, and later *Black*, had previously been preferred.

The Africans like a grin and a laugh A remark which spelt trouble for Sir Paul Hasluck (1905–), GOVERNOR-GENERAL of Australia 1969–74. He said of the Liberal Prime Minister John Gorton: "He won the affection of the African leaders with his grin. The Africans like a grin and a laugh." The comment was widely seen, particularly by the opposition, as patronizing and insensitive.

Africanization (1) The process by which newly-independent African countries replace Europeans in official posts by their own nationals. (2) The emotive and hostile term used by President Andrew Johnson and others for radical Republican moves during RECONSTRUCTION to give blacks the right to vote.

Afro-Caribbean The favoured term in 1980s British politics for Britons of African extraction, principally those whose families had migrated from the West Indies since World War II. Left-wingers use the word Black to include descendants of all "non-European" immigrants including those from the Indian subcontinent and even, in some circumstances, Turkey.

Agadir crisis The dispute between France and Germany in the run-up to WORLD WAR I triggered by Germany's despatch of the warship *Panther* in July 1911 to the Moroccan port of Agadir. Germany claimed to be protecting its interests in response to the arrival of French troops in Morocco. The affair raised tensions throughout Europe; Lloyd George in his MANSION HOUSE SPEECH warned both countries that Britain, too, had interests in the region. This brought an angry response from Berlin and fears of a German attack on the Royal Navy. The dispute was settled by a Franco-German agreement signed on 4 November, but hostility between the two nations remained – and the crisis had brought France and Britain closer together.

Age of Reason The religio/political treatise published in Paris in 1794–95 by the English radical writer Thomas Paine (1737–1809), which had a considerable impact in continental Europe and in the new American Republic, its title encouraging a new wave of intellectual ferment. In it, he set out his beliefs with such frankness that he was called a "dirty little atheist"; Paine, who had been brought up in a Quaker home, wrote: "The only idea man can affix to the name of God is that of a 1st. cause of all things."

> Tom Paine invented the name of the Age of Reason; and he was one of those sincere but curiously simple men who really did think that the age of reason was beginning, at about the time when it was really ending.
> G. K. CHESTERTON.

agency An office performing a function of government, subordinate to but not totally controlled by a Cabinet department. In Britain the number of such agencies was limited until the 1980s; they are now proliferating fast (*see* NEXT STEPS AGENCIES). In America they have long been numerous; the first was the Federal Trade Commission, set up in 1887. President Carter complained on taking office that there were 17 separate agencies with responsibility for migratory birds.

> A government agency is the nearest thing to eternal life we'll ever see on this earth. RONALD REAGAN.

Alphabet agencies The plethora of bodies set up by President Franklin D. Roosevelt to implement the NEW DEAL, which became known by their initials. The most important were the NRA (National Recovery Administration), **RFC** (Reconstruction Finance Corporation), **AAA** (Agricultural Adjustment Administration or "Triple A"), **PWA** (Public Works Administration) and **WPA** (Works Progress Administration).

agenda (Lat. to be done) The schedule for the conduct of a meeting, setting out in order the issues to be raised.

agenda-setting Co-ordinated NEWS MANAGEMENT by a party to ensure that the issues debated at a particular time, even by other parties, are those it wishes to discuss and on which it believes it will score most heavily.

hidden agenda An undeclared programme which a party or government conceals behind a more innocuous statement of what it plans to do. Since the early 1980s it has been a normal campaigning tactic to accuse one's opponents of having such an agenda, whether or not there is evidence. In Britain's 1983 election a number of leaked documents, notably on family policy, led the CONSERVATIVES' opponents to assert with a degree of corroboration that Margaret Thatcher had such an agenda.

agent One of the cornerstones of British political life, the person employed by a party at CONSTITUENCY level to develop the local organization, supervise fund-raising, organize campaigning, see that electoral law is observed and make sure the vote is got out. Most Conservative agents are salaried officials, most Labour and Liberal Democrat agents are part-time volunteers.

agent-general The quasi-diplomatic representative of one of Canada's provinces in Britain or an Australian state.

Agent Orange A powerful defoliant used by the US military during the VIETNAM WAR to strip away tree cover from areas where large Communist troop concentrations were believed to be hiding. Sprayed from the air, it poisoned many civilians and its use was widely condemned by environmentalists and human rights groups.

agent-provocateur A person who infiltrates a political party or movement in order to disrupt it, or encourage it to take steps that push it into conflict with the authorities, destroy its basis of support or lead to its becoming discredited.

Parliamentary agent In Britain, a lawyer who specializes in preparing Private BILLS for submission to Parliament, or in collating and lodging objections to them.

Agitate, educate, legislate! The motto of the Women's Christian Temperance Union, which from the mid-19th century became one of the principal forces for PROHIBITION; it was strongest in America, Britain and its emerging White colonies.

agitator (Lat. a stirrer-up) A person who stirs up dissatisfaction, unrest and support for radical action among the public or specific parts of it. The term was in use by the early 19th century, as now not entirely as a compliment; the Irish patriot Daniel O'Connell (1775–1847) was described as "the great agitator". Shortly before the 1976 Presidential election the pastor of PLAINS, Georgia, Baptist church embarrassed Democratic contender Jimmy CARTER by announcing that members had voted to ban "niggers and Civil rights agitators."

> Those who profess to favour freedom, and yet deprecate agitation, are men who want rain without thunder and lightning. They want the ocean without the roar of its waves. FREDERICK DOUGLASS (*c.* 1817–95).

agitprop (Russ. *agitatsiya propaganda* agitation PROPAGANDA) Dramatic, literary, media or artistic activity designed to promote Communist ideology, both within the system and worldwide. The term was coined by Georgy Plekhanov and elaborated by LENIN in *What Is To Be Done* (1902). "Agitation" implied the use of political slogans and half-truths to exploit mass grievances and mould public opinion; "propaganda" in this context meant using rational, scientific and historic arguments to train and INDOCTRINATE Communist party members. In 1920 the Soviet Party's CENTRAL COMMITTEE established a Department of Agitation and Propaganda, which remained in charge of this activity until the collapse of the party and the Soviet state in 1991.

Agnew resignation The departure from office of Richard Nixon's Vice-President, Spiro T. Agnew (1918–), on 10 October 1973, which paved the way for the unelected Gerald FORD to become President of the United States. Agnew, a hero of HARD-HAT conservatives, pleaded no contest to a charge of evading income tax as Baltimore County executive, Governor of Maryland and Vice-President. US attorneys found evidence that until not long before, Agnew had been receiving bribes and kickbacks in plain envelopes from Baltimore County engineers and other contractors. Two days later, and barely a week before the SATURDAY NIGHT MASSACRE which brought WATERGATE to a head, Nixon nominated Ford, then House MINORITY LEADER, to succeed Agnew. The outgoing VEEP was sentenced to three years' probation and fined $10,000 – a sentence criticized as light but defended as being in the national interest. During his political career Agnew had gained a reputation for blunt public utterances, some of which, like his comments on the INNER CITIES, were regarded as outright GAFFES. Insisting on his probity, Agnew had told supporters:

> I have often been accused of putting my foot in my mouth, but I have never put my hand in your pocket.

agonizing reappraisal A change in policy stemming from a painful acceptance that the original plan has failed. The phrase is attributed to the US SECRETARY OF STATE John Foster Dulles, who told the North Atlantic Council in Paris on 14 December 1953:

> If EDC [the European Defence Community] should fail, the United States might be compelled to make an agonizing reappraisal of its basic policy.

agrarian parties Political parties which give farmers and the peasantry an organized voice and a coherent programme. They have had the greatest success in Central and Eastern Europe, but have also had some impact in the US Farm Belt (*see* Farmer-LABOR) and in Canada's prairie provinces.

agreement to differ In UK politics, an acceptance that members of a government cannot reach unanimity on a single divisive issue, but that that issue is not of such importance as to bring the government down. The first such agreement – though not referred to as such at the time – was the readiness of ASQUITH's government in 1913 to accept that while a majority wanted VOTES FOR WOMEN, the Prime Minister himself would not drop his opposition to female suffrage. The term was first used in respect of the readiness of Liberal FREE TRADERS to serve in the 1931 NATIONAL GOVERNMENT, despite its commitment to maintain tariffs. A further example was the continuance of Harold WILSON's Labour government in 1975, when a minority of the Cabinet was actively campaigning for a "No" vote in the EC REFERENDUM while the majority backed the "Yes" campaign.

> We agree on everything, including the fact that we don't see eye to eye. HENRY KISSINGER and GOLDA MEIR.

air. Air Force One The name of the aircraft used on official business by the PRESIDENT of the United States. The title was bestowed on successive models of Boeing (originally a 707) from the early 1960s; George BUSH in 1990 traded up to a 747-200B. The aircraft includes VIP office and sleeping accommodation, a secure communications network, and space for staffers and a travelling press pool. Its title reflects the Air Force's prime role in transporting the President (*see also* MARINE ONE). The plane that flies the VICE-PRESIDENT is known as **Air Force Two**. Asked what he liked about it, Dan QUAYLE said: "You don't have to have a ticket, and you never lose your luggage."

air raid shelter A politician who chooses, or is chosen, to share the responsibility of others for some calamity, and thus enable them to hang on. The phrase was first, and famously, used by Lloyd George on 7 May 1940 in the Commons debate that led to the fall of CHAMBERLAIN's government. After CHURCHILL had made a speech defending the government's conduct of the war, the former Liberal premier observed:

> The Right Honourable Gentleman must not allow himself to be converted into an air raid shelter to keep the splinters from hitting his colleagues.

John MAJOR, apparently unaware of its original context, used the phrase in Cabinet on 17 September 1992 after Britain had withdrawn from the ERM and devalued the pound (*see* BLACK WEDNESDAY). He insisted that Chancellor Norman Lamont, who was under heavy outside pressure to resign, should not be made to act as an "air raid shelter" for policies agreed by the entire government.

al-Fatah (Arab. the victory) The Palestinian guerrilla and political organization which has occupied the leadership of the PLO since 1969. Founded in Kuwait in 1958 by Yassir Arafat (1929–) to fight for the return of Palestine to the Arabs, it carried out its first guerrilla action from Jordan in 1964. Expelled from Jordan in the BLACK SEPTEMBER of 1970, it withdrew to Lebanon where it carried on the guerrilla campaign until the Israeli invasion of 1982. For a time from 1983 al-Fatah was split between factions in Tripoli, Lebanon and Tunis; but it regrouped, building support in the GAZA STRIP and WEST BANK, to launch the INTIFADA in 1987.

Alabama claim An episode which soured US–British relations in the aftermath of the CIVIL WAR. The *Alabama* was a cruiser built for the Confederacy at Birkenhead despite Britain's supposed NEUTRALITY. The ship, with the *Florida* and *Shenandoah*, pillaged Union merchant shipping, inflicting heavy losses which led to an outcry in the North against Britain, diplomatic protests and claims for compensation, which were ignored in London. In 1869 negotiations opened on this and other outstanding issues; an initial settlement was rejected by the US Senate, but in 1871 the Treaty of WASHINGTON, submitting the claims to an international tribunal, was ratified. The tribunal met in Geneva in 1872; it refused to accept US claims for indirect damages caused by the *Alabama* and other British-built Confederate vessels, but awarded $15.5 million for direct damages, which Britain promptly paid.

Albany. Albany Plan The plan for a devolved federal union of Britain's American colonies put forward in 1754 by Benjamin FRANKLIN. A conference was convened at Albany, the future New York State capital, and the plan presented to it; though it was unanimously adopted, none of the colonies would accept it. Both the colonial legislatures and the British authorities believed the plan would give too much power to the other.

Albany Regency The political organization in New York State in the 1820s and 1830s which was one of the earliest US political MACHINES and a constituent of the embryo DEMOCRATIC PARTY. Its principal organizer was Martin van Buren (*see* OLD KINDERHOOK) for whom it served as a stepping-stone to the Presidency. With van Buren in the White House, the invincibility of the Regency was dealt a severe blow by the election of the WHIG W. H. Seward as governor of New York in 1838.

albatross An incubus or handicap to a government or political party; the term stems from Coleridge's poem *The Ancient Mariner*, in which the mariner brings a curse on his ship by shooting the albatross that has flown over it, bringing luck to the crew. The word was put to its most damning use at the time of the SUEZ CRISIS when Aneurin Bevan (*see* NYE) called Selwyn (later Lord Selwyn) Lloyd, Foreign Secretary from 1955 to 1960, "a putrefying albatross around the neck of this government".

Aldermaston marches The four-day marches between TRAFALGAR SQUARE and the Atomic Weapons Research Establishment at Aldermaston, Berkshire, between 1958 and 1963 which put CND on the map and made the cause of nuclear disarmament respectable to the British public. The first began in London and terminated at Aldermaston; in subsequent years Trafalgar Square was the destination, and the scene of a mass RALLY attracting up to 100,000 people.

aldermen In England and Wales, senior members of a local authority who were elected by that body and not by the voters; aldermanic seats were abolished in the local government reorganization of 1974. In America, ward representatives on some city councils are styled aldermen.

Algérie Française (Fr. Algeria is French) The rallying-cry of the opponents of French withdrawal from Algeria who first brought General DE GAULLE to power in 1958, then turned against him when he pressed ahead with independence. At times of protest, Paris echoed with the sound of car horns sounding the slogan as three quick blasts and two slow. *See also* FOUR GENERALS; OAS.

alienation The process by which certain groups of the public become detached from and hostile to the political process, seeing it as incapable of meeting their needs or solving their problems. In its extreme forms a cause of civil unrest or even REVOLUTION, alienation has been particularly associated with ethnic groups who feel the system is rigged against them or simply ignores them, groups who have chosen to disengage like Britain's New Age Travellers, and the UNDERCLASS as a whole.

All-Ireland Court *See* SUNNINGDALE.

Alliance The umbrella under which Britain's LIBERAL PARTY and SDP fought the General Elections of 1983 and 1987, winning 23 seats in the first and 22 in the second. It was not a purely electoral machine, the two parties having started to work together – and share out candidacies – within months of the SDP's formation in 1981. The Alliance was always under strain; in 1983 the SDP leader Roy Jenkins started out as "Prime Minister designate", but the Liberal leader David Steel had his role reduced at the ETTRICK BRIDGE summit; in 1987 Steel and Dr. David Owen, who was now leading the SDP, pursued differing strategies; the comedian Rory Bremner christened them "the quack and the dead". Immediately after that election Steel called for a merger of the two parties, thus triggering a split in the SDP which wrecked the Alliance, though eventually producing a united party under Paddy Ashdown (*see* LIBERAL DEMOCRATS).

> Two cocks in one pen never did agree.
>
> Derbyshire voter to Alliance canvasser, 1983.

> They have a new colour. They call it gold. It looks like yellow to me. MARGARET THATCHER, 1987.

Alliance for Progress A partnership for economic and social improvement between the United States and the countries of Latin America, proposed by President KENNEDY in March 1961 and accepted by all Latin states except Cuba at a conference in Punta del Este, Uruguay, five months later. America agreed to foot most of the bill for a series of projects to raise living standards, and Kennedy became a popular figure in the southern continent. The Alliance eventually ran out of steam, partly because of concern among private investors at the instability of several recipient states.

> An alliance between one millionaire and many beggars.
>
> FIDEL CASTRO, 1964.

Peace, commerce and honest friendship with all nations, entangling alliances with none One of the guidelines set for American policy by Thomas JEFFERSON in his first INAUGURAL ADDRESS, on 4 March 1801.

Atlantic Alliance *See* ATLANTIC.

Triple Alliance *See* TRIPLE.

Allighan case The expulsion from the House of Commons on 30 October 1947 of Gary Allighan, Labour MP for Gravesend, for breaching the "PRIVILEGE and decorum" of the House. Allighan wrote in *World's Press News* that MPs gave confidential information to strangers while drunk, and took money for tip-offs to the Press; he was also held to have "persistently misled" the investigating committee, thus committing a CONTEMPT OF THE HOUSE. The vote to expel him was 187–75.

Allons, enfants de la patrie (Fr. let's go, children of our country) The opening words of the MARSEILLAISE, written in 1792 by Claude Joseph Rouget de Lisle (1760–1836).

Allotment Act *See* DAWES.

ALP The widely-used abbreviation for the Australian LABOR Party.

alternate A person designated to take the place of a DELEGATE if that delegate is unable to carry out his or her duties.

alternatives The staple diet of politics, despite Margaret Thatcher's claim that none exist (*see* THERE IS NO ALTERNATIVE; TINA). The UK CABINET SECRETARY Burke Trend reckoned: "The acid test of any political question is 'What is the alternative?'", while Henry KISSINGER declared that "the absence of alternatives clears the mind marvellously".

alternative vote *See* VOTE.

Alton Bill The Bill to reduce the final date for termination of a pregnancy from 28 weeks to 18, promoted at Westminster in 1987–88 by the Liverpool Liberal MP David Alton (1951–). Though there was widespread support for some reduction, it ran out of Parliamentary time because Alton and his fellow PRO-LIFE campaigners refused to accept any compromise on the time limit.

ambassador The highest-ranking diplomatic representative of one country stationed in another; most countries send career diplomats, but America's ambassadors are often POLITICAL APPOINTEES. Also a representative of the President appointed to conduct international negotiations or act as a roving envoy.

> An honest man sent abroad to lie for the Commonwealth.
>
> Sir HENRY WOTTON (1568–1639).

ambush In a legislature, a vote suddenly called by a party lacking numbers, which hopes to catch its opponents unawares and defeat them. Ambushes are often staged in mid-evening, when complacent members of the majority are away at dinner.

Amen Corner A section of corridor in New York City's Fifth Avenue Hotel where Republican TAMMANY HALL managers met to review policy and tactics. It was originally the corner at the west end of London's Paternoster Row where monks would finish their *Pater Noster* (Lord's Prayer) when they processed to St. Paul's Cathedral on Corpus Christi Day.

amendment A change made to a piece of legislation: a BILL during its passage through a legislature, a MOTION under debate or, most portentously, the US CONSTITUTION since its enactment. Twenty-seven amendments (the first ten of them in the BILL OF RIGHTS) have so far been enacted. An amendment to the Constitution may originate with Congress – as all have so far – or with a National CONVENTION called at the request of two-thirds of the States. Two-thirds of both Houses of Congress must support the amendment, and to take effect it must then be RATIFIED by three-quarters of the State legislatures (which means 38 States) or by special constitutional conventions in as many states. A state may not reverse a vote to ratify, but can reconsider a vote not to.

> Amendments to the constitution ought to not be too frequently made; [if] continually tinkered with it would lose all its prestige and dignity, and the old instrument would be lost sight of altogether in a short time.
>
> President ANDREW JOHNSON, 22 February 1866.

dilatory amendment An amendment put forward with the intention of delaying debate; in the US CONGRESS, a ruling that an amendment is dilatory will prevent its being debated.
killer amendment In the US Congress, an amendment whose adoption would wreck the purpose of the measure being debated.
manuscript amendment At Westminster, an amendment put forward in writing during debate for acceptance by the CHAIR, as opposed to one appearing on the ORDER PAPER. Such amendments are usually accepted only when it is clear the proposal being debated does not reflect the will of the House; a rare example was the acceptance of a manuscript amendment from Tony BENN during the debate on the ZIRCON affair when the Labour left-winger remarkably persuaded backbench Tories that the Government was seeking to abridge their rights.
marshalled amendments A list of amendments put forward when debate on a Bill is imminent, which groups them in the order in which they will be debated rather than the order in which they were TABLED.
non-germane amendment An amendment not relevant to the purposes of a Bill, specifically when inserted by the US SENATE into a measure originally passed by the HOUSE OF REPRESENTATIVES.
wrecking amendment The Westminster counterpart of the KILLER AMENDMENT.
amendment tree A structure of amendments put forward by the promoter of a Bill, which effectively prevents its opponents from destroying the package; perfected in the US Senate by Robert Dole, it ties supporters to the Bill by giving them a chance to back amendments protecting their pet programmes. *See also* ANTHONY AMENDMENT; BOLAND AMENDMENT; CUNNINGHAM AMENDMENT; ERA; ROOKER-WISE AMENDMENT; STEIGER AMENDMENT and the relevant numbers for amendments to the US Constitution.

America. America First (1) The ISOLATIONIST campaign to keep America out of WORLD WAR II, which kept up an onslaught against US involvement between Hitler's invasion of Poland in September 1939 and Japan's attack on PEARL HARBOR. **The America First Committee** embraced pro-Nazis, Communists (until Hitler's attack on Russia) and ordinary Americans who felt the war was none of their business. (2) The slogan of the ultra-conservative Pat Buchanan in his campaign against George BUSH in the 1992 Republican primaries; though it faltered after the first half-dozen contests, Buchanan's charge that Bush had neither ideas nor ideology played its part in the President's ultimate defeat.
large America The vision of America's IMPERIALISTS, and specifically the supporters of McKINLEY in the 1900 Presidential election; supporters of William Jennings Bryan (*see* PRAIRIE AVENGER), who opposed the acquisition of overseas territories, were said to favour a "small America".
Middle America *See* MIDDLE.
Voice of America (VOA) The overseas radio broadcasting network of the US Information Agency; it was founded in 1942 for PROPAGANDA purposes but now promotes a favourable image of America through a balanced worldwide output of news and entertainment. VOA broadcasts from Washington, in English and 41 other languages, reaching an estimated weekly audience of 120 million. It is often confused with **Radio Free Europe/ Radio Liberty**, the Munich-based organization funded by Congress but run by private US citizens, whose role after the COLD WAR is in doubt.

come home, America The theme of George McGovern's ACCEPTANCE SPEECH at the 1972 Democratic convention in Miami Beach. His aim was to touch a deeper chord with the people than the radical platform devised by convention delegates whom Shirley MacLaine described as "a couple of high schools, a grape boycott, a BLACK PANTHER rally and four or five politicians who walked in the wrong door". McGovern appealed for America to rediscover its virtues and values – but interminable floor action meant that he did not deliver it until 3 a.m., thus missing his PRIME TIME audience.

It's morning again in America The confident theme of Ronald Reagan's ACCEPTANCE SPEECH after being nominated for a second term by the Republicans' Dallas convention in 1984. It was the high point of the FEELGOOD FACTOR; public satisfaction won Reagan a LANDSLIDE victory over Walter Mondale (*see* NORWEGIAN WOOD), but within months the longest HONEYMOON in US political history was over.

The frontier of America is on the Rhine A comment reputedly made by Franklin D. Roosevelt to Senators during a White House meeting on 31 January 1939, which enraged America's ISOLATIONISTS. FDR disowned the remark, describing it as "a deliberate lie", but Americans who were convinced he was leading them into war saw it as confirming their worst fears, while the UK and French governments were heartened by his apparent commitment to oppose any German advance. However Neville CHAMBERLAIN observed around this time: "It is always best and safest to count on nothing from the Americans but words."

No one can kill Americans and brag about it. No one Ronald Reagan's truculent declaration in April 1986 in support of the LIBYAN BOMBING in retaliation for the alleged involvement of Colonel Gaddafi's agents in the bombing of a disco in Berlin, in which several US service personnel were killed.

there is nothing wrong with America that cannot be cured by what is right with America The key phrase of the INAUGURAL ADDRESS delivered by Bill Clinton (*see* COMEBACK KID) after being sworn in as 42nd President of the United States on 20 January 1993.

American plan The campaign waged by US business at the height of the RED SCARE after World War I, aimed at convincing the public that COLLECTIVE BARGAINING and the CLOSED SHOP were "un-American". Its backers included the American Bankers Association and National Association of Manufacturers. By 1920 there were American Plan Associations in every state of the Union, 46 of them in Illinois. The campaign succeeded in blocking most legislative moves to strengthen union rights, but subsided as the threat of revolution evaporated and America took a more conservative turn.

American revolution The overall term used by politicians and historians for the welling-up of political consciousness and communal feeling in Britain's American colonies which culminated in the Declaration of INDEPENDENCE in 1776, the war which secured America's freedom and the devising by the Founding FATHERS of the political system that endures to this day. Looking back, John ADAMS reckoned that "the revolution was in the mind of the people, and this was effected from 1760 to 1775, before a drop of blood was shed at Lexington". The revolution produced many memorable phrases. When Britain first closed the port of Boston in 1774, Benjamin FRANKLIN wrote: "You may reduce their cities to ashes, but the flame of liberty in North America shall not be extinguished". But Dr. Samuel Johnson regarded much of the talk of principle as humbug, asking: "How is it that we hear the loudest yelps for liberty from the drivers of negroes?" When the colonists finally lost patience with what they saw as a string of provocations, Thomas Paine declared: "The period of debate is closed. Arms as the last resort decide the contest." The Lutheran pastor Peter Muhlenberg reputedly told his congregation in Woodstock, Virginia: "There is a time for all things, a time to preach and a time to pray, but those times have passed away. There is a time to fight, and that time has now come." And early in 1777 PITT THE ELDER said portentously: "If I were an American as I am an Englishman, while a foreign troop was landed in my country, I would never lay down my arms – never, never, never!"

> These are times that try men's souls. The summer soldier and the sunshine patriot will, in this crisis, shrink from the service of their country; but he that stands it now deserves the love and thanks of man and woman.
>
> THOMAS PAINE, December 1776.

> Americans of the revolutionary generation proved themselves the most creative statesmen in modern history, perhaps in all history.
>
> HENRY STEELE COMMAGER, 1970.

> No other revolution, worthy of the name, ended so happily.
>
> HUGH BROGAN.

Daughters of the American Revolution *See* DAR.

American System The combination of TARIFFs, a national bank and improved transportation put forward by Henry Clay (1777–1852) as SPEAKER of the House of Representatives between 1823 and 1825. The plan, intended to enable farms and factories to exchange their goods more easily and lessen dependence on European products and markets, prompted the enactment of America's first protective tariff in 1824, but failed to win Clay the Presidency the following year. As Speaker, Clay presided over the election by the House of his friend John Quincy ADAMS, who had trailed Andrew Jackson in the popular vote; when Adams made Clay Secretary of State, Jackson's supporters became convinced a CORRUPT BARGAIN had been struck.

Americanism A word brandished by US politicians, especially in the late 19th century and first half of the 20th, though its meaning – beyond a general patriotism – was never defined. Theodore Roosevelt came closest, terming Americanism as "the virtues of courage, justice, honor, truth, sincerity and hardihood – the virtues that made America." But President HARDING confessed: "I don't know much about Americanism, but it's a damn good word to carry an election." And Sen. Boies Penrose defined it candidly as "something to get votes with." With McCARTHYISM, defined by its founder as "Americanism with its sleeves rolled up", the word gained more sinister connotations; the Republican Sen. Margaret Chase Smith observed: "Those who shout the loudest about Americanism in making character assassinations all too frequently ignore some of the basic principles of Americanism: the right to criticize, the right to hold unpopular beliefs, the right to protest, the right to independent thought." And Malcolm X (*see* X) was to state: "I am not an American. I am one of 22 million Black people who are victims of Americanism."

amnesty A general order for the release of prisoners or the pardoning of as yet unpunished offenders, either as an act of clemency on some specific occasion or as a deliberate act of policy. Most controversially, President CARTER announced a partial amnesty for DRAFT DODGERS from the VIETNAM WAR, some of whom had fled to Canada to avoid prosecution. The Provisional IRA for many years convinced its bombers that, even if caught, they would serve only a minimum sentence because the UK government would be bombed into granting an amnesty; it has never done so.

Amnesty International A pressure group, founded in and run from the UK, which monitors the detention of POLITICAL PRISONERS throughout the world, keeps their plight in front of public opinion and campaigns for their release.

General Amnesty Act The Act pushed through the US Congress in 1872 by a coalition of Democrats and Republicans who felt RECONSTRUCTION was going too far, which restored political privileges to all but 500 of the leading former CONFEDERATES; by 1876 only three States were still controlled by radical Republicans elected with Black votes.

anarchism The political philosophy which asserts that human society would function best without any organized government, and that no government can be legitimate unless its actions are truly consented to by those they affect. The 17th-century thinker Thomas Hobbes anticipated the attraction of anarchism, writing in LEVIATHAN: "No man believes that want of government is any new kind of government." Anarchism was pioneered by early 19th-century thinkers including Pierre-Joseph Proudhon, who wrote in 1850: "Our idea of anarchism is launched: non-government is developing as non-property did before." Thirty years later Prince Peter Kropotkin declared: "Permanent revolt by word of mouth, in writing, by the dagger, by the rifle, dynamite . . . everything is good for us which falls outside legality." Such comments created the Victorian stereotype of the anarchist as a bomber from east of the Elbe; anarchists were banned from the United States after one of their number, the American-born Leon Czolgosz, assassinated President McKinley in 1900, and SACCO AND VANZETTI were almost certainly executed for their beliefs. Yet the US anarchist Emma Goldman wrote in 1910: "Anarchism is the only philosophy which brings to man the consciousness of himself," and it remains to many of its adherents a noble creed, though with its innocence bruised by the experience of Spain's sizable anarchist movement at the hands of the Communists during the SPANISH CIVIL WAR.

> Christ was an anarchist who succeeded.
>
> ANDRÉ MALRAUX (1901–76).

> I don't bother to vote. I'm an anarchist anyway. I don't think it makes any difference who has his duke in the till.
>
> ROBERT MITCHUM.

anarcho-syndicalists Anarchist workers who believe in seizing control of their industries through strikes and violence. The movement (*see also* SYNDICALISM), was strong in Republican Spain.

anarchy The total breakdown in order stemming from the absence of an effective government, not to be confused with anarchism, which aims for peace and harmony. Jeremy Bentham (1748–1832) declared that "tyranny and anarchy are never far asunder", while Napoleon saw opportunistically that "anarchy is always the stepping-stone to absolute power".

Lawlessness is lawlessness. Anarchy is anarchy. Neither race nor color nor frustration is an excuse for either lawlessness or anarchy.
US Solicitor-General THURGOOD MARSHALL, 15 August 1966.

ANC African National Congress. The body which led the struggle against APARTHEID within South Africa, and hopes as the representative of the largest number of Black South Africans to become its first fully democratic government. It was formed at Bloemfontein in 1912 as the South African Native National Congress by the Zulu clergyman J. W. Dube "to protect the interests of all coloured peoples in South Africa". Gaining inspiration from the campaigning of MAHATMA Gandhi in South Africa, it formed a common front in 1926 with the Indian community. From 1948 when the NATIONAL PARTY was elected and began to erect the structure of apartheid, the ANC led the non-White resistance, from 1952 to 1967 under the moderate leadership of Chief Albert Luthuli. Together with the more militant PAC, it was banned in 1960, and increasingly turned to violence through its military wing, UMKHONTO WE SIZWE, whose leader Nelson Mandela was arrested in 1962 and jailed for life for sabotage (*see* RIVONIA TRIAL). Oliver Tambo, with strong support from South Africa's hard-line Communist Party, led the ANC from exile during a quarter of a century in which the movement was harassed by Pretoria's undercover squads, maintaining a political organization within the country and conducting occasional guerrilla action. When F.W. de Klerk signalled the end of apartheid, the regime opened secret talks with the ANC and in 1989 Mandela – whose continued imprisonment had sparked world-wide protests – was released to a hero's welcome. Despite his age he took over the leadership from the ailing Tambo, and in 1992 led the ANC into the CODESA talks on a democratic future for the country. However, these were marred by a series of bloody clashes with the tribalist Zulu INKATHA movement, which Pretoria had encouraged as a "safe" non-Marxist alternative to the ANC (*see* BOIPATONG MASSACRE); Mandela temporarily broke off the CODESA talks, but faced growing pressure from younger militants to resume the armed struggle and go for absolute power.

We are not a political party. We are a government in waiting. NELSON MANDELA, 1991.

Andean Pact The agreement signed at Cartagena, Colombia, in 1969 between Bolivia, Chile, Colombia, Ecuador, Peru and Venezuela to enable them to compete with Latin America's more industrialized economies. Chile withdrew in 1977, but rejoined in 1990; Ecuador temporarily withdrew in the early 1980s over a border dispute. The pact (*Acuerdo de Cartagena*) established an Andean Council, a Parliament of five members from each member state meeting in turn in each, and a Court of Justice. Progress on economic development has been made since the introduction in 1984 of an Andean peso to reduce dependency on the dollar, with projects for agriculture, transport, social welfare and education. In 1989 an Andean SUMMIT committed members to closer political links and nuclear ARMS CONTROL.

Anglo-. Anglo-Irish Agreement The agreement concluded in November 1975 between Margaret Thatcher's UK government and the FINE GAEL/Labour coalition headed by Garret FitzGerald which, for the first time, gave the Republic a formal say in the affairs of NORTHERN IRELAND on behalf of its Catholic minority. A regular inter-governmental conference was established to discuss security, political and legal questions and cross-border co-operation, and a joint secretariat comprising officials of the two governments was established in Belfast. The Agreement enraged Ulster LOYALISTS, and the two Unionist parties condemned it as a betrayal and a first step toward the reunification of Ireland over their heads, the more so as Mrs. Thatcher had always taken a stridently pro-Unionist line. For Enoch Powell (*see* POWELLITE), who until now had idolized her, it was the final breach; when she defended the Agreement, he commented: "There you have it, straight from Jezebel's own mouth." There were widespread Loyalist protests and violence the following spring, coupled to an ULSTER SAYS NO campaign in which all the Official Unionist MPs resigned their seats and fought BY-ELECTIONS; all but one were re-elected. The campaign died down, but the Agreement, while improving relations with London and Dublin, showing that Britain was looking for progress and reducing grassroots support for SINN FEIN, did nothing to check the IRA's terrorist campaign for a united Ireland.

Anglo-Saxons The term of abuse used by many French politicians and officials, and President DE GAULLE in particular, for the British and the Americans. The Anglophone world has long been baffled by the resentment shown toward it by the French establishment, apparently combining feelings of cultural contempt and nationalist envy. This resentment surfaced forcibly at the close of 1992 when France endeavoured to sabotage the URUGUAY ROUND of GATT negotiations, at least in part because it could not stomach the role played by Britain in bringing the EC–US talks to a successful conclusion.

Angry Brigade A radical group with ANARCHIST sympathies which instigated a sporadic campaign of bombings and firearms attacks on ESTABLISHMENT targets in the UK in the late 1960s and early 1970s. In most respects a relatively ineffective counterpart to the equally middle-class BAADER-MEINHOF GANG, some of its members were imprisoned for a bomb attack on the home of the Employment Secretary Robert Carr (later Lord Carr of Hadley) in 1971.

animal. Animal Farm One of the most vicious satires on STALINISM, written in 1945 by the British novelist George Orwell (Eric Blair, 1903–50). It was set in a farm where the animals seize control from the farmer and set up a COMMUNE based on equality, only for a pig named Napoleon to grab absolute power under the slogan **All animals are EQUAL, but some are more equal than others**. Any illusions Orwell, a Socialist, may have had about Communism were shattered when he fought in the SPANISH CIVIL WAR and saw at first hand the way the Communists undermined and destroyed their leftist allies; he wrote *Animal Farm* after watching a wartime cinema newsreel praising Stalin as a loyal ally of Britain. The book enraged the KREMLIN and was banned in most Communist countries; it has survived the eclipse of Communism as a parable against all forms of exploitative TOTALITARIANISM.

Animal Liberation Front The militant UK group, acting on behalf of animals but with an entirely human membership, which from the late 1970s has staged numerous acts of violence in protest at cruelty toward captive animals, and animal husbandry in general. Based largely in the West Country, but active throughout the country, its targets have included research laboratories from which animals have been released, and shops which have been firebombed for selling furs and other animal products. Few of the bombers have been caught.

annexation The forcible incorporation of one nation's territory into another; most notoriously NAZI Germany's takeover of the bulk of Poland in September 1939. In almost the same sense, it had been used almost a century before of the courtship by the 52-year-old President Tyler (*see* OLD VETO) of the 23-year-old Washington belle Julia Gardiner, who became his second wife and bore him seven children to add to his previous eight.

Annexation Manifesto The declaration printed by the *Montreal Gazette* in October 1849, signed by more than 300 English-speakers from the city, which called for "a peaceful and friendly separation from [the] British connexion and a union upon equal terms with the great North American Confederacy of Sovereign States". This was one of the few occasions on which a demand for the union of Canada with the United States was put forward with enough vigour to be taken seriously in London.

Annexationists The IMPERIALIST advocates of American acquisition of the Republic of Hawaii which had been declared in 1894, who got their way in 1898 when Congress annexed the islands by joint resolution. They argued for annexation because Hawaii might otherwise fall under foreign (Japanese) control; it would give America a Pacific naval base and offer opportunities for investment. The election of President McKINLEY, a protest by Japan against annexation and the outbreak of the SPANISH-AMERICAN WAR all hastened the step. Hawaii did not gain STATEHOOD until 1959.

Annie's Bar The dingy bolt-hole in the bowels of the Palace of WESTMINSTER, close to the Parliamentary barber's shop, accessible only to MPs and LOBBY journalists, where they can unwind together and exchange political gossip. The original *Annie's*, off the Members' LOBBY, was destroyed when a German bomb hit the Commons CHAMBER on 10 May 1941. The post-war Labour government, at the urgings of its teetotal Chief WHIP William Whiteley who feared Ministers would LEAK confidences too easily, refused to reopen it. It was 1969 before *Annie's* reopened below stairs on the initiative of Robert Maxwell, then chairman of the Commons Catering Committee; Annie, the pre-war barmaid, returned to pull a first ceremonial pint for the Conservative leader Edward Heath. The new *Annie's* fulfilled its purpose for almost a quarter of a century, despite a high correlation between the hard core of MPs frequenting it and those DESELECTED by their constituencies. But in 1992 a firm of American consultants recommended its closure as part of a drive to maximize catering income by making better use of space. *See also* BARLOW MEMORIAL AWARD.

> A useful if well-lubricated workshop for MPs and journalists alike. IAN AITKEN, Evening Standard.

Annuit Coeptis (Lat. he will complete what he has undertaken) One of the many Latin mottoes with Masonic connections inscribed on the insignia of the United States at their inception, and appearing to this day on the dollar bill.

annunciator The system of closed-circuit television in the Palace of Westminster that enables MPs and Peers in other parts of the building to know what is taking place in each

Chamber. When either House is sitting, the annunciator lists the item of business under discussion, who is speaking and how long they have been on their feet. Each system also shows when there is a DIVISION in the other House or in a STANDING COMMITTEE. The system was installed in 1968, replacing an earlier, less widespread, system of piano-keys typing out the name of the member speaking on a continuous paper strip; this had been in service since the 1870s.

another place An alternative to "the OTHER PLACE" as a term used by members of one House at Westminster when referring to the other.

Anschluss (Ger. union, connection) The takeover of Austria by Germany in March 1938, viewed by Hitler and many inhabitants of both countries as a reunification unjustly denied by the Treaty of VERSAILLES after the break-up of the Austro-Hungarian Empire. In 1934 Austrian NAZIS mounted a COUP aimed at unifying the countries; it was put down but Germany continued to interfere in Austria's affairs. Then, in February 1938, Hitler summoned Austria's Chancellor Kurt von Schuschnigg to the EAGLE'S LAIR at Berchtesgaden and demanded that he bring Nazis into his Cabinet. Schuschnigg tried to call a PLEBISCITE on Austrian independence, and resigned when he was frustrated. German troops entered Vienna amid scenes of jubilation on 13 March 1938 and the Anschluss was proclaimed. After Germany's defeat in WORLD WAR II, the victorious Allies ruled out continuation of the union in December 1945 by recognizing the second Austrian Republic.

Anthony amendment The NINETEENTH AMENDMENT to the US CONSTITUTION, also known as the WOMEN'S SUFFRAGE AMENDMENT, that guaranteed women the vote when it was RATIFIED on 26 August 1920. Named after the ABOLITIONIST, Suffragist and temperance campaigner **Susan B. Anthony** (1820–1906), it was first introduced in 1878 by Sen. Aaron Sargent of California. However, it took the advances made by women in WORLD WAR I to persuade Congress to follow a growing number of states, culminating in New York in 1917 after a campaign by the Suffragist Carrie Catt, and grant them the vote. The House backed the amendment on 10 January 1918 amid scenes of counterproductive militancy, and the Senate finally capitulated on 18 August 1920.

anti-. anti-clericalism Opposition to the Roman Catholic church exerting too great an influence over government and public life; a particular force in Republican France.

anti-Communist A COLD WAR campaigner against Communism; also the profession given by one of the accused in the WATERGATE burglary trial. John Foster Dulles maintained that the world was "divided into two kinds of people: Christian anti-communists and the others"; Ronald Reagan declared:

> A Communist reads Marx and Lenin. An anti-Communist understands Marx and Lenin.

Anti-Dühring The book attacking the "reformist" wing of Germany's Social Democratic Party which Friedrich Engels (1820–95) published in 1878; it was directed against the faction's intellectual leader, Eugen Dühring. The ideas set out in it, including that of the withering away of the STATE, made an important impact on a new generation of Socialists.

Anti-Federalists (1) The opponents of RATIFICATION of the US CONSTITUTION in 1787–88; they argued that equal representation for each State in the Senate would disadvantage the most populous states, and that over-large electorates for members of the House would encourage corruption in Congressional elections. (2) The name chosen by UK opponents of moves toward a more centralized European Community in which the COMMISSION would exercise greater power; some self-styled anti-Federalists are in fact ANTI-MARKETEERS.

Anti-Imperialist League The group formed in November 1898 by opponents of US territorial and colonial expansion. It was particularly opposed to the ANNEXATION of the Philippines, but was unable to stop an enterprise that cost more lives than the SPANISH-AMERICAN WAR as Filipinos led by Aguinaldo put up three years of resistance. One of the League's leaders was the PRAIRIE AVENGER William Jennings Bryan, who argued that America had become a world power "without the use of sword or Gatling gun". He said:

> Our form of government, our traditions, our present interests and our future welfare all forbid our entering upon a career of conquest.

anti-intellectualism The strand in politics that deplores the influence of academics and other thinkers on shaping policy and responding to events. The White House aide Jack Valenti said of Lyndon B. Johnson:

> He doesn't like cold intellectuals around him. He wants people who will cry when an old lady falls down in the street.

anti-Marketeers Opponents of UK entry to and membership of the EUROPEAN COMMUNITY; after 20 years of membership and with controversy over Europe as sharp as ever, they frequently masquerade as EURO-SCEPTICS.

Anti-Nazi League A coalition of ANTI-RACIST groups founded in the late 1970s by the UK SOCIALIST WORKERS' PARTY to challenge organizations like the BRITISH MOVEMENT and NATIONAL FRONT on the streets. Though it professed to be a mass movement and gained the backing of a few celebrities, it developed into a group of White radicals and Asian militants whose confrontations with racist demonstrators led to violence, and arrests on both sides.

anti-Racism Organized opposition to RACISM, either through the formation of political or VIGILANTE groups to resist racist demonstrators or attacks, or through public bodies laying down policies on avoiding discrimination against ethnic minorities, and ensuring what they see as sensitive – and critics view as provocative – teaching in schools.

Anti-Saloon League The organization, formed in 1893, which was the driving force for PROHIBITION in America. Combining opposition to liquor with evangelical Protestantism, it had by late 1917 persuaded more than half of the states, with two-thirds of America's population, to ban the liquor traffic; that December Congress passed the EIGHTEENTH AMENDMENT.

anti-Semitism Hatred of and opposition to Jews and all things Jewish, raised into an obscene art form by the NAZIs for whom Heinrich Himmler declared:

> Anti-Semitism is exactly the same as de-lousing. Getting rid of lice is not a question of ideology, it is a matter of cleanliness.

Yet it is also present in most societies that consider themselves civilized. The US academic J. M. Cameron wrote in 1982: "Anti-Semitism circulates in the European bloodstream like a permanent infection"; the 19th-century German writer Treitschke declared: "Wherever he finds his life sullied by the filth of Judaism the German must turn from it, and learn to speak the truth boldly about it," and in 1990 a Western journalist in Warsaw was told: "Why should there not be anti-Semitism in Poland when there are so few Jews left? We have traffic jams, and there are hardly any cars." Even Ulysses S. GRANT was not immune. In 1862 he issued an infamous order – immediately rescinded by LINCOLN – which read:

> The Jews, as a class violating every regulation of trade established by the Treasury Department and also departmental orders, are hereby expelled from the [War] Department within 24 hours from the receipt of this order.

August Bebel called anti-Semitism "the Socialism of fools", while Lloyd George declared: "Of all the bigotries that savage the human temper there is none so stupid." But it has mainly been left to Jews themselves to combat anti-Semitism. When Disraeli was insulted in the Commons by Daniel O'Connell, he replied:

> Yes, I am a Jew, and when the ancestors of the Right Honourable Gentleman were brutal savages in an unknown island, mine were priests in the Temple of Solomon.

A similar riposte was made to an anti-Semitic US Senator by Sen. Judah Philip Benjamin (1811–84); he responded:

> The gentleman will please remember that when his half-civilized ancestors were hunting the wild boar in Silesia, mine were princes of the earth.

Anti-Trust Laws The legislation under which various US administrations have sought to break the power of Monopolies and Trusts and to create a framework for genuine economic competition. It is policed by the Anti-Trust division of the Justice Department. Popular pressure to weaken the Trusts, and especially those controlling many of America's railroads, came to a head in 1889 after years when the Senate, in particular, had been widely perceived to be in their pocket. President Benjamin Harrison recommended Congressional action and in 1890 the SHERMAN ACT was passed. Few prosecutions followed until Theodore Roosevelt became President, and the scope of the law was broadened by the CLAYTON ANTITRUST ACT of 1914.

anti-war movement The loose coalition of radical and liberal groups opposed to the VIETNAM WAR. Large and at times unruly rallies were held in New York and Californian centres from 1965; and in 1967, as the protests grew in size, Dr. Martin Luther KING proposed a merger of the anti-war and CIVIL RIGHTS movements. The movement played a key if unofficial part in the ending of Lyndon B. Johnson's Presidency. In the fall of 1969 millions demonstrated against the war across America, Vice-President AGNEW dismissing them as "an effete corps of snobs who characterized themselves as INTELLECTUALS". The most tragic event of the anti-war campaign occurred with the KENT STATE shootings in May 1970, and the following April 2000 Vietnam veterans rallied against the war in Washington, many throwing their medals on to the Capitol steps. Protests and CIVIL DISOBEDIENCE tailed off as the withdrawal of US troops began.

Anyone for Denis? The farce based on life at NUMBER TEN Downing Street in the early years of Margaret Thatcher's government, which was staged at the Whitehall Theatre *c.* 1982 with Angela Thorne as the Prime Minister and John Wells as her husband, Denis; it ran for a considerable time. The title was a play on the old cliché "Anyone for tennis?"; in the play Mrs. Thatcher was portrayed as a forceful master in her own home and her husband as an amiable buffer with a taste for gin who had shrewdly developed his own techniques for survival. The tone of the play owed a considerable amount to the DEAR BILL column in PRIVATE EYE; Wells was co-author of both.

ANZUS Treaty A mutual defence treaty signed in 1951 by Australia, New Zealand and America, under which each pledged to defend itself against the common danger (of Communist aggression) and declared that an attack on any signatory was a threat to all. From the mid-1980s the pact became a dead letter as New Zealand refused to accept any US ships without an undertaking that they carried no nuclear arms, and Australia also went through an anti-nuclear phase.

apartheid (Afrik. apartness) The policy of racial SEGREGATION implemented by the NATIONAL PARTY in South Africa between its coming to power in 1948 and the reforms pushed through by President F.W. de Klerk from 1989. It was denounced by almost every other country in the world, prompting virtual ostracism of South Africa in the worlds of sport and culture and widespread, but not consistently enforced, trade SANCTIONS. At home it was bitterly resisted both by liberal Whites (*see* BLACK SASH) and both moderate and militant Africans and Coloureds (*see* ANC; BLACK CONSCIOUSNESS; PAC). Such resistance led to the TREASON and RIVONIA trials, the imprisonment of key activists like Nelson Mandela, and also to the SHARPEVILLE massacre and other atrocities. Segregation already existed in 1948, but the National Party extended and codified it through measures including the POPULATION REGISTRATION ACT of 1950 and the GROUP AREAS ACT; movement of non-Whites was controlled by the notorious PASS LAWS. Other laws banned mixed marriages, established separate education, and prohibited non-White participation in government. The policy also encouraged African tribalism, to keep Black South Africans from drifting to the cities and developing a middle class and political organization, and as a form of "divide and rule"; this same policy lay behind the encouragement given the Zulu INKATHA movement to take on the ANC as apartheid was dismantled. From 1970 most Africans were held to be citizens of tribal BANTUSTANS or Homelands, which were declared independent and generally given the poorest land. However millions were by now living in townships from which they poured daily to work in the cities; it was here that the outlawed ANC developed its strength. Apartheid began to wither in the 1980s as the demand for labour outstripped the availability of qualified Whites, and as world pressure and internal resistance began to bite. Yet while the ANC was legalized in 1990 and the CODESA talks began on a multiracial constitution, doubts remained as to whether the Afrikaner establishment would yield up power without a fight.

> We did what God intended us to do.
> Prime Minister Dr. HENRIK VERWOERD, 1961.

> We don't want apartheid liberalised. We want it dismantled. You can't improve something that's intrinsically evil. Archbishop DESMOND TUTU, 1985.

> All oppression is repugnant, but there is an obscenity about oppression based on no more than the colour of a person's skin.
> Australian Prime Minister MALCOLM FRASER, Lusaka, August 1979.

apathy Lack of interest by the electors, much decried by politicians but useful to them when potentially unpopular policies fail to spark opposition, and consequently a danger if a fanatical minority is in sight of power. Edmund BURKE maintained that "the only thing necessary for the triumph of evil is for good men to do nothing", and US Treasury Secretary Bill Simon that "bad politicians are sent to Washington by good people who don't want to vote". After the 1989 European elections, Ireland's TANAISTE Brian Lenihan observed: "There was so much apathy that Pat O'Connor only voted once." O'Connor, Charles HAUGHEY's election agent, was known as Pat Pat O'Connor because he had once been convicted of voting twice.

> I am not prepared to go about the country stirring up apathy. WILLIAM WHITELAW (*see* WILLIE, *attr.*).

apologize One of the hardest things for politicians to do, but which will be required of them if they breach Parliamentary etiquette or are to survive the exposure of personal misjudgment or wrongdoing. Joseph Chamberlain's motto was "Never apologize, never explain, never retract;" Spiro Agnew's "Apologize now. It will save time later." UK Transport Secretary Paul Channon, son of CHIPS, described his post as "the only job I know where you are expected to apologize to others when they are late for your meetings". In the Chamber an apology to the CHAIR can be a humiliating experience, but a gifted speaker can turn it to advantage. When Barbara Castle, Transport Secretary in the late 1960s, complained that Iain Macleod had accused her of not knowing what she was doing, Macleod's apology was damning:

> It seems that during the previous debate I suggested the Right Honourable Lady did not know what she was doing. I ask the House to consider what they would have thought of me if I had suggested that she did know what she was doing.

apologist A writer, pamphleteer or speaker who concentrates on justifying the actions and policies of a particular régime, party or group.

Apostles The semi-secret and self-perpetuating dining club formed by undergraduates at Trinity College, Cambridge, in the mid-1930s; seen at the time as a harmless exercise in snobbery, it turned out during the BLUNT CASE to have been one of the most fertile recruiting grounds for Soviet spies.

apparatchik An originally Soviet term for a BUREAUCRAT, *apparat* being the Communist Party machine; it has come to imply someone who carries out robotically any task they are instructed to perform. Not surprisingly, it has gained world-wide currency. When Robert H. BORK was asked by Senators during his abortive CONFIRMATION hearings if he would ever resign as a Justice of the Supreme Court, he told them:

> I don't want to be regarded as an apparatchik, an organization man who does whatever the organization wants.

appeasement The word used by Neville CHAMBERLAIN for his dealings with Hitler (notably at MUNICH) in the late 1930s, which has become a byword throughout the world for weakness in the face of bullying. Chamberlain's hope at the time was to mollify Hitler and concede enough of other nations' territory to satisfy NAZI ambitions; the justification now advanced is that he bought valuable time for Britain to defend itself when war, inevitably, broke out. Sir Robert Vansittart (1881–1957), permanent secretary at the Foreign Office, wrote at the close of 1936 when the threat was already forming:

> Time is the very material commodity which the Foreign Office is expected to provide in the same way as other departments provide OTHER war material.

The policy was bitterly opposed by CHURCHILL, who cuttingly described an appeaser as "one who feeds a crocodile, hoping it will eat him last". And on 13 March 1940, during the phoney war, Lloyd George told the Commons:

> It is the old trouble – too late in dealing with Czechoslovakia, too late with Poland, and certainly too late with Finland. It is always too late, or too little, or both. That is the road to disaster.

Appeasement has had a bad press ever since. During the Truman administration, Sen. William Jenner attacked General George Marshall (*see* MARSHALL AID) as "an errand boy, a front man, a stooge, or a conspirator for this administration's crazy assortment of COLLECTIVIST cut-throat crackpots and communist FELLOW-TRAVELING appeasers". And as the SUEZ CRISIS approached in 1956, the Conservative MP Sir Godfrey Nicholson told the Commons:

> Appeasement has never won a race yet. It is a bad horse, bred by good intentions out of paralysis of will.

Appomattox courthouse The crossroads in Virginia, 20 miles north-east of Lynchburg, where America's CIVIL WAR formally ended on 9 April 1865, though some fighting continued elsewhere until July. Robert E. Lee handed his sword to Ulysses S. Grant and the two Generals agreed terms: his 27,800 CONFEDERATE troops to return home, with their horses for the spring ploughing and rations from Union stores, and a promise that no Confederate soldier, from Lee downwards, would face punishment provided they kept to the terms of their parole. LINCOLN's reaction was that it was "providential" Congress was out of session; he told his Cabinet on 14 April: "We should get the Union re-established before Congress comes together in December." That evening he was assassinated.

apportionment The allocation of seats in the US HOUSE OF REPRESENTATIVES between the various states, on the basis of the 10-yearly census. The Bureau of the Census works out how many of the 435 Representatives each State is entitled to, and its computation becomes law unless Congress changes the formula.

Apprentice Boys of Derry One of the most prestigious events in the ORANGE calendar in Northern Ireland is the Apprentice Boys' procession at the height of the MARCHING SEASON. Both a gesture of defiance towards the Catholic majority in the city and a reaffirmation of LOYALIST determination, it commemorates the arrival of food supplies on 28 July 1689 to relieve the siege of Derry by Catholic forces loyal to the ousted King James II. The siege has come, with the Battle of the BOYNE, to occupy a central place in Unionist mythology. The city's military governor, Robert Lundy, advised surrender as the JACOBITE forces – which were not over-strong – closed in, and fled when his advice was rejected; at the end of the commemoration each year he is burned in effigy. For two months, 30,000 Protestant refugees held out within the city's walls before being relieved, an event Loyalists now hail as decisive to the survival of their community.

appropriations The allocation by the US Congress of funds for spending on particular projects, a task co-ordinated by Committees in the House and Senate overseeing a network of sub-committees (13 in the House) for each area of expenditure. The system and process provide endless opportunities to alter the Administration's budgetary priorities.

> All were agreed on one point, however. If Congress would make a sufficient appropriation, a colossal benefit would result. MARK TWAIN.

approval rating The barometer of public confidence in a political leader provided by OPINION POLLS. Voters are asked whether they are satisfied or dissatisfied with a particular politician's performance, and the approval rating is the positive figure given, *i.e.* 67% support is converted by SPIN DOCTORS into a "67% approval rating". For a leader in trouble, an approval rating below 30% is not unknown; at times like that, the spin doctors are nowhere to be seen.

après moi le déluge (Fr. after me, the flood) A saying associated with most ABSOLUTE rulers who have considered themselves indispensable, but in fact said after the Battle of Rossbach in 1757 by Madame de Pompadour (1721–1764), the mistress of King Louis XV of France, who was widely blamed for the Thirty Years' War. It was used a century later by the Austrian statesman Metternich.

April Fool! One of the most unexpected moments in the US HOUSE OF REPRESENTATIVES came early in April 1941, when Rep. Robert Fleming Rich, a grumpy PROHIBITIONist Republican from Pennsylvania, rose to his feet. Rich so often intervened with bad-tempered cries of "Where are we going to get the money?" that colleagues would roar the words in unison when he stood up. This time, Rich got his own back: he simply exclaimed: "April Fool!" and sat down again, to tumultuous applause.

Arab. Arab boycott *See* BOYCOTT.

Arab League An organization of states, originally 22 in number, founded in 1945 to foster economic, political and cultural co-operation throughout the Arab world. The League has experienced divisions on many issues, notably the status of Israel, the formation of a Palestinian state, the Lebanese civil war (for which it established an Arab deterrent Force in 1976), and the crisis precipitated between Arab nations by Iraq's invasion of Kuwait in 1990 and the subsequent GULF WAR.

Aras na Uachtarain The formal title, in Irish, of the official residence of Ireland's President in Phoenix Park, Dublin.

arbitration The process whereby an inter-governmental, commercial or industrial dispute is referred to a third party who will consider the arguments put to him by both sides and then propose a decision, which in many cases will be binding. **Pendulum arbitration** is a process advocated by some industrial relations lawyers, and formerly by Britain's SDP, under which the arbitrator is obliged to accept one side's case *in toto*; the purpose is to ensure that each submits realistic demands, instead of inflating them in the hope of gaining more.

Archivist of the United States The Federal official who not only supervises the National Archives containing America's most historic documents, but is charged with submitting any AMENDMENT to the Constitution approved by a two-thirds vote of both Houses of Congress to the States for RATIFICATION.

Ard Fheis (Ir. high summit) The title given in the Irish Republic for the annual CONFERENCES of most political parties.

are. Are you better off than you were four years ago? Ronald Reagan's most telling line in his televised DEBATE with Jimmy CARTER in Cleveland on 28 October 1980; it was reputedly written for him by David Gergen.

Are you now, or have you ever been, a member of the Communist Party? The stock question asked by Rep. J. Parnell Thomas (1895–1970) at sittings of the House UN-AMERICAN ACTIVITIES Committee between 1947 and 1957.

Arena (Sp. *Alianza Republicana Nacionalista*, National Republican Alliance) The right-wing party in El Salvador whose candidate, Alfredo Cristiani, came to power in the central American country's March 1989 Presidential election. To the surprise of Western liberals (and of the Salvadorean far right), Cristiani not only took tough action against the left-wing FMLN guerrillas, who had boycotted the elections, but cracked down on the DEATH SQUADS linked to the military; this raised hopes, which have persisted, that the CONTADORA peace plan for the region could eventually succeed.

Argentinian firecracker The stage name of the striptease dancer Fanne Foxe (Annabell Battistella), with whom the veteran Arkansas Congressman Wilbur Mills (1910–92) had a highly public dalliance which cost him the chairmanship of WAYS AND MEANS. Mills, who served 38 years in Congress, had wielded awesome power from his chair for 17 years; when he caught POTOMAC FEVER in 1971, one colleague asked him: "Wilbur, why do you want to run for President and lose your grip on the country?" Then, at 2 a.m. on 7 October 1974, 38-year-old Ms. Foxe jumped out of his car and threw herself into Washington's Tidal Basin; she was rescued by police patrolmen who had just booked Mills for speeding and driving without lights. Mills was re-elected the following month after warning his constituents against "drinking champagne with foreigners", but that December he appeared on stage with Ms. Foxe at the Boston Burlesque Theater, and admitted that he was an alcoholic – something colleagues had known for years. In May 1977, after several attempts to dry out, he was stripped of his chairmanship. Mills served out his term, then took a well-paid job as a tax consultant; Ms. Foxe made a low-budget movie that was pulled from a Washington cinema after one night.

Argumenti i Fakti (Russ. arguments and facts) The weekly paper that served as the organ of GLASNOST in Soviet Russia as Mikhail Gorbachev's reforms got under way from 1986. Its circulation rocketed into the millions as readers wrote in with complaints about the way the system was operating, and ideas for making it work better.

aristocracy (Gr. government by the best) (1) A system of government in which the "best" – those of a superior social class – take the decisions. Aristotle termed it "that form of government in which education and discipline are qualifications for suffrage and office-holding"; the 19th-century Russian revolutionary Alexander Herzen saw it rather differently: "a more or less civilized form of cannibalism". (2) The privileged social class itself, the **aristocrats**, in Britain being identified with hereditary PEERS and their families. Mirabeau, from across the Channel, saw it as "the intermediary between the King and the people, just as a sporting dog is the intermediary between the sportsmen and the hare", and Heinrich Heine referred to aristocrats in general as "asses who talk about horses". Yet the most vitriolic comments were made by Lloyd George, when the HOUSE OF LORDS was trying to wreck his PEOPLE'S BUDGET. He said:

> An aristocracy is like cheese; the older it is, the higher it becomes.

and

> A fully-equipped DUKE costs as much to keep up as two Dreadnoughts, and Dukes are just as great a terror – and they last longer.

It is wrong to assume that the word "aristocracy" means nothing in America. Despite the absence of a titled nobility, there has been no shortage of self-important people eager to fill the vacuum. Ralph Waldo Emerson described each such "aristocrat" as "a democrat ripe and gone to seed".

> An aristocrat in a republic is like a chicken whose head has been cut off. It may run about in a lively way, but in fact it is dead. NANCY MITFORD (1904–73), *Noblesse Oblige*.

Arlington National Cemetery The 500 acres of Virginia hillside facing across the POTOMAC to WASHINGTON where many of the great of America are buried – together with 163,000 dead from every one of the nation's wars. President TAFT, L'Enfant, the planner of Washington, William Jennings Bryan (*see* PRAIRIE AVENGER), Abraham LINCOLN's son Robert, John F. KENNEDY and Robert F. Kennedy are all buried there. JFK's tomb with its eternal flame lies close to the Custis-Lee Mansion, built in 1802 by George WASHINGTON's adoptive son and later the home of Robert E. Lee, whose memorial the house now is. The cemetery was designated in 1864, an act later held illegal by the Supreme Court which ordered the Lee family to be compensated. The first burial, on 13 May 1865, was of a Confederate prisoner who had died in hospital; the Memorial Amphitheatre to America's dead in World War I was dedicated in 1920, and the Tomb of the Unknown Soldier in 1932.

Armalite and ballot box The twin strategy of the Provisional IRA: aiming to force Britain to give up control over NORTHERN IRELAND through a campaign of violence, and making electoral gains in Nationalist areas through Provisional SINN FEIN, its POLITICAL WING. The Armalite is the US-made rifle which is the Provisionals' basic weapon.

armed conflict The term used by Anthony EDEN to describe the Anglo-French intervention at SUEZ in 1956, which he insisted was not an act of war. Eden told the House of Commons on 4 November 1956:

> We are not at war with Egypt. We are in a state of armed conflict.

armistice The cessation of hostilities while a peace settlement is negotiated. **Armistice Day** was 11 November 1918, the day WORLD WAR I ended; it is commemorated in Britain as **Remembrance Day** on the nearest Sunday. *See also* CENOTAPH.

armoured train The train in which TROTSKY toured the infant Soviet Union to rally the RED ARMY during the CIVIL WAR with the WHITES that followed the BOLSHEVIK revolution. Covered with thick steel plate as protection against artillery fire and plastered with revolutionary slogans, it served as Trotsky's mobile military headquarters, and was guarded by troops hand-picked for their loyalty and commitment.

arms. arms control The generic term of the various processes by which the international community, and specific nations, have endeavoured to halt and reverse the ARMS RACE. It has embraced apparently interminable negotiations in Geneva involving the SUPERPOWERS and various combinations of other countries, depending on whether nuclear or conventional weapons are involved and which potential theatres of conflict are concerned. It has led over the years to the CFE, INF, SALT and START agreements. In America such negotiations have since 1961 been the province of the Arms Control and Disarmament Agency (ACDA), though in the early years of the Reagan administration the negotiating process was in the hands of HAWKS rather than disarmers.

arms crisis The upheaval in the Irish Republic in 1970 when two FIANNA FAIL Cabinet Ministers, Charles HAUGHEY and Neil Blaney, and the TD Kevin Boland, stood trial for alleged GUN-RUNNING to the IRA. All were acquitted, Haughey denouncing the process as a "political trial"; nevertheless the Ministers were dismissed by the TAOISEACH, Jack Lynch.

arms for hostages The notion behind the IRAN-CONTRA affair: the idea that by supplying Iran with arms, America could obtain enough leverage in Teheran to secure the release of Western HOSTAGES held by Islamic militants in Beirut.

arms race The race between the SUPERPOWERS throughout the COLD WAR to establish a clear lead over each other in nuclear weaponry, both in terms of quantity and effectiveness.

> We have a three to one advantage over the Russians, which I understand means we have the potential to kill all the Russians twice and they have the potential to kill us one and a quarter times.
>
> Sen. EUGENE McCARTHY, 1968.

> The Soviets have been quite single-minded. They increased their defense expenditures as we increased ours. And they increased their defense expenditures as we decreased ours.
>
> US Defence Secretary HAROLD BROWN, 1979.

> The nuclear arms race has no military purpose.
>
> Earl MOUNTBATTEN of Burma, Strasbourg, 1979.

> We have gone on piling weapon upon weapon, missile upon missile, new levels of destructiveness upon old levels. . . . Like the victims of some kind of hypnotism, like men in a dream, like lemmings heading for the sea, like the children of Hamelin marching blindly behind their Pied Piper.
>
> GEORGE F. KENNAN, 1982.

right to keep and bear arms *See* RIGHT.

Army-McCarthy hearings *See* McCARTHY.

Arnold. Benedict Arnold US shorthand for a turncoat or traitor. The original Benedict Arnold (1741–1801) was a major-general in the Revolutionary army who, given the command of West Point in 1780, conspired with the British to surrender the garrison. When his intrigue was discovered, he fled to the British and fought for them until 1781, when he took refuge in England.

Arthur, Chester *See* ELEGANT ARTHUR.

Aryanism The basic test imposed on all Germans by the NAZIs in the mid- to late 1930s, to establish racial purity and disqualify all those with any element of Jewish descent from participating in the Master Race. A certificate of Aryanism was required for any official post, and lack of it meant exclusion from the professions and eventually from society. Hitler had foreshadowed the drawing of such a distinction in MEIN KAMPF, which stressed the supremacy of the Aryan (originally an Indo-Persian) race.

As of now, I am in control here in the White House, pending the return of the Vice-President The statement issued by Secretary of State Alexander Haig on 30 March 1981 shortly after John Hinckley's attempt to assassinate President Reagan. With George BUSH flying back to Washington from Texas, it was intended to show the people that the situation was under control despite the serious injuries the President had suffered, and that there was no cause for panic. However, Haig exceeded his constitutional powers, and the statement was seen by other senior members of the Administration as a grab for power. They praised Haig publicly for his prompt action, then sidelined him.

Ascendancy The ethos of 18th-century Ireland under Anglo-Irish Protestant domination, prior to the NINETY-EIGHT and the UNION with England. The social elite looked back on it as a golden age; the average Irish family as a period of spectacular irrelevance to real life and their day-to-day problems.

ASEAN Association of South East Asian Nations. The grouping of states at the west of the PACIFIC RIM, formed in 1967 to promote collective economic and political stability. Founded by Indonesia, Malaysia, the Philippines, Thailand, Singapore and Brunei, ASEAN has become a steadily stronger voice in the world with the rapid development of its members' economies.

ASIO Australian Security Intelligence Organization. The agency, formed in 1949, that seeks to protect Australia and its institutions from internal and external threat.

Overseas intelligence gathering is handled by an offshoot, ASIS (Australian Secret Intelligence Service). ASIO was set up because of suspected Soviet penetration of the Department of External Affairs in Canberra, and the PETROV CASE was an early success. Until 1968 it was run with an iron hand by Sir Charles Spry, who had lobbied for its creation. Close links were established with the CIA and MI5, and at least one MI5 officer joined it because he believed his own agency was penetrated by Soviet agents. ASIO went through a controversial patch in the 1970s when Labor Ministers accused it of keeping them under surveillance – one, Lionel Murphy, having its headquarters raided in a vain search for hostile files; there was also an embarrassing incident when agents "hijacked" a Sydney hotel as part of a training exercise without the police or hotel management being informed. ASIO has since regained its equilibrium.

Asquith, Herbert Henry (1st Earl of Oxford and Asquith, 1852–1928), Prime Minister (Liberal) from 1908 to 1916 and the last head of a purely Liberal government. A Yorkshire-born barrister, he became MP for East Fife in 1886 and six years later was HOME SECRETARY under Gladstone, whose biographer Sir Philip Magnus rated him "the best Home Secretary of the century". In opposition he was a LIBERAL IMPERIALIST during the BOER WAR, and on the party's return to power in 1905 took part in the RELUGAS COMPACT which aimed to make Asquith, rather than Campbell-Bannerman, effective head of the government; a fellow-member of the Compact, Lord Haldane, wrote: "From the beginning [he] meant to be Prime Minister." Campbell-Bannerman hung on, yet made Asquith Chancellor; on C-B's death early in 1908 he was the obvious successor. Asquith's Cabinet included such vibrant figures as Lloyd George (*see* L. G.) and the young CHURCHILL, and kept up a reforming programme including DISESTABLISHMENT of the Welsh church, the foundations of the WELFARE STATE, and the curbing of the powers of the HOUSE OF LORDS when it resisted the PEOPLE'S BUDGET. Asquith was ready to force the creation of hundreds of Liberal peers to get the Budget through, telling King George V:

> I hold my office not only by favour of the Crown, but by the confidence of the people, and I should be guilty indeed of treason if in this supreme moment of a great struggle I were to betray their trust.

His government was also dogged by agitation for VOTES FOR WOMEN, which Asquith opposed, the slide toward war with Germany (*see* WE WANT EIGHT AND WE WON'T WAIT), growing industrial unrest and steadily-increasing tension in Ireland as HOME RULE legislation was finally enacted. Asquith faced down the CURRAGH MUTINY, but the situation in Ireland was explosive when war broke out in Europe. Asquith was appalled by the implications of war, and disconcerted by the attention it brought him, saying:

> I have never before been a popular character with the man in the street, and in all this dark and dangerous business it gives me scant pleasure.

He was not a great war leader, prosecuting the conflict conscientiously but without imagination; Lady Tree once tellingly asked him at dinner: "Mr. Asquith, do you take an interest in the war?" He also moved only slowly to form a wartime COALITION, his biographer Roy Jenkins writing: "Although he had always been a moderate in politics, he hated the idea of bringing Tories into his Cabinet," and after two years of stalemate on the battlefield Lloyd George conspired with the Conservatives to oust him. His colleague Lord Grey lamented: "He took no trouble to secure his own position or to add to his general reputation."

Asquith remained leader of the Liberal Party, and his insistence on keeping the position as L. G. flirted with the Tories opened up a damaging and probably fatal split. Asquith remarked:

> Now that Lloyd George calls me a lunatic and Carson calls me a traitor, I begin to feel sure that I must be on the right lines.

Episodes such as the MAURICE LETTER and the HONOURS SCANDAL distanced the two men still further, and after the coalition broke up in 1922 each Liberal faction lost heavily at the polls, with Labour moving up to take power. Asquith lost his seat in 1918, but returned in 1920 after a spectacular BY-ELECTION victory at Paisley, where he was finally unseated in 1923. He did not finally give up the party leadership until 1926, by which time he had taken a PEERAGE.

Asquith was renowned for his mental precision, Churchill writing: "His mind opened and shut smoothly and exactly, like the breech of a gun," and Lord Robert Cecil reminiscing that "he brought to Cabinet meetings the cold calculation he displayed at the bridge table". His stamina was renowned, his son Cyril writing: "He could stand more in the way of late hours and airless meetings than any other public man. It was a matter of indifference to him whether he inhaled cigar smoke or oxygen." His obsession with detail was also legendary; Lloyd George observed:

> Asquith worries too much about small points. If you were buying a large mansion he would come to you and say:

"Have you thought there is no accommodation for the cat?"

This trait could land him in trouble. Once a HECKLER, referring to an episode when he was Home Secretary, called out: "Why did you murder the miners at Featherstone in '92?" Instead of denying the charge as he was entitled to, he replied: "It was not '92, it was '93."

Asquith was not regarded as a great speaker, W. T. Stead terming him "a forensic gladiator who never made a heart beat quicker by his words, and who never by any possibility brought a lump into his hearers' throats". Yet he was well-read and articulate, though John Morley described him as "unduly cassant". He knew that he could seem a plodder, once saying to his second wife, the socialite Margot Tennant:

Character is better than brains, and loyalty more valuable than either, but I shall have to work with the material that has been given to me.

She said of his public image: "His modesty amounts to a deformity," but also described him as "a cold, unsympathetic man, loved by none, admired by a few". Asquith became a heavy drinker; Lord Alfred Douglas christened him **Old Squiffy** and the word stuck to describe anyone who over-indulged. Yet Bonar Law remarked: "Asquith, when drunk, could make a better speech than any of us sober." His biographer Roy Jenkins (*see* WOY) observed that "there was always in his character a surprising but strong streak of recklessness", and this showed in the stream of mildly compromising notes he wrote to the young Venetia Stanley – even from the Government front bench – until her marriage.

Bland and wicked, and with only a nodding acquaintance with the truth. LADY CUNARD.

Arthur Balfour is wicked and moral. Asquith is good and immoral. CHURCHILL.

The inveterate lack of ideals and imagination seems really unredeemed; when one has peeled off the brown paper wrapping of phrases and compromise – just nothing at all. LYTTON STRACHEY.

For twenty years he has held a season ticket on the line of least resistance, and gone wherever the train of events has carried him, lucidly justifying his position at whatever point he has happened to find himself.
LEO AMERY in the House of Commons, 1916.

With him died the best part of the classical tradition in English politics. ROY JENKINS.

assassination Political murder, described by George Bernard Shaw as "the extreme form of censorship". Its victims over the centuries have included Julius Caesar, the British Prime Minister Spencer Perceval, Abraham LINCOLN, Archduke Franz Ferdinand at SARAJEVO, John F. KENNEDY and his brother Robert, Dr. Martin Luther KING, MAHATMA Gandhi, Indira Gandhi and the former Swedish premier Olof Palme. The word derives from the *assassins*, a fanatical Islamic sect founded at the end of the 11th century who terrorized Persia and Syria for over 200 years; those who carried out their missions were rewarded with gifts of hashish, hence the name. Under EXECUTIVE ORDER 12333, signed by President Reagan in 1981, "no person employed by or acting on behalf of the US government shall engage in or conspire to engage in assassination" of foreign leaders, no matter how hostile they are to America's interests.

absolutism tempered by assassination *See* ABSOLUTISM.

character assassination Efforts by a person's political opponents to destroy his or her reputation so that he or she is removed as a potential threat.

association The term used by Britain's Conservatives and Liberal Democrats to describe their organization in each CONSTITUENCY; one of their MPs will talk of "my Association". Labour's equivalent is the CLP.

Aswan High Dam The massive construction project in Egypt whose funding precipitated the SUEZ CRISIS of 1956. The Eqyptian leader Colonel Nasser NATIONALIZED the Suez Canal Company to finance the construction of the dam after America withdrew its offer of funds; the Eisenhower administration felt Cairo was establishing over-close ties with Moscow. The $1 billion dam was finally opened in 1971; the temple of Abu Simbel had to be raised before the waters rose. It created Lake Nasser, the world's largest reservoir controlling the irrigation of over 3 million acres.

at. at a stroke *See* STROKE.

at-large A US term for the election of a legislator or official by all the voters of a state or city, instead of simply by those of a DISTRICT or WARD. At-large elections to the House of Representatives – save for those States electing only one member – were abolished in 1967.

Atlantic. Atlantic Alliance A commonly-used term for NATO, emphasizing America's role in the defence of western Europe.

Atlantic Charter The eight-point declaration of principles on which peace was to be based after the defeat of the AXIS powers in WORLD WAR II, agreed by President Roosevelt and Winston CHURCHILL on 14 August 1941 at secret meetings on warships off the Newfoundland coast. Conclusion of the Charter, comparable to WILSON's FOURTEEN POINTS but less ambitious, was cited by Axis leaders as evidence that FDR had already taken

America into the war; its commitment to "final destruction of the Nazi tyranny" was hard to reconcile with US neutrality. Churchill hoped that it would "make Japan ponder", but four months later PEARL HARBOR was attacked. The Charter also made first mention of the UNITED NATIONS, a term originated by Roosevelt to avoid the impression that he was concluding an alliance without the permission of Congress.

Atlanticist A Western European committed to close strategic, diplomatic and cultural co-operation with America; the term is used as a mild pejorative by left-wingers for enthusiastic supporters of NATO and, implicitly, of nuclear weapons.

atomic bomb The bomb depending on nuclear fission, whose successful detonation in New Mexico on 16 July 1945 confronted humanity with the prospect of being exterminated by the hand of its leaders. The basic technique developed by the MANHATTAN PROJECT was to bring together sufficient quantities of fissile material (a critical mass) to prompt a self-sustaining uncontrolled chain reaction. When J. Robert Oppenheimer (1904–67), the director of the project, saw the awesome power of the first explosion and its MUSHROOM CLOUD, he thought of a quotation from the *Bhagavad Gita*:

> I am become Death, the shatterer of worlds.

A number of senior scientists on the project were so horrified at their creation that they suggested its destructive power should be publicly demonstrated to the Japanese. Oppenheimer and key figures in the Truman administration opposed this, and the bomb was first dropped on HIROSHIMA on 6 August. Three days later another was used against NAGASAKI, after which Japan capitulated. These are the only two occasions on which nuclear weapons have been used in warfare, though the threat was ever-present during the COLD WAR, once the Soviet Union had produced its own bomb in 1949. Britain from 1952, France from 1960, China (1964) and India (1974) also have nuclear weapons, and Israel, Pakistan, South Africa and possibly Brazil, Algeria and Taiwan have the capability; Iraq was close to achieving it when forced by the UNITED NATIONS to destroy its nuclear plants after the GULF WAR.

> If only I had known, I would have become a watchmaker.
> ALBERT EINSTEIN, 1945.

> The greatest thing in history. HARRY S TRUMAN, 1945.

See PAPER TIGER.

Atoms for Peace The programme pioneered by the Eisenhower administration to loan US uranium to nations willing to use it for peaceful purposes.

> There is no evil in the atom – only in men's souls.
> ADLAI STEVENSON.

Attlee, Clement (later Earl) Attlee (1883–1967), the apparently uncharismatic man of few words who led Britain's LABOUR PARTY for 20 years, served with distinction as CHURCHILL's wartime deputy, and from 1945 to 1951 led the great reforming government that created the WELFARE STATE. An Oxford-educated lawyer converted to Socialism by experience of the East London slums, Attlee returned from World War I with the rank of major to become Mayor of Stepney. Elected to Parliament in 1922, he held junior posts under RAMSAY MACDonald prior to the GREAT BETRAYAL of 1931; one of the relatively few Labour MPs to hold their seats in the subsequent election, he was elected leader in 1935 "for the remaining weeks of the Parliamentary term" in place of George Lansbury. Hugh Dalton categorized the contest between Attlee and Herbert Morrison as "a choice between a nonentity and a drunk". Labour's fortunes recovered a little at the 1935 election, and by the outbreak of war Attlee had done much to restore its morale. In 1940 his refusal to take Labour into a COALITION under anyone other than Churchill was decisive; Attlee became a key member of the War CABINET, deputizing for Churchill whenever he was out of the country. Churchill respected Attlee, but found his readiness to stand up to the great man disconcerting, saying: "He combines a limited outlook with strong qualities of resistance."

With Germany defeated in May 1945, Attlee withdrew Labour from the coalition and precipitated an election; the party chairman Harold Laski was convinced he would lead it to defeat (*see* THANK YOU FOR YOUR LETTER), but in the event Labour won a LANDSLIDE victory. Attlee took office facing formidable problems: a crippled economy, run-down industries, a serious housing shortage, bloated armed forces to demobilize, Imperial commitments far beyond Britain's capacity to sustain, the incipient COLD WAR and crisis in the Middle East. He also had to meet the high expectations of the voters, especially the ex-servicemen who had voted Labour in millions, and to keep the peace between such giants in his Cabinet as Morrison, Ernest Bevin (*see* BEVIN BOYS) and Aneurin Bevan (see NYE). The late 1940s under Attlee's leadership were the heyday of democratic Socialism as key industries were NATIONALIZED, the National Health Service (NHS) established and India granted its independence. Attlee saw Britain through a crippling

FUEL CRISIS in 1947 and serious economic difficulties culminating in DEVALUATION in 1949. He pressed ahead with the development of an independent nuclear DETERRENT, backed the establishment of NATO and GERMAN REARMAMENT (unpopular with his left wing), joined in the KOREAN WAR and acquiesced in the foundation of ISRAEL, to which the party, though not all his Ministers, was warmly committed. The 1945 Government had its embarrassments, including the BUDGET LEAK and the GROUNDNUT SCHEME, but never lost a seat in a by-election and increased its vote in 1950. But it now had only a tiny majority and was running out of steam; Attlee called a further election at the end of 1951, and lost. He stayed on as leader for more than three years, taking the heat from the campaigning of the BEVANITES for more left-wing policies, but retired in 1955 once he was certain Morrison would not succeed him. Attlee went to the House of Lords with an EARLDOM; in later years he spoke out strongly against Britain joining the EUROPEAN COMMUNITY.

Attlee is famed for his lack of obvious charisma. His only obvious interest, apart from his family, was cricket. He himself admitted: "I have none of the qualities which create publicity," and "I am a diffident man. I find it hard to carry on a conversation." Once, taking a colleague to a restaurant and finding himself without cash, he observed: "I could pay by cheque. Trouble is, I'm not known here." His political opponents were scathing. Churchill once reputedly commented: "An empty taxicab drew up at the House of Commons and Mr. Attlee got out," and said: "Mr. Attlee is a very modest man. But then, he has much to be modest about." He denied ever having called him "a sheep in sheep's clothing", but one anonymous Westminster wit did say:

> The door of 10 Downing Street opened and the cat put out Mr. Attlee.

In 1945 Bevan wrote in *Tribune*: "He brings to the fierce struggle of politics the tepid enthusiasm of a lazy summer afternoon at a cricket match," and two years later the *Economist* editorialized: "Mr. Attlee touches nothing that he does not dehydrate." George Orwell was even more uncomplimentary, writing:

> He reminds me of a dead fish before it has had time to stiffen.

Attlee was also famed for his economy with words. He would dismiss Ministers with the sole comment: "I'm making some changes. Not up to it." When his Food Minister John Strachey wanted to publish a book of poems, Attlee wrote to him: "Can't possibly publish. Lines don't scan." When confronted by a hostile meeting of the PLP in 1952 he announced: "King dead – meeting adjourned." And when approached in retirement by a young Labour CANVASSER he simply said: "Already a member." Almost his longest recorded comment was his advice to young Labour MPs about contact with the PRESS BARON Lord Beaverbrook: "He is a magnet to all young men, and I warn you that if you talk to him no good will come of it."

> He would never use one syllable where none would do. Among the longest comments I ever extracted from him was: "Wouldn't serve any useful purpose."
> DOUGLAS JAY.

> Feed a grub with royal jelly and it may become a queen.
> CHURCHILL.

> Labour's greatest triumph was scored under Attlee, who had the charisma of an average building society branch manager. ERIC HOBSBAWM, 1983.

> Charisma? He did not recognise the word except as a clue in his beloved *Times* crossword. JAMES MARGACH.

> Few thought he was even a starter.
> There were many who thought themselves smarter.
> But he ended PM
> CH and OM
> An Earl, and a Knight
> Of the Garter. ATTLEE.

Attorney-General In America, the head of the Justice Department and an important member of the CABINET, the post having become more politicized in the 20th century. In Britain, the Government's chief Law Officer, with both political and legal functions, who attends the Cabinet as required and may also lead the prosecution in major trials.

audace. l'audace, et encore de l'audace, et toujours de l'audace (Fr. daring, still more daring, and always daring) This motto of the FRENCH REVOLUTION was first uttered by Danton (1759–94) in a speech to the Legislative Committee of General Defence on 2 September 1792.

Au H_2O One of the slogans of Barry Goldwater's 1964 Presidential campaign, representing the chemical symbols for gold (*Au*) and water (H_2O).

audience The regular weekly meeting at Buckingham Palace (usually on a Tuesday evening) at which the UK Prime Minister briefs the Sovereign on current political events; the term applies to all such meetings, and also to personal consultations between the Sovereign and the Heads of Government of COMMONWEALTH countries which are still monarchies. The term is also used to describe meetings between individuals and the Pope.

Augean stables The ultimate in a corrupt political system, requiring drastic action to cleanse it. The term stems from the labours of

Heracles in Greek mythology, one of which involved the cleansing of the stables of King Augeas which were feet deep in dung deposited over 30 years by 3000 oxen; the hero achieved this by diverting a river through the premises.

Ausgleich (Ger. compromise) The accommodation made by the Habsburg Emperor Franz Josef I in 1867, which technically created the dual monarchy of Austria-Hungary. Under pressure from his Hungarian subjects to accept their separate identity, he accepted the crown of St. Stephen and recognized the integrity of Hungary's borders in return for the Budapest Parliament acknowledging his responsibility for foreign affairs and defence. The *Ausgleich*, which lasted until the collapse of the empire in 1918, was partly designed to prevent Bismarck drawing Hungary into Prussia's ambit.

autarky A political and social system that depends on a rigorous commitment to economic self-sufficiency.

authoritarianism A system of government depending on the exercise of overweening power by the State.

authority (1) The existence or exercise of legitimate power. Fidel Castro said after the Cuban revolution:

> We hope that in the future few if any men will have the authority, which we, the creators of this revolution, have had, because it is dangerous for men to have so much authority.

(2) An appointed or elected body empowered to exercise certain powers over a community or section of the population.

autocrat A leader who rules personally without powerful lieutenants or any pretence of a representative government; TSARIST Russia was long regarded as the ultimate autocracy, Count Sergei Uvarov (1786–1855) describing the system as "the main condition of Russia's political existence".

> I shall be an autocrat, that is my trade. And the Good Lord will forgive me – that is his.
>
> CATHERINE THE GREAT (1729–96).

autonomy Self-government for a people or region falling nominally within the borders of a wider nation. The Russian Republic includes a number of "autonomous regions", essentially for non-Russian peoples.

Avanti! (Ital. forward!) The newspaper of Italy's Socialist party, traditionally produced in Milan, which from 1911 to 1914 was edited by Mussolini (*see* DUCE) until his expulsion from the party for advocating war with Austria.

AWACS Air Warning and Control System. The modified Boeing 747 jumbo jets developed by the US Air Force in the early 1970s to provide a continual radar watch for potentially-hostile incoming flights and to guard against nuclear attack, gaining valuable minutes in launching a counter-attack. America sold the planes to a number of its NATO allies – though not until the mid-1980s to Britain, which first spent almost £1 billion on developing the rival Nimrod before concluding that its avionics could not be made reliable. In one trial Nimrod flight, the radar "detected" a tanker crossing the North Sea at 400 knots and another aircraft that turned out to be the bowl of the plane's own lavatory. In 1981 the Reagan administration also sold several AWACS to Saudi Arabia, overcoming bitter Congressional resistance mounted by AIPAC, the pro-Israeli lobbying group. AWACS should not be confused with the jumbo that provides the President with an emergency command post from which he can conduct a nuclear war if the WHITE HOUSE is threatened, or is destroyed after he has managed to escape.

Axis The alliance between FASCIST Italy and NAZI Germany concluded by Mussolini and Hitler in October 1936. It was formed after Italy's invasion of Abyssinia in 1936 made clear that Mussolini had contempt for the LEAGUE OF NATIONS, and paved the way for both leaders openly to flout the League. Mussolini said:

> This Berlin–Rome connection is not so much a diaphragm as an axis, around which can revolve all those states of Europe with a will towards collaboration and peace.

In 1937 it became the Rome–Berlin–Tokyo Axis. *See also* PACT OF STEEL.

Ayatollah (Pers. token of God) The word in Iran for an authoritative holy man, but used throughout the world for Ruholla Khomeini (1900–89), the militant Shi'ite cleric whose followers brought down the Shah in January 1979, and who for the next ten years ruled Iran as a ruthless mediaeval theocracy. Khomeini was acclaimed an Ayatollah in 1950, but was arrested and exiled from the holy city of Qum for attacking the Shah's westernizing policies, especially the emancipation of women. Ejected from Iraq by Saddam Hussein in 1978, he settled in Paris just as the Shah was losing his grip; a month after the Shah's overthrow he was given a hero's reception in Teheran by three million people. For a year he ruled Iran alone, imposing strict observance of Islamic law and fomenting the occupation of the Embassy of the United States, which he termed the GREAT SATAN, to start the

HOSTAGE CRISIS. From 1980 Iran was nominally in the hands of an elected government, but Khomeini still exerted immense influence, though he mellowed enough to accept a ceasefire in the first GULF WAR in 1986, saying: "I have drunk poison." The kidnappers of Western hostages in Beirut were loyal to Khomeini, if not acting on his instructions, but the Ayatollah was not directly involved in the IRAN-CONTRA AFFAIR. In the last year of his life he sowed the seeds for further strain between Iran and the West by handing down a FATWA ordering all good Muslims to murder the UK-based author Salman Rushdie, whose book *The Satanic Verses* he considered blasphemous.

aye. aye, lad, but never forget – Monty had a picture of Rommel in his bloody caravan The crushing retort delivered by an elderly reporter from *The Guardian* to Winston Churchill, grandson of the war leader, fighting his first election campaign at Manchester Gorton in 1967. Churchill, who was to win a seat at the next attempt, had told a BY-ELECTION press conference how encouraged he was that skilled workers in a local engineering plant had his picture from his ELECTION ADDRESS over their machines.

as many as are of that opinion say "Aye" The call made by the Speaker of Britain's House of Commons straight after PUTTING THE QUESTION. If the shout of "Aye" is followed by a shout of "No", the Speaker will call:

> DIVISION - CLEAR THE LOBBIES! The Ayes to the right, the Noes to the Left.

At the end of that division he or she will hear and repeat the vote, and then declare either **"The Ayes have it"**, or "The Noes have it".

In the US House of Representatives the words used by the Speaker for a VOICE-VOTE are very similar. The Chair says: "As many as are in favor say 'Aye'. As many as are not in favor say 'No'." If the result is not clear-cut, the Chair then says that a division has been demanded and adds: "As many as are in favor will rise and stand until counted." As at Westminster, the result is announced by the TELLERS and then repeated by the Speaker.

Azania An alternative name for South Africa, used by some nationalists and especially by the Pan-Africanist Congress (PAC), whose military wing (*compare* POLITICAL WING) is the **Azanian People's Liberation Army**. It was originally the name of an Iron Age civilization that occupied the area between A.D. 500 and 1500. Evelyn Waugh used the name *Azania* for the imaginary African kingdom in his novel *Black Mischief* (1932).

B

B. B and K. Headline-writers' tag for the joint Soviet leaders, Prime Minister Marshal Nikolai Alexandrovich Bulganin (1895-1975) and First Secretary Nikita Sergeyevich Khruschev (1894-1971), on their visit to Britain in 1956. *See* CRABB AFFAIR.

B1 bomber The aircraft project which symbolized the determination of the Carter administration to rein in defence projects it considered poor value, and of the Reagan administration to push the boat out. Rockwell International sought to ensure the supersonic successor to the B52 would go ahead by allocating work to plants and subcontractors in 48 states and more than 400 of the 453 Congressional districts. When President Carter cancelled the project at prototype stage in 1977, Congress fell just short of an OVERRIDE. The company kept its key workers together in the hope of a Republican victory, lobbied hard and was given the order to restart soon after Reagan entered the White House. The B1's production run was eventually limited; defence experts are divided over whether it has been of great enough use to justify its immense cost.

> I've been getting some flak about ordering the production of the B1. How did I know it was an airplane? I thought it was vitamins for the troops. RONALD REAGAN.

B-Specials The armed special constabulary which over half a century earned a reputation for brutalizing the Catholic minority in NORTHERN IRELAND. They were formed in 1920 almost entirely of Protestants, including many former members of the ULSTER VOLUNTEER FORCE and other PARAMILITARY bodies. The B-Specials acted as Ulster's Home Guard during World War II, and performed many non-controversial duties. But with the upsurge of CIVIL RIGHTS activity in 1968 many of the B-Specials, and elements of the Royal Ulster Constabulary, took the law into their own hands and attacked first the largely peaceful Civil Rights demonstrators (*see* BURNTOLLET) and then Catholic areas of Belfast. The outcry caused by their activities led the UK government to order their disbandment in 1970 following the highly-critical Hunt report on the policing of Ulster.

> Pubescent youths, old men and thugs.
> BRIAN WESLEY, *Sheffield Morning Telegraph*, reporting from Derry, 1969.

Baader-Meinhof gang The popular name for the RED ARMY FACTION, first and most notorious of the urban GUERRILLA groups that plagued West Germany from 1968. Founded by Andreas Baader (1943–77), his lover Ulrike Meinhof (1934–76), Horst Mahler and Gudrun Esslin, and consisting mainly of radicalized former middle-class students, it turned to violence against organs of NATO and the West German state, which it termed the **"Strawberry Reich"**, following the attempted assassination of the leftist former student leader Rudi Dutschke. Its most spectacular coup was Meinhof's rescue of Baader from prison in Berlin on 14 May 1970. Meinhof was arrested in Hannover in 1972 and hanged herself in prison in 1976; in revenge, the gang murdered Attorney-General Siegfried Bruback. Meinhof was described in her funeral eulogy as "the most significant woman in German politics since Rosa Luxemburg". Baader too committed suicide after the failure of the Mogadishu aircraft hijack in October 1977, a joint operation with Palestinian extremists which had been designed to free him. Gang members who had kidnapped Hans-Martin Schleyer, head of Daimler-Benz, killed him as a reprisal; after this the gang went into sharp decline, with most of its members either dead or in prison and the young backing away from revolution. By 1985 membership was estimated at 20 hardcore activists, 200 militants willing to help in guerrilla attacks and 2000 supporters who would protect other members if required.

> Don't argue – destroy.
> Slogan of the Red Army Faction.

Baath Party (Arab. renaissance) The militant party, founded in Damascus in 1943 by Michel Aflaq, which advocates the formation of a single Arab socialist nation. It took power in Syria as "the leading party in State and society" in 1963, then became the base of Saddam Hussein's regime (*see* BUTCHER OF BAGHDAD) in Iraq – with the two governments becoming mortal enemies.

back. back me or sack me The definitive challenge by a leader to a rebellious party. In 1977 James Callaghan (*see* SUNNY JIM) told Britain's Labour Party conference: "Either back us or sack us."

backbench revolt Dissent by backbenchers. against their government or party's policies, pursued if necessary to the point of abstention or a "No" vote.

backbencher Member of a legislature who (at Westminster) does not hold a Ministerial post or Opposition portfolio or (in the US Congress) is not a party office-holder or committee chairman or RANKING MEMBER. The back benches lie behind the Treasury bench or Opposition front BENCH.

background The basis on which information is given to journalists by political SOURCES, in order to explain the full picture rather than for direct use, and certainly not for attribution. **backgrounder**, a briefing conducted on this basis; **deep background**, on a strictly confidential and purely explanatory basis.

backing winners The keynote of an INTERVENTIONIST industrial policy under which an agency of the state invests in or takes charge of sectors of industry which it believes can thrive with government help. In Britain, it was a central element of LABOUR PARTY policy from the mid-1980s as its commitment to NATIONALIZATION waned.

backlash A bitter, probably violent reaction by a community or ethnic group against a perceived threat. It as originally used in the late 1950s of action by Whites in the southern US and major industrial cities against increased Black assertiveness and visibility; in a non-racial sense it has also applied to strong pressure for tougher action against criminals in response to an upsurge in crime.

backstabber An unreliable "ally" capable of betrayal. In Britain the term dates back at least to this 1906 quote from the *Westminster Gazette*: "I will tell you my idea of a false friend and backstabber – to sweat the workman for a personal profit and fawn on him for political profit, to promise old-age pensions for votes and having got the votes, to refuse them." The former White House CHIEF OF STAFF Donald Regan told the Congressional committee investigating the IRAN-CONTRA AFFAIR that he was not so worried about "spears in the breast" from his questioners as "knives in the back" from his ex-colleagues.

backwoodsman A lone political figure with reactionary opinions, specifically a PEER who seldom attends the House of Lords but can be relied on to oppose change if persuaded to travel up to vote. Originally, in America, a backwoodsman was an inhabitant of remote, impenetrable country.

bad for Britain, bad for Europe and bad for the whole free world Harold Macmillan's view of DE GAULLE's NON in January 1963 to his application for Britain to join the Common Market (EC). In 1950 Macmillan had said of the Labour Government's rejection of the SCHUMAN PLAN: "This has been a black week for Britain; for the Empire; for Europe; and for the peace of the world."

Bad Godesberg declaration The statement in which West Germany's SPD finally broke with MARXISM and embraced the MARKET ECONOMY. The party congress at Bad Godesberg, just outside Bonn, in 1959 that endorsed the statement was a watershed in the SPD's fortunes, paving the way for electoral recovery.

Bad Godesberg meeting The talks between Hitler and Neville CHAMBERLAIN at the Hotel Dreesen, Bad Godesberg, on 22–23 September 1938, which paved the way for MUNICH. Hitler rejected an Anglo-French proposal for some Czech concessions on the SUDETEN question, and Chamberlain flew back to London after being warned from there by Halifax, his Foreign Secretary, that opinion was hardening against further APPEASEMENT.

badge messenger At Westminster, one of the team of uniformed messengers, male and middle-aged or over, who preside over the galleries of the House of Commons and tour the building to locate MPs and give them messages. They are identified by the gilt badges that hang from their necks.

bag and baggage The keyword of Gladstone's attack on Turkey's BULGARIAN ATROCITIES. On 5 May 1877 he told the House of Commons:

> Let the Turks now carry off their abuses in the only possible manner, namely by carrying off themselves. Their Zaptiehs and their Mindirs, their Bimbashis and their Yuzbachis, their Kaimakams and their Pashas, one and all, bag and baggage, shall, I hope, clear out from the province they have desolated and profaned.

The sentiments were not original: in 1829 Palmerston had written: "I confess I should not be sorry some day or other to see the Turk kicked out of Europe and compelled to go and sit cup-legged, smoke his pipe, chew his opium and cut off heads on the Asiatic side of the Bosphorus."

baggage The ideological impedimenta of belonging to a political party or grouping, which prevent an individual's rejection of outdated or unpopular ideas and their replacement by new ones.

Baghdad pact A treaty for military and economic co-operation signed by Iraq and Turkey in 1955 and later joined by Iran, Pakistan and Britain to create a front against

Soviet southward ambitions. Its initial purpose was frustrated by the refusal of America (out of deference to pro-Israel sentiment) and Egypt (before SUEZ) to join. In 1959 Iraq withdrew, America became an associate member and the signatory states became **CENTO** (Central Treaty Organization). By the fall of the Shah of Iran in 1979 the pact was dormant; CENTO was subsequently dissolved.

Bailie Vass A nickname for SIR ALEC Douglas-Home coined by PRIVATE EYE after the Aberdeen *Evening Express* transposed picture captions of the then Prime Minister and a so-named local official. During the 1964 election the magazine issued car stickers reading:

> Up your ass with Bailie Vass!

Baird nomination The first embarrassment of the Clinton administration: the failure of the President's nominee as Attorney-General, Zoë Baird, to secure CONFIRMATION by the Senate. On the eve of Clinton's inauguration on 20 January 1993, it emerged that Ms. Baird, a law partner of Secretary of State Warren Christopher, had hired an ILLEGAL Peruvian immigrant couple to drive and look after her children. Although Ms. Baird and her husband had paid $12,000 in back taxes and a $2900 penalty to the Immigration and Naturalization Service, Senate critics argued that no one could be appointed to head the Justice Department who had been caught in such an illegality. To compound Clinton's embarrassment, his second nominee, Judge Kimba Wood, turned out to have used a Trinidadian illegal as a babysitter in 1986; her nomination too was withdrawn.

Baker. Bobby Baker affair Baker (1928–) was a notorious Washington INFLUENCE PEDDLER whom even President Johnson, who told him: "You're like a son to me," could not save from jail. He arrived in Washington with $60 in his pocket from Pickens, South Carolina, aged just 14, to be a Congressional PAGE, and two decades later was making $300,000 a year on a salary of $19,600 as secretary to the Senate MAJORITY LEADER. Indicted in 1966 for pocketing $80,000 of a $100,000 "campaign contribution" he had solicited, he was convicted of fraud, larceny and tax evasion and sentenced to one to three years. Paroled in 1972, Baker returned to Washington to manage his assets. When sentenced, Baker said:

> Like my bosses and sponsors in the Senate, I was ambitious and eager to feather my personal nest.

But after his release he insisted:

> I made mistakes, and I'm going to admit those mistakes. But I was put in jail for something that didn't happen. If having girlfriends and drinking whisky is immoral, then I'm guilty. But nobody was buying Bobby Baker.

Baker, James (1930–) The linchpin of the Reagan and Bush administrations: White House CHIEF OF STAFF 1981–85, Treasury Secretary 1985–88, Bush's campaign manager in 1988, SECRETARY OF STATE 1989–92 and last-minute manager of the Bush re-election campaign in the fall of 1992. A highly accomplished political manager, he showed his finesse in handling the GULF WAR and the collapse of the SOVIET UNION, but was unable to present Bush in a positive enough light to get him re-elected. Mike Deaver termed him "the most cautious human being I have ever met", Sen. Richard Lugar praised him as "patient to a fault", while Sen. Howard Baker said early on: "Jim Baker has a lot of great traits, but one is he can carry on a 30-second conversation." Hedrick Smith reported: "Many in Washington said he would have saved Reagan from the IRAN-CONTRA disaster had he remained as chief of staff in Reagan's second term." During the Bush administration he was widely seen as his obvious successor, David Brock writing: "Baker has long thought of himself as Bush's better."

Baker amendments The amendments to the PANAMA CANAL TREATIES required by Senate MINORITY LEADER Howard Baker as the price for his eleventh-hour support. One allowed US military intervention in Panama, the other secured 20 extra US fighter planes for Israel and a Saudi promise not to use its American-made planes against Israel.

Baker v. Carr A landmark decision of the US SUPREME COURT, which held in 1962 that town-dwellers in Tennessee were being denied "equal protection of the laws" through the rurally-dominated state legislature's failure to REAPPORTION itself.

Bakke case The 1978 milestone case in which the US SUPREME COURT set limits to the use of AFFIRMATIVE ACTION. Allan Bakke sued the University of California for denying him a graduate school place when ethnic minority candidates with inferior records were being admitted, and won.

balance. balance of payments The difference between a country's imports and exports, with allowance made for "invisible earnings" such as insurance or tourism. Deficits in Britain's balance of payments were the cause of repeated STERLING crises during the late 1960s, but far larger deficits are now accepted as a matter of course.

balance of power (1) The theory that war is less likely when potential combatants, or opposing alliances, are of equal strength. The doctrine was first applied to 18th-century

Europe, its earliest recorded use being by WALPOLE in the Commons on 13 February 1741. It was responsible for the Alliance system which kept the powers of Europe in rough equilibrium except when disrupted by Napoleon, the Kaiser and Hitler, and was both a reason for the COLD WAR and the reason why it did not lead to nuclear conflict. Throughout those centuries it had its critics, John Bright in the mid-19th century denouncing its requirement for vast armies as "a gigantic system of outdoor relief for the aristocracy", and Clement ATTLEE saying between the World Wars:

> We ought to give up altogether the old traditional doctrine of the Balance of Power – that balance of armed strength we used to support for so many years. That is obsolete now. The way to get peace is not through the Balance of Power but through the LEAGUE [OF NATIONS].

Yet President Nixon was stating more than the obvious when he said in 1972:

> The only alternative to a balance of power is an imbalance of power.

(2) In a legislature or other elected authority, the balance between the parties or blocs. If two parties are of equal strength and there is one unaligned member, that member holds the balance of power.

balance of terror A nuclear-age variant of the doctrine of balance of power, based simply upon the assumption that the consequences of nuclear war were too horrifying for either side to risk starting one. Implicit in the phrase was the implication that they just might.

balanced Budget The aim of successive US administrations, increasingly unlikely to be achieved since the GREAT SOCIETY and the VIETNAM WAR pushed Federal spending ahead of resources. Franklin D. Roosevelt (*see* FDR) promised a balanced budget in 1932 but let spending rip under the NEW DEAL; Ronald Reagan ridiculed Jimmy CARTER for failing to balance the budget, then presided over a rocketing deficit. In 1992 George BUSH backed a **Balanced Budget Amendment** to the Constitution, but the House of Representatives narrowly rejected it.

> The Budget should be balanced, the treasury should be refilled, public debt should be reduced, the arrogance of officialdom should be tempered and controlled, assistance to foreign lands should be curtailed lest Rome become bankrupt, the mobs should be forced to work and not depend on government for subsistence. CICERO (*attr.*).

Baldwin, Stanley 1st Earl Baldwin of Bewdley (1867–1947). One of 20th-century Britain's most durable political leaders, leader of the Conservative Party from 1923 to 1937 and three times Prime Minister (May–December 1923, 1924–29, 1935–37). He started his Ministerial career in Lloyd George's coalition government, which he was instrumental in terminating, was crucial in advising George V to send for RAMSAY MACDonald after his own defeat at the close of 1923, and served for four years in MacDonald's NATIONAL GOVERNMENT which he eventually dominated. His priorities were at first sight Victorian; he once recalled: "When the call came to me to form a government, one of my first thoughts was that it should be a Government of which Harrow [school] would not be ashamed." He was consistently underrated; Lord Curzon, who had assumed he and not Baldwin would succeed Bonar Law, dismissed him as "a man of no experience, and of the utmost insignificance". But he was a skilled political operator, saying: "I would rather be an opportunist and float than go to the bottom with my principles round my neck." His strength was in doggedness rather than flair, G. M. Young writing: "Baldwin always hits the nail on the head, but it doesn't go in any further." Lord Beaverbrook, his greatest critic, declared: "His successive attempts to find a policy remind me of the chorus in a third-rate revue. His evasions appear in different scenes and in new dresses, and every time they dance with renewed and despairing vigour. But it is the same old gig." CHURCHILL scorned his government as "decided only to be undecided, resolved to be irresolute, adamant for drift, solid for fluidity, all-powerful to be impotent". Of his speaking style, Aneurin Bevan commented: "Murmurs of admiration break out as this second-rate orator trails his tawdry wisps of mist over the Parliamentary scene." But Harold Macmillan felt that "Baldwin was never quite sure that anybody was right, especially himself".

Baldwin's final premiership was dominated by his disavowal of the APPEASEMENT-minded HOARE-LAVAL PACT, a belated REARMAMENT programme and his sympathetic handling of the 1936 ABDICATION crisis – of which he remarked:

> When I was a little boy in Worcestershire reading history books, I never thought that I should have to interfere between a King and his mistress.

Lord Home, an MP at the time, asserted: "When the history of the century is written Baldwin will top the list in domestic achievement – and his handling of the Abdication crisis will tip the balance, for he saved our Constitutional monarchy." On his retirement Churchill observed: "The candle in that great turnip has gone out." And in his later years he was vilified for his supposed failure to prepare Britain for war (*see* YEARS THE LOCUSTS HAVE EATEN). The Beaverbrook press claimed he was refusing to give up his house's iron gates for the war effort; when the ageing Baldwin heard the crowd jeer him, he asked: "Why do they hate me so?"

Balfour Declaration The promise of a national home for the Jews in Palestine, made in 1917 by the British Conservative statesman Arthur Balfour (1848–1930), which has dictated the history of the Middle East ever since. Made in a letter to the ZIONIST leader Lionel Walter (2nd Baron) Rothschild (1868–1937), it was conditional on the rights of existing non-Jewish residents of Palestine being maintained and the rights of Jewish citizens in other countries also being respected. Dean Inge (1860–1954) commented, probably unfairly,

> When he launched his scheme for peopling Palestine with Jewish immigrants, I am credibly informed that he did not know there were any Arabs in the country.

The declaration was repudiated by the British Government in 1939, but Jewish immigration to that point and the flight from Europe during and after the HOLOCAUST turned it into reality. (The term is also used for the statement made by the 1926 Imperial Conference on the nature of the emerging COMMONWEALTH – *see* Statute of WESTMINSTER.) Balfour made the declaration on a Jewish state when Foreign Secretary in Lloyd George's Coalition. He had himself been Prime Minister from 1902 until his defeat in 1905 after splitting the Tory party on the TARIFF issue, resigning the leadership in 1911 ostensibly on health grounds but in fact because of growing internal criticism. Balfour owed his early advancement to being a nephew of Lord SALISBURY, but when he took office, according to Roy Jenkins, "he amazed the House by the ruthlessness of his policy and the tenacity of his debating. His soubriquet changed from 'Pretty Fanny' to 'Bloody Balfour'." Gladstone termed him "Artful Arthur", but he was also an infuriating dilettante; he once exclaimed: "Nothing matters very much, and very few things matter at all." Lloyd George described his impact as "no more than the whiff of scent on a lady's pocket handkerchief"; to J. M. KEYNES Balfour was "the most extraordinary *objet d'art* our society has ever produced". CHURCHILL described him as "a powerful, graceful cat walking delicately and unsoiled across a rather muddy street".

Balfour must go The watchword of a series of whispering campaigns aimed at Balfour's removal from the Tory leadership. Its origin was "The Saloon Must Go", adopted in 1895 as slogan of America's PROHIBITIONist Anti-Saloon League. Suitably modified, it was used in 1930 against BALDWIN by the PRESS BARONS Beaverbrook and Rothermere; in the early 1960s **Marples Must Go**, directed against Ernest Marples, then Minister of Transport, was daubed on Britain's first motorway bridges. In a few places it can still be seen.

Mr. Balfour's poodle Lloyd George's dismissive term for the HOUSE OF LORDS, responding in the Commons on 26 June 1907 to a claim that the Upper House was acting as "the watchdog of the nation" in rejecting the ASQUITH government's programme. L.G. said:

> No mastiff, it is the Rt. Honourable Gentleman's poodle, it fetches and carries for him, barks and bites anybody he sets it on to.

Balkanization The breaking up of a large and relatively stable political unit into ill-assorted and feuding parts. The term derives from the warfare and instability that broke out in the Balkans – continuing to this day – once the decay of the Ottoman Empire gave its peoples their independence.

ballot The paper used to cast one's VOTE in secret; the process of holding a vote conducted by this method, which generally replaced the SHOW OF HANDS during the 19th century. Also a process of drawing lots, as in the ballot for Parliamentary time for Private Members' BILLS at Westminster.

the ballot is stronger than the bullet Abraham LINCOLN's declaration in a speech on 18 May 1858. He also said:

> To give the victory to the right, not bloody bullets, but peaceful ballots only, are necessary.

give us the ballot The theme of one of Dr. Martin Luther KING's definitive speeches, in Washington. He said:

> Give us the ballot, and we will no longer have to worry the federal government about our basic rights.

ballot box The box, normally made of metal, in which the papers are cast, and kept until they are counted; hence the symbol of democracy.

> The ballot box is a most inadequate mechanism of change.
> SIMONE DE BEAUVOIR.

ballot-rigging A corrupt practice that occasionally afflicts trade unions, generally when two rival factions (often one Communist, one anti-Communist) are struggling for control. Notorious examples include the Communist ballot-rigging within Britain's Electrical Trades Union, exposed in the late 1950s, and in Australia's Federal Iron Workers' Association a decade earlier. In more recent, but unproven, cases staff at a union headquarters were said to be suffering "a severe outbreak of writer's cramp" just before the ballot closed.

absentee ballot A system under which voters unable to reach the POLLS may vote by post or by PROXY. During America's CIVIL WAR eleven states enabled soldiers in the Union army to vote by mail; the right was first extended to civilians by Vermont in 1896.

Australian ballot An American name for the secret ballot, which 33 states had adopted by 1892. In the UK the secret ballot was introduced by the **Ballot Act**, 1872.
down the ballot Someone standing for a relatively minor post, in American elections where a complete set of office-holders is being chosen and all appear on the same ballot paper in order of importance.
on the ballot Another way of describing a candidate for office; it is an abbreviation of "on the ballot paper".
on the – th ballot The point at which a Presidential candidate is finally nominated at a party CONVENTION where no obvious FRONT-RUNNER has emerged during the PRIMARIES.

Balmoral The family home in Scotland of the British sovereign, purchased by Prince Albert for Queen Victoria in 1848. For most of the decade after his death she lived in seclusion in the castle, remotely situated at the top of Deeside, until Disraeli tempted her back to public life. Every September, the Prime Minister travels to Balmoral to spend a few days with the Royal family.

> Siberia. CAMPBELL-BANNERMAN.

baloney A favourite American term for nonsense or rubbish, common from the 1920s and popularized by Al Smith, Governor of New York, when he said in a 1936 campaign speech: "No matter how you slice it, it's still baloney." Its origin is commonly assumed to be the bologna sausage – hence the slicing – but this is not proven. On 9 February 1943 Rep. Clare Boothe Luce (1903–87), in her MAIDEN SPEECH, coined the word **globaloney** to describe the internationalist post-war theories of Vice-President Henry Wallace.

Bamboo Curtain The veil of secrecy and suspicion drawn between Communist China and its SATELLITE COUNTRIES and the non-Communist nations of both the West and the Far East. The term is analogous to the IRON CURTAIN.

ban. Ban the Bomb! The definitive slogan of CND and other movements opposed to nuclear weapons and nuclear war. It originated in the early 1950s with the Communist-front WORLD PEACE COUNCIL, but was taken up by CND at the first ALDERMASTON MARCH.
banning order The restriction on political activity imposed on both Black and White dissidents in South Africa under the Internal security Act of 1977. "Banned" people were prevented from appearing in public or expressing political opinions, and in some cases were required to live in remote areas.

banana. banana republic A derisive term for a poverty-stricken country without a stable civilian government, run by a corrupt dictatorial clique and subservient to outside (*e.g.* US) commercial interests; it first applied to certain states in Latin America but is now used to describe any poor country whose government is a laughing-stock. It had its origin in Minor Keith's United Fruit Company, which in the 1870s built railroads in Costa Rica and grew bananas to generate traffic for them, and developed a stranglehold on much of central America. In 1954 President Eisenhower permitted the CIA to overthrow Guatemala's government to protect United Fruit's operations.

> Louisiana is a banana republic which should declare bankruptcy, secede from the Union and apply for foreign aid. Rep. KEVIN REILLY (1928–).

In his MAIDEN SPEECH in the House of Commons in July 1992 Michael Fabricant, Conservative MP for Mid-Staffordshire, noted that the constituency was shaped like a banana – and went on to call it his banana republic.
banana skin An unnoticed fact or political issue which suddenly breaks surface to cause a politician or government great embarrassment. The term became commonplace in Britain in the early 1980s when Margaret Thatcher's government (*see* IRON LADY) hit a series of unexpected difficulties; deputy Prime Minister William Whitelaw (*see* WILLIE) was deputed to watch out for banana skins.

Bandung conference The conference of 29 African and Asian states in 1955 at Bandung in West Java, Indonesia, at which the policy of NON-ALIGNMENT was agreed. The conference took a strongly anti-COLONIALIST line.

bandwagon effect The process by which a party or movement attracts support by virtue of its growing success or popularity; at the point of BREAKTHROUGH, well-known people not previously identified with the movement will rally to it in order to boost their own careers or prestige. The bandwagon is the vehicle which pulls or conveys the band in a circus procession.

bank. bank rate *See* MINIMUM LENDING RATE.
bankers' ramp The conspiracy theory offered by LABOUR PARTY loyalists to explain the collapse of RAMSAY MACDonald's second government in 1931 (*see* GREAT BETRAYAL). Britain's banks were supposed to have deliberately pushed the economy into crisis to split the party and bring about the formation of the NATIONAL GOVERNMENT. That September, Hugh Dalton (1887–1962) told a meeting at Bishop Auckland:

The Labour Party . . . would not stand idly by and see our social services butchered to make a bankers' holiday.

Bantustan A manufactured name for a manufactured entity: South Africa's Black homelands. It was derived by the architects of APARTHEID from *Bantu*, one of the peoples in question; and *-stan*, a state (as in Hindustan, Pakistan). The first to be created was Transkei in 1973; it received full "independence" in 1976.

bar of the House At Westminster, the point at the far end of the Chamber of the HOUSE OF COMMONS to the Chair, to which those alleged to have committed CONTEMPT of the House are summoned. A new member must wait at the Bar of the House until summoned to take the Oath. The Bar comprises two rods which can be drawn across from the end of benches opposite the Chair to form the boundary of the House.

I knew that if I ever lost 500 men without the clearest necessity, I should be brought upon my knees to the bar of the House of Commons.

The DUKE OF WELLINGTON.

In the US CAPITOL, the bar is a similar point at the rear of the House of Representatives chamber where, in bygone days, members had to present themselves during a QUORUM CALL; they now report direct to the Clerk.

Barber boom The period of apparent runaway prosperity in Britain in 1972–73 under Edward Heath, whose Chancellor of the Exchequer Anthony (later Lord) Barber (1920–) was given credit at the time. He received corresponding blame when the economy went abruptly into reverse as INFLATION took hold; Enoch POWELL blamed Barber for failing to control the MONEY SUPPLY.

Barlow memorial award The highly unofficial award made each spring in the 1980s by denizens of ANNIE'S BAR in the Palace of Westminster, to the teller of the most obscene and tasteless story heard there. It commemorated Sir Frank Barlow (d. 1979), a noted raconteur who worked for Labour leaders from Attlee to Callaghan and retired as secretary of the Parliamentary party. Winners include police officers from the MEMBERS' LOBBY, a senior correspondent from *The Times* and several Conservative MPs. The shortest winner, entered by PC Ken Thomas in 1982, was:

Q: Why do you bind sellotape round a hamster?
A: So it doesn't split when you fuck it.

barnstorming A highly energetic campaign by a politician, combining a large amount of travel with a crowded programme of rousing speeches. The term has its origin in the travelling theatre, which set up stage in farmers' barns.

Baron (1) In Britain, the formal title of the lowest degree of hereditary LORD and of all life PEERS. When the veteran Labour MP Bill Blyton told his wife he had been elevated to the Lords and was "Baron Blyton now", she replied: "Thou's been barren these forty years!" (2) In the US Congress, the barons were the conservative Democrats who until the early 1970s chaired almost every committee under the SENIORITY rule, and thus wielded immense power.

barracking Systematic chanting from sections of the audience at a meeting, or from the opposing side of a legislature, to unsettle or shout down the person who is attempting to speak.

barricades A traditional feature of popular uprisings, particularly in Paris, with obstacles dragged into the street to form a barrier against any attempt by riot police or troops to move in and "restore order". In Paris the slogan *Aux barricades!* (to the barricades!) has marked the start of numerous challenges either to an occupying force (notably the Germans in 1944) or to the authority of the State.

Barry, Kevin The 18-year-old Dublin medical student whose execution by the British on 1 November 1920 produced a backlash of support for Irish independence and gave rise to one of the Republic's most moving patriotic songs. Barry took part in an IRA raid for arms on a military convoy in Church Street in which six soldiers died. Captured at the scene, he was court-martialled and hanged at Mountjoy prison. His sacrifice and execution aroused deep feeling, and scores of his fellow-students immediately joined the IRA. In the House of Commons the hanging was condemned by Labour's J. H. Thomas. The song written to commemorate Barry's death has become part of Irish folklore, for committed Republicans and liberal patriots alike. Its first verse is:

In Mountjoy jail one Sunday morning
High upon the gallows tree,
Kevin Barry gave his young life
For the cause of liberty.

Base rate *See* MINIMUM LENDING RATE.

Basic Law The "temporary" legal framework set by the BUNDESTAG on 23 May 1949 for the government of the German Federal Republic, the state (WEST GERMANY) formed in the former American, British and French zones. It has survived to be the constitution of the unified German state. Drawing heavily on the lessons of suffering under the NAZIs, it guarantees human freedoms, sexual equality and the right of asylum for any foreigner seeking it. Politically, it established a liberal but ADVERSARIAL democracy, with power-sharing between the centre and the LÄNDER. Amendments to the Basic Law may be made by a two-thirds vote of the Bundestag, but most of its fundamentals are ENTRENCHED.

Bastille The notorious prison fortress in Paris, the storming of which by the mob on 14 July 1789 marked the start of the FRENCH REVOLUTION. Lafayette sent the key of the Bastille to George WASHINGTON, who received it as "a token gained for liberty". The freeing of prisoners was an anti-climax; the mob of over 5000 found only seven – four forgers, two madmen and an Irish lord imprisoned for 30 years for debt. But **Bastille Day** became Republican France's great national holiday, and the occasion for an outpouring of patriotic fervour.

> How much the greatest event it is that ever happened in the world! and how much the best.
>
> CHARLES JAMES FOX (1749–1806).

baton round The name given by security forces in NORTHERN IRELAND to plastic bullets in the late 1970s, after the projectiles had killed a number of rioters and demonstrators. *See also* rubber BULLET.

battle. battlebus The self-contained mobile election headquarters used by (Sir) David Steel (1938–), leader of Britain's Liberal Party, in the 1979 and subsequent General Elections. It included facilities for writing and duplicating speeches and press handouts, telephoning senior party figures, relaxation and servicing the travelling press, some of whom were aboard. The idea quickly caught on with leaders of other parties when they took to the road to campaign.

battleground states The states where a US Presidential election is determined, because they hold the decisive votes in the ELECTORAL COLLEGE. Which states they are varies a little from election to election because the appeal of each TICKET differs, but the battleground generally includes the states of the industrial Midwest: Illinois, Michigan and Ohio.

Battling Bob The nickname won by Sen. Robert la Follette (1855–1925) of Wisconsin. A popular hero in the Midwest by the end of the 19th century, la Follette twice broke with the Republicans to offer a POPULIST alternative to the two established parties. In 1911 he formed the National Progressive Republican League, which formed the base for Theodore Roosevelt's BULL MOOSE candidacy the following year. Again, in 1924, he led his followers out of the Republican Party to run for the Presidency as a PROGRESSIVE. He won 5 million votes but carried only his home state, and died the following year.

Bay Street Boys The clique of White merchants who ran the Bahamas like a private club until 1967, when Lynden Pindling and his Progressive Liberal Party broke their power. Sir Lynden, as he became, ruled for 25 years, becoming unaccountably rich as allegations of corruption and collusion with drug traffickers spread. In 1992 he in turn was ousted by Hubert Ingraham's Free National Movement.

Be it enacted . . . The formal statement that a BILL has been passed into law, which appears immediately after the statement of the measure's purpose. An ACT of the US Congress carries the rubric: "Be it enacted by the Senate and House of Representatives of the United States of America in Congress assembled"; the traditional wording for UK laws is: "Be it enacted by the Queen's most excellent Majesty, by and with the advice and consent of the Lords Spiritual and Temporal, and Commons, in this present Parliament assembled, and by the authority of the same, as follows . . ."

beam-splitter The almost invisible TELEPROMPTER which enables a politician to pick up the next phrase of a speech, giving an impression of spontaneity and control when in fact the occasion has been carefully rehearsed. Margaret Thatcher and Ronald Reagan were the first masters of this type of autocue.

bean soup An institution of the House restaurant in the US Capitol for over a century, and on the menu every day since 1904 when Speaker Joseph Cannon (*see* FOUL-MOUTHED JOE) found none was on offer. The waiter told him the chef had thought the weather too clammy to serve it up, but Cannon told him: "Hell and thunderation! I had my mouth set for bean soup. Get me the chef." Cannon castigated the chef, then told him: "From now on, hot or cold, rain, snow or shine, I want bean soup on the menu every day." And so it has been, to the delight of many.

Bear, the To Westerners, the menacing image conjured up by a strong Russia, in Tsarist times, under Communism and even at times under the democracy that has succeeded it. The image has been in use, especially by cartoonists, since at least the early 19th century.

beard and sandals The deprecatory nickname for the ENVIRONMENTALIST fringe of Britain's

Liberal Party, which gained a reputation for turning up in strength at the annual party assembly and embarrassing the party leadership with its whimsical line. In 1986 this faction was blamed for an anti-nuclear motion that wrecked the joint defence policy of the SDP/Liberal ALLIANCE and was widely blamed by both for the parties' poor showing in the following year's election and the subsequent break-up of the Alliance. Many of this tendency subsequently joined the GREEN Party, giving it a firmly idealistic identity but rendering it unelectable in the process. At the Greens' 1991 conference the chair called "the man in the beard in the back row" to the rostrum, and several dozen people came forward.

beast. Beast of Bolsover The nickname earned over two decades at Westminster by **Dennis Skinner** (1932–), the consistently left-wing MP for Bolsover in Derbyshire. Skinner, a miner for 21 years who described himself in *Who's Who* as coming from "good working-class stock", entered Parliament in 1970 and quickly became known for his fiery pursuit of class warfare and his support for the rebel CLAY CROSS COUNCILLORS, several of whom were his relatives. Skinner's outspokenness and his refusal to compromise led to numerous clashes with the SPEAKER and demands for him to leave the Chamber. His sustained interruption of the SDP leaders Roy Jenkins and Dr. David Owen, whom he regarded as traitors, did much to limit their effectiveness in the Commons. A committed Parliamentarian and a forceful member of Labour's National Executive, Skinner earned respect among Tories for his incorruptibility and his refusal to be diverted or to kow-tow to his own party leadership. Indeed Margaret Thatcher's most memorable lines in her farewell speech as Prime Minister were based on a Skinner interruption.

Beast of Buffalo The Republicans' nickname in the 1884 election for **Grover Cleveland** (1837–1908), who overcame the tag to be elected 22nd President of the United States (Democrat, 1885–89). He was also the 24th, coming back in 1892 to oust Benjamin Harrison and serve until 1897. A lawyer who quickly became active in the Democratic Party, he was elected mayor of Buffalo, governor of New York and President in less than four years. Corpulent and with a walrus moustache, he exuded firmness, Samuel Tilden stating: "He has so much backbone that it sticks out in front." But there was also a skeleton in his cupboard; though he arrived a bachelor, he had fathered an illegitimate child in Buffalo (*see* MA, MA, WHERE'S MY PA?). During his first term he married the attractive 21-year-old ward of his former law partner; rumours that he beat her reinforced the "beast" image. Narrowly elected over James G. Blaine, who was widely branded as corrupt, Cleveland's first term was marked by reforms to depoliticize the civil service and by a drive against favourable treatment for any special interest. Though he was welcomed by the great industrial Trusts, the railroad magnate and fraudster Jay Gould telling him: "I feel that the vast business interests of the country will be safe in your hands," his administration saw the creation of the initially toothless Interstate Commerce Commission. He also vetoed a Bill to distribute $10,000 worth of grain to drought-stricken Texas farmers, declaring:

> Federal aid in such cases encourages the expectation of paternal care on the part of the Government and weakens the sturdiness of our national character.

He ran for re-election in 1888 purely on his record, telling critics: "What is the use of being elected or re-elected unless you stand for something?" But the country did not see it that way – although he won the popular vote, Benjamin Harrison carried the ELECTORAL COLLEGE. Four years later he got his revenge, but his second term was marred by the DEPRESSION of 1893. At its height he had to have much of his cancerous upper jaw replaced by one of vulcanized rubber, the operation being performed in secret at sea to avoid heightening the economic panic. Cleveland was an industrious President, the White House usher Ike Hoover saying: "It was work, work, work all the time." He also had simple tastes, once confiding: "I must go to dinner, but I wish it was to eat a pickled herring, a Swiss cheese and a chop at Louis' instead of the French stuff I shall find."

> His huge carcass seemed to be made of iron. There was no give in him, no bounce, no softness. He sailed through American history like a steel ship loaded with monoliths of granite. H. L. MENCKEN.

bed. bed-sit brigade In Britain, the dedicated left-wingers (from the MILITANT TENDENCY and a range of BENNITE and hard LEFT groups) who in the late 1970s and early 1980s moved into constituencies with a moribund local Labour Party to work for the DESELECTION of the sitting Labour MP. Party moderates gave them the label because they often rented bed-sitting rooms for the duration of their campaign.

Bedchamber crisis The constitutional crisis that broke in Britain in 1839 when on the fall of Melbourne's WHIG ministry the young Queen Victoria refused to part with her ladies of the bedchamber, many of whom were wives, sisters or daughters of leading Whigs. The

Queen's resistance prevented Sir Robert Peel (*see* PEELITES) forming a TORY government, and her confidant and mentor Viscount Melbourne, who still had a narrow majority, was recalled; only after an election did Peel return to power.

> I have no doubt that Melbourne is as passionately fond of the Queen as he might be of his daughter if he had one, and the more so because he has the capacity for loving without anyone to love. It is become his province to educate, instruct and form the most interesting mind and character in the world. CHARLES GREVILLE, *Memoirs*.

Bedtime for Bonzo The 1951 movie in which Ronald Reagan starred with a chimpanzee, giving rise to numerous jokes, regrettably all obvious, when he embarked on a political career.

Beeching report The report produced in 1962 by the senior ICI executive Dr. Richard (later Lord) Beeching (1913–85) which caused a furore by advocating the closure of more than half of Britain's railway system. Commissioned by Ernest Marples, Transport Minister in the Macmillan government, it was largely implemented by the Labour government which came to power in 1964.

beef mountain *See* MOUNTAIN.

beer. beer and sandwiches at Number Ten Harold WILSON's practice of inviting trade union leaders to NUMBER TEN Downing Street to resolve potentially damaging industrial disputes, with a national strike on occasions averted after marathon talks when beer and sandwiches were served. Its adoption in the 1966 seamen's strike (*see* TIGHTLY KNIT GROUP OF POLITICALLY-MOTIVATED MEN) and subsequent disputes was scorned by the Conservatives; Edward Heath (who relented) and Margaret Thatcher (who did not) both insisted they would never indulge in such tactics. *Compare* Coffee and Danish at the WHITE HOUSE.

we have been borne down in a torrent of gin and beer Gladstone's lament on the Liberals' heavy defeat in the 1874 general election; the Conservatives had been heavily backed by the BEERAGE.

Beerage A derogatory collective term for the heads of the brewing industry who from the late 19th century gave unquestioning support to Britain's CONSERVATIVE PARTY, and frequently received seats in the House of Lords as their reward. The link between the brewers and the Tories, which persists to this day, was forged in part when the LIBERAL PARTY in the 1870s began to represent the NONCONFORMIST CONSCIENCE by taking an increasingly hostile attitude to drink.

Beirut airport bombing The devastating attack on the main US barracks in the Lebanon on 23 October 1983 that left 241 marines dead, hastening America's withdrawal the following February from the MULTINATIONAL FORCE endeavouring to keep the peace there. The attack, by an Islamic suicide truck bomber, was followed by one on the French peacekeeping barracks which killed 58 troops. The atrocity, which a special commission blamed partly on lax security, was seized on by critics of the Reagan administration to argue that the marines should never have been sent to so unstable and dangerous a country. However Reagan kept public anger in check by ordering US troops into GRENADA two days later. He insisted he would not CUT AND RUN by pulling the Marines out of Beirut, but signed the order on 1 February 1984, just as his press secretary Larry Speakes was denouncing Democrats demanding a pullout as "unpatriotic". In April 1983, 63 people had died when the US Embassy in Beirut was bombed by Islamic JIHAD; a new Embassy was found and in September 1984 that, too, was bombed, with 40 deaths.

Belgrano affair The most controversial incident of the FALKLANDS WAR, the sinking on 2 May 1982 of the Argentine cruiser *General Belgrano* (the former USS *Phoenix*, a survivor of PEARL HARBOR) by the British submarine HMS *Conqueror*. A long-running political argument began in Britain, not because 323 Argentine sailors had died but because, contrary to what Margaret Thatcher and defence ministers told the Commons, the *Belgrano* had been steaming away from the Falklands for eight hours when torpedoed. Naval staff officers apparently gave Ministers the misleading information, and the politicians when they discovered the facts (in Mrs. Thatcher's case two years later) felt obliged to defend the service. The inconsistencies that crept into official explanations led the Labour MP Tam Dalyell to launch a campaign to prove that the sinking had been engineered to torpedo the PERUVIAN PEACE PLAN. The Prime Minister, in a 1983 election PHONE-IN, was put on the rack over the *Belgrano* by a Bristol housewife, Mrs. Diana Gould, her hesitant answers leaving lasting doubts about her veracity. The gradual emergence of a cover-up which heartened the conspiracy theorists led to the PONTING AFFAIR, in which a senior MoD civil servant was prosecuted under the OFFICIAL SECRETS ACT for LEAKing information about the sinking to Dalyell and the *Observer* newspaper; he was acquitted. The *Belgrano* campaigners suffered a reverse on the tenth anniversary of the sinking when the ship's commander, Captain Hector Bonzo, told *The Times*:

> The attack on the *Belgrano* did not violate the laws of a military conflict. If I had been a British commander confronted by the enemy ship, I would have done exactly the same.

Believe! Obey! Fight! A slogan of Mussolini's FASCIST movement which sums up its members' commitment, its AUTHORITARIAN structure and its belligerence.

Belknap scandal The juiciest of the scandals that gave the Grant (*see* GRANTISM) administration a probably unjustified reputation for corruption. Secretary for War William W. Belknap resigned abruptly in 1876 to escape IMPEACHMENT, after it was found that he had taken bribes to grant the right to sell supplies to the Indians. The story broke in a Congressional hearing on 29 February when Caleb Marsh, a trader at Fort Sill in the Indian territories, testified to having paid $25,000 over six years to Carrie and Puss Belknap, the attractive, vivacious sisters whom Belknap had married in turn. Belknap resigned amid rumours that he had attempted suicide, but although cleared by the Senate he spent the rest of his life in disgrace; however the stylish Puss Belknap continued to captivate Washington society and the press.

bell. on the bell *See* ON.

below the gangway In the HOUSE OF COMMONS at Westminster, the seats at the end of the Chamber away from the CHAIR. On both sides of the House, the gangway runs backward to separate the Front BENCH from the *hoi polloi*; on the Government side the first seat at the front below the gangway was occupied in retirement from 1955 until 1964 by Sir Winston CHURCHILL, and for even longer, from 1979, by Sir Edward Heath. Sir Edward shared the bench with senior Tory backbenchers, some of them right-wingers who were no friends of his, sharing the description of BOVVER BOYS bestowed on the left-wing occupants of Labour's below-gangway front bench.

bench. bench of bishops The bench next to the Government front bench in the HOUSE OF LORDS where the two Anglican Archbishops and the 24 bishops with places in the Upper House are seated.

back benches The seats in the HOUSE OF COMMONS occupied by all those MPs who are not members of the Government, or official Opposition SPOKESMEN. A Minister who leaves office is said to be "returning to the back benches", even if he takes his seat on the front bench BELOW THE GANGWAY. *See also* BACKBENCHER.

front bench The seats on either side of the HOUSE OF COMMONS, close to the CHAIR and facing the DESPATCH BOX, where members of the CABINET and SHADOW CABINET sit as of right, to be joined by junior Ministers and spokesmen when the business of the House requires. The term also applies collectively to the entire Opposition team of shadow Ministers and spokesmen.

Treasury Bench The official term for the Government front bench in the House of Commons, reflecting the Prime Minister's formal title as First Lord of the TREASURY.

Benelux The collective term by which Belgium, the Netherlands and Luxembourg are known. It originated in the customs union the three countries formed in 1948, and remains in use because of the many issues on which the three act as one within the EUROPEAN COMMUNITY.

benign neglect The stance toward the problems of Black Americans, both economic and in relation to CIVIL RIGHTS, adopted by the Nixon administration; a settled climate in which "Black capitalism" could supposedly thrive was preferred. The phrase was first used in a memorandum to Nixon by Daniel Patrick MOYNIHAN, later an influential if maverick Democratic Senator, which was leaked to the press in March 1970. Moynihan advised:

> The time may have come when the issue of race could benefit from a period of benign neglect. The subject has been too much talked about. The forum has been too much taken over by hysterics, paranoids, and boodlers on all sides. We may need a period in which negro progress continues and racial rhetoric fades. The administration can help bring this about by paying close attention to such progress – as we are doing – while seeking to avoid situations in which extremists of either race are given opportunities for martyrdom, heroics, histrionics or whatever.

Benn. Bennery A derogatory term for the combination of POPULISM, WORKERS' CONTROL and (to its critics) dangerous eccentricity which Tony (Anthony Wedgwood) **Benn** (1925–) pursued as UK Industry Secretary in 1974–75 before being moved by Harold WILSON to the less controversial Energy portfolio in his Labour government. Benn championed increased NATIONALIZATION, State involvement in private industry and the conversion of loss-making factories into workers' CO-OPERATIVES with a schoolboyish zeal and a patrician manner which led the novelist Malcolm Bradbury to term him "the Bertie Wooster of Marxism". His policies earned him bitter enemies in the Tory Party and Fleet Street; Benn himself said: "If I rescued a child from drowning, the press would no doubt headline the story: 'Benn Grabs Child'." The Liberal Cyril Smith (*see* BIG CYRIL), asserted: "He did more to British industry in one speech than the combined effects of the Luftwaffe and the U-boats did in the whole of the last war."

Yet Benn was to earn even greater vituperation seven years later from right-wingers in his own party when hard LEFT **Bennites**, campaigning for "party democracy", provoked the GANG OF FOUR into leaving Labour to start the SDP. He himself came within a whisker in 1981 of ousting Denis Healey as deputy party leader. Healey, when told of Benn's challenge, said: "Yes, and tomorrow he is parachuting into Scotland to hold peace talks with the Duke of Hamilton" (*see* HESS MISSION).

Benn's career has been a paradox, combining sudden enthusiasms and U-turns as he moved from right to left (notably on nuclear policy and Europe) with a strong belief in the rights of Parliament (*see* ZIRCON) and the individual. But his greatest legacy is a change in the law so that heirs to PEERAGES can renounce their titles and remain eligible to sit in the House of Commons. Elected an MP for Bristol in 1950, Benn succeeded to the Viscountcy of Stansgate when his father died in 1960; his seat was declared vacant, he fought a BY-ELECTION, won it, but was barred from the Commons. He instigated legislation to make peerages disclaimable for life, and on its passage was re-elected to his old seat. The change in the law had a dramatic effect within months, when Lord Hailsham renounced his peerage in a bid for the Tory leadership; another peer, Lord Home, was chosen and gave up his title to become SIR ALEC Douglas-Home. Benn served as Postmaster-General, Minister of Technology and Minister of Power in the 1964–70 Wilson government; Bernard Levin wrote: "He threw himself into the Sixties technology with the enthusiasm (not to say the language) of a newly-enrolled Boy Scout demonstrating knot-tying to indulgent parents." In opposition Benn moved leftward, championing on the party's National Executive a markedly more Socialist PLATFORM adopted in 1973. On Labour's sudden return in 1974, Benn was given first Industry and then Energy, where he oversaw the birth of North Sea oil; he had not yet turned against nuclear power. Once a pro-European, he was a leader of the anti-EC faction in the Wilson–Callaghan Cabinet, and of the "No" campaign in the 1975 referendum on Britain's continued membership. When Labour lost power in 1979, Benn emerged as leader of the left, infuriating first Callaghan and then his successor as leader, Michael Foot. He posed Neil KINNOCK fewer headaches, as he lost his seat in 1983, and by the time he returned as MP for Chesterfield, the trauma of Labour's worst defeat for half a century and the decline of the hard LEFT had weakened his support. But he continued in the Commons as an effective, and in many ways respected, BACKBENCHER.

Tomfool issues, barmy ideas, a kind of ageing, perennial youth who immatures with age. HAROLD WILSON.

Less of a wide-eyed Trot than a very English phenomenon; a descendant of the Puritans and the Nonconformists and, despite his doubts about the Almighty, 19th-century Christian socialists. JOHN MORTIMER.

He has had more conversions on the road to Damascus than a Syrian long-distance lorry driver. JIMMY REID.

Berkeley rules The rules on which the first election for the Conservative leadership was held in 1965, Edward Heath defeating Reginald Maudling by 150 votes to 133, with other candidates well behind, to succeed SIR ALEC Douglas-Home. They were devised by and named after Humphry Berkeley (1926–), who at the time was Conservative MP for Lancaster; after losing his seat he was first a Labour and then an SDP candidate. Previously the leader had "emerged" after consultations within the MAGIC CIRCLE of the party hierarchy. The Berkeley rules produced a leader but were felt to be flawed, so Sir Alec devised a more thorough system, first used when Margaret Thatcher defeated Heath a decade later.

Berlaymont The building in the heart of BRUSSELS that houses the EUROPEAN COMMISSION; with its three wings curving from a central core, it has come to represent both the power and the bureaucracy of the EC. Within the Berlaymont, an official's status is determined by the number of windows in his or her office; a COMMISSIONER has up to 32. The Commission had to move temporarily from the building in the early 1990s so that large quantities of potentially lethal asbestos could be removed.

Berlin. Berlin airlift The response of Britain and America to the blockade that STALIN imposed on 24 June 1948 on all road, rail and canal links from the West through the Soviet zone of Germany to West Berlin. He hoped to force the Allies out of Berlin, on which he had already tried to impose the Soviet currency, and incorporate West Berlin into East Germany, but he was foiled by an airlift by over 1000 planes which for 321 days met the needs of over two million West Berliners, bringing in over 2.5 million tons of cargo including fuel, and flying out its exports. Shooting down the planes would have meant war; Stalin was not prepared to go this far. So in May 1949 he relented and the links were reopened, in return for four-power talks on the future of Berlin.

Berlin crisis The crisis in the summer of 1961 which culminated in the building of the Berlin Wall. The Soviet leader Nikita S. Khruschev challenged the Western powers – Britain, America and France – to sign a

German peace treaty by the end of the year or see the USSR conclude a separate treaty with East Germany, not recognizing the status of West Berlin. The allies stood firm and both sides built up their forces until the KREMLIN backed down, but then East Germany began building the Berlin Wall.

Berlin Wall The wall which from 13 August 1961 until 9 November 1989 sealed off West Berlin from the Communist-controlled territory of East Germany and East Berlin that surrounded it. Erected to prevent East Germans fleeing to the West – 30,000 crossed in the previous month – it consisted in its final form of two walls of concrete two metres high, separated by a no man's land tens of metres wide which could be raked by gunfire from border police in watchtowers. Crossing was possible at a handful of checkpoints for road (*see* CHECKPOINT CHARLIE), rail, canal and metro traffic, but in practice only citizens of the occupying powers (Britain, America, France and the Soviet Union) and handpicked West Berliners who paid for the privilege were allowed through. The building of the wall brought East–West tension over Berlin to a head; John F. KENNEDY confessed that "a wall is better than a war", but spoke out strongly against it in his ICH BIN EIN BERLINER speech. The wall was opened amid scenes of jubilation as the East German Communist regime collapsed; its leader Erich Honecker was later put on trial for having ordered the shooting of escapers, though freed on health grounds early in 1993. The wall itself, apart from short stretches kept as memorials to the dozens shot trying to escape, was broken up for souvenirs.

Congress of Berlin The international negotiations in June – July 1878 which stabilized the Balkans, where Turkish influence was declining, until the war of 1912–13. Russia gained territory from the Turks after intervening to protect the Christian population of Bulgaria, and Britain took control of Cyprus.

Bermuda agreements The agreements between British and US Transport Secretaries which since 1946 have regulated air traffic between the two countries, governing the number of airlines permitted to fly the routes and the destinations to which they may fly. The agreements are open to renegotiation, with each side wanting greater scope for its own airlines but reluctant to reciprocate. In 1977 a new **Bermuda II** agreement was only concluded after the US authorities had given orders for UK planes to be turned back at midnight if final concessions were not made.

Berrigans The two radical New England Catholic priests who throughout the 1970s and into the 1980s were leading lights in the militant ANTI-WAR and peace movements. In 1970 Fr. Daniel and Fr. Philip Berrigan were jailed for burning DRAFT cards in protest at the VIETNAM WAR. Daniel was released in February 1972; Philip, who with Sister Elizabeth McAlister had been caught smuggling letters into prison, was freed that December. The sentences did not deter them from mounting further high-profile protests.

Berufsverbot (Ger. prohibition of vocation) The regulation barring political radicals – suspected communists and extreme leftists – from holding office in the West German civil service and educational system. It was enforced with particular vigour during the 1970s when East German efforts to infiltrate the bureaucracy of the West coincided with the upsurge of terrorism. However, liberals saw the prevention of at times harmless individuals from earning a living, particularly as teachers and minor officials, as an affront to HUMAN RIGHTS.

best. Best and the Brightest, the The book by the *New York Times* writer David Halberstam (1972) which catalogued the destruction of the high hopes of the KENNEDY administration and Johnson's GREAT SOCIETY in the morass of the VIETNAM WAR. The title emphasized the way in which some of the finest minds in America, brought together to high purpose by two Democratic Presidents, either created or were unable to prevent the war that tore America apart and destroyed its self-confidence.

why not the best? *See* WHY.

you do your worst, and we will do our best Winston CHURCHILL's challenge to Hitler in a speech on 14 July 1941, immediately after Germany's invasion of Russia.

Bevan. Bevanites The left-wing supporters of Aneurin Bevan (*see* NYE) who caused serious problems for the leadership of Britain's LABOUR PARTY in the early and mid-1950s. Shortly before the 1951 election Bevan resigned from ATTLEE's Cabinet in protest against the imposition of NHS charges. The Bevanites emerged as a faction in March 1952 when 57 Labour MPs broke with the leadership to vote against the new Conservative government's defence policy. The vote led to the imposition of tight party discipline, with anyone who defied decisions of the Parliamentary Party (*see* PLP) facing expulsion. Led by Bevan, Michael Foot (*see* WURZEL GUMMIDGE), Tom Driberg and Richard CROSSMAN, the group had strong support in the constituency parties and several seats on Labour's National Executive, though only

Bevan won election to the SHADOW CABINET. In 1954 they broke with the leadership over GERMAN REARMANENT after a narrow 113–104 party vote to approve it; Bevan resigned from the Shadow Cabinet. The next year Bevan had the WHIP withdrawn after 62 MPs ABSTAINed on Labour's official amendment to the Defence White Paper and he interrupted Attlee's speech. Right-wingers led by Herbert Morrison wanted Bevan out of the party, but the NEC by one vote accepted a compromise from Attlee under which Bevan stayed in, provided he apologized. After Labour's defeat in the 1955 election and Attlee's retirement, Bevan stood for the leadership, winning 70 votes to Hugh GAITSKELL's 157 and 40 for Morrison. He polled more strongly for the deputy leadership, and was actually elected party treasurer. However SUEZ soon united the party against the Government, after Gaitskell's initial support for tough action. The Bevanites never regained their strength as an irritant, and when the party next split, over UNILATERALISM, Bevan, now Shadow Foreign Secretary, sided with the leadership.

An uneasy coalition of well-meaning emotionalists, rejects, frustrates, crackpots and FELLOW-TRAVELLERS, making Fred Karno's army look like a Brigade of Guards.
HUGH DALTON.

Beveridge report The report produced in 1942 by the UK economist William Henry (later Lord) Beveridge (1879–1963) which paved the way for the post-war WELFARE STATE. Nominally the result of a review set up by the Ministry of Heath in 1941, the *Report on Social Insurance and Allied Services* was almost entirely Beveridge's work. He advocated the reorganization of social insurance to provide a minimum national income, and depended on three assumptions: a National Health Service (NHS), family allowances and a Government guarantee of FULL EMPLOYMENT. It was recognized even by CHURCHILL as a basis for action, but was adopted most enthusiastically by LABOUR as a central feature of its post-war programme. After 1945 Labour implemented many of its recommendations, but Beveridge's advocacy of WORKFARE was quietly ignored. Beveridge was given full credit by Labour, though he himself was an active Liberal.

Bevin boys Young men conscripted during World War II to work in Britain's coal mines under the Emergency Powers (Defence) Act of 1940. Ernest Bevin (1881–1951), Minister of Labour and National Service, directed in 1943 that one in ten men called up between the ages of 18 and 25 should go down the mines; the scheme continued for a time after the war. Bevin had been orphaned at seven and was a Baptist preacher before becoming a trade-union organizer, starting a meteoric rise during which he created the Transport and General Workers' Union from 32 separate bodies, serving as its General Secretary for almost 20 years; he was an influential figure in the 1926 GENERAL STRIKE. He was himself conscripted into Churchill's wartime coalition, his success in organizing the labour market establishing him as one of Labour's election-winners in 1945; Angus Calder wrote: "Bevinism in industry was symbolised by the growing understanding of the value of music and entertainment in helping people to work faster." Bevin as a union leader had always been influential in the Labour Party; at its 1935 conference he destroyed George Lansbury's PACIFIST campaign by accusing him of "trailing your conscience around from conference to conference asking to be told what to do with it"; when Lansbury's friends complained, he told them: "He has been going around in saint's clothes for years, waiting for martyrdom; I set fire to the faggots." As Alan Bullock put it, Bevin "often bullied in a good cause; he was a bully all the same".

Bevin described himself as "a turn-up in a million", and few would disagree. He went on to serve as Foreign Secretary in Attlee's government until forced to resign through ill-health early in 1951; he took a firm line with the Russians at the start of the COLD WAR, standing up to Stalin over BERLIN, and NATO was his lasting creation. Kingsley Martin wrote: "Bevin always treated the Soviet Union as if it were a breakaway faction of the Transport and General Workers' Union." In the process, as Harold Macmillan pointed out, "he imposed on an unwilling and hesitant party a policy of resistance to Soviet Russia and to Communism." Bevin was less happy with the birth of Israel, agreeing reluctantly to a Jewish state he was sure would solve none of the region's problems; nor was he keen on a united Europe. Nor was he happy speaking in the Commons, once saying: "I gets up when they nudges me and I sits down when they pulls me coat." And Michael Foot recalled: "A speech from EB on a major occasion had all the horrific fascination of a public execution." Yet he is rated one of the great Foreign Secretaries; asked once to define his policy, Bevin said: "My policy is to be able to take a ticket at Victoria Station and go where I damn well please."

There was no other position in the Foreign Office, unless it was that of a rather truculent liftman on the verge of retirement . . . which it would have been possible to imagine his filling.
ROY JENKINS.

Like Churchill he seemed a visitor from the 18th

> century – of the company of Chatham and Samuel Johnson, men of strong hearts and strong opinions.
> Obituary, *The Times*.

> He thought he was Palmerston wearing Keir Hardie's cloth cap, whereas he was really the Foreign Office's Charlie McCarthy. KONNI ZILLIACUS MP (Lab.).

bicameral system A legislature which has two chambers rather than one (a UNICAMERAL system), providing checks and balances and lessening the risk of elective dictatorship. At the birth of the United States, Benjamin FRANKLIN wrote that "a plural legislature is as necessary to good government as a single EXECUTIVE".

Biffo The nickname at Westminster both for John Biffen, a Cabinet Minister under Margaret Thatcher from 1979 until 1987 (*see* SEMI-DETACHED), and for the flamboyant Tory backbencher Geoffrey Dickens (*see* HORSEFACE). The Labour MP Joe Ashton gave Dickens the name, saying that it stood for "Big Ignorant Fool From Oldham". It originates in the comic character Biffo the Bear.

big. Big Ben The popular nickname for the clock tower at the northern end of the Palace of WESTMINSTER, overlooking Parliament Square and Westminster Bridge. Parties are occasionally permitted to climb the stairs of the tower, which contains several suites of members' offices that have never been used. The name should correctly refer only to the 13-tonne bell that chimes the hours. Big Ben took its name from Sir Benjamin Hall, Commissioner of Works when the bell was installed in 1859. It was first cast at Stockton in 1856, but on arrival by sea it developed a 4 ft. crack and was recast at Whitechapel; it cracked again and the Astronomer-Royal solved the problem by having a lighter hammer fitted.

Big Bill The popular name for William Hale Thompson (1867–1944), three times Mayor of Chicago, who was noted for his anti-British views. He once threatened to punch King George V on the nose if he ever visited Chicago. *See also* WOBBLIES.

Big Brother An all-pervading political authority able to keep all its citizens under continual observation and intrude into their lives in every respect. It comes from one of the most powerful phrases in George Orwell's novel NINETEEN EIGHTY-FOUR, whose central characters are constantly reminded that their deviations from the official line may be being watched. The allusion was implicitly to the Soviet Union, but it could apply to many other societies.

> The posters that were plastered everywhere . . . BIG BROTHER IS WATCHING YOU the caption said, while the dark eyes looked deep into Winston's own.
> *Nineteen Eighty-four*, p. 1.

Big Cyril The popular nickname for **Sir Cyril Smith** (1928–), Liberal MP for the Lancashire town of Rochdale from 1972 to 1992. A vast man weighing 25 stones, Smith's habit of speaking his mind did not make him a natural party man, but as the jovial proprietor of a spring-making company who lived with his old mother, he was a vastly popular media personality.

Big Four The four Allied leaders – Woodrow WILSON, Clemenceau (*see* the TIGER), Lloyd George (*see* L.G.) and Orlando of Italy – who set punitive peace terms for Germany and redrew the map of Europe at VERSAILLES after WORLD WAR I.

big government One of the great targets of US conservatives, a sprawling government machine that becomes the master, not the servant, of the people.

> If the government is big enough to give you all you want, it is big enough to take it all away.
> Sen. BARRY GOLDWATER'S ACCEPTANCE speech at the 1964 Republican convention.

Big Idea The critical new dimension to a party's policy that can capture the voters' imagination and ensure victory. Much sought by strategists, especially in Britain's LABOUR PARTY prior to its defeat in 1992.

Big Mo A US term for the critical momentum that will carry a political campaign through to victory. The phrase was coined in the late 1970s; in 1980 George BUSH claimed to have the "Big Mo" after beating Ronald Reagan in the Iowa CAUCUSes.

> He was clobbered by Reagan in the New Hampshire primary and the "big Mo" turned into the "big No".
> PAUL F. BOLLER, *Presidential Campaigns*.

bilaterals Talks or negotiations involving two heads of government or Ministers, often taking place on the fringes of an international conference of a larger number of leaders. In Britain the term also applies to the haggling over cash between the CHIEF SECRETARY to the Treasury and individual spending Ministers during the annual PESC round.

Bilderberg The international conferences, named after the Bilderberg Hotel at Arnhem where the first conference was held in 1954, which have brought Western politicians, industrialists and trade unionists together to promote closer transatlantic understanding. They were started by Joseph Retinger, a Pole who settled in England after World War II, and were chaired by Prince Bernhard of the Netherlands until his disgrace in the LOCKHEED SCANDAL. They have been denounced by CONSPIRACY THEORISTS in America as part of a left-wing conspiracy to rule the world and subvert the United States.

bilingualism A policy of giving more or less equal weight to two languages in a particular jurisdiction, for instance French in various provinces of Canada. When Bill Clements, governor of Texas from 1987 to 1991, tried to learn Spanish to promote bilingualism, one state legislator remarked:

> Good, now he'll be bi-ignorant.

Bill An item of proposed legislation, when presented to a legislature and during its passage, at the end of which it becomes an ACT. Speaker John Nance Garner (*see* CACTUS JACK) used to tell SPONSORS:

> Hell, don't tell me what the Bill says. Just tell me what it does.

Bill of Rights (1) The Bill passed at Westminster after the GLORIOUS REVOLUTION of 1689 which declared that James II (VII of Scotland) had ABDICATED, established William III (William of ORANGE) and Mary II as joint monarchs, barred Roman Catholics from ascending the THRONE and remedied a number of James's perceived abuses, for instance by making it illegal to keep a standing army in peacetime. (2) The first ten AMENDMENTS to the US CONSTITUTION, proposed in 1789 and ratified on 15 September 1791. They added several basic safeguards to the Constitution, starting with FREEDOM OF SPEECH and also including the RIGHT TO KEEP AND BEAR ARMS, immunity from search without proper warrant, protection against self-incrimination and a guarantee of due process, the right to a speedy and public trial and a strict construction of the powers of the Federal government. Drafted and campaigned for by James MADISON, the Bill met opposition from Alexander HAMILTON who asked: "Why declare that things shall not be done which there is no power to do? Why, in short, have a Bill of Rights?" But Thomas JEFFERSON declared:

> A Bill of Rights is what the people are entitled to against every government on earth, general or particular, and what no just government should refuse or rest on inference.

(3) In the UK, a package of legislation to protect the rights of the individual which has long been campaigned for by the Liberal (since 1988 Liberal Democrat) party and progressive judges and lawyers, and since 1992 has been Labour Party policy also. A central feature would be the incorporation of the European DECLARATION OF HUMAN RIGHTS into English law.

Bill 101 The law put forward by Quebec's PQ government after its election in 1976 which made French the province's sole official language and imposed severe restraints on the use of English in business, education and many other fields of life. Its enaction caused a number of Anglophones to leave Quebec for the United States or English-speaking Canadian provinces, but did not prove the first step to the province's separation from Canada, as its promoters had hoped.

clean Bill In the US HOUSE OF REPRESENTATIVES, a Bill which is reported by the relevant committee without any amendments having been made.

companion Bill A Bill introduced in one House of the US Congress that is identical to one put forward in the other.

enrolled Bill A Bill as finally approved by both Houses of Congress, if necessary after a House-Senate CONFERENCE, for signature by the President. The wording and punctuation have to be exactly as decided, with all AMENDMENTS accurately reflected. The enrolled Bill is printed on parchment paper, with the Clerk of the House or Secretary of the Senate certifying in which House it originated, it is examined for accuracy by the Committee on House Administration or the Secretary of the Senate, and is then signed by the SPEAKER of the House and the VICE-PRESIDENT or PRESIDENT PRO TEM before transmission by the Committee to the White House.

Finance Bill The Bill incorporating the detailed taxation and other provisions of the UK BUDGET. Immediate tax changes are made in BUDGET RESOLUTIONS voted on at the close of the Budget debate, but the Finance Bill which can run to hundreds of pages, is only brought forward once the technical work is complete, with debate (including late-night sessions in COMMITTEE) usually concluding four months after the Budget. The finance Bill does not have to be debated or approved by the House of Lords.

non-contentious Bill At Westminster, a measure over which there is no disagreement and for which only a limited amount of TIME need be allocated.

Paving Bill *See* PAVING.

Private Bill (1) In the US Congress, a Bill affecting an individual rather than the public at large, for instance to deal with an individual immigration or naturalization case or to settle a claim by or against the Federal Government. (2) At Westminster, a Bill brought forward by an individual, a company or a public body. The majority deal with the construction and regulation of railways, harbours and markets, but occasionally Bills enabling a couple within the prohibited degrees to marry (usually a step-parent and stepchild) are promoted in the House of Lords. The procedure for dealing with a Private Bill involves a different committee process from Government legislation. *See also* HYBRIDITY.

Private Member's Bill A Bill promoted at Westminster by a BACKBENCH MP; most are minor changes in the law suggested by Government departments or pressure groups, but the procedure has also been used to promote major reforms to the law on abortion and obscenity and to try to force through FREEDOM OF INFORMATION and abolish the Sunday observance laws. TIME for such Bills to be debated is allocated on several Fridays, and in an average year around a dozen Private Members' Bills, including some originating in the Lords, reach the Statute Book.

Public Bill (1) At Westminster, any piece of legislation put forward by the Government. (2) In the US Congress, one that affects the public generally, regardless of who promotes it.

Reported Bill A Bill that has been considered and endorsed by a Committee of either House of Congress, and is placed on the relevant CALENDAR for future debate. It is accompanied by a "committee report" from one of the committee's members, which describes the scope and purpose of the Bill and the reasons for recommending approval; these reports are used by the courts and other agencies, if the measure is passed, to ascertain the meaning intended by Congress.

Billygate A considerable embarrassment caused to President CARTER by his beer-swilling redneck brother Billy, arising from a free trip to Libya he unwisely accepted. On his return, Billy founded a Libyan-Arab-Georgia Friendship Society; but he got more attention in January 1979 by urinating on an airport runway while waiting to greet a Libyan delegation. The Justice Department demanded that he register as a foreign agent, which he at first refused to do, saying of Jewish protesters: "They can kiss my ass." The President, aware that his Jewish support was compromised, asserted that his brother was seriously ill; Billy checked into an alcohol rehabilitation clinic, and a Senate investigation concluded that Billy had done little for the $200,000 the Libyans had paid him. However the damage was done, the President admitting to "bad judgment" in asking his brother to intercede with Libya to press for the release of the Teheran HOSTAGES.

> I got a mamma (*see* MIZ LILLIAN) who joined the PEACE CORPS and went to India when she was 68. I got one sister who's a Holy Roller preacher. I got another sister who wears a helmet and rides a motorcycle. And I got a brother who thinks he's going to be President. So that makes me the only sane person in the family.
> BILLY CARTER, 1976.

binding. Solomon Binding As with LAURA NORDER, not a person but a political idea: the "solemn and binding" agreement the trade unions offered Harold WILSON's government in 1969 in return for the abandonment of the reforms advocated in IN PLACE OF STRIFE. There was widespread scepticism, which was to prove justified, over the unions' ability or readiness to put their house in order, and before long the phrase had turned into this fictitious individual.

Bingham Report (1) The report, concluded in September 1978, of the inquiry into SANCTIONS-BUSTING to supply the Smith regime in Rhodesia, which was headed by Thomas Bingham QC. The inquiry, set up the year before by the Labour Foreign Secretary Dr. David OWEN, embarrassed the Government when it was suggested that Harold WILSON had known about the continued supply of oil to Rhodesia by Shell-BP and Total, despite denials at the time. Bingham concluded that some breaches had been committed, but moves to set up a fuller inquiry petered out. (2) The report on the collapse of the Bank of Credit and Commerce International submitted in 1992 by the by-now Lord Justice Bingham. He largely exonerated the authorities and the Bank of England against charges that prompter action to close down a bank being defrauded on a massive scale would have saved thousands of depositors from bankruptcy – not to mention Scotland's tiny Western Isles Council which lost £23 million in the crash.

bipartisanship Co-operation between normally-opposed parties in pursuit of a common aim deemed to be non-controversial. The virtual unanimity achieved may not mean that the policy is the right one, the Victorian Liberal MP G. W. Erskine Russell writing:

> When the government of the day and the opposition of the day take the same side, one can be almost sure that some great wrong is at hand.

Britain's main parties have generally followed a bipartisan policy toward NORTHERN IRELAND, while the US Congress has at times adopted one on key foreign policy issues, Sen. Arthur H. Vandenberg loftily declaring:

> To me bipartisan means a mutual effort, under our indispensable two-party system, to unite our official voice at the water's edge so that America speaks with the maximum authority. . . . It does not involve the remotest surrender of free debate in determining our position.

> I don't intend to be in on the crash-landing unless I can be in on the take-off. HAROLD STASSEN (*attr.*).

> If you're going to lie down with the dogs, you're going to get fleas. Rep. TRENT LOTT, House Minority WHIP.

Birch. John Birch Society An ultraconservative US secret society founded on 9 December 1958 by Robert H. W. Welch

(1899–1985), a retired Boston candy manufacturer, to combat Communism and other potential threats to the American way of life. The society is named in honour of Captain John Birch, a Baptist missionary and US Army intelligence officer killed by Chinese Communists in August 1945. Welch regarded John Birch as the first US victim of the COLD WAR.

I don't believe I have any moral justification for repudiating them. RONALD REAGAN.

Birmingham campaign The non-violent campaign for racial INTEGRATION and CIVIL RIGHTS mounted by Dr. Martin Luther KING and the Southern Christian Leadership Council in the spring of 1963 to break one of the stongest bastions of SEGREGATION. Huge demonstrations were mounted day after day, and television viewers across America saw BULL Connor, the Alabama city's commissioner of public safety, turn dogs and firehoses on the protesters, including children. Hundreds of arrests were made, but new recruits filled the gaps until the city's businessmen capitulated and offered to end segregation in restaurants and discrimination in jobs. Mass demonstrations by Black Americans in support of President KENNEDY's Civil Rights Bill, and for its strengthening, spread across America, and culminating in the MARCH ON WASHINGTON FOR JOBS AND FREEDOM.

Now is the time to lift our national policy from the quicksand of racial injustice to the solid rock of human dignity.
MARTIN LUTHER KING, letter from Birmingham city jail, 16 April 1963.

Birmingham Six The six Irish residents of Birmingham who were convicted in July 1975 of the bombings of the *Mulberry Bush* and *Tavern in the Town* pubs in the city the previous November which killed 21 people and injured almost 200. The bombings prompted the Labour government to rush through the Prevention of TERRORISM Act. Those convicted were Hugh Callaghan, Patrick Hill, Gerrard Hunter, Richard McIlkenny, William Power and John Walker, five of whom had been arrested as they boarded the Belfast boat off a train that left Birmingham just before the explosions. Though the trial judge said they had been convicted on the clearest evidence, doubts were raised over the forensic evidence and the conduct of the police in obtaining statements – one of which subsequently appeared to have been forged – and confessions. A campaign gradually got under way on their behalf, and after the Court of Appeal had twice rejected moves to overturn the convictions, they were finally set free on 14 March 1991, having been in custody for over 16 years. The furore over this and a series of other miscarriages of justice, most of them in trials of alleged IRA terrorists, raised deep concerns about the workings of the legal system and the police, and prompted the establishment of a ROYAL COMMISSION on Criminal Justice.

Bismarck, Prince Otto von *See* IRON CHANCELLOR.

bisque A variant of a PAIR at Westminster, an arrangement under which an MP is excused from attending the House by party WHIPS; the name has nothing to do with soup, coming from the game of croquet when a player can agree to miss his turn. The practice was introduced in the 1983–87 Parliament when a Conservative majority of almost 150 left many Tory MPs without a pair; it has been little used since the 1992 election, when the majority was cut to 21.

Bitburg affair The furore around President Reagan's visit to the Kolmeshohe German war cemetery at Bitburg in May 1985. Planned as a gesture of reconciliation, the trip backfired politically when US officials, and then the press, belatedly discovered that the cemetery included graves of 47 men from the *Waffen SS*. Jewish groups, 53 senators, 390 members of the House and Nancy Reagan herself all urged the President not to go, but he went ahead rather than stage a public snub to his host, Chancellor Kohl. The President acknowledged that "some old wounds have been reopened", and with dignity undid much of the damage.

black. Black and Tans The irregulars enlisted by Lloyd George's government in 1920 to supplement the Royal Irish Constabulary as political disorder reached its height; though withdrawn a year later, they left behind a lasting reputation for indiscriminate brutality against Irish Nationalists. The name came from a pack of hounds in Co. Limerick, and was applied to them because of their mixed black and tan uniforms, there being a shortage of police uniforms.

Black Caucus The organization which since 1967 has brought together Black members of the US Congress, to co-ordinate action on matters of common interest and CIVIL RIGHTS in particular.

Black Codes The laws to restrict the liberties of freed slaves, introduced by states in America's South in 1865–66 to blunt the edge of RECONSTRUCTION after the CIVIL WAR. Marriages between them were at last permitted and the right to hold property granted, but conditions of work little short of slavery were laid down, freedmen having to hire themselves out by the year. While the Codes deprived most Black people of the vote, they failed to bring back the old plantation system, as in the end the labourers could not be compelled to work as before.

Black Consciousness The moderate anti-APARTHEID movement founded in South Africa by Steve Biko (1946–77), who was to die of head injuries in police custody. The film *Cry Freedom* (1987) paid tribute to his life and vision.

> The most potent weapon in the hands of the oppressor is the mind of the oppressed. STEVE BIKO.

Black Hand Gang (1) (Serbo-Croat: *Ujedinjenje Ili Smrt*, Unity or Death) The popular name for the Serb secret society responsible for the assassination of Archduke Franz Ferdinand at SARAJEVO in 28 June 1914, which led directly to the outbreak of WORLD WAR I. The Gang, headed by Colonel Dragutin Dimitrievic of Serbian military intelligence, aimed to recover lands that had historically belonged to Serbia. (2) A criminal society, once active in New York, largely made up of Italians.

Black is beautiful The BLACK POWER slogan current in America from 1966 and attributed to Stokely Carmichael.

blackleg (1) In industrial disputes, an abusive term used by strikers for a person who has carried on working. (2) The word which, used by Sen. John Randolph of Virginia in 1826, provoked Speaker Henry Clay into challenging him to a duel. At that time it meant a dishonest gambler. The duel took place by the POTOMAC upstream from Washington on 8 April; after two exchanges of shots inflicted no injuries, Randolph and Clay shook hands and buried their differences.

blacklist A list of individuals considered unsuitable for employment because of their political views or personal lives. It was used in the days of McCARTHYISM for people barred from Hollywood's motion picture industry for alleged links with the Communist Party, and is used by some employers to prevent the employment of militant trade unionists.

Black Monday (1) The US SUPREME COURT's action on 27 May 1935 in declaring the National Recovery Administration (NRA) UNCONSTITUTIONAL, which appeared to strike a deadly blow at the NEW DEAL. President Roosevelt thought so, declaring that the Court had reinstated the "HORSE AND BUGGY definition of interstate commerce". Its ruling in what became known as the Sick CHICKEN CASE was in fact followed by a fresh burst of New Deal activity and the re-enactment of much of the legislation struck down, but it reminded the Roosevelt administration that it had to act within the Constitution. (2) The plunge in share prices on 19 October 1987, when the Dow Jones average on Wall Street fell by 23% and London and most other markets followed suit. Caused by computerized selling of stock in New York, it was thought likely to lead to RECESSION, but reflationary measures taken to avert this, especially in Britain, produced OVERHEATING instead.

Black Muslims The Islamic sect, founded in 1931, that has flourished among urban Black Americans since the mid-1960s; the most famous Black Muslims have been Malcolm X and the boxer Muhammad Ali, who was stripped of his title when he refused to fight in VIETNAM. As well as the mainstream sect itself, a number of splinter groups have also been established, several of them thriving.

Black Panthers A US Black revolutionary organization founded in October 1966, which was briefly notorious for demanding the release of all Black prisoners from US gaols and for a series of dramatic shootouts with the police which killed 25 of their members. The origin of the name was probably the black panther adopted as an emblem in 1965 by the SNCC, and used by a group of BLACK POWER candidates who contested Alabama elections in 1966. A Black Panther Party emerged in California the following year led by Huey Newton and Eldridge Cleaver, preaching total separation from White society and urging Blacks to take up arms in "self-defense". In October 1968 Newton was jailed for manslaughter for involvement in one of the shootouts, prompting a "Free Huey" campaign. And in December 1970 the Panthers' Chicago leader was shot dead in his bed by police officers; his head of security was a police agent, recruited under J. Edgar Hoover's COINTELPRO programme. The movement lapsed in the 1970s, after internal rifts and the arrest, defection or death of leading members.

> The panther is a fierce animal, but he will not attack until he is backed into a corner. Then he will strike out. HUEY NEWTON.

Black Power A slogan first used by the US Black leader Stokely Carmichael during a confrontation with police at Greenwood, Mississippi, on 16 June 1966, subsequently adopted by a variety of Black and radical organizations. It implied a rejection of both INTEGRATION as a political goal and the pacifism of the CIVIL RIGHTS movement led by Dr. Martin Luther KING, who was deeply suspicious of the word "power". As such, it sparked keen debate among Black Americans, gradually gaining ground at the expense of less militant campaigning, and alienated many White liberals. This applied particularly to the clenched-fist Black Power salute, dramatically given by the sprinters Tommie Smith and John Carlos during the US National Anthem at their medal ceremony at the 1968 Mexico Olympics; they were expelled from the games and ordered home.

> To ask Negroes to get in the Democratic Party is like asking Jews to join the NAZI party.
> STOKELY CARMICHAEL.

> The slogan "Black Power" and what has been associated with it has set the Civil Rights movement back considerably in the United States over the period of the last several months.
> Sen. ROBERT KENNEDY, 8 December 1966.

black propaganda *See* PROPAGANDA.

Black Rod The Royal appointee, generally a former military man, who controls the functioning and security of the HOUSE OF LORDS, his counterpart in the Commons being the SERJEANT-AT-ARMS. His most visible function is to convey messages from the Lords to the Commons, and to ask them to attend the State Opening of Parliament and the PROROGATION ceremony; to demonstrate their independence, the Commons shut the door on him and he has to knock for admission. On 13 November 1979 Labour MPs, incensed that Michael Heseltine (*see* TARZAN) had announced council-house rent increases in a WRITTEN ANSWER, too late for debate, physically prevented Black Rod entering to bring the session to an end.

Black Sash The organization of White liberal women in South Africa which, throughout the time of APARTHEID, staged dignified VIGILs against the policy and the RACISM it stood for.

Black Sections The groups set up in various constituency LABOUR parties, mainly in London, in the mid-1980s by left-wingers determined that ethnic minority members should have separate representation in the party. Their advocates hailed them as essential to the involvement of Black and Asian Britons in mainstream politics; their opponents, mainly in the trade unions, denounced them as a form of APARTHEID in reverse. Labour's National Executive and party conference refused to endorse the sections, and ultimately the compromise of a political society within the party open to all ethnic minority members was decided.

Black September A Palestinian terrorist group founded in 1972, the name commemorating the expulsion of the PLO from Jordan in 1970. The MUNICH OLYMPICS MASSACRE of 1972 was staged by the group, as well as several HIJACKINGs and assassinations; one of its activists, Leila Khaled, was arrested in London in the early 1970s and deported lest the group stage terrorist attacks in Britain. King Hussein of Jordan was at the top of its assassination list, and Australia's pro-Israeli trade union leader (and later Prime Minister) Bob Hawke (*see* SILVER BODGIE) was also believed to be a target.

Blackshirts Mussolini's Italian FASCISTS, named after the distinguishing garments they wore. A similar uniform was adopted by the British Union of Fascists under Sir Oswald Mosley (*see* MOSLEYITES). It was also a name for the German SS (*Schutzstaffeln*) led by Himmler. *See also* BLUESHIRTS; BROWNSHIRTS.

> Before the organisation of the Blackshirt movement, free speech did not exist in this country.
> Sir OSWALD MOSLEY.

Black Thursday The name given to 24 October 1929, the day when the GREAT CRASH on Wall Street began. After some selling the previous day, a record 12.9 million shares were dumped on the market, ruining thousands of investors and some brokers, even though a consortium led by the Morgan banking house moved in to steady prices. The market steadied on Friday, but selling began after a statement from President HOOVER, intended to reassure but worded so as to hint that the stock market might be less sound than the economy as a whole. And on **Black Tuesday**, 29 October, the bottom fell out of the market. 650,000 shares in US Steel were unloaded in the first three minutes, company after company collapsed, and by the close 16.4 million shares had been sold, at a loss of $10 billion.

Black Wednesday The day, 17 September 1992, which saw the UK DEVALUE the pound and pull out of the Exchange Rate Mechanism (ERM). With the pound sliding against the mark after tensions between Chancellor Norman Lamont and the BUNDESBANK, the Bank of England raised interest rates from 10% to 12% and then to 15% in a vain attempt to halt the slide. With at least $8 billion of Britain's currency reserves (more than twice the cost of the GULF WAR) spent on this ultimately futile exercise, Lamont pulled sterling out of ERM and the pound began a 45-pfennig fall against the mark; interest rates reverted to 12% and returned to 10% later in the week. Black Wednesday did considerable political damage to John MAJOR's government and brought almost universal calls for Lamont's resignation, but he stayed on till the following spring (*see* JE NE REGRETTE RIEN) – partly because Major loyally stressed that the failed policy had been his. It also cast a large shadow over Britain's presidency of the EC. However the medium-term effect of devaluation was to break away from the savagely deflationary policies of the Bundesbank and offer some hope of economic recovery – and by early 1993, with interest rates down to 6%, many

Conservative MPs were speaking of **Golden Wednesday**.

> Now we've ALL been screwed by the Cabinet!
>
> The *Sun*.

Baa, Baa, Black Sheep Press reports in 1987 that London's Labour-controlled Islington council had banned the rhyme in its nursery schools as RACIST marked the high-point of controversy over the activities of the "loony LEFT" in the capital. The council denied it had banned the rhyme, but some nurseries in other parts of inner London were found to have done so.

Blair House The four-storey yellow brick Georgian mansion across Pennsylvania Avenue from the WHITE HOUSE. The house where Robert E. Lee refused the Union command before the CIVIL WAR, it was bought by the Federal Government during World War II as a guest house for visiting dignitaries, an action hotly opposed by Congressional Republicans. It is used by incoming Presidents the night before their INAUGURATION, most recently by Bill Clinton on 19–20 January 1993. It has also housed the President himself when the White House has been under reconstruction. While Harry S Truman was staying there on 1 November 1950 two Puerto Rican gunmen, Oscar Collazo and Griselio Torresola, burst in and tried to shoot him; Torresola was shot dead by SECRET SERVICE agents, Collazo was caught and sentenced to death but REPRIEVED by the President. During World War II the Soviet foreign minister Vyacheslav Molotov (*see* NIET!) arrived at Blair House with brown bread, sausages and a pistol in his suitcase, and asking to see Virginia's Luray Caverns.

The accord between America and the EUROPEAN COMMUNITY on oilseeds and farm subsidies, reached in December 1992 in the teeth of resistance from France, was concluded there. Known as the Blair House Agreement, it was designed to facilitate an early resolution of the URUGUAY ROUND of GATT talks.

blame game politics The art of ensuring that when a policy misfires, the blame falls on someone else. In Washington the SEPARATION OF POWERS enables the President to blame Congress for manifest failures, though he sometimes finds it convenient to blame his STAFF. Ronald Reagan, prior to the IRAN-CONTRA AFFAIR, was widely seen as a master of the art. *See also* PREPARE THREE ENVELOPES.

blanket protest The protest staged by convicted IRA terrorists in Northern Ireland's MAZE PRISON from 1980 as a demand for the same POLITICAL STATUS as had been enjoyed by unconvicted suspects held during INTERNMENT. Prisoners "on the blanket" refused to wear prison clothes, wrapping themselves in grey prison blankets. The campaign escalated into a DIRTY PROTEST and eventually a hunger STRIKE in which several prisoners died, before it was abandoned in return for some limited freedoms.

bleeding-hearts An unflattering term for political LIBERALS, stemming from their tendency to agonize over the human condition. It was popularized in the 1930s by the US newspaper columnist Westwood Pegler (1864–1969). "Bleeding-heart liberals" were targeted as one of a number of suspect groups in 1947 by the House Committee on UN-AMERICAN ACTIVITIES, and in October 1968 Pierre TRUDEAU, as he prepared to invoke Canada's WAR MEASURES ACT, said of critics of his crackdown on Quebec SEPARATIST terrorism:

> There are a lot of bleeding hearts around who just don't like to see people with helmets and guns. All I can say is go and bleed – it is more important to keep law and order in society than to be worried about weak-kneed people.

blip A sudden downturn (or upturn) in the economy or one of its indicators that should not be taken as indicating a long-term trend. The term is sometimes used by politicians to put a less serious gloss on one set of bad figures; when the UK economy in early 1989 began the downturn that three years later had become a serious recession, Chancellor Nigel Lawson described the first adverse indicators as a blip.

Blitzkrieg (Ger. lightning war) (1) The devastating motorized advance of German armies through the Low Countries and into France in early May 1940, which rewrote the war manuals; Hitler tried the same tactics against Soviet Russia the next summer, with great initial success. The German air assault on London and other British cities following the Battle of Britain, in which the HOUSE OF COMMONS chamber was destroyed on 10 May 1941, was known as the Blitz. And when Israeli tanks launched a devastating attack on the country's Arab neighbours at the start of the 1967 SIX-DAY WAR, *Time* magazine headlined it "The Blintzkrieg". (2) The crash COLLECTIVIZATION programme ordered by East Germany's Communist leader Walter Ulbricht in 1959–60.

block captain One of the essential functionaries in US MACHINE POLITICS, being responsible for delivering votes in a city block to the ruling party, and keeping an ear open for those in need of help or PATRONAGE.

blockade A naval operation to discourage and, if necessary, prevent ships conveying supplies to a nation or community under siege. General Franco's navy staged a blockade of Republican Spain during the SPANISH CIVIL WAR which enterprising captains including Potato Jones (Captain D. I. Jones, 1870–1962) attempted to break. A US blockade to prevent Soviet ships carrying nuclear missiles reaching Cuba brought the CUBAN MISSILE CRISIS to a head.

blood. Blood and Iron The phrase that epitomizes the militarism that lay behind the rise of Prussia under Bismarck (*see* IRON CHANCELLOR) and Germany's subsequent headlong rush toward WORLD WAR I. Bismarck is credited with being its author; on 30 September 1862 he told the Prussian Chamber:

> The great questions of our day cannot be solved by speeches and majority votes ... but by iron and blood.

Yet the phrase was not original; the 1st-century Roman orator Quintilian actually used the words *sanguinem et ferrum* – blood and iron.

blood, sweat and tears The slightly-modified public recollection of Winston CHURCHILL's dramatic first speech as Prime Minister to the House of Commons on 13 May 1940; he was taking office after the fall of Neville Chamberlain as the German BLITZKRIEG was sweeping toward Paris. Churchill's exact words were:

> I would say to the House, as I said to those who have joined this Government: "I have nothing to offer you but blood, toil, tears and sweat."

Churchill may actually have meant to say "blood, sweat and tears", which would have been a quotation from Byron. Indeed some radio listeners thought that was what he did say when his speech – re-delivered – was broadcast later.

Bloody Sunday (1) The riot that broke out in London's TRAFALGAR SQUARE on 13 November 1887 during a demonstration by the unemployed, which prompted William Booth, founder of the Salvation Army, and others to campaign for better conditions for the capital's poor. It culminated in Cunninghame Graham, a Scottish laird and radical MP, and the future Liberal Cabinet Minister John Burns being charged and convicted of unlawful assembly. (2) The murderous attack by TSARIST troops on 22 January 1905 on a deputation of workers and peasants led by Father Gapon as they marched to the Winter Palace in St. Petersburg to present a petition to the "Little Father". Hundreds of unarmed people were killed. (3) The killing by the IRA on 21 November 1920 of 11 Englishmen thought to be spies. The BLACK AND TANS retaliated by killing 12 spectators at a football match at Croke Park, Dublin, that afternoon. (4) The greatest single error by British security forces in Northern Ireland since the current troubles began, the shooting by paratroops on 30 January 1972 of 14 Catholic anti-INTERNMENT marchers in the Bogside area of Londonderry. The demonstration had been banned and the troops had itchy trigger fingers, and disaster ensued. The atrocity provoked riots in Dublin in which the British embassy was burned down, and drove many hitherto law-abiding Nationalists into the arms of the IRA. At Westminster, wrote the Labour MP Phillip Whitehead:

> Bernadette Devlin [*see* FIDEL CASTRO IN A MINISKIRT] bore down on the huge bulk of the Home Secretary [Reginald Maudling] like a pocket battleship, and battered him into something approaching wakefulness.

Bloody Sunday did untold damage to Britain's image throughout the world – especially in America where fund-raising for the Provisionals (*see* NORAID) rocketed.

rivers of blood *See* RIVERS.

there are worse things than bloodshed, and slavery is one of them The stirring words of the Irish nationalist revolutionary Padraic Pearse (1879–1916) in his book *The Coming Revolution* (1913). Three years later, Pearse led the EASTER RISING in Dublin, delivering the Proclamation of Independence as head of the "Provisional Government of the Irish Republic". He surrendered on 19 April and was executed on 3 May. Pearse wrote:

> We may make mistakes in the beginning and shoot the wrong people, but ... there are many things worse than bloodshed, and slavery is one of them.

waving the bloody shirt *See* WAVING.

bludger An Australian term for an idler on unemployment pay, the equivalent of "scrounger" in Britain, or the US "welfare queen". Gough WHITLAM's Labor government was accused by the Liberal opposition of encouraging "dole bludgers" while increasing tax burdens on the MIDDLE CLASS.

blue The campaign colour (with a couple of regional exceptions) of Britain's CONSERVATIVE PARTY, hence the expression "true blue" for a totally committed TORY. The Progressive Conservatives who governed Ontario continuously from 1943 to 1984 were known as the **Big Blue Machine**.

Blue and the Gray The rival combatants in America's CIVIL WAR: Blue for the Union and Gray for the Confederacy. In 1938, seventy-three years after the end of hostilities, 1845 survivors of the two armies – 1359 from the North and 486 from the South – gathered at GETTYSBURG, scene in 1863 of one of the war's most hard-fought engagements, for a final reunion, at which President Roosevelt unveiled a memorial of Eternal Light. Despite their extreme age, just one Veteran died on the final day and six more on the way home; the last lived on until 1949.

blue books At Westminster, the report of a Commons SELECT COMMITTEE or other document issued by the House; those produced by the Lords are coloured red.

blue-collar An originally US term for manual, as opposed to clerical (white-collar) workers.

blue helmets The universal nickname for United Nations PEACEKEEPING troops, who wear a blue helmet with the letters *UN* in place of their national uniform headgear.

Blue Laws The Sunday observance laws current in a number of American States, and especially those regulating the Sunday opening of shops and stores.

blue-ribbon panel or commission The Washington term for a group of eminent Americans appointed by the President or a Federal agency to inquire into or resolve a particular issue. The UK equivalent is the GREAT AND THE GOOD.

blue-rinse brigade An uncomplimentary term for the massed ranks of women constituency activists in Britain's CONSERVATIVE PARTY who assemble at its conferences; "blue-rinse" refers to their coiffure and is only coincidentally of political significance.

Blueshirts The FASCIST "National Guard" founded in Ireland on 20 July 1933 by General Eoin O'Duffy (1892–1944), Commissioner of the Garda (police) until his dismissal that year by de Valera. Outlawed within a month, it had grown out of the Army Comrades' Association founded the year before. O'Duffy became President of FINE GAEL two months after founding the Blueshirts, but resigned the next year and in 1935 founded the National Corporate Party. In the SPANISH CIVIL WAR a Blueshirt battalion led by O'Duffy fought alongside Franco's troops; on his death O'Duffy was accorded a State funeral.

Blue Streak The missile developed by the UK to deliver its independent DETERRENT, which was cancelled in 1960 when President Eisenhower agreed to supply Britain with the POLARIS submarine-launched missile and the air-delivered SKYBOLT. Two years later, the KENNEDY administration cancelled Skybolt, embarrassing Harold Macmillan, who had negotiated the original deal in BERMUDA. UK politicians and scientists had hoped Skybolt would become the basis of a British space programme, but it had run into technical difficulties during tests at the Woomera range in Australia and Ministers would not pay to keep the project alive.

blue water navy One of the attributes of a WORLD POWER, a navy able to command the great oceans as well as patrolling home waters. The term has a Victorian ring, but was first used between the World Wars by UK Admiralty officials who favoured building large ships to be deployed in distant parts of the world; in consequence Britain went into World War II with no landing craft. The phrase was used again in the 1960s and 1970s by the Soviet Admiral Gorchkov as his fast-expanding navy broadened its horizons.

Blunt case The belated exposure in 1979 of Sir Anthony Blunt (1907–83) as the FOURTH MAN in the BURGESS AND MACLEAN affair. Blunt, a distinguished art historian and former surveyor of the Queen's pictures, had been recruited at Cambridge in the 1930s by Soviet intelligence while a member of the APOSTLES. He had been a Soviet agent during the war while working for MI5, and in 1951 arranged Burgess and Maclean's flight to the Soviet Union. In 1964 he confessed his treachery, but he was guaranteed immunity from prosecution in return for telling all he knew. When Margaret Thatcher heard this on coming to power, she insisted, against the advice of senior civil servants, on making a detailed explanation to the House of Commons of what many MPs saw as a classic Establishment COVER-UP; in the ensuing furore, Blunt was stripped of his KNIGHTHOOD. In November 1979 the Attorney-General, Sir Michael Havers, told MPs that when confronted with his treachery, Blunt

> maintained his denial. He was offered immunity from prosecution. He sat in silence for a while. He got up, looked out of the window, poured himself a drink and after a few minutes he confessed. Later he co-operated, and he continued to co-operate. That is how the immunity was given and how Blunt responded.

Blythe, William Jefferson The original name of Bill Clinton (*see* COMEBACK KID), who was born on 19 August 1946 three months after his father, William Blythe, was killed in a car crash. When he was 15, the future President of the United States took the surname of his step-father, Roger Clinton. For another President who changed his name, *see* Leslie KING.

B'nai Brith (Heb. Sons of the Covenant) The oldest Jewish organization in the world, founded in New York in 1843, which exercises considerable political influence through the respect in which it is held by Jewish and Gentile politicians alike. *B'nai Brith* is closely identified with the the **Anti-Defamation League**, which it established in 1913 to counter anti-Jewish prejudice.

BND *Bundesnachrichtendienst* (Ger. Federal Information Service) The internal and overseas security and intelligence organization set up by the former West German government in

1956, and now serving the reunited nation; its headquarters is at Pullach. The BND absorbed the Gehlen organization, the covert force created after the war by Reinhold Gehlen, a former section head in Hitler's *Abwehr* who was trusted by the Americans.

board. Board of Education The informal gatherings of HOUSE Democratic and Republican leaders that took place most afternoons around 5 p.m. in a first-floor Capitol hideaway from 1928 until the death of Speaker Sam RAYBURN in 1961. They started with a chance meeting between Speaker Nicholas LONGWORTH and Minority Leader John Nance Garner (*see* CACTUS JACK), which developed into a regular session to get round PROHIBITION and keep the wheels of House BUSINESS rolling. Sometimes Longworth played his Stradivarius, on other occasions members would play poker; always they drank bourbon and what Garner called "branch water". The name was coined by Rep. Albert McDuffie of Alabama, a regular attender, because the Speaker would take in young Congressmen to "educate" them into voting his way; Garner, who took over as host on becoming Speaker in 1931, explained:

> We pay the tuition by supplying the liquor.

Rayburn carried on the tradition when he became Speaker in 1940, even inviting Vice-President Truman. It was from one such session on 12 April 1945 that Truman was called to the White House to be told by Eleanor Roosevelt that her husband was dead and he was now President. Apart from a hiatus from 1952 till 1954 when the teetotal Republican Joe Martin interrupted his reign, Rayburn stayed in the chair until his death.

Board of Trade *See* TRADE.

boat. boat people The flood of refugees from VIETNAM who, following the final Communist victory in 1975, crowded on to anything that would float to head for a new life in America – or anywhere else that would have them. Many drowned when their overloaded craft sank, others were murdered or raped by pirates, but tens of thousands made it to a mixed welcome in other Southeast Asian countries. As conditions in Vietnam improved, neighbouring states became less welcoming, and in the late 1980s the British authorities in Hong Kong attempted – against US opposition – to REPATRIATE some of the 40,000 boat people in camps in the colony who were ruled to be migrants and not genuine refugees.

Boatman Jim The nickname of **James Abram Garfield** (1831–81), 20th President of the United States (Republican, Mar.–Sep. 1881), who had worked as a boy on the Ohio Canal. A CIVIL WAR general, professor and eight-term Congressman, Garfield was elected Speaker in 1878. President GRANT declared him "not possessed of the backbone of an angleworm", but after his narrow victory over Winfield Hancock (his Electoral College margin was wider) he disproved this. He took on the powerful Sen. Roscoe Conkling, naming William H. Robertson to run the New York Custom House instead of a Conkling nominee and saying:

> This will settle the question of whether the President of the United States is registering clerk of the Senate or the Executive of the United States.

Garfield was shot at a Washington train station on 2 July 1881 by Charles Guiteau, a disappointed office-seeker, and died 11 weeks later; even the medical expertise of the day should have saved him but doctors mistakenly tried to recover the bullet.

> How could anyone be so cold-hearted as to want to kill my baby?
> Garfield's mother.

Bobbetty The nickname of Lord Cranborne (Robert Cecil), later the 5th Marquess of SALISBURY (1893–1972). Appointed a junior Minister at the Foreign Office by BALDWIN, he resigned with Anthony EDEN over APPEASEMENT, and abstained in the vote on the MUNICH AGREEMENT. He served as Leader of the Lords under CHURCHILL, Eden and Macmillan, but moved increasingly to the right, threatening to quit over Churchill's overtures to Russia after Stalin's death, and finally resigning in 1957 over the release of Archbishop Makarios from detention (*see* ENOSIS). His role in determining the succession to Eden early in 1957 was crucial (*see* WAB OR HAWOLD?).

Bodenstown The burial place, on the Liffey west of Dublin, of Wolfe Tone, the Irish patriot who brought French Forces to assist the rebellion of NINETY-EIGHT. Each year it is the scene of the **Bodenstown Parade**, staged by SINN FEIN as a rally for hard-line Republicans.

Boer War The conflict between 1899 and 1902 in which British forces subdued the independent Afrikaner states of what is now South Africa, paving the way for the country's unification under the British flag; it is sometimes known as the Second Boer war, the first having been fought in 1880–81. It saw the humiliation of the British Army by Boer commandos on several occasions, and gave a foretaste of the brutality of 20th-century warfare. British victory was only secured after harsh measures, including the confinement of Boer women and children to CONCENTRATION CAMPS, where

20,000 died. The Liberal opposition leader Sir Henry Campbell-Bannerman (*see* C-B) was moved to say:

> When is a war not a war? When it is carried out by methods of barbarism in South Africa.

The war created a serious split in the Liberal Party, some of the LIBERAL UNIONISTS realigning themselves with the Conservatives, and the radicals being denounced as PRO-BOER. The KHAKI ELECTION, held with victory apparently near, brought a comfortable victory for Lord SALISBURY's ruling Conservative/Unionists.

> A war that has been forced upon this country.
> Sir EDWARD GREY.

> When you enter a war purely for the purpose of plunder, I know of nothing which is more degrading to the country or more hideous in its effects on the mind and character of the people engaged in it. LLOYD GEORGE.

See also CHURCHILL; DEFEAT; MAFFICKING; VEREENIGING TREATY.

Bogside The area outside the walls of the Protestant (London) Derry where Catholics first settled in the 17th century. It became a stronghold of Republicanism after the "Battle of the Bogside" when Loyalists, backed by the B-SPECIALS, besieged it on 13 August 1969 at the start of the present TROUBLES.

Boipatong massacre The attack on African National Congress (ANC) supporters at Boipatong, in South Africa's *Vaal*, on 17 June 1992 which left 39 people dead. It was carried out by hostel-dwelling supporters of INKATHA; a judicial inquiry ruled that although the security forces could have done more to prevent the killings, they had not actually instigated them. Together with the massacre of 28 ANC demonstrators at Bishu on 7 September by the Ciskei security forces, they heightened tension between the ANC and both Inkatha and the Pretoria government to the point where a successful outcome by the CODESA process looked remote.

Bokassa diamonds The scandal surrounding a gift of diamonds to France's President Valéry Giscard d'Estaing from the self-styled Emperor Bokassa I of Central Africa. The transaction was unearthed by the satirical magazine *Le* CANARD ENCHAÎNÉ; Giscard at first denied it, then said that the diamonds had only been small ones. His benefactor, Jean-Bédel Bokassa, a French colonial soldier 1939–60, had overthrown Central Africa's first President, David Dacko, in 1966 and after ten years of autocratic rule crowned himself Emperor and commissioned a gigantic palace; its cold stores contained the carcases of opponents on whom he was alleged to have feasted. In 1979 Giscard, perhaps embarrassed by the disclosure of the gift, sent in French paratroops to restore Dacko. Bokassa fled, but returned in 1986; two years later he was sentenced to life imprisonment for crimes including a massacre of 100 schoolchildren, yet was acquitted of cannibalism.

Boland amendment The Congressional sanction, voted in 1982, against the Reagan administration providing training or military supplies to the Nicaraguan CONTRAS. The amendment to the Defense Appropriation Act, named after Rep. Edward Boland of Massachusetts, Chairman of the House Intelligence Committee, was passed unanimously by the House because members feared the CIA was secretly helping the Contras in their war against the SANDINISTA government. The next year, still suspecting the CIA was conducting a "secret war", Boland pushed through a second amendment setting a ceiling on funding for the Contras and urging the President to negotiate. With the exposure of the IRAN-CONTRA affair at the end of 1986, both the TOWER COMMISSION and Congressional hearings showed that the Boland amendment had been flagrantly violated.

boll weevils The 50 or so Conservative Southern Democratic members of the House of Representatives whose Conservative Democratic Forum is a cohesive and influential voting bloc. They took the name from the cotton weevil which bores from within, signifying their intention of making their presence felt in the Democratic caucus as a whole – even though many were elected by running against the party's national platform on defence spending and budget deficits. The support of the boll weevils was critical to Ronald Reagan's ability to win Congressional votes early in his presidency.

Bolsheviks (Russ. the majority) The hard-line Russian advocates of proletarian (*see* PROLETARIAT) revolution who broke with the MENSHEVIKS in 1903, and planned and agitated in exile, during which LENIN reputedly said:

> Give us a child for eight years and it will be a Bolshevik forever.

In 1917 the Bolsheviks, with Mensheviks and liberals, first overthrew the TSARIST system and then, in the OCTOBER REVOLUTION, crushed their domestic opposition to win total power. Despite their name the Bolsheviks were the majority only of the Russian Social-Democratic Labour Party from which they stemmed. Once in power, Lenin and STALIN preferred to call themselves Communists, and "Bolshevik" soon became a term of abuse from the West. In Britain, the word **Bolshie** came to be applied to any bloody-minded and unco-operative individual, especially in the field of trade unionism.

> A Socialist who wants to do something about it.
> GEORGE BERNARD SHAW.

> Czarism in overalls.
> GEORGE JEAN NATHAN (1882–1958).

> Nature has no cure for this sort of madness, though I have known a legacy from a rich relative work wonders.
> F. E. SMITH (Lord BIRKENHEAD), 1927.

Bolshevism run mad The description accorded to Labour's REFLATIONARY election programme in 1931 by Philip Snowden, Chancellor in the NATIONAL GOVERNMENT, who had been a member of the party until the GREAT BETRAYAL shortly before.

Bomb, the Shorthand throughout the 1950s and into the 1960s for the ATOMIC BOMB, and the threat to world peace and survival that it represented, as in the CND's simplest slogan BAN THE BOMB.

bomb North Vietnam back into the Stone Age The election pledge delivered in 1968 by George Wallace's RUNNING-MATE, the former Air Force general Curtis Le May (1906–90). While the Wallace ticket won considerable support from HARD-HAT voters for its policies on race and VIETNAM, Le May's comments on the war frightened off many potential supporters and were seized on by opponents to depict him as a war-crazed nut. What Le May in fact said was that the Communist North must stop its infiltration of South Vietnam or "we're going to bomb them back into the Stone Age".

Bomber Thorpe The accolade bestowed on the UK LIBERAL PARTY leader Jeremy Thorpe (*see* THORPE CASE) in 1966 after he called for the RAF to bomb Rhodesia in order to end the state of UDI declared the previous year by the Smith regime.

the bomber will always get through Stanley BALDWIN's chilling phrase that encouraged Britons in the 1930s to imagine that there was no defence against aerial bombardment, and thus strengthened the mood against REARMAMENT. On 10 November 1932 Baldwin told the Commons:

> I think it is well also for the man in the street to realise that there is no power on earth that can protect him from being bombed. Whatever people may tell him, the bomber will always get through.

bombing halt The pause in the bombing of North Vietnam ordered by Lyndon B. Johnson on 31 March 1968 when he announced his decision not to run again for the Presidency. He hoped that it would lead to a negotiated end to the VIETNAM WAR, but the conflict was to continue into the Nixon administration's second term.

Boneless Wonder The nickname for the UK Prime Minister RAMSAY MACDonald, cruelly awarded him by Winston CHURCHILL. In the Commons on 28 January 1931, Churchill said:

> I remember when I was a child being taken to the celebrated Barnum's Circus. . . . The exhibit which I most desired to see was the one described as "the Boneless Wonder". My parents judged that the spectacle would be too revolting for my youthful eyes, and I have waited fifty years to see the Boneless Wonder sitting on the Treasury bench.

bonfire of controls The cull of expendable wartime controls and restrictions on business and the consumer which the young Harold WILSON, President of the Board of Trade in ATTLEE's government, announced early in 1949. Wilson abolished controls which required the issuing of 900,000 licences a year, and over six weeks completely abolished the rationing of clothes. This break with Austerity contributed to Labour's narrow re-election in 1950. However Labour's continued identification with post-war drabness and shortage was a feature in the party's eventual defeat in 1951, after Wilson had resigned from the Cabinet.

Bongo-Bongo Land The description of THIRD WORLD countries which landed the devil-may-care British politician Alan Clark (1928–) in hot water *c.* 1987, prompting accusations of racism. Clark, an aristocratic military historian who held middle-ranking posts under Margaret Thatcher and John MAJOR, was given to languidly outrageous comments; he once evoked a protest from the Philippine Embassy by voicing regret that the nobility now had to have their children brought up by Filipinos rather than home-grown help. After his retirement in 1992 he precipitated the MATRIX-CHURCHILL affair, and in 1993 produced a shrewd but ribald autobiography.

Bonus Army The mass of unemployed World War I ex-servicemen who converged on Washington in 1932 as a "Bonus Expeditionary Force" and refused to go home until Congress authorized immediate payment of the 20-year bonus for veterans it had voted in 1924. By mid-June 15,000 were camped on the MALL in tarpaper shacks and packing crate huts; most left in the following month after President HOOVER refused to meet them, but some 2000 refused to disband. Believing they might resort to violence, Hoover on 28 July sent General Douglas MACARTHUR with infantry, cavalry and tanks to drive them from the capital, leaving two veterans dead; this contributed to his defeat by Franklin D. Roosevelt later that year. When Bonus Army members returned to press the new administration for action, Eleanor Roosevelt, at FDR's suggestion, took coffee out to them and joined in "There's a long, long trail".

> Hoover sent the Army – Roosevelt sent his wife.
> ANON. Bonus Army veteran.

boom The high-point in the economic cycle, a time of growth, plenteous money and near-full employment. The term can suggest that the economy is running out of control. Inevitably a boom is followed by an economic slowdown, but if the situation has been badly handled it can lead, as occurred in Britain in the late 1980s, to RECESSION – or even depression and slump.

boondoggle The useless spending of public money on make-work projects, originally with reference to the US government's NEW DEAL expenditure in the 1930s to combat the GREAT DEPRESSION. In his 1987 State of the UNION address, President Reagan told Congress:

> We can carve out the boondoggles and PORK.

The word's political use derives from a 1935 investigation of public relief in New York City, when a Mr. Robert Marshall testified that he taught "boon doggles":

> Making belts in leather, or maybe belts by weaving ropes, or it might be belts by working with canvas, maybe a tent or a sleeping bag. In other words it is a chamber of horrors where boys perform crafts that are not designed for finesse and fine work, but simply for a utility purpose.

It was a Frontier word for time taken up in leatherwork – boondoggles are the plaited lanyards or things worn by many Boy and Girl Scouts.

Bork nomination The furore over President Reagan's nomination to the SUPREME COURT in 1986 of Robert H. Bork (1927–), an ultraconservative law professor and former circuit judge. Fervent objections from liberal and other groups who saw Bork as a right-wing extremist led Congress to question him closely on his consistent opposition to CIVIL RIGHTS legislation and his refusal to accept a "right to privacy". In his 30 hours of testimony Bork managed to alienate even some conservatives, and the Senate rejected his confirmation early in 1987 by 58 to 42 – the largest margin for a Supreme Court nominee. Reagan denounced the hearings as a "lynch mob".

borough. pocket borough In Britain's Parliamentary system, a town so firmly under the control of a patron or family (or now a party) that it will always return their nominee without question. A common phenomenon before the 1832 REFORM ACT, the term has survived to describe a handful of Conservative-held seats where the constituency ASSOCIATION still respects a patron's choice of candidate.

rotten borough Again in the unreformed House of Commons, a constituency where the electorate was small enough and corrupt enough for a candidate to ensure his election by the payment of lavish bribes – unless his opponent paid even more.

boss (1) In America, the head of a political MACHINE; also a term of abuse for one powerful caucus by another. The word comes from the Dutch *baas*, meaning master or foreman, and was popularized by servants who, after the AMERICAN REVOLUTION, did not want to address anyone as "Master". It was in political use by the 1860s, and remained so for a century. Those given the name included:

Boss (Richard) **Croker** of New York. Asked why he stayed silent when the STAR SPANGLED BANNER was sung, an aide said: "He doesn't want to commit himself."

Boss (John F., HONEY FITZ) **Fitzgerald** of Boston, grandfather of President KENNEDY. Fitzgerald was twice elected Mayor through the activities and loyalty of his Irish-descended DEAROS, providing a colourful administration riddled with GRAFT.

Boss (Sen. Thomas) **Platt** of New York, who sought to gag the reforming governor Theodore Roosevelt, by getting him elected in 1896 as McKINLEY's Vice-President. His plans backfired when McKinley was shot six months after his inauguration and Roosevelt became President.

Boss Tube A facetious but apt 1980s term for the immense influence of television ("the tube") over American public opinion.

> Television has largely replaced the political parties as the middleman between candidates and voters. Boss Tube has succeeded Boss Tweed of Tammany Hall, Boss Crump of Memphis, and the DALEY MACHINE in Chicago.
> HEDRICK SMITH, *The Power Game*.

Boss (William March) **Tweed** Perhaps the most notorious of all TAMMANY bosses, Tweed controlled every political appointment in New York during 20 years as Commissioner of Public Works, taking $200 million in kickbacks. On one occasion the books were cooked to show that a plasterer had earned $138,137.50 for two days' work. He was toppled in 1870 by his fellow Democrat Samuel Tilden through articles in *Harper's Weekly*, accompanied by Thomas Nast's celebrated cartoons; after a series of trials he was imprisoned, escaped to Cuba and was recaptured, dying in jail in 1878. Tweed summmed up his political philosophy as:

> As long as I count the votes, what are you going to do about it?

(2) South Africa's Bureau of State Security, its principal intelligence organization which

during the 1970s, in particular, waged a ruthless campaign against opponents of APARTHEID at home and worldwide.
(3) **the Boss** A common political nickname used for, among others, the Irish Prime Minister Charles HAUGHEY; Franklin D. Roosevelt; Margaret Thatcher; and FIRST LADY Bess Truman (by her husband).

Boston. Boston massacre The attack by British Redcoats on snowball-throwing Bostonians on 5 March 1770 which left four civilians dead. It sparked radical passions throughout New England which were partly responsible for Lord North's new government in Britain repealing a range of unpopular duties imposed in 1768 – except those on tea.
Boston police strike The stoppage in 1919 by three-quarters of the Boston force over their right, denied by the police commissioner, to affiliate to the American Federation of Labor (*see* AFL-CIO). Governor Calvin Coolidge sent in the state militia to prevent a breakdown in law and order; though the situation was already under control, one of SILENT CAL's rare statements won popular approval:

> There is no right to strike against the public safety by anybody, anywhere, anytime.

Boston Tea Party The incident popularly taken as the start of the AMERICAN REVOLUTION, when on 16 December 1773 Bostonians led by Samuel Adams and dressed as Indians dumped the cargo of three tea ships into the harbour in protest at the tax on tea and the East India Company's monopoly over its shipment. Chanting "Boston harbour a teapot tonight", they boarded the ships by moonlight and tipped 342 chests of tea over the side. When news of the Tea Party reached Britain the next month, a series of Coercive Acts curbing the freedoms of the colonies were quickly passed, together with the QUEBEC ACT. These, in turn, provoked the convening of the CONTINENTAL CONGRESS.

> The boldest stroke which had yet been struck in America.
> Mass. Governor THOMAS HUTCHINSON.

> The question is whether the destruction of this tea was necessary. I apprehend it was absolutely and indispensably so. . . . To let it be landed would be giving up the principle of taxation by Parliamentary authority, against which the Continent has struggled for 10 years.
> JOHN ADAMS.

Boundary Commission (1) The body set up after the PARTITION of Ireland in 1921 to delineate the border between NORTHERN IRELAND and the Irish Republic. The founders of the Republic confidently expected that it would include Nationalist areas of the SIX COUNTIES contiguous with the South, but the exercise was rendered void when UNIONIST leaders in the North made it clear they would not accept the Commission's recommendations. (2) The impartial body which determines UK Parliamentary boundaries at each REDISTRIBUTION; there are separate Commissions for England, Wales, Scotland and Northern Ireland.

Bourbons The nickname acquired by the arch-conservative, White-supremacist Democratic Party leaders who gained control of America's Solid SOUTH after the end of RECONSTRUCTION. A combination of former planters and southern Whites who had done well out of Reconstruction, their determination to turn back the clock by depriving Blacks of their limited rights brought a natural comparison with the Royal house of France (and several other countries) whose stiff-necked inability to countenance change cost several of them their heads or their thrones. It was of the original Bourbons that Talleyrand wrote:

> They have learned nothing and forgotten nothing.

bourgeois An originally French term for the middle class; the word entered the English language in the 16th century, but only became derogatory with its adoption by MARX and Engels to represent the class enemy, and those who lacked the imagination to embrace revolutionary theories. In the *Communist Manifesto* (1848) they wrote:

> The essential condition for the existence and the sway of the bourgeois class is the formation and augmentation of capital, the condition for wage labour. What the bourgeoisie therefore produces is its own gravediggers. Its fall and the victory of the proletariat are equally inevitable.

And in a maybe less serious vein,

> The bourgeois, not content with having the women and daughters of their wage-slaves at command . . . find it capital amusement to seduce each other's wives.

Since then *bourgeois* has been the standard Communist term for any idea or behaviour that differs from their own.

> The European bourgeoisie has its reasons to be frightened. The proletariat has its reasons to rejoice.
> LENIN on Russia's defeat by Japan at Port Arthur, 1895.

> The political art of the British bourgeois consists in shortening the revolutionary beak of the proletariat, thereby not enabling him to pierce the shell of the capitalist state. TROTSKY.

> To carry out socialist work in a bourgeois democracy is impossible.
> Spanish Prime Minister FRANCISCO LARGO CABALLERO (1869–1946).

petit-bourgeois An even more dismissive variant of "bourgeois" used by Marx for the small-minded middle class.

bovver boys' bench At Westminster, the front bench BELOW THE GANGWAY on the Opposition side of the House of Commons, which is home to a huddle of left-wingers who are vocal interrupters but shrewd debaters. Dennis Canavan, Bob Cryer and Dennis Skinner (*see* BEAST OF BOLSOVER) have been three of the most formidable.

Bow Group A group of young liberal Tories formed in the late 1950s which has had a considerable impact on party thinking, though at times in the 1980s it moved to the right of centre. It takes its name from Bow in East London, where the group held its inaugural meeting, addressed by Geoffrey HOWE, in a room over a pub; its magazine, which at times has been equally influential, is titled *Crossbow*. Several Ministers in the Heath, Thatcher and Major governments were Bow Groupers at an early stage in their careers. *Compare* RIPON SOCIETY.

box. the box, in the HOUSE OF COMMONS, is the enclosure level with the CHAIR where officials from the relevant Government department sit during debates.

doing the boxes For Ministers in UK Governments, the task of going through the (usually red) boxes of official papers which they are expected to read, and where necessary sign, each night when they get home.

pick a box The system used in Australia since 1984 for electing members of the SENATE. The BALLOT paper is divided by a thick black line; above it are printed boxes giving a choice of parties, and below it boxes for candidates. A voter may either place the figure 1 in a square above the line, voting one party's TICKET, or numbering all candidates' squares in order of preference.

Boxer Rebellion The rising against foreigners in China in 1899–1900, in which the secret society of "Boxers" took a leading part. Its Chinese name was *Gee Ho Chuan*, signifying "righteousness, harmony and fists", implying training in martial arts to build character. The Boxers tore up railway lines, sacked Christian churches, attacked foreign missions and murdered some 300 foreigners before they were suppressed by an international force put together by America and the European colonial powers. The rising created conditions for a grab for what was left of independent China by those powers, but America extended its OPEN DOOR POLICY and bought them off for a time.

boy. Boy David The nickname given to **David** (later Sir David) **Steel**, leader of Britain's LIBERAL PARTY 1976-88, by condescending figures in the Conservative and Labour leaderships. The son of a former Moderator of the General Assembly of the Church of Scotland, Steel was the "baby" of the Commons when elected at a BY-ELECTION in 1965, but he quickly made a reputation by pushing through a Private Member's BILL to legalize abortion. As party leader, he safely navigated the Liberals through the trauma of the THORPE CASE, negotiated the LIB-LAB PACT with Labour and extricated the party from it, and encouraged the formation of the SDP; but he retained a boyish demeanour. Steel fought two elections in ALLIANCE with the SDP; in the first (1983) he reduced the role of the SDP's Roy Jenkins at the ETTRICK BRIDGE summit, and in the second (1987) he was handicapped by vicious satire from SPITTING IMAGE making him look David Owen's junior partner. Immediately after the election he called for a merger of the two parties, triggering splits in both parties. Steel stood down as leader when the LIBERAL DEMOCRATS were formed, but remained the new party's foreign affairs spokesman.

Boy Orator of the Platte A nickname for the American POPULIST William Jennings Bryan (*see* PRAIRIE AVENGER) in his first (1896) campaign for the Presidency. The tag turned out to be two-edged, Sen. Joseph Foraker pointing out that the Platte river in Nebraska was "six inches deep, and six miles wide at the mouth".

Boy Patriots The Parliamentary opponents who harried Robert WALPOLE towards the close of his 21-year ministry; an influential member from 1736 was the prodigy William Pitt (*see* PITT THE ELDER).

boycott The organized shunning of an individual, event or business in protest at the politics they represent, or as a protest at the involvement of others who are considered beyond the pale. The term originated in the avoidance of Captain Boycott, a County Mayo landowner, by Irish land reformers led by Charles Stewart PARNELL; on 19 September 1880 Parnell told a meeting in Ennis:

> When a man takes a farm from which another has been evicted, you must show him on the roadside when you meet him; you must show him in the streets of the town; you must show him in the fair and the market place; and even in the house of worship, by leaving him severely alone – by putting him into a moral Coventry, by isolating him from his kind as if he were a leper of old. You must show him your detestation of the crimes he has committed.

The boycott became a widely-used weapon, by CIVIL RIGHTS campaigners against the segregated bus line in Montgomery, Alabama; by the Arab states against companies doing business in Israel; by countries opposed to APARTHEID against Olympic and Commonwealth Games attended by states whose teams had continued to play in South Africa; by US athletes against the 1980 Moscow games in protest at the invasion of Afghanistan; by anti-apartheid groups against South African goods, and by US liberals against fruit produced by non-unionized migrant labour – and for a time against Coors beer.

Boyne, Battle of the The decisive engagement on 1 July 1690 between Protestant forces loyal to William of ORANGE and Catholic supporters of the ousted King James II. The battle, on the banks of the River Boyne three miles west of Drogheda, had wide European implications and involved, as well as Irish fighters on both sides, French, German and Walloon troops for James and English, Germans and Danes for William. SECTARIAN rivalry and tension already existed, especially in ULSTER, yet the Protestant victory set the agenda for centuries of bitterness, provocation and violence which continue to this day. In LOYALIST areas of Belfast, larger-than-life pictures of **King Billy** adorn gable ends of houses even now, and his victory is a critical part of the folk-memory and of communal pride – as well as a provocation to Catholics.

Bradlaugh case The furore caused in the 1880s by the refusal of Charles Bradlaugh (1833–91), the radical Liberal elected for Northampton in 1880 at the fourth attempt, to take the Parliamentary OATH. Bradlaugh's insistence on being allowed to AFFIRM (as may now be done) caused an uproar in the Commons; he was refused his seat, and the scenes were repeated twice more in April 1881 and March 1882 when the voters re-elected him (*compare* BENNERY). He was formally excluded from the House in 1884 but the next year won yet another election; this time the Speaker, exasperated by the intransigence of all parties, seated Bradlaugh despite bitter protests. His refusal to take the oath was not his only breach of Victorian conventions; to the horror of the Queen he was an advocate of birth control, and he was living in sin with the redoubtable feminist Annie Besant.

Brady Bill The measure seeking to impose a moderate degree of GUN CONTROL brought forward in Congress after Ronald Reagan's press secretary Jim Brady received serious head wounds in John Hinckley's attempt on the President's life on 30 March 1981. Despite widespread sympathy among the public and on Capitol Hill – and campaigning by Brady and his wife – the bid to ban "Saturday Night Special" handguns such as Hinckley's was blocked after intensive lobbying by groups including the NRA, and the opposition of the President himself.

brain. Brain(s) Trust The group of unofficial advisers on economic and social reform on whom Franklin D. Roosevelt relied in the 1932 election campaign and into the opening years of the NEW DEAL; they also acted as speechwriters. James Kieran of the *New York Times* nicknamed the group the Brains Trust because its members were academics, among them the Columbia University Professors Raymond Moley (its organizer), Adolph Berle and Rexford Tugwell. FDR modified the nickname to *Brain Trust* and used it himself.

> This country is being run by a group of college professors. This brain trust is endeavoring to force Socialism on the American people. Sen. HENRY D. HATFIELD.

brainwashing The psychological techniques employed on US officers and men taken prisoner by the Communists during the KOREAN WAR, so that they would spout anti-American propaganda on their release. The phrase acquired a political connotation in 1967 when Governor George Romney of Michigan, the favourite of liberal Republicans for the next year's Presidential campaign, claimed in a Detroit TV interview that he had been "brainwashed" by the US military on a trip to VIETNAM. Richard Nixon seized on Romney's gaffe, renounced his decision to retire from politics just before Romney's withdrawal from the race in February 1968, and went on to win the Presidency.

> Romney convinced many Americans that he didn't have a brain worth washing.
>
> DAVID WALLECHINSKY and IRVING WALLACE, *The People's Almanac.*

Brandt Commission The international commission convened by the UNITED NATIONS in 1977 under the former West German Chancellor Willy Brandt (1913–92) which raised the alarm over the plight of the THIRD WORLD. In its report, NORTH-SOUTH: *A Programme for Survival 1980*, it recommended urgent steps for fairer and greater trade between the rich "North" and the poor "South". World leaders reviewed the report at the CANCUN SUMMIT, but did not act on its recommendations. In 1983 the Commission produced a second report which warned of "conflict and catastrophe" if the imbalance were not addressed.

bread and circuses (Lat. *panis et circenses*) The bribing of the mass of the population with its own money to keep a government in office. The term stems from the practice of governments in ancient Rome of staging lavish public entertainments for the public and providing them with free food as a means of averting popular discontent.

break. breaking the mould The process which the founders of Britain's SDP hoped to precipitate, with voters abandoning traditional class-based party loyalties when given the chance to create a new political system. The dream lasted six years; the SDP/Liberal ALLIANCE collapsed after the 1987 election, and by 1992 the traditional two-PARTY system had almost reasserted itself.

breakthrough Under the FIRST PAST THE POST system, the point at which a party starts converting growing electoral support into seats. In Britain the LIBERAL DEMOCRATS would require around 35% before each extra percentage point pays a handsome dividend in seats; in Scotland the breakthrough point for the SNP is probably even higher because of the size of most Labour majorities.

Bretton Woods A conference at Bretton Woods, New Hampshire, in 1944 attended by America, the UK and Canada, which led to the establishment of the International Monetary Fund (IMF) and WORLD BANK. The Bretton Woods system, as it became known, involved a world monetary structure pegged to the dollar and governed, in the last resort, by the US TREASURY. The creation of the IMF provided a valuable safety-net for STERLING, but at an initially heavy cost to Britain that hindered her post-war recovery. The system collapsed in 1971 when Germany floated the mark and the Nixon administration followed suit by floating the dollar.

Brewster case The landmark INFLUENCE-PEDDLING case in Washington that forced LOBBYISTs to avoid offering money in the same conversation as they asked a legislator for his or her vote on a particular issue. In 1971 former Sen. Daniel Brewster of Maryland was convicted of unlawfully accepting $24,500 in campaign funds in return for his vote on postal-rate legislation.

Brezhnev Doctrine The policy, associated with the Soviet leader Leonid Brezhnev (1906–82), under which the Soviet Union reserved the right to intervene, with its WARSAW PACT allies, in the domestic affairs of SATELLITE states in defence of Socialism and its own global interests. The crushing of the PRAGUE SPRING of 1968 was an example of the Brezhnev Doctrine in practice; defending it in a speech to the Polish Communist Party congress on 12 November 1968, Brezhnev said:

> When internal and external forces which are hostile to Socialism try to turn the development of any Socialist country towards the restoration of a capitalist regime . . . it becomes not only a problem of the people concerned, but a common problem and concern of all Socialist countries.

The COLD WAR lasted as long as the KREMLIN was ready to impose the doctrine; in 1989 Mikhail Gorbachev (*see* GORBYMANIA) made it clear the doctrine no longer applied, and the Communist regimes of eastern Europe were swept from power.

Brighton. Brighton bombing The most devastating attack by the IRA on the UK's political leadership, which came within a whisker of assassinating Margaret Thatcher (*see* IRON LADY) and her entire CABINET. On the final night (11 October) of the 1984 Conservative party conference, a bomb planted weeks before exploded in the Grand Hotel around 3.20 a.m. immediately above the room where Mrs. Thatcher and her husband were awake. The Prime Minister and most of her senior colleagues had a miraculous escape, but five people (including the Conservative MP Sir Anthony Berry) were killed and two Cabinet ministers, Norman Tebbit (*see* CHINGFORD SKINHEAD) and John Wakeham suffered very serious injuries; Wakeham also lost his wife. Marks & Spencer opened its Brighton store to clothe survivors who had fled in their pyjamas; the conference continued as scheduled with Mrs. Thatcher going ahead with her closing speech that afternoon. Anti-terrorist checks at the conference had been lax because the police were mainly concerned with possible violent protests by striking miners; the IRA commented chillingly on its near-miss: "WE ONLY HAVE TO BE LUCKY ONCE." Mrs. Thatcher showed great coolness amid the rubble, but that weekend at Chequers wept over "a DAY I WAS MEANT NOT TO SEE".

like Brighton pier – all right as far as it goes, but inadequate for getting to France Neil KINNOCK's description of the Conservatives' ambivalent policy on Europe, from a House of Commons speech on 2 February 1981.

brinkmanship The art of going to the verge of war, but not into it; specifically the taking of the toughest line possible short of war by America and its allies against the Soviet Union during the COLD WAR. The word was coined by, and used as criticism of, US Secretary of State John Foster Dulles (1888–1959); in 1956 he stated that the US had three times gone to the brink with the Soviet Union, adding: "If you are scared to go to the brink, you are lost." Dulles's attitude scared many in the West; Adlai Stevenson scorned it as **the art of positive brinking**.

Britain. Britain is no longer a world power; all they have got are generals and admirals and bands. The verdict of General George Brown, chairman of the US JOINT CHIEFS OF STAFF, in an interview in October 1976. The comment aroused some adverse reaction in Britain, but nothing like as strong as that to Dean Acheson's "lost an EMPIRE and not yet found a role" 14 years previously.

I'm backing Britain The slogan coined by the publisher, Labour MP and eventual mass fraudster Robert Maxwell in 1968 to encourage the public to buy British-made goods. It inspired frantic activity and self-sacrifice on behalf of some workers and a forgettable song from Bruce Forsyth, but had no lasting impact. *See also* GREAT BRITAIN.

British. British disease The combination of industrial unrest, low productivity and economic decline which the nations of continental Europe detected in Britain in the 1960s and 1970s, and which they held out as a grim warning to their own people. In 1963 Tony Benn (*see* BENNERY) defined the British disease as "galloping obsolescence".

British Empire *See* EMPIRE.

British Gazette The newspaper produced by the UK Government during the 1926 GENERAL STRIKE, belligerently edited by Winston CHURCHILL, then Chancellor of the Exchequer. Churchill called the strikers "the enemy" and called for their "unconditional surrender". The TUC countered with its own publication, the *British Worker*. Churchill himself did not take the exercise entirely seriously; many years later in the Commons, he taunted Labour MPs:

> If ever you inflict on us another General Strike . . . [INTERRUPTION] . . . I swear that we will inflict on you . . . another *British Gazette*!

British Movement One of the many small but nauseating RACIST and NEO-FASCIST groups which proliferated in less affluent parts of Britain during the 1980s. A splinter from the NATIONAL FRONT, it was most evident in Southeast London and parts of Central Scotland till upstaged by the British National Party (BNP).

British North America Act The legislation passed by the Westminster Parliament in 1867 that established Canada as a DOMINION and a CONFEDERATION, initially of Quebec, Ontario, Nova Scotia and New Brunswick. It remained the basis for Canada's Constitution until PATRIATION in 1982.

the British are coming! The warning sent out by night-riders from Boston on 18 April 1775 when General Thomas Gage sent 700 British infantrymen secretly (he hoped) to capture or destroy a military store at Concord, 20 miles away, so as to deny it to rebel farmers. They were met at the village of Lexington by 75 volunteers, or MINUTEMEN; shots were fired (by whom is unknown) and in the ensuing exchanges the Redcoats left eight Americans dead and ten wounded. The British went on to Concord, found the stores had been hidden from them, and on the way back to Boston suffered heavy losses from sharpshooters. Lexington marked the opening of the War of INDEPENDENCE, and the cry "the British are coming!" entered history.

broad church A party or movement containing highly disparate elements stretching across the political spectrum. The term was used by Tony BENN to justify the right of the MILITANT TENDENCY and other hard LEFT groups to operate within the UK LABOUR PARTY.

broadcast. election broadcast In the UK, a Party Political Broadcast (PPB) transmitted during an election campaign. Every party fielding more than a certain number of candidates nationally, or in a particular region, is allocated a certain amount of time on radio and television, broadcast political advertisements being banned. Such broadcasts are the only occasions when spokesmen for Provisional SINN FEIN are allowed to speak on the air; at all other times their remarks have to be read by actors.

Ministerial broadcast A broadcast made by the Prime Minister, Chancellor or occasionally another member of the Cabinet to announce, justify or otherwise comment on some major development. The OPPOSITION has the right to reply in a broadcast of corresponding length and prominence. Apart from the annual BUDGET broadcasts and exceptional events such as John MAJOR's broadcast on the eve of the coalition offensive in the GULF WAR, such broadcasts have become a rarity.

party political broadcast *See* PPB.

public service broadcasting The concept of broadcasting as a means of educating, entertaining and informing the nation, free of advertising and the dictates of commercialism. This was the principle behind the formation of the BBC, which was slightly eroded by the Thatcher government in the late 1980s.

broccoli The vegetable whose too-frequent presence on the White House menu provoked a public outburst from George BUSH. The President's comments infuriated America's farmers, and trailer-loads of broccoli were delivered, unsolicited, to the White House. Staffers arranged their distribution to the needy in the Washington/Baltimore area. One of Hillary Clinton's first actions as FIRST LADY was to restore broccoli to the menu. *Compare* SWEETBREADS.

Broederbond (Afrik. brotherhood) The semi-secret and highly conservative society to which most members of South Africa's Afrikaner ESTABLISHMENT belong, and which was for long a force for cohesion and reaction within the ruling NATIONAL PARTY and a cornerstone of APARTHEID.

broker A state or leader who seeks to resolve differences between others, acting as an impartial MEDIATOR, is said to be brokering a settlement. **honest broker** is a term sometimes used to describe themselves by leaders in this position. At the Congress of BERLIN in 1878 Bismarck (*see* IRON CHANCELLOR), declared:

> If we are to negotiate peace, I imagine an essentially modest role, that of honest broker, who really intends to do business.

When Harold WILSON offered his good offices to bring about an end to the VIETNAM WAR, cynics at home said this was because while he might not be honest, Britain couldn't be broker.

power broker A largely US term for the men in SMOKE-FILLED ROOMs who determine who is put forward to govern. Hedrick Smith, in *The Power Game*, wrote:

> The most influential voices in Congress are power brokers back home.

brokered convention In US politics, a CONVENTION where there is deadlock between the delegations representing rival candidates, and the outcome is finally determined by party bosses in a SMOKE-FILLED ROOM.

Brookings Institution Perhaps Washington's most influential THINK TANK. Based near Dupont Circle, this generally liberal body recruits distinguished Fellows from the worlds of politics and political science, diplomacy, economics and journalism, giving them the opportunity to develop their ideas. Apart from producing its own assessments of events and policies, Brookings brings together experienced figures from public life to exchange opinions and judgments, both formally and informally.

brother The brotherhood of man has long been an ideal, and in the 20th century has developed connotations both of trade-union SOLIDARITY and of the breaking down of barriers between racial groups.

> We do not want men of another color for our brothers-in-law, but we do want them for our brothers.
>
> BOOKER T. WASHINGTON.

Brother, let me take you out of your misery! Neil KINNOCK's caricature of the outdated approach adopted by Britain's trade-union leaders to prosperous manual workers, which, when delivered at Labour's 1987 conference, was widely seen as a dig at the T&G leader Ron Todd.

Brothers, we're on our way! The exuberant motto of the deputy Labour leader George BROWN (*see below*) in 1963–64 as the party moved toward its expected return to power under Harold WILSON, newly united and with the Conservatives in disarray. As it was, Labour only scraped home with a majority of six.

Brown. Brown v. Topeka Board of Education The landmark US SUPREME COURT judgment on 17 May 1954 that overturned its previous position that SEPARATE BUT EQUAL facilities should be provided for the races, and declared SEGREGATED education to be UNCONSTITUTIONAL. A Black child, Linda Brown, had been turned away from an all-White school; the court unanimously struck down a Kansas law that required segregated classrooms, declaring that "separate education facilities are inherently unequal", and that such laws in 17 states were a denial of the FOURTEENTH AMENDMENT. Chief Justice Earl WARREN stated that segregating Black children from others solely because of their race "generates a feeling of inferiority as to their status in a community that may affect their hearts and minds in a way unlikely ever to be undone". In 1955 the Court ordered that DESEGREGATION of public schools should begin "with all deliberate speed", but it was years before the goal was achieved.

> I don't belive that you can change the hearts of men with laws and decisions. President EISENHOWER.

> The law may not change the heart – but it can restrain the heartless. Dr. MARTIN LUTHER KING.

don't just say Brown, say hopeless! A punning Conservative bumper sticker directed against George (later Lord George) Brown (1914–85), the colourful deputy to Harold WILSON in the Labour governments from 1964. The slogan, directed at Brown's stewardship of economic policy as head of the short-lived Department of Economic Affairs and his frequent DRINK-induced GAFFES, was a play on the popular bread advertisement "Don't just say brown, say Hovis!"

John Brown's Body The rhyme commemorating the ABOLITIONIST hanged in 1859 after leading the raid on HARPER'S FERRY which became the marching-song of the North in America's CIVIL WAR and reverberated around the world. Written either by Thomas Bingham Bishop or Charles Sprague Hall, it went:

> John Brown's body lies a-mouldering in the grave (3 times),
> His soul is marching on!

The Battle Hymn of the Republic (MINE EYES HAVE SEEN THE GLORY OF THE COMING OF THE LORD) was written to the same melody –

the hymn tune *Gone to be a soldier in the army of the Lord*.

Brownshirts Hitler's NAZI *Sturmabteilung* (stormtroopers) or SA, formed in 1921. Under Ernst Röhm the Brownshirts, named after their uniform, staged street brawls with the Nazis' opponents and became a mass movement. Its size and lack of accountability to Hitler worried the FÜHRER and on 30 June 1934 Röhm and other leaders of the SA were murdered on his orders in the NIGHT OF THE LONG KNIVES, power passing to the SS.

Bruges To Tory ANTI-MARKETEERS and EUROSCEPTICS, the symbol of resistance to a Federal Europe, stemming from Margaret Thatcher's speech in the ancient Belgian town on 20 September 1988 in which she scorned the centralizing Socialism of Jacques DELORS and defended national SOVEREIGNTY. Mrs. Thatcher, in a speech which also applauded the SINGLE MARKET, declared:

> We have not succeeded in rolling back the frontiers of the state in Britain, only to see them reimposed at a European level.

Bruges Group A group of mainly Conservative opponents of closer European union, set up to support Mrs. Thatcher's aims after the Bruges speech, which was an irritant to John MAJOR during the negotiation of the MAASTRICHT TREATY, but was weakened when some of its members stood against Conservative candidates as "anti-Federalists" at the 1992 General Election.

Brundtland Report The report published in 1988 by the UN World Commission on Environment Development, chaired by the Norwegian Labour Prime Minister Mrs. Gro Harlem Brundtland (1939–). It argued for "sustainable development", stressing that only under strict conditions can economic growth be reconciled with the dictates of the environment. It stressed the critical importance for global survival of preserving such a balance in the Amazon basin, sub-Saharan Africa and other regions.

Brussels The headquarters city of the EUROPEAN COMMUNITY, and to critics of the EC a symbol for excessive BUREAUCRACY and ludicrous DIRECTIVES. One of the most counter-productive election slogans of recent times was the Conservatives' "Don't vote and you'll live on a diet of Brussels" in the 1989 campaign for the European Parliament. It was intended to convey that Labour gains would leave Britain subject to a regime of Socialist regulation through the EC; instead many electors took it as an invitation to abstain.

Bryan, William Jennings *See* BOY ORATOR; PRAIRIE AVENGER.

buck. The buck stops here The hand-lettered sign that President Truman kept on his desk in the OVAL OFFICE.

a bigger bang for a buck President Eisenhower's aim in pressing for shrewder and more economical defence spending, as opposed to the escalating budget pressed for by the MILITARY-INDUSTRIAL COMPLEX.

buck the market *See* MARKET.

bucking the trend A phrase describing an election result which runs against the apparent trend of public opinion polls, or which, in a particular DISTRICT or CONSTITUENCY, is out of line with results in other elections held at the same time.

Buckingham Palace *See* PALACE.

Budget (1) At Westminster, the financial statement presented annually by the CHANCELLOR – customarily in March, but from 1993 in November – in which he sets out his taxation régime for the year ahead. This is subsequently legislated for in the FINANCE BILL. For some years prior to 1993 the public spending programme was presented in a separate autumn STATEMENT. Harold Macmillan described **Budget Day** as "rather like a school speech day – a bit of a bore, but there it is". Since the early 18th century considerable tradition and mystique have grown up around the Budget: the Chancellor's appearance on the steps of NUMBER ELEVEN Downing Street, holding the **Budget Box** containing his speech; the glass of water or stronger liquid on the DESPATCH BOX, and his Ministerial BROADCAST explaining his plans that night.

> The immediate judgment on a Budget is almost invariably wrong. IAIN MACLEOD (1913–70).

(2) In Washington, the Administration's spending plans presented to Congress at the end of each January; TAX-WRITING is undertaken by the Congress, which also makes changes of its own to the Budget. The end product for almost all of the past twenty years has been an increased Budget deficit; Norman Ornstein concluded that "historically, Congress was certainly an accomplice in increasing deficits – but Presidents were the masterminds".

> If the definition of a good Budget proposal is to distribute dissatisfaction, ours is a real winner. RONALD REAGAN.

> In government the Budget is the message. I. F. STONE.

> I didn't know much about Budgets – but I knew more than the rest of them.
> DAVID STOCKMAN, President Reagan's Budget Director.

(3) The name of Sir Geoffrey HOWE's dog while his master was Chancellor (1979–83). While Sir Geoffrey was Foreign Secretary, it was superseded by SUMMIT.

Budget leak (1) Claims in 1936 that details of the NATIONAL GOVERNMENT's Budget had been leaked to a private individual who had used the information to make money. The report of an official tribunal that investigated the allegations led to the resignation of the Colonial Secretary, J. H. Thomas. (2) The incident which forced the resignation of Hugh Dalton (1887–1962) as Chancellor of the Exchequer in ATTLEE's government. On his way through the LOBBY of the Commons to present his Budget on 13 November 1947, Dalton told John Carvel, a correspondent from the London evening paper *The Star*:

> No more on tobacco, a penny on beer, something on dogs and [football] pools but not on horses, increase in Purchase Tax, but only on items now taxable, Profits Tax doubled.

An astonished Carvel phoned the scoop to his office, and the paper ran a "Stop Press" announcement of tax changes before the Chancellor was able to inform the Commons – though no one there or in the City would have seen it. This grave breach of protocol by the garrulous Dalton left him with no option but to resign. He returned to the Cabinet in 1948 as Chancellor of the Duchy of Lancaster, but never regained his influence.

Budget resolutions In the UK HOUSE OF COMMONS, the resolutions put to the vote at the end of the (usually four-day) debate straight after the Budget. They include the basic changes in taxes and EXCISE DUTIES which are to take effect immediately or at the start of the new tax year. The more detailed provisions of the Budget are legislated for in the FINANCE BILL in the subsequent months. In the US Congress, "concurrent resolutions on the Budget" are passed each year to co-ordinate the revenue and spending decisions to be taken by the various committees involved in the budgetary process. Action on the resolutions, which set spending levels and direct the committees to achieve them, has to be completed by 15 April.

Congressional Budget Office (CBO) The office established by the Budget and IMPOUNDMENT Control Act of 1974 to produce for Congress independent analysis of the economy and of the Administration's Budget proposals. The change ended the situation in which the President and his staff could make assertions about the economy and the implications of their Budget that Congress was unable to challenge. The CBO has made a sizable impact on the balance of power in Washington by challenging efforts by administrations of both parties to massage the figures.

mini-Budget A package of economic and tax measures presented by a Chancellor at a different time from his formal Budget, usually in response to a sudden worsening in the state of the UK economy. Tory and Labour Chancellors have brought in mini-Budgets, but Conservatives claim Labour did it most and, since 1979, have prided themselves on avoiding them – if only because BLACK WEDNESDAY occurred during a Parliamentary recess.

Office of Management and Budget *See* OMB.

People's Budget *See* PEOPLE.

bugging The tapping of private telephone conversations by the security and INTELLIGENCE services, and others with less authority or justification. In Britain, tapping is supposed only to happen under a warrant from the Home Secretary; in SPYCATCHER Peter Wright said of MI5 in the mid-1970s:

> We bugged and burgled our way across London.

And in the mid-1980s hints of further abuses, coupled with a ruling from the European Court, led to the passing of the Interception of Communications Act which codified the arrangements for tapping.

In America the exposure of the FBI's COINTELPRO campaign and abuses by the CIA and the Nixon administration led eventually to Congressional OVERSIGHT of intelligence matters. In 1966 Justice William O. Douglas had warned:

> We are rapidly entering the age of no privacy, where everybody is open to surveillance, at all times, where there are no secrets from government.

And the next year President Lyndon Johnson declared:

> Every man should know that his conversation, his correspondence and his personal life are private. I have urged Congress – except where the national security is at stake – to take action to that end.

Buggins' turn A UK term for the culture in which the leadership of a political organization devolves on the next person in line, regardless of ability. A politer US word is SENIORITY.

build-down One of the proposals for nuclear ARMS CONTROL and disarmament put forward in America in the early 1980s. Pressed strongly from early 1983 by Sen. Sam Nunn of Georgia, it would have involved cutting the size of both US and Soviet arsenals at the same time as they were being "modernized" (older weapons being replaced by newer and more effective ones). President Reagan was tempted by the idea, which won the backing of 45 Senators, but it ran into resistance from the PENTAGON and was not seriously pressed by US arms negotiators in Geneva, where the Russians walked out soon after over the deployment of CRUISE MISSILES in Europe.

Bulgarian atrocities The massacre of Christians in Bulgaria by the Turks in 1876 that gave Gladstone (*see* GRAND OLD MAN) an ideal platform for a bout of righteous campaigning. Gladstone did not begin the agitation, but brought it to a head with his pamphlet *The Bulgarian Horrors*, which sold 200,000 copies in its first month. Disraeli was his target, not because of any suggestion that he condoned the massacres, but because he was determined to prevent Russia moving in to fill any vacuum left by Turkey. Russia attacked Turkey in April 1877 and made sweeping gains which Disraeli was able to moderate at the Congress of BERLIN in July 1878. Gladstone was still able to extract some capital from the issue in his MIDLOTHIAN CAMPAIGN of 1880. *See also* BAG AND BAGGAGE.

bull. Bull Connor The usual name for Eugene Connor, the REDNECK Commissioner of Public Safety for BIRMINGHAM, Alabama, who in the spring of 1963 gained national notoriety for setting his police force and fire hoses against CIVIL RIGHTS demonstrators led by Dr. Martin Luther KING, and making mass arrests. For five years prior to these demonstrations, Connor had harassed and bugged local civil rights activists led by the Rev. Fred Shuttlesworth, and had threatened to close White-owned stores that agreed to serve Blacks. He predicted that "blood would run in the streets" before Birmingham was integrated.

> At his disposal were a large police force, vicious attack dogs, electric cattle prods, the WHITE CITIZENS' COUNCIL, the KU KLUX KLAN, and the established institutions of Southern White society.
>
> ALDON D. MORRIS, *Origins of the Civil Rights Movement*.

bullhorn The portable instrument known to UK politicians and campaigners as a loud-hailer or megaphone, used to make a speaker's voice audible at impromptu outdoor meetings or to marshal DEMONSTRATIONS.

Bull Moose The breakaway POPULIST ticket on which Theodore Roosevelt (*see* TEDDY), disillusioned with his successor President TAFT, made a comeback in 1912. After a stirring series of PRIMARY victories, he formed a PROGRESSIVE PARTY and with California governor Hiram Johnson as his running-mate, he won 27.5% of the popular vote, splitting the REPUBLICAN PARTY, pushing Taft into third place and handing the election to Woodrow WILSON. Roosevelt had coined the phrase as far back as 1900, when he wrote to Sen. Mark Hanna:

> I am as strong as a bull moose, and you may use me to the limit.

bullet A bold dot in the margin of the CONGRESSIONAL RECORD denoting items that have been inserted by members and are not transcripts of words uttered in the Chamber.

bullet point or **bull point** The key point that a politician is anxious to get across in a speech.

bite the bullet To brace oneself and take a difficult decision. President BUSH said of Bill Clinton's attitude to the GULF WAR:

> I bit the bullet, and he bit his nails.

I am simply a bullet fired by the Colne Valley workers against the established order The comment made by Victor Grayson, the charismatic Socialist who later disappeared without a trace, on winning the historic 1907 by-election for Labour in this Yorkshire stronghold of Liberalism. Grayson also declared: "If the people have no shrapnel, they have broken bottles."

rubber bullet A projectile made from hard rubber fired from a special weapon, used in riot control. The rubber bullet, or BATON ROUND, was developed by UK government scientists for use against rioters in NORTHERN IRELAND and was based on the wooden police baton that could be fired from a gun, as used by the Hong Kong police for riot control in the late 1960s. The rubber bullet was supposed to be bounced off the ground as opposed to being fired directly into crowds but it, and its successor the **plastic bullet** (a solid PVC cylinder), have been responsible for the deaths of 12 people, six of them children, in Northern Ireland since 1970.

Bullock Report The report to the UK government in 1976 by a committee headed by the historian Professor Alan Bullock that recommended a degree of industrial democracy, with representatives of the workforce on company boards. The Labour government was eager for such representation, but trade union leaders insisted that the board members should be appointed by them, not elected by the workers as a whole.

Bullshot of the Year award The award made for many years by members of Congress playing paddleball – a cross between squash and tennis – in the RAYBURN BUILDING gym to the player who supposedly cheats and argues most; it has been in fact a mark of esteem, requiring the holder to chair the gym's annual dinner.

Bullying-manner The nickname of Sir Reginald Manningham-Buller (later Lord Dilhorne, 1905–1980), inverting his surname, which he gained as ATTORNEY-GENERAL between 1954 and 1962. When Manningham-Buller led the prosecution against the Eastbourne G. P. Dr. John Bodkin Adams in 1957 for allegedly murdering an elderly woman patient for her money, Mr. Justice (later Lord) Devlin described him and Adams as "the two most self-righteous men in England"; Adams was acquitted after a 17-day trial at the Old Bailey.

Bundesbank Germany's powerful CENTRAL BANK. Based at Frankfurt, it is independent of the Federal government and has as its overriding priority under its statutes the control of INFLATION. In 1992 its tough interest-rate policy resulting from the cost of German reUNIFICATION and an ensuing rise in prices created strains in the Exchange Rate Mechanism (ERM) that culminated first in DEVALUATION of the Italian and Spanish currencies, and then in BLACK WEDNESDAY when the UK devalued and withdrew from the mechanism.

Bundesrat The indirectly-elected upper house of the German legislature, comprising representatives of the 16 LÄNDER. Each Land has four, five or six votes, which must be cast as a block.

Bundestag The powerful lower house of the German legislature, whose main functions are to pass laws, elect the CHANCELLOR and keep the Federal government in check. Elected every four years, it can only be dissolved prematurely when the Federal President is convinced there are "exceptional circumstances". Since the reUNIFICATION of Germany in 1990 it has had 662 members.

Bundist A NAZI supporter, generally of German origin, in America prior to the US entry into World War II. The name came from the *Deutschland-Amerika Bund*, the Nazi-backed organization which campaigned for closer links with Germany, and for staying out of the war.

bunker mentality A syndrome in which a leader considers him- or herself under siege, develops a persecution complex and steadily isolates him- or herself from contact with all but most trusted aides and advisers. The phrase has its origin in the *Führerbunker* where Hitler spent the final days of his life, ordering phantom divisions into action as the Russians closed in on Berlin. It was used most appropriately of the Nixon White House; the mood first appeared soon after Nixon's inauguration in reaction to violent demonstrations against the VIETNAM WAR, but returned in full force as WATERGATE began to threaten the survival of the administration.

bunkum Irrelevant nonsense advanced as an argument. The word derives from Buncombe County in North Carolina, whose Congressman, Felix Walker (*see* OLD OIL-JUG), made a tedious speech in the House debate in 1820 on the MISSOURI COMPROMISE and declared that he was speaking "for Buncombe". The name stuck – unfortunately for the Revolutionary War hero Colonel Edward Buncombe after whom the county was named. The word has also been contracted to **bunk**.

bunkum and balderdash The trademark of Margaret Thatcher's press secretary Bernard Ingham (*see* YORKSHIRE RASPUTIN), who would use the phrase in LOBBY meetings about any news report or question he considered fanciful.

Bureau The body which supervises the running and expenditure of the EUROPEAN PARLIAMENT; it comprises the Parliament's President and 14 Vice-Presidents, all elected by the Parliament every 2½ years. When political decisions are to be made, the chairmen of the party groups also attend. Five quaestors (all MEPs) advise the bureau on administrative and financial matters.

bureaucracy Government by unfeeling paper-shufflers, or the dead hand of OFFICIALDOM itself. The word **bureaucrat** was first used in 1842 when Count Karl von Nesselrode, Minister to Tsar Nicholas I, was described in a letter as "bureaucrat to the great autocrat". Bureaucracy has ever since been a target for politicians, who either berate "faceless bureaucrats" for blocking their decisions or complain that its efficiency makes it over-powerful. Balzac termed it "the giant power wielded by pigmies", Lord Grimond "the antithesis of democracy"; JFK described dealing with bureaucracy as "like trying to nail jelly to the wall" and Sen. Eugene McCarthy warned that "an efficient bureaucracy is the greatest threat to liberty".

> The nearest thing to immortality on earth is a government bureau. JAMES F. BYRNES, *Speaking Frankly* (1947).

> We declared our independence 200 years ago, and we are not about to lose it now to paper shufflers and computers. PRESIDENT FORD.

> Bureaucrat: a Democrat who holds some office that a Republican wants. Vice-President ALBEN BARKLEY.

Burgess and Maclean The two British FOREIGN OFFICE diplomats, Guy Burgess (1911–63) and Donald Maclean (1913–83), who worked undetected as Soviet agents during World War II and the COLD WAR that followed, before defecting suddenly to the Soviet Union in 1951. Both were privileged and members of a group of mainly homosexual young men recruited at Cambridge University in the 1930s (*see* APOSTLES). Burgess, an alcoholic, was a relatively junior official; Maclean, as a member of MI6 with access to classified information who had aroused US suspicions while working in Washington, could do more damage. They defected after being warned by another agent, the THIRD MAN Harold (Kim) Philby (1912–88), that the net was closing in on them; their flight was arranged by Anthony BLUNT, unmasked three decades later as the FOURTH MAN. Burgess, Maclean and eventually Philby led a melancholic existence in Moscow, nostalgic for home but insisting that the sacrifice had been worthwhile.

Burke. Burke's address to the electors of Bristol One of the standard texts of Parliamentary democracy, establishing that a member of a legislature is a representative elected to exercise his or her judgment, and not a DELEGATE. It was delivered on 3 November 1774 by the radical Edmund Burke (1729–97), who said:

> Your representative owes you, not his industry only, but his judgment; and he betrays, instead of serving, you if he sacrifices it to your opinion.

He was unlikely in any event to have reflected the views of his constituents; he once confided:

> I believe in any body of men in England I should have been in the minority.

Burke, a Dublin-born WHIG, condemned Lord North's handling of the American colonies and lost his Bristol seat in 1780 for supporting a relaxation of the laws against Catholics. He was re-elected the same year for Malton, sitting until 1794. He took an active part in the IMPEACHMENT of Warren Hastings, and ended his career with vitriolic and increasingly desperate attacks on the FRENCH REVOLUTION, by which time he was close to becoming a TORY. Burke left behind him a great reputation as an orator, but his contemporary Sheridan observed:

> When posterity read the speeches of Burke, they will hardly be able to believe that, during his lifetime, he was not considered a first-rate speaker, nor even a second-rate one.

Thomas Paine considered Burke's oratory superficial, saying: "He pities the plumage, but forgets the dying bird." Yet Dr. Johnson was captivated:

> You could not stand five minutes with that man beneath a shed, while it rained, but you must be convinced you had been standing with the greatest man you had ever seen.

Burke's great rival in later years was Charles James Fox; he said of Fox's passion for Revolutionary France: "He is like a cat – fond of the house tho' the family be gone." Fox wrote: "Burke was a damned wrong-headed fellow, through his whole life jealous and obstinate", adding: "He never would support any measure, however convinced in his heart he might be of its utility, if it had first been proposed by another."

> Though equal to all things, for all things unfit,
> Too nice for a statesman, too proud for a wit.
>
> OLIVER GOLDSMITH.

> As he rose like a rocket, he fell like a stick.
>
> THOMAS PAINE.

Burke Act *See* DAWES.

burn. burn, baby, burn! One of the most incendiary slogans of US Black militants from the mid-1960s. Spiro AGNEW once attacked Black community leaders in Baltimore as "ready-mix, instantaneous, circuit-riding, Hanoi-visiting, caterwauling, riot-inciting, burn-America-down type of leaders".

burn everything English but their coal! The slogan coined by the disillusioned Irish cleric Jonathan Swift (1667–1745) which, with its combination of violence and BOYCOTT, greatly appealed to later Republican revolutionaries.

burning the house to roast the pig Justice Felix Frankfurter's verdict on the anti-obscenity laws of various States when the US SUPREME COURT declared them UNCONSTITUTIONAL in 1957.

book-burning The ultimate word for intolerance by a regime or faction devoted to stamping out culture as a whole or views with which it disagrees. The NAZIs held bonfires of books that conflicted with their "perverted science". When in 1948 Rep. John Taber took the Library of CONGRESS to task for publishing a monthly list of new Soviet books, his leftist New York colleague Vito Marcantonio suggested he appropriate "a reasonable amount of money for the burning of books".

Burntollet One of the violent incidents which marked the start of the current TROUBLES in Northern Ireland and pushed the CIVIL RIGHTS movement into the arms of the waiting IRA. It occurred on 4 January 1969, when a PAISLEYITE mob ambushed a "People's Democracy" march from Belfast to Derry at Burntollet Bridge, while the police stood by.

Burr-Hamilton duel The tragic episode on 11 July 1804 when the brilliant but much-detested Alexander HAMILTON was shot dead by JEFFERSON's Vice-President, Aaron Burr (1756–1836). New England FEDERALISTs opposed to the LOUISIANA PURCHASE because it would dilute their influence were preparing to SECEDE from the Union and turned to Burr for help. He agreed to run for Governor of New York and then lead the state into a new Northern confederation. Hamilton heard of the plot and revealed it; Burr already hated Hamilton for turning the tied ELECTORAL

COLLEGE against him three years before by calling him "a cold-blooded Catiline . . . a profligate, a voluptuary . . . no doubt insolvent", and challenged him to a duel. The confrontation with pistols took place beside the Hudson at Weehawken, New Jersey. When the command "Present!" was given, Burr fired, and Hamilton shot over him as he fell forward, his supporters later claiming he had fired to miss. A grand jury in Bergen, New Jersey, indicted Burr for murder, and he fled to Georgia and South Carolina, journeying 400 miles through swamps by canoe and hatching a plot to separate New Orleans from the Union. Hamilton left behind seven children and debts of $55,000, and Burr was dogged for the rest of his life by the anonymous rhyme:

> Oh Burr, Oh Burr, what has thou done,
> Thou hast shooted dead Great Hamilton.
> You hid among a bush of thistle
> And shooted him with a great hoss pistol!

bus. a bus driven by the Marx Brothers A Spanish diplomat's description of Italy's PRESIDENCY of the EUROPEAN COMMUNITY in the second half of 1990; officials in Rome were furious, but blamed the British who they mistakenly thought had originated it.

buses for Cuba The export deal that strained relations between the UK and America *c.* 1961. It involved the sale of buses built by Leyland to Fidel Castro's regime in Cuba, the subject of a US trade EMBARGO. The tension was eased somewhat when the ship carrying one consignment of buses sank in the Thames estuary.

are those your own buses? The remark reputedly made by Nicholas Ridley (*see* GERMAN RACKET) when, as Transport Secretary, he visited a London bus garage to see how the industry worked. It was during Ridley's tenure of the Department of Transport, 1983–86, that bus services outside London were DEREGULATED.

The Boys on the Bus The classic account of how the media covers a US Presidential election, written in 1972 by Timothy Crouse while covering George McGovern's campaign for *Rolling Stone.* As well as being hysterically funny in places, it remains arguably the best book ever written about political journalism, even though many of the names and faces have changed. *See also* ZOO PLANE.

If you see me at the back of the bus One of the most popular songs among the FREEDOM RIDERS who campaigned for the DESEGREGATION of bus services in America's Deep South; written by Pete Seeger, it originated in the MONTGOMERY BUS BOYCOTT when Mrs. Rosa Parkes refused to sit in the seats reserved for Blacks at the back of the bus.

Man on the Clapham omnibus *See* MAN.

Number 11 bus One of the great hypothetical questions at Westminster is who would take over as leader of either main party "if they were run over by a number 11 bus", route 11 being one of those that pass the end of DOWNING STREET. During Margaret Thatcher's first term, a weekend television programme polled Tory BACKBENCHERS on whom they would like to take over should such a mishap occur; for some time afterward, government WHIPS were trying to ascertain who had replied: "The bus driver." Lord Carrington, Mrs. Thatcher's first Foreign Secretary, had more basic doubts about the scenario. "The bus wouldn't dare," he said.

busing The process under which children are transferred by bus from one part of an American city to another in order to ensure that each school contains an ethnic mix; it reached its height in the early 1970s, and has since declined. Busing, ordered by the courts in some cities to end virtual SEGREGATION of neighbourhood schools, actually heightened racial tension in some places by enraging White parents who objected to their children being bused to predominantly Black schools. Working-class parents who had moved to "better" neighbourhoods because of the local schools now felt they had to give their children a private education to maintain that advantage; in the 1972 Presidential election both Richard Nixon and (initially) George Wallace attracted votes by attacking busing. *See also* SCHOOLS YOU CAN WALK TO.

Bush, George Herbert Walker (1924–), 41st President of the United States (Republican, 1989–93). George Bush came to the Presidency after eight years as Ronald Reagan's Vice-President with a glittering résumé: son of a distinguished New England Senator, a DFC as the youngest Navy pilot of World War II, successful Texas oilman, two-term Congressman, twice-defeated Senatorial candidate, US Ambassador to the UNITED NATIONS (1971–73), Chairman of the Republican NATIONAL COMMITTEE (1973–74), unofficial Ambassador to China (1974–75), and director of the CIA (1976–77). He ran against Reagan for the Republican nomination in 1980 (*see* Voodoo ECONOMICS), and eight years later defeated Michael Dukakis to become the first Vice-President since Van Buren to win "promotion" to the executive mansion. Yet during his 1988 campaign doubts were raised, notably by conservatives, about the depth of conviction of this patrician New Englander. George F. Will wrote:

> The unpleasant sound Bush is emitting, as he traipses from one conservative gathering to another, is a thin, tiny 'arf – the sound of a lapdog.

Meanwhile Sen. Robert Dole identified these doubts with a TV commercial reciting Bush's résumé while the camera panned across a forest path to show no footsteps had been left in the snow. But Bush doggedly insisted:

> If Carter can do it with no credentials, I can do it with these fantastic credentials; the fact that nobody else knows it is kind of discouraging.

and went on to conduct a campaign exceeded in negativism only by the one he was to lose four years later. He pilloried the wooden Dukakis as a "liberal", accusing him of favouring FLAG-BURNING and being soft on criminals (*see* Willie HORTONISM), and went on to win a convincing victory.

Bush took office, declaring in his INAUGURAL address: "We must hope to give [our children] a sense of what it means to be a loyal friend, a loving parent, a citizen who leaves his home, his neighborhood and town better than he found it", and his aim was to be remembered as "the education President". Yet it soon became clear that his main interest, as his record suggested, was in foreign affairs. He pressed ahead with ARMS-CONTROL agreements with the collapsing Soviet Union; sent US troops into PANAMA in May 1989 to overthrow the hated strongman Manuel Noriega who had just rigged a Presidential election and to arrest him on drug-trafficking charges; through Secretary of State James BAKER he took a far tougher line with the ISRAELI government over its reluctance to co-operate in the PEACE PROCESS; and in August 1990, stiffened by a visiting Margaret Thatcher, committed US forces to drive the invading Iraqis out of Kuwait. The following February Bush gave the go-ahead to Operation Desert Storm, in which US, British, French and allied Arab forces delivered what appeared to be a knockout blow to Saddam Hussein, then halted when they had fulfilled objectives set by the UN; in the summer of 1991 his position seemed impregnable. However Saddam survived, giving the impression that Bush had passed up the chance to finish him off; the US economy was also turning down; and the President, a fitness fanatic, was having problems with his health. First mild heart trouble was diagnosed, causing the *National Jewish Post and Opinion* to gloat: "Bush's heart problem was visited on him by God for his treatment of Israel," and then, on a visit to Tokyo at the start of 1992, he vomited over the Japanese Prime Minister at a State banquet. By now it was apparent that, apart from Bush's own basic decency and sincerity, his greatest asset was his grandmotherly wife Barbara, who could mix it with the best of them. When Bush was seeking re-election as Vice-President in 1984, she had said of his opponent Geraldine Ferraro:

> My husband and I have no intention of hiding our wealth – not like that four million dollar – I can't say it, but it rhymes with "rich".

An early PRIMARY challenge in 1992 by the conservative columnist Pat Buchanan did enough damage to make Bush look vulnerable, and while the Democrats struggled to find a nominee before the emergence of Bill Clinton, the intervention of H. Ross PEROT to mock him as a failure heightened the impression. Bush suddenly found himself called upon to justify the domestic achievements of his administration, but the jibe of former Democratic Sen. Paul Tsongas that he was "America's foreign minister" struck home, and the more Bush tried to depict himself as macho, the more the voters were reminded of the WIMP FACTOR. His own comments such as "just a splash of tea, please", when offered a drink in a workmen's canteen heightened the impression; Texas State Senator Carl Parker commented:

> Reagan can portray a real macho guy. Bush can't. He comes off looking like Liberace.

When Bush's otherwise loyal predecessor observed from retirement that he "doesn't seem to stand for anything", he was identifying another problem. When the Mafia don John Gotti was jailed by a New York court during the primary campaign, Washington jokers asked the difference between him and Bush, and replied: "At least Gotti has one conviction."

Bush was also handicapped by his ability to murder the English language. Mary McGrory summed it up when she wrote:

> He has an arm's length relationship with the English language. The only speech part that he has mastered completely is the *non sequitur*.

And he himself admitted, giving a toast in 1989 to the then Pakistani Prime Minister Benazir Bhutto:

> Fluency in English is something that I'm not often accused of.

His howlers were notorious. He said in a 1988 campaign speech in Detroit that "America's freedom is the example to which the world expires". He caused consternation at a Republican rally at Twin Falls, Idaho, in 1988 by declaring: "For 7½ years I have worked alongside him [Reagan], and I am proud to be his partner. We have had triumphs, we have made mistakes, we have had sex. . . ." Of the Alaska pipeline he said: "The caribou love it. They rub up against it, and they have babies." He told one startled audience: "I hope I stand for anti-bigotry, anti-Semitism, anti-Racism", and once declared his intention to "make sure that everybody who has a job wants a job". He was also a master of the banal. On a trip to a refugee camp in Pakistan he observed: "Oh boy, this brings the Afghan war close to home"; and he asked the Jordanian chief of staff Zeid Ben Shaker: "Tell me general, how dead is the Dead Sea?"

Bush could also be downright tactless. He described his three half-Mexican grandchildren in Houston as "the little brown ones over there". But above all he was capable of total gibberish. At a press conference on 4 December 1990 he told one questioner:

> I know what I've told you I'm going to say, I'm going to say. And what else I say, well, I'll take some time to figure out – figure that out.

His finest effort came when he visited a Union, New Jersey, high school and told bewildered students:

> I'm delighted that Barbara Bush is with me today, and I – she got a good, clean bill of health yesterday from Walter Reed Hospital, I might add – and then – But I'm taking another look at our doctor. He told her it's okay to kiss the dog – I mean – no, it's okay to kiss your husband, but don't kiss the dog. So I don't know exactly what that means.

After early reverses in the 1992 campaign, Bush said: "I've been very kind and gentle. I'll still be kind, and I'm now debating how gentle to be"; but he told David FROST: "I will do what I have to do to get re-elected." There followed an even more negative campaign than the Republicans had mounted in 1988, with NEGATIVE RESEARCH about Clinton's private life put to the fullest use, and Tory strategists imported from England mounting an attack on Clinton's tax plans that considerably embarrassed John MAJOR once the votes were counted. Two weeks before the election, Bush seemed in with a chance, but it slipped away from him as the Clinton campaign rebutted all charges against it and Perot (who had dropped out of the campaign altogether for two months) won enough Republican waverers to put Clinton into the White House. Bush in defeat was gracious and dignified, raising the suspicion that he had never really wanted a second term that much, and after a genial handover to the Clintons, he and Barbara helicoptered to retirement in Texas.

> I was smart enough to recognize a bad marriage and get out of it. I'm smart enough to recognize a bad President and get out of that.
> CINDY RIOUX-MATTA, Ridgewood, N. J., September 1992.

> Bush and his advisers misread the year, the country and his opponent. ELIZABETH DREW, *New Yorker*.

> Bush had two faults. He didn't care for domestic politics, and he didn't care for people.
> CHARLES WHEELER, BBC television.

See also CONCENTRATION CAMPS; KENNEBUNKPORT; MILLIE; PEARL HARBOR; READ MY LIPS. NO NEW TAXES.

business The term used in many legislatures for the volume of legislation and other items that have to be fitted into the time available for its necessary tasks to be completed. At Westminster the **business of the House** has a particular importance, as the Government feels obliged to get it through, and the Opposition's role is to make selective attempts at delay, the balance being maintained by negotiations through the USUAL CHANNELS.

business as usual The declaration that WORLD WAR I would not be allowed to interfere with Britain's daily life, made by Winston CHURCHILL in a speech at London's GUILDHALL on 9 November 1914, two months after the conflict had begun. The First Lord of the Admiralty said:

> The maxim of the British people is "Business as usual".

business managers The team at Westminster comprising the Government WHIPs and the Leader of each House who endeavour to ensure that legislation flows smoothly, that the committee system is fully manned and produces no shocks, and that Opposition delaying tactics arising from misunderstandings between the parties are avoided.

business statement At Westminster, a statement from the Leader of the House announcing a change in the programme of business for the coming days. The routine business statement every Thursday gives rise to **business questions.**

next business A device common to the STANDING ORDERS of many UK elected bodies and organizations: the opportunity to end a debate that is getting nowhere by moving "next business" and passing to the following item on the AGENDA.

a man I can do business with The words with which Margaret Thatcher is supposed to have indicated to fellow Western leaders, notably Ronald Reagan, that Mikhail GORBACHEV was serious about ending the COLD WAR. What she actually said after meeting him at CHEQUERS at the end of 1985 was: "I like Mr. Gorbachev. We can do business together." The IRON LADY may not have realized that, in 1961, Earl ATTLEE reminisced of STALIN:

> He was clearly a pretty ruthless tyrant, but a man you could do business with.

I never knew a pollytician go wrong until he's been contaminated by contact with

a businessman. A classic *bon mot* from "Mr. Dooley", the Irish-American cog in a political MACHINE created by the humorist Finley Peter Dunne (1867–1936).

Less government in business, and more business in government One of the campaign pledges of Warren HARDING when he won the US Presidency in 1920. The TEAPOT DOME scandal that ensued was probably not what he had in mind.

lose the business The setback suffered by Government BUSINESS MANAGERS in the UK House of Commons when dissidents on one side or the other keep one day's sitting going until the following lunchtime, forcing the abandonment of whatever was due to have been discussed that day. On very rare occasions, such tactics on a Monday or Wednesday night have wiped out Prime Minister's QUESTION TIME.

opposed private business The time allotted in the UK House of Commons by the Chairman of WAYS AND MEANS for the debate of Private Bills to which objection has been raised; until the passage of the 1992 Transport and Works Act these normally concerned new railway, light rail or dock schemes, plus occasional local Bills to regulate market trading.

the business of America is business The statement for which President Coolidge (*see* SILENT CAL) is best known; apart from being his longest, it sums up the ethos of America in the 1920s and explains the Republicans' tenure of the White House from 1920 until the onset of the GREAT DEPRESSION. *See also* NEXT BUSINESS *above*.

Butcher of Baghdad A widely-used western nickname for **Saddam Hussein** (1937–), the BAATHist President of Iraq from 1979. It was bestowed after his invasion of Kuwait in August 1990, and the alleged atrocities that followed in the run-up to the second GULF WAR. A party member since 1957 and a participant as an army officer in the revolution of 1968, Saddam consolidated his power with a series of ruthless PURGES, chemical warfare against rebellious Kurds in Northern Iraq and repeated military offensives against the Shi'ites and Marsh Arabs of the South. Saddam also instigated the first Gulf War of 1980–88, in which 1.5 million people died; at this stage he was abetted by the West, which saw him as a bulwark against the Islamic fundamentalism of the AYATOLLAH.

Butler Education Act The landmark Act passed in 1944 which established the structure of state education in England and Wales for the post-war period, much of it surviving the COMPREHENSIVIZATION of the late 1960s and even the Baker Act of 1988 (*see* GERBIL). The brainchild of R.A. (RAB) Butler, President of the Board of Education, it turned out to be the most significant item of legislation for peacetime passed at Westminster during World War II. Butler's greatest achievement was in resolving the argument that had rumbled on for decades over how the Church of England's schools could be incorporated into the State system, and what proportion of the cost of Roman Catholic education the State would meet. The one fly in the ointment was that a combination of YOUNG TURK Tories and Labour MPs inflicted a one-vote defeat on the Government over equal pay for teachers – the Churchill coalition's first Commons defeat in four years.

Butskellism The moderate CONSENSUS POLITICS that reigned at Westminster in the early 1950s, when CHURCHILL's Conservatives undid very little of Labour's work of NATIONALIZATION and left the WELFARE STATE intact. In particular it reflected continuity in economic policy, with the Tory Chancellor R.A. Butler picking up where Labour's Hugh Gaitskell had left off. The word first appeared in *The Economist* on 13 February 1954:

> Mr. Butskell is already a well-known figure in dinner table conversations in both Westminster and Whitehall, and the time has come to introduce him to a wider audience.

butter mountain *See* MOUNTAIN.

by-election (1) In the UK political system, an election held outside the normal cycle or (for a Parliamentary seat) other than during a General Election. A Parliamentary by-election is set in motion by the Speaker issuing a WRIT for the poll to take place. As by-elections afford the most obvious, and at times the most dramatic, test of a Government's popularity and that of the various parties, considerable media attention is devoted to them, and they are thus that much more keenly fought. *See also* EATANSWILL, MINDER, ORPINGTON MAN. (2) The MID-TERM Congressional elections held in the United States, in OFF-YEARS when there is no Presidential contest.

C

C. C-B The nickname of Sir **Henry Campbell-Bannerman** (1836–1908), Britain's Liberal Prime Minister from 1905 to 1908. He was born a Campbell in Glasgow, adding the name Bannerman in 1872 as the price for receiving a family inheritance. Elected an MP in 1968, he became Gladstone's Chief Secretary for Ireland in 1884, strongly supporting his HOME RULE policy. As Secretary for War he was the occasion of the fall of ROSEBERY's government; the Liberals were defeated in a snap division over Campbell-Bannerman's alleged failure to supply sufficient CORDITE to the Army. Rudyard Kipling termed him:

> The mildly nefarious
> Wildly barbarious
> Beggar that kept the cordite down.

And Joseph Chamberlain said as C-B's career recovered: "I sometimes think that cordite has entered his soul." Even before the cordite vote, the *Spectator* was terming him "the dark horse of the Gladstonian party on whom a great many knowing people are inclined to put their money". And as the Liberal Party tired of the chaos it suffered under Rosebery and Harcourt, it turned in 1899 to C-B as its leader. The *Nation* later editorialized:

> He came to the rescue of the Liberal Party when it was a mere hulk, floating captainless and rudderless.

Immediately he was confronted with the BOER WAR which split the party and led to his being perceived by Tories and some of his own party as unpatriotic; his former associate Lord Milner dismissed him as "merely too revolting". But he held the Liberals together, and when Balfour's government fell apart in 1905 he was ready to take power, winning a landslide election victory.

Senior and ambitious colleagues wanted him to take a PEERAGE and give them the real power (*see* RELUGAS COMPACT); they persuaded Edward VII to offer him a peerage, which he did with the words: "We are not as young as we were, Sir Henry." But C-B stood his ground, developed an ascendancy over the Commons (*see* ENOUGH OF THIS FOOLERY!) and for three years, until halted by cancer, led a successful reforming government.

He paved the way for the social reforms of the ASQUITH ministry, and for the curbing of the powers of the HOUSE OF LORDS, but his greatest achievement was reconciliation between Whites in South Africa, with English-speakers and Afrikaners who had been at war just before uniting in self-government under the British flag. Their future leader Jan Smuts saw him as "almost commonplace to the superficial view, but a real man, shrewd and worldly-wise". Queen Victoria regarded C-B as "a good, honest Scotchman", Beatrice Webb dismissed him as "a quite stupid person for a leader – well suited to a position of wealthy squire or a sleeping partner in an inherited business". Indeed he was widely regarded as stuffy, if cultured, and indolent. W. T. Stead wrote: "If he could only be induced to become a vegetarian, and to read only one French novel a month, he might become famous in history as the man who created the modern British Army." The Times described him as "not prone to excess of activity", and he himself wrote: "I am a great believer in bed, in constantly keeping horizontal. The heart and everything else go slower, and the whole system is refreshed." But the appearance was deceptive, the King's private secretary Arthur Ponsonby recalling: "He had an acute sense of humour which I should never have suspected from the dull colourless figure by which he seemed to be represented publicly." Margot Asquith hailed him as "essentially a *bon vivant*, a *boulevardier* and a humorist", though she dismissed his election address as "quite good, but not as striking as Robespierre's". Sir Gordon Voules reminisced: "He had an extraordinarily methodical mind which enabled him to get through the maximum of work with the minimum of labour." And the Irish politician and journalist T. P. O'Connor said: "He had wit as ready as his opponents, he had immense force of character; above all he had unfathomable, unreachable depths of imperturbability." In Cabinet he was crisp and to the point, John Morley recalling: "He always knew his mind, and we were all aware that he knew it." Yet he was personally modest, Ponsonby writing: "He was constantly forgetting he was Prime Minister. He would ask why people crowded round when he went out shopping alone." Though the radical Lord Haldane once dismissed him as "that dear old Tory", he was radical enough to cause controversy even after his death, the reactionary Lord Lansdowne writing: "Personally, I hold a very strong view as to the impropriety of erecting a monument to Sir Henry Campbell-Bannerman in [Westminster] Abbey."

> The man about whom almost all is forgotten.
>
> NICOLAS BENTLEY.

C-span The cable television channel founded by Brian Lamb in 1979 which carries (frequently live) coverage of proceedings in the US Congress and election campaigns, and has also brought QUESTION TIME at Westminster to US viewers. Congressmen have found C-span's live coverage of the House when it goes into Special ORDERS an ideal way of winning publicity; its coverage of the 1985 Senate hearing on "porn-rock" brought a flood of requests for tapes. By early 1993 58 million homes could receive it.

C2s In Britain, the critical 29% of the population who are skilled manual workers and their families, and whose votes win or lose elections. Margaret Thatcher's success in capturing the C2s from Labour was critical to her victory in 1979 and the Conservatives' re-election in 1983, 1987 and 1992; after the second of those defeats Labour readjusted its policies and campaigning in a bid to recover the C2s which almost until polling day in 1992 looked like succeeding. The classification is one of six indicators of social class produced in 1962 by the Institute of Practitioners in Advertising: A (upper middle class: professional and managerial, 3%); B (middle class: administrative and professional, 14%, *see* ABs); C1 (lower middle class: supervisory and clerical, 22%); C2 D (working class: semi-skilled and unskilled, 18%), and E (lowest level: pensioners and casual workers, 14%). *See also* DEs.

Ça ira (Fr. that will go its way) Benjamin Franklin's off-the-cuff remark in Paris in 1776–77, on America's War of Independence, which was taken up in the FRENCH REVOLUTION as the opening line of its most militant song: "*Ça ira* (3 times), *les aristos* A LA LANTERNE!" (string up the aristocrats on the nearest lamp-post!)"

cabal A clique, or group of intriguers. The origin is widely said to be the initials of the Ministry appointed by Charles II in 1670: Clifford, Ashley, Buckingham, Arlington, Lauderdale. But it actually comes from the French *cabale*, an intriguing faction, and Hebrew *cabala*, secret knowledge.

Cabinet (1) The group of senior Ministers or departmental heads in charge of a government through regular, usually weekly, meetings. From the French *cabinet*, a small room. In Britain, an inner core of PRIVY COUNCILLORS on whom the monarch relied for advice in the late 17th century, it became a formal group of MINISTERS two centuries before its existence was recognized by statute in 1937. Macaulay wrote: "A man in office, and out of the cabinet, is a mere slave." And Aneurin Bevan (*see* NYE) advised:

> There are only two ways of getting into the Cabinet. One is to crawl up the staircase of preferment on your belly; the other way is to kick them in the teeth. But for God's sake don't mix the two methods.

In Britain and principal COMMONWEALTH countries, the Cabinet comprises senior Ministers who are members of the legislature. In America, where the term was first used by James MADISON in 1793, it has a less crucial role, has no statutory basis and consists of politically-appointed department heads (*see* SEPARATION OF POWERS). Abraham LINCOLN put his Cabinet in perspective by announcing: "One aye, seven nays; the ayes have it." A century later TRB wrote: "Ike has picked a Cabinet of eight millionaires and a plumber." Henry KISSINGER reckoned that "every President since Kennedy seems to have trusted his White House aides more than his Cabinet"; while Ronald Reagan said of his Cabinet:

> Ronald Reagan slept here.

Cabinet committee A sub-group of Ministers covering a field of government activity (the economy, foreign affairs), sometimes but not always chaired by the head of government.

Cabinet government In the UK, the doctrine of governing by ministerial agreement, rather than at the *fiat* of the Prime Minister. Sir Geoffrey HOWE felt Cabinet government was "all about trying to persuade one another from within"; Richard CROSSMAN concluded that "the post-war epoch has seen the final transformation of Cabinet government into Prime Ministerial government". By the end of his service under Margaret Thatcher, Howe volubly agreed. The Australian Prime Minister Malcolm Fraser gave a reason:

> A willingness to consult your senior colleagues indicates a willingness not to proceed with the decision.

Cabinet Minister In Britain, a Minister who sits by right in the Cabinet.

Minister of Cabinet rank A Minister who has Cabinet status, though not the salary, and attends as required.

Cabinet Office In WHITEHALL, the small Government department closely linked to

NUMBER TEN which supervises the machinery of government.

Cabinet officer In America, a member of the Cabinet.

Cabinet papers The documents circulated to and stemming from UK Cabinet meetings; by convention no incoming government may see its predecessor's papers, and former Ministers wishing to refresh their memory have to apply to see their own.

Cabinet room The location of cabinet meetings. In NUMBER TEN on the first floor overlooking the garden, in the WHITE HOUSE since 1934 in the West Wing overlooking the ROSE GARDEN, each chair bearing a brass plaque with its occupant's name.

Cabinet Secretary In Britain, the very senior official, often the head of the civil service, who services the Cabinet and keeps its minutes. In America (1) the secretary to the Cabinet, a relatively junior White House appointment; (2) an individual member of the Cabinet.

Cabinet War Rooms The complex of rooms off WHITEHALL, beneath the Treasury from where CHURCHILL and his staff commanded the British war effort for much of the period from 1940 until 1945 when London came under aerial attack.

blubbering Cabinet Gladstone's last Cabinet meeting on 1 March 1894 when several ministers broke into tears at the GRAND OLD MAN's departure.

inner Cabinet In Britain, a nucleus of Ministers occasionally formed by the Prime Minister on a semi-permanent basis to tackle particularly important or sensitive questions.

kitchen cabinet An informal group of friends or advisers on whom a leader relies to an extent resented by others; the term was first applied to the entourage of President Andrew Jackson (*see* OLD HICKORY), and in Britain to Harold WILSON.

reporting Cabinet A meeting which hears reports from Ministers on events and policy development, rather than taking decisions.

Second Eleven Cabinet A pejorative term for Britain's Bonar Law administration (*see* UNKNOWN PRIME MINISTER), which included several forgettable members.

Shadow Cabinet *See* SHADOW.

War Cabinet The small group of senior Ministers charged with prosecution of a war.

(2) In the EUROPEAN COMMISSION and continental Europe, the team of officials and advisers working to a Prime Minister, Minister or European Commissioner.

chef de Cabinet The leader of such a team, and that politician's principal representative.

Cable Street, battle of The violent disorder in October 1936 stemming from a march through a largely Jewish quarter of London's East End and attacks on Jewish shops by Sir Oswald Mosley's BLACKSHIRTS. It led to the passing of the **Public Order Act**, which banned the wearing of political uniforms.

Cactus Jack Nickname for John Nance Garner (1868–1967), the Texan who was SPEAKER of the House of Representatives 1931–33 and Franklin D. Roosevelt's Vice-president in his first two terms (1933–41); Garner had tipped the nomination to FDR at the 1932 Democratic Convention.

cadre An individual or small group providing activist, militant leadership, especially in a MAOIST or Communist movement. From the Latin *quadrum*, square, originally the framework of a regiment.

Cairns group A group of 17 nations led by Australia, set up to champion freer world trade in farm produce during the URUGUAY ROUND of GATT negotiations. It took its name from the town in Queensland where the group first met.

calendar In the US CONGRESS, the various schedules, printed daily, of BILLs down for debate in either House. The House of Representatives has five. The **Union Calendar** and the **House Calendar** are the main ones, listing public Bills that have been favourably reported. The **Consent Calendar** contains bills transferred from those calendars on the initiative of any member wishing to expedite their progress. If no objection is raised three days running when the Consent Calendar is read, the Bill passes; any objection strikes it from that calendar. There are also a **Private Calendar** and a **Calendar of Motions to Discharge Bills**, and each committee has its own **Legislative Calendar.**

calendar days Those days on which the US House of Representators is in session.

Calendar Wednesday Each Wednesday, unless the House decides otherwise, the STANDING COMMITTEEs are called in turn and may call up for consideration any reported Bill pending on the House or Union Calendar. After no more than two hours of debate divided equally between supporters and opponents, a simple majority of members present will pass the measure.

Californi(c)ation The devastation of unspoilt areas of America's West Coast states with unplanned urban sprawl: industrial development, speculative housing, shopping malls and other benefits of the southern Californian way of life. As in the 1970s environmentalist sticker

> Don't Californicate Oregon.

Caligula's horse A politician promoted to an office way above his abilities, and operating as a cipher. After the Roman Emperor Caligula, who threatened to make his horse Incitatus CONSUL to spite the Senate. When President John Quincy ADAMS appointed Richard Rush Secretary of the Treasury, Rep. John Randolph commented:

> Never were abilities so much below mediocrity so well rewarded; no, not when Caligula's horse was made consul.

And in 1865 the *New York World* described President Andrew Johnson as

> An insolent, drunken brute, in comparison with whom Caligula's horse was respectable.

In 1935 Sen. Carter Glass of Virginia was so offended by Sen. Huey (KINGFISH) Long that he accused the voters of Louisiana of going one further and making the posterior of a horse a US Senator.

call. Call Me God, Kindly Call Me God, God Calls Me God WHITEHALL slang for the three great Civil Service (esp. diplomatic) honours awarded by the Crown: **CMG** (Commander of the Order of St. Michael and St. George), **KCMG** (Knight Commander) and **GCMG** (Knight Grand Commander). The unofficial titles were cited by Anthony Sampson in his *Anatomy of Britain*.

call-in The US word for PHONE-IN.

call up In the US HOUSE OF REPRESENTATIVES, the Speaker's action in bringing up a Bill for a vote. In Britain, CONSCRIPTION, as practised throughout the 1950s.

Callaghan, (Leonard) James *See* SUNNY JIM

Cambridge Mafia The group of late 1950s and 1960s Cambridge graduates who formed a key element in Margaret Thatcher's Cabinets. It included Sir Leon Brittan (*see* WESTLAND AFFAIR), Kenneth Clarke, Sir Norman Fowler, John Selwyn Gummer, Michael Howard, David Howell, Norman Lamont and Sir John Nott. Former office-holders in CUCA (the University Conservative Association), the Cambridge Union or the BOW GROUP, their outlook was mainly practical rather than ideological.

Camelot The mythical kingdom of the 6th-century English King Arthur as portrayed in the Lerner-Loewe musical of that name, evoked to describe the glittering memory of the brief KENNEDY Presidency and the hope and glamour it brought to Washington. Though the term has now come to imply scepticism, it was coined by Jacqueline Kennedy (*see* JACKIE O) who recited the song:

> Don't let it be forgot
> That there was once a spot, for one brief shining moment
> That was known as Camelot.

She explained after her husband's assassination:

> Camelot had suddenly become the symbol of those thousand days when people the world over saw a bright new light of hope shining from the White House. For myself, I have never been able to see a performance of *Camelot* again.

Camp David The Presidential retreat in Maryland's Catoctin mountains, 50 miles north-west of Washington. Created by Franklin D. Roosevelt in 1942 as *Shangri-La*, Eisenhower renamed the cluster of cabins, where he could relax and converse with distinguished guests, after his grandson.

Camp David agreement The agreement that ended the 31-year state of war between Israel and Egypt, reached there in 1979 after days of intensive talks between Jimmy CARTER, Menachem Begin and Anwar Sadat. The agreement brought mutual diplomatic RECOGNITION between the two countries and the return of Sinai to Egyptian rule, but did not, as hoped, presage a wider Middle East settlement. Begin termed it: "A great day in the annals of two ancient nations. It is thanks to our fallen heroes that we could have reached this day." And Sadat prayed: "Let there be no more war or bloodshed between Arabs and Israelis. Let there be no more suffering or denial of rights. Let there be no more fear or loss of face."

campaign (1) The gruelling, wounding and often costly contest for a political office, or the duration of the electoral process and an individual candidate's part in it. President TAFT declared it "the most uncomfortable four months of my life". Adlai Stevenson reckoned: "The hardest thing about any political campaign is how to win without proving that you are unworthy of winning"; he also said that "you learn more about yourself while campaigning for just one week than in six months spent with a psychiatrist". The more ruthless Richard Nixon said: "You don't win campaigns on a diet of dishwater and milktoast." Rosalynn Carter felt that "nothing is more thrilling than the urgency of a campaign", while Governor Mario Cuomo mused:

> You campaign in poetry – you govern in prose.

campaign button The small, round lapel badge which has been a commonplace of US elections, starting with the Harrison-Van Buren campaign of 1840.

campaign contributions The financial life-blood of US electoral politics, and historically a rich vein for corruption – "good old-fashioned GRAFT in a very thin disguise" as the reformer Mark Green put it. In the late 19th century Sen. Boies Penrose told businessmen:

> You send us to Congress; we pass laws under which you make money; and out of your profits you further contribute to our campaign funds to send us back again to pass more laws to enable you to make more money.

Theodore Roosevelt was convinced "the need for collecting large campaign funds would vanish if Congress provided an appropriation for the proper and legitimate expenses of each of the great national parties". And as pressure for such funds for Presidential campaign funding finally paid off, Hubert Humphrey said:

> Campaign financing is a curse. It's the most disgusting, demeaning, disenchanting, debilitating experience of a politician's life.

(2) An organized attempt to rally public opinion for a particular cause, or the body promoting such a campaign.

Campaign for Democratic Socialism In Britain, a GAITSKELLITE group which sought to counter left-wing influences in the LABOUR PARTY in the early 1960s, specifically by supporting NATO and nuclear weapons.

Campaign for Labour Party Democracy The hard LEFT group which broke the hold of Labour MPs over the party, provoked the GANG OF FOUR into leaving it and founding the SDP, and in 1981 almost secured the election of Tony BENN as deputy Labour leader.

Campaign for Nuclear Disarmament *See* CND.

Campaign Group The group of hard LEFT Labour MPs which split from the TRIBUNE GROUP in 1982 to form a rival and more uncompromising body. This BENNITE faction began strongly but quickly shrank as a reaction set in to the left-wing policies and splits that had caused Labour's 1983 election defeat. It later added "Socialist" to its name. Andrew Marr, in the *Independent* described the maverick Labour MP and Scots laird Tam Dalyell as "possibly the only member of the Campaign Group to keep peacocks."

single-issue campaign *See* ISSUE.

Campbell case The episode in which the Attorney-General in RAMSAY MACDonald's first UK Labour government initiated, then withdrew, a prosecution for incitement to mutiny against John Campbell, acting editor of the Communist DAILY WORKER. The former liberal Prime Minister Herbert ASQUITH's call for a SELECT COMMITTEE inquiry into whether political pressure had been applied was carried 364–198 in the Commons in October 1924, forcing MacDonald to call an election. The case created the climate for the ZINOVIEV LETTER to do Labour great electoral damage, with the Conservatives deriving all the benefit.

Campbell-Bannerman, Sir Henry *See* C-B.

Campobello The Roosevelt family's summer home in New Brunswick where in 1921 FDR contracted the polio that left him paralysed.

can of worms An issue which becomes more complex and damaging, the more thoroughly it is investigated. President Nixon used the expression to John Dean on 15 September 1972 about the original WATERGATE indictments.

Canada. Canada Act (1) The Westminster legislation of 1791 which divided the old province of Quebec into two, effectively creating English-speaking Ontario. (2) The Westminster legislation, passed in 1982, that finally PATRIATED the Canadian constitution and removed the last vestiges of rule from London. It was passed after fierce argument over whether the necessary degree of unanimity in Canada existed.

Canada First The movement founded in 1868 which during the next decade gained wide support for a policy of national assertiveness built on PROTECTIONISM and "a voice in the treaties concerning Canada".

O Canada! Canada's national anthem, approved by Parliament in 1967 to replace GOD SAVE THE QUEEN, and officially adopted on 27 June 1980 under the National Anthem Act. It was written in French by Judge Adolphe-Basil Routhier, to music by Calixa Lavallée, and first performed in QUEBEC city on 24 June 1880. It was not heard in English Canada until 1901, when it was sung in Toronto for the future King George V; the present English translation was written in 1908 by Robert Stanley Weir (1858–1926), with slight amendments after the 1967 debate. The English version begins:

> O Canada!, Our home and native land!
> True patriot love in all thy sons command.
> With glowing hearts we see thee rise,
> The True North strong and free!
> From far and wide, O Canada, we stand on guard for thee.
> God keep our land glorious and free!
> O Canada, we stand on guard for thee.
> O Canada, we stand on guard for thee!

Canal Zone The 10-mile-wide US enclave carved out of Panama in 1903 when that state itself was formed from the northern tip of Colombia (as a result of a revolution with which Washington connived), to include and protect the Panama Canal. Jurisdiction reverted to Panama in 1979 under the PANAMA CANAL TREATIES, and sovereignty – and the canal – will revert in 2000. At its inception Theodore Roosevelt said: "I took the Canal Zone and let the Congress debate it. And while the debate goes on, the canal does too." Roosevelt wanted a legal pretext for his actions, but Attorney-General Philander Chase Knox (1853–1921) told him: "Mr. President, do not let so great an achievement suffer from any taint of legality." And during the 1978 Senate debates on the Treaty, Sen. Strom Thurmond, echoing Ronald Reagan, declared:

> We bought it. We paid for it. It is ours.

Canard Enchaîné, Le (Fr. the chained duck) France's cutting satirical weekly, which over the decades has destroyed several political careers, reduced many politicians to figures of ridicule and occasionally, as with the BOKASSA DIAMONDS, broken highly-significant stories.

Cancun summit The NORTH-SOUTH summit of world leaders at the Mexican resort of Cancun in October 1981 to approve the BRANDT COMMISSION Report on the THIRD WORLD. While the report gained general endorsement, there was little positive action.

candidate Someone in the process of election for a public office. The *New York Times* once declared: "The best character that can be given any candidate is that he is so rich he does not need to steal"; just as cynically George O. Ludcke rhymed: "The candidate never wore diapers as a baby way back when;/ It seems that no one could ever pin him down, even then." And Sen. Eugene McCarthy reckoned: "It is dangerous for any national candidate to say things that people might remember." Most politicians hate being a candidate. Adlai Stevenson said: "A presidential candidate has to shave twice a day – and I didn't like that." And Walter Mondale (*see* NORWEGIAN WOOD), at first declining to run in 1984, declared: "I don't want to spend the next two years in Holiday Inns." But Jimmy CARTER put a better face on it:

> The advantage of being a presidential candidate is that you have a much broader range of issues to be fuzzy on.

Manchurian candidate Someone who has been programmed (*i.e.* by a foreign power) to obey orders without thinking. The term originated with Richard Condon's 1959 novel of that name, and the 1962 film by John Frankenheimer, about a US prisoner of war who returns from Korea unaware that he has been BRAINWASHED as an assassin by the Chinese.

paper candidate One who is put forward purely "on paper" and does not fight an active campaign.

prospective candidate A person who has been SELECTED to fight a seat, but will only be ADOPTED at the start of the campaign.

The Candidate The 1972 film in which Robert Redford plays a candidate created by advertising and PR men, and is elected a Senator for California. In the final line of the film, the victorious Redford asks:

> What do we do now?

Cannon Building In Washington, the first of the HOUSE office buildings erected to the south of the Capitol. Named after Rep. Joe Cannon of Illinois, Speaker 1903–11 (*see* FOUL-MOUTHED JOE), work on it began in 1903.

Cannon's precedents *See* PRECEDENTS.

Can't pay – won't pay The slogan used in Britain – especially in London and Scotland – in 1990–92 by militant campaigners against the POLL TAX.

cantonization The breaking-up of a state into smaller units usually based on ethnic differences, as when Serbs and Croats, though not Muslims, tried to dismember Bosnia in 1992. A *canton* is one of the units of the Swiss Confederation.

Canuck letter The Republican-engineered cause of Sen. Edmund Muskie's exit from the 1972 Presidential race, in which he had been expected to be a FRONT-RUNNER. Canuck is an abusive term for a French Canadian, and was used in a letter to William Loeb, ultra-right publisher of the Manchester, New Hampshire, *Union Leader*. The letter said a Muskie aide had told a meeting in Florida of his native Maine: "We don't have Blacks but we do have Canucks", and urged the audience to "Come to New England and see." The letter had in fact been concocted by the Nixon camp's dirty tricks department as part of its RATFUCKING operation; deputy White House communications director Ken Clawson privately boasted of being the author, then publicly denied it. Loeb published the letter, together with a front-page editorial headed "Senator Muskie insults Franco-Americans", two weeks before the NEW HAMPSHIRE PRIMARY in which thousands of former French Canadians were eligible to vote. Muskie lost his composure and burst into tears when attacking Loeb's editorial on the STUMP, and his campaign began to fall apart – as the Republicans had hoped.

canvass, to In America, to scrutinize the ballots cast at an election to ensure the count has been fair.

canvassing The practice of all political parties, mainly at election time, under which

ACTIVISTS call on as many voters as possible to locate their support. In Britain canvassing has consisted almost entirely of banging on doors, though telephone canvassing is now creeping in; in America it is generally done by telephone (*see* PHONE BANK).

CAP The EUROPEAN COMMUNITY's Common Agricultural Policy, under which around 70% of the EC Budget is devoted to subsidizing farmers – large-scale producers, peasants and part-timers – creating the opportunity for massive fraud by agricultural big business. Based on promoting the over-production of inferior produce, it has become an increasing irritant to relations with the United States, and an obstacle to a more liberal GATT agreement.

Cap the Knife The nickname earned by **Caspar Weinberger** (1917–) when serving as cost-cutting and tax-reducing Director of Finance to Governor Ronald Reagan of California. It was later amended to **Cap the Ladle** in a 1981 Herblock cartoon because of the enormous sums Weinberger obtained and disbursed for military projects as Reagan's Secretary of Defence. In December 1992 the outgoing President BUSH gave Weinberger a PARDON on the eve of his trial for allegedly giving false testimony over the IRAN-CONTRA scandal, amid signs that Bush would be firmly implicated.

> The first person in history to overdraw a blank check.
> Sen. ROBERT DOLE.

Cape to Cairo The driving slogan of late 19th-century British IMPERIALISM, and in particular the expansionist plans of Cecil Rhodes (1853–1902), who dreamed of constructing a railway entirely on British land from South Africa to the Mediterranean.

capital (1) The money and other resources necessary for the ownership of business, and that ownership personified. Karl MARX asserted that capital "comes into the world dripping from hand to foot, from every pore, with blood and dirt"; Abraham LINCOLN argued less emotively that "capital is only the fruit of LABOR, and could never have existed if labor had not first existed".

capitalism The form of economic organization which predominates in the industrialized West, and which has seen off COMMUNISM, its mortal foe. It combines private property, a free MARKET and the vast majority of the workforce in private, wealth-creating employment. The original theory of capitalism posited an entirely free market in which small entrepreneurs hired individual workers to achieve the maximum output for the lowest price; increasingly that model has been distorted by the growth of monopolies and MULTINATIONALS.

To the left, capitalism is inherently flawed and dangerous. The French Socialist Jean Jaurès (1859–1914) asserted that "capitalism carries within itself war, as clouds carry rain". PANDIT Nehru believed that "the conflict between capitalism and democracy is inherent and continuous". Arthur Scargill, Marxist leader of Britain's National Union of Mineworkers, declared: "Life under capitalism has convinced me that there is no moral or political justification for the continuation of the free enterprise system." And Neil KINNOCK, long before his dash to make Labour ELECTABLE, wrote in 1975:

> We cannot remove the evils of capitalism without taking its source of power – ownership.

KEYNES reckoned that "capitalism, wisely managed, can probably be made more efficient for attaining economic ends than any alternative system yet in sight, but that in itself it is in many ways extremely objectionable". And CHURCHILL made this comparison:

> The inherent vice of capitalism is the unequal sharing of blessings; the inherent virtue of Communism is the equal sharing of miseries.

popular capitalism The economic regime advocated by Margaret Thatcher in the 1980s. It hinged on the bulk of the population becoming shareholders as State industries were PRIVATIZED, and on the growth of small business as opposed to large, unionized concerns.

capitalist An owner of capital, and an advocate or an integral part of the capitalist system; a term of abuse widely used by COMMUNISTS.

> The capitalists are so hungry for profits that they will sell us the rope to hang them with. LENIN (*attr.*)

> The peace of the world has been preserved not by statesmen but by capitalists.
> DISRAELI on the impact of Rothschild loans to Italy and Russia, 1863.

capitalist-roader A standard charge by Chinese Communist leaders against anyone who steps out of line. It was originally used by the MAOISTS against allegedly BOURGEOIS rivals (often pro-Soviet) whom they accused of wanting elements of a MARKET economy, but the tables were turned when the leadership after Mao's death denounced the GANG OF FOUR as capitalist-roaders.

Capital Territory The 2400 sq. km. enclave carved from New South Wales in 1911 to contain the Australian federal capital of Canberra; in 1915 land at Jervis Bay on the New South Wales coast was added to provide a port. Canberra was planned by the US architect

Burley Griffin, who won an international competition in 1911; by 1986 its population had reached 285,000. Parliament first met there in 1927. In 1988 the Commonwealth Parliament granted it self-government; the following year it elected a Labor government under Rosemary Follett, Australia's first woman chief minister.

Capitol The building dominating Washington that houses the US CONGRESS; also the comparable buildings in each of the 50 State capitals. The Capitol was designed by William Thornton (1759–1828) and subsequently heavily modified – particularly through the construction of a high, rather than a low, dome – and extended. George WASHINGTON laid the cornerstone on 18 September 1793; the first wing was ready for use late in 1800. On 24 August 1814 the still-uncompleted Capitol was burned by the British in reprisal for the burning by US troops of the Parliament House at York (Toronto). Rear-Admiral George Cockburn gave the order, asking his men:

> Shall this harbour of YANKEE democracy be burned?

The damage was quickly repaired, the original building being completed on 6 December 1819. But construction was still under way during the CIVIL WAR; Abraham Lincoln justified the work by saying: "If people see the Capitol going on, it is a sign that we intend the UNION shall go on." The Capitol, which for 134 years also housed the SUPREME COURT, now stands 287 ft. 5½ in. high, is 350 ft. wide and more than 751 ft. long. It has 540 rooms, and its floor area covers 16½ acres.

> We have built no national temples but the Capitol.
> Rep. RUFUS CHOATE (1799–1859).

Carbonari (Ital. charcoal-burners) The radical secret society which agitated in the early 19th century for a republican form of government and also served as a spur to national unification. It was founded in the Kingdom of Naples, where it was ruthlessly suppressed after disorder in 1813. It spread rapidly throughout Italy, prompting risings against the Bourbons in 1820 and throughout the divided country in the following decade. It faded away before the RISORGIMENTO got under way, but paved the way for it.

card-carrying member Technically a paid-up member of any political organization, but in practice a sinister term from the days of McCARTHYISM for a member of the US COMMUNIST Party. The phrase came to life on 3 October 1950 when McCarthy charged that there were "57 card-carrying members of the Communist Party" in the State Department and demanded action against them from President Truman. In the 1988 Presidential election campaign George Bush resurrected the inference behind the term when he accused the Democratic nominee Michael Dukakis of being "a card-carrying member of the American Civil Liberties Union".

careerist A politician dedicated to his or her own advancement at the expense of any commitment to principle or to colleagues.

caretaker government An administration appointed until a government with full authority can be elected and sworn in. In Britain, CHURCHILL formed a caretaker government in May 1945 after Labour withdrew from the wartime coalition; it resigned two months later when Labour won a LANDSLIDE election victory.

CARICOM The Caribbean Community, formed in 1973 by former British colonies in the region to co-ordinate economic and foreign policy. Its founder-members were Antigua, Barbados, the Bahamas, Belize, Dominica, Grenada, the Grenadines, Guyana, Jamaica, Montserrat, St. Kitts aand Nevis, St. Lucia, St. Vincent, Trinidad and Tobago.

caring but daring One of the slogans for the "new politics" of Britain's SDP adumbrated by Dr. David OWEN after he became its leader in 1983. Another was "tough but tender". Owen's aim was to demonstrate that the SDP was not a "soggy" party of BLEEDING-HEART liberals.

Carlos *See* JACKAL.

Carlton Club The club in St. James's, London, which is the embodiment of the CONSERVATIVE PARTY's Establishment and the continuity of its traditions.

Carlton Club revolt The decision taken by Conservative backbenchers on 19 October 1922, meeting at the club, to force their leaders to break with Lloyd George's Coalition. The pretext was L. G.'s handling of the CHANAK CRISIS. Lloyd George resigned, and the Conservatives took power under Bonar Law.

> The cabin boys have taken over the ship.
> F. E. SMITH (Lord Birkenhead, 1872–1930).

Caroline The aircraft, named after his daughter who was then aged almost three, in which John F. KENNEDY campaigned for the Presidency in 1960.

carpetbagger Originally a derogatory term for the Northern Whites who headed south after the CIVIL WAR; some genuinely wanted to establish a fair society, more sought political advancement and self-enrichment during

RECONSTRUCTION. The newcomers earned the name because of the cheap travelling bags made of carpeting with which many of them, especially bankers, arrived – and frequently vanished. It has come to apply to anyone who arrives to start a political career in a town where he or she has no roots.

carrot and stick The combination of incentives and penalties which a government is able to use on recalcitrant groups in society. When the latter are used there are often cries of "all stick and no carrot". The term relates to the two methods of getting a donkey to move, the inference being that the group in question is being as obstinate as an ass.

carry In a US Presidential election, a candidate carries each state where he or she obtains the most votes, and thus wins its support in the ELECTORAL COLLEGE.

Carswell nomination The furore surrounding President Nixon's nomination in 1970 of federal judge G. Harrold Carswell (1917–) of Florida to the SUPREME COURT. The Senate, after furious protests by civil rights groups, rejected Carswell by 51–45 because of his allegedly RACIST views and actions (he had broadcast a White supremacist speech in 1948), as well as an undistinguished judicial record. Carswell was one of several conservatives Nixon nominated to eliminate the liberal bias of the WARREN COURT; his nomination of Warren E. Burger as Chief Justice was approved, but with four vacancies occurring it took him some time to find candidates acceptable to the Senate.

> Even if he is mediocre, there are a lot of mediocre judges and people and lawyers. They are entitled to a little REPRESENTATION too, aren't they?
>
> Sen. ROMAN HRUSKA (1904–).

Carter. Carterized To be weakened to the point of ridicule. A word stemming from the crisis-ridden tenure of **Jimmy** (James Earl Jr.) **Carter** (1924–), 39th President of the United States (Democrat, 1977–81). It was much used in Washington in the early Reagan years when the Carter Presidency appeared the nadir of America's fortunes, but was heard less as history put it into perspecive; a Carter administration reunion late in 1989 attracted a favourable press. A peanut farmer, born-again Southern Baptist, former Naval officer and one-term Governor of Georgia, Carter capitalized on public disillusion with Washington after WATERGATE to come from nowhere and win the 1976 Democratic nomination. His issues director Stuart Eizenstat reckoned Carter "the most conservative of the Democratic candidates in the '76 campaign". In his ACCEPTANCE speech he declared: "We have been shaken by a tragic war abroad, and by scandals and broken promises at home. Our people are searching for new voices, and new ideas and new leaders." Carter was one of the most overtly religious Presidents, teaching Sunday school and insisting: "We should live our lives as though Christ was coming this afternoon." From the outset he told the American people: "I will never lie to you," and at times embarrassingly he did more than most Presidents to keep his word. He was strongly supported throughout by his wife Rosalynn (*see* STEEL MAGNOLIA), who shared his beliefs and took an active interest in government; her own special issue was mental health.

Carter started way ahead of Gerald FORD but a lacklustre campaign punctuated by his LUST IN MY HEART *Playboy* interview and a claim to have seen a UFO, coupled with public doubts about an "outsider" in the White House, led to him only scrambling victory. Once elected, he had problems putting together an administration and his early weeks in the White House foreshadowed frayed relations with the Democratic Congress. Nelson Pollsby wrote: "Nothing in his prior experience as a politician, certainly nothing in his experience of the nomination process, led him to the view that he needed to come to terms with the rest of the Democratic Party." Republican Rep. James Leach said: "There was something about him that brought out an instinct to do battle", and Hedrick Smith wrote: "He circled his wagons with young Georgians inexperienced in Washington and suffered the consequences." Carter himself reminisced:

> I treated the Congress as if they were the Georgia legislature, and they treated me as if I was governor of Georgia.

But White House staffer Mark Siegel was more acid: "Congress was the enemy. The Carter people regarded TIP O'Neill as a horse's ass, and if you call someone a horse's ass in the White House, do you know how fast that gets back to that someone?"

Carter frankly and disconcertingly shared his doubts about America's strength, telling a Kentucky town meeting in 1979: "I thought a lot about our Nation and what I should do as President. And Sunday night before last, I made a speech about the two problems of our country – energy and malaise." But he also showed a disconcerting assertiveness, saying: "People who meet with me had better know the subject, because I know it." He did indeed involve himself more than other Presidents in the minutiae of government. Roy Jenkins reckoned that "his weakness did not lie in his brain, which was quick, orderly and fact-absorbing. His faults, such as they were, were mainly ones of style." Carter's press secretary Jody Powell wrote: "He would rather spend the next hour on the ifs, ands or buts of the decision he had to make, than on the selling of the decision." Hedrick Smith's verdict was blunter:

> He slaved like an indentured servant and the public watched him sink in the morass of detail.

An early initiative on energy (*see* MORAL EQUIVALENT OF WAR) was mauled by Congress, and his Biblical rectitude was dented by the Bert LANCE AFFAIR; his powerful commitment to HUMAN RIGHTS was contradicted by his fulsome support for the Shah of Iran. Carter's greatest successes were in foreign affairs: the CAMP DAVID AGREEMENT and the PANAMA CANAL TREATIES. But he was dogged by INFLATION as the world economy went into recession, and torpedoed by the HOSTAGE CRISIS with Iran (*see* OCTOBER SURPRISE). Weakened in his bid for re-election in 1980 by a challenge from Sen. Edward KENNEDY and the intervention of liberal Republican Rep. John Anderson, he was outgunned by Ronald Reagan. The GREAT COMMUNICATOR landed a number of campaign blows, saying: "his foreign policy is like the sorry tapping of Neville Chamberlain's umbrella on the cobblestones of MUNICH", but concentrating mainly on the economy. Carter also opened himself to ridicule by saying in a Presidential DEBATE: "I had a discussion with my daughter Amy the other day before I came here to ask her what the most important issue was. She said she thought nuclear weaponry and the control of nuclear arms." After a predictably heavy defeat, Carter concentrated on charitable works and the Carter Center for trouble-shooting in crisis areas like the Sudan.

> He finished up less like the captain of a ship than a frantic white-water canoeist. DAVID BRODER.

carthorse The public image for several decades of Britain's Trades Union Congress (*see* TUC), as evoked in the 1930s by the NEW STATESMAN and *Manchester Guardian* cartoonist David Low (1891–1963).

Casa Rosada (Sp. Pink House) The Presidential palace in the heart of Buenos Aires from whose balcony successive Argentine leaders – notably Juan PERÓN and his charismatic wife Eva (*see* EVITA) have whipped up their supporters to strengthen their position. The process was reversed after Argentina's defeat in the FALKLANDS WAR of 1982 when the military dictator General Leopold Galtieri (1926–) was booed off the balcony, paving the way for the return of democracy.

casework The work of a legislator in dealing with individual constituents' complaints and problems. In Britain it is carried out by MPs themselves, often through weekend SURGERIES; in the US Congress STAFFERS carry the burden.

> It means having your staff track down missing Social Security checks, inquire about sons and husbands in the armed services, help veterans get medical care, pursue applications for small-business loans.
> HEDRICK SMITH, *The Power Game.*

cash. Cash and Carry Act An Act passed by the US Congress in November 1939 at the urging of President Roosevelt, to limit the harm done by the NEUTRALITY ACTS to the countries threatened by Nazi Germany at the start of WORLD WAR II. It enabled participants in the war to buy US arms, provided they paid immediately and transported the arms themselves.

cash limits The budgeting principle embraced by Margaret Thatcher's UK government in the early 1980s. Under it a cash total was set for each department and each programme, and cost rises due to INFLATION had to be absorbed within the programme itself.

casual vacancy A vacancy in an elected body which has to be filled at a time when no elections are scheduled, as a result of the death, resignation or even expulsion of a member.

casus belli (Lat. the occasion of war) An act or incident justifying a resort to war; the grounds for waging war or a dispute falling short of conflict.

Cat and Mouse Act The popular name for the Prisoners (Temporary Discharge for Ill-Health) Act of 1913, put through by the Liberal Home Secretary Reginald Mackenna to prevent imprisoned SUFFRAGETTES achieving martyrdom by going on hunger STRIKE. Prisoners too weak to tolerate further FORCE-FEEDING were released on licence, but were subject to re-arrest once they had regained their strength. To play cat and mouse is to toy with a creature in one's power.

catch-all The pejorative term attached by investigative journalists and campaigners for civil liberties to the notorious Section 2 of Britain's 1911 OFFICIAL SECRETS ACT, which outlawed the unauthorized communication of any official information to anybody by a Crown servant. Theoretically, it was even an offence for a civil servant to tell a friend what was on the menu in the departmental canteen. The section, under which over 2000 differently-worded charges could be brought, was totally discredited by the time a far less comprehensive and draconian measure replaced it in 1989.

Catherine Place meeting The informal gathering of Ministers late on 20 November 1990, at the home of the deputy Chief Whip Tristan Garel-Jones, which concluded that Margaret Thatcher (*see* IRON LADY) would have to step down as Prime Minister. Diehard Thatcherites are convinced the meeting was called to plot against her after her failure to eliminate Michael Heseltine in the first round of the Tory leadership ballot. Apart from Garel-Jones, who went on to run Douglas Hurd's leadership campaign, those present included Norman Lamont, who was to head John MAJOR's campaign after Mrs. Thatcher withdrew, and four other members of the Cabinet. Some felt she would lose in a second ballot, others that she might win but would be fatally weakened. They reported their views to the Chief Whip, and to Mrs. Thatcher's staff; the Prime Minister polled individual Cabinet members herself, and within 36 hours she resigned.

Cato Street conspiracy A plot by some 50 followers of the socialist radical Thomas Spence (1750–1814) led by Arthur Thistlewood, to assassinate Lord Liverpool's Cabinet at a dinner on 22 February 1820 and declare a republic. The group had been penetrated by a government spy, and its members were arrested before they could leave their base in Cato Street off London's Edgware Road; the principal conspirators were tried for TREASON and hanged.

caucus A closed meeting of a party group, usually to agree a line to be adhered to and candidates to be supported; also the organized members of a party in a legislature. The verb **to caucus** means to go into a meeting where party matters will be resolved. The term emerged in early 18th-century Boston with the **Caucus** (or Caucas) **Club**, where the politically-involved gathered to choose candidates for office before their presentation to the voters; H. L. Mencken traced the word to the Algonquin Indian for "counsellor". It was in common use by 1824, when Republican members of Congress attempted to instal William H. Crawford as the party's Presidential candidate. The *Baltimore Morning Chronicle* reported: "The poor little political bird of ominous note and plumage, denominated a *CAUCUS*, was hatched at Washington on Saturday last."

> The difference between a caucus and a cactus is that a cactus has all the pricks on the outside.
>
> Rep. MORRIS UDALL (1922– , *attr.*).

Iowa caucuses The small gatherings of registered voters at the close of the year before a Presidential election at which Iowa's DELEGATE selection process for the Democratic National Convention the following summer is begun. They attracted little attention until Jimmy CARTER won headlines and invaluable momentum there in 1975, stealing a march on rivals who had been waiting for the NEW HAMPSHIRE PRIMARY. His initiative effectively extended the Presidential campaign by two to three months.

Caudillo (Sp. leader, chief) The title taken by the dictator General **Francisco Franco** (1892–1975) after the victory of his Nationalist forces in the SPANISH CIVIL WAR. As leader of the FALANGE, Franco gave the term a similar meaning to DUCE or FÜHRER, the titles chosen by his counterparts Mussolini and Hitler. The title died with Franco, there being no room for such a figure in the CONSTITUTIONAL MONARCHY that replaced his Fascist state.

cause A goal whose achievement takes on the nature of a struggle or a crusade, and becomes a way of life to the exclusion of everything else. Most worked-for revolutions, and the continuing drive for a united Ireland, have been referred to by their adherents simply as "the cause". Thomas Paine wrote of the AMERICAN REVOLUTION: "It is not a few acres of ground, but a cause, that we are defending, and whether we defeat the enemy in one battle or by degrees, the consequences will be the same"; he also remarked that:

> A bad cause will ever be supported by bad means and bad men.

Theodore Roosevelt declared that:

> No man is worth his salt who is not ready at all times to risk his well-being, to risk his body, to risk his life in some great cause.

The term implies not only sacrifice, but long struggle and setbacks, Wendell Willkie once saying:

> I would rather lose in a cause I knew some day would triumph, than triumph in a cause that I know one day will fail.

CBI Confederation of British Industry. The body which represents most of Britain's large companies, in the manufacturing, utility and transport sectors, in their dealings with and LOBBYing of government. Formed in 1965 to succeed the Federation of British Industry (FBI), it has 250,000 members. Unlike the rival, more ideological Institute of Directors it campaigns for direct help for industry from the State.

CCF Co-operative Commonwealth Federation. The forerunner of Canada's New Democratic Party (NDP) founded at Regina in 1933 by farm, labour, socialist and intellectual groups and veterans of the PROGRESSIVE movement.

With J. S. Woodsworth as leader it made immediate inroads and within a year was the official opposition in British Columbia and Saskatchewan. Anti-war in the 1930s but a reluctant supporter of Canadian involvement in World War II, the CCF benefited from wartime regimentation to become Ontario's second party in 1943 and win power in Saskatchewan under T. C. Douglas the next year – holding it until 1966. By then, in 1961, the CCF had merged with the Canadian Labour Congress to form the NDP.

> No CCF government will rest content until it has eradicated capitalism and put into operation the full programme of socialized planning which will lead to the establishment in Canada of the Co-operative Commonwealth. REGINA DECLARATION, 1933.

ceasefire An agreement between two warring armies to halt hostilities while efforts are made to negotiate a peace settlement. In some cases, as with the KOREAN WAR, a ceasefire or armistice will remain in force for decades without the war being formally ended or a peace agreement reached.

Cecchini report The European COMMISSION's economic justification for the SINGLE MARKET, named after Paolo Cecchini, who chaired the team of EC officials who put it together in 1987–88. Published in 16 volumes after a two-year study in which 11,000 businesses were questioned, it put a compelling case for the 1992 package by estimating the costs of continuing with an "uncommon market" at $243 billion a year. It predicted that completion of the single market would "trigger a supply-side shock to the Community economy as a whole" and lead to lower prices, greater competition, lower government deficits, reduced inflation and "very substantial job creation".

cell A tiny unit of membership in a REVOLUTIONARY or terrorist movement, self-contained so as to maintain secrecy and limit any damage caused by infiltration. The cell was a basis of communist organization in hostile environments, and is the most secure unit for a terrorist group.

Celtic fringe The mountainous and coastal constituencies of the Scottish Highlands and Islands, west Wales and Devon and Cornwall – bastions of Celtic culture and frequently of language – which just kept Liberalism alive at Westminster from the 1920s to the 1960s, when the party's chance of winning seats in the rest of the country was negligible (*see* TELEPHONE BOX). The radical tradition of these areas patchily resisted the rise of Labour, initially because of the continuing appeal of Lloyd George, himself the ultimate Celt (*see* WELSH WIZARD).

Cenotaph (Gr. *kenos*, empty; *taphos*, tomb) The obelisk erected in WHITEHALL to commemorate the dead of WORLD WAR I, before which the leaders of the nation stand in tribute each Remembrance Sunday (the Sunday nearest to Armistice Day, 11 November). Designed by Sir Edwin Lutyens, the Cenotaph was dedicated at the first such ceremony in 1920. The two-minute silence at 11 a.m. is the most solemn moment of the year, recalling the United Kingdom's "glorious dead" in all the wars of the 20th century; in 1981 there was a furore when the Labour leader Michael Foot laid his wreath in what was described by one Labour MP as a DONKEY JACKET instead of the conventional dark suit.

censure A disciplinary measure taken by a legislature, which denotes strong disapproval of a member's statement or action, but stops short of suspension or EXCLUSION. One such was the censure of Sen. Thomas Dodd by the US Senate in June 1967 for using CAMPAIGN CONTRIBUTIONS to settle personal bills; he kept his seat and his SENIORITY. The word "censure" is not always the one used; Sen. Joseph McCARTHY was "condemned" by the Senate, while erring members of the House are REPRIMANDED. Members of the UK House of Commons may also be censured, the POULSON AFFAIR in the early and mid-1970s being a rare instance.

vote of censure A motion put down by the OPPOSITION at Westminster in order to mount a concerted attack on the Government over a specific issue or set of issues; unlike a vote of No-CONFIDENCE, which covers a Government's entire performance, its success will not necessarily bring about the fall of the Prime Minister, or force a General Election.

CENTO *See* BAGHDAD PACT.

central. central banks The national banks of the CAPITALIST world which between them endeavour to control, subject to MARKET forces, the relative levels of currencies and of interest rates – and through them seek to maintain world prosperity and economic stability. America's FED is independent though its chairman is Federally-appointed, Germany's BUNDESBANK exerts an even more stubborn independence; the Bank of England, owned by the State since 1946, reaches its decisions in consultation with the TREASURY.

> The job of a central banker is not easy at the best of times. It has been said that he must always exude confidence, without actually lying. DENIS HEALEY.

Central Committee The main executive committee of the Soviet COMMUNIST PARTY, elected by the party congress. The main power resided in the POLITBURO and the Secretariat.

Central Council The two-day annual business meeting of Britain's CONSERVATIVE PARTY, held each March, which also affords the party leader and senior spokesmen a chance to enthuse the constituency RANK AND FILE and make speeches aimed at the electorate at large, some five weeks before the local elections.

Central Office The headquarters organization of the Conservative Party, based at Conservative Central Office in SMITH SQUARE, Westminster. Headed by the party chairman, it constitutes one of three legs of the movement: the voluntary party in the country, Central Office, and the Parliamentary party which elects the Tory leader.

Central Policy Review Staff *See* THINK TANK.

Central Powers The collective term used during WORLD WAR I for the ultimately-defeated central European alliance of Germany and Austria-Hungary.

centre The MIDDLE GROUND in politics, whose generally moderate adherents all but the most ideologically-based parties have wooed in the hope of winning power.

> Anyone who throws away the centre sacrifices his capacity to govern. WILLY BRANDT (1913–92).

A **centrist** party is one that occupies the middle ground, frequently needing to form COALITIONs with other parties to gain a share in power and as often wooed by them. **Centre-left** and **Centre-right** emerged in the late 1970s as terms for politicians and parties with an obvious political slant, but not driven by an uncompromising ideology.

Ceres Socialist Studies, Research and Education Centre. A radical left-wing ginger group which for over a quarter of a century has pressed adventurous policies on France's Socialist Party. In particular, it has offered an alternative to the increasingly moderate course steered by President Mitterrand from the mid-1980s. One of its leading lights has been Jean-Pierre Chevènement (1939–), intermittently secretary of CERES since 1965, who resigned as Defence Minister in protest at France's involvement in the GULF WAR. *Ceres* was the Roman goddess of creation, and her image, bearing a sheaf of corn, has long been a symbol of the French republic.

CETA Comprehensive Employment and Training Act. The Act passed in 1973 under which US Federal funds are made available to state and local governments to provide jobs and training for the unemployed.

CFE Conventional Forces in Europe. The agreement between 22 NATO and WARSAW PACT countries, signed in PARIS on 20 November 1990, which marked the end of COLD WAR tension by dictating huge cuts in the weaponry and forces of the opposing alliances. It was concluded at the CSCE conference in Vienna the previous week after US Secretary of State James Baker and the Soviet Foreign Minister Eduard Shevardnadze had resolved the final differences between the superpowers. CFE imposed the heaviest cuts in Soviet weaponry – tanks, artillery, armoured vehicles, helicopters and aircraft – and ended the Warsaw Pact's heavy superiority in troop numbers.

> The most substantial and far-reaching agreement for the reduction of armaments which has yet been achieved.
> MARGARET THATCHER, reporting to the House of Commons.

CFR Confidential – Final Revise. The pre-publication copies of WHITE PAPERS and other UK government publications (except where market-sensitive), circulated to the LOBBY under EMBARGO so that the media has time to report correctly on detailed and complex findings and recommendations.

CGT *Confédération Générale du Travail*, General Confederation of Labour. France's largest and most militant trade-union grouping, allied to the Communist Party; it is strongest in traditional industries such as coal and the railways. The trade union movement is fragmented between the CGT, the Catholic CFDT (*Confédération Française du Travail*), and the Socialist *Force Ouvrière* (Workers' Force).

chair (1) the Chair. In a legislature, the authority represented by the SPEAKER or chairman. It is a convention for members to address the Chair and not each other. (2) A term pioneered in 1980s Britain by leftist or POLITICALLY CORRECT groups to supersede the use of "chairman", which they saw as sexually discriminatory, and avoid the alternatives of **chairwoman** or **chairperson**.

behind the Chair The space at the rear of the House of Commons CHAMBER where MPs of opposing parties can converse informally without being observed, and where deals are frequently struck.

empty chair The tactic of one nation leaving its place in an international body or conference vacant, either as a protest at a course of action being followed or in an effort to prevent decisions being reached. It has generally proved counterproductive: the Soviet Union's withdrawal from the SECURITY COUNCIL in 1950 left it unable to VETO UN participation in the KOREAN WAR, and France's refusal to participate in meetings of the EC COUNCIL OF MINISTERS in 1966 failed to produce the endorsement of GAULLIST aims that it had hoped for; instead it produced the LUXEMBOURG COMPROMISE.

by your leave, Mr. Speaker, I must borrow your chair a little King Charles I's opening words when he arrived in the House of Commons on 4 January 1642, accompanied by troops, to have the FIVE MEMBERS arrested. Speaker Lenthall made way for the King, who told Members he valued their privileges, but that the five had committed treason, and "I must have them wheresoever I find them". He then observed: "I SEE ALL THE BIRDS ARE FLOWN", and with the Speaker refusing to give him any information he left the House. The episode was a landmark on the road to England's CIVIL WAR.

Chairborne Division A World War II British Service pejorative for the army of military officers and BUREAUCRATS who prosecuted the war from WHITEHALL. It was a none-too-subtle comparison with the combatant *Airborne Division*.

Chairman Mao Mao Tse-Tung (or Mao Zedong, 1893–1976), the co-founder in 1921 of China's Communist Party who after 28 years of struggle including the LONG MARCH finally overthrew Chiang Kai-Shek's Kuomintang government (*see* KMT) in 1949, then ran China as an autocracy for almost a quarter of a century. At first friendly with STALIN, Mao broke with Moscow to launch his first experiment in back-to-basics Communism, the GREAT LEAP FORWARD, in 1958. He survived its unpopularity to try again with the extremist CULTURAL REVOLUTION between 1966 and 1969; at its heart was the LITTLE RED BOOK containing Mao's thoughts (*see below*). Chairman Mao was by now the centre of a PERSONALITY CULT of which Stalin would have been envious; a memorable feature was his supposed swim across the Yangtse. After the XENOPHOBIA of the Cultural Revolution he also established links with Western leaders to annoy the KREMLIN. Mao remained in apparent total control until his death aged 83, though it is suggested that his wife Chiang Ching (or Jiang Qing) (*see* GANG OF FOUR) was responsible for some of his most extreme policies.

the thoughts of Chairman Mao The often-banal and mainly negative statements on the merits of revolution set out in the LITTLE RED BOOK, which elevated Mao's personality cult to its highest point. They were memorized and chanted by MAOISTS throughout the world.

> The best weapon is not the aircraft, heavy artillery, tanks or the atom bomb. It is Mao Tse-Tung thought; the greatest fighting force is the man armed with Mao Tse-Tung thought.
>
> LIN PIAO, speaking to the Army on the eve of the Cultural Revolution, 1965.

chamber The hall, generally purpose-built, where a legislature meets. The seats are either set out in rows facing each other, as at Westminster, to facilitate ADVERSARIAL POLITICS, or in a semicircle (see HEMICYCLE), as in the US CAPITOL and in Continental legislatures where the politics of COALITION prevails.

Chamber of Deputies The formal title of the more powerful House in a number of legislatures, notably that of France.

> A broken mirror in which the nation cannot recognize its own image.
>
> LÉON GAMBETTA, French Prime Minister 1881–82.

Old Senate Chamber The original meeting-place of the US Senate, where in 1800 John Adams addressed the first Joint Session of Congress. In 1810 the Chamber was subdivided through the interposition of an extra floor, with the Senate taking the upper portion. After the Capitol was burnt by the British in 1814, Benjamin Latrobe rebuilt the Chamber as larger and more ornate; the Senate reoccupied it on 6 December 1819. It was here that Daniel Webster delivered his most memorable speeches, and Charles Sumner launched his near-murderous caning of Preston Brooks (*see* Crime against KANSAS). In 1859 the Senate moved to its present chamber and the SUPREME COURT moved upstairs to the Old Senate Chamber, remaining there for three-quarters of a century until their own building was ready. The Old Senate Chamber is now open to the public, restored to its 1850s condition.

second Chamber A general term for the less influential chamber in a BICAMERAL system, at Westminster the HOUSE OF LORDS. It is also used by UK politicians in debates about what more democratic form of Upper House could replace the Lords.

Chamberlain, (Arthur) **Neville** (1869–1940), Prime Minister (Conservative) 1937–40. The Premier who led Britain reluctantly into WORLD WAR II but is best remembered as the architect of APPEASEMENT. The son of the charismatic IMPERIALIST Joseph Chamberlain, he went into industry in his native Birmingham, became Lord MAYOR and entered Parliament in 1918. At first he was overshadowed by his half-brother Austen, who warned him portentously: "Neville, you must remember that you don't know anything about foreign affairs." He was a successful Minister of Health 1923–29; he was offered the Exchequer, but rejected it, writing: "What a day! two salmon in the morning, and the offer of the Exchequer in the afternoon." He took the job in the 1931 NATIONAL GOVERNMENT, over the next six years establishing himself as Stanley BALDWIN's natural successor despite a lack of CHARISMA. Harold Nicolson wrote: "He has the mind and manner of a clothes brush," and Aneurin Bevan described his speaking style as "like a visit to Woolworth's: everything in its place, and nothing over sixpence". Bevan said of Chamberlain as Chancellor: "The worst thing that I can say about democracy is that it has tolerated him for four and a half years," and when he succeeded Baldwin, Bevan commented:

> In the funeral service of capitalism the honeyed and soothing platitudes of the clergyman are finished and the cortège is now under the sombre and impassive guidance of the undertaker.

Chamberlain became Prime Minister at just the point when Hitler's expansionism and massive military build-up were becoming obvious; according to his critics he sought to co-exist with a threat he never understood, while his supporters assert that he aimed to buy time while the UK too rearmed. In 1938 he flew to Germany to sign the MUNICH AGREEMENT, now viewed as a national disgrace but then hailed as a triumph. The columnist Godfrey Winn wrote: "Praise be to God and to Mr. Chamberlain. I find no sacrilege in coupling those two names." But Hitler said patronizingly:

> He seemed such a nice old gentleman, I thought I would give him my autograph as a souvenir.

Churchill told him bluntly: "You were given the choice between war and dishonour. You chose dishonour – you will have war", and noted: "In the depths of that dusty heart there is nothing but surrender." Hitler's move into Prague the next March forced Chamberlain to face reality, saying: "I have decided that I cannot trust the Nazi leaders again"; he gave a GUARANTEE to Poland, but dragged his feet over a defensive pact with the Soviet Union, enabling the Germans to conclude the cynical HITLER-STALIN PACT. When Hitler invaded Poland in September 1939, Chamberlain declared war (*see* I HAVE TO TELL YOU . . .). He reshaped his government to bring CHURCHILL back from the wilderness (*see* WINSTON IS BACK), but after a period of Phoney WAR was left woefully exposed by the loss of Norway; his declaration that HITLER HAS MISSED THE BUS did not help. On 7 and 8 May Chamberlain came under withering fire from Tory critics (*see* YOU HAVE SAT HERE LONG ENOUGH) in a debate on the conduct of the war; the stubborn and insular Chamberlain said plaintively: "I have friends in this House," but the Government's majority was slashed from 240 to 81. Chamberlain hung on, Hugh Dalton saying: "He seems determined to stick to office, like a dirty old piece of chewing gum on the leg of a chair;" Brendan Bracken said that shifting him was "like trying to get a limpet off a corpse". But when two days later Hitler launched his BLITZKRIEG against the Low Countries he made way for Churchill. He stayed in the Government, but died of cancer six months later.

> Had he retired or died in 1937, he would have gone down in history as a great social reformer and a great administrator. HAROLD MACMILLAN.

> No better than a Mayor of Birmingham, and in a lean year at that. LORD HUGH CECIL.

> He saw foreign policy through the wrong end of a municipal drainpipe. LLOYD GEORGE.

champagne socialist *See* LIMOUSINE LIBERAL.

Chanak crisis The crisis in October 1922 that caused the fall of Lloyd George's coalition government. It was precipitated by the entry of the Turks, aiming to take part of Thrace from Greece, into the British- and French-held neutral zone of Chanak, on the Asiatic side of the Dardanelles. Conservative members of the Cabinet felt that L. G. had sided with Greece by reinforcing the British garrison in Chanak; mistrust of his leadership led to the CARLTON CLUB REVOLT of 19 October, the break-up of the coalition and the formation of the 1922 COMMITTEE. Lloyd George had also called for the DOMINIONS to hold Chanak against the Turks, enraging the Canadian Prime Minister Mackenzie King who refused to "play the imperial game".

chancellery. Chancelleries of Europe A phrase, used mainly in the late 19th and early 20th centuries, for the apparently-unshakable centres of European power. **Chancellery** (*Kanzlerei*) was, and is, the word in German-speaking nations for the offices of the head of government.

spy in the Chancellery The scandal in 1974 that forced the resignation of Willy BRANDT (1913–92) as Chancellor of West Germany. It was discovered that Gunther Guillaume, one of his senior aides, had for many years been spying for the East Germans.

Chancellor (1) In German-speaking countries, the head of government. When Germany was reunified in 1990, the West German Chancellor Helmut Kohl who presided over the process became known as **Chancellor of all the Germans**. (2) Shorthand for

Chancellor of the Exchequer, a position with mediaeval origins. Since the 18th century the Chancellor has been the senior Cabinet Minister in charge of UK economic and tax policy, and delivers the annual BUDGET.

> Can there be a more lamentable figure than a Chancellor of the Exchequer, seated on an empty chest, by the pool of bottomless deficiency, fishing for a budget?
>
> Sir ROBERT PEEL on the WHIGS, 1841.

> The Chancellor of the Exchequer is a man whose duties make him more or less of a taxing machine. He is trusted with a certain amount of misery which it is his duty to distribute as fairly as he can.
>
> ROBERT LOWE (later Viscount Sherbrooke), House of Commons, 11 April 1870.

Chappaquiddick The incident on 28 July 1969 which enveloped Sen. Edward KENNEDY in a lasting fog of scandal and implausibility, and almost certainly prevented him becoming President. Late that night Kennedy was driving 28-year-old Mary Jo Kopechne, who had been one of his brother Robert's campaign team, away from a party on Chappaquiddick Island, off Martha's Vineyard in Massachusetts. Kennedy inexplicably drove away from the ferry, and off a narrow bridge into the water; he escaped but Miss Kopechne did not. The car, with her body, was found before Kennedy was; he had returned to the mainland – swimming, by his own account – but did not report the accident until the next morning, 10 hours later. Kennedy later said:

> I regard as indefensible the fact that I did not report the accident to the police immediately.

Kennedy staffers realized the damage his conduct could do to his Presidential prospects and to the dynasty, and set in motion a damage limitation exercise that critics termed a COVER-UP; Kennedy himself appealed for public understanding with a dramatic account of how he had dived to save Mary Jo. He was given a two-month suspended sentence for failing to report the accident; a closed inquest did not follow up critical questions and exonerated him from her death. Efforts to reopen the case through grand jury hearings proved abortive. But for Chappaquiddick, according to Sen. Edmund Muskie, Kennedy could have had the 1972 nomination "for the asking". As it was, Kennedy was confronted with placards reading: "Swim, don't run in '72." The scandal was still a powerful issue when he made his unsuccessful run in 1980. And when it was revealed on his marriage to Victoria Reggie in 1992, that he proposed while snorkelling, the British humorist Ned Sherrin said:

> I don't see how she could hear underwater. Perhaps the car windows were still up.

> *Q:* Would you let Nixon sell you a used car?
>
> *A:* Yes, but I sure wouldn't let Teddy drive it.
>
> ANON. Washington, 1969.

> Senator Kennedy killed that girl the same as if he put a gun to her head and pulled the trigger.
>
> Det.-Lt. GEORGE KILLEN, Massachusetts State Police.

chargé d'affaires (Fr. responsible for business). In diplomatic language, the senior official at an EMBASSY in the absence of the AMBASSADOR, or when no ambassador has been appointed because of poor relations between the countries in question.

charisma The exceptional quality in a political leader that attracts others and enables him or her to influence them, for good or ill. It was originally a religious term, the Greek word for the "gift of grace" attributed to the early Christian saints. A politician's lack of charisma can give rise to comment; at one UK Conservative conference, a speaker said of David Bookbinder, Labour leader of Derbyshire County Council: "He thinks Charisma is the day after 24 December." George BUSH recognized his own deficiency, telling the 1988 Republican convention in New Orleans: "I'll try to hold my charisma in check." He also said during that campaign:

> I think I'm a charismatic son of a gun, but I'm not going to depend entirely on that to win.

Charlemagne Prize The most prestigious international prize recognizing an individual's contribution to European unity; it commemorates Charlemagne (Charles the Great), the Frankish king who in the 8th century united Western Europe under his rule to end the Dark Ages and create the Holy Roman Empire. The prize is conferred on Ascension Day each May in the German city of Aachen, which was Charlemagne's imperial capital. Winners since 1945 include CHURCHILL, Sir Edward Heath (*see* GROCER) and Roy (later Lord) Jenkins (*see* WOY).

Charlottetown Accord The agreement concluded on 28 August 1992 by the leaders of Canada's provinces in an effort to break the deadlock over the country's constitution. It would have given new powers to Quebec reflecting its **distinct society,** including more seats in the House of Commons than warranted by its population, and more say in the Senate for the western provinces. It was negotiated for Brian Mulroney's Conservative government by Constitutional Affairs Minister Joe Clark (*see* JOE WHO?). It was put to a REFERENDUM on 26 October 1992 – and rejected.

charter. Charter Movement (1) One of the groups in the US DEMOCRATIC PARTY which was influential in transforming its national organization *c.* 1970 and ensuring that its CONVENTION was no longer in the pocket of MACHINE politicians. In the convention that ensued in 1972, Blacks and women were properly represented for the first time – but so were radicals from the ANTI-WAR and PROTEST MOVEMENT who pushed through a platform well to the left of Presidential nominee George McGovern and helped guarantee his defeat by Richard Nixon. (2) A ginger group in Britain's CONSERVATIVE PARTY which throughout the 1980s agitated for full publication of the party's accounts, a party structure that took notice of the views of constituency associations, and the election of the party chairman – traditionally appointed by the Tory leader – by constituency activists.

Charter 77 A group of DISSIDENTS formed in Prague in 1977 (designated "Year of Rights for Political prisoners") to monitor abuses of HUMAN RIGHTS by the Czech Communist authorities. Their Charter demanded that the government abide by UN covenants and the HELSINKI ACCORDS. Hundreds of people of all classes signed it, many subsequently suffering harassment, imprisonment or exile; among those imprisoned was the writer Václav Havel, who was to be elected President of Czechoslovakia after the collapse of Communism in 1989. Charter 77 was wound up in November 1991.

Charter 88 A UK "dissident" group set up in 1988 with a title cheekily linking it to its Czech forebear, and advocating basic constitutional reforms including a written Constitution, PROPORTIONAL REPRESENTATION and a BILL OF RIGHTS guaranteeing individual freedoms. When the group was founded, Neil KINNOCK dismissed its members as "wankers, whiners and whingers"; four years later his wife Glenys joined it.

Chartists The mass movement comprising both industrial workers and intellectuals which demanded radical political reforms in early Victorian England; its campaign was most active from 1838 to 1849. It was based in the new but largely unrepresented industrial areas of Birmingham, Clydeside, South Wales, Tyneside and West Yorkshire, a fact that diminished its impact on Parliament. Its objectives were set out in a **People's Charter**, a great PETITION presented at Westminster on 14 June 1839; they included universal male SUFFRAGE, the secret BALLOT, the abolition of property qualifications for the franchise and payment of Members of Parliament. With the exception of a call for annually-elected Parliaments, almost all the Chartist programme had been adopted by 1910. The Chartists' effective end came in 1848 when, with Europe aflame with revolution, they staged a mass demonstration at Kennington Common on 10 April; a baker's shop was looted and Wellington mobilized troops to prevent them marching on Westminster. In driving rain they quietly dispersed and the movement died away.

Chartwell The private country home near Westerham, Kent, of Sir Winston CHURCHILL, now open to the nation. The Churchills moved to Chartwell in 1922, Winston's daughter Sarah describing it as "wildly overgrown and untidy, containing all the mystery of houses that had not been lived in for many years". It became in the words of one visitor "an astonishing combination of private home, Grand Hotel and a Government department". With the cost of its upkeep creating considerable financial pressure, Chartwell was the nerve-centre of Churchill's campaign against APPEASEMENT and for preparedness for war; in the grounds he perfected his hobby of bricklaying by constructing elegant walls.

Chatham House rules The regime under which politicians, diplomats, academics, strategic experts and journalists meet to pool ideas at Chatham House, the home in St. James's Square, London, of the Royal Institute of International Affairs. The information is exchanged to ensure that all concerned are better informed, and is thus not supposed to be attributed to a particular source.

chattering classes A UK, and specifically London, term for the intermeshing community of left-of-centre and middle-class intellectuals, especially writers, dramatists and political pundits, who believe their views should carry enormous weight and have considerable access to the BBC and much of the media. Originally the term was coined in the first years of Margaret Thatcher's ascendancy to disparage the liberal INTELLIGENTSIA who raged impotently about Thatcherism around the dinner tables of North London. It was popularized by Alan Watkins, the *Observer*'s political correspondent, who widened its meaning to include people of all complexions united only by their chattering.

> The Beatles, James Bond – that's the sort of thing we export to France best, while they send us their ideas. We do not even recognize our ideas merchants over here; we prefer to turn the spotlight on the glitterati, the chattering classes, the *cognoscenti*. . . .
>
> *The Independent*, 20 March 1991.

chauvinist A person excessively devoted to his or her country or race, and showing unreasoning hostility and disdain for others. The word stemmed from the soldier Nicholas Chauvin, a Frenchman whose devotion to Napoleon was so excessive that he became a laughing-stock; from 1831 his name was linked to a JINGOIST character in French vaudeville. The term **white chauvinist** was recorded *c.* 1930 and **male chauvinist** *c.* 1950; the derivative **male chauvinist pig** surfaced around 1970.

Ché The name by which Ernesto Guevara (1928–67) was known to the generation of leftists and students throughout the world who hung his portrait, with his beret bearing a single star, in their living-rooms. A well-to-do Argentine physician and writer who became a Marxist GUERRILLA leader, he joined Fidel Castro and played a leading role in the Cuban revolution before leaving Cuba secretly in 1965. The next year he appeared in Bolivia, which he considered ripe for revolution, and joined an embryo guerrilla movement; he was betrayed, wounded, captured and finally shot on 9 October 1967 by US-trained counter-insurgency forces. His book *Guerrilla Warfare* became required reading for all aspiring revolutionaries.

check against delivery The phrase printed on the advance text of almost every political speech in Britain, urging journalists not to file it to their newspapers until they have checked that the words have actually been uttered.

Checkers The dog around whom Richard Nixon (*see* TRICKY DICK) constructed the tear-jerking broadcast that kept him on the Republican ticket in 1952 after disclosures that millionaire backers had given him an $18,000 SLUSH FUND. Newspaper editorials urged the Presidential nominee Dwight D. Eisenhower to drop Nixon as his RUNNING-MATE, and IKE himself was hedging. Then, on 23 September, Nixon went on live television and claimed that the fund was to meet "necessary expenses" and "expose Communism". He denied that his wife Pat had a mink, applauding her for having a REPUBLICAN CLOTH COAT, listed his highly-mundane assets and added that he had received another gift:

> A little cocker spaniel dog in a crate that [was] sent all the way from Texas. Black and white spotted. And our little girl – Trisha, the 6-year-old one – named it Checkers. And you know, the kids love the dog, and I just want to say this right now, that regardless of what they say about it, we're gonna keep it!

Supportive telegrams poured into Republican headquarters and the nation's radio and TV stations, and the next day Eisenhower embraced Nixon and declared him "completely vindicated as a man of honor". WATERGATE still lay 20 years ahead.

Checkpoint Charlie The nickname given to the main crossing-point for foreigners between East and West Berlin before the demolition of the BERLIN WALL. Standing at the junction of the Friedrichstrasse and Zimmerstrasse, it was a barometer of the level of East-West tension; when this was strained, East German border guards would cause long delays. Checkpoint Charlie has been immortalized in many spy novels and films as one of the places where intelligence agents were supposed to be exchanged. In 1990, at the end of the COLD WAR, Checkpoint Charlie was removed intact to be preserved in a museum. The term has been extended to mean any crossing point between divided communities, for example between the Christian East and Muslim West of Beirut in the late 1970s and 1980s.

checks and balances The principle that dominated the creation of America's system of government by the FOUNDING FATHERS; the notion, particularly associated with John ADAMS, that each arm of government created must to a large extent cancel out the ability of the others to act against the best interests of the people. Americans anxious to advance radical changes or just see things happen have fumed at the way the WHITE HOUSE, HOUSE and SENATE can work against each other, and the restraints arising from the separation of EXECUTIVE, JUDICIARY and LEGISLATURE; the historian Richard Hofstadter termed them "a harmonious system of mutual frustration", but they have survived two centuries.

> A majority held in restraint by constitutional checks and balances and always changing easily with deliberate changes of popular opinions and sentiments is the only sovereign of a free people.
>
> ABRAHAM LINCOLN's first INAUGURAL ADDRESS, 4 March 1861.

> People . . . prefer divided government. They just don't want one party of scoundrels in there. People believe in checks and balances. The POLLSTER LOUIS HARRIS.

Cheka The original political police agency of the SOVIET UNION, established by Lenin in December 1917. At first known as *Vecheka*, it was intended to investigate sabotage and counter-revolutionary activity – but instead indulged in the arrest, imprisonment and execution of anyone considered an enemy of the state. It was disbanded in 1922 to be replaced by the GPU, which the following year became the notorious OGPU.

Chequers The official country seat of British Prime Ministers, in Buckinghamshire near Princes Risborough. It was presented to the nation for this purpose by Sir Arthur and Lady Lee (Lord and Lady Lee of Fareham) in 1917, and first officially used by Lloyd George in 1921. Every Prime Minister plants a tree of their choice in the grounds, and on their retirement their stained-glass coat of arms is placed in a window of the house's Long Gallery.

> A wonderful place in which to hold a family party, especially as the staff enter into the spirit of the occasion.
> JAMES CALLAGHAN.

Chernobyl The nuclear disaster in the Ukraine in 1986 – the world's worst until then – which contaminated much of Europe and revived the public concern over the safety of nuclear power that had first peaked after THREE MILE ISLAND. On 26 April the number 4 reactor in the Chernobyl nuclear power station blew up, killing some 250 people almost immediately and leaving many civilians living nearby and heroes of the clear-up to suffer slow and painful deaths; the fire and escape of radioactive materials were finally ended by entombing the reactor in concrete. The Soviet authorities were at first silent about the disaster, which is believed to have contaminated 2 million people in Belarus and the Ukraine; when a sharp increase in radiation was first detected in Sweden a leak nearer at hand was suspected. 135,000 people were evacuated from a 35 km. (22 mile) zone around the installation – the area to which the POLITBURO said radiation was confined; farm produce across much of Eastern Europe was destroyed, and radioactive rain over Wales and north-west England left some flocks of sheep unfit for market six years later. The accident was attributed to an unauthorized experiment that went wrong, poor design of the reactor building and the slow response of the station's staff to early danger signs. Though Western countries issued reassuring statements about the safety of their own installations, immense damage was done to nuclear-energy programmes throughout the world, many being cancelled or cut back as a result of public disquiet.

Chevaline The secret project for upgrading and improving the penetration of Britain's POLARIS nuclear missiles so that they could knock out Soviet ABM defences. The proposal was initiated by the Heath government in 1971, but the crucial decision was taken later by a group of Labour Ministers without the knowledge of the full Cabinet. Chevaline eventually cost the taxpayer £2.25 billion – by which time the Russians had agreed not to extend their ABM system.

Chevening The magnificent 17th-century house near Westerham in Kent which is the official country residence of Britain's FOREIGN SECRETARY, and also plays host to the annual strategy meeting of the CHANCELLOR and TREASURY Ministers and officials before he goes into his pre-Budget PURDAH. For 250 years Chevening, designed by Inigo Jones, was the home of the Earls of Stanhope. In the early 1970s the last of the line left it to the nation for use by a senior member of the Cabinet; the original intention was for the LORD CHANCELLOR to have it. In 1988 Sir Geoffrey HOWE was reluctant to give it up when Margaret Thatcher wanted to move him from the Foreign Office; as compensation, Chancellor Nigel Lawson was asked to give up DORNEYWOOD for the duration of Sir Geoffrey's period as DEPUTY PRIME MINISTER.

Chicago. Chicago convention The Democratic national CONVENTION in Chicago from 25 to 29 August 1968, at the height of the VIETNAM WAR, which was accompanied by ANTI-WAR protests brutally suppressed by police sent in by Mayor Richard DALEY, who had vowed that "no one is going to take over the streets". One clash between police and chanting and brick-throwing protesters ended with what was officially termed a "police riot" which put 101 demonstrators, a number of reporters and 49 police in hospital. Many of the demonstrators were young idealists who had hoped that, by a miracle, the anti-war Sen. Eugene McCarthy might yet be nominated over Vice-President Hubert Humphrey. The WALKER REPORT blamed the language of more militant protesters – the words "Fuck the PIGS" were regularly chanted – for provoking the police. One witness told the Walker committee:

> It seemed to me that only a saint could have swallowed the rude remarks to the officers. However, they went to extremes in clubbing the YIPPIES. I saw them move into the park, swatting away with clubs at girls and boys in the grass.

The images seen by over 50 million television viewers of the disruption and violence, and the peaceful divisions on the war in the convention, had a serious impact on Humphrey's Presidential campaign, and on the image of the Democrats – and of Mayor Daley – for years after.

Chicago Seven The group of anti-war leaders charged with violating the anti-riot provisions of the 1968 Civil Rights Act during the Chicago Convention. The seven – Abbie Hoffman, Jerry Rubin, Tom Hayden, Rennie Davis, David Dellinger, Lee Weiner and John Froines – were convicted in February 1969 of conspiracy to cross State lines and institute a riot. The BLACK PANTHER leader Bobby Seale, also charged in the case, was bound and gagged with chains after calling the judge a pig; eventually all charges were dropped and convictions reversed on appeal. The label Chicago Seven, used by their supporters and the press, set a trend for the naming of the victims of alleged legal persecution on both sides of the Atlantic (*see also* BIRMINGHAM SIX). By the mid-1970s graffiti were appearing in London reading: "Free the Heinz 57".

We were invented. We were chosen by the Government to serve as scapegoats for all that they wanted to prevent happening in the 1970s. TOM HAYDEN

Chicago School The group of economists led by Milton Friedman (1912–), Professor of Economics at the University of Chicago 1948–82, which devised and, where possible, attempted to implement the theory of MONETARISM.

chicken. a chicken in every pot The slogan attributed to King Henry IV of France (1553–1610), who is reputed to have said:

I want there to be no peasant in my kingdom so poor that he is unable to have a chicken in his pot every Sunday.

Herbert HOOVER took it a stage further, promising "A chicken, two chickens in every pot with Hoover". John F. KENNEDY commented of the place where he made the promise:

No Presidential candidate has dared to come back to this community since.

chicken littles A Washington term for politicians who are reluctant to take or countenance any bold but risky step. It comes from the fairy tale in which Chicken Little was convinced that the sky was falling down.

We just had too many Chicken Littles in Congress in the last week who seemed to become hysterical over covert aid [to the Nicaraguan CONTRAS].
Unnamed Reagan administration official, *New York Times*, 15 April 1984.

rubber chicken (1) An object much loved by clowns and practical jokers in America, and likely to be produced at an unexpected moment. One day in 1977 the STATE DEPARTMENT spokesman Hodding Carter became so enraged during his morning briefing at provocative questions from the ultra-conservative priest and columnist Lester Kinsolving that, after the question: "Does the UN have a branch office in northern Philadelphia?" he produced a rubber chicken from under his lectern and threw it at him. (2) Rubber chicken is said by US politicians, and others, to be the staple menu of FUND-RAISERS and other party dinners. Those who frequently speak at them are said to be on the **rubber chicken circuit**.

sick chicken case The case in which the US SUPREME COURT finally imposed Constitutional limits on Franklin D. Roosevelt's NEW DEAL. It concerned the powers of the National Recovery Administration (NRA), which critics had increasingly branded as "Hitlerian" and a farcical BUREAUCRACY. In the case of *Schechter Poultry Corporation v. United States*, the NRA was accused of exceeding its powers over inter-state commerce by interfering in the trade in kosher fowls in the New York area. As Schechter had offended the NRA by allegedly selling an "unfit chicken" to a butcher, the proceeding became known as the "sick chicken case", and on BLACK MONDAY, 27 May 1935, the Court declared the NRA – which had already been reorganized – unconstitutional.

some chicken, some neck The defiant statement on Britain's prospects in World War II made by CHURCHILL to the Canadian Parliament on 30 December 1941. He told them:

When I warned them [the French government] that Britain would fight on alone whatever they did, their Generals [Gen. Weygand] told their Prime Minister and his divided Cabinet: "In three weeks England will have her neck wrung like a chicken". Some chicken! Some neck!

chief. Chief Justice The presiding member of America's SUPREME COURT, appointed by the President with the ADVICE AND CONSENT of the Senate on the same basis as the other eight, though paid rather more. The main difference from the other justices is one of prestige, as a strong Supreme Court will be remembered by the name of the Chief Justice, as in the WARREN COURT.

chief of staff (1) In the WHITE HOUSE, the principal aide of the President, whose task is to run the STAFF and who thus enjoys considerable control over ACCESS to the President, and substantial political influence. This can pit the Chief of Staff against the SECRETARY OF STATE and other senior Cabinet members and officials who feel their own influence is being challenged. (2) The head of one of the armed services, who sits with his counterparts on (in Washington) the JOINT CHIEFS of Staff or (in London) the Defence Staff.

You may take the most gallant sailor, most intrepid airman, or the most audacious soldier, put them at a table together – what do you get? The sum of all their fears!
CHURCHILL.

Chief Secretary Not a bureaucrat, but the second Cabinet Minister at the British TREASURY after the CHANCELLOR OF THE EXCHEQUER. The Chief Secretary's main responsbility is the allocation and control of public spending, through the annual PESC round resulting in the Autumn STATEMENT.

chief whip *See* WHIP.

chienlit (Fr. crap-in-the-bed) The barrack-room word with which President DE GAULLE stunned the French public when he used it in a televised appeal for the restoration of order during the ÉVÈNEMENTS of 1968. Trawling back into the vocabulary of the troops from his early days as a young officer, the normally staid de Gaulle declared:

Réforme: Oui! Chienlit: Non!

Chiltern Hundreds The technicality under which a member of the UK HOUSE OF COM-

MONS resigns his or her seat. Theoretically an MP cannot resign, but can be disqualified by accepting an OFFICE OF PROFIT UNDER THE CROWN. The two sinecures traditionally used are that of steward or bailiff of the three Chiltern Hundreds of Stoke, Desborough and Burnham, and that of Steward of the MANOR OF NORTHSTEAD. Though billed as "offices of profit", holding them does not generate any income, but when application is made for one of them, a person's membership of the House automatically lapses.

China. China card The use by America *c.* 1978 of closer links with China as a means of putting pressure on the Soviet Union to pursue a more moderate foreign policy and make concessions in ARMS CONTROL talks. The gambit at first seemed productive, but was capped by the Soviet invasion of Afghanistan and the subsequent failure of the Senate to ratify the SALT II agreement. *See also* ORANGE CARD; RACE CARD.

China lobby The powerful pressure group that mobilized in Washington after the defeat by Mao Tse-Tung's Communists of Chiang Kai-Shek's NATIONALIST CHINESE in 1949 to ensure total US backing for his claim to be China's lawful ruler, commit America to defend Taiwan (then Formosa) against any Communist attack, and work for the overthrow of the RED CHINESE regime in Peking. Its driving force was Henry Luce, the publisher of *Time*, who had been born in China and idolized the upright but incompetent GENERALISSIMO Chiang, but questions were raised as to the involvement of Chiang's government in LOBBYing. The China lobby, and its slogan of **Who lost China?** with its inference of betrayal, was a great embarrassment to the Truman administration, which was about to take the full force of McCARTHYISM. Chiang's longevity, and the fervour of his supporters, enabled the China lobby to keep an armlock on US policy in the region for over two decades. Ironically it was Richard Nixon, who as a Senator had shouted: "Who lost China?" loudest, who opened links with Peking (*see* Ping-Pong DIPLOMACY).

Chingford skinhead One of the politer nicknames for **Norman** (later Lord) **Tebbit** (1931–), the former airline pilots' union official who sloughed off a reputation as a right-wing BARRACKER in the Commons to become a respected Trade and Industry Secretary and Employment Secretary under Margaret Thatcher. At the height of his powers and influence, though still with a reputation for going for the jugular, he was seriously injured in the 1984 BRIGHTON BOMBING which left his wife paralysed. He over-came great pain to fight his way back and become party chairman for the 1987 election. Despite the eventual LANDSLIDE victory the experience was not a happy one; his relations with Mrs. Thatcher deteriorated and he retired from the government, re-emerging from the Lords in 1992 to campaign against the MAASTRICHT TREATY. Tebbit was the epitome of the social group to whom Mrs. Thatcher appealed strongest – hard-working, patriotic, ruthless in their judgments on others – and as he took on the trade unions he became a hero to the upwardly mobile; indeed he used the phrase as the title of his biography. Labour politicians hated him, particularly when, as a backbencher, he shouted to the ailing left-wing MP Tom Litterick: "Why don't you go and have another heart attack?"; Michael Foot branded him a SEMI-HOUSETRAINED POLECAT. Labour MPs considered his appointment as Employment Secretary a provocation to the unions, Eric (later Lord) Varley saying:

> Putting Norman Tebbit in charge of industrial relations is like putting Dracula in charge of the blood transfusion service.

Yet trade unionists knew where they stood with him, and many came to respect him. At one of his first meetings with shipyard shop stewards after joining the government he floored them by saying: "The first thing you should know is that there's nothing I'd like better than to pin the lot of you to the wall"; productive talks followed.

Tebbit could seldom resist using a tongue which, in the words of one Labour MP, would have killed him with acid poisoning had he bitten it; he told Dennis Skinner (*see* BEAST OF BOLSOVER): "Far better to keep your mouth shut and let everyone think you're stupid than open it and leave no doubt," and Neil KINNOCK: "I'm older than you, sonny, and you can take on men when you grow up." Pressed on the subject, the subsequent Tory chairman Chris Patten observed:

> We all try to be as nice as Mr. Tebbit.

Yet he regarded himself as a man of honour, humanity and conscience, and sued the *Guardian* columnist Hugo Young for suggesting he had declared that no-one with a conscience could vote Conservative.

> *Woman Heckler*: Gizza job!
> *Tebbit*: Madam, you're dirty, you're filthy, you're unkempt, you're foulmouthed and disgusting – why should anyone in their right mind give you a job?

Chips The nickname of **Henry Channon** (1897–1958), the wealthy Conservative backbencher whose diaries are one of the delights of 20th-century British political literature. He became MP for Southend in 1935, and after his death in 1958 the seat passed to his son Paul, who went on to be the most civilized member of the Thatcher Cabinet. The height of Chips' career was a spell as PPS to R.A. (RAB) Butler, but his delight was the backstairs gossip of the Commons – which he retailed with a Pepysian eye and a snobbish flourish – and the confidences of the great over dinner at 5 Belgrave Square, where he lived in great style.

CHOGM COMMONWEALTH Heads of Government Meeting. The gathering of Prime Ministers or Presidents from all the countries of the Commonwealth, held every two years in a member capital with the leader of the host government in the chair and the Queen, as Head of the Commonwealth, presiding. A regional CHOGM, without the Queen present, is also held by Pacific members of the Commonwealth. When CHOGM assembled in Harare, Zimbabwe, in 1991, officials asserted that the initials stood for:

> Cheap holidays on Government money.

Chowder and Marching Society A fraternity of 15 Republican Congressmen which has flourished since 1949, and which is widely seen as grooming those invited to join it for leadership. It was the base for the revolt of YOUNG TURKS that in 1965 ousted Rep. Charles Halleck as MINORITY LEADER and installed Gerald FORD. Founder-members included Ford and the young Richard Nixon.

Christ. Christ and Carrots The nickname, coined by CHURCHILL, for Sir Stafford Cripps (1889–1952), the lawyer who became a fanatical and ascetic Christian Socialist, wartime ambassador to Moscow and a successful Chancellor in the ATTLEE government. Briefly Solicitor-General under RAMSAY MACDonald, he campaigned during the 1930s for a POPULAR FRONT – getting himself expelled from the Labour Party – and against APPEASEMENT. Churchill appointed him to Moscow, where Stalin never warmed to "this man who eats nuts and lectures me on Communism", and in 1942 made him LEADER OF THE HOUSE, and later Minister for Aircraft Production. Attlee made him President of the Board of Trade, and Chancellor in 1948 when Hugh Dalton resigned over the BUDGET LEAK. His self-denying manner echoed the mood of post-war austerity, and he managed to secure the unions' agreement to WAGE RESTRAINT, but he had to resign through ill-health a year after DEVALUING in September 1949. Denis Healey rated Cripps, with Ernest BEVIN, the most powerful member of the Labour Cabinet, but wrote that in the 1930s he had been "a political ninny of the most superior quality". Churchill said of Cripps: "He has all the virtues I dislike and none of the vices I admire", and also declared: "There, but for the grace of God, goes God." CHIPS Channon noted after Cripps dined with him in June 1950, eating "three scraped carrots, some salad and an orange":

> I felt as if I had breathed the dark, fetid atmosphere of beyond the tomb.

Christian Democrats The centre-right and predominantly Roman Catholic parties that are a permanent feature of politics in most Continental European countries except France. They have had the greatest success in Italy, where they have had a share in government since World War II despite an increasing reputation for jobbery, inertia and corruption, and in Germany, where they are allied with the more conservative Bavarian CSU (Christian Social Union). The European People's Party, the second largest grouping in the EUROPEAN PARLIAMENT, is an alliance of Christian Democrats and like-minded parties including Britain's CONSERVATIVES.

Christian Socialism *See* SOCIALISM.

Christmas tree In the US Congress, a tax Bill designed to gain a winning coalition of support because it contains something for everybody. It is constructed in such a way that if one provision is removed, the rest of the package becomes unworkable.

Christophe The Beverly Hills hairdresser whose $200 haircut for President Clinton in May 1993, which closed the runway of Los Angeles Airport, caused the "COMEBACK KID" considerable embarrassment.

Church House The administrative headquarters of the Church of England on the far side of Westminster Abbey from the Houses of Parliament. During World War II the HOUSE OF LORDS sat in its Convocation Room in 1940–41 and 1944, either when their own House was threatened by bombing or so that the Commons, whose own house had been destroyed, could sit in the Lords' chamber.

Churchill, Sir Winston (Leonard Spencer) (1874–1965), the larger-than-life if sometimes wrongheaded figure and one of the greatest orchestrators of the English language, who dominated half a century of British politics and came out of the wilderness to lead the nation to victory in WORLD WAR II, being Prime Minister (Conservative) 1940–45 and 1951–55. Born at Blenheim Palace, the son of Lord Randolph Churchill (*see* FOURTH PARTY; ULSTER WILL FIGHT) and the glamorous American Jennie Jerome, he fought in the Sudan, and was a war correspondent in

South Africa, escaping from a Boer prison; the "Wanted" poster read:

> Englishman, 25 years old, about five feet eight inches tall, indifferent build, walks with a forward stoop, pale appearance, reddish brown hair, small and hardly noticeable moustache, talks through his nose – cannot pronounce his "s"s properly.

He entered the Commons in 1900 as Tory MP for Oldham, crossing the FLOOR to the Liberals in 1904. He served as Colonial Under-Secretary under Campbell-Bannerman, and as President of the Board of Trade and Home Secretary to ASQUITH (*see* SIDNEY STREET SIEGE; TONYPANDY) before becoming First Lord of the Admiralty. A year into World War I, he was forced out by the Conservatives because of his support for the disastrous Gallipoli campaign; H. A. L. Fisher wrote to Bonar Law that Churchill was "a bigger danger than the Germans by a long way in what is now happening in the Dardanelles". Churchill's wife "Clemmie" had begged Asquith to keep him, writing:

> Winston may in your eyes and in those with whom he has to work have faults, but he has the supreme quality which I venture to say very few of your present or future Cabinet possess – the power, the imagination, the deadliness to fight Germany.

He resumed soldiering on the Western Front until Lloyd George recalled him as Minister of Munitions in 1917; from 1919 he was Secretary for War, being involved in the British intervention against the BOLSHEVIKS in Russia and the Irish crisis of 1919–21, then Colonial Secretary. In 1922 Churchill, who was edging away from the Liberals, lost his seat at Dundee, where he had moved in 1908; he wrote: "In a twinkling of an eye, I found myself without office, without a seat, without a party and without an appendix." Two more defeats ensued before he was elected in November 1924 as "Constitutionalist" MP for Epping, becoming Chancellor in BALDWIN's second Government and putting Britain back on the GOLD STANDARD, Sir Oswald MOSLEY declaring:

> Faced with the alternative of saying goodbye to the gold standard, and therefore to his own employment, and goodbye to other people's employment, he characteristically selected the latter course.

Churchill, who rejoined the Conservatives in 1925, published the BRITISH GAZETTE during the 1926 GENERAL STRIKE; Asquith termed him "a Chimborazo or Everest among the sandhills of the Baldwin Cabinet". He resigned from the FRONT BENCH in 1931 over Tory support for the granting of DOMINION status to India, and from 1932 spoke out from the BACK BENCHES with increasing concern against the threat from NAZI Germany – backing this up with numerous newspaper articles written to finance an expensive family lifestyle; F. E. Smith had called him "a man of simple tastes, always prepared to put up with the best of everything". Baldwin was tempted to recall him to the Cabinet, but wrote:

> Anything he undertakes he puts his heart and soul into. If there is going to be war, we must keep him fresh to be our war Prime Minister.

Churchill was involved in the ABDICATION CRISIS of 1936, endeavouring to keep King Edward VIII on the throne. By now he was a fervent campaigner against APPEASEMENT, telling critics: "I decline to be impartial as between the fire brigade and the fire," and in September 1938 narrowly escaped censure by his constituency association for attacking the MUNICH AGREEMENT, but as Hitler renewed his demands pressure grew for his return to the Government. When war was declared on 3 September 1939, CHAMBERLAIN recalled him as First Lord of the Admiralty (*see* WINSTON IS BACK), and his greatest days began. When Hitler's occupation of Norway brought criticism of Chamberlain to a head the following May, Churchill loyally backed him (*see* AIR RAID SHELTER), but when Chamberlain fell days later, was the obvious choice to succeed him, Labour refusing to serve under anyone else. Churchill took over a nation on the brink of defeat (*see* BLOOD, SWEAT AND TEARS), but set a bulldog example, steadied the ship through Dunkirk and the Battle of Britain and then as FORMER NAVAL PERSON established a close relationship with President Roosevelt prior to PEARL HARBOR in the hope of bringing America into the war; FDR told him: "It is fun to be in the same decade with you."

Below Whitehall in the CABINET WAR ROOMS Churchill worked long hours as he presided over the war in a way that led General Wavell to complain: "Winston is always expecting rabbits to come out of empty hats," and urged on an unprecedented mobilization of the people. He frequently conducted business from his bath, Lord Boothby recalling:

> At intervals he turned a somersault, exactly like a porpoise, and when his head reappeared at the other end of the bath, he continued precisely where he left off.

When FDR entered his bathroom, Churchill shouted: "Come in, Mr. President. England has nothing to hide from her allies." He was also partial to brandy, saying: "I have taken more out of alcohol than alcohol has taken out of me." And above ground he kept up civilian morale with his hat, cigar and V-sign; he said later: I WAS NOT THE LION. BUT I SUPPLIED THE ROAR.

He frequently made long and dangerous flights to meet Roosevelt and other Allied leaders, telling the US Congress on one visit to Washington: "If my father had been American and my mother British, instead of the other way round, I might have got here on my own." He also got on well with STALIN; Robert Lewis Taylor wrote:

> The Russians were enormously impressed by Churchill at the table. His appetite for caviar and vodka convinced them they were fighting on the right side.

Yet he managed to keep a grip on the House of Commons except for a brief period in 1943, being much helped by the Labour leader Clement ATTLEE, a loyal and capable deputy who once told him: "I must remind you that a monologue is not a decision," and who complained: "The trouble with Winston is that he nails his trousers to the mast, and can't climb down." A frustrated Aneurin Bevan said of this period:

> He refers to victory as to a disaster, as if it came from God, but to a victory as though it came from himself . . . the PM wins debate after debate, and loses battle after battle. The country is beginning to say that he fights debates like a war, and a war like a debate.

As US and Soviet military might told, Churchill lost influence in strategic terms, but he emerged from the war a towering world figure. On 8 May 1945 the crowds cheered him to the echo as they celebrated victory over Germany, and Labour's LANDSLIDE win in the election two months later, with Japan still undefeated, was an immense shock. He wrote:

> On the night of the tenth of May [1940], at the outset of this mighty battle, I acquired the chief power in the State, which henceforth I wielded in ever-growing measure for five years and three months of world war, at the end of which time, all our enemies having surrendered unconditionally or being about to do so, I was immediately dismissed by the British electorate from all further conduct of their affairs.

Churchill confided: "I feel very lonely without a war," but after a spell painting in Morocco and being lionized in formerly Nazi-occupied Europe, he revived the Tory party – which he had never much cared for – in opposition, ran Labour close in 1950 and became Prime Minister again in 1951 at the age of 77. He also managed, with help from researchers, to complete two formidable literary works: his *History of the Second World War* and *History of the English Speaking Peoples*. "Winnie" in his last administration was less decisive and interested in detail, being consumed by a desire to end the nuclear ARMS RACE before retiring; after Stalin's death in 1953 he believed just one SUMMIT could do it, but was disappointed. Harold Macmillan wrote in 1954:

> He is now quite incapable – mentally as well as physically – of remaining Prime Minister. He thinks about one thing all the time – this Russian visit and his chance of saving the world – until it has become an obsession.

He suffered a severe stroke in office with few colleagues realizing, and the public – which was lied to – unaware, but eventually bowed to the inevitable and resigned as Prime Minister on 6 April 1955, Macmillan saying of his final Cabinet: "Now that he has really decided to go we are all miserable. Anthony [Eden] made rather a flat speech, then we all shuffled out."

The Queen – the sixth sovereign under whom he had served in Parliament – paid tribute by coming to Downing Street to dine. Churchill stayed in the Commons until 1964 as FATHER OF THE HOUSE, but spent most of an honoured retirement reminiscing with friends, notably Lord Beaverbrook, painting on the Côte d'Azur, or resting and building walls at CHARTWELL with "Clemmie". He died at his London home on 24 January 1965; he had said: "I am ready to meet my maker, but whether my maker is ready for the great ordeal of meeting me is another matter," but his last words were: "Oh, I am so bored with it all." Churchill was given the greatest State funeral seen in 20th-century Britain; he is buried at Bladon, near Woodstock.

Above all, Churchill is remembered as an orator, through his wartime speeches in the Commons and the radio broadcasts in which they were repeated – sometimes by the actor Norman Shelley. When the diarist/MP Harold Nicolson congratulated him on being a born orator, Churchill replied: "Not born in the very least – just hard, hard work." Yet J. L. Garvin called him "one of the born organists of the English language", F. E. Smith asserted that "Winston has devoted the best years of his life to preparing his impromptu speeches", and Lionel Curtis wrote: "In private conversation he tries on speeches like a man trying on ties in his bedroom to see how he would look in them." Bevan declared: "He never spares himself in conversation. He gives himself so generously that hardly anybody else is permitted to give anything in his presence;" but he also asserted that "the mediocrity of his thinking is concealed by the majesty of his language". John F. KENNEDY put his achievement most concisely:

> He mobilized the English language, and sent it into battle.

Churchill could also be caustic about his political contemporaries. He said of Joseph Chamberlain: "Mr. Chamberlain loves the working-class man: he loves to see him work;" Austen Chamberlain: "He always plays the game – and he always loses it;" Earl Jellicoe: "the only man on either side who could lose the war in an afternoon"; George Bernard Shaw: "The world has long watched with tolerance and amusement the nimble antics and gyrations of the unique, double-headed chameleon while all the time the creature was anxious to be taken seriously;" MAHATMA Gandhi: "a half-naked fakir", who "should be bound hand and foot and trampled by an enormous elephant ridden by the VICEROY"; the future Queen Elizabeth II: "At the age of two she had an authority and reflectiveness astonishing in an infant"; John Foster Dulles: "a bull who carries his own china with him"; Field-Marshal Montgomery: "in defeat, unbeatable; in victory, unbearable"; and the Conservative MP Arthur Bossom: "neither one thing, nor the other". When the flamboyant homosexual Labour MP Tom Driberg married, Churchill observed of his choice of wife: "Buggers can't be choosers." He also detested modern art, causing a stir in 1949 in a broadcast Royal Academy speech by asking Sir Alfred Munnings:

> If you met Picasso coming down the street, would you join me in kicking his backside?

And when he was presented with a Graham Sutherland portrait by the House of Commons to mark his 80th birthday, he said: "It makes me look as if I were straining a stool"; Lady Churchill quietly destroyed the painting, which Sutherland considered his masterpiece.

At Westminster Churchill is venerated for stories of his REPARTEE, most of them true. He once infuriated Nancy, Lady Astor to the point where she exclaimed: "If I were married to you, I'd put arsenic in your coffee." Churchill replied: "Nancy, if you were my wife, I'd drink it." After he rejoined the Conservatives, an indignant lady told him: "I do not like your new politics, or your moustache." Churchill responded: "Madam, pray do not disturb yourself – you are not likely to come into contact with either." And one night at Westminster he is said to have bumped into the Labour MP Bessie Braddock, who told him: "Winston, you're drunk, bloody drunk!" Churchill unsteadily fixed his gaze on her and said: "Bessie, you're ugly – bloody ugly! But I'll be sober in the morning."

At the end of his Parliamentary career he was in the SMOKING ROOM when a pompous Tory complained to all and sundry that the policeman outside had not held up the traffic for him. "He said he didn't know who I was," he complained. At this Churchill roused himself from apparent slumber and asked him: "All right, then, who *were* you?" Another time he was gently reminded that his fly buttons were undone, and reassured his benefactor: "Dead birds don't fall out of nests." In the late 1950s, one young Tory MP pointed out Churchill apparently dozing in the corner and said: "Of course the old man's a bit past it now." Suddenly a voice boomed out: "They say he's lost his hearing, too."

> By his father he is an Englishman, by his mother an American. Behold the perfect man. MARK TWAIN.

> A slippery gentleman, a fraudulent and dishonest politician and no friend of the workers.
> G. H. STUART, his Independent opponent at Dundee, 1908.

> He would make a drum out of the skin of his mother in order to sound his own praises. MARGOT ASQUITH.

> It's a pity that Winston hasn't a better sense of proportion, and also a larger endowment of loyalty. . . . I am really fond of him, but he will never get to the top in English politics, with all his wonderful gifts. ASQUITH, 1915.

> Winston has written four volumes about himself and called it *World Crisis*. ARTHUR BALFOUR.

> He would go up to the Creator and say that he would like very much to meet his Son, of Whom he had heard a great deal, and, if possible, would like to call on the Holy Ghost. LLOYD GEORGE.

> 50 per cent genius, 50 per cent bloody fool. ATTLEE.

> One layer was certainly 17th century. The 18th century in him is obvious. There was the 19th century and a large slice, of course, of the 20th century; and another, curious layer which may possibly have been the 21st. ATTLEE.

> Eating words has never given me indigestion.
> CHURCHILL on his changes of tack.

> Always in the wrong, always surrounded by crooks, a most unsuccessful father – simply a radio personality who outlived his prime. EVELYN WAUGH.

> Churchill was fundamentally what the English call unstable – by which they mean anybody who has that touch of genius which is inconvenient in normal times.
> MACMILLAN.

> To be alive with him was to have dined at the table of history. CASSANDRA (William Connor).

Churchill arch The arch leading from the Members' LOBBY into the CHAMBER of the House of Commons, which still bears the scars of the bomb that wrecked this part of the Palace of Westminster in 1941. In the debate in January 1945 on rebuilding the House, Churchill called for the damaged arch to be kept "as a monument to the ordeal which Westminster has passed through in the Great War, and as a reminder to those who will come centuries afterwards, that they may look back from time to time upon their forebears who 'kept the bridge in the brave days of old'". To the left of the arch is Churchill's statue, its black toecap shined bronze by generations of Conservative MPs touching it for good luck.

Churchill of Asia The term US Secretary of State Dean Rusk once unwisely used for South Vietnam's President Ngo Dinh Diem, whose administration became so venal, unpopular and harmful to the war effort that on 1

November 1964 he was killed in a COUP which had US backing.

Churchill Room *See* HARCOURT ROOM.

churning An opinion POLLSTERS' term for the movement of likely votes between parties during an election campaign.

CIA Central Intelligence Agency. A department of the US government set up by President Truman under the 1947 National Security Act to conduct intelligence operations abroad; headed by Allen Dulles, it was based on the wartime OSS. Much of the work at its headquarters at McLean, Virginia, consists of analysis of information from countries throughout the world, to watch out for potential sources of tension that might harm US interests; it was through the CIA that Washington had prior warning in 1963 of what became the CUBAN MISSILE CRISIS. Its clandestine overseas ventures are mainly designed to monitor and undermine left-wing groups and regimes, and its brief in the 1950s and 1960s included the overthrow and even the assassination of anti-American leaders. After a series of public relations disasters in the Caribbean, Cuba (*see* Bay of PIGS) and Chile, Congress placed the CIA on a tight rein in the mid-1970s. In 1982 the BOLAND AMENDMENT tightened the control by barring the PENTAGON and the CIA from training or giving supplies to anyone trying to overthrow the SANDINISTA regime in Nicaragua, but the CIA under the Reagan appointee William J. Casey went ahead with COVERT OPERATIONS until the subterfuge was detected, Congress retaliating by cutting off all US aid to the CONTRAS. The CIA's internal counter-intelligence activities are limited, and operate in conjunction with the FBI; since alleged abuses during WATERGATE they have to be sanctioned by the ATTORNEY-GENERAL.

> No American who works for the CIA is a spy. A spy is a foreign agent who commits treason.
>
> JIM KEEHNER, CIA psychologist, *New Times*, 1976.

Cicciolina. la Cicciolina (Ital. the little plump one) Ilona Staller (1955–) Hungarian-born sex-show performer and pornographic film actress, elected to the Italian parliament in 1987 for the small RADICAL Party on the slogan "less nuclear energy, more sexual energy". She handed the banner on to others after marrying the US artist Jeff Koons.

CITES The Convention on International Trade in Endangered Species, the agreement under which most countries have banned the trade in elephant ivory, rhinoceros horn, and in rare animals or products made from them. The Convention was signed at Bern, Switzerland, in November 1976, and the signatories meet every two years to review progress, most recently in Kyoto in 1992.

Citizen The form of address decreed to be used by every Frenchman and woman to each other during the FRENCH REVOLUTION. Extreme anti-clerics still use it toward priests as an insult.

Citizen's Charter The initiative pioneered by John MAJOR as his Government's BIG IDEA, under which every branch of the public service was expected to set standards for its dealings with individual citizens, and compensate them if the targets were not met. Unveiled in 1991 and pursued after the 1992 election, it led to hospitals undertaking to see patients within a certain time of their arriving, officials dealing with the public wearing name tags, the railways compensating passengers for persistent late running of trains, and Government departments promising to reply to letters within a fixed period. Opposition politicians denounced it as a gimmick and no substitute for higher spending on those services, but Major insisted that the public was fed up with second-best treatment and deserved better.

second class citizen A member of an ethnic, economic or other group placed at a disadvantage by discriminatory treatment from the State. The phrase reflects the fundamental assumption that all the citizens of any country must have equal rights. Wendell Willkie, in *An American Program* (1944) wrote: "The constitution does not provide for first and second class citizens," and Dwight D. Eisenhower, desegregating the US armed forces, declared: "There must be no second class citizens in this country."

the humblest citizen of all the land, when clad in the armour of a righteous cause, is stronger than all the hosts of error One of the grandest phrases of William Jennings Bryan (*see* BOY ORATOR; PRAIRIE AVENGER) during his three POPULIST campaigns for the Presidency.

the most important office, that of private citizen The dictum of US Supreme Court Justice Louis Brandeis (1856–1941) that confirmed the fundamental rights of the individual over the State or any other overweening organization.

city on the hill One of the most popular images of a better society conjured up by US Presidential candidates. John F. KENNEDY and Walter Mondale (*see* NORWEGIAN WOOD) both used it; Ronald Reagan first harnessed it in 1976, and relied heavily on it in his 1984 re-election campaign. Mario Cuomo, Democratic Governor of New York, dismissed Reagan's right to talk of a "shining city on a hill", saying that the President was ignoring the "despair in the slums" and that America under his leadership was in reality a "tale of two cities". The phrase has a long pedigree, having first been used in 1630 by John Winthrop, governor of the Massachusetts Bay Colony; in *A Modell of Christian Discourse*, Winthrop wrote:

> For we must consider that we shall be as a City upon a hill. The eyes of all people are upon us. Soe that if we shall deal falsely with our God in this work we have undertaken, and so cause him to withdraw his present help from us, we shall be made a story and a byword throughout the world.

Needless to say, few if any politicians have dwelt on the retributive part of Winthrop's message.

Civic Forum The Czech DISSIDENT movement that toppled the Communist regime in Czechoslovakia late in 1989; its Slovak counterpart was PUBLIC AGAINST VIOLENCE. A coalition of 12 groups united to form Civic Forum on 19 November, two days after street protests began; their spokesman was the dissident playwright Václav Havel, who had been released from prison that May. They forced the resignation of prime minister Miloš Jakeš on 24 November, while Alexander Dubček, exiled hero of the PRAGUE SPRING, was addressing a rally of 250,000 people in WENCESLAS SQUARE. The protests continued and on 9 December the hard-line president Gustav Husák finally resigned, with Havel nominated to succeed him and Dubček as chairman of the Federal Assembly; when elections were held the following May, Civic Forum and its allies won a convincing majority. Havel was subsequently elected President by popular vote.

civil. civil defence The protection of civilians from the consequences of warfare, and particularly from nuclear war and the radiation resulting from it. Civil defence was a political issue throughout the COLD WAR, with Governments offering schemes of varying degrees of adequacy to enable at least some of the population to survive a nuclear holocaust, and anti-nuclear campaigners accusing them of fooling the public into imagining that there was any hope of survival. Communist China's precautions have been the most thorough, with entire underground cities excavated in case of a Soviet nuclear attack; the UK government for a long time considered a shallow trench covered by earth and a spare door quite adequate.

civil disobedience Deliberate flouting of the law in order to make a political point or secure a change in the law being broken. The term was first used by David Thoreau in 1849, and the practice was developed most enthusiastically by MAHATMA Gandhi, first in South Africa and later in India. Since World War II it has been used by CIVIL RIGHTS protesters in America's Deep South, by militant nuclear disarmers in Britain (*see* COMMITTEE OF 100), in South Africa against APARTHEID, and in countless other circumstances by groups who believe they are fighting an injustice.

> It has been the teaching of the Church throughout the ages that when government degenerates into tyranny, laws cease to be binding on its subjects.
>
> Bishop TREVOR HUDDLESTON, South Africa, 1952.

> I will not pretend to obey a Government that is organizing a mass massacre of mankind.
>
> BERTRAND RUSSELL (1872–1970), speaking in Birmingham, 15 April 1961.

civil liberties An alternative term for HUMAN RIGHTS, especially in relation to an individual's right to fair treatment by the police.

Civil List The sum paid annually by the UK Treasury to the Sovereign to finance the performance of her official duties, and those undertaken by certain members of the ROYAL FAMILY. It has been the subject of sporadic political controversy, most recently in 1992 when it was disclosed that a past formula on inflation-proofing had led to its increasing at a far greater rate than the cost of living. Such discontent is nothing new; in 1884 Henry Labouchère (*see* LABBY) wrote:

> Nothing has more conduced to shake that decent respect for the living symbol of the State, which goes by the name of Royalty, than the ever-recurring rattle of the money-box.

Civil Rights The term given in US politics for a century and a half to the securing for Black Americans of the fundamental rights guaranteed to all under the CONSTITUTION, in the face of at times violent opposition from RACISTS and SEGREGATIONISTS. (It has also been used by minorities elsewhere in campaigns to end discrimination against them, notably by Catholics in NORTHERN IRELAND in the late 1960s.) The first **Civil Rights Act**, conferring citizenship and equal rights on Black Americans, was passed in 1866, but proved a dead letter after the end of RECONSTRUCTION. For decades the battle for Civil Rights was fought through the courts by the NAACP and other groups, and in Congress where segregationist Southern Senators FILIBUSTERed hour after hour against interventionist Federal legislation. The mass Civil Rights movement dates from the 1950s, when Blacks and White liberals combined under the leadership of Dr. Martin Luther KING and others to demand VOTING RIGHTS, EQUAL

OPPORTUNITIES and an end to segregation on housing, education and other facilities. And in 1964 the Senate finally lost patience with obstructionist tactics and ended the filibuster to hand President Johnson a radical if overdue Civil Rights Act. Signed by LBJ on 2 July, it integrated public facilities such as restaurants and hotels, ended job discrimination on grounds of race, sex or religion, and barred racial discrimination in any federally assisted undertaking.

Civil Service In Britain, America and other English-speaking countries, the BUREAUCRACY that actually runs the country, carrying out what it understands to be the decisions of government. Civil servants range from the MANDARINS of WHITEHALL and the career diplomats who staff the STATE DEPARTMENT to thousands of clerks in humble social security offices. Although Adlai Stevenson was once moved to remark that "your public servants serve you right" and Ronald Reagan had plenty to say about bureaucracy, the greater influence of civil servants in Whitehall through the absence of POLITICAL APPOINTEES at the highest level has made Britain's Civil Service a particular subject of controversy. Lord Vansittart once remarked that "the soul of our service is the loyalty with which we execute ordained error", but few politicians are ready to take the blame. Lord Samuel described the Civil Service as "a difficulty for every solution", R.A. (RAB) Butler as "a bit like a Rolls-Royce – you know it's the best machine in the world, but you're not quite sure what to do with it", and Shirley Williams as "a beautifully designed and effective braking mechanism".

> You don't need brains to be Minister of Transport because the civil servants have them.
>
> ERNEST MARPLES (1907–78).

> A faceless mortal riding like a flea on the back of the dog, Legislation. ANON.

> Men who write minutes, make professional assessments, who are never attacked face to face, who dwell in the Sargasso sea of the civil service and who love the seaweed that conceals them. CASSANDRA (William Connor).

civil war The ultimate trauma for a nation: a war between two factions, each intent on governing it and each believing in the justice of its cause. Whoever wins, the bloodshed and bitterness leave scars that take generations to heal. England experienced a civil war from 1642 to 1649 when Parliament rose up against the autocratic King Charles I and, after its victory, tried and executed him; Russia after the BOLSHEVIK revolution of 1917 was convulsed by a civil war between REDS and WHITES, which the Reds eventually won; Ireland after PARTITION was riven by a bloody struggle between supporters of the newly-created IRISH FREE STATE and those who would only accept the independence of all 32 counties. But the most traumatic of all convulsed America from 1861 until 1865.

Stemming from the desire of the CONFEDERATE States to SECEDE from the UNION, the war inflicted prodigious casualties on both sides: from FORT SUMTER to APPOMATTOX, 359,000 Union soldiers and 258,000 Confederates died, and the economy of the South was destroyed. In the process Abraham LINCOLN had EMANCIPATED the slaves of the South, whose continued servitude was one of the causes of the war. Slavery did not return, but after the false dawn of RECONSTRUCTION a new form of repression was inflicted on Black Southerners, which did not lift significantly until the middle of the 20th century.

> In your hands, my dissatisfied fellow-countrymen, and not in mine, is the momentous issue of civil war . . . you can have no conflict without being yourselves the aggressors.
>
> LINCOLN's first INAUGURAL ADDRESS, 4 March 1861.

> My paramount object in this struggle is to save the Union, and is not either to save or destroy slavery.
>
> LINCOLN, August 1862.

> My opinion is that the Northern states will somehow manage to muddle through. JOHN BRIGHT (1811–89).

> The Republic needed to be passed through chastening, purifying fires of adversity and suffering; so these came and did their work and the verdure of a new national life springs greenly, luxuriantly from their ashes.
>
> HORACE GREELEY, *Greeley on Lincoln*, (1893).

Spanish Civil War *See* SPANISH.

Civis Romanus Sum The doctrine used by Palmerston (*see* PAM) to justify Britain's use of naval force against Greece in the case of Don PACIFICO in the House of Commons on 25 June 1850. He fought off Parliamentary censure by declaring:

> As the Roman, in days of old, held himself free from indignity when he could say *Civis Romanus Sum*, so also a British subject, in whatever land he may be, shall feel confident that the watchful eye and strong arm of England will protect him against injustice and wrong.

> Historically it is an anachronism and a blunder, legally it is an injustice and a wrong, politically it is a folly and a crime. Sir WILLIAM HARCOURT, 1868.

claptrap Vacuous rubbish delivered as a political speech. The word dates from the early 19th century, originally describing language intended to win applause (clap-trap).

Clarion, the The newspaper founded by the English Socialist Robert Blatchford, and the Clarion Fellowship that stemmed from it, which throughout the first half of the 20th century sought to broaden the minds of the people and inspire them to intelligent left-wing ideals. The movement brought many people into the Labour Party through a range of activities ranging from political discussion to rambling, cycling and even a youth hostel; its greatest influence was either side of World War I, but it lived on into the 1960s.

Clark memorandum The declaration by the HOOVER administration in 1930 that America had given up the right to intervene in the internal affairs of a Latin American country through the "exercise of an international police power". This clarification of the MONROE DOCTRINE, welcomed in the nations concerned, had been drafted two years before by Under-Secretary of State J. Reuben Clark. In 1931 Secretary of State Henry Stimson went one step further and renounced President WILSON's policy that new Latin American governments would only be RECOGNIZED if they met certain moral criteria.

class The basis of MARXIST and COMMUNIST political theory and activity, and in a different sense a preoccupation of most politicians. Social class has long been the basis of politics, as one has usually been dominant and one or more have generally been excluded from power. In an ideal democracy, class would become irrelevant, building on Lord Acton's dictum: "The danger is not that a particular class is unfit to govern. Every class is unfit to govern." Traditionally society was said to be divided into the haves and the have-nots, with the middle class (to which 92 per cent of Americans say they belong) and other more subtle subdivisions conveniently ignored. Yet it was basically true for Mirabeau to write:

> Society is composed of two great classes: they who have more dinner than appetite, and they who have more appetite than dinner.

MARX and Engels were not the first political theorists to develop the idea of class, but they were the first to put it at the centre of their ideology. Marx wrote in 1852:

> What I did that was new was to demonstrate: (1) that the existence of classes is merely linked to particular phases in the development of production; (2) that class struggle necessarily leads to the dictatorship of the PROLETARIAT; (3) that this dictatorship itself constitutes the transition to the abolition of all classes and to a classless society.

To some, the existence of social differences is an abomination in itself. William Morris wrote in 1883 that "the most grinding poverty is a trifling evil compared with the inequality of classes".

class consciousness The MARXIST notion that a true revolutionary must be aware of the potential of his or her class to change the system, and feel SOLIDARITY with its other members, which will itself inspire action.

class struggle Another basis of Marxism and the movements that sprang from it: the notion that the classes are historically pitted against each other and that in the end the proletariat shall and must triumph. LENIN wrote that "the proletariat will inevitably have to wage a class struggle for Socialism against even the most democratic and republican BOURGEOISIE and petty bourgeoisie". When the Bolsheviks eventually took power in Russia, deputy Prime Minister Vyshinsky, accused of maintaining the Tsarist naval policy of looking for warm-water ports, told his critics:

> The class struggle does not alter geography.

class war (1) Another term for class struggle. Stanley BALDWIN once said: "If there are those who want to fight the class war, we will beat them by the hardness of our heads and the largeness of our hearts." (2) A militant UK ANARCHIST group in the 1980s, with a penchant for disrupting snobbish events like the Henley regatta.

The New Class The book written in 1953 by the Yugoslav Communist Milovan Djilas which argued that Soviet-style Communism, instead of producing a classless society, had in fact produced a new class system every bit as objectionable as the one it replaced. From a society dominated by ARISTOCRATS and the rich, Communism had moved to one where party officials, the heads of State industries and senior BUREAUCRATS enjoyed a superior standard of living and special privileges, which they defended by using the SECRET POLICE against anyone they perceived as a threat. Djilas, a former minister in TITO's government, was explaining where Marxism had gone wrong rather than breaking with it; nevertheless his writing earned him several terms in prison.

ruling class A term used by Marxists and many others for the clique of the wealthy and the well-born that believes it is naturally entitled to wield authority in many countries. Marx and Engels wrote in the COMMUNIST MANIFESTO that "the ruling ideas of each age have ever been the ideas of its ruling class". Their English RADICAL contemporary John Bright declared: "We must oust the dominant class or they will destroy us," and Malcolm Muggeridge, around the time of the PROFUMO AFFAIR, wrote:

> There is nothing on earth so edifying or more ludicrous than the spectacle of the ruling class on the run.

classless society One of the stated aims of Communism, not necessarily achieved as Djilas (*see above*) pointed out. America is supposed to be a classless society, but is not (*see* ARISTOCRACY, MIDDLE CLASS); in Britain LABOUR leaders, notably Harold WILSON, have made the classless society their aim and John MAJOR, on becoming Prime Minister, did the same, though he soon qualified his initial statement:

> When I have talked of a classless society or an opportunity society, I mean that it just does not matter whether you come from a tiny, scruffy back-to-back in a pretty poor housing area or from one of the best mansions in one of the best parts of town.

classify. classified documents Sensitive papers whose circulation is limited and which it is often an offence to divulge. Depending on how confidential they are, they will be marked TOP SECRET or EYES ONLY, *secret* or for those with a wider circulation, *restricted. See also* OFFICIAL SECRETS ACT.

classified results A UK media term for a complete list of election results DECLARED by a particular time, given in alphabetical order.

clause A portion of a piece of legislation which deals with a particular aspect of the subject, and covers a specific point or proposal.

Clause Five meeting The meeting of the LABOUR PARTY's (SHADOW) CABINET and National Executive (NEC) which historically took place on the eve of a UK General Election campaign to settle the contents of the party MANIFESTO.

Clause Four The most controversial section of the LABOUR PARTY's Constitution, which for the past 30 years has been seen by modernizers as an ALBATROSS because of its commitment to NATIONALIZATION and which is seen by the left as a touchstone of the party's SOCIALISM. Hugh GAITSKELL's efforts to abandon it after Labour's defeat in 1959 were thwarted, and no leader since has thought it wise to risk another confrontation over it, though Roy Hattersley (*see* HATTERJI) called for its abolition in February 1993. The precise text, however, contains qualifications which make it less than the demand for immediate action that some leftists claim. Drafted in 1918 by Sidney Webb and revised in 1926, it reads:

> To secure for the workers by hand or by brain the full fruits of their industry and the most equitable distribution therefor that may be possible upon the basis of the common ownership of the means of production, distribution and exchange. . . .

Intriguingly, the wording is close to that used by Abraham LINCOLN in a discussion on the TARIFF in 1847. His closing phrase was:

> To [secure] for each laborer the whole product of his labor, or as nearly as possible, is a most worthy object of any good government.

Clause 27 The clause inserted into the Thatcher government's 1988 Local Government Bill by Tory BACKBENCHERS that outlawed the propagation of homosexuality in schools. In the final Act it was **Clause 28**. The MPs behind the amendment argued that it was necessary because some LOONY LEFT councils were encouraging gay teachers to tell their classes that homosexuality was not only normal but desirable; GAY RIGHTS groups saw it as a homophobic attack and the first step toward a legal crackdown on their basic rights. Since the Bill became law the clause has not been the basis for any prosecutions, but its proponents say it has had a deterrent effect.

commerce clause The portion of Article I, section 8 of the US CONSTITUTION that sets limits on the right of the Federal government to regulate interstate trade. Of vital commercial importance, it was tested in the Sick CHICKEN CASE of 1935. Clause 3 states that:

> The Congress shall have power . . . to regulate commerce with foreign nations; and among the several states; and with the Indian tribes.

sweeping clause Also known as the NECESSARY AND PROPER CLAUSE. Clause 18 of the same article of the Constitution, which states:

> The Congress shall have power . . . to make all laws which shall be necessary and proper for carrying into execution the foregoing powers, and all other powers vested in this Constitution in the Government of the United States, or in any department or office thereof.

Clay Cross councillors The symbol of resistance to the Heath Government's 1972 Housing Finance Act, which prevented councils from providing subsidized housing at knockdown rents. Labour councils embarked on a policy of NON-IMPLEMENTATION, but most reluctantly voted to conform. The left-wing council of the Derbyshire mining village of Clay Cross was left facing the music; those who voted not to implement the Act were SURCHARGED by the DISTRICT AUDITOR and barred from office. A campaign by the local MP Dennis Skinner (*see* BEAST OF BOLSOVER) on behalf of the councillors, who included his brother and cousins, failed to earn them a complete remission when Labour took office in 1974.

Clayton Antitrust Act The Act of 1914 by which the WILSON administration moved against big business, outlawing MONOPOLY practices and establishing a Federal Trade Commission to prevent them recurring. It outlawed anti-competitive pricing in interstate trade, large purchases by corporations of each other's stock, and interlocking directorates in major inter-state trading concerns; it also curbed the use of injunctions in labour disputes and permitted peaceful PICKETING.

clean your teeth in the dark The phrase that dogged the career of Patrick (later Lord) Jenkin (1926–) after he exhorted the public to do just that during the THREE-DAY WEEK of early 1974. Jenkin, as newly-appointed

Minister for Energy, was exhorting the public to save electricity as a MINERS' STRIKE reduced power supplies to a minimum. He went on to serve under Margaret Thatcher as Secretary for, in turn, Social Services, Industry and the Environment before leaving politics in 1985, but his *bon mot* was never entirely forgotten.

Clemenceau, Georges *See* TIGER.

clenched fist The salute, given with arm raised and where possible by every member of a large crowd, that has long been a feature of Communist and other left-wing movements, especially in Continental Europe and the THIRD WORLD. It is a sign of SOLIDARITY with workers and revolutionaries throughout the world.

clerk. Clerk of the House The term used for the officer in charge of recording the transactions of the HOUSE OF COMMONS at Westminster and HOUSE OF REPRESENTATIVES in Washington. In the House of Lords the responsibility rests with the **Clerk of the Parliaments,** and in the US Senate with the **Secretary of the Senate.**

committee clerk The clerk who attends meetings of the committees of an elected body, preparing the AGENDA, taking MINUTES and giving advice on procedure when asked.

Cleveland, Grover *See* BEAST OF BUFFALO.

cliché A hackneyed phrase which nevertheless has a readily-identified meaning; political speakers are much scorned by their peers for using them, especially when they are an alternative to any statement of substance. The classic example of a cliché-ridden speech was reputedly delivered in the Irish Parliament by Sir Boyle Roche (1743–1807); it included the sentence:

> Mr. Speaker, I smell a rat; I see him forming in the air and darkening the sky; but I'll nip him in the bud.

Anthony EDEN came in for particular criticism; CHURCHILL is supposed to have once said of his speeches: "They consist entirely of clichés – clichés old and new – everything from 'God is Love' to 'Please adjust your dress before leaving'". Ernest BEVIN was even blunter, describing them as: "Clitch, clitch, clitch." However Eden had some support from Adlai Stevenson, who voiced the generality that

> One man's cliché can be another man's CONVICTION.

forever poised between a cliché and an indiscretion The silky phrase used by Harold Macmillan to describe the dilemma of Britain's FOREIGN SECRETARY. In the Commons on 27 July 1955, Macmillan said:

> Nothing he can say can do very much good, and almost anything he may say may do a great deal of harm. Anything he says that is not obvious is dangerous; whatever is not trite is risky. He is forever poised between the cliché and the indiscretion.

Clinton, Bill (William Jefferson) *See* COMEBACK KID.

Cliveden set The clique of APPEASEMENT-minded politicians and journalists who gathered for weekend parties in the late 1930s at Cliveden, the country home of Lord and Lady Astor near Maidenhead, Berkshire. The name first appeared in Claud Cockburn's iconoclastic left-wing journal *The Week*, but the strength of the legend may have become exaggerated despite a certain softness toward Hitler among some upper-class right-wingers. A second Cliveden set with rather different priorities emerged in the early 1960s, giving rise to the PROFUMO AFFAIR; it was at Cliveden that John Profumo first met Christine Keeler.

close. closed rule A resolution by the US HOUSE OF REPRESENTATIVES that it will give immediate consideration to a reported Bill, and will limit or prevent floor AMENDMENTS.

closed shop In industrial relations, the situation in which all employees of a particular company or at a certain plant are required to be members of a trade union. Trade unionists argue that the closed shop assists COLLECTIVE BARGAINING and avoids a situation where non-union members can gain preferential treatment and weaken the union's effectiveness. Management sees the closed shop as giving the unions a stranglehold, and the practice was outlawed in Britain by the Thatcher government in the early 1980s (*see* STEP BY STEP).

closure The procedure introduced by Britain's House of Commons in 1881 to end disruption by PARNELLITE members pressing for Irish HOME RULE. James, later Lord, Bryce, wrote:

> It marked the end of the old, dignified, constitutionally regular and gentlemanly House of Commons.

To obtain the closure, the sponsor of a Bill (usually the Government) must be able to find 100 members to vote for it; if carried, the proposal under debate is immediately put to the vote. Should the closure on a Private Member's BILL fail, it is said to have been TALKED OUT.

kangaroo closure A procedure in the US Congress to enable a whole section of a Bill to be voted on without debate.

cloture The procedure introduced by the US SENATE in 1919 to end the chaos caused by unlimited FILIBUSTERS. The immediate cause was the delaying tactics of a group of Senators known as the "wilful eleven" who had blocked essential business on the eve of America's entry into World War I. Under pressure from Sen. Thomas Walsh of Montana, a provision (Rule 22) was adopted for any 16 Senators to petition for an end to debate on any "pending measure"; two days later it would be put to the vote. If passed by a two-thirds majority (later three-fifths), the cloture would take effect and each senator could then speak for no more than an hour, including the raising of any procedural points. Cloture was successfully moved on very few occasions – and never between 1927 and 1962 as the rule was gradually whittled away, nor on any CIVIL RIGHTS measure until the landmark Bill of 1964 when Senators' patience with obstruction by Southern conservatives finally ran out. Since then, aided by a liberalization of the rules in 1975, cloture has been achieved some 70 times. A further delaying tactic, the post-cloture filibuster, was outlawed in 1979.

cloud cuckoo land The ultimate term of scorn for the fantasy world in which some politicians accuse others of living. Originally the name given by Aristophanes in *The Birds* to a city in the sky built by feathered creatures, it was much used in various contexts by Hitler, using the German *Wolkenkuckucksheim*. More recently, Margaret Thatcher harnessed it to describe the world inhabited by advocates of closer European union.

CLP Constituency Labour Party. The basic unit of organization in the UK LABOUR PARTY. It is made up of WARDS and branches, and sends delegates to the regional party and Labour's annual conference. Its governing bodies are the GMC (General Management Committee) and the smaller constituency executive.

CND Campaign for Nuclear Disarmament. The movement that mobilized mass opposition to Britain's independent nuclear DETERRENT, and nuclear weapons in general, during the late 1950s and early 1960s and again in the early 1980s. Founded in 1958 by a group including Bertrand Russell and Canon John Collins, Dean of St. Paul's Cathedral, its demonstrations and annual ALDERMASTON MARCHES were a feature of national life for five years or so, fading after the conclusion of the TEST-BAN TREATY. Politically, CND's success and organization assisted the campaign for UNILATERALISM which in 1960 briefly captured the Labour Party (*see* FIGHT, FIGHT AND FIGHT AGAIN). In 1961 Russell and other militant nuclear disarmers who feared CND was losing its edge launched the COMMITTEE OF 100, which carried out a brief campaign of CIVIL DISOBEDIENCE. CND, now led by Monsignor Bruce Kent, enjoyed a new lease of life 20 years later as controversy grew over America's planned deployment of CRUISE MISSILES in Britain; a new generation took part in huge demonstrations and Labour once again went unilateralist. It subsided once again in 1990 after the end of the COLD WAR and with Cruise being withdrawn in return for destruction of the Soviet SS20s; Labour repudiated unilateralism after its election defeat in 1987.

> A load of peanuts who aren't worth a tinker's cuss.
> HUGH GAITSKELL.

coalition (1) A government comprising members of two or more parties, formed because no one party has an outright MAJORITY, or to tackle a national emergency. The alternative to a coalition is a MINORITY GOVERNMENT or a HUNG PARLIAMENT. In Britain the two main parties are fundamentally opposed to coalitions, echoing Disraeli's statement (*see* DIZZY) that "England does not love coalitions", though Edward Heath flirted with the idea in 1974; the LIBERAL DEMOCRATS positively advocate them. There have been just two in peacetime this century: under Lloyd George (L. G.) from 1918 until 1922 in the aftermath of World War I, and the NATIONAL GOVERNMENT from 1931 until 1935 to combat the economic crisis. ASQUITH, Lloyd George and CHURCHILL all led wartime coalitions, Asquith observing: "Nothing is so demoralising to the tone of public life, or so belittling to the stature of public men". On the continent of Europe, coalitions are far more common, being the basic form of government in Italy, Belgium and the Netherlands, and having governed Germany for long periods since World War II. (2) An international grouping in pursuit of a common object, notably the coalition formed under US leadership to carry out UN-authorized military action against Iraq in the GULF WAR. (3) The binding-together of diverse strands in a political party. *See* BROAD CHURCH.

> Every political movement, whether conservative or liberal, owes its success to its ability to maintain a coalition between the greedy and the idealistic.
> MURRAY KEMPTON.

Grand Coalition The government formed by West Germany's two main parties, the Christian Democrats (CDU) and Social Democrats (SPD), with Kurt Georg Kiesinger (1904–88) as CHANCELLOR, which held office from 1966 to 1969.

Great Coalition The broad government of both GRITS and Bleus (Tories) formed in Canada in 1864 under John Macdonald, at the urging of George Brown, editor of the *Toronto Globe*, to prepare the way for CONFEDERATION.

Rainbow coalition *See* RAINBOW.

coat-tail effect The means by which an unpopular or unknown candidate can benefit from the presence on the same TICKET, or even in the same party, of a highly popular and charismatic figure. The candidate is said to have been elected "on the coat-tails" of the other, *i.e.* to have been dragged in by him or her.

COCOM The Co-ordinating Committee for Multilateral Export Controls, the trading arm of the West in the COLD WAR. A Paris-based body set up to prevent advanced Western technology, especially with a military potential, falling into Communist hands. It continues to function with slightly slackened guidelines, and is seen by some Europeans as a PROTECTIONIST device to maintain US control over the trading practices of firms in other Western countries.

co-decision A EUROPEAN COMMUNITY term for the joint decision-making process of the European COMMISSION and the EUROPEAN PARLIAMENT, in which the Commission remains dominant despite a slight shift in the balance under the MAASTRICHT TREATY.

Cod Wars The skirmishes between Icelandic gunboats and British trawlers which broke out in 1972 when Iceland unilaterally increased its territorial waters from 12 to 50 miles. Britain sent in warships to support the trawlers against having their nets cut as they stayed in their traditional fishing grounds, but eventually conceded Iceland's right to impose a limit. When the Conservative MP John Watson told a meeting in Yorkshire: "Things will improve now – we're sending in the Royal Navy," a HECKLER replied: "And how many bloody fish are they going to catch?"

Code Napoléon The comprehensive and neatly-organized corpus of laws introduced in France by Napoleon Bonaparte, which forms the basis of French law to this day.

coded message An apparently innocuous remark by a politician that conveys a definite – and usually critical – meaning for those at whom it is aimed. Such messages are frequently used to make criticism without rendering the speaker liable to charges of disloyalty; Peter Walker, who survived for years as a WET in Margaret Thatcher's government, was a past master of the art.

codification The transformation of a disorganized mass of written and unwritten law into clear and orderly STATUTES. In Britain the process is known as CONSOLIDATION.

CODESA The talks on replacing South Africa's APARTHEID constitution with a multi-racial democracy begun in 1991 by President de Klerk, between 19 groups including the ANC and INKATHA; the letters stand for *CO*nvention for the constitution of a *DE*mocratic *S*outh *A*frica. The talks were deadlocked by May 1992 over the issue of federalism; the ANC broke off negotiations in June after the BOIPATONG MASSACRE, but later reopened direct contact with the National Party government which produced a POWER-SHARING agreement early in 1993.

coercion The repressive Irish policy adopted by Britain, especially under Disraeli from 1874 till 1880 and, briefly, by Gladstone before his conversion to HOME RULE. It met the popular upsurge for land reform with measures that one PARNELLITE called "an open declaration of war on every man in Ireland". Mass meetings, CIVIL DISOBEDIENCE, rent strikes and sporadic violence were countered by special magistrates backed up by heavy troop reinforcements. Based on the belief that resistance would collapse if a small number of troublemakers could be isolated, the system kept a degree of order, at an immense political price. Gladstone's Irish Secretary W. E. FORSTER was the architect of the stiffest measures, passed in 1881 despite stiff Parnellite resistance; the repercussions led to his being dropped from the Cabinet. A further Crimes Bill was passed in 1882 after the PHOENIX PARK MURDERS.

cohabitation In France's FIFTH REPUBLIC, a situation in which a President of one party and a Prime Minister and government of another co-exist in office. The term, with its Gallic sexual inference, originated during the period 1986–88 when a right-wing government headed by Jacques Chirac "cohabited" with the Socialist President François Mitterrand. Cohabitation came back into vogue after the National Assembly elections of March 1993, when Mitterrand had to accept a centre-right government under Édouard Balladur.

cohesion The EC term for policies designed to raise the economies of the poorer member states – Greece, Ireland, Spain and Portugal – toward the level of the rest, largely through large-scale transfers of funds. The Edinburgh summit in December 1992 was deadlocked for many hours over Spain's demand for the largest-possible cohesion fund, before a compromise was reached.

COINTELPRO *Co*unter-*Intel*ligence *Pro*gram. The campaign initiated by FBI director J. Edgar Hoover in 1968 against "Black Nationalist-Hate Groups"; it grew into an operation by 41 of the Bureau's field offices to undermine or discredit any organization he regarded as subversive. The campaign relied heavily on the bugging of prominent Black activists, starting with Dr. Martin Luther KING, and the "exposure" of their sexual activities. In the years leading up to COINTELPRO, Hoover told FBI agents he aimed to prevent the coalition of militant Black nationalist groups into a "real MAU MAU in America, the beginning of a true Black revolution", and "prevent the rise of a 'Messiah' who could unify and electrify the militant Black nationalist movement". Hoover saw Dr. King and Malcolm X as potential Messiah figures; by the time COINTELPRO was fully under way, both had been assassinated.

COLAs In America, the annual *C*ost *O*f *L*iving *A*djustments paid to increase social security benefits. Soon after Ronald Reagan took office in 1981, several Senate Democrats offered him a COLA freeze to reduce the Budget deficit by up to $38 billion. Reagan refused it, saying he was pledged not to cut social security benefits – only to put forward a plan of his own two months later slashing the benefits themselves. The ensuing furore did Reagan considerable political damage. The plan was dropped – and it was 1983 before a far more modest and BIPARTISAN package was adopted.

cold. Cold War The period of tension between East and West, stopping just short of conflict between the SUPERPOWERS, which began within months of YALTA and the end of WORLD WAR II and ended with the breaching of the BERLIN WALL 44 years later. The period – particularly from 1948 to the mid-1960s – was dominated by the fear of nuclear annihilation. The term was first used by Bernard M. Baruch (1870–1965) in a speech to the South Carolina legislature on 16 April 1947:

> Let us not be deceived – we are today in the midst of a cold war. Our enemies are to be found abroad and at home.

Baruch himself credited the phrase to Herbert B. Swope, former editor of the *New York World*.

The mood of the Cold War had been set in 1946 by Dean Acheson. Though later pilloried as "soft on Communism", Acheson said:

> We have got to understand that all our lives the danger, the uncertainty, the need for alertness, for effort, for discipline – will be upon us. This is new to us. It will be hard for us.

And in 1949 Harold Macmillan said:

> With Communists we cannot say it with flowers . . . the Cold War must be fought with as much energy and singlemindedness as the shooting war.

Eventually the ability of America's economy to keep up in the ARMS RACE and the dire economic plight of the Soviet Union, coupled with the rise of Mikhail Gorbachev, brought the Cold War to an end.

> By the Grace of God, America won the Cold War.
> GEORGE BUSH, 1992.

cold peace The Norwegian Trygve Lie (1896–1968), who became the first Secretary-General of the UNITED NATIONS, used this term in 1949 to describe the combination of high tension and lack of actual conflict that characterized the early stages of the Cold War.

cold warrior A US/British term for an enthusiastic advocate of belligerent competition with the Soviet Union.

collaborator or **collaborationist** The ultimate insult in countries occupied by Nazi Germany during WORLD WAR II. It described someone who had co-operated willingly with the invaders; many collaborators paid for that co-operation with their lives – often without trial – once the country had been liberated.

collective. collective bargaining The process under which an employer and a trade union, or groups representing both, negotiate wages and conditions for the workers as a whole. The unions are able to back up their claims with the sanction of industrial ACTION; as the alternative would be for each employee to negotiate his or her own conditions of service with little ability to stand up to management, collective bargaining is one of the main reasons for joining a union. Governments may be worried by both the economic impact of the deals arrived at and the power unions wield in unfettered bargaining; attempts to introduce wage and price controls, and legislation to impose checks on union power, are seen by the unions as intrusions into "free collective bargaining".

collective leadership A system in which a nation or a party is ruled jointly by several individuals, rather than by a single leader. It does not have an impressive track record; recent examples include federal Yugoslavia prior to its disintegration in 1991–92, and the Liberal–SDP ALLIANCE.

collective responsibility The doctrine, enshrined in Britain's UNWRITTEN CONSTITUTION, under which every member of the CABINET is equally responsible for decisions taken by it, whatever view they expressed at the time. Traditionally any Minister who could not approve a decision had to resign unless there was an AGREEMENT TO DIFFER; in recent times, except for WESTLAND, the tradition has been honoured in the breach.

collective security The principle underlying both the LEAGUE OF NATIONS and the UNITED NATIONS, whereby the nations of the world act together to maintain the peace and to respond to threats to it. The phrase was coined in 1932 by the Czech Foreign Minister Eduard Beneš (1884–1948) at the League of Nations; a French delegate is said to have protested:

> Impossible; it's not French.

collectivism The theory that a nation's economy, and indeed many aspects of its society, should be operated for the community as a whole with the individual being subordinated. It appealed to Communists and Fascists alike, but is also echoed in the policies of all but the most conservative parties.

> If the nineteenth century was the century of individualism, this will be the century of collectivism, and hence the century of the State. MUSSOLINI.

collectivization The process of forcing peasants and larger farmers (*see* KULAKS) on to state-owned collective farms, pioneered by STALIN in the late 1920s and followed in much of Communist eastern Europe after World War II. In some countries it was accompanied by the killing or imprisonment of those who were expropriated. Though Soviet leaders trumpeted the achievements of the collective farms for half a century, their productivity was frequently low and the quality of their produce indifferent. However, they linger on in several post-Communist countries, notably Hungary. *See also* BLITZKRIEG.

College of Cardinals In the US Congress, the semi-reverent collective nickname for the chairmen of the House's 13 APPROPRIATIONS Committees. It reflects the immense power they exercise over the budgetary and legislative process.

Colombey-les-deux-Églises The tiny French village to which General DE GAULLE retired in 1946 after the failure of his efforts to put together and lead a government of national unity, and where he remained until called back to be President of the FIFTH REPUBLIC in 1958. He retained an immense fondness for Colombey, settling there again on his resignation in 1969 and dying there the following year. Colombey is in the Haute-Marne department of north-eastern France, 8 miles east of Bar-sur-Aube.

> What other consolation can be sought when one has faced history? DE GAULLE, 1969.

Colombo Plan An agreement to foster economic development in South and South-East Asia, concluded at Colombo, Ceylon (now Sri Lanka), in 1951. There are annual meetings to discuss economic development plans such as irrigation and hydro-electric schemes, and a permanent office to give technical assistance.

Colonels, the The right-wing military junta led by Georgios Papadopoulos (*see* PAPA DOP) (1919–) which overthrew Greece's constitutional monarchy in 1967 and in the ensuing seven years became a byword for ruthlessness, and a target for world-wide left-wing odium. Costa-Gavras' film *Z*, portraying the murder of the former opposition deputy Gregory Lambrakis, showed the régime's sinister side to the full. Its lasting, though unintended, effects were the PARTITION of Cyprus and the end of the Greek monarchy. With King Constantine in exile in Britain, the monarchy was abolished in 1973 and Papadopoulos appointed President, but the army ousted him the same year. The Colonels fell after they backed a right-wing coup in Cyprus against the government of Archbishop Makarios, aimed at uniting the country with Greece. The coup, led by Nikos Sampson, was staged after Makarios demanded the removal of Greek officers sent by the Colonels to fan feeling for ENOSIS; it was abortive, but gave Turkey the pretext to occupy the north of the island to protect Turkish Cypriots. The junta collapsed on 23 July 1974 amid riots in Athens, and ex-premier Constantine Karamanlis was called from exile to head a civilian government. The monarchy was formally abolished in a referendum after the return of democracy, and 20 of the colonels put on trial; Papadopoulos was sentenced to death for treason, soon commuted to life imprisonment.

colonialism The policy of keeping control of a nation's dependent territories for the purpose of exploiting them. Throughout the 1950s and 1960s the term was used abusively by MOSCOW-LINE and NON-ALIGNED countries to denounce both the retention of colonies by former imperial powers such as Britain and France, and the foreign policy of the United States.

colony The overseas dependencies of a state, especially those to which emigrants have travelled to replicate the home country's economic system and forms of government, while excluding the indigenous people from power. Colonies were first established by the Greeks, Romans and other Mediterranean nations in classical times, but it was Britain who adopted the policy most comprehensively in Africa, Asia, the Caribbean and elsewhere. John Ruskin, lecturing in 1870, declared: "This is what [England] must do, or she will perish: she must found colonies as fast and as far as she is able, formed of her most energetic and worthiest men." But even the IMPERIALIST Disraeli saw disadvantages, which led him to state:

> These wretched colonies will all be independent, too, in a few years, and are a millstone round our necks.

self-governing colony The ultimately self-defeating constitutional arrangement under which a colony is permitted to govern itself, having the potential to embarrass the nation nominally responsible for it. Rhodesia prior to UDI, and Gibraltar in its opposition to any contacts with Spain have both made Britain pay dearly for this misguided exercise in DEVOLUTION.

colour (or color) bar A term widely used in the 1940s and 1950s for racial SEGREGATION, and specifically the exclusion of Black people from premises deemed by the authorities or their proprietors to be "Whites only".

columnist A newspaper or magazine writer who has a column of his or her own, in America often syndicated to papers across the country, which is filled either with personal comment (Walter Lippmann, Peter Jenkins), polemics (Lester Kinsolving, Bernard Levin) or exposés (Jack Anderson, who did much to unmask ITT's efforts in the early 1970s to subvert the political process in Chile). In Washington, where columnists exert particular influence, much of the revelatory material comes from embittered sources within the political system or the military.

combined development TROTSKY's theory explaining why the first successful Socialist revolution occurred in a backward agrarian country rather than in an advanced capitalist one, as had been predicted.

come. Come home, America *see* AMERICA.

Comeback Kid The nickname chosen for himself by Governor **Bill Clinton** (1916–) of Arkansas as he recovered from a shaky start in the PRIMARIES to take the 1992 Democratic nomination – and go on to win the Presidency. George BUSH disputed the name in the closing stages of the campaign, declaring:

> We're not running against the comeback kids, we're running against the Karaoke Kids – they'd sing any tune to get elected.

Clinton was almost knocked out of the running prior to the NEW HAMPSHIRE PRIMARY when Gennifer Flowers, a blonde club singer, claimed they had had a passionate 11-year affair; the charges were revived throughout the campaign but Clinton's handling of them – virtual denials coupled with acknowledgment of past "difficulties" in his marriage to his talented wife Hillary – ensured they never killed off his candidacy. He also overcame Republican charges that while a Rhodes Scholar at Oxford he had taken drugs, and a leading role in the movement against the VIETNAM WAR. Clinton admitted: "When I was in England, I experimented with marijuana a time or two and I didn't like it. I didn't inhale." As a negative campaign even by 1988 standards neared its height (or depth) the Bush campaign director Mary Matalin made the deadpan observation:

> We have never said to the press that Clinton is a philandering, pot-smoking draft dodger.

Overriding the appeal of Ross PEROT, Clinton and his running-mate Sen. Albert Gore (*see* OZONE MAN) won a comfortable margin in the ELECTORAL COLLEGE; defeated Vice-President Dan QUAYLE said graciously:

> If he runs the country as well as he ran his campaign, we'll be all right.

However once in office, Clinton saw his political abilities called in question (*see* BAIRD NOMINATION, CHRISTOPHE) and his apparent indecision led to a slump in his APPROVAL RATING.

Comecon Council for Mutual Economic Assistance. The international grouping set up by STALIN in 1949 to promote economic development and trade between the Soviet Union and the Communist countries of eastern Europe, except for Yugoslavia. Until 1953 it was largely a propaganda vehicle to cover Soviet exploitation of its SATELLITES. Later it did promote genuine mutual co-operation and development. In 1989, with the collapse of Communism in eastern Europe, Comecon announced that it would take account of market forces, but the grouping was speedily left meaningless by events.

Cominform Communist Information Bureau. An international organization set up in 1947 under Soviet control to issue propaganda encouraging world Communist solidarity, and co-ordinate the activities of communist parties – and subversion – in countries not under Soviet control. Its members were the parties of the Soviet Union, Bulgaria, Czechoslovakia, France, Hungary, Italy, Poland, Romania and Yugoslavia. In 1948 Yugoslavia was expelled for not following Soviet instructions; the Cominform was dissolved in 1956 to improve relations between the Kremlin and President TITO.

Comintern Communist International. An organization of world communist parties founded by LENIN in 1919 to hasten the world-wide revolution of the proletariat. Regarded as highly sinister in the West, it was dissolved by Stalin in 1943 as a gesture toward his wartime capitalist allies.

Anti-Comintern Pact An agreement signed by Germany and Japan on 25 November 1936, and by Italy the following year, ostensibly to counter the activities of the Comintern. For Japan, the pact reinforced her expansionist plans, hastening her invasion of China in 1937. The agreement, viewed as ominous by the Western democracies and the Soviet Union, foreshadowed the 1940 TRIPARTITE PACT between the three AXIS countries.

comity The international custom under which some effect is given to the laws of one state within the territory of another. America has at times – notably under President CARTER's Attorney-General Griffin Bell – invoked the principle with vigour, giving other states the impression that it expects US law to override that of other states in those territories.

Commander-in-chief The supreme position accorded to the PRESIDENT in relation to America's armed forces. The US constitution reads:

> The President shall be commander in chief of the Army and Navy of the United States and of the militia of the several states, when called into the actual service of the United States.

Presidential control over the armed forces is not unlimited, Congress having a significant role in the declaration of war. However the President does have the power to send US troops anywhere in the world, and theoretically could take the field in active command, though he has never actually done so.

> Any president as commander-in-chief faces no more solemn decision than whether to send American troops into battle, knowing they will not all return.
>
> JOHN F. KENNEDY.

commie An abusive term for a supposed or actual COMMUNIST, common in America after World War II but which has outlived the age of McCARTHYISM. The word, more insulting than "Communist", has been applied not only to genuine Marxist-Leninists but more loosely to any foreigner, outsider, liberal or person with unconventional views.

commissar Under the early Soviet system, an official with at least as great a responsibility to the Party as to the state. In the RED ARMY, commissars from the Party were attached to each unit to ensure ideological soundness among the troops. Until 1946, Ministers in the Soviet government held the title **People's Commissar**.

Commission, European The EXECUTIVE BRANCH of the EUROPEAN COMMUNITY, comprising 15,000 officials, most of them based in BRUSSELS. As the sole authority to initiate EC legislation and the body responsible for its enforcement by prosecution in the EUROPEAN COURT, the Commission enjoys immense power and is thus a target for EURO-SCEPTICS. Its bureaucracy is divided into 23 Directorates-General (DGs), and a range of auxiliary units, such as for legal and translation services. At its head are 17 **Commissioners** appointed by member states, one of whom serves as President; normally reasonably senior national politicians, they take an oath to serve the Community rather than their own state. They serve for four years (five under the MAASTRICHT TREATY) and can only be removed, en bloc, by a vote of the European Parliament. This power has never been exercised.

committee A group of individuals, often part or even the whole of a legislature or other elected body, convened to consider a particular matter or range of matters. Committees in their various forms are essential to the workings of government, but can become the weapons of inert BUREAUCRACY. At best a committee can be highly effective in arriving at conclusions, apportioning blame or drafting legislation; at worst it can kill an imaginative proposal, producing a platitudinous report or a clumsy FUDGE.

> A cul-de-sac down which ideas are lured and quietly strangled.
>
> SIR BARNETT COCKS, Clerk of the House of Commons (1907–88).

> A group that keeps MINUTES and loses hours.
>
> MILTON BERLE.

> A group of the unwilling, chosen from the unfit, to do the unnecessary. ANON (US).

> The best committee is a committee of two, when one is absent. E. V. LUCAS (1868–1938).

> A camel is a horse designed by a committee. ANON.

> If Moses had been a committee, the Israelites would never have got across the Red Sea.
>
> Salvation Army General WILLIAM BOOTH.

In many legislatures, the US Congress in particular, committees provide both the legislative and political engine-room.

> A good committee assignment [for a Congressman] can make the difference between a brief and obscure service in the House and the kind of influence that means tenure for decades. *New York Times*

> When internally unified and buttressed in parliamentary privilege by special rules, they can almost at will dominate the business of the parent chamber.
>
> STEPHEN BAILEY.

committee clerk *See* CLERK.

committees of correspondence The committees formed by discontents in Massachusetts on the eve of the AMERICAN REVOLUTION, which eventually usurped the government of the colony. The first was set up by the Boston TOWN MEETING at the urging of Samuel Adams (1722–1803); by 1774, 300 communities had joined the network. The BOSTON TEA PARTY stemmed from an initiative against Britain's Tea Tax by the Massachusetts correspondence committee.

committee of dukes and earls The nickname given to the grouping of all 15 Senate committee chairman pulled together in 1981 by MAJORITY LEADER Sen. Howard Baker to maximize support for the programmes of the newly-elected President Reagan.

Committee of 100 The militant network formed *c.* 1961 by members of Britain's Campaign for Nuclear Disarmament (CND) who felt the movement's non-confrontational tactics were doomed to failure. Members took part in mass SIT-DOWNS and other acts of CIVIL DISOBEDIENCE; a number were sent to prison, including the aged philosopher Bertrand Russell (1872–1970).

Committee of the whole House At Westminster, a sitting of the House of Commons, chaired by the Chairman of WAYS AND MEANS rather than the Speaker, to hear the Chancellor deliver his BUDGET and to tackle the COMMITTEE STAGES of Bills involving Constitutional issues, and key sections of the FINANCE BILL. The US House of Representatives can form itself into a **Committee of the Whole** (short for Committee of the Whole House on the State of the Union), with a QUORUM of 100, to consider all measures on the Union CALENDAR – tax and appropriation Bills – and any other matter on resolution of the House.

Committee on the Present Danger A pro-defence pressure group launched in the early days of the Carter administration by Washington insiders who felt that America was adopting a dangerously relaxed military posture at a time when the Kremlin under Brezhnev was posing new threats and challenges, notably deployment of the SS20 missile which CRUISE missiles were developed to counter.

committee room (1) In the US CAPITOL, the Palace of WESTMINSTER and elsewhere, the small rooms to medium-sized halls, depending on the size and prestige of the body, where committees sit to carry out their business.

> Congress, with its committee rooms, is Congress at work.
> WOODROW WILSON.

(2) The basic unit of the electoral machine in Britain; the offices in each POLLING DISTRICT which on election day serve as a party's headquarters and the base from which its workers get out the vote. The NCR or READING pads will be put out, street by street, on a table, alongside a heap of leaflets making a last-minute appeal to vote and a list of voters who will need transport to the polls. The average committee room will be in the living-room of a party supporter sited conveniently close to the POLLING STATION, or sometimes in a disused shop or office.

Committee Stage At Westminster, the stage of a Bill between the Second and Third Reading when the measure is considered LINE BY LINE and amendments are taken. In the Commons, the work is done by a STANDING COMMITTEE except for Constitutional measures and key sections of the FINANCE BILL; protracted debate by the opposition may lead the Government to seek use of the GUILLOTINE. In the Lords, Committee stages are conducted on the FLOOR of the House.

in committee The House of Commons is said to be in committee when the Speaker has left the chair and the MACE is off the table. The discussion of a Bill or other matters by a committee rather than by the whole House is also said to take place in committee.

common. Common Agricultural Policy *See* CAP.

Common Cause A public-interest lobby founded in the late 1960s which campaigns to keep America a democracy by limiting the scope for outside interests to exert financial influence over politicians. It advocates Federal funding for elections, and has long fought to curb the influence of lobbyists and reform the laws on campaign funding; its joint campaign with the People's Lobby in 1974 led to California introducing tough State laws. Common Cause has pressed for stricter observance of existing campaign financing laws, and for an end to the Congressional free-mail privilege which it says enables INCUMBENTS to raise three times as much funding as challengers. It has taken a strong stand against the activities of PACs, reporting in 1985 that many members of the Senate Finance Committee and House Ways and Means Committee were receiving campaign funds from PACs eager to win tax breaks for their areas of business. It also helped force an end to the rigid SENIORITY system for House chairmanships in 1975, by sending every member of the Democratic Caucus a "report card" on the record of each committee chairman.

Common European home The phrase used by Mikhail GORBACHEV (1931–) for the tension-free Europe he hoped could develop following the end of the COLD WAR. Unfortunately for him the Soviet Union, and his own position within it, was abolished before the policy could bear fruit.

Common Market The original colloquial UK term for the EUROPEAN (Economic) COMMUNITY; it is now only used by diehard opponents of British membership.

> Neither we nor the Common Market are so affluent that we can long afford to shelter high cost farms or factories from the winds of foreign competition.
>
> JOHN F. KENNEDY.

> Given a fair wind, we will negotiate our way into the Common Market, head held high – not crawl in. Negotiations? Yes. Unconditional acceptance of whatever terms we are offered? No. HAROLD WILSON, 20 March 1966.

Common roll In the various constitutions devised by Britain for COLONIES nearing or achieving independence, a common electoral roll was one on which both Whites and indigenous people were included on an equal basis. There was normally a further roll giving subjects of the colonial power a guaranteed number of seats; as independence neared, this built-in advantage was eliminated.

Common Sense The revolutionary tract written in Philadelphia by the recent English immigrant Thomas Paine (1737–1809) and published on 10 January 1776. In it he argued:

> Can we but leave posterity with a settled form of government, an independent constitution of its own, the purchase at any price will be cheap.

Within three months of that momentous year it had sold 100,000 copies – at a time when there were only 2 million Americans. Eventually 500,000 were sold worldwide, but Paine made a loss; he promised the original printer, Robert Bell, that he would subsidize any loss on a first edition of 1000 copies, with any profit divided between Bell and the supply of mittens for the Continental army. Bell insisted he had made no profit on the first edition, and refused Paine any payment for the second. George WASHINGTON reckoned the pamphlet "worked a powerful change in the minds of many men", but in 1819 John ADAMS fumed:

> What a poor, ignorant, malicious, short-sighted crapulous mass is Tom Paine's *Common Sense*.

Commoner, Great *See* GREAT.

Commons, House of *See* HOUSE OF COMMONS.

Common Wealth An idealistic left-wing political party which enjoyed some success in Britain during and shortly after World War II. A merger of Sir Richard Acland's **Forward March** and the **1941 Committee**, formed by followers of J. B. Priestley's radio talks, it won seats in wartime BY-ELECTIONS where no Labour candidate stood against the defending Tories. It fielded 23 candidates in the 1945 General Election but only one was elected alongside Labour's victorious horde. The party did not survive, most of its members being absorbed by Labour.

Commonwealth (1) The (British) Commonwealth. The grouping of nations under the leadership, though not the SOVEREIGNTY, of the British crown, which comprises almost all the nations of Britain's former EMPIRE. Its potency as a unified trading force was weakened by Britain's attempts from 1962 to join the EC. The Commonwealth has its own secretariat which assists joint diplomatic and development initiatives, and its Prime Ministers meet every two years in a member capital (*see* CHOGM). The term was in use long before the Empire formally came to an end with Britain's withdrawal from India.

> There is no need for any nation, however great, leaving the Empire, because the Empire is a Commonwealth of nations. LORD ROSEBERY.

(2) The Republic established in England, with Oliver Cromwell at its head, following the execution of King Charles II in 1649. It survived until 1660, being governed by the military for the final five years following the disbandment of its increasingly argumentative Parliament (*see* RUMP). (3) The official title of Australia since 1901, and the term used to personify the federal power. (4) The formal status and title of Massachusetts, dating back to colonial times. (5) The status accorded to Puerto Rico by the United States; it falls short of STATEHOOD, support for which is limited because of fears on the island that federal aid might be less generous and the people's obligations greater.

Commonwealth of Independent States The grouping of former Soviet republics set up in late 1991 under Russian leadership in an effort to maintain common services and prevent harmful fragmentation. At the time of going to press, it was still not clear which components of the former Soviet state would remain members; the Baltic States, Belarus, Georgia and the Ukraine had all gone their own way and some others might follow.

New Commonwealth Member states of Britain's Commonwealth other than the White-ruled DOMINIONS; conversely, all those states ruled by their indigenous peoples. The term came into use in the 1970s to describe the nations of the Caribbean, Africa and the Indian subcontinent whose citizens were migrating in force to Britain, leading both to poor living conditions among many who had arrived, and RACISM from some British people and politicians. *See* POWELLITES; RIVERS OF BLOOD.

White Commonwealth (1) The great DOMINIONS of the former British EMPIRE, in which Whites mainly of British origin formed the majority and held power. The governments of the UK, Australia, Canada and New Zealand earned the epithet in the 1960s when at times they and the newly-independent colonies were on opposite sides of the political fence. (2) The LOBBY correspondents of Britain's serious broadsheet press - then *The Times*, the *Daily Telegraph*, the *Guardian* and the *Financial Times* - who on occasion up to the early 1980s were invited to Downing Street for briefings not extended to the popular tabloids.

communautaire A French term meaning "in the spirit of the European Community", which is applied to any policy or action which, in the view of the beholder, will further the interests of the EC rather than national ends. The test is ruthlessly subjective, frequently being used in the negative sense by one nationally-motivated politician about the actions of another, or by the COMMISSION against anyone trying to inject common sense into its policies.

acquis communautaire The body of existing EC law, especially the *status quo* a state must accept as a basis for negotiations on its ACCESSION to membership.

commune A basic unit of local government, an experiment in collective living (*see* KIBBUTZ), and, specifically, the revolutionary authority set up in Paris in 1870 after France's defeat in the FRANCO-PRUSSIAN WAR. Seen by MARX and others as foreshadowing more permanent revolutions, it was suppressed within months by troops sent by the government of the embryo THIRD REPUBLIC under Thiers, which was based at VERSAILLES. Participants in the Paris Commune were not Communists but **Communards.**

communiqué The official statement issued at the end of a round of negotiations, frequently concocted by officials before the talks have even begun and often deliberately inconclusive.

> Communiqués are like bikinis. What they reveal is alluring, but the essential points remain hidden.
>
> KARL GUNTHER VON HASE (1917–), West German government spokesman, 1967.

communism The ideal of revolution to overthrow CAPITALISM in the interests of the Proletariat, leading to the withering away of the STATE, which Karl MARX set out with Engels in the *Communist Manifesto* of 1848. But also the use (and frequently misuse) of power and the cavalier interpretation of MARXISM-LENINISM by nominally Communist governments from 1917. Either way, it has been one of the great forces of history since the mid-19th century, notably through efforts to implement it in Soviet Russia and its SATELLITES, and in China. Marx himself termed communism "the definitive resolution of the antagonism between man and nature". He and Engels wrote that "the theory of Communism may be summed up in one sentence: Abolish all private property". Its advocates - some of whom later changed their minds - have had other justifications for it: "exploitation of the strong by the weak" - Pierre Joseph Proudhon; "the completion of Socialism" - William Morris; "the more communism, the more civilization" - George Bernard Shaw; "SOVIET power plus the electrification of the whole country" - LENIN; "the logical consequence of Christianity" - Albert Camus.

To some, Communism has appeared the lesser of two evils; in 1949 the Labour MP Tom O'Brien declared that Britons "would rather run the risk of civilising communism than be kicked around by the pot-bellied money magnates of the US". Others have seen its triumph as inevitable, Nikita Khruschev telling Sir William Hayter in 1956: "Every year humanity takes a step towards communism. Maybe not you, but at all events your grandson will surely be a communist." Yet Communism has always had a ruthless, disciplinarian backbone which caused many party loyalists to forfeit their lives in pointless and bloody PURGES. Mao Tse-Tung wrote: "Communism has nothing to do with love. It is an excellent hammer which we use to destroy our enemy." And Khruschev, in his memoirs, wrote:

> We had no use for the teachings of the Gospels, if someone slaps you, turn the other cheek. We had shown that anyone who slapped us on our cheek would get his head kicked off.

The strongest foes of Communism have always been its rivals on the left; as early as 1868 the ANARCHIST Bakunin wrote presciently: "I detest communism because it is the negation of liberty. I am not a communist because communism concentrates and absorbs all the powers of society into the state." Political liberals, too, have detested it, partly because they objected to being tarred with the same brush. Communism has been condemned as "the death of the soul" and "the corruption of a dream of justice" - Adlai Stevenson; "one big phone company" - Lenny Bruce; "successful FASCISM" - Susan Sontag, and "a race in which all the competitors come in first with no prizes" - Lord Inchcape. And James Baldwin wrote of America: "There will never be a communist government in this country, and for this reason. No gospel founded on hate will ever seize the hearts of our people."

The difference between Communism and SOCIALISM has caused many arguments. The left-wing Spanish general José Miaja Menant said: "The socialists talk first, then act. If the communists talk, they do so after acting." And numerous writers have described Communism as "socialism in a hurry". Russian Communism, in its 74 years of power, came in for particularly savage criticism. Half a century before the BOLSHEVIK revolution, Alexander Herzen identified it as "TSARIST autocracy turned upside down"; at its height Clement Attlee termed it "the illegitimate child of Karl Marx and Catherine the Great"; and in its latter days Alexander Solzhenitsyn wrote: "For us in Russia communism is a dead dog, while for people in the West it is still a living lion." Albert Camus wrote: "Fascism represents the exaltation of the execution by the executioner – Russian communism represents the exaltation of the executioner by the victim." Stalin's subject peoples in Eastern Europe were even more caustic; Lech Walesa remarked that "communism has done very much for us – exactly the opposite of what they wanted".

> Like PROHIBITION – it's a good idea but it won't work.
> WILL ROGERS.

> A spectre is haunting Europe, the spectre of communism.
> Opening words of the COMMUNIST MANIFESTO.

> Those who wait for the USSR to reject Communism must wait until a shrimp learns to whistle.
> NIKITA S. KHRUSCHEV (1894–1971).

> Capitalism is the exploitation of man by man. Communism is the reverse.
> Polish joke.

Communism with a human face *See* SOCIALISM.

Goulash Communism The somewhat liberalized communism (though still with rigid police surveillance) which operated in Hungary from the late 1970s under Janos Kadar (1912–89), who had taken office as a hardliner after the crushing of the HUNGARIAN UPRISING. With the benefit of hindsight, it paved the way for the rapid transition to democracy and a market economy which followed Kadar's retirement and death (*see* DEMOCRATIC FORUM), but at the time there was no telling how much relaxation the KREMLIN would tolerate. Khruschev had anticipated the phrase in 1964, saying:

> If we should promise people nothing better than revolution, they would scratch their heads and say: "Isn't it better to have good goulash?"

Suppression of Communism Act The legislation passed by South Africa's National Party government in 1950 to hamper resistance to APARTHEID, enabling it to detain, imprison or exile anyone whose views it found uncomfortable under the pretext that he or she was a Communist. The legislation, later renamed the **Internal Security Act**, drove the Communist Party underground, some of its leaders joining the African National Congress (ANC).

> Christ in this country would most likely have been arrested under the Suppression of Communism Act.
> Archbishop JOOST DE BLANK, 1963.

communist An adherent of Communism, a candidate for preferment (or purging) in a MARXIST-LENINIST state and an object of fear and hatred in America. The revolutionary duty of the Communist fuelled Western distrust; Khruschev said that a Communist had "no right to be a mere onlooker", while Mao Tse-Tung wrote: "We communists are like seeds and the people are like the soil. Wherever we go we must unite with the people, take root and blossom among them." CHURCHILL reckoned that "a communist is like a crocodile; when it opens its mouth you cannot tell whether it is trying to smile or preparing to eat you up", a lesson the Czech democrat Eduard Beneš would have done well to learn; the year before the Communist takeover in Prague, he said naively: "If ever we have trouble with the communists in my country, I pick up that telephone and get on to my friend STALIN." Lyndon B. Johnson could see good reason to declare: "We don't propose to sit here in our rocking chair with our hands folded and let the communists set up any government in the Western hemisphere." Yet Communist intentions and capabilities could both be overestimated; in 1967 Ambassador Edwin O. Reischauer told a Congressional hearing: "Communists are not supermen at all, but men with feet of clay which extend almost all the way up to their brains." Ronald Reagan was even more dismissive, saying: "A communist is someone who has read the works of Marx and Lenin; a capitalist is someone who understands the works of Marx and Lenin." Adherence to Communism, like other left-wing views, is seen by some as a natural phase; Clemenceau is reputed to have said: "My son is 22 years old. If he had not become a communist at 22, I would have disowned him. If he is still a communist at 30, I will do it then." Yet distinctions have always been made between Communists and other left-wingers, the UK Labour leader John Clynes (1869–1949) saying: "A communist is no more a left-wing member of the Labour Party than an atheist is a left-wing member of the Christian church."

One who has nothing, and wishes to share it with the world. ANON.

One cannot be a communist and preserve an iota of one's personal integrity. MILOVAN DJILAS.

If I had to do it again I would not even be a communist, and if Lenin were alive today he would say the same.
Bulgarian ex-president TODOR ZHIVKOV (1911–), 1990.

communist bloc Those countries in Eastern Europe which were occupied by Soviet troops after WORLD WAR II, with the installation of Communist governments, and became SATELLITES of the Soviet Union. The bloc comprised all the signatories of the WARSAW PACT; Yugoslavia was also considered a member at times, despite TITO's disagreements with Stalin. The bloc held together as long as the KREMLIN was ready to use force to maintain it (*see* BREZHNEV DOCTRINE), but it disintegrated in a matter of months in 1989 when it became evident Mikhail Gorbachev was ready to loosen the ties.

Communist Manifesto The 40-page pamphlet written by Marx and Engels, and published in London in 1840, which encapsulated the Marxist analysis of history and set out the case for the "forcible overthrow of all existing social conditions". Though the *Manifesto* was not immediately successful, it was to become the ideological basis of 150 years of Communist activity.

Communist Party of Great Britain (CP for short) Formed in 1920 and disowned by the Labour Party not long after, it was never a mass movement, at most securing two seats in Parliament; it nevertheless exercised considerable influence, notably in the TRADE UNIONS. It suffered a damaging split at the time of the HITLER-STALIN PACT in 1939; that was soon healed when Russia entered the war, but a second wave of defections in 1956 after Soviet troops crushed the HUNGARIAN UPRISING fatally weakened the party and it disintegrated in the late 1980s. The MORNING STAR stuck to the pro-Soviet line as the party flirted with EUROCOMMUNISM, but the newspaper survived the relaunch of the rump of the party in 1991 as the DEMOCRATIC LEFT.

Its relationship to democratic institutions is that of the death watch beetle; it is not a party, it is a conspiracy.
ANEURIN BEVAN.

Communist Party of the Soviet Union (CPSU) The party which presided over 74 years of power following the OCTOBER REVOLUTION, until Boris Yeltsin ordered its dissolution following the KREMLIN COUP of 1991.

The party is the rallying-point for the best elements of the working class. STALIN.

Communist Party of the United States The party formed legally in 1929 after previous legitimate and clandestine parties had fallen foul of both Moscow and the Federal authorities. A MOSCOW-LINE body which never itself gained significant public support, it nevertheless attracted enough FELLOW-TRAVELLERS in the immediate post-war period to pave the way for McCARTHYISM. Harassment of declared Communists culminated in a 1954 Act of Congress which claimed to outlaw the party; this was overthrown by a court decision in 1961, and in 1965 the provisions of the McCARRAN ACT requiring Communists to register was also ruled UNCONSTITUTIONAL. The party resumed overt activity in 1966 and has run Presidential candidates, but their support has been negligible.

community. Community Charge *See* POLL TAX.

community politics The basis for the revival of Britain's LIBERAL PARTY from the 1960s through activism at local government level, with councillors winning and holding seats by concentrating on basic problems affecting the voters. *See also* Pavement POLITICS.

Compact of government The document drawn up by the Pilgrim Fathers aboard the *Mayflower* on 21 November 1620, once it became clear they would make landfall far north of Virginia and outside the jurisdiction of any government. 41 men signed the compact, soon afterward electing Deacon John Carver as governor. The signatories agreed that they

solemnly and mutually in the presence of God and one of another, Covenant and Combine ourselves together into a Civil Body Politic . . . and by virtue hereof to enact, constitute and frame such just and equal laws, as shall be thought most meet and convenient for the general good of the Colony.

Company, the The nickname for the CIA long used by its operatives, which entered the public domain during the VIETNAM WAR.

comparability The question of how, and to what extent, pay for workers in the PUBLIC SECTOR should match that in private industry and commerce. Long a thorny question for governments, it culminated in Britain in the Clegg Commission report in 1979 which recommended "catching-up" pay rises of over 20%. Margaret Thatcher's Conservatives promised to pay whatever the commission recommended, and stuck to their promise even though it proved highly INFLATIONary. Public-sector pay has since been determined by a combination of statutory formulae (the police), advisory review bodies ("top people", the armed forces, doctors and dentists, nurses and teachers) and negotiation limited by strict curbs set on the funds available.

compassion fatigue The phenomenon complained of by both charities and caring politicians, under which the public feels it has simply exhausted its ability to show sympathy for those in the greatest need in the wake of one disaster or tragedy after another.

competition policy A policy designed to remove restrictions on business and create a LEVEL PLAYING FIELD between potential competitors, so that the MARKET may operate fairly. It can also involve the removal of subsidies which give one particular company, or a nation's entire industry, an unfair advantage. Introduction of a competition policy was one of the first steps taken by Margaret Thatcher's UK government, legislation being passed in 1980. The Conservative European COMMISSIONER Sir Leon Brittan (1939–) ran into heavy opposition, particularly from France and Spain, when he started to create a similar policy for the EC in the early 1990s.

composite A MOTION or resolution formed by reconciling a number of others which make much the same point or points in different ways. Composite motions are a particular feature of UK LABOUR PARTY or trade union conferences, the compositing process taking several days before the publication of the final AGENDA; in debate on a major policy issue, there may be three or four composites setting out differing lines of thinking or action, each moved and seconded by the organizations which tabled motions incorporated into that composite.

comprehensivization In Britain, the highly-controversial process, starting in the mid-1960s, under which central government encouraged or acquiesced in the ending of selective education from the age of 11, with all-ability comprehensive schools replacing grammar schools, technical schools and secondary moderns. Parents fought hard to save the grammar schools, where the brighter children were perceived as receiving a better education; rather fewer took up the cudgels for the comprehensives. A quarter of a century on, some grammar schools survive, as does selection by some education authorities. Though comprehensivization is claimed by Comnservatives as a Labour aberration from the "swinging sixties", Margaret Thatcher when Education Secretary 1970–74 is said to have signed the death warrants of more grammar schools than any other minister.

compromise The process of finding a single course of action which advocates of two contradictory policies can both accept, ideally by each giving ground. Burke declared that "all government is founded on compromise and barter", and Speaker Joseph Cannon that "all legislation is the result of compromise"; no wonder Gerald Ford described compromise as "the oil that makes governments go". The West German Chancellor Ludwig Erhard described compromise as "the art of dividing a cake in such a way that everyone believes he has the biggest piece", though G. K. Chesterton observed: "Compromise used to mean that half a loaf was better than no bread. Among modern statesmen it seems to mean that half a loaf is better than a whole loaf." To hardened CONVICTION POLITICIANS, compromise is the ultimate sin. LENIN wrote: "If compromise continues, the revolution disappears," and Golda Meir said of compromise with Arabs pledged to destroy ISRAEL:

> We intend to remain alive. Our neighbours want to see us dead. This is not a question that leaves much room for compromise.

compromise candidate A candidate who has few strong supporters of his or her own but emerges as acceptable to a majority when backers of two or more candidates of equal strength are deadlocked. When the Democrats chose Franklin Pierce (*see* HANDSOME FRANK) as their Presidential nominee after 48 deadlocked ballots, Sen. Stephen Douglas warned: "Hereafter no private citizen is safe."

compromise of 1850 The resolutions put to the US Senate by the ageing Henry Clay on 29 January 1850 to head off the break-up of the UNION; they were enacted that September. Clay appealed to the North and South to pull back from the "edge of the precipice", adding to his argument by brandishing fragments of George WASHINGTON's coffin. His plan involved admitting California as a non-slave state, organizing New Mexico and Utah as TERRITORIES without settling their slave status, settling the dispute over Texas's boundary with neighbouring states and paying the Texas Republic's debts, ending the slave trade in the District of Columbia and enacting a stricter Fugitive Slave Law. The compromise eased the tension for a time, but created strains that broke up the WHIG party in 1852, after which US politics rapidly POLARIZED.

compromise of 1877 The creation by the US Congress of a 15-member commission to adjudicate on the outcome of the 1876 Presidential election, with Democrats agreeing to be in a minority in return for a promise that the Republican Rutherford Hayes, if elected, would end RECONSTRUCTION by pulling Federal troops out of the South. The commission "investigated" alleged vote fraud in three key states, then voted 8 to 7 on straight party lines for Hayes, the apparent loser in the election; he became known as OLD 8 TO 7.

Connecticut compromise *See* CONNECTICUT.
Luxembourg compromise *See* LUXEMBOURG.
Missouri compromise *See* MISSOURI.

comrade The term by which Communists and other members of disciplined left-wing organizations referred to each other; it was also used in some of the more ideological trade unions. In meetings they would refer to each other as Comrade X or Comrade Y. Right-wingers still scornfully refer to the labour movement generally, and the left in particular, as "the comrades".

Comstock Act The legislation passed by Congress in 1873 which made it illegal to send obscene materials through the mail. Anthony Comstock (1844–1915), a lifelong crusader against drink and pornography, formed the New York Society for the Suppression of Vice to campaign for the measure. Once it was passed, he had himself appointed an agent for the US Post Office, and in his first year claimed to have seized 200,000 pictures and photographs, 100,000 books, over 60,000 condoms, 5000 decks of playing cards and 30,000 boxes of aphrodisiacs; much of the material was innocent. Comstock was proud of having hounded 16 people to their deaths through his campaigning.

concede To admit defeat in an election; originally a US term, it is now in general use. A **concession speech** is one in which a candidate formally tells his or her supporters that his or her rival has won.

concentration camps Specially-constructed camps in which POLITICAL PRISONERS or members of a particular ethnic or cultural group are held without trial, with the chance that they may never be released. The term originated during the BOER WAR, when the British held a large number of Afrikaners in such camps. In Germany, NAZI rule from 1933 brought the establishment of camps to detain socialists and communists, and later Jews, gipsies and homosexuals. This did not deter the Roosevelt administration from referring to the RELOCATION CAMPS in which Japanese-Americans were INTERNED after PEARL HARBOR as concentration camps. In WORLD WAR II the Nazi camps at Belsen, Buchenwald, Dachau and Ravensbruck in Germany were augmented by Auschwitz and Treblinka in occupied Poland. The cruelty of the guards, use of slave labour, extreme malnutrition and medical experiments on prisoners made them the most notorious establishments in world history – though in some ways the régime in the Soviet GULAG was as monstrous. The conversion of some into extermination camps in which over 20 million died of disease, starvation and deliberate murder (including 6 million Jews; *see* FINAL SOLUTION) has left an ineradicable stain on world history; the survivors played a major role in the building of the state of Israel and in both post-war reconciliation and perpetuating the memory of the HOLOCAUST. Recent US leaders have found this hard to assimilate; Vice-President George BUSH, visiting Auschwitz in September 1987, did not utter the usual expressions of horror and remorse; instead he declared:

> Boy, they were big on crematoriums, weren't they?

Ronald Reagan, anxious to head off criticism of his visit to the German war cemetery at BITBURG by going to a concentration camp, told Cabinet members: "As horrible as these places were, there were impulses of compassion." His CHIEF OF STAFF Mike Deaver told colleagues: "Oh, Christ, don't let this get out. I can see the headlines now: 'Reagan says concentration camps are hotbeds of humanity!'"

> Camps to turn anti-social members of society into useful members by the most humane means possible.
>
> JOSEF GOEBBELS, 1934.

> The generation of Buchenwald and the Siberian labor camps cannot talk with the same optimism as its fathers.
>
> HENRY KISSINGER.

conchies *See* CONSCIENTIOUS OBJECTORS.

concordat An agreement between a national government and the Vatican under which the Roman Catholic church is given preferential rights and privileges and the status of Catholic education is assured. One such was the LATERAN TREATY between Mussolini and the Church, which secured the Vatican's broad support for the FASCIST regime. The term has come to be used for any solemn and binding agreement between powerful forces; James Callaghan (*see* SUNNY JIM) used it of the formula devised in the autumn of 1964, after the election of Harold Wilson's first government, to define the responsibilities of the Treasury under himself and George BROWN's newly-formed Department of Economic Affairs.

condominium The exercise of sovereignty by two nations jointly over a territory; a prime example was the joint colonial authority exercised over the New Hebrides until the mid-1980s by the UK and France.

Conducator (Romanian. leader) The title bestowed upon himself by Nicolae Ceauşescu (1918–89), the Communist President of Romania from 1967 until his death. Ostensibly at loggerheads with Moscow, Ceauşescu was lionized by Western leaders while pursuing domestic policies of the utmost cruelty and erecting extravagant monuments to his dubious glory. When the anti-Communist tide of 1989 finally reached Romania he was captured despite bitter resistance by the SECURITATE, and with his wife was tried and shot on Christmas Day.

Confederacy The eleven Southern slave states which SECEDED from the United States, starting with South Carolina in December 1860, to form the **Confederate States Of America**, and were re-incorporated in the UNION after suffering defeat in the four-year CIVIL WAR. Created on 4 February 1861 and with a Constitution close to that of the US, its President was Jefferson Davis (1808–89), who declared at his INAUGURATION two weeks later:

> All we ask is to be let alone.

Confederation The creation of the Canadian state under the BRITISH NORTH AMERICA ACT of 1867; Ontario, Quebec and the Maritimes were founder-members, with other provinces free to join. Dr. (later Sir) Charles Tupper, Conservative premier of Nova Scotia, said in 1860 that "Confederation would give us nationality", and his Ontario counterpart John Macdonald: "Instead of looking on us as a merely dependent colony, England will have in us a friendly nation."

> Flora Macdonald [MP for Kingston and later External Affairs Minister] is the finest woman to walk the streets of Kingston since Confederation. JOHN DIEFENBAKER.

Articles of Confederation The instrument drawn up by the second CONTINENTAL CONGRESS in 1781 for the government of the infant America, and which applied until the adoption of the Constitution eight years later. It involved a loose league of independent states, each of which had one vote in a one-house legislature. Despite many shortcomings – Congress could not levy taxes and all 13 states had to agree to any AMENDMENT – this structure held long enough for final victory to be achieved in the Revolutionary War, and for a more ordered system to be created.

New England Confederation The union formed in 1643 by the colonies of Massachusetts Bay, Plymouth, Connecticut and New Haven. Its main purpose was to co-ordinate campaigns against the Indians, but it also had authority over boundary disputes, fugitive criminals and slaves. Though not oustandingly successful, it operated until 1684.

conference (1) The process by which the two Houses of the US Congress resolve their differences over an item of legislation by setting up a committee of MANAGERS representing interested members of both. The resulting panel of **conferees**, often referred to as the **third House of Congress**, may only narrow the differences until a COMPROMISE is reached; it may not add any new material of its own, or in a tax or spending Bill step outside the range of figures in dispute. Its House and Senate members meet separately, deciding by majority vote, until each panel agrees. If they have failed to do so after 20 CALENDAR days, the HOUSE may discharge its conferees and appoint new ones.
(2) A gathering of international leaders or representatives convened to discuss a particular problem or range of problems, in many cases with the hope of arriving at a settlement.

> The conference lasted six weeks. It wasted six weeks. It lasted as long as a carnival, and like a carnival it was an affair of masks and mystification. Our Ministers went to it as men in distressed circumstances got to a place of amusement – to while away the time, with a consciousness of impending failure.
> DISRAELI reporting to the House of Commons in 1864.

> We can lick any nation in the world, but we can't come back from a conference in Costa Rica with our shorts on.
> WILL ROGERS.

(3) In Britain, the annual gatherings, generally by the seaside or in spa towns and lasting most of a week, held by the various political parties. For LABOUR and the LIBERAL DEMOCRATS they are policy-making events at which the leadership can expect a bumpy ride. James Callaghan once remarked that at Labour conferences "policy will be made by those who feel most keenly." CONSERVATIVE conferences are customarily STAGE-MANAGED unless an issue of exceptional divisiveness, like the recognition of UDI in Rhodesia or the MAASTRICHT TREATY, gets out of hand. Tory leaders prior to Margaret Thatcher only appeared at the conference toward the end of the week; CHURCHILL held court at a hotel some distance away before appearing to make the final speech. Arthur BALFOUR once said that he would no more think of taking advice from the Conservative party conference than of taking it from his valet; Denis Thatcher, after his wife's resignation, declared in 1991:

> Thank goodness I won't have to go to that bloody thing this year.

conference season The portion of the British political year from the start of September until the second week of October during which all the parties hold their conferences, and when members of the political media are almost continually on the road. It opens with the Trades Union Congress (TUC), followed after a short gap by the LIBERAL DEMOCRATS, the GREENS and the Scottish National Party (SNP). The LABOUR PARTY customarily holds its conference in either Brighton or Blackpool at the end of September, and the CONSERVATIVES the following week in the resort that did not play host to Labour; each makes occasional detours to Bournemouth.

as I said at the Blackpool conference One of Harold WILSON's favourite phrases, given added currency when repeated by impressionists like Mike Yarwood.

confidence. confidence-building measures Steps to reduce international tension and encourage the confidence of governments in each other's peaceful intentions by such methods as inspection of military facilities and the installation of HOT LINES. In Europe the CSCE has taken a leading part in promoting such steps.

no-confidence motion A motion tabled by opponents or critics of a government which, in the WESTMINSTER SYSTEM, will force the resignation of that government if carried. In the UK House of Commons the traditional wording is "That this House has no confidence in Her/His Majesty's Government". Just such a motion, tabled originally by the SNP, was carried by one vote on 28 March 1979, forcing James Callaghan's Labour government to call an election which it lost. But the passage of no-confidence motions is rare; the instance in 1979 was the first of precisely that kind for over a century.

vote of confidence *See* VOTE.

confidentiality The duty to remain silent about official matters required by both the British and the US governments during the 1980s from present and former employees. In Britain Margaret Thatcher applied it specifically and with enthusiasm to ex-members of the security services after Peter Wright's embarrassing revelations about the activities of MI5 in SPYCATCHER, so that any further disclosures would be punishable. The Reagan administration was more concerned about LEAKS by current officials, and in 1985 prosecuted a PENTAGON official, Samuel Loring Morrison, for passing classified photographs to *Jane's Defence Weekly*. Reagan, also in 1983, attempted to make any book, article or speech by 200,000 present or former government employees subject to "pre-publication review" and make thousands of officials subject to lie-detector tests; after protests in Congress the administration instead made an undertaking to submit to pre-publication review a condition for access to intelligence material.

confirmation The process under which the President's nominee to hold a particular senior political, official or judicial post must be approved by the US SENATE. The ensuing hearings give Senators a chance to expose areas of ignorance, especially among campaign contributors who have been offered ambassadorships, to probe outrageous opinions that may make a candidate unsuitable, or to expose wrongdoing which should disqualify him or her from office. It also gives opponents of the administration an opportunity to weaken the President by rejecting a nominee who may be perfectly well qualified. SENATORIAL COURTESY also requires Senators to block the appointment of anyone to a post in the Home STATE of a Senator who objects to the choice. The process of ADVICE AND CONSENT has torpedoed the careers of several nominees for Cabinet posts, such as Bert LANCE and Sen. John Tower; it has also led to the rejection of several nominees for the Supreme Court (*see* BORK; CARSWELL; HAYNSWORTH) and in 1992 produced the torrid Clarence THOMAS hearings.

> They don't have the guts to say "This guy is a dud because he doesn't agree with us", so they put him through this ritual of being pecked to death by ducks.
>
> Sen. ALAN SIMPSON on the Senate Judiciary Committee's rejection of William Bradford Reynolds as associate Attorney-General, 1985.

confrontational politics or style The search by a leader or party for "enemies" to take on and crush in order to reinforce their own political standing, as opposed to a desire to govern without unnecessary conflict. The term was widely used of Margaret Thatcher (*see* IRON LADY), who was perceived as regularly needing foes to take on, engage in a gargantuan struggle and then humiliate; the FALKLANDS WAR and the 1984–85 MINERS' STRIKE gave her two such adversaries in General Galtieri and Arthur Scargill (*see* KING ARTHUR), and the rest of Europe and the trade unions generally were always fair game.

Congress (1) The collective term for the two houses of the LEGISLATURE of the United States: the HOUSE OF REPRESENTATIVES (for which alone the term is sometimes used) and the SENATE. It met in 1789–90 in New York, and from 1790 until 1800 in Philadelphia before moving to Washington and the first completed portions of the CAPITOL. Congress has played its full part in governing the country, being in Woodrow WILSON's words "the country in miniature". Yet, possibly for that reason, it has also attracted savage criticism and a rich vein of ridicule both from its own members and from outside observers. Will Rogers cracked: "Every time they make a joke it's a law. And every time they make a law it's a joke." Harry S Truman reminisced:

> When I came to Washington, for the first six months I wondered how the hell I ever got here. For the next six months I wondered how the hell the rest of them ever got here.

And much more recently Sen. Alan Simpson conceded: "The reputation of the Congress is lower than quail crap."

Members of Congress have long defended their right to say and do exactly what they like. Davy Crockett, when he arrived in the House, declared:

> I am now here in Congress . . . I am at liberty to vote as my conscience and judgment dictate to be right, without the yoke of any party on me, or the driver at my heels, whip in hand, commanding me to go ge-wo-haw, just at his pleasure.

And in the 1970s Rep. William Ford put it another way:

> A person has a constitutional right, when elected to Congress, to be a damn fool and act like one.

But the overriding imperative is to make sure the current TERM is followed by at least one more; as Rep. Frank E. Smith put it,

> All members of Congress have a primary interest in being re-elected. Some members have no other interest.

The effects of Congressional decisions on the people are hard to assess, but their impact on the WHITE HOUSE is great and immediate. This was established by the late 19th century when Thaddeus Stevens explained:

> Though the President is COMMANDER-IN-CHIEF, Congress is his commander and, God willing, he shall obey.

And in modern times the POLLSTER Louis Harris concluded that "the more Congress stands up to the President, the more people like it". Such pressures led Theodore Roosevelt to exclaim:

> Oh, Lord, if only I could be President and Congress too for just ten minutes!

President Eisenhower said in exasperation: "I simply will not have those monkeys telling us what we can and cannot do", but Ronald Reagan thought he had the answer, saying:

> It isn't necessary to make the Congress see the light – make them feel the heat.

His solution was simple: "We can lecture our children about extravagance until we run out of voice and breath. Or we can cure their extravagance by simply reducing their allowance."

Eisenhower's assessment of members' individual quality has been shared by many others. Rep. Sam Steiger conceded that "there are members of Congress you wouldn't hire to wheel a wheelbarrow". J. Peter Grace of Reagan's cost-cutting panel stated baldly: "Two thirds of them are clowns." And Reagan himself once commented:

> If Congress wants to bring the Panamanian economy to its knees, why doesn't it just go down there and run the country?

Plenty has also been said about the probity of members of Congress. Mark Twain observed:

> There is no distinctly native American criminal class except Congress.

Rep. Adam Clayton POWELL, condemning his own exclusion, said: "There is no one here who does not have a skeleton in his closet", while Jack Newfield damningly observed:

> The arrest rate for members of the 95th Congress was higher than the arrest rate among unemployed Black males in Detroit.

Those who have watched debates in Congress have been more concerned about their prolixity; Woodrow WILSON defensively explained that "Congress in session is Congress on public exhibition, while Congress in its committee rooms is Congress at work", and this is by and large true. Boris Marshalov, a Russian visiting the House in the 1930s, observed:

> Congress is so strange. A man gets up to speak and says nothing. Nobody listens – then everybody disagrees.

Speaker Thomas Reed regretted that "they never open their mouths without subtracting from the sum of human knowledge", and Raymond Clapper commented: "What you hear in Congress is 99 per cent tripe, ignorance or demagoguery." However Speaker Sam RAYBURN maintained:

> Too many critics mistake the deliberations of the Congress for its decisions.

At the very outset, Thomas JEFFERSON lamented: "When Congress will rise no mortal can tell, not from the quantity but the dilatoriness of its business," and the reason was apparent, Benjamin FRANKLIN explaining: "Their nature, by training, is to argue and procrastinate – yet we persist in electing lawyers to Congress." John ADAMS reputedly observed that "one useless man is called a disgrace, two are called a law firm and three or more become a Congress", and in the mid-20th century Ralph Nader commented:

> Almost half the Congress is composed of lawyers, who make up less than one-third of one per cent of the population. Blue-collar workers may get to Congress, but usually as tourists passing through the guided tours.

A body of men who meet to repeal laws. AMBROSE BIERCE.

For the most part illiterate hacks whose fancy vests are spotted with gravy and whose speeches, hypocritical, unctuous and slovenly, are spotted also with the gravy of political patronage. MARY McCARTHY.

Usually only scandal, longevity or death distinguishes a member from the pack. MARY McGRORY.

The Congress does not like to take responsibility. And after it has taken an important action, it usually likes to take a rest. ELIZABETH DREW.

The last plantation. Sen. JOHN GLENN.

The term "a Congress" is used for the body that assembles on the 3 January after each biennial election of members to the House, and sits for the ensuing two years. Each is known by a number, the Congress elected in 1992 being the 103rd Congress.

> I've never seen a Congress yet that didn't eventually take the measure of the President it was dealing with.
> LYNDON B. JOHNSON.

Congress shall make no law . . . The opening phrase of the FIRST AMENDMENT to the US Constitution which guarantees FREEDOM of religion and OF THE PRESS.
billion-dollar Congress The 52nd Congress which in 1891–92 appropriated the first ever peacetime billion-dollar budget, at the urging of President Benjamin Harrison who was promoting development at home with naval and mercantile expansion. When critics used the term derogatorily, Speaker Thomas Reed (*see* CZAR) responded: "This is a billion-dollar country."
Continental Congress *See* CONTINENTAL.
do-nothing Congress The phrase which President Truman, staring apparent defeat in the face, pinned on his opponents on Capitol Hill in the 1948 election campaign. During his frenetic WHISTLE-STOP tour, GIVE 'EM HELL HARRY told crowds across the country:

> That notorious do-nothing Republican 80th Congress has stuck a pitchfork in the farmer's back. . . . These Republican gluttons of privilege want a return of the Wall Street dictatorship. Your typical Republican reactionary is a very shrewd man with a calculating machine where his heart should be.

Library of Congress The greatest repository of knowledge in Washington, if not in America, it has developed from Congress's own source of reference to a national library sited since 1897 in its own building a stone's throw from the EAST FRONT of the CAPITOL. Congress in 1800 appropriated $5000 for "such books as may be necessary", but they were used for kindling by British troops when they burned the Capitol in 1814. The following year Thomas JEFFERSON sold to Congress his own library which he said contained no "branch of science which Congress would wish to exclude from their collections; there is, in fact, no subject to which a Member of Congress may not have occasion to refer". After the CIVIL WAR the Library expanded rapidly, outstripping its quarters in the Capitol, and in 1886 Congress appropriated funds for a new building.
Radical Congress The Congress elected in 1866 which advocated an aggressive process of RECONSTRUCTION, came within a whisker of IMPEACHing President Andrew Johnson and tried to prosecute CONFEDERATE leaders under the FOURTEENTH AMENDMENT.
Sense of Congress resolution A resolution passed by either or both of the Houses of Congress which expresses an opinion or asserts the desirability of a particular course of action, but is of no legal force because the matter in question requires either detailed legislation or action by the President.
Congressional Budget Office *See* BUDGET.
Congressional Club The principal fund-raising mechanism that enabled the ultra-Conservative Republican Sen. Jesse Helms (1921–) to secure re-election in North Carolina time after time and to promote candidates and right-wing causes that he favoured. His campaign in 1984, costing $16.4 million, was at the time the most expensive ever for the Senate; it led Sen. Howard Baker to call Helms "the Nelson Rockefeller of political fund-raising". Helms and his Senate backers were felt by some to have taken a needlessly CONFRONTATIONAL line on minor issues in order to keep up the temperature so that funds continue to flow into the Club from their right-wing supporters.
Congressional government Woodrow WILSON's expression for the dominance that Congress is able to exercise over the WHITE HOUSE in peacetime, compared with the extra power the President can exert in time of war.
Congressional investigations The inquiries set up by committees of Congress into everything from alleged racketeering in labour unions and overcharging by defense contractors to the McCARTHYITE probes after World War II into alleged Communist infiltration of the State Department and motion picture industry. Woodrow Wilson termed the bodies launching such probes "smelling committees".

> A legalized atrocity where Congressmen, deprived of their legitimate food for thought, go on a wild and feverish man-hunt, and do not stop at cannibalism.
> WALTER LIPPMANN.

Congressional liaison The efforts made by every WHITE HOUSE to build Congressional support for the President and his policies. Some Presidents, notably Lyndon Johnson, have been conspicuously successful; others, notably Jimmy CARTER, have struggled. The Washington observer and liberal Democrat Mark Green termed the procedure "LOBBYING by the executive".
Congressional Medal of Honor The popular term for the medal awarded by the President "in the name of the Congress of the United States" to Americans who have given outstanding service to the nation. It was authorized by Congress in 1862 for Union enlisted men who showed bravery in CIVIL

WAR engagements. In 1863 Secretary of War Edwin Stanton approved awards to all 300 men of the 27th Maine Regiment who re-enlisted, but it has since been given more sparingly. Harry S. Truman said at a presentation of the medal to 14 service personnel in October 1945:

> I would rather have that medal than be President of the United States.

But when offered it 20 years later, he turned it down, saying he had done nothing to merit it.

Congressional oversight *See* OVERSIGHT.

Congressional Quarterly The prestigious journal, now a weekly, that recounts and analyses the actions and performance of Congress and its members; it can be found in Congressional, government, LOBBYISTs' and media offices throughout Washington, and much further afield. Founded in 1945 by Henrietta and Nelson Poynter, editor and publisher of the *St. Petersburg*, Florida *Times*, it soon became and has remained a Washington fixture, not least because of its success in fighting off any rival. **CQ**, as it is known, comprises a weekly report mailed to subscribers every Saturday, and an annual Almanac covering the legislative year; it is also a publishing house producing books in many fields of politics and public policy.

Congressional Record The official record of proceedings in both Houses of Congress, and of the state of BILLs in progress. First published in 1883 and a successor to earlier freelance publications, it has a daily paperback circulation of over 30,000 and is also bound annually in hardback. As well as verbatim reports of debates it includes in its back section, which is often two-thirds of the whole, extraneous material of CONSTITUENCY interest – even poetry and recipes – inserted by Members; Speaker Champ Clark reckoned that while it was undesirable to have such items appearing in the Record, it was better than having to listen to them. Once **read into the Record**, copies could then be circulated to constituents at the taxpayers' expense. Nowadays anything not actually said by a member is marked with a BULLET. Until 1978 Congressmen could also insert into the record speeches they had not delivered; under the PRIVILEGE TO REVISE AND EXTEND they can still massage those actually made before they appear in print.

> More a work of fiction than one of fact.
>
> Sen. SAM ERVIN.

Congressman A member of the US HOUSE OF REPRESENTATIVES. Although the two Houses are equal in status, Congressmen are generally accorded less respect and media interest than Senators. Rep. Clem Miller once said that "to the congressman, publicity is his lifeblood", but Max Ways was largely correct when he wrote in *Fortune*: "Journalists who will risk life and limb to find out what the President had for breakfast wouldn't walk around the corner to hear a Congressman deliver a reasoned explanation of his vote." And when a temporary stenographer asked: "Is there anything lower [in precedence] than a Congressman?", Rep. Otha Wearin told her: "If you read my mail long enough you'll find out there probably isn't." The tone was set long ago; in 1869 a Cabinet officer (probably Interior Secretary Jacob Dolson Cox) told Henry Adams:

> You can't use tact with a Congressman. A Congressman is a hog – you must take a stick and hit him on the snout.

This prompted Adams to ask: "If a Congressman is a hog, what is a Senator?" Despite the lack of public and media respect, Rep. Otis Pike could fairly assert that "Congressmen are treated, in Washington at least, like little tin Jesuses". Will Rogers joked that "it is not the original investment in the Congressman that counts – it is the upkeep", and plenty of opportunities for GRAFT exist – some being taken. Mark Twain declared that "to my mind Judas Iscariot was nothing but a low, mean, premature Congressman", and the controversial lobbyist Paula Parkinson said of Congressmen in the mid-1980s: "Only 15 per cent of them are genuine." Yet the bulk are honest and conscientious, their performance tempered largely by the requirement to get re-elected every two years. This long ago produced the observation from Speaker Joe Cannon (*see* FOUL-MOUTHED JOE):

> Some Congressmen keep their ears so close to the ground that they can get both ears on the ground. Only two other animals can do that – a donkey and a jack rabbit.

> I have tried to live my life so that I will never become a Congressman.
>
> WILL ROGERS.

Congressperson The term for a female member of Congress introduced by the feminist Rep. Bella Abzug, a New York Democrat who served 1970–76.

Congress (2) A conference, either of an organization, such as Britain's annual Trades Union Congress (*see* TUC) or of national representatives, for example the 1948 **Congress of Europe** in the Hague, chaired by CHURCHILL, which paved the way for western European union, and the 1815 **Congress of Vienna** which determined the future of Europe after the final defeat of Napoleon.

Congress of People's Deputies The popularly-elected body established in the SOVIET UNION in the late 1980s under the reform programme of Mikhail Gorbachev, which survived after 1991 – still with its largely ex-Communist membership – as the national assembly of the Russian republic.

Congress Party The movement founded in 1885 which, led by MAHATMA Gandhi and Jawaharlal Nehru, led former British India to independence in 1948, though with Pakistan splintering away in the process. Under first Nehru and then his family's NEHRU DYNASTY it became India's dominant party after Independence, surviving factional splits to govern as the Congress (I) Party and first losing power only in 1979.

Coningsby Benjamin Disraeli's most successful novel, which sold 50,000 copies in America alone. First published in 1844, the future Conservative leader said that he wrote it "to vindicate the just claims of the Tory party to be the popular political confederation of the country", but it was also a satire on PEEL. Apart from the book's hero Henry Coningsby, a model for YOUNG ENGLAND, Disraeli (*see* DIZZY) introduced Tadpole and Taper, two of his most memorable characters.

Connecticut compromise The compromise accepted by the PHILADELPHIA CONVENTION in July 1787, under which seats in the House of Representatives were to be allocated by population, and in the Senate equally for each State. To placate the larger States, the power to introduce MONEY BILLS was restricted to the House of Representatives.

conquer. Conquer or die! The general order issued by George WASHINGTON to America's revolutionary army on 2 July 1776, as INDEPENDENCE was declared. He told his troops:

> The time is now near at hand which must probably determine: whether Americans are to be Freemen or Slaves; whether they are to have any property they can call their own; whether their Houses, and Farms, are to be pillaged and destroyed, and they consigned to a State of Wretchedness from which no human efforts will probably deliver them. The fate of unborn Millions now depend, under God, on the Courage and Conduct of this army – Our cruel and unrelenting Enemy leaves us no choice but a brave resistance, or the most abject submission; that is all we can expect – We have therefore to resolve to conquer or die.

conquered provinces theory The argument advanced during the US CIVIL WAR by leading Republicans including Sen. Benjamin Wade and Rep. Thaddeus Stevens, that by having engaged in the "crime" of SECESSION, the southern States had placed themselves outside the protection of the Constitution and must after the war be treated as "conquered provinces" which Congress had the power to govern. Abraham LINCOLN insisted that as the right to secede did not exist, the Confederate states had never left the Union. In December 1863 he put forward a plan for RECONSTRUCTION that would help all but the most intractable Confederates to resume their place in the Union. However after Lincoln's assassination the conquered provinces theory reappeared in Congress's own aggressive Reconstruction programme.

conscience The still, small voice for right which speaks within every human and which troubles most politicians, who find decisions confronting them that conflict with their conscience. The CBS commentator Elmer Davis once reported:

> Senator H. Alexander Smith of New Jersey spent the day wrestling with his conscience. He won.

conscience clause The provision invoked by Labour MPs at Westminster when they break with the PARTY LINE on a matter on which they feel strongly, and where they reckon an issue of conscience is involved. It was cited particularly by left-wingers voting against the DEFENCE ESTIMATES because of their opposition to nuclear weapons. The party leadership has long insisted, however, that while the WHIPS are tolerant on genuine issues of conscience, no such clause exists in any party code.

prisoner of conscience A POLITICAL PRISONER detained solely because of his or her opinions, with no suggestion that they have indulged in violent or subversive activity. This has not prevented some convicted TERRORISTS claiming to be prisoners of conscience.

conscientious objector A person who refuses to join the armed forces because their conscience prevents them from killing. Both Britain and America behaved harshly toward CONCHIES in World War I; President WILSON recognized the right of men to object to military service on non-religious grounds in March 1918. He also saved the life of Pvt. Richard Stierheim, sentenced to be shot after deserting three times in France because he refused to kill; Stierheim's sentence was commuted because of his heroism in saving wounded colleagues under fire. In WORLD WAR II the Allies took a more sympathetic line, providing a variety of forms of alternative war service for those with genuine objections. The VIETNAM WAR produced both conscientious objectors, and DRAFT-DODGING on a massive scale.

> War will exist until that distant day when the conscientious objector enjoys the same reputation and prestige as the warrior does today. JOHN F. KENNEDY.

conscription The compulsory recruitment of individuals for military service, practised by most countries in time of war and by many in Europe, for a limited period, in peacetime. The decision by government to conscript, or DRAFT, young men in wartime has frequently provoked political controversy, notably in

America during the VIETNAM WAR and in French-speaking Canada both in World War I and in 1944 when Mackenzie King finally ran out of troops and was forced to send conscripts to Europe.

> How many French soldiers, or even British soldiers, would they send to America if Canada was attacked by the United States?
> HENRY BOURASSA, *Le Devoir* (Montreal), 1916.

consensus Those points of coincident rather than negotiated agreement between parties which a **consensus politician** will work to develop as a basis for action and support, and a CONFRONTATIONAL politician will shy away from. In the UK consensus politics reached their height in BUTSKELLISM but lingered until their repudiation by Margaret Thatcher. *See also* BIPARTISANSHIP.

> A consensus politician is someone who does something he doesn't believe is right because it keeps people quiet.
> JOHN MAJOR, 4 January 1991.

> When a line of action is said to be supported by "all responsible men", it is nearly always dangerous or foolish.
> HAROLD MACMILLAN.

> If you can find something everyone agrees on, it's wrong.
> Rep. MAURICE UDALL.

conservative A traditionalist who opposes change that he or she sees as destabilizing, who disapproves of State intervention in the economy but believes it should set and enforce moral standards. In America the term does not necessarily imply party affiliation; many conservative Democrats are well to the right of liberal Republicans. Franklin D. Roosevelt defined a conservative as "a man with two perfectly good legs who has never learned to walk", Woodrow WILSON as "a man who just sits and thinks, mostly sits", Eibert Hubbard as "a man who is too cowardly to fight and too fat to run", Frank Vanderlip as "a man who thinks nothing new ought to be adopted for the first time", Mort Sahl as "someone who believes in reform, but not now", William F. Buckley as "a fellow who is standing athwart history yelling 'Stop!'", and Philadelphia's Mayor Frank Rizzo as "a liberal who got mugged the night before".

> When a nation's young men are conservative, its funeral bell is already rung. HENRY WARD BEECHER (1813–87).

> Some fellows get credit for being conservatives when they are only stupid. KIN HUBBARD (1868–1930).

In Britain, the word conservative has been almost coterminous with the party of that name.

While there have been exceptions, conservatives and radicals are usually considered opposites. Ralph Waldo Emerson wrote:

> Men are conservatives after dinner, or before taking their rest; when they are sick, or aged. In the morning, or when their intellect or their conscience has been aroused; when they hear music, or when they read poetry, they are radicals.

However Woodrow Wilson reckoned that "the most conservative persons I have ever met are college undergraduates. The radicals are men past middle life." The comparison in the British political world is as often with socialists. The Australian Prime Minister Robert Menzies (*see* MING) once told Britain's Labour ex-Chancellor Hugh Dalton: "You are a most extraordinary phenomenon, a Socialist with wit." Dalton replied: "You are a more extraordinary phenomenon still, a Conservative with intelligence."

Conservative Party (1) The party of the traditionalist right in Great Britain (it has only organized in Northern Ireland since the late 1980s) which since the 1920s has alternated with Labour; it stands for the monarchy, law and order and Free ENTERPRISE with a minimum of state interference in business. The name "Conservative" was first used in 1830 by John Wilson Croker (1780–1857); he wrote in the *Quarterly Review*:

> We now are, as we always have been, decidedly and conscientiously attached to what is called the TORY, and which might with more propriety be called the Conservative, party.

Based on the legacy of such Tory statesmen as BURKE, PEEL and Disraeli (*see* DIZZY), despite his early claim that "a Conservative government is an organised hypocrisy", it has in the 20th century generally championed evolutionary rather than revolutionary change: reform where necessary, but always within the existing framework of the state and society. The eleven-year premiership of Margaret Thatcher (*see* IRON LADY) was an exception, with an aggressive and CONFRONTATIONAL radical programme being pursued. The traditional Conservative stance makes the party attractive not only to those content with the existing order but to those suspicious or afraid of the more radical policies of its opponents (until the 1920s the LIBERAL PARTY, since then LABOUR). Though primarily a middle-class organization, the modern Conservative Party has always enjoyed considerable working-class support. Often it has vigorously opposed change only to accept it once enacted by others, a phenomenon Mrs. Thatcher scorned as the RATCHET EFFECT. Examples include the PEOPLE'S BUDGET (1909), the curtailment of the power of the House of Lords (1911), the WELFARE STATE (1945–48) and the independence of India (1947). The party has always enjoyed the backing of the landowning aristocracy and of successful businessmen, but during the 20th century the balance has tipped firmly to the latter.

Since the 1950s its leaders have ceased to be Old Etonians like Harold Macmillan (*see* SUPERMAC) and SIR ALEC Douglas-Home, the firmly middle-class Edward Heath (*see* GROCER), Margaret Thatcher and John MAJOR reflecting a shift from the party of estate owners to the party of estate agents. When Douglas Hurd was criticized for being an Old Etonian during the 1990 leadership contest the change was confirmed; Hurd himself exploded: "I thought I was running to be leader of the Conservative Party, not some demented Marxist outfit." Up to 1963 the party's leader "emerged" (*see* MAGIC CIRCLE); since then he or she has been elected; the Party Chairman who controls Conservative CENTRAL OFFICE is an appointee of the leader. The heart of the party lies in the constituencies, internal party affairs being decided by the NATIONAL UNION.

The rise of Labour after World War I could have overwhelmed the Conservatives as well as the Liberals, but for two factors: the enfranchisement of women which swelled the Tory vote at a critical time, and the defection of frightened Liberal voters to the Conservatives. This shift added the middle-class liberal commitment to personal freedom and equal opportunity to the traditional Tory virtues of maintaining the social system at home and the Empire abroad. An inter-war Tory supremacy eventually emerged from the husk of the NATIONAL GOVERNMENT, under BALDWIN and then CHAMBERLAIN, before World War II brought a return to COALITION government under CHURCHILL, whose relations with the party he had left and rejoined were seldom good. At the close of World War II the Conservatives were routed in a Labour landslide reflecting a desire for social change; in opposition they regrouped, accepting many of Labour's changes and paving the way for a bout of moderate BUTSKELLISM when Churchill returned to power in 1951. Post-war prosperity helped the Tories increase their majority under EDEN in 1955 and, despite the trauma of SUEZ, under Macmillan in 1959 (*see* YOU'VE NEVER HAD IT SO GOOD). Then the tide turned, working-class voters moving away as the economy faltered, and the PROFUMO AFFAIR and other scandals making the Tory government look tired after what a revived and reunified Labour Party called THIRTEEN WASTED YEARS. Douglas-Home just failed to hold on at the 1964 election, and eighteen months later the party, now under Heath, went down to a heavy defeat. In 1970, however, Heath pulled off a shock win in an election Harold WILSON seemed set to win easily. He went on to succeed where Macmillan failed and take Britain into the EUROPEAN COMMUNITY, before being brought down by the MINERS' STRIKE of 1974. Heath lost his majority in February, and went down to a narrow but outright defeat by Wilson in October, and the following February Mrs. Thatcher ousted Heath as leader. She shifted the party immediately to the Right, and after a nail-biting four years finally forced an election by defeating Labour in a no-CONFIDENCE vote in March 1979. Two months later Mrs. Thatcher was in Downing Street and the party began a lengthy term in office, winning landslide victories over Labour in 1983 and 1987 while the Thatcher government pressed ahead with trade union reform, PRIVATIZATION and radical change to every aspect of society, winning the FALKLANDS WAR and crushing the miners in the process; the Thatcher agenda – minus the hated POLL TAX – was continued in a minor key by John Major, who succeeded her when Tory MPs turned against her in 1990 and won a 21-seat majority in April 1992, despite a deep RECESSION. One legacy of Mrs. Thatcher was a deep split in the party on Europe, which caused Major considerable trouble over ratifying the MAASTRICHT TREATY.

The Conservatives' opponents have had plenty to say about them: J. S. Mill branded them as "by the law of their existence the stupidest party", the left-wing Labour MP Eric Heffer as "a load of kippers – two-faced with no guts", and an unsourced car sticker *c.* 1983 as "the cream of Britain – thick, rich and full of clots". *See also* TORY.

> The trade union for the nation as a whole.
>
> EDWARD HEATH.

> Like a bird, it has a right wing and a left wing, but its brains are in the middle. ANON. Conservative MP.

> The only thing wrong with the Tory party is the people who are in it. JOHN LYDON.

> Conservatives do not worship democracy. For them majority rule is a device. Sir IAN GILMOUR.

(2) The centre-right party, also known since 1942 as the PROGRESSIVE CONSERVATIVES, that has alternated with the LIBERALS as the government of Canada since the early days of CONFEDERATION. The party of MacDonald, Borden, Bennett and DIEFenbaker, it took power most recently in 1984 when Brian Mulroney (1939–) ousted Pierre TRUDEAU's Liberals, remaining in office after a change of leader in 1993. It has traditionally supported the COMMONWEALTH, a favourable climate for business, and close ties with America including FREE TRADE (*see* NAFTA).

> The day the Canadian Pacific busts, the Conservative Party busts the day after.
>
> JOHN HENRY POPE (1824–89).

Conservative Party at prayer A commonly-used term for the Church of England with its ESTABLISHMENT image, originating in a speech in 1917 by a Congregational minister Agnes Maude Royden (1887–1967), when she said:

> The Church should no longer be satisfied to represent only the Conservative Party at prayer.

Life's better under the Conservatives – Don't let Labour ruin it! The slogan with which Harold Macmillan (*see* SUPERMAC) won a landslide victory for the Conservatives in the 1959 general election. *See also* YOU'VE NEVER HAD IT SO GOOD.

conservatism The philosophy of conservatives, also a term for fiscal caution. Abraham LINCOLN termed it "adherence to the old and tried against the new and untried", Benjamin Disraeli "an unhappy crossbreed, the mule of politics that engenders nothing", Gladstone "distrust of the people tempered by fear", Thorstein Veblen "the maintenance of conventions already in force" – and William F. Buckley Jr. "the politics of reality". Thomas Arnold maintained that "conservatism destroys what it loves, because it will not mend it", Disraeli that it "discards prescription, shrinks from principle, disavows progress, having rejected all respect for antiquity, it offers no redress for the present and makes no preparation for the future".

> Conservatism, I believe, is mainly due to want of imagination. GRANT ALLEN (1848–99).

> Conservatism goes for comfort, reform for truth.
> RALPH WALDO EMERSON.

> What brought conservatism into existence was the French revolution. LORD HUGH CECIL, *Conservatism* (1912).

Consolidated Fund Bill At Westminster, the Bills introduced three times a year to give statutory confirmation to Parliament's granting of money to the Government. The final Consolidated Fund Bill of the year becomes the APPROPRIATION Act. The procedure for debating such Bills allows MPs to stay up all night debating a series of topics of their own choice; until the late 1980s it was possible to prolong debate and wipe out the next day's business.

consolidation (1) The passage of a Bill to re-enact in simpler and coherent form the surviving sections of a number of long-standing Acts of Parliament on one subject, other parts of which have been repealed. *See also* CODIFICATION. (2) The underpinning of political gains recently made, instead of pressing ahead with further radical initiatives. After 1948 Herbert Morrison persuaded ATTLEE's Labour Cabinet to pause after its first burst of NATIONALIZATION – the Bank of England, coal, electricity, gas and the railways – instead of pressing ahead with further acquisitions, as left-wing MPs wanted. And in 1986 John Biffen angered Margaret Thatcher by calling for "consolidation" of the social changes already pushed through by her government, rather than embarking on a fresh burst of radical measures; she went ahead regardless and the following year dropped Biffen from her Cabinet.

conspiracy theorist Someone who believes that almost any event in politics is the result of some deep-seated conspiracy by dark and sinister forces, in preference to accepting the simple explanation on offer. Sometimes the conspiracy theorists are right – the problem is that the public seldom finds out the truth. The greatest number of conspiracy theories have attached to the shooting of President KENNEDY, with the WARREN COMMISSION's conclusion that Lee Harvey Oswald killed him and was the sole assassin still vigorously contested. The sinking of the BELGRANO comes a close second.

constituency (1) The section of the population from whom a politician or movement draws their support or to which it will appeal. (2) The geographical area whose inhabitants elect a member to the Westminster Parliament.

constituents Those who reside in the area represented by a member of a legislature, regardless of whether they voted for him or her – or indeed at all. When in the 18th century Alderman Sawbridge of Billingsgate – an area renowned for coarse language – delivered an unusually blunt speech, Lord North declared:

> The Honourable Gentleman speaks not only the sentiments but the very language of his constituents.

There was a time when constituents could be dismissed, Sir Henry Campbell-Bannerman (*see* C-B) saying after one speech to his:

> I had nothing to say to my constituents on Friday, and I think I effectively said it.

And when a horde of new Labour MPs arrived at Westminster after the LANDSLIDE of 1945, one old Tory hand declared:

> Who the hell are these people? They look like a lot of damned constituents.

Members of the US Congress have many more constituents each, and are expected to do more for them (*see* WHAT HAVE YOU DONE FOR ME LATELY?). Rep. Joseph Bryns Jr., a Tennessee Democrat, was unseated in 1940 after saying he "wouldn't come home to shake hands with the clodhoppers"; "Clodhopper Clubs" backing an Independent opponent sprang up all over the district. Much of the contact is maintained through vast amounts of mail under the FRANKING PRIVILEGE; Rep. John Dowdy made the headlines when a constituent in east Texas who had shotgunned his wife and said he was glad he did it received a condolence card from the Congressman in prison. Rep. William Ayres also used to send out condolences to the bereaved in his Akron district until he got a letter reading:

> I received your letter expressing sympathy concerning the passing of my late husband. If you have known how mean that SOB was to me you would have sent me a letter congratulating me on being rid of the bastard.

Increasing ease of travel has meant that mail is no longer the only contact between members of Congress and constituents, with more and more turning up in Washington. Rep. Morris Udall lamented:

> The jet plane wrecked everything. It used to be when a constituent came in, it was a big deal.

Replies to idiotic constituents have created a rich vein of humour, whether or not the recipients have appreciated the joke. One Congressman received a letter from a man threatening to emigrate to Canada if he voted a particular way; he simply wrote back: "Bon Voyage!" And just before World War II Rep. Stephen McGroarty reputedly blew his top with one constituent impatient for action, writing:

> One of the countless drawbacks of being in Congress is that I am compelled to receive impertinent letters from a jackass like you in which you say I promised to have the Sierra Madre mountains reforested and I have been in Congress two months and haven't done it. Will you please take two running jumps and go to Hell.

When the President of Pakistan presented a thoroughbred horse to Jacqueline Kennedy (*see* JACKIE O) and the US Air Force flew it to her free, Sen. Stephen Young of Ohio got an enraged letter from a constituent demanding a horse for himself, delivered in the same way. He wrote back:

> I am wondering why you should need a horse when there is already a jackass at your address.

There is also an all-purpose reply used on both sides of the Atlantic to "nut letters", which are often closely written in green ink on both sides of the paper or typed single-space with comments scrawled in the margins. It reads:

> I feel I should let you know that a lunatic has stolen your headed notepaper.

Back in 1744 the British MP Anthony Henley, urged by constituents to oppose the Excise Bill, wrote back:

> May your houses be as open and common to all excise officers, as your wives and daughters were to me when I stood for your rascally Corporation.

Edmund BURKE, standing firm against voters in his Bristol constituency, told them:

> I did not obey your instructions. No, I conformed to the instructions of truth and nature, and maintained your interest, against your opinions.

In 1906 the humorist and Liberal MP Hilaire Belloc told constituents in Manchester who complained that he was a Catholic:

> If you reject me on account of my religion, I shall thank God that he has spared me the indignity of being your representative.

But sometimes the constituents get the last laugh. One ten-year-old boy asked the Labour MP John Evans:

> Did you used to have a proper job before you came here?

See also HORSEFACE.

constitution The rules under which a country is governed, either written as with the Constitution of the United States, or unwritten as with the "British Constitution", which is based on a combination of legislation, Common Law and accepted tradition.

The Constitution of the United States, devised at the PHILADELPHIA CONVENTION of 1787 and which took effect on 4 March 1789, is described in its own Article VI as "the supreme law of the land . . . any thing in the Constitution or laws of any State notwithstanding". The process of drafting it carried severe risks, John JAY pointing out that

> The Americans are the first people whom Heaven has favored with the opportunity of deliberating upon, and choosing, the forms of government under which they shall live.

Benjamin FRANKLIN left the Convention fearing the document was not perfect:

> I confess that there are several parts of this Constitution which I do not at present approve, but I am not sure I shall never approve them.

At the same time he professed astonishment that so diverse an assembly should have devised "this system approaching so near to perfection as it does". Yet Alexander HAMILTON insisted that "the system is the best that the present views and circumstances of the country will permit", and George WASHINGTON warned:

> Should the states reject this excellent constitution, the probability is, an opportunity will never again offer to cancel another in peace – the next will be drawn in blood.

Moreover James MADISON foresaw that America's constitution had the potential to be a blueprint for others throughout the world. He wrote:

> The free system of government we have established is so congenial with reason, with common sense, and with a

universal feeling, that it must produce approbation and a desire of imitation.

The Constitution has stood the test of time – which would not have surprised Wendell Phillips as he claimed that "all that is valuable in the United States Constitution is a thousand years old". Americans' reluctance to tamper with it is explained by Andrew Jackson's assertion that "perpetuity is stamped upon the Constitution by the blood of our fathers". Abraham LINCOLN warned against radical changes to it, saying:

Don't interfere with anything in the Constitution. That must be maintained, for it is the only safeguard of our liberties.

It has in fact been amended just 26 times in two centuries – the first ten amendments constituting the BILL OF RIGHTS, ratified on 15 December 1791, and 14 passed since Lincoln's warning.

The task of interpreting the Constitution, and whether the actions of the Federal and State governments and courts accord with it, rests with the SUPREME COURT. Thomas JEFFERSON termed the Constitution "a mere thing of wax in the hands of the judiciary, which they may twist and shape into any form they please", and Charles Evans Hughes, a politician who later became Chief Justice, declared:

The Constitution is what the judges say it is.

We have no common oracles but the Constitution.
Rep. RUFUS CHOATE, 1833.

Your Constitution is all sail and no anchor.
THOMAS BABINGTON MACAULAY, to Henry Randall on US universal male suffrage, 1857.

A covenant with death and an agreement with hell.
WILLIAM LLOYD GARRISON, *The Liberator*, 11 July 1856.

Our Constitution is color-blind.
Justice JOHN HARLAN, dissenting opinion in *Plessy v. Ferguson*, 1896.

Whenever the Constitution comes between men and the virtue of the White women of South Carolina, I say to hell with the Constitution.
Governor COLEMAN BLEASE (1868–1942).

We must remember that any oppression, any injustice, any hatred, is a wedge designed to attack our Constitution.
FRANKLIN D. ROOSEVELT, to the American Committee for the Protection of Foreign-Born, January 1940.

As the British constitution is the most subtile organism which has proceeded from the womb and the long gestation of progressive history, so the American constitution is, so far as I can see, the most wonderful work struck off at a given time by the brains and purpose of men.
GLADSTONE, *North American Review* (1878).

The English Constitution The classic work of political theory – and practice – written by Walter Bagehot (1826–77) and published in 1867. In some respects it remains a valuable commentary on the workings of the UK system of government. The most celebrated dictum from it is:

The sovereign has, under a constitutional MONARCHY such as ours, three rights – the right to be consulted, the right to encourage, the right to warn.

living Constitution The term used by US jurists and politicians for the total body of law governing the operations of America's system of government, including not just the Constitution as amended but lasting enactments of Congress, major Presidential decisions and landmark decisions by the courts.

unwritten constitution The rules by which a nation is governed, when they have not been codified into a single document. The classic example is the British constitution, which is a mixture of legislation, common law and custom and practice.

our constitution is the will of the Führer The philosophy that governed the operation of the NAZI state, as stated by Hans Frank, Hitler's lawyer (*see* FÜHRER) who became Governor-General of Poland and was hanged at NUREMBERG.

constitutional Referring to an executive act or item of legislation falling within the Constitution; in America the question of what is constitutional is a matter for the SUPREME COURT. On 6 July 1935 Franklin D. Roosevelt wrote to Rep. Samuel Hill of a NEW DEAL measure (probably the WAGNER ACT): "I hope your committee will not permit doubts as to constitutionality, however reasonable, to block the suggested legislation." The sentence caused an uproar when published in the Press, but Roosevelt insisted it had been taken out of context and he had no intention of defying the Supreme Court which, six weeks before, had dealt a serious blow to New Deal programmes on BLACK MONDAY.

Constitutional convention *See* PHILADELPHIA CONVENTION.

constitutional monarchy *See* MONARCHY.

constitutional nationalist The term used in NORTHERN IRELAND for the mainly Roman Catholic Social Democratic and Labour Party (SDLP), which is committed to the reunification of Ireland by peaceful means; it draws a distinction from SINN FEIN and the IRA, which see violence as legitimate in pursuit of a united Ireland.

Constitutionalist The party label on which Winston CHURCHILL stood at Epping in the November 1924 general election, as his journey from the Liberals back to the Conservative Party neared its end. Despite not formally being a Tory, he joined BALDWIN's Cabinet as Chancellor, and the following year rejoined the party.

constructive engagement The policy followed toward South Africa by the Reagan administration, under which US diplomacy aimed at securing the end of APARTHEID by persuasion and involvement rather than SANCTIONS and MEGAPHONE DIPLOMACY. Liberals claimed that this amounted in practice to tacit acceptance of the Pretoria government's internal policies.

consul Originally one of the two chief magistrates of Republican Rome; from 1799 until 1804 one of the three heads of the French republic, Napoleon being "first consul"; now an agent for a government (not necessary one of its nationals) who assists its citizens and trading interests in a foreign city. A **consulate** is the office from which a consul works; the consular section of an EMBASSY issues visas, and passports to nationals of its own country living abroad.

> A person who having failed to secure an office from the people is given one by the Administration on condition that he leave the country. AMBROSE BIERCE.

consultancy An arrangement under which an MP at Westminster keeps a watching brief for the interests of a company or other organization in return for payment; such consultancies, which have to be listed in the REGISTER OF INTERESTS, are in a few cases as lucrative as the Member's Parliamentary salary and there have been occasions when a Member has listed his occupation as "consultant".

Contadora plan The group of Latin American countries that since 1983 has been working, with considerable success, for an end to conflicts in Central America, especially Nicaragua and El Salvador. It takes its name from a meeting on Contadora island of representatives of Mexico, Colombia, Panama, Venezuela and Panama, backed by a "support group" of Argentina, Brazil, Peru and Uruguay. The Reagan administration and Nicaragua's SANDINISTAS both refused to back the draft Contadora agreement; but the "Esquipulas II" peace plan launched in 1987 with Contadora support by President Arias of Costa Rica led to a release of prisoners and direct talks between the Sandinistas and the CONTRAS. These failed, but paved the way for elections in 1990, after the Bush administration halted direct military funding to the Contras, in which Violetta Chamorro's National Opposition Union ousted the Sandinistas. A number of formulae for ending the guerrilla war in El Salvador were also advanced, despite US disapproval. The conflict continued to flare sporadically, but the ARENA government elected in 1989 (after elections the FMLN guerrillas boycotted) took firm action against guerrillas and right-wing DEATH SQUADS alike.

containment One of the fundamental aims of US policy during the COLD WAR, the prevention of Soviet expansion by an alliance of encircling states pledged to resist any aggression. The word and the principle were first put forward in 1947 by George Kennan, then head of the State Department's policy planning staff, in an article in *Foreign Affairs* signed "Mr. X"; in it Kennan wrote:

> The Russians look forward to a duel of infinite duration.

The Truman administration speedily adopted the policy, going beyond Kennan's thinking to create challenging military alliances. Containment worked best in Europe, where NATO held a line stretching from Arctic Norway to Turkey; the establishment of the ANZUS, CENTO and SEATO alliances was intended to contain the threat of a Communist advance on all sides, but proved less durable. Though America became even more alarmed at the prospect of a Communist upsurge in Latin America, the traditional political climate of the region (*see* GRINGO FACTOR) ruled out a system of alliances and led to the US taking unilateral action (*see* CUBAN MISSILE CRISIS, IRAN-CONTRA AFFAIR).

contempt. contempt of Congress The offence that either House of Congress may deem to have been committed if an individual refuses to testify before a Congressional committee or does so and commits perjury (the most frequent instance), holds Congress up to ridicule or impedes its activities. Neither House has the power to punish those it holds in contempt; instead it must pass a citation for contempt enforceable by its SERGEANT AT ARMS, or (as more frequently occurs) seek an indictment through the Justice Department and the courts.

contempt of the House The serious charge which the UK HOUSE OF COMMONS is, by custom, able to bring against anyone alleged to have interfered with its workings. The boundaries between contempt and Breach of PRIVILEGE are blurred, but generally a contempt would be committed if an individual or organization acted in the face of a specific decision. Refusal to appear before a SELECT COMMITTEE when summoned is a contempt of the House. Those judged to have committed a contempt are ordered by the SERJEANT-AT-ARMS to attend the BAR OF THE HOUSE to explain themselves; until 1750 they had to kneel.

Contents The name given to Peers voting for a proposition in the HOUSE OF LORDS. Those voting against are **Not Contents**.

continent. Continental Congress The gathering of representatives from Britain's 23 American colonies which convened twice to propose first an association of the colonies and then to declare INDEPENDENCE. It directed the conduct of the Revolutionary war and drafted the Articles of CONFEDERATION. The first Congress, in Carpenter Hall, Philadelphia, in 1774, was attended by representatives of every colony except Georgia. It warned Britain any attempt to subdue Massachusetts would be resisted by the other colonies, demanded repeal of the Coercive Acts (*see* BOSTON TEA PARTY) and the QUEBEC ACT, and imposed a BOYCOTT of British-made goods. It also questioned the authority of Parliament over America, directly appealing to the Crown and the British people for the redress of grievances; the petitions were rejected.

The second Congress met on 10 May 1775 with all the colonies represented, on 23 June it appointed George WASHINGTON commander-in-chief of the American forces and on 2 July 1776 passed the resolution to declare independence – "that these United Colonies are, and of right ought to be, free and independent states" – with New York abstaining. It continued sitting until 1781.

continentalism The question of whether there is room for two separate nations in North America – the inference being that there is not – which has overshadowed Canadian politics for two centuries and in the 1840s motivated some US politicians to advocate the absorption of Canada as part of the United States' MANIFEST DESTINY, Daniel Webster saying:

> A large portion of the people believe that a desire for the conquest and final retention of Canada is the mainspring of public opinion.

contingency reserve The sum included in a BUDGET which is not earmarked for spending on any particular project or service, but is kept in reserve to meet the cost of unexpected needs.

Contras (Lat. *contra*, against) The US-backed GUERRILLA group which throughout the 1980s fought for the overthrow of Nicaragua's SANDINISTA government headed by Daniel Ortega, whose election in 1984 they disputed. Many of its members had been supporters of the dictatorial President Anastasio Somoza (1925–80), who was ousted by the Sandinistas in 1978; some had been members of his hated Presidential guard, and others were the retainers of former landowners whose estates the Sandinistas had expropriated. The Contras were based in Miami, Honduras and Costa Rica, and backed by the Reagan administration in defiance of Acts of Congress (*see* BOLAND AMENDMENT; IRAN-CONTRA AFFAIR). Peace talks under the auspices of the CONTADORA GROUP and President Arias of Panama led to a prisoner exchange in 1987, but later broke down. However direct US funding for the Contras ended with the election of President BUSH in 1988, and in 1990 the Sandinistas were ousted peacefully at an election won by a Centre-Right coalition led by Violetta Chamorro.

> We will not betray you. We will do everything we can to win this great struggle. RONALD REAGAN.

> If you want to squander $440 million be my guest, but not a heritage of honor. Why sacrifice that for this grubby, sleazy little operation?
> Sen. LOWELL WEICKER (Rep.), 18 March 1987

convenor A Scottish term for the chairman or leader of an organization, specifically a local authority or political grouping.

convention (1) A TREATY signed by a number of nations, generally to set enforceable standards of conduct, as with the GENEVA CONVENTIONS or VIENNA CONVENTION. (2) In America, a conference of a political party, and specifically the gathering at which a party devises its PLATFORM and selects its Presidential NOMINEE. The first was held at Baltimore in September 1831 by the Anti-Masonic Party. In 1992 Arkansas Sen. Dale Bumpers, after listening to Bill Clinton's ACCEPTANCE SPEECH, said of convention speeches in general:

> You gotta throw the corn where the hogs can get to it.

> A chess tournament disguised as a circus.
> ALISTAIR COOKE (1908–).

> The dirty work at political conventions is always done between midnight and dawn. RUSSELL BAKER (1925–).

brokered convention *See* BROKER. **Constitutional convention** *See* PHILADELPHIA.

National Convention In America, a gathering that can be convened to AMEND the Constitution in a particular way if two-thirds of the States petition the Congress for it. This method of amendment has never been used, but during the 1980s there was strong pressure from the PRO-LIFE movement for a convention to promulgate a Constitutional amendment outlawing abortion.

National Union Convention The mid-term convention in 1866 at which President Andrew Johnson's supporters, eager to head off extreme programmes of RECONSTRUCTION, endorsed the besieged President's policies and declared that the Southern states had a right to representation in Congress.

conventional warfare or weapons Warfare that does not involve nuclear weapons, and the weapons with which it is fought. *See also* CFE.

convergence A EUROPEAN COMMUNITY term for the ideal world in which the economies of the weaker member states will strengthen to "converge" with those of the soundest, with levels of unemployment, inflation and other INDICATORS drawing closer together. Convergence is seen by advocates of a SINGLE CURRENCY as both achievable and necessary; sceptics argue that it will simply never happen and that consequently a single currency for the entire EC, as foreshadowed by the MAASTRICHT TREATY, is a dead duck.

Convict # 2273 The name chosen for himself by Eugene Debs (1855–1926), Socialist candidate in America's 1920 Presidential election, who at the time was serving a 10-year sentence under the Espionage Law for an anti-war speech delivered to his party's Ohio state convention two years before (*see* FREEDOM OF SPEECH). Debs's sentence was commuted by President Harding the following year.

convictions The basic beliefs and ideals that are supposed to motivate a politician; in the 1992 Presidential campaign George BUSH was accused by critics of having fewer convictions than the jailed Mafia boss John Gotti. A **conviction politician** is one who is driven by these beliefs and is loth to COMPROMISE, Margaret Thatcher (*see* IRON LADY) prided herself on being one such. She said:

> It must be a conviction government. As Prime Minister I could not waste time having internal arguments.

Cook County The subdivision of Illinois which includes Chicago and its immediate suburbs, and which has been governed almost as a whole through Cook County Democratic Party MACHINE. As the DALEY MACHINE it not only gave Chicago effective government but acquired a reputation for over-enthusiastic delivery of the vote to whichever Presidential candidate Mayor Daley was backing. In 1960 John F. KENNEDY's knife-edge victory over Richard Nixon rested on a few thousand votes in Cook County which swung Illinois, and a similar number in LBJ's Texas, about which there were also suspicions.

cool, calm and elected The goal set by Margaret Thatcher for the Conservatives' 1983 election campaign when she addressed Tory MPs and candidates at its start; the phrase was a play on "cool, calm and collected". She was successful on all counts; after a campaign with few shaky moments, the Conservatives were re-elected with a LANDSLIDE majority of 144.

Keep Cool and keep Coolidge The slogan on which President Coolidge (*see* SILENT CAL) won re-election in his own right in 1924 by an equally convincing margin over the Democrat John W. Davis and the Progressives' Robert (BATTLING BOB) La Follette.

cooling-off period In some codes of industrial relations law, notably the US TAFT-HARTLEY ACT, a fixed period during which a union, having given notice of a strike, must suspend its action to allow tempers to cool and a settlement to be explored.

Coolidge, Calvin *See* SILENT CAL.

co-operate. co-operation procedure The process, created by the SINGLE EUROPEAN ACT, for the approval of EC legislation. It involves a complex network of consultation between the European COMMISSION, which initiates legislation, the EUROPEAN PARLIAMENT and the Council of Ministers, which takes its final decision by qualified MAJORITY vote.

co-operative An enterprise which is owned and managed jointly by the workers (*see* OWENITES; ROCHDALE PIONEERS). In Britain the **Co-operative Party** (founded 1917) is a separate political movement whose membership is compatible with that of the Labour Party, a number of whose MPs it sponsors; the party is also closely involved with the co-operative retail movement. The 1974–79 Labour government, especially early on when Tony BENN was Industry Secretary, backed a series of co-operatives born from the ashes of failed businesses, among them the Meriden motor-cycle works and the *Scottish Daily News*, but none survived.

co-option The appointment of members of a committee by the committee itself or by other bodies, after any directly-elected places have been filled.

Copperheads The minority of northern Democrats who, during the US CIVIL WAR, campaigned for peace and at times verged on TREASON; the name comes from a particularly devious species of American snake. They managed to control the party's platform for the 1864 election – demanding an immediate ARMISTICE and making no mention of SLAVERY – but not the Presidential candidate, Gen. George McLellan rejecting their policies. By the time voting took place the Confederates were on the run, and the Copperhead platform contributed to McLellan's heavy defeat by LINCOLN.

co-presidency The arrangement which Ronald REAGAN considered before choosing a RUNNING-MATE in 1980. It would have applied had he picked former President Gerald FORD; despite the appeal of a dream TICKET, Reagan rejected the idea partly because he was unwilling to give the Vice-President a direct stake in the power of the Presidency.

Cordite vote The episode on 21 June 1895 that brought the fall of ROSEBERY's government; it was defeated 132–125 in a snap House of Commons vote after the usually sure-footed Sir Henry Campbell-Bannerman (C-B), Secretary for War, had botched the government's defence against charges – never proven – that there was insufficient cordite for the Army.

A chance blow, but a fatal one. CAMPBELL-BANNERMAN.

A well-manoeuvred assassination.
AUGUSTINE BIRRELL MP (Lib.).

cordon. Cordon rule The equivalent in the US Senate of the House's RAMSEYER RULE, setting out the precise form in which a Bill must be REPORTED.

cordon sanitaire (Fr. sterile strip) A strip of territory, or belt of states, seen by a country or countries on one side as protection from those beyond, which they regard as potential aggressors. In February 1946 Harold Macmillan suggested that the Soviet Union was preoccupied, defensively, with creating "a new cordon sanitaire ... of states made SATELLITE and dependent" between itself and the West.

CORE Congress of Racial Equality. One of the spearheads of America's CIVIL RIGHTS movement from the early 1960s, when Black and White activists tested SEGREGATION laws in the Deep South, notably through SIT-INS and the FREEDOM RIDES in 1961. CORE, a previously small organization founded in Chicago in 1942, and led from 1961 by its co-founder James Farmer, may have owed its name to the old Southern saying:

White man get the apple, nigger get the core.

COREPER Committee of Permanent Representatives. The group comprising the Ambassadors to the EUROPEAN COMMUNITY of each member state that meets regularly in Brussels and keeps the business of the COUNCIL OF MINISTERS moving between formal sessions.

Corn Laws The PROTECTIONIST legislation over which PEEL split Britain's old TORY party, and which was widely believed to have exacerbated the IRISH POTATO FAMINE. Introduced by Lord Liverpool's government in 1815, it banned corn imports when the price reached 80 shillings a quarter. There were riots in London when it was introduced, and serious bread shortages when it was invoked in 1820 led to its amendment eight years later, with the imposition of heavy duties. By 1839 Melbourne was declaring the Laws "the maddest scheme that had ever entered into the imagination of man to conceive"; in the early 1840s the Anti-Corn Law League began winning Parliamentary seats. When news of the famine reached London, Peel tried and failed to reverse the Tory position by persuading the Cabinet to suspend the laws; in January 1846 he formed an alliance with the embryo Liberals to phase out the duties over three years, and by the end of May Parliament had passed the repeal legislation.

corporate. corporate donors Businesses and their top executives who make sizable donations to party or campaign funds.

corporatism A system in which the state works hand in glove with large companies and trade unions in pursuit of a single goal. It is disliked both by right-wing politicians who see it as violating both the principles of the MARKET and the right of a government to govern; and by the Left and militant TRADE UNIONISTS who see it as smothering workers' rights. A particular form of corporatism, stemming from the turn-of-the-century theories of Emile Durkheim, lay at the heart of Mussolini's FASCIST state and, even more so, the state and economic structure erected by the Franco regime in Spain (*see* FALANGE).

Corrective Party The UK party started in the late 1980s by the anti-prostitution law campaigner Lindi St. Clair (1952–), otherwise known as Miss Whiplash, which received an enormous amount of publicity but very few votes. Miss St. Clair claimed to have a file on well over 100 MPs and peers who had come to her for "corrective" flagellation; shortly afterward her empty car was found at Beachy Head, a well-known suicide spot. However, after several days of police inquiries, she was discovered on a cruise liner off Florida.

Corrie Bill The first serious attempt by a BACKBENCHER to tighten David Steel's liberal Abortion Act of 1967; promoted in 1979 by John Corrie (1935–) Conservative MP for Bute and North Ayrshire, it gained a SECOND READING but was strangled in Committee the following summer. *See also* ALTON BILL.

corruption A concomitant of politics through the centuries, the remarkable thing being how many men and women without wealth have rejected offers of lucre and done what they believed to be right. The historian Gibbon termed corruption "the most infallible symptom of constitutional liberty", George WASHINGTON maintained that "few men have the virtue to withstand the highest bidder", while Mayor Richard DALEY declared: "You know that if I had ever been corrupted, I wouldn't still be around."

When I want to buy up any politician I always find the anti-monopolists the most purchasable – they don't come so high. WILLIAM VANDERBILT (1821–1885).

corrupt bargain The name given by angry supporters of the defeated Andrew Jackson (*see* OLD HICKORY) to John Quincy ADAMS' election as President in 1824. Adams had finished behind Jackson, but with no majority in the ELECTORAL COLLEGE the election passed to the House of Representatives. Speaker Henry Clay swung two key States, though not quite a majority, to Adams – who then made Clay Secretary of State. The Jacksonians insisted a deal had been struck – a deal, as John Randolph put it, "between the BLACKLEG and the puritan" – which it probably had not. But they had their revenge in 1828 when Jackson brushed Adams aside.

The Judas of the West has closed the contract and will receive the thirty pieces of silver. His end will be the same. Was there ever such a bare faced corruption in this country before?
JACKSON, letter to W. B. Lewis, 14 February 1825.

Federal Corrupt Practices Act The Act passed in 1925 which made a first attempt to control campaign spending and contributions; its aim was limited, and its effect even more so – as it did not apply to PRIMARIES. House and Senate candidates were expected to file reports of their spending, but if filed at all these were fragmentary. Donations of $100 or more had to be reported – so donations of $99.99 became common – but campaign committees only had to name their contributors if they operated in two or more states. In 1972 it was superseded by the Federal Election Campaign Act, which was marginally more effective.

More loophole than laws. LBJ.

Cortès The two-chamber Parliament of democratic Spain, which in 1977 replaced the single-chamber *Cortès* of Franco's FALANGIST state. It comprises a Congress of Deputies, and a less powerful Senate.

COSLA Convention of Scottish Local Authorities. The body representing all of Scotland's councils – the regions and districts and the single-tier authorities that were to replace them in the mid-1990s. Comprising council leaders of all parties, it exerts considerable influence over government through its contacts with the Scottish Office and its Ministers.

Cosmic Bob The nickname given to Nebraska's Sen. Bob Kerrey (1943–) because of his interest in the ethereal. It haunted him when he made a brief run for the Democratic Presidential nomination in 1992.

council. Council of Europe *See* EUROPE.

Council of Ministers The political driving force of the EUROPEAN COMMUNITY, at least when it is able to agree. The Council comprises all the EC's heads of government or their representatatives, and provides the COMMISSION with a working brief. It takes two forms: the Council proper, which holds SUMMIT meetings at least every six months which decide such critical matters as the provisions of the MAASTRICHT TREATY, and the more frequent meetings of Ministers in specific fields such as finance (ECOFIN), agriculture or transport. *See also* COREPER.

Council of All Ireland *See* SUNNINGDALE.

council tax The local tax introduced by John MAJOR's government to replace the notorious POLL TAX, which took effect throughout Great Britain in April 1993. Unlike the poll tax or COMMUNITY CHARGE, which was a flat-rate charge on almost all adults, the council tax is property-based. Homes are valued in a number of bands, and a charge is set by each local authority which varies according to those bands. There is a reduction of 25% for a single householder, and those on social security also pay a lower council tax. One unexpected phenomenon was the number of householders appealing that their home was in too *low* a band because of the social stigma they felt was implied.

count The tallying of votes once an election has taken place, conducted in the advanced democracies with considerable safeguards to avoid fraud. In most cases the count begins as soon as ballot papers can be got to central counting points; in some remote parts of Britain (plus cities with unimaginative officials) it does not begin until the following morning. In Ireland the complicated formula of PROPORTIONAL REPRESENTATION may require the count to go on for several days in a closely-fought constituency. The count has given rise to abuses in many countries; in 1977 the Nicaraguan dictator Anastasio Somoza boasted to his opponents:

You won the election. But I won the count.

The term is also applied in America to the JOINT SESSION of Congress on the 6 January after a Presidential election, to count the votes of the ELECTORAL COLLEGE; if no candidate has a majority, the House then chooses the President from the three having the largest number of electoral votes, and the Senate the Vice-President from the two leading candidates for that office.

counted out At Westminster, the fate of a sitting of the House of Commons when not enough MPs are available to "keep a HOUSE".

counter-espionage One of the roles of internal security agencies such as America's FBI, Britain's MI5 and Germany's BND: the detection of foreign spies with a view to their arrest and the destruction of the organization behind them.

counter-inflation strategy A term used by politicians either for a PRICES AND INCOMES POLICY or for the curbing of the MONEY SUPPLY.

counter-insurgency The combating of GUERRILLA movements by government forces, a term which was frequently used by Americans to describe the nature of the VIETNAM WAR in its early stages.

country. country member In Australia, a Member of the House of Representatives representing an outback constituency who since 1952 has received higher allowances than his or her city counterparts.

Country Party The right-wing though originally "non-political" farmers' movement in Australia which had already won 11 seats in federal elections when it constituted itself a political party in 1920. In 1923 it went into coalition with the LIBERALS, and remained their junior partner, even though as the **National Party** (the name it adopted in 1982) it became Australia's largest, with 140,000 members. It provided three Prime Ministers, each for less than two months: Earle Page (1939), Arthur Fadden (1941) and John McEwen (1967–68).

a country fit for heroes A phrase popularized by Lloyd George in a speech on 24 November 1918, a fortnight after the end of WORLD WAR I, in which he set goals for Britain's returning servicemen that proved hard to achieve. What L. G. actually said was:

> What is our task? To make Britain a fit country for heroes to live in.

Lloyd George's sincerity was later questioned by G. K. Chesterton in his verse *A Land Fit for Heroes*, with the ironic subtitle *Refutation of the Only Too Prevalent Slander that Parliamentary Leaders are Indifferent to the Strict Fulfilment of their Promises and the Preservation of their Reputation for Veracity*:

> They said (when they had dined at Ciro's)
> The land would soon be fit for heroes;
> And now they've managed to ensure it,
> For only heroes could endure it.

Ask not what your country can do for you – ask what you can do for your country One of the key phrases of John F. KENNEDY's INAUGURAL address on 20 January 1961, which became a text for the NEW FRONTIER and such innovations as the PEACE CORPS. What JFK said was:

> And so, my fellow Americans: ask not what your country can do for you – ask what you can do for your country. My fellow citizens of the world: ask not what America will do for you, but what together we can do for the freedom of man.

The words were not entirely original; the funeral oration for John Greenleaf Whittier contained a similar exhortation, Oliver Wendell Holmes made the juxtaposition in a speech in 1884, and after World War I, in *The Voice of the Master*, Khalil Ghibran (1883–1931) wrote:

> Are you a politician asking what your country can do for you or a zealous one asking what you can do for your country? If you are the first, then you are a parasite; if the second, then you are an oasis in the desert.

Even the far from eloquent President HARDING said, in a speech in St. Louis in 1923,

> I like people in the cities, in the States and in the nation to ask themselves now and then: "What can I do for my city?", not "How much can I get out of my city?".

die for one's country The ultimate sacrifice, urged on many young men by their political leaders when war looms. In classical times Horace wrote: "Sweet and glorious it is to die for one's country", and the sentiments have all too frequently had to be repeated. The American Nathan Hale, facing execution as a spy by the British in 1776, is said to have proudly stated: "I only regret that I have but one life to give for my country;" unfortunately for romantics, the diary of a witness recalls his actual words as:

> It is the duty of any good officer to obey any orders given him by his commander-in-chief.

The day before Indira Gandhi (*see* NEHRU DYNASTY) was assassinated in 1984, she stated:

> Even if I die in the service of this nation, I would be proud of it. Every drop of my blood, I am sure, will contribute to the growth of this nation and make it strong and dynamic.

And the UK Labour leader Neil KINNOCK, in a powerful party conference speech in 1987, said of nuclear war:

> I would die for my country, but I would not let my country die for me.

go to the country A traditional UK phrase for the action of a Prime Minister in calling a GENERAL ELECTION. When defeated on a no-CONFIDENCE motion in February 1979, James Callaghan (*see* SUNNY JIM) defiantly told the Commons:

> We shall take our case to the country.

I have no country to fight for; my country is the earth, and I am a citizen of the world The internationalist credo of Eugene

Debs (1855–1926), the US Socialist presidential candidate and PACIFIST (*see* CONVICT #2273).

I vow to thee, my country The English patriotic verse, ranking with LAND OF HOPE AND GLORY and JERUSALEM, written by Sir Cecil Spring-Rice (1858–1918) and sung to the Jupiter theme from Gustav Holst's *The Planets* suite. The opening couplet runs:

> I vow to thee, my country – all earthly things above –
> Entire and whole and perfect, the service of my love.

Mother Country The term traditionally used to describe England in Australia, and to a lesser extent the other DOMINIONS of the COMMONWEALTH. It has been heard much less since the 1960s as Australia asserts its national identity, and more and more of its citizens are non-British in origin.

my country, right or wrong One of the great statements of simple PATRIOTISM, first uttered as a toast in 1816 by the American Stephen Decatur (1779–1820). He proclaimed:

> Our country! In her intercourse with foreign nations, may she always be in the right, but our country, right or wrong!

The argument did not pass unchallenged. In 1872 Sen. Carl Schurz countered:

> The Senator for Wisconsin cannot frighten me by exclaiming: "My country, right or wrong". In one sense I say so, too. My country, and my country is the great American republic, my country right or wrong: if right, to be kept right, and if wrong, to be set right.

But G. K. Chesterton (1874–1936) was wholly opposed, saying:

> Our country, right or wrong, is something no patriot would think of saying except in a desperate case. It is like saying: "My mother, drunk or sober!"

My country, 'tis of thee The US patriotic anthem, known as *America*, written in 1831 by Samuel Francis Smith (1808–95), a young Boston clergyman, and set by him (unwittingly) to the same tune as GOD SAVE THE KING; it stands second in popularity only to The STAR SPANGLED BANNER. The first of four verses runs:

> My country, 'tis of thee,
> Sweet land of liberty,
> Of thee I sing:
> Land where my fathers died,
> Land of the pilgrims' pride,
> From every mountainside,
> Let freedom ring.

What this country needs is a good 5 cent cigar The classic dictum of Woodrow WILSON's Vice-President Thomas Marshall (1854–1925), delivered from the Chair in the Senate while Sen. Joseph Bristow of Kansas was making an interminable speech on "What this Country needs".

county (1) In America, the administrative subdivisions into which almost every State is divided. (2) In Britain, the traditional large-scale unit of local government; in the 1970s the Scottish counties were replaced by larger regions as the upper tier, and the English and Welsh county boundaries were heavily redrawn. **Metropolitan Counties** were created covering the major English conurbations outside London, and **Shire Counties** for predominantly rural areas (though often containing one large city); the Metropolitan Counties were abolished some 12 years later, the district councils becoming UNITARY AUTHORITIES.

County Hall The stately building on the South Bank of the Thames, facing the Houses of Parliament across Westminster Bridge, which from 1933 to 1986 was the headquarters of first the LCC (London County Council) and from 1965 the GLC (Greater London Council). Designed by Ralph Knott and extended in 1963, County Hall symbolized London to many inhabitants of the capital, but was left largely empty after the abolition of the GLC by Margaret Thatcher's government (*see* RED KEN). Moves in 1992 to secure it as a new headquarters for the London School of Economics (LSE) failed, and a Japanese firm went ahead with plans to reopen it as a hotel.

coup (d'état) (Fr. blow to the state) The sudden and often violent overthrow of the established political system by a faction anxious to seize power for itself. A coup may be mounted by civilians, or by the military.

> *Q*: What has one wing, is armed to the teeth and produces milk?
> *A*: A right wing military coup.
>
> 1960s Scottish ANARCHIST joke.

In May 1968 Cecil King, megalomaniac chairman of Britain's *Daily Mirror*, explored the scope for a military coup to oust the government of Harold WILSON. On 8 May he invited Earl Mountbatten to form a government of national unity once such a coup had taken place. Sir Solly Zuckerman, the government's chief scientific adviser who was also at the meeting, described the plan as "rank treachery", adding: "All this talk of machine-guns at street corners is appalling. I am a public servant and I will have nothing to do with it. Nor should you, Dickie." Mountbatten then told King his plan was "simply not on".

Coupon election The General Election held in Britain in December 1918, immediately after victory in WORLD WAR I. The Lloyd George coalition of Conservatives and much of the

LIBERAL PARTY gave a "coupon" to all candidates pledged to support it, and scored a crushing victory over the orthodox Liberals led by ASQUITH (who lost his seat, denouncing the "coupon" as "a wicked fraud"). The coalition won 478 seats, its opponents 229, including 63 Labour, Asquithian Liberals 28 and SINN FEIN 73. Though L. G. remained as Prime Minister for a further four years, the election spelt the end of the Liberal Party as a major force. *See also* HANG THE KAISER!; HARD FACED MEN WHO HAVE DONE WELL OUT OF THE WAR.

court. court dress The fancy garb that members of Britain's PRIVY COUNCIL traditionally had to wear for its meetings; the practice was relaxed in 1924 when the first Labour government took office, and has since died out.
court-packing The stratagem briefly advocated by Franklin D. Roosevelt in reaction to the US SUPREME COURT's invalidation of much of his NEW DEAL legislation in 1935–36 (*see* BLACK MONDAY; Sick CHICKEN CASE). On 5 January 1937 FDR, without consulting Congressional leaders, unveiled a plan to overthrow the nine-man Court's conservative majority by appointing up to six new justices if those aged over 70 did not voluntarily retire. Congress, including many of the President's supporters, was outraged at what it saw as a dictatorial attempt to subvert the Constitution. Conservative Democrats threatened to withdraw support from the New Deal, and the Senate rejected the court plan by 70–22. However the Court got the message, and in the summer of 1937 reversed itself to declare the WAGNER ACT constitutional. With the death soon after of several conservative justices and their replacement by liberals, the conflict with the White House subsided, but FDR paid a heavy political price.

cover-up The action by those in authority of concealing their actions in order to escape scrutiny, criticism or censure. The most notorious example was the WATERGATE cover-up practised by the Nixon White House, but there have been many others; in Britain WESTLAND was widely reckoned to fall into that category. Ironically Nixon himself (*see* TRICKY DICKY) had accused President Truman of a cover-up during America's 1952 election, saying as McCARTHYISM hit its stride:

> Mr. Truman, Dean Acheson and other Administration officials for political purposes covered up this Communist conspiracy and attempted to halt its exposure.

covert operations Operations carried out by a security or intelligence agency outwith the knowledge not only of the populus of the state where they are taking place but of all but a handful of officials of the government for whom they are supposed to be acting. Covert operations by the CIA, including plans to ASSASSINATE a number of hostile or inconvenient foreign leaders, led to Congress imposing OVERSIGHT on the agency; however even specific legislation (*see* BOLAND AMENDMENT) could not prevent the IRAN-CONTRA AFFAIR, described by the CIA director William Casey as the "ultimate covert operation".

Coxeyites The army of several hundred jobless men who marched on Washington in April 1894 as the full effects of the DEPRESSION of 1893 were felt. Led by "General" Jacob Coxey, a horsebreeder and quarry owner, 20,000 had set off the previous autumn from Massillon, Ohio, and other centres to present Congress with a PETITION demanding inflation of the currency and a Federal programme of public works. Welcomed and fed by farmers as they set off, they met a cooler reception in the East and only 600 completed the journey. The protest evaporated after Coxey and two aides were arrested – for walking on the Capitol lawn.

CP Universal shorthand in political circles for Britain's COMMUNIST PARTY, which preferred to refer to itself as the **CPGB**, the Soviet party being known as the **CPSU**.

Crabb affair The mysterious episode that overshadowed the visit to Britain of the Soviet leaders Bulganin and Khruschev in May 1956. It hinged on the disappearance of Commander Lionel "Buster" Crabb, a Royal Navy frogman, who disappeared while exploring the underside of the Soviet cruiser *Ordjonikidze*, in which B AND K had arrived, in Portsmouth Harbour. The UK government persistently claimed that he had been working independently and was not under orders. However reporters from *The Times* discovered that senior detectives had called at Crabb's hotel, removed all record of his stay, and ordered staff not to discuss it. The incident was never fully explained: there was speculation that he had DEFECTED to the Soviet Union, drowned by accident, or been killed by British agents when it was realized that intelligence interest in the visiting flotilla might prove politically embarrassing. Anthony EDEN, repeatedly questioned by Labour MPs about the episode, told the Commons:

> It would not be in the public interest to disclose the circumstances in which Commander Crabb is presumed to have met his death.

cradle. from the cradle to the grave The ethos of Britain's WELFARE STATE in its ultimate form, as proposed in the BEVERIDGE REPORT and largely created by the 1945

Labour government. (*see also* NHS; WOMB TO TOMB)

the hand that rocks the cradle can rock the system The slogan on which the left-wing feminist lawyer Mary Robinson stood for the Presidency of the Irish Republic in 1990, pulling off a shock victory that November over the former FIANNA FAIL TANAISTE Brian Lenihan. It represented Mrs. Robinson's belief that the women of Ireland were ready to take a more active role in politics than they had traditionally accepted, and was designed to convince them they could make the difference. However she was also helped by the scandal that broke during the campaign over the claim – strongly denied – that Lenihan in 1982 had rung President Hillery at ARAS NA UACHTARAIN to dissuade him from granting a DISSOLUTION to the Fine Gael *Taoiseach* Garret FitzGerald.

crash through, or crash The phrase that came to exemplify the increasingly desperate and ultimately doomed efforts of Gough WHITLAM's Australian Labor government to revive the economy, get its policies implemented and remain in office. Whitlam had once told colleagues: "You must crash through, or crash", and the words became the title of the definitive book on his ministry by Laurie Oakes. However Whitlam himself was cautious, and the risks were taken by members of his Cabinet, several of whom had to be sacked for exceeding their brief. *See also* KERR SACKING; LOANS SCANDAL; MOROSI AFFAIR.

Great Crash *See* GREAT.

credibility gap The discrepancy between what a politician claims to be the case and the facts of the matter. The phrase is credited to future President Gerald FORD, who when House MINORITY LEADER in 1966, contrasted the Johnson administration's denial of greater US involvement in the VIETNAM WAR with the evidence available. The following year the veteran COLUMNIST Walter Lippmann wrote:

> In order to avoid the embarrassment of calling a spade a spade, newspapermen have agreed to talk about the credibility gap. This is a polite euphemism for deception.

credit. Créditistes The allies in Quebec of Canada's SOCIAL CREDIT party, who made a major breakthrough in 1962, winning 26 seats in the House of Commons, ebbed and flowed and were eliminated in 1980.

Crédit Mobilier affair One of the greatest of the scandals that plagued the GRANT administration, involving Congressional leaders and Vice-President Schuyler Colfax, whom Grant dropped from the ticket when the scandal broke in 1872. Rumours of graft involving the *Crédit Mobilier*, the construction company that had built the Union Pacific Railroad, were upheld by a Congressional investigation the next year. It found that Rep. Oakes Ames, a Massachusetts Democrat who owned the company with his brother and had amassed a $10 million fortune through contract-padding, had handed out Crédit Mobilier stock to legislators (including Colfax, when Speaker in 1867–68, and on a small scale the wife of Henry Wilson, who replaced him as Vice-Presidential nominee) at less than market value to smooth the passage of measures benefiting railroad interests. Voters exasperated with corruption in high places took their revenge at the 1874 Congressional elections, overturning the Republican majority. Exposure of the WHISKEY RING and the BELKNAP SCANDAL still lay ahead.

credit squeeze The use of tighter credit to stop the economy OVERHEATING, through controls on lending to businesses and private individuals by banks, finance houses and other financial institutions.

CREEP Committee for Re-Election of the President. The organization set up to finance the re-election of President Nixon in 1972, which was revealed in the WATERGATE scandal as the conduit for illegal and unethical payments – including to the burglars themselves.

Crichel Down The scandal in 1954 which brought the ultimate in principled resignations, Sir Thomas Dugdale, UK Minister of Agriculture, resigning after conduct by his civil servants was criticized. CHURCHILL described his action as "chivalrous in a high degree", and would not accept the resignations of the rest of his ministerial team including Lord Carrington. The case stemmed from the compulsory purchase of 725 acres of Dorset farmland in 1938 from three owners for a wartime airfield, and the refusal of the Ministry of Agriculture to let them buy it back, insisting it could be farmed more efficiently as a whole. Lt.-Cdr. George Marten, son-in-law of one of the owners, launched a campaign against the decision, backed by his MP and the National Farmers' Union. An inquiry by Sir Andrew Clark QC publicly blamed several named civil servants, but Sir Thomas decided that it was his duty to resign – though he may have gone because he agreed with the officials' decision. A bitter Commons debate over Crichel Down on 20 July 1954 clearly established standards for MINISTERIAL RESPONSIBILITY which have not always been honoured since.

cricket test The test of a non-White Briton's loyalty to England, raised in 1991 by Norman

Tebbit (*see* CHINGFORD SKINHEAD), which aroused accusations of RACISM and briefly threatened to reopen the political debate about **immigration**. Interviewed by a US newspaper, Tebbit suggested that many, even in the second generation, would support the visiting cricket team from their country of origin when it played in England, rather than the home team whose nationality they held.

crime. Crime against Kansas *See* KANSAS.

Crime of '73 The term used by advocates of FREE SILVER in the late 19th century for the Coinage Act passed by Congress in 1873, which ended the minting of silver dollars and effectively put America back on the GOLD STANDARD. The Act was later blamed by advocates of bimetallism for a shortage of coin in circulation, and consequently for falling farm and commodity prices.

Crimean War The Anglo-French war against Russia from 1854–56, which was fought on the Crimean peninsula in the Black Sea. It arose partly from British fear of Russian influence in Turkey and partly from Russia's suppression of the revolutions of 1848. Best known for the **Charge of the Light Brigade**, its legacies were the routine use of the rifle in warfare, long-overdue reforms to introduce competence into the British Army's command structure, and the field nursing techniques pioneered by Florence Nightingale at her hospital at Scutari, Turkey. *See also* EASTERN QUESTION.

> Are we to be the Don Quixotes of Europe, to go about fighting for every cause where we find that someone has been wronged?
>
> RICHARD COBDEN, House of Commons, 22 December 1854.

> The Angel of Death has been abroad throughout the land. You may almost hear the beating of his wings.
>
> JOHN BRIGHT, House of Commons, 23 February 1855.

crisis, what crisis? The highly compromising remark the Labour Prime Minister James Callaghan (*see* SUNNY JIM) is supposed to have made about the WINTER OF DISCONTENT on his return to Heathrow from the Guadeloupe economic summit on 10 January 1979. It was, in fact, a headline in the *Sun*, paraphrasing Callaghan's reply when asked if he did not agree Britain was in a state of mounting chaos from industrial unrest, but that was enough in a pre-election atmosphere with the Government apparently losing its grip. He replied:

> I don't think that other people in the world would share the view that there is mounting chaos.

And the *Sun* did the rest.

When written in Chinese, the word "crisis" is comprised of two characters – one represents danger and the other represents opportunity The comment made by John F. KENNEDY in 1959 which showed his readiness to indulge in BRINKMANSHIP if he thought it could benefit America and the world.

cronyism The award of jobs and contracts by a political leader to close friends, rather than on merit and through fair competition. Harold Ickes, Franklin Roosevelt's Interior Secretary and a thorn in the flesh of several corrupt politicians, was an early user of the term when he declared: "I am against government by crony." And in May 1952 Walter Lippmann wrote:

> The Truman administration appeared to be foundering in a mess of corruption, cronyism, extravagance and so forth.

cross. crossbencher In the HOUSE OF LORDS, a PEER without party affiliation who sits on the Cross Benches, sideways on to the Government and Opposition benches and facing the WOOLSACK. "Crossbencher" is also the title of the long-running speculative political column in the *Sunday Express*.

cross-border security The name given by UK, Ulster and Irish politicians to the efforts of the London and Dublin governments to co-ordinate the actions of their security forces on either side of the border between NORTHERN IRELAND and the Irish Republic. Such co-operation against IRA and other terrorists has grown steadily closer, though embarrassing misunderstandings still do occur and there have been occasions when British troops or helicopters have "inadvertently" strayed into or over the Republic. Conclusion of an EXTRADITION agreement between the UK and the Republic, and subsequent steps to make it work, have had a considerable effect, but hard-line UNIONISTS in the North still complain that the security forces there are not allowed to cross the border in **hot pursuit**.

Cross of Lorraine The two-barred patriarchal and archiepiscopal cross which was adopted by DE GAULLE as the emblem of the FREE FRENCH during World War II, because it had also been the emblem of Joan of Arc. When CHURCHILL's patience with France's exiled would-be leader was wearing thin, he confided:

> The heaviest cross I have to bear is the Cross of Lorraine.

Crossman diaries The *Diaries of A Cabinet Minister* kept, and eventually published, by the UK Labour politician Richard Crossman (1907–74). An Oxford don whose book, *Government and the Governed*, was a textbook of how the British constitution should perform, Crossman's diaries of life in Harold

WILSON's Cabinet from 1964 to 1970 are a classic, though not for the reasons intended. They do expose very clearly the workings of government, but also portray their author as a man obsessed by the need to be part of the "inner Cabinet" Wilson was always toying with setting up, and a minister whose political antennae were not as acute as he imagined. Crossman is best remembered as a LEADER OF THE HOUSE who tried to introduce daytime sittings in the Commons, and – until frustrated by Michael Foot and Enoch POWELL – reform the HOUSE OF LORDS, and also as the Health Secretary who, to Labour's dismay, announced increased health charges on the day of the 1969 local elections.

Crown, the The British monarchy personified in the State. The Cabinet Secretary Sir Robert Armstrong (*see* ECONOMICAL WITH THE TRUTH) advised civil servants that

> The Crown means and is represented by the government of the day.

The fount of power in the British state is also described as the **Crown in Parliament**: the nexus between the legislature and the nominal head of the executive.

> The myth of the king in Parliament has lasted for centuries, and it is not quite done for yet. It cannot be defended on any grounds except that it happens to be the way the British do things.
>
> HUGH BROGAN, *Penguin History of America.*

Crown Agents The agency of the UK government, supposed to organize bulk purchasing for the smaller COMMONWEALTH governments, which became the subject of a major scandal in 1977. A committee under Mr. Justice Fay confirmed rumours that it had lost some £270 million of clients' money through rash involvement in property and fringe banking, without proper monitoring from the Ministry of Overseas Development, the Treasury or the Bank of England.

Crown immunity The legal doctrine under which many of the operations of the UK government have been immune from criminal or regulatory sanctions. Its scope was limited in the mid-1980s after strong Parliamentary objections to a situation where no action could be taken to enforce hygiene regulations in NHS hospitals where patients were dying from food poisoning caused not by their condition but by the state of the kitchens.

Crown prince In most monarchies, the formal title for the heir to the THRONE; in Britain a male heir is designated PRINCE OF WALES, a female heir receiving no specific title in advance of her accession.

demise of the Crown The formal term for the death of a King or Queen, and the constitutional consequences flowing from it. These are strictly limited nowadays, with no requirement for Parliament to be dissolved.

The influence of the Crown has increased, is increasing and ought to be diminished The classic Parliamentary motion tabled on 6 April 1780 by John Dunning, later Baron Ashburton (1731–83) in protest at what was seen as the increasingly AUTOCRATIC rule of King George III. Its passage is seen as a turning point, ending a period when the House of Commons had been relatively supine and marking the beginning of its role as a contemporary democratic legislature.

CRS France's national riot police, who are bused into any city when large demonstrations or political unrest are expected, and which have a well-deserved reputation for meeting force with force (and on occasions getting their retaliation in first). At moments of domestic crisis, such as the ÉVÈNEMENTS of 1968, parts of Paris have become a battleground between rioters hurling paving-stones and CRS detachments in riot gear using batons on every cranium within reach and setting off tear gas.

cruel. cruel and unusual punishment The phrase in the US CONSTITUTION (the 8th Amendment in the BILL OF RIGHTS) under which the SUPREME COURT in 1972 declared the death penalty to be UNCONSTITUTIONAL. Taken by 5 to 4 after President Nixon had already begun to dilute the liberalism of the WARREN COURT, the ruling was reversed seven years later (*see* GILMORE case).

Cruella de Ville The nickname given by Conservative MPs at Westminster to **Edwina Currie** (1946–), the colourful and outspoken colleague who had a brief and controversial career in 1986–88 as a junior Health Minister and later turned down a post in John MAJOR's government. The name was originally that of a glamorous villainess in the Walt Disney film *101 Dalmatians*. Mrs. Currie first attracted attention by brandishing a pair of handcuffs at a Conservative Party conference, and in 1983 was elected MP for South Derbyshire. From that moment she was enveloped in publicity, though in a libel case in 1991 she insisted:

> I am not, and never have been, interested in publicity for myself.

As a BACKBENCHER, despite her obvious talent, she made both noise and enemies. Tory colleagues rushed to criticize her, saying: "Empty vessels make the most noise" – Ann Winterton; "She has done for our party what King Herod did for baby-sitting" – Andrew Mackay; "She has been to the Tory party what the Bishop of Durham is to the Church of England" – Richard Holt; "She is so conceited

I'm sure she has her X-rays retouched" – Anon.; "At Christmas I would rather hang her and kiss the mistletoe" – Anon.; "She is writing a book. It is called 'Famous People who have met me'" – Anon. Margaret Thatcher's decision to appoint her junior Health Minister was recognition of her undoubted talents, and she took to the job with enthusiasm, telling North-Eastern men to stop eating so many chips because it gave them heart disease, conducting a campaign against heavy smoking (including by her boss, Health Secretary Kenneth Clarke), and saying as the AIDS scare grew:

> My message to the businessmen of this country when they go abroad on business is that there is one thing above all that they can take with them to stop them catching AIDS – the wife.

But her most controversial moment came when evidence emerged that a number of people eating eggs were catching *Salmonella*, a severe form of food poisoning. With the public already nervous, Mrs. Currie told a television interviewer on 3 December 1988:

> Most of the egg production in this country, sadly, is now infected with *Salmonella*.

Apart from not being true, the statement caused a public panic, egg consumption slumping. It enraged the poultry industry, Tory MPs with farm constituencies and John MacGregor, the Minister of Agriculture; and a fortnight later Mrs. Currie resigned. She resumed her career on the back benches in slightly muted form, but after the 1992 election made it clear Europe was her priority, turning down a MINISTER OF STATE's job at the Home Office.

> When she goes to the dentist, he's the one who needs the anaesthetic. FRANK DOBSON MP (Lab.).

Cruise missiles The low-flying winged missiles driven by an air-breathing turbofan, which are one of the most versatile and effective elements of America's nuclear and conventional arsenal; they have a speed of some 885 m.p.h. They are guided by an inertial system that is updated during flight by matching the contours of the land they overfly with maps stored in their computer memories. Cruise missiles were a subject of great political controversy in Western Europe in the early 1980s when America deployed ground-launched versions with nuclear warheads to counter the Soviet SS20; heated campaigns against deployment (*see* GREENHAM WOMEN) failed, and they were finally withdrawn under the INF agreement of December 1987, which also committed the Soviet Union to withdraw and destroy its medium range missiles. The sea-launched *Tomahawk* missile survived some spectacular failures in initial testing off the coast of California to be used with devastating impact in the GULF WAR, reporters in Baghdad telling enthralled TV audiences that they could be seen following the street pattern and almost stopping at red lights. There is also an air-launched version, which the CARTER administration deployed from B52 bombers as an alternative to developing the B1 BOMBER.

crypt (1) In the House of Commons, the chapel under ST. STEPHEN's Hall which survived the fire of 1834 and now serves as a place of occasional worship for MPs. Christenings of members' children, the occasional wedding and memorial service are held there, and the Moderator of the General Assembly of the Church of Scotland preaches there each year during his official visit to London. (2) The vault beneath the ROTUNDA of the US CAPITOL, which houses a photographic exhibition of the Capitol's history, the LADIES IN A BATHTUB statue and a huge head of Lincoln by Gutzon Borglum. In the centre of the floor is a compass stone, marking the point from which all Washington streets are lettered and numbered. Beneath the crypt lies the tomb that was intended for George Washington, who was eventually buried at MOUNT VERNON. It now contains the bier on which Lincoln's coffin rested in the Rotunda. From 1820 to 1828, in anticipation of Washington's arrival, the floor of the Rotunda lay open so that the public could look down into the tomb. The opening was sealed, and the full crypt created, because damp from below was harming the paintings in the Rotunda.

crypto-Communist or Fascist Someone who is actually a Communist or Fascist, but keeps their true allegiance a secret and postures as a member of a less extreme grouping. In one intemperate moment near the end of her Premiership, Margaret Thatcher surprised MPs on both sides of the Commons by calling Neil KINNOCK a "crypto-Communist".

CS Gas A potent form of tear gas used by France's CRS on rioting students during the ÉVÈNEMENTS of 1968, by the security forces against rioters in NORTHERN IRELAND, especially between 1969 and 1972, by a protester over Ireland who threw a canister into the CHAMBER of the House of Commons, and by Iranian students who in 1978 rioted on the ELLIPSE against a visit to Washington by the Shah of Iran.

CSCE Conference on Security and Co-Operation in Europe. The security framework established under the 1975 HELSINKI

ACCORDS, involving 35 European countries plus America and Canada. At conferences in Belgrade (1977), Madrid (1980) and Vienna (1986–89), progress was made on CONFIDENCE-BUILDING measures and procedures, and with the sudden end of the COLD WAR, CSCE emerged with the potential to provide security and stability for NATO and former WARSAW PACT countries alike. It speedily spawned the European Bank for Reconstruction and Development (1980) and the CHARTER OF PARIS, but proved powerless to check the civil war in former Yugoslavia.

CSU Christian Social Union. The conservative, Catholic party in Bavaria, led for many years by Franz-Josef Strauss (*see* SPIEGEL AFFAIR), which generally operates as an ally of Germany's more moderate Christian Democrats.

Cuba. Cuban missile crisis The moment in 1962 when the SUPERPOWERS came closer to war, and the world to nuclear destruction, than at any other point in the COLD WAR. It stemmed from America's discovery from aerial photographs that Soviet experts were building offensive missile bases in Fidel Castro's Cuba, thus posing a direct threat; US Ambassador Adlai Stevenson displayed them to great effect at the UNITED NATIONS. On 22 October President KENNEDY ordered a naval QUARANTINE against ships transporting offensive military equipment to Cuba, and demanded the removal of the bases. Two Soviet ships bound for Cuba were stopped by US warships, searched for war materials and then allowed to continue when nothing was found. Kennedy and the Soviet leader Nikita Khruschev were EYEBALL TO EYEBALL, with the risk of war if the Kremlin stood its ground. After critical days of suspense, it was Khruschev who blinked first, first offering to dismantle the bases and pull out its missiles in return for the withdrawal of NATO missiles from Turkey; Kennedy rejected the offer, and Khruschev eventually settled for a US commitment not to invade Cuba (*see* Bay of PIGS). The crisis subsided; the bases were removed to the PENTAGON's satisfaction on 8 November, and the US naval blockade was lifted on 20 November. The world breathed an almost audible sigh of relief.

> I guess this is the week I earn my salary.
> JFK to his staff.

> The Cuban missile crisis enabled the United States to pull defeat out of the jaws of victory. RICHARD NIXON.

> They talk about who won and who lost. Human reason won. Mankind won. KHRUSCHEV, November 1962.

> We achieved a spectacular success without having to fire a single shot.
> KHRUSCHEV, *Khruschev Remembers* (1971).

Fair Play for Cuba Committee The pro-Castro organization which Lee Harvey Oswald, supposed assassin of JFK in DALLAS, joined in New Orleans in 1962. It shared its premises with a CIA-backed group running guns to Castro's opponents.

It is our destiny to have Cuba and it is folly to debate the question The declaration made by Sen. Stephen Douglas in 1858, 37 years before a revolt against Spanish rule gave America the chance its IMPERIALISTS had been waiting for. The ANNEXATION of Cuba had in fact been contemplated in Washington since the JEFFERSON administration. *See* PLATT AMENDMENT; SPANISH-AMERICAN WAR.

Cullom committee The special committee, appointed by the US Senate in 1885, which paved the way for the first Federal legislation to curb inter-state commerce, and specifically the monopolistic practices of the railroads. The committee, chaired by the Republican Sen. Shelby M. Cullom of Illinois, held hearings throughout the nation, then produced a 2000-page report concluding that the regulation of inter-state trade would have near-unanimous public support. The Interstate Commerce Act of 1887 stemmed directly from it, though more effective legislation took considerably longer.

culture. Cultural revolution The Great Proletarian Cultural Revolution which took place in 1966 under the direction of CHAIRMAN MAO Tse-Tung, arguably doing even more damage than his GREAT LEAP FORWARD. Intended to invigorate revolutionary fervour and avoid stagnation and REVISIONISM, it involved replacing leaders of the old guard, abolishing the formal education system (many universities closed) and mobilizing students as RED GUARDS. For almost ten years, until Mao's death, there was social and political turmoil in which foreigners were reviled and millions of urban "BOURGEOIS reactionaries" were sent to the country to be "re-educated" by manual labour.

> In history it has always been those with little learning who have overthrown those with too much learning.
> MAO TSE-TUNG.

Culture of Contentment The book published in 1992 by the veteran Canadian-born US liberal economist John Kenneth Galbraith (1908–) which argued that the norm for the West was becoming a nation's prosperous two-thirds governing the underprivileged rest. Galbraith maintained that traditionally the prosperous one-third governed, with the rest of the population exerting pressure for reform and greater equality; with prosperity more evenly spread, the pressure on government was less. Government, wrote Galbraith, was now "accommodated not to reality or common need, but to the beliefs of the contented, who now form the majority of those who vote".

Cunningham amendment The amendment attached in 1978 to the Labour Government's Scotland Bill which provided that a "Yes" vote in a REFERENDUM on DEVOLUTION would be invalid unless half of Scotland's registered electors had supported it. It was the brainchild of the Labour (later SDP) MP George Cunningham (1931–), a fiercely anti-devolutionist Scot representing a London constituency. In the event there was a narrow "Yes" majority on 1 March 1979 – around 80,000 out of 2,380,000 who voted. With a low turnout of 63.8%, only 32.9% of registered voters were in favour; in none of Scotland's administrative regions was the 40% threshold surmounted. The Callaghan government fell in with the amendment by deciding against further action on HOME RULE; the SNP reacted by putting down a no-CONFIDENCE motion. Margaret Thatcher's Conservatives threw their weight behind the motion and defeated the Labour government by one vote, and in the ensuing General Election an anti-Devolution government was elected and most of the SNP lost their seats (*see* TURKEYS VOTING FOR AN EARLY CHRISTMAS).

Curragh Mutiny The threat in March 1914 by British cavalry officers stationed at the Curragh (a military training camp in Co. Kildare, west of Dublin) to resign if they were ordered to coerce Ulster into accepting Irish HOME RULE. The threat hardly constituted a mutiny; the greater threat to ASQUITH's government lay with Sir Edward Carson and Bonar Law, who had said that they would lead the UNIONISTS and Conservatives in armed resistance to ensure that Ulster was governed from London, not Dublin (*see* ULSTER VOLUNTEERS). Nevertheless the "mutiny", caused partly by lack of firmness and consistency from the Minister of War Colonel J. E. B. Seely (*see* THROW TO THE WOLVES) heightened an already charged atmosphere, and had WORLD WAR I not unexpectedly intervened, the threat could have reasserted itself.

> The Army will hear nothing of politics from me, and I expect to hear nothing of politics from the Army.
>
> ASQUITH, speaking in his Fife constituency, 6 April 1914.

Currie, Edwina *See* CRUELLA DE VILLE.

Customs scandal The scandal that broke in Canada in 1925 over the revelation by a Commons committee of extensive corruption in the Customs Department. Stemming from efforts to evade PROHIBITION in the United States, a system of "rum-running" across the border and along the coast had developed into a wholesale system of evasion on a range of commodities. The committee reported "not merely the tacit connivance of a multitude of Customs officials but in many cases their active co-operation in making a wholesale mockery of the Customs laws of Canada". Faced with the threatened desertion of 24 Progressive MPs to deny him a majority, the Liberal Prime Minister Mackenzie King advised the GOVERNOR-GENERAL, Lord Byng, to dissolve Parliament. As there had been an election within the past year and King had not been defeated in the Commons, Byng refused. King then resigned and the Conservative Arthur Meighen was asked to form a government, only for it to be defeated within a week. An election did then ensue, and King fought it on his (incorrect) contention that Byng was bound to accept his advice and that the Imperial power was interfering in Canada's internal affairs. The Customs Affair was thus forgotten as it turned into what became known as the **Constitutional Crisis of 1926**, and King was returned with a clear majority.

cut and run To abandon one's duties and pull out of a struggle one is honour-bound to continue; early in his administration President Nixon refused to "cut and run" by pursuing any policy over the VIETNAM WAR that looked like a US withdrawal. In Britain, where the Prime Minister picks the date of an election, it is a time-honoured tactic for the Opposition to claim, any time in the last two years of a PARLIAMENT, that the Government is about to "cut and run" and call an election because it knows the economy is about to deteriorate. When no election is called, the Opposition then asserts that it has frightened the Prime Minister out of calling an election because the Government knows it would have lost. The term has a cricketing origin: the batsman "cuts" the ball fine of the off stump and immediately starts a run.

cycle of deprivation The theory advanced by Sir Keith Joseph (*see* MAD MONK) and others that poverty is self-perpetuating, even when the conventional methods of the WELFARE STATE are used as an attempted remedy, and that its elimination may be beyond the ability of any government to achieve.

czar An alternative spelling of the Russian TSAR, which is used in America (especially Washington) to describe an all-powerful figure. It became the nickname of House

Speaker Thomas Reed (1839–1902), reflecting his aggregation of power to himself, and was also applied to his successor Joseph Cannon (*see* FOUL-MOUTHED JOE), who exerted total power by gaining control of the RULES COMMITTEE. It is also used of a powerful industrialist or BUREAUCRAT; during the two World Wars it was used in Washington for the heads of key agencies prosecuting or policing the war effort.

D

D-Notice Defence Notice. The system under which the British media censors itself in peacetime about sensitive (and supposedly-sensitive) security matters. It operates through occasional requests to the media from a special secretariat at the Ministry of Defence not to publish specific items for reasons of security. Two or three D-notices are usually current at any time, mostly requiring secrecy about a particular training exercise or military project. The system, introduced in 1911 and policed by a committee of editors, has been generally adhered to despite left-wing denunciations of it as a self-policing form of censorship that compromises the Press. However the system's advocates say it has avoided a more formal and draconian restrictive régime.

Dail Eireann The legislature of the Irish Republic, established in 1918 by SINN FEIN members of the UK Parliament who refused to take their seats at Westminster. On independence from Britain the *Dail* (pronounced Doil, in the Irish language; Assembly of the Irish) was legitimized in the Constitution of 1922 as the lower house of the Republic's legislature.

Daily Worker The newspapers which served as the official organs of the US and UK COMMUNIST Parties. They were published respectively in Chicago from 1924 to 1968, and in London from 1930 to 1966, when it changed its name to the *Morning Star*, eventually breaking with the Party's EUROCOMMUNIST line.

Daley machine The Democratic organization and city government in Chicago (COOK COUNTY), ruthlessly but efficiently controlled by Richard J. Daley (1902–76), Mayor from 1955 to 1976 and last of the big city BOSSes. It was usually able to control Democratic politics in Illinois, and to deliver the state to the Presidential nominee of Daley's choice; in 1960 Daley was widely believed to have stolen Illinois for the Democratic ticket and thus ensured the election of President Kennedy. He reacted to this charge, and others, by declaring: "I resent the insinuendoes." His son (also Richard) served as Mayor 15 years after his father's death – but with a much more open and uncorrupt political organization. *See* CHICAGO CONVENTION; MACHINE POLITICS.

Dallas The Texas city which became on 22 November 1963 the scene of the assassination of President John F. KENNEDY. According to the WARREN COMMISSION Kennedy, who was travelling through the city in a MOTORCADE, was shot by Lee Harvey Oswald from an upper window of the TEXAS SCHOOL BOOK DEPOSITORY. Jacqueline Kennedy (*see* JACKIE O) was with the President, as were Governor John Connally of Texas, who was shot and wounded, and Mrs. Connally who, a few moments before, had told the President:

> You certainly can't say the people of Dallas haven't given you a warm welcome.

DAR Daughters of the AMERICAN REVOLUTION. A patriotic and largely non-partisan (if conservative) group, they acquired notoriety in 1939 when they refused to allow the black singer Marian Anderson to perform in their Constitution Hall. Instead the Interior Department gave her the best stage in Washington – the steps of the Lincoln Memorial – and 75,000 people including a host of celebrities turned out on Easter Sunday to hear her sing.

Das Kapital (Ger. CAPITAL) Karl Marx's definitive work on "scientific" economics, the first volume of which appeared in 1867, and one of the basic texts of MARXISM. The second and third volumes were completed by Friedrich Engels from Marx's notes, appearing in 1885 and 1894. Many world leaders, among them Harold WILSON, have complained that it is almost unreadable.

> A collection of atrocity stories designed to stimulate martial ardour against the enemy. BERTRAND RUSSELL.

dash for growth The sudden and desperate adoption of REFLATIONary policies by a government that needs to deliver economic growth, particularly if an election is looming. In the short term the result is generally an upsurge in economic activity leading to a fall in unemployment and boom conditions, but before long the economy is OVERHEATING and the brakes have to be applied in the form of higher interest rates or taxation.

date. a date which will live in infamy Franklin D. Roosevelt's furious and unforgettable description of Japan's attack on PEARL HARBOR on 7 December 1941. It comes from his speech to a JOINT SESSION of Congress the following day in which he sought a declaration of war – which was granted with just one vote against. FDR's actual words were:

> Yesterday, December 7, 1941 – a date which will live in infamy – the United States of America was suddenly and deliberately attacked by naval and air forces of the Empire of Japan.

Davis, Jefferson (1808–89) President of the CONFEDERATE States of America, 1861–65. A Kentucky-born West Point graduate and cotton planter, Davis was elected to Congress in 1845, fought in the 1846–47 MEXICAN WAR, served as a Senator 1847–50 and Secretary for War 1853–57. As leader of the STATES' RIGHTS Party he urged Congress in 1860 not to outlaw slavery. When the Confederate states seceded, Davis was nominated President for a six-year term; introducing him at Montgomery in 1861 as President-elect, William Yancey declared: "The man and the hour have met!" However his Vice-President, Alexander Stephens, described him as "weak and vacillating, timid, petulant, peevish, obstinate but not firm". His UNION adversaries detected a greater fault, Winfield Scott writing: "He is not a cheap Judas. I do not think he would have sold the Savior for thirty shillings; but for the successorship to Pontius Pilate he would have betrayed Christ and the apostles and the whole Christian church." On the Confederate defeat, Davis was charged with treason by the victorious Union, but released under amnesty in 1868.

> The only American with whose public character BENEDICT ARNOLD need not fear comparison.
>
> THEODORE ROOSEVELT.

Dawes. Dawes Act The measure passed by the US Congress in 1887 which granted 160 acres and US citizenship to heads of Indian families who would abandon their tribal allegiance, with land freed up on reservations being sold to White settlers. The Act – also known as the **Allotment Act** – benefited the Whites more than the Indians, who were to lose 86 million acres of their best land in the next half-century, so fresh incentives were offered in 1906 under the **Burke Act**.

Dawes plan The American scheme implemented in 1924 to break the deadlock between France and Germany over the non-payment of REPARATIONS. It began the revival of a Germany economy stricken by inflation and the burden of reparations – and hence of post-war Europe – but ultimately proved inadequate and was replaced by the YOUNG PLAN. A key element was a massive international loan. It earned its author Brig.-Gen. Charles Gates Dawes (1865–1951) the NOBEL PEACE PRIZE (jointly) and nomination as Coolidge's Vice-President.

day. A day I was meant not to see Margaret Thatcher's reaction to the BRIGHTON BOMBING in October 1984 in which she narrowly escaped assassination by the IRA. She said that when she was sitting in church three days later, she suddenly realized that "this was a day I was meant not to see".

go ahead, make my day The threat uttered by Clint Eastwood (and backed up by a gun) as Dirty Harry in the 1983 film *Sudden Impact*. Ronald Reagan took it up in March 1985, telling a business conference when Congress was pressing for tax increases:

> I have my veto pen drawn and ready for any tax increase that Congress might even think of sending up. And I have only one thing to say to the tax increasers – "Go ahead, make my day."

DEs In the sociological and pollsters' scale of social groups from A to E, unskilled and casual workers and their families; for a full explanation *see* C2s.

de Gaulle, General Charles André Joseph Marie (1890–1970) Leader of the FREE FRENCH during World War II, and President of France 1958–69. The inspiration of the GAULLIST movement, with his rigid concept of the destiny of France and his own destiny to lead it. "When I want to know what France thinks, I ask myself," he said. He had this certainty even as a young officer when he declared: "Such as I am, I cannot fail to be, at a given moment, in the centre of the stage." A 1922 War College report termed him:

> intelligent – brilliant – resourceful. He spoils his undoubted talents by his excessive assurance, his contempt for other people's point of view and his attitude of a king in exile.

Having predicted Germany's BLITZKRIEG, the towering de Gaulle escaped to Britain when it happened to lead France's fightback. CHURCHILL found him exasperating, declaring: "The hardest cross I have to bear is the CROSS OF LORRAINE." When de Gaulle was proving particularly inflexible, Churchill minuted: "I have every sympathy with General de Gaulle and his violent tantrums, but let us conquer some of his country before we start squabbling about how it is to be governed." To Harold Macmillan, de Gaulle had "all the rigidity of a poker without its occasional warmth". Leaders of the other ANGLO-SAXON peoples for whom de Gaulle developed a life-long resentment felt the same, US Ambassador Robert Murphy calling him "a Frankenstein monster of which we ought to welcome the opportunity to rid ourselves". Yet when Germany was defeated, de Gaulle could justifiably claim:

> I was France.

After the LIBERATION of France, when he made a courageous walk down a *Champs Elysées* still open to German snipers, he was France's obvious leader. But Communist and other opposition denied him power. He then founded the RPF (Rally of the French People), the first Gaullist party, but its support slipped from an initial 40% and in 1953 he gave up the leadership and retired to COLOMBEY-LES-DEUX-ÉGLISES. He was called back in 1958 after successive governments failed to resolve the Algerian conflict and de Gaulle's supporters in the army were rumoured to be planning a military coup (*see* THIRTEEN PLOTS OF MAY 13); as the crisis came to a head he announced:

> Now I shall return to my village and there will remain at the disposition of the nation.

De Gaulle was duly installed as President of the FIFTH REPUBLIC, declaring: "The national task that has been incumbent on me for 18 years is hereby confirmed." He then gave Algeria its independence, to the fury of of the hard-line officers who had hoped their revolt which hastened his return would reap dividends. The result was the OAS campaign to assassinate him; of one narrow miss he declared:

> They really are bad shots.

He justified his U-turn on Algeria by saying: "In politics it is necessary either to betray one's country or the electorate. I prefer to betray the electorate."

In power de Gaulle presided over an upsurge of prosperity and technology, formed a new ENTENTE with West Germany and blocked Macmillan's efforts to get Britain into the EUROPEAN COMMUNITY. It was in this period that Franz-Josef Strauss said of de Gaulle: "He is not a genius, just a political cosmonaut, continually in orbit." The British revue duo Michael Flanders and Donald Swann were blunter:

> This old man thinks he's St. Joan.

De Gaulle survived the ÉVÈNEMENTS of 1968 though only after flying to Germany to ensure French forces there were loyal; at the height of the unrest he was asked for permission to detain Jean-Paul Sartre and replied: "How can you arrest Voltaire?" But the following year he made a REFERENDUM on regional government a matter of CONFIDENCE and resigned when defeated.

De Lorean affair The scandal surrounding the collapse of a car plant in Catholic West Belfast founded in 1978 by John Z. de Lorean (1925–), with over £80 million in backing from the UK government. De Lorean, a former vice-president of General Motors, planned a revolutionary gull-winged stainless steel car largely for the US market. The Labour government was anxious to back it, as mainly Catholic West Belfast was a blackspot for unemployment and IRA terrorism. De Lorean chose Northern Ireland after an aide told him: "the worse the area, the more financing they'll give us"; the initial advance alone was £53 million. Margaret Thatcher's government continued to back the project and the first car was produced in 1981, but there were problems over price and quality, sales were slow and on 19 October 1982 the plant closed with the loss of 2500 jobs. Fewer than 10,000 cars were built; one achieved fame in the 1985 film *Back to the Future.* The day the receivers moved in, de Lorean was arrested in Los Angeles on a charge of bankrolling a 59 lb. cocaine shipment; he was acquitted two years later. De Lorean was subsequently charged with defrauding US investors in de Lorean of $4.9 million, and cleared in December 1986. The one proven fraud was committed by Colin Chapman, head of Britain's Lotus Cars, and its finance director Fred Bushell; in 1992 Bushell was jailed for 3 years in Belfast and fined £2.2 million for defrauding the company, with Chapman, of £10 million over a decade. The UK government sued de Lorean to recover its stake, and in August 1992 after selling his New York penthouse, de Lorean handed over £5 million. But £30 million in loans from the UK taxpayer were still missing.

Deacon US Secret Service code name for President CARTER.

dead. dead calf At the height of the 1979 UK election campaign, Margaret Thatcher, while electioneering in a cattle market, picked up a calf and awkwardly held it for the photographers. Her husband Denis, seeing this, exclaimed in the hearing of reporters:

> Unless she's careful, we're going to have a dead calf on our hands.

dead Labour A Cardiff CONSTITUENT's unfortunate description to Speaker George Thomas (later Lord Tonypandy) of the political allegiance of her deceased mother who was laid out in the front room when he called.

dead on arrival (1) There is a tradition/legal fiction that a member of Parliament cannot die in the PALACE OF WESTMINSTER. Any who does is taken to a hospital where it is announced that they are "dead on arrival". (2) Any legislation from the WHITE HOUSE which from the outset stands no chance of being accepted by the Congress.

dead parrot The draft constitution for a unified UK LIBERAL and Social Democratic party which was instantly rejected when put to the parties' MPs early in 1988. It was named after the Monty Python television sketch in which John Cleese complains to a pet shop owner that the parrot he had just bought was dead. Margaret Thatcher compared the LIBERAL DEMOCRATS, product of the eventual Liberal/SDP merger, with a dead parrot in her 1990 party conference speech; when they won the Eastbourne BY-ELECTION from the Tories shortly after, Conservative party chairman Kenneth Baker declared:

> The parrot has twitched.

dead sheep, savaged by a Chancellor of the Exchequer Denis HEALEY's withering retort to his Tory SHADOW, Sir Geoffrey Howe, in a Commons debate on June 14 1978. Healey said: "That part of his speech was rather like being savaged by a dead sheep." He insisted the phrase was not original, and that CHURCHILL had once dismissed an attack by ATTLEE as "like being savaged by a pet lamb".

Dear Bill The column in the UK satirical magazine PRIVATE EYE throughout the Thatcher years and occasionally after, purporting to be a letter from the Prime Minister's husband Denis to his old golfing friend Bill – Lord Deedes, Editor of the *Daily Telegraph*. Downing Street insiders said it gave an alarmingly accurate insight into the workings of that government and the volcanic nature of its leader.

Dearos The Boston supporters of Boss John "HONEY FITZ" Fitzgerald (1863–1951), grandfather of John F. KENNEDY. The name came from his description of his power base as "Dear old North End".

death. Death of a Princess A BBC television drama-documentary built around the alleged execution of a Westernized Saudi princess for an affair with a married man. When shown on 9 April 1980, it caused a near-rupture in relations between Britain and Saudi Arabia, whose government ordered the British ambassador home.

Death on the Rock Another UK television programme, this time on the shooting by undercover SAS personnel of three intending IRA bombers – Mairead Farrell, Daniel McCann and Sean Savage – in Gibraltar on 6 March 1988. The programme, shown on ITV on 28 April, caused a political storm by disputing the UK government's claim that they had been killed in self-defence; it contended that two of the three had been shot after putting their hands up. The programme was broadcast despite calls for it to be banned, and a 19-day inquest eventually returned a verdict of "lawful killing" despite continuing discrepancies in evidence.

death squad A Latin American contribution to Western civilization. It comprises members of the military or the police under a usually right-wing dictatorship who travel round out of uniform and in unmarked cars, wiping out opponents of the regime and anyone else against whom they have a grudge. The concept has found some adherents in Africa and Asia.

deaths in the chamber An occasional feature of all legislatures. In the US HOUSE OF REPRESENTATIVES former President John Quincy ADAMS suffered a fatal stroke at his desk in 1848, in 1932 Rep. Edward Eslick, a Democrat from Tennessee, dropped dead in mid-speech and in 1940 Rep. Morris Edelstein, a New York Democrat, died as soon as he had finished denouncing an anti-Semitic speech by John Rankin of Mississippi. On 10 February 1983 Michael Roberts, a Welsh Office Minister, collapsed at the DESPATCH BOX in Britain's House of Commons and died. In the late 1940s Rep. Adolphe Sabath, octogenarian chairman of the House RULES COMMITTEE, pretended to be dying so as to prevent the Georgia Democrat Eugene Cox moving an alteration to the rules. Cox momentarily believed his insistence on his proposal had killed Sabath – then saw the chairman open an eye once the crisis was over.

merchants of death A popular term for arms manufacturers and exporters, first heard in 1934 during an investigation of the industry by the United States Senate.

Deaver syndrome The *Washington Post*'s term for the practice of former high US government officials rapidly cashing in on their contacts after leaving office. It gained its name from the scandal surrounding Mike Deaver, who within a year of resigning as President Reagan's deputy chief of staff in 1985 had lined up six-figure LOBBYING contracts to represent Canada, Mexico, Singapore, Korea, Puerto Rico, CBS, TWA, Philip Morris and Rockwell International. Accused of violating laws barring high office-holders from lobbying within a year of leaving their job, he was eventually convicted on three charges of perjury. *See* REVOLVING DOOR; SLEAZE FACTOR.

debate A structured exchange of views in a legislature or other elected body, either as part of the passage of a Bill or on a specific question, generally but not always culminating in a vote. Also a similarly-structured exchange between two individuals or two bodies of opinion on television or in a debating society.

floor debate In the US Congress, a debate by the entire House or Senate, rather than by a committee.

Great Debate In the UK, a national discussion on educational standards launched in 1978 by James Callaghan (*see* SUNNY JIM) and Education Secretary Shirley Williams.

Lincoln-Douglas debates The great debates between Abraham LINCOLN and Sen. Stephen Douglas in 1858 when they were contending for Douglas's Illinois seat in the Senate. They met seven times throughout the state, speaking to crowds of up to 15,000 and attracting national publicity; slavery was the dominant issue. Douglas won the vote, but Lincoln made the lasting impact.

presidential debate A direct confrontation between candidates for the US Presidency on national television; the first was between Richard Nixon and John F. KENNEDY in 1960 (*see* FIVE O'CLOCK SHADOW). President Eisenhower feared Kennedy would come out on top because "Nixon was widely known; Kennedy was not". Nixon scored better in the three debates that followed, partly because a crash course of milkshakes made him look less cadaverous. But fewer voters watched them, the die having been cast. Such debates became a regular feature of Presidential campaigns with the Ford-Carter debates of 1976. In 1980 Raquel Welch termed the Carter/Reagan debates "The one with the fat lips v. the one with no lips." And Nixon told Reagan: "Since I've never won a debate, let me tell you now not to lose one."

Debategate The mystery/scandal in 1980 when briefing papers prepared for President CARTER prior to their television debates fell into the hands of the Reagan campaign team. The Carter camp claimed the loose-leaf folder was stolen; the Reaganites said it had been sent to them anonymously. William J. Casey, Reagan's campaign manager and subsequently head of the CIA, fell under suspicion of having secured the papers, though he denied it.

Decent Interval The title of a 1977 book by Frank Snepp, awarded the CIA's Medal of Merit for his work as an analyst in VIETNAM, exposing the chaos and incompetence of the final stages of the American presence. Snepp, who had to resign from the CIA to publish the book, argued that the Nixon administration, and in particular Dr. Henry KISSINGER, had cynically abandoned the people of South Vietnam to the Communists under the guise of a lasting peace, and that warnings of the final North Vietnamese offensive in 1975 were systematically ignored. He argued that only the heroism of a few young Embassy staff and the ingenuity of the Defense Attaché had prevented the US Embassy in Saigon falling into Communist hands. The phrase "decent interval" has come to mean any situation in which a government creates a scenario which after a suitable period can be quietly and cynically unravelled.

decentralization The practice of moving administrators and departments out of the national capital to provincial centres in order to benefit regional economies.

declaration A portentous announcement, in particular the result of an election.

Declaration of Conscience The statement made in the Senate on 1 June 1950 by Margaret Chase Smith (1897–) and six other anti-McCARTHY Republicans, emphasizing the rights of any American to criticize, hold unpopular beliefs, protest and think freely.

(Second) Declaration of Havana Fidel Castro's violent and revolutionary speech in January 1962 after Cuba's suspension from the OAS in which he appealed to the peoples of Latin America to rise up against IMPERIALISM.

Declaration of Independence *See* INDEPENDENCE.

Declaration of Interdependence John F. KENNEDY's aim, echoing the Declaration of INDEPENDENCE, of a mutually beneficial ATLANTIC partnership "between the new union now emerging in Europe and the old American union".

Declaration of Intent Statements made by the leaders of the UK trade union movement to work with a Labour government to exercise wage restraint in return for pressure to keep prices down. They are generally made to avoid the imposition of a PRICES AND INCOMES POLICY at times of economic crisis.

Declaration of war The formal announcement that a state is opening hostilities against another.

overnight declaration The announcement of an election result the day after polling, generally where the count has not begun until that morning.

Universal Declaration of Human Rights *See* HUMAN.

declare an interest *See* INTEREST.

deep. deep doodoo, in A euphemism for "in deep shit" – meaning "in very serious trouble". It was frequently used by George BUSH – and first quoted by the *Wall Street Journal* in 1986; Vice-President Bush, asked what would happen to a Chinese official who was too friendly with Americans, said:

> He would have been in deep doodoo.

deep freeze scandal The episode in which Brig.-Gen. Harry Vaughan, President Truman's top military aide, hinted to a Milwaukee deep freeze manufacturer, Harry Hoffman, that he and the President needed new freezers for their homes. Hoffman sent one to Vaughan, one to Truman for his house in Missouri, and also freezers to four key Truman aides. Only Treasury Secretary Fred Vinson sent his back. Acceptance of the freezers was not illegal – only gifts from foreign governments are barred by the Constitution – but Truman's opponents hailed it as a sign of flawed judgment, or worse.

deep throat The unnamed source, high in the Nixon administration, who in parking-garage meetings with Bob Woodward gave the *Washington Post* much of the information it needed to unravel the WATERGATE story. The name came from the early-1970s pornographic film in which a girl played by Linda Lovelace was supposed to have a clitoris in her throat, and put it to exhaustive use. Nixon's acolytes made frantic efforts to identify the source of such damaging leaks, but two decades later his identity has still not been divulged.

defeat Many politicians would agree with the US trade union leader Walter Reuther that "if you're not big enough to lose, you're not big enough to win". But rejection by the voters still hurts, and they take it in very different ways. Winston CHURCHILL, on his government's surprise defeat in 1945, commented: "If this is a blessing, it is certainly very well disguised." And George BROWN, losing his seat in Britain's 1970 election, was even more philosophical, saying: "That's how democracy democts." But the mask often slips, Reginald Maudling (*see* POULSON AFFAIR) saying after Edward Heath beat him for the Tory leadership: "What have I to look forward to but to sit here and get pissed?" Gladstone (*see* GRAND OLD MAN), appropriately, took just the opposite view of the Liberals' 1874 election defeat: "We have been borne down in a torrent of gin and beer." US politicians have taken defeat just as well, and just as badly. Adlai Stevenson, after Eisenhower beat him to the presidency, laconically remarked: "A funny thing happened to me on the way to the White House." But future Speaker Champ Clark, losing his House seat in 1894, inveighed: "What was the cause of my defeat? A system of grossest lies, a complete and unlimited use of the boodle of this country, a subsidized press, a lot of conscienceless demagogues that never ought to have even a name, a host of mountebanks and jugglers sent us down." And Walter Mondale (*see* NORWEGIAN WOOD) chillingly conveyed what it feels like to lose a Presidential election:

> At about 11.30 p.m. on election night, they just push you off the edge of the cliff – and that's it. You might scream on the way down, but you're going to hit the bottom and you're not going to be in office.

Defeat at a CONVENTION has a particular poignancy. In 1980 Edward KENNEDY rallied his troops, declaring: "For me, a few hours ago, this campaign came to an end. For all those whose cares have been our concern, the work goes on, the cause endures, the hope still lives, and the dream shall never die." And four years later Gary Hart observed: "This is one Hart that you will not leave in San Francisco." But Richard NIXON (*see* TRICKY DICK) has the last word on electoral setbacks: "A man is not finished when he is defeated. He is finished when he quits."

If we win, nobody will care. If we lose, there will be nobody left to care Winston CHURCHILL's sanguine assessment of Britain's prospects in a speech to a SECRET SESSION of the House of Commons on 25 June 1941, at the height of WORLD WAR II.

snatch defeat from the jaws of victory To throw away an apparently impregnable position; the opposite of the original "snatch victory from the jaws of defeat". The term may first have been used by the NEW DEALER Paul Porter about the 1948 Presidential campaign of Thomas DEWEY.

victory has a thousand fathers, but defeat is an orphan An observation attributed to John F. KENNEDY.

We are not interested in the possibilities of defeat; they do not exist An assertion first made by Queen Victoria about Britain's prospects in the BOER WAR, repeated by Margaret Thatcher (*see* IRON LADY) over the FALKLANDS. During "black week" in December 1899, when British forces suffered a number of reverses, Queen Victoria told Foreign Secretary A. J. BALFOUR:

> Please understand that there is no one depressed in this house. We are not interested in the possibilities of defeat. They do not exist.

DEFCON Defense Condition. The stages of alert on to which US forces are placed as war becomes more likely. The lower the number, the greater the state of readiness, hence the PENTAGON phrase "raising the DEFCON". DEFCON 5 is the normal peacetime condition; with DEFCON 4 some Air Force crews are on 12 to 15 minutes' notice for takeoff; DEFCON 1 would be declared if hostilities were imminent or already under way.

defector A citizen – frequently an employee or agent – of one state who flees to another, transferring his allegiance, out of repugnance at his own country's policies or regime.

defence (US spelling **defense**) The most basic function of a government. James Wilson declared to the PHILADELPHIA CONVENTION on 11 December 1787: "A government without the power of defence? That is a solecism." 188 years later Gerald FORD observed: "A strong defense is the surest way to peace. Strength makes detente attainable, and we cannot rely on the forbearance of others to protect this nation." Spending on defence has exercised the political community for centuries. The *Kingston Whig* once editorialized: "An excellent figurehead for battleships would be a formal design of a weeping taxpayer." And George Jean Nathan (1882–1958) asked: "What would our government think of a citizen who spent 93 per cent of his income on ammunition?" President Eisenhower, despite or perhaps because of his military background, added a moral dimension: "Every gun that is fired, every warship launched, every rocket fired signifies a theft from those who hunger and are not fed, from those who are cold and are not clothed. [But] this is the best way of life to be found on the road the world has been taking." Marshal of the Royal Air Force Sir John Slessor countered: "The most important social service that a government can do for its people is to keep them alive and free." But Monsignor Bruce Kent of CND added a nuclear argument: "Preparing for suicide is not a very intelligent means of defence."

Defence Estimates The global budget for Britain's armed forces debated by Parliament every year, which was habitually opposed by Labour left-wingers, especially in the late 1950s when CND first made its impact.

defence review A formal and infrequent reassessment of Britain's military commitments and resources, customarily carried out in the search for economies.

Defence policy? I didn't know that you had one. I now observe that Labour are all for sanctions imposed by the League of Nations and that you will fully support them; and that if this leads to hostilities, you will wage war with bows and arrows The acerbic response of Australia's Robert Menzies (*see* MING) in 1936 to an attempt by Sir Stafford Cripps to explain the UK Labour Party's then neo-PACIFIST policies to him.

Millions for defense, but not one cent for tribute The anti-French slogan taken up by the American public at the height of the X, Y AND Z FEVER; it was first uttered by Robert Goodloe Harper.

defenestration The beguilingly obscure term for the barbaric practice of throwing one's political opponents out of an upper window. This was the probable explanation for the death of the Czech Foreign Minister Jan Masaryk, who mysteriously plunged from his office window late in 1948 as Communist pressure on that country's democrats reached its height.

deflation The opposite of INFLATION, the contraction of the economy through the removal of money from circulation. At times of OVERHEATING, deflationary policies may deliberately be pursued; the difficulty arises if the degree of deflation is too great and a RECESSION or HARD LANDING ensues.

deflator The formula applied to planned future levels of spending to allow for the expected rate of inflation.

Delaney amendment An amendment to America's Food, Drug and Cosmetic Act prohibiting the use of substances that cause cancer. The amendment, promoted in 1970 by Rep. James J. Delaney (1901–), stated that "no additive shall be deemed to be safe if it is found, after tests which are appropriate for the evaluation of food additives, to induce cancer in man and animals." It caused controversy in the 1970s because the Food and Drug Administration interpreted it strictly, irrespective of the dose involved. For instance, in 1970 they banned the use of cyclamates, artifical sweetening agents widely used in the food industry, on evidence that massive doses caused bladder tumours in rats. In 1977, they invoked the amendment again to ban the sweetener saccharine.

delaying power The power of Britain's HOUSE OF LORDS to delay, but not reject, legislation passed by the Commons. The PARLIAMENT ACT of 1911 empowered the Lords to delay a Bill for two years before being OVERRIDDEN; the 1949 Act reduced the period to one year.

delegate An individual sent by one organization as its representative to meetings of another. In America, a state's representative at a nominating CONVENTION, often committed to a particular candidate, sometimes not. Also the non-voting members of the HOUSE OF REPRESENTATIVES elected for the District of Columbia, American Samoa, Guam and the Virgin Islands (and, before STATEhood, Hawaii).

delegate count The running tabulation of delegates won by Presidential hopefuls during the PRIMARY season, kept and published by America's main news organizations.

delegation (1) The process of a chief executive or official at any level permitting subordinates to take action on his or her behalf. Public authorities may well delegate powers to sub-committees or other bodies. Not every decision-maker finds it easy to delegate; President James Knox Polk (1795–1849) lamented:

> I prefer to supervise the whole operations of the Government myself rather than entrust the public business to subordinates, and this makes my duties very great.

(2) A party representing a government or organization which travels to meet its counterparts abroad.

delenda est Carthago (Lat. Carthage must be destroyed) The statement with which Cato the Elder (234–149 B.C.) opened every speech in the Roman Senate. It has become synonymous with any campaign by a lone voice, based on persistent repetition of one simple statement.

Delhi Pact (1) The agreement between MAHATMA Gandhi, leader of the CONGRESS Party, and Lord Irwin, VICEROY of India, in 1931 which addressed some of the movement's grievances about British rule. It marked a truce in Congress's campaign of CIVIL DISOBEDIENCE and established Congress as the principal conduit of Indian opinion for the ROUND TABLE CONFERENCE. Winston CHURCHILL said of talks in India in early 1931 following the conference:

> It is alarming and odious to see Mr. Gandhi, a seditious Middle Temple lawyer, now posing as a fakir of a type well-known in the East, striding half-naked up the steps of the vice-regal palace while he is still conducting a defiant campaign of CIVIL DISOBEDIENCE, to parley on equal terms with the representative of the King-Emperor.

(2) The agreement signed in April 1950 by the Indian Prime Minister Jawaharlal Nehru (*see* PANDIT) and his Pakistani counterpart Liaqat Ali Khan. Prompted by communal RIOTS and massive two-way migration of religious minorities after PARTITION, it ensured the rights of Muslim and Hindu minorities in their respective countries.

Delors report The report, presented to EUROPEAN COMMUNITY heads of government in April 1989, which gave a critical push toward economic and monetary union (EMU). It took its name from Jacques Delors (1925–) the PRESIDENT of the EC Commission and an ardent advocate of a more centralized community, who sat on the drafting group with a fellow Commissioner, the 12 CENTRAL BANK governors and three outside experts. It proposed three stages toward monetary union: completion of the SINGLE MARKET, creation of an independent EUROFED controlling a proportion of national currency reserves, and the irrevocable locking of exchange rates which would create a single currency, managed by the Eurofed. The strategy was broadly endorsed in the MAASTRICHT TREATY.

Delors II The ambitious plan put forward by Jacques Delors for substantial increases in the EC budget from 1993 to 1999, financing it by an increase in OWN RESOURCES, with special emphasis on COHESION funding for the "poor four" members and on STRUCTURAL FUNDS for improving the infrastructure. A scaled-down version was adopted at the Edinburgh summit in December 1992, with Delors claiming he had got 80% of what he wanted.

Up yours, Delors! The ultimate in CHAUVINIST press campaigns, launched by Britain's the *Sun* newspaper on 1 November 1990 as the strains between Margaret Thatcher and Jacques Delors over moves to closer European union reached their *dénouement*. The campaign was a combined attack on Delors for his perceived vision of a Europe governed by *diktat* from Brussels, and on the French for attempts to sabotage UK farm exports. It began:

> UP YOURS, DELORS!
> At midday tomorrow *Sun* readers are urged to tell the French fool where to stuff his ECU.
> *The Sun* today calls on its patriotic family of readers to tell the feelthy French to FROG OFF.
> They INSULT us, BURN our lambs, FLOOD our country with dodgy food and PLOT to abolish the dear old pound.
> Now it's your turn to kick THEM in the Gauls.

demagogue A POPULIST who is able to whip up ugly sentiments through obsessive mob oratory. Ambrose Bierce cynically defined a demagogue as "a political opponent". In America the word has become a verb: in the late 1970s House MAJORITY LEADER Jim Wright declared: "Thou shalt not demagogue with thy colleagues," and in 1986 Labor Secretary Bill Brock said: "The Democrats are making a mistake by demagoguing this issue."

démarche In diplomacy, an initiative involving an approach to one or more other governments.

demo 1970s shorthand for a **demonstration**. A MARCH or RALLY, with participants carrying their slogans on banners, to protest against a policy or event, or to advocate a cause. The focus is on the mass who turn out to demonstrate, rather than on any speakers who address them.

> Quite small and unattended demonstrations can be made to look like the beginnings of a REVOLUTION if the cameraman is in the right place at the right time.
> GOUGH WHITLAM.

democracy (1) A system of government in which SOVEREIGNTY is vested in the people. Over the centuries it has been seen in many lights: "A government in the hands of men of low birth, no property and unskilled labour" – Aristotle; "The meanest and worst of all forms of government" – John Winthrop; "There never was a democracy yet that did not commit suicide" – John Adams; "Were our state a pure democracy, in which all its inhabitants should meet together to transact all their business, there would yet be excluded from their deliberations 1. infants, 2. women, 3. slaves" – Thomas JEFFERSON; "a government of bullies tempered by editors" – Ralph Waldo Emerson; "Democracy is only a dream. It should be put in the same category as Arcadia, Santa Claus and Heaven" – H. L. Mencken; "the art and science of running the circus from the monkey cage" – Mencken; "the worship of jackals by jackasses" – Mencken; "the theory that common people know what they want, and deserve to get it good and hard" – Mencken; "government by orgy, almost orgasm" – Mencken; "All the ills of democracy can be cured by more democracy" – Al Smith; "a form of government you have to keep for four years, no matter what it does" – Will Rogers; "a process by which the people are free to choose the man who will get the blame" – Lawrence J Peter; "an institution in which the whole is equal to the scum of the parts" – Keith Preston; "information is the currency of democracy" – Ralph Nader; "Speed of action was never the absolute goal of democracy, because a king is faster than a Congressman on any given day" – Sen. William Cohen; "A democracy can only exist until the voters discover that they can vote themselves largesse from the public treasury" – Lord Woodhouselee; "an aristocracy of blackguards" – Lord Byron; "Democracy will prevail when men believe the vote of Judas as good as that of Jesus Christ" – Thomas Carlyle (*attr.*); "the bludgeoning of the people by the people, for the people" – Oscar Wilde; "it substitutes election by the incompetent many for appointment by the corrupt few" – George Bernard Shaw; "the worst form of government except all those others that have been tried from time to time" – CHURCHILL "Democracy is no harlot to be picked up in the street by a man with a tommy gun" – Churchill; "Democracy means government by discussion, but it is only effective if you can stop people talking" – ATTLEE; "Democracy means choosing your dictators, after they've told you what it is you want to hear" – Alan Coren; "A state which recognizes the subordination of the minority to the majority" – LENIN; "The Soviet people want full-blooded and unconditional democracy" – Mikhail Gorbachev; "Democracy is a truth in America. In Europe it is a falsehood" – Metternich; "In a democracy the people elect a leader in whom they have confidence. The elected leader says: 'Shut up and obey me'" – Max Weber; "As long as people are people, democracy, in the full sense of the word, will always be no more than an ideal" – Václav Havel.
(2) a democracy. A nation where the conditions of democracy are seen to apply.

arsenal of democracy In a broadcast on 29 December 1940, President Franklin D. Roosevelt responded to PEARL HARBOR and Germany's declaration of war on America with a determination to make the United States "the great arsenal of democracy". The phrase was not original; in 1928 Josef Goebbels had written: "We [NAZI deputies] enter Parliament in order to supply ourselves, in the arsenal of democracy, with its own weapons."

guided democracy The regime which governs the internal workings of Britain's CONSERVATIVE PARTY, notably through the selection of anodyne motions for debate at its annual conference to ensure that criticism of the leadership is kept to a minimum. *See* STAGE-MANAGEMENT.

New Democracy The centre-right party which, since 1989, has formed the government of Greece under the premiership of Constantine Mitsotakis (1918–).

people's democracy A term used by Communists to describe the system of government in the former Soviet Union and its SATELLITES.

> It's the same difference as between a jacket and a strait jacket.
> RONALD REAGAN.

social democracy *See* SOCIAL.

The world must be made safe for democracy Woodrow WILSON's declaration to a JOINT SESSION of Congress on America's entry into WORLD WAR I, on 2 April 1917. John F. KENNEDY built on the phrase during the COLD WAR, declaring: "If we cannot now end our differences, at least we can make the world safe for diversity."

democratic centralism Another term used by Communists to justify a political system in which all decisions are taken at the centre, with those governed expected to fall into line.

democratic deficit The absence of ACCOUNTABILITY in many fields within the European Community, which the MAASTRICHT TREATY was devised partly to redress by giving the EUROPEAN PARLIAMENT a greater supervisory role over the Commission.

Democratic Forum The centre-right party, led by Joszef Antall (1932–) which headed the first democratic government in Hungary after the collapse of Janos Kadar's Communist regime in 1989. The Democratic Forum was founded at Lakitelet in September 1987, becoming a political party the following year.

Democratic Left (1) The new name adopted in 1991 by the continuing remnants of Britain's COMMUNIST PARTY. (2) The title adopted prior to Ireland's 1992 elections by the WORKERS' PARTY, formerly Official SINN FEIN.

Democratic Party One of America's two great political parties, and in the main the more liberal. It has its roots in the vision of Thomas JEFFERSON and the populism of Andrew Jackson (*see* OLD HICKORY), after whose election in 1828 the party took shape, getting van Buren, Polk, Pierce and Buchanan into the White House. Yet in 1860 the POPULIST Ignatius Donnelly could declare: "Like a mule, it has neither pride of ancestry nor hope of posterity." The New Hampshire anti-slaver Sen. John Hale was more personal, saying: "I never said that all Democrats were rascals – only that all rascals were Democrats." The CIVIL WAR split the Democrats and left the party seriously weakened; it did not elect another President until Cleveland (*see* BEAST OF BUFFALO) in 1884. The party regained stability as a coalition of the northern urban masses, mid-western populists and southern conservatives, even though Speaker Thomas Reed asserted that "the Democratic Party is like a man riding backward in a railroad car; it never sees anything until it has got past it." The great crusades of William Jennings Bryan (*see* PRAIRIE AVENGER) failed to win majority support, and Woodrow Wilson's election in 1912 was helped by a Republican split. The next year Rep. John Jacob Rogers said:

> The Southern Democrats are in the saddle and the Northern Democrats must tag along as best they may, no matter what ill may betide.

The post-war ISOLATIONIST tide weakened the Democrats, but as the GREAT DEPRESSION bit, Franklin D. Roosevelt's INTERVENTIONIST NEW DEAL paved the way for a 20-year Democratic presidency (though not always control of Congress) and the renewal of the mass party as Black voters switched to it. The Democrats had always been the White ethnic party, Ray Miller saying in 1948 when running for governor of Ohio:

> Canada and Australia have as much opportunity, as many natural resources and as much land, but your mothers and mine came here because this country supports God, and because of the Democratic Party which has always supported God.

The Democrats suffered from the impact of McCARTHYISM, but John F. KENNEDY proved the coalition's strength in 1960 by becoming the first Catholic president, and in 1964 Lyndon Johnson's welfarist GREAT SOCIETY swept the board. The VIETNAM WAR wrecked party unity, producing the spectacle of the 1968 CHICAGO CONVENTION amd the hijacking of the 1972 platform and delegate selection by ANTI-WAR and other radical groups. Nevertheless the Democrats generally retained control of Congress – with control slipping away from the Southern Conservatives from the early 1970s as the SENIORITY system was dented.

Disillusion with Washington after WATERGATE enabled the more conservative Jimmy CARTER to reunite the coalition and win in 1976, only for his administration's failures and Ronald Reagan's appeal to BLUE-COLLAR voters to give the Republicans a near-stranglehold in 1980. Jeane Kirkpatrick saw a dilemma for the party in the Reagan years:

> The Democrats are in a real bind. They won't get elected unless things get worse, and things won't get worse unless they get elected.

Reagan himself said of the Democrats: "They have gone so far left, they have left America," and "We need more Democrats in the Senate like Custer needed more arrows." Even the Democrat Rep. Pat Schroeder confessed: "Spine transplants are what we really need to take Reagan on." Yet under Reagan and George BUSH the Democrats rebuilt their strength in Congress; and in 1992 Bill Clinton (*see* COMEBACK KID) regained the Presidency. Though he stopped short of embracing Jesse Jackson's RAINBOW COALITION, Clinton built an electoral base embracing labor, White ethnic, Jewish, Black and Hispanic support and liberal voters generally, yet reaching out for enough of the middle ground – notably the REAGAN DEMOCRATS – to win power.

The nature of the Democrats' support, and until the 1980s the greater ideological content of its programme, has made it a more overtly fissile party than the Republicans. In 1901 Finley Peter Dunne wrote:

> When ye see two men with white neckties go into a street car an' set in opposite corners while wan mutters "thraiter" an' th' other hisses "miscreant", ye can bet they're two Dimmycratic leaders thryin' to reunite th' gran' ol' party.

Will Rogers insisted: "I am not a member of any organized political party. I am a Democrat," and he also remarked: "You've got to be an optimist to be a Democrat, and you've got to be a humorist to stay one." And Speaker Jim Wright described the party as "a mixture, an amalgam, a mosaic, call it a fruitcake". At times it can be downright suicidal; Rep. Morris Udall once said:

> When the Democratic Party forms a firing squad, we form a circle.

Democratic-Republican Party The faction formed by Thomas JEFFERSON and his supporters to contest the 1798 Congressional elections and the Presidential election of 1800, which took Jefferson to power.

Democratic Socialism *See* SOCIALISM.

Democratic Study Group (DSG) The powerful informal caucus of Liberal Democrats in Congress, originally founded by Rep. Eugene McCarthy and 79 others after the landslide of 1958 to push through the party programme despite the opposition of conservative committee chairmen. The DSG's persistent efforts over more than a decade for greater democracy was a major factor in opening up Congressional committee chairmanships to election and greater accountability.

Democrats The centrist party in Australia founded in 1977 by the Liberal MHR Don Chipp. While efforts to merge with other small parties were abortive, it has remained in existence with around 5% of the popular vote and has won occasional seats, mainly in Victoria and New South Wales.

demonstration *See* DEMO.

denationalization The return of a NATIONALIZED industry from public to private ownership. The term was coined by UK Conservatives in their campaigning prior to their return to power in 1951, when they reversed the nationalization of steel and road haulage. Since the early 1980s the word PRIVATIZATION has superseded it.

denazification The process carried out by the victorious Allies from 1945 in what became West Germany. Its aim was to punish NAZI leaders and ensure that other party activists were excluded from the country's post-war administration.

deniability A US term, current during WATERGATE but not a product of it, for the conduct of a particular issue so that those responsible can subsequently deny all knowledge of it.

One picture is worth a thousand denials The motto of the White House Photographers' Association, reflecting the snapper's advantage when anything that appears in print can – plausibly or otherwise – be denied by those in power.

Denning Report The report of the inquiry by Lord Denning, Master of the Rolls (1899–) in 1963 into the security aspects of the PROFUMO AFFAIR. When published that autumn, the report disappointed the Labour opposition who hoped it would contain enough compromising material to finish off the Conservative government; however Harold Macmillan (*see* SUPERMAC) retired through ill health shortly after and the Tories narrowly lost power the following year. Denning concluded that the liaison between the former War Minister John Profumo and the call-girl Christine Keeler had posed no threat to national security despite Keeler's parallel association with a Soviet naval attaché. More disappointingly, he found no evidence to support rumours about the involvement of other ministers. Denning's criticism of security arrangements did lead Macmillan's successor, SIR ALEC Douglas-Home, to establish a standing committee on security.

densepack *See* MX.

département One of the administrative units into which Republican France has been divided since 1800. Until 1964 the number was set at 89; it has since risen to 96.

dependency A territory dependent on another for its government, lacking any of its own; as in the former Falkland Islands Dependencies, none of which were permanently inhabited.

dependency culture A phrase first used by sociologists in the late 1970s, and soon after by politicians, for the sector of society which is entirely dependent for its needs on welfare benefits and other forms of public assistance, and in time becomes conditioned to having no work and no hope of, or desire for, any other income.

dependency theory The doctrine, common among radicals in the 1960s and 1970s, that the United States and the former colonial powers had not relaxed their control over the THIRD WORLD, and were now using their economic power and those nations' weakness to exert unfair advantage over them in terms of trade. At its extreme, the theory even argues that foreign aid is harmful because it develops Third World economies in a way that ties them even more firmly to the needs of the donors.

deposit The sum which a candidate in a British Parliamentary election has to lodge with the RETURNING OFFICER, to be repaid if he or she attains a certain share of the poll. Imposed to discourage frivolous candidacies, the deposit was set at £150 until 1985, with the threshold for return being 12.5% of the votes cast; since then it has been £500, but is only forfeit if the candidate polls less than 5%. A candidate who is within a few votes of saving his or her deposit will frequently call for a RECOUNT.

depression A very severe and lasting downturn in the economy, the resulting stagnation causing even greater dislocation and hardship than a RECESSION. It usually follows a boom, and brings both high unemployment and weak prices. The GREAT DEPRESSION of the 1930s was the most widespread and severe of recent times.

Deputy (Fr. *député*) A member of France's NATIONAL ASSEMBLY.

Deputy Prime Minister A position seldom made formal in Britain's governmental structure, Sir Geoffrey HOWE during 1989–90 being a rare exception. From 1979 to 1987 William (later Lord) Whitelaw (*see* WILLIE) was Margaret Thatcher's unofficial deputy, as deputy leader of the Conservative Party; R. A. Butler (*see* RAB) was unofficial deputy to Eden and then Macmillan – a fact which probably robbed him of the Premiership when each retired. Labour's deputy leaders have seldom enjoyed such prestige, though George BROWN held the title of First Secretary of State for a time in the mid-1960s as deputy to Harold Wilson.

deregulation The policy of removing controls from a field of commercial activity, for example commercial airlines (*see* OPEN SKIES) or bus transport, in the hope of improving consumer choice and weakening trade union influence.

Dergue The hard-line Marxist government of Ethiopia under Colonel Mengistu Haile Mariam which ruled the country from 1977, three years after officers including Mengistu overthrew Emperor Haile Selassie, until May 1991, when Mengistu fled the country as a rebel alliance closed in on Addis Ababa. The Dergue's rule was notable for its attempts to impose a Marxist-Leninist economy and political system at a time when much of the country was gripped by desperate famine, and its unsuccessful efforts to defeat SEPARATIST guerrillas in Eritrea and Tigre.

derogation The exemption that a member country of the EC may seek from a piece of Community legislation which it considers harmful to its interests. A derogation will normally only be granted by the EUROPEAN COURT if it would not impact on any other Community member.

descamisados (Sp. shirtless ones) The working-class and lower middle-class masses who gave vocal support to Argentina's dictator Juan PERÓN, in return for benign social policies, outright handouts and expropriation of unpopular foreign capitalists. When his popularity seemed threatened, his charismatic wife Eva (*see* EVITA) would whip up the descamisados into a state of frenzy from the balcony of the CASA ROSADA, the Presidential palace in Buenos Aires.

desegregation The ending of the provision of separate facilities for people of different races. The breaking down of the COLOUR BAR throughout the United States, and especially in the South, was the immediate aim of the CIVIL RIGHTS movement that reached its height in the 1970s – and of the Kennedy/Johnson administration. The process was begun with President Truman's desegregation of the armed forces, and hastened by the 1954 Supreme Court decision outlawing segregated public schools in BROWN V. TOPEKA BOARD OF EDUCATION.

deselection The removal by a constituency Labour Party (CLP) of a sitting member of Parliament by refusing to reselect him or her as their candidate for the next General Election. The battle over the automatic right of a constituency to deselect deeply divided the party *c.*1978–81, and the victory of the CAMPAIGN FOR LABOUR PARTY DEMOCRACY (CLPD) was one reason for the breakaway of the GANG OF FOUR to form the SDP. The adoption of deselection by the party conference has led to relatively few MPs being ousted – perhaps 20 at the three subsequent elections – but forced many others to put up a desperate fight to keep the party nomination, which hampered the duties they were elected to fulfil. Meanwhile a number of sitting Conservative MPs have been removed by their constituency associations with just as much acrimony.

desk. clearing one's desk A euphemism for resigning, being dismissed or expecting to be dismissed, used particularly of Government Ministers (in America Cabinet Secretaries and senior White House staffers) whose careers are suddenly terminated. Sometimes the staff of a senior functionary will clear his or her desk if he or she appears certain to be replaced; it was rumoured that civil servants in the office of William Ross (Lord Ross of Marnock), Secretary of State for Scotland under Harold Wilson, cleared his desk three times when they expected him to be moved or sacked in a RESHUFFLE, only to have to put his papers back hurriedly.

banging of desk lids The traditional way in which Conservative BACKBENCHERS at Westminster show their approval for comments made at the weekly meetings of the 1922 COMMITTEE.

despatch box In the UK HOUSE OF COMMONS, the brassbound oak boxes on which Ministers and senior Opposition spokesmen may lean when speaking. They contain Bibles for use in swearing-in new members.

> The Right Honourable Gentleman's red face looming over the despatch box is a pretty terrifying sight. I was not sure at one stage whether it was indignation, claret or a faulty sun lamp.
>
> PETER SNAPE MP (Lab.) on Cecil (now Lord) PARKINSON.

> His delivery at the despatch box has all the bite of a rubber duck.
>
> LADY FALKENDER (*see* LADY FORKBENDER) on John (now Lord) Moore.

The term is also used, not entirely correctly, for the (usually) red boxes in which Ministers carry official papers (*see* doing the BOXES).

despot, despotism A tyrant, a state governed by a tyrant. Daniel Webster declared: "Whenever a government is not a government of laws, it is a despotism, let it be called what it may." Bertrand Russell saw a niche for it, writing: "Mankind need government, but in reasons where anarchy has prevailed they will, at first, submit only to despotism." And Oscar Wilde asserted:

> There are three kinds of despot: the despot who tyrannizes over the body; the despot who tyrannizes over the soul; [and] the despot who tyrannizes over the soul and body alike. The first is called the prince. The second is called the Pope. The third is called the People.

In the early days of American independence, Thomas JEFFERSON warned Lafayette: "We are not to be expected to be transported from despotism to liberty in a feather bed."

> Despotism and oppression never yet were beaten except by heroic resistance.
>
> LAJOS KOSSUTH, Hungarian revolutionary (1802–94).

> No despot is ever going to give up his throne because you ask him to give it up, or because you beg him to go away. The final word is always an act of war.
>
> MEHDI BAZARGAN, Prime Minister of Iran, 1979.

destabilization Action by one nation or political grouping to undermine the stability of another, for example by promoting dissent or unrest within it.

détente The policy of limited disengagement and PEACEFUL CO-EXISTENCE between the SUPERPOWERS, though without any reduction in Soviet influence over its SATELLITES, pioneered by Leonid BREZHNEV (1906–82). He put it forward to rebuild bridges after the crushing of the PRAGUE SPRING in 1968, and to separate Soviet–US relations from the VIETNAM WAR; President Nixon and Henry KISSINGER responded, and SUMMIT meetings and other contacts produced a THAW. The ARMS RACE continued, but Nixon and Brezhnev did conclude the first SALT agreement; Jimmy CARTER and Brezhnev signed a second, but the Senate would not RATIFY it. The Soviet invasion of Afghanistan in 1979 finally discredited the process.

deterrence The doctrine that a nation can prevent (specifically nuclear) attacks on itself by possessing overwhelming retaliatory strength. Campaigners for nuclear disarmament have argued that the theory is flawed, but advocates of deterrence point out that the COLD WAR ended after over 40 years without any nuclear weapons having been fired. The success of deterrence also depended on a firm and consistent political stance rather than the sending-out of confusing signals about what actions would provoke retaliation, the US Defense Secretary Robert McNamara writing in 1968: "One cannot fashion a credible deterrent out of an incredible action."

> Only when our arms are sufficient without doubt can we be certain that they will never be deployed.
>
> JOHN F. KENNEDY, 1961.

independent deterrent The possession by the UK of nuclear weapons under purely British command, maintained by governments of all parties from the late 1940s, Labour's anti-nuclear phases never coinciding with its periods of office. To nuclear disarmers the possession of such a deterrent by a relatively small nation was a dangerous farce and an invitation to proliferation (*see* NON-PROLIFERATION) among others, but advocates of the policy argued that Britain's possession of nuclear weapons ensured it a place at the top table. *See* NAKED INTO THE CONFERENCE CHAMBER.

> For honourable members opposite the deterrent is a phallic symbol. It convinces them that they are men.
>
> GEORGE (later Lord) WIGG (1900–76), speaking from the Labour front bench, March 1964.

Deutschland. Deutschland einig Vaterland (Ger. Germany one Fatherland) The popular slogan under which Germany moved toward reUNIFICATION on 3 October 1990, less than 11 months after the breaching of the BERLIN WALL.

Deutschland Über Alles (Ger. Germany above all) The patriotic poem adopted as the German national anthem after World War I, which has remained the ultimate expression of German patriotism, although other less assertive anthems were chosen for the two separate Germanies between 1949 and 1990. The anthem, written in 1841 by Heinrich Hoffmann von Fallersleben (1798–1876), is sung to Haydn's *Imperial Anthem*, the tune being familiar to Anglophones as

> Glorious things of thee are spoken,
> Zion, City of our God.

The verses now sung reflect the culture of the post-war Federal Republic:

Einigkeit und Recht und Freiheit
für das Deutsche Vaterland!

(Unity, justice and freedom
for the German Fatherland.)

Deuxième Bureau (Fr. Second Bureau) The French agency which counters internal subversion, broadly comparable with Britain's MI5 but with a more combative role. External threats are a matter for the SDECE.

Dev The popular nickname for Eamonn de Valera (1882–1975), the New York-born participant in Ireland's EASTER RISING who became a leader of the forces against PARTITION, the founder of FIANNA FAIL, TAOISEACH 1932–48, 1951–54 and 1957–59, and President 1959–73. His American birth saved him from execution after the Rising, he escaped from Lincoln prison in 1919 and raised $1 million in America for the IRA. A founder member of DAIL EIREANN, he fought in the Civil War of 1922–23, was imprisoned, but renounced violence in 1924. As Prime Minister he repudiated Ireland's allegiance to the British Crown in 1937, kept the Republic neutral during World War II and angered British opinion by sending official condolences on Hitler's death. Highly intelligent and devoutly religious, his premiership covered the period immediately before the emergence of Ireland as not only a sovereign state, but a modern one.

Lloyd George: [Negotiating with him is] like picking up mercury with a fork.
De Valera: Why doesn't he use a spoon?

devaluation The unilateral reduction in the value of one's currency compared with others. Unsuccessful attempts to avoid it have caused British Governments considerable anguish, and the economy much pain, in 1948–49, 1964–67 and 1992; the CHANCELLORs forced to devalue were Sir Stafford Cripps, James (later Lord) Callaghan and Norman Lamont. *See also* POUND IN YOUR POCKET.

The sky is darkening with the wings of chickens coming home to roost.

LORD CALLAGHAN on BLACK WEDNESDAY, 16 September 1992.

deviationism The term used by STALINISTS and other disciplinarian Communists for any variation from the line laid down by the Party; it was used both against genuine advocates of another course and anyone the leadership wished to get rid of.

devolution The handing over of power from a centralized government to a state's constituent parts. The term is used specifically of successive proposals to devolve power from the Parliament at WESTMINSTER to elected assemblies for Scotland and Wales. In Scotland the argument over the merits of independence, advocated by the SNP; devolution, supported by Labour and the Liberal Democrats; and the status quo of a single Parliament, backed by most Conservatives, has been raging for a quarter of a century. It has partly been over whether devolution would weaken or strengthen the UNION between England and Scotland. Pressure for devolution first peaked in 1974, when the SNP polled over 30% of votes in Scotland and won 11 Parliamentary seats; Labour hastily dropped its opposition to a Scottish assembly, and pushed through the SCOTLAND BILL for a REFERENDUM on devolution. (There was a parallel measure for Wales, whose assembly was to have fewer powers.) The referendum was eventually held in February 1979; a narrow majority in Scotland voted for devolution, but under the CUNNINGHAM AMENDMENT requiring a "Yes" vote by 40 per cent of registered electors, the proposal fell. Welsh voters rejected devolution outright after an energetic "No" campaign by Neil KINNOCK. Margaret Thatcher was strongly opposed to devolution, and the IRON LADY held the line rigidly against it as the number of Conservative MPs in Scotland plunged to 9 out of 72; Labour after 1979 championed a Scottish Parliament and Welsh Assembly, and in Scotland a **Constitutional Convention** devised a HOME RULE plan in 1991 with strong cross-party support. Scotland, especially, went into the 1992 election expecting its own Parliament; 75% of Scots voted for devolution or independence, but John MAJOR rallied enough support for keeping the Union unchanged to win back two seats. His pre-election promise to "take stock" on how Scotland was governed led to a limited package of administrative reforms early in 1993. Meanwhile SCOTLAND UNITED sought to capitalize on popular frustration at being deprived of a Scottish Parliament, and 25,000 demonstrators protested during the Edinburgh summit in December 1992.

Power devolved is power retained. ENOCH POWELL.

Devonshire declaration The statement made in 1923 by the Duke of Devonshire, Colonial Secretary in BALDWIN's government, which made it inevitable that White settlers in Kenya and Britain's other East African possessions would one day find themselves under Black rule. Devonshire laid down that the interests of the colony's native peoples had to be "paramount"; the settlers protested strongly, but the policy stuck. Independence under Black rule was granted 40 years later, after the MAU MAU rising, which if anything hastened it. By contrast the Whites in

Southern Rhodesia were granted self-government at the time of the Devonshire declaration, creating the built-in obstacle to MAJORITY RULE which enabled Ian Smith to declare UDI in 1965.

DEW line Distant Early Warning line. A network of radar stations, mostly in the Canadian Arctic, established during the COLD WAR and intended to give America early warning of attack by Soviet missiles or aircraft. It was under the control of NORAD.

Dewey. Dewey defeats Truman The headline carried by early editions of the *Chicago Tribune* on 3 November 1948, based on the assumption that Thomas E. Dewey (1902–71) had ousted the incumbent President Truman, as the pollsters had predicted. Truman's GIVE 'EM HELL campaign confounded all the pundits, and the re-elected President did not allow the paper to forget its embarrassing "scoop", which was emulated by the *Washington Post*. Dewey, the Republican governor of New York, was sincere, but his lack of CHARISMA had been cruelly pointed out even before he ran against Franklin D. Roosevelt in 1944, Samuel Grafton asking: "If a young man is as cold as this at 37, will he reach absolute zero at 50?" David Brinkley wrote of his platform style: "He spoke so euphoniously that each word emerged polished and glowing like a jewel nestling on its own little velvet pillow," and Richard Rovere noted: "He comes out like a man who has been mounted on castors and given a tremendous shove from behind." Alice Roosevelt Longworth and Grace Flandreau are both credited with saying of Dewey: "How can you vote for a candidate who looks like the bridegroom on a wedding cake?" And when Dewey ran a second time, against Truman, Mrs. Longworth observed: "You can't make a soufflé rise twice." Nevertheless post-war malaise and disillusion with the Democrats made him clear favourite for the Presidency – but he had reckoned without Truman.

> Just about the nastiest little man I've ever known. He struts sitting down. Mrs. DYSKSTRA.

DHSS Department of Health and Social Security. The UK government department responsible for the National Health Service (*see* NHS) and all other aspects of the WELFARE STATE, from 1968 until 1988 when it was split into a Department of Health and a separate Department of Social Security (**DSS**). Throughout almost all its life it was based in the award-winning but monstrous Alexander Fleming House at the Elephant and Castle, two miles south of Westminster; in its last couple of years its Ministers and key staff operated from Richmond Terrace, in WHITEHALL within a stone's throw of the Commons and DOWNING STREET. As a single department it was the largest employer in Europe after the RED ARMY.

> It was in reality Harold Wilson's folly, put together for no greater purpose than satisfying the ministerial ambitions of Dick CROSSMAN. PETER HENNESSY, *Whitehall*.

dialectical materialism A quasi-MARXIST doctrine (known in Soviet Russia as *DiaMat*) which holds that development and change in societies and economies can only be caused by technical changes in the methods of production. Many leftists use the term more generally for the general process of Marxist thought.

dictator A ruler with absolute power; originally a figure in ancient Rome deliberately entrusted with just such powers at times of crisis. Applied particularly to the monolithic leaders of the inter-war period – Hitler, Stalin, Mussolini, Franco and others – the term developed sinister and obsessional connotations. Hitler wrote: "The man who is born to be a dictator is not compelled. He wills it." Margaret Thatcher, at the time of the FALKLANDS, declared: "When you stop a dictator there are always risks. But there are greater risks in not stopping a dictator." And Chile's ruthless General Pinochet lamented of his poor world image:

> It's not that I am a dictator. It's just that I have a grumpy face.

dictatorship The form of goverment presided over by a dictator. MACHIAVELLI was using the word's original, less sinister sense when he wrote: "Those republics which in time of danger cannot resort to a dictator will generally be ruined when grave occasions occur." Ignazio Silone defined a 20th-century dictatorship as "a regime in which people quote instead of thinking", and Walter Winchell as "a place where public opinion can't even be expressed privately". And Franklin D. Roosevelt warned:

> Dictatorships do not grow out of strong and successful governments, but out of weak and helpless ones.

dictatorship of the proletariat *See* PROLETARIAT.

elective dictatorship The alarmist term used by Lord Hailsham (1907–) for the potential of a UK government with a clear majority in the HOUSE OF COMMONS to do whatever it wishes. Lord Hailsham, who sat on the Tory Front BENCH in one House or other from 1945 to 1987, was voicing concern about the ability of a Labour government to implement its programme – not the potential for a Conservative administration to be equally ruthless.

die. Fight and die! The chilling order given by Stalin to units of the RED ARMY as German forces closed in on Moscow toward the end of 1941. At that year's commemoration of the OCTOBER REVOLUTION, Soviet troops taking part in the parade through RED SQUARE marched straight on to the front line. Many never returned, but the line was held.

I am as content to die for God's eternal truth on the scaffold as any other way John BROWN's declaration at his trial on 31 October 1859 for treason, criminal conspiracy and murder for leading the raid on HARPER'S FERRY two weeks before. He was hanged on 2 December.

If a man hasn't discovered something he will die for, he isn't fit to live Martin Luther KING's definition of the purpose of life. *See also* die for one's COUNTRY.

It is better to die on your feet than live on your knees The motto coined by Emilio Zapata during the Mexican Revolution of 1910, and later broadcast by LA PASIONARIA on Republican radio during the SPANISH CIVIL WAR.

Diehards The nickname given to Tory rebels in the HOUSE OF LORDS who, in 1911, rejected the advice of their party leader, A. J. BALFOUR, and pledged to "die fighting" the constitutional changes which became the PARLIAMENT ACT, limiting the Lords' veto over Bills passed by the Commons. Their revolt caused Balfour to resign the Tory leadership in November 1911.

Dief the Chief The nickname coined by Canada's PROGRESSIVE Conservatives for John **Diefenbaker** (1895–1979), the Saskatchewan lawyer who in the late 1950s revitalized the party as a radical, almost POPULIST force. Party leader from 1956 to 1967, he won a narrow victory in the 1957 election and two years later led his party to Canada's greatest LANDSLIDE: 208 Conservative, 49 LIBERAL, 8 CCF. His term of office – ended in defeat by Lester Pearson's Liberals in 1963 – was dominated by a show of independence, coupled with co-operation, in dealings with the United States. Though it was Diefenbaker's government that concluded the NORAD agreement, he frequently irritated Washington. Diefenbaker once mistakenly thought President KENNEDY had called him a s.o.b, but when the complaint was lodged, Kennedy said:

> I didn't think he was a son of a bitch. I thought he was a prick.

Dien Bien Phu The village in north Vietnam, surrounded by hills, which was the site of the ignominious defeat of French forces by the VIET MINH in May 1954 which ended colonial rule in Vietnam. After eight years of indecisive conflict which had cost 50,000 French lives, General Henri Navarre chose Dien Bien Phu in November 1953 as a land-air base for offensive operations against the Viet Minh; his hope was to tempt them into the open for a decisive battle they would lose. But within a month the Viet Minh commander, General Vo Nguyen Giap (later the architect of America's defeat in the VIETNAM WAR) had surrounded the 15,000-strong garrison with over 40,000 men and heavy artillery in the mountains overlooking the base. The final battle began on 12 March 1954; the French found themselves under bombardment with nothing visible to shoot at, and then the guerrillas closed in for hand-to-hand combat. Dien Bien Phu eventually fell on 7 May, the day before the opening of the international peace conference at GENEVA. President Eisenhower wisely resisted French appeals for support during the siege, but the lessons of the defeat were ignored by his successors. Dien Bien Phu has become a byword for an untenable position defended with pointless determination; Roy Jenkins (*see* WOY) described the first WILSON government's defence of the $2.80 sterling rate for three years until a forced DEVALUATION as "a sort of British Dien Bien Phu".

Diet The Japanese Parliament under the country's democratic post-war constitution. The **House of Representatives** has 512 members, elected every four years; the upper house (**House of Councillors**) has 252: of these 100 are elected by the party LIST SYSTEM under proportional representation, and 152 from the prefectural districts, half elected every five years.

Dieu et mon Droit (Fr. God and my Right) The motto of the Kings and Queens of England, which appears on the Royal coat of arms.

Diggers The small group of extreme religious and social radicals under Gerrard Winstanley (1609–60) who began digging and planting the common at St. George's Hill, Surrey, in 1649, after the overthrow and execution of Charles I, with the aim of giving the land back to the people. The Diggers, who formed groups of 20 to 30, were soon suppressed by the Cromwellian army leaders, but Winstanley set out his vision of a true COMMONWEALTH in 1652; in it private family life and ownership were respected, but there would be no money or wages. The Digger philosophy has been invoked by a number of later revolutionary and UTOPIAN movements.

Dikko affair The diplomatic incident between Britain and Nigeria prompted by UK Customs officials' discovery of Omaru Dikko, Nigeria's former Transport Minister, drugged and in a crate at London's Stansted Airport on 5 July 1984. With him in other crates were three Israelis, one an anaesthetist, who were charged with kidnapping and administering drugs. The Nigerian authorities had been eager to try Dikko on corruption charges, and when frustrated by the EXTRADITION process, arranged for him to be kidnapped by the country's National Security Organization and sent home in the DIPLOMATIC BAG. Britain protested at the violation of its sovereignty, and allowed Dikko to stay. Some weeks later, the Labour MP Peter Snape reduced the Commons to laughter by saying of Britain's Transport Secretary, Nicholas (later Lord) Ridley (*see* GERMAN RACKET):

> The Nigerians have kidnapped the wrong Minister of Transport.

Dilke case *See* THREE-IN-A-BED.

Dillingham Report The 42-volume report published in 1911 which concluded that "old" Protestant and Nordic immigrants from western and northern Europe were better suited for settlement in America than the "new", Catholic migrants from Mediterranean countries. The report, from a committee chaired by Sen. William P. Dillingham of Vermont, was commissioned by Congress because of an upsurge of RACIST feeling against non-WASPs, fuelled by a spate of pseudo-scientific literature on the "inferiority" of other races. A series of illiberal immigration laws followed, based partly on Dillingham's "findings": the 1917 Immigration Act, passed despite Woodrow WILSON's VETO, the 1921 QUOTA Act and the Johnson-Reed Act of 1921. Their combined effect was to cut immigration from an average 862,514 in the years prior to 1914 to a ceiling of 150,000 – with oriental immigration banned altogether.

dining clubs The semi-formal and often highly secret gatherings of MPs at Westminster which meet regularly in the private rooms of restaurants and the homes of well-heeled politicians. Such groups may be comprised of the like-minded, or have a particular social cachet; the most raucous members are unlikely ever to be asked to join one, which is why CHURCHILL and F. E. Smith founded the OTHER CLUB. Dining clubs are particularly influential in Conservative politics, particularly if, as happened in 1990, their members form the campaign teams of rival leadership candidates. Far fewer Labour MPs form such groups, but there are notable exceptions (*see* SUPPER CLUB).

diplomacy The art of conducting relations between governments, and the process of resolving disputes through personal contact between emissaries. The Canadian Prime Minister and NOBEL PEACE PRIZE winner Lester Pearson described diplomacy as "letting someone else have your way"; Henry KISSINGER defined it as "the art of restraining power", and the US writer Isaac Goldberg as "to do or say/the nastiest things in the nicest way". STALIN, with typical cynicism, declared that "sincere diplomacy is no more possible than dry water or wooden iron". The purpose of diplomacy is to achieve just settlements while averting war, but at the start of the FALKLANDS WAR the British Tory MP Julian Amery accused the FOREIGN OFFICE of failing to distinguish between diplomacy and foreign policy. Yet diplomacy and war are inextricable; Frederick the Great declared that "diplomacy without armaments is like music without instruments", Chou En-Lai termed diplomacy "the continuation of war by other means", and Tony BENN argued that "all war represents a failure of diplomacy".

> Protocol, alcohol and Geritol. ADLAI STEVENSON.

gunboat diplomacy A show of strength by a COLONIAL or other self-important power against a weak nation to ensure that its aims and view of the world prevail. The name arose from Britain's practice during the 19th century of despatching a gunboat to any overseas territory where the natives were getting restless, or receptive to overtures from another colonial power.

megaphone diplomacy A 1980s term for belligerent and uncompromising statements made by a nation's leaders in the usually vain belief that they will make another country change its policies.

> Megaphone diplomacy leads to a dialogue of the deaf.
> Sir GEOFFREY (later Lord) HOWE.

open diplomacy *See* OPEN.

panda diplomacy Communist China's practice, in CHAIRMAN MAO's last years and since, of cultivating relations with Western countries by making their leaders gifts of giant pandas, which have then been passed on to zoos.

ping-pong diplomacy The means by which the Nixon administration finally opened contacts with Communist China, through the exchange of table-tennis teams. The pandas came later.

shuttle diplomacy The technique, perfected in the Middle East by Henry KISSINGER, by which an intermediary in an international dispute travels repeatedly between the capitals in question in an effort to bridge the gap.

diplomat A representative of one country stationed in another to conduct relations with its government, or based at home to liaise with diplomats from elsewhere. Because diplomacy is a diplomat's stock in trade, the word has also come to refer to anyone who is able to handle a tricky situation with inexhaustible tact.

> A real diplomat is one who can cut his neighbour's throat without having his neighbour notice it.
>
> UN Secretary-General TRYGGVE LIE (1896–1968).

> One who is disarming, even if his country isn't.
>
> UK Defence Secretary MALCOLM RIFKIND.

> A diplomat these days is nothing but a head waiter who's allowed to sit down occasionally.
>
> PETER USTINOV, *Romanoff and Juliet*.

diplomatic bag The receptacle in which documents and larger items are carried between a country's EMBASSY abroad and its home government. Under international conventions, the diplomatic bag is immune from inspection by customs and its confidentiality is respected. However there have been instances of countries using the diplomatic bag to transport weapons and explosives to revolutionaries abroad, or even (*see* DIKKO AFFAIR) to kidnap their citizens abroad and smuggle them home.

diplomatic corps The body of overseas diplomats stationed in any one of the world's capitals. The longest-serving is the **doyen**.

diplomatic immunity *See* IMMUNITY.

diplomatic list The list produced by a government containing either the names of its own diplomats or the names and seniority of the DIPLOMATIC CORPS in its capital, and in some cases listing their wives as well.

diplomatic relations Formal contact between nations marked by the presence of their diplomats in each other's country; diplomatic relations normally attract attention only when they are strained or broken off. When they are broken off, the contacts are kept going by INTERESTS SECTIONS in other countries' embassies. *See* RECOGNITION.

> The reason for having diplomatic relations is not to confer a compliment, but to secure a convenience.
>
> CHURCHILL, 1949.

> Diplomatic relations are merely practical conveniences and not measures of moral judgment.
>
> Gov. NELSON ROCKEFELLER, reporting to President Nixon on Latin America, 1969.

diplomatic toothache An "illness" which a leader is said to be suffering from when he wishes to avoid a particular person or occasion without delivering the insult of cancelling it. Originally the phrase was **diplomatic cold,** stemming from claims by Gladstone and the Marquess of Hartington in 1885 that they were suffering from colds when they wished to duck out of a series of speaking engagements; the next day they admitted to being "much better". The Soviet leader Nikita Khruschev invented the diplomatic toothache in the late 1950s when he wanted to avoid pre-arranged meetings with Western leaders visitng Moscow.

activities inconsistent with his/her/their diplomatic status The phrase used by a host government when declaring a foreign diplomat PERSONA NON GRATA for espionage – or alleged espionage in the case of a TIT FOR TAT EXPULSION.

direct. direct mail The technique for large-scale fundraising and mobilization of opinion pioneered and perfected by US conservative and single-ISSUE groups, and tried with moderate success in Britain in the late 1980s by the Conservatives and, subsequently, other parties. It has enabled PRESSURE GROUPS in America to build up computer banks of supporters who, at the touch of a button, can be solicited to send in funds or write to a politician who might be influenced to vote for or against a particular proposition. As early as the 1950s Marvin Liebman had compiled a list of 1,000,000 names, initially of supporters of NATIONALIST CHINA, and the technique was perfected in the 1970s by Richard Viguerie. It has also enabled parties and campaigns to target and mobilize voters who can be appealed to over particular issues, *e.g.* Jewish or Italian voters or owners of imported cars. In Britain the reputation of direct-mail campaigns has suffered because of the number of appeals sent to well-known politicians on the other side, or to computer-invented persons like "Mr. PhD", "Mrs. OBE" or even "Mr. Deceased", but they have raised considerable sums of money for all the parties.

direct rule The imposition of central authority on a portion of a country after the breakdown of local or regional government. The term is applied particularly to the government of Northern Ireland since 1972, when the UK government abolished the devolved Parliament at STORMONT – and the province's pre-existing local authorities. A Northern Ireland Office headed by a Cabinet Minister – initially William Whitelaw (*see* WILLIE) – was set up, with the aims of combating terrorism, removing the discrimination against Catholics that had played into the hands of the IRA, and governing the province until new democratic structures could be established.

directive A mandate from the EUROPEAN COMMUNITY to national governments, requiring them to enact legislation implementing the policy in question by a particular date, usually within two or three years. If a government fails to do so, the COMMISSION may compel it to legislate by taking legal action through the EUROPEAN COURT OF JUSTICE. Before a directive is issued, a draft will have been debated by ECOSOC and the EUROPEAN PARLIAMENT, and a final decision on enactment taken by the COUNCIL OF MINISTERS.

Directory The Republican government of France established under the constitution of 1795, when power was vested in five "Directors", one of whom retired every year. After a sickly four-year existence, it was ended by Napoleon's COUP of 18 *Brumaire* (9 November) 1799. *See also* X, Y and Z FEVER.

dirigisme Rigid control by central government of the economy, and other areas of daily life. The term originated in the centralizing policies pursued by Louis XIV and his minister Jean-Baptiste Colbert (1619–83), which are echoed in France to this day; however the term now has a much wider application.

Dirksen. Dirksen's three laws of politics The principles for a lengthy political career put forward, only half in jest, by Sen. Everett Dirksen (1896–1969). They were:

> 1. Get elected. 2. Get re-elected. 3. Don't get mad, get even.

Dirksen was a much-respected Republican from Illinois who served as Senate MINORITY LEADER from 1959 and whose body lay in state in the ROTUNDA of the Capitol after he died in harness; his daughter Joy married Howard Baker, who became Senate MAJORITY LEADER with the Reagan landslide of 1980. Dirksen's long Congressional career – 16 years in the House, 19 in the Senate – included recording a hit single, *Gallant Men*, waging a protracted campaign to have the marigold declared America's national flower, and appearing on television to defend a Congressional pay increase, saying: "Senators have to eat, too." His oratorical style earned him the nickname "the Wizard of Ooze".

Dirksen building The Senate office building north-east of the Capitol named after Sen. Dirksen; the second of three bearing the names of prominent Senators, it was opened in 1958, but only named after his death.

dirty protest The action taken by convicted IRA prisoners in Northern Ireland's H-BLOCKS in the late 1970s and early 1980s in support of their claim for POLITICAL STATUS. It involved their refusal to use prison sanitation, and their smearing of excrement over their cell walls until special cleansing squads moved in to spray them clean with disinfectant. The dirty protest, and the parallel BLANKET PROTEST, failed to shift the authorities, so Bobby Sands and other Republican hard-liners embarked on a HUNGER STRIKE – also unsuccessful – in a desperate bid to achieve victory.

Disappeared, the (Sp. *Desparecidos*) The 7500 Argentines, many of them political DISSIDENTS or suspected MONTONEROS, who vanished between 1976 and 1982 and are presumed dead at the hands of DEATH SQUADS controlled by the military JUNTA which fell after the FALKLANDS WAR. The fate of the Disappeared is one of the darkest pages in Latin America's record on human rights; one of the brightest is the bravery of the parents who demonstrated outside the CASA ROSADA in Buenos Aires for news of those who had vanished, and stage VIGILS to this day.

disarmament The process of dismantling the armaments of one or every nation, attempted with brief success after World War I and with hardly any after World War II, but seriously attempted by the SUPERPOWERS after the end of the COLD WAR. *See also* ARMS CONTROL; CFE; CND; INF; MULTILATERALISM; SALT; START; UNILATERALISM.

> The notion that disarmament can put a stop to war is contradicted by the nearest dogfight.
>
> GEORGE BERNARD SHAW.

World Disarmament Conference A conference of 60 nations held in Geneva from 1932 to 1934, which proved fruitless as each GREAT POWER demanded a tariff of cuts in weaponry that would strengthen its own hand. The first session from February to July 1932 was marked by disparate approaches from France, Germany and America. At the second from February to October 1933, a British proposal to cut European troops by nearly 500,000 was opposed by NAZI Germany. The impasse proved insurmountable, and after a brief session in 1934 the Conference broke up. A vivid caricature of the national positions was given by the French author Gabriel Chevallier in the opening sequence of his comic novel *Clochemerle*.

discharge a committee In the US HOUSE OF REPRESENTATIVES, the procedure under which the full House may move to debate a BILL which is stuck in committee for more than a month. When a majority of members sign a motion for discharge, the proposer can seek RECOGNITION on the second or fourth Monday of a month, for a 20-minute debate followed by an immediate vote.

Disco Dick The nickname given by the Canadian press to Richard Hatfield, the Conservative premier of New Brunswick from 1970 to 1987, because of his flamboyant lifestyle.

discrimination. positive discrimination is the deliberate preferment of candidates for jobs or college places from groups felt to lack the normally-required qualifications because they have been held back through discrimination (*see* BAKKE CASE). Pursued in America from the 1970s to reverse the harm done by SEGREGATION and the denial of facilities to Black people, it is now practised in a number of countries. Strongly opposed by conservatives, it is known as **reverse discrimination** to those who feel they have been overtaken because they are White or male. *See also* APARTHEID.

racial discrimination The act of distinguishing between members of different ethnic or social groups, usually as a means of giving advantages to Whites or males at the expense of others. In the summer of 1941 pressure from Black trade unionists to end the COLOUR BAR that was reserving war jobs for Whites compelled Franklin D. Roosevelt to issue EXECUTIVE ORDER 8802, which declared that contractors should exercise

> No discrimination on grounds of race, color, creed or national origin.

> Discrimination is a hellhound that gnaws at negroes in every waking moment of their lives, to remind them that the lie of their inferiority is accepted as the truth in the society dominating them.
>
> Dr. MARTIN LUTHER KING, Atlanta, 16 August 1967.

> That's part of American greatness, is discrimination. Yes, Sir. Inequality, I think, breeds freedom and gives a man opportunity.
>
> LESTER MADDOX,
> Segregationist Governor of Georgia (1915–).

disestablishment The ending of the position of the Church of England as the country's established church, enjoying a privileged position in the life of the nation and with the Sovereign as its SUPREME HEAD. Traditionally the Conservative Party has strongly supported the maintenance of the established church, which became known as "the CONSERVATIVE PARTY AT PRAYER", and the Liberals opposed it (ASQUITH's Liberal government disestablished the Church in Wales); Labour had no enthusiasm for the status quo, but did not wish to risk the controversy aroused by changing it. Disestablishment remained a latent issue until 1992, when the separation of the Prince and Princess of Wales led politicians and bishops to question whether the links between Church and State might have to be broken to enable Prince Charles eventually to become King.

dishonour and disrepute The key words of the resolution condemning Sen. Joseph McCARTHY's actions as "unbecoming a member of the United States senate", which the Senate (belatedly in the view of many Americans) passed by 69 votes to 22 in December 1954. McCarthy had been exposed as a bully during the ARMY-McCARTHY HEARINGS that summer, and his hold on the nation's fears and prejudices was broken. Fellow Senators were finally emboldened to distance themselves from him, and the resolution marked the end of the Wisconsin Senator's influence. He died of drink in 1957.

disinformation The deliberate spreading of falsehoods in order to mislead an enemy or rival political force. In 1986 the *Washington Post* revealed that President Reagan had approved such a strategy against Libya's leader Colonel Gaddafi with the aim of toppling him. A memo to Reagan from his NATIONAL SECURITY ADVISER John Poindexter (*see* IRAN-CONTRA AFFAIR) proposed a plan combining "real and illusory events – through a disinformation program – with the basic goal of making Gaddafi think there is a high degree of internal opposition to him within Libya, that his key trusted aides are disloyal, that the US is about to move against him militarily".

disqualification The barring of a person from holding elective office, generally because they have been convicted of some form of corruption or electoral irregularity. In Britain the disqualification of a local councillor for the irregular approval of spending is often accompanied by a SURCHARGE to retrieve some of the money paid out.

Disraeli, Benjamin *See* DIZZY.

dissident The word used from the late 1960s for a critic of the STALINIST rigidity of the Soviet Union and its East European SATELLITES who was ready to risk imprisonment or exile by campaigning for change. The term was first applied to intellectuals in the Soviet Union – some of them REFUSENIKS – who denounced the status quo under Brezhnev, using the underground press or SAMIZDAT, to argue for greater freedoms. With the formation of CHARTER 77 in Czechoslovakia it gained a wider application.

dissident triangle In Washington, the informal alliance between critics in the PENTAGON of waste, GOLD-PLATING and the misdirection of spending, members of Congress who are on the lookout for such issues, and the media which thrive on LEAKS from both. It is pitted against the IRON TRIANGLE of Pentagon brass-hats, defence contractors and Congressional supporters of programmes that mean jobs back home.

dissolution In the UK and DOMINIONS and in Ireland, the termination of a Parliament by proclamation so that a GENERAL ELECTION may be held. The Sovereign (or President) would normally grant a request from the Prime Minister for a dissolution, unless an election had only recently been held and it appeared that another leader might command a majority. A **double dissolution** is the process under which the GOVERNOR-GENERAL of Australia may dissolve both the House and the Senate for the simultaneous holding of elections to both.

dissolution honours *See* HONOUR.

distinct society *See* MEECH LAKE.

district The area represented by a US CONGRESSMAN.

district auditor In Britain, the Government-appointed accountancy watchdog who supervises spending by local authorities, and has the power to declare an item of spending *ultra vires* and recommend the imposition of a SURCHARGE on the offending councillors. The district auditor not only examines the accounts of authorities, but investigates complaints about the way they spend public money from individual taxpayers.

District of Columbia The administrative title of America's Federal city of WASHINGTON, designated in 1801 on a site selected by George Washington. Originally it was ten miles square, spanning the Potomac, but the smaller portion taken from Virginia was later returned. Until the early 1970s the District was governed by Congress; its inhabitants have the right to vote in Presidential elections and elect a non-voting DELEGATE to the House, but are still without a voice in the Senate. The city is governed by its mayor and council from the **District Building** at 1350 Pennsylvania Avenue, next to the Department of Commerce. Until World War II the vast majority of Washingtonians lived within the District Line, as its boundary is known, but now barely a fifth of the conurbation's population of nearly 4 million does so.

Ditchers *See* HEDGERS AND DITCHERS.

division A Westminster term for a vote in either House. In the Commons at the appropriate time the SPEAKER puts the QUESTION, shouts: "Division! Clear the lobbies!", and electric **division bells** are rung throughout the PRECINCTS of the House and in those premises away from it that are ON THE BELL. From the time they start ringing, MPs have ten minutes to get into the Division LOBBIES before the Speaker names the TELLERS and orders the lobby doors locked until the voting figures are declared – generally around 13 minutes after the Question was put. The Tellers report the outcome aloud to the Speaker (or deputy) who then repeats it. In the HOUSE OF LORDS, peers have one minute less to reach the Division Lobbies. MPs anxious to show their disapproval have tried many ways of disrupting a division. The most formal and accepted is to don a top hat kept for the purpose and raise a Point of ORDER; one method that has proved more effective but angers the Chair is to queue to use the lavatory in one of the Division Lobbies, so that the counting of votes is protracted.

division list A list showing how each member of the House voted, produced by clerks within minutes of the result of the division being announced.

Dixie The affectionate name of CONFEDERATES for the American South, and the name of the tune its soldiers whistled on the way into battle and which remains the South's unofficial anthem. There is a dispute over the origin of the name; most likely it stems from the MASON-DIXON LINE which was the boundary between the free and SLAVE STATES before the Civil War. The name Dixie has also been attributed to the "dix" or $10 notes issued by a New Orleans bank soon after the LOUISIANA PURCHASE, or to "Dixie's Land", the name supposedly given to a farm near New York by slaves sent there from Charleston by their master, Johann Dixie. The song was written by Dan Decatur Emmett, a Northerner, in 1859, for a show put on at the Mechanics' Hall on Broadway, New York, by Bryant's black-faced Minstrels; he was paid $300 for it. Its opening lines were:

> I wish I was in the land of cotton,
> Old times there are not forgotten,
> Look away, look away, look away, Dixieland.
> In Dixieland where I was born
> Bright 'n'early on a frosty morn,
> Look away, look away, look away, Dixieland.
>
> I wish I was in Dixie, hooray, hooray,
> In Dixieland I'll take my stand
> To live or die in Dixie.
> Look away, look away, look away, Dixieland.

The song caught on throughout America, but the Confederates claimed it with fervour and a stirring version was played at Jefferson DAVIS's Inauguration. Southern sympathizers whistled it to embarrass supporters of the Union, but President LINCOLN loved it and, when the Confederates laid down their arms at the end of the Civil War, he startled die-hard Northerners by saying:

> That's a fine-looking band you have there, Colonel. Let's hear it play Dixie!

Dixiecrats The Southern Democrats who fielded the SEGREGATIONIST Governor Strom Thurmond of South Carolina (1902–) as a Presidential candidate in 1948, further reducing the chances of President Truman who also faced a left-wing challenge from the PROGRESSIVE former Vice-President Henry Wallace. The Dixiecrats walked out of the Democratic Convention after Northern Liberals led by Mayor Hubert Humphrey of Minneapolis (*see* HAPPY WARRIOR) inserted a commitment to CIVIL RIGHTS into the party platform. Thurmond won 1,176,125 votes, carrying Alabama, Mississippi, South Carolina and Louisiana, but could not prevent Truman, with over 24 million, registering a surprise victory (*see* DEWEY). Thurmond went on to serve over 35 years in the US Senate, ending as a Republican; his motto was:

> The longer you stay, you realize that sometimes you can catch more flies with honey than with vinegar.

Dixville Notch The small community in New Hampshire which traditionally casts the first collective vote of the US Presidential election. Once its electorate of around 20 provided a very crude straw poll as to the likely outcome; it now consistently produces a Republican majority, so receives less attention.

Dizzy The universal nickname for **Benjamin Disraeli** (1804–81), first Earl of Beaconsfield, twice Prime Minister (February–December 1868, 1874–80), the most romantic politician of the Victorian age who set the tone of the modern CONSERVATIVE PARTY. Disraeli, from a Jewish family that had converted to Anglicanism, entered Parliament in 1837 with a growing reputation as a novelist; this did him few favours, when he delivered his MAIDEN SPEECH that December, he struggled to make himself heard and finally shouted: "Though I sit down now, the time will come when you shall hear me." Originally he styled himself a Radical, declaring in an unsuccessful bid for Parliament in 1832:

> I am a Conservative to preserve all that is good in our Constitution, a radical to remove all that is bad, I seek to preserve property and to respect order, and I equally decry the appeal to the passions of the many or the prejudices of the few.

But though he flirted with the CHARTISTS, he was elected as a TORY; a string of sycophantic letters to PEEL failed to win him a place in the Government when they came to power in 1841. Disraeli retaliated by forming YOUNG ENGLAND, and by creating blistering satires on his leader in CONINGSBY and SYBIL; in this period he declared:

> I am neither Whig nor Tory. My politics are described in one word and that word is England.

Five years later he launched a devastating attack on Peel for betraying his party over the CORN LAWS that sped him into the wilderness and placed Disraeli among the founders of the Conservative Party as the Tories split. He received mixed reviews as Chancellor under Lord Derby from 1852 and was succeeded by Gladstone, and resigned from Derby's second administration in 1859 because he did not consider it radical enough. The third time he fared better, piloting through as Chancellor the 1867 REFORM Bill that greatly expanded the electorate. He served briefly as Prime Minister in 1868, remarking: "I have climbed to the top of the greasy pole." But it was after 1874 that he established the relationship with Queen Victoria that drew her out of her seclusion since the death of Prince Albert and made him her favourite – in sharp contrast with Gladstone. On his appointment he launched a charm offensive, writing of himself to the Queen:

> He can offer only devotion. It will be his delight and duty to render the transaction of affairs as easy to Your Majesty as possible; and in smaller matters he hopes he may succeed in this; but he ventures to trust that, in the great affairs of state, Your Majesty will deign not to withhold from him the benefit of Your Majesty's guidance.

Disraeli bought a half-interest for Britain in the Suez Canal, and with his greatest Imperial flourish had the Queen declared EMPRESS of India. His final diplomatic triumph was the Congress of BERLIN in 1878, which secured PEACE WITH HONOUR in the Balkans and Cyprus for Britain. But soon afterward the economy turned down, and when Gladstone launched his MIDLOTHIAN CAMPAIGN Beaconsfield's Conservatives went down to a massive defeat.

Disraeli's dazzling personality charmed some, mesmerized many and outraged a few. John Bright said: "He is a self-made man – and he adores his maker," and Daniel O'Connell launched a series of ANTI-SEMITIC tirades against him, declaring:

> His life is a living lie. He is the most degraded of his species and kind, and England is degraded by having upon the face of her society a miscreant of his abominable, foul and atrocious nature.

O'Connell also said: "He possesses just the qualities of the impenitent thief who died upon the cross, whose name, I verily believe, was Disraeli." Yet Dizzy could give as good as he got, describing Lord Liverpool as "the arch-mediocrity who presided, rather than ruled, over a Cabinet of Mediocrities"; John Wilson Croker: "A man who possessed, in very remarkable degree, a restless instinct for adroit baseness"; Lord John Russell: "If a traveller was informed that such a man was LEADER OF THE HOUSE of Commons, he might begin to comprehend how the Egyptians worshipped an insect"; Lord Aberdeen: "His temper, naturally morose, has become licentiously peevish. Crossed in his cabinet, he insults the

House of Lords and plagues the most eminent of his colleagues with the crabbed malice of a maundering witch"; John Bright: "that hysterical old spouter"; the diarist Charles Greville: "The most conceited man I've ever met, though I've read Cicero and known Bulwer-Lytton"; Sir Stafford Northcote: "A complete Jesuit"; and Joseph Chamberlain: "He looks and speaks like a cheesemonger". Gladstone described him as "the greatest master of Parliamentary sarcasm and irony for the past two centuries", and Michael Foot, who named his dog *Dizzy* as a tribute, regarded him as "the greatest comic genius who ever installed himself in Downing Street". He was also a master of spontaneity: Lord George Hamilton recalled that "in the middle of a sentence his teeth fell out and he caught them up with extraordinary rapidity . . . turned round apparently to ask a question of his neighbour, put them in and resumed his speech at the exact word where he had left off".

> Dizzy has the most wonderful courage, but no physical courage. When he has his shower-bath I always have to pull the string.
> Disraeli's wife MARY-ANN.

> His face was lividly pale, and from beneath two finely arched eyebrows blazed out a pair of intensely black eyes. Over a broad, high forehead were ringlets of coal-black glossy hair. There was a sort of half-smile, half-sneer playing about his beautifully-formed mouth, the lips of which were curved, as we see it in portraits of Byron.
> ANON. quoted by MONEYPENNY AND BUCKLE, *Life of Disraeli* (1910).

> Disraeli very generously purchased the Panama Canal from the Khalif and presented it to Queen Victoria with a huge bunch of PRIMROSES (his favourite flower) thus becoming Lord Beaconsfield and a romantic minister.
> W. C. SELLAR and R. J. YEATMAN, *1066 and All That* (1930).

> The soul of Dizzy was a chandelier.
> EDWARD CLERIHEW BENTLEY, *A Ballad of Souls*.

DLP In Australia, the right-wing and largely Catholic party that broke away from LABOR during the split of 1955–57 as GROUPERS left or were expelled from the ALP; it was formally founded in Canberra, with backing from the Catholic hierarchy, in August 1957. At its peak in 1958, the DLP polled over 8% of the Federal vote for the House of Representatives, but after 1972 when it still polled 5.2%, it collapsed; its last elected representatives at federal and State level lost their seats in 1974.

DMZ De-militarized Zone. An area between two armies or states in a military confrontation, which it is agreed shall contain no troops or military installations. The DMZ between North and South Vietnam was an example.

doctor. Doctor Death An unflattering nickname for Dr. David OWEN, leader of Britain's SDP, intended to reflect on his ruthlessness and political impact rather than his prowess in his previous role as a neurologist. When a LIBERAL DEMOCRAT strategy committee in 1990 was considering if there were votes to be gained by playing up Paddy Ashdown's past with the Special Boat Squadron, one member observed that Ashdown must have killed more people than any other UK politician, a voice at the back called out:

> What about the Doctor?

Doctor's mandate The MANDATE to deal with the financial crisis arising from the onset of the GREAT DEPRESSION, sought by Ramsay MacDonald's NATIONAL GOVERNMENT in the October 1931 UK General Election. No comprehensive MANIFESTO was offered, as the partners in the coalition differed on other matters, notably the Conservatives and Liberals over TARIFF REFORM. The Coalition parties – NATIONAL LABOUR, Tories and Liberals – won 554 out of 610 seats, and Labour just 52.

Doctors' Plot An alleged conspiracy by a group of leading Soviet doctors to murder prominent political and military figures in STALIN's government. The nine doctors were arrested in January 1953 and charged with poisoning a former Leningrad party leader, Andrei Zhdanov, and acting as US intelligence agents. Stalin's death on 5 March led to the charges being dropped, and some police officers were later executed for fabricating evidence against the doctors. Fears that Stalin had intended the case to be the pretext for an anti-Jewish PURGE, raised because six of the accused were Jewish, were confirmed by Khruschev in 1956.

Dod *Dod's Parliamentary Companion*, the squat, blue-bound volume published annually which lists – with photographs – the members of both Houses at Westminster with biographies, election results, details of UK government agencies and the rules of Parliamentary procedure. Until 1960 much of the information about the House of Lords appeared in a separate *Dod's Peerage, Baronetage and Knightage*. In 1990 a parallel *European Companion* covering the EUROPEAN PARLIAMENT, COMMISSION and member Governments was also introduced. Dod was first published in 1832 by Charles Roger Phipps Dod (1793–1855), son of an Irish clergyman, who headed *The Times* staff in the PRESS GALLERY.

Dogger Bank incident The tragic and startling attack by ships of the Russian Baltic fleet on Hull trawlers off the Dogger Bank in the North Sea in October 1904. Two of the British vessels were sunk, with the loss of their skippers. Apparently the Russians, en route to fight Japan, mistook the fishing craft for Japanese torpedo boats. After an international inquiry in Paris, Russia agreed to pay Britain £65,000 in compensation.

dogs The canine world has more to do with politics than one might imagine, quite apart from the dogs owned by politicians (*see* FALA, HIM AND HER; MILLIE). Lord Avebury (*see* ORPINGTON MAN) decided after his conversion to Buddhism to donate his body to Battersea dogs' home, and dogs are even capable of political comment; the guide dog of the Labour front-bencher David Blunkett was once violently sick while his colleague Bryan Gould was unveiling a policy document at a press conference. Blunkett also remarked, after allegations of vote-rigging at one Labour conference: "Next time the dog and me will be the SCRUTINEERS." On the campaign trail, the ULSTER UNIONIST leader James Molyneaux was followed into a constituent's house by a strange dog which wrecked the place while they made polite conversation. When he got up to leave, the farmer's wife asked: "Aren't you taking your dog with you?" Moreover, "going to the dogs" is a term frequently used by politicians in opposition to describe the country's fate. The Conservative MP Greg Knight was once told by a voter he couldn't get to the polls because he was going to the dogs (greyhound racing). Knight replied:

> The whole country is going to the dogs, so you'd better come and vote for me.

Not long after World War II, the Labour MP Wilfred Paling accused CHURCHILL in the Commons of being a "dirty dog". Churchill, with a huge grin, turned to him and said: "Yes – and you know what dogs do to palings."

dog licence speech Harold WILSON's outburst against left-wing Labour MPs on 2 March 1967 after they had failed to support his government's defence WHITE PAPER. Not normally a man to utter threats against his own party, Wilson cut loose at a meeting of the PLP to warn of disciplinary action if they continued to rebel; whether he could have enforced it is another matter, but the speech angered much of the party. He told them:

> Every dog is allowed one bite, but a different view is taken of a dog that goes on biting all the time. He may not get his licence returned when it falls due.

either way you get the dog back The argument used by Lloyd Bentsen in running for the Vice-Presidency in 1988 while not relinquishing his seat in the Senate. He told of the Texan vet who set himself up as a taxidermist; when a man called at the surgery with a sick dog and asked why he was following both trades, the vet told him:

> Either way you get the dog back.

Bentsen got the dog back, and served four more years as a Senator before being appointed Treasury Secretary in the Clinton administration.

running dogs Communist, and especially MAOIST, jargon for someone who carries out another's bidding, especially a lackey of CAPITALISM. It is a literal translation of *zou gou*, used by CHAIRMAN MAO when he said:

> People of the world, unite and defeat the US aggressors and their running dogs.

It was taken up, with some of his other picturesque phrases such as PAPER TIGER, by devotees of his LITTLE RED BOOK.

dollar. dollar-a-year men The industrialists and corporate lawyers, more than 1000 in all, brought to Washington by Franklin D. Roosevelt's Office of Production Management (OPM, established in January 1941) to mobilize war production. They got their name because the Federal government paid them just $1 per year, with their peacetime employers paying the rest of their salary. NEW DEALERS complained that too many were Republicans inimical to the Administration, but the OPM's joint head, General Motors president William Knudsen told FDR:

> There is no Democrat rich enough to take a job at a dollar a year.

dollar diplomacy The name that has stuck to the TAFT administration's policy of forcing nations in the Caribbean and the Far East to accept US businessmen and investments, and then using the Navy and the Marines to protect these interests. The policy, not entirely reversed by the WILSON administration, did America lasting damage in both regions.

constant dollars The budgeting term for the listing of sums as if the value of the dollar were constant, instead of in current dollars which allow for INFLATION.

I was alarmed at my doctor's report. He said I was as sound as the dollar One of Ronald Reagan's deepest digs at the CARTER administration's economic policies – while at the same time brushing aside concerns about his age and health. *The* GREAT COMMUNICATOR delivered it in a campaign speech in Jersey City on 1 September 1980.

tax dollars A US term for money paid and collected in taxes.

dominion A fully-independent member of the British EMPIRE (later COMMONWEALTH) with the British Monarch as its HEAD OF STATE, and equal in status with the United Kingdom. The term was first used to describe the newly self-governing Canada in the BRITISH NORTH AMERICA ACT of 1867; it was applied after 1919 to Newfoundland (until its union with Canada), Australia, New Zealand and South Africa (until it left the Commonwealth). The IRISH FREE STATE, on its creation, was also declared a Dominion. The autonomy of the Dominions became complete in 1931 with the Statute of WESTMINSTER. The term is nowadays seldom used.

Dominion of New England A grouping of colonies formed in 1643 to plan joint campaigns against the Indians, and which had jurisdiction in disputes over boundaries, fugitive criminals and slaves. Comprising Massachusetts Bay, Plymouth, Connecticut and New Haven, it lasted until 1684.

domino theory The theory prevalent in US foreign policy throughout the COLD WAR, and especially during the VIETNAM WAR, to justify US intervention in S.E. Asia to contain the spread of Communism. The argument went that if Communism were not resisted in one country, not only that country would be "lost" but also its neighbours. President Eisenhower explained at a press conference on 7 April 1954:

> You have a row of dominoes set up, you knock over the first one, and what will happen to the last one is that it will go over very quickly.

The domino theory was turned into a moral imperative by the KENNEDY and Johnson administrations, justifying involvement in Vietnam to prevent Laos, Cambodia, Thailand and the rest of Southeast Asia following suit.

donkey The emblem of America's DEMOCRATIC PARTY, a respectable version of the JACKASS.

donkey jacket The garment the Labour leader Michael Foot (*see* WURZEL GUMMIDGE) was said by critics, including the Labour MP Walter Johnson, to have worn for the 1981 Remembrance service at the CENOTAPH in WHITEHALL. Foot and his wife insisted that it was a perfectly respectable coat.

donkey vote In Australian elections, a vote cast by simply numbering a House ballot paper straight down and the Senate paper down each group of candidates and across from left to right. The practice was a result of the twin requirements, from 1934, that every elector turn out to vote and that they number every space on the ballot paper; between 1940 and 1984 the law was amended to ensure no party could benefit, by requiring the position of party groups on each paper to be chosen by lot. *See also* FOUR AS.

Donovan Report The report to Harold WILSON's UK government in 1968 of the Royal Commission on Trade Unions and Employers' Associations, chaired by the senior judge Lord Donovan. It focused on ways of reducing the high incidence of unofficial strikes in British industry, recommending a move toward agreements negotiated at plant rather than national level. Donovan also advocated an Industrial Relations Commission to investigate problem areas of industry, and Labour Tribunals to examine individuals' grievances against companies or unions. The report was criticized by the Conservatives for rejecting legally enforceable collective agreements and criminal sanctions on unofficial strikes and PICKETING. The Labour Cabinet quietly shelved it – then came up with an alternative: IN PLACE OF STRIFE.

don't. Don't get mad, get even *See* DIRKSEN

Don't-knows In OPINION POLLS, those listed as saying they do not know whom they will vote for; some polls omit them and round up the other totals to 100%. The KNOW-NOTHINGS were a US political party.

Don't let the buggers get you down The message inscribed on a watch sent to the disgraced tycoon Asil Nadir early in 1992 by the Northern Ireland Minister Michael Mates (1934–) just before Nadir jumped bail on fraud charges and fled to Turkish-occupied Northern Cyprus. John MAJOR told the Commons the gift, though foolish, was "not a hanging offence", but Mates was forced to resign on 24 June. Major confirmed Mates's assertion that he had done nothing improper in supporting Nadir; Mates went on to allege in the Commons that the Serious Fraud Office and other agencies had victimized Nadir and been partly responsible for the fall of his Polly Peck empire.

Don't mourn, organize! The last words of the US union pioneer Joe Hill before his execution by a Utah firing squad on 18 November 1915. Hill, who had also written most of the WOBBLIES' songs, had been convicted on the flimsiest of evidence of murdering a Salt Lake City grocer and ex-policeman; he was executed despite pleas for a REPRIEVE or a retrial from President WILSON and many others. Hill's exact words, in a letter to Bill HAYWOOD, were: "Don't waste any time mourning – organize!" They became a rallying-cry for union activists and the left throughout the world.

Don't tread on me! The motto on the very first flag of the rebel American colonies, which showed a coiled snake. The inference was clear: if Britain trod on the colonies it would suffer a poisonous bite.

dontopedalogy A word coined by Britain's Prince Philip, consort of Queen Elizabeth II, for "opening one's mouth and putting one's foot in it". The Prince, noted in the 1950s for his outspoken if mainly non-political comments, put it together from the Greek words for a tooth and a foot. More recently one Conservative MP observed of a tactless colleague:

> He only opens his mouth to change feet.

doomsday. Doomsday clock An image of a clock contained in each issue of the *Bulletin of Atomic Scientists* (founded 1945) that points to the time remaining before the nuclear holocaust. In 1945 the time was set to 11.52, at the height of the COLD WAR it was moved to 11.58, but with the collapse of Communism in Russia and Eastern Europe, it was put back to 11.50. A similar clock at the Worldwatch Institute in Washington reflects ecological pressures on the planet from population.

doomsday scenario The concern voiced by some Labour politicians in Scotland prior to the 1987 and 1992 General Elections that if the UK as a whole continued to elect Conservative governments, voters in Scotland where Labour held over two-thirds of the seats would decide their votes were wasted and switch to the pro-independence SNP.

DORA The popular name for Britain's Defence of the Realm Acts, which imposed many restrictions on individual freedoms for the duration of WORLD WAR I. Their application to munition factories and the drink trade caused particular irritation. The abbreviation passed into common speech after being used in the law courts by Mr. Justice Scrutton. In numerous press cartoons Dora was portrayed as a long-nosed, elderly female, personifying crabbed restriction. However the legislation did have a purpose; commending it to the Commons in 1915, Lloyd George declared:

> Instead of BUSINESS AS USUAL, we want victory as usual.

Dorneywood The country house, near Burnham Beeches outside Slough, owned by the National Trust, which is used for entertaining, informal conferences and weekend relaxation by Britain's Chancellor of the Exchequer. From the 1950s to 1970s the house, of no great antiquity, served the same function for the FOREIGN SECRETARY, who now has the use of CHEVENING.

double. double-dipping A Washington term for the practice of senior military officers and civil servants who retire on a sizable pension, then find another job (often still in the public service) so that they effectively receive two incomes.

double whammy A phrase for two blows which between them deliver a knockout, which entered US politics in the 1980s and Britain's political vocabulary during the 1992 election campaign. It caught on after being used just before the campaign by the Conservative chairman Chris Patten (*see* GOBSMACKED); Speaker Bernard Weatherill commenting when pressed: "I'm not an expert in rhyming slang. I've no idea what a wham is." On election night Scottish Secretary Ian Lang, re-elected when he had expected to lose both his seat and his job, told jubilant supporters in his Galloway constituency:

> Scotland has rejected SEPARATISM. Britain has rejected Socialism. It's a double whammy!

doughnutting The practice, in televised legislatures, of supportive members crowding round a colleague speaking in an otherwise deserted chamber, to draw attention to themselves and give the impression that the speaker is highly popular. The area in the view of the camera is known as the **doughnut**. The words originated in the Canadian Parliament during the 1980s, catching on quickly at Westminster when televising of its proceedings began at the end of the decade.

Douglas-Home rules The rules for electing a leader of Britain's CONSERVATIVE PARTY, under which Margaret Thatcher was ousted in 1990. Drawn up by Lord Home (*see* SIR ALEC) as a refinement of the original BERKELEY RULES, they were first tried in 1989 when Sir Anthony Meyer mounted his STALKING-HORSE challenge to Mrs. Thatcher. They dictate a two-stage election process, the first effectively being a referendum on the existing leader (who must win more than half the votes of all Tory MPs and have a clear lead of more than 15% over the nearest challenger). Mrs. Thatcher's narrow failure to open up such a lead over Michael Heseltine was interpreted as a moral defeat, and brought her withdrawal from the more open second stage as her support crumbled. The party establishment reacted to the outcome by advocating changes to make the overthrow of a leader more difficult, but little was actually done.

dove The opposite of HAWK, but a word with a far shorter pedigree. The dove of peace became a symbol – widely used, but exploited by the Communists – after Pablo Picasso presented his drawing of one to the World Congress of Intellectuals in Wroclaw, Poland, in 1948. It entered the US political vocabulary during the CUBAN MISSILE CRISIS, Charles Bartlett and Stewart Alsop writing in the *Saturday Evening Post* on 20 December 1962:

> The hawks favored an air strike to eliminate the Cuban missile bases . . . The doves opposed the air strikes and favored a BLOCKADE.

But the word really caught on during the VIETNAM WAR, being used particularly by

Sen. Robert F. KENNEDY for opponents of US involvement. It was also applied from the mid-1970s to moderate politicians in Israel – mainly from the LABOUR party – who opposed the LIKUD government's policy of provocative confrontation with the Arabs.

Downing Street The narrow cul-de-sac in Westminster between WHITEHALL and Horse Guards' Parade, less than 400 yards from PARLIAMENT SQUARE, near the end of which lie NUMBER TEN, the official residence and office of Britain's Prime Minister, NUMBER ELEVEN, where the Chancellor of the Exchequer lives, and NUMBER TWELVE, the office of the Government chief WHIP. Until 1979 access was open to all, but as the threat from the IRA grew it was cordoned off first by a token fence and, since 1989, by high security gates; these withstood an onslaught the following March by rioters against the POLL TAX. However they could not prevent the IRA attack in February 1991, when terrorists came close to wiping out John MAJOR's Cabinet by firing a mortar at Number Ten over the Cabinet Office, from the other side of Whitehall.

doyen *See* DIPLOMATIC CORPS.

draft (1) A US term for the action of the leaders of a political party, or a CONVENTION, in adopting as a candidate someone who was not in the race and who may have been reluctant to run. When in 1980 Rep. Morris Udall was asked if he would accept a draft for the Democratic nomination – not that one was on offer – he replied:

> Only on three conditions: 1. If a star rose in the East; 2. If three men on camels rode up demanding that I run; 3. If their names are CARTER, Mondale and KENNEDY.

(2) A text of a speech, document or treaty put together for consideration and still open to change; as a verb, the process of putting together a report, communiqué or other text. At the 1989 CHOGM in Kuala Lumpur, the Australian Foreign Minister Sen. Gareth Evans brought a frustratingly long drafting session on SANCTIONS against South Africa to a standstill when he remarked in the presence of several Islamic colleagues:

> Geez, we're not trying to draft the fucking Koran!

(3) The draft, the form of CONSCRIPTION used in the United States which, in its highly selective form, aroused great controversy during the VIETNAM WAR. Thomas JEFFERSON told James MONROE in 1813: "We must train and classify the whole of our male citizens, and make military instruction a regular part of collegiate education", but Daniel Webster asked the following year: "Where is it written in the Constitution . . . that you may take children from their parents, and parents from their children, and compel them to fight the battles of any war in which the folly or wickedness of government may engage it?"

> White people sending black people to fight yellow people to protect the country they stole from red people.
>
> GEROME GRAGNI and JAMES RADO.

> The only way we'll ever get a volunteer army is to draft 'em.
>
> Rep. F. EDWARD HÉBERT (1901–79).

The issue of **draft-dodging** is not a new one; in the CIVIL WAR over 600,000 out of 776,829 men called up either paid someone else to serve for them, paid $300,000 to be passed over, or were declared medically unfit. But it aroused strong feelings during the Vietnam War; some opponents of the war simply refused (*see* HELL, NO, WE WON'T GO!), some vanished (often to Canada) and those with influential connections used them to secure a safe berth. President CARTER aroused controversy by declaring partial AMNESTY, and the issue still raises its head as candidates for national office have their efforts to avoid active war service revealed. Dan QUAYLE came under heavy fire for having secured a safe berth in the Indiana National Guard; Republicans were even more fiercely critical of Bill Clinton (*see* COMEBACK KID) for having demonstrated against the war while a Rhodes Scholar at Oxford.

Drang Nach Osten (Ger. push to the east) The belief that Germany's destiny requires an eastward extension of its boundaries. It was a powerful element in the policies of the newly-created German REICH after 1870 and, coupled with Germany's supposed need for LEBENSRAUM, had an echo in Hitler's eastward expansion of the late 1930s.

Dreikaiserbund (Ger. league of three emperors) The agreement reached in Berlin in 1872 between the newly-proclaimed Kaiser Wilhelm I and the Emperors of Austria and Russia to maintain the status quo in Europe, work together amicably over the Balkans as the Ottoman Empire broke up, and promote reform while suppressing Socialism. The *Dreikaiserbund* was dealt a severe blow in 1878 at the Congress of BERLIN, at which Russian ambitions for the region were passed over in favour of an Anglo-Austrian plan. The alliance was renewed at meetings every three years, but from that point Russia moved into the ambit of Republican France, setting the battle-lines for WORLD WAR I.

Dreyfus case The miscarriage of justice in the 1890s stemming in part from ANTI-SEMITISM, which became a *cause célèbre* reflecting immense discredit on France's military hierarchy. In 1894 Captain Alfred Dreyfus (1859–1935), an artillery staff officer of Jewish peasant origins, was convicted by court-martial of betraying military secrets to Germany and sent to Devil's Island. He was convicted on the evidence of a letter, the *bordereau*, signed "D", which had been retrieved from the German embassy. No-one knew the spy's identity, but to Dreyfus's aristocratic colleagues he was the perfect scapegoat. In 1898 Clemenceau (*see* TIGER) and Emile Zola took up his case, Zola writing his famous open letter J'ACCUSE. In 1899, as a result of the pressure, Dreyfus was retried and again condemned, but was pardoned shortly after. In 1906 the proceedings were finally quashed, and Dreyfus awarded the LEGION OF HONOUR.

> Military justice is to justice as military music is to music. CLEMENCEAU.

> Truth is on the march. Nothing can stop it now. ZOLA.

Dries (1) In early 20th-century America, the supporters of PROHIBITION. (2) In the Conservative Party under Margaret Thatcher, the most loyal supporters of her rigorous early economic policies and strongest opponents of the WETS.

drink One of the great perils of political life, with the long, late hours in a legislature, and temptations of being away from home and under pressure making alcohol an attractive comforter. Its effect on many political careers has been tragic; it has also given rise to harmless and hilarious episodes. At Westminster some of these arise from the fiction that no MP can be drunk if he is in the CHAMBER of the Commons, and that to suggest otherwise is a CONTEMPT OF THE HOUSE; as the Conservative MP Kenneth Warren put it:

> members of Parliament are never drunk. They are indisposed.

Some politicians mind more than others when accused of overindulging. In 1957 Aneurin Bevan (*see* NYE), Richard CROSSMAN and Morgan Phillips, general secretary of the LABOUR PARTY, sued the *Spectator* for libel for reporting that they had been drunk at a Socialist meeting in Venice. They were awarded £2500 each, but Crossman wrote in his *Diaries* that Phillips, at least, had been "dead drunk most of the conference". A senior Labour figure who cared less about his reputation was George BROWN, who once said:

> Many British statesmen have either drunk too much or womanised too much. I never fell into the second category.

Brown's unstable behaviour with the drink taken was legendary (*see* TIRED AND EMOTIONAL). When Foreign Secretary *c.* 1967, he was at an Embassy reception in Lima, Peru, when he espied a remarkable creature in flowing red attire, and asked it to dance. The apparition refused, and when Brown asked why, replied:

> First, you are drunk. Second, this is the Peruvian national anthem. And third, I am the Cardinal Archbishop of Lima.

Abuse of liquor has long been frowned upon by MIDDLE AMERICA, but from the earliest days it has been a problem in Washington. Thomas JEFFERSON once confided: "Were I to commence my administration again, the first question I would ask respecting a candidate would be: 'Does he use ardent spirits?'" Even some Presidents were susceptible; the WHIGS hailed Franklin Pierce (*see* HANDSOME FRANK) as "the hero of many a well-fought bottle" and Ulysses S. GRANT was a renowned heavy drinker when commander of the Union forces. When politicians complained to Abraham LINCOLN, he reputedly told them: "Find out what the brand is and I'll give it to my other generals." Congress has seen its fair share of excess; Sen. Wayne Morse (*see* LONE RANGER) reminisced: "There has never been one night session of the Senate in my experience that hasn't witnessed at least one Senator making a fool of himself and disgracing the Senate." Yet some of the culprits have been able to laugh at themselves; at one Washington party Speaker TIP O'Neill toasted Sen. Thomas Dodd with:

> Here's to the second nastiest drunk in town!

To be sure, I never drank there much meself The reply of the Independent Irish Republican MP Frank Maguire to a House of Commons policeman in 1974 when told "Mr. Maguire, had you heard the Duke of Gloucester has gone?" The policeman was referring to the death of that member of the Royal family; Maguire assumed the IRA had blown up another London pub.

Yes – er, no. Unless I was drunk at the time The response, according to PRIVATE EYE, of the Labour MP Michael O'Halloran to party officials who questioned him about alleged irregularities in his selection to fight the Islington North seat prior to the BY-ELECTION in 1968 that took him to Westminster.

You are drunk. Leave the room at once The message passed to a baffled Chancellor Austen Chamberlain over a dinner for most of Bonar Law's Cabinet given in 1921 by the Tory hostess Mrs. Ronnie Greville. The butler had been drinking heavily and was unsteady on his feet; Mrs. Greville wrote the note and handed it to him, whereupon he beamed, placed it on a silver salver and delivered it to Chamberlain. *See also* ADULTERY; ASQUITH; CHURCHILL.

dropping the pilot The caption of one of the most celebrated political cartoons carried by the usually humorous magazine *Punch* (1841–1992). Drawn by Sir John Tenniel in the issue of 28 March 1890, it depicted the aged Bismarck leaving a ship for the pilot's launch after being "dropped" by the young Kaiser Wilhelm II. The cartoon summed up precisely the headstrong German ruler's desire to break with the past and make his own way – a course that led to war 24 years later. However he and his father's IRON CHANCELLOR were reconciled soon after.

Dublin Castle Under British rule, the seat of government of the VICEROYS of Ireland, and thus a symbol much resented by nationalists. The Castle was taken over for purposes of State by the Republic of Ireland, the state apartments being lovingly maintained and part of the building turned into a conference suite that has housed three EC SUMMITs and a media centre for the visit of Pope John Paul II in 1979.

Dublin Post Office The focal point of the EASTER RISING in 1916.

Duce, il (Ital. leader) the title chosen for himself by **Benito Mussolini** (1883–1945), first as leader of the FASCIST movement and, from 1924 when the King accepted him as Prime Minister, effective head of the Italian state. An early Fascist slogan was:

> The Duce is always right.

Originally a left-winger, and editor of the Socialist paper AVANTI! until his expulsion from the party for demanding war with Austria, Mussolini progressed from strident nationalism to founding the world's first significant Fascist party. Capitalizing on the reservoir of discontent after WORLD WAR I, it pioneered the mixing of uniforms and mildly fatuous ceremonial with policies of nationalism, POPULISM and CORPORATISM; it lacked much of the menace of NAZISM and was only actively ANTI-SEMITIC toward the end, but was rather more corrupt. Elected to Parliament in 1921, Mussolini said in his MAIDEN SPEECH:

> I shall adopt a reactionary line throughout my speech, which will be . . . anti-Socialist and anti-Democratic in substance.

After the Fascists seized the initiative with the MARCH ON ROME in 1922, Mussolini was made Prime Minister to head off conflict between Communists and conservatives, telling Parliament:

> I could have transformed this grey assembly hall into an armed camp for BLACKSHIRTS, a bivouac for corpses. I could have nailed up the doors of Parliament.

He survived an assassination attempt in 1926, saying to his followers:

> If I advance, follow me. If I retreat, kill me. If I die, avenge me.

Mussolini took total power in 1928, creating a ONE-PARTY STATE. He secured the backing of the Vatican by concluding the LATERAN TREATY, and grandly revived Rome's Imperial ambitions (George Seldes titled his biography of Mussolini *Sawdust Caesar*) by invading Abyssinia in 1935 in contempt of the LEAGUE OF NATIONS. His success led to the conclusion of the AXIS with Germany and prompted Hitler to embark on his own campaign of conquest; the two leaders also joined forces to back Franco in the SPANISH CIVIL WAR. Mussolini's relationship with Hitler was close for one not based on mutual respect. Mussolini said of the Nazis:

> I should be pleased, I suppose, that Hitler has carried out a revolution on our lines. But they are Germans, so they will end by ruining our idea.

And as Hitler, unaided, rolled up the map of Europe, Mussolini confided: "The Italians will laugh at me. Every time Hitler occupies a country, he sends me a message." In return, the Germans (as later, *see* ITALIAN TANKS) despised Italy's military prowess – Mussolini did not enter World War II until 1940, and the Nazi invasion of Russia was fatally delayed when Mussolini had to be rescued in the Balkans. Yet after his opponents on the Fascist Grand Council staged a COUP against him in 1943 following the Allied invasion of Italy to restore constitutional government, Hitler sent crack commandos under Otto Skorzeny to free him from captivity and restore him as *Duce* of the limited SALO REPUBLIC. In the closing days of the war he was captured with his mistress Clara Petacci by Communist PARTISANS; they were both shot and their bodies put on display, hanging upside down, in the centre of Milan. The Duce's last words were said to be:

> But, Mr. Colonel . . .

> The King presupposes subjects, Il Duce, followers.
> IGNAZIO SILONE, *The School for Dictators* (1939).

> I have a great personal admiration for Mussolini, who has welded a nation out of a collection of touts, blackmailers, ice-cream vendors and gangsters.
> Letter in the *Saturday Review*.

> This whipped jackal frisking by the side of the German tiger. CHURCHILL, House of Commons, April 1941.

The only journalist, so far as I know, to become a dictator.
JAN MORRIS, *Daily Telegraph*, 1978.

He made the trains run on time. ANON.

Yes, I have a tremendous admiration for Caesar. Still, I myself belong rather to the class of the Bismarcks.
MUSSOLINI, in conversation with Emil Ludwig.

Uno Duce, una Voce *See* HAUGHEY.

Duchy of Lancaster The ancient Royal estate, almost coterminous to the English county of Lancashire, whose CHANCELLOR still sits in the UK CABINET. The Sovereign, even when a woman, is described in the county as the Duke of Lancaster. The Chancellor accompanies the monarch on visits to Lancashire, but his or her main duties are those of a Minister Without PORTFOLIO.

due process clause The clause from the FIFTH AMENDMENT in the US BILL OF RIGHTS which guarantees the due process of law – the right to full and fair legal procedures – to all citizens. More cases have probably been decided by the SUPREME COURT on the basis of this clause than any other part of the constitution. It is repeated in the FOURTEENTH AMENDMENT, ratified in 1868, which binds the States as well as Federal institutions to guarantee due process to all.

Duma (Russ. council) The Russian Parliament established in the wake of the REVOLUTION OF 1905, which TSAR Nicholas II was determined not to allow meaningful power. He proposed the first Duma in his OCTOBER MANIFESTO of 1905, but had curtailed its powers before it met in May 1906; all its decisions could be VETOed by the Tsar, and the Tsar could pass laws when it was not sitting. Moreover, Ministers were ultimately answerable to the Tsar, not the Duma. When the first Duma nevertheless proved radical and demanded land reforms, it was dissolved in July 1906. The second Duma, convened in March 1907, lasted only three months. Next the electoral system was rigged to ensure more conservative third and fourth Dumas (1907–12 and 1912–17) which generally supported the government. During World War I opposition to the monarchy again swelled in the Duma; after the Tsar was deposed in 1917, a Duma Provisional Committee formed the first Provisional GOVERNMENT.

Dumbarton Oaks The conference held in Washington from August to October 1944 involving Britain, America, the Soviet Union and China to discuss the formation of what became the UNITED NATIONS. It was named after the Georgetown mansion where it was held. There was general agreement over the basic structures, such as the GENERAL ASSEMBLY, SECURITY COUNCIL and secretariat. More contentious were the issues of membership – the Soviet Union wanted seats for all its 16 republics – and the right of VETO in the Security Council. These questions were reconsidered at YALTA in February 1945, and the SAN FRANCISCO CONFERENCE fixed the UN's final form.

dumping The export of manufactured goods, food or commodities to a country at below cost price in order to undercut other trading nations and that country's domestic suppliers. One of the reasons for the GATT system is to curb dumping by ensuring not only free but fair trade; where GATT makes no provision, nations retaliate against dumping by imposing stiff TARIFFS.

social dumping A term used by countries with high labour costs or costly social benefits for the practice of MULTINATIONALS switching production to cheaper locations. It was used by French Ministers early in 1993 when Hoover switched much of its European production from Dijon to Cambuslang, near Glasgow, on the ground that UK wages and social security costs were far less.

Dunkirk spirit The spirit repeatedly invoked by Harold WILSON in the mid-1960s when urging the British people on to greater sacrifice and effort to pull the nation's economy round. It sought to emulate the country's success at snatching survival, if not victory, from the jaws of defeat in June 1940 when over 300,000 troops were evacuated from the beaches of Dunkirk under the noses of Germany's *Luftwaffe* as Nazi troops advanced through northern France. Even where the reaction to Wilson's appeals was detectable, it did not lead to an upsurge in Britain's economic fortunes; recovery only began with DEVALUATION, which Wilson had long resisted, in November 1967.

economic Dunkirk The alarming estimate of the prospect facing America given to Ronald Reagan immediately after his election as President in 1980 by David Stockman, who was named budget director soon after, and the conservative Rep. Jack Kemp. Stockman made a deliberately pessimistic pitch at a time when the economy was barely in RECESSION in order to instil urgency into the new administration, and prompt Reagan to go for serious cuts in the Budget proposed by the CARTER administration.

Durham Report The report to the British government by John Lambton, first Earl of Durham (*see* RADICAL JACK, 1792–1840) which paved the way to Responsible GOVERNMENT for the Canadian colonies. Durham was despatched to Canada as GOVERNOR-GENERAL in 1838 after the Mackenzie and Papineau rebellions of the year before. He reported:

> I expected to find a contest between a government and a people; I found two nations warring in the bosom of a single state: I found struggle not of principles but of races.

Durham concluded that Britain was going too far in APPEASING French-Canadians, and that unless a fairer balance was struck, the Anglophone business community would look to the United States. To avert this, he recommended a union of Upper and Lower Canada (Ontario and Quebec) as a democracy that would be under English-Canadian dominance. This was provided for in an Act of Union in 1840. The Report was deeply unpopular with French Canadians and did much to unite them; Conservatives in Upper Canada were as opposed to democratic rule.

during pleasure The euphemism used in the HOUSE OF LORDS for the period in the evening when PEERS adjourn for dinner. Occasionally a short debate on a non-controversial subject is staged to avoid giving the impression that "everything stops for tea".

duty. If we believe a thing to be bad, and have a right to prevent it, it is our duty to prevent it and damn the consequences The terms in which Lord Milner (1854–1925) set out the resolve of himself and the other DIEHARDS to oppose the PEOPLE'S BUDGET put forward by Lloyd George, regardless of the consequences for the HOUSE OF LORDS of doing so. He made the declaration in a speech in Glasgow on 26 November 1909.

Let us therefore brace ourselves to our duty A key phrase of the rallying speech made by CHURCHILL in the House of Commons on 18 June 1940, after DUNKIRK but with the Battle of Britain ahead and invasion by Germany expected shortly. Churchill said:

> Let us therefore brace ourselves to our duties, and so bear ourselves that if the British Empire and its Commonwealth last for a thousand years, men will still say: "THIS WAS THEIR FINEST HOUR."

E

E Pluribus Unum (Lat. one out of many) The motto on the device forming the Great SEAL of the United States, and the other emblems of the nation. It is written on a scroll held in the beak of the American EAGLE.

eagle A traditional symbol of strength, hence of the power of a nation. The emblem of the United States, and before it of Russia, Prussia, Austria-Hungary, Imperial France, Rome, the Kings of Babylon and Persia and the Ptolemies of Egypt. America's national bird is the bald eagle; H. G. Wells wrote:

> Every time Europe looks across the Atlantic to see the American eagle, it observes only the rear end of an ostrich.

The eagle is also a symbol of dominance, CHURCHILL saying after VE Day: "The [German] eagle has ceased to scream, but the parrots will now begin to chatter."

eagle's lair or nest The Berghof, HITLER's redoubt 1829 m. (6000 ft.) up a mountain near Berchtesgaden in southern Germany, close to the Austrian border. The FÜHRER received many important guests here.

Earl A senior, hereditary rank in the British PEERAGE (from O.E. *eorl*), with an automatic seat in the HOUSE OF LORDS. An **earldom** is offered to the most distinguished former Prime Ministers; the last to accept was Macmillan (Earl of Stockton).

Early Bird The PENTAGON's confidential daily news sheet, officially called *Current News*, which in 16 pages distils the overnight news reports of greatest relevance to the department and its followers in the White House, Congress, the military and the intelligence community.

Early Day Motion *See* EDM.

Earth Summit The meeting of world leaders in Rio de Janeiro in June 1992, sponsored by the United Nations, to gain agreement on global steps to save the environment. It was undermined by President Bush's initial refusal to attend and his insistence, once there, on withholding US support from a Biodiversity Treaty to save endangered species. The summit did take some steps to curb global warming, but stopped short of setting firm limits on carbon emissions which ENVIRONMENTALISTS had argued were essential.

east. Eastern Question The overriding foreign policy issue for European states in the second half of the 19th century, stemming from the gradual collapse of the Ottoman Empire and its efforts to retain control in the face of rising Balkan nationalisms, the perceived interests of Austria-Hungary, Britain, France and Germany, and the ambitions of Russia in the region. It came to a head in the CRIMEAN WAR and the Balkan crisis of 1876–78, ending only with the establishment of the modern Turkish state in 1923.

east front The aspect of the US CAPITOL facing the Washington Monument, and the scene of many Presidential inaugurations. The cornerstone of the Capitol was laid on the east front by George Washington on 18 September 1793; the first portion was completed in 1800. The EAST FRONT was extended to its present length of 751 ft. by 1867, then built out 32½ ft. between 1959 and 1961 to create extra office space.

Easter Rising The uprising in Dublin on Easter Monday 1916 against British rule, which paved the way for the creation of the Irish state. 1600 volunteers of the IRISH REPUBLICAN BROTHERHOOD ("a minority of a minority" – R. F. Foster) led by Patrick Pearse and James Connolly captured positions in the city, notably Dublin Post Office where Pearse read a "proclamation of the Republic", and held out for a week. 450 people, including 116 soldiers and 16 police, were killed and 2614 wounded. Fifteen leaders of the rising were executed, the revulsion caused greatly strengthening nationalist feeling.

> A terrible beauty is born. W. B. YEATS.

eat crow To be forced to swallow one's own words. The phrase originated in the 19th-century US joke about a man who claimed he could eat anything; when forced to eat roast crow, he declared: "Yes, I can eat crow! . . . but I'll be darned if I hanker after it." Popularized in the 1872 Presidential election when Horace Greeley, who split from the Republican party to run against GRANT, was nicknamed "boiled crow" by his foes; those who "ate crow" were ready to swallow their reservations and vote for Greeley. After Truman's shock re-election in 1948, the *Washington Post* advertised a banquet at which political reporters and POLLSTERS would be treated to "breast of tough old crow, en glace".

Eatanswill The fictitious, corrupt and Rabelaisian BY-ELECTION in Dickens' *Pickwick Papers* which has come to epitomize the squalid, corrupt side of political life in England before the BALLOT Act.

EC *See* EUROPEAN COMMUNITY.

ECOFIN The EC's council of economics and finance ministers, which normally meets once a month in Brussels or in the country holding the PRESIDENCY. It has supervised the development of economic and monetary union (EMU).

economical with the truth *See* TRUTH.

economics The theoretical study of the production and distribution of wealth, inextricably linked to politics. Thomas Carlyle described it as "the dismal science"; to George Meany it was "the one profession where you can gain great eminence without ever being right". Eugene W. Baer reckoned that "what's good politics is bad economics; what's bad politics is good economics"; while Lyndon B. Johnson observed:

> Making a speech about economics is a bit like pissing down your leg. It seems hot to you, but it never does to anyone else.

economic advisers A prerequisite of all rulers, but loved by few of them. President Truman begged: "Give me a one-handed economist. All my economists say 'on the one hand . . . on the other'."

> Mitterrand has a hundred mistresses; one of them has AIDS but he doesn't know which one. Bush has a hundred bodyguards; one of them is a terrorist, but he doesn't know which one. I have a hundred economic advisers. One is smart, but I don't know which one.
> MIKHAIL S. GORBACHEV.

Economic and Monetary Union (EMU). The process of unifying the economies of the EC member states, the subject of testing negotiations in an inter-governmental council (IGC) before the 1991 MAASTRICHT summit.

economic blizzard CHURCHILL's term for the financial crash of 1931, following a series of European bank collapses, which ensured the GREAT DEPRESSION.

economic cycle The cycle in an economy consisting successively of BOOM, RECESSION, DEPRESSION, recovery and boom.

Economic League A UK right-wing organization with links to the CONSERVATIVE PARTY, which specializes in circulating BLACKLISTs of alleged union troublemakers to employers.

economic miracle (Ger. *Wirtschaftswunder*) Germany's free-market economic recovery following World War II.

Economic Report of the President The annual assessment of the US economy prepared by the President's Council of ECONOMIC ADVISERS;

economic Royalists Franklin D. Roosevelt's tag early in his second term for big business and its Republican backers in Congress, whom he blamed for a revival of unemployment. He used the phrase to push further NEW DEAL legislation through Congress – though without the same impact on the economy as his initial measures.

economic warfare Strategic and financial measures used to back up a military campaign and weaken an enemy's economy, as in the UK's WORLD WAR II Ministry of Economic Warfare.

matchstick economics The pursuit of economic policy by the uninitiated using simple logic, from the statement by SIR ALEC Douglas-Home:

> When I read economic documents, I have to have a box of matches and start moving them into position, to illustrate and simplify the points to myself.

voodoo economics George BUSH's pejorative for REAGANOMICS during the 1980 Republican primaries. Bush's criticisms, conjuring up images of sleight of hand, mumbo-jumbo and deception, did not prevent Reagan selecting him as his RUNNING-MATE.

> It's the only memorable thing I've ever said, and I've regretted saying it. GEORGE BUSH.

economist (1) A proponent or analyst of economic theory and its application to national economic systems. Ronald Reagan described an economist as "the only professional who sees something working in practice and seriously wonders if it works in theory", and said:

> A friend of mine was asked to a costume ball. He slapped some egg on his face and went as a liberal economist.

(2) In ASQUITH's peacetime Cabinet, the faction which argued for economy in spending and, in particular, against an accelerated Dreadnought building programme (*see* WE WANT EIGHT AND WE WON'T WAIT).

economy (1) An economy or the economy: the operation of a nation's finances, wealth creation, production, exchange and employment.

> It is much easier to manage an economy if you can use electrodes on the most sensitive parts of those who refuse to co-operate. DENIS HEALEY.

> Government's view of the economy can be summed up in a few short phrases. If it moves, tax it. If it keeps moving, regulate it. And if it stops moving, subsidize it.
> RONALD REAGAN.

black economy The portion of the economy operated, largely by the self-employed, out of reach of the tax authorities.
command economy An economy in which orders are given by the centre and the system is expected to meet set targets, regardless of economic forces. A key feature of Soviet COMMUNISM.
commanding heights of the economy The phrase coined by Aneurin Bevan (*see* NYE) for the areas of activity Labour had to NATIONALIZE to bring about fundamental change.
mixed economy An economy in which elements of SOCIALISM and CAPITALISM co-exist. The term was particularly used of Britain from the late 1940s, when state controls, the WELFARE STATE and NATIONALIZED INDUSTRIES interacted with a classic PRIVATE SECTOR.
permanent war economy An economy permanently distorted by the demands of military spending and procurement, regardless of whether the nation is actually at war.
siege economy An inherently weak economy isolated by a government from external pressures in order to protect and restructure it.
It's the economy, stupid! The sign hung in the WAR ROOM at Clinton campaign headquarters in LITTLE ROCK during the 1992 Presidential campaign by James Carville, Bill Clinton's campaign manager and strategy adviser. He was anxious to drive home the message to campaign staff that, whatever other issues were raised, the election would be decided on the state of America's economy and the candidates' commitment to tackling it.
(2) Prudence in the handling of money.

> Everyone is always in favour of general economy and particular expenditure. ANTHONY EDEN.

ECOSOC (1) The UN Economic and Social Conference. (2) The EC's Economic and Social Committee, a body drawn from all walks of life, which can submit "opinions" on proposed Community legislation.

Ecu The European Currency Unit (the *écu* was also a 17th-century French silver coin). The notional currency, based on a "basket" of 10 currencies and with a fluctuating value of approximately $1, which is the base for the European Monetary System (EMS).
hard Ecu John MAJOR's proposal when Chancellor for a fixed-value Ecu which could gain credibility against national currencies and conceivably supplant them. It was put forward in an unsuccessful effort to head off early moves by other EC states toward a common currency.

Eden, (Robert) **Anthony** Eden, later the Earl of Avon (1897–1977), UK Prime Minister (Conservative) 1955–57. From a landed Co. Durham family, Eden was wounded three times in World War I before making an early entry into politics. In 1935 BALDWIN made him Foreign Secretary, the youngest-ever; handsome and dashing, Aneurin Bevan called him "the juvenile lead", but Bertrand Russell remarked: "Not a gentleman. He dresses too well." To Bonar Thompson he was "the best advertisement the Fifty Shilling Tailors ever had". In 1938 he resigned over CHAMBERLAIN's dealings with Fascist Italy, and the – not wholly correct – legend of Eden as the man who stood against the dictators was born. A. J. P. Taylor was to write:

> Eden did not face the dictators; he pulled faces at them.

CHURCHILL brought him back to government in 1940, serving again as Foreign Secretary 1941–45 and 1951–55 and becoming his heir-apparent. But Churchill hung on, leading Eden to remark: "I have been Foreign Secretary for 10 years. Am I not to be trusted?" Harold Macmillan wrote: "Winston thought Anthony would wreck it. That's the reason he held on so long." When Churchill went, there was some unease. Lord Swinton wrote of Eden: "He will be the worst Prime Minister since Lord North", while Macmillan observed: "It really may be that he has been Prince of Wales too long."

So it turned out. To start with he did well, increasing the Tory majority in a SNAP ELECTION campaign when, said Macmillan, "he never put a foot wrong". Malcolm Muggeridge felt it was all too easy: "They asked for a leader and were given a public relations officer: here is the news, and this is Anthony Eden reading it." R. A. Butler (*see* RAB) agreed with a reporter that he was "the best Prime Minister we have", but privately he described the sensitive Eden as "half mad baronet, half beautiful woman"; the Labour MP Sir Reginald Paget was as cruel: "an overripe banana – yellow outside, squashy within". Yet he could be crushing in the Commons. When the notorious homosexual Tom Driberg asked him about the government's "flirtations with kings", he retorted to gasps: "I do not know how far the Honourable Gentleman is an expert in flirtations, or in what kind of flirtations".

Then came SUEZ, which, said Brendan Bracken, changed Eden from "charming milksop to blood-lusting monster". Suez was all Eden's work, with the Prime Minister casting

Egypt's Colonel Nasser in the same mould as Hitler. As controversy grew, the military planners vacillated and America turned against the operation, his stock plummeted. Robert Blake was to write: "He was the last Prime Minister to believe that Britain was a great power, and the first to confront a crisis which proved she was not." And Harold WILSON concluded: "When he did say boo, he said it to the wrong goose and too roughly." Suez left Eden bitter toward US Secretary of State John Foster Dulles, who had been ambivalent at critical stages; he termed him: "as tortuous as a wounded snake, with much less excuse". Eden's health began to deteriorate – he had never been well – and early in 1957 he resigned. Lord Carrington concluded that "Anthony had clearly gone mad", but he lived to a ripe and lucid old age.

EDM Early Day Motion. In the UK HOUSE OF COMMONS, a motion tabled by (usually) BACKBENCH MPs which appears in the later, blue, pages of the full daily ORDER PAPER known as the VOTE. Seldom debated, they are mainly tabled to show the strength of support for a particular cause or complaint, the test being the number of signatories. Occasionally an EDM, generally one on cruelty to animals, attracts the signatures of more than half the House – a considerable feat as Ministers never sign.

EDP (previously known as E or EA). Economic and Domestic Policy. The principal UK CABINET committee dealing with the economy. Membership of it is prized, and sometimes demanded, by Ministers keen to influence economic policy.

EFL External Financing Limit. In Britain, the amount a NATIONALIZED industry receives in a year in Government subsidy, grants and authorized borrowing.

EFTA The European FREE TRADE Association. Founded in 1960 with Britain in the lead for western European nations which wanted free trade without the EC's political and economic union. It has become a "transit lounge" for countries wanting to join the Community – Denmark, Portugal and the UK have so far done so. Current members are Austria, Finland, Iceland, Liechtenstein, Norway, Sweden and Switzerland.

egg. egghead An INTELLECTUAL preoccupied with erudite matters (supposedly requiring a larger, balding head). British slang post-1910, it caught on in the US after World War II with Adlai Stevenson branded as such by his opponents. Stevenson retaliated: "Eggheads of the world unite – you have nothing to lose but your yolks," and *Via Ovicapitum Dura Est* – "the way of the egghead is hard".

eggs As a weapon, found by protesters to be a messy, non-explosive and cheap form of ammunition.

> Those who scream and throw eggs are not the real unemployed. If they were really hard up, they would be eating them. NORMAN TEBBIT.

like playing tennis with a dish of scrambled eggs The vivid description by the Conservative MP Sir Harold Nicolson (1886–1968) in 1943 of trying to debate in the House of Commons with Nancy, Lady Astor, who despite her vigorous style found it hard to keep to the point.

Most of the egg production of this country, sadly, is now infected with salmonella The statement in December 1989 by UK junior Health Minister Edwina Currie (*see* CRUELLA DE VILLE) which sparked a national panic and cost her her job.

You can't make an omelette without breaking eggs Robespierre's justification for the carnage of the FRENCH REVOLUTION. Anthony Eden turned it round, saying: "If you've broken the eggs, you should make the omelette."

Eichmann trial The trial of (Karl) Adolf Eichmann (1906–62), one of the architects of Hitler's FINAL SOLUTION for the Jews, on WAR CRIMES charges in Israel in 1961. Eichmann, who had organized the logistics of shipping Jews to death camps and setting up gas chambers, escaped from Allied custody in 1945 and fled to Argentina. Fifteen years later he was abducted by Israeli agents and put on trial in a bulletproof glass booth; he was convicted of the murder of thousands of Austrian Jews, and hanged.

eighteen. 1848, year of revolution The year when urban crowds throughout Europe rose up against despotism, though not all their gains were permanent. They overthrew King Louis-Philippe of France, forced the abdication of the Austrian emperor and the fall of his chief minister Metternich, briefly created republics in Rome (under Garibaldi) and Hungary, and won constitutions from the kings of Prussia and Naples. Only in Spain, where the dictatorship stood firm; Russia, which brutally put down the Hungarian revolt; and Britain where a massive but peaceful CHARTIST demonstration was the height of pressure, did the *status quo* survive.

18½-minute gap The celebrated gap in one of the most incriminating WATERGATE tapes, found when they were released to Congress. Experts concluded that there had been a deliberate erasure, but Rose Mary Woods,

Nixon's secretary, claimed the gap was accidental. In an entertaining Congressional hearing she demonstrated how she could have inadvertently wiped the tape clean by pressing the wrong pedal on her dictating machine.

Eighteenth Amendment The amendment to the US CONSTITUTION which, in tandem with the VOLSTEAD ACT, introduced PROHIBITION. Ratified on 29 January 1919 (only Connecticut and Rhode Island resisting), it banned the manufacture, sale and transportation of liquor, but not drinking or purchase; the Volstead Act did that. The amendment was repealed by the 21st Amendment, which was proposed on 20 February 1933 and ratified that December.

Ein Volk, Ein Reich, Ein Führer (sometimes *Ein Reich, Ein Volk* . . .) (Ger. One people, one nation, one leader) The slogan of the NAZI party, first used at the September 1934 NUREMBERG RALLY.

Eire The Irish Gaelic name for the island of Ireland, and the Irish nation; from 1937 the official title of the Southern Irish State.

Eisenhower. Eisenhower Commission The commission set up by President Eisenhower (*see* IKE) under his brother Milton to investigate the causes and prevention of violence.

Eisenhower Doctrine Eisenhower's promise in January 1957 to commit economic or military aid to Middle Eastern countries under threat from Communist aggression. Though denounced by Egypt and Syria in the wake of SUEZ, it became an integral part of American foreign policy.

elastic clause *See* NECESSARY.

elect To choose representatives by a democratic process, or to secure the election of a particular candidate. John F. KENNEDY said at the height of the 1960 Presidential campaign:

> With the money I'm spending I could elect my chauffeur.

electability The quality of fitness for election, and more particularly the suitability of a candidate in the eyes of the voters.

election The actual process of choice, comprising the CAMPAIGN, the BALLOT, the COUNT and the DECLARATION. Edmund BURKE asked: "What is it we all seek in an election? You must first possess the means of knowing the fitness of your man, and then you must retain some hold upon him by personal obligation or dependence." And Walt Whitman declared: "I know nothing grander, better exercise, better digestion, more positive proof of the past, the triumphant result of faith in humankind, than a well-contested American national election." To Stanley BALDWIN elections were a regrettable necessity: "I hate elections but you have to have them. They are medicine." But Baldwin's urbane backbencher Henry "CHIPS" Channon described an election as "like a violent love affair". George Bernard Shaw cynically termed them "a moral horror, as bad as a battleground except for the blood; a mudbath for every soul concerned with it". Gerald Lieberman wrote: "Elections are held to delude the populace into believing that they are participating in government." And Richard CROSSMAN saw a Royal perspective: "For the Queen an election simply means that just when she has begun to know us, she has to meet another terrible lot of politicians."

election address In a UK election, a candidate's formal communication with the voters, introducing him- or herself and setting out his or her policies and claims to be elected, which the Post Office will deliver in the FREE POST.

Elections are about something more important than choosing between a man with a pipe and a man with a boat Enoch POWELL's view of Britain's General Elections of 1966, 1970 and 1974 (February and October), fought out between Labour under the pipe-smoking Harold WILSON and the Conservative Edward Heath who was an ocean-going yachtsman (*see* MORNING CLOUD).

direct elections The term used for the 1979 elections to the EUROPEAN PARLIAMENT, when MEPs were for the first time elected directly by the voters instead of being appointed from national legislatures.

free elections The democratic right guaranteed at YALTA for the Soviet-occupied nations of Eastern Europe, but reneged on by STALIN and his successors.

general election In a Parliamentary system, the election of the main house of the legislature, which determines whether the Government remains in office or is replaced by a new administration led by a different party. In America, a coincident Presidential, congressional and local election.

mid-term election The elections for the US Congress (all the HOUSE OF REPRESENTATIVES, part of the SENATE) which fall halfway through a Presidential Term. *See* OFF-YEAR.

snap election *See* SNAP.

special election *See* SPECIAL.

See also COUPON ELECTION; KHAKI ELECTION.

electioneering The process of conducting a partisan election campaign; the production, not necessarily during an election, of arguments and stunts which have more to do with getting elected than with a constructive approach to the problems of the moment.

elector Someone eligible to vote.

Electoral College (1) In the US political system, the body comprising delegations from all 50 states (plus the District of Columbia) which meets after the Presidential election actually to select the President. There are 538 votes in the college, 270 being a winning total; if no candidate reaches it, the election is handed to the HOUSE OF REPRESENTATIVES. Each state's delegation is weighted according to population, the number of votes being the number of Senators and Congressmen combined. Alaska and Delaware are among several states with 3 votes; California has 54. Each state casts all its votes for the winning candidate in that state. A nominee piling up large votes in key states could thus emerge victorious from the Electoral College despite running second in the popular vote.

> It affords a moral certainty that the office of President will never fall to the lot of any man who is not in an eminent degree endowed with the requisite qualifications.
> ALEXANDER HAMILTON.

(2) in Britain, the body representing trade unions (40%), MPs (30%) and constituency parties (30%), set up under BENNITE pressure by the LABOUR PARTY in 1981–82 to elect its leaders. Its creation gave impetus to the breakaway SDP; by 1992 when John Smith was elected leader, the college's preponderance of union BLOCK VOTES stood discredited.

Electoral Commission The body set up by the US Congress in 1877 to resolve the disputed election between Rutherford Hayes and Samuel Tilden; while Tilden won the popular vote, competing sets of returns were submitted by four states which left Tilden one vote short in the ELECTORAL COLLEGE. The Commission divided on straight party lines, giving each state, and the Presidency, to Hayes by an eight-to-seven vote – hence his nickname OLD EIGHT TO SEVEN.

electoral pact A deal between parties under which each stands down some of its candidates in return for support from the other.

electoral reform The umbrella term for moves from a FIRST PAST THE POST system toward PROPORTIONAL REPRESENTATION.

Electoral Reform Society The UK body which promotes study of improved voting systems, and also supervises and conducts ballots for a number of trade unions.

electoral register *See* REGISTER OF ELECTORS.

electoral truce An agreement by the parties to suspend normal electoral politics at a time of national emergency. In Britain, the Conservatives, Labour and the Liberals operated such a truce during WORLD WAR II. In theory it should have led to the candidate from the party previously holding a seat being returned unopposed at a BY-ELECTION; in practice minor candidates frequently forced a contest and occasionally even won.

electorate The number of electors in each electoral district; also the general body of VOTERS, of which most politicians are highly wary. Sen. Henry F. Ashurst wrote: "The electorate suspects and distrusts men of superb intellect, calmness and serenity"; of the Australian electorate Don Aitkin commented: "Whatever politicians, activists and manipulators propose, it is the phlegmatic, indifferent, ingrained electorate which disposes."

> You have to give the electorate a tune they can whistle.
> ENOCH POWELL.

Elegant Arthur The nickname of **Chester Alan Arthur** (1830–86), 21st President of the United States (Republican) from 1881 to 1885. A lawyer and Republican leader in New York State, Arthur was dismissed by President Hayes in 1878 as collector of customs after a patronage scandal; Democrats knew him as a "spoilsman's spoilsman". He had never run for office until party bosses nominated him in 1880 as James Garfield's running-mate to appease the New York boss Roscoe Conkling. Arthur himself declared that "the office of Vice-President is a greater honor than I ever dreamed of attaining", but on Garfield's death within months of taking office he found himself in the White House. One New York associate exclaimed:

> Chet Arthur! President of the United States? Good God!

Arthur came to office regarded, in Woodrow WILSON's words, as "a nonentity with side-whiskers". But he proved an unexpected success, his failure to win re-election in 1884 ironically stemming from his refusal to indulge in CRONYISM. He also kept himself to himself; he once told an inquisitve temperance campaigner: "Madam, I may be President of the United States, but my private life is nobody's damn business." When he left the White House, Alexander K. McClure wrote:

> No man entered the Presidency so profoundly and widely distrusted, and no one ever retired more generally respected.

elephant The long-standing emblem of the US REPUBLICAN PARTY. Though identified by the Democrats as representing ponderous conservatism, the elephant has understandably been the cause of less satirical comparison than the Democrats' own DONKEY or JACKASS.

> The Republicans are thinking of changing the Republican Party emblem from an elephant to a condom, because it stands for INFLATION, halts production and gives a false sense of security while one is being screwed.
> JOSEPH ROSENBERGER, 1974.

elephant on the doorstep The slightly baffling description given by UK Welsh Secretary John Morris of the Welsh people's decisive "No" to DEVOLUTION in the 1979 referendum. He said:

> If you find an elephant on the doorstep, you know what it is.

rogue elephant A politician who bucks party discipline, setting off on rampages that are frequently destructive of his or her own side's prospects.

élitists A small and carefully-selected group of people, who believe themselves entitled to participate in government or decision-making.

> A very inbred group of very rich people who go around telling everybody else what to do and how to suffer.
>
> New York Mayor ED KOCH.

Ellipse The oval, grassed area due South of the WHITE HOUSE and separated from its gardens by E Street. In 1978 it was the scene of a riot by Iranian students protesting at an official visit by the Shah; teargas emitted in clashes with the police overcame the crowd attending the WELCOMING CEREMONY on the White House lawn.

Ellis. Ruth Ellis case The final instance of a woman being hanged in the UK, the accompanying controversy and revulsion playing a major part in the eventual abolition of the death penalty. Ruth Ellis was sentenced to death for shooting her lover, who was having an affair with another woman; she had recently suffered a miscarriage. The HOME SECRETARY, Gwilym Lloyd George, refused to exercise the Royal Prerogative of mercy and reprieve her, despite immense political pressure, and she was hanged at Holloway prison on 13 July 1955.

Ellis Island The gateway to America for millions of immigrants from Europe, and hence a symbol for the welcome they received in the New World. The island in Upper New York Bay was America's main immigration station from 1892 to 1943, and was then used until 1954 as a detention centre for illegal aliens. The Statue of Liberty close by with its high-minded motto GIVE ME YOUR TIRED, YOUR POOR, YOUR HUDDLED MASSES contrasted with the impersonal procedures and casual brutality of its staff. It is now part of the Statue of Liberty National Monument.

Élysée. Élysée Palace The official residence and seat of power in the heart of Paris of the President of France.

Élysée Treaty The agreement between President DE GAULLE and the West German Chancellor Konrad Adenauer in 1963 which formalized the close Franco-German co-operation that steered the EUROPEAN COMMUNITY for the next quarter-century.

emancipation The grant or restoration of CIVIL RIGHTS to groups from which they have been deliberately and systematically withheld, often through some form of servitude. From the Latin *e*, out of; *manceps*, one who holds property.

Emancipation Proclamation The proclamation read by Abraham LINCOLN to his Cabinet on 22 July 1862, and signed formally on 1 January 1863, which declared freedom to slaves in all rebel states. He told the Cabinet:

> I have got you together to hear what I have written down. I do not wish your advice about the main matter – that I have determined for myself.

The proclamation freed few slaves – the rights of slaveowners in loyal states were confirmed, and the emancipation of slaves in the South could not be enforced. But it effectively turned the UNION's cause into that of ABOLITIONISM, rallying Northern support for the CIVIL WAR, and had an immense international impact, stemming pressure in Europe to recognize the CONFEDERACY. On the advice of Secretary of State William Seward, Lincoln delayed the proclamation until after the battle of Antietam, so that it could appear a sign of strength, not desperation.

> An arbitrary and despotic measure in the cause of freedom. GIDEON WELLES (1802–78).

emancipation of the serfs The ending of the Feudal System in Tsarist Russia, though not the plight of its peasantry. Under a ukase of Alexander II published in 1861, 23 million serfs were released from their obligations in March 1863.

Catholic emancipation One of the burning issues of early 19th-century UK politics, as tentative steps were taken to end the centuries-old ban on Roman Catholics in English public life and grant basic religious rights to the people of Ireland. By-election victories in Ireland for Catholics who would not take the Anglican oath, and an energetic campaign by Canning, paved the way for reform; the critical legislation was passed in 1829 after Wellington had prevailed on George IV to lift his veto on the Cabinet discussing the issue.

> Under a pure despotism a people may be contented, because all are slaves alike; but those who, under a free government, are refused equal participation, must be discontented. PALMERSTON.

embargo (1) An arrangement under which a public body supplies the media with information, subject to the requirement that it is not published or broadcast before a certain time.

(2) A prohibition on trade (or certain types of trade) with a country held to have committed a hostile or repugnant act. Originally a Spanish term for a ban on shipping between two countries, it has come to apply to an officially-imposed restriction on any form of trade. The grain embargoes on the Soviet Union imposed by Presidents FORD and CARTER lost both men critical votes among mid-Western farmers – especially Carter who prior to the invasion of Afghanistan in 1979 had promised never to take such action.

Great Embargo The embargo on all trade between the United States and Europe, passed by Congress in December 1807. Promoted by JEFFERSON as an alternative to all-out war with Britain which had been harassing US shipping and press-ganging its sailors, the embargo aimed at starving both Britain and France into respecting America's trading rights. As with later embargoes, however, its main effect was to cripple American grain farmers and merchants. The embargo became a major issue in the 1808 election but MADISON, who backed it, was elected anyway; three days before leaving office, Jefferson repealed the Act.

> Our ships all in motion once whitened the ocean;
> They sailed and returned with a cargo.
> Now doomed to decay they are fallen a pray
> To Jefferson, worms and EMBARGO.
>
> New Hampshire Federalist song.

embassy (1) The building housing the AMBASSADOR of one country and his or her staff in the capital of another. (2) A term from the earlier days of DIPLOMACY for a mission despatched by a government to negotiate with another.

light up an Embassy A 1960s UK cigarette advertisement, which became a slogan of far-left and revolutionary groups.

emergence The term used up to the 1960s to describe the process by which the leader of Britain's CONSERVATIVE PARTY was chosen. *See* MAGIC CIRCLE.

emergency. Emergency Banking Act One of the first measures pushed through Congress by Franklin D. Roosevelt on taking office in 1933. FDR immediately ordered closure of America's banks, and kept them closed for five days while legislation based on plans prepared by the HOOVER administration was enacted. It gave explicit Federal backing to banks found to be solvent, and prevented the weakest from reopening; the Federal Government took on powers to regulate the entire banking system.

emergency debate A debate in a legislature which takes priority over business on the calendar because of its urgency. In Britain's House of Commons, an application for such a debate is made to the Speaker under Standing Order 20 (formerly Standing Order 9); such applications are rarely granted, but they give the member making the application a chance to state the case briefly on the floor of the House.

emergency financing The process used to keep the US government functioning when – as frequently happens in the fall – Congress has failed to pass a BUDGET Bill containing appropriations for the continued payment of Federal employees.

emergency powers Powers taken by a government, with the backing of legislation, to keep services running or maintain order during a period of unrest.

Emergency Provisions The regulations under which Britain conducts DIRECT RULE of NORTHERN IRELAND and the security and legal system created since 1969 to combat TERRORISM.

state of emergency The condition declared by a government, usually without the need for legislation, to enable it to tackle a natural disaster, damaging industrial dispute or outbreak of violence. Generally it involves drafting in the military to do tasks normally done by civilians, and abridging individual property rights in order to maintain services and public order.

Eminent Persons' Group The seven-strong group of COMMONWEALTH statesmen, headed by the former Australian Prime Minister Malcolm Fraser and the former Nigerian President General Olusegun Obasanjo, set up to advance political reform in South Africa as pressure for an end to APARTHEID peaked in the 1980s. It was decided on at the Nassau CHOGM meeting in October 1985, and visited South Africa the following year. Mainly concerned with the political situation, it gained a cool reception from South Africa's White government and in its report back urged a stiffening of SANCTIONS; the 1987 Vancouver CHOGM agreed to tighter sanctions, with Margaret Thatcher (*see* IRON LADY) dissenting. The Group's mission and the policy it represented is given some credit for the subsequent abandonment of Apartheid.

emperor or **empress** A sovereign who reigns over a number of diverse nations (a king or queen reigns normally only over a single nation or ethnic group).

empire A grouping of nations under the rule of an emperor or empress.

Empire Free Trade An unsuccessful campaign (1929–31) to establish free trade throughout the BRITISH EMPIRE (*see below*). The crusade was launched in their newspapers by the PRESS BARONS Lords Beaverbrook and Rothermere, who founded a (completely unsuccessful) United Empire Party to gain a Parliamentary platform. The campaign foundered on the reluctance of the DOMINIONS to grant free entry to British goods, and collapsed with the onset of the GREAT DEPRESSION.

Empire loyalists Devotees of the ideals of the British Empire who remain committed to them despite the Empire's transformation into the COMMONWEALTH. In Britain the League of Empire Loyalists was a right-wing group which directed vitriolic criticism against Conservative governments in the late 1950s for granting independence to Britain's COLONIES. In Canada the United Empire Loyalists are a respectable group who uphold the interests of English-speaking Canada and its ties with the Crown.

Austro-Hungarian Empire The empire ruled by the Habsburg dynasty which covered much of middle Europe until Austria's defeat in WORLD WAR I. It covered not just the lands of the Dual MONARCHY but Bohemia, Slovakia, Croatia, Slovenia and parts of present-day Poland and Romania. Lombardy and Venetia were given up in 1859 and 1866 respectively, but gains were made in the Balkans; the annexation of Bosnia in 1908 indirectly caused World War I (*see* SARAJEVO). The empire was held together from 1848 to 1917 by the Emperor Franz Josef, but the following year the defeat of Austria and its German ally paved the way for dismemberment of the Empire and its transformation into NATION STATES. The publication of WILSON's FOURTEEN POINTS marked the death of the empire; the last emperor, Karl, gave up power on 11 November 1918. His dynasty survives. *See* WHO ARE WE PLAYING?

British Empire The empire, arguably the greatest the world has seen, which came into being on 1 January 1877, when Queen Victoria was proclaimed Empress of India, and formally gave way to the COMMONWEALTH in December 1958. The title stemmed from Britain's upgraded role in India, a device adopted by Disraeli to play a supreme compliment to his Queen. Campbell-Bannerman objected: "We cannot add to the lustre and dignity of the Crown of this realm, the most ancient and august in Europe, by tricking it out in a brand new title." But the ethos of Empire spurred Britain, and its rivals, to consolidate Imperial possessions throughout the world. Joseph Chamberlain (1836–1914), the high priest of IMPERIALISM, proclaimed in 1904: "The day of small nations has long passed away. The day of Empire has come." And on another occasion he asked: "England without an Empire? can you conceive it?" Among Imperialists the Empire was seen wholly as a force for good: a means of mutual security and economic development as well as the supreme expression of British power. Lord Curzon, VICEROY of India (1859–1925), declared: "There has never been anything so great in the world's history than the British Empire, so great an instrument for the good of humanity." The Canadian Prime Minister Alexander Mackenzie (1822–92) said: "I am anxious that its glory should be unsullied, that the power should never be abridged and that the English supremacy shall last until the end of time, because it means universal freedom, universal liberty, emancipation from everything degrading." Australia's Prime Minister William Hughes (1864–1952) reckoned that "without the Empire we shall be tossed like a cork in the cross-current of world politics. It is at once our sword and our shield." And in 1927 the future King George VI, opening Australia's first Canberra Parliament, stated:

> The British Empire has advanced to a new conception of autonomy and freedom, to the idea of a system of British nations each freely ordering its own individual life, but bound together in unity by allegiance to the Crown, and co-operating in all that concerns the commonweal.

Yet there were always critical voices, and as Britain's power began to ebb they became stronger; Jaraprakash Narayan (1902–79), a founder of India's CONGRESS PARTY, asserted that "lies are one of the central pillars of the British Empire".

Apart from the PARTITION of Ireland, the granting of Indian independence in 1948 was the first sign that the Empire would not endure. In 1930 CHURCHILL had claimed:

> The loss of India would mark and consummate the downfall of the British Empire. From such a catastrophe there would be no recovery.

As the break-up accelerated, South Africa's hardline Premier Albert Herzog blamed Western decadence, saying: "The vast British Empire built up over hundreds of years has been reduced to ruins largely through the influence of television." But as it neared its end, David Ormsby-Gore (Lord Harlech, 1918–85) suggested:

> In the end it may well be that Britain will be honoured by the historians more for the way she disposed of her empire than for the way in which she acquired it.

evil empire The epithet bestowed upon the SOVIET UNION by Ronald Reagan in a speech to Evangelical church leaders in March 1983; he also categorized the Soviet state as "the focus of evil in the modern world". Despite his subsequent "bomb Russia" gaffe (*see* OPEN MIKE), Reagan reversed his position during his second term in SUMMIT contacts with

Mikhail Gorbachev as the COLD WAR neared its close.

empire on which the sun never sets, the The archetypal slogan of the late Victorian IMPERIALISTS, which in fact originated before the days of empire. Christopher North (John Wilson, 1785–1854), the Scots poet and essayist, wrote in 1829 in his *Noctes Ambrosianae* of "His Majesty's dominions, on which the sun never sets". The expression had been used centuries before of the Spaniards, Captain John Smith writing in 1631: "Why should the brave Spanish soldier brag the sun never sets in the Spanish dominions?" Moreover, its use has outlasted the British Empire, an IRA protest placard against Prince Charles's visit to New York in 1981 reading:

> The sun never sets on the British Empire because God doesn't trust the Brits in the dark.

Empire Strikes Back, The The title of the highly-successful sequel to the 1977 space adventure film *Star Wars*, taken up by *Newsweek* magazine in 1982 as its cover headline when Britain despatched its naval TASK FORCE to recapture the FALKLANDS.

How is the Empire? The supposed last words of King George V as he lay dying in 1936. A more plausible tale is that when the King's doctor told him he would soon be well enough to visit Bognor Regis, he exclaimed: **"Bugger Bognor!"** and died.

lost an empire and not yet found a role The comment about Britain made on 6 December 1962 by the former US SECRETARY OF STATE Dean Acheson (1893-1971), which enraged Fleet Street and some UK politicians. Acheson made his assertion that Britain was "just about played out" at the time of that country's greatest uncertainty over where in the world its future lay – and only weeks before DE GAULLE delivered his first NON to Britain's membership of the EC.

EMS European Monetary System. The system for stabilizing European currencies in the short term, and in the long term for establishing a single currency unit for the whole of the EUROPEAN COMMUNITY. Devised by Roy Jenkins (*see* WOY) when President of the European Commission and adopted by the 1978 Copenhagen summit, the EMS comprises a European Monetary Co-Operation Fund, to which all EC members belong, and an Exchange Rate Mechanism (*see* ERM) which Britain belatedly joined in October 1990 (*see* MADRID CONDITIONS) and left on BLACK WEDNESDAY in September 1992.

Ems telegram The calculated insult to France with which Bismarck engineered the start of the FRANCO-PRUSSIAN WAR. It arose from the CORTÈS's choice of the Prussian Prince Leopold of Hohenzollern, to fill the vacant Spanish throne. France threatened war unless the candidature were withdrawn and the prince backed down, to Bismarck's disappointment. Then the French Foreign Minister Gramont sent an emissary, Count Benedetti, to get confirmation of the withdrawal from King William of Prussia at Ems. The King said he understood Prince Leopold had withdrawn, but refused to elaborate; he then telegraphed an account of the meeting to Bismarck. The IRON CHANCELLOR issued the telegram to the Press with a gloss making it appear Benedetti had insulted the King, and had been sharply rebuffed. On 14 July 1870 the telegram was published; the French realized they had been tricked, but with the Parisian crowd chanting "A Berlin!", had no alternative but to go to war – and a humiliating defeat.

EMU European Monetary Union. One of the two main goals of the MAASTRICHT TREATY, embracing for all member states except Britain a firm commitment to a SINGLE CURRENCY by 1997. Political union is the other aim.

ENA (Fr. *École Nationale d'Administration*, National School of Administration) The technocratic forcing-house which produces France's governing CADRE of future ministers and senior civil servants and imbues them with the basics of the self-interested policy pursued by all French governments. It was founded by General DE GAULLE in 1945 to extirpate the spinelessness shown by the VICHY bureaucracy in COLLABORATING with Nazi Germany.

Enabling Act A piece of legislation passed by a democratically-elected legislature which gives those in power the authority to take sweeping action without further, specific approval. Hitler used this device to seize control of the key organs of the German state after coming to power in the WEIMAR REPUBLIC by more or less democratic means. TROTSKYIST groups in Britain have argued that a Labour government elected on a DEMOCRATIC SOCIALIST platform should pass an Enabling Act to set up a Marxist state.

enabling state The phrase used from the late 1980s to describe a structure in which the State has the power and the duty to help its citizens fulfil their potential, rather than to leave them exposed to market forces or determine everything for them. One of its main exponents has been the UK Liberal Democrat leader Paddy Ashdown (1941–).

endorsement A public declaration of support for a candidate running for office, given by an influential political figure, a labour union or some other interest which believes such support will strengthen the candidate's chances.

> I well remember my first campaign. My opponent called me a cream puff. That's what he said. Well, I rushed out and got the bakers' union to endorse me.
>
> Sen. CLAIBORNE PELL (1918–).

enemies Every politician has enemies, but their attitudes toward them differ from Abraham Lincoln's (attributed) "I am going to destroy them. I am going to make them my friends" to the 19th-century Spanish general Ramon Maria Narvaes, who said on his deathbed: "I do not have to forgive my enemies. I have had them all shot." Robert F. KENNEDY's watchword was "always forgive your enemies – but never forget their names," while Richard Lamm (1935–), governor of Colorado said philosophically: "I have no permanent enemies – only people I have yet to persuade," and Steve Bell, a Congressional aide, warned: "When you dig a grave for your enemy, dig two – one for yourself." Mao Tse-Tung, drawing on his experience of guerrilla war, wrote: "You must despise your enemy strategically, but respect him tactically;" he also declared: "We should support whatever the enemy opposes and oppose whatever the enemy supports." Speaker Joe Cannon warned: "Never attempt to buy the favor of your enemies at the expense of your friends," and the TEAMSTERS' leader Jimmy Hoffa gave as his philosophy: "You keep your door open to your enemies. You know all about your friends."

enemies list A list of President Nixon's perceived adversaries drawn up in 1971, the year before WATERGATE, after White House counsel John Dean had circulated a memo suggesting ways "we can use the available Federal machinery to screw our political enemies". Tactics included harassment of Nixon's critics by the Internal Revenue Service. The list included Carol Channing, Bill Cosby, Jane Fonda, Paul Newman and Tony Randall, CBS correspondent Daniel Schorr and the Black congressman John Conyers of Michigan, against whom was written: "Has known weakness for White females."

enemy within, the The phrase used by Margaret Thatcher to charge Arthur Scargill's striking mineworkers (*see* KING ARTHUR) with attempting to destroy British society. Speaking at a private meeting with Conservative MPs on 19 July 1984, she said that Argentina's General Galtieri had been the enemy without during the FALKLANDS conflict, and the striking miners and dockers now constituted the enemy within. The phrase had been used by *The Economist* several months before in almost the same context; Mrs. Thatcher was accused by Labour MPs of questioning the miners' patriotism.

naked to mine enemies The Shakespearean phrase used during the WATERGATE investigation by Sen. Sam Ervin, when he told Herbert Porter, who eventually served 27 days in jail for lying to the FBI:

> Had I not served by God with half the zeal
> I serv'd my King, he would not in mine age
> Have left me naked to mine enemies.

Shakespeare, in *Henry VIII*, put the words into Thomas Wolsey's mouth, having him say them to his assistant, Thomas Cromwell.

own worst enemy During Britain's 1945–51 Labour government, an MP in the Commons tea room is said to have remarked of Aneurin Bevan: "NYE's his own worst enemy," only for Ernest BEVIN to break in: "Not while I'm alive, he ain't." The retort, if uttered, was not original; around 1939 the Southern conservative Sen. Walter George declared: "Roosevelt is his own worst enemy;" South Carolina's "Cotton Ed" Smith replied: "Not so long as I am alive!"

We love him most for the enemies he has made The slogan coined by General Edward Bragg of Wisconsin when he NOMINATED Grover Cleveland (*see* BEAST OF BUFFALO) for the Presidency at the 1884 Republican convention; it referred to his independence of TAMMANY HALL and his readiness to fight corruption. Supporters of Franklin D. Roosevelt resurrected the slogan in 1936 to show their contempt for opponents of the NEW DEAL.

your enemies are behind you A newly-elected MP was reputedly shown the CHAMBER of the House of Commons by a senior colleague. When he saw the opposition benches the newcomer remarked: "I see that is where the enemy sits," but the old hand told him:

> They are your adversaries. Your enemies are behind you.

England The kingdom united under King Alfred of Wessex in the late 9th century, which became the major and dominant part of the UNITED KINGDOM after conquering Wales in the 13th century, gaining uneasy control over Ireland and uniting with Scotland in 1707. The name is used carelessly by some English and US politicians for the entire United Kingdom, as in PITT THE YOUNGER's "England has saved herself by her exertions, and will, as I trust, save Europe by her example" and Napoleon's "England is a nation of shopkeepers".

Young England *See* YOUNG.

Speak for England! *See* SPEAK.

English disease, the The term adopted in Continental Europe in the early 1960s for

Britain's unique mixture of poor economic performance and suicidally militant trade unionism. Use of the expression spread worldwide – but subsided in the 1980s as the Thatcher government sorted out the unions and prosperity briefly returned. It had first been used by the French *c.*1500 – to describe syphilis.

engrossment In the US Congress, the process of preparing a copy of a BILL in the precise form in which it has passed the HOUSE. The task is carried out by the Enrolling Clerk who receives all relevant papers, some of them often in longhand, and prepares a comprehensive version including all the amendments carried. The engrossed Bill is printed on blue paper, at which point it becomes an ACT of the House, and a certificate that it has been passed is signed by the Clerk of the House. A reading clerk delivers it to the Senate, where it is received in a convoluted ceremony in which it is recognized by the PRESIDING OFFICER.

enlargement The term used for the process of accepting new states into the EUROPEAN COMMUNITY ever since its expansion from the original six members was first contemplated.

> It would not be in the interests of the European Community that its enlargement should take place except with the full-hearted consent of the Parliament and people of the new member countries. EDWARD HEATH, 1970.

Enoch factor The electoral pull exercised by Enoch POWELL in the February 1974 General Election, when he stood down as a Conservative MP and urged his supporters to vote Labour in protest at the Heath government's taking Britain into the EUROPEAN COMMUNITY. Three days before the poll. Powell told a meeting at Shipley:

> I was born a Tory, am a Tory and shall die a Tory . . . I never heard that it was any part of the faith of a Tory to take the institutions and liberties, the laws and customs which his country has evolved over centuries and merge them with those of eight other nations into a new-made artificial state.

The resulting electoral shift, notably in Powell's native West Midlands, was one factor in the Tories' narrow defeat. In the October election he stood and was elected as an ULSTER UNIONIST; the Enoch factor, though less pronounced, contributed to Labour achieving a small overall majority.

Enosis (Gr. union) The political union of Greece and Cyprus, the goal of most Greek Cypriots (*see* EOKA) in the 1950s prior to independence from Britain. Archbishop Makarios, later President of Cyprus, was exiled to the Seychelles for supporting Enosis; ironically the coup backed by the Greek COLONELS in 1974 which came close to overthrowing him was designed to achieve it.

Enough of this foolery! The crushing rejoinder by Campbell-Bannerman to a series of pedantic interventions from Arthur BALFOUR in the Commons on 12 March 1906 which finally established C-B's Parliamentary supremacy.

entente. Entente Cordiale (Fr. cordial understanding) The agreement between Britain and France, reached in April 1904 and sealed by Edward VII's visit to Paris in 1906, which revolutionized relations between the two neighbours and the diplomacy of Europe. It repaired the damage between them over FASHODA and paved the way for their alliance in WORLD WAR I. It had been set in motion in 1902 by the French Premier Delcasse, who found a willing listener in Colonial Secretary Joseph Chamberlain whose contacts with Germany had broken down. The entente was one of the lasting achievements of the BALFOUR government; though its conclusion was later said by critics to have made war with Germany inevitable, France was at times to doubt Britain's will to turn it into a full-blooded alliance. The term was first used by King Louis Philippe in 1843, when he spoke to Parliament of:

> The sincere friendship which unites me to the Queen of Britain and the cordial understanding which exists between my government and hers.

Franco-German entente The close relationship, through joint leadership of the European Community, which the West German Chancellor Konrad Adenauer (1876–1967) developed with France in the 1950s to heal the wounds caused by World War II. Chancellor from 1949, Adenauer cemented the entente during the five years (1958–63) when he and DE GAULLE led their respective countries.

Triple Entente The informal agreement between the UK, France and Russia to seek means of settling their outstanding COLONIAL differences. It was based on the ENTENTE CORDIALE, which settled Anglo-French differences in Egypt and Africa, and the Anglo-Russian agreement of 1907 over Persia, Tibet and Afghanistan. The Triple Entente became a military pact in 1914, forming the nucleus of the Allied powers in WORLD WAR I.

enterprise A watchword of conservatives and (economic) liberals, the force which they believe will flourish in a free MARKET and which they are equally convinced will be stifled by any form of Government intervention. To make the point more forcefully, they often refer to it as **free enterprise**.

> We must beware of trying to build a society in which nobody counts for anything except a politician or an official, a society where enterprise gains no rewards and thrift no privilege. CHURCHILL, 1943.

> If enterprise is afoot, wealth accumulates whatever may be happening to thrift; and if enterprise is asleep, wealth decays, whatever thrift may be doing.
> JOHN MAYNARD KEYNES, *General Theory of Employment*.

enterprise culture The society which free-marketeers aim to create, with anyone capable of creating wealth knowing that the means exist for them to do so. The term became current in the 1980s as Margaret Thatcher and Ronald Reagan sought to break free of the COLLECTIVIST attitudes of the previous four decades.

entitlements In US politics, the categories of government spending – some 40% of the whole – which go in social security and other payments to whoever is qualified to receive them. The other categories are defence, interest on the NATIONAL DEBT, and the basic operation of government (stretching out to education, housing, mass transit and the environment).

entrenched provisions or powers Functions bestowed, usually on another elected body, by one piece of legislation and which cannot be taken away by another. The granting of entrenched powers is held by critics to violate the doctrine that one Parliament or Congress cannot bind its successors. The argument was foreseen by Thomas JEFFERSON in a letter to James MADISON on 6 September 1789:

> The question – whether one generation of men has the right to bind another – seems never to have started either on this [France] or on our own side of the water. I set out on this ground "that the earth belongs in usufruct to the living, that the dead have neither powers nor rights over it".

It was widely raised during the arguments over DEVOLUTION in the 1970s and 1980s, with opponents of a Scottish Assembly or Parliament objecting to the creation of an elected body with powers that could not be taken away later by Westminster.

entryism The process by which members of a political movement committed to one set of aims instal themselves as members and officers of a larger party devoted to different purposes, and then subvert it. The technique was perfected by the MILITANT TENDENCY, who for two decades from the mid-1960s infiltrated Britain's LABOUR PARTY and through it secured the election of TROTSKYIST councillors and even members of Parliament. *See* UNDERHILL REPORT.

environmentalism The political force which has grown most in influence since the late 1960s, giving rise to the GREEN movement and greater concern for the planet and all its occupants among most other political parties. The issue was recognized on both sides of the Atlantic in 1970 when President Nixon set up the Environmental Protection Agency (EPA), and Edward Heath a Department of the Environment – though this took little interest in "green" issues for some time. Resistance to concern over the environment goes back almost a century to when Speaker Joe Cannon said:

> Not one cent for scenery.

James Watt, Ronald Reagan's Secretary of the Interior, took the same view, once saying:

> America's lands may be ravaged as a result of the actions of the environmentalists.

Rep. Morris Udall retaliated that Watt and EPA administrator Anne Burford had

> done for the environment what Bonnie and Clyde did for the banks.

EOKA (Gr. *Ethniki Organisos Kipriakou Agonos*, National Organization of Cypriot Struggle) The movement founded in 1955 to pursue the political goal of ENOSIS. Led by George Grivas (codename Digenis) and supported up to a point by Archbishop Makarios, it conducted a guerrilla campaign against the occupying British forces. It disbanded on independence in 1959, but was re-formed in 1971; its impact has been minimal since the failure in 1974 of a pro-Enosis coup backed by the Greek COLONELS.

EPIC plan End Poverty in California. The campaign for ending the hardship of the GREAT DEPRESSION through widespread state enterprise on which the formerly Socialist author Upton Sinclair (1878–1968) sought and won the Democratic nomination for governor in 1934. The radical nature of his campaign, backed by his bestselling book *I, Governor*, and its runaway success galvanized business, the Hearst press and the Republican Party, who spent $10 million to ensure Sinclair's defeat. Despite a hysterical campaign against him, Sinclair polled 37% of the vote, and his running-mate Sheridan Downey was elected to the US Senate in 1938.

equal. equal opportunity or opportunities The regime under which a government or other body makes a conscious effort to assist ethnic or other groups which it believes need encouragement to catch up. It applies particularly to recruitment policy, with an equal opportunity employer making special efforts to attract women, members of ethnic minorities or the disabled to a workforce in which they are under-represented. It is arguable whether such an approach gives a positive edge to applicants from such groups; AFFIRMATIVE ACTION unquestionably does (*see* BAKKE CASE).

> There are many things in life that are not fair, that wealthy people can afford and poor people can't. But I don't believe that the Federal Government should take action to try to make these opportunities exactly equal, particularly when there is a moral factor involved.
>
> President CARTER on the funding of abortions for the poor, 12 July 1977.

equal pay The principle under which women receive the same pay as men for doing the same work; established in America for decades and in Britain since Labour's 1975 Equal Pay Act, it is nevertheless widely flouted by employers.

> Legislation to apply the principle of equal pay for equal work without discrimination because of sex is a matter of simple justice.
>
> President EISENHOWER, State of the UNION message, 5 January 1956.

Equal Rights Amendment *See* ERA.

equal time The principle that each side in a political argument should receive equal exposure on radio or television to put their case. It is built into broadcasting standards on both sides of the Atlantic; in America the ability of candidates to buy advertising time weakens its effect, in Britain the REPRESENTATION OF THE PEOPLE ACTS impose rigid controls. *See* FAIRNESS DOCTRINE; Ministerial BROADCAST; PARTY POLITICAL BROADCAST.

All men are created equal One of the axioms of American democracy, set out by Jefferson in the second paragraph of the Declaration of INDEPENDENCE. It took the SUPREME COURT well over a century to construe the words as meaning that Black Americans were entitled to the same fundamental rights as Whites. The phrase has its variants. The revolutionaries in George Orwell's ANIMAL FARM put forward the slogan: **"All animals are equal – but some animals are more equal than others."** And Lord Mancroft (1917–) wrote:

> All men are born equal, but quite a few get over it.

There never will be complete equality until women themselves help to make laws and elect lawmakers The rallying-cry of the American suffragist Susan B. ANTHONY, written in 1897.

The idea of equality should now be regarded as out of date, since it leads only to confusion and hampers a precise examination of the problem The definitive MARXIST explanation of how "Scientific SOCIALISM" differs from classic LIBERALISM, delivered by Engels in a letter to August Bebel on 28 March 1875.

Equality State The nickname earned by the state of Wyoming because of its pioneering adoption of women's SUFFRAGE. Wyoming granted women the vote in 1869, even before being given STATEHOOD, and elected the first woman governor.

ERA Equal Rights Amendment. The amendment to the US Constitution, championed most forcefully by the women's movement in the 1970s, which was designed to give women explicit protection from discrimination. It stated:

> Equality of rights under the law shall not be denied or abridged by the United States or by any state on account of sex.

First proposed in 1923, it was passed by Congress in 1972 but lapsed in 1982, having fallen three short of the 38 states needed to RATIFY it. Its opponents, headed by Phyllis Schlafly and backed by the religious Right, argued that it ignored the biological differences between the sexes, would harm the institutions of marriage and the family, and was redundant because of protection already offered by the 5TH and 14TH AMENDMENTS.

> The Equal Rights Amendment is a must.
>
> BETTY FORD, 1975.

Era of good feelings The name given to James MONROE's two Presidential terms, from 1817 to 1825, partly because of the eclipse of the two-party system; when he ran for re-election in 1820, he did not even need to be nominated and only one vote was cast against him in the ELECTORAL COLLEGE. The phrase was coined early in Monroe's administration when he made a goodwill visit to Boston; his popularity later waned, particularly in New England which fell on hard times, but the memory of "good feelings" lingered.

ERM Exchange Rate Mechanism. The central structure of the European Monetary System (*see* EMS), in which governments commit themselves to maintain the value of their currencies within agreed limits of fluctuation (2.25% from parity in the narrow bands for the most committed states and 6% in the looser broad band for Italy). If a currency's market rate reaches the upper or lower limits, other member nations are obliged to restrain or support it; if that fails, the country in question must adjust interest rates. If more drastic action is needed, member states may agree a REALIGNMENT; the alternative is withdrawal from the ERM to revalue or DEVALUE. Britain adopted this latter course on BLACK WEDNESDAY, 16 September 1992, when the pound crashed through the floor of the ERM despite two interest rate rises totalling 5%. Margaret Thatcher's government, with John MAJOR as Chancellor, had joined the ERM in October 1990 as a means of fighting INFLA-

TION despite warnings from her economic adviser Alan Walters that the system was "half-baked". Lower inflation was achieved, but a surge in German interest rates following reUNIFICATION hamstrung the UK economy and with sterling weakening, recriminations broke out with the BUNDESBANK which hastened the slide and forced Chancellor Norman Lamont to withdraw.

> When Margaret Thatcher is dead and opened, it will be those three letters that will be lying in her heart.
> NICHOLAS RIDLEY.

Erskine May The book which has become the ultimate authority on Parliamentary procedure at Westminster. It takes its name from Thomas Erskine May (1815–86), Clerk of the House of Commons from 1871 to 1876) who in 1844 published his *Treatise on the Law, Privilege, Proceedings and Usage of Parliament*. Updated and revised by his successors, the "Bible" of the Commons has passed through 21 editions; the most recent, edited by Clifford Boulton, appeared in 1989.

Ervin Committee The popular name for the Senate Select Committee on Presidential Campaign Activities, which between May and August 1973 held televised hearings on the WATERGATE affair. It was chaired by the 76-year-old Democratic Sen. Sam Ervin of North Carolina, who cast off his reputation as an arch-conservative to emerge as an avuncular but no-nonsense defender of the Constitution. The hearings produced crucial revelations about the involvement of top White House aides in Watergate and the COVER-UP, and ultimately of President Nixon (*see* TRICKY DICK) himself. It was at one of the Ervin hearings that the existence of the tapes which ultimately destroyed Nixon first came to light.

escalation The dramatic increase in the scale of action or response, a word first used to describe the rapid upgrading of US involvement in the VIETNAM WAR by the Johnson administration soon after the 1964 Presidential election. Prior to that Johnson had pursued the "limited" war he had inherited from President KENNEDY; in the election campaign the Democrats savaged Sen. Barry Goldwater for advocating a greatly increased US military involvement.

Essex man A young man of braying coarseness and Neanderthal right-wing opinions, widely supposed to be more easily found in the county of Essex, immediately north-east of London, than elsewhere. The term was invented in October 1990 by the political columnist Simon Heffer, a native of Essex who shared his creation's views on Europe, and caught on rapidly; the term **Essex girl**, denoting white-stilettoed promiscuity, appeared as if by magic soon after. Essex man had the last laugh in the 1992 General Election when David Amess's Tory win at Basildon, a haunt of the species, pointed the way to John Major's unexpected outright victory.

establish. Established Church A branch of the Christian church which has a formal and privileged position in a nation's life. The Roman Catholic church enjoys this position in a number of states through a CONCORDAT; in England the Church of England, with the sovereign as Supreme Governor, is similarly favoured. Indeed the sovereign is an Anglican in England and a Presbyterian in Scotland, where the Calvinist Church of Scotland enjoys official status. The Anglican church in Wales was DISESTABLISHED early in the 20th century, and there has at times been pressure for the English church to be put on the same footing as all other denominations.

Establishment, the The term used since the late 1950s for the influential hierarchy or inner circle in the community, and particularly the informal grouping of academic, cultural and governmental figures who impose social attitudes on the public. The word originated in Britain, and was reflected in the opening in London *c.* 1961 of a satirical club of that name. But it is now applied throughout the world.

> The establishment is made up of little men, very frightened. Rep. BELLA ABZUG (1920–).

> We must realize that today's establishment is the new George III. Whether it will continue to adhere to his tactics, we do not know. If it does, the redress, honored in tradition, is also revolution.
> Justice WILLIAM O. DOUGLAS, 1970.

> Eastern establishment types, ideological eunuchs whose most comfortable position is straddling the fence.
> Vice-President SPIRO AGNEW, speaking in New Orleans, 19 October 1969.

ETA (Basque *Euzkadi ta Azkatasuna*) The militant SEPARATIST movement which since 1975 has conducted a terrorist campaign throughout Spain for an independent state centred on Bilbao. The Spanish government placated some moderate Basques in 1980 by giving the region, known to its people as *Euzkadi*, their own Parliament, but the violence has continued – though at a lesser level since France began deporting known ETA members operating on its side of the border to Spain.

eternal flame The memorial to President KENNEDY in ARLINGTON NATIONAL CEMETERY, which stands immediately over his grave.

ethics. Ethics Committees The bodies formed by both Houses of the US CONGRESS in the early 1970s in a partly-successful attempt to force basic standards of probity on their members. Mark Green wrote of the Senate committee:

> The Senate took to its new offspring with all the glee of a father who has found an illegitimate child dropped on his doorstep.

The House Committee got off to an unpromising start, COMMON CAUSE chairman John Gardner calling it "the worst kind of sham, giving the appearance of serving as a policeman while extending a marvelous protective shield over members of Congress". One chairman of the committee, Rep. Richardson Preyer, explained: "It's not much fun sitting in judgment on your colleagues;" his successor Rep. John Flynt set the guideline that "a member should be in flagrant abuse of his office for the House to act". Speaker TIP O'Neill stiffened the regime somewhat, telling Rep. David Obey when a code of ethics was mooted: "If you're going to write one, go all the way. I want a damn good code I can be proud of."

Ethics in Government Act The legislation passed by Congress in 1978 which, in the wake of WATERGATE, sought to outlaw a range of abuses and conflicts of interest including the practice of former Federal officials becoming LOBBYISTS and immediately lobbying their former agencies.

ethnic cleansing The infamous practice adopted by Serb forces in Bosnia in 1992 by which an area was captured and its non-Serb inhabitants either expelled, deported to CONCENTRATION CAMPS, or killed in cold blood. Ironically the term had previously been used by Kurt Waldheim, later UN GENERAL SECRETARY and President of Austria, in a report to Goebbels when a staff officer with NAZI forces in Yugoslavia.

ethnic monitoring The practice by which government agencies keep a check on the number and proportion of their staff from various ethnic minorities.

ethnic purity An unfortunate phrase used by Democratic Presidential nominee Jimmy CARTER during a campaign visit to a Polish area of Cleveland in 1976. Carter used it to praise the cohesiveness of a community that was resisting the influx of other ethnic groups, including Blacks; his opponents seized on it as a sign of illiberal attitudes and, at worst, RACISM. Carter, who later withdrew his remarks, said:

> I see nothing wrong with ethnic purity being maintained. I would not force a racial integration of a neighborhood by government action.

ethnic vote A collective term for the vote from a particular racial group that can be mobilized for one party or candidate; it is based on the assumption, not always correct, that most members of a particular minority will vote the same way.

Ettrick Bridge coup The replacement of the SDP leader Roy Jenkins (*see* WOY) by the Liberal leader David Steel (*see* BOY DAVID) as chief campaigner for the ALLIANCE in the middle of Britain's 1983 General Election campaign. The change was made at a meeting on 29 May at Steel's home at Ettrick Bridge in the Scottish borders. The Liberals strongly wanted such a change, believing the experienced but urbane Jenkins, officially the Alliance's PRIME MINISTER DESIGNATE, was not making a strong enough impact; most Social Democrats resisted it, detecting unnecessary panic. In the end a statement was issued saying that Steel would take a higher profile in the final ten days of the campaign. Dr. David OWEN, who admired Steel's decisiveness at the time, later called it a "ruthless and savage deed".

Euratom The European Atomic Energy Community, formed in 1958 by the six founder-members of the European Economic Community (France, Germany, Italy, BENELUX, *see* EUROPEAN COMMUNITY) to promote peaceful uses of atomic energy; it shared the Community's Parliament and courts. Its functions included joint research projects, safety and health in nuclear installations, and creation of a common market in nuclear materials and technology. In 1967 Euratom was merged with the EEC and the EUROPEAN COAL AND STEEL COMMUNITY to form the present-day EUROPEAN COMMUNITY.

Eureka stockade The skirmish at Ballarat, Victoria, on 3 December 1854 between 150 gold prospectors and a force of troopers and police which became Australia's most celebrated rebellion, and a landmark in the securing of popular rights. It was the culmination of diggers' grievances over exorbitant licences for prospecting, police brutality, lack of the vote and a ban on prospecting in Crown lands. Tension rose with the murder of James Scobie, a digger, in October and the subsequent acquittal of his alleged killers. On 11 November diggers formed the Ballarat Reform League to petition for redress of grievances; Lieutenant-Governor Charles Hotham responded but on 28 November the arrival of troop reinforcements brought further clashes. The diggers organized into military companies and elected Peter Lalor, a League activist, as commander-in-chief. They built the stockade, and 150 diggers were inside when the police surrounded it. They refused to come out, opened fire, and were routed in just 15 minutes; 25 diggers and five troopers died.

Lalor went into hiding until an AMNESTY was declared; a number of the diggers were accused of treason, but none was convicted. The following year reforms were enacted that remedied many of the prospectors' grievances.

Euro. Eurocommunism The variant of COMMUNISM, not differing greatly from Democratic SOCIALISM, which the Communist parties of Italy and Spain followed from the late 1970s in order to retain their popular support and Parliamentary representation. The party leaderships, to the irritation of the KREMLIN, concluded that both the repressive ethos of Soviet Communism and the failure of Eastern Europe to match the prosperous West required them to follow a different road, with Communism only an ultimate aim. Their example was followed by Communists in some other Western countries, though conspicuously not in France, where STALINISM remains alive and well, though the party's support has shrunk.

Eurocrats Shorthand for the BUREAUCRATS who staff the European COMMISSION.

Eurofed A handy term for the European CENTRAL BANK that would be set up under the MAASTRICHT TREATY as the EC moved toward a single currency. The name stems from the similarities the organization, as an independent central bank, would have with the FED in Washington.

Eurogroup The gatherings of defence ministers from the 14 European member states of NATO (including France) which were instigated in 1968 by Denis Healey with the consent of President Nixon. Healey wrote in 1989:

> Differences on strategic policy have prevented it from providing that European pillar inside NATO for which I originally hoped; but it has been of some value in developing common European projects for arms and equipment.

Europhilia A derogatory term for excessive zeal for European union, coined by critics of the MAASTRICHT TREATY after Denmark rejected it in a REFERENDUM and France came within an ace of doing so. The echo of "necrophilia" is intentional, the critics aiming to imply that a united Europe was dead anyway.

Euro-sceptics The group in the UK CONSERVATIVE PARTY, whose spiritual leader was Margaret Thatcher, who resisted closer European integration before and after the signature of the MAASTRICHT TREATY and caused the government of John MAJOR immense discomfiture. Their high point came in November 1992 when they came within three votes of defeating the Government over proceeding to RATIFY the Treaty; Labour voted with the sceptics and only the votes of all but one of the Liberal Democrats saved Major from a possibly terminal defeat.

Europe (1) Apart from its correct geographical use, a shorthand term used in Britain for the rest of the EC. The Euro-MP Fred Tuckman was told by a constituent while CANVASSING: "Europe – but that's abroad!" And Christopher Monckton defined Europe as "Now, an area geographically to the left of Russia. After MAASTRICHT, an area politically to the left of Russia." The word acquired this sense in the late 1950s when **"going into Europe"** (joining the EC) was first contemplated.

> This "going into Europe" will not turn out to be the thrilling mutual exchange supposed. It is more like middle-aged couples with failing marriages meeting in a darkened bedroom in a Brussels hotel for a group grope.
> E. P. THOMPSON, during the 1975 REFERENDUM campaign.

Occasionally US officials have used the word in this sense, to denote the EC. On one occasion Henry KISSINGER, frustrated by the Community's disunity, asked:

> If I want to ring Europe, who do I call?

(2) To US politicians, the continent from which they sought to distance themselves by declaring INDEPENDENCE, but which has commanded their attention for much of the 20th century. At the birth of the nation, WASHINGTON declared: "Europe has a set of primary interests, which to us have none, or a very remote relation. Hence it must be unwise to implicate ourselves, by artificial ties, in the ordinary vicissitudes of her politics." And JEFFERSON observed: "It is a maxim with us, and I think it a wise one, not to entangle ourselves with the affairs of Europe." Ralph Waldo Emerson deemed this impossible, saying: "Europe extends to the Alleghenies; America lies beyond." ISOLATIONISTS resisted the commitment of US troops in WORLD WAR I and any commitment to preserving peace thereafter; in 1935 Sen. Schall of Minnesota declared: **"To hell with Europe!"** The COLD WAR and KOREAN WAR made such involvement inevitable; Gen. Douglas MACARTHUR declared: "If we lose the war to Communism in Asia, the fall of Europe is inevitable", and John F. KENNEDY said:

> The United States cannot withdraw from Europe, unless and until Europe should wish us gone.

Europe à la carte Picking and choosing from the MAASTRICHT TREATY the elements a member state feels it can live with. A pejorative term used by Jacques DELORS and European FEDERALISTS as Denmark attempted to negotiate better terms after the rejection of the treaty in a REFERENDUM.

Europe des Patries (Fr. Europe of the NATION STATES) The GAULLIST ideal for the EUROPEAN COMMUNITY, of a loose organization of sovereign states in which France could pursue its national interests, as opposed to a FEDERAL Europe. DE GAULLE himself did not originate the phrase; it was first used by Michel Debré on 15 January 1959 on his inauguration as Prime Minister. The doctrine was perfected in the Fouchet Plan of 1961 for closer political co-operation between nation-states, and reflected in the European policy of successive French governments over the next three decades, culminating in France's attempts to sabotage the URUGUAY ROUND of GATT negotiations.

Europe of the regions The notion of the EUROPEAN COMMUNITY as a conglomeration of sub-states like the Basque country, Bavaria and Scotland rather than a grouping of formally-constituted nations.

Concert of Europe The vague post-Napoleonic consensus of the crowned heads of Europe in favour of maintaining the political and diplomatic *status quo*.

Council of Europe The loose grouping of democratic nations established at the Hague in May 1948 which has provided a broad framework for European unity. Many of the ideas that were eventually institutionalized in the EC were first aired at the Council's first assembly at Strasbourg in August 1949, which CHURCHILL dominated – particularly in making sure West Germany was invited to join. However Britain's coolness to closer union ensured that the Council did not itself develop into that union. The Strasbourg-based council developed instead as a 23-nation body embracing EC, EFTA and other free nations, whose activities in such fields as culture and human rights supplemented the tighter groupings. After the fall of Communism in 1989 Czechoslovakia, Hungary and Poland were swiftly admitted, and other East European states have since joined.

> A Council of Europe must inevitably embrace the whole of Europe, and all the main branches of the European family must some day be partners in it. CHURCHILL.

two-speed Europe The system advocated by some FEDERALIST members of the EC, and feared by poorer or less integrationist nations, under which the most enthusiastic advocates of closer union (notably Germany, BENELUX and France) would press ahead with MAASTRICHT-style economic and political union and on toward a United States of Europe while others like Britain, Denmark and Greece lagged behind.

united Europe The goal of politicians nobly and otherwise inspired from the days of CHARLEMAGNE. Goebbels declared for the NAZIs: "The aim of our struggle must be to create a unified Europe." The post-war West German Chancellor Konrad Adenauer stated: "We must free ourselves from thinking in terms of nation states. The countries of western Europe are no longer in a position to protect themselves individually; not one of them is any longer in a position to protect European culture." And John F. KENNEDY told America's allies: "Far from resenting the rise of a united Europe, this country welcomes it."

Fortress Europe *See* FORTRESS.

sick man of Europe The phrase coined by Tsar Nicholas I of Russia in 1853, when he said of Turkey in a letter (written in French) to Sir George Seymour:

> We have on our hands a sick man, a very sick man; it will be, I tell you quite frankly, a great misfortune if one of these days he should slip away from us, especially before all necessary arrangements can be made.

At the 1990 Labour Party conference Glyn Ford, leader of the party's MEPs, called Britain the **thick man of Europe** because of its education policies. Environmental groups have frequently called Britain the **dirty man of Europe** because of what they categorize as its poor record on GREEN issues.

the lamps are going out all over Europe The melancholy observation by the Liberal Foreign Secretary Sir Edward Grey (later Viscount Grey of Fallodon, 1862–1933) on 3 August 1914, the eve of the outbreak of WORLD WAR I. He added: "We shall not see them lit again in our lifetime" – and indeed the Europe Grey knew has never been re-created even though Serb leaders have been eager for a re-run of 1914.

we are part of the community of Europe – we must do our duty as such One of the most-quoted (and wrongly attributed) remarks by a British politician. It was actually made by Lord SALISBURY in a speech at Caernarvon on 11 April 1888; however imaginative or slipshod reference-book compilers have also attributed it to Gladstone and Lloyd George – and in one case both.

European (1) A generic term for anyone of Caucasian origin, used especially in Africa and former British possessions generally.

> New Zealand Europeans, and I am not saying this in a bitter way, are peasants. What we have here is aristocratic Maoris and peasant Europeans.
> NZ Internal Affairs Minister PETER TAPSELL (a Maori), 1985.

(2) Pertaining to Europe. Also one committed to the European ideal and regarding him- or herself as a citizen of the entire continent. To such folk it is a particular compliment to be called a good European. However John

MAJOR, during the negotiations on the MAASTRICHT Treaty, observed:

> The good European sometimes says No.

European Coal and Steel Community The community founded in 1952 by France, Germany, Italy and the BENELUX countries, which was the driving force for the creation of the EUROPEAN COMMUNITY; it co-existed with the original EEC until 1967 and still technically exists, having expanded with the Community itself. The ECSC was the brainchild of the French Foreign Minister Robert SCHUMAN; Britain under Labour refused to join the founders, and the Conservatives elected at the end of 1951 concurred. This is widely regarded as the moment when Britain lost its golden chance to enter a united Europe on equal or even advantageous terms.

European Commission *See* COMMISSION.

European Commission or **Convention on Human Rights** *See* HUMAN RIGHTS.

European Community (EC) The organization of European states created in 1967 from the merger of EURATOM, the EUROPEAN COAL AND STEEL COMMUNITY and the European Economic Community (EEC), given its lasting shape by the Treaty of ROME in 1957. The original members were the BENELUX countries, France, Italy and West Germany; the UK (at the third attempt), Denmark and the Republic of Ireland joined in 1973, Greece in 1981 and Spain and Portugal in 1986. In early 1993 Austria, Finland and Sweden opened negotiations on membership. The Community has developed as the world's largest trading bloc (prior to the conclusion of NAFTA), and has done much to harmonize commercial laws and product specifications; it also speaks on most world issues with a single voice. Most of the Community's continental members see it as a means of achieving complete political and economic union; Britain and Denmark, and much of the population in France, sees those goals as unrealistic and undesirable. The consequent strains have hampered collaboration on more immediate matters. While the entire community agreed the SINGLE MARKET which took effect at the end of 1992, the MAASTRICHT TREATY on closer union was a toughly-fought compromise between advocates of a United States of Europe and those wanting to retain national sovereignty; Britain and Denmark did not accept its goal of a single currency by 1999.

> The EC is about business, not politics.
>
> Professor WALTER HALLSTEIN, President of the Commission 1958–67.

> The EC is an economic giant, but still acts like a political pygmy.
>
> DAVID MARTIN MEP (Lab.), report to the European Parliament on closer union.

In Britain, the question of membership has aroused deep emotions, when the Community was first mooted in 1951, when DE GAULLE said NON in 1963, when Harold WILSON's application was vetoed by France in the late 1960s, during the 1975 REFERENDUM and after Denmark's rejection of the MAASTRICHT TREATY. CHURCHILL said: "We will be with Europe, but not of it, and when they ask us why we take that view, we will say we dwell in our own land." Macmillan cautioned that membership would be "a bracing cold shower, not a relaxing Turkish bath"; Hugh GAITSKELL warned outright that joining would mean "the end of a thousand years of history".

European Council The official term for the SUMMITs of EC heads of Government held twice a year in the country holding the PRESIDENCY, and for special meetings held in between, for instance in Birmingham in October 1992.

European Court of Justice The supreme court of the European Community, which determines whether its organs have acted within their powers and whether member states are violating EC law. The court, consisting of 13 judges and 6 advocates-general, derives its authority from the Treaty of ROME.

> The Court has been responsible for an upheaval in European justice, which has accelerated the shift in power from national to Community institutions.
>
> *The European.*

European Defence Community The proposal for a single Western European army – including a rearmed West Germany – under a European Assembly and Defence Council of Ministers, put forward by the French Minister René Pleven in 1950. A parallel to the SCHUMAN PLAN for the EUROPEAN COAL AND STEEL COMMUNITY, it initially gained a general welcome, but Britain soon had reservations and France followed; America was keen to see Europe pull its weight, and John Foster Dulles threatened an AGONIZING REAPPRAISAL of its policy toward NATO if France did not participate. Nevertheless the French NATIONAL ASSEMBLY blocked the plan, and after further discussions on a more limited "multilateral force" it died.

European Economic Area A FREE TRADE area embracing both the EUROPEAN COMMUNITY, the EFTA countries and other Western and Eastern European states, devised as a step toward closer union; the Area was referred to as a "transit lounge" for states aiming to join the EC. Its birth was placed in jeopardy at the last moment in December 1992 by Switzerland's rejection of the plan in a referendum.

European Free Trade Area *See* EFTA.

European Monetary System *See* EMS.

European Parliament The representative body, first proposed by France and Belgium after World War II and institutionalized in the Treaty of ROME, which has gradually acquired a role in Community legislation and budgeting, and in exerting checks on the Commission. At first nominated by national legislatures, it has since 1979 been directly elected; the elections are held every five years. There are 518 members (to be increased to 576 from 1994), sitting in trans-national party groups rather than in national caucuses. The Parliament meets for a week every month, mainly at Strasbourg, but once a year in Brussels; it is headed by a President with considerable influence and ceremonial functions, and has a comprehensive committee structure. Its powers will be slightly increased under the MAASTRICHT TREATY.

> When you open that Pandora's box you will find it full of Trojan 'orses. ERNEST BEVIN on the original plan.

> This place needs a laxative. BOB GELDOF, 1985.

European People's Party The grouping in the European Parliament comprising CHRISTIAN DEMOCRATS from throughout the Community and, since 1992, MEPs from the UK CONSERVATIVE PARTY. It is the Parliament's second largest group, after the Socialists.

Evans. Timothy Evans case The miscarriage of justice in England which did more than anything else finally to induce Parliament to abolish the death penalty for murder. In 1966 campaigning by the journalist Ludovic Kennedy persuaded Mr. Justice Brabin that Timothy Evans, hanged 15 years before for killing his baby daughter, was "probably innocent", though Brabin felt Evans might "possibly" have been guilty of killing his wife, with which he had not been charged. The real murderer was John Christie, who shared 10 Rillington Place in North Kensington with the Evanses, and after Evans's execution was hanged for the murder of six other women whose bodies were found at the house. By the time Brabin reported, the SILVERMAN BILL had been passed, partly as a result of the Evans case, and hanging abolished. Doubts about Evans's guilt had been voiced as early as 1953 when the bodies were found, but were dismissed as unfounded by an inquiry held by Scott Henderson QC.

Évènements (Fr. events) The understated word by which the French remember the social and political upheavals of May and June 1968, when President DE GAULLE's government came within a whisker of collapsing in the face of an upsurge of militant and often violent protests by students and workers. The students flooded out of their universities to erect BARRICADES, hurl paving stones at the CRS (who responded in kind) and occupy key buildings like the *Théâtre de l'Odéon*. The student uprising, ostensibly for a greater say in how their colleges were run, coincided with widespread industrial unrest, but the student radicals and France's more conventional trade unions only momentarily formed common cause. De Gaulle secretly left Paris at a crucial moment to assure himself of the backing of French generals in West Germany, then waited for the uprising to burn itself out (*see also* CHIENLIT). When he resigned the following year, it was over his defeat in a relatively unimportant constitutional REFERENDUM.

Evita The popular nickname by which Maria Eva de Perón (1919–52), wife of the dictator Juan PERÓN, became known to the adoring Argentine masses. A radio actress born in poverty, she married Perón in 1945 and immediately formed a rapport with the poor and needy – as well as revealing great rabble-rousing abilities which were a boon to her husband, who kept her body in a glass coffin at the CASA ROSADA until his overthrow three years after her death from cancer at the age of 32. Her charitable work, perceived beauty and early death all contributed to the popular myth surrounding her name. Her life became the subject of one of the most successful stage musicals of all time – *Evita* by Andrew Lloyd Webber and Tim Rice, which opened in London in 1978.

> If a woman like Eva Perón with no ideals can get that far, think how far I can go with all the ideals that I have. MARGARET THATCHER, 1980.

exchange. exchange controls Restrictions on the amount of a nation's currency that may be taken out for use or investment elsewhere. They are normally imposed in an attempt to husband scarce reserves or prevent a speculative run on the currency that would force DEVALUATION. Members of the EUROPEAN COMMUNITY are supposed to be phasing them out, though Spain, in particular, continues to impose restrictions on a wide range of foreign currency transactions.

exchange of letters The ritual that is gone through when a Minister resigns or is dismissed from a Government. Traditionally they comprise a letter from the Prime Minister saying how sad they are that he or she is leaving, but quite understand, and a letter from the outgoing Minister saying how sorry they are to be going. Consequently the letters are closely scrutinized for clues as to what has really happened. When Norman Lamont (*see* JE NE REGRETTE RIEN) was ousted as CHANCELLOR in May 1993, he pointedly sent John Major an impersonal fax.

Exchange Rate Mechanism *See* ERM.

excise duties Taxes levied on certain commodities, notably alcoholic spirits, whose production is kept under close supervision by the State. **Excisemen** – the class so roundly cursed by Robert Burns – were the collectors of the taxes, and also patrolled against smugglers. The UK agency collecting excise duties – now including VAT – is known as the Customs and Excise.

exclusion The action of a legislature in preventing an elected member from taking his or her SEAT. Charles BRADLAUGH was repeatedly barred from the Victorian House of Commons for refusing to take the OATH; Adam Clayton POWELL was excluded from the House of Representatives in 1967 for alleged misuse of Congressional travel funds and being under indictment for contempt of court – the first time the House had taken such action in 46 years. Powell described his exclusion as "LYNCHING Northern style"; he was readmitted, minus SENIORITY, in 1969 after winning two more elections.

executive. Executive, the One of the three arms of government, co-existing with the JUDICIARY and the LEGISLATURE; it is also known as the **executive branch**. In America the Executive is personified in the PRESIDENT and also includes Cabinet secretaries and the rest of the ADMINISTRATION; in Britain it comprises the PRIME MINISTER and Cabinet (who are also part of the Legislature) and the CIVIL SERVICE. Writing of the Roman Empire, Edward Gibbon wrote:

> The principles of a free constitution are irrecoverably lost when the legislative power is nominated by the executive.

Hence the FOUNDING FATHERS' insistence on a complete SEPARATION OF POWERS in America. Benjamin FRANKLIN justified the system of CHECKS AND BALANCES by stating:

> The executive will always be increasing here, as elsewhere, till it end in MONARCHY.

Yet, as was seen with WATERGATE and as BACKBENCH MPs and civil libertarians in Britain have long asserted, no check will totally prevent the Executive gathering new powers to itself.

> The Constitution supposes, what the History of all Governments demonstrates, that the Executive is the branch of power most interested in war; and most prone to it. MADISON, letter to JEFFERSON, 1798.

> The contest, for ages, has been to rescue liberty from the grasp of executive power.
> DANIEL WEBSTER, speaking against Andrew Jackson in the Senate, 27 May 1834.

executive agreement An agreement under which the President may enter into agreements with foreign governments on behalf of the United States without having to submit them afterward to the SENATE. He can act under powers given by Congress, for example to conclude reciprocal trade agreements, or as chief executive and COMMANDER-IN-CHIEF, as when Franklin D. Roosevelt concluded the LEND-LEASE agreement with Britain in 1940.

executive communication In Washington, a letter from the President, a Cabinet member or head of an independent agency transmitting the draft of a proposed BILL to the SPEAKER of the House or the President of the Senate. A wave of such letters customarily follows the President's State of the UNION message.

executive mansion A formal term for the WHITE HOUSE, and also the Governor's Mansion in each of America's 50 states.

Executive Office *See* OLD EOB.

Executive Order An order issued by the President dictating a particular way in which the Federal government is to act or be organized. For instance in 1941 Franklin D. Roosevelt, following pressure from Black trade unionists, issued Executive Order 8802 requiring all defence contractors to abstain from racial discrimination. Compliance is another matter; during the IRAN-CONTRA scandal it emerged that Colonel Oliver North's COVERT OPERATION to support the Nicaraguan Contras lacked the written Presidential authority required by Ronald Reagan's own Executive Order 12333.

executive privilege The doctrine on which President Nixon (*see* TRICKY DICK) relied in his efforts to avoid Congressional investigation of WATERGATE, and to which the Supreme Court eventually set strict limits. It was first claimed by JEFFERSON when he refused to answer a subpoena to appear in court and present documents relating to Aaron BURR's trial for treason. When Nixon called for the Senate Judiciary Committee's Watergate hearings to take place *in camera* on grounds of executive privilege, Sen. Sam ERVIN responded:

> That is not executive privilege. That is executive poppycock.

executive session A mainly US term for the secret session of a legislature or other deliberative body. In the US SENATE, executive sessions are usually confined to discussion of executive nominations – which used frequently to mean appointments to remote post offices – and treaties.

exhausted volcanoes Disraeli's withering denunciation of Gladstone's first Cabinet after four years in office, delivered in a speech in Manchester on 3 April 1872. It was almost two years more before DIZZY was to oust them at a general election. He said:

> As I sat opposite the TREASURY BENCH, the Ministers reminded me of one of those marine landscapes not very unusual on the coasts of South America. You behold a range of exhausted volcanoes. Not a flame flickers on a single pallid chest. But the situation is still very dangerous. There are occasional earthquakes, and ever and anon the dark rumbling of the sea.

exocet To destroy a project or a political argument with a sudden and deadly move. The term originated in the FALKLANDS WAR when the Argentine air force used the French *Exocet* (flying fish) missile with lethal effect. The most notable casualty was HMS *Sheffield*, which was sunk with a number of the ship's company.

Experience Counts The slogan on which Richard Nixon (*see* TRICKY DICK) and Henry Cabot Lodge fought the 1960 Presidential campaign. It was designed to capitalize on Nixon's service for two terms as Vice-President to the popular and trusted Eisenhower, and to imply that, compared with the experienced and responsible Nixon, the youthful John F. KENNEDY was unqualified for the White House. It glossed over the fact that Nixon and Kennedy had both first been elected to Congress in 1946, and that at 47 Nixon was only four years older. Experience is a quality claimed as essential by those already in high office, and dismissed as an irrelevance by challengers who lack it. In Britain's 1987 and 1992 elections, the victorious Conservatives made much of the fact that the Labour leader Neil KINNOCK had never held even the most junior Ministerial office. But when H. Ross PEROT was challenged by George BUSH on his lack of experience during one of the 1992 PRESIDENTIAL DEBATES, he replied:

> They've got a point. I don't have any experience in running up a $4 trillion deficit.

experiment. The country needs, and unless I mistake its temper, the country demands, bold, persistent experiment The philosophy set out by Franklin D. Roosevelt as Governor of New York as he mounted his successful campaign for the Presidency in 1932. The words come from his book *Looking Forward*, published after the votes were in.

the Noble Experiment The name given to PROHIBITION by its most ardent and high-minded advocates.

experimental aircraft The expression used by Roy Jenkins (*see* WOY) for the proposed new party that was later launched as the SDP. He caught headlines with it in a speech to the Parliamentary PRESS GALLERY at Westminster on 9 June 1980, when he was still PRESIDENT of the European Commission. Jenkins said of creating a new party:

> The likelihood before the start of most adventures is that of failure. The experimental plane may well finish up a few fields from the end of the runway. If that is so, the voluntary occupants will have only inflicted bruises or worse upon themselves. But the reverse could occur and the experimental plane soar into the sky. If that is so, it could go further and more quickly than few now imagine, for it would carry with it great and now untapped reserves of political energy and commitment.

expletive deleted The phrase used in the published transcripts of the WATERGATE tapes to cover for the profanities repeatedly used by Richard Nixon and his aides in plotting the cover-up. As the unexpurgated version became available, MIDDLE AMERICA was scandalized at least as much by the sleazy language of the nation's chief executive as by what he and his henchmen had done. From 1974, when the tapes were published and Nixon resigned, "expletive deleted" came into general use as an alternative to an obscenity or blasphemous comment.

expulsion The ultimate disgrace for a legislator: irrevocable ejection from the assembly in which he or she has sat, on a vote by their fellow-members. The expulsion of a member is uncommon in the US Congress and rarer still at Westminster; when it does occur, it generally follows conviction for a serious offence in a criminal court or some grave breach of discipline or PRIVILEGE. *See also* EXCLUSION.

extra-Parliamentary action Political activity based on campaigning, marches and DEMOS in Britain's major cities, rather than through pressure for change in Parliament. In the early 1980s the Hard LEFT adopted it as a tactic and as an aim for the Labour Party, prompting a bitter dispute with Labour's then leader Michael Foot (*see* WURZEL GUMMIDGE). In one of the pivotal moments of his leadership Foot, stung by a challenge from an SDP member, repudiated Peter Tatchell, the party's selected candidate for the 1983 Bermondsey BY-ELECTION, because he had advocated extra-Parliamentary action. Tatchell, a gay Australian Marxist, duly lost the ultra-conservative working-class constituency to the Liberals – a result that paved the way for the ALLIANCE's recovery in the run-up to that year's General Election and Labour's crushing defeat. Ten years on, the seat was still in Liberal Democrat hands.

extra-territorial jurisdiction The extent to which the writ of a government or a nation's courts runs beyond its boundaries. It has become a matter of international and political controversy first through sporadic US attempts to enforce the doctrine of COMITY and more recently because governments are anxious to bring to justice TERRORISTS and perpetrators of major environmental disasters who have harmed their nationals but are based in another jurisdiction.

extradition The legal process under which a suspect for a crime committed in one jurisdiction who has been detained in another is transferred by its courts to stand trial where the offence was committed. When conducted between American States it is known as interstate rendition. The extradition of IRA suspects from the Irish Republic to stand trial in Britain has been a sporadic irritant to relations between the two countries. After a string of cases where the Irish courts refused to hand over anyone who claimed the offence had been "political", the Dublin government changed the law to override such arguments. A few suspects were then extradited before a series of squabbles broke out over cases where certain Irish courts released them, saying that the UK authorities had not technically complied with the extradition law; British politicians accused some judges of hiding behind small print to frustrate the fight against terrorism. After a further tightening of Irish law, a delicate matter because of politicians' need to make it clear the Republic's SOVEREIGNTY was not being compromised, more extraditions have taken place.

extremism. extremism in defence of liberty is no vice The phrase which haunted Barry Goldwater's Presidential campaign in 1964 and contributed to the Republican ticket's heavy defeat; Goldwater himself attributed it to Cicero when defending Rome against Catiline. Delivered in his ACCEPTANCE SPEECH at the Republicans' San Francisco convention on 16 July 1964, it starkly highlighted Goldwater's LIBERTARIAN beliefs and frightened many liberal Republicans, who detected an echo of the John BIRCH Society's philosophy, into backing Lyndon Johnson. Goldwater was unrepentant, telling a protesting ex-President Eisenhower: "When you landed your troops in Normandy, it was an exceedingly extreme action taken because you were committed to the defense of freedom." A grinning IKE replied: "I never thought of it that way." Goldwater's actual words were:

> I would remind you that extremism in defense of liberty is no vice. And let me also remind you that moderation in the pursuit of justice is no virtue.

Johnson scornfully countered with:

> Extremism in the pursuit of the Presidency is an unpardonable vice. Moderation in the affairs of the nation is the highest virtue.

extremist One who advocates and pursues an extreme course of action to achieve his or her political ends.

> You show me a Black man who isn't an extremist and I'll show you one who needs psychiatric attention.
>
> MALCOLM X.

> What is objectionable, what is dangerous about extremists is not that they are extreme, but that they are intolerant.
>
> ROBERT F. KENNEDY.

eye. eyeball to eyeball The supreme moment of international tension when the leaders of the SUPERPOWERS have each deployed their full strength and are waiting to see whether the other will raise the stakes by initiating nuclear conflict or back down. The phrase originates from the closest shave of all for world peace, the CUBAN MISSILE CRISIS of 1962. When the Soviet leader Nikita Khruschev backed away from all-out war, US Secretary of State Dean Rusk observed:

> We're eyeball to eyeball – and I think that the other fellow just blinked.

eyes only The designation of a document so secret that only the recipient is permitted to read it; the phrase is an American abbreviation of the British **for your eyes only**.

F

Fabian Society The principal intellectual grouping within the UK LABOUR PARTY, which was instrumental in its formation. Founded in 1884, the Society seeks to achieve SOCIALISM by constitutional, non-revolutionary means. It took its name from the tactics of the Roman general Quintus Fabius Maximus.

> For the right moment you must wait, as Fabius did most patiently when warring against Hannibal, though many times censured for his delays, but when the time comes you must strike hard, as Fabius did, or your waiting will be in vain and fruitless.
>
> FRANK PODMORE, the Fabians' co-founder.

The society's influence was greatest up to the 1920s, with Sidney and Beatrice Webb and George Bernard Shaw its leading lights.

face-saving Maintaining or restoring one's public image in circumstances that could damage it.

> While you're saving your face, you're losing your ass.
>
> LYNDON B. JOHNSON.

faction A political grouping, normally informal and by inference involved in dispute or controversy with another. Also the state of discord between factions.

failure

> It is hard to fail, but it is harder still never to have tried to succeed. THEODORE ROOSEVELT.
>
> All political lives, unless they are cut off in mid-stream at a happy juncture, end in failure, because that is the nature of politics and of human affairs. ENOCH POWELL.

fair. Fair Deal President Truman's sequel to Franklin D. Roosevelt's NEW DEAL. Introduced after his upset 1948 re-election victory, it comprised national health insurance, help for the elderly, more federal housing, aid to education and an anti-LYNCHING law. Only the housing construction bills and increases to Social Security and the minimum wage got through Congress.

> This program symbolizes for me my assumption of the office of President in my own right. HARRY S TRUMAN.

a fair day's wage for a fair day's work A basic demand of TRADE UNIONS throughout the 19th century, widely seen as fair and reasonable.

> "A fair day's wage for a fair day's work": it is as just a demand as governed men ever made of governing. It is the everlasting right of man.
>
> THOMAS CARLYLE (1795–1881).

fairness doctrine The principle under which the US Federal Communications Commission imposes limits on political partisanship and requires airtime to be given to opposing viewpoints.

Fala President Franklin D Roosevelt's Scots terrier, nicknamed "the informer" in wartime because it insisted on being taken for walks from the President's train (*see* Ferdinand MAGELLAN), and the sight of the dog and its secret service escort alerted reporters to the VIP traveller's identity. In 1944 Republican allegations that Roosevelt had sent a destroyer to fetch Fala back from a visit to the Aleutians where he had supposedly been left behind caused a minor Washington scandal.

> His Scotch soul was furious – he has not been the same dog since. FDR.

Falange (Gr. *phalanx*, a compact body of troops) The NEO-FASCIST, NATIONALIST movement founded in 1932 by José Antonio Primo de Rivera, son of the Spanish dictator. Later adopted by General Franco as the official, ruling party of the state forged by his victory in the SPANISH CIVIL WAR; it was disbanded in 1977 after his death. The Falange (spelt **Phalange**) is also a right-wing Christian party and MILITIA in the Lebanon. The term **Falangist** is occasionally used as a pejorative for any movement dominated by conservative Roman Catholics, as by Jimmy Reed, then a Communist, in 1974 to describe the Labour Party on Clydeside.

Falklands war The conflict started by the Argentine invasion of the Falkland Islands (*see* MALVINAS), a British COLONY in the South Atlantic, on 2 April 1982, and culminating in the Argentine surrender at Port Stanley on 11 June. It was brought about by UK naval cuts which left the islands almost undefended and a perception in Buenos Aires that, in the words of Argentina's military dictator General Galtieri, "the British won't fight". When Argentine forces landed, the Falklands' governor, Rex Hunt, told their commander: "It is very uncivilized to invade British territory." In the electric emergency Commons debate on the invasion, the Conservative MP Julian Amery declared: "We have suffered the inevitable consequences of unpreparedness and feeble counsel." The war embraced a UK political crisis culminating in the resignation of Lord Carrington as Foreign Secretary, the despatch of a naval TASK FORCE by Margaret Thatcher's government, intensive US diplomacy by Secretary of State Alexander Haig, the PERUVIAN PEACE PLAN, the sinking of the Argentine Cruiser General BELGRANO and the recapture of South Georgia (*see* REJOICE!, REJOICE!). After accepting the final Argentine surrender the British commander, Maj.-Gen. Jeremy Moore, sent home the message: "The Falkland Islands are once more under the government desired by their inhabitants. God save the Queen!" The Argentine defeat led to the collapse of the Galtieri regime and a return to democracy under President Raul Alfonsin – and Mrs. Thatcher's LANDSLIDE victory in the 1983 general election.

> A fight between two bald men over a comb.
>
> JORGE LUIS BORGES.

Falklands factor The electoral bonus to Mrs. Thatcher's Conservatives prior to and during the 1983 election campaign from Britain's military success.

fall like a ripe fruit The VIET CONG based their protracted guerrilla campaign for control of South Vietnam on the belief that they would erode support for the US-backed government to the point where Saigon would "fall like a ripe fruit" into their hands.

Falls, the The Falls Road in West Belfast, which runs from the city centre to Andersonstown through the core of the city's Catholic community and of support for the Provisional IRA.

Fame is the Spur The British author Howard Spring's 1940 novel in which Hamer Shawcross becomes a pioneer of the LABOUR PARTY as a young idealist, but compromises and eventually joins RAMSAY MACDonald in breaking with the party to form an alliance with the Conservatives. *See* GREAT BETRAYAL.

family. Family Assistance Plan The programme put to Congress by Richard Nixon early in his first term for what was effectively a national welfare system. It would have established a federally guaranteed income, albeit at a maximum $1600 a year for a family of four with no other means, which would have particularly benefited poor families in the South. Devised by Daniel Patrick MOYNIHAN, the plan passed the House but was stifled in the Senate by a coalition of conservative Republicans and Democrats, and Liberals who disliked its work requirements. Nixon himself did not fight hard for the plan once it ran into trouble.

Family Compact In Canada, the tightly-knit group of families whose landholdings were granted by successive Governors who dominated what was to become Ontario during the first third of the 19th century, pursuing rigidly conservative policies.

family values One of the watchwords of Republican campaigning in the run-up to the 1992 US Presidential election. The stated message was that the Republicans stood for the nuclear American family; the unstated message that single parenthood was responsible for crime and riots (the Rodney KING riot had recently occurred). The issue caught light when Vice-President Dan QUAYLE enraged liberals by saying of a popular TV show starring Candice Bergen:

> It doesn't help matters when prime time TV has Murphy Brown, a character who supposedly epitomises today's highly paid intelligent professional woman, mocking the importance of fathers by bearing a child alone and calling it just another lifestyle choice.

spend more time with my family The classic reason now given by politicians for resigning from office, originally a sincere statement of the pressures of political life; Rep. Gary Myers, announcing that he would not seek re-election in 1978 but return to his old foreman's job in a Pennsylvania steel plant, said:

> The amount of time it takes to do this job is just not compatible with how much time I want to spend with my family. I wanted to know my kids before it was too late.

But the phrase came to be code for getting out before being pushed; Nicholas Ridley, not long before he did resign as Trade and Industry Secretary in 1990 (*see* GERMAN RACKET), told Labour MPs who were baiting him:

> I don't want to spend more time with *my* family.

fanatic An advocate of a cause who loses all sense of proportion and resorts to extreme methods. CHURCHILL's definition was "one who won't change his mind and won't change the subject"; Franklin P. Jones preferred "one who sticks to his guns whether they're loaded or not". Keats versified: "Fanatics have their dreams, wherein they weave/A paradise for a sect".

> From fanaticism to barbarism is only one step.
>
> DENIS DIDEROT (1713–84).

> Without fanaticism, one cannot accomplish anything.
>
> EVA PERÓN (1919–52).

Fannie Mae Affectionate mnemonic for the US Federal National Mortgage Authority.

FAO The United Nations Food and Agriculture Organization, based in Rome.

faraway. a faraway country of which we know nothing Neville CHAMBERLAIN's notorious reference to Czechoslovakia, in a radio broadcast on 27 September 1938 acquiescing in Germany's annexation of the SUDETENLAND. It was regarded by his critics, then and even more so later, as the ultimate in APPEASEMENT; since World War II British Prime Ministers have habitually apologized to the Czechs for this attitude. Chamberlain said:

> How horrible, fantastic, incredible it is that we should be digging trenches and trying on gas-masks here because of a quarrel in a faraway country between people of whom we know nothing.

farm. Farm Belt The American states radiating out from the mid-West that are largely dependent on agriculture, and on Federal support for farmers. Its people have long been attracted by POPULIST Presidential candidates.

Farmers' Platform The programme adopted as the basis for political action by discontented Canadian farmers in WORLD WAR I. Developed by the Canadian Council of Agriculture between 1916 and 1918, it was also known as the New NATIONAL POLICY; it called for reforms including drastic TARIFF cuts and lower freight rates, public ownership of utilities and control of natural resource exploitation, higher taxes on the rich and political changes including REFERENDA and RECALL, PROPORTIONAL REPRESENTATION and votes for women. Only this last was rapidly realized.

buying back the farm In Australia, the WHITLAM government's policy, spearheaded by F. X. Connor, of reclaiming national resources that had been sold overseas.

like a farmer with terminal cancer trying to borrow on next year's crop The devastating description by Hunter S. Thompson in *Rolling Stone* of a flagging Sen. Edmund Muskie campaigning in the 1972 Florida Democratic Primary.

vote yourself a farm The slogan of America's National Reform Association, founded in 1842, which advocated giving 160 acres of land to anyone willing to farm them.

Fascism The right-wing TOTALITARIAN/CORPORATIST ideology and political system devised by MUSSOLINI which was largely adopted by Hitler and Spain's General Franco. The name comes from the Latin *fasces*, the bound rods and arrows that were the symbol of authority in ancient Rome and in some more recent democracies. Mussolini founded his party in 1919; it took power after the MARCH ON ROME in 1922. Based on a ruthless, uniformed political party, on POPULISM, DEMAGOGY and leader-worship, fascism promoted an intense NATIONALISM (RACISM in Hitler's case) which, with territorial claims, was a principal cause of WORLD WAR II. Mussolini declared that "Fascism is a religion. The twentieth century will be known in history as the century of fascism." But he also said more candidly:

> Our programme is simple. We wish to govern Italy.

He held that "for the fascist, everything is in the state, and nothing human or spiritual exists, much less has value, outside the State". And he warned that "Fascism believes neither in the possibility nor the utility of perpetual peace". Alfredo Rocco praised it as "the unconscious awakening of our profound racial instinct", while José Antonio Primo de Rivera, before the outbreak of the SPANISH CIVIL WAR, hailed Fascism as "a way of knowing everything – history, the state, the achievement of the proletarianization of public life, a new way of knowing the phenomena of our epoch". LENIN saw Fascism as "capitalism in decay", Upton Sinclair as "capitalism plus murder", and Aneurin Bevan as "the future refusing to be born". John Strachey coined the slogan **Fascism means war**, while G. D. H. Cole declared: "Fascism is nonsense, and that is perhaps the gravest indictment of all". Only in Spain did an entirely Fascist state survive the war, though PERONISM in Argentina was closely related. Though small fascist parties and movements survive in many countries, the name is now used mainly as a term of abuse. *See also* COMMUNISM; MOSLEYITES; NAZI.

> Benito Mussolini governed Italy with a new theme of government which, while it claimed to save the Italian people from Communism, raised himself to dictatorial power. As Fascism sprang from Communism, so Nazism developed from Fascism.
>
> WINSTON CHURCHILL, *The Gathering Storm*, ch. i.

> If Fascism came to America, it would be on a program of Americanism.
>
> Sen. HUEY (KINGFISH) LONG (1893–1935).

neo-fascist An individual or organization with similar style or objectives to fascism

proto-fascist An organization that is developing fascist tendencies.

Fashoda The crisis in 1898 when Britain and France disputed control of the upper Nile, and therefore of a sizable part of Africa. It began when French troops under Major Marchand marched from the Congo into the Sudan, halting at Fashoda. British forces under Kitchener confronted them, and after a period of great tension, with the nations on the brink of war, the French withdrew, confirming Britain's supremacy in the region.

fat cats Large-scale, and by inference smug and complacent, contributors to political campaigns. The term was coined in the mid-1920s by Frank R. Kent of the *Baltimore Sun*.

> I've always wondered why the Democrats call supporters of the Republican party "fat cats" but their own contributors are called "public spirited philanthropists".
> RONALD REAGAN.

father. Father of his Country Reverential name for George WASHINGTON, first used on a calendar published in Philadelphia in 1778, before the independence of the US had been finally secured and 11 years before he became their first President.

Father of the A-bomb Dr Edward Teller (b. Hungary 1908), who worked in World War II on the ATOMIC BOMB, and in 1949-51 helped produce the US hydrogen bomb (*see* H-BOMB). He believed world security depended on stockpiling nuclear weapons.

Father of the Constitution The title unofficially bestowed on James MADISON for his part in drafting both the US CONSTITUTION and the BILL OF RIGHTS, and writing the FEDERALIST papers.

Father of the House The longest-serving member of a legislature. In the UK House of Commons, the Father of the House takes the CHAIR before members have been sworn in to elect a new SPEAKER.

Founding Fathers The men who formed the United States and devised its constitution. Improbably, President HARDING was the apparent originator of the phrase. On 22 February 1918 he told a patriotic gathering in Washington: "It is good to meet and drink at the fountain of wisdom inherited from the founding fathers of the Republic." And in his INAUGURAL ADDRESS on 4 March 1921, he said:

> Standing in this presence, mindful of the solemnity of this occasion, feeling the emotions which no one may know until he senses the great weight of responsibility for himself, I must utter my belief in the divine inspiration of the Founding Fathers.

fatwa The Arabic term for an edict imposed by a religious leader. It became known worldwide in 1989 when the AYATOLLAH Khomeini (1902–89), spiritual and effective secular leader of Iran, offered a cash reward to any Muslim who assassinated Salman Rushdie (1947–), the British author of Indian Muslim origin, for alleged blasphemy in his novel *The Satanic Verses*. The *fatwa* read:

> The author of *The Satanic Verses* book, which is against Islam, the Prophet and the *Koran*, and all those involved in its publication who were aware of its content, are sentenced to death. I ask all Muslims to execute them wherever they find them.

The pronouncement caused a diplomatic and political storm, with fundamentalist Muslims in many countries including the UK rioting and burning Rushdie's books in protest at the publication. Rushdie was forced into hiding under the protection of the Metropolitan Police, whom the book also ridiculed.

favourite son A candidate, often for the American Presidential nomination, put forward by a party BOSS or MACHINE, and stuck to by his home-state delegates regardless of the merits or strengths of the other contenders in the hope of striking a deal. Originally a term of approbation (used of Washington when he visited Portsmouth, New Hampshire, in 1789) it became by the 1820s a term of irony, referring to a beneficiary of nepotism or PATRONAGE.

FBI Federal Bureau of Investigation. The agency of the US Department of Justice founded in 1908 to investigate violations of federal law, becoming under J. Edgar Hoover, director 1924–72, a force against organized crime in the 1930s and an instrument of McCARTHYISM in the 1950s.

FCO Foreign and Commonwealth Office. The nerve-centre of British diplomacy, sandwiched in WHITEHALL between DOWNING STREET and the TREASURY. Founded as the FOREIGN OFFICE in 1782, it absorbed in the late 1960s its junior partner, the Department for Commonwealth Relations, formerly known as the Colonial Office.

FDR The popular nickname for **Franklin Delano Roosevelt** (1882–1945), author of the NEW DEAL, America's WORLD WAR II leader and its 32nd and longest-serving President (Dem., 1933–1945). A patrician and 5th cousin of Theodore Roosevelt, he joined a smart New York law firm, married his 4th cousin Eleanor and at 28 won a spectacular State senate campaign. At 30 he was picked by Woodrow WILSON, who called him "the handsomest young giant I have ever seen", as Assistant Secretary of the Navy. His wartime performance won him the Democratic Vice-Presidential nomination in 1920; he boosted his reputation despite the ticket's heavy defeat. Then, in August 1921, he was paralysed by polio while vacationing at CAMPOBELLO. Crippled from the waist down, he fought his way back to fitness, boasting: "Maybe my legs aren't so good – but look at those shoulders!" In 1924 he came back with a stirring speech to nominate Al Smith (*see* HAPPY WARRIOR) for the Presidency, and four years later was elected Governor of New York. In 1932 he ran for the White House, his wife saying: "If the polio didn't kill him, the Presidency won't." FDR himself confided: "If you have spent two years in bed trying to wiggle your big toe, then anything else seems easy"; Paul Conklin wrote:

> Polio made the aristocratic Roosevelt into an underdog. For him it replaced the LOG CABIN.

Roosevelt won the Democratic nomination on the fourth ballot and, despite being scorned by HOOVER as "a chameleon on plaid", he swept to power, carrying all but six states. Many pundits were convinced he was not up to the job; Walter Lippman wrote: "He is a pleasant man who, without any important qualifications for the office, would like to be President. Here is a man who has made a good governor, who might be a good cabinet officer, but who simply does not measure up to the tremendous demands of the office of President;" and Murray Kempton: "I have always found Roosevelt an amusing fellow, but I would not employ him, except for reasons of personal friendship, as a geek in a common carnival." FDR set his sights low, saying: "I have no expectation of making a hit every time I come to bat. What I seek is the highest possible batting average."

Roosevelt was elected on a promise to balance the Budget, but with the GREAT DEPRESSION crushing the US economy, he declared in a ringing inaugural speech: "The only thing we have to fear is fear itself"; 400,000 Americans wrote him letters of appreciation. He closed the banks, promised a HUNDRED DAYS of decisive action and pushed legislation through Congress for numerous Federal agencies to get the country working again. The powers he took spawned the Washington bureaucracy and led H. L. Mencken to write: "I am advocating making him King in order that we may behead him if he goes too far beyond the limits of the endurable. A president, it appears, cannot be beheaded, but kings have been subject to the operation since ancient times." His first term appalled Republicans, but he pressed on, confident as Richard Hofstadter put it "that even when he was operating in unknown territory he could do no wrong, commit no serious mistakes".

In 1936, having made some impact on the Depression, FDR was re-elected by an even greater majority. Republicans denounced his programmes as "Socialism", but the women of New York's GARMENT DISTRICT caught the mood in a poster reading: "We love him most for the ENEMIES HE HAS MADE". FDR said:

> I should like to have it said of my first administration that in it the forces of selfishness and lust for power met their match. I should like to have it said of my second administration that in it those forces met their master.

But he found his second term tougher. Unemployment crept up again and the Supreme Court declared key New Deal legislation UNCONSTITUTIONAL (*see* BLACK MONDAY). Roosevelt threatened COURT-PACKING legislation, but backed off when Congress baulked. He kept on creating new agencies to kick-start the economy, Earl Goldman writing: "Restless and mercurial in his thinking, a connoisseur of theories but impatient with people who took theories seriously, he trusted no system except the system of endless experimentation." FDR attracted some trenchant critics: Georgia's Govenor Eugene Talmadge, who called him "that cripple in the White House", Hugh Johnson – "the man who started more creations since Genesis – and finished none", Alice Roosevelt Longworth – "Franklin is two-thirds mush and one-third Eleanor", and the ISOLATIONIST Sen. Burton Wheeler – "a warmonger". Anthony EDEN saw him in these years as "a conjuror skilfully juggling with balls of dynamite", but H. L. Mencken commented: "If he became convinced tomorrow that cannibalism would get him the votes he so sorely needs, he would begin fattening a missionary in the White House backyard come Tuesday". It was the outbreak of war in Europe that got America back to work, turning it into the great "Arsenal of DEMOCRACY".

Roosevelt was re-elected in 1940 by a slimmer margin, promising not to take America into another war but quietly doing what he could to help Britain. After PEARL HARBOR (*see* A DATE THAT WILL LIVE IN INFAMY) he galvanized America into an unprecedented military and industrial effort. Isolationist opposition almost ceased, but FDR had to set up new agencies to get American industry to deliver the goods at a fair price. He also alienated labour's leaders by his determination to get results; the United Mineworkers' John L. Lewis said: "It ill-behooves one who has supped at labor's table and who has been sheltered in labor's house to curse with equal fervor and fine impartiality both labor and its adversaries when they become locked in deadly embrace."

From his inauguration, FDR cast a spell over most of the American people through his dynamism and his FIRESIDE CHATS, and his magnetism increased in wartime. Hugh Brogan wrote that "he was better able to respond to people in numbers, at a distance, than to the needs of his intimates", and his relationship with Eleanor (*see* FIRST LADY OF THE WORLD) had been purely political since before his paralysis; each genuinely supported the other's campaigning, but he looked elsewhere to meet his sexual needs. Yet to those meeting him he exuded dynamism. He once told Orson Welles: "There are only two great actors in America. You are the other one," and Winston CHURCHILL felt that "meeting him is like opening a bottle of champagne". When Madame Chiang Kai-Shek asked him not to stand up when she entered the room, he chuckled: "My dear child, I couldn't stand up if I had to." He would tell inattentive White House guests: "I murdered my grandmother this morning", and say to bores: "The ablest man I ever met is the man you think you are." He also had powerful lungs; Harry S. Truman remarked: "With Roosevelt you didn't need a phone. All you had to do was raise the window and you could hear him." FDR won and held an adoring following among White and Black Americans alike, though he did little to advance the cause of CIVIL RIGHTS. Harold Macmillan recalled: "Apparently unconscious of conditions either in Harlem or the Deep South, he expressed concern about the low standard of living in many of the West Indian islands."

During the war Roosevelt cemented a solid relationship with Churchill, and believed he could handle STALIN. But by YALTA, after winning a record fourth term with a further-reduced majority, his powers were failing. On his return he made his only public reference to his disability, telling Congress: "I hope that you will pardon me for the unusual posture of sitting down. It makes it a lot easier for me not having to carry about 10 lbs. of steel around on the bottom of my legs." And within weeks he was dead, suffering a cerebral haemorrhage at WARM SPRINGS while sitting for a portrait. After a train journey back to Washington along a track lined with grieving sharecroppers, FDR was buried in his garden at HYDE PARK. His death dumbfounded America, and momentarily raised NAZI hopes of deliverance, Goebbels writing: "This was the Angel of History! We felt its wings flutter through the room. Was this not the future we awaited so anxiously?"

> The only man we ever had in the White House who would understand that my boss is an s.o.b.
>
> ANON. American worker, 1945.

> He saved the capitalist system by simply forgetting to balance the books. ALISTAIR COOKE (1908–).

> The greatest American we have ever known and the greatest champion of freedom who has ever brought aid and comfort from the New World to the Old.
>
> CHURCHILL.

fear. Fearless talks The talks aboard the British cruiser of the same name in October 1968 which marked the second and last attempt by Harold WILSON to persuade Ian Smith to end UDI and return Rhodesia to legality.

Let us never negotiate out of fear, but let us never fear to negotiate One of President John F. KENNEDY's most celebrated dicta on COLD WAR diplomacy.

The only thing we have to fear is fear itself The most memorable phrase of Franklin D. Roosevelt's inaugural speech on 4 March 1933. He declared:

> The only thing we have to fear is fear itself – nameless, unreasoning, unjustified terror which paralyzes needed efforts to convert retreat into advance.

The phrase had its origins in *Proverbs* 3:25 ("Be not afraid of sudden fear"), Montaigne ("The thing of which I have most fear is fear"), Francis Bacon ("Nothing is terrible except fear itself") and Thoreau ("Nothing is so much to be feared as fear").

featherbedding The granting of over-generous subsidies (especially to certain categories of farmer) and wage settlements by governments or public-sector bodies.

Fed (1) Northern Clubs Federation Bitter, one of the beers on draught in the bars of the Palace of Westminster, originally ordered at the urging of North-Eastern Labour MPs and now a firm favourite. (2) The Fed. Abbreviation for the US FEDERAL RESERVE system.

federal. Federal Election Commission The body set up by the US Congress in 1974 to oversee new laws on campaign conduct and financing, and administer campaign subsidies (*see* MATCHING FUNDS). Originally it was appointed jointly by the President and Congress, but the SUPREME COURT ruled that as the FEC was executive and not legislative, the President should appoint all its members, subject to the consent of the Senate.

Federal Government The central government of the United States, based in WASHINGTON and exercising the powers reserved to it, rather than to the STATES, under the US CONSTITUTION. When the Republic was created, Alexander HAMILTON argued for a strong centre, declaring: "The three great objects of government, agriculture, commerce and revenue, can only be secured by a federal government." But in recent times Ronald Reagan said: "We all need to be reminded that the Federal Government did not create the states – the states created the Federal Government."

> An American may through a long life never be reminded of the Federal Government, except when he votes in Federal elections, lodges a complaint against the post office, or is required to pay duties of customs or excise.
>
> LORD BRYCE, British Ambassador in Washington 1907–13.

Federal Hall The two-storey building in New York, in Wall Street at the head of Broad Street, where the US CONGRESS first met on 4 March 1789. Though heavily modernized by l'Enfant, the planner of WASHINGTON, it was used for only one session before Congress decamped to Philadelphia; it was pulled down in 1816.

Federal period The period between 1781 and 1789 when the Articles of CONFEDERATION served as America's constitution, the country being little more than a league of 13 sovereign states.

Federal Register The daily bulletin, published in Washington, in which the US Government published Presidential proclamations, EXECUTIVE ORDERS, and other regulations and notices.

Federal Reserve America's CENTRAL BANKing system created by Woodrow WILSON's Federal Reserve Act, 1913. The nation is divided into 12 Federal Reserve Districts, with a federal reserve bank in each acting as the lender of last resort; presiding over them is a board of governors (*see* FED) with an independent chairman. This can regulate the amount of money in circulation and sets the level of interest rates.

Federalism Originally the doctrine advanced by HAMILTON and MADISON for a strong federal government in the United States stopping short of a unitary state, instead of a loose confederation of states with a weak centre. When Canada was formed, Lord Acton wrote: "A great democracy must either sacrifice self-government to unity, or preserve it by federalism. The co-existence of several nations under the same state is the best, as well as the best security of its freedom." In the EUROPEAN COMMUNITY, self-styled Federalists want the whole governed by elected representatives of all the member states and/or their component regions. But Margaret Thatcher and her supporters take the term to mean direct rule by non-elected bureaucrats in BRUSSELS.

New Federalism, the President Reagan's unsuccessful initiative in 1982 to transfer major federal programmes and revenues to the States.

Federalist In Europe, a Federalist will describe him- or herself as one who aims for a democratic United States of Europe. But to the opponents of closer union, it is a term of abuse.

> One who wants Britain to be governed by everyone but the British. CHRISTOPHER MONCKTON.

Federalist (Papers), The The 85 essays in support of ratification of the US CONSTITUTION published in New York newspapers in 1787–78 under the name "Publius". The real authors were Alexander HAMILTON, John JAY and James MADISON.

Federalist Party The party formed in the early days of the United States to pursue Federalism (*see above*) against advocates of a weak national government. It was dominant during the administrations of WASHINGTON and John ADAMS, but the party faded after JEFFERSON's election in 1800 and ceased to be a force after 1830.

anti-Federalists The contemporary collective term for those who opposed the adoption of the US CONSTITUTION after its completion in 1787.

Federast The ultimate term of abuse for European Federalists by their (mainly British Conservative) opponents. A corruption of "pederast".

feelgood factor The feeling of national wellbeing which President Reagan (*see* GREAT COMMUNICATOR) was credited with generating during his first term, after the uncertainties of the CARTER years. More generally, the mood all political leaders would like to generate so as to ensure their re-election.

fellow-traveller A person in sympathy with a political party (usually the Communists) but not a CARD-CARRYING MEMBER. The term (Russ. *poputchik*) was coined by TROTSKY, appeared in English in 1936 in an article by Max Lerner ("*Mr. Roosevelt and his Fellow-Travelers*") and became a commonplace in the late 1940s and 1950s at the height of worldwide concern over Communist influence (*see* McCARTHYISM; UN-AMERICAN ACTIVITIES). By 1957 the lexicographer Eric Partridge was writing: "it shows signs of being employed so widely and so indiscriminately that it becomes mere vogue and probably discredited".

> He is but one of a reputed short list of seven fellow-travellers under threat of expulsion.
>
> *Time and Tide*, 1 May 1948, on the Labour Party's expulsion of one of its members.

feminism The demand for widespread political and social reform to remove restraints on women's capacity to lead a fulfilling life, which emerged in late-1960s America and has spread to most of the world. With its roots in earlier movements such as the SUFFRAGETTES, the movement has as its basis the demand for equal political, social and economic rights with men, and in many countries has achieved significant advances. More militant, often left-wing groups have tried to create an alternative society, even in extreme cases excluding men. In many campaigns, notably that of the GREENHAM WOMEN, feminists have made common cause with anti-nuclear or environmental groups. *See also* NOW; WOMEN'S RIGHTS.

fence-sitting A classic term for refusing to take sides in a political argument. Lloyd George said of Sir John Simon (1873–1954): "He has sat on the fence so long that the iron has entered his soul." Vice-President Spiro AGNEW denounced the Eastern ESTABLISHMENT as "ideological eunuchs, whose most comfortable position is straddling the fence". And the 300-lb. Liberal MP Sir Cyril Smith (*see* BIG CYRIL) once declared:

> If the fence is strong enough, I'll sit on it.

Fenians An Irish Nationalist movement founded in New York in 1857, taking its name from Fionn MacCumhail, a hero of Irish legend. It spread rapidly across America, then to Ireland, where it absorbed the Phoenix Society, eventually developing into the IRISH REPUBLICAN BROTHERHOOD, the militant Republican body which paved the way for the EASTER RISING and the IRA. In the late 1860s London was rocked by a chain of **Fenian outrages**, the most serious being the Clerkenwell bombings of 13 December 1867, when a bungled attempt to blast Fenian prisoners free with a barrel of gunpowder caused several deaths. Over the years "Fenian" has become a term of abuse for any Irish Nationalist by opponents of the movement.

Fianna Fail (Ir. warriors of Ireland) The Republican party formed in 1926 by the arch-Nationalist Eamonn de Valera (*see* DEV) to oppose the PARTITION of Ireland which had resulted in the IRISH FREE STATE. Formed of men who had been on the losing side in the Civil War, Fianna Fail refused at first to take its seats in the DAIL. But in 1932 it formed a government under de Valera, and since then has been in power except from 1948–51, 1973–77 and 1982–87, alternating with coalitions led by FINE GAEL. From 1989–92 it governed in coalition with the Progressive Democrats (*see* PDs), and from January 1993 with LABOUR. Fianna Fail has placed a high emphasis on economic self-sufficiency and reviving the Irish language, and while it remains committed in theory to a united Ireland it enjoyed, under Jack Lynch, Charles HAUGHEY and Albert Reynolds, generally good relations with British leaders.

> *Interviewer* (John Bowman of RTE): Surely you are aware that Fianna Fail are on record as saying they will never enter coalition?
>
> *Labour leader Frank Cluskey*: Yeagh, but Fianna Fail are also on record as saying they would never enter *Dail Eireann*. 1981 election campaign.

Fidel. Fidel Castro in a miniskirt The verdict of the ULSTER UNIONIST MP Stratton Mills (1932–) on the electrifying MAIDEN SPEECH in 1969 of Bernadette Devlin (1947– , later McAliskey). The fiery Miss Devlin, a radical student CIVIL RIGHTS campaigner, was elected a "Unity" MP for Mid-Ulster at the age of 21 just as years of discrimination against Catholics were starting to produce a backlash, but before the IRA had resumed its terror campaign. The speech was described by those present as the most dramatic début by an MP for decades. Miss Devlin held her seat in 1970 but was not re-elected in 1974; she subsequently founded the Irish Republican Socialist Party and contested (as an independent) elections in both Ulster and the Irish republic.

Fidelistas The devoted followers of Fidel Castro (1927–) who from 1956 waged a guerrilla campaign from the Cuban mountains against the corrupt Batista regime, then joined him in taking power in February 1959. As Castro's regime became more rigidly Marxist and pro-Soviet, a number of the original *Fidelistas* were executed or imprisoned, or fled to the United States. *See also* GRANMA; Bay of PIGS.

Fifteenth Amendment The amendment to the US CONSTITUTION, ratified in March 1870, which guaranteed Black Americans the right to vote. It stipulated that that right was not to be abridged by the Federal or State authorities "on account of race, color, or previous condition or servitude". The amendment, too radical even for many Northerners, was a cornerstone of RECONSTRUCTION, and when that process was reversed in the late 1870s the amendment ceased to be a guarantee.

fifth. Fifth Amendment The fifth of ten amendments to the US CONSTITUTION contained in the BILL OF RIGHTS, ratified in December 1791. Its critical and controversial provision is that "nor shall [any person] be compelled in any criminal case to be a witness against himself". As a result, generations of mobsters called to testify before Congressional committees have "taken the Fifth". So, too, did many alleged Communists at the height of McCARTHYISM; those who did invoke the amendment to avoid self-incrimination became known as **Fifth-Amendment Communists.**

Fifth Columnist A member of a community or group with loyalties to a state or body determined to destroy it, who at the appropriate moment will undermine or strike against the order of which he or she appears to be part. The term was originally applied during the SPANISH CIVIL WAR by General Emilio Mola to citizens of Republican Madrid loyal to General Franco. When asked in October 1937 which of his four army columns would capture Madrid, he replied: "The fifth column."

Fifth Republic The government of France introduced by General DE GAULLE in 1958 to replace the Fourth Republic, which had staggered from one crisis to another under a series of unstable coalitions since the end of World War II. The Fifth Republic remedied this by placing power essentially in the hands of the President, with the Prime Minister operating in the shadow of the ÉLYSÉE. Despite muscle-flexing by the right-wing Premier Jacques Chirac during the years of COHABITATION, this has remained essentially true.

fifty. Fifty-first state The term applied to Britain in the late 1950s and early 1960s by left-wingers, and some others, who thought it was too much under US domination and lacked a credibly independent foreign and defence policy. Prior to the statehood of Alaska and Hawaii in 1959, Britain was categorized as the **forty-ninth state**.

Fifty-four Forty or fight! The slogan on which James Knox Polk (1795–1849) was elected President of the United States in 1844. It staked a claim to all of what was then known as the OREGON territory as far north as Alaska. In 1827 America and Britain had agreed to share the territory after Russia and Spain had abandoned claims to it; when it became clear the lands were not worthless as originally thought, America pressed its claim. However Polk compromised, and on 15 June 1846 the Oregon Treaty was signed, with the US accepting its northern border as the **49th Parallel** – well south of the line Polk's supporters had pressed for.

fight, fight and fight again The most celebrated phrase from the long battle within Britain's Labour Party over UNILATERALISM. It was spoken by Labour's leader Hugh GAITSKELL during a passionate speech on 5 October 1960 to the party's Scarborough conference after it had voted to commit Labour to scrap Britain's nuclear weapons unconditionally. Gaitskell said:

> It is not in dispute that the vast majority of Labour Members of Parliament are utterly opposed to unilateralism and neutralism. So what do you expect them to do? Change their minds overnight? . . . There are other people, too, not in Parliament, in the Party, who share our convictions. What sort of people do you think they are? What sort of people do you think we are? Do you think we can simply accept a decision of this kind? Do you think that we can become overnight the PACIFISTS, unilateralists and FELLOW TRAVELLERS that other people are? . . . There are some of us, Mr. Chairman, who will fight and fight and fight again to save the party we love. We will fight and fight and fight again to bring back sanity and honesty and dignity, so that our party, with its great past, may retain its glory and its greatness.

Fighting French *See* FREE FRENCH.

filibuster (Sp. *filibustero,* corruption of the Dut. *vrij buiter,* a freebooter) A speech prolonging debate on a measure to the point where it becomes procedurally impossible for its progress to continue; a technique honed to perfection in the US SENATE until reform of the rules reduced its capacity to thwart the will of the majority. Filibusters were originally more common in the House, but in 1841 it passed the ONE-HOUR RULE which limited speeches to that maximum. That same year, the Senate rejected such a change, and the filibuster became part of its workings. No limit at all was imposed until 1917, when filibusters by ISOLATIONIST Senators against WILSON's war preparations led to the CLOTURE being provided for. Between 1927 and 1962 the cloture was never achieved and filibusters, normally by Southern conservatives, invariably succeeded. Only after the cloture was invoked in 1964 to pass a CIVIL RIGHTS Bill did matters change; since 1975 filibusters have been rare.

In 1881 Sen. George F. Edmunds justified the filibuster thus: "It is of greater importance to the public interest that every Bill in your calendar should fail than that any Senator should be cut off from the right of expressing his opinion." More recently filibusters became as much a matter of pride as of ideology, Sen. Allan Allender saying: "I held the title of longest filibuster for two or three years, until another idiot [Sen. Wayne Morse] beat my record." But Rep. Clare Boothe Luce had the last word:

> They say women talk too much. If you have worked in Congress you know that the filibuster was invented by men.

post-cloture filibuster A fresh procedural device which briefly revived the filibuster from 1975 to 1979. Sen. James Allen of Alabama discovered that while speeches were now limited to one hour each after cloture, time-consuming items such as ROLL CALL votes, QUORUM calls and the like did not fall within the limit. After two Democratic senators filed 508 amendments to a gas deregulation Bill, keeping the Senate up all night for the first time in 13 years, MAJORITY LEADER Robert C. Byrd persuaded Vice-President Mondale to rule such amendments dilatory and Out of ORDER.

Final Solution (Ger. *Endlösung*) The chilling euphemism used by the NAZIs for their grotesque policy of exterminating European Jewry. Though implicit in Hitler's MEIN KAMPF, it was 1941 before Goering ordered Heydrich to prepare for "a total solution of the Jewish question in those territories of Europe which are under German influence". Schedules were set by Nazi leaders at a conference at Wannsee, Berlin, in 1942; the details were left to Adolf EICHMANN, who almost 20 years later was executed for GENOCIDE by the Israelis. Most Germans at the time would not have known that the policy involved such a monstrous programme of mass extermination, but once the elaborate apparatus for rounding-up and transporting Jews eastward to death camps began to function, the truth about the HOLOCAUST must have dawned on many.

Financial Management Initiative (FMI) A WHITEHALL efficiency exercise set in motion by Sir Derek RAYNER early in the Thatcher administration. A seven-strong team of civil servants and management consultants, reporting in May 1982, recommended stimuli for Civil Service efficiency comparable to the disciplines of the private sector. Everyone from PERMANENT SECRETARIES downward was expected to define and understand their function, clear responsibilities for spending money were to be set, and managers should have better information about costs, training and access to expert advice. The exercise was based on Michael Heseltine's MINIS, and Mrs. Thatcher ordered all her Ministers to implement it, despite protests from Sir Frank Cooper, the powerful Permanent Secretary at the Ministry of Defence, that the idea of Ministers as managers was "nonsense". FMI was implemented by Rayner's successor Sir Robin Ibbs; the concept of NEXT STEPS AGENCIES was just one of its fruits.

Fine Gael (Ir. tribe of the Gaels) The party founded by William T. Cosgrave and other members of DAIL EIREANN who supported the Treaty of 1921 that created the IRISH FREE STATE. Considered more conservative but less GREEN than FIANNA FAIL, Fine Gael nevertheless declared a republic and withdrew Ireland from the COMMONWEALTH in 1948 during its coalition with Labour. It was a Fine Gael government, led by Garret FitzGerald, which sought to break the deadlock over Northern Ireland by negotiating the 1975 ANGLO-IRISH AGREEMENT, and trying to remove some of the more overtly Catholic features of the Republic's constitution to make it seem less threatening to Northern Protestants.

fine-tuning The regulation of an economy by making small changes to taxation, interest rates, money supply, *etc.*, so as to steer a steady middle course between RECESSION and OVERHEATING.

Finland. Finland Station speech The speech made by LENIN on 16 April 1917 at the Finland Station in Petrograd on his return from exile in Switzerland, as the old order in Russia began to collapse; by November of that year his BOLSHEVIKs had taken power. *To the Finland Station*, by Edmund Wilson, is a classic account of the Bolshevik Revolution and the forces behind it. In his speech Lenin told supporters:

> Dear comrades, soldiers, sailors and workers! I am happy to hail in you the victorious Russian revolution! . . . The hour is not far off when at the summons of our comrade, Karl Liebknecht, the German people will turn their weapons against their capitalist exploiters. The sun of the world socialist revolution has already risen!

Finlandization The process of turning the neighbour of a Communist state into a muted semi-client, even if it is politically independent and has a wholly democratic political system. It derives from the position of Finland and the course followed by its governments, especially during the four decades after World War II. Although Finland was a capitalist democracy, its leaders conducted their affairs in close consultation with the superpower next door. *See also* WINTER WAR.

fire. The Fire Next Time The best-known work of the Black American author James Baldwin (1924–87). Published in 1963, it gave an apocalyptic view of the America's future if White attitudes to race remained unchanged. He wrote:

> White people in this country will have quite enough to do in learning how to accept and love themselves and each other, and when they have achieved this – which will not be tomorrow and may very well be never – the Negro problem will no longer exist, for it will no longer be needed.

firebell in the night Thomas JEFFERSON's emotive phrase for the capacity of the issue of SLAVERY to wreck the American UNION. In a letter to John ADAMS on 22 April 1820 over the MISSOURI COMPROMISE, Jefferson wrote:

> This momentous question, like a firebell in the night, awakened and filled me with terror. I considered it at once as the knell of the Union.

fireside chat A broadcast in which a political leader talks easily and intimately to the people. The term was coined in 1933 when Franklin D. Roosevelt, eight days after taking office, gave a frank, confiding radio talk about America's problems and his plans for solving them; projecting himself to sound like a family friend, he continued the talks throughout his Presidency. His successors have sought to emulate him, Ronald Reagan coming closest to success. Some have conspicuously failed; Mark Russell said of Sen. Henry "SCOOP" Jackson:

> He gave a fireside speech – and the fire went out.

first. First Amendment The first of ten amendments to the US CONSTITUTION ratified in December 1791 which constitute the BILL OF RIGHTS. It guarantees what have become the most sacred freedoms of the American people, reading:

> Congress shall make no law respecting an establishment of religion, or prohibiting the free exercise thereof; or abridging the freedom of speech, or of press; or the right of the people peaceably to assemble, and to petition the government for a redress of grievances.

The Supreme Court has customarily given those claiming the right to freedom of speech the benefit of the doubt; the one exception is obscenity. The liberal Justice William Douglas maintained: "'Congress shall make no law' does not mean 'Congress may make some laws'", but more recently Justice William Brennan wrote: "Implicit in the history of this amendment is the rejection of obscenity as utterly without redeeming social importance." The Burger Court in 1973 ruled that states could ban any works that, taken as a whole, appeal to prurient interests, portray sexual conduct in an offensive way, and do not have serious literary, artistic, political or scientific value. Outside the Bible Belt, these constraints have rarely been exercised.

first among equals (Lat. *primus inter pares*) A term central to the concept of CABINET GOVERNMENT, defining the position of the PRIME MINISTER in relation to other members of the Cabinet. Jeffrey Archer used it in 1983 as the title of a novel chronicling the struggle between four contrasting politicians to reach NUMBER TEN. The phrase was probably first used by the Liberal statesman John (later Lord) Morley (1838–1923), who wrote in his 1889 life of WALPOLE:

> Although in Cabinet all its members stand on an equal footing, speak with equal voice, and on the rare occasion when a division is taken, are counted on the fraternal principle of one vote, yet the head of the Cabinet is *primus inter pares*, and occupies a position which, so long as it lasts, is one of exceptional and peculiar authority.

First Division The highest ranks of Britain's Civil Service, numbering some 2000 officials and including Whitehall's MANDARINS. Its trade union, the **First Division Association**, is a prestigious affiliate of the TUC.

First Family, the A satirical record lampooning the KENNEDY family and its life in the White House which topped America's best-sellers *c.* 1962.

first in war, first in peace, first in the hearts of his countrymen The tribute paid to George WASHINGTON on his death in a Congressional speech on 26 December 1799 by Henry "Light Horse Harry" Lee.

First Lady The wife of the President of the United States. The term was known early in the life of the nation, Zachary Taylor (1784–1850) saying of Dolley Madison: "She was truly our First Lady for half a century," but it only came into general use after 1900. Though the First Lady has no Constitutional status, she occupies a niche in the life of the nation and much is expected of her. Grace Coolidge subordinated her own identity, saying: "This was the wife of the President of the United States and she took precedence over me," and Eleanor Roosevelt warned the First Ladies who followed her: "You will feel that you are no longer clothing yourself – you are clothing a public monument." Jacqueline Kennedy (*see* JACKIE O) bridled at first, saying: "The one thing I do not want to be called is First Lady. It sounds like a saddle horse," but she gave way on the use of the term, at least: "People have told me 99 things that I have to do as First Lady – and I haven't done one of them."

First Lady of the World The title earned by Eleanor Roosevelt (1884–1962), who after the death of her husband Franklin D. Roosevelt in 1945 toured the world as an ambassador for peace and the needy. Though she and her husband had been close to divorce before he contracted polio in 1921, she campaigned vigorously for him and on social issues until his death in 1945. When Roosevelt was elected in 1932, she told friends: "Now I'll have no identity," but soon proved herself wrong. She started by stating: "If any SECRET SERVICE man shows up and starts following me around, I'll send him right back where he came from." FDR called her "my eyes and ears", declaring: "My missus goes where she wants to, she talks to everybody and does she learn something!" Despite being, in her husband's words, "the originator, discoverer and inventor of the Household Economy for Millionaires", she had a remarkable ability to communicate with the most disadvantaged of people – and to articulate their hopes where it counted. More liberal than FDR, she even brought her feisty lobbying to the dinner table, her daughter Anna once having to interject: "Mother, can't you see you're giving Father indigestion." Eleanor Roosevelt herself said: "I used to tell my husband that if he could make me understand something, it would be clear to all the other people in the country." And despite evidence to the contrary, she insisted: "I never urged on [FDR] a specific course of action, no matter how strongly I felt." She had none of the glamour of Jacqueline Kennedy, Joe Alsop writing: "Her hats had the look of having been found under the bed." But after her wartime tour of the South Pacific theatre, Admiral William F. Halsey reported:

I marveled at her hardihood, both physical and mental. She also accomplished more good than any other person, or any group of civilians, who passed through my area.

After the death of her husband, she embarked on a new career as a humanitarian on the world stage, remarking: "When you cease to make a contribution you begin to die." And as chairwoman of the UN HUMAN RIGHTS Commission, she made a unique contribution.

No woman has ever so comforted the distressed or distressed the comfortable.

CLARE BOOTHE LUCE (1903–87).

She would rather light candles than curse the darkness, and her glow has warmed the world.

ADLAI STEVENSON at the United Nations, 9 November 1962.

First Mama The CB radio callsign given to Betty FORD during her husband's tenure of the White House, 1974–77.

first past the post The electoral system in which any number of candidates compete for a single post, and the one with the highest number of votes is elected even if he or she has only gained a small proportion of the total.

First Reading The initial stage of a Bill's progress through a legislature, generally a formality.

First Strike The opening shot in a nuclear war, which the aggressor hopes will destroy the attacked nation's capacity to retaliate. First-strike weapons are usually not protected by missile silos and "hardened" shelters and are designed, as their name implies, to destroy the enemy's planes, submarines and missiles. Second-strike weapons, to be used in the event of a surprise attack to "take out" first-strike weapons or if the target nation does manage to retaliate, are heavily protected. *See* NO FIRST USE.

fiscal. fiscal drag The process under which, in a system of Progressive TAXATION, an increase in income can take a taxpayer into a higher tax bracket. The effect is to increase revenue without increasing taxes.

fiscal 199- Washington shorthand for a financial year.

fiscal policy Measures used by governments to influence economic activity, particularly by manipulating the levels and allocation of taxes and spending. They are often used in conjunction with monetary policy to achieve set goals.

Too often in recent history liberal governments have been wrecked on the rocks of loose fiscal policy.

FRANKLIN D. ROOSEVELT, 1933.

Fishbait The nickname of William Mosley Miller (1912–87), Doorkeeper to the US HOUSE OF REPRESENTATIVES for 28 years. Despite the diminutive stature which earned him the name, the feisty Mississippi-born Miller was no respecter of persons. President Truman warned the future Queen Elizabeth II of this before she visited the Capitol; "Fishbait" greeted her with a cordial: "Howdy, Ma'am," then called down from the rostrum to the Duke of Edinburgh's party: "Hey, pass me up the prince!" When "Fishbait" retired, he published an autobiography under that title casting harsh judgments on many Congressional figures.

five. Five Members The five members of the Long Parliament - Pym, Hampden, Haselrig, Strode and Holles - whom Charles I attempted to arrest for treason on 4 January 1642. The King's arrival with troops in the House of Commons (*see* I SEE THE BIRDS ARE FLOWN) was a crucial moment on the road to Civil War.

five minute rule The limit imposed by the US House of Representatives on questioning of a witness by any one member of the APPROPRIATIONS Committee during hearings on the BUDGET. Once all members have asked their questions, further time may be allowed.

five o'clock shadow The stubble on Richard Nixon's chin whose sinister appearance before the cameras was blamed in part for John F. KENNEDY's perceived victory in their first Presidential DEBATE, in Chicago on 26 September 1960. The phrase comes from a 1950s razor-blade commercial.

He looked like a man with shaving and perspirational problems, glumly waiting for the commercial to tell him how not to offend.

ROGER BUTTERFIELD, historian.

I paid too much attention to what I was going to say and too little to how I would look. RICHARD NIXON.

Five Year Plan In the Soviet Union and subsequently in some other countries, plans for developing the whole of a nation's economy in a co-ordinated effort over five years. The first Five Year Plan was launched by STALIN in 1928, with the aims of making the Soviet state self-supporting, mechanizing agriculture, promoting literacy, *etc.* Five Year Plans were to be promulgated for the next six decades, but especially after World War II there was an increasing divergence between the goals set and the advances achieved.

flag-burning The most controversial form of protest in America, seen by most as highly unpatriotic. It is also long-standing, going back at least to the start of the 20th century. Largely because it was so provocative, anti-VIETNAM WAR militants set fire to the STARS AND STRIPES as an easy way of gaining publicity. A less widespread recurrence in the mid-1980s led to Congressional efforts to ban such protests, and consequent litigation over whether such legislation would violate the FIRST AMENDMENT.

> If you want a symbolic gesture don't burn the flag – wash it.
>
> NORMAN THOMAS, US Socialist leader (1884–1968).

> You flag-burning pigs should not have the right to coexist with us devout, God-fearing Americans.
>
> Letter to the QUAYLE QUARTERLY from Dominick Swinhart, Olympia, Washington.

flags and furloughs Democratic nominee Michael Dukakis's characterization of the successful Republican tactics in the 1988 Presidential election. It stemmed from George Bush's call for legislation to outlaw FLAG-BURNING, and his linking of Dukakis with the furlough granted in Massachusetts to the rapist murderer Willie HORTON.

Flat, the The modest living quarters of the PRIME MINISTER on the top floor of 10 Downing Street. They were carved out of the building for Clement ATTLEE in 1945; until then family rooms in NUMBER TEN existed cheek-by-jowl with offices.

flexible response The strategic doctrine that in the event of war a state should have a graduated range of responses to attack open to it, instead of simply the MASSIVE RETALIATION of a full-scale nuclear counterthrust, which was the West's initial stance during the COLD WAR. Its basis is that the option to make a less cataclysmic response may prevent the war ending in global annihilation; as such it requires far more sensitive planning and more careful targeting of weapons. The doctrine was formally adopted by NATO in 1968, with the implicit rider that the West would use nuclear weapons first if its conventional forces were defeated. The term was also applied to the KENNEDY administration's range of options – military, diplomatic and presentational – for countering Soviet ambitions; in July 1961 JFK said

> We intend to have a wider choice than humiliation or all-out nuclear action.

flier In America, a handbill distributed to voters in support of a candidate, party or campaign – or against them.

flip-flop Repeated reversals of policy or stance which make a political leader look capricious, unreliable and not worthy of re-election. The term surfaced in the 1976 US Presidential election campaign in counter-charges between Gerald FORD and Jimmy CARTER; it was frequently used against Carter during his Presidency, and has stayed in the political vocabulary ever since.

FLN (Fr. *Front de Libération Nationale*, National Liberation Front) The Algerian nationalist group that won the war of independence from the French, and subsequently formed the country's government. Formed in 1954 from three earlier groups, it was the political wing of the ALN (*Armée de Libération Nationale*) which waged an increasingly successful guerrilla campaign, and set up a Provisional GOVERNMENT in Tunis. In 1962 President DE GAULLE conceded independence after referenda in both France and Algeria, and the FLN under Ben Bella (1916–) became the governing and sole political party; multi-party politics was not restored until 1989.

float. floater Originally an American term for voters who sold their support to the highest bidder, and when bought would campaign energetically for them. As **floating voter**, it has been used in Britain since the 1950s for an elector with no firm loyalty to any one party, whose change of allegiance could be decisive. As a group, floating voters (*see also* SWING VOTERS) are heavily wooed by all parties.

floating currency A currency whose value fluctuates in response to forces in world markets, instead of being held at or close to a fixed parity as a tenet of national policy.

floor In any legislature, the body of the CHAMBER where members exchange views and business is transacted. The word is frequently used to emphasize that open debate is being conducted by the full membership "on the floor of the House", rather than by a small group in COMMITTEE.

floor leader In America, a member of a campaign team who marshals DELEGATES supporting a particular candidate on the floor of a party CONVENTION, and works to maximize their number.

crossing the floor The action of a member of the UK HOUSE OF COMMONS in resigning from his or her own party and joining the party on the opposite side of the Chamber. It was most recently done by Christopher Brocklebank-Fowler, MP for NW Norfolk, who in 1981 left the Conservative benches in mid-debate and walked across to the SDP benches; he stood for the SDP in 1983 and lost his seat. When Sir Hartley Shawcross, Attorney-General in the 1945–51 Labour government, showed signs of the right-wing views which ultimately led him to quit the party, he was nicknamed **Sir Shortly Floorcross**.

> The Right Honourable and Learned Gentleman has twice crossed the floor of this house, each time leaving behind a trail of slime.
>
> LLOYD GEORGE on Sir John Simon.

have the floor To have the leave of the CHAIR to speak, free of interruption.

taken on the floor of the House Describing the consideration of a measure by the full House, most likely sitting In COMMITTEE, rather than by a separate committee.

yield the floor The action of a legislator who has the floor, but permits another member to INTERVENE. The phrase is most frequently used in the US SENATE.

FLQ (Fr. *Front Libération du Québec*) A Quebec SEPARATIST terrorist organization which operated in Montreal and Quebec city from 1963 till its suppression in 1970. It graduated from mail-box bombings in Montreal's Anglophone suburbs to robbery and murder. In October 1970 the FLQ kidnapped Pierre Laporte, a Quebec politician, and British trade commissioner James Cross; when Pierre TRUDEAU and Quebec's Premier Bourassa refused to negotiate, Laporte was murdered. After a massive manhunt leading to 400 arrests, Cross was found, Laporte's murderers prosecuted and Cross's kidnappers allowed safe passage to Cuba.

fly-posting The (illegal) practice in Britain of sticking election and other political posters to shop windows, bus shelters, walls and trees without permission – sometimes obscuring the other side's propaganda. The political parties are infrequently implicated because all their posters have to bear an imprint saying who has published them.

focus group A representative group of voters gathered by a party's POLLSTERS to test their reactions to themes and issues that campaign professionals have thought of highlighting. In 1988 Jim Pinkerton, research director to the BUSH campaign, tried out issues that might destroy Michael Dukakis on a focus group in Paramus, New Jersey.

> The focus group may be a perfect symbol of what has happened to democracy in America. Insofar as "the people" are consulted by political leaders these days, their reactions are of interest not as a guide to policy but simply as a way of exploring the electorate's gut feelings, to see which kind of (usually divisive) message might move them most.
>
> E. J. DIONNE Jr., *Why Americans Hate Politics*.

Foggy Bottom The nickname given to the area in Washington where the STATE DEPARTMENT was relocated during World War II. It stems from the thick, swirling haze which hung over the swamps that stretched from the POTOMAC to the Lincoln Memorial and H Street North-West, but has also come to apply to the impenetrability of State's bureaucracy and culture. This sense was popularized by James Reston of the *New York Times* in 1947; Richard Nixon exploited it to the full at the height of McCARTHYISM by attacking

> the striped-pants faggots in Foggy Bottom.

Fontainebleau agreement The deal struck between leaders of the EUROPEAN COMMUNITY on 25 June 1984 at Fontainebleau, near Paris, which guaranteed Britain a rebate on its substantial net contribution to the EC budget. It was the conclusion of five years of acrimonious argument between Margaret Thatcher and almost all the rest of the Community at 12 European summits (*see* "I want my MONEY back"). Under the mechanism agreed, Britain has received 66% of the difference between what it pays to the Community and what it receives.

Foot, Michael *See* WURZEL GUMMIDGE.

Football, the The briefcase containing the secret codes needed to launch America's nuclear weapons, which aides to the President carry with him everywhere he goes, 24 hours a day.

Too much football without a helmet *See* TOO.

force. Force Acts Three Enforcement Acts passed by Congress in 1870–71 to implement RECONSTRUCTION in the face of White Southern resistance. The Act of May 1870 imposed stiff penalties for violations of the FOURTEENTH and FIFTEENTH AMENDMENTS giving Black Americans full voting rights and disqualifying former Confederate officials. The Act of February 1871 placed congressional elections under Federal control, and the KU KLUX KLAN Act of April 1871 gave the President military authority to suppress violence in the South – which GRANT used immediately to put down the Klan in South Carolina.

Force de Frappe (Fr. strike force) France's name for its independent nuclear DETERRENT, which it has possessed since the late 1950s; unlike Britain, France has not incorporated its nuclear force into NATO's command structure, or signed the NON-PROLIFERATION TREATY.

force-feeding The method adopted by prison authorities in various countries at various times to keep hunger-STRIKERS alive. It was most notoriously used in Britain against SUFFRAGETTE prisoners (*see* CAT AND MOUSE ACT).

force majeure (Fr. greater force) The diplomatic and strategic term for the use of single-minded and ruthless force used by one power against another. It is often cited as an excuse not to honour one's obligations, the essence of *force majeure* being that its application was so great and unexpected that resistance was useless.

Ford, Gerald Rudolf (1913–), 38th President of the United States (Republican, 1974–

77). At the start of Nixon's second term, Gerald Ford was House MINORITY LEADER; twenty months later he was President after Nixon's resignation over WATERGATE. Less than three years later he was out of office, defeated by Jimmy CARTER in a vote of no confidence in a WASHINGTON Ford had begun to cleanse. Ford's name at birth was Leslie KING; like Bill Clinton (*see* BLYTHE) he later took his stepfather's name. He became a high-school football star in Grand Rapids, Michigan – Lyndon Johnson later claimed he had "played too much football without a helmet" – going on to study law at Michigan (where he was Most Valuable Player) and Yale before serving in the Navy. In 1948 he was elected to Congress for his home district, and married Betty Bloomer, an intelligent, glamorous home-town divorcee. She later said: "I wish I'd married a plumber. At least he'd be home by 5 o'clock," but their marriage was close and happy, despite Betty Ford's troubles with alcohol and pills after leaving the White House, which she faced with honesty and courage. Ford built up a reputation for integrity, and for solidity rather than brilliance (*see* WALK AND CHEW GUM AT THE SAME TIME). And in 1965 Republican YOUNG TURKS in Congress turned to him as their natural leader. Ford was a loyal supporter of Nixon, and when Spiro AGNEW resigned in October after pleading "no contest" to kickback charges, was an obvious safe choice as Vice-President. He was sworn in on 6 December 1973 – and eight months and three days later was President after witnessing the trauma of Nixon's fall at first hand. He said then:

> If you have not chosen me by secret ballot, neither have I gained office by secret promises. I have not campaigned either for the Presidency or the Vice-Presidency. I have not subscribed to any partisan platform. I am indebted to no man, and to only one woman – my dear wife – as I begin this very difficult job.

Ford immediately caused an outcry by giving Nixon a PARDON, but the wounds of Watergate began to heal. He had a bruising fight with Ronald Reagan for the 1976 Republican nomination, and on LABOR DAY was well behind Jimmy CARTER. Yet a robust campaign, based mainly on keeping America "number one" in defence, ate into the gap and Ford went down to a respectably narrow defeat. Carter, in his INAUGURAL speech, paid this tribute:

> For myself and for our nation, I want to thank my predecessor for all he has done to heal our land.

Ford was widely ridiculed for his limitations, and was himself modest and self-deprecating, saying: "I'm a Ford, not a LINCOLN." Betty Ford observed: "Jerry and I are ordinary people who enjoy life and aren't overly impressed with ourselves," adding in bewilderment: "People have written to me objecting to the idea of a President of the United States sleeping with his wife." Ford took pride in being "the first Eagle Scout vice-president of the United States", and once in the White House observed: "I guess it just proves that in America anyone can be President." He also lapsed into his sporting past, saying: "I only wish I could take the entire United States into the locker room at half time." Politically he described himself as "a moderate on domestic issues, a conservative in fiscal affairs and a dyed-in-the-wool internationalist in foreign affairs"; he stood up to the Reaganite right by keeping Henry KISSINGER as Secretary of State. His contacts on the HILL were excellent; he once said: "My motto toward the Congress is communication, conciliation, compromise and co-operation."

His GAFFES, saying "if Lincoln were alive today he would be spinning in his grave", or claiming at the height of the 1976 election that Poland was "not under Soviet domination", did raise doubts. Larry King commented: "He is so average one almost expects it to be deliberate;" David Frye wrote: "Gerry Ford looks like the man in the science fiction movie who is the first to see the creature." And the Rev. Duncan Littlefair of Grand Rapids observed: "Ford isn't a bad man, but he's dumb. He shouldn't be dumb either – he went to school just like everyone else." However Rep. Barber Conable spoke for many when he said: "Ford has a slow mind, but he has backbone." And when the Senate was confirming Ford as Vice-President, the Democratic Sen. Alan Cranston declared: "I doubt if there has ever been a time when integrity has so surpassed ideology in the judgement of a man for so high an office in the land." The public took time to appreciate these qualities; during Ford's brief Vice-Presidency, one anonymous joker wrote:

> A year ago Gerald Ford was unknown throughout America. Now he is unknown throughout the world.

Ford to City: Drop Dead The unforgettable front-page headline in the *New York Post* on 30 October 1975, when President Ford rejected the city's application for Federal aid when it was on the edge of bankruptcy. The headline was the creation of the *Post*'s Bill Brink and Mike O'Neill.

Ford's Peace Ship The ship despatched to Europe in December 1916 by the automobile magnate Henry Ford (1863–1947), after PACIFISTS took him up on a pledge to give up half his fortune to shorten the carnage of WORLD WAR I by a single day. The company of pacifists, journalists and Ford's staff feuded on the *Oscar II's* 13-day crossing from Hoboken, New Jersey, to Christiania in Norway; five days after their arrival Ford went home, saying he had seen few signs of peace. A few of the pacifists pressed on to campaign in Europe, but the episode discredited pacifism in America.

Ford's Theatre The theatre on Washington's E Street where Abraham LINCOLN was assassinated by John Wilkes Booth on 14 April 1865. It survives as a historic exhibit and place of pilgrimage.

Fordney-McCumber tariff The TARIFF imposed by Congress under the HARDING administration that put the stiffest duties to date on imported goods - and, within a short time, produced an unprecedented budgetary surplus. By closing US markets to Japan, it also began the economic and political build-up which culminated in PEARL HARBOR. By 1930 even this tight regime - which included the power for a President to vary the tariff on particular goods by 50% either way - was not enough for PROTECTIONISTS in Congress, who imposed the even stiffer SMOOT-HAWLEY TARIFF.

foreign. foreign aid One of the most controversial components of US policy, with many voters and members of Congress seeing it as an unjustified waste of public money that could be spent to better effect at home. Bernard Rosenberg described it as "taxing poor people in rich countries for the benefit of rich people in poor countries". **Foreign Aid Bills** have controversial and even irrelevant provisions attached to them on their way through Congress, which may prevent them being signed into law; this troubles the administration and the State Department who see aid as a crucial tool of diplomacy, but delights POPULISTS.

> Nobody shoots Santa Claus. AL SMITH, 1936.

> Is this nation stating it cannot afford to spend an additional $600 million to help the developing nations of the world become strong and free and independent - an amount less than this country's annual outlay for lipstick, face cream and chewing gum?
> President KENNEDY, New York, 8 November 1963.

> The United States is not just an old cow that gives more milk, the more it is kicked in the flanks.
> Secretary of State DEAN RUSK, testifying to Congress, 4 June 1967.

Foreign Office *See* FCO.

Foreign Office view The assessment of international events and how Britain should react to them which is arrived at in the Foreign Office; by inference it differs from the position of the Government as a whole and of Downing Street. Differences between NUMBER TEN and the Foreign Office frequently occur, and occasionally prove irreconcilable.

> The Ministry of Agriculture looks after farmers. The Foreign Office looks after foreigners. NORMAN TEBBIT.

foreign policy The stance toward the other nations of the world adopted by the government of a particular nation. On the outbreak of the FALKLANDS WAR the Conservative MP Julian Amery accused the FOREIGN OFFICE of being unable to tell the difference between DIPLOMACY and foreign policy. In America, there has been a 200-year argument between Congress and the White House, and between the White House and the STATE DEPARTMENT, over who should conduct foreign policy and what course should be followed; at the outset Thomas JEFFERSON wrote: "The transaction of business with foreign nations is executive altogether".

> Just like Canadian foreign policy, all piss and wind.
> DEAN ACHESON (1893-1971).

> The purpose of foreign policy is not to provide an outlet for our own sentiments of hope and indignation; it is to shape real events in a real world.
> PRESIDENT KENNEDY in Salt Lake City, 26 September 1963.

> *Questioner*: How will the Reagan administration change American foreign policy?
> *Jeane Kirkpatrick*: We've taken down our "kick me!" signs.

> English policy is to float largely downstream, occasionally putting out a diplomatic boathook.
> Lord SALISBURY (*attr.*), 1877.

> Fear is no basis for foreign policy.
> MARGARET THATCHER.

like being in a foreign country The unkind and somewhat racist description of Home Office QUESTION TIME in the Commons, *c.* 1984, which a Cabinet member conveyed to Margaret Thatcher. The Home Secretary at the time was Leon (later Sir Leon) Brittan, and his Labour Shadow Gerald Kaufman; both men were of Baltic Jewish descent and Kaufman's rhetoric in particular had an edge reminiscent of an ancient feud.

Former Naval Person The codename adopted by Winston CHURCHILL in his secret correspondence with Franklin D. Roosevelt prior to America's entry into WORLD WAR II. It referred to Churchill's previous post (at the start of both World Wars) as First Lord of the Admiralty (*see* WINSTON IS BACK). Roosevelt chose the codename POTUS, short for President of the United States. The talks were kept secret because they involved greater preparedness for war than FDR felt he could reveal during the 1940 election campaign; a German spy in the US Embassy in London with some access to transcripts was detected before he could do much damage.

Forster. Forster's Education Act The Act passed by Gladstone's Liberal government in 1870 which for the first time gave Britain a school system over and above that provided by churches and charities. It was promoted by William Edward Forster (1818–86), nicknamed "Buckshot", who was brought up a Quaker and married the daughter of Dr. Arnold, headmaster of Rugby. His system of "board schools" was neither universal nor free, and was criticized by Nonconformists whose taxes were diverted to fund poor pupils in Anglican schools. Yet the Act was one of the great Victorian measures of reform and public provision – and a far cry from Forster's later disasters in Ireland (*see* KILMAINHAM TREATY).

Fort Sumter The engagement in South Carolina which marked the start of America's CIVIL WAR. The fort in Charleston harbour and its garrison of 84 were cut off by land when South Carolina SECEDED from the Union on 20 December 1863; on 9 January the merchant steamer *Star of the West*, bringing UNION reinforcements to the fort, was fired on by militia cannon and twice hit. But the war began in earnest at 4.30 a.m. on 12 April, when CONFEDERATE batteries, after a one-hour ultimatum, opened fire from Cummings Point. The bombardment from four sides lasted 34 hours before the fort's commander, Major Anderson, surrendered; 4000 rounds had been fired but no one was killed until the last gun of a 50-gun victory salute blew up and killed Daniel Hough, who thus became the first casualty of the war. Abraham LINCOLN, inaugurated President on 4 March, was reckoned to have manoeuvred the South into attacking the beleaguered garrison, thus throwing the onus for starting the war on to the Confederacy.

Fortas resignation The first-ever resignation of a justice of the US SUPREME COURT. Fortas, who had been Lyndon B. Johnson's principal legal adviser and was appointed by him to the court in 1965, was forced to quit on 15 May 1969 after allegations that he had accepted money from a foundation that was under investigation, and after the House Judiciary Committee had been requested to inquire into his alleged "failure of good behavior". Fortas's resignation led directly to President Nixon's notorious HAYNSWORTH NOMINATION.

fortress. Fortress Europe The term used by critics of closer EUROPEAN COMMUNITY for a European Community which, they claim, will become more prosperous by trading within its borders while at the same time erecting barriers to commerce with the world outside.

Fortress Falklands A pejorative for Margaret Thatcher's policy after the FALKLANDS WAR of building up a strong military presence on the islands to deter any fresh Argentine attack. Critics of the policy argued that it would prevent any kind of *rapprochement* with Argentina – not that the islanders wanted one. A new airport, under RAF control, was constructed at Mount Pleasant, 25 miles from Port Stanley, and forces of several thousand from all three services – two or three times the islands' population – stationed on the Falklands. Gradually those forces have been reduced, though a strong defensive capability remains. They have not prevented relations being restored with Argentina, though the dispute over the islands is unresolved.

forty. Forty acres and a mule! The slogan of those freed slaves in the former CONFEDERATE States who organized to press the Federal government for ownership of enough land to enable them to support themselves. A certain amount of land was made available from 1886 under the Southern Homestead Act, but it was not very fertile and little was taken up. Increasingly the freedmen drifted back on to the old plantations as sharecroppers.

forty-shilling freeholders Those Englishmen who, prior to the 1832 REFORM ACT, qualified for the vote in certain constituencies because their property had a rental value of £2 a year; the right dated back to 1343. Under the Act a £10 threshold was introduced throughout, but existing forty-shilling freeholders retained the vote.

forty-ninth parallel The line of latitude that forms the land border between the western United States and Canada. To the north lie British Columbia, Alberta, Saskatchewan and Manitoba; to the south Washington state, Idaho, Montana, North Dakota and western Minnesota. It was accepted in 1818 as the boundary as far west as the Rockies; beyond that it was undefined. By 1844 waves of American settlers arriving on the Oregon Trail were pressing for total US control of the Pacific west and a border west to the north, and James Polk was elected president on the slogan FIFTY-FOUR FORTY OR FIGHT. In the event both countries agreed in 1846 on the extension of the 49th parallel to the coast.

forty-ninth state *See* FIFTY-FIRST STATE.

Foul-mouthed Joe One of many nicknames for **Joseph Cannon** (1836–1926), SPEAKER of the US House of Representatives from 1903 to 1911. To his supporters an avuncular UNCLE JOE (he was first elected Speaker aged 67), he was renowned for his profane language and was said by his opponents to be in the hands of liquor interests. But their real objection was to his tyrannical control of Congress; he appointed himself chairman of the RULES COMMITTEE and blocked any Bill he did not personally support. In 1910 "INSURGENTS" in his own Republican Party ousted him from the committee, thus breaking his power.

four. Four A's The device used by the LABOR Party in New South Wales in 1937 to get its candidates into the most advantageous place on the BALLOT paper for elections to the Australian SENATE, which led to a change in the law. A party was entitled to group all its candidates together on the paper, and Labor put forward four candidates whose names began with "A" – Amour, Armstrong, Arthur and Ashe – to secure the left-hand spot, where voters were most likely to make their mark. All four were elected; three years later the law was changed so that the parties drew lots for where their groups would appear on the paper. *See* DONKEY VOTE.

Four Generals, revolt of the The revolt in Algeria in 1961 against President DE GAULLE's policy of granting the territory independence, led by four generals who had backed his rise to power in the belief that he would stick to a policy of ALGÉRIE FRANÇAISE, and now felt betrayed. The four – Edmond Jouhaud, Raoul Salan, Maurice Challe and André Zeller – made their move on 22 April after a period of unrest among Algeria's French community; the bulk of the army stayed loyal and de Gaulle quelled the revolt in a few days.

4-H club The hard core of Conservative Republicans in the Senate who during Ronald Reagan's Presidency exerted critical influence over legislation and appointments. The four were Jesse Helms of North Carolina, Orrin Hatch of Utah, Gordon Humphrey of New Hampshire and Chic Hecht of Nevada. They formed the nucleus of the Steering Committee of 15 to 20 Republicans who lunched every Tuesday to set the conservative agenda in the Senate.

Four Horsemen The four powerful Irish-American politicians who in the mid-1970s took charge of the sensitive issue of NORTHERN IRELAND, encouraging the British Government to act fairly and positively toward the Catholic minority while reining in pressure from within their own community to support the Provisional IRA. The four were Speaker TIP O'Neill, Sen. Edward KENNEDY, Sen. Daniel Patrick MOYNIHAN and Hugh Carey, Governor of New York State.

Four legs good, two legs bad The slogan with which the animals seized control from their human master in George Orwell's ANIMAL FARM. *See also* All animals are EQUAL, but some are more equal than others.

four-minute warning Popular shorthand in the 1950s and 1960s for the length of time the British public would have to prepare for a Soviet nuclear attack. So brief a warning aroused fears which formed a potent recruiting weapon for CND; it also gave rise to numerous suggestions of how one would spend those four minutes, many of them ribald and some physically impossible.

Four more years! The slogan chanted by supporters of a US President who want him elected for a further TERM. During Margaret Thatcher's 11-year ascendancy in Britain, the derivative "five more years" or even "ten more years" was heard at election times. The TWENTY-SECOND AMENDMENT which since 1952 has limited a President to two terms means that the chant is only appropriate when an INCUMBENT is completing his first term. When Ronald Reagan heard it in 1988, he told the crowd: "Since the Constitution has something to say about what you have just been chanting, I'll assume you're suggesting that I live four more years."

> *Dan Quayle* (September 1992): Four more years!
> *Crowd*: Four more months!

Four Policemen The belief of Franklin D. Roosevelt that after WORLD WAR II responsibility for world peace and order would rest with America, the Soviet Union, Britain and China. With France, these nations came after FDR's death to form the PERMANENT FIVE members of the UN SECURITY COUNCIL. Roosevelt believed giving the major powers pre-eminent status would avoid the pitfalls experienced by the LEAGUE OF NATIONS, and make Congress more likely to accept the new order. He had even told Molotov that all other nations than the four should be disarmed. YALTA marked the high-point of the policy, before it became blindingly evident that STALIN would act ruthlessly in pursuit of his own interests.

four-power agreement The regime under which military governments from the four victorious powers in World War II – America, the Soviet Union, Britain and France, continued to exert a degree of control over Berlin after the division of the former German capital between east and west, co-existing with the East and West Berlin civil authorities. Even after the building of the BERLIN WALL, troops from each power were not only responsible for a sector of the city but were able to travel in each other's zone. The Soviet war memorial, for instance, was in West Berlin, and Spandau Prison, where Rudolf HESS was held, remained under four-power control until his death in 1987. The four-power agreement was terminated in 1990 following the reunification of the city; **four plus two talks** involving the former allies and the east and west German authorities dismantled the old regime in the city and prepared the way for total German control.

four score and seven years ago The opening phrase of Abraham Lincoln's GETTYSBURG ADDRESS.

fourteen. Fourteenth Amendment The amendment to the US CONSTITUTION ratified in July 1868, over the objections of President Andrew Johnson, which guaranteed citizenship to Black Americans by stipulating that citizenship applied to every person born within its boundaries. The decision in the Dred SCOTT case that they could not become US citizens was thus repealed; an accompanying Civil Rights Act spelt out that citizen rights were possessed by everyone born in the US, "of every race and color, without reference to any previous condition of slavery or involuntary servitude".

fourteenth Mr. Wilson The riposte of Lord Home (*see* SIR ALEC) on taking office as Prime Minister in October 1963 to charges by Harold WILSON that "the whole process of democracy has ground to a halt with a Fourteenth Earl". Home replied:

> I suppose, if you come to think of it, Mr. Wilson is the forteenth Mr. Wilson.

fourth. Fourth Estate A phrase first coined by Edmund BURKE for the influential position of the Press in the British political community; the Estates (*see* THIRD ESTATE) were the representatives of the aristocracy, the Church and the Commons in the pre-Revolutionary French National assembly. According to Thomas Carlyle,

> Burke said that there were Three Estates in Parliament; but in the Reporters' GALLERY yonder, there sat a Fourth Estate, more important far than they all.

Fourth International The world body established by TROTSKY in the 1930s in an effort to unite all left-wing parties in an anti-Fascist POPULAR FRONT, which developed into the the representative body of world Trotskyism. The original aim failed because Soviet Communism through the Third International, alarmed at the rise of NAZISM, itself reached out to the democratic Left.

fourth man The suspected fourth Soviet agent involved in the defection of BURGESS AND MACLEAN, and in the espionage that had preceded it. The term came into use after Kim Philby was identified in 1963 as the THIRD MAN; it was another 17 years before Margaret Thatcher dramatically disclosed that there had indeed been a fourth man – Sir Anthony BLUNT.

Fourth Party The Conservative splinter group headed by Lord Randolph Churchill which from 1880 to 1885 conducted an aggressive and at times humiliating campaign against Sir Stafford Northcote for his lacklustre leadership of the party in the Commons. Churchill, Drummond Wolff, Sir John Gorst and at times the young Arthur BALFOUR, conducted their campaign from BELOW THE GANGWAY, being given particular ammunition by Northcote's vacillating handling of the BRADLAUGH CASE; Churchill was adamant that having refused to take the oath, Bradlaugh had no right to sit in the Commons. The Fourth Party's highly opportunistic campaigning got Churchill into SALISBURY's government, but did not finish Northcote.

Fourth Republic The French Republic established in 1946 in place of the provisional governments that had ruled since the LIBERATION and the collapse of VICHY. Essentially a continuation of the THIRD REPUBLIC (1870–1940), not least in the chaotic instability of its governments, it limped on until DE GAULLE returned in 1958 to establish the more stable FIFTH REPUBLIC.

Fox resignation The resignation of Francis Fox (1939–) as Canada's Solicitor-General in 1978 after a scandal involving his private life. It acquired a historic cachet because Fox's resignation speech to the House of Commons in Ottawa was the first such in a (largely) Anglophone legislature to be delivered live on television. His dignity and frankness earned him respect, and in 1980 Pierre TRUDEAU brought Fox back into the Government as Minister of Communications; he stayed in the Cabinet until the Liberals were defeated in 1984, then returned to private practice.

fox-shooting The destruction by a third party of an individual, policy or opportunity on which a political faction had hoped to capitalize. In the world of hunting, shooting the fox is the ultimate treason as it deprives the hunt of the thrill of the chase and, probably, the hounds of their prey. In a political sense it goes back at least to November 1947, when on Hugh Dalton's resignation over the BUDGET LEAK, the Conservative MP Nigel Birch observed:

> My God, they've shot our fox!

franc-tireurs (Fr. sharp-shooters or snipers) One of the elements in the French RESISTANCE during World War II, specifically a Communist grouping known as the *Franc-tireurs et Partisans*. In a political sense a *franc-tireur* is a lone operator who traps his or her opponents with deadly questions or interruptions.

Françaises, français The words with which President DE GAULLE prefaced his broadcasts to the French people, and which became his trademark. He usually accompanied them by opening his hands and holding them out, palms upwards.

France The focus of intensive pride among its fractious inhabitants, and a source of perpetual bafflement to the Anglo-Saxons. Despite its intense centralism, DIRIGISME and national pride, even an exasperated DE GAULLE once observed:

> No one can simply bring together a country that has 265 kinds of cheese.

Lamartine partly explained the constant ferment when he wrote: "France is revolutionary or she is nothing at all. The revolution of 1789 is her political religion." Sir Robert Peel, in a remark that would have seemed topical at almost any time in the century after he made it, asserted that "the modern history of France is the substitution of one crisis for another," and Metternich observed: "When France has a cold, all Europe sneezes." The British have always regarded the French with a mixture of bafflement, resentment and amusement; Churchill, after one of his many difficulties with de Gaulle, told MPs in 1942: "The Almighty in his infinite wisdom did not see fit to create Frenchmen in the image of Englishmen." And when legislation to decriminalize homosexual acts between consenting males was being debated, Viscount Montgomery of Alamein declared:

> This sort of thing may be tolerated by the French, but we are British, thank God.

> When discussing France's international policy, one should not imagine that its object is to react to events or to determine our position in relation to the actions of other powers. It pursues objectives of its own, France's objectives. President VALÉRY GISCARD d'ESTAING, 1980

France has lost the battle, but she has not lost the war DE GAULLE's assertion in 1940 as he issued his rallying-call from London for loyal Frenchmen to join the FREE FRENCH and fight on.

francization The programme for stamping out the use of the English language in Quebec, embarked on by the province's PQ government after its election victory in November 1976. Its cornerstone was BILL 101 which, among other things, required Anglophone businesses to establish their own francization programmes, going far beyond such simple but irritating steps as removing English-language signs. Francization drove some Anglophones out of Quebec, led others – and members of other ethnic groups who had opted to speak English – to use French more actively, but failed to produce a majority for SEPARATISM in the 1980 referendum.

franchise The right to VOTE in ELECTIONS, which has been steadily extended in most developed countries from a small elite of propertied men to the totality of the adult population of both sexes.

Franco, General Francisco *See* CAUDILLO.

Franco-Prussian war The brief but decisive conflict in 1870 when Napoleon III challenged the military machine built up by King Wilhelm I. France declared war; it ended in total Prussian victory, the end of the THIRD EMPIRE, the convulsion of the Paris COMMUNE and the creation of the German state under Wilhelm I, who took the title of Kaiser.

frank. frank exchange of views A polite DIPLOMATIC term for a serious disagreement at a meeting between leaders or emissaries.

to be perfectly frank and honest One of the phrases by which Harold WILSON is remembered, because of his frequent use of it in television interviews. Another was "as I said at the Blackpool CONFERENCE".

appalling frankness The phrase with which Stanley BALDWIN confessed to the Commons on 12 November 1936 that he had not advocated REARMAMENT earlier to meet the threat from NAZI Germany because such talk would have lost the Conservatives the 1935 General Election. *See* YEARS THE LOCUSTS HAVE EATEN.

franking privilege The right of members of the US CONGRESS to send out mail to CONSTITUENTS at the public expense. Its use was a scandal as early as 1869, with some Congressmen even posting all their dirty laundry home free of charge, and public opinion forced its abolition in 1873. However it was soon reintroduced – minus the worst excesses, though well-known politicians throughout the 20th century have been accused of abusing it. In 1983 the Supreme Court rejected a plea from COMMON CAUSE that the franking privilege was UNCONSTITUTIONAL because it favoured INCUMBENTS. Its use to mail political propaganda and raise funds has snowballed with the advent of DIRECT MAIL, around 4 million items being generated each working day by the 535 voting members of Congress. The annual bill exceeds $100 million; in 1984 one Senator, Pete Wilson of California, sent $3.8 million worth of free mail. The only limits on its use for ELECTIONEERING are that no mass mailing may be sent within 60 days of an election, and that the word "I" may not appear more than eight times on a page, which can also contain no more than two personal photos.

> A matter strictly between a member of Congress and his conscience. US Post Office spokesman, 1966.

Franklin The breakaway state created in 1784 by 10,000 frontiersmen in the WATAUGA territory as America's migrant population moved westwards. The area had been ceded by North Carolina to the infant Federal government to administer, and its inhabitants banded together to defend and govern themselves. After four years the territory was forcibly reincorporated into North Carolina. It was named in honour of the FOUNDING FATHER **Benjamin Franklin** (1706–90), the printer and inventor who from 1747 had been active in the movement that led to INDEPENDENCE. He was sent to England to protest at the taxing of the American colonies without their consent, was a signatory of the Declaration of Independence, secured French support for the new nation and from 1785 to 1787 was America's Minister in Paris, where he was known (mistakenly) as "*Le Bon Quacker*". He signed the Treaty of peace with Britain, presided over the infant state of Pennsylvania for three terms, and chaired the PHILADELPHIA CONVENTION which drafted the US Constitution. When he finally retired from politics in 1789, George WASHINGTON wrote to him:

> If to be venerated for benevolence, if to be admired for talents; if to be esteemed for patriotism; if to be beloved for philanthropy, can gratify the human mind, you must have the pleasing consolation that you have not lived in vain.

Franklin once reputedly remarked: "Where liberty is, there is my country"; the epitaph he wrote for himself read:

> The body of Benjamin Franklin, printer
> Like the cover of an old book
> Its contents worn out
> And stript of its leather and guilding
> Lies here food for the worms!
> Yet the work itself shall not be lost
> For it will, as he believed, appear once more
> In a new and more beautiful edition
> Corrected and amended
> By its Author.

> I succeed him; no-one could replace him. JEFFERSON.

> Antiquity would have raised altars to this mighty genius who, to the advantage of mankind, compassing in his mind the heavens and earth, was able to restrain alike thunderbolts and tyrants. MIRABEAU.

> Benjamin Franklin, incarnation of the peddling, tuppenny YANKEE. JEFFERSON DAVIS.

Franklin D. One of the many nicknames for Franklin D. Roosevelt (*see* FDR). In the late 1930s a small boy is supposed to have told his father that when he grew up he would like to be President; his father replied: "What about Franklin D.?"

Franks Report The findings of the inquiry set up under the diplomat and academic Lord Franks (1905–) by Margaret Thatcher to examine claims that her government had been caught unawares by the Argentine invasion of the FALKLANDS in 1982, and that the ensuing war had been avoidable. Franks and his committee of senior PRIVY COUNCILLORS concluded that though a hardening of Argentina's attitude in the three weeks prior to the invasion had not been recognized in London,

> We would not be justified in attaching any criticism or blame to the present Government for the Argentine JUNTA's decision to commit an act of unprovoked aggression.

The report noted that Lord Carrington, who resigned as Foreign Secretary after the invasion, had repeatedly urged the Defence Secretary, John Nott, in 1981–82 not to withdraw the ice patrol ship *Endurance*, lest the Argentines take it as a sign of British weakness; in the Commons James Callaghan had urged Mrs. Thatcher to countermand the order, which he termed an "error that could have serious consequences", but she refused, quoting Nott's view that "other claims on the defence budget should have greater priority".

> It itemises one unfortunate misjudgment after another, producing a catalogue of errors and missed opportunities which provide the raw material for a formidable indictment. But . . . it was a classic establishment job. It studiously recoiled from drawing the large conclusions implicit in its detailed findings. HUGO YOUNG, *One Of Us*.

fraternal delegate A DELEGATE who attends the CONFERENCE of one organization as the representative of another that is friendly to it. *Frater* is Latin for BROTHER; particularly in the Labour, Co-operative and trade union movement, it is customary for leaders of each to appear at the others' gatherings to deliver fraternal greetings. There is an apocryphal story of a trade union official in hospital receiving a letter from his branch extending fraternal greetings for a speedy recovery, and adding:

> The motion was carried by six votes to four with five ABSTENTIONS.

free. Free at last! Free at last! Thank God almighty – we are free at last! The words from a Negro spiritual with which Dr. Martin Luther KING closed his I HAVE A DREAM speech in Washington on 28 August 1963, and which appear as his epitaph in Atlanta's South View Cemetery.

Free Democrats Germany's LIBERAL party, founded after World War II, which has governed in coalition with, in turn, the CHRISTIAN DEMOCRATS and the SPD; in 1990 it won 79 seats in the first BUNDESTAG of reunited Germany with 11% of the vote, and continued its coalition with the CDU.

free elections The process promised by STALIN at YALTA for the countries of eastern Europe "liberated" from NAZI occupation, and which was either prevented by Soviet influence or speedily negated by a Communist takeover. Throughout the 1950s, free elections in Poland and its neighbours were insisted on by the West as a prerequisite for a post-war peace settlement.

free enterprise *See* ENTERPRISE.

Free French The movement founded by General DE GAULLE to continue the military struggle against Nazi Germany after the collapse of France in 1940. Later rechristened the **Fighting French**, its troops liberated Paris in 1944, but also found themselves fighting VICHY forces in the Middle East.

free market *See* MARKET.

Free Nelson Mandela *See* GRAFFITI.

free post The facility offered to every candidate in a UK Parliamentary election, with the Post Office making one free delivery to every household. Generally a candidate will send out his or her ELECTION ADDRESS by this means.

Free Silver The policy on which the POPULIST PARTY was launched to fight America's 1892 elections; it involved INFLATING the currency by the free and umlimited coinage of silver at a ratio of 16 oz. of silver to one ounce of gold. It also formed the basis four years later of the electrifying first campaign for the Presidency of William Jennings Bryan (*see* BOY ORATOR), who in the House in 1893 had advocated it as a panacea. The idea of breaking with the GOLD STANDARD by the coining of plentiful silver captivated the farmers and miners of the West and South, but made little impact on the industrial workers of the East and Midwest.

Free Soilers The faction who seceded from the 1848 Democratic Convention to form their own party to campaign against any Westward extension of slavery, which was a forerunner of America's REPUBLICAN PARTY. Their slogan was **Free Soil, Free Speech, Free Labor and Free Men**, what most of them wanted was not an end to slavery but land and opportunities for White pioneers from the Eastern states and the "oppressed and banished of other lands". They nominated former President Martin van Buren (*see* OLD KINDERHOOK) as their Presidential candidate, but won only 10% of the vote.

Free Staters In the Irish Civil War (1922–23), supporters of the Provisional GOVERNMENT of the IRISH FREE STATE set up under the Anglo-IRISH TREATY OF 1921. Led by Michael Collins (1890–1922), they were opposed by the Republicans under Eamonn de Valera (*see* DEV), who repudiated the treaty because it left NORTHERN IRELAND outside the Irish state and still demanded an OATH OF ALLEGIANCE to the British crown. Collins died in an ambush in 1922, but the severe measures taken by the Free State government forced the Republicans to abandon the armed struggle in 1923 – though the IRA was to resume operations later.

free trade A regime under which nations trade with each other unimpeded by TARIFFS and other barriers. It was traditionally the policy of Britain's LIBERAL PARTY. Between 1929 and 1931 the PRESS BARONS Lords Beaverbrook and Rothermere promoted an unsuccessful campaign for EMPIRE FREE TRADE. Free trade within its borders is one of the basics of the EUROPEAN COMMUNITY (*see also* EFTA; EUROPEAN ECONOMIC AREA). A free trade agreement between the United States and Canada took effect in 1989, and was extended to Mexico in 1992 to complete the North American Free Trade Area (NAFTA).

> The only policy which is technically sound and intellectually right. JOHN MAYNARD KEYNES.

free vote A vote in a legislature where the party WHIPS are off and members are free to vote as they please, or as their conscience dictates. At Wesminster free votes generally apply either to matters where there is no party view, or social or ethical questions such as abortion.

free world A COLD WAR term for the members of the ATLANTIC ALLIANCE ranged against the SOVIET UNION and its SATELLITES, and for the pro-Western countries that sided with it on world issues.

> The free world is not just a fortress. It is a promised land. ANTHONY EDEN, 1953.

freebie A trip, usually overseas, on which a legislator travels at someone else's expense, generally to encourage him or her to look favourably on the country in question, its government or its policies.

Freedmen's Bureau The Bureau of Refugees, Freedmen and Abandoned Lands created by the US Congress in March 1865 to provide the South's newly-EMANCIPATED former slaves with the basics of life and to protect their civil rights, and to care for former plantation land left abandoned. In February 1866 Congress passed a Bill giving the Bureau an indefinite life as part of its aggressive programme for RECONSTRUCTION; President Andrew Johnson attempted to VETO both this and a further Bill later that year extending the Bureau's powers. The Bureau eventually expired in 1872.

freeloader A politician with a reputation for accepting any form of free hospitality: food, drink or overseas trips. The word apparently originated during World War II and thus may be of military, rather than political, provenance.

freedom The aspiration of enslaved peoples and the stock-in-trade of democratic politicians and revolutionary leaders. Rousseau declared that "man was born free, and everywhere he is in chains", while Jean-Paul Sartre more gloomily asserted: "Man is condemned to be free." Abraham LINCOLN said of slavery: "Those who deny freedom to others deserve it not for themselves;" the ABOLITIONIST Frederick Douglass that "he who would be free must strike the first blow". To John F. KENNEDY "freedom is indivisible, and when one man is enslaved, all are not free"; Malcolm X militantly asserted: "Nobody can give you freedom. Nobody can give you equality or justice or anything. You just take it." Once gained, freedom has to be preserved; as Adlai Stevenson put it, "We inherited freedom. We seem unaware that freedom has to be remade and re-earned in each generation of man." Eisenhower, who defeated him for the Presidency, asserted that "only our individual faith in freedom has kept us free". But General Douglas MACARTHUR warned that "no man is entitled to the blessings of freedom unless he be vigilant in its preservation", and Kennedy added the caution that "if the self-discipline of the free cannot match the iron discipline of the mailed fist, the threat to freedom will continue to rise".

Adlai Stevenson asserted that "a free society is a society where it is safe to be unpopular", and dissent and freedom march hand in hand. MAHATMA Gandhi taught that freedom "is not worth having if it does not connote freedom to err", Rosa Luxemburg maintained that "freedom is always and exclusively freedom for the one who thinks differently", and, at the other end of the political spectrum, Charles Evans Hughes agreed, saying: "When we lose the right to be different, we lose the privilege to be free." With dissent comes tolerance, Richard Nixon cautioning: "We can maintain a free society only if we recognize that in a free society no one can win all the time." With freedom also comes law. G. D. H. Cole wrote that "man in society is not free where there is no law; he is most free where he co-operates best with his equals in the making of laws", and Lord SALISBURY maintained: "If one man imprisons you, that is tyranny; if two men, or a number of men imprison you that is freedom." The law should also prevent violations of freedom; PITT THE YOUNGER warned that "necessity is the plea for every infringement of human freedom. It is the argument of tyrants; it is the creed of slaves." Another obstacle – to the achievement of freedom – is sheer poverty. Adlai Stevenson maintained that "a hungry man is not a free man", Lord Boyd Orr that "if people have to choose between freedom and sandwiches, they they will take sandwiches".

> The English people imagine themselves to be free, but they are wrong. It is only during the election of members of Parliament that they are so.
>
> JEAN-JACQUES ROUSSEAU (1712–78), The SOCIAL CONTRACT.

> If we wish to be free . . . we must fight! I repeat it, Sir, we must fight! An appeal to arms and to the God of Hosts, is all that is left us.
>
> PATRICK HENRY to the Virginia Convention, 23 March 1775.

> He who dies for freedom dies not for his country alone but for the whole world.
>
> KHRISTO BOTEV, Bulgarian revolutionary (1848–76).

> The progress of freedom depends more upon the maintenance of peace, the spread of commerce, and the diffusion of education than upon the labours of Cabinets and Foreign Offices.
>
> RICHARD COBDEN, House of Commons, 26 June 1850.

> All the resources of a SUPERPOWER cannot isolate a man who hears the voice of freedom; a voice that I heard from the very chamber of my soul.
>
> NATHAN (Anatoly) SHCHARANSKY after his release from the GULAG, 11 May 1986.

freedom of assembly The right of individuals to meet and discuss whatever is of interest to them; in America it is guaranteed by the FIRST AMENDMENT.

freedom of association The right of individuals to form organizations, such as political parties and trade unions, to promote their mutual aims.

freedom of conscience or thought The right to believe what one chooses, without fear of punishment or persecution by the State. American liberals believe that McCARTHYISM was a direct challenge to this principle; Adlai Stevenson declared that "to strike freedom of the mind with the fist of patriotism is an old and ugly subtlety".

> Without freedom of thought there can be no such thing as wisdom, and no such thing as public liberty without freedom of speech. BENJAMIN FRANKLIN, 1722.

> It behoves every man who values liberty of conscience for himself, to resist invasions of it in the case of others.
>
> Thomas JEFFERSON, 1799.

> If there is any fixed star in our constitutional constellation, it is that no official, high or petty, can prescribe what shall be orthodox in politics, nationalism, religion or other matters of opinions, or force citizens to confess by word or act their faith therein.
>
> Justice ROBERT H. JACKSON, 1943.

Diversity of opinion is the essence of freedom.
LORD DEVLIN, *Report on The Press* (1967).

Freedom of Information Act The Act passed by the US Congress in 1974 over President Ford's VETO which gave citizens and the media access to a wide range of information held by the Government and documentation on how decisions were reached; an agency is obliged to reply within 14 days. The Act greatly increased the ACCOUNTABILITY of government and created a better-informed public, but most seismic journalism in Washington is still the result of LEAKS. In Britain there have been persistent efforts by backbench MPs to promote a Freedom of Information Act, the Liberal MP Clement Freud being foiled in 1979 by the fall of the Labour government after his Bill had passed initial hurdles in the Commons. Margaret Thatcher was strongly opposed, as for long were Whitehall MANDARINS who wanted to maintain Britain's traditional culture of secrecy (*see* OFFICIAL SECRETS ACT). A Freedom of Information Act is now Labour Party policy, and John MAJOR has considerably relaxed restrictions on making information available to the public.

I question very seriously whether a secret intelligence agency and the Freedom of Information Act can co-exist for very long. CIA Director WILLIAM J. CASEY, 1982.

Information, free from interest or prejudice, free from the vanity of the writer or the influence of the Government, is as necessary to the human mind as pure air and water to the human body.
WILLIAM REES-MOGG, 1970.

freedom of the press The right of the media to publish news and comment without fear of suppression or prosecution. Again this is protected in America by the FIRST AMENDMENT (*see* CONGRESS SHALL MAKE NO LAW); in Britain the laws on libel and contempt have exerted some kind of restraining influence, but the Calcutt Report in 1993 proposed stiff penalties for invading the privacy of individuals. *See also* POWER WITHOUT RESPONSIBILITY; The PRICE OF PETROL HAS GONE UP BY A PENNY.

Our liberty depends on the freedom of the press, and that cannot be limited without being lost.
Thomas JEFFERSON.

Freedom to publish means freedom for all and not for some. Justice HUGO BLACK (1886–1971).

Reading about one's failings in the daily papers is one of the privileges of high office in this free country of ours.
Govenor NELSON ROCKEFELLER, 29 November 1972.

The liberty of the press is the Palladium of all the civil, political and religious rights of an Englishman.
The anonymous pamphleteer JUNIUS (*fl.* 1769–72).

The press is easier squashed than squared. CHURCHILL.

freedom of speech The right of individuals to say what they think without fear of prosecution or victimization. The right is enshrined in the FIRST AMENDMENT and in the Common Law of England, but there is perpetual argument over the point at which freedom becomes licence. Oliver Wendell Holmes considered that "the most stringent protection of free speech would not protect a man in falsely shouting 'fire' in a theatre and causing a panic". To this end most democratic countries have legislation making it an offence to utter blasphemy or obscenities, or to stir up racial hatred. As Adlai Stevenson put it,

Every man has the right to be heard, but no man has the right to strangle democracy with a single set of vocal chords.

My people and I have come to an agreement that satisfies us both. They are to say what they please, and I am to do what I please.
FREDERICK THE GREAT (1712–86).

Without free speech the search for truth becomes impossible. CHARLES BRADLAUGH (*attr.*).

I realize that, in speaking to you this afternoon, there are certain limitations placed upon the right of free speech. I must be exceedingly careful, prudent, as to what I say, and even more careful and prudent as to how I say it. I may not be able to say all I think, but I am not going to say anything I do not think.
The anti-war speech delivered by EUGENE DEBS (CONVICT #2273) to the Socialist Party of Ohio on 6 June 1918 which earned him a 10-year prison sentence, commuted by President HARDING in 1921.

Freedom of speech is the greatest safety, because if a man is a fool, the best thing to do is encourage him to advertise the fact by speaking.
WOODROW WILSON, 1919.

The right to be heard does not automatically include the right to be taken seriously.
Sen. HUBERT HUMPHREY.

freedom fighters A term used by fighters for national independence, regarded by themselves as PATRIOTS, by those not involved as GUERRILLAS and by their foes as TERRORISTS.

Freedom Riders Young members of CORE, Black and White, who in 1961–62 travelled by bus through America's Deep South, defying SEGREGATION in bus stations and other public facilities. The first ride, which left Washington for New Orleans on 4 May 1961, ended in the burning of a bus in Annniston, Alabama, a riot in MONTGOMERY and the riders' arrest in Jackson, Mississippi. Drivers refused to take them further and they finished their journey by plane. Subsequent Freedom Rides led to scores of riders being jailed for alleged breaches of the law; in Montgomery that December, 737 marchers protesting at the prosecution of 11 Freedom Riders were arrested. By then the Interstate Commerce Commission had banned segregation on buses and in terminals.

freedom under the rule of law The basic philosophy of Margaret Thatcher (*see* IRON LADY) which she repeatedly articulated as

Prime Minister both as an aim for the oppressed peoples of the world, and the main theme of her policies at home.

Four Freedoms *See* ROOSEVELT.

Freemason's apron One of the most intriguing aspects of the PROFUMO AFFAIR was the rumour of an orgy attended by many celebrities at which a man presided, dressed only in a Freemason's apron. The identity of the man was never established beyond a doubt, but one Cabinet minister had to submit to bodily examination before being cleared of involvement.

freeze. nuclear freeze The idea that both SUPERPOWERS should halt the increase in their nuclear weaponry, first put forward by the Republican Sen. Mark Hatfield as an amendment to the SALT II treaty in 1979. It prompted a mass movement in America that was echoed in Europe; President Reagan, who opposed a freeze, claimed three years later that the author of the freeze was Leonid Brezhnev.

wage or price freeze The halting of wage or price increases, or both, in order to curb inflation. Such freezes have occasionally been tried, both in Britain (before Margaret Thatcher came to power) and in America (by the Nixon administration). They have been successful in the short term, but have bottled up inflationary pressures and industrial unrest.

Freikorps A post-World War I manifestation of German MILITARISM and right-wing thuggery. First appearing in December 1918, after Germany's defeat, and consisting of ex-soldiers (officers and men), unemployed youths and others, by 1919 there were some 65 groups throughout Germany. The Government used them to beat up left-wing agitators; once they had acquired a taste for such bullying violence, they soon chose their targets for plundering and vandalism. Ernst Röhm, a *Freikorps* commander, became head of the BROWNSHIRTS, and many of the groups were later absorbed by the NAZI party. *See also* KAPP PUTSCH.

FRELIMO (Port. Front for the Liberation of Mozambique) The MARXIST independence movement and subsequent governing party founded in 1962 by Eduardo Mondlane (1920–69). It fought a ten-year war (1964–74) against Portuguese rule, which succeeded after a leftist military COUP against the right-wing Lisbon government; a counter-coup by Whites in Mozambique failed. Portugal's African colonies were granted independence in June 1975 and Samora Machel (1930–86), who had become FRELIMO's leader when Mondlane was assassinated in 1969, became Mozambique's first President. FRELIMO in power gradually modified its Marxist line, but was subjected to an increasingly vicious guerrilla campaign by a new enemy, RENAMO.

French British politicians have always spoken French at their peril; CHURCHILL was aware of this, once warning a delighted audience in Strasbourg's town square:

> *Prenez garde! Je vais parler Français.*
> [Beware – I am going to speak French.]

Churchill's use of French was picturesque. He once told DE GAULLE: *"Markez mes mots. Si vous me doublecrosserez, je vous liquidaterai."* And when, intending to tell radio listeners in Occupied France that his past had been divided into two, he reputedly said: *"Mon derrière est divisé en deux parties"*. [My bottom is divided into two parts.]

Neville CHAMBERLAIN's wife made an equally unfortunate GAFFE. Declining a dinner invitation from the French Ambassador, she said: *"Mon mari est toujours occupé dans le Cabinet avec beaucoup, beaucoup de papier"* [My husband is always stuck in the lavatory with lots and lots of paper.]

By comparison, Edward Heath's French grammar and vocabulary were sound, but his excruciating vowels did the ENTENTE no service. *See also* SIMULTANEOUS TRANSLATION.

French Community An association of former French COLONIES formed in 1958 by the constitution of the FIFTH REPUBLIC, when DE GAULLE was called back to become President of France. It replaced the former French Union, which was itself the replacement of the French Colonial Empire, and was supposed to maintain cultural and economic uniformity; by 1970 it had all but ceased to exist.

French Revolution The turbulent and at times bloody upheavals that began with the Tennis Court OATH and the fall of the BASTILLE in 1789, followed in 1793 by the execution of Louis XVI and Marie Antoinette. PITT THE YOUNGER described the King's execution as "the foulest and most atrocious deed the world has yet had occasion to attest"; Burke said of the Queen's:

> I thought ten thousand swords must have leaped from their scabbards to avenge even a look that threatened her with insult. But the age of chivalry is gone.

Robespierre asserted that "the government of the Revolution is the despotism of liberty against tyranny", and embarked on the Reign of TERROR when the Revolution, in Vergniaud's words, devoured its children. The revolutionary fires subsided in the DIRECTORY, before Napoleon declared himself

First Consul and subsequently Emperor. The Revolution aroused terror among England's ruling class and conservatives in Parliament, though Charles James Fox hailed it as "the most stupendous and glorious edifice of liberty which has been erected on the foundations of human integrity in any time or country", and Wordsworth wrote:

> Bliss it was in that dawn to be alive,
> But to be young was very heaven.

It was seen in America as an echo of that country's own recent and successful struggle for its INDEPENDENCE. Its ideals were founded on Thomas Paine's RIGHTS OF MAN, and while many of its innovations did not survive, little of the old order it destroyed was ever reinstated, giving Napoleon a *tabula rasa* on which to construct new systems of law and measurement.

> A clap of thunder for the wicked.
>
> LOUIS DE SAINT-JUST (1767–94).

> Merely the herald of a far greater and much more solemn revolution, which will be the last . . . The hour has come for the founding of the Republic of Equals – that great refuge open to every man.
>
> FRANÇOIS-ÉMILE BABEUF (1760–97).

> It was the best of times, it was the worst of times, it was the age of wisdom, it was the age of foolishness, it was the epoch of belief, it was the epoch of incredulity, it was the season of Light, it was the season of Darkness, it was the spring of hope, it was the winter of despair; we had everything before us, we had nothing before us, we were all going direct to Heaven, we were all going direct the other way . . .
>
> CHARLES DICKENS, *A Tale of Two Cities*.

> The PENDULUM swung furiously to the left because it had been drawn too far to the right.
>
> THOMAS BABINGTON MACAULAY.

freshman A Washington term for a newly-elected member of Congress. George WASHINGTON advised newcomers: "Speak seldom, but to important subjects . . . make yourself perfectly master of the subject. Never exceed a decent warmth, and submit your sentiments with diffidence." Speaker Champ Clark reckoned that "a new Congressman must start at the bottom and spell up", and Speaker Sam Rayburn told newcomers:

> Learn your job. Don't even talk until you know what you're talking about. If you want to get along, go along.

Friedmanism The MONETARIST doctrine developed and promoted by the US economist Milton Friedman (*see* CHICAGO SCHOOL) which contradicted KEYNESIANISM and encouraged a free-MARKET economy. Friedmanism was influential in the birth of THATCHERISM, determining UK government policy in the IRON LADY'S early years of power.

friends Often a greater danger to a politician than ENEMIES. The British politician George Canning wrote in the early 19th century: "Save, oh save me from the candid friend"; Gladstone exclaimed: "Standing up to one's enemies is admirable, but give me the man who can stand up to his friends." President HARDING confided as the TEAPOT DOME scandal broke: "My friends – they're the ones that keep me walking the floors at nights", and Alva Johnson said of New York's Mayor La Guardia: "Anyone who extends to him the right hand of friendship is in danger of losing a couple of fingers." And in Ireland Charles HAUGHEY's press secretary P. J. Mara reflected that "sometimes you have to sacrifice your friends to placate your enemies".

my good friend In the US SENATE, the customary way of referring to a Senator of the same party.

my honourable friend The way one member of the House of Commons refers to another from the same party; a PRIVY COUNCILLOR is referred to as "my Right Honourable friend", and a Queen's Counsel (senior barrister) as "my (Right) Honourable and learned friend".

Friends of the Earth An environmental pressure group in Britain, uncompromising but less militant than GREENPEACE, which campaigns for recycling and the use of renewable forms of energy, and against waste and the destruction of the natural habitat.

fringe. fringe meeting During the UK CONFERENCE SEASON, a meeting held close to the conference hall by a faction of the party or outside pressure group. The aim is to attract participants in the conference, and if possible attention from the media.

lunatic fringe A graphic expression for EXTREMIST members of an otherwise moderate and sane organization or community who express in outrageous fashion views that are a caricature of those held by the majority. It was coined by Theodore Roosevelt, who wrote in 1913 of the PROGRESSIVE Party:

> There is apt to be a lunatic fringe among the votaries of any forward movement.

from each according to his ability, to each according to his needs A slogan that has become one of the axioms of 20th-century Socialism, which was used by Karl MARX in his *Critique of the Gotha Programme* (1875). He wrote:

> Only in a higher phase of communist society . . . can the narrow horizon of bourgeois right be crossed in its entirety, and society inscribe on its banners: "From each according to his ability, to each according to his needs!"

Marx did not originate the phrase. Five years before, 47 ANARCHISTS tried at Lyon after the failure of their uprising signed a declaration written by Michael Bakunin (1814–76) which stated:

> We wish, in a word, equality – equality in fact as corollary, or rather, as a primordial condition of liberty. From each according to his faculties, to each according to his needs; that is what we wish sincerely and energetically.

Fronde A political party that flourished in France *c.* 1648–53 in opposition to Cardinal Mazarin and his court party, during the minority of King Louis XIV. Its members were called *Frondeurs* (*fronde*, a sling) because they were compared to urchins who throw stones in the street and run away when anyone in authority appears.

front. front line states The Black-ruled states in southern Africa, notably Zambia and Tanzania, whose leaders maintained pressure on Britain from 1965 to 1980 for action to end Rhodesia's UDI. Through the COMMONWEALTH and the OAU, they mobilized international opposition to Ian Smith's regime through the maintenance of SANCTIONS, and also gave backing to the GUERRILLA groups whose leaders eventually gained power by democratic means after the LANCASTER HOUSE AGREEMENT.

front-loading In Washington, particularly in the PENTAGON, the budgetary tactic of pressing for a large increase in funding for the coming year, by promising to take less later. Regardless of whether the promise is kept, the effect of such funds being granted is that capital projects can be begun which should prove impossible to halt.

front organization A political movement which appears to be independent but is in fact directed by, and acting on behalf of, another. For instance the WORLD PEACE COUNCIL was not a purely PACIFIST movement, but an instrument of Soviet Communism.

front porch campaign A campaign in which the candidate stays at home and selected groups of voters are brought to him, instead of his making extensive travels. The technique was pioneered by "BOATMAN JIM" Garfield in 1880 and perfected in 1888 by Benjamin Harrison (*see* WHITE HOUSE ICEBERG), who ousted President Cleveland by staying at home in Indianapolis and receiving thousands of visitors, to whom he made short speeches on the TARIFF; Harrison's campaigning style cannot have been decisive, as Cleveland (*see* BEAST OF BUFFALO) refused to go on the stump either, sending his 75-year-old RUNNING-MATE Allen Thurman to tour the country instead. McKINLEY in 1896 and 1900 also won election through a front-porch campaign, but after that the BARNSTORMING of Theodore Roosevelt changed the nature of US electioneering for good. *See also* ROSE GARDEN STRATEGY.

front-runner The candidate in an election who is estimated by the OPINION POLLS and political PUNDITS to be ahead at a given moment.

Frost. Frost interviews The first major interviews given by ex-President Nixon (*see* TRICKY DICK) after the disgrace of WATERGATE. They were conducted by the UK broadcaster David Frost (*see* THAT WAS THE WEEK THAT WAS) in 1977 at Nixon's SAN CLEMENTE compound in California, and transmitted by Metromedia television. The first, dealing with Watergate, attracted a massive audience; subsequent programmes covering foreign policy and other aspects of the Nixon administration achieved much lower ratings. *See* I GAVE THEM A SWORD.

FTPO For the President Only. The daily intelligence bulletin circulated in Washington containing such sensitive information that fewer than 20 people apart from the President are permitted to see it on a need-to-know basis. Senior Administration officials sometimes have to read through a numbered copy of the four- or five-page document with an armed guard standing by to collect it.

Fuchs case One of the most serious breaches of Western nuclear security prior to and at the start of the COLD WAR. It concerned Klaus Fuchs (1911–88), a German-born British physicist (known by the UK authorities to be a Communist) who worked on the ATOMIC BOMB during World War II in both the UK and America – and from 1943 passed details of the research to Soviet agents. In 1950 after the defection of a Soviet cipher clerk in Ottawa exposed him and implicated several other spies, Fuchs, who saw himself as an idealist, was arrested, confessed to espionage and was sentenced to 14 years' imprisonment. He was released in 1959 and emigrated to East Germany, resuming his research and remaining there until his death. *See also* ROSENBERGS.

fuck The ultimate UNPARLIAMENTARY word, which has nevertheless been heard in debate in both Houses at Westminster, though not – as far as the PARLIAMENTARIAN of the House of Representatives is aware – in the US Congress. It was apparently first uttered on 15 November 1783 in the HOUSE OF LORDS by the Earl of Sandwich, who was mischievously quoting the rhyme

> . . . life can little more supply
> Than just a few good fucks and then we die.

from the *Essay on Woman*, attributed to John WILKES but probably written by his friend Thomas Potter. Though some peers cried: "Go on! Go on!", the majority were scandalized and the House resolved to prosecute Wilkes for "a most scandalous, obscene and impious libel". Sandwich had not forgiven Wilkes for smuggling a baboon dressed as the Devil into a Black Mass celebrated by the Hell Fire Club, where it jumped on the Earl's back, giving him the fright of his life.

The first recorded use of the word in the House of Commons came on 3 February 1982 in a debate on the harmless-sounding Local Government (Miscellaneous Provisions) Bill when the left-wing Labour MP Reg Race informed members that in a sex shop in his constituency, there was a list of prostitutes with the message:

> Phone them and fuck them!

The deputy Speaker called Race to order, but passed no comment; the next day Speaker George Thomas (Lord TONYPANDY) said the word would be Unparliamentary as long as he was Speaker, adding: "None of us would use it in our homes." He also privately rebuked the Editor of HANSARD, who had printed the word as "f . . .", for letting even this hint of obscenity appear. Ironically, the only other known use of the word came in 1988, when a radio microphone picked it up in an aside from an exasperated Speaker Bernard Weatherill. On the margins of a Commons committee debating charges for dental examinations, the Government whip David Lightbown had two short, sharp words for the Tory backbencher Jerry Hayes for pointing out that Mrs. Thatcher had committed the party not to introduce them. Asked what the words were, Hayes said:

> We had a conversation about sex and travel.

Once in the late 1970s, the Canadian Prime Minister Pierre TRUDEAU was accused by furious Tories of uttering the "F-word" during heated exchanges in the House of Commons. Trudeau insisted he had actually said: "Fuddle-duddle!"

fudge An unsatisfactory solution to a problem that in fact solves nothing, cobbled together as an uneasy compromise to avoid facing up to reality. This use of the word is said – implausibly – to originate with a Captain Fudge, who in the 17th century always brought back to England a "cargo of lies" about the reason for his ship's poor condition. Fudge's existence is proved by a letter dating from 1664, but the rest of the story is not.

fudge and mudge Dr. David OWEN's phrase for the inability of the LABOUR PARTY to stand up to the wrecking tactics of its extreme Left, frustration with which led the GANG OF FOUR to quit the party early in 1981 and found the SDP. Dr. Owen said at the party's Blackpool conference in October 1980:

> We are fed up with fudging and mudging, with mush and slush.

Fudge factory A derogatory term for the US STATE DEPARTMENT used by those who consider it a temple of APPEASEMENT and compromise.

fuel crisis The desperate shortage of energy in Britain early in 1947 caused by a combination of bitterly cold weather for months on end which immobilized coal stocks, and soaring demand which put strain on a power network debilitated by war and lack of investment. With the need for heat at its greatest, savage power cuts had to be imposed, families shivered in their homes, thousands of workers were laid off as industrial production halted; Emmanuel Shinwell (*see* MANNY), Minister of Fuel and Power in the ATTLEE government, was widely criticized. Ministers had known since the previous November that a severe winter might prove disastrous, and Hugh GAITSKELL had voiced the fear that "as an administrator, Shinwell is hardly a starter". The Conservatives seized their opportunity with the slogan:

> Starve with Strachey. Shiver with Shinwell.

John Strachey was Minister of Food, and was in charge of the equally austere rationing programme.

Führer (Ger. leader) The title – "Führer of the People" – adopted by **Adolf Hitler** (1889–1945) on the death of President von Hindenburg in August 1934, when he finally assumed total power and declared the Third REICH. It was also held briefly after Hitler's suicide on 30 April 1945 by Grand Admiral Karl Dönitz, who presided over Germany's final surrender. The title reflected the almost mystical supremacy over and leadership of the German people that Hitler regarded as his destiny, which galvanized a country whose morale had been shattered by war and internal division and led to its Wagnerian nemesis as the Russians advanced on his BUNKER in a devastated Berlin. Hitler himself had said: "I go to the way that providence dictates with the assurance of a sleepwalker", "I am convinced nothing will happen to me, for I know the greatness for which Providence has chosen me", and "I know of no statesman in the world today who with greater right than I can say that he is the representative of his people". The Austrian-born housepainter's belief in his destiny developed at the end of World War I, in which he won two Iron Crosses with the Bavarian Army and was temporarily blinded in a gas attack. Already steeped in the ANTI-SEMITIC culture of Vienna, he became convinced that Germany had not been militarily defeated, but had been betrayed by its leaders, and joined the fiercely anti-Bolshevik German Workers' Party as its seventh member. In 1921 he ousted the Munich locksmith Anton Dexter as leader of what was now the NATIONAL SOCIALIST German Workers' party (NSDAP), and began his hypnotic campaign against Marxism and the Treaty of VERSAILLES. After the failure of the MUNICH BEER HALL PUTSCH in 1923, he was imprisoned for nine months with Rudolf HESS, using the time to dictate the text of MEIN KAMPF, the book that presaged uncannily the policies he was eventually to follow. On his release he began cultivating German industrialists, who backed him as a bulwark against Marxist revolution, and in 1926, as the NAZIS' violent confrontations with Communists increased, he formed the SS (*Schutzstaffel*) as his personal force. Hitler's support increased rapidly with the onset of the GREAT DEPRESSION, and with the Nazis close to a majority in the REICHSTAG he mounted a campaign for the Presidency in 1932 in which he polled strongly against Hindenburg. Of his campaigning technique he was to write:

> I learned the use of terror from the Communists, of slogans from the Catholic church, and the use of PROPAGANDA from the democracies.

By now the WEIMAR REPUBLIC was floundering, not least because of Nazi DESTABILIZATION, and in January 1933 Hindenburg – who privately referred to him as "that Bohemian corporal" – finally appointed him CHANCELLOR. The REICHSTAG Fire gave him the pretext to suppress all other political parties, and in June 1934 he eliminated his rivals within the movement including his veteran colleague Ernst Röhm in the NIGHT OF THE LONG KNIVES.

As *Führer* he set in motion a programme of rapid rearmament and systematic violations of Versailles. When his REMILITARIZATION of the Rhineland in 1936 proved to him that Britain and France would not baulk him, he began the systematic persecution of political opponents and Jews that would lead to the HOLOCAUST, and started an aggressive programme of territorial expansion. This began with the ANSCHLUSS with Austria in March 1938 and the steady annexation of Czechoslovakia, starting notoriously with the MUNICH AGREEMENT that September. The stop-go nature of Hitler's advance in the face of APPEASEMENT lulled many abroad into a false sense of security; Beverly Nichols wrote:

> Herr Hitler has one of the endearing characteristics of Ferdinand the Bull. Just when the crowd expects him to be most violent, he stops and smells the flowers.

Sir John Simon, after meeting the *Führer*, concluded:

> If Joan of Arc had been born in Austria and had borne a moustache, she might have conveyed much the same impression.

Lloyd George, also briefly captivated by him, had declared: "I don't think Hitler is a fool; he is not going to challenge the British Empire," but he and others changed their tune as the threat became obvious. Hitler alarmed the West by forming the PACT OF STEEL with Italy, though Alan Bullock was to write: "He showed surprising loyalty to Mussolini, but it never extended to trusting him." He also provided decisive help to the Nationalists in the SPANISH CIVIL WAR, though when he eventually met General Franco (who was to keep out of World War II), he said: "Rather than go through that again, I would prefer to have three or four of my teeth yanked out." In August 1939 he concluded the HITLER-STALIN PACT (also known as the Nazi-Soviet and Ribbentrop-Molotov Pact) to pre-empt Russia from joining forces against him with Britain and France, and within ten days invaded Poland, triggering World War II. The exiled former Kaiser Wilhelm II warned:

> The machine is running away with him as it ran away with me.

His initial successes were devastating: Poland overcome in days, Norway the following spring, and then the BLITZKRIEG that rolled up the Low Countries and France and brought German troops to the English Channel. CHURCHILL, who denounced Hitler as "that bloodthirsty guttersnipe", and "Herr SCHICKLGRUBER", became Prime Minister, and a personal duel to the death began. Thwarted in his invasion plans by the *Luftwaffe*'s failure to win the Battle of Britain, he resorted to the bombing of British cities, and the following spring turned eastward to take Yugoslavia and Greece after a botched Italian invasion before launching his offensive against Russia. By the end of the year he was at the gates of Moscow and Leningrad, and for the next two years was in sight of toppling STALIN, but the line held and eventually the RED ARMY began moving remorselessly west as the German forces took huge casualties. With the turn of the tide, Hitler's insane genius as a gambler turned against him, as did those generals who had never been comfortable with Nazi ideology and the atrocities they knew the regime was committing; up to then they had always been subdued by success and by Hitler's towering rages when anyone ventured to disagree. On 20 July 1944 the STAUFFENBERG PLOT came within an ace of killing him; badly shaken, he reacted with bloody retribution (*see* PEOPLE'S COURTS). Always dependent on drugs, his need increased as defeat drew near, and at the end he gathered his entourage around him in the bunker, married his lover Eva Braun, helped her take poison and then shot himself; their bodies were burned in the yard of the CHANCELLERY. Instead of a Reich to last a thousand years, Hitler left behind a Germany shattered by war which was to be divided by its conquerors, the Bolsheviks he had fought so passionately rampant in eastern Europe, and the stain of the greatest campaign of GENOCIDE the world has ever seen.

> I believe that I am acting in accordance with the will of he Almighty Creator – by defending myself against the Jew, I am fighting for the work of the Lord.
>
> HITLER, *Mein Kampf.*

> I could not bear it if I ever had to despair of this man. This man has everything needed to be king.
>
> JOSEF GOEBBELS, *Diaries*

> If Hitler had put his energies into promoting nuclear physics instead of persecuting the Jews, the first atomic bomb could well have exploded over London instead of Hiroshima. DAVID IRVING, *The Virus House.*

> The people Hitler never understood, amd whose actions continued to exasperate him to the end of his life, were the British.
>
> ALAN BULLOCK, *Hitler: A Study in Tyranny.*

full. full dinner pail One of the slogans which delivered the Presidency to William McKINLEY, Governor of Ohio, in his 1896 contest with William Jennings Bryan. It emphasized the prosperity that returned to the US economy as the campaign unfolded, blunting Bryan's POPULIST challenge. The Republicans used the message "McKinley and the full dinner pail!" again in 1900 to secure his re-election. It was revived in the 1928 campaign by Herbert HOOVER, who went a stage further to claim:

> The slogan of progress is changing from the full dinner pail to the full garage.

full employment A situation in which a job is available for everybody seeking work, which is the ideal for almost all political parties in Western democracies, though only those on the Left regard it as achievable. In the 1950s, unemployment reached record lows throughout the West and it seemed that a political consensus on the maintenance of something close to full employment had been attained. In the late 1970s the US labour movement institutionalized the aim in the HUMPHREY-HAWKINS FULL EMPLOYMENT ACT, and Britain's LABOUR PARTY still holds it out as a goal that must be worked for even if it cannot be wholly achieved.

full faith and credit clause Article IV, section 1 of the US CONSTITUTION, designed to prevent anyone "beating the law" by moving out of a state before a court action can be brought against him or her, and which also guarantees the validity of a marriage anywhere in the Union. It stipulates that

> Full faith and credit shall be given in each State to the public acts, records and judicial proceedings of every other state.

Fulton report The report of the committee on reforming the culture of WHITEHALL set up by Harold WILSON in February 1966 under Lord Fulton, Vice-Chancellor of Sussex University; its terms of reference were to "examine the structure, recruitment and management, including training, of the Home Civil Service" and make recommendations. Fulton reported in June 1968 that the Civil Service was a 19th-century organization facing 20th-century problems, in which the cult of the all-rounder or gifted amateur led to specialist experts being ignored. He proposed a Civil Service Department under the Prime Minister, a Civil Service College, greater emphasis on career management, the hiving off of some functions to other bodies and a lessening of secrecy. Many, but not all, of the proposals were implemented, but Fulton did not bring as much of a revolution as had been intended. This has led to a what Peter Hennessy termed a "debate of almost theological poportions" about what and how much had gone wrong, and whether Fulton had been sold short by conservative Whitehall MANDARINS or lack of vision within the Labour government of the day.

Fulton speech The speech made by Winston CHURCHILL at Fulton, Missouri, on 5 March 1946 in which he warned that an IRON CURTAIN was descending across Europe "from Stettin on the Baltic to Trieste on the Adriatic". For convenience's sake, many historians have marked this speech, delivered in the presence of President Truman who had read it beforehand, as the start of the COLD WAR.

fund-raiser On both sides of the Atlantic, a person who raises money for political parties, candidates and campaigns; in America also, a dinner or other event staged to raise funds for a political object (*see also* RUBBER CHICKEN CIRCUIT). In parts of the country still controlled by a political machine, municipal employees are expected to spend hundreds of dollars a plate to attend such functions, in gratitude for the PATRONAGE shown to them. The most expensive fund-raisers can cost thousands of dollars to attend; John F.

KENNEDY told one such gathering in Denver in 1960:

> I am grateful to you all. I could say I am deeply touched, but not as deeply touched as you have been in coming to this dinner.

future. the future is . . . black The assertion of the Black US author James Baldwin (*see The* FIRE NEXT TIME), made in August 1963 on the eve of Dr. Martin Luther KING's I HAVE A DREAM speech in Washington.

I have seen the future, and it works The eventually notorious comment made after a visit to BOLSHEVIK Russia in 1919 by the US journalist and reformer Lincoln Steffens (1866–1936); originally he told the financier Bernard Baruch: "I have been over into the future, and it works." William Bullitt, a diplomat who travelled with him, claimed Steffens had been rehearsing the phrase even before he got to Moscow to meet LENIN.

Let us face the future The slogan under which Clement ATTLEE led Britain's LABOUR PARTY to a LANDSLIDE election victory over CHURCHILL's Conservatives in July 1945.

the only limit to our realization of tomorrow will be our doubts of today The key phrase of the last speech drafted by Franklin D. Roosevelt. He drafted it at WARM SPRINGS in early August 1945 for the forthcoming conference to organize the UNITED NATIONS, but died with it undelivered.

Your future is in your hands The campaign slogan of Churchill's CONSERVATIVES in Britain's 1950 General Election, when they trimmed Labour's majority from 146 to 5, making an early second election and a Tory return to power almost inevitable.

G

G7 Group of Seven. The West's leading industrial nations – America, the UK, Germany, Japan, France, Canada and Italy – whose leaders have met for an economic SUMMIT each year since 1976. Their meetings have become steadily more political, and since 1991 when Mikhail Gorbachev attended an extra session, they have also been a bridge to the East. The **G6** is the same collection of countries, minus Italy, who concluded the LOUVRE ACCORD in 1987.

gadfly A questioner, persistent to the point of irritation; often a maverick politician repeatedly probing on a single issue and with a cutting edge to his or her questions. The origin is the insect of that name, from the O.E. *gad*: a goad.

Gadsden purchase The agreement of 1853 under which the United States bought a strip of what is now southern Arizona from Mexico for $10 million. It was negotiated by James Gadsden on behalf of President Pierce. The land was required so that a transcontinental railroad serving the southern states could be constructed on US territory throughout.

gaffe An unfortunate statement bringing ridicule on the person making it. Some are harmlessly amusing, others are capable of endangering or even ending a political career. (The origin of the word is French.) There are plenty of celebrated examples, and some that deserve wider exposure. At Westminster, Harold WILSON referred to the then Australian Prime Minister, in his presence, as "Mr. Whit Goughlam". The veteran Tory woman MP Dame Irene Ward once asked a Minister who announced that sailors would get new uniforms ahead of female personnel: "How long is he going to hold up the skirts of the Wrens for the convenience of the sailors?" The Conservative MP Geoffrey Dickens, at the height of media exposure of his private life, brought proceedings to a standstill by declaring: "Mr. Speaker, I seek to do a favour for every woman in the United Kingdom"; Nicholas Ridley's career as Transport Secretary nearly came to an end when, after the 1987 Zeebrugge ferry disaster, he said of the environment minister William Waldegrave: "He is navigating with his bow doors closed." The Tory MP Tim Janman got off on the wrong foot when he celebrated his election by loudspeakering to cows in a field: "I should like to thank the cows of Bowers Gifford for voting Conservative"; he was unaware that a number of female electors were within earshot. And John Wakeham, answering questions as Leader of the House, raised a boffo in the Commons by saying of Mrs. Thatcher:

> The Prime Minister is making herself available to President Gorbachev.

The best-known gaffe in American politics is apocryphal – of the out-of-town politician campaigning in New York City who asked: "Where are the Bronx?" In the 1960 Presidential campaign Richard Nixon appeared to insult his wife by saying in his DEBATE with John F. KENNEDY: "They can't stand pat." In 1976 Earl F. Butz, Gerald Ford's Agriculture secretary, was forced to resign after admitting saying of Black Americans: "All they want is loose shoes, a tight pussy and a warm place to shit." FORD himself dropped a terminal gaffe debating that year with Jimmy CARTER, when he insisted: "There is no Soviet domination of eastern Europe – and there never will be under a Ford administration." And Ford's campaign manager Rogers Morton torpedoed the Republican effort by declaring: "There is no point in rearranging the furniture on the deck of the *Titanic*." At the 1980 Democratic Convention it was Carter's turn, delivering a reverent tribute to a great American whom he named "Hubert Horatio Hornblower". In 1983 James Watt, Secretary of the Interior in the Reagan administration, made his position untenable by confiding that he had formed an advisory group comprising "a Black, a woman, two Jews and a cripple – and we have talent". In an inadvertently sexist gaffe the following year, Ed Rollins, Reagan campaign chief, described Walter Mondale's selection of Rep. Geraldine Ferraro as his running-mate as "the biggest political bust of recent years". And in 1988 George BUSH managed to slight Ronald Reagan by saying of Governor George

Deukmejian: "He will go down as *the* great governor of California."

Gag rule The rule adopted in 1836 by the US HOUSE OF REPRESENTATIVES which provided that all petitions against slavery "be laid upon the TABLE", with no action taken; thousands were flooding in and proving highly divisive. Ex-President Rep. John Quincy ADAMS refused to vote on the rule, terming it "a direct violation of the Constitution of the United States", and for the next eight years conducted a one-man campaign to evade or repeal it. Eventually, in December 1844, Adams got the rule repealed by 180 votes to 80. In his diary that night, Adams wrote: "Blessed, forever blessed, be the name of God!"

Gaitskell. Gaitskellites The right-wing faction in Britain's LABOUR PARTY who rallied behind the party leader, **Hugh Gaitskell**, first against Aneurin Bevan (*see* BEVANITES) in the mid-1950s, next against Harold WILSON's leadership challenge and finally against the UNILATERALISTS (*see* FIGHT, FIGHT AND FIGHT AGAIN). Hugh Todd Naylor Gaitskell (1906–63) first made his mark in the FUEL CRISIS of 1947 when he declared: "personally, I have never taken a great many baths myself". He succeeded Sir Stafford Cripps as Chancellor of the Exchequer in 1950, being dubbed "**Mr. Rising Price**" by Iain Macleod. Harold Macmillan (*see* SUPERMAC) saw him as "a pupil of Mr. [Hugh] Dalton. He has imitated his rather pedantic style, tedious expositions of the obvious, weak gestures and irritating smile." His moderate approach was pursued after 1951 by the Conservative R. A. (RAB) Butler (*see* BUTSKELLISM). But Henry (CHIPS) Channon reckoned: "Gaitskell has a Wykehamist voice and manner, and a thirteenth-century face." Gaitskell succeeded ATTLEE as Labour leader in 1955, holding the office until his sudden death in 1963, by which time he had pre-equipped the party for power – though he had failed to persuade the party to ditch its NATIONALIZATION policies as set out in CLAUSE FOUR. As Labour leader Bevan denounced him as "a desiccated calculating machine" – though he later insisted he was merely setting out the requirements for the job. And Macmillan remarked: "He is going through all the motions of being in government when he isn't in government. It is bad enough having to behave like a government when one is in government." Roy Jenkins, a strong supporter, concluded:

> All his struggles illustrated some blemishes as well as exceptional strength. He would not have been a perfect Prime Minister, but he was that very rare phenomenon, a great politician who was also an unusually agreeable man.

gallery The area from where visitors – "strangers" in the House of Commons – may observe the proceedings of a legislature.
press gallery The galleries overlooking each House of Parliament, and each chamber in the Capitol, and the rooms adjacent, from which journalists report their proceedings. At Westminster, also the body of journalists, *etc.*, accredited to Parliament (*see also* LOBBY).

Gallipoli The peninsula in the Dardanelles where in 1915 Allied troops made a disastrous attempt to open a second front against Turkey. British, French and ANZAC troops sustained heavy losses – 25,000 dead, 13,000 missing – over 10 months after commanders failed to order a rapid advance from the beachheads. The affair created national trauma and pride in Australia and New Zealand, but seemed for a time to have finished the career of Winston CHURCHILL, who as First Lord of the Admiralty had backed the expedition.

Gallup poll *See* OPINION POLLS.

Gang of Four (1) Mao Tse-Tung's name for the Shanghai-based hard-core radicals of the CULTURAL REVOLUTION, led by Mao's widow Jiang Qing. The four – Zhang Chunqiao, Yao Wenyuan, Wang Hongwen and Jiang Qing – attempted to perpetuate Mao's policies in China after his death, but were arrested and disgraced in 1976. (2) In Britain, the four former senior Labour figures who launched the SDP in 1981: Roy Jenkins, Dr. David Owen, Bill Rodgers and Mrs. Shirley Williams.

GAO Abbreviation for America's **General Accounting Office**, the arm of Congress which investigates how effectively public money is spent.

garden. garden girls Elite secretarial staff at NUMBER TEN Downing Street, at least one of whom always travels with the Prime Minister. When Lloyd George first established the CABINET OFFICE, the secretaries were housed in a temporary building in the garden of No. 10.
gardening leave WHITEHALL euphemism for home leave taken by, or forced on, a civil servant whose position has become untenable.

Garfield, James Abram *See* BOATMAN JIM.

garment district The former sweatshop area of New York City, now highly-unionized and the base of the International Ladies' Garment Workers' Union, which Democratic presidential nominees traditionally visit for a euphoric reception from the workers. It lies between 20th and 41st Streets and 6th and 8th Avenues.

Garter, Order of the In England and Wales, the highest order of KNIGHTHOOD, in the personal gift of the CROWN. Non-hereditary, it was instituted by Edward III *c.* 1348. Limited to members of the Royal family and 25 Knights, now distinguished (and usually retired) figures from politics and other walks of life. Holders of the Garter take the initials KG. *See* HONI SOIT QUI MAL Y PENSE.

> I could not accept the Order of the Garter from my sovereign, when I have received the Order of the Boot from the people.
>
> WINSTON CHURCHILL to George VI after his defeat in 1945 (he took the Garter in 1953).

Garveyism The doctrine of Black self-pride and self-help promoted in America just after WORLD WAR I by Marcus Garvey (1887–1940). Garvey, a Jamaican, condemned White America as corrupt and RACIST and urged Blacks to set up their own institutions pending a return to Africa. His Universal Negro Improvement Association raised Black consciousness and spawned a number of enterprises, including a Black Star Steamship Line. But they were financially unsound and in 1925 Garvey was jailed for mail fraud. He was deported on his release and the movement collapsed.

Gastarbeiter (Ger. guest worker) The immigrant workers from Turkey, Yugoslavia and elsewhere who migrated to EUROPEAN COMMUNITY countries, especially West Germany, to fill shortages of unskilled labour during the boom years, often becoming permanent residents despite official efforts to limit their stay and deny them full rights.

GATT The General Agreement on Tariffs and Trade, the Geneva-based world organization which has worked since 1948 to break down trade barriers by eliminating tariffs and quotas. Over 90 nations are signatories to the treaty under which it operates. *See* CAIRNS GROUP; KENNEDY ROUND; MULTI-FIBRE AGREEMENT; TOKYO ROUND; URUGUAY ROUND.

Gauleiter The high-ranking administrator of a *Gau*, or province, in NAZI Germany. Often appointed directly by Hitler, a *Gauleiter* was responsible for all economic and political activities in his area, civil defence and sometimes policing. The word has become a term of abuse for any ruthless and machine-minded figure at mid-level in the chain of authority.

Gaullism The uniquely French philosophy behind the post-war movement founded and led by General/President DE GAULLE, and which has outlived him healthily. Based on vigorous assertion of the national interest and French military independence, Gaullism also breaks with other right-wing ideologies in requiring heavy state intervention in industry. Its tenets have been widely adopted even by elements of the French Socialist party.

> I have myself only become a Gaullist little by little.
>
> DE GAULLE.

gavel In many legislatures and deliberative bodies, the small hammer banged by the chairman to call members to order. The ivory gavel first used by John ADAMS to call the US SENATE to order broke apart 165 years later in the hand of Vice-President Nixon. The Indian government provided a replica, but the original still rests on the vice-president's desk.
gavel-to-gavel Television or radio coverage of a Parliamentary event, conference or convention which covers the entire proceedings live.

Gay Lib or gay rights The movement for equal rights for homosexuals which took its cue from the impact of the FEMINIST movement in the late 1960s. The **Gay Liberation Front**, founded in New York City in 1970, was the forerunner of many political, social and economic pressure groups.

Gaza Strip A disputed belt of land, 42 km. long and 6 to 10 km. wide, on the Mediterranean coast between Israel and Egypt. Ruled by Egypt from 1948 after the UN partition of Palestine, briefly held by Israel in 1956, and seized again in 1967 (*see* SIX-DAY WAR) to become one of the OCCUPIED TERRITORIES. Heavily-populated, the Strip is a strong point of the INTIFADA against continued Israeli rule.

GCHQ Government Communications Headquarters. The nerve-centre at Cheltenham of SIGINT (Signals Intelligence), the worldwide eavesdropping network which is a key element of British intelligence-gathering. Worldwide it meshes in with other British listening posts; much of the information gathered is shared with the United States. Occasional espionage charges against GCHQ staff – notably Geoffrey Prime in 1983 – are thus a cause of concern to Washington. So was a trade union campaign of disruption in 1981, which led Mrs. Thatcher in 1984 to ban union membership and activity at GCHQ, occasioning a bitter controversy which ran on for years.

GDP Gross Domestic Product. The value of all goods and services produced by an economy over a given period of time, excluding net exports. The most reliable estimate of a nation's economic state.

GDR The former German Democratic Republic, better known as East Germany. It comprised the zone of Germany occupied by the Soviet Union in the wake of Hitler's defeat. The Communist state was formally created in 1949 in response to the establishment of a democratic regime (the Federal Republic) covering the British, French and US zones.

> Communism fits Germany like a saddle fits a cow.
> STALIN, 1944.

general. General Accounting Office *See* GAO.

General Assembly The forum of the UNITED NATIONS in which every member state has equal influence by virtue of its single vote. It sits in New York for three months every year from the third Tuesday in September. It elects the ten non-permanent members of the SECURITY COUNCIL, and can make pronouncements or recommendations – a two-thirds majority is required for important matters. But immediate issues are almost entirely the province of the Security Council.

General Strike A stoppage of work by the entire unionized workforce of a nation or city, in some countries a regular form of protest and display of SOLIDARITY; in Britain the unique stoppage from 3 to 12 May 1926 when the TUC called out key workers in support of miners resisting a pay cut. It was brought about by a lockout of miners on 30 April, itself the culmination of a long and bitter struggle (*see* NOT A PENNY OFF THE PAY, NOT A MINUTE ON THE DAY). The strike affected the railways, road transport and industries including iron and steel, building, gas, electricity and printing. Stanley BALDWIN's government enacted a STATE OF EMERGENCY and called in troops and civilian volunteers to maintain essential services; the TUC had promised to maintain vital food supplies. Baldwin's object, claimed Sir Oswald MOSLEY, was "to make working class bees without a sting who were to gather honey for the rich, but be deprived of the right to defend themselves". With national newspapers off the streets, the Government produced its own BRITISH GAZETTE, belligerently edited by Chancellor Winston CHURCHILL; the TUC countered with its own *British Worker*. Though making a considerable impact, the strike was not total, and with the TUC losing the political battle it was reluctantly called off. The miners stayed out another six months before being starved back to work on the owners' terms.

> The General Strike has taught the working class more in four days than years of talking would have done.
> Earl BALFOUR.

general will, the The doctrine of Rousseau that "the body politic, therefore, is also a moral being possessed of a will, and this general will, which tends always to the preservation and welfare of the whole". Come the French Revolution, Robespierre declared: "Our will is the General Will." And in the 20th century Herbert Marcuse asserted: "The General Will is always wrong."

generalissimo The supreme commander, especially of a force drawn from two or more nations or services. Also the supreme leader of certain authoritarian regimes. In modern times the title has been applied to Marshal Foch (1851–1929) who commanded the Allied forces in France in 1918; to Joseph STALIN, who was made generalissimo of the Soviet forces in 1943; to General Franco, who proclaimed himself generalissimo of the Spanish army in 1939; and to Marshal Chiang Kai-Shek (1888–1975), leader of the KMT, who was in power in China from 1927 to 1949, and subsequently in NATIONALIST CHINA.

Geneva. Geneva Agreement The settlement signed in Geneva on 21 July 1954 between the warring parties in Indochina, which was intended to end conflict between French and VIET MINH forces in VIETNAM and ensure the evacuation of Communist troops and GUERRILLAS from Laos and Cambodia. The agreements, signed also by America, the Soviet Union, Britain and China, were signed as a "midnight or never" deadline set by the French was about to expire – but US Secretary of State John Foster Dulles did so with the worst possible grace out of pique at France's admission of defeat. A CEASEFIRE line was established along the 17TH PARALLEL; although this was not intended as a territorial boundary, Vietnam became divided into the North under Viet Minh control and the South under an American-backed anti-Communist regime. The FREE ELECTIONS envisaged for the whole of Vietnam never took place, and the stage was set for the VIETNAM WAR.

Geneva Conventions Four conventions, the first submitted in 1864 by the International Committee of the Red Cross to a conference of diplomats in Geneva, which govern the conduct of war. The best-known covers the humane treatment of prisoners of war.

Geneva disarmament conference The conference involving 31 nations held in Geneva between 2 February 1932 and late 1934 to discuss general disarmament. The high point of international efforts to avoid a repetition of WORLD WAR I, it began with brave hopes, but was dogged by the conflicting interests of the participants and, particularly, France's insistence on a guarantee of security from German invasion. France eventually won a conditional guarantee, but then the NAZIs came to power and on 14 October 1933 the Germans walked out. The conference rejected a number of worthy initiatives, including one from America to ban all offensive weaponry; by the close most nations had concluded that rearmament was their only guarantee of security.

Geneva Protocol A Protocol for the pacific settlement of International Disputes, proposed to the LEAGUE OF NATIONS in 1924 by RAMSAY MACDonald and the French premier, Edouard Herriot. Requiring all disputes to be settled by compulsory ARBITRATION by the Permanent Court of International Justice (*see* WORLD COURT) or other League bodies, it was unanimously endorsed by the League Assembly on 2 October 1924. But MacDonald's government fell soon after (*see* ZINOVIEV LETTER), and Stanley BALDWIN's incoming administration disowned the Protocol, paving the way for its demise.

Geneva summit (1) The first SUMMIT conference in the correct meaning of the word, with the leaders of America, Britain, France and the Soviet Union meeting in July 1955 in an effort to reduce world tension in the depths of the COLD WAR. They rejected war as an instrument of national policy, agreed to set up economic, cultural and economic contacts and had abortive talks on DISARMAMENT and German reUNIFICATION. Though the meeting was largely inconclusive, its good-natured tone did ease the climate for a time. (2) The first meeting, in November 1985, between President Reagan (*see* GREAT COMMUNICATOR) and Mikhail GORBACHEV. The two leaders clashed on Reagan's insistence on America developing STAR WARS, and the meeting was generally inconclusive, showing no sign of the two men's future friendship.

genocide The attempted destruction of a national, ethnic or religious group by another, designated a crime under international law by the UN GENERAL ASSEMBLY in 1948. The word, from the Greek *genos*, race; and Latin *caedere*, to kill, was invented by Professor Raphael Lemkin of Duke University, and was used in drafting the official indictment of WAR CRIMINALS in 1945.

Gens du pays (Fr. people of the land) The romantic nationalist song written by Gilles Vignault which became the anthem of Quebec's SEPARATIST movement in the 1970s. Its first verse and chorus, translated from the French, are:

> The time that it takes to say: "I love you"
> Is all that is left us at the end of our days.
> The wishes one's made, the flowers one's sown
> Each of them the harvests in oneself
> In the fragrant gardens of passing time.
>
> People of the land, it is your turn
> To be free to talk of love.

gentleman. gentleman's agreement An informal understanding, stopping short of a written agreement but still regarded as binding. The term was first applied to the deal struck in 1907 between America and Japan restricting the flow of Japanese emigrants to the US (*see* YELLOW PERIL). It was also used to describe an agreement between Anthony EDEN and the Italian government in 1936 regulating Italian activities in the Mediterranean; Mussolini did not honour his side of the bargain.

Gentlemen, I think we had better start again somewhere else John MAJOR's comment to his Cabinet on 2 February 1991 when an IRA mortar-bomb fired from the other side of WHITEHALL exploded in the garden only yards away. No one was hurt by the blast from the bomb – one of three – but it came unnervingly close to its target, and damage to NUMBER TEN was worse than was publicly admitted.

Our government of gentlemen Josef Goebbels's wildly inappropriate term for Germany's NAZI rulers. He was speaking in October 1933, soon after Hitler took power.

Gentlewomen The term used by colleagues to describe the first women members of the US HOUSE OF REPRESENTATIVES. Rep. Nicholas Longworth (Speaker 1924–30) directed from the Chair that the phrase be used; it survived a quarter of a century until Congresswomen convinced male colleagues that they found it patronizing.

geopolitics The joint application of power politics and geography, pioneered in Germany by F. Ratzel and Karl Haushofer and in Britain by Sir Halford Mackinder (1861–1947). Geopolitical arguments were used by the NAZIs to back up their demand for LEBENSRAUM.

Georgia mafia The coterie of advisers, led by White House policy chief Hamilton Jordan, whom the newly-elected Jimmy CARTER brought to Washington in 1977. Most had worked for him during his single term as governor of Georgia, but despite many qualities had little knowledge of national politics prior to Carter's campaign for the presidency. They were unfairly lampooned for their down-home manners (*see* TWIN PYRAMIDS OF THE NILE). But their lack of understanding of Washington's ways, and especially of the Congress, caused the Carter administration lasting difficulties.

> I treated the Congress as if they were the Georgia state legislature. And they treated me as if I was Governor of Georgia. JIMMY CARTER.

GERBIL The Great Education Reform BILL which was the political legacy of Kenneth

Baker (1935–), Britain's Education Secretary from 1986–89 and holder of a series of other Cabinet posts. The measure, passed in 1988, was seen as the most significant since the BUTLER ACT, introducing a National Curriculum and paving the way for self-management of schools outside local authority control. The acronym is appropriate – the gerbil is one of the most common classroom pets in primary schools.

German. a German racket The description of closer European union which forced the EURO-SCEPTIC **Nicholas** (later Lord) **Ridley** (1929–93) to resign as Margaret Thatcher's Trade and Industry Secretary in the summer of 1990. Ridley, a tetchy but sophisticated aristocrat who was both a talented artist and a trained engineer, made the comments, and others about the Germans, in an interview with the *Spectator*; he later maintained that at the time he thought the interview had finished. He was reluctant to resign and Mrs. Thatcher, to whom he was very close, was loth to let him go, but after 48 hours he went. Ridley's apparent arrogance (*see* strut from a SEDENTARY POSITION) and his chain-smoking had been manna to the Labour opposition; Gordon Brown, accusing him of seeking to dismantle the Department of Trade and Industry, told the Commons:

> Eventually he will be seated alone at his desk – no in-tray, no out-tray, just an ashtray.

German rearmament *See* REARMAMENT.

German reunification *See* UNIFICATION.

German revolution The attempt by the SPARTACISTS to seize power in Germany and establish a Communist state, which began with an uprising in Munich on 7 November 1918, two days before the ABDICATION of the Kaiser. It was put down by the National Guard of the infant WEIMAR REPUBLIC early in 1919 with the loss of many lives, including that of Rosa Luxemburg, one of German Communism's prime movers.

> We are fighting for the gates of heaven.
>
> KARL LIEBKNECHT.

gerrymander To rig electoral boundaries in order to ensure that one's own party is elected, whatever its level of support. The term originated in Massachusetts in 1812 when the state legislature created a Congressional DISTRICT in Essex County that looked on the map like a dragon or salamander. Since Governor Elbridge Gerry (1744–1814) was thought to favour the stratagem, the name stuck.

Gestapo (Ger. *Geheime Staatspolizei*, secret state police) The ruthless and dedicated backbone of the NAZI state, which acquired sinister notoriety throughout Europe. Formed by Hermann Goering, it was later controlled by Heinrich Himmler, under whom it was responsible for terrorizing first the German people and then the peoples of occupied territories. It was declared a criminal organization by the NUREMBERG tribunal in 1946; Himmler had committed suicide as the Allies closed in on Berlin.

In June 1945 CHURCHILL, in an election broadcast, equated Labour with the Gestapo – a remark blamed by some for the scale of his surprise defeat. He said the Socialists "would have to fall back on some kind of Gestapo, no doubt very humanely directed in the first instance". ATTLEE blamed the PRESS BARON Lord Beaverbrook for Churchill's intemperate language, saying:

> The voice was the voice of Churchill, but the mind was the mind of Beaverbrook.

get. get in (1) In HOUSE OF COMMONS parlance, to get into a debate; to be called by the Speaker. (2) To be elected to a legislature. Speaker Bernard (later Lord) Weatherill (1920–) remarked some time after the Tory LANDSLIDE of 1983:

> A number of people got in by mistake at the last election.

Get your tanks off my lawn The archetypal rebuff from a Labour Prime Minister to trade union leaders seeking to coerce the government into following their agenda. It was delivered by Harold WILSON to the engineers' leader Hugh (later Lord) Scanlon during the controversy in 1969 over the trade union reform White Paper IN PLACE OF STRIFE.

Gettysburg Address The brief speech delivered by Abraham LINCOLN at Gettysburg, Pennsylvania, on 19 November 1863, at the ceremony to dedicate the national cemetery on the battlefield where UNION forces had defeated General Robert E. Lee's CONFEDERATE army the previous July. He delivered the speech, drafted by himself over the previous 11 days, immediately after a 2-hour dedication speech by Edward Everett, which had left the crowd of 15,000 restless. Lincoln, who was unknowingly nursing smallpox, spoke for barely three minutes, and while he was interrupted three times by applause the true import of a speech which set the parameters for America's second century was not immediately grasped. The *Chicago Times* reputedly (the cutting has not been found) commented:

> The cheek of every American must tingle with shame as he reads the silly, flat and dishwatery utterances of the man who has to be pointed out to intelligent foreigners as the President of the United States.

For over a century, however, the speech has been accepted as a masterpiece in its own right and a model for the future of the nation. Indeed in 1992 David Gates asked: "How did Lincoln manage to re-invent America in 272 words?" Lincoln's entire speech ran as follows:

> Four score and seven years ago our fathers brought forth on this continent a new nation, conceived in Liberty, and dedicated to the proposition that all men are equal.
>
> Now we are engaged in a great civil war, testing whether that nation, or any nation so conceived and so dedicated, can long endure. We are met on a great battlefield of that war. We have come to dedicate a portion of that field, as a final resting-place of those who here gave their lives that the nation might live. It is altogether fitting and proper that we should do this.
>
> But, in a larger sense, we cannot dedicate, we cannot consecrate, we can not hallow this ground. The brave men, living and dead, who struggled here, have consecrated it, far above our poor power to add or detract. The world will little note, nor long remember what we say here, but it can never forget what they did here. It is for us, the living, rather to be dedicated here to the unfinished work which they who fought here have thus far so nobly advanced. It is rather for us to be here dedicated to the great task remaining before us, that from these honored dead we take increased devotion to that cause for which they gave the last full measure of devotion; that we here highly resolve that these dead shall not have died in vain, that this nation, under God, shall have a new birth of freedom; and that government of the people, by the people, and for the people, shall not perish from the earth.

gherao (Hindi *gherna*, to besiege) A form of protest or Direct ACTION popular in India, which has been exported to other parts of the world by migrant communities. It consists of gathering outside the home of a politician or industrialist against whom the crowd have a grievance, serenading him or her with the maximum amount of cacophonous noise and refusing to leave until the demands of the protesters are met.

ghetto Originally the area, sometimes walled, in a European city where the Jewish community either chose or were compelled to live. The name comes from the Ital. *ghetto*, foundry; the Venetian ghetto was constructed on the site of a former foundry. Since the 1960s it has also come to be used for the sections of America's INNER CITIES where a largely Black UNDERCLASS has grown up, unable to escape either through lack of opportunities or obstacles to grasping them.

ghetto mentality A state of mind which shows an incapacity to break out of a cycle of poverty and deprivation.

ghetto of national sentimentality The stark phrase used by Harold Macmillan to describe the mind-set of opponents of his initiative to take Britain into the EUROPEAN COMMUNITY.

GI Bill The legislation under which former US service personnel (GI, Government Issue) receive medical and educational benefits and guaranteed mortgages on returning to civilian life. The Service Readjustment Act, also termed the GI Bill of Rights, was passed by Congress in June 1944 to assure combatants in WORLD WAR II a secure future; over a million veterans received a virtually free college education, though some had to live in gymnasiums and even tugboats. Despite fears that the measure would turn America's colleges into a "hobo jungle", it was immensely successful and remains substantially in force despite costing billions of dollars a year.

Gilmore. Gary Gilmore case The case which triggered the resumption of capital punishment in America in 1977 after almost a decade. Gilmore was executed by firing squad in Utah on 17 January after frenetic appeals by others against his murder conviction and sentence, despite his own determination that the shooting go ahead. The Supreme Court, in 1976, had qualified its earlier decision that the death penalty was CRUEL AND UNUSUAL PUNISHMENT. Civil liberties groups and the NAACP fought the sentence because they feared it would be followed by widespread executions of 400 other men and women on Death Row, particularly Blacks, who had not been fairly tried. Gilmore's final words to the squad were:

> Let's do it!

Ginsburg nomination The controversy in 1987 surrounding President Reagan's nomination of Judge Douglas Ginsburg for the SUPREME COURT. Ginsburg, Reagan's second choice for the Court after the rejection of Judge Robert BORK, stood down after admitting he had smoked marijuana while a lecturer at Harvard Law School. As Nancy Reagan had recently launched a "Just Say No" campaign against drugs, the nomination proved highly embarrassing to the White House despite Ginsburg's strong legal qualifications.

Giovinezza (Ital. youthfulness) The official anthem of Italy's FASCIST party. Written by Giuseppe Blanc in 1909, it was originally titled *Commiato* (Farewell), and adopted by Turin University. In 1926 Blanc reissued the song with words by Salvatore Gotta, under the title *(la) Giovinezza*. This followed a legal battle to stop a plagiarized version of his original, published in 1918 by Marcello Manni.

Gipper, the One of Ronald Reagan's nicknames, stemming from his portrayal of the original Gipper – American football star George Gipp (1895–1920) – in the 1940 film *Knut Rockne – All American*. Gipp played for Rockne's legendary Notre Dame team but died of pneumonia at the height of a brilliant career. On his deathbed Gipp told Rockne:

> Someday, when things look real tough for Notre Dame, ask the boys to go out there and win one for the Gipper.

Reagan repeatedly used the phrase "win one for the Gipper", until it became his own. And when he arrived at the Senate as President, SERGEANT AT ARMS Nordy Hoffman, a veteran of the Rockne team, greeted him with: "Hiya, Gipper!"

Girondists The moderate republican party during the FRENCH REVOLUTION, so called because their initial leaders were Deputies from the Gironde, the DÉPARTEMENT centred on Bordeaux.

give. Give 'em hell Harry The most picturesque of many nicknames for Harry S Truman (1884–1972), 33rd President of the United States (Democrat, 1945–53). It stemmed from his feisty manner, his colourful comments about his opponents, and his come-from-behind victory in the 1948 Presidential campaign. During his WHISTLE-STOP tour, Truman stepped up his rhetoric against Thomas DEWEY, and the crowds shouted: "Give 'em hell, Harry!" He himself remarked: "I never give 'em hell; I just tell 'em the truth and they think it's hell." But he never pulled his punches. Truman's most famous onslaught was against Paul Hume, the *Washington Post* music critic who in 1950 panned a song recital by his daughter Margaret. The President wrote to him:

> I have just read your lousy review buried in the back pages of the paper. You sound like a frustrated old man who never made a success, an eight-ulcer man on a four-ulcer job, and all four ulcers working. I have never met you, but if I do you'll need a new nose and plenty of beefsteak and perhaps a supporter below . . . Westbrook Pegler, a guttersnipe, is a gentleman compared to you. You can take that as more of an insult than a reflection of your ancestry.

One of his greatest targets was Richard Nixon (*see* TRICKY DICK). In the 1960 campaign Truman said on the STUMP that "anyone who voted for Nixon and Lodge ought to go to hell" and that "Nixon never told the truth in his life". Under pressure, he denied the first statement but said: "They can't challenge the second." In his old age, he told Merle Miller: "Nixon's a shifty-eyed goddam liar and everyone knows it."

Truman reminisced: "My choice early in life was either to be a piano player in a whorehouse or a politician. And to tell the truth there's hardly any difference." Asked for his secret of success, he replied: "Never kick a fresh turd on a hot day", and when a friend complained to his wife Bess that Truman was indelicately using the word "manure", she replied: "It's taken me 25 years to get him to say 'manure'".

The son of a prosperous Missouri farmer, John Anderson "Peanuts" Truman, his main childhood interest was indeed piano playing. He was also bookish, saying in his retirement: "Without my glasses I was blind as a bat and, to tell the truth, I was a bit of a sissy. If there was any danger of getting into a fight, I always ran. I guess that's why I'm here today". A slump in family fortunes ruled out a college education, and until the age of 33 he marked time, helping with the farm and taking on white-collar jobs. Then came WORLD WAR I. He volunteered for the Army, won officer status and came home from France a much-commended Captain. Armed with new confidence, Truman went into business (*see* HABERDASHER HARRY), but it failed. He turned to politics, and with the aid of the PRENDERGAST MACHINE was elected a judge, and in 1934, despite having built a reputation for honesty, was elected to the US Senate. By 1940 Tom Prendergast was in jail for tax evasion and Roosevelt was backing a rival candidate, but Truman stumped the state, driving his own car, to win a narrow re-election. His second Senate term put him on the map; after an angry speech from him complaining about wartime waste and graft, the Senate set up the TRUMAN COMMITTEE. Its work kept him in the headlines, and by 1944 Washington reporters were putting him second only to Roosevelt in promoting the war effort. With Roosevelt seeking a fourth term, Truman was offered the vice-presidency but replied: "Tell him to go to hell. I'm for Jimmy Byrnes." Democratic national committee chairman Bob Hannegan said that President Truman was "the contrariest Missouri mule I've ever dealt with", and he only agreed to join the ticket when FDR said:

> If he wants to break up the Democratic party in the middle of a war, that's his responsibility.

Truman's three months as Vice-President were no preparation for the White House, despite FDR's failing health. Martha G. Kempton wrote that he "scarcely saw President Roosevelt, and received no briefing on the development of the atomic bomb or the unfolding difficulties with Soviet Russia". On 12 April 1945 he was called from the Capitol to be told by Eleanor Roosevelt that her husband was dead. Truman said to White House reporters: "Boys, if you ever pray, pray for me now. I don't know whether you fellows ever had a load of hay fall on you, but when they told me what had happened, I felt like the moon, the stars and the planets had fallen on me".

There were many to say he would fail. The union leader Al Whitney declared: "You can't make a president out of a ribbon clerk." Admiral Ernest King wrote him off as "a pipsqueak haberdasher", and the TVA chairman David Lilienthal wrote: "The country and the world don't deserve to be left this way, with that THROTTLEBOTTOM Truman at the head of the country at such a time." But he imposed his authority, steered America through the last months of war and authorized the dropping of atomic bombs on HIROSHIMA and NAGASAKI. Averell Harriman said: "I had talked with Mr. Truman for only a few minutes when I began to realize that the man had a real grasp of the situation. What a surprise and a relief that was!" And Churchill told him: "I must confess, Sir, I loathed your taking the place of President Roosevelt. I misjudged you badly. Since that time you, more than any man, have saved Western civilization." The problems of peace proved great, even though the economy continued to thrive. The start of the COLD WAR, the nuclear issue, and the formation of the state of ISRAEL which led Ernest BEVIN to comment "he would lick any Jewish arse that promised him a hundred votes", were some of his preoccupations. He was also careless in his appointments, leading to accusations of graft and drift. The Republicans controlled Congress, and Washington COLUMNISTS were scathing. Walter Lippmann wrote in 1946: "Mr. Truman is not performing, and gives no evidence of his ability to perform, the function of Commander-in-Chief. At the very center of the Truman administration there is a vacuum of responsibility and authority." And two years later Arthur Krock commented: "The president's influence is weaker than any president's has been in modern history." Truman replied: "Whenever the press quits abusing me I know I'm in the wrong pew." But he also remarked: "Why in Hell does anyone want to be a head of state? Damned if I know." And on a surprise after-lunch visit to the Senate when he took his old seat, he confessed: "Right here is where I've always wanted to be, and the only place I've ever wanted to be. The Senate – that's just my speed and style." He knew his strengths, saying: "I'm proud that I'm a politician. A politican understands government, and it takes a politician to run a government." And he said of his presence in the White House: "Sure it's a big joke, but I don't know anyone who can do it better than I can." Of all presidents, he was one of the most unspoiled, once saying:

> Three things can ruin a man: money, power and women. I never had any money, I never wanted power and the only woman in my life is up at the house right now.

Truman started the 1948 campaign well behind; even the Democratic Convention was lukewarm. Sen. Robert Taft, MR. REPUBLICAN, set his party's tone when he declared: "It defies all common sense to send that roughneck ward politician back to the White House." But Truman stumped the country relentlessly, beat Dewey convincingly despite the intervention of the left-wing former Vice-President Henry Wallace, and enjoyed a lavish inauguration budgeted by Republicans who had expected their man to win – and who still took both houses of Congress. Yet his second term was less happy. His administration was dogged by charges of INFLUENCE-PEDDLING, and by the HISS CASE and other controversies that gave rise to McCARTHYISM; when Secretary of State Dean Acheson, hounded as a "COMMIE-LOVER", offered to resign for standing by Hiss, Truman told him: "Dean, always be shot in front – never behind." The KOREAN WAR set fresh challenges, culminating in Truman's electrifying decision to fire General MACARTHUR. He decided not to seek a further term, and went home to Independence, Missouri. Asked the first thing he did in retirement, he said: "I took my suitcases up to the attic." And pressed on his record as a President, he said: "I did my damnedest and that's all there is to it." In retirement he campaigned actively for Democratic candidates and kept up a stream of comment – mainly directed against Nixon. In 1971 he rejected the CONGRESSIONAL MEDAL OF HONOR, saying: "I do not consider that I have done anything which should be the reason for any award, Congressional or otherwise."

> He ended up one of the greatest presidents of this century.
> CHARLES KRAUTHAMMER.

> I wasn't one of the great Presidents, but I had a good time trying to be one.
> TRUMAN.

> The last authentic American, with all the characteristic faults and virtues of his breed, to occupy the White House.
> MALCOLM MUGGERIDGE.

> One of the most extraordinary human beings who ever lived.
> DEAN ACHESON.

Give me your tired, your poor, your huddled masses The inscription on the base of the Statue of Liberty which epitomized 19th-century America's role as a refuge for the oppressed of Europe. It came from a sonnet, *The New Colossus,* written specially by Emma Lazarus (1849–1887):

> "Keep, ancient lands, your storied pomp!" cries she
> With silent lips. "Give me your tired, your poor,
> Your huddled masses yearning to breathe free,
> The wretched refuse of your teeming shore.
> Send these, the homeless, tempest-tossed to me,
> I lift my lamp beside the golden door."

Her sentiments were an echo of George WASHINGTON's letter to newly-arrived Irish immigrants in December 1782:

> The bosom of America is open to receive not only the Opulent and respectable Stranger; but the oppressed and persecuted of all Nations and Religions; whom we shall wellcome to a participation of all our rights and privileges, if by decency and propriety of conduct they appear to merit the enjoyment.

Give us the tools, and we will finish the job CHURCHILL's call to America for assistance in the blackest days of WORLD WAR II, made in a broadcast from London on 9 February 1941. Churchill promised Roosevelt: "We shall not fail or falter; we shall not weaken or tire."

give way The request made to an MP in mid-speech in the House of Commons by another who wishes to INTERVENE. By tradition it is up to the member on his or her feet to decide whether to give way or keep talking, but persistent refusal can cause angry scenes.

Gladstone, William Ewart *See* GRAND OLD MAN.

glasnost (Russ. openness) One of the keywords of the reform programme introduced by Mikhail GORBACHEV in 1986 after becoming General Secretary of the Soviet Communist Party the previous year. It implied the acceptance of free speech, an end to the persecution of DISSIDENTS and an opening-up of the Communist system of government to criticism. Together with PERESTROIKA (reconstruction), its adoption signalled a final break with STALINISM, a relaxation of nearly seven decades of internal repression, economic reform and, through the lessening of international tension that followed, an end to the COLD WAR. *Glasnost* and *perestroika* also stimulated reform movements and nationalism in the SATELLITE states of eastern Europe. The pace of change ultimately brought the eclipse of Gorbachev through Boris Yeltsin's defeat of the 1991 KREMLIN COUP, and the disintegration of the Soviet Union itself.

Glass-Steagall Act The legislation passed by the US Congress in June 1933 which built on the emergency measures pushed through after Franklin D. Roosevelt's inauguration. It separated commercial banking from investment banking, increased the FED's power to prevent excessive speculation by member banks, and created the Federal Deposit Insurance Corporation (FDIC) to guarantee bank deposits up to $5000 (later raised) in the event of the institution's failure.

GLC Greater London Council. The authority covering the entire capital which formed the upper tier of the local government structure created in 1963, the 32 London boroughs forming the lower. The GLC replaced the London County Council (LCC) but covered a far wider area reflecting suburban growth. It had largely strategic planning and housing functions, eventually taking control of London Transport. But under the Labour administration of Ken (RED KEN) Livingstone in the early 1980s it pursued radical policies on transport, race and other issues that brought it into conflict with Margaret Thatcher's government. Despite a vigorous campaign led by the charismatic Livingstone, the GLC was abolished in 1986.

Gleichschaltung (Ger. co-ordination) The NAZI's policy of integrating all aspects of German social and economic life into their movement. For instance, all trade unions were merged in 1933 into a German Labour Front (*Deutsche Arbeitsfront*). Other fronts created under this policy included a German Milk Front and German Shoe Front.

Gleneagles agreement The undertaking entered into by COMMONWEALTH Heads of Government in 1977 to ban official sporting links with South Africa until steps were taken to dismantle APARTHEID. The meeting took place at the luxurious Gleneagles Hotel, a golfing resort in Scotland between Stirling and Perth.

gloire. la gloire (Fr. glory) The obsession, combining pride, arrogance, self-interest, CHAUVINISM, cynicism and a desire to put noses out of joint, that has governed France's dealings with the rest of the world, and especially the ANGLO-SAXONS, for the second half of the 20th century and especially since the Presidency of DE GAULLE. It manifests itself not only in a ruggedly independent foreign policy (*see* QUAI D'ORSAY) but in a commitment to grandiose architectural projects and advanced home-grown technology, regardless of expense.

Glorious Revolution The upheaval in 1688–89 when the Catholic King James II fled from England as Parliament and the nobility prepared to welcome the Protestant Prince William of ORANGE. The Convention Parliament which met in 1689 not only confirmed William and his wife Mary, who had the better claim, as joint Sovereigns, but barred Roman Catholics from the succession; it also reasserted the country's traditional liberties. The Revolution was triggered by James's action against Protestant clerics, and the birth of a Catholic male heir. *See also* APPRENTICE BOYS OF DERRY; Battle of the BOYNE.

Gnomes of Zurich Harold WILSON's name for the Continental speculators who he claimed were undermining the pound in the period between Labour's return to power in 1964 and the DEVALUATION of sterling three years later. It apparently originated with George (later Lord George) BROWN, Secretary for Economic Affairs, in the sterling crisis of November 1964 and was picked up by the Prime Minister, who spoke in the Commons of

> All these financiers, all the little gnomes of Zurich and the other financial centres, about whom we keep on hearing.

The dating of this phrase to 1956 by several dictionaries of quotations appears based on someone else's misprint.

> What most infuriated George Brown, and Labour MPs such as John Mendelson and Ian MIKARDO . . . was that the men they disparaged as the "gnomes of Zurich" were really giants.
>
> T. R. FEHRENBACH, *The Gnomes of Zurich*.

gobbledygook A term coined in 1944 by the Texas Democrat Rep. Maury Maverick (1895–1954) to denote the long-winded and virtually unintelligible jargon used by BUREAUCRATS and others instead of plain English. As chairman of the Smaller War Plants Corporation, Maverick was so infuriated by phrases like "maladjustments co-extensive with problem areas" that he issued a formal order:

> Be short and say what you're talking about . . . No more patterns, effectuating, dynamics. Anyone using the words activation and implementation will be shot.

As the word caught on in Washington, Maverick explained its origin:

> Perhaps I was thinking of the old bearded turkey gobbler back in Texas who was always gobbledy-gobbling and strutting with ludicrous pomposity. At the end of this gobble there was a sort of gook.

gobsmacked Originally Liverpool slang for being left gaping in disbelief, from the colloquial *gob*, mouth, this word was made part of Britain's political vocabulary in 1991 by Chris Patten, then chairman of the CONSERVATIVE PARTY. His use of the word to describe his reaction to a Labour Party statement on the Health Service caused much press comment, and Patten was saddled with it in coverage of the following year's election campaign.

God. God Save the King or **Queen** The National Anthem of the UNITED KINGDOM since the late 18th century. Attributed by some to Henry Carey (*c.* 1690–1743), it was in print by 1745 and set to a traditional tune (the same as for *My Country, 'Tis of Thee*). Of the three verses, only the first is normally sung:

> God save our Gracious Queen,
> Long live our noble Queen,
> God save the Queen.
> Send her victorious,
> Happy and glorious,
> Long to reign over us,
> God save the Queen!

With God on our Side One of the most celebrated PROTEST SONGS of the early 1960s. Sung by Bob Dylan, it reflected on the patriot's claim always to be acting on the side of right, and how the Germans, against whom Americans had fought with such divine backing, now had God on their side since becoming part of the "Free West".

going. going for the Park In Irish politics, the colloquial term for running for the Presidency; the Presidential residence (ARAS NA UACHTARAIN) is in PHOENIX PARK on the western edge of Dublin.

going native The process by which a politician or official despatched to represent a country in a hostile environment takes on the views of those he or she has been sent to tame. The term is used especially of those British European COMMISSIONERS who switch from being EURO-SCEPTICS to enthusiastic advocates of closer union within months of arriving in BRUSSELS.

when the going gets tough, the tough get going A slogan said to have been coined, or first used, by Joseph P. KENNEDY, as an exhortation to strive harder in the face of adversity. It was used as a publicity slogan for the film *Jewel of the Nile* in 1985; the next year it was the title of a hit song by Billy Ocean.

Golan Heights A strategically-important hilly area on the Israeli-Syrian border, designated as a buffer zone between the countries in 1949 and bitterly contested in the Arab-Israeli conflicts of 1956, 1967 and 1973. During the 1950s and 1960s Israeli settlements spread eastwards into the area, provoking constant clashes. In the SIX DAY WAR, over 100,000 Syrians fled when the Israeli army stormed the Heights. The Syrians regained some of the territory during the YOM KIPPUR WAR of 1973. The remainder was again designated a buffer zone by the UN in 1974, but was annexed by Israel in 1982 in defiance of UN RESOLUTION 242. Together with the WEST BANK and GAZA STRIP, the continued Israeli occupation of the Heights has been an obstacle to the PEACE PROCESS, but in September 1992 Israel told Syria it was ready to discuss concessions; these Damascus rejected as inadequate.

gold. gold-plating The spending of infinitely more on an item by a Government department than it would cost if purchased privately. Though it occurs throughout the world, it has been highlighted most in the PENTAGON through the exposure of excesses in Congress, by WHISTLE-BLOWERS and by Sen. William Proxmire's GOLDEN FLEECE awards. Prize items have included a $640 toilet seat, a $1118 plastic cap for a stool leg, a nut costing $2063, a coffee maker modestly priced at $7622 and a $9606 wrench.

Gold Standard A monetary system based on keeping the currency at the value of a fixed weight of gold. The UK adopted it from 1821, but suspended gold payments in 1914; John Maynard Keynes in 1924 described it as "already a barbarous relic" but CHURCHILL as Chancellor returned to it ("at far too high a rate" – Nicholas Ridley) in 1925; the NATIONAL GOVERNMENT's Philip Snowden finally abandoned it in the crisis of 1931. America adopted it by the Coinage Act of 1873, and abandoned it in 1933 (*see* GREAT DEPRESSION). The strains caused by the Gold Standard prompted William Jennings Bryan's legendary 1896 ACCEPTANCE speech:

> You shall not press down upon the brow of labor this crown of thorns; you shall not crucify mankind upon a cross of gold.

go for gold A phrase with two meanings: to opt for the most lucrative course of action or (from the awarding of gold medals to Olympic winners) to seek the greatest prize. It can be traced back to 1832 when the English radical leader Francis Place (1771–1854) sought to block the formation of a Tory government under the Duke of Wellington with the slogan: "To stop the Duke, go for Gold." George Bernard Shaw (1856–1950) wrote at the turn of the century:

> You have to choose (as a voter) between trusting to the natural stability of gold and the natural stability of the honesty and intelligence of members of the government. As long as the capitalist system lasts – go for gold.

The slogan was taken up by Ronald Reagan in his re-election campaign in 1984, the year of the Los Angeles Olympics – and in Britain's 1987 election by the SDP/Liberal ALLIANCE, which had chosen gold as its party colour.

Golden Fleece The "award" made regularly during his long Senate career by William Proxmire of Wisconsin (1915–) to highlight federally-funded projects which appear a waste of the taxpayers' money. One instance was the spending of $97,000 on a study on *The Peruvian brothel – a sexual dispensary and social arena*. Much of his campaigning was directed against GOLD-PLATING and cost overruns on defence projects.

golden share The critical share retained by government in a PRIVATIZED industry in order to keep a degree of control, or prevent the concern passing completely out of its influence. Although keeping a 51% share would have made certain, the UK government generally settled for far less as the whole purpose of privatization was to remove the dead hand of government. The golden share has in practice been as little as 20%.

Goldfine affair *See* Sherman ADAMS affair.

Goldilocks A widely-used and somewhat patronizing nickname for Michael Heseltine (*see* TARZAN).

GOM *See* GRAND OLD MAN.

Good Neighbour policy The policy toward Latin America embarked on in 1933 by President Franklin D. Roosevelt to allay fears that America was bent on total domination of the continent. Its measures – withdrawal of forces from Haiti, renunciation of the PLATT AMENDMENT and the right to intervene unilaterally anywhere in the hemisphere, removal of trade barriers and a common defence policy – were foreshadowed by FDR in his first INAUGURAL ADDRESS on 4 March 1933:

> In the field of world policy, I would dedicate this nation to the policy of the good neighbour.

goose. Goose Green A settlement in the FALKLANDS which in May 1982 saw fierce fighting during the British assault on the occupying Argentine forces; outnumbered three to one, the British force lost 17 men dead; 250 Argentine troops were killed – some, it was later claimed, in cold blood – and 1200 taken prisoner. At the height of the 1983 election campaign Neil KINNOCK caused a furore by saying of Margaret Thatcher's despatch of UK forces in a broadcast interview:

> To prove that she has guts, they had to lose theirs at Goose Green.

goose-step The style of marching perfected by the NAZI soldiery which sent a sinister message across Europe in the late 1930s. The legs are moved from the hips, the knees being kept rigid and each leg swung as high as possible. In Germany the goose-step (*Stechschritt*) was introduced as a full-dress and processional march in the army of Prussia's Frederick the Great; it was adopted with gusto under the THIRD REICH, and survived in East Germany's army – and some other Soviet bloc forces – until shortly before reunification in 1990. At the height of the AXIS, the Italian army adopted the goose-step as the *passo Romano*, but it attracted ridicule and was dropped; the British army once tried the step in recruit drill, but it never caught on.

GOP Universally-used shorthand for America's REPUBLICAN Party, standing for **Grand Old Party**; its use dates from the 1880s. Adlai Stevenson renamed them "Grouchy old pessimists".

Gorbachev. Gorbymania Public adulation in the West for the last Soviet leader, **Mikhail**

Sergeyevich Gorbachev (1931–), in response to his reform programme (*see* GLASNOST; PERESTROIKA). He was elected Communist party leader in 1985 on the death of Constantin Chernenko, the veteran Andrei GROMYKO telling the POLITBURO: "This man, comrades, has a nice smile, but he has iron teeth." Gorbachev received a rapturous welcome on international visits, especially to West Germany, as he moved to end the COLD WAR. His popularity was fostered by the Western media, which nicknamed him "Gorby". But at home his reforms, particularly to the economy, ran into the sand; he faced down the KREMLIN COUP of August 1991, but was out of a job four months later when the Soviet state collapsed.

Gordon. Gordon riots The riots in London in 1780, headed by Lord George Gordon, which aimed to force repeal of legislation passed in 1778 to ease discrimination against Roman Catholics. They were the last of the great outbreaks of anti-Catholic violence which convulsed London over two centuries since the Counter-Reformation. Gordon was mentally unstable, and by his death in 1793 had veered from extreme Protestantism to convert to Judaism. Dickens gave a vivid description of the riots in *Barnaby Rudge*.

Gordon telegram The angry, scathing telegram Queen Victoria despatched to Gladstone when news reached London on 5 February 1885 of the fall of Khartoum and the death of Major-General Charles Gordon at the hands of the Mahdi's horde. Gladstone was given the uncoded telegram by an embarrassed stationmaster at Carnforth, Lancs. as he started back to London from Holker Hall (pronounced Hooker), seat of the Marquess of Hartington, Secretary for War. Gordon had been sent to Khartoum to evacuate the Sudan, but stayed and demanded assistance; a relief force under Wolseley was sent, but arrived just too late. Another telegram at the height of the crisis was left unopened for hours in the servants' hall at Holker because Hartington had not given instructions to be woken before noon. The loss of Khartoum caused a wave of public indignation against Gladstone's government; the Queen's was all the greater as she had never cared for the GRAND OLD MAN.

Gosplan Acronym for *Gos*udarstvennyy *Plan*ovyy Komitet, the State Planning Committee of the Soviet Union established in 1921. It was entrusted in 1927 with formulating the first FIVE-YEAR PLAN for Soviet economic development. This was delivered in 1929, after STALIN had purged *Gosplan* of its more cautious members to obtain a more optimistic projection. The committee continued to form the apex of the economic planning system, its strictures affecting all reaches of Soviet industry and its decisions being implemented through industry ministries.

govern To direct or regulate the affairs of a nation. To the 19th-century French revolutionary Pierre-Joseph Proudhon, "to be governed is to be watched over, inspected, spied on, directed, legislated at, regulated, docketed, indoctrinated, preached at, controlled, assessed, weighed, censored, ordered about, by men who have neither the right nor the knowledge nor the virtue". Thomas Paine averred that "that government is best that governs least", and Thoreau "that government is best that governs not at all"; DE GAULLE that "one cannot govern with 'buts'", and Pierre Mendès-France that "to govern is to choose". Napoleon reckoned that "the great art of governing consists in not letting men grow old in their jobs", while John JAY reputedly said: "The people who own the country ought to govern it".

> Which is the best government? That which teaches us to govern ourselves. GOETHE.

government (1) The art or technique of governing. Thomas JEFFERSON wrote that "the care of human right and happiness, and not their destruction, is the first and only legitimate object of good government"; George WASHINGTON that "government is not reason, it is not eloquence, it is force; like fire, a troublesome servant and a fearsome master". Spinoza (1632–77) stated that "the aim of government is liberty", Jefferson that "the whole of government is the art of being honest" and George Bernard Shaw that "the art of government is the organization of idolatry". Theodore Roosevelt concluded that "the bulk of government is not legislation but administration", Sen. John Sharp Williams that "most bad government has grown out of too much government", and the US political writer Kenneth Crawford (1902–83) that

> the cocktail glass is one of the most powerful instruments of government.

(2) The institution that administers a country. Henry Ward Beecher termed it "the worst thing, next to anarchy", and Thomas Paine "even in its best state, a necessary evil . . . like dress, the badge of lost innocence". But James MADISON pointed out that "if men were angels, no government would be necessary", and asked: "What is government itself but the greatest of all reflections on human nature?" LINCOLN said: "The legitimate object of government is to do for a community of people whatever they need to have done, but can not do at all, or cannot so well do for themselves

in their separate, individual capacities." But he also admitted: "The first necessity that is upon us is of proving that popular government is not an absurdity." Walt Whitman cynically observed that "it is only the novice in political economy who thinks it is the duty of government to make its citizens happy", but Governor William Scranton (1917–) pointed out: "The value of government to the people it serves is in direct relationship to the interest citizens themselves display in the affairs of state." And Stephen Miller noted: "The more government tampers with the daily lives of its citizens, the less authority it ends up having." In a similar vein, Tom Wicker commented: "Government expands to absorb resources and then some", and Robert Strauss observed from the inside: "Everyone in government is like a bunch of ants on a log floating down the river." Ronald Reagan, a great foe of BIG GOVERNMENT, had most to say: "Government is not the solution to the problem – government is the problem;" "Government is a referee; it shouldn't try to be a player in the game;" and

> Government is like a big baby – an alimentary canal with a big appetite at one end and no sense of responsibilty at the other.

The argument in Britain has not always paralleled that in America. Edmund BURKE described government as "a contrivance of human wisdom to provide for human wants. Men have a right that these wants should be provided for by this wisdom." Macaulay wrote: "The business of government is not directly to make the people rich, but to protect them in making themselves rich," while Lord Melbourne at much the same time declared: "The whole duty of government is to prevent crime and to preserve contracts." Lord KEYNES wrote: "The important thing for government is not to do those things which individuals are doing already and to do them a little better or a little worse, but to do those things which at present are not done at all," and Lord BEVERIDGE: "The object of government in peace or in war is not the glory of rulers or of races, but the happiness of the common man." The Canadian Prime Minister Mackenzie King described government as "organized opinion", and TROTSKY termed it "an association of men who do violence to the rest of us".

(3) a government. Any collection of individuals who govern a country at a particular time, usually under the lead of a certain party in office for a set period.

> Every government carries a health warning. ANON.

> Every country has the government it deserves.
> JOSEPH DE MAISTRE (1753–1821).

William Penn wrote: "Governments, like clocks, go from the motion men give them, and as governments are made and moved by men, so by them are they ruined too"; a century later Benjamin FRANKLIN declared: "In free governments the rules are the servants and the people their superiors and sovereigns," and George Washington: "In a free and republican government you cannot restrain the voice of the multitude." President Cleveland insisted that "while the people should patriotically and cheerfully support their government, its functions do not include the support of the people"; Garfield that "all free governments are managed by the combined wisdom and folly of the people"; William Jennings Bryan that "the chief duty of governments, in so far as they are coercive, is to restrain those who would interfere with the inalienable rights of the individual". But TAFT pointed out: "We are all imperfect. We cannot expect a perfect government." Madison had put down a marker for the media, writing: "A popular government, without popular information or the means of acquiring it, is but a Prologue to a Farce or Tragedy – or perhaps both;" almost a century later Wendell Phillips declared: "We live under a government of men and morning newspapers;" in 1980s Britain Bernard Ingham (*see* YORKSHIRE RASPUTIN) was to write: "Confidentiality is the nature of all governments." H. L. Mencken reckoned that "the worst government is the most moral", Justice Louis Brandeis that "if a government is a lawbreaker, it breeds contempt for the law". Elihu Root (1845–1937) pointed out: "We are apt to forget how little it is possible for any government to do", Harry S Truman that "Whenever you have an efficient government you have a DICTATORSHIP" (though in Britain Lloyd George maintained: "What is a government for except to dictate? If it does not dictate, it is not a government"). John F. KENNEDY warned: "No government is better than the men who comprise it;" Milton Friedman that "Governments never learn. Only people learn;" and Ronald Reagan that "Governments tend not to solve problems – only rearrange them."

> Lord, the money we do spend on government, and it's not one bit better than the one we got for one third of the money 20 years ago. WILL ROGERS.

> Every government is run by liars, and nothing they say should be believed. I. F. STONE.

> A government is the only known vessel that LEAKS from the top. JAMES RESTON.

In 18th-century Britain, Dr. Johnson wrote that "any government is ultimately and essentially absolute", and Adam SMITH that "there is no art which one government sooner learns of another than that of draining money from the pockets of the people". George Grenville, speaking in 1769 against the expulsion of John WILKES, told the Commons: "A wise government knows how to enforce with temper, or conciliate with dignity, but a weak one is odious in the former and contemptible in the latter." A century later, Gladstone declared that "the history of governments is one of the most immoral parts of history", adding: "It is the duty of the government to make it difficult for people to do wrong, easy to do right." Lord SALISBURY wrote: "The best form of government (setting aside the issue of morality) is one where the masses have little power, and seem to have a great deal." George Bernard Shaw was first to appreciate that "a government which robs Peter to pay Paul can always depend on the support of Paul", and Lord Keynes admitted: "I work for a government I despise for ends I think criminal." Philip Snowden, shaken by experience, declared: "It would be desirable if every government, when it came into power, should have all its old speeches burned;" while the author Joyce Cary struck a chord when he wrote:

> The only good government is a bad one in a hell of a fright.

Voltaire laid down that "governments need to have both shepherds and butchers", while Thoreau maintained: "The objections which have been brought against a standing army . . . may also . . . be brought against a standing government." The 1950s British politician Lord Eccles maintained that "all governments are selfish, and French governments are more selfish than most;" Australia's Frank Crean that

> The man in the street doesn't care who the government is once the election is over. It's just somebody to criticize.

(4) The government. A specific administration, either the bureaucratic structure or the politicians supposedly in charge of it. Theodore Roosevelt told the people: "The government is us, we are the government, you and I;" and Calvin Coolidge: "The government is not self-existent. It is maintained by the effort of those who believe in it;" but Woodrow Wilson branded the government of the US "a foster child of special interests". Will Rogers simply said: "I don't make jokes. I just watch the government and report the facts." Sen. Edmund Muskie told the voters: "You have the God-given right to kick the government around. Don't hesitate to use it;" and Ronald Reagan matched him with: "Today if you invent a better mousetrap, the government comes along with a better mouse."

> The ten most frightening words in the English language are: "Hello, I'm from the Government and I'm here to help." RONALD REAGAN.

(5) Government, compared with ADMINISTRATION. In America the term "administration" refers more to a specific political regime than to the practice of government. Abraham Lincoln stated: "One is perpetual, the other is temporary and changeable. A man may be loyal to his government, and yet oppose the particular principles and methods of administration." In Britain, the term "administration" applies purely to the practice of government, not to those who conduct it.

government girls The young women who flocked into WASHINGTON from all over America just before and after America's entry into World War II, to perform clerical and other duties in the vastly expanded Federal bureaucracy.

Government House In most British COLONIES, the formal residence and/or headquarters of the Governor who headed the colonial administration.

government-in-exile A government set up outside the territory of the nation it aims to represent, either because that country has been invaded by an outside power or because those forming the regime believe the *de facto* government does not represent the people.

government-in-waiting A body of politicians who confidently expect to take power when elections are held, and concentrate their actions on preparing to govern.

Government of National Unity (GNU) The proposal put forward by Edward Heath during Britain's October 1974 election to heal the wounds and check growing POLARIZATION in UK politics by forming a government reaching out beyond his Conservative Party. It was an extraordinary proposal to put forward during an election campaign, and many felt Heath, who had lost power that February over his confrontation with the miners, was not the person to propose it. Yet although Labour had taken the initiative in eight months of minority government, Heath kept their gains to a minimum.

big government *See* BIG.

Cabinet government *See* CABINET.

caretaker government *See* CARETAKER.

central government The institution of government from a nation's capital, as opposed to local or devolved government.

Congressional government *See* CONGRESS.

Federal government *See* FEDERAL.

good government The governing of a nation, and the operation of its civil service and public bodies, on a basis of probity, merit, competence and fairness. Long a general principle, it gained a specific application from 1990 as Lynda (later Baroness)

Chalker, UK Overseas Development Minister under Margaret Thatcher and John MAJOR, began making aid for THIRD-WORLD states and co-operation with poorer COMMONWEALTH countries conditional on its observance – notably through action to curb corruption and embrace democracy. An early gain was the staging of democratic elections in Kenya by President Daniel Arap Moi, who had previously operated a one-PARTY state.

Her Majesty's Government The formal name for the UK government, as in "This House has no CONFIDENCE in Her Majesty's Government." It is often abbreviated to **HMG**.

> It is the duty of Her Majesty's Government not to flap or falter. HAROLD MACMILLAN.

invitation to form a government The form of words used to describe the Sovereign's contact with the winner of a UK GENERAL ELECTION. The victor drives to Buckingham Palace (after the outgoing Prime Minister has resigned if there is a change of government), and then KISSES HANDS on appointment.

machinery of government The mechanism, particularly at the higher levels of a civil service, which translates the politicians' decisions into action.

> Lord Hailsham said the other day that the machinery of government was creaking. My Lords, it is not even moving sufficiently to emit a noise of any kind.
>
> VICTOR MONTAGU, Earl of Sandwich, House of Lords, 20 April 1963.

open government *See* OPEN.

petticoat government A patronizing term sometimes used by men for a government dominated by women. It originally had a more direct and justified meaning, describing the vice-like grip on power exercised in the WHITE HOUSE by Edith Bolling Galt Wilson (1872–1961) (*see* PRESIDENTRESS) for 17 months from October 1919, as her husband Woodrow WILSON slowly recovered from a debilitating stroke. Mrs Wilson took total control of access to the President, decided which matters should be brought to his attention, and then emerged to give her account of what he had decided. Vice-President Thomas Marshall abetted her by showing no desire to take on Presidential duties, and Mrs. Wilson herself always denied having taken on herself the running of the country. But an outraged Sen. Albert Fall declared:

> We have a petticoat government! Mrs. Wilson is President!

provisional government A government established after the collapse of a country's political system, or following a REVOLUTION, to administer it until more lasting political structures can be established.

puppet government A regime in one country controlled by another, or a nominal civilian government in a state controlled by the military.

responsible government The term used in 19th century Canada, and later in other parts of the BRITISH EMPIRE, for the achievement of a large degree of self-government in place of almost total control from London. It was granted to Canada in 1846 in the wake of the DURHAM REPORT.

> Give us this truly British privilege, and colonial grievances will soon become a scarce article in the English market.
>
> JOSEPH HOWE, the Nova Scotia politician and editor.

> It is neither possible nor desirable to carry on the government of any of the British provinces in North America in opposition to the opinion of the inhabitants.
>
> LORD GREY, Colonial Secretary, 1846.

government of the people, by the people, for the people The most memorable phrase of Abraham Lincoln's GETTYSBURG ADDRESS on 19 November 1863, which ended:

> . . . that government of the people, by the people, and for the people, shall not perish from this earth.

It was not entirely original, Daniel Webster having spoken in 1830 of "the people's government made for the people, made by the people, and answerable to the people", and Theodore Parker in 1850 of "government of all the people, by all the people, and for all the people". It has also spawned numerous variants; Oscar Wilde wrote of "the bludgeoning of the people by the people for the people", Lincoln Steffens declared that "city government is government of the people, by the rascals, for the rich", and Winston CHURCHILL described ATTLEE's Labour administration as "government of the duds, by the duds, for the duds".

Go back to your constituencies, and prepare for government The rallying-cry of the UK LIBERAL leader David Steel to the party at its 1981 Llandudno assembly. In the first flush of enthusiasm for the ALLIANCE with the recently-formed SDP, Steel declared that he was the first Liberal leader for half a century who could make such a claim. His hopes were blunted by infighting between the parties over who should fight which Parliamentary seats, and the outbreak of the FALKLANDS WAR the following spring.

God reigns and the government in Washington still lives The key phrase from the dramatic speech made by Rep. (later President) James Garfield (*see* BOATMAN JIM) to calm a panicky New York crowd on 17 April 1865, two days after Abraham LINCOLN's assassination.

I'm surprised that a government organization could do it that quickly President

CARTER's comment, during a visit to Egypt, on being told that it took 20 years to build the Great Pyramid.

the negation of God erected into a system of government Gladstone's ringing denunciation of the government of Naples, stemming from the persecutions instigated by the BOURBON kings. He made it in 1851 in a letter to Lord Aberdeen.

the smack of firm government The decisive phrase in an article criticizing Anthony EDEN's premiership which appeared in the normally-friendly *Daily Telegraph* on 3 January 1956. Written by Donald McLachlan, it accused Eden of indecisiveness and half-measures:

> There is a favourite gesture of the Prime Minister's; to emphasise a point he will clench one fist to smack the open palm of the other hand – but the smack is seldom heard. Most conservatives, and almost certainly some of the wiser trade union leaders, are waiting to feel the smack of firm government.

Eden, angered by this and other charges that he was losing his grip, used a tough line with Egypt over SUEZ as a first to chance to prove his critics wrong; it proved his undoing.

Governor (1) The executive head of a British COLONY or other overseas territory, responsible to the Crown.

> Unlike my predecessors, I have devoted more of my life to shunting and hooting than to hunting and shooting.
>
> Sir FRED BURROWS (1887–1973), former President of the National Union of Railwaymen, on his appointment as the last British governor of Bengal.

(2) Most American colonies were ruled by a governor, and the title was inherited by the elected head of each State government.

> A governor plays in the minor leagues.
>
> Speaker TIP O'NEILL.

Governor-General The representative of the Sovereign who acts in place of the HEAD OF STATE in the DOMINIONS of the COMMONWEALTH, notably Australia and Canada.

Well may we say "God save the Queen", because nothing will save the Governor-General The comment of Australia's outgoing Labor Prime Minister Gough WHITLAM, on hearing the proclamation dissolving Parliament for the 1975 election following his removal from office by the Governor-General Sir John Kerr (*see* KERR SACKING).

Governor Moonbeam One of many nicknames for Gov. Edmund G. "Jerry" Brown of California (1938–), reflecting his readiness to embrace eccentric policies alongside a genuinely concerned populism. *See also* SPACE CADET.

GPU *Gosudarstvennoye Politicheskoye Upravlenye* (Russ. State Political Administration) The Soviet state security organization, created in 1922 out of the Bolshevik SECRET POLICE, the CHEKA. Its function was to identify "counter-revolutionaries" and monitor their activities. It was renamed **OGPU** (*Obedinennoye Gosudarstvennoye Politicheskoye Upravlenye*; United State Political Administration) in 1924, and was absorbed into the newly formed NKVD in 1934. *See also* KGB.

Gracie Mansion The official residence of the Mayor of New York City (*see* HIZZONER), sited at 88 East End Avenue, NY 10028.

Gracious Speech or **Speech from the Throne** The formal title to the QUEEN's SPEECH, delivered by the Sovereign or her representative at the opening of each SESSION of Parliament at Westminster and in her DOMINIONS.

gradualism The variety of SOCIALISM which spurns revolution, maintaining that change achieved through the democratic process could in time bring the major changes sought. It has consistently been advocated by the FABIANS, whose leading light Sidney Webb (later Lord Passfield) told the 1925 Labour Party conference:

> Let me insist on what our opponents habitually ignore, and indeed what they seem intellectually incapable of understanding, namely the inevitable gradualness of our scheme of change.

graffiti (Ital. scribbings on walls) One of the oldest forms of PROPAGANDA and protest, used in particular by supporters of outlawed movements to get their point across. The Soviet intervention in Czechoslovakia following the 1968 PRAGUE SPRING produced some celebrated examples, among them "Red Brothers, go back to your reservations", and "Russian circus in town. Do not feed the animals." The art of graffiti extends to doctoring slogans already daubed by an opponent. "No Pope here!" has been capped by "Lucky Pope"; "MOSLEY for Peace" adapted by prefixing it with the word "Shoot", and "Free Nelson Mandela/Astrid Proll" by adding "with every 4 gallons".

graft The use of public office for self-enrichment. In US MACHINE POLITICS some practitioners have readily admitted to graft – but insisted that it has all been "honest graft". The TAMMANY HALL stalwart George Washington Plunkitt (1842–1924) explained "honest graft" thus:

> I'm tipped off, say, that [my party] are going to lay out a new park at a certain place. I see my opportunity and I take it. I go to that place and I buy up all the land that I can. . . . Then the board of this or that makes the plan public, and there is a rush to get my land, which nobody cared for before. Ain't it perfectly honest to charge a good price and make a profit on my investment and foresight?

Gramm-Rudman Act The Act passed by Congress in 1985 in a desperate effort to check and reverse the growth in the Federal budget deficit. It was sponsored by Sen. Phil Gramm, a Texas Democrat-turned-Republican, Sen. Warren Rudman, a New Hampshire Republican, and the Democratic Sen. Ernest F. Hollings of North Carolina. Democratic leaders ridiculed it as "government by veg-o-matic", and Reagan's former budget director David Stockman termed it "mindless, destructive gimmickry". The Act required automatic cuts in Federal programmes if the Budget exceeded certain levels year by year, and ordered annual reductions in the deficit to zero by 1991; Gramm declared: "We are shooting real bullets," but though the trigger mechanism had some effect the deficit continued to rise.

> The gloomers and doomers are talking as if it'll close down the entire federal government. Hmmmmm.
>
> RONALD REAGAN.

> Not a model of political responsibility but an exercise in the politics of evasion.
>
> HEDRICK SMITH, *The Power Game*.

Gramm-Stockman Bill The "budget" drafted in March 1980 by Gramm, still then a Democrat, and Stockman to show how REAGANOMICS could work in practice. It included a 10% cut in individual tax rates and a depreciation-based cut for business, foreshadowed Reagan's massive cuts in welfare, public service jobs and REVENUE SHARING with states and cities, and also capped spending on a range of other benefits and programmes that Reagan never seriously tackled. The Bill won 140 Republican supporters in the House and 30 Democrats, giving Reagan and Stockman a solid base when they did move.

grand. Grand Coalition *See* COALITION.

Grand Old Man A semi-affectionate nickname for **William Ewart Gladstone** (1809–98), Liberal Prime Minister four times between 1868 and 1894. It was often abbreviated to GOM; the Conservative leader Sir Stafford Northcote reversed it to MOG: Murderer of Gordon, after the fall of Khartoum (*see* GORDON TELEGRAM). A serious figure in a serious age, Gladstone nevertheless got on badly with Queen Victoria, who met her match in him and greatly preferred his raffish Conservative rival Disraeli (*see* DIZZY). The Queen objected that "he speaks to me as if I were a public meeting", and wrote: "He can persuade himself that everything he takes up is right even though it be calling black white and wrong right." PARNELL described him as "like the brass knocker on a coffin", while Lord Derby observed that "Gladstone's jokes are no laughing matter". Even Gladstone's wife told him: "If you weren't such a great man you'd be a terrible bore." Walter Bagehot was probably close to the truth when he wrote: "He has the soul of a martyr with the intellect of an advocate." Gladstone, an Anglican, himself said:

> Politics would be an utter blank to me were I to make the discovery that we were mistaken in maintaining their association with religion.

The son of a Liverpool merchant, he was elected to Parliament in 1832 as a TORY, first holding ministerial office in 1834 when just 25; Macaulay saw him as "the rising hope of those stern and unbending Tories". But he broke with the Tories over the CORN LAWS, and in 1852 became Chancellor in Lord Aberdeen's coalition. By 1865 he was firmly a Liberal, serving as Leader of the House under Lord John Russell; after two years in opposition he formed his first government in 1868. From then on he alternated first with Disraeli and then with Salisbury, spending his time in opposition studying theology and the classics, cutting down trees at his HAWARDEN estate, and finding time for an interest in fallen women that may have been ambivalent. His other idiosyncracy was filling his hot water bottle with tea, which he drank cold the next morning. As might be imagined, Disraeli had plenty to say about Gladstone. "He has not a single redeeming defect"; "honest in the most odious sense of the word"; "a sophisticated rhetorician inebriated by the exuberance of his own verbosity". "If he fell in the Thames," Disraeli told the Commons, "that would be a misfortune. And if anyone pulled him out, that, I suppose, would be a calamity."

His governments lasted from 1868–74, 1880–85, February to August 1886, and 1892–94. Though not an IMPERIALIST, as Khartoum showed, he nevertheless presided over much of Britain's imperial expansion; yet his record bears out the Earl of Kimberley's prediction: "Foreign affairs are uncongenial to him. He will never shine when they occupy the first place in importance." The craggy Gladstone is best remembered as a reformer at home. His first government DISESTABLISHed the Church of Ireland, ended religious tests in universities, laid the foundations of a national education system and brought in the secret BALLOT. Gladstone declared: "All the world over, I will back the masses against the classes;" and T. H. Huxley wrote: "If working men were today to vote by a majority that two and two make five, Gladstone would believe it, and find them reasons for it that they had never dreamed of." In 1875 Gladstone "retired", saying: "At the age of 65, and after 42 years of a laborious public life, I think myself entitled to retire." But he bounced back in 1880 with the MIDLOTHIAN CAMPAIGN in which, at 71, he showed devastating power as an orator, condemning the Tory government for a weak reaction to Turkey's BULGARIAN ATROCITIES (*see* BAG AND BAGGAGE). He described the resounding Tory defeat that ensued as "like the vanishing of some vast magnificent castle of Italian romance". In office again Gladstone, branded by Lord Randolph Churcill as "an old man in a hurry", extended the FRANCHISE, but he had now resolved that "my mission is to pacify Ireland" and was increasingly preoccupied with HOME RULE, a policy which wrecked his second and third administrations. When he took office the third time the Queen, a stripling of 72, wrote:

> The danger to the country, to Europe, to her vast Empire, which is involved in having all these great interests entrusted to an old, wild, incomprehensible man of 82½, is very great.

Henry Labouchère (*see* LABBY) agreed, calling him "an aged fetish, thinking of nothing but Home Rule, senilely anxious to retain power, and fancying he can do so by tricking and dodging everyone". Gladstone finally retired in 1894 at the "Blubbering CABINET"; his biographer Sir Philip Magnus noted: "He received not one syllable of thanks for all his years of faithful and honourable service, and the Queen's letter was so curt as to be almost insulting." In her diary the Queen wrote: "Mr. Gladstone has gone out, disappeared all in a moment." Gladstone remained a powerful voice in the country up to his death, seeing off his successor, ROSEBERY. Asked why he clung to power so long, he said: "Why, to keep Mr. [Joseph] Chamberlain out, of course." Of his own impact on history, he remarked: "My name may have buoyancy enough to float upon the sea of time."

> I do not object to Gladstone always having the ace of trumps up his sleeve, but merely to his belief that God put it there. LABOUCHÈRE.

> Posterity will do justice to that unprincipled maniac Gladstone – extraordinary mixture of envy, vindictiveness, hypocrisy and superstition, and with one commanding characteristic – whether Prime Minister or Leader of the Opposition, whether preaching, praying, speechifying or scribbling – never a gentleman. DISRAELI.

> They told me Mr Gladstone read Homer at school, which I thought served him right. Sir WINSTON CHURCHILL.

> The W. G. Grace of politics. Earl ATTLEE.

Grand Old Party *See* GOP.

Granma The 58-foot yacht on which Fidel Castro sailed from Tuxpan, Mexico, with 82 followers on 24 November 1956 to begin the Cuban revolution. It was bought the month before from an American couple named Ericson for $15,000. The expedition was timed to coincide with a rising against President Batista in Santiago de Cuba; that went ahead, but the *Granma* beached on 1 December not at Niquero as planned but the inconvenient Playa de los Colorados. The rebels lost many of their weapons, were betrayed, and dispersed into the Sierra Maestra. Nevertheless the *Granma* expedition was a preliminary to Castro's eventual triumph, and is commemorated in FIDELISTA legend; *Granma* became the name of one of the regime's leading newspapers.

Grant. Grantism A late 19th-century term for nepotism, the SPOILS SYSTEM and corruption at the top. It derived from the amount of cronyism and abuse uncovered during the administration of **Ulysses S. Grant** (1822–85), 18th President of the United States (Republican, 1869–77). While the corruption unquestionably existed, the link with Grant was not entirely fair; while he did appoint too many friends and relatives to office, much of the corruption came to light because Grant ordered its exposure. A regular soldier whose career was hampered by heavy drinking, he rose swiftly in the CIVIL WAR to become General-in-chief of the UNION armies and led them to ultimate victory. Grant said of his success: "The art of war is simple enough. Find out where your enemy is. Get at him as soon as you can. Strike at him as hard as you can, and keep moving on." His conduct of the war was nevertheless controversial. Mary Todd Lincoln termed him "a butcher", and former President John Tyler was even harsher: "A scientific Goth, resembling Alaric, destroying the country as he goes and delivering people over to starvation. Nor does he bury his dead, but leaves them to rot on the battlefield." The President, under pressure to remove him, explained: "I cannot spare this man. He fights." Taxed with Grant's drinking which he had by now largely cured, LINCOLN said: "Find out what the brand is and I'll give it to my other generals." After the trauma of Lincoln's assassination and of Andrew Johnson's brief presidency, Grant was the pre-eminent choice for the 1868 elections, even though William Clafin observed: "Early in 1869 the cry was for 'no politicians', but the country did not mean 'no brains'." Grant easily defeated the Democrat Horatio Seymour; newly-enfranchized Southern Black voters boosted his majority. Political stability returned, with RECONSTRUCTION continuing, though at a more modest pace; Grant dismissed its liberal Republican proponents as "narrow-headed men, whose eyes are so close together they can look out of the same gimlet hole without winking". In the White House Grant sponsored development of the West (*see* GREAT

BARBECUE) but did not exude an aura of total control, a visitor detecting "a puzzled pathos, as of a man with a problem before him of which he does not understand the terms". And Joseph Brown declared: "The people are tired of a man who has not an idea above a horse or a cigar." Yet despite growing evidence of corruption, Grant won a landslide re-election over Horace Greeley in 1872. After his Presidency, he lost $16 million on Wall Street; his best-selling *Memoirs* were written to help pay off the debt after he had turned down an offer of millions from the Showman Phineas T. Barnum. Grant attempted a comeback in 1880, but the Republican convention blocked him; he said: "Since my name is up, I would rather be nominated. But I will do nothing to further that end."

> He combined great gifts with great mediocrity.
> WOODROW WILSON.

GRAPO An extreme leftist Spanish terrorist organization, which operates in concert with the Basque separatist movement ETA. Car-bombings and shootings of senior military figures and supposed "COLLABORATORS" with the Madrid "establishment" are its speciality; its victims have included a woman doctor.

grass. The grass grows green on the battle-field, but never on the scaffold Winston Churchill's warning after the EASTER RISING of 1916 that the execution of its leaders would lead to their martyrdom and prolong Ireland's agony.

grassroots The RANK AND FILE of party activists and supporters in the country, whose views have to be taken into account by those they get elected and by the party leadership.

grassy knoll The open slope that John F. KENNEDY's limousine was about to pass when he was assassinated in DALLAS on 22 November 1963. Topped by a wooden fence with trees just behind, it is claimed, by those who do not believe that Lee Harvey Oswald in the TEXAS SCHOOL BOOK DEPOSITORY was the sole assassin, to be the point from which the fatal shots were fired. Among their arguments is that some of Kennedy's wounds were consistent with a bullet fired from in front of him, *i.e.* from the knoll. Two police patrolmen from the Presidential motorcade were so sure it was that they ran up the knoll and saw another "police officer" behind the fence. They were then called away; the man they saw was later photographed in a uniform – but not a Dallas police uniform. That mystery has never been explained.

gravy train A situation in which one can make financial and other gains for a minimum of effort and at other people's advantage. The phrase has been used of a number of governmental systems where the rewards are great and responsibilities and ACCOUNTABILITY limited; EURO-SCEPTICS have frequently used it of the EUROPEAN PARLIAMENT at Strasbourg, where members' allowances are generous and attendance peaks during the asparagus season. At the height of the PROFUMO AFFAIR, Christine Keeler said:

> I'm on the gravy train with a second class ticket.

great. great and the good The virtually closed circle of individuals, few of them known to the general public, who are called upon by successive British governments to advise on how policy or issues should be handled. The phrase, now widely used to describe Britain's apparently effortless governing élite, was originated by Anthony Sampson in 1965. He wrote:

> A secret tome of The Great and The Good is kept, listing everyone who has the right, safe qualifications of worthiness, soundness and discretion; and from this tome came the stage army of COMMITTEE people.

Such a list is indeed kept in DOWNING STREET, and from it are appointed members of ROYAL COMMISSIONs, heads of inquiries and appointees to QUANGOS.

> Nor ought one exclusively to rely on the Civil Service Department's famous "List of the Great and the Good", all of whose members . . . are aged fifty-three, live in the South-East, have the right accent and belong to the Reform Club.
> Lord ROTHSCHILD.

Great Barbecue The process under which President GRANT offered vast tracts of unsettled land in the West to the railroad companies as an inducement to them to shoulder the immense cost of building lines across the continent.

Great Betrayal The name still used in Britain's LABOUR PARTY for the collapse of RAMSAY MACDonald's Labour Government in 1931 and its immediate replacement by a NATIONAL GOVERNMENT, also under MacDonald, in alliance with the Conservatives, which pursued policies of strict financial orthodoxy and left Labour a shattered rump. MacDonald told his Labour Cabinet as the unions resisted planned cuts in unemployment pay: "If we yield to the TUC now, we shall never be able to call our bodies or souls or intelligence our own." Some of MacDonald's colleagues thought the National Government was a temporary move rather than a permanent split, Chancellor Philip Snowden bitterly writing later: "I expected that . . . we should be able to resume our former co-operation in the Labour Party when the emergency legislation had been passed."

What would you make of a Salvation Army that took to its heels on the Day of Judgment? Sir OSWALD MOSLEY.

Great Britain The largest of the British Isles, comprising the mainlands of England, Scotland and Wales; the official title of the Kingdom from the 1707 Act of Union until the partition of Ireland in 1921, when it became the UNITED KINGDOM of Great Britain and Northern Ireland.

Great Commoner A name bestowed on a series of charismatic political figures who have either had the interests of the people at heart or are seen as having spurned the chance to opt out of representative politics and join the aristocracy. PITT THE ELDER was the first, and William Jennings Bryan (*see* PRAIRIE AVENGER) and Sir Winston CHURCHILL are among others to have earned the title.

Great Communicator The nickname of **Ronald Wilson Reagan** (1911–), the former B-movie actor who became Governor of California and at the age of 69 was elected 40th President of the United States; his two terms in the White House (1981–89) were marked by radical CONSERVATISM and FEELGOOD politics. From a poor Irish family in Illinois, Reagan became a radio sportscaster after graduating from college, and in 1937 signed with Warner Brothers, going on to make 54 movies (*see* the GIPPER). Initially a liberal Democrat and supporter of the NEW DEAL, Reagan was president of the Screen Actors' Guild from 1947 to 1952, standing out against the worst excesses of McCARTHYISM. J. K. Galbraith recalled: "I once started a trade union with Ronald Reagan. He was quite a lot to the left of me then. A real firebrand." But he began to shift after marrying his second wife Nancy (his first was his fellow film star Jane Wyman); as his career branched into television, he declared himself a Republican in 1962, worked for the party's 1964 campaign, and was elected governor of California two years later. At the start of that campaign Jack L. Warner said incredulously: "No, Jimmy Stewart for Governor, Reagan for best friend." Though both he and his opponents later depicted his tenure of the statehouse as rigidly conservative, it was in fact relatively mild. He flirted with a challenge for the Presidency in 1968, then built support on the conservative wing of the Republican Party which in 1976 enabled him to run President FORD close for the nomination. Four years later he was an obvious choice, and after defeating George BUSH for the nomination, he routed Jimmy CARTER, whose campaign was dogged by the HOSTAGE CRISIS and high levels of INFLATION.

At his INAUGURATION, Reagan pledged to "restore the great, confident roar of American progress and growth and optimism". He hit the ground running with a dramatic programme of REAGANOMICS: tax and spending cuts, coupled with a military build-up; these and other initiatives were backed initially by a majority of both Houses of Congress. Reagan's combination of tough talk towards America's enemies, his inference that everything was now under control but that anything wrong in Washington was nothing to do with him, and his canny ability to touch the public mood – even over a disaster like the later BEIRUT AIRPORT BOMBING – made him immensely popular. That popularity touched a record high after the attempt on his life in Washington on 30 March 1981. Seriously wounded, he told the surgeons: "Please assure me that you are all Republicans," and said to Nancy: "Honey, I forgot to duck." When his aide Lyn Nofziger told him: "Everything in Washington is working normally," Reagan replied: "What makes you think I'd be happy about that?" Reagan's greatest attribute was his ability to make the Presidency look easy, instead of the treadmill it had been for his predecessor. Simon Hoggart described him as "the first man for 20 years to make the Presidency a part-time job, a means of filling up a few of the otherwise blank days of retirement". He himself said: "They say hard work never hurt anybody, but I figure why take the chance?" and observed: "Over there in the White House there's a fellow that puts a piece of paper on my desk every day that tells me what I'm going to be doing every 15 minutes. He's the most powerful man in the world." And well into his second term he quipped: "The last few weeks have been really hectic, what with Libya, Nicaragua, the Budget and taxes. I've really been burning the midday oil." And after one crisis he joked: "I've laid down the law to everyone from now on about everything that happens, that no matter what time it is, wake me – even if it's in the middle of a Cabinet." The Reagans restored the pomp of the WHITE HOUSE which had been banished by the Carters, adding a touch of showbiz glitter. Hedrick Smith wrote: "He rekindled the ceremonial magic of the presidency;" but Gore Vidal remarked: "There's a lot to be said for being *nouveau riche*, and the Reagans mean to say it all." Nancy was credited with considerable influence, but Reagan said: "The idea that she's involved in government decisions . . . and being some kind of dragon lady, there is nothing to that." Yet she could freeze out a White House staffer she disliked; when she and CHIEF OF STAFF Don Regan were at loggerheads, Reagan joked: "Nancy and Don tried to patch things up. They met privately over lunch, just the two of them and their food tasters." Intellectuals resented his popular touch, bemoaning his lack of interest in culture; Jonathan Hunt joked: "In a disastrous fire in President Reagan's library both books were destroyed. And the real tragedy was that he hadn't finished coloring one." Political observers were more worried by an imprecision which was to cost him dear in the IRAN-CONTRA scandal. James David Barber called him "the first modern President where contempt for the facts is treated as a charming idiosyncracy", while House Majority Leader Jim Wright observed:

> It pains me to have to correct inaccuracies uttered by the President about meetings which I attended and he did not. Maybe it's not an intentional lie. If not, it's amnesia.

The liberal cartoonist Herblock noted: "It didn't matter whether the words were factual – it only mattered that they were presented well and sounded good." And David Stockman, his budget director in the golden days of REAGANOMICS, remarked: "If he didn't understand the big picture, how could he take the right decisions?" His ability to mis-speak himself was legendary. In 1976 he had told a Republican women's rally that "Simpson slew the Philippines with the jawbone of an ass"; he said to Britain's Shadow Foreign Secretary Denis Healey: "Nice to meet you, Mr. Ambassador;" and called Princess Diana "Princess David". More seriously, he sidestepped questions about the SLEAZE FACTOR which blighted his administration by professing ignorance of all such matters.

Reagan's stock peaked when America intervened in GRENADA in 1983, and with the economy finally showing signs of an upturn, he was re-elected in 1984 by a large majority over Walter Mondale (*see* NORWEGIAN WOOD), who belaboured his handling of the economy, saying: "Let's tell the truth. Mr. Reagan will raise taxes and so will I. He won't tell you. I just did." Reagan's age could have told against him, but he turned it into a joke, telling college students: "When I was attending college – now I know many of you probably think that was back when there were dinosaurs roaming the earth – actually there weren't, it was about the time Moses was parting the Red Sea." He also declared: "Just to show you how youthful I am, I intend to campaign in all 13 states." He was well-nigh unbeatable, TIP O'Neill confiding:

> Reagan is the most popular figure in the history of the US. No candidate we put up would have been able to beat Reagan this year.

To O'Neill Reagan was an enigma. He found him "warm and congenial, but his policies hurt people", and termed him "President HOOVER with a smile", but conceded that "every time you compromise with him, he gets 80 per cent of what he wants". When O'Neill pressed him hard over one measure, the President told him: "You can get me to crap a pineapple, but you can't get me to crap a cactus."

Reagan had promised of his second term: "I learned a lesson in my former profession. We're saving the best stuff for the last act." But this was not the case. He lost his way with Congress, adopted softer but costlier economic policies as Reaganomics stalled, and dropped his talk of the Soviet Union being an Evil EMPIRE, holding four SUMMIT conferences with Mikhail Gorbachev; at REYKJAVIK he stunned his advisers by briefly agreeing to work for total nuclear disarmament, but eventually the two SUPERPOWER leaders did conclude an INF agreement. Reagan, strongly supported by Margaret Thatcher with whom he developed a close friendship, kept up America's macho image by ordering air strikes against LIBYA in retaliation for its alleged role in the bombing of a disco in Berlin used by US troops; he said of Colonel Gaddafi: "He's not only a barbarian but he's flaky." He also stood by the CONTRAS in Nicaragua despite Congressional votes to cut off funding, but the efforts of underlings to finance it led to the Iran-Contra affair in 1986–87 which seriously dented his reputation for competence and questioned his veracity. He insisted: "I'm not smart enough to lie," but his various accounts were inconsistent. Reagan managed to dissociate himself from the worst of the wrongdoing, but never again exuded the total aura of power.

At the same time the economy was thriving – even if it meant the first ever three trillion dollar budget. And while he handed over to Bush at the 1988 election, he would almost certainly have been re-elected despite his age, had the Constitution permitted it, despite having had two operations for cancer. He quipped: "Since I got to the White House, I got two hearing aids, a colon operation, and was shot. I've never felt better in my life." He even paved the way for Reagan nostalgia, saying: "Do you remember when I said that bombing would begin in five minutes? When I fell asleep during an audience with the Pope? Those were the good old days." In retirement he remained popular, though eyebrows were raised in some quarters at the size of lecture fees he was paid in Japan; he got a rousing welcome when he joined Bush's unsuccessful re-election campaign in 1992. *See also* GREAT RONDINI.

> He has never been a good manager or strategist. His great political talent is as a visionary leader, painting themes and values broadbrush and in bold colors and thereby capturing the public imagination.
>
> HEDRICK SMITH, *The Power Game.*

Reagan may be remembered less as the engine of late 20th century conservatism than as its jaunty, if somewhat wayward, caboose. KEVIN PHILLIPS.

This nice, amiable King Victoria.
Rep. NEWT GINGRICH (Republican).

Ronald Reagan must love poor people. He's creating so many more of them. Sen. EDWARD KENNEDY.

Q: What do the USA and McDonald's have in common?
A: Both are run by a clown named Ronald.
Letter in the *Los Angeles Times*.

Great Crash The collapse of the New York stock market on 24 October 1929 which paved the way for the GREAT DEPRESSION and burst the economic bubble on which President HOOVER had been elected.

great debate *See* DEBATE.

Great Depression The world economic crisis between 1929 and 1935, triggered first by the GREAT CRASH on Wall Street in 1929, then by economic instability in Europe and finally in 1931 by the failure of several major banks. It ended the post-war boom of the 1920s, forced the West off the GOLD STANDARD, and plunged America and the other industrialized nations into an era of business failures, mass unemployment, urban and rural poverty and hardship. In Germany it propelled the NAZIS to power and paved the way for WORLD WAR II, in Britain it brought the formation of the NATIONAL GOVERNMENT (*see* GREAT BETRAYAL); America avoided such instability through Franklin D. Roosevelt's NEW DEAL, which while not restoring prosperity gave the country hope and negated the worst effects of the slump. World-wide recovery did not occur until the outbreak of war.

In the old days we could send out people from the cities to the country. If they went out today they would meet another army of unemployed coming back from the country to the city.
J. S. WOODSWORTH, Canadian CCF leader.

Great Emancipator One of many nicknames that became attached to Abraham LINCOLN, stemming from his signature of the EMANCIPATION PROCLAMATION and the freeing of the slaves after the Union's victory in the CIVIL WAR.

Great Engineer The most complimentary nickname awarded to President HOOVER, because of the talents that led him to make his fortune in a career in engineering, then perform administrative miracles as American food Administrator in WORLD WAR I and subsequently shine as Coolidge's Secretary of Commerce. The magic deserted him once he reached the White House, but he was to mobilize humanitarian relief again in World War II.

Great Leap Forward A radical economic and social reorganization in China, introduced by CHAIRMAN MAO in 1958, that was intended to transform the country into an industrialized society in the shortest possible time. The policy, which owed much to romantic MAOIST notions of inspiring the peasants and harnessing their latent skills, sought to bypass the lengthy process of developing heavy industry by concentrating on labour-intensive small-scale industries and agriculture. Traditional customs and living patterns gave way to a new system based on communes, but at the cost of major economic disruption compounded by bad harvests and the withdrawal of Soviet technical help. By early 1960 the Great Leap Forward was being modified, with elements of individual incentive and land ownership reintroduced. The Chinese leadership blamed the policy's failure on poor implementation by over-zealous CADRES plus bureaucratic ineptitude; opponents argued for a more conventional approach to industrialization.

Great Patriotic War The Soviet name for the theatre of WORLD WAR II in which the USSR was fighting for its life after Hitler's invasion in June 1941. STALIN played down the Communist nature of his regime to stress old-fashioned Russian patriotism, briefly reviving the Orthodox church to assist him. After 1945 the KREMLIN used the memory of the Great Patriotic War to bind the people to it and justify its own LEGITIMACY; the trauma of the bitter shared experience did much to prolong the Soviet system.

Great Powers A loose term for the four or five nations that at any given moment dominate the world's affairs; Hitler once declared: "Germany will either be a world power, or no power at all." Since World War II Britain has lost great power status, though she retains considerable influence; Margaret Thatcher said in the 1979 election campaign:

Unless we change our ways and our direction, our greatness as a nation will soon be a footnote in the history books, a distant memory of an offshore island lost in the mist of time like CAMELOT, remembered mainly for its noble past.

In 1987 Paul Kennedy, English-born Dilworth Professor of History at Yale, published *The Rise and Fall of the Great Powers*, which chronicled the predominance in turn of the Habsburgs, the British Empire, the United States and the Soviet Union, and predicted America's eclipse by Japan; the book was an instant best-seller.

There never was a nation great until it came to the knowledge that it had nowhere in the world to go for help.
CHARLES DUDLEY WARNER (1829–1900).

Great Removal The mass removal westward of Indian peoples from their lands in the

1830s so that Whites could settle them. In the most shameful episode of the Jackson administration, 60,000 members of the "five civilized tribes", among them the Cherokees and Choctaws, were ousted under the Indian Removal Act of 1830 from lands guaranteed to them under treaty, suffering hardship and often death before they arrived in the "Indian territory" of Oklahoma and other less hospitable lands.

Great Rondini Another nickname for Ronald Reagan, deriving from his ability to shrug off responsibility for any action or situation which looked likely to cause him political damage. *See* HOUDINI.

Great Satan The term for the United States used by Iran's AYATOLLAH Khomeini (1900–89) in whipping up Islamic fundamentalist fervour against the West.

Great Society The phrase used by President Lyndon Johnson (*see* LBJ) to describe his vision of the caring America he tried to create until the VIETNAM WAR sidetracked him. He first outlined it in a speech at Ann Arbor, Michigan, on 22 May 1964:

> In our time we have the opportunity to move not only toward the rich society and the powerful society, but upward to the Great Society. The great Society rests on abundance and liberty for all. It demands an end to poverty and racial injustice, to which we are totally committed in our time.

Johnson borrowed the phrase from the title of a 1914 book by the economist Graham Wallas. It had been used previously by Aneurin BEVAN, who wrote in 1952:

> Personal relations have given way to impersonal ones. The Great Society has arrived and the task of our generation is to bring it under control.

In the 1964 election, the Johnson platform followed up with anti-poverty programmes, expanded social security schemes and legislation to strengthen voting rights; LBJ won a LANDSLIDE victory, and followed up by getting through Congress the largest volume of welfare legislation in history. However critics later asserted that the Great Society had brought a huge increase in social security payments, rather than in real opportunities.

> The greatest outpouring of programs since the New Deal.
> HEDRICK SMITH, *The Power Game.*

> The Great Society lost its greatness in the jungles of Indo-China. Sen. GEORGE MCGOVERN, 1973.

Great Unrest The wave of strikes, especially in coal, steel, the railways and the docks, which afflicted Britain between 1911 and 1914, leading Foreign Secretary Edward Grey to observe: "We are dealing with a condition of civil war." The strikes took place as the Liberal government was acting to remove some of the irritants that caused them, passing the PEOPLE'S BUDGET and reversing the TAFF VALE JUDGMENT. They reflected the growing strength of the labour movement, which within a dozen years, and after World War I, was to bring both the first LABOUR government and the GENERAL STRIKE.

Great War The original name for WORLD WAR I, used until the outbreak of WORLD WAR II.

the greatest happiness of the greatest number The definition of the basis for successful government put forward by the English philosopher Jeremy Bentham (1748–1832). Bentham wrote:

> The greatest happiness of the greatest number is the foundation of morals and happiness.

The phrase echoed Thomas JEFFERSON's "life, liberty and the pursuit of happiness", but was not original. In 1725 the Irish philosopher Francis Hutcheson had written: "That action is best which procures the greatest happiness for the greatest numbers."

Greater East Asian Co-Prosperity Sphere Japan's plan for a new political order in Southeast Asia, drawn up in 1941 as the justification for its programme of conquest. It envisaged concentrating industry in Japan, northern China and Manchuria, with other countries in the region supplying raw materials and forming part of the consumer market. By a combination of military conquests and political alliances the plan was embarked on, but it collapsed with Japan's defeat in 1945. However it did fragment COLONIALISM in the region and foster aspirations for independence in such nations as Burma, the future Indonesia and Vietnam.

Greater London Council *See* GLC.

green (1) The colour adopted by the ENVIRONMENTALIST political movement, and the name of the parties which scored major successes in the 1980s, especially in Germany. (2) The traditional colour of Irish nationalism, the phrase **wearing of the green** going back two centuries. The extent of an Irish politician's "greenness" depends on how enthusiastic he or she is for a united Ireland. (3) The sacred colour of Islam, as in the GREEN MARCH.

Greenback Party The US party advocating the continued use of paper money first circulated during the Civil War (**greenback** = paper dollar) and opposing the GOLD STANDARD, which flourished among Western farmers before merging into the FREE SILVER movement. Founded in 1875, it won over 1 million votes in the 1878 Congressional elections, taking 14 seats in the House, but the Gold Standard was reimposed in 1879. The Greenbackers (sometimes as Greenback-

Labor) fought four Presidential elections from 1876 to 1888; their nominee in 1880, General James Weaver, was to be the candidate of the POPULIST PARTY 12 years later.

greenhouse effect The effect that occurs in the Earth's atmosphere which leads to some of the energy of the sun's radiation being retained by the Earth as heat, causing the temperature of the planet to rise (**global warming**). It is caused by the increasing emission of greenhouse gases, notably carbon dioxide. Coupled with the depletion of the ozone layer (*see* MONTREAL PROTOCOL; OZONE MAN), it poses one of the greatest threats to the future of the Earth and its inhabitants, and national governments and international bodies have since the mid-1980s been under heavy political pressure to act.

Green March The march into the colony of Spanish Sahara in October 1975 by 350,000 Moroccans armed only with copies of the *Koran* to claim the territory for King Hassan. They penetrated only a few miles, halting when they encountered the Spanish Foreign Legion, but a token party reached the capital of El Aaiun (Layoune). While the march appeared on the ground to have ended in failure, negotiations in Madrid with the post-Franco government led to Spain giving up the territory, the majority passing to Morocco and a portion briefly to Mauritania. The transfer irritated Algeria and offended a section of the territory's population of 70,000-odd, who formed the POLISARIO FRONT to fight for its independence. The march, hundreds of miles from the nearest city and sources of supply, was a masterpiece of logistics; just seven participants died – all through drowning when marchers who had never seen the sea walked straight in before military guards could stop them.

Green Paper A document issued by the UK Government containing proposals for future action, put out for consultation. It compares with a WHITE PAPER, which contains firm proposals for legislation. Such proposals allowing some room for manoeuvre are known as **white with green edges**.

Greenpeace The high-profile environmental movement originating in British Columbia in 1971 and now based in Amsterdam, which aims to persuade governments to change industrial and other activities that threaten the environment and the Earth's natural heritage. It supports NON-VIOLENT action, and has gained wide attention by its efforts to protect whales, prevent the killing of baby seals, and thwart nuclear dumping at sea. When acting against French underground nuclear tests in the South Pacific in 1985 their ship, RAINBOW WARRIOR, was sunk by a French saboteur. *See also* FRIENDS OF THE EARTH; SAVE THE WHALES.

green pound The artificial exchange rate used within the Common Agricultural Policy (CAP) to protect UK farmers from currency fluctuations. Each member nation has its own "green currency".

green revolution The Western-backed initiative to boost farm production in the THIRD WORLD which since the 1950s has produced huge increases in output, but has been blamed for tilting the economic balance in favour of large farmers and encouraging the growth of crops for export rather than domestic use. Supported by the WORLD BANK, the increased use of machinery, fertilizers, pesticides and high-yielding hybrid grains has had a particular impact in India.

green shoots The phrase used by Chancellor Norman Lamont in October 1991 for the first signs of economic recovery which boomeranged on John MAJOR's government the following year when the economy turned sharply downwards. John Smith, on his election as Labour leader on 18 July 1992, said:

> You don't have to be a paid-up member of the Royal Horticultural Society to know that the Chancellor's green shoots and his promised recovery are as far away as ever.

Big Green A radical INITIATIVE for tighter environmental laws which was defeated by California voters in 1992.

Greenham women The group of anti-nuclear UK feminists who in September 1981 set up a Peace Camp outside the US Air Force base at Greenham Common, near Newbury, to protest against the planned deployment there of CRUISE MISSILES. The camp became a focus for repeated demonstrations, breaches of the perimeter fencing and harassment of military convoys, but could not prevent the missiles arriving on schedule in 1983. The protesters were hailed by activists in CND as the front line in the struggle against nuclear war; their detractors sought to depict them as a bunch of bedraggled lesbians. The cruise missiles were eventually removed in 1988–89, not through the activities of the campers but because of the INF agreement between the SUPERPOWERS. The closure of the camp was announced in 1990, but took some time to implement.

Grenada The invasion of the Caribbean island by US forces on 25 October 1983 to overthrow ultra-leftists led by Bernard Coard who had seized power six days earlier from the NEW JEWEL MOVEMENT, murdering Premier Maurice Bishop and other leaders. President Reagan feared that the new regime would align itself with Cuba as a base for subversion and revolution in the region, making use of the British-financed airport then under construction; Reagan claimed the airport was being built by Cuban soldiers, but few Cubans were found. The invasion revealed shortcomings in liaison between US forces which led Congress to bang heads together; one Marine commander had to telephone an Air Force base in Georgia with his credit card to direct bombing attacks, because the two services had insisted on developing incompatible radio systems. While the invasion was welcomed on the island, it was condemned by the UNITED NATIONS and also produced one of the few strains between Reagan and Margaret Thatcher. Queen Elizabeth II, Grenada's nominal head of state, had not been consulted and British ministers felt they had been lied to by Washington about the decision to attack.

> Notre Dame v. the Little Sisters of St Mary's.
>
> ANON. US officer.

grey. Gray Panthers A semi-humorous name (punning on the BLACK PANTHERS) for the US pressure group organized from the 1970s to promote the rights of the retired and elderly.

grey eminence A shadowy figure behind those really in power, and the author of their policies. The term was originally used of the Italian-born Cardinal Mazarin (1602–61), chief minister to King Louis XIV of France from 1642.

Grey Wolves An extreme right-wing Turkish terrorist group, with Bulgarian Communist connections, which was implicated in the attempted assassination of Pope John Paul II in St. Peter's Square in May 1981.

Gridiron Club The élite of 60 political writers whose annual dinner at the Capitol Hilton gives 600 Washingtonians the chance to poke fun at one influential figure from each party. Every President since Benjamin Harrison has attended the Gridiron at least once; Ronald Reagan termed one of his receptions "the most elegant LYNCHING I have ever seen". Sheila Tate, press secretary to Nancy Reagan who managed to reverse a previously-negative image at one Gridiron dinner, reckoned that "for an event that has almost no television coverage and almost no press coverage, it is the most influential three or four hours".

> One of the high tribal rites of Washington insiders . . . a gathering of political celebrities that combines snob appeal with Hollywood glitter.
>
> HEDRICK SMITH, *The Power Game.*

> About as much fun as throwing cowshit at the village idiot. President LYNDON B. JOHNSON.

gridlock A Washington term for a situation in which legislation is making no progress because of conflicts within Congress and between legislators and the Administration. The word originated in the field of traffic engineering, describing the indefinite traffic jam which could develop because of a blockage at one point in a city's grid system.

Grieve for Solihull! The double-edged slogan on which Sir Percy Grieve QC fought and won the Midland seat for the Conservatives at six General Elections from 1964 to 1979.

gringo The pejorative Latin American term for Americans, in use at least since the MEXICAN WAR of 1846–7. The origin is unknown; one suggestion is that Mexican soldiers heard the YANKEE invaders singing "green grow the rushes, O". The **gringo factor** is the difficulty America has to overcome in its dealing with Central American countries because of suspicion of its motives.

Griswold-Lyon brawl The second most dramatic fight in the US Congress, after the beating of Sen. Charles Sumner over the Crime Against KANSAS. In 1798, the FEDERALIST Rep. Roger Griswold of Connecticut accused Vermont's Rep. Matthew Lyon of cowardice during the Revolutionary war, and Lyon spat in his face. A move to expel Lyon failed, and a fortnight later Griswold attacked him with his cane; Lyon retaliated with a pair of fire tongs and the two rolled across the FLOOR of the House until other members separated them.

Grits The forerunners of Canada's LIBERAL PARTY, the word still being a nickname for the Liberals. They originated in the 1840s as the **Clear Grits** (grit = determination), a radical faction in Upper Canada (Ontario) who wanted a truly democratic constitution. Their slogan of REP. BY POP. alarmed French Canadians and POLARIZED national politics into a two-party system (Grit v. CONSERVATIVE).

Grits and Fritz A nickname for the 1976 Democratic Presidential ticket of Jimmy CARTER and Sen. Walter Mondale (*see* NORWEGIAN WOOD). Carter earned the name "grits" because of Northerners' belief that Georgians ate nothing else than this variant of porridge, and "Fritz" was Mondale's nickname in the Senate.

Grocer The nickname attached by the satirical magazine PRIVATE EYE to (Sir) **Edward Heath** (1916–), Prime Minister of the United Kingdom (Conservative) from 1970 to 1974 and the leader who took Britain into the EUROPEAN COMMUNITY. (Colleagues called him Ted.) Margaret Thatcher, whom he came to loathe, was ironically referred to by some as the **Grocer's Daughter**, but this was a reference by President Giscard d'Estaing to her bourgeois nature (*fille d'épicier*) rather than any suggestion of parentage or continuity. It did, however, spark the anonymous couplet

> She was only a grocer's daughter
> But she showed Sir Geoffrey HOWE.

As applied to Heath, the epithet stemmed from his classless origins, the white-coated efficiency he sought to promote and the haggling over food prices that accompanied Britain's push to join the EC. When the Portuguese dictator Dr. Marcello Caetano visited Heath in Downing Street, he was greeted by a placard reading:

> Grocer meets Butcher.

Born in Kent and educated at Oxford – once dating Jane Wyman, who became Ronald Reagan's first wife, on a US debating tour – Heath had a distinguished wartime Army career before becoming editor of the *Church Times*. Elected an MP in 1950, the technocratic Heath was a WHIP within a year, becoming Harold Macmillan's Chief Whip, and from 1959 Minister of Labour, Lord Privy Seal and Trade and Industry Secretary. When SIR ALEC Douglas-Home resigned as Conservative leader in 1965, Heath stood in the party's first leadership election (*see* BERKELEY RULES) and won. Defeated convincingly by Harold WILSON in 1966 (*see* ACTION, NOT WORDS), he rebuilt the Tory team despite its being branded YESTERDAY'S MEN, and unexpectedly defeated Wilson's bid for a third term in 1970; Wilson had scornfully dismissed him as

> A shiver looking for a spine to run up.

The essentially liberal Heath came to office committed to an abrasive free-enterprise Toryism (*see* SELSDON MAN), but after two years of refusing to support LAME DUCKS was forced into the original U-TURN to rescue the Rolls-Royce aero engine company by NATIONALIZING it. The U-turn led Norman Tebbit (*see* CHINGFORD SKINHEAD) to observe that "his government rarely persisted with any of its announced policies once the going got tough – except on Europe", while Enoch POWELL maintained that "he executed somersaults with the unselfconsciousness of the professional civil servant". Powell added: "Ted believes there is an answer to all problems which can be worked out by proper bureaucratic means."

Heath's great achievement was to take Britain into Europe, the Treaty of ACCESSION taking effect at the start of 1973. He also had to confront the worst of terrorism in NORTHERN IRELAND, abolishing STORMONT and imposing DIRECT RULE by a UK Cabinet Minister. Heath set out to reform the trade unions where Labour had failed with IN PLACE OF STRIFE, but the INDUSTRIAL RELATIONS ACT proved over-legalistic and unenforceable (*see* PENTONVILLE FIVE). There was also industrial strife, including a miners' strike in 1972 (*see* SALTLEY) over Heath's efforts to impose a tough PRICES AND INCOMES POLICY. After the U-turn Heath's government decided on a DASH FOR GROWTH, and briefly, during the BARBER BOOM of 1973, prosperity seemed at hand. Then the combination of rising inflation, an Arab oil embargo after the YOM KIPPUR WAR and another miners' dispute threw the economy into reverse. The miners' dispute escalated into a strike, and Heath ordered a THREE-DAY WEEK, then, early in 1974, called an election on the theme of WHO GOVERNS BRITAIN? The gamble failed, the Conservatives losing their Commons majority and having to give up power to Labour after Heath failed to agree a COALITION with the Liberal leader Jeremy THORPE. In October 1974 Wilson went for an overall majority and Heath, advocating a GOVERNMENT OF NATIONAL UNITY, kept Labour's gains to a minimum. In February 1975 Heath submitted himself to re-election by his party's MPs; Margaret Thatcher (*see* IRON LADY) stood against him where others held back and was elected on the second ballot. Heath had paid the price for his remoteness, Julian Critchley commenting:

> His parsimony when it came to handing out the twice-yearly honours to clapped-out MPs was bitterly resented . . . he was also reluctant to flatter the simple.

The fact and manner of his removal by an ungrateful party soured Heath, and the way Mrs. Thatcher moved the party to the Right outraged him. Penny Junor commented:

> Ted Heath disliked two things almost above all else: people who disagreed with him, and women. Margaret Thatcher was both.

For over a decade, until Mrs. Thatcher's own overthrow in 1990, Heath glowered at her from the front bench BELOW THE GANGWAY, selectively pouring scorn on her economic policies and her strident attitude to Europe. Mrs. Thatcher herself said:

> When I look at him, and he looks at me, I don't feel that it is a man looking at a woman. More like a woman looking at another woman.

Heath's attitude aroused bitterness among Thatcherites, Robert Jones MP observing:

> Margaret Thatcher and Ted Heath both have a great vision. The difference is that Margaret Thatcher has a dream that Britain will one day be great again, and Ted Heath has a vision that Ted Heath will one day be great again.

Nicholas Fairbairn, even more bluntly, called him "a little boy sucking his misogynist thumb and blubbing and carping in the corner of the front bench below the gangway". Heath bore the carping with a mixture of irascibility and humour. HECKLED when he attempted to put his views to the 1981 party conference, he told his opponents:

> Please don't applaud. It may irritate your neighbour.

Efforts to broker peace between Heath and Thatcher failed, and the stand-off did the party considerable damage. Yet Heath in the early 1980s had few supporters; at times it seemed he was only welcome in Peking. Mrs. Thatcher's keen supporter George Gardiner observed that "receiving support from him in a by-election is like being measured by an undertaker". Heath came in from the cold when John MAJOR succeeded Mrs. Thatcher, though he raised some hackles by visiting Saddam Hussein to urge the freeing of British hostages just before the GULF WAR. At the 1992 election he became FATHER OF THE HOUSE; that year he also became a Knight of the GARTER.

Heath was not only single-minded but the only single man in modern times to occupy NUMBER TEN; an anonymous wag said that "every time Ted has a bath he looks down on the unemployed". Heath himself said: "PITT THE YOUNGER was a great British Prime Minister. He saved Europe from Napoleon. I don't know whether he would have done it any better or quicker had he been married." He was also a keen ocean yachtsman (*see* MORNING CLOUD), and a competent orchestral conductor who recorded Elgar's *Cockaigne* overture. He once said:

> Music means everything to me when I'm alone. And it's the best way of getting that bloody man Wilson out of my hair.

> That grammar school twit.
>
> ALF GARNETT (Warren Mitchell), *Till Death Us Do Part*, BBC television, 1966.

> He became leader before his party was ready for him.
>
> JAMES MARGACH, *The Abuse of Power*.

> If only he had lost his temper in public the way he does in private, he would have become a more commanding and successful national leader. WILLIAM DAVIS.

> He had some of the best ideas of any post-war Prime Minister. He was a very radical person.
>
> Dr. DAVID OWEN.

> *Heath*: Other countries have far greater problems than we have.
> *James Wellbeloved MP* (Lab.): No, they haven't. We've got you.

Gromyko. Gromyko of the Labour Party The nickname adopted for himself by **Denis Winston** (later Lord) **Healey** (1917–), a dominant Labour figure at Westminster for three decades, though never party leader. He was comparing himself with the durable **Andrei Gromyko** (1909–89), who was at the centre of Soviet foreign policy-making from 1944, attending the YALTA and POTSDAM conferences, until 1985 when he stood down as Foreign Minister, remaining on the POLITBURO till his death. As the old regime in the Kremlin crumbled, Healey said to a Soviet welcoming committee: "Same old Mafia again, I see!"

Yorkshire-born of Irish descent, Healey had a distinguished war record, serving as a beachmaster at Anzio, and made an impact when he addressed Labour's 1945 victory conference in his major's uniform. He graduated via TRANSPORT HOUSE to Parliament in 1952, and though a pre-war Communist, settled on the centre-right of the party as a foe of UNILATERALISM. Elected to the Shadow Cabinet in 1959, he served as Defence Secretary throughout the 1964–70 WILSON government; PRAVDA branded him "the atomic maniac", but his critical decisions were to abandon the TSR2 aircraft and Britain's commitments East of SUEZ. In 1974 Wilson made him CHANCELLOR, and he survived a gruelling five years at the Treasury. He confronted INFLATION nearing 30%, and weathered a party and Cabinet crisis over the spending cuts needed to secure a standby credit from the IMF. The Conservatives ridiculed him for dashing back from Heathrow en route for Manila to speak from the floor at Labour's conference. With his beetling eyebrows, scorn for his critics as "silly billies" and love of playing a pub piano on television, Healey became a national celebrity – carefully concealing a formidable intellect and a Milanese's love of opera. But he was less popular in his own party. Lady Falkender termed him a "political thug" and Roy Jenkins "one of the most insensitive know-alls of British politics"; Simon Hoggart wrote: "One feels that if he were ill, the Parliamentary Labour Party would agree to send a get-well card by 154 votes to 127 with 28 abstentions". The comedian Bob Monkhouse was even blunter: "I saw a headline which read: 'Denis Healey caught with his pants down'. That's a shame – it will make it easier to hear what he's saying." But Healey was more than a match for his critics; he dismissed Sir Keith Joseph as "a mixture of Hamlet, Rasputin and Tommy Cooper", and his assertion that he had been "savaged by a DEAD SHEEP" did lasting damage to Sir Geoffrey HOWE.

By 1979 Healey, now Labour's deputy leader, had overcome the worst of inflation and edged towards MONETARISM, but his pay policy was derailed by the WINTER OF DISCONTENT. James Callaghan (*see* SUNNY JIM) told him he would stay on for 18 months "to take the shine off the ball for you", but by now the blustering Healey was loathed by the increasingly-powerful Left, and in 1980 Michael Foot (*see* WURZEL GUMMIDGE) unexpectedly defeated him for the leadership. With the formation of the SDP, Healey, his power base weakened, fought back inside the Labour Party against unilateralism and the hard LEFT, surviving by a whisker a 1981 deputy leadership challenge from Tony BENN. At the 1984 Chesterfield by-election when supposedly campaigning for Benn, he said in an ice-skating analogy:

> Healey without Benn would be like Torvill without Dean – I can't get the bugger off my back.

He stepped down as deputy leader in 1983, but remained Shadow Foreign Secretary till 1987, going to the Lords in 1992.

Grosvenor Square demonstration The height of the protest campaign in Britain against the VIETNAM WAR, on 27 October 1968. 30,000 demonstrators massed peacefully against the war in Hyde Park, London, and 5000, headed by the then revolutionary Tariq Ali, made for the US Embassy in Grosvenor Square. The police held back the mostly good-natured crowd, but the event has since acquired a symbolism for violent protest that was not evident at the time.

Groundnut Scheme The hastily organized and badly-planned scheme by Britain's post-war Labour government to clear large areas of hitherto unproductive land in Tanganyika to grow groundnuts. The venture, started in 1947, was abandoned three years later at a cost of £30 million to the taxpayer. It was an electoral embarrassment to the LABOUR PARTY, and the phrase "groundnut scheme" came to mean any extravagant enterprise with little or no chance of succeess.

group In a UK local authority, the collective term for the members of each party; the LEADER of the council will be the leader of the controlling party group.

Group Areas Act One of the cornerstones of APARTHEID, the legislation introduced in 1950 by South Africa's ruling NATIONAL PARTY under which residential and business areas were designated exclusively for particular racial groups. It had the effect of expelling Africans, Coloureds and Asians from many suburbs and causing expropriation of their property. For the White minority, the Act served to consolidate their economic and political power. President F.W. de Klerk's promise early in 1990 to repeal or radically reform the Act was a critical step in his government's relaxation of apartheid.

Group of Ten *See* PARIS CLUB.

grouper A member of one of the Industrial Groups formed in Australia's LABOR PARTY in the late 1940s, mainly by Catholics, to combat Communist influence in the party and the trade unions. Tension between Groupers and the rest of the party culminated in the accusation from H. V. Evatt, the party's then leader, that Labor had lost the 1954 Federal elections because of "the attitude of a small minority of members, located particularly in Victoria, who [have] become increasingly disloyal to the Labor movement and the Labor party". When Labor split in 1955, many Groupers were expelled or left to found the DLP. From then on, the battle between Left and Right rendered the distinction obsolete.

grouse-moor image The phrase describing the upper-class leadership of Britain's CONSERVATIVE PARTY that did it considerable damage in the early 1960s. Built on press photographs of Harold Macmillan (*see* SUPERMAC) shooting on the grouse moors and the "emergence" of the even more aristocratic Lord Home (*see* SIR ALEC) to lead the party when he retired, it enabled Harold WILSON, who used it readily, to present himself as a young, dynamic and classless alternative. The last of the breed, William Whitelaw (*see* WILLIE) caused a stir in the mid-1980s when he inadvertently shot two beaters; fortunately neither was seriously injured.

GRUNK The magnificent initials of the Royal United National Khmer Government – *Gouvernement Royale Unifiée Nationale Khmer* – which ruled parts of Cambodia in the early 1970s under the leadership of Prince Sihanouk (1922–). Sihanouk, who had governed alone from 1941, was overthrown in 1970 by a right-wing coup while abroad, but formed GRUNK in alliance with the KHMER ROUGE; Sihanouk increasingly became a figurehead and in 1975 the Khmer Rouge overthrew the US-backed government of Lon Nol to begin the return to YEAR ZERO.

Grunwick The photographic processing factory in Northwest London which became an industrial and political battleground in 1976–77 when Asian workers fighting for higher pay were sacked for joining a trade union. They quickly gained widespread union support, and members of James Callaghan's Labour Government took part in several peaceful demonstrations. When post office workers blacked delivery of mail to the factory, the right-wing National Association for Freedom (or NAFF), of whom Margaret Thatcher was an enthusiastic supporter, won a court ruling that this breached the Post Office Act. This encouraged the firm's equally hard-line owner, George Ward, who was determined not to give in under any circumstances. In the summer of 1977 the dispute turned violent after the conciliation service ACAS had recommended recognition of the union, APEX, and Grunwick, backed by NAFF, resisted. Brent Trades Council called a mass picket, and activists from the SOCIALIST WORKERS' PARTY (SWP) moved in to stage a violent attack on the police that horrified millions of television viewers. From that point on the Grunwick workers had no chance, and hardliners in the Conservative Party had the issue they were praying for to justify a policy of tough curbs on the unions; by the 1979 election the WINTER OF DISCONTENT was to give them another.

GS rating Government Service. The rankings into which the US CIVIL SERVICE is divided; they run from GS-1 at the base of the pyramid to GS-14, grades above which have been replaced by the Senior Executive Service, membership of which is much sought by political HOLDOVERS. Most recruits start at grade GS-3.

Guadalupe Hidalgo, Treaty of The treaty between the United States and Mexico, signed on 2 February 1848, that formally ended the MEXICAN WAR. Under it Mexico gave up the lands that became the states of California, Arizona, Utah, Nevada, New Mexico and part of Colorado, and formally renounced its sovereignty over Texas. The settlement, under which Mexico received just $15 million, left lasting resentment south of the Border.

guarantee An undertaking by one country to protect or come to the aid of a second, smaller one if it is attacked – as a deterrent to aggression by another power. Britain's guarantee to Poland against attack by Germany in 1939 is an example of one that failed to deter, but was honoured nevertheless.

gubernatorial Refers to matters relating to the GOVERNOR of an American STATE; for instance, an election for Governor is known as a **gubernatorial election**.

GUBU The disastrous chain of events for Ireland's FIANNA FAIL party in the autumn of 1982 that led to the heavy defeat of Charles HAUGHEY's government in that November's election; the party was to stay in opposition for five years. GUBU stands for **"grotesque, unbelievable, bizarre and unprecedented"** – words used by Haughey himself that August when a well-known murder suspect was arrested in the flat of the Attorney-General, Patrick Connolly. The journalist and diplomat Conor Cruise O'Brien coined the acronym GUBU to refer to Haughey's style of government – and it haunted Fianna Fail to defeat. Haughey's problems also included a backlash against his refusal to back Britain over the FALKLANDS, which ended his relationship with Margaret Thatcher, and a MACHIAVELLIAN offer of an EC Commissioner's job to a FINE GAEL TD so that Fianna Fail could win his seat at a BY-ELECTION – which it failed to do.

Guernica The symbol of the brutality of General Franco's conduct of the SPANISH CIVIL WAR, and a foretaste of what Hitler had in mind for the rest of Europe. Guernica, a historic town near Bilbao which until 1876 housed the Basque Parliament, was flattened on 26 April 1937 by German bombers sent by Hitler to assist Franco's forces. The town was bombed indiscriminately, and civilian survivors mercilessly strafed; Goering admitted that the German objective was to test the effectiveness of saturation bombing. The carnage shocked the world, and Pablo Picasso commemorated the event in his famous painting, *Guernica*, completed two months after the attack.

guerrilla (Sp. little war) Irregular warfare carried on by small groups acting independently, especially by patriots (*see* PARTISANS; RESISTANCE) when their country is being invaded. The word was first used for the Spanish and Portuguese action against the French in the Peninsular War (1808–14). In the 20th century guerrilla warfare has been employed by many movements of national liberation or hoped-for revolution, some successful in achieving power, some able to destroy the economy and spread misery without the popular support to take control, others becoming romantic failures. The VIETNAM WAR demonstrated the difficulty a large-scale army backed by technology has in combating elusive guerrillas with a degree of popular support. *See also* WAR OF THE FLEA.

> The peaceful population is a sea in which the guerrilla swims like a fish. MAO TSE-TUNG.

> The conventional army loses if it does not win. The guerrilla wins if he does not lose. HENRY KISSINGER, 1969.

urban guerrilla The phrase invented by the Brazilian revolutionary Carlos Marighella (1911–65) which caught on in the 1960s as radical and MAOIST groups began to take their struggle into the teeming cities. Marighella wrote a manual for the urban guerrilla, in which he argued that if terrorists use revolutionary violence, the government will be forced to intensify repression. The notion that the forces of authority can be provoked from a political to a military solution was seized on by the BAADER-MEINHOF GANG, and more recently the Provisional IRA. Marighella wrote:

> It is necessary to turn political crisis into armed crisis by performing violent actions that will force those in power to transform the military situation into a political situation. That will alienate the masses who, from then on, will revolt against the army and the police and blame them for this state of things.

Guildhall speech The major speech which Britain's Prime Minister delivers each November as the guest of the Lord MAYOR of London, in which he or she reviews the state of world affairs and elaborates on the Government's foreign policy.

guillotine (1) The device which made beheading swift and reliable and gave the FRENCH REVOLUTION its cutting edge. Invented by the French doctor Joseph Ignace Guillotin (1838–1814), it accounted first for King Louis XVI and Queen Marie Antoinette and then, during the Reign of TERROR, for hundreds who fell foul of the leaders of the Revolution, and eventually for Robespierre himself. The guillotine was not abolished in France until 1981, the last execution by it being in 1977. (2) A procedural device for curtailing debate in a legislature. At Westminster debate on a Bill is recommended for the guillotine if Government BUSINESS MANAGERS consider the Opposition is delaying it unreasonably in STANDING COMMITTEE of the COMMONS; a timetable for further debate is put to the whole House and voted on.

guilt. guilt by association A phrase much used in America in the heyday of McCARTHYISM, reflecting the readiness of campaigners against alleged Communists to assume that anyone who had had any dealings with such people must also be guilty, without their having the chance to clear their name.

Guilty Men The polemic published in London in the summer of 1940 by Gollancz, under the name of *Cato*, which directed withering criticism against those members of CHURCHILL's coalition government who had made war more likely by pursuing policies of APPEASEMENT. The book, which became an immediate best-seller when the newsagents W. H. Smith tried to ban it, was actually written by Frank Owen, editor of the *Evening Standard*, Peter Howard, a *Sunday Express* columnist, and Michael Foot (*see* WURZEL GUMMIDGE), who was then the *Standard*'s leader writer.

Gulag The word that the Russian novelist Alexander Solzhenitsyn (1918–) branded on the conscience of the world to represent the nightmare world of forced labour camps to which DISSIDENTS and many loyal members of Soviet society were sent to break their spirit. It entered the English language from Solzhenitsyn's trilogy *The Gulag Archipelago* (1974–78); Solzhenitsyn was expelled from the Soviet Union when the manuscript was discovered. GULAG is the initials of *Glavnoye Upravlenye Ospravitelno-Trudovykh Lagerey* (Chief Administration of Corrective Labour Camps), the section of the KGB in charge of such camps.

gulf. Gulf Co-operation Council The grouping of Arab oil-producing states adjoining the Gulf, formed in 1981 primarily to co-ordinate petroleum, investment and customs policies, as well as general economic, social and cultural matters. Its members are Bahrain, Kuwait, Oman, Qatar, Saudi Arabia and the United Arab Emirates.

Gulf War (1) The conflict between Iran and Iraq that began with Iraq's invasion of West Iraq in 1980 and ended without benefit to either side in 1988. It brought the deaths of hundreds of thousands of combatants, toxic gas attacks by Iraq, and Iranian rocket attacks on Iraqi cities.

> It couldn't have happened to two nicer guys.
>
> HENRY KISSINGER.

(2) The conflict between Iraq and an American-led COALITION supported by the UNITED NATIONS, precipitated by Iraq's invasion of Kuwait on 2 August 1990. Critically, the Soviet Union, a traditional backer of Iraq, raised no objection to the West intervening. Saddam Hussein (*see* BUTCHER OF BAGHDAD) refused UN demands to withdraw and placed foreign hostages at potential targets as a HUMAN SHIELD to deter attacks; he also launched Scud missile attaches in ISRAEL. On 17 January 1991 Allied aircraft began attacking Baghdad, and on 24 February Allied ground troops drove into Kuwait and South Iraq. Kuwait was liberated, the Iraqis offering only token resistance but severely damaging the emirate's oil installations. Coalition forces pulled up inside Iraq as their remit from the UN did not extend to overthrowing Saddam; a ceasefire was agreed and the UN passed the MOTHER OF ALL RESOLUTIONS to maintain SANCTIONS until Iraq had dismantled its nuclear and chemical weapons capability and stopped persecuting its Shi'ite and Kurdish populations. The coalition's failure to finish off Saddam caused lasting problems, requiring them to establish safe havens for the Kurds and a NO-FLY ZONE to protect the Shi'ites in the south from bombing and strafing by Iraqi jets; Saddam also repeatedly harassed UN

nuclear inspectors. Early in 1993 the US, Britain and France launched renewed air strikes in an effort to bring Saddam to heel. Meanwhile Kuwait's ruling Al-sabah family reneged on its wartime promises to introduce democracy.

> Saddam Hussein is a man without pity. Whatever his fate may be, I for one will not weep for him.
>
> JOHN MAJOR, February 1990.

> The coalition will give Saddam Hussein until noon Saturday to do what he must do – begin his immediate and unconditional withdrawal from Kuwait.
>
> GEORGE BUSH, 22 February 1991.

Gulf of Tonkin resolution The resolution passed by the US Congress on 7 August 1964 which granted President Lyndon Johnson emergency powers to take any action necessary to repel or prevent attacks on US forces in VIETNAM, and support America's allies on request. Voting was 98 to 2 in the Senate and unanimous in the House. The Administration took the resolution as *carte blanche* to wage an undeclared war in Southeast Asia without further, more specific reference to Congress. It stemmed from what was erroneously reported as an uprovoked attack by North Vietnamese torpedo boats on the US destroyers *Maddox* and *C. Turner Joy*, to which LBJ had retaliated with a 64-bomber raid on military targets in the North; it later emerged that the *Maddox* had been on a spying mission in northern waters, supported by South Vietnamese patrol boats.

gun. gun control One of the keenest-fought issues in the US Congress in the three decades since the assassination of President KENNEDY, with the NRA and other gun-owners' groups having successfully lobbied against significant Federal controls on gun ownership, citing the RIGHT TO KEEP AND BEAR ARMS. Modest restrictions were enacted after the shooting of Sen. Robert Kennedy in 1968; the NRA has pressed for the relaxation of these, as well as blocking the BRADY BILL promoted after President Reagan's narrow escape from death.

Gunpowder Plot The celebrated attempt by Guy Fawkes to blow up the HOUSES OF PARLIAMENT at Westminster on 5 November 1605, the day King James I was due to open a new session. Barrels of gunpowder were found under the HOUSE OF LORDS the night before the ceremony, and Fawkes – who aimed to oust the Protestant dynasty imported from Scotland – was put to a grisly death. Justifying the plot, he said:

> A desperate disease requires a desperate remedy.

gun-running The illicit supply of weapons to an opposition or guerrilla group, for use in terrorism or an all-out rebellion. The most celebrated gun-running of the 20th century was that conducted by the ULSTER VOLUNTEERS who were organizing to stage a military challenge to HOME RULE. It reached its height on 24 April 1914 when 800 Volunteers massed at Larne to unload weapons from two steamers, the *Mountjoy* and the *Millswater*. During World War I Sir Roger Casement was executed by the British for running guns to Irish Republicans; in 1970 two Irish Cabinet ministers, Charles HAUGHEY and Neil Blaney, were acquitted of assisting the running of guns to the IRA, and in the mid-1980s the Provisionals received several shipments of SEMTEX and missiles from Libya via the *Eksund* before the ship was intercepted by French coastguards.

guns or butter? A common phrase either side of World War II for the choice facing a nation of whether it devotes its resources to armaments or to the well-being of its people. It became associated with the wartime speeches of Hitler's PROPAGANDA chief Josef Goebbels, but he had used it as early as January 1936, when he said in a speech in Berlin:

> We can do without butter but, despite our love of peace, not without arms. One cannot shoot with butter, but with guns.

Later in the year Goering took up the theme, saying:

> I must speak clearly. There are those in international life who are hard of hearing. They listen only if the guns go off. We have no butter, my good people, but I ask you, would you rather have butter or guns? Should we import lard or metal ores? Let me tell it to you straight: preparedness makes us powerful. Butter merely makes us fat!

Guomindang *See* KMT.

guru (Hindi. venerable) A term borrowed from Hinduism, where a *guru* is a revered teacher, and applied from the early 1970s to the pioneer of an ideology who becomes the focus of reverence by its adherents. Examples are Milton FRIEDMAN and Sir Keith Joseph (*see* MAD MONK) for MONETARISTS, and Ted Grant (*see* MILITANT TENDENCY) and Tony Cliff (*see* SWP) on Britain's far Left. Although he might have disputed it, preferring the title MAHATMA, Gandhi was the *guru* of the non-violent movement.

Gypsy Moths The liberal North-Eastern Republican Congressmen who rebelled against the Reagan administration's drive in 1981 for large spending cuts, and whom Reagan's budget director David Stockman blamed in part for his failure to balance the books; however he conceded that the sheer implausibility of REAGANOMICS was the real culprit. The Gypsy Moths pressed with considerable success for the restoration of cuts in Amtrak, MEDICAID, programmes for the poor and unemployed and aid for "frost belt" industrial plants, while angering the BOLL WEEVILS, also essential to a Reagan majority in the House, by demanding higher taxes on oil. Two dozen of them also threatened to oppose the budget unless there were significant cuts in defence spending.

H

H. H-Blocks The accommodation blocks at the MAZE PRISON, Long Kesh, near Belfast – named after their layout – in which convicted LOYALIST and REPUBLICAN terrorists are held, and from which 38 IRA men staged a mass breakout on 25 September 1983, stabbing a warder to death. The breakout brought a highly critical report from Sir James Hennessy, chief inspector of prisons, and the prison governor resigned. But Northern Ireland Ministers rejected calls for them, too, to go. Nineteen prisoners were still at large six months later and went on to play a major part in IRA campaigns; most were later rearrested on the Continent and in America, though two remained unaccounted for almost 10 years later. The H-blocks were the scene of the IRA's BLANKET PROTEST and, in 1981, a traumatic series of HUNGER STRIKES.

H-Bomb The thermonuclear device, first tested by the US at Eniwetok in 1952, which generated far more devastating power than the original A-BOMB. It was based on energy released by the fusion of light atomic nuclei; the A-bomb worked through fission, with heavy nuclei splitting apart. Its development gave a new twist to the ARMS RACE and also gave birth to the anti-nuclear movement.

> There is an immense gulf between the atomic and hydrogen bombs. The atomic bomb, with all its horrors, did not carry us outside the scope of human control . . . but [with] the hydrogen bomb the entire foundation of human affairs was revolutionised and mankind placed in a situation both measureless and laden with doom.
>
> CHURCHILL.

Habeas Corpus (Lat. You are to produce the body) One of the basic rights enshrined in MAGNA CARTA; confirmed under Charles II in the Habeas Corpus Act, and Article 1, section 9 of the US Constitution. The principle is that no one can be detained indefinitely or without charge; anyone held by the State can issue a writ demanding to be brought before a court for reason to be given why they are being held. LINCOLN suspended Habeas Corpus during the CIVIL WAR, but in 1866 the Supreme Court ruled that he had no authority to do so; in England *Habeas Corpus* has been weakened in practice. But it remains a fundamental of English and American justice.

Haberdasher Harry A nickname for President Truman (*see* GIVE 'EM HELL HARRY); he had opened a haberdasher's store in Kansas City after World War I but it failed after two years.

Had enough? The Republican slogan in America's 1946 mid-term elections – the first since Franklin D. Roosevelt's death – which gave the party control of both houses of Congress for the first time since 1930.

Haganah The Jewish force that operated to protect Jewish settlements in Palestine from 1920 until the declaration of the State of ISRAEL in 1948, when it became the basis of the country's armed forces. It avoided the terrorist tactics of the STERN GANG and the IRGUN. Haganah was banned under the British mandate, leading to clashes with the British as well as Arabs after World War II.

Hail to the Chief The musical greeting traditionally accorded to the PRESIDENT of the United States. The words are from the *Boat Song* in Sir Walter Scott's *Lady of the Lake*, the tune by James Sanderson. It came into use around 1828, was insisted on by Julia Tyler (FIRST LADY 1844–45), "retired" by Jimmy CARTER in a bid to end the IMPERIAL PRESIDENCY and reinstated by Ronald Reagan. During WATERGATE, satirists corrupted it to **Hail to the Thief**.

half-breeds The liberal US REPUBLICAN faction who, during Rutherford Hayes's presidency, rallied round Sen. James G. Blaine of Maine to back Hayes's southern policy and civil service reforms against the STALWARTS. *See also* OLD 8 TO 7.

Halitosis Hall The derogatory term for Britain's HOUSE OF COMMONS used frequently by the Denis Thatcher character in *Private Eye's* DEAR BILL letters.

halitosis of the intellect The classic insult delivered to Sen. Huey (KINGFISH) Long in the 1930s by Harold L. Ickes, head of FDR's Public Works Administration. Ickes said:

> The trouble with Sen. Long is that he is suffering from halitosis of the intellect. That's presuming Emperor Long has an intellect.

Hallstein doctrine The policy, adopted by the Federal Republic of Germany in 1955, that recognition of East Germany (*see* GDR) by another state was a hostile act against the Bonn government. The purpose was to maintain the isolation of the GDR, which Bonn maintained was not a legally constituted state but a barrier to German reunification. Though named after Dr. Walter Hallstein, State Secretary of the West German Foreign Office and later PRESIDENT of the European Commission, the doctrine was actually devised by Wilhelm Grewe, the country's ambassador to the US.

Hamas The REJECTIONIST group of Islamic militants who managed to derail the Middle East PEACE PROCESS in December 1992. Hamas kidnapped and murdered an Israeli army sergeant, and the Israeli government reacted by rounding up 415 alleged Hamas supporters in the OCCUPIED TERRITORIES and expelling them over the border into Lebanon. Lebanon refused to take them and the expellees – all men – were stranded in no man's land in midwinter; a handful were later allowed home as they had been detained by mistake. The PLO immediately pulled out of peace talks that had been under way in Washington.

Hamilton, Alexander (1755–1804) Washington's wartime aide-de-camp, co-framer of the US CONSTITUTION and principal author of the FEDERALIST (51 of 85 issues). As Secretary of the Treasury from 1789 until he resigned in 1795, he constructed the financial base of the new Republic.

> He smote the rock of the national resources, and abundant streams of revenue gushed forth. He touched the dead corpse of the Public Credit, and it sprung upon its feet. The fabled birth of Minerva, from the brain of Jove, was hardly more sudden or more perfect than the financial system of the United States as it burst forth from the conceptions of Alexander Hamilton.
>
> DANIEL WEBSTER (1782–1852).

Hamilton was less successful with his own finances, having paid out well over $1000 to the blackmailers James and Maria Reynolds, after being seduced into an adulterous relationship with Maria. On a political level his opponents, who knew little of this, declared: "When a little Alexander dreams himself to be Alexander the Great, he is very apt to fall into miserable intrigues." And his fellow-Federalist John ADAMS termed him "that bastard son of a Scotch pedlar". But to his opponent Thomas JEFFERSON, who recalled that "Hamilton and myself were daily pitted in the Cabinet like two cocks", Hamilton was "a colossus . . . he is a host within himself". Hamilton engineered Adams's defeat in the REVOLUTION OF 1800, but instead of securing the presidency for himself got Jefferson elected. He retired from politics, and in 1804 was killed in the BURR-HAMILTON DUEL.

> The Republic is his monument.
>
> Sen. ARTHUR H. VANDENBERG (1884–1951).

hammer and sickle The twin emblem of world COMMUNISM, as firmly identified with it as the RED STAR. Adopted by the Soviet Union in 1923, they symbolize productive work in the factory and on the land.

Hampstead set The close friends of Hugh GAITSKELL, UK Labour Party leader 1955–63, who like him were mainly Oxford-educated intellectuals living in Hampstead. The group, which included Anthony Crosland, Denis Healey, Douglas Jay, Roy Jenkins and Frank Pakenham (later Lord Longford) were accused by BEVANITES of undue influence over Party affairs.

Hancock, John A person's signature, from the bold hand with which John Hancock (1737–93) became the first signer of America's Declaration of INDEPENDENCE, saying:

> There, I guess King George will be able to read that.

hand. handbagging Pejorative for Margaret Thatcher's negotiating tactics (*see* IRON LADY) and treatment even of her colleagues. At one Cabinet committee meeting Nicholas Ridley said: "Why don't we start? The handbag is here." And US Secretary of State George Shultz presented her with a handbag at his retirement party, telling her:

> You are the only person so far to whom has been awarded The Order of the Handbag.

The term has been ruled UNPARLIAMENTARY in Ireland's DAIL. In 1992 Maire Geoghegan-Quinn, Minister of Transport, was accused of handbagging the board of *Aer Lingus*. She objected that the term was a sexist hangover from Thatcherite Britain, and a man acting the same way would have been praised for decisiveness. The Speaker agreed.

handbell The "Victory bell" rung by party chairman Lord Hailsham (Quintin Hogg, 1907–), at the Conservatives' 1957 conference during a morale-boosting speech aimed at rallying the party after SUEZ. Ever since, a handbell has been presented to the chairman of the conference. Together with the flat cap he wore as Macmillan's Minister for the North-East, it became his trademark. Hailsham told the conference:

> Let us say to the Labour Party: "Send not to ask for whom the bell tolls – it tolls for them!"

Handsome Frank The nickname of **Franklin Pierce** (1804–69), 14th President (Democrat, 1853–57) of the United States. A New Hampshire lawyer with a fine physique, colourful dress and a touch of personal vanity, Pierce was a Congressman at 25 and a Senator at 33, but returned to private practice after one Senate term until the MEXICAN WAR, when he served as a Brigadier-General. He was nominated in 1852 as a COMPROMISE CANDIDATE after 48 ballots at the Democratic convention had produced deadlock. In the Presidential campaign supporters of the WHIG Winfield Scott termed Pierce, always a hard drinker, "the hero of many a well-fought bottle" – inferring cowardice in battle; in fact Pierce was thrown from his horse and injured in his only engagement. On his inauguration after defeating Scott, he appealed: "You have summoned me in my weakness – you must sustain me by your strength." Stephen Douglas was even blunter, declaring: "Hereafter, no private citizen is safe," and his friend Nathaniel Hawthorne told him: "Frank, I pity you, indeed I do, from the bottom of my heart." The Pierce administration brought trade RECIPROCITY with British North America, treaty links with Japan, but the seeds of the CIVIL WAR in the repeal of the MISSOURI COMPROMISE and passage of the KANSAS-NEBRASKA ACT. Pierce himself was a LAME DUCK, his former secretary B. B. French maintaining in 1856: "Whoever may be elected, we cannot get a poorer cuss than now disgraces the Presidential chair."

> Pierce didn't know what was going on, and even if he had, he wouldn't have known what to do about it.
>
> HARRY S TRUMAN.

hang. hang me first, and let him speak afterwards The plea of a prisoner about to be hanged in public in 1874 when J. C. S. Blackburn, a candidate for Congress in Kentucky, offered to speak when the condemned man had no last words.

Hang the Kaiser! A POPULIST slogan in Britain and France at the close of WORLD WAR I, and one of the slogans on which the Lloyd George COALITION won the COUPON ELECTION. It branded Germany's *Kaiser* (Emperor) Wilhelm II (1859–1941) as the principal architect of the war; in the event, he was exiled to Holland.

we must indeed hang together, or most assuredly we shall hang separately Benjamin FRANKLIN's remark to his fellow-revolutionary John HANCOCK, at the signing of the Declaration of INDEPENDENCE, 4 July 1776. It reflected the fate that awaited them should America lose the Revolutionary War.

hangers and floggers Shorthand for the powerful lobby for LAW AND ORDER on the right of Britain's CONSERVATIVE PARTY which campaigned in the 1950s for the return of flogging and, from the moment of its abolition in 1966, the return of capital punishment.

Hangman Foote The mid 19th-century US Senator Henry Foote of Mississippi. He gained his nickname for threatening to hang a New England senator from the tallest tree in his state. In 1850, Foote pulled a loaded revolver in the Senate on Sen. Thomas Hart Benton of Missouri, the only Southern senator to oppose an extension of slavery. Benton cried: "Let him fire!", but colleagues overpowered Foote.

Hansard The **Official Report** of proceedings at Westminster in the two Houses of Parliament. It is named after Thomas Curson Hansard, son of the government printer Luke Hansard, who produced the first reliable reports of debates from 1803. Previously such reports had been treated as a breach of privilege.

> History's ear, already listening. Lord SAMUEL, 1949.

Happy Nickname of Margaretta Rockefeller, socialite wife of Nelson Rockefeller (*see* ROCKY), governor of New York and Gerald Ford's Vice-President. The name was reportedly given in 1927 by her French nursemaid; bouncing the baby on her knee when she heard that Charles Lindbergh had achieved the first nonstop flight from New York to Paris, the maid saw she was responding with happy gurgles and smiles.

Happy days are here again Franklin D. Roosevelt's 1932 campaign theme song and the anthem of the NEW DEAL. Written in 1929 by Milton Ager (words) and Jack Yellen (music), it was adopted at the Democratic Convention after FDR's aide Edward Flynn rejected *Anchors Aweigh* as "a dirge".

> Happy days are here again!
> The skies above are clear again!
> Let's all sing a song of cheer again –
> Happy days are here again!

Happy Warrior, the Originally the nickname of **Al** (Alfred Emmanuel) **Smith** (1873–1944), Governor of New York and Democratic presidential nominee in 1928. It was accorded him at the 1924 Democratic CONVENTION by Franklin D. Roosevelt, who described him in his unsuccessful nominating speech as "the Happy Warrior of the political battlefield."

More recently the name has belonged to Sen. **Hubert Horatio Humphrey** (1911–78), the lifelong liberal with strong LABOR connections. A Democratic Senator for Minnesota from 1946 to 1964, he served as Lyndon B. Johnson's VICE-PRESIDENT, then ran for the Presidency himself against Richard

Nixon in 1968. His apparently no-hope candidacy for a party hopelessly split over the VIETNAM WAR ran Nixon close after he belatedly distanced himself from Johnson's war policy. He tried again in 1972 and 1976, but failed to win the nomination. He died in 1978 after a heroic fight against cancer.

HHH had a powerful social conscience. He was the co-architect of the HUMPHREY-HAWKINS FULL EMPLOYMENT ACT which set full employment as a national goal, and in 1966 he told a local government convention in New Orleans: "I'd hate to be in those [slum] conditions, and I'll tell you that if I were in those conditions, you'd have more trouble than you already have because I've got enough spark left in me to lead a mighty good revolt." But the radical Left suspected him, Hunter S. Thompson attacking him in 1972 as "a treacherous, gutless old WARD-HEELER who should be put in a goddam bottle and sent out with the Japanese current". Humphrey was a rapid speaker; Barry Goldwater once said: "He talks so fast that listening to him is like trying to read *Playboy* magazine with your wife turning the pages." Goldwater also claimed Humphrey had been "vaccinated with a phonograph needle". But Humphrey retorted: "I've never thought my speeches were too long – I've enjoyed them."

> Above all, Hubert was a man with a good heart. He taught us all how to hope and how to live, how to win and how to lose, he taught us how to live and, finally, he taught us how to die.
>
> Vice-President WALTER MONDALE's funeral eulogy, Washington, 15 January 1978.

> According to Gandhi, the seven sins are wealth without works, pleasure without conscience, knowledge without character, commerce without morality, science without humanity, worship without sacrifice and politics without principle. Well, Hubert Humphrey may have sinned in the eyes of God, as we all do, but according to those definitions of Gandhi's, it was Hubert Humphrey without sin.
>
> President JIMMY CARTER's funeral eulogy, St. Paul, 16 January 1978.

Don't worry, be happy The unofficial theme song of George BUSH's successful 1988 campaign for the Presidency. It won a Grammy award for the singer Bobby McFerrin.

Harambee! (Swahili. Let's all pull together) The slogan for Kenyan independence and national unity of Jomo Kenyatta (1889–1978), from 1964 the republic's first president, and his KANU party. *See also* MAU MAU; UHURU.

Harare declaration The declaration committing members of the COMMONWEALTH to GOOD GOVERNMENT free of corruption and human rights abuses, which was agreed at the 1991 CHOGM in Harare, Zimbabwe, at the instigation of John MAJOR.

Harcourt Room For decades, the restaurant at Westminster adjoining (and below) the riverside terrace of the HOUSES OF PARLIAMENT where MPs could entertain guests. It was named originally after Lewis "Loulou" Harcourt, 1st Viscount and son of the Victorian Liberal statesman Sir William, but renamed the **Churchill Room** in 1991 amid protests by over 100 MPs. The room featured a harpist who performed in apparent violation of regulations banning music in the Palace of Westminister.

> *Peer 1*: We could do with this in the Lords.
> *Peer 2*: Most have got a harp already. We are only waiting for the wings.

hard. hard cider candidate The US WHIGS' name for their 1840 Presidential candidate William Henry Harrison (1773–1841), whom they contrasted with the "oriental splendour" of the incumbent Martin van Buren. Harrison defeated him but caught cold during his inauguration and died 31 days later. *See also* LOG CABIN.

hard faced men who have done well out of the war Stanley BALDWIN's verdict on the businessmen and other prosperous non-combatants who took their seats in the Commons after the COUPON ELECTION of 1918 to seek vengeance on Germany. His actual words were: "A lot of hard-faced men who look as if they had done very well out of the war."

hard-hats The conservative construction workers whose support President Nixon and, even more, Vice-President Spiro AGNEW cherished during the closing stages of the VIETNAM WAR. Wearing their safety helmets, they demonstrated for continuing the war and against anti-war protesters.

hard landing An economically bleak ending to a boom cycle stemming from over-severe measures taken to check it. As Nigel Lawson sought to damp down the UK's boom in 1988, commentators speculated on whether the corrective measures would bring a "hard landing" or a less painful "SOFT LANDING". The former were right.

hard left *See* LEFT.

Harding, Warren Gamaliel (1865–1923) 29th President of the United States (Republican, 1921–23). A low-profile Senator from Ohio chosen in the original SMOKE-FILLED ROOM to break the deadlocked 1920 Republican Convention, Harding defeated James M. Cox in a LANDSLIDE through his appeal for NORMALCY after the WILSON era. Harry Daugherty explained that Harding was nominated because "he looked like a President", and there could have been few other reasons. Harding himself said: "I am not fit for this office and never should have been here", and his father once told him:

If you were a girl, Warren, you'd be in the family way all the time. You can't say "No."

Indeed he had a string of extramarital affairs, one producing an illegitimate daughter; a second mistress was sent on a world cruise during the election. His presidency was banal; Harding himself said: "I am a man of limited talents from a small town. I don't seem to grasp that I am President." Woodrow Wilson had warned that "he has a bungalow mind", and Sen. William McAdoo recorded: "His speeches leave the impression of an army of pompous phrases moving over the landscape in search of an idea. Sometimes these meandering words would actually capture a straggling thought and bear it triumphantly a prisoner in their midst until it died of servitude and overwork"; H. L. Mencken more tartly observed: "He writes the worst English I have ever encountered. It is so bad that a sort of grandeur creeps into it". Mencken's overall verdict on Harding was "a tinhorn politician with the manner of a small town doctor and the mien of a ham actor". Harding died suddenly in San Francisco as the corruption in his administration (*see* TEAPOT DOME) was becoming evident, Samuel Hopkins Adams declaring: "Few deaths are unmingled tragedies. Harding's was not; he died in time."

He was not a bad man. Just a slob.
ALICE ROOSEVELT LONGWORTH.

harmonization In the EUROPEAN COMMUNITY, the process of bringing member states' taxation systems, industrial specifications, professional qualifications, *etc.*, into line to assist creation of the SINGLE MARKET.

Harper's Ferry The most celebrated incident which preceded the US CIVIL WAR. On 16 October 1859 the ABOLITIONIST John Brown and 18 followers seized the Federal arsenal at Harper's Ferry on the upper POTOMAC and issued a proclamation to the slaves to rise up. US troops under Robert E. Lee forced the raiders to surrender; Brown was taken to Richmond, tried and hanged.

Harrison, Benjamin *See* WHITE HOUSE ICEBERG.

Hart Building The most opulent of the six office buildings constructed around the US CAPITOL to provide 1 million square feet of office space and other facilities for the Senate. With a planned rooftop dining room, third gymnasium, 16-foot ceilings and a basketball court, it proved so costly (*c.* $150 million) that the House suspended APPROPRIATIONS for a time. It was completed in the early 1980s.

hat in the ring To throw one's hat in the ring is to declare one's availability, or candidacy, for office. It originated with Theodore Roosevelt, who said when launching his 1912 BULL MOOSE campaign:

I am stripped to the buff and my hat is in the ring.

Hatch Act The legislation, enacted in 1939, which barred US civil servants, other than policymaking officers, from participating in party political campaigns. The Act also imposed tentative curbs on campaign financing.

hatchet-man A ruthless demolisher of political opponents, by inference acting with the approval of apparently more civilized colleagues. In the 1976 vice-presidential DEBATE, Sen. Walter Mondale said Sen. Robert Dole had "richly earned his reputation as a hatchet man" by asserting that 1.6 million Americans had been killed in "Democratic wars". The phrase originated in 19th-century America, describing hired killers from China.

Hatterji The nickame of **Roy Sydney George Hattersley** (1932–), writer, gourmet, Yorkshire nostalgist and, from 1983 to 1992, deputy leader of the Labour Party. The only son of two Sheffield Labour councillors (one a former Catholic priest), Hattersley was a youthful success in local government before being elected MP for Birmingham Sparkbrook in 1964. The constituency's high Indian and Pakistani population and a party conference reference to "my Asians" earned him the soubriquet; one Labour colleague went further, describing him to the author as a "closet Muslim". Harold Wilson marked him out for early promotion, and he became a junior employment minister in 1967. He was a Foreign Office minister from 1974 and joined the Cabinet as Prices Secretary in 1976. In opposition from 1979 he fought hard against the BENNITE Left when many colleagues were defecting to the SDP. Neil KINNOCK defeated him for the leadership in 1983, but Hattersley served under him in what was claimed as the Dream TICKET. After Labour's fourth successive defeat in 1992, he retired to the back benches. His critics saw him as, in Dr. David OWEN's words, "the acceptable face of opportunism"; Professor John Vincent asserted that "there are lies, damned lies and Roy Hattersley", and Norman Tebbit asked: "Would you want him as your bank manager?". But Hattersley, on the right of the party, was consistently pro-European and above all loyal to Labour, though his image of it was sometimes the party of the late 1940s. He was also lampooned for his appetite and, unmeritedly by the TV puppet satire *Spitting*

Image, for reputedly spraying those around him when he spoke. Ironically the Tory MP Jock Bruce-Gardyne had once said:

> He has a voice like the last splash of a soda syphon.

Hattersley could be a robust debater. He once described the Tory deputy premier William (later Viscount) Whitelaw (*see* WILLIE) as "one of the last representatives of a dying Tory tradition, possession of land, enthusiasm for shooting small birds and antipathy for reading books". He could also hold his own in Labour's bruising internecine conflicts. Prior to the 1983 election he clashed with party leader Michael Foot:

> *Hattersley*: You have betrayed us [by refusing to change the block voting system]. What kind of leadership is this?
> *Foot*: Don't talk to me like that. I'll have your head off. I'll have the skin off your back.
> *Hattersley*: You couldn't knock the skin off a rice pudding.

But he often got as good as he gave. Once, when he was in full flight denouncing a Tory attack on the Callaghan government as "an unprecedented example of the triumph of tactics over principle", Norman St. John Stevas (later Lord St. John) brought the house down by asking: "Has the Rt. Honourable Gentleman ever considered his own career?" And after his retirement as deputy leader the Tory party chairman Sir Norman Fowler described Hattersley as

> The only man to move from the Cabinet table to the restaurant table and consider it a promotion.

Hattonistas The MILITANT TENDENCY supporters on Merseyside of Derek Hatton (1948–), deputy leader of Liverpool City Council from 1983 to 1986. The name was a parallel with the SANDINISTAS. Through Militant sympathizers in the Labour Party and local government trade unions, the sharply-dressed and convivial Hatton controlled the council. But his challenges to the Thatcher government in defiance of Labour policy led Neil KINNOCK to denounce him in a dramatic scene at Labour's 1985 conference. Kinnock spoke scornfully of

> The grotesque chaos of a Labour council – a Labour council – hiring taxis to scuttle around a city handing out redundancy notices to its own workers.

He was subsequently expelled from the Labour Party, disqualified by the courts from serving on the council because of unjustified spending, and eventually prosecuted – but acquitted – for alleged corruption.

Haughey factor The reluctance of middle-class Irish voters to support FIANNA FAIL so long as **Charles Haughey** (1925–) was its leader. FINE GAEL strategists identified this and played on it in successive elections in the 1980s. Haughey was the most charismatic politician of his age, his rise to power only briefly interrupted by the ARMS CRISIS of 1970. Elected a TD in 1957, he was a Cabinet Minister from 1960 to 1970, returned in 1977 and in 1979 became TAOISEACH on the retirement of Jack Lynch. Tougher than expected against TERRORISM, he enjoyed an initially very warm relationship with Margaret Thatcher, one British official describing their first meeting as "almost a seduction"; but she turned against him when Ireland blocked EC support for Britain over the FALKLANDS. He headed Fianna Fail governments from 1979 to 1981, February–December 1982 (*see* GUBU), and 1987–1992 (from 1989 in coalition with the Progressive Democrats) (PDs).

Haughey once said: "I do not contemplate defeat." He also asked: "What would I be doing if I wasn't leading Fianna Fail? It's my life." His critics agreed. Declan Hilberd wrote that "his only philosophy appeared to be the retention of power". To Fianna Fail TD Charlie McCreevy, Haughey was "only at his best when his back is to the wall". Conor Cruise O'Brien went further, noting: "His admirers thought he resembled the Emperor Napoleon, some of whose better known mannerisms he cultivated." According to his unofficial biographer Stephen Collins, "he never wore a watch or carried anything apart from cash in his pockets. If he needed to know the time or wanted anything, he asked a minion who was expected to respond promptly." To Dublin journalist Tim Pat Coogan, he was "the epitome of the men in the mohair suits".

Vincent Browne concluded that "faced with almost all challenges, except leadership challenges, his instinct has been to back off or fudge". Yet he could be ruthless. One anonymous TD confided: "Give him enough rope and he'll hang you." After the WHIP was withdrawn from the future PD leader Desmond O'Malley, Haughey's press secretary P. J. Mara said: "*Uno* DUCE. *Una Voce*. There'll be no more nibbling at my leader's bum." And Haughey once described his own Cabinet as "only a crowd of gobshites". His Fine Gael adversary Garret FitzGerald asserted, in turn, that Haughey "comes with a flawed pedigree". Yet Haughey's stature was immense. New York's Governor Hugh Carey called him "the Harry Truman of Irish politics". To Sen. Edward KENNEDY he was "a great personal friend". And many Irish people backed him all the way. Conor Cruise O'Brien wrote: "They knew perfectly well that he was a rogue, and liked him the better for it." And when he resigned, a letter in the *Irish Times* termed him

> The only honest gangster ever to run Ireland.

Havana conference A conference of American states held in Havana in 1940 to consider the impact and implications of WORLD WAR II, which at that point was confined to western and central Europe. The participants agreed on the "No Transfer" principle under which control over colonies in the Americas could not be transferred between non-American states; this meant that they would oppose any move by Germany to take over British and French possessions.

Hawarden Kite The LEAK in December 1885 by Herbert Gladstone, son of the GRAND OLD MAN, of his father's intention to go for Irish HOME RULE: a Dublin parliament under the Crown and Westminster. The kite thus flown took its name from Gladstone's home at Hawarden, in North Wales just west of Chester. It did considerable political damage to the LIBERAL PARTY, precipitating a split over Home Rule.

> It marked the withdrawal from the Liberal party of the aristocratic element.
>
> JOHN (later Viscount) MORLEY (1838–1923).

Hawke, Robert *See* SILVER BODGIE.

hawks Active supporters of a war policy, and of a belligerent stand on other issues. The term originated with the **war hawks,** Thomas JEFFERSON's term for the party who in 1798 were pressing for conflict with Britain. It was used of Henry Clay, John C. Calhoun and their frontier supporters of the 1812 war with Britain, and of advocates of a military settlement of the 1840s dispute over the US border with Canada. The term "hawk" on its own – and its opposite, DOVE – dates from the VIETNAM WAR; it was popularized by Robert F. Kennedy.

Hay-Pauncefote treaty The treaty signed by America and Britain in 1901 which freed each country from its pledge never to build a canal across Central America on its own or colonize any part of the region. It enabled America to build the PANAMA CANAL, provided all nations should have equal use, and created the CANAL ZONE. The **Hay-Herran Treaty** with Colombia, two years later, gave America a 99-year lease over the Canal Zone. When the Colombian senate refused to RATIFY it, the province of Panama seceded and, with US support, formed a separate Republic which agreed to the creation of the Zone. The treaties with Britain, Colombia and Panama were all concluded by John Hay (1838–1905), who was Theodore Roosevelt's Secretary of State.

Hayes, Rutherford *See* OLD 8 TO 7.

Haymarket riot The outbreak of violence in Chicago on 4 May 1886 arising from a mass meeting of strikers at the McCormick Harvester Company. When police tried to break up the meeting, called to protest against their tactics, a bomb was thrown, killing seven police officers. Both sides opened fire, leaving two strikers dead and a number of police and civilians injured. The bomb-thrower was never found, but eight anarchists were convicted of inciting the crowd and four were hanged. The incident severely damaged the American labour movement, and began the eclipse of the KNIGHTS OF LABOR, even though they were not responsible for it.

Haynsworth nomination The first of President Nixon's defeats by the Senate over nominations to the SUPREME COURT. Federal appeal judge Clement Haynsworth Jr., a Southern Democrat, was Nixon's second nomination after Chief Justice Warren Burger as he moved to reverse the liberal thrust of the former WARREN COURT. Nominated to replace the resigning Justice Abe FORTAS, Haynsworth was strongly opposed by CIVIL RIGHTS campaigners and organized labour for his views, but the Senate rejected him in 1969 by 55 to 45 because he had tried cases involving businesses in which he held small amounts of stock. It was only the second time in the 20th century that such a nomination had been rejected. Nixon fought hard to get Haynsworth confirmed, winning one Senator's vote by channelling a $3 million urban grant through his office instead of that of the local Congressman.

Hays, Wayne Hays affair The scandal that erupted in 1976 after the *Washington Post* reported that Rep. Wayne Hays of Ohio, 65-year-old chairman of the House Administration Committee, had been keeping Elizabeth Ray, a former Virginia beauty queen, on the payroll of a subcommittee as a $14,000-a-year clerk in return for sexual favours. Miss Ray, 33, had gone to the paper after Hays suddenly remarried, telling her: "You'll be Mistress No. 1" She admitted: "I can't type. I can't file. I can't even answer the phone," and said of Hays:

> He did to me what Nixon did to the country.

Hays was one of the most feared figures on Capitol Hill, but the scandal brought his resignation from Congress. It triggered a rash of disclosures about other legislators, but the New York Congresswoman Bella Abzug was not among them. She said:

> I was never worried about any sex investigation in Washington. All the men on my staff can type.

Haywood case The trial in 1907 of three union leaders for allegedly assassinating former Idaho governor Frank Steunenberg, who was elected as a "friend of miners", but called in the troops to Coeur d'Alene in 1899 to break a strike. A local man, Harry Orchard, confessed under investigation to the bombing and incriminated the "inner circle" of the World Federation of Miners. Its secretary, Bill Haywood, president, Charles Moyer, and George Pettibone, a BLACKLISTed miner, were extradited to Idaho. The arrests produced a rare unity among US labour and Socialist bodies, and a vigorous campaign was launched to save the three; President Roosevelt remarkably declared the three to be "undesirable citizens" before the case was heard. After a year on Death Row awaiting trial, they were acquitted following a brilliant 11-hour defence speech by Clarence Darrow.

he. He asked to see me again. I think he wants me for my body The comment made by Ken Livingstone (*see* RED KEN), leader of the Greater London Council (GLC), *c.* 1981 after a meeting with Transport Secretary Norman Fowler to discuss his revolutionary "Fares Fair" policy for the London Underground.

He is to the arts what James "Bonecrusher" Smith is to lepidoptery One of many derogatory comments made during the 1980s by the Labour MP Tony Banks against Terry Dicks (1937–), right-wing Tory MP for Hayes and Harlington. Another, anonymous, member said of Dicks: "He was born ignorant and has been losing ground ever since."

He may be a blackguard, but not a dirty blackguard The verdict of Sir Neville Henderson, pre-war British Ambassador in Berlin, on the leading NAZI Hermann Goering. Henderson's remark, in a speach at Sleaford, typified the views of one of the champions of APPEASEMENT.

He reminds every woman of her first husband A charge levelled against a number of US Presidential hopefuls, starting probably with Thomas Dewey.

He seen his opportunities and he took 'em The epitaph on George Washington Plunkitt (1842–1924), a one-time butcher's boy of poor Irish stock who rose through mastery of TAMMANY HALL to become a millionaire. At one point in 1870 he was drawing three salaries, as an assemblyman, alderman and police magistrate. His "office" was an Italian's shoeshine stand in the basement of the old county court office.

He shines and stinks like rotten mackerel at moonlight The stinging insult delivered by John Randolph (1773–1833), Virginian leader of the Jeffersonians in the House of Representatives, against his political foe Edward Livingstone.

He that will not work shall not eate The charge made by Captain John Smith (1580–1631) in 1608 to the Jamestown colony of which he was governor. The phrase became the embodiment of the Protestant WORK ETHIC.

He thinks manual labour is a Spanish peasant The dismissive rebuke directed against an allegedly-remote Conservative minister in the 1950s by the left-wing Labour MP Fenner (later Lord) Brockway (1888–1988).

He who is not with us is against us An axiom of STALIN's style of government, lifted from Christ's statement in *Luke* xi, 23 that "He who is not with me is against me." Stalin must have remembered it from his days as a seminarian – even if he forgot most of the other basics of Christianity. The Hungarian Communist leader Janos Kadar (1912–89) was also quoting Christ when he reversed the phrase to produce the less confrontational "He who is not against us is with us."

He would, wouldn't he The most celebrated saying from the PROFUMO AFFAIR. It was made on 29 June 1963 by the 19-year-old Mandy Rice-Davis when, during the trial of the osteopath Stephen Ward, she was told that Lord Astor had denied charges she had made.

head. head of Government A collective term covering PRIME MINISTERS in countries where there is a largely ceremonial monarch or President, and Presidents who themselves head the EXECUTIVE, as in the United States.

head of State The formal leader of a country, who may like Britain's sovereign wield only limited, though ultimate, power or who may, as with the French or American President, be in everyday political charge of the nation.

headbanger A dogmatic left- or right-winger whose views are not only extreme but eccentric. The term originally applied in the 1970s to fans of heavy metal music who shook their heads violently in time to it.

Healey, Denis Winston *See* GROMYKO OF THE LABOUR PARTY.

Hear, Hear! The standard expression of agreement with a point made in Parliamentary debate. At WESTMINSTER it frequently comes out as a low rumble.

hearing A COMMITTEE session called to take evidence from one or more individuals or organizations, and to question them on it. Hearings are generally part of a process leading either to the CONFIRMATION of an office-holder, the production of a report or (sometimes) the approval of legislation.

heart. hearts and minds The watchword for America's campaign to secure the backing of the civilian population in VIETNAM for Western, democratic values and the rejection of Communism. Eventually it was the Johnson administration's failure to capture the hearts and minds of many Americans for its Vietnam policy which doomed the war effort. One reason may have been the attitude of the military, one of whom told a visiting journalist:

Get them by the balls, and their hearts and minds will follow.

In the Nixon White House, this became the motto of the Watergate PLUMBERS. Previously the phrase "hearts and minds" was linked with President Theodore Roosevelt, who told the young Douglas MACARTHUR that he had won the leadership of the nation through his ability "to put into words what is in their hearts and minds but not in their mouths."

a heartbeat away from the presidency *See* PRESIDENCY.

Heath, Edward *See* GROCER.

heavy manners The slogan adopted by the Jamaican Prime Minister Michael Manley (1923–) during his unsuccessful re-election campaign in 1980; it reflected the stiff austerity needed to pull the island out of economic crisis. Manley, son of Jamaica's independence Prime Minister Norman Manley, won power for his National People's Party on a radical Socialist programme in 1972, and was re-elected in 1976, blaming rising unemployment on US efforts to DESTABILIZE his regime. Defeated in 1980 and 1983 by Edward Seaga's Jamaica Labour Party, he returned on a LANDSLIDE in 1989 to follow more moderate policies.

heckler An attender at a political meeting who endeavours to throw the speaker off his or her stride with barbed interruptions. Heckling is a tradition throughout the English-speaking world, but has been dealt a serious blow by the decline in large public meetings as television takes over, and by the tight security which discourages most leading politicians from speaking to large gatherings which could prove hostile or a shelter for terrorists. In 1966 the US film maker Joseph Strick took a crew to film the heckling at a number of British election meetings, prompting claims that he was encouraging such interruptions; the film he eventually produced was a showcase of politicians triumphing over hecklers and being severely rattled by them. Most of the great recorded exchanges between hecklers and politicians involve the rout of the heckler; one classic came when Richard Nixon responded to an interrupter: "The jawbone of an ass is just as dangerous as it was in Samson's time." Others include:

Heckler: Vote for you? I'd sooner vote for the Devil. *John Wilkes*: And what if your friend is not standing?

Heckler: Speak up, I can't hear you. *Disraeli*: Truth travels slowly, but it will reach you in time.

Heckler: Say Missus, how many toes are there on a pig's foot? *Nancy, Lady Astor*: Take your boots off, man, and count them yourself.

Churchill (when thrown a cabbage): I asked for the gentleman's ears, not his head.

Heckler: Rubbish! *Harold Wilson*: I'll come to your special interest in a minute, Sir.

Heckler: What about Vietnam? *Wilson*: The government has no plans to increase expenditure in Vietnam.

Heckler: Why are you talking to savages [in Rhodesia]? *Wilson*: We don't talk to savages. We just let them come to our meetings.

Heckler: You are two-faced! *Geoffrey Dickens*: Would I be wearing this face if I had two?

Norman Tebbit to Heckler: Calm down, my lad. *Heckler*: You're not my dad. *Tebbit*: I would quit while you're ahead, son. It's obvious I'm the only father you'll ever know.

Pompous Tory MP: I will have you know that I have asked no fewer than 97 Parliamentary Questions. *Heckler*: Ignorant bastard!

MP to heckler: What if everybody was like you and the whole country decided to run away from its problems? *Heckler*: At least we'd all be running in the same direction.

Heckler: War criminal! *Mayor Ed Koch*: Fuck off!

Heckler: Pig! *Ronald Reagan*: I'm very proud to be called a pig. It stands for pride, integrity, guts.

Heckler: I wouldn't vote for you if you were St. Peter. *Sir Robert Menzies*: If I were St. Peter you wouldn't be in my CONSTITUENCY.

Heckler: Tell us what you know, Bob. It won't take long. *Menzies*: I'll tell you everything we both know. It won't take any longer.

Heckler: I could swallow you in one bite. *Saskatchewan Premier Tommy Douglas*: If you did, you'd have more brains in your belly than in your head.

See also REPARTEE.

hedgers and ditchers The rival groups into which the Conservative majority in the HOUSE OF LORDS split in 1911 over the Liberal government's Bill to curtail the powers of the Upper House. The "Hedgers" under Lord Lansdowne were prepared to acquiesce rather than risk the mass creation of Liberal peers to ensure the Bill's passage. The "Ditchers" led by Lord Halsbury were prepared to die in the last ditch rather than yield. The Hedgers, the "Judas group", prevailed and the Bill passed by 131 votes to 114, ending the power of the Lords over MONEY BILLS and giving it a DELAYING POWER only over other legislation.

See Mr. BALFOUR's POODLE; PARLIAMENT ACTS.

hegemony (1) Domination by one nation over others or over a region; Communist China consistently accused Soviet Russia of trying to exercise "hegemony" over the rest of the Socialist world. (2) The theory of the Italian ideologue Antonio Gramsci (1891–1937) that private "civil society" exercises hegemony, while political society (the state) exercises domination. The effect being that the capitalist CONSENSUS structure is harder to destroy than the "autocratic" state.

Hell. Hell, no, we won't go! One of the most popular chants of campaigners against the VIETNAM WAR, especially those facing the DRAFT.

Give 'em hell Harry *See* GIVE.

If Hitler invaded Hell, I would make at least a favourable reference to the Devil in the House of Commons CHURCHILL's explanation in his book *The Grand Alliance* of his readiness to give STALIN his full support after Hitler invaded Russia in June 1941. Echoing the speech he made at the time, he wrote:

> I have only one purpose, the destruction of Hitler, and my life is much simplified thereby.

I told them to go to Hell Mikhail Gorbachev's account of what happened when the instigators of the KREMLIN COUP in August 1991 came to see him, under house arrest in his Black Sea villa.

The farmers of Kansas must raise less corn and more hell The slogan of the POPULIST movement which arose in America's Midwest during the recession of 1892. It was coined in a speech in 1890 by the Irish-born farmers' leader Mary Ellen Lease, who also said:

> The people are at bay! Let the bloodhounds of money who have dogged us thus far beware!

You may all go to Hell. And I will go to Texas The embittered reaction of the frontiersman Davy Crockett (1786-1836) on losing his seat in Congress.

Helsinki. Helsinki accords or **Final Act** The unexpectedly positive outcome in 1975 of two years of negotiation by 35 nations on a Soviet initiative for a **European Agreement on Security and Co-operation**, with special reference to confirming post-1945 frontiers. The Final Act included proposals to prevent accidental East–West confrontations, for economic and technical co-operation and reaffirming basic human rights. Helsinki backfired on the still repressive Soviet regime, with DISSIDENTS forming a group to monitor its own observance of human rights, and CHARTER 77 in Czechoslovakia following suit. Out of Helsinki has grown the CSCE mechanism for confidence-building and averting conflict in Europe.

Helsinki summit The SUMMIT in September 1990 between George Bush and Mikhail Gorbachev which showed an unprecedented openness and closeness between the SUPERPOWERS. The first to be convened as the result of an international crisis since the end of the COLD WAR, it ended with both leaders pledging themselves to any action, including force, to remove Saddam Hussein's invading forces from Kuwait. *See* GULF WAR.

hemicycle A semi-circular chamber designed for a Continental-style, non-ADVERSARIAL legislature. The term is used particularly of the chamber in Strasbourg, France, where the EUROPEAN PARLIAMENT holds most of its plenary sessions; it is also used by the COUNCIL OF EUROPE. A further hemicycle has been built in Brussels, where most MEPs would prefer to meet.

Hepburn Act The legislation passed by the US Congress in 1906 which greatly increased the powers of the Interstate Commerce Commission, giving it the benefit of the doubt in disputes with the railroads and thus subjecting the railroads to effective regulation for the first time. It gave the ICC power to reduce unreasonably high and discriminatory rates, subject to JUDICIAL REVIEW, and barred the railroads from transporting goods in whose production they had an interest.

Herbert Divorce Act The 1937 **Matrimonial Causes Act**, a divorce reform measure originating in a Private Member's BILL from the humorist and writer Sir A. P. Herbert (1890–1971), who had been elected as an Independent MP in 1935. The Act extended the grounds for divorce to include desertion (for more than three years), insanity (of over five years' duration) and cruelty. It also made adultery by a husband as great a cause for divorce as adultery by a wife, and made it possible for a wife to divorce her husband for rape, sodomy or bestiality.

here. here, borrow these The words of a Birmingham councillor *c.* 1979, offering his false teeth to a woman who said she could not go to vote becase she had lost hers.

here we are again, with both feet planted firmly in the air The scathing comment of Hugh (later Lord) Scanlon (1913–), President of Britain's Amalgamated Union of Engineering Workers, in 1973 on his union's attitude to joining the EUROPEAN COMMUNITY.

Here we go, here we go, here we go! The song of the Yorkshire MINERS as they spearheaded their union's year-long strike in 1984–85. Set to the tune "The STARS AND STRIPES Forever", the words were repeated for each line. The chant was taken up both by football supporters and by other left-wing demonstrators.

Heritage Foundation A campaigning right-wing THINK TANK and pressure group formed in Washington in the early 1970s by the former Capitol Hill staffers Frank Weyrich and Ed Feulner. Its aim was to achieve rapid political gains by feeding ideas directly to conservative groups and receptive members of Congress. It was one of the most effective elements in the new RIGHT, which capped the election of Ronald Reagan with a radical agenda, and remained an ideological force throughout the 1980s.

Herrenvolk The German word meaning broadly "master race", which in NAZI usage implied the superiority of the German peoples.

Heseltine, Michael *See* TARZAN.

Hess. Hess mission The bizarre solo flight to Scotland in May 1941 by Hitler's deputy **Rudolf Hess** (1894–1987), apparently to discuss peace terms with the Duke of Hamilton, whom he had met at the 1936 Berlin Olympics. Hess was captured and detained in the Tower of London, the last prisoner to be held there; Berlin Radio announced that the Deputy FÜHRER had been suffering from "hallucinations". In May 1946 the WAR CRIMES judges at NUREMBERG rejected his plea of insanity, and Hess was sentenced to life imprisonment. He was held in Berlin's Spandau prison, from 1966 as the sole occupant, until allegedly committing suicide. The last Nazi detainee acquired the nickname **Prisoner of Spandau**, because some CONSPIRACY THEORISTS believed, on the basis of discrepancies in the medical records, that he was not Hess but a "double" substituted by the Nazis prior to his flight or by the Allies at some later stage.

> One of those cases where imagination . . . is baffled by the facts as they present themselves. CHURCHILL.

Hezbollah (Arab. Party of God) The militant Iranian-backed SHI'ITE Muslim faction which from the early 1980s conducted a GUERRILLA campaign against the Israelis, and Christian and rival Muslim militias, and a campaign of HOSTAGE-taking against Westerners in Beirut. In 1985 members of *Hezbollah* hijacked a jet with 104 American passengers shortly after takeoff from Athens, killing a US naval diver; the final 39 hostages were released after 17 days, in return for the subsequent release by Israel of over 700 mostly Shi'ite Lebanese and Palestinian detainees.

HHS Health and Human Services. The department of the US Federal Government that succeeded the Department of Health, Education and Welfare (HEW, formed 1953) when President CARTER gave Education a department of its own in 1980. Its brief is to oversee all government agencies concerned with the health and social and economic welfare of the people.

high. High Contracting Parties The formal diplomatic term used in TREATIES to describe the nations who have concluded the agreement.

high crimes and misdemeanours One of the grounds for IMPEACHMENT, which has been listed in such proceedings from the trial of Warren Hastings in 1788–95, to the articles of impeachment prepared against Richard Nixon by Congress in 1974.

high ground, to take the To set the terms of a political debate by taking a morally unimpeachable position.

Highgate Cemetery The Victorian cemetery in north-central London where Karl MARX is buried, his grave and memorial being a place of pilgrimage for Communists from throughout the world.

Royal Highness A courtesy form of title for the closest relatives of a monarch, confined in the UK since 1917 to the children of the sovereign, grandchildren in the male line, the wives of sons and male line grandsons and the eldest son of the eldest son of the PRINCE OF WALES. Following the ABDICATION of King Edward VIII in 1936, he was denied his wish that Wallis Simpson, the woman for whom he had given up the throne, should be styled "Her Royal Highness" as well as Duchess of WINDSOR.

hijacking A common and effective form of political attention-seeking, involving the seizure of an aircraft in flight, the taking of its passengers as hostages and a hoped-for safe passage for the culprits to a country where they will not be punished, or will even receive a friendly welcome. The origin of the word is obscure but H. L. Mencken listed it as US criminal slang. It first achieved a political dimension on 1 May 1961 when a National Airlines plane bound for Miami was hijacked to Havana by an armed passenger. A rash of political misfits and criminals in America began commandeering airliners on internal flights and ordering the pilot at gunpoint to fly to Cuba; that September President KENNEDY made hijacking a Federal crime punishable by death. It subsequently became the stock-in-trade of Arab terrorists and their European and Japanese associates, and of disaffected individuals in the collapsing Soviet Union.

Hill, the Washington shorthand for CAPITOL HILL, and for all the activities of CONGRESS that take place there. As in "he's worked on the Hill for the last 15 years" or, "she's been posted to their Washington bureau to cover the Hill".

Him and Her The two beagles which President Lyndon Johnson (LBJ) picked up by the ears on the White House lawn in 1964 while entertaining bankers. Self-styled arbiters of Washington taste eized on the episode as proof of the Texan's gaucheness and social unacceptability.

Hiroshima The Japanese city and military base which was virtually obliterated on 6 August 1945 by the first ATOMIC BOMB ever dropped in warfare, as America sought to hasten the end of WORLD WAR II. Over 160,000 people, the vast majority civilians, were killed or suffered terrible burns, and many more doomed to ultimately-fatal radiation sickness. President Truman justified the attack by asserting that "military objectives and soldiers and sailors are the target, and not women and children"; but he also said: "The force from which the sun draws its power has been loosed against those who brought war to the Far East." The flash of the explosion was seen 170 miles away, and a MUSHROOM CLOUD of black smoke rose over where the city had stood to a height of 40,000 feet. Hiroshima – and NAGASAKI which was also destroyed by a US atomic bomb before Japan surrendered – remains a solemn and humbling warning of the fate confronting mankind in the event of a nuclear war, and a powerful symbol to advocates of NUCLEAR DISARMAMENT.

> We have resolved to endure the unendurable and suffer what is insufferable. Emperor HIROHITO.
>
> The genius of Einstein leads to Hiroshima.
> PABLO PICASSO.

His. His Accidency The nickname accorded Chester Arthur (*see* ELEGANT ARTHUR) by his critics when he succeeded to the Presidency in 1881 on the assassination of President Garfield. It surfaced again twenty years later when Theodore Roosevelt (*see* TEDDY) became President after McKinley's assassination; Roosevelt was upset by such references and resolved to win a Presidential term in his own right, which – unlike Arthur – he duly did.

His chain gang Excellency The name given by Harold L. Ickes, Secretary of the Interior throughout Theodore Roosevelt's presidency, to the UNRECONSTRUCTED Governor Talmadge of Georgia.

His Fraudulency The title bestowed on Rutherford Hayes (*see* OLD 8 TO 7) by opponents who never forgave him or the Republican Congress for depriving Samuel Tilden, who appeared to have beaten him convincingly, of the Presidency in 1876. They also called him **Rutherfraud Hayes**.

His Highness the President of the United States, and Protector of their Liberties The original title chosen by the US Senate for the head of the new nation; they abandoned it when the House of Representatives insisted on his simply being named "President".

His Rotundity The nickname accorded by Ralph Izard, one of the first US Senators, to Vice-President John ADAMS because of his love of pomp and titles; another suggestion was **His Superfluous Excellency**.

His Shadowship The nickname gained by the Rev. Jesse Jackson after his election as "Shadow Senator" for the DISTRICT OF COLUMBIA. The District has a non-voting DELEGATE to Congress and no representation in the Senate, and Jackson was elected unofficially to keep a watching brief – gaining a new power base in the process.

Hiss case The case in 1948–50 involving alleged espionage by a Communist sympathizer in the State Department, which made Richard Nixon's name and paved the way for McCARTHYISM. It also led to a series of Congressional investigations into the Department that profoundly embarrassed the Truman administration and Secretary of State Dean Acheson. It stemmed from allegations against **Alger Hiss** (1904–), a former official at State, by Whittaker Chambers, an ex-Communist and former editor of *Time* magazine, before the House Committee on UN-AMERICAN ACTIVITIES. Nixon, a member of the committee, pursued the allegations with tenacity. Hiss strenuously denied them, and in August 1948 sued Chambers for slander. When challenged for supporting evidence, Chambers produced copies of classified State Department papers he claimed had come from Hiss. Chambers even led investigators to his Maryland farm, where he produced three rolls of microfilm hidden in a pumpkin – the infamous "pumpkin papers". Hiss was indicted and appeared before a grand jury on charges of perjury – for his denial of passing papers to Chambers. The trial resulted in a hung jury, but at a retrial in January 1950 – the month before McCarthy opened his campaign – Hiss was convicted and imprisoned for five years. He was released in 1954. Many believed Hiss a victim of the anti-communist hysteria then sweeping America; others were convinced of his guilt.

history. history will absolve me! (Sp. *la historia me absolvera*) The declaration made by Fidel Castro at his trial in July 1953 for leading an attack on the Moncada barracks in Cuba in an attempt to overthrow the Batista regime.

dustheap of history *See* MENSHEVIKS.

I shall not fail before the bar of history, and it is there that I demand to be heard The challenge laid down by President Adolphe Thiers (1797–1877) to the French CHAMBER OF DEPUTIES on 24 May 1873 when facing the CONFIDENCE motion which led to his resignation.

today I am a trillionth part of history The claim made by Arthur Bremer (1950–) after his attempt to assassinate Governor George Wallace of Alabama in a Laurel, Maryland, shopping mall on 15 May 1972. Bremer, who had stalked Wallace during the Democratic primary campaign, fired several shots at Wallace which left him paralysed; he had to abandon his campaign for the Presidency, but stayed on as governor.

Hitler. Hitler has missed the bus One of the worst recorded examples of political timing: Neville CHAMBERLAIN's complacent speech on 4 April 1940 declaring that NAZI Germany had lost the initiative in WORLD WAR II. Five days later Hitler (*see* FÜHRER) invaded Norway; the BLITZKRIEG followed and by mid-May Chamberlain was out of office. Chamberlain told the Conservative CENTRAL COUNCIL:

> Whatever may be the reason – whether it was that Hitler thought he might get away with what he had got without fighting for it, or whether it was that after all the preparations were not sufficiently complete – however, one thing is certain: he missed the bus.

Hitler-Stalin pact The NON-AGGRESSION PACT concluded by Germany and the Soviet Union on 23 August 1939 which freed Hitler's hands to attack Poland, thus starting WORLD WAR II. Also known as the Nazi-Soviet Pact or the Ribbentrop-Molotov Pact, it was signed in Moscow by Germany's foreign minister Joachim von Ribbentrop and the Soviet foreign affairs commissar Vyacheslav Molotov (*see* NIET!). The two countries agreed not to support any third party that launched an attack on the other, and to consult on matters of mutual interest. But more significant was a secret PROTOCOL that effectively partitioned Europe into German and Soviet spheres, enabling Stalin to acquire eastern Poland as a strategic buffer when Germany made its move the following week. The readiness of the two arch-enemies to conclude such a deal stunned the world, and wrongfooted Britain, which had been making desultory contacts with a view to concluding a similar treaty with the Soviet Union. When the pact was announced, a FOREIGN OFFICE spokesman in London opined:

> Isms have become wasms.

Hitler Youth (Ger. *Hitler Jugend*) The main boys' organization of NAZI Germany, established in 1933 to encompass all the country's existing youth clubs; its equivalent for girls was the League of German Girls (*Bund Deutscher Mädel*). In 1935 Baldur von Schirach was appointed Reich Youth Leader, and the following year all other youth organizations were banned. The Hitler Youth embodied the vehement anti-intellectualism of the FÜHRER, who wanted its members to be "swift as the greyhound, tough as leather and hard as Krupp steel". Boys were admitted to the Hitler Youth at 14, normally after three or more years in its junior division, the *Deutsches Jungvolk* (German Young People). At 18 they graduated to the NATIONAL SOCIALIST Party, and so into the adult echelons of Nazism, having been INDOCTRINATED by Hitler's demented philosophy.

Hizzoner A colloquial name for the Mayor of any major American city, and specifically of New York; it is a corruption of "His Honour".

HMG *See* Her Majesty's GOVERNMENT.

Ho Chi Minh. Ho Chi Minh City The name given by the victorious North Vietnamese to Saigon, formerly capital of South Vietnam, after its fall on 30 April 1975 – the final action of the VIETNAM WAR. Ho Chi Minh (1890–1969), a founder-member of the French Communist Party and President of North Vietnam from 1954 to 1969, had led first the struggle against the Japanese, then the VIET MINH against the French and finally the North Vietnamese/VIET CONG campaign to defeat the South and its US allies.

Ho Chi Minh Trail A network of routes running south from North Vietnam, through eastern Laos into Cambodia and South Vietnam, along which the VIET CONG moved guerrillas and military hardware to supply their campaign in the south. The trail, parts of which date back to the late 1940s, comprises a mixture of footpaths, tracks and roads through the mountains and jungles, largely built and maintained by manual labour. Some stretches were suitable for trucks, but most were passable only by bullock cart, by bicycle or on foot. Supplies could take up to six months to pass the full length of the trail. Despite intensive US bombing and efforts by the South Vietnamese army to cut their supply lines, the North Vietnamese and Viet Cong kept the trail open throughout the war; this proved a crucial factor in their ultimate victory.

Ho, Ho, Ho Chi Minh! One of the most provocative chants of anti-VIETNAM WAR demonstrators in America, not only opposing US involvement in the war but actually encouraging the other side.

Hoare-Laval Pact One of the first instances of APPEASEMENT in the years prior to WORLD WAR II: secret proposals for ending the conflict caused by Italy's invasion of Abyssinia (Ethiopia) in 1935, formulated that December by the UK Foreign Secretary Samuel Hoare and his French opposite number, Pierre Laval. They granted substantial territorial concessions to Italy, plus a zone of exclusive economic interest; the LEAGUE OF NATIONS would protect Abyssinian sovereignty over remaining areas. The pact was LEAKed to the press on 9 December, causing a storm of protest in Britain. By 18 December the British Government had been forced to repudiate the pact, and Hoare resigned, to be succeeded by Anthony EDEN; Laval was executed as a COLLABORATOR by the French after the war. Unhindered and with the League unable to enforce effective SANCTIONS, Mussolini proceeded to complete the conquest of Abyssinia and form the AXIS with Germany.

> No more coals to Newcastle – no more Hoares to Paris.
> King GEORGE V.

holdover An official in the US government who attempts to hang on to his or her job after a change of administration, despite being a POLITICAL APPOINTEE of the outgoing President. Only occasionally are such functionaries asked to stay on by the new administration, so during a TRANSITION period, there is a rush by appointees who want to stay put to have themselves reclassified as career civil servants; few succeed, but it can take the best part of a year to prise out the most determined holdovers.

Hollywood East A derogatory name for WASHINGTON during the Reagan presidency, with movie stars regular visitors at the White House and the public face of the presidency oriented strongly toward television (*see* GREAT COMMUNICATOR; video PRESIDENCY).

Hollywood Ten The group of ten screenwriters, film producers and directors who refused to confirm or deny their affiliation to the US Communist Party during the investigations of the House UN-AMERICAN ACTIVITIES Committee in 1947. They were Alvah Bessie, Herbert Biberman, Lester Cole, Edward Dymytryk, Ring Lardner Jr., John Howard Lawson, Albert Maltz, Sam Ornitz, Adrian Scott and Dalton Trumbo. All were briefly imprisoned for contempt of court in 1950, and on their release were BLACKLISTED and unable to work in Hollywood for several years as McCARTHYISM thrived; many never returned to the industry.

Holocaust (Gr. *holos*, whole; *kaustos*, burnt) The extermination of six million Jews in CONCENTRATION CAMPS by the NAZIS under Hitler between 1940 and 1945, a crime whose enormity has barely been grasped by humanity, yet which has prompted both the existence and HAWKish policies of the state of Israel, and post-war Germany's reluctance to flex its muscles on the world stage. Holocaust Day is observed in Israel on 27 Nisan (19 or 20 April). The word originally referred to a sacrifice to the Greek gods in which the victim was burned whole. It later came to mean slaughter or destruction on an immense scale, especially by fire, and has also been applied to nuclear warfare. *See* EICHMANN TRIAL; FINAL SOLUTION.

> There were many ways of not burdening one's conscience, of shunning responsibility, looking away, keeping silent. When the unspeakable truth of the holocaust became known at the end of the war, all too many of us claimed that they had not known anything about it, or even suspected anything. Whoever refuses to remember the inhumanity is prone to new risks of infection.
> RICHARD VON WEISZÄCKER, President of West Germany, on the 40th anniversary of the end of World War II, 1985.

Holt drowning The mysterious death of Australia's Liberal prime minister Harold Holt on 17 December 1967, which gave rise to intense speculation over his fate. Holt, a keen and strong swimmer, went into the water off Cheviot Beach in Victoria, on a coastline hazardous to bathers. The sea "churned up" around him and he disappeared; no body was ever found. The prime minister's death caused political turmoil, and speculation about sharks and suicide. The most remarkable theory came 15 years later, in Anthony Grey's book *The Prime Minister was a Spy*; according to Grey, Holt had swum out to a submarine and been spirited away to Communist China, having completed a nefarious career on behalf of Mao's regime. The theory was based on Holt's evident desire to accommodate Chinese wishes on various occasions; it also hinted that ASIO knew more about his disappearance than was generally supposed. However Holt's son ridiculed the theory, saying:

> My father didn't even like Chinese food.

Holy Loch An inlet of the Firth of Clyde west of Glasgow, 2.5 miles long, which from 1961 to 1992 was the British base for US POLARIS submarines. Holy Loch, not far from Dunoon, was from the outset a focus of anti-nuclear protests, both from CND and from militant Scottish nationalists who saw the base as an affront to their country's dignity. Various forms of CIVIL DISOBEDIENCE, including SIT-INs at Ardanadam Pier, continued for a number of years; but when the PENTAGON took the decision to close the base in 1991 many local people viewed it with regret.

home. Homelands *See* BANTUSTAN.

Home Rule The term originally used by 19th-century campaigners for the restoration of self-government to Ireland, and also sporadically for movements then and since for DEVOLUTION for Scotland and Wales. The phrase was coined by Isaac Butt (1813–70), who began the campaign for Dublin to regain the Parliament it had lost in 1800, though with Ireland remaining part of the British kingdom. Butt mobilized most of Ireland's MPs at Westminster into a Home Rule party, which PARNELL inherited and radicalized. Then, in 1885, Gladstone had a "seismic conversion" to Home Rule (*see* HAWARDEN KITE), his pursuit of which twice caused the fall of Liberal governments. ASQUITH got a Home Rule Bill through Parliament amid growing tension (*see* CURRAGH MUTINY, ULSTER VOLUNTEERS), but the outbreak of World War I left it a dead letter and the EASTER RISING paved the way for outright independence of the mainly Catholic South. The cause of Home Rule for Scotland, with a devolved Parliament in Edinburgh is over a century old; the inability of Westminster to deliver it has produced periodic surges of support for the SNP.

> Scottish Home Rule involves English Home Rule. Only by local parliaments and local executives in each of the three kingdoms can we settle Home Rule at all.
>
> Sir HENRY CAMPBELL-BANNERMAN.

Home Rule is Rome Rule One of the early slogans of the ULSTER UNIONISTS. *See also* ULSTER WILL FIGHT.

Home Secretary The senior UK Cabinet Minister in charge of the Home Office, with responsibility in England and Wales for law and order, the police, prisons, emergency planning, charities, local bye-laws, elections, race relations and data protection and shopping hours, throughout the UK for drugs, immigration, extradition and gambling, and also for the Channel Islands and Isle of Man. The counterpart of a Continental Minister of the Interior, the Home Secretary formerly held the power of life and death over convicted murderers.

Homestead Act The Act passed by Congress in 1862 which provided 160 acres of land in the West for any current or prospective US citizen who was the head of a family, provided they paid a small fee and lived there for five years. By 1890, 48 million acres had been distributed – most of it to 375,000 homesteaders, but with millions of acres snapped up fraudulently by developers and railroad companies. VETOED by President Buchanan in 1860, it was signed by LINCOLN two years later.

urban homesteading The granting of houses in run-down areas of America's INNER CITIES for a nominal sum to middle-class families prepared to renovate them and rebuild the community. Pioneered in the early 1970s by Baltimore's Mayor William Donald Shaefer, it caught on in many other cities – though in some places it ended in failure.

Honest Abe One of Abraham LINCOLN's many nicknames, awarded him by Washingtonians who had been appalled by the graft and scandal surrounding his predecessor James Buchanan.

Honey Fitz The nickname of Mayor **John F. Fitzgerald** of Boston (1863–1951), the Boston-Irish MACHINE politician who was grandfather of the KENNEDY brothers Joe Jr., John (JFK), Robert (RFK) and Edward. A Democratic congressman 1895–1901, he was elected mayor in 1905. Ousted in 1907 by a GOOD GOVERNMENT coalition, he returned in 1909; he would have run again in 1911, had not his young challenger John Michael Curley threatened to expose his relationship with a cigarette girl. The name "Honey" came both from his charm and the fine voice with which he sang *Sweet Adeline* on party occasions; he sang it again and danced a jig at the age of 85 when his grandson was elected to Congress. JFK returned the compliment by naming his Presidential yacht the Honey Fitz.

> Our present mayor has the distinction of appointing more saloon keepers and bartenders to public office than any previous mayor. ANON. Boston clergyman.

honeymoon The period following a newcomer's election to high office during which he or she enjoys public goodwill and popularity; it ends after a few months when unpopular decisions have been taken or certain qualities turn out to be lacking. Gerald FORD, after assuming the Presidency, told Congress: "I do not want a honeymoon with you; I want a good marriage."

> It doesn't matter what kind of majority you come in with. You've got just one year when they treat you right.
>
> President LYNDON JOHNSON.

Honi Soit Qui Mal Y Pense (Fr. evil be to him who evil thinks) The motto of the Order of the GARTER, founded by King Edward III in 1348 or 1349.

honky A term for a White person popularized in the 1960s by militant Blacks; it carries an implication of ignorance or gullibility. Many Americans heard it first in television interviews with the provocative H. "Rap" Brown.

honour. honor guard The small, smartly uniformed marching party which in America accompanies the STARS AND STRIPES on most ceremonial occasions, and even at many sporting events; one will also guard the bier on the death of a great American. A guard of honour is the party of troops that a visiting political leader reviews on arriving to meet another head of government or state.

the (Right) Honourable Gentleman or Lady or Member In the UK HOUSE OF COMMONS, the way in which a member from one party refers to a (senior) member of another. One on the same side of the House is my Honourable Friend. The prefixes "and gallant" and "and learned" are used for former Commissioned officers in the services, and Queen's Counsel, respectively.

Honours List The collection of more than 700 awards made twice yearly by the Sovereign – at New Year and on their "official birthday" in July – to persons put forward by the Prime Ministers of the UK and certain COMMONWEALTH countries as deserving recognition. They range from senior civil servants and diplomats who receive theirs automatically (*see* CALL ME GOD) through party officials and workers to charity workers and postwomen and telephone engineers. A few nominees reject honours, but generally they mean a lot to those who receive them; however the system is widely seen as archaic, socially stratified and, in the case of awards for political and public service, open to abuse. John MAJOR recognized this in 1992 when he suggested reforms to open it up. In addition to these twice-yearly lists, there are also **Dissolution Honours**, recommended for retiring members of a Parliament, **Resignation Honours**, proposed by an outgoing Prime Minister (*see* LAVENDER LIST), and lists of Working PEERS to top up the House of Lords.

> I wonder what you thought of the Honours List. I have never ceased to congratulate myself that I did not figure among the rabble.
>
> NEVILLE CHAMBERLAIN, New Year, 1918.

Honours scandal The controversy that broke in June 1922 over Lloyd George's blatant use of the honours system to reward wealthy contributors to his LLOYD GEORGE FUND, and in particular the unscrupulous South African millionaire Sir James Robinson, without regard to their personal reputations or actual philanthropic credentials. Sir James was honoured for "Imperial and public services", but it emerged that the Colonial Secretary had not been consulted, and that the company he was supposed to be chairing had been liquidated in 1905; he refused the peerage as the agitation grew. A committee of inquiry set up to investigate the alleged sale of honours was told that anyone could buy a barony for £50,000, a baronetcy for £25,000 or a knighthood for £15,000 – payable to "party funds" which meant Lloyd George's own kitty. As a result of the scandal the Honours (Prevention of Abuses) Act was passed in 1923 – which led to the conviction of Maundy Gregory (1877–1941) ten years later for selling honours at this time – and a Political Honours Scrutiny Committee of senior PRIVY COUNCILLORS, which still weeds out unsuitable nominees, was established. Lloyd George's refusal to yield control of the fund contributed to the downfall of his coalition government (*see* CARLTON CLUB REVOLT), even though he gave a share of it to the Conservatives.

Hoover. Hoover Commission The commission set up by Congress in 1947 to reorganize the EXECUTIVE Branch of government, under **Herbert Hoover** (1874–1964), who had been America's 31st President (Republican, 1929–33). It recommended 36 proposals for change to President Truman, all of which Congress accepted save for a plan to create a single department for health, education and welfare; this was, however, adopted in 1953, the year Hoover was asked by Eisenhower to head a second Commission whose proposals were also implemented.

Hoover Depression The Democrats' name for the GREAT DEPRESSION, pinning the responsibility firmly on President Hoover. The link was exploited by Franklin D. Roosevelt in his 1932 campaign for the Presidency; he declared:

> The present administration has either forgotten or does not want to remember the infantry of our economic army.

Yet the name had already stuck. The homeless of the Depression had named their shanty towns **Hoovervilles**, the newspapers under which they slept became **Hoover blankets**, broken-down motor vehicles hauled by mules **Hoover wagons** and empty pockets turned inside out **Hoover flags**.

Hoover himself came to the Presidency with a reputation as the GREAT ENGINEER, which indeed transcended his ill-fated term in the White House. As a mining engineer he had built up an international business empire and a personal fortune. In World War I he headed the American relief administration, skilfully co-ordinating aid for starving Europeans. He told critics of food aid for Russia:

> Twenty million people are starving. Whatever their politics, they shall be fed.

After the war he served in the Cabinets of HARDING and Coolidge (*see* SILENT CAL), nominally as Secretary of Commerce but with wider influence, earning the nickname "assistant Secretary of everything else". When Coolidge stood down (*see* I do not choose to RUN), the Republicans turned to Hoover with what Elmer Greene called his "unprecedented reputation for public service as an engineer, administrator and humanitarian", as a potential President, though he had never run for public office. He told them: "You convey too great a compliment. . . . In no other land would a boy from a country village, without inheritance or influential friends, look forward with unbounded hope – I am indebted to my country without any human power to repay." In the 1928 election Hoover heavily defeated Al Smith (*see* HAPPY WARRIOR) for the Presidency with his declarations that

> We in America are nearer to the final triumph over poverty than ever before in the history of any land.

Hopes were high that this was so, but after eight months of OVERHEATING, Wall Street was hit by the GREAT CRASH and the rest of his term was dogged by misfortune. Hoover created a number of weapons that could have eased the Depression, but was reluctant to use them, dismissing INTERVENTION on the ground that "prosperity cannot be restored by raids upon the public treasury". He also surprised many in Washington by his preoccupation with minutiae and an apparent inability to see the big picture. Secretary of State Henry Stimson said that "a private meeting with Hoover is like sitting in a bath of ink", while Bernard Baruch observed: "Facts to Hoover's brain are as water to a sponge; they are absorbed into every tiny interstice," and Will Rogers joked:

> It's not what he doesn't know that bothers me, it's what he knows for sure just ain't so.

The Presidency took its toll of Hoover, Raymond Moley writing in 1932: "He seems to me to be close to death. He has the look of being done, but still of going on, driven by some damned duty." With FDR conducting a positive and energetic campaign, Hoover found the Depression an ALBATROSS and he carried only six of the 48 states. From the White House he went back to business and humanitarian work, and in World War II again headed America's relief effort before heading the HOOVER COMMISSIONS; in 1947 the Hoover Dam, on the Colorado river at the Nevada–Arizona border, which had been started during his Presidency, was named after him.

> The greatest engineer in the world. He drained, ditched and damned the United States in three years.
>
> Kansas farmer, 1932.

> Such a little man could not have made so big a depression.
>
> NORMAN THOMAS.

Hoover moratorium The concession made by President Hoover in June 1931, allowing European nations to suspend repayment of intergovernmental war debts for one year, to help ease their plight during the GREAT DEPRESSION.

hopper The receptacle at the side of the Clerk's desk in the Chamber of the US HOUSE OF REPRESENTATIVES where any member may at any time place a BILL he or she wants to introduce. Pending legislation is described as being "in the hopper".

horse. horse and buggy A US politicians' term for an outdated way of operation, most notably used by Franklin D. Roosevelt after the Supreme Court's rejection of the NRA on BLACK MONDAY. FDR said:

> Is the United States going to decide, are the people of this country going to decide, that their federal Government shall in the future have no right under any implied power or any court-approved power to enter into a solution of a national economic problem, but that national economic problem must be solved only by the States? We thought we were solving it, and now it has been thrown right straight in our faces. We have been relegated to the horse-and-buggy definition of interstate commerce.

Horseface The name inadvertently given to one of his constituents *c.* 1980 by the irrepressible Conservative MP Geoffrey Dickens (*see* BIFFO). One weekend as he toured his constituency on the Yorkshire–Lancashire border, he was followed everywhere by a middle-aged woman. A few days later he received a letter from her; she apologized if she had been a nuisance, but said she had wanted to see her MP in action, was most impressed and would tell all her friends to vote for him. She asked Dickens if she could have a photograph of him; below her signature was the word "Horseface". Dickens signed a photograph: "To Horseface with very best wishes," bought a frame for it and dropped it in a House of Commons mailbox. A few minutes later his secretary came in and said: "Did you see the letter from that woman? I wrote 'Horseface' at the bottom in case you'd forgotten who she was."

horse-trading Hard bargaining between politicians, with each being ready to make concessions if the other does. The term originates in the tough bargains driven with farmers by horse-dealers, and by farmers with each other.
dark horse A candidate with no apparent prospects of victory who comes through to make an unexpectedly strong showing. The term was first used of James Polk (1795–1849), whose election to the White House in 1844 was engineered by ex-President Andrew Jackson. Though he had made a bid for the vice-presidency in 1840, Polk was one of the least-known candidates in the field, but defeated Henry Clay to become America's 11th President. Polk (*see* FIFTY-FOUR FORTY OR FIGHT!), was exhausted by a single term, dying four months after leaving office, but he carried out the expansionist policy objectives he set for himself.
stalking horse *See* STALKING.
don't swap horses while crossing a stream The phrase with which Abraham LINCOLN argued during the 1864 election campaign against a change of President with the CIVIL WAR not yet won. In a speech on 9 June, he spoke of:

> An old Dutch farmer, who remarked to a companion once that it was best not to swap horses in mid-stream.

In the 1920s the British Conservative F. E. Smith reacted to calls for a change in the Tory leadership by declaring:

> We must not swap donkeys crossing the stream.

It's the horse that comes in first at the finish that counts One of the many homespun ways in which President Truman (*see* GIVE 'EM HELL HARRY) dismissed OPINION POLLS during the 1948 election campaign which put his Republican challenger Thomas DEWEY ahead by a wide margin. Truman won.

Horton. Willie Hortonism The use of RACISM as a subliminal weapon in election propaganda. The phrase stems from the issue which gave George BUSH his comfortable margin over the Democratic nominee Michael Dukakis in the 1988 Presidential election, but also heightened concerns about negative and misleading campaigning that were to rebound on Bush four years later. At the height of the campaign, the Republicans aired campaign advertisements claiming that Dukakis, as governor of Massachusetts, was directly responsible for the fact that a Black convict named Willie Horton had raped a White woman in Maryland while on furlough from a Massachusetts prison. The commercial attracted furious Democratic complaints of racism and of being grossly misleading, as Dukakis had had no direct involvement with the case. However it succeeded in making Dukakis, against whom Bush was using LIBERAL as a term of abuse, look weak on crime; the governor made matters worse for himself by giving a feeble answer when asked when he would do if a man broke into his home and attacked his wife.

> You can't find a stronger metaphor, intended or not, for racial hatred in this country than a Black man raping a White woman. And that's what the Willie Horton story was. SUSAN ESTRICH, Dukakis campaign manager.

> Why should you let a guy like that, who has no chance for parole, out for a weekend with no supervision?
> LEE ATWATER, Bush campaign manager.

hostage. hostage crisis The humiliation for America which (together with INFLATION) brought down the CARTER administration. It arose from the seizure of the US Embassy in Teheran on 4 November 1979 by student supporters of the AYATOLLAH Khomeini, who detained 52 diplomats and other staff in protest at the overthrown Shah's presence in America for medical treatment. The plight of the hostages, and America's shame, increased when an effort to rescue the hostages by helicopter in April 1980 broke down in incompetence in the desert 200 miles short of its goal; Secretary of State Cyrus Vance, who had opposed the mission, resigned. President Carter had pledged himself not to campaign for re-election until the hostages were freed, but eventually entered the contest as Sen. Edward F. KENNEDY mounted a strong challenge. The hostage crisis eventually hurt Kennedy as the Iranians hailed him as an "American prophet", leading to the *New York Times* headline: "Teddy is the Toast of Teheran". By now the Ayatollah and his fanatical supporters saw the crisis as a trial of strength, and were determined not to let Carter off the hook, though he never gave up negotiating. The deal was almost in place as Carter prepared to leave the White House, and despite the pain he kept his sense of humour. After President-elect Reagan called on him for a briefing, Carter told his right-hand man Hamilton Jordan: "I briefed him on what was happening to the hostages. He mostly listened, but when I finished he said: 'What hostages?'" They were finally released through Algerian MEDIATION immediately after Reagan was sworn in, Carter flying to Germany to welcome them. *See also* OCTOBER SURPRISE.

> The hostages became a concrete metaphor for the nation's sense of impotence.
> HEDRICK SMITH, *The Power Game.*

hostage taking The action of Iranian-backed Shi'ite Muslim extremists in taking hostage

Americans, Britons and other Westerners who had stayed on in Beirut despite the complete breakdown in law and order in the early 1980s. At one time over 26 were held in darkened rooms in and around the city. Though some were detained as alleged spies, there seemed no logic to their seizure, and their captors appeared to have no idea what to do with them. Three were killed, and the rest eventually released after anything up to five or six years in captivity. The detention of the hostages led to Syria sending troops into Beirut to restore order and impose Damascus's influence, and also created the backdrop for the IRAN-CONTRA affair with its sub-plot of ARMS FOR HOSTAGES, in which the subsequent British hostage, the Archbishop of Canterbury's envoy Terry Waite, was allegedly implicated. By 1992 all, save for two Germans held by a splinter group, had been released.

> Freeing hostages is like putting up a stage set – which you do with the captors, agreeing on each piece as you slowly put it together. Then you leave an exit through which both the captor and the captive can walk with sincerity and dignity.
>
> TERRY WAITE, 3 November 1986 (before his own captivity).

hot line The direct link between the WHITE HOUSE and the KREMLIN which, since 30 August 1963, has provided a means of instant communication to avert "accidental" nuclear war; the contact is generally between senior members of the US and Soviet/Russian national security staffs. Initially a telex circuit, it has been steadily upgraded over the years. Communication has not been continuous; at one point in the late 1960s it was interrupted when a mechanical digger in Finland sliced through the line.

Hotel Cecil The name given by its Liberal opponents to Lord SALISBURY's second government (1886–92), because of the number of his relatives who served in it. Among them was the future Prime Minister Arthur BALFOUR, who went to Ireland as Chief Secretary; Balfour was "Bob" Salisbury's nephew and his appointment is said to have spawned the phrase **Bob's your uncle** for an action that suddenly solves a problem.

Houdini A politician who develops an ability to escape from every conceivable difficulty without suffering any damage. The original Great Houdini (real name Erik Weiz, 1874–1926) was the world's most celebrated escapologist, who even managed to escape from the condemned cell in Washington jail. The term has been applied to many political leaders, including President Franklin Roosevelt (FDR) and – up to WATERGATE – Richard Nixon (*see* TRICKY DICK). Ronald Reagan, who deserved the title even more until the IRAN-CONTRA AFFAIR, was known as the GREAT RONDINI.

House. the House At Westminster, shorthand for the HOUSE OF COMMONS though only applied to the premises; in Washington, for the HOUSE OF REPRESENTATIVES.

House Bank scandal An episode in 1992 which brought considerable discredit on the House of Representatives. It stemmed from the disclosure that a number of members had used the House bank run by the SERGEANT AT ARMS to run up overdrafts that would have been denied them anywhere else. The bank was closed after sustaining sizable losses, but there was widespread criticism that its practices would have been illegal in the outside world. Three Democratic members who had come in for heavy adverse comment were unseated that November, including Rep. Gerry Sikorski of Minnesota who had run up 697 overdrafts.

House Divided speech The courageous – some feared suicidal – speech on the future of the UNION delivered by Abraham LINCOLN on 16 June 1858 at the close of the Republican CONVENTION in Springfield, Illinois, which nominated him to run for the US Senate against Stephen Douglas. The key words are a paraphrase of Mark 3:25. Lincoln said:

> A house divided against itself cannot stand. I believe this government cannot endure, permanently half slave and half free. I do not expect the Union to be dissolved – I do not expect the house to fall – but I do expect it will cease to be divided. It will become all one thing, or all the other.

House Magazine The weekly journal that chronicles events and personalities at Westminster for members of both Houses when they are sitting. It is privately produced under the supervision of an all-party board of MPs and peers. It is instantly recognizable by the cartoon of a member which usually adorns the cover.

House of Commons The principal, elected house of the Westminster Parliament (and also of the Parliament of Canada), traditionally held out as a model for democratic assemblies throughout much of the English-speaking world. Its origins date back to 1258, when Simon de Montfort, leading the barons against King Henry III, summoned representatives of the towns together. Kings, too, convened such Parliaments, with PEERs sitting with representatives of the boroughs and the counties. During the 1350s the Lords and Commons began to sit separately, and later that century the Commons settled at WESTMINSTER – using ST. STEPHEN'S Chapel from 1549/50. They had a SPEAKER from at least 1376, and by 1455 it was accepted that for a Bill to become law, the consent of the Crown, Lords and Commons was necessary. In 1642 Parliament went to war against King Charles II, defeating, trying and, in 1649, executing him. Though the Monarchy was restored in 1660, Parliament had gained the right to tax and spend, and thus held ultimate power. The Commons were decisive in ousting James II in the GLORIOUS REVOLUTION of 1688–89, and in 1707 the ACT OF UNION brought in representatives of Scotland; Irish members followed in 1801. With the birth of a democratic America, the FRENCH REVOLUTION and the Industrial Revolution, the Commons came to look (and be) increasingly unrepresentative, and the 1832 REFORM ACT gave the new cities their first voice, abolishing the worst ROTTEN BOROUGHS. In 1834 the Palace of Westminster was razed to the ground, and in the late 1840s the Commons moved into the Chamber they occupy today – though completely rebuilt since, after taking a direct hit from a German bomb in 1941. Though the electorate was steadily extended, universal adult suffrage was only achieved with the "Flapper VOTE" of 1928.

The House of Commons, elected at most every five years and now with 651 members, sits from (generally) November to November, with approximately three months' RECESS from August to October and brief breaks at Christmas, Easter and Whitsun; its sittings begin at 2.30 p.m., except on Friday when the House meets at 9.30 a.m. Though critics doubt that it can effectively control the EXECUTIVE, the process of QUESTION TIME and the establishment in 1979/80 of departmental SELECT COMMITTEES have kept it a powerful instrument, even though many of its procedures are arcane and much of the debating serves little practical purpose. Recent Speakers, starting with Bernard Weatherill from 1983, have gone out of their way to confirm that in the CHAMBER Ministers enjoy no advantages over BACKBENCHERS.

Members of the House, and those watching from the Galleries, have had no shortage of views on it: "better than a play" – King Charles II; "a parcel of younger brothers" – PITT THE YOUNGER; "four-fifths comprised of country squires and great fools" – Richard Brinsley Sheridan; "a parcel of button-makers, pin-makers, horse jockeys, gamesters, pensioners, pimps and whoremasters" – James Otis; "I never saw so many shocking bad hats in all my life" – The Duke of Wellington; "an elaborate conspiracy to prevent the real clash of opinion which exists outside from finding an appropriate echo within its walls" – Aneurin BEVAN; "hours and hours of exquisite boredom" – Bevan; "a palace of illogicalities" – George BROWN.

Party combat is not all, and away from the clash of debate and committee work, the Commons has a culture of its own. Lloyd George remarked that "to anyone with politics in his blood, this place is like a pub to a drunkard", and Henry CHIPS Channon noted: "I love the House of Commons so much that if I were to be offered a peerage, I should be tempted to refuse it. Only tempted, of course;" but Shirley Williams, who never liked it, described it as "not so much a gentlemen's club as a boys' boarding school".

In the Commons, modest backbenchers rub shoulders with the mighty. Disraeli declared that "we come here for fame!" but Beverly Baxter noted: "A great many persons are able to become members of this House without losing their insignificance." ASQUITH maintained that "the first duty, if not the only duty, of a private member of the House of Commons is to speak as little and vote as often as he can", and Augustine Birrell, who served in his Cabinet, wrote: "I know of no place where the great truth that no man is necessary is brought home to the mind so remorselessly, and yet so refreshingly." In the same vein Palmerston concluded:

> The House of Commons allows itself to be led, but does not like to be driven, and is apt to turn against those who attempt to drive it.

See also HALITOSIS HALL.

> When in that House MPs divide,
> If they've a brain and cerebellum too.
> They have to leave their brains outside
> And vote just as their leaders tell 'em to.
>
> W. S. GILBERT, *Iolanthe.*

> Today for the first time I really liked it; boredom passed and a glow of pleasure filtered through me. But I wish I understood what I was voting for.
>
> HENRY CHANNON, 1936.

> A writer of crook stories ought never to stop seeking new material. EDGAR WALLACE, standing for election.

> When you stand up to speak, the bench in front of you seems to catch you just below the knee and gives you the impression that you are about to fall headlong over.
>
> HAROLD MACMILLAN.

House of Keys The 24-strong directly elected lower house of TYNWALD, the Isle of Man parliament; eight of its members also serve on the appointed **Legislative Council**.

House of Lords The dazzlingly ornate gilded chamber at the south end of the Palace of Westminster, and the Upper House of Parliament that meets there. In theory 921 hereditary and LIFE PEERS and a clutch of bishops could crowd on to its red leather benches (those in the Commons are green), but in practice 300 is a very high turnout. The Lords, presided over by the LORD CHAN-

CELLOR, are widely seen as an anachronism, and the deliberate good manners and relaxed nature of the proceedings, coupled with the age of many peers attending, and the fact that no member will have to seek re-election, make a mellow contrast with the Commons. However the Lords have carved out a rôle for themselves as a REVISING CHAMBER, and the presence of a number of eminent scientists and experts gives it an authoritative edge that the Commons may lack. Reform of the House of Lords has been argued throughout the 20th century, but has usually broken down over the difficulty that electing it would compromise the ultimate supremacy of the Commons. However the introduction of Life Peers from the 1950s has given it more of a cutting edge, and its powers have been reduced under the PARLIAMENT ACTS, so that it cannot prevent the BUDGET being implemented and may only delay legislation passed by the Commons for a year; the 1991 WAR CRIMES Act was passed after the Commons voted to OVERRIDE the Lords. The House of Lords is also a court, its Judicial Committee being England's ultimate court of appeal. *See also* Mr. BALFOUR'S POODLE; WOOLSACK; Working PEERS.

Most comments made about the Lords emphasize the unrepresentativeness, age and political impotence of its members. To the 18th-century Earl of Chesterfield it was "that hospital of incurables", to Campbell-Bannerman "a mere annexe of the Unionist party"; to Lloyd George "500 men, ordinary men, chosen accidentally from among the unemployed"; to Viscount Samuel "the only institution in the world which is kept effective by the persistent absenteeism of most of its members"; to Clement ATTLEE "a glass of champagne that had stood for five days"; to the Methodist preacher Lord Soper "good evidence of life after death"; to Michael Foot "the only club in the world where the proprietor pays for the drinks"; to Tony BENN "the British Outer Mongolia for retired politicians"; and to Frank Field "a model of how to care for the elderly". When the Earl of Arran (1910–83) was asked why the House had been packed for a Bill on reforming the law on homosexuality and half-empty for one to protect badgers, he replied:

> There are no badgers in the House of Lords.

> I am dead – dead but in the Elysian Fields.
> DISRAELI on his elevation as Earl of Beaconsfield.

> A severe though not unfriendly critic of our institutions once said that the cure for admiring the House of Lords was to go and look at it. WALTER BAGEHOT (1826–77).

> The House of Peers, throughout the war
> Did nothing in particular,
> And did it very well. W. S. GILBERT, *Iolanthe.*

> There are no credentials. They do not even need a medical certificate. They need not be sound either in body or mind. They only require a certificate of birth – just to prove that they were the first of the litter. You would not choose a spaniel on those principles.
> LLOYD GEORGE delivering his PEOPLE'S BUDGET, 1909.

> If like me you are over 90, frail, on two sticks, half dead and half blind, you stick out like a sore thumb in most places, but not in the House of Lords. Besides, they seem to have a bar and a loo within 30 yards in any direction.
> The Earl of STOCKTON (SUPERMAC).

House of Representatives The larger house of the US CONGRESS, though co-equal in power with the SENATE (also the lower and more powerful house of Australia's Federal parliament); it has greater powers over finance, but none over treaties and Presidential appointments. Comprising Representatives elected every two years by Congressional DISTRICTS roughly equal in population, it has had 435 voting members since 1912; there is also a non-voting DELEGATE from the District of Columbia and similar members with a watching brief for America's overseas TERRITORIES. A member must be at least 25 years old, have been a US citizen for seven years and live in the State for which he or she was elected. The most powerful member is the SPEAKER, who not only presides over the House but is its political leader, overshadowing, though working with, the MAJORITY LEADER. The House has met in its present Chamber since 16 December 1857; before then it met for half a century in what is now the STATUARY HALL along the corridor. The House does much valuable work, especially in committee, but the requirement to seek re-election every two years creates an atmosphere of permanent ELECTIONEERING which accentuates the contrast with the more measured pace of the Senate. Vice-President Alben Barkley made another comparison with the Senate:

> When I was in the House I was told that the difference between the House Foreign Affairs Committee and the Senate Foreign Relations Committee was that Senators were too old to have affairs – they only had relations.

It is tempting to see the House as a stepping stone to the Senate and even the Presidency, but many legislators choose to spend a lifetime as Congressmen or women, serving their constituents.

The House has for four decades had a Democratic majority, leading Hedrick Smith to term it "the Gibraltar of the Democratic party". It has had for longer a not entirely justified reputation as a haven of eccentricity and a willing target for INFLUENCE-PEDDLING; Walter Winchell called it "the House of Reprehensibles", and one anonymous observer christened it "a large body of egos surrounded on all sides by LOBBYISTS". Speaker Thomas Reed was convinced that "the House has more sense than anyone in it", though he also believed it was "no longer a deliberative body". And members have frequently complained, as in most legislatures, about the difficulty of getting anything done or having their own views taken seriously. Congresswoman Bella Abzug complained during the VIETNAM WAR: "I'm tired of listening to a bunch of old men who are long beyond the draft age standing there and talking about sending our young men over to be killed in an illegal and immoral war", and Rep. Dante Fascell said more measuredly: "Being in the House is sometimes like trying to push a wheelbarrow up a hill with ropes and handles".

> Composed of very good men, not shining but honest and reasonably well-informed, and in time they will be found to improve, and not to be much inferior in eloquence, science and dignity to the British Commons.
>
> FISHER AMES, 1789.

> I find speaking here and elsewhere almost the same thing. I was about as badly scared, and no more than when I speak in court.
>
> ABRAHAM LINCOLN after his MAIDEN SPEECH.

> There is something peculiar in the temper of the House. A clear strong statement of a case, if made too soon or late, fails. If well made at the right time it is effective. It is a nice point to study the right time.
>
> Rep. (later President) JAMES GARFIELD, 1874.

> To be quite blunt about it, I'm not impressed with the overall caliber of members of the House.
>
> Vice-President DAN QUAYLE.

House-Senate conference *See* CONFERENCE (1).

Journal of the House or Senate The official records of the proceedings of each House, published at the end of each session under the direction of the Clerk of the House and the Secretary of the Senate.

keeping a house At Westminster, the ability to keep enough members in and around the Chamber to prevent the House being COUNTED OUT and enable business to continue.

losing the house Making a speech in the Chamber that loses the attention of other members; the term is used particularly of Ministers and Leaders of the Opposition at Westminster who have the opportunity to make an impact in a crucial debate, but throw it away with a tedious or off-key speech.

Houses of Parliament The new Palace of WESTMINSTER erected on the site of the jumble of Parliamentary buildings destroyed in the fire of 1834. The idea of moving to a more salubrious site was considered, but Wellington (*see* IRON DUKE) insisted:

> You must build your House of Parliament upon the river, so that the populace cannot exact their demands by sitting down round you.

Tsar Nicholas I described the completed building as "a dream in stone"; when it was rebuilt almost in replica after severe damage in World War II, Clement ATTLEE observed:

> The British have the distinction above all other nations of being able to put new wine into old bottles without bursting them.

Hoverthorpe The nickname bestowed by the UK media on the Liberal leader Jeremy THORPE (1929–) when in the late summer of 1974 with a General Election imminent he campaigned by landing on seaside beaches in Devon from a hovercraft to woo the holidaymakers' vote.

Howe resignation The event which triggered the overthrow of Margaret Thatcher, the resignation on 1 November 1990 of Sir Geoffrey (later Lord) Howe (1926–). Howe (*see* DEAD SHEEP, MOGADON MAN) had become increasingly disenchanted with the IRON LADY since, having loyally supported her for a decade, she demoted him from FOREIGN SECRETARY to LEADER OF THE HOUSE and (in name only) Deputy Prime Minister. His discontent became greater as she took a steadily harder line against the moves toward closer European union that were to culminate in the MAASTRICHT TREATY, and dug in her heels against eventual membership of the ERM until Howe and Chancellor Nigel Lawson threatened to resign. His resignation was provoked by Mrs. Thatcher's statement to the Commons after the Rome EC summit (*see* NO, NO, NO!) in which she departed from her text to attack not only closer union but the "Hard ECU" plan of Chancellor John MAJOR. Sir Geoffrey's resignation alone Mrs. Thatcher might have survived, but on 13 November he stunned the Commons with a PERSONAL STATEMENT amounting to a devastating indictment of her style of government. On Europe, he said:

> If some of my former colleagues are to be believed, I must be the first Minister in history to resign because he was in full agreement with Government policy.

And of Mrs. Thatcher's attitude to her Ministers' efforts to negotiate in Europe, he described it as:

> like sending your opening batsmen to the crease only for them to find, the moment the first balls are bowled, that their bats have been broken by the team captain.

The trauma inflicted on the Conservative Party by Sir Geoffrey's speech led Michael Heseltine (*see* TARZAN) to declare himself a candidate in the leadership election which, coincidentally, was imminent. And just over two weeks later, Mrs. Thatcher left NUMBER TEN – to be replaced by Major.

HUD The US department of Housing and Urban Development, established by Congress in 1965 at the prompting of President Lyndon Johnson. To demonstrate his commitment to CIVIL RIGHTS, Johnson appointed as its first head Robert C. Weaver, who thus became the first Black Cabinet Secretary. The name is always pronounced "Hud".

Hughes loan The $200,000 secret loan from the billionaire Howard Hughes to Richard Nixon's brother Donald, which became an issue in the Republican's campaign for the Governorship of California in 1962. When Nixon visited Chinatown in San Francisco, he was handed a fortune cookie, opened it – and found the motto "What about the Hughes Loan?" Nixon was furious at the stunt, staged by the prankster Dick Tuck. He lost the election to the Democrat "Pat" Brown, then announced his retirement from politics (*see* Last PRESS CONFERENCE.

Hughligans The group of Conservative MPs led by Lord Hugh Cecil (hence their name) and F. E. Smith who staged bitter protests in the House of Commons in 1911 as the ASQUITH government pushed through the PARLIAMENT ACT to curb the powers of the HOUSE OF LORDS. For half an hour they barracked the Prime Minister at the DESPATCH BOX with cries of "Traitor!" Of Lord Hugh, Asquith's daughter Lady Violet Bonham Carter wrote half a century later:

> [He] screamed: "The King is in duress!", and in his frenzied writhings seemed like one possessed. His transformation, and that of many other personal friends, was terrifying. They behaved, and looked, like mad baboons.

human rights The basic freedoms of humanity to live, express themselves and hold opinions without fear of persecution by the State or from any other quarter. These rights are constantly under threat from TOTALITARIAN regimes, and occasionally in democracies as well. The concept dates back to antiquity, but was championed by thinkers in the 18th century including America's FOUNDING FATHERS who upheld the rights to "life, liberty and the pursuit of happiness". Alexander Hamilton, in *The Farmer Refuted*, wrote:

> The sacred rights of mankind are not to be rummaged for among old parchments or musty records; they are written, as with a sunbeam, in the whole volume of human nature, by the hand of the divinity itself; and cannot be erased or obscured by mortal power.

Even in the age of Empire, the rights of those being conquered had their champions. At the height of his MIDLOTHIAN CAMPAIGN, Gladstone told an audience:

> Remember the rights of the savage, as we call him. Remember that the happiness of his humble home, remember that the sanctity of life in the hill villages of Afghanistan, among the winter snows, is as inviolable in the eye of Almighty God as can be your own.

Theodore Roosevelt took up the banner of human rights in his opposition to America's PLUTOCRATS; in 1910 he said in Paris: "Human rights must have the upper hand, for property belongs to man and not man to property." Human rights also began at home for Eleanor Roosevelt (*see* FIRST LADY OF THE WORLD); on 27 March 1958 she told the UN Commission on Human Rights:

> Where, after all, do universal human rights begin? In small places, close to home – so close and so small that they cannot be seen on any map of the world.

The phrase came into its own after the election of Jimmy CARTER as President in 1976. Carter made the promotion of human rights throughout the world a principal aim of his administration, declaring them "the soul of our foreign policy". Many conservatives objected that he was interfering in the domestic affairs of other countries and harming America's influence abroad, but his campaign struck a positive chord in much of the THIRD WORLD and behind the IRON CURTAIN. However the Black Congresswoman Barbara Jordan felt it necessary to remind him:

> Human rights apply equally to Soviet DISSIDENTS, Chilean peasants and American women.

The worldwide drive for human rights had already produced the HELSINKI ACCORDS of 1975 which, although not immediately honoured by the Soviet Union and its SATELLITES, set a yardstick against which their conduct was measured, and against which democratic governments were judged after the collapse of Communism.

European Convention on Human Rights The document drawn up by the Council of EUROPE in 1950, and signed by all member states, which commits them to protect and develop human rights; it was extended in 1989 to cover torture and loss of liberty. Most countries have incorporated it into their national laws; the UK has yet to do so. The Council also formed a **European Commission on Human Rights** to investigate complaints by governments, organizations or groups that their rights have been abused; cases that cannot be resolved are passed to the European Court of Justice for a decision.

Universal Declaration of Human Rights The text adopted by the UNITED NATIONS General Assembly in 1948 setting out fundamental rights and freedoms to which all are entitled. They include the right to life, liberty, freedom from servitude, fair trial, marriage, ownership of property, freedom of thought and conscience, and freedom of expression. They also include the rights to vote, to work and to be educated. Article 1 reads:

> All human beings are both free and equal in dignity and rights.

human shield The detention and location of HOSTAGES from one country by the leadership of another at potential military targets in the hope that the government whose nationals are held will be deterred from attacking them. The tactic was first employed during the GULF WAR of 1990–91 by the Iraqi leader Saddam Hussein, who had 700 US, British, French, German and Japanese nationals (and captured aircrew) sent to installations that were most liable to attack. In the event, none was killed, but Saddam's readiness to use civilians in this way in violation of the GENEVA CONVENTIONS confirmed the international view of him as a ruthless psychopath.

Humphrey-Hawkins Full Employment Act The measure promoted in the late 1970s by Sen. Hubert Humphrey (*see* HAPPY WARRIOR) and Rep. Gus Hawkins of California, which put the Federal Government under moral pressure to stimulate the economy and combat widespread unemployment. Widely seen at the time as Democratic members of Congress paying their dues to Big LABOR, it was inevitably a dead letter. The Act imposed a number of duties on the Federal government, and requires the chairman of the FED to report twice yearly to Congress on the state of the economy.

hundred. Hundred Days A term used by many political leaders who have wished to appear dynamic for an initial dramatic burst of executive action to put the nation right. The original "hundred days" was Napoleon's brief return to power between his escape from Elba and his final defeat at the Battle of Waterloo (1815). It was first invoked in its present sense by Mussolini, with Franklin D. Roosevelt, John F. KENNEDY and Harold WILSON among incoming leaders to follow suit. Wilson said in a 1964 campaign speech:

> We are going to need something like that which President Kennedy had after years of stagnation – a programme of a hundred days of dynamic action.

FDR's "hundred days of dynamic action", from 9 March to 16 June 1933, was the most dramatic and successful, with an unprecedented torrent of legislation aimed at averting economic collapse, checking the GREAT DEPRESSION and laying the ground for the NEW DEAL. He began it by calling Congress into emergency session, closing the banks and making the first of his FIRESIDE CHATS. Roosevelt launched a "second hundred days" of New Deal legislation after BLACK MONDAY, 27 May 1935, when the Supreme Court declared the NRA unconstitutional; this time a Social Security Act was at its heart.

Hundred Flowers policy The short-lived policy of liberalization in China instituted by CHAIRMAN MAO Tse-Tung in 1957. Mao set it out in a speech to the Supreme State conference in Peking on 17 February:

> The policy of letting a hundred flowers blossom and a hundred schools of thought contend is the policy for promoting the flourishing of the arts and the progress of science.

Mindful of the recent HUNGARIAN UPRISING and Khruschev's denunciation of STALIN, Mao was trying to "resolve the contradictions" becoming increasingly apparent within the Chinese Communist state. Critics of the regime saw the speech as a green light, and a barrage of complaint was directed at the Peking regime, especially from liberals and anti-communists. Party bosses became alarmed and on 8 June a policy change was signalled by the publication of Mao's speech in amended form. This was followed in July by a crackdown on the most outspoken critics. *See also* CULTURAL REVOLUTION.

hung Parliament A newly-elected Parliament in which no party has an overall MAJORITY, and in which the largest party has to decide whether to govern on its own or do a deal with smaller groups. A hung Parliament was the aim of the Liberal/SDP ALLIANCE, outside its moments of greatest euphoria, and remains the LIBERAL DEMOCRATS' best hope of power, but when one has seemed likely (as in 1992) the voters have shied away from it. The last hung Parliament to be elected was in February 1974, when after abortive negotiations between the outgoing Tory Prime Minister Edward Heath (*see* GROCER) and the Liberal leader Jeremy THORPE, Labour under Harold WILSON formed a minority government; it won an election outright that October but lost its majority at by-elections and bought time through the LIB-LAB PACT. A **hung council** is one on which no party enjoys overall control. It is usual for negotiations after inconclusive elections to produce a more or less stable COALITION between two parties, generally the Liberal Democrats and Labour or, less frequently, the Conservatives.

Hungarian uprising The popular revolt against Soviet control of Hungary that cost over 30,000 lives in the autumn of 1956. It started on 23 October – now Hungary's most sacred national day – when police tried to break up a student demonstration in Budapest for the reinstatement of Imre Nagy, the reformist leader ousted in April 1955 by the hardline Matyas Rakosi. Rakosi's policy of limited liberalization while strengthening ties with Moscow became untenable in the face of mounting pressure for radical change, intensified by Destalinization (*see* STALIN) in the Soviet Union and the Poznan revolt in Poland on 28 June; on 18 July he was forced to resign. MOSCOW-LINE Communists struggled to contain the situation under the equally repressive Erno Gero, but the students set off widespread anti-Soviet riots. In Budapest, Soviet flags were burned and Stalin's statue destroyed.

Hungary's own police and army backed the uprising, while members of the notorious SECRET POLICE (AVO) were hunted down. Nagy was installed as Prime Minister on 24 October and promised the withdrawal of Soviet troops. But fighting was intense, especially in East Hungary, and by 30 October some 10,000 lives had been lost. Nagy announced that Hungary had quit the WARSAW PACT and was now NEUTRAL. He appealed for UNITED NATIONS intervention, but no outside assistance was forthcoming; deep splits between Western nations over the SUEZ operation were given as the excuse for allowing the KREMLIN a free hand, but America had privately indicated after the rising in Poland that it would not intervene militarily in such cases.

The Soviet counterstrike began on 4 November with the bombing and military takeover of Budapest, the troops were invited in by Nagy's co-leader Janos Kadar (1912–89), who had fled to the east as tension rose. By 12 November most of the country was under Soviet control, and Hungary had a puppet GOVERNMENT under Kadar. An estimated 190,000 Hungarians had fled to Austria by the end of 1956. On 18 November Nagy was tricked into leaving his refuge in the Yugoslav embassy, taken to Romania and shot. The Kadar government imposed its authority on the country and the uprising was extinguished everywhere, except in the hearts of the Hungarian people. Kadar eventually loosened the reins, and in the month of his death, July 1989, Nagy was reinterred with a moving State funeral. By the turn of the year, Hungary was a democracy.

Hunger March *See* JARROW CRUSADE.

hunger strike *See* STRIKE.

Hurry Upkins The nickname given by Londoners to **Harry Hopkins** (1890–1946), President Roosevelt's emissary to London in the months before America entered World War II (*see* FORMER NAVAL PERSON; LEND-LEASE; POTUS). It reflected both the breakneck pace of his missions and also Britons' desire for America to "hurry up" and join in the war. In March 1941 Hopkins reported to FDR that the UK's two main needs were food and refrigerated cargo vessels, and that German bombing of gas mains had created a demand for food that did not need cooking. He was back in August – when he also made a three-day secret visit to Moscow for talks with STALIN on supplying US war *matériel* to help combat Germany's invasion of the Soviet Union.

hustings, the A general term for ELECTIONEERING, but specifically a platform from which all the candidates in an election address the voters; formerly a booth where votes were collected.

Hyannis Port The compound of white clapboard cottages in an exclusive and otherwise quiet resort on Massachusetts' Cape Cod coast that served as JFK's summer White House, and both the vacation home and the tribal centre of the KENNEDY DYNASTY. Kennedy's father Joseph would divide his time between there and Palm Beach, Florida. At times of decision or of crisis, notably in the wake of CHAPPAQUIDDICK, the Kennedy clan and their advisers would mass in the Hyannis compound to consider the next move, while the world's media massed at police barriers nearby.

Hybridity Hyslop The nickname earned by the Conservative MP **Robin Maxwell-Hyslop** (1931–), who in 1976 delayed Labour's legislation to NATIONALIZE Britain's aircraft and shipbuilding industries for a year by pointing out that the government had inadvertently promoted a **Hybrid Bill.** Such a Bill, because it combines general questions of policy with specific reference to particular commercial undertakings, has to be dealt with by special and complicated Parliamentary procedures. The Speaker's ruling in favour of Maxwell-Hyslop was a blow to Labour, which was nursing a Commons majority of 3, and a tonic for Margaret Thatcher's Conservatives, but the Bill eventually went through.

Hyde Park The 187-acre estate and birthplace of Franklin D. Roosevelt, in New York state 4 miles north of Poughkeepsie; it is now a historic landmark. It took its name from its builder Edward Hyde, Lord Cornbury, the eccentric cross-dresser who governed New York 1702–08. In 1939, before FDR bowed to pressure to run for a third TERM, he wrote:

> I want to go back to Hyde Park. I want to take care of the trees. I want to make the farm pay. I want to finish my little house on the hill.

Hymietown The word that did lasting damage to the Presidential ambitions of the Rev. Jesse JACKSON, alienating many Jewish voters and New Yorkers. On 13 February 1984 the *Washington Post* revealed that when talking to Black reporters, Jackson had referred to Jews as "Hymies" who only wanted to talk about Israel, and to New York City as "Hymietown". Jackson hedged for two weeks before acknowledging that he had been accurately quoted; he insisted he had not been ANTI-SEMITIC but was merely using language that was common in Chicago when he was young. Then Louis Farrakhan, leader of the "Nation of Islam", weighed in by denouncing the reporter who had broken the story as a traitor worthy of death. Jackson managed to mend a number of his fences in time for a more serious challenge in 1988; in the long run his closeness to Farrakhan probably did him more harm with White voters than his "Hymie" comments.

hyperinflation *See* INFLATION.

hypocrite Someone who pretends to be what they are not, or whose speeches run counter to their actions. Abraham LINCOLN typified a hypocrite as "the man who murdered his parents, [then] pleaded for mercy on the grounds that he was an orphan"; Adlai Stevenson as "the kind of politician who would cut down a redwood tree, then mount the stump and make a speech for conservation". The word "hypocrite" is UNPARLIAMENTARY; "hypocrisy" is not.

I

I accuse *See* J'ACCUSE.

I address you neither with rancor nor bitterness in the fading twilight of my life, with but one purpose in mind. To save my country General Douglas MACARTHUR's opening words to a JOINT SESSION of Congress on 19 April 1951, eight days after President Truman dismissed him from command of US forces in KOREA. His audience hailed the speech as one of the most memorable in the history of Congress, but Truman dismissed it as "nothing but a bunch of damn bullshit". *See also* OLD SOLDIERS NEVER DIE.

I am a novel principle – here to be endured The Conservative MP Nancy, Lady Astor, the first woman to take her seat in the House of Commons, making her MAIDEN SPEECH in 1919. (Countess Constance Markievicz (Sinn Fein, Sligo) had been elected in 1918, but stayed away in accordance with her party's policy of BOYCOTTing Westminster.)

I am not a crook Richard Nixon's declaration on 17 November 1973 as the WATERGATE affair gathered pace. He said:

> I made my mistakes, but in all my years of public life I have never profited, *never* profited from public service. I have earned every cent. And in all my years of public life I have never obstructed justice. . . . I welcome this kind of examination because people have got to know whether or not their President is a crook. Well, I am not a crook.

I am the man, the very fat man, who waters the workers' beer The chorus of a comic song, popular from the 1930s, parodying but also sympathetic with left-wing denunciations of capitalist exploitation.

I, being the (acting) returning officer for the – constituency, hereby give notice that the number of votes cast for each candidate is as follows . . . And I therefore declare that the said – has been duly elected to serve in Parliament for the – constituency The formal DECLARATION of the result of a UK Parliamentary election.

I'd much rather have that fellow inside the tent pissing out than outside the tent pissing in The reason given by President Lyndon B. Johnson for not firing FBI director J. Edgar Hoover. Hoover, who had hung on well beyond retirement age and at his death had run the bureau as his personal fief for 48 years, was detested by most leading politicians – but also feared as through his own private intelligence-gathering he was in a position to blackmail most of them – as he threatened to when President Nixon tried to force his retirement.

I disapprove of what you say, but will defend to the death your right to say it The most celebrated statement attributed to Voltaire (1694–1778). The closest he is known to have come to it is: "I detest what you write, but I would give my life to make it possible for you to continue to write", written to Abbé le Riche in 1770.

I do solemnly swear (or affirm) that I will faithfully execute the office of President of the United States, and will to the best of my ability preserve, protect and defend the Constitution of the United States The OATH of office required of the President under Article II, clause 7 of the US Constitution.

I gave them a sword Richard Nixon's view of WATERGATE and his resignation as President in the 1977 FROST INTERVIEWS. It encapsulated both his own acceptance that he had been the architect of his own downfall, and his continuing belief that the liberal and media ESTABLISHMENT was against him. Nixon told his interviewer:

> I gave them a sword. And they stuck it in and they twisted it with relish. And I guess if I'd been in their position I'd have done the same thing.

I have a dream The culmination of Dr. Martin Luther KING's address from the Lincoln Memorial to a crowd of over 200,000 at the close of the "MARCH ON WASHINGTON FOR JOBS AND FREEDOM" on 28 August 1963. His powerful oratory was interspersed with cries of "Dream some more!" from the crowd. The occasion finally forced the KENNEDY administration to take a more active stance in support of civil rights.

> Now is the time to rise from the dark and desolate valley of segregation to the sunlit path of racial justice. . . . There will be neither rest nor tranquility in America until the Negro is granted his citizenship rights . . . No, we are not satisfied and we will not be satisfied until justice rolls down like water and righteousness like a mighty stream. . . . I say to you today, even though we face the difficulties of today and tomorrow, I still have a dream. It is a dream that is deeply rooted in the American dream. I have a dream that one day this nation will rise up, live out the true meaning of its creed: We hold these truths to be self-evident, that all men are created equal. I have a dream that one day on the red hills of Georgia the sons of former slaves and the sons of former slave-owners will be able to sit down together at the table of brotherhood. I have a dream that my four little children will one day live in a nation where they will not be judged by the color of their skin but by the content of their character. I have a dream today. . . . I have a dream that one day every valley shall be exalted, every hill and mountain shall be laid low. The rough places will be made plain and the crooked places will be made straight. . . . Free at last, free at last, thank God almighty, free at last.

The final phrases form his epitaph.

I have been to the top of the mountain Dr. King's speech to striking Memphis sanitation workers on 3 April 1968, the eve of his assassination. In it he compared himself to Moses, who had been shown the Promised Land even though he might not enter it.

> I don't know what will happen now. We've got some difficult days ahead. It doesn't really matter with me now, because I've been on the mountain top. I won't mind. Like anybody, I would like to lead a long life. Longevity has its place. But I'm not concerned about that now. I just want to do God's will. And he's allowed me to go up to the mountain. And I've looked over, and I've seen the promised land. I may not get there with you, but I want you to know tonight that we as a people will get to the promised land. Well, I'm happy tonight. I'm not worried about anything. I'm not fearing any man. Mine eyes have seen the glory of the coming of the Lord!

I have neither eyes to see, nor tongue to speak here, but as the House is pleased to direct me The definitive statement of the freedom of the HOUSE OF COMMONS from outside interference, delivered by Speaker William Lenthall (1591–1662) on 4 January 1642 when King Charles II demanded to know where the FIVE MEMBERS could be found. *See also* I SEE ALL THE BIRDS ARE FLOWN.

I have to tell you that no such undertaking has been received The words with which Neville CHAMBERLAIN told Britain that WORLD WAR II had begun. In a radio broadcast from 10 Downing Street on 3 September 1939, Chamberlain said:

> This morning, the British ambassador in Berlin handed the German Government a final note stating that, unless we heard from them by 11 o'clock, that they were prepared at once to withdraw their troops from Poland, a state of war would exist between us. . . . I have to tell you that no such undertaking has been received, and that consequently this country is at war with Germany.

I have too great a soul to die like a criminal The claim of John Wilkes Booth, assassin of Abraham LINCOLN. The words were not his last; those were "Useless, useless", as he was dragged by Federal troops, mortally wounded, from a burning farmhouse where he had been cornered.

I hereby resign the office of President of the United States The full text of the letter which Richard Nixon wrote to Secretary of State Henry KISSINGER on 8 August 1974, when IMPEACHMENT as a result of his role in WATERGATE had become inevitable.

I, John Brown, am now quite certain that the crimes of this guilty land will never be purged away but with blood The final statement of the leader of the ABOLITIONIST raid on HARPER'S FERRY before being hanged at Richmond, Virginia, on 2 December 1859.

I may have signed my death warrant The prophetic remark of the Irish patriot Michael Collins (1890–1922) as he signed the Treaty with Britain in December 1921 establishing the IRISH FREE STATE. When the document was signed, the Lord Chancellor, Lord Birkenhead (1872–1930), said: "I may have signed my political death warrant tonight." Collins, commander-in-chief of the government forces in Ireland's CIVIL WAR and a reluctant participant in the Treaty talks, replied: "I may have signed my actual death warrant." He was killed by Republicans in an ambush in Co. Cork on 22 August 1922.

I offer neither pay, nor quarters, nor provisions; I offer hunger, thirst, forced marches, battles and death. Let him who loves his country in his heart, and not with his lips only, follow me The rallying call of the Italian patriot Giuseppe Garibaldi (1807–82) in his struggle to unite his country under liberal rule (*see* RISORGIMENTO). He delivered it in a speech to his surrounded Legion in Rome on 2 July 1849.

I refer the honourable member to the reply I gave some moments ago At Westminster, the standard reply given by the Prime Minister in the House to each Open QUESTION asking him or her their engagements for the day, once the initial answer has been given.

I see all the birds are flown Charles I's comment on 4 January 1642 after arriving in the House of Commons to arrest the FIVE MEMBERS – John Pym and four others – against whom he had issued writs for high TREASON. When rumours of the action against the Five reached Westminster, the House asked them to leave, lest soldiers be sent in to remove them forcibly. No sooner had they left than the King arrived. He took the Speaker's CHAIR, surveyed the House and then delivered a speech apologizing for "this occasion of coming unto you", asserting that "I must have them wheresoever I find them" and asking the House to hand them over when they returned. "I never did intend any Force but shall proceed against them in a legal and fair way, for I never meant any other", he said. He then asked Speaker Lenthall where the Five were, and Lenthall refused to answer unless the House so directed. The King then left, with the House in disorder, and the CIVIL WAR had come a step nearer.

I see the river Tiber foaming with much blood *See* RIVERS OF BLOOD.

I shall not seek, and I will not accept . . . Lyndon B. Johnson's announcement in March 1968 that he would be stepping down from the Presidency. LBJ decided not to run again because of the divisions occurring in the Democratic party over his VIETNAM WAR policy; the anti-war Sen. Eugene McCarthy had run strongly against him in the early PRIMARIES. His surprise announcement came at the end of a broadcast on Vietnam. Johnson said:

> It is true that a HOUSE DIVIDED against itself cannot stand. There is a division in the American house now, and believing as I do, I have concluded that I should not permit the presidency to become involved in the partisan divisions that are developing in this political year. Accordingly, I shall not seek, and I will not accept, the nomination of my party for another term as your President.

I stand here with a deep sense of the improbability of this moment The reaction of Spiro T. AGNEW (1918–) when Richard Nixon nominated him for the Vice-Presidency at the 1968 Republican CONVENTION. Liberals were quick to assert that Agnew was right and the purpose of his being a heartbeat away from the Presidency was preposterous. It seemed even more so in October 1973, when Agnew resigned under a cloud.

I, too, was a carpenter A remark attributed to the British Labour left-winger Eric Heffer (1922–91), reflecting both his high self-opinion and his deep religious faith. Heffer, one of the most popular members of the House of Commons, represented Liverpool Walton for 27 years until his death from cancer; on one of his last appearances in the CHAMBER John Major, newly-installed as Prime Minister, earned the rare COMPLIMENT of a round of applause by crossing the floor of the House to shake his hand.

I wanted to dance, but couldn't find any nice ladies to dance with The despairing account by the UNITED NATIONS secretary-general Javier Perez de Cuellar (1920–) of his final visit to Baghdad in January 1991, which he undertook in an effort to prevent the second GULF WAR.

I warn you not to be ordinary . . . Neil KINNOCK's apocalyptic warning at the close of the 1983 election campaign of the impact of THATCHERISM on all but the most privileged members of society. Despite Labour's heavy defeat, the speech had a great effect and contributed to his choice as party leader after the poll. Speaking at Bridgend on 7 June 1983, Kinnock declared:

> If Margaret Thatcher wins on Thursday, she will be more a leader than a Prime Minister. That power produces arrogance and when it is toughened by Tebbitry and flattered and fawned upon by spineless sycophants, the boot-licking tabloid Knights of Fleet Street and placemen in the QUANGOS, the arrogance corrupts absolutely.
>
> If Margaret Thatcher wins on Thursday –
> I warn you not to be ordinary.
> I warn you not to be young.
> I warn you not to fall ill.
> I warn you not to get old.

ICBM Inter-Continental Ballistic Missile. Those missiles with a range in excess of 5500 km. *i.e.* capable of reaching the former Soviet Union when fired from the US or *vice versa*. *See* ABM TREATY; FIRST STRIKE; MIRV; NUCLEAR WAR; SALT; START AGREEMENTS.

ice axe The ultimate symbol of betrayal and brutal removal of one's opponents, from the murder of TROTSKY in Mexico in 1940 on the orders of STALIN. Trotsky was killed with an ice-axe by Ramon Mercader, a Spaniard whose mother was the mistress of an NKVD general. The murder was regarded as savage even by Stalin's standards, and gave a new lease of life to Trotskyists' hatred of Soviet Communism.

Ich. Ich bin ein Berliner (Ger. I am a Berliner) President KENNEDY's defiant identification with the people of West Berlin when he spoke in the free enclave on 26 June 1963 at the height of Cold War tension. He said:

> Two thousand years ago the proudest boast was *civis Romanus sum*. Today, in the world of freedom, the proudest boast is *Ich bin ein Berliner*. . . . All free men, wherever they may live, are citizens of Berlin, and, therefore, as a free man, I take pride in the words *Ich bin ein Berliner*.

The phrase is not strictly correct, grammatically or factually: mischievous Germans point out that a *Berliner* is actually a doughnut. When Jimmy Carter was to visit Germany in 1978, his adviser Gerald Rafshoon jokingly suggested he go to Frankfurt and make a similar pronouncement.

Ich dien (Ger. I serve) The motto of the PRINCE OF WALES.

idealism The aim for total perfection, often refusal to compromise with reality. Aldous Huxley dismissed it as "the noble toga that political gentlemen drape over their will to power". Woodrow Wilson asserted that "America is the only idealistic nation in the world", but Speaker Joe Cannon (*see* FOUL-MOUTHED JOE) said: "You can't make a silk purse out of a sow's ear, and you can't change human nature from intelligent self-interest into pure idealism – not in this life, and if you could what would be left for paradise?".

I have never been an idealist. That implies that you aren't going to achieve something. ARTHUR SCARGILL.

ideology The driving philosophy behind a political or social movement, generally of an abstract and dogmatic nature. A formulator or proponent of an ideology is an **ideologue**.

As a citizen I would hesitate, or not like to see, any political party outlawed on the basis of its ideology. We have spent 170 years in this country on the basis that democracy is strong enough to stand up and fight against the inroads of any ideology.
RONALD REAGAN, for the Screen Actors' Guild, answering Rep. Richard Nixon in 1947.

ideological warfare The battle of rival ideologies, specifically between left and right, or totalitarianism and democracy.

if. If it ain't broke, don't fix it A dictum of Henry FORD, picked up by Margaret Thatcher as an argument against unnecessary Government intervention.

If it's not hurting, it's not working Chancellor John Major's defence of high interest rates as a means of bringing down inflation, October 1990. *Compare* THERE ARE NO GAINS WITHOUT PAINS.

If pressed further . . . The phrase sometimes placed in documents used by WHITEHALL officials to brief the press, indicating more information that may be given under persistent questioning.

If you can't beat or **lick 'em, join 'em** A favourite saying of Sen. James E. Watson (1864–1948), taken up by Sen. Everett DIRKSEN. The reverse, "if you can't join them, beat them" was said by the Danish Foreign Minister Uffe Elleman-Jensen in May 1992 when, after Denmark's rejection of the MAASTRICHT TREATY, the Danish football team was co-opted into the European football championship at the last minute in place of war-torn Yugoslavia – and beat Germany to win the competition.

If you can't convince them, confuse them A favourite saying of President Truman.

If you can't stand the heat, get out of the kitchen Another Trumanism, directed at those politicians without the nerve to take tough decisions – and at himself on deciding not to seek re-election in 1952. Truman himself attributed it to Maj.-Gen. Harry Vaughan. It was frequently quoted by Harold WILSON.

If you don't constantly sharpen your knife, it will rust A justification of continued REVOLUTIONARY violence from Mao Tse-Tung (*see* CHAIRMAN MAO).

IGs Inter-departmental groups that meet to co-ordinate US government policy, especially those in the field of foreign affairs which are generally under the chairmanship of STATE.

He who controls the key IGs, controls the flow of options to the President. Dr. HENRY KISSINGER.

IGCs The two Inter-Governmental Conferences, comprising ministers or officials of the 12 EC member states, set up at the Rome summit in December 1990 to negotiate European political and economic union. The drafts they produced formed the basis of the MAASTRICHT TREATY, concluded a year later.

Ike The universal nickname for **Dwight David Eisenhower** (1890–1969), Supreme Allied Commander Europe in WORLD WAR II and 34th President of the United States (Republican, 1953–61). He was elected on the slogan **I Like Ike**. A career army officer, he told his wife Mamie when they married: "My country comes first and always will. You come second." Eisenhower made a world reputation by preparing and commanding the massed force which on 6 June 1944 landed on the Normandy beaches of occupied France, then pressed on to victory. On D-Day he told US troops:

The eyes of the world are upon you. The hopes and prayers of liberty-loving people everywhere march with you.

With the war over, Republicans and Democrats courted him as a Presidential candidate, but Eisenhower had no overweening political ambitions. He once said: "I can think of nothing more boring for the American people than to have to sit in their living rooms for a whole half hour looking at my face on their television screens," and on another occasion remarked: "Once in a while I get to the point, with everybody staring at me, where I want to go back indoors and pull down the curtains." But he eventually accepted the Republican nomination for 1952, against the Democrat Adlai Stevenson who commented: "If I talk over people's heads, he must be talking under their feet." Of his ideology, Eisenhower said: "I'm no reactionary. Christ on the Mountain! I'm as idealistic as hell." His candidacy amused General Douglas MACARTHUR, who described him as "the best clerk I ever fired". Ike hit back: "I studied dramatics under him for 12 years."

Eisenhower was a laid-back President, Sen. Robert Kerr terming him "the only living unknown soldier". His public image was of a leader who stood back and occupied himself with golf, even putting in the OVAL OFFICE; he did have squirrels trapped on the White House lawn because they interfered with his practice. Emmet John Hughes wrote: "As an intellectual he bestowed upon the games of golf and bridge all the enthusiasm and perseverance that he withheld from books and ideas." But David Halberstam had an explanation: "A subtle man, and no fool. He did not like to be thought of as brilliant; people of brilliance, he thought, were to be distrusted." Eisenhower himself said:

> At last I've got a job where I stay home nights, and by golly I'm going to stay home.

Eisenhower stood aside from many of the contentious issues of the day. He declined to take on Sen. Joseph McCARTHY, saying: "I refuse to get into the gutter with that man;" belatedly the Senate itself saw him off. His first term brought the landmark BROWN case on Civil Rights, but it was the Supreme Court and not the White House that acted. Nevertheless he was a man of principle, in George Kennan's words "the nation's Number One Boy Scout". He made vigorous efforts to prevent the COLD WAR turning into nuclear conflict, and refused to back the Anglo-French military adventure at SUEZ. On leaving office, he warned of the threat to democracy from the MILITARY-INDUSTRIAL COMPLEX. His tenure was sullied only by the Sherman ADAMS affair. Eisenhower's predecessor Harry S Truman was not impressed with his performance, saying: "Eisenhower wasn't used to being criticized, and he never did get it through his head that this is what politics is about. He was used to getting his ass kissed." Yet the overall tone was of prosperous torpor, especially after Eisenhower suffered second-term heart attacks and lowered his profile to the point where one wit cruelly observed:

> Things have never been the same since Ike died.

illegals Illegal immigrants to the United States who have evaded all controls and found jobs, their vulnerability to detection creating a subculture. At first the term applied mainly to "illegals" from Central America; later other groups, notably the Irish, adopted it.

Illinois baboon or **gorilla** Just two of the many nicknames for Abraham LINCOLN, stemming from his height, stark, hirsute face and long arms.

ILO International Labour Organization. The body originally established in 1919 as an organ of the LEAGUE OF NATIONS, which regulates labour practices throughout the world, with government, employer and union representatives from each country. One of the last survivals of the Treaty of VERSAILLES, the ILO is now an agency of the UNITED NATIONS.

> It cannot enforce decisions, but it can publicly humiliate disobedient members.
>
> BLANCHE D'ALPUGET, biographer of Robert Hawke.

ILP Independent Labour Party. The party founded in 1893 by Keir Hardie (*see* QUEER HARDIE) and others, as a forerunner of Britain's LABOUR PARTY. An ILP of sorts, with a left-wing slant, continued to exist after Labour's formation, with five rebel MPs claiming allegiance to it in 1929. It remained AFFILIATED to Labour until 1932; when forced to choose, most of its members went with Labour but a tiny rump has continued.

I'm. I'm all right, Jack The phrase which characterized industrial relations in 1950s Britain, and the title of a film in which Peter Sellers played a Communist shop steward. The film made a considerable impact, but such was the strength of the trade unions that it was over 20 years before a law was successfully passed to curb wildcat strikes. The phrase dates back to 1910, when Sir David Bone (1874–1959) had a character in his seafaring novel *The Brassbounder* say: "It's 'Damn you, Jack – I'm all right' with you chaps."

I'm so pleased to be here in – The standard opening for one of the most frequent political GAFFES, especially during frantic election campaigning. The speaker proudly announces that he or she is in one town (or country) and has to be reminded that they are in fact somewhere else. SIR ALEC Douglas-Home had a tendency to do this; his wife got round the problem by whispering "Peking, Alec, Peking", or whatever the correct venue might be. Examples are legion. In the 1940 Presidential campaign Wendell Wilkie began a speech with the words "Now we are in Chicago", to be told by a heckler: "No, you're in Cicero". Wilkie made matters worse (with Chicago voters) by replying: "Well, all right, this is Cicero. To hell with Chicago!" In 1980 Jimmy CARTER told a crowd in Gerald Ford's home town of Grand Rapids that he was pleased to be in Cedar Rapids; Ford capped him in the gaffe stakes by saying Carter didn't know Michigan was one of the 48 states. Ronald Reagan once welcomed Premier Lee Kuan Yew of Singapore to the White House with the words "Welcome to Singapore!" In the 1984 campaign George Bush told a crowd in Green Bay, Wisconsin how much he liked the Minnesota Vikings. Margaret Thatcher once praised the delights of Malaysia while visiting Indonesia. And during Britain's 1992 campaign Paddy Ashdown arrived in Cornwall with the words: "It's nice to be in Devon again."

image-makers The unseen marketing executives who aim to groom politicians so that they appear warm, decisive and acceptable on television, and expand that image into advertising campaigns and campaign strategy generally.

IMF International Monetary Fund. A specialized agency of the UNITED NATIONS established by the BRETTON WOODS conference (1944) to promote international trade by easing liquidity problems and stabilizing exchange rates. Based in Washington, the IMF makes funds available to countries experiencing short-term BALANCE OF PAYMENTS difficulties, and also supervises economic reform and restructuring in countries moving away from a Command ECONOMY. Deposits of gold or domestic currency are made by member states, who can then borrow automatically up to the limit of their reserve. In 1970 SPECIAL DRAWING RIGHTS (SDRs) were introduced to allow members to borrow in convertible currencies from other members, and SDRs became the IMF's unit of account. In Britain, the IMF was at the centre of a political crisis in 1976 when the Labour government was split over swingeing spending cuts demanded before it would authorize a £2.3 billion standby credit to stabilize sterling; Prime Minister James Callaghan (*see* SUNNY JIM) asked a hostile meeting of Labour MPs: "Do you want us to go on?" The IMF, egged on by the US Treasury, got £2 billion of cuts; it later turned out that the available data were faulty and they had probably not been necessary. The exercise alienated Chancellor Denis Healey (*see* GROMYKO OF THE LABOUR PARTY) from the Left (probably costing him the leadership in 1980) and also gave the Tories a stick with which they beat Labour relentlessly until their own economic crisis 16 years later.

immobilisme A French term for the paralysis in decision-making resulting from unstable COALITIONS and frequent changes of government. It related particularly to the politics of the THIRD (1870–1940) and FOURTH (1946–58) REPUBLICS, which left France without a stable EXECUTIVE, with all power vested in the NATIONAL ASSEMBLY, from which governments were formed. While in this respect similar to the Westminster system, it was handicapped by the multi-party system reflecting the complex structure of French society, and a form of PROPORTIONAL REPRESENTATION which encouraged unstable coalitions.

> Neddy, I've been talking to one of the French governments . . .
>
> PETER SELLERS as Gritpype Thynne in *The Goon Show*, BBC radio, *c.* 1957.

immunities The exemption from civil legal action for the consequences of industrial disputes, which Britain's trade unions enjoyed from the remedying of the TAFF VALE JUDGMENT by Campbell-Bannerman's government in 1906 until the Thatcher government (*see* IRON LADY) removed it in its STEP BY STEP industrial legislation of the early 1980s.

diplomatic immunity The privilege accorded to DIPLOMATS under which they and their households are exempt from taxes, customs duties and prosecution for all but serious criminal offences when serving in another country. The right is guaranteed by the VIENNA CONVENTION.

impeachment The trial by the LEGISLATURE of an office-holder, even a HEAD OF STATE, and his or her removal from office if members so vote. Impeachment was a valued weapon of the Westminster Parliament as it sought to prevent abuses of power. In 1769 John Hatsell wrote: "Impeachments are the groans of the people, and carry with them a greater supposition of guilt than any other accusation." The most celebrated came in 1788, when the enemies of Warren Hastings, former Governor-General of India, had him brought before the House of Lords; he was acquitted after a seven-year trial, but was reduced to poverty. Edmund BURKE, leading the charge, declared:

> I impeach him in the name of the people of India, whose rights he has trodden under foot, and whose country he has turned into a desert. Lastly, in the name of human nature itself, in the name of both sexes, in the name of every age, in the name of every rank. I impeach the common enemy and oppressor of all!

America's FOUNDING FATHERS included impeachment in the Constitution as a sanction against "Treason, Bribery, or other HIGH CRIMES AND MISDEMEANORS". Benjamin FRANKLIN argued that without such a process against an alleged wrongdoer, "recourse was had to assassinations, in which he was not only deprived of his life but of the opportunity of vindicating his character". And in 1970 – just two years before WATERGATE – Rep. Gerald Ford stated: "An impeachable offense is whatever the House of Representatives considers [it] to be at a given moment in history; conviction results from whatever offense or offenses two-thirds of the other body considers to be sufficiently serious to require removal of the accused from office."

The procedure is for the HOUSE OF REPRESENTATIVES to draw up a Resolution of Impeachment, and if it is passed, for the SENATE to conduct the trial; a two-thirds vote is required for conviction. Over two centuries the House has instituted more than 50 impeachments, though only a dozen have reached the Senate. There have been only five convictions, all of Federal judges – such as Harry Claiborne in 1986 for tax evasion.

Two Presidents have faced impeachment – the first for political reasons, the second for judicial. Andrew Johnson was impeached in 1868 by supporters of RECONSTRUCTION, which he strongly opposed. Joseph Medill noted: "Like an aching tooth, everyone is impatient to have the old villain out," and Rep. Thaddeus Stevens declaimed: "He is surrounded, hampered, tangled on the meshes of his old wickedness. Unfortunate, unhappy man, behold your doom!" Johnson faced his critics head-on, saying: "Let them impeach and be damned!" The House voted a resolution of impeachment by 126 to 47 – but the vote in the Senate fell one short and Johnson served out the term to which LINCOLN had been elected. Benjamin Wade, PRESIDENT PRO TEM of the Senate, had been so certain of a vote to impeach that he had even named his own Cabinet. Sen. Edmund Ross, who tipped the vote against conviction and paid the price with the voters, warned prophetically:

> Conditions may arise some day when the exercise of the power to impeach and remove the President may be quite as essential to the preservation of our political system as it threatened to become in this instance destructive of that system.

So it proved in 1974, when the WATERGATE plot and COVER-UP were traced straight back to Richard Nixon despite his denials. On 27 July the House Judiciary Committee voted 27 to 11 to recommend impeachment, and Nixon resigned the following week to avoid the embarrassment of a trial. As the revelations of wrongdoing gathered pace late in 1973, Sen. George Aitken said: "May I now pass on to this Congress advice which I received recently from a fellow Vermonter – either impeach him or get off his back."

One recent successful impeachment took place in September 1992 when the Brazilian Congress removed President Fernando Collor on charges of massive corruption.

imperial. Imperial Conferences The conferences held in London between the Prime Ministers of the DOMINIONS of the BRITISH EMPIRE between 1907 and 1946. They had their origins in the Colonial Conference held in 1887 on the occasion of Queen Victoria's Golden Jubilee. Since 1948, Commonwealth conferences (*see* CHOGM) have replaced the Imperial Conferences.

Imperial Preference A system for encouraging trade between the countries of the British Empire, and particularly between them and Britain, by applying preferential TARIFFs, or none at all. The issue was live early as 1903, when Joseph Chamberlain said: "If you are to give a preference to the colonies, you must put a tax on food". The system was finally negotiated at the 1932 Imperial Economic Conference in Ottawa; after 1948 it applied to the Commonwealth. It was gradually dismantled as a result of the anti-PROTECTIONIST conditions imposed by GATT in 1947 and by Britain's entry into the EC in 1973. Commonwealth preference was finally abandoned in 1977.

Imperial Presidency *See* PRESIDENCY.

imperialism The upsurge of feeling for overseas expansion and the seizure of colonial possessions that swept the great nations of western Europe, and America, at the end of the 19th century. Originally the word for supporting an emperor, imperialism took on its new meaning in Britain after Disraeli had Queen Victoria proclaimed Empress of India, with Africa its main focus and Joseph Chamberlain its most enthusiastic advocate; similar aims were pursued by France (*see* FASHODA), Germany and to a lesser extent Belgium and Italy. American Imperialism reached its crescendo in the SPANISH-AMERICAN WAR and the election of McKINLEY; Sen. Mark Hanna was its driving force. Lord Rosebery, the founder of Liberal Imperialism in Britain, argued that "imperialism – sane imperialism – is nothing but a larger patriotism".

The eclipse of the great empires (except the British) in WORLD WAR I and the rise of COMMUNISM turned the words imperialism and COLONIALISM into terms of abuse; LENIN termed it "the monopoly stage of capitalism". And as imperialism retreated, its detractors grew shriller. In 1958 Nelson Mandela declared: "The Communist bogey is an American stunt to distract the attention of the peoples of Africa from the real issue facing them, namely American imperialism;" Egypt's President Nasser dismissed Israel as "nothing more than one of the consequences of imperialism".

> The struggles waged by the different peoples against US imperialism reinforce each other and merge into a torrential worldwide tide of opposition to US imperialism. . . . Since World War II, US imperialism has stepped into the shoes of German, Japanese and Italian fascism and has been trying to build a great American empire by dominating and enslaving the whole world.
>
> LIN PIAO (1908–71), Chinese Minister of Defence.

In its time (1898) the ultimate argument of the imperialists was spelt out by Hilaire Belloc (1870–1953) when he wrote:

> Whatever happens, we have got
> The Maxim gun, and they have not.

dollar imperialism The term used by Communist and NON-ALIGNED leaders during the COLD WAR to denounce what they saw as economic exploitation of the developing world by US interests.

impoundment Withholding by a US President of funds APPROPRIATED by Congress for programmes of which he does not approve, pending a Bill from the Administration setting different budget priorities. The limited power Presidents had traditionally exercised to balance the books was turned by Richard Nixon into an instrument of policy, directed mainly against social programmes, and was severely restricted by Congress in 1974.

in. In God We Trust The motto stamped on US coins since the 1950s, reflecting an upsurge in religious feeling at the time and a belief that the words did not violate the FIRST AMENDMENT's stipulation that "Congress shall make no law respecting an establishment of religion".

In Place of Fear The title of Aneurin BEVAN's 1952 book setting out the case for radical disarmament, which became part of the credo of Labour's Bevanites.

In Place of Strife The White Paper proposing controls over the trade unions which Employment Secretary Barbara Castle produced in January 1969 for Harold WILSON's Labour Government. Mrs. Castle was assisted by a small drafting group including Tony BENN, later a vehement opponent of curbs on the unions, and Peter Shore. Its central proposal, to outlaw unofficial strikes with the Government itself taking unions and strikers to court, infuriated the unions and split the Cabinet, which had had little chance to discuss it. Home Secretary James Callaghan led the opponents; he described Mrs. Castle, who wanted legislation that summer, as "galloping ahead with all the reckless gallantry of the Light Brigade at Balaclava". Cabinet resistance grew, and when the TUC agreed to police unofficial disputes itself, Wilson dropped the plan to legislate.

> The unions were blameworthy for failing, despite Barbara Castle's warning, to make their own programme of reforms effective. . . . This, coupled with the excesses of some activists in the 1970s, led inexorably to. . . . legislation and the intervention by the courts in their affairs. JAMES CALLAGHAN.

In your heart you know he's right The slogan on which Arizona's Republican Senator Barry Goldwater (1909–) fought an ultra-conservative campaign for the Presidency in 1964 and went down to a LANDSLIDE defeat by Lyndon Johnson. The Democrats parodied the slogan as: **In your guts you know he's nuts,** and Hubert Humphrey said: "He'd have been a great success in the movies – working for 18th-Century Fox." Goldwater had sought the Presidency despite active discouragement from John F. KENNEDY, whom he would have faced but for DALLAS; when Goldwater took JFK's photograph and sent him a copy, the President signed it: "For Barry Goldwater, whom I urge to follow the career for which he has shown so much talent – photography." Goldwater was half-Jewish and philosophical about it, saying: "I told Paradise Valley I was half-Jewish – could I play the back nine?" But I. F. STONE commented: "It was hard to listen to him and realize that a man could be half Jewish and yet appear twice as dense as the average Gentile." Goldwater also crossed swords with the veteran columnist Walter Lippmann; when he complained: "I won't say the papers misquote me, but I sometimes wonder where Christianity would be today if some of those reporters had been Matthew, Mark, Luke and John", Lippmann shot back: "The Senator might remember that the Evangelists had a more inspiring subject." Conservatism made a return with Ronald Reagan, and Goldwater survived his defeat to serve as a distinguished Senator until 1986; he exercised great influence over WATERGATE, defending Richard Nixon till the die was cast against him and and then telling the President the game was up.

inauguration The ceremony at which the PRESIDENT of the United States is sworn in by the CHIEF JUSTICE of the Supreme Court at the start of his four-year term. Until 1932 the President was inaugurated in March, four months after being elected; since the start of Franklin D. Roosevelt's second term the inauguration has taken place on 20 January, unless that day falls on a Sunday. The ceremony itself is usually held in the open air on either the EAST or WEST FRONT of the CAPITOL. After taking the OATH OF OFFICE, the President delivers the **Inaugural Address**; this is followed by a parade down Pennsylvania Avenue to the White House – President Carter and his wife got out and walked, mingling with the crowd – and in the evening there is an Inaugural Ball. In fact there are several such balls, with contributors to the victor's campaign having the best chance of a ticket.

incomes policy An element of economic policy designed to keep growth in wages under control, either by securing voluntary agreement between employers and unions, or by legislation. It has a better chance of success when parallel action is taken to restrain prices, creating a PRICES AND INCOMES POLICY. Governments on both sides of the Atlantic operated such policies in the late 1960s and well into the 1970s, but they lost favour in Britain and America with the election of Margaret Thatcher and Ronald Reagan.

incumbent A current holder of an elective office who is seeking, or intends to seek, re-election. An incumbent, unless personally unpopular, generally enjoys an advantage over challengers known as the power of the incumbency. While an incumbent UK Prime Minister has the great advantage of being able to pick the date of a GENERAL ELECTION, the benefits are even stronger in America where an incumbent President can allocate funds to SWING DISTRICTS and States, and a Senator or Congressman can use their FRANKING PRIVILEGE to deluge electors during their term with mail carefully pitched to gather votes. These and other advantages are reckoned to be worth $500,000 in campaign funds to each incumbent; the effect is that at each Congressional election only a handful of members of the House are unseated.

> In Congress today we have neither a Democratic nor a Republican party. Rather we have an Incumbency Party which operates a monopoly.
> FRED WERTHEIMER, *Common Cause*.

independence The state of being a nation with sovereignty resting in itself; the goal of COLONIAL peoples throughout the ages and notably of a growing proportion of the American population in the late 18th century.

> The country shall be independent, and we are all satisfied with nothing short of it. SAMUEL ADAMS, 1774.

Independence Day The anniversary of the date on which a nation achieved its independence, in America's case 4 July 1776 when the last draft of the Declaration of Independence was reported to the CONTINENTAL CONGRESS and voted on. Though 4 July soon became the nation's greatest holiday, John ADAMS reckoned independence from two days before when a resolution for independence was carried, writing:

> The second day of July, 1776, will be the most memorable epoch in the history of America. It ought to be commemorated, as the Day of deliverance by solemn acts of devotion to God Almighty. It ought to be solemnized with pomp and Parade, with Shews, Games, Sports, Guns, Bells, Bonfires, Illuminations from one end of this Continent to the other from this Time forward forever more.

Independence, Missouri The town, now an eastern suburb of Kansas City, which for more than 70 years was the home of President Harry S Truman (*see* GIVE 'EM HELL HARRY) and to which he and his wife retired on leaving the White House in 1953. Truman is buried in the courtyard of the library named after him in Independence, which also contains a replica of the OVAL OFFICE.

Declaration of Independence The document on which America's nationhood and freedoms are founded. It proclaimed the secession of Britain's 13 American colonies, and blamed the break on the "injuries and usurpations" of King George III which were designed to bring about an "absolute tyranny". The Declaration, which received only brief mention in the London papers, was suggested by Thomas Paine and drafted by Benjamin FRANKLIN, John ADAMS, Roger Sherman, Robert Livingston and Thomas JEFFERSON, whose language shines through it. No one actually signed it on 4 July; most of the 56 signers did over the next two months, but six added their names some time later, Thomas McKean in 1781, and Livingston never signed. *See* John HANCOCK; Life, LIBERTY AND THE PURSUIT OF HAPPINESS; We Hold These TRUTHS TO BE SELF-EVIDENT; WHEN, IN THE COURSE OF HUMAN EVENTS.

> It gave liberty not alone to the people of this country, but hope to all the world. ABRAHAM LINCOLN.

> In 1776, the Americans laid before Europe that noble Declaration, which ought to be hung up in the nursery of every king, and blazoned on the porch of every royal palace. HENRY THOMAS BUCKLE, 1861.

> The rights of man, through MAGNA CARTA, the Bill of Rights, the HABEAS CORPUS, trial by jury and the English common law find their most famous expression in the American Declaration of Independence.
> WINSTON CHURCHILL at FULTON, Missouri, 1946.

Independent (1) **registered Independent**. In America, a voter who wishes to specify formally that they are neither a Republican nor a Democrat, though at times they may vote for either party's candidates.

> The guy who wants to take the politics out of politics.
> ADLAI STEVENSON.

(2) In Britain, a local councillor who has been elected as an individual candidate and not under a party label, even though in some cases he or she may belong to a party (usually the Conservatives). Some local authorities, especially in rural areas, are still controlled by Independents, though their number has fallen steadily since World War II.

index-linking A system by which increases in pay, social security benefits and the like are determined by the increase in the cost of living. In Britain during the rapid INFLATION of the 1970s, the index-linking of civil service pensions was claimed by some to be a reward for failure to devise a workable policy to keep prices under control.

Indian. Indian Mutiny The uprising in 1857 by native sepoys under British command, which was sparked by an order that troops use the new Enfield rifle, which had cartridges greased by pig or cow fat that had to be bitten off before loading. This offended Muslims and Hindus alike, most troops issued with the rifle refused to use it and some were jailed in Meerut. Their comrades mutinied, freed them and then carried out mass atrocities against Britons, including women and children, in Cawnpore, Delhi and Lucknow. The public at home was outraged both by the atrocities and by the measured way in which the Governor, Lord Canning, tried to restore order without unnecessary bloodshed. Once the Mutiny had been crushed, the post of Governor was abolished and those portions of India under British rule made the responsibility of a Secretary of State in the Cabinet.

Indian Reorganization Act The law put through Congress in 1934 by Secretary of the Interior Harold Ickes (1874–1952) which finally turned the tide for what was left of the native American peoples. It undid much of the damage done by the well-meaning DAWES ACT, halted the pillage of Indian lands by commercial interests and White settlers, allocated funds for land acquisition, recognized tribal authority while encouraging modernization of tribal government, and supported Indian education.

The only good Indian I saw is a dead Indian The regrettably immortal comment of General Philip Sheridan (1831–88) at Fort Cobb in January 1869, when told he would be meeting a good Indian chief.

indicator A statistic – for instance the level of production in an industry like housebuilding – which is taken, with others, to show the current level of economic activity and point to trends for the near future. In America a specific index of **key indicators** is published regularly by the Federal government.

lagging indicator Data – such as unemployment figures – which reflect past trends in the economy rather than pointing to how it is developing at present, or will develop in the future.

indoctrination The instilling of a political ideology in someone, implicitly by continuous repetition, by duress or subliminal means.

Industrial Relations Act The legislation introduced by Edward Heath's government in 1971 in an effort to curb the excesses of Britain's trade unions. Though introduced by the liberal Employment Secretary Robert Carr, it was heavily influenced by Sir Geoffrey HOWE and other Tory lawyers. Based on the TAFT-HARTLEY ACT, it involved a more rigid and legalistic approach than Labour's abortive IN PLACE OF STRIFE; its centrepiece was a National Industrial Relations Court (NIRC). Unions lost all IMMUNITIES against legal action unless they agreed to register, and were held responsible in law for the activities of their members. The unions and the Labour Party strongly resisted passage of the legislation, and once it took effect the NIRC found its authority repeatedly flouted. The Act finally lost credibility when the Official Solicitor had to intervene to get the PENTOVILLE FIVE released from prison; they had defied the court's order for them to end secondary PICKETING, but their imprisonment led to a wave of sympathy strikes and the threat of public disorder.

Industry Act forecasts The predictions of economic growth, unemployment and the rate of inflation which a UK Chancellor of the Exchequer makes each year in his Autumn STATEMENT. They were first required by the 1975 Industry Act, which also established the TREASURY MODEL to make the predictions.

INF treaty Intermediate Nuclear Forces Treaty. The first accord to provide for comprehensive ARMS CONTROL, signed by Presidents Reagan and Gorbachev in Washington in December 1987. It ended the round of the ARMS RACE in which the Soviet Union had deployed SS20 medium-range nuclear missiles throughout eastern Europe from the mid-1970s, and America had matched them, to the fury of anti-nuclear campaigners – with CRUISE and PERSHING missiles. The US undertook to destroy 358 missiles and the Soviets 573; as some of the Soviet missiles carried three warheads, the advantage to the West was even greater than the numbers suggest.

infantile leftists The pejorative used by LENINIST leaders for self-styled Communists who lack the discipline and restraint to toe the party line, but rush into indiscriminate revolutionary action without considering the long-term interests of the movement.

inflation The rate of increase in the level of prices, reflecting an increase in the MONEY SUPPLY not accompanied by economic growth. Save for the GREAT DEPRESSION when prices actually fell, inflation has been latent throughout the 20th century and has at times – in Germany in the 1920s when a suitcase of notes was needed to buy a loaf, Britain in the 1970s and Latin America most of the time – been a rampant and DESTABILIZING force. High inflation for any length of time attacks the value of savings, while **hyperinflation**, of 50% or more each month, renders the conduct of a money-based economy almost impossible. The MONETARIST Milton FRIEDMAN, whose views greatly influenced Margaret Thatcher, argued that inflation was

> The one form of taxation that can be imposed without legislation.

The only cure, he wrote, was "a slower rate of increase in the quantity of money".

> Inflation in the Sixties was a nuisance to be endured, like varicose veins or French foreign policy. BERNARD LEVIN.

> Having a little inflation is like being a little pregnant.
> LEON HENDERSON (1895–1986).

influence peddling The Washington word for what anywhere else would be called bribery and corruption. In terms of the US Congress, it involves the gaining of influence by LOBBYISTS and others through the judicious distribution of favours in the hope – or expectation – that this will be reciprocated. A classic example was KOREAGATE, but there are many others.

Information Scandal The scandal in South Africa in 1978–79 which first brought down the Minister of Information, Mr. Connie Mulder, then forced the retirement of B. J. Vorster first as Prime Minister (in September 1978, on grounds of ill health) and then as State President on 4 June 1979. It revolved around covert Government funding of pro-APARTHEID media, approved by Mulder – who said Vorster had known all about it. Dr. Eschel Rhoodie, former Secretary for Information, fled abroad and gave interviews defending his use and control of the secret funds, which financed a failed takeover bid for the anti-National Party SAAN newspaper group, and then set up the pro-government *Citizen*; property was also purchased in South Africa, France and Miami. Supreme Court Justice Mostert tabled charges of corruption, and these were investigated by a commission under Mr. Justice Erasmus. The Erasmus Commission severely criticized Vorster's judgment, saying he shared responsibility with Mulder for the department's ineptitude; he immediately resigned as President. Unusually for a scandal which provided South African liberals with political capital, **Muldergate** inflicted considerable damage on the Afrikaner political establishment.

informed source *See* SOURCES.

Ingham, Bernard *See* YORKSHIRE RASPUTIN.

initiative A procedure by which electors can directly bring about a change in the law, used at various times by 22 American states – starting with South Dakota in 1898. The combination of initiative and public referendum, pioneered by Oregon in 1902, was seen as a means of circumventing MACHINE POLITICS. Usually the signatures of 10% of voters are required for a proposal to be submitted to either the state legislature or the people for approval. Even if an initiative is defeated by popular ballot, the campaign for it can bring about a change in legislators' attitudes.

Inkatha (*Inkatha Yenkululeko Yesizwe*, National Cultural Liberation Movement) The political movement, led by Chief Mangosouthu Gatsha Buthelezi (1928–), which has spearheaded in more senses than one the claims of the Zulus for a special position in post-APARTHEID South Africa. Originally founded in 1928 as a mainly cultural organization, it was revived by Buthelezi in the 1970s as a political force. While opposing apartheid, Inkatha has pursued a less radical approach than the African National Congress, opposing SANCTIONS and foreign disinvestment and preferring some form of POWER-SHARING to Black majority rule. It has thus been promoted by the governing NATIONAL PARTY (which dubs it the Freedom Party) as a potential electoral ally and a counterweight to the ANC. It has combined assertions of Zulu strength with an at times violent struggle with the ANC. It took part initially in the CODESA talks, but withdrew, and has also demonstrated against any attempt to prevent its members carrying the "cultural symbols" of clubs and spears with which they have launched sporadic murderous attacks on ANC supporters (*see* BOIPATONG MASSACRE). *Inkatha* is the Zulu word for the grass coil Zulu women use to carry loads on their heads; its strength depends on the weaving together of many strands.

INLA Irish National Liberation Army. A small but ultra-radical Irish republican terrorist group, best known for its assassination in 1979 of Margaret Thatcher's Northern Ireland spokesman and close confidant Airey NEAVE. INLA's political wing was the **Irish Republican Socialist Party**, whose Belfast stronghold was known as the "planet of the ISPS".

inner cities The densely populated and increasingly run-down central areas of cities throughout the West where bad housing, deteriorating public services, poverty, deprivation and a concentration of ethnic minorities can produce an UNDERCLASS and serious social tension. In America from the 1960s, and Britain from the early 1980s, frustration heightened by tension with the police has spilled over into sporadic RIOTS.

> When you've seen one inner-city slum, you've seen them all.
>
> Vice-President SPIRO AGNEW, campaign speech in Detroit, 18 October 1968.

> We've got a big job to do in some of those inner cities.
>
> MARGARET THATCHER at Conservative CENTRAL OFFICE after her 1987 election victory.

inoperative The immortal word used at the height of WATERGATE by Richard Nixon's press secretary Ron Ziegler to categorize previous statements from him which had been exposed as untrue. On 17 April 1973 as the conspiracy and the White House's involvement began to break surface, Nixon told reporters that "serious" charges had come to light and members of his staff would not be immune from prosecution. Ziegler, who had previously denied there was anything to investigate, was then relentlessly grilled by the White House press corps. Eventually, pressed for the 18th time as to whether all previous statements had been untrue, he told them:

> This is an operative statement. The others are inoperative.

inside the Beltway The phrase used by Washington insiders for the culture of government and its attitudes. The Beltway is the 64-mile Interstate Highway 495, which circumnavigates the capital ten miles from the White House; most government activity takes place within it, and most of those involved live inside it. Outside the Beltway, beyond the first few miles of suburbs and shopping malls, lies real America.

Institutional Revolutionary Party (PRI) The originally radical party which since 1929 (1946 under its present name) has formed the self-perpetuating government of Mexico. Although Mexico has had a fully-democratic US-inspired constitution since 1917 with a President elected for a single term every six years, the PRI has somehow always retained power, regardless of its level of popularity. Since President Carlos Salinas de Gortari, elected in 1988, set out a genuinely multi-party agenda, the PRI has lost a number of provincial elections.

insular cases The series of SUPREME COURT judgments between 1901 and 1903 which settled the status of the various island TERRITORIES America had acquired. They established the principle that the Constitution need not apply in full to residents of US possessions outside the continental United States; this left Congress free to administer each territory virtually as it chose.

insurgency *See* COUNTER-INSURGENCY.

Insurgents The independent-minded liberal Republicans who won election to Congress in the early 1900s independent of, and sometimes in opposition to, the local party MACHINE. Spurning the party's Congressional leadership which they saw as a tool of big business, they pressed a radical agenda including TARIFF reforms, and when Speaker Joe Cannon (*see* FOUL-MOUTHED JOE) blocked them, they combined with the Democrats to strip him of his near-absolute power. Their leaders included Sen. Robert La Follette of Wisconsin, and Reps. George Norris of Nebraska and Jonathan Dolliver of Iowa.

insurrection A popular and apparently spontaneous uprising against the established government.

> When the government violates the people's rights insurrection is for the people, and each part of the people, the most sacred of rights and the most indispensable of duties.
>
> LAFAYETTE to the French National Assembly, 20 February 1790.

> Insurrection, by means of guerrilla bands, is the true method of warfare for all nations desirous of emancipating themselves from a foreign yoke.
>
> GIUSEPPE MAZZINI (1805–72).

> Insurrection is an art, and like all arts it has its laws.
>
> TROTSKY.

integrationist One who believes that members of different races should be encouraged to live side by side; integration is the opposite of SEGREGATION. The extent of integration desirable, and the means of achieving it (*see* BUSING) has been a matter of debate among Americans of all shades since the 1950s. James Baldwin asked: "Who needs to be integrated into a burning house?" and Sen. Barry Goldwater declared: "Forced integration is just as wrong as forced segregation." But the Georgia CIVIL RIGHTS campaigner Julian Bond explained:

> What we mean by integration is not to be with [whites] but to have what they have.

intellectuals A respected political vanguard in continental Europe, a key constituent of the revolutionary Communist movement ("workers, peasants and intellectuals") and a term of abuse in England; Hugh Dalton dismissed them as "semi-crooks, diabetics and under-sized semites". Intellectuals have not had a much better press in America (*see* EGG-HEADS).

> The "Communism" of the English intellectual is something explicable enough. It is the patriotism of the deracinated.
>
> GEORGE ORWELL.

intelligence Information gained about another country, usually an actual or potential enemy, or a group considered subversive, by a process of espionage, BUGGING or deduction. Many politicians are suspicious of this twilight world; US Secretary of State Henry Stimson, who closed his department's code-breaking Black Chamber in 1929, justified his action by saying: "Gentlemen do not read each other's mail."

intelligence community An especially American term for all those engaged in gathering intelligence for a particular government; it refers specifically to the CIA and NATIONAL SECURITY AGENCY, based on opposite sides of Washington. The community is reckoned both by itself and those who fantasize about it to have a culture and attitudes entirely of its own.

intelligentsia An originally Russian term for the intellectual or cultured classes, who were supposed to be in the forefront of political liberalism and reform.

interdependence The way in which each of the world's nations is dependent on the others for a balanced economy and continuing peace. *See* DECLARATION OF INTERDEPENDENCE.

interest. interest groups Sections of society which may be concerned about a particular area of policy; for instance all those affected by a decision to reduce the subsidy to dairy farmers, or to impose taxes on a particular sphere of commerce.

interests Matters which a nation considers to be its business, and in which it reserves a right to intervene. Palmerston said of Victorian Britain: "The sun never sets on the interests of this country." He is also reputed to have said: "a nation has no friends, only interests," but he actually told the Commons on 1 March 1848:

> We have no eternal allies, and we have no eternal enemies. Our interests are eternal and perpetual, and those interests it is our duty to follow.

interests section The section of a country's EMBASSY in a foreign capital which represents the interests of a third nation, usually because that nation and the host country have broken off diplomatic relations.

conflict of interest A situation where an elected representative has commercial or other interests which could prevent them forming an impartial view on a matter that has to be decided. Anyone in this position is supposed to declare an interest; in Britain it is a criminal offence for a local councillor to fail to do so.

declaring an interest The action of a legislator or member of an elected body in stating, when a subject is under discussion, that they have a financial interest in it. Failure to declare an interest when appropriate will render a member liable to disciplinary action, or even prosecution.

outside interests Business or other activities by an elected representative which bring in remuneration and impose demands on his or her time, but do not necessarily impose a conflict of interest.

register of interests A list kept by most legislatures in which each member is supposed to record his or her business connections and outside sources of income. Some are more fully honoured than others; for years completion of the register in the UK House of Commons was voluntary, because Enoch POWELL refused to sign it on principle.

special interests Commercial and other groups that are anxious to secure reliable support from politicians, paying for it if necessary. The ANTI-TRUST LAWS were an early attempt to weaken the power of such interests; President Clinton's proposals to limit PAC contributions are a modern example.

> When I have to choose between voting for the people or the special interests, I always stick to the special interests. The people forget.
>
> Sen. HENRY F. ASHURST, (1874–1962).

vested interests Those entrenched personal, class or corporate interests, usually but not necessarily financial, which act within a social and political system to prevent change that might have implications for them.

intern *See* INTERNMENT.

internal settlement The formula put forward in 1978 and implemented by Ian Smith (1919–) for a multi-racial Rhodesia achieved with safeguards for the Whites and without ending UDI; his hope was that Britain and other countries would reckon that MAJORITY RULE had been achieved, and restore RECOGNITION to the country. It involved renaming the country **Zimbabwe-Rhodesia**, and holding elections from which ZANU-PF would be excluded to produce a non-militant Black government; one was duly elected in 1979 under Bishop Abel Muzorewa (1925–). However even the incoming Margaret Thatcher was persuaded a RETURN TO LEGALITY had not been achieved, and UDI was eventually ended and majority rule achieved by the 1980 LANCASTER HOUSE AGREEMENT. In the ensuing elections, Muzorewa's party won only three seats.

Internal Security Act *See* SUPPRESSION OF COMMUNISM ACT.

international. International Brigades The foreign volunteers who fought for the Republicans against General Franco in the SPANISH CIVIL WAR (1936–39). There were seven brigades, divided by nationality; most came from Europe – many from Britain, including the novelist George Orwell and the poet W. H. Auden – but there was also an Abraham LINCOLN brigade from America. Recruitment was largely organized by the Communist Party (though not all volunteers were Communists); the Brigades included intellectuals and writers, adventurers, the unemployed and ordinary workers. They were involved in the defence of Madrid in November 1936, and reinforced Republican forces to defend the Jarama Valley and Guadalajara the following spring. In 1938 the brigades suffered heavy losses in the Ebro Valley.

International Court of Justice *See* WORLD COURT.

International Development Agency *See* WORLD BANK.

International Labour Organization *See* ILO.

International Monetary Fund *See* IMF.

Internationale, the The rousing march, first heard during the PARIS COMMUNE of 1871, which became the anthem of world Communism and is still played in China whenever there is a pretext. It opens:

> Arise, ye starvelings, from your slumber!
> Arise, ye prisoners of want!

internationalism The belief that no nation can develop and exist alone, and either that all nations have common interests or that they should take joint action. An **internationalist** is both someone with such an outlook, or one who accepts the policies of one of the Internationals that have concerted World Marxism.

> We deny your [Socialist] internationalism because it is a luxury which only the upper class can afford; the working people are hopelessly bound to their native shores.
> MUSSOLINI.

internment The detention of members of a political movement or ethnic group by a government unable or unwilling to bring criminal charges against them. "Internment camps" were used by the "UNION" side in America's CIVIL WAR, thousands of "enemy aliens" were interned by the UK government during WORLD WAR II, while the US government even interned Japanese-Americans in RELOCATION CAMPS. The most controversial – and counter-productive – use of internment was in Ireland; the UK and Irish governments both used it to end an IRA terrorist campaign in the 1950s, and on 9 August 1971 the UK authorities, against Army advice, had 342 IRA suspects in ULSTER rounded up in a bid to curb an upsurge in IRA activity. Many of the wrong people were detained, and 23 people died in the ensuing riots. The number of internees swelled, and with it the protests, culminating in BLOODY SUNDAY the following January. Internment was ended in 1976, but marches against it are still staged as if it were continuing.

interregnum (Lat. between reigns) The period between the termination of one government or form of government and the inauguration of another.

interruption The word that appears (bracketed) in HANSARD when there is a disturbance in the House of Commons, or when some comment brings proceedings to a standstill. It also applies to interjections designed to interrupt a speech, which have not been recognized by the Chair as a formal INTERVENTION. The Conservative MP Oliver Stanley (1896–1950) once said of a tiresome interrupter:

> I wish the Honourable Gentleman's interruptions were as inaudible as they are unintelligible.

intervention (1) In the House of Commons and other assemblies, a contribution – often a challenge or question – from one member in the middle of a speech made by another, made after the person speaking has agreed to GIVE WAY. (2) The action of a CENTRAL BANK in buying, or more infrequently selling, its own currency in order to halt a slide in exchange rates. (3) In the EC's Common Agricultural Policy (CAP), the purchase by member states of farm produce, in order to keep market prices up to pre-set minima.

> Purchase by Eurocrats of local farm produce which no one else wants at prices no one else will pay, for storage in conditions no one else would accept and eventual subsidised export to countries no one else would dream of subsidising.
> CHRISTOPHER MONCKTON.

interventionism (1) In America, a social policy which actively assists one disadvantaged (often ethnic) group in preference to others. Ronald Reagan was elected governor of California in 1966 after accusing the Democrat "Pat" Brown of excessive interventionism to assist the state's Black population. (2) An activist industrial policy under which a national government supports its industries, intervening in management decisions, giving assistance or incentives and even investing in particular companies. Anathema to THATCHERITES, it has been pursued zealously by successive French governments. Michael Heseltine (*see* TARZAN) told the Conservative Party Conference on 7 October 1992:

> If I have to intervene to help British companies – like the French government helps French companies, or the German government helps German companies, or the Japanese government helps Japanese companies – then I tell you, Mr. Chairman, I'll intervene – before breakfast, before lunch, before tea and before dinner. And I'll get up the next morning and I'll start all over again.

Heseltine's credibility was undermined the next week when he announced the closure of

31 coal mines without prior consultation – a decision that aroused a political storm and was later ruled illegal by the High Court.

Intifada (Arab. uprising) The campaign of CIVIL DISOBEDIENCE and RIOTS staged by the PALESTINIAN inhabitants of OCCUPIED TERRITORIES from December 1987 in protest at Israel's failure to grant them autonomy. Shops were closed for long periods, and bands of Palestinian men and boys threw rocks and stones at Israeli soldiers. They retaliated by firing on the demonstrators, killing over 300 Palestinians in the first year of the Intifada while themselves suffering a dozen fatalities.

introduction (1) In the House of Commons, the procedure by which a newly-elected member takes his or her seat. Waiting at the BAR of the House until called by the SPEAKER, the new member steps up to the CHAIR to take the OATH OF ALLEGIANCE or to affirm, signs the register and shakes the Speaker's hand. (2) The start of a BILL's passage through the US CONGRESS, either being sent formally to each House by the ADMINISTRATION or placed in the HOPPER beside the Clerk's table in the HOUSE.

Invergordon Mutiny The mutiny in the Royal Navy's Atlantic Fleet at the naval base in the Cromarty Firth, Scotland, on 15 November 1931. Ratings led by Able Seaman Len Wincott refused to prepare ships for sea in protest at cuts in pay ordered by the NATIONAL GOVERNMENT, which had been announced over the radio in advance of official notification. The Board of Admiralty defused the crisis by agreeing to keep the cuts below 10%. However the incident accelerated the financial crisis that led to the UK abandoning the GOLD STANDARD on 21 September 1931.

invisibles "Invisible earnings" from tourism, shipping and insurance which have to be taken into account when calculating a nation's BALANCE OF PAYMENTS. In Britain's case they have traditionally made an alarming deficit look slightly more palatable, though in the late 1980s they began to slip from their customary monthly total of around £600 million.

IRA Irish Republican Army (also, confusingly, IRA stands in America for Individual Retirement Account). The body which, with varying degrees of moral legitimacy, has conducted a violent campaign for the independence of all Ireland's 32 counties and regards itself as the true government of the Irish Republic. Its slogan is *Tiocfaidh ar La* (Our Day will come). The IRA was founded in 1919 as a GUERRILLA force largely reorganized by Michael Collins from veterans of the EASTER RISING and the former Irish Volunteers, and confronted the Royal Irish Constabulary and the BLACK AND TANS until PARTITION. Collins joined the Free State government, but a faction of the IRA carried on the fight. It went underground after the short and bloody civil war, and was banned by Dublin in 1936 as sporadic attacks continued. A campaign of bombings in London and Coventry was halted by the outbreak of World War II, and during the 1950s there were sporadic but largely bloodless raids on British Army barracks and symbolic bombings of telephone boxes. When civil unrest broke out in NORTHERN IRELAND in 1969 the IRA did not immediately mobilize, British troops being welcomed as deliverers by the Catholic population. But heavy-handedness by STORMONT, the violence of the B-SPECIALS and misjudgments by the SECURITY FORCES culminating in the atrocity of BLOODY SUNDAY gave the IRA a fertile recruiting ground and a grievance on which to act. The movement split into the **Officials**, who opposed a campaign of all-out violence and eventually renounced it, becoming the WORKERS' PARTY, and the PROVISIONALS, who stepped up the struggle with indiscriminate bombings and shootings aimed at cowing the people of Ulster and terrorizing Britain into withdrawing its troops; what would happen then was never spelt out, as extremists among the LOYALIST majority in the north showed their readiness to fight back ruthlessly. IRA ACTIVE SERVICE UNITS, operating with increasing discipline and sophistication, have been responsible for well over 2000 deaths, their actions including the 1974 BIRMINGHAM pub bombings which killed 21 people, the murder of Lord Mountbatten off the coast of Co. Sligo in 1979, the attempted assassination of Margaret Thatcher and her Cabinet in the 1984 BRIGHTON BOMBING, the Remembrance Day bombing in Enniskillen (1987), attacks on British military bases in Germany and England (1989) and a nearly-successful mortar bomb raid on John MAJOR's Cabinet in NUMBER TEN Downing Street. In 1992 the IRA shifted its emphasis to weakening the UK economy, notably through a bombing in the City of London just after the General Election that killed three people and did millions of pounds' worth of damage, causing insurers to panic. The IRA has enjoyed considerable support from Irish-descended Americans, Canadians (*see* NORAID) and Scots, but its political wing SINN FEIN has had limited success in Northern Ireland and has repeatedly been humiliated in the South. *See also* FALLS; INLA; NO GO AREA; OWN GOAL; PARAMILITARY; REPUBLICAN; SECTARIANISM;

SHOOT TO KILL; STALKER REPORT; WE ONLY HAVE TO BE LUCKY ONCE.

They blow up policemen, or so I have heard
And blame it on Cromwell and William the Third.
MICHAEL FLANDERS.

Iran-Contra Affair The scandal in 1986–87 that tarnished Ronald Reagan's second term as President, creating serious doubts both over his credibility and his control over key members of his administration. Also known as **Irangate,** it concerned a plan devised by Marine Lieut.-Col. Oliver North, on the staff of NATIONAL SECURITY ADVISER Admiral John Poindexter, to supply Israeli arms to the AYATOLLAH's regime in Iran, with whom America had had no relations since the captivity of the Teheran HOSTAGES, and use the proceeds to ship arms to the right-wing CONTRAS in Nicaragua, in defiance of Congressional resolutions to give them no such assistance. The deal also aimed to enlist the violently anti-American regime in Teheran to press for the release of seven US hostages held by Shi'ite extremists in Beirut. Exposure of the deal in a Lebanese magazine in November 1986 brought the firing of North and the resignations of Poindexter and White House CHIEF OF STAFF Donald Regan who, echoing Harry S. Truman, said: "The buck doesn't even pause here;" former National Security Adviser Robert McFarlane, who had gone to Teheran bearing a cake from the President, attempted suicide. An unrepentant North declared: "I thought that using the Ayatollah's money to support the Nicaraguan resistance was a good idea", but Secretary of State George Shultz fumed: "We are signalling to Iran that they can kidnap people for profit." The bizarre nature of the dealings baffled many Americans, but North explained: "We were always stuck dealing with intermediaries who really couldn't be trusted." North, who insisted that "throughout I believed that the President had indeed approved such activity", became a hero of the militant Right, as did his glamorous, loyal secretary Fawn Hall, who asserted: "Sometimes you have to go above the written law, I believe," but the episode did lasting damage to Reagan. The President at first denied everything, then said he had known nothing about it, then justified what had been done and finally ordered the arms trading to stop. Washington wits asked:

What did Reagan know and when did he forget it?

The TOWER COMMISSION reported in March 1987 that Reagan had failed to supervise his staff properly, and that the Administration's policies toward both Iran and the Contras were underpinned by deception and a disregard for Federal laws. Former Secretary of State Ed Muskie said:

We were appalled by the absence of the kind of alertness and vigilance to his job and to these policies that one expects of a president.

A Senate committee chaired by Sen. Daniel Inouye was less charitable; it disbelieved claims by North and Poindexter that they had kept Reagan in the dark, and held that if the President did not know about questionable and illegal acts by his staff in such a sensitive area, he should have done. Inouye described the case as

A chilling story, a story of deceit and duplicity and the arrogant disregard of the rule of law. It is a story of withholding vital information from the American people, from the Congress, from the Secretary of State, from the Secretary of Defense, and according to Admiral Poindexter, from the President himself.

Poindexter had said:

I made a very deliberate decision not to ask the President, so I could insulate him from the decision and provide some future deniability for him even if it leaked out.

North had told senators: "I don't think that there's another person in America that wants to tell this story as much as I do," but took the FIFTH AMENDMENT. Charges were brought against several of the conspirators including North, who was convicted in 1988 of obstructing a Congressional investigation, falsifying documents and accepting an illegal gift; he was sentenced to two years' probation, 1200 hours of community service and a $150,000 fine, but on appeal won a retrial which proved abortive. Poindexter was sentenced to, but did not serve, six months in prison. George BUSH, then Vice-President, may also have been closely implicated; one of his last acts in the White House was to PARDON former Defense Secretary Caspar Weinberger (*see* CAP THE KNIFE) on the eve of his trial on perjury charges. It was widely believed that Weinberger might have been forced under oath to confirm that Bush had been involved, despite his denials.

The ultimate irony, the ultimate COVERT OPERATION.
CIA director WILLIAM CASEY.

The most stunning case of the surreptitious accumulation of STAFF power in recent presidencies.
HEDRICK SMITH, *The Power Game.*

I never carried out a single act, not one, in which I did not have authority from my superiors. OLIVER NORTH.

This is going to make a great movie one day.
RONALD REAGAN.

Iran-Iraq war *See* GULF WAR.

Ireland. Ireland would not be a difficult country to govern – were it not that all the people were intractable and all the

problems insoluble The conclusion reached by the Liberal politician John (later Viscount) MORLEY (1838–1923) after several spells as Chief Secretary for Ireland. His bafflement was typical of the English attitude in the years between the fall of PARNELL and the EASTER RISING. Morley's contemporary Viscount Esher declared that "if the Irish were Mahommedans or Hindus, we should have no difficulty with them", and Lord SALISBURY asked: "Is it not just conceivable that there is no remedy that we can apply for the Irish hatred of ourselves?" Even in the 1980s Charles HAUGHEY could say: "It seems that the historic inability in Britain to comprehend Irish feelings and sensibilities still remains." The following reputed exchange shows the gulf in attitudes:

> *Winston Churchill*: The situation in the United Kingdom is serious but not hopeless.
> *Taoiseach*: The situation in my country is hopeless, but not serious.

England's difficulty is Ireland's opportunity An early 20th-century Irish nationalist slogan revived in the late 1980s by leaders of Provisional SINN FEIN.

New Ireland Forum The multi-party body set up by Garret FitzGerald's FINE GAEL-LABOUR coalition in 1983 to devise a future form of government for NORTHERN IRELAND that all democratic nationalist parties in the island (*i.e.* not Sinn Fein) could agree. It sought a formula to put to the UK government as a means of breaking the constitutional deadlock. Its report, published in May 1984, expressed a preference for a unitary Irish state, but showed readiness to consider a federal solution, or joint authority with Britain over the SIX COUNTIES. However Charles Haughey upstaged the launch by playing up the report's references to a united Ireland. Margaret Thatcher was cool about the Forum's proposals, but the Republic's readiness to be constructive paved the way for the ANGLO-IRISH AGREEMENT the following year.

Young Ireland *See* YOUNG.

Irish Free state The TWENTY-SIX COUNTIES of southern Ireland that were granted DOMINION status within the Empire under the provisions of the IRISH TREATY of 6 December 1921. Its first premier, W. T. Cosgrave (1880–1965), was replaced in 1932 by Eamonn de Valera (*see* DEV), founder of FIANNA FAIL, who had fought against the establishment of the state. In 1937 the Free State was renamed Eire; it stayed neutral during World War II, but remained a member of the Commonwealth until 1949 when it became known officially as the Republic of Ireland.

Irish National Caucus A group formed in Washington in 1977 by Fr. Sean McManus, a priest from "one of the English-occupied counties of Ireland", to lobby for a united Ireland. It has gained the support of up to 100 members of Congress with its campaigning for Ireland to be "one nation, indivisible under God" regardless of the views of the majority in the North. The Caucus has been particularly effective in discouraging US investment through rigid application of the MACBRIDE PRINCIPLES. It stops short of supporting the IRA, but has created fertile ground in America for militant Irish Republicanism. The British government regards it as a dangerous and highly tendentious manipulator of half-truths; the Caucus accuses London of spending millions of pounds to counteract its influence and perpetuate discrimination against Catholics in Ulster.

Irish National Volunteers An irregular force raised by the IRISH REPUBLICAN BROTHERHOOD in November 1913 to counteract the ULSTER VOLUNTEERS. It had attracted over 150,000 recruits by June 1914, but then split into two: the majority, the National Volunteers, following the moderate nationalist leadership of John Redmond, and the minority Irish Volunteers joining the radical Eoin MacNeil. The outbreak of World War I gave this latter group the initiative as it campaigned against the war and CONSCRIPTION, and by 1919 the Irish Volunteers had evolved into the IRA.

Irish potato famine The disaster from 1845 caused by the collapse of the potato crop, on which western Ireland had become totally dependent. Caused by blight, it left thousands starving, prompted mass emigration by embittered survivors whose descendants are among the IRA's strongest supporters, and fed resentment among those who stayed against the London government and absentee landlords for failing to alleviate it. It also hastened the repeal of the CORN LAWS.

Irish Question The problem which dogged British politicians from 1844, when Disraeli defined it, until PARTITION in 1921 – and now survives in another form. Disraeli told the Commons on 16 February 1844:

> Consider Ireland. One says that it is a physical question; another a spiritual. Now it is the absence of the aristocracy, now the absence of railways. It is the Pope one day and potatoes the next. Thus you have a starving population, an absentee aristocracy, and an alien Church, and in addition the weakest EXECUTIVE in the world. That is the Irish Question.

Having defined the question, solving it was another matter. In *1066 and All That* (1930), W. C. Sellar and J. S. Yeatman wrote:

> Gladstone spent his declining years trying to guess the answer to the Irish Question. Unfortunately whenever he was getting warm, the Irish secretly changed the question.

And in 1919 Keith Fraser MP told the House of Commons:

> I have never met anyone in Ireland who understood the Irish Question, except one Englishman who had been there only a week.

Irish Republican Army *See* IRA.
Irish Republican Brotherhood The pledge-bound secret organization founded in 1858 which became known as the FENIANS. Its aim was war with England, and it originally hoped that Irish-American soldiers demobilized after the CIVIL WAR would fight for Ireland's freedom; in fact its offshoot *Clan na Gael* rallied US opinion and raised money. By 1873 it had abandoned secrecy and switched to militant political campaigning, joining forces with PARNELL and advocates of HOME RULE. However it retained its Military Council, and with the outbreak of World War I its 1660 members in Ireland prepared again for the fight, and it played a large part in the EASTER RISING of 1916.
Irish Republican Socialist Party *See* INLA.
Irish Treaty The agreement concluded on 6 December 1921 by Lloyd George and the leaders of SINN FEIN, ending English rule over the 26 southern counties of Ireland. It granted DOMINION status to what became known as the IRISH FREE STATE. Hard-line Nationalists rejected the treaty and waged a bloody civil war which claimed the life of many including Michael Collins, an organizer of the EASTER RISING and signatory of the Treaty who took a key role in the new nation's government.
The Irish was born to rule One of the basics of MACHINE POLITICS in America's cities, as set out by the TAMMANY HALL grafter George Washington Plunkitt (1842–1924). Though Irish-Americans did not invent the political machine or the corruption that it bred, they made the system their own, creating many municipal advances along with its sleazier features.
Uncrowned King of Ireland *See* UNCROWNED.

Irgun Zvai Leumi (Heb. National Military Society) A Jewish terrorist organization founded in 1931; it was active in Palestine 1946–48. Its most notorious act was the KING DAVID HOTEL BOMBING on 22 July 1946. It claimed responsibility for over 200 acts of terrorism against the British and Arabs before being disbanded in 1948, when members took an oath of loyalty to the newly founded Israeli state.

iron. Iron Butterfly The nickname given to **Imelda Marcos**, wife of the Philippines' president Ferdinand Marcos (1917–89), who revelled in power, built up the world's largest collection of unworn shoes, went into exile with him when ousted by PEOPLE POWER in 1986, and after his death returned in 1992 in an unsuccessful bid for the presidency. A beauty and singer in her youth, her vanity was only matched by her desire for power and riches; until their downfall, she and her husband would croon to each other adoringly on election platforms. After they fled, crowds flocked to the Presidential mansion to view Imelda's collection of gowns, corsets and shoes; when she appeared in a New York court charged with looting the Philippine treasury, her counsel termed her a **"world class shopper"**. The nickname "Iron Butterfly" had originally been used of the US singer and film star Jeannette Macdonald (1901–65).
Iron Chancellor Prince **Otto von Bismarck** (1815–98), the mastermind of the rise of Prussia and the creation of the German state. From 1862 he increased the influence of his master King Wilhelm I, bringing the SCHLESWIG-HOLSTEIN QUESTION to a head, fomenting a brief and victorious war with Austria and provoking the FRANCO-PRUSSIAN WAR through the EMS TELEGRAM. With Wilhelm installed as *Kaiser*, Bismarck became Chancellor of the Second REICH and set out to create a modern industrial state with universal suffrage and even welfare benefits. The only person in Europe to match Bismarck's influence was Queen Victoria; she called him "the most mischievous and dangerous person alive"; after an audience with her, Bismarck exclaimed: "What a woman!" He presided over the 1878 Congress of BERLIN and survived two assassination attempts, but broke with the young Kaiser Wilhelm II in 1890 (*see* DROPPING THE PILOT); they were reconciled in 1894. Bismarck's last words were

> I do not want a lying official epitaph. Write on my tomb that I was the faithful servant of my master, the Emperor William, King of Prussia.

> He lied with consistency and enjoyment, although unlike LENIN he did not actually prefer lying to telling the truth.
> EDWARD CRANKSHAW.

> He had been as ruthless and unscrupulous as any other politician. What had distinguished him was his moderation.
> A. J. P. TAYLOR.

Iron Curtain The line between the free and Communist states of Europe imposed by the Soviet Union after World War II. It blocked the movement of people and ideas between East and West for over 40 years until the breaching of the BERLIN WALL in 1989 signalled the collapse of Communism. The phrase was popularized by CHURCHILL in his FULTON SPEECH (5 March 1946):

> From Stettin on the Baltic to Trieste on the Adriatic, an iron curtain has descended across Europe.

Hitler's PROPAGANDA chief Josef Goebbels had used almost the same words on 23 February 1945. The phrase goes back at least to 1817, when it appears in the Earl of Munster's journal. Queen Elizabeth of the Belgians in 1914 spoke of a "bloody iron curtain" between her and the Germans, Ethel Snowden used it in 1920 with reference to BOLSHEVIK Russia, and Lord D'Abernon in 1925 with regard to the proposed LOCARNO Pacts.

Iron Duke The affectionate nickname for **Arthur Wellesley, 1st Duke of Wellington** (1769–1852), who led Britain's armies to victory against Napoleon in eight years of campaigning culminating with the battle of Waterloo (1815), which he termed a "damned close run thing". Of the eve of battle the diarist Creevey noted: "Lord W. was at the Ball tonight, as composed as ever." First elected an MP in 1807, he was rewarded after Waterloo with a dukedom and was Prime Minister 1827–30 and briefly in 1834, also being Minister without Portfolio under PEEL 1841–46; of this last spell he said: "I have no small talk and Peel has no manners." In office the Irish-born Duke strongly opposed the REFORM Bill but supported Catholic EMANCIPATION; he said of his policies:

> I have invariably objected to all violent and extreme measures, which is not exactly the mode of acquiring influence in a political party in England, particularly one in opposition to government.

Wellington was a peppery character. When threatened with the publication of letters about a love affair, he told his blackmailer: "PUBLISH AND BE DAMNED". When a man mistook him for the painter George Jones, he replied: "Sir, if you believe that, you will believe anything." And when in his old age Queen Victoria asked him what would clear sparrows from the glasshouses of the Great Exhibition, he told her: "Sparrowhawks, Ma'am." He had had far less respect for the Prince Regent, of whom he said: "He speaks and swears so like Falstaff that damn me, if I wasn't ashamed to walk into a room with him."

> It is incredible what popularity environs him in his latter days. He is followed like a show everywhere he goes and the feeling of the people for him seems to be the liveliest of all popular sentiments, yet he does nothing to excite it, and scarcely seems to notice it.
>
> CHARLES GREVILLE, 1847.

> The Duke, getting on for 80, wrote Baroness Burdett Coutts 850 letters, but was distinctly rattled when she proposed marriage. The Duke retreated in disorder.
>
> DIANA ORTON, *A Biography of Angela Burdett Coutts.*

> The Duke of Wellington has exhausted nature and has exhausted glory. His career was one long unclouded day.
>
> *The Times* obituary, 16 September 1852.

Iron Guard The Romanian FASCIST party founded in 1927 by Cornelieu Zelca Codreanu, which carried out a number of terrorist atrocities in the 1930s. By 1938, when King Carol tried to suppress it, the Iron Guard, which was never fully backed by Germany's NAZI party, was backed by 17% of voters.

Iron Lady The name bestowed upon **Margaret** (later Lady) **Thatcher** (1925–), UK Prime Minister 1979–90, in her early days as Conservative leader by a Soviet Defence Ministry newspaper. Responding to a Commons speech on the Soviet threat to the west, *Red Star* on 24 January 1976 accused her of trying to revive the COLD WAR in face of the "peace-loving policy of the Soviet Union". The attack backfired, making it appear that the KREMLIN saw Mrs. Thatcher as a formidable threat. A week later she struck back, telling a dinner in London:

> I stand before you in my green chiffon evening gown, my face softly made up, my fair hair gently waved. The Iron Lady of the Western world. Me? A cold war warrior? Well, yes, if that is how they wish to interpret my defence of values and freedoms fundamental to our way of life.

The British press were quick to retranslate the phrase as the **Iron Maiden**, a medieval instrument of torture; Clive James wrote:

> She deserves credit for her iron guts, even if you think her brains are made of the same stuff.

Born Margaret Hilda Roberts in the monochrome Lincolnshire town of Grantham, she showed the temperament that would make her Britain's first woman Prime Minister and a world force at the age of nine, when on winning her first school prize, she said: "I wasn't lucky. I deserved it." She gained an Oxford science degree; Dame Janet Vaughan described her as "a perfectly good second-class chemist". She went into industry, a 1948 ICI personnel report terming her "headstrong, obstinate and dangerously self-opinionated". She fought her first seat at Dartford in 1950 and 1951, meeting her businessman husband Denis at the selection meeting. She qualified as a barrister, brought up twins and in 1959 was elected MP for Finchley. She made an immediate impact and in 1961 became a junior Minister in Harold Macmillan's government. In opposition from 1964 she climbed the political ladder through hard work, and in 1970 Edward Heath (*see* GROCER) made her Education Secretary (*see* MILK-SNATCHER). After Heath lost the February 1974 election, she began her obvious move to the Right under the influence of Sir Keith Joseph (*see* MAD MONK). Early the next year she stood against Heath for the Conservative leadership when others held back, and was elected. In four years as Leader of the Opposition, with the collapse of the Labour Government always possible, she moved the party rightwards – but did not easily establish command in the House. After Labour's defeat in a no-CONFIDENCE vote, she fought a spirited election campaign and on 4 May 1979 the Tories were returned to power with a majority of 43.

She offered a healing administration (*see* WHERE THERE IS DISCORD) and in office coupled a MONETARIST economic policy and a determination to move rightwards on LAW AND ORDER with an unexpectedly open mind on Rhodesia, refusing to endorse Ian Smith's INTERNAL SETTLEMENT. The unions she froze out, almost from the start:

> *Syd Bidwell MP* (Lab.): Are you aware that Mr. Len Murray, general secretary of the TUC, insists that when he sees you, it is like having a dialogue with the deaf?
> *Mrs. Thatcher*: I had no idea that Mr. Murray was deaf.

Scorning past Tory feebleness, she ground down the Cabinet WETS and surrounded herself with loyalists; when the economy seemed to be running into trouble, she insisted: "The LADY'S NOT FOR TURNING". She adopted a bulldog attitude toward the EUROPEAN COMMUNITY, whose fellow-leaders she lectured relentlessly (*see* I want my MONEY back); Sir Ian Gilmour, one of the first wets to go, said:

> She will insist on treating other heads of government as if they were members of her cabinet.

She was hostile to the Soviet Union, of whose evil she was convinced, and began a very close working relationship with President Reagan. As the Conservatives moved Right and Labour moved Left the SDP was formed, making inroads into the moderate Tory vote; defeat at the next election looked on the cards when the FALKLANDS WAR transformed the political landscape. In June 1983, with her opponents evenly split, Mrs. Thatcher won re-election with a stunning majority of 144. Her second term was marked by a campaign of PRIVATIZATION, by a turnround in the economy, Mrs. Thatcher's recognition that in Mikhail Gorbachev the Soviet Union had a leader who would end the COLD WAR, and the ANGLO-IRISH AGREEMENT. But it also brought the BRIGHTON BOMBING of October 1984 in which she narrowly escaped death, the year-long MINERS' STRIKE in which she crushed the National Union of Mineworkers led by Arthur Scargill (*see* KING ARTHUR), and the WESTLAND affair which nearly brought her downfall, and left lasting doubts about the ethics of her inner circle. The business activities of her son Mark magnified those doubts. In June 1987 Mrs. Thatcher led the Conservatives to a record third term, with a reduced but still huge majority of 102. With the economy booming until late 1988, she now seemed untouchable; the dismantling of the PUBLIC SECTOR accelerated and she set a triumphalist tone in home policy – epitomized by her advocacy of the POLL TAX – and foreign affairs. Standing out at a Commonwealth conference against tighter SANCTIONS on South Africa, she said:

> If it is 48 against one, I feel sorry for the 48.

And when her daughter-in-law had a baby, she incurred ridicule by proclaiming: "We are a grandmother" (*see* ROYAL WE). Fissures opened between Mrs. Thatcher and Chancellor Nigel Lawson on the economy, which began to deteriorate, and Sir Geoffrey HOWE, her most senior Minister, on Europe, and while her BRUGES speech did not split the party her refusal to contemplate closer union did (*see* NO, NO, NO!). A STALKING-HORSE challenge to her leadership in 1989 by Sir Anthony Meyer sounded a warning she ignored; Sir Geoffrey's resignation over Europe triggered a challenge by Michael Heseltine (*see* TARZAN) in November 1990. She fell four votes short of the margin she needed, and after defiantly declaring: "I fight on, I fight to win", resigned on 28 November, to be succeeded by John MAJOR, her favoured candidate. She said of her defeat: "It's a funny old world", and of him:

> He won't falter and I won't falter. It's just that I shan't be pulling the levers there. But I can be a very good back seat driver.

She left Downing Street in tears and found retirement hard to take, saying wistfully: "Home is where you go when you have nothing else to do." Before long she had gathered a coterie of hard-line devotees; she and they fired off criticism of Major's government on economic policy and Europe that made his job all the harder. Edwina Currie (*see* CRUELLA DE VILLE) declared:

> She is in danger of becoming the Tony BENN of the Tory Party – old and mad and silly and wrong.

She left the Commons at the 1992 election and took a LIFE PEERAGE, remaining active in speaking out against the MAASTRICHT TREATY.

Margaret Thatcher aroused very strong feelings: "A man with tits" – the feminist Labour MP Maureen Colquhoun; "the plutonium blonde" – Arthur Scargill; "a brilliant tyrant surrounded by mediocrities" – Harold Macmillan; "she thinks Sinai is the plural of sinus" – Jonathan Aitken; "a cross between Isadora Duncan and Lawrence of Arabia" –

Daily Telegraph; "a heady mixture of whisky and perfume" – Dr. David Owen; "David Owen in drag" – the *Rhodesia Herald*; "that bloody woman" – Edward Heath; "she who must be obeyed" – Julian Critchley; "clearly the best man among them" – Barbara Castle; "crocodile tears with crocodile teeth" – Neil KINNOCK; "the Enid Blyton of economics" – Richard Holme; "the best man in England" – Ronald Reagan; "the eyes of Caligula and the lips of Marilyn Monroe" – François Mitterrand; "the grocer's daughter" – Valéry Giscard d'Estaing; "she is of such charming brutality" – Helmut Kohl; "she is trying to wear the trousers of Winston Churchill" – Leonid Brezhnev. Denis Healey was rudest about her, calling her "the lady with the blowlamp", "a Pétain in petticoats", "Miss Floggie", "Rhoda the Rhino", and "the Castro of the Western world, an embarrassment to all her friends. All she lacks is the beard", and saying: "The Prime Minister tells us that she gave the French President a piece of her mind – not a gift I would receive with alacrity," and: "Mrs. Thatcher is doing for monetarism what the Boston Strangler did for door-to-door salesmen".

MAGGIE was adored in the constituencies, Julian Critchley writing: "She seemed to share the views so often expressed by party workers and, worse, to articulate them." But the liberal CHATTERING CLASSES loathed her. Keith Waterhouse declared: "I cannot bring myself to vote for a woman who has been voice-trained to speak to me as though my dog has just died." She won the votes of the C2s, but was loathed in Scotland (*see* SERMON ON THE MOUND). She was suceptible to flattery from flashy, middle-aged men; the party ESTABLISHMENT had backed her believing they could control her, but she turned away from them and encouraged not just an ENTERPRISE CULTURE but, at the height of the boom, a Philistine get-rich-quick element, some of whom ended in prison when the recession bit. Harold Macmillan observed:

> She has taken our party from the Etonians and given it to the Estonians.

Nor did she do women any favours; saying: "I owe nothing to WOMEN'S LIB", she believed other women could succeed on their own. Feminists said:

> She may be a woman but she isn't a sister.

The relationship between Mrs. Thatcher and the one woman she had to defer to was reputedly fraught, Anthony Sampson writing: "The weekly meetings between the Queen and Mrs. Thatcher – both of the same age – are dreaded by at least one of them." She had not expected to become Prime Minister until male resistance evaporated; in 1969 she said: "No woman in my time will be Prime Minister or Chancellor or Foreign Secretary – not the top jobs. Anyway, I would not want to be Prime Minister; you have to give yourself 100 per cent"; and in 1972:

> I don't think it will come for many, many years. I don't think it will come in my lifetime.

Mrs. Thatcher's firm anti-Communism and her support for DISSIDENTS in Eastern Europe earned her warm support at the end behind the former IRON CURTAIN. Robin Oakley wrote: "She may have lost Scotland and Wales for the Tories, but she could have had Eastern Europe any time she wanted"; Alexander Dubček simply called her "the kind lady".

Mrs. Thatcher's husband Denis (*see* ANYONE FOR DENIS) gave her financial security and moral support; he was also an unreconstructed right-winger (*see* DEAR BILL) who advocated resuming sporting links with South Africa. US SECRETARY OF STATE George Shultz said: "If I were married to her, I'd be sure to have the dinner ready when she got home", and Denis, asked who wore the trousers in the house: "I do, and I also wash and iron them."

Mrs. Thatcher's overriding attribute was her strength of determination. While she lacked an obvious sense of humour, she could win laughs with her stridency. When she took office James Callaghan told her: "May I congratulate you on being the only man in your team?" She struck back: "That's one more than you've got in yours." Yet she insisted: "I'm not hard – I'm frightfully soft. But I will not be hounded." And she said:

> I am extraordinarily patient – provided I get my own way in the end.

At the same time she wanted to be stood up to, saying: "I love argument. I love debate. I don't expect anyone just to sit there and agree with me. That's not their job." And of her critics she said: "I always cheer up immensely when an attack is particularly wounding because that means that they have not got a single political argument left."

> She sounded like the *Book of Revelation* read out over a railway public address system by a headmistress of certain age wearing calico knickers. CLIVE JAMES.

> The nanny seemed to be extinct until 1975 when, like the coelacanth, she suddenly and unexpectedly reappeared in the shape of Margaret Thatcher.
> SIMON HOGGART, The *Observer*.

> Margaret Thatcher plays, I suspect, to an unseen gallery of headmistresses, economists and the Madame Tussaud version of Winston Churchill.
> KATHARINE WHITEHORN, The *Observer*.

> She has turned the British bulldog into President Reagan's poodle. DAVID STEEL.

Trying to tell her anything is like making an important phone call and getting an answering machine.

DAVID STEEL.

If you want to change her mind, you don't use argument – you look for a transplant surgeon.

GMB Union Leader JOHN EDMONDS.

Bawling out trade unionists, the unemployed, foreigners and other miscreants has been part of her enduring appeal to the British public.

JULIAN BARNES.

She's democratic enough to talk down to anyone.

AUSTIN MITCHELL MP (Lab.).

Her power produces arrogance and when it is toughened by Tebbitry and flattered and fawned upon by spineless sycophants, the boot-licking tabloid knights of Fleet Street and placemen in the quangos, the arrogance corrupts absolutely.

NEIL KINNOCK.

When the undertakers come to lay her out, they will find a colonel's uniform on underneath.

RENEE SHORT MP (Lab.).

I hope she will go on until the end of the century looking like Queen Victoria.

NORMAN TEBBIT.

I wish the old cow would resign.

Northern Ireland Minister RICHARD NEEDHAM, November 1990.

She was constitutionally always right. Power never corrupted her.

NICHOLAS RIDLEY.

A towering Prime Minister who left her country in a far better position than she found it.

JOHN MAJOR.

Paddy Ashdown is the first trained killer to be a party leader . . . Mrs. Thatcher being self-taught.

GILBERT ARCHER, President of Edinburgh Chamber of Commerce, 1992.

See A DAY I WAS MEANT NOT TO SEE; JIM IS VERY, VERY SORRY; REJOICE! REJOICE!; THERE IS NO ALTERNATIVE; TINA.

Iron Triangle A Washington term for the interlocking network of the military services, the defence contractors and the members of Congress whose home districts benefit from military spending. The relevance of a project to the security of the nation is not their highest priority.

cast-iron man The nickname of John C. Calhoun (1772–1850), who was Andrew Jackson's Vice-President and ran for the Presidency against John Quincy Adams in 1824. It was given him by the English economic writer Harriet Martineau:

The cast-iron man, who looks as if he had never been born, and could never be extinguished.

irredentism A campaign for areas outside a nation state's borders but with the same language and culture to be joined to that state. The term comes from *Italia irredenta*, unredeemed Italy, the patriotic movement formed after the virtual union of Italy in 1866 to incorporate Italian-speaking lands still outside, notably the South Tyrol and the northern Adriatic coast. Italy's determination to win these lands from the Austro-Hungarian empire brought it into World War I in 1915; the VERSAILLES conference granted Italy most of the territory, though not Rijeka (Fiume) which Gabriele d'Annunzio seized in 1919.

Iskra (Russ. spark) The revolutionary newspaper edited by LENIN in London in the early 1900s, and the group that sprang from it, devoted to "the preservation of orthodox Marxism".

island. an island of coal surrounded by fish The shorthand term for Britain coined by Aneurin Bevan (*see* NYE). At Labour's victory conference in Blackpool on 18 May 1945, Bevan said:

This island is almost made of coal and surrounded by fish. Only an organizing genius could produce a shortage of coal and fish at the same time.

isolationism The belief that America should not involve itself in the affairs of Europe, which became a potent political force prior to the US entry into World War I, after it when the Senate rejected the LEAGUE OF NATIONS, and from the late 1930s when WORLD WAR II was inevitable. Franklin D. Roosevelt reckoned that the retreat to the isolationism of the late 1930s "was started not by a direct attack against international co-operation, but against the alleged imperfections of the peace"; he warned that if isolationists had their way, Americans could become "a people lodged in prison, handcuffed, hungry and fed through the bars from day to day by the contemptuous unpitying masters of other continents". However the isolationist Sen. Robert Taft (*see* MR. REPUBLICAN) said: "The President confuses the defense of Britain with the defense of the United States."

We do not want the racial antipathies or national antagonisms of the Old World transformed to this continent – as they will, should we become a part of European politics.

Sen. WILLIAM BORAH, 1936.

It is not possible for this nation to be politically internationalist and economically isolationist. This is just as insane as asking one Siamese twin to high dive while the other plays the piano.

ADLAI STEVENSON.

splendid isolation Britain's position in relation to Europe in the late 19th century, which some EURO-SCEPTICS a century later would have liked to re-create. The phrase is commonly credited to the Liberal Unionist George (later Viscount) Goschen (1831–1907), who said on 26 February 1896:

We have stood alone in that which is called isolation – our splendid isolation, as one of our colonial friends was good enough to call it.

And, indeed, the previous month the Canadian statesman Sir George Foster (1847–1931) had spoken in the House of Commons in Ottawa of the days when the great Mother Empire stands splendidly isolated in Europe. . . .

Israel The Jewish state, created in 1948 for a people that had suffered and been divided for centuries, building on the BALFOUR DECLARATION of a generation before. Its foundation, and entire history, is set against a backdrop of tension with the country's Arab neighbours, lightning wars generally won by Israel, Palestinian terrorism and the INTIFADA, Israeli resistance to international pressure to give LAND FOR PEACE, and almost automatic support from America. The relationship with America was summed up by General Moshe Dayan's comment to Secretary of State Cyrus Vance: "Whenever you accept our views, we shall be in full agreement with you." US loyalty was stretched to the limit as LIKUD governments took what was seen in Washington as a dangerously aggressive line, to the point where Secretary of State James BAKER declared:

> Mr. [Yitzhak] Shamir wants to talk peace: our telephone number is area code 202-456-1414.

> The Jews and Arabs should sit down and settle their differences like good Christians.
>
> WARREN R. AUSTIN (1877–1962, *attr.*).

> It took the Jewish people 2000 years to found a state, then along comes a lunatic like [Menachem] Begin and puts everything at risk.
>
> German Chancellor HELMUT SCHMIDT, 1981.

> An outlaw state. The Rev. JESSE JACKSON.

> *Christopher Mayhew MP* (Lab.): The Arabs never said they would drive the Jews into the sea. I will give £5000 to anyone who can ever prove that such a statement was made.
> *Jewish Tory MP*: If I hear six, perhaps we could do business.

issues The particular matters of controversy that attract or polarize the voters during an election campaign.

> Issues are like snakes. They just refuse to die. They keep coming back, time after time.
>
> Sen. HOWARD BAKER (1925–).

> Voters do not decide issues. They decide who will decide issues. GEORGE F. WILL (1941–).

issues-orientated campaign A campaign in which party leaders address specific problems facing the nation, instead of concentrating on personalities or indulging in airy rhetoric.

pocket-book issues A US term for issues raised during an election that concern the individual's economic well-being.

single-issue campaign A campaign or organization that seeks to influence public opinion on one specific theme, for instance abortion or gay rights.

it. It's Scotlands Oil. The slogan launched by the Scottish National Party (SNP) in September 1972 which drove home the message to discontented Scots that the wealth of North Sea oil was not reaching them. The SNP registered strong gains in the two 1974 General Elections, frightening the Labour Party into committing itself to DEVOLUTION.

It's shapely, it wiggles and its name is Ainsley Gotto The phrase that came to haunt Australia's LIBERAL Prime Minister John Gorton and contributed to his replacement on 10 March 1971. Miss Gotto, his English-born private secretary, known as "the shape", was felt by members of his Ministry to wield excessive influence. Picked from the typing pool when just 21 to be Gorton's secretary, she was soon seen as the "power behind the throne"; the key phrase was coined by Dudley Erwin when, sacked as Air Minister in 1969, he was asked why Gorton had got rid of him.

It's the hinge that squeaks that gets the grease The justification put forward by Malcolm X for revolutionary, rather than peaceful, action by Black Americans to secure their rights.

It's Time! One of the shortest-ever election slogans, and one of the most successful. It was aired in Australia's 1972 election campaign by Gough WHITLAM's LABOR PARTY as it strove to end 13 years of Liberal/Country Party rule. The slogan was just part of a promotional package put together by the ALP's Federal secretary, Mick Young, with help from marketing and advertising executives. It gained the ALP eight seats – and won the election.

Italy. Italian tanks The story told by the West German Chancellor Helmut Schmidt (1918–) at a military college passing-out ceremony that brought a formal protest from the Italian government. The story, which Schmidt had first heard as a young man in the *Luftwaffe*, went something like this:

> I hear that our Italian allies have just ordered a new generation of tank, specifically designed for their needs. It is fitted with four reverse gears . . . and one forward, in case the enemy attack from behind.

Italy is a geographical expression The assertion made by the Austrian statesman Prince Metternich (1773–1859) after the revolutions of 1848 had failed to unite the country. Within 13 years, Italian national unity had been proclaimed, but by the 1990s the LOMBARD LEAGUES were arguing that it had broken down, proving Metternich right.

ITT scandal A series of interlocking revelations in the early 1970s of the involvement of the corporate giant ITT (International Telephone and Telegraph) in both US and overseas politics. In 1972 the *Washington Post* columnist Jack Anderson published a memo written by Dita Beard, an ITT LOBBYIST, indicating that the corporation had agreed to underwrite the cost of that year's Republican CONVENTION to the tune of $400,000 in return for the settling of ANTI-TRUST suits by the Nixon administration. ITT also channelled funds through the CIA to support the right-wing opposition to Chile's President Salvador Allende because he was committed to NATIONALIZING ITT's 70% stake in the Chilean telephone Company (*Chitelco*). After the stake was expropriated, ITT drew up an 18-point plan to create disorder in Chile, culminating in a COUP against Allende, which was adopted by the Nixon administration. Allende was overthrown and shot by right-wing officers on 11 September 1973.

Iveagh House The elegant former home of the Iveagh (Guinness) family on St. Stephen's Green, Dublin, which now houses Ireland's Foreign Ministry. Charles HAUGHEY once referred to its occupants as "dog handlers".

Izvestia (Russ. news) The official national newspaper of the Soviet government from 1917, when it was established in Petrograd as an organ of the revolution, to 1991, when the state disintegrated and the Communist Party was outlawed. Transferred to Moscow in 1918, its circulation had grown to 1.5 million by 1932, and in the decades after World War II was considerably higher. It represented the government's views, especially on foreign policy and international relations; reproduced official documents at length; and was intended to educate and inform the public in the light of official policy.

J

J'accuse (Fr. I accuse) The title of the first of two open letters from Emile Zola to the President of the French Republic demanding justice in the DREYFUS CASE. Each paragraph of the letter, published in *L'Aurore* on 13 January 1898, began with the phrase. Clemenceau later claimed to have coined the phrase and written most of the letter.

Jackal, the Journalists' nickname for **Illich Ramirez Sanchez** (1949–), also known as **Carlos**, the Cuban-trained son of a wealthy Venezuelan lawyer who has worked as an assassin for various terrorist groups in the Middle East, Europe and Asia. The name is taken from Frederick Forsyth's 1970 novel *The Day of the Jackal*, in which a professional assassin codenamed "The Jackal" is hired by leaders of the OAS to kill President DE GAULLE. Sanchez joined the Popular Front for the Liberation of Palestine in the late 1960s and masterminded attacks including the 1972 Lod Airport massacre at Tel Aviv in which 25 people were machine-gunned to death, and the kidnapping of eleven oil ministers in 1975 during the OPEC meeting in Vienna; he introduced himself as "the famous Carlos". He operated from safe havens in Iraq, South Yemen, Hungary and Yugoslavia, but since the end of the COLD WAR has lived in Syria with his wife Magdalena Kopp, a former member of the BAADER-MEINHOF GANG.

jackass A stupid or ignorant person, applied politically in America at least from 1820 when Rep. John Randolph of Virginia told Rep. Tristam Burges (Rhode Island) who had spoken of his alleged impotence: "You pride yourself upon an animal faculty, in respect to which the slave is your equal and the jackass infinitely your superior." Sen. William Borah of Utah (1865–1940) was known by opponents as "Son of the Wild Jackass". The term is collectively used by critics of the Congress, as in "the great American jackass". The jackass was also the precursor (derogatorily) of the DONKEY as symbol of the DEMOCRATIC PARTY, in a Thomas Nast cartoon of 1870. To Republicans the two coincide, as in Richard Nixon's "if the economy may be turning down . . . the Democrats could nominate a jackass and probably win".

jackboot, under the Originally a term for NAZI occupation and control of a nation, used now more loosely for any under AUTHORITARIAN foreign domination. From the jackboots (large leather boots extending over the knee) which were first worn by 17th-century cavalry troopers, but gained notoriety as part of the uniform of Nazi stormtroopers (*see* GOOSE-STEP).

Jackie O Nickname for **Jacqueline Kennedy Onassis** (1929–), the stylish widow of President John F. KENNEDY who in 1968 married the Greek shipping magnate Aristotle Onassis (1906–75), denting in the eyes of many Americans the legend of CAMELOT. Even in her husband's lifetime President DE GAULLE had predicted: "I can see her in about 10 years on the yacht of a Greek petrol millionaire." On Onassis's death she gave up her life of Mediterranean luxury and began a career in publishing in New York City. She had set the tone for the glittering Kennedy years in Washington; the events of 22 November 1963, when she rode beside her husband in the DALLAS motorcade, had made her the world's most celebrated widow.

> *Sir Alec Douglas-Home*: I wonder what would have happened if it had been Khruschev, and not Kennedy, who had been assassinated
> *Mao Tse-Tung*: I do not think that Aristotle Onassis would have married Mrs. Khruschev.

Jackson. Andrew Jackson *See* OLD HICKORY. **Jesse Jackson** (1941–) The Baptist minister and former aide of Dr. Martin Luther KING who in the 1984 and 1988 Democratic PRIMARIES became the first serious Black challenger for the US Presidency. In his first campaign he told Black voters in New York: "I cast my bread on the waters long ago. Now it is time for you to send it back to me – toasted, and buttered on both sides." His electoral weapon was the RAINBOW COALITION, Jackson telling the 1984 Democratic Convention: "My constituency is the desperate, the damned, the disinherited, the disrespected, and the despised." His campaign transcended the races but earned him the distrust of many Jews (*see* HYMIETOWN); New York Mayor Ed Koch said of him:

> As a person, there is much to admire in him. As a potential President of the United States, there is much to fear.

Jackson-Vanik Amendment The amendment to President Nixon's 1973 Trade Bill by Sen. Henry Jackson (*see* SCOOP) and Rep. Charles Vanik, which linked Most Favoured NATION status for the Soviet Union to the level of Jewish emigration. President FORD signed the Act in 1975; the Kremlin responded by ignoring the incentive and reducing the flow of emigrants still further. *See also* REFUSENIKS.

Jacobins In the FRENCH REVOLUTION, the revolutionary party led until his execution by Robespierre who between November 1789 and November 1794 fought for a national parliament as the sole sovereign power. It was at the time, and remains, a general term for democratic radicals, but in France specifically refers to the advocates of rigid centralization.

Jacobites The adherents of the line of King James II of England (and VII of Scotland), ousted from the throne and exiled in 1688 after the birth of a Roman Catholic male heir. Support for the KING OVER THE WATER remained widespread, especially in Scotland, well into the 18th century, peaking with the rebellions of 1715 and 1745.

jam. jam tomorrow Promises of better things to come which never arrive; from the saying: "Jam yesterday, jam tomorrow, but never jam today."

jamming Electronic procedures by which (usually Communist) dictatorships prevent their peoples receiving radio broadasts from overseas.

Jameson Raid The incursion into independent Transvaal at the turn of 1895–96 by a detachment of police from what is now Zimbabwe, led by Dr. Leander Starr Jameson (1853–1917), which stoked IMPERIALIST feeling in Britain prior to the BOER WAR. The intruders, who were supposed to link with a revolt of "Uitlander" mineworkers and overthrow President Kruger (*see* OOM PAUL), were captured by the Boers and repatriated. The episode caused a major crisis for Lord SALISBURY's Conservative government, though the complicity of Colonial Secretary Joseph Chamberlain was not proved until after his death. Jameson was tried in London and imprisoned for 15 months. *See also* KRUGER TELEGRAM.

Jar Wars A campaign set up in 1986 by the Reagan administration to stamp out illegal drug taking and dealing. Its name was analogous to the space adventure film *Star Wars* (1977); all government personnel were required to supply urine samples, in jars or bottles, to be tested for the presence of drugs.

Jarrow Crusade The October 1936 "Hunger March" by workers from Jarrow, on the Tyne, to London in protest at the closure of Palmer's shipyard which left two-thirds of the town's workers unemployed. The march was organized by Jarrow council and led by the town's Labour MP, Ellen ("Red Ellen") Wilkinson. After 26 days on the road, she presented a petition in the Commons for government aid to ease unemployment in depressed regions. Now a central part of Labour's mythology, it was at the time shunned by the party establishment – but enthusiastically supported by many of the general public.

jaw To talk, often to excess. House of Representatives Speaker Thomas Reed (1839-1902) described the dandyish Westerner J. Hamilton Lewis as "a thing of beauty and a jaw forever"; Lewis had pointed out a newspaper headline calling Reed "a thing of beauty and a joy forever".

Jaw, jaw is better than war, war The peacemaking phrase widely attributed to Churchill, but in fact the *New York Times* headline based on his comment at the White House in 1954 that "talking jaw to jaw is better than going to war".

jawboning Tough talk by a political leader to bring powerful interests into line with his policies. Notably used of JFK's success in bringing steel industry chiefs to heel and rescind an announced price increase.

Jay. Jay's Treaty A treaty between the US and Great Britain negotiated in 1795 by Chief Justice **John Jay**. Inspired by HAMILTON, it aimed to resolve problems caused by Britain's abuse of American neutrality during its war with revolutionary France. It secured British withdrawal from Detroit and other north-western forts, but was attacked by Washington's opponents as a sell-out because it ignored British violations of American neutrality at sea and the impressment of US sailors into the Royal Navy; the treaty only scraped through Congress.

Je ne regrette rien (Fr. I have no regrets) The title of the song by Edith Piaf which Chancellor Norman Lamont used on 23 April 1993, during the Newbury BY-ELECTION, to justify his heavily-criticized stewardship of the economy. The Conservatives lost the seat, and on 27 May Lamont was sacked by John MAJOR (see EXCHANGE OF LETTERS).

Jefferson, Thomas (1743–1826) Third President of the United States (1801–09). A Virginian lawyer and plantation-owner, he was the author at 33 of the Declaration of INDEPENDENCE, governor of Virginia 1779–81, Minister to France, and Secretary of State from 1789. Defeated for the Presidency by John ADAMS in 1796, he served as his vice-President, then was elected President as a Republican (*i.e.* anti-FEDERALIST) in the REVOLUTION OF 1800. An ardent Francophile and the ultimate all-rounder, his inventions included an automatic door, the dumbwaiter, the thumbtack and a machine that duplicated his letters as he wrote them; he said: "Science is my passion, politics my duty." James Parton described him as "a gentleman who could calculate an eclipse, survey an estate, tie an artery, plan an edifice, try a cause, break a horse, dance a minuet and play the violin". And President KENNEDY told a gathering of Nobel laureates:

> I think this is the most extraordinary collection of talent, of human knowledge, that has ever been gathered at the White House – with the possible exception of when Thomas Jefferson dined alone.

Jefferson was not always seen in such a light; on his election, the *Connecticut Courant* editorialized: "Murder, robbery, rape, adultery and incest will be openly taught and practised. The air will be rent with the cries of distress, the soil soaked with blood and the nation black with crimes. Where is the heart that can contemplate such a scene without shivering with horror?" Martha Washington is said to have called him "one of the most detestable of mankind, the greatest misfortune our country has ever experienced", while HAMILTON wrote: "The moral character of Jefferson was repulsive. Continually puling about liberty, equality and the degrading curse of slavery, he brought his own children to the hammer, and made money of his debaucheries"; this was a reference to Jefferson's rumoured liaison after the death of his wife with his mulatto slave Sally Hemings.

Jefferson has gone down in history as a noble figure, committed to liberty. He himself said: "I have sworn upon the altar of God, eternal hostility against every form of tyranny over the mind of man", and again: "That peace, safety and concord may be the portion of our native land, and be long enjoyed by our fellow-citizens, is the most ardent wish of my heart, and if I can be instrumental in procuring or preserving them, I shall think that I have not lived in vain." Nor was he wedded to politics. He once observed that "the happiest moments of my life have been the few which I have past at home in the bosom of my family. . . . Public emploiment contributes neither to advantage nor happiness. It is an honorable exile from his family and affairs." And toward the end of his long life he remarked: "I have sometimes asked myself whether my country is the better for my having lived at all."

> The principles of Jefferson are the definitions and axioms of a free society. LINCOLN.

Jefferson-Jackson Day The annual commemoration by America's DEMOCRATIC PARTY of the two Presidents it regards as its founders – Jefferson and Andrew Jackson (*see* OLD HICKORY). It is usually celebrated on or around 15 March (Jackson's birthday in 1767) or 13 April (Jefferson's in 1743). In some states, such as Virginia, it can also be marked on Washington's birthday, 22 February.

> The Democratic Party's annual political rain dance. DAVID BRINKLEY.

Jefferson's decalogue of canons Ten rules "for observation in personal life" written by Jefferson in 1825. The first is: "Never put off till tomorrow what you can do today."

Jenkins Hill The original name of the HILL on which the US CAPITOL was built.

Jenkins, Roy *See* WOY.

Jerusalem The anthem of the Christian and non-Marxist elements of English SOCIALISM, as well as of non-political bodies like the Women's Institute. Setting the goal of re-creating the holy city of Jerusalem in the soul of England, the Scottish MEP Janey Buchan has termed it "a call to action". It was written by William Blake (1757–1827), and later set to music by Thomas Parry.

> And did those feet in ancient time
> Walk upon England's mountains green?
> And was the holy Lamb of God
> On England's pleasant pastures seen?
> And did that countenance divine
> Shine forth upon those clouded hills?
> And was Jerusalem builded here
> Among those dark Satanic mills?
>
> Bring me my bow of burning gold!
> Bring me my arrows of desire!
> Bring me my spear! O clouds, unfold!
> Bring me my chariot of fire!
> I will not cease from mental fight,
> Nor shall my sword sleep in my hand,
> Till we have built Jerusalem
> In England's green and pleasant land.

New Jerusalem The ideal – exemplified by the hymn – to which 19th-century socialists, and many since, aspired. During a party conference debate on GAY RIGHTS in 1986, one delegate said: "I joined the Labour Party to build Jerusalem, not Sodom and Gomorrah." And Margaret Thatcher in 1992 asked: "When will they [Labour] learn that you cannot build Jerusalem in Brussels?"

Jewish. Jewish Agency Set up in 1929 by Chaim Weizmann to encourage Jewish settlement in Israel. In its early years it took a conciliatory stance, raising funds for the Jewish national home in Palestine (*see* BALFOUR DECLARATION), overseeing immigration and helping to ease resulting tension with Palestinian Arabs, establishing the Youth Aliyah programme to resettle Jewish orphans fleeing the Nazis, and representing Jewish interests at the LEAGUE OF NATIONS. From 1935 under the leadership of David Ben Gurion it gradually abandoned its ancillary roles to become an uncompromising instrument of militant ZIONISM. In 1948 it became officially identified with the World Zionist Organization.

Jewish Defence League A militant VIGILANTE group set in New York City in the late 1970s by Rabbi Meir Kahane, to defend Jews against attack by other and to cow potential attackers into keeping well clear. The aggressive conduct of the JDL caused controversy among American Jews as well as in the community at large. Kahane moved to Israel in the mid-1980s and adopted a strodently provocative anti-Arab line that embarrassed even the hard-line LIKUD government; eventually Kahane was murdered by an Arab.

JFK The initials of John Fitzgerald KENNEDY, by which the President was widely known. Their use was encouraged, as it drew comparison with his Democratic predecessor FDR. Since December 1963, after Kennedy's assassination, the initials have also applied to New York City's main airport, formerly Idlewild.

Jihad In Islam, a Holy War against the unbeliever. The Jihad is frequently invoked by Muslim leaders in both religious and secular causes.

Islamic Jihad A hard-line Shi'ite group in Lebanon, involved in the 1980s in both terrorism and the kidnapping of Western HOSTAGES.

Jim. Jim Crow laws Legislation, especially in America's southern states, depriving Black people of civil rights. The term probably originated in the 1828 minstrel song *Jim Crow* by Thomas D. Rice; it came to stand for segregation, as in the **Jim Crow car** (a railroad car for Blacks only) and even as a reference to Black people as such.

Jim is very, very sorry Margaret Thatcher's comment in 1980 about her Employment Secretary James Prior, one of the most effective of the Cabinet WETS. Prior had criticized British Steel's handling of a lengthy strike to journalists, and when word of the briefing leaked out Mrs. Thatcher was asked by an interviewer if she would sack him. She replied: "We all make mistakes. I think it was a mistake, and Jim Prior was very, very sorry indeed." Prior, who had not apologized, was furious.

Boatman Jim *See* BOAT.

Sunny Jim *See* SUNNY.

jingoism Extravagant, populist IMPERIALIST feeling, notably in late 19th-century Britain. It was summed up by, and possibly stemmed from, the 1878 music hall song by G. W. Hunt:

> We don't want to fight, but, by jingo if we do,
> We've got the ships, we've got the men, we've got the money too.
> We've fought the Bear before, and while Britons shall be true,
> The Russians shall not have Constantinople.

Practitioners of Jingoism, on both sides of the Atlantic, were known as **Jingoes**.

Jix The nickname of **William Joynson-Hicks**, the 1st Viscount Brentford (1865–1932), Home Secretary in BALDWIN's 1924–29 Conservative government. A noted puritan, he was prominent in Parliament's blocking the adoption by the Church of England of its revised Prayer Book in 1928.

> Regarded by most as a preposterous figure.
> ROBERT RHODES JAMES.

jobs for the boys The exercise of CRONYISM, appointing one's friends and associates to key or lucrative positions on taking office. The phrase dates back at least to the 1930s.

Joe Who? Nickname for **Joe** Charles Joseph **Clark** (1939–), the Conservative who defeated Pierre TRUDEAU in 1979 to become Canada's youngest Prime Minister, but lost power a year later. As PC leader he acquired a bad press on the campaign trail: he was said to carry a turkey with him "in case he needs spare parts". In 1983 he lost the party leadership to Brian Mulroney, who the following year appointed him External Affairs Minister; in 1992, as Constitutional Affairs Minister, he attempted through the CHARLOTTETOWN ACCORD to end the deadlock over how to amend the Constitution that had begun with PATRIATION and remained unsolved by MEECH LAKE.

> No shirt is too young to be stuffed. ANON.

Johnson, Lyndon Baynes *See* LBJ.

Join the Army, see the world, meet interesting people and kill them A 1960s PACIFIST variant of the WORLD WAR II recruiting slogan "Join the Army and see the world".

joint. Joint Chiefs (of Staff) The principal military advisers to the President of the United States in the structure created by the National Security Act of 1947. The chairman is America's highest-ranking military officer; the other chiefs, appointed for four-year terms, are the Army chief of staff, the Navy's director of naval operations, the chief of staff of the Air Force and, on matters concerning his service, the commandant of the Marine Corps.

> A facade of jointness.
> Joint Chiefs Chairman, General DAVID JONES.

joint session A meeting of the two houses of the US CONGRESS, generally to hear an address by the President or a distinguished foreign visitor. Until 1976, when the House rebelled, every visiting head of government was accorded this privilege.

joint sitting In Australia, a combined sitting of the two Houses of Parliament which under certain circumstances may pass legislation rejected by the SENATE, thus overriding the upper house's VETO. A joint sitting in 1974 to pass six of the Labor government's measures the Senate had blocked was the first sitting of the Australian Parliament to be televised. In Britain, the term is used for the occasional functions in the Royal Gallery of the House of Lords when MPs and peers are addressed by a visiting foreign dignitary; they do not amount to a formal session.

Joint tax On CAPITOL HILL, the Joint Committee on Taxation, a non-partisan committee staff which services both the Senate Finance Committee and the House WAYS AND MEANS Committee. Its highly-skilled members assist legislators in putting together workable tax packages for submission to their respective committees.

Joseph, Sir Keith *See* MAD MONK.

Journal, the The official record of each House of the US CONGRESS, the Senate having four such. Each gives a sketchy account of the business done, in contrast to the voluminous CONGRESSIONAL RECORD. In the Senate, reports of House-Senate CONFERENCES cannot be presented while the Journal is being read.

Judaea and Samaria The name given by militant ZIONISTS, including the LIKUD party, to the WEST BANK. They claim Biblical authority for its incorporation into the state of Israel and the creation of Jewish settlements there on previously Arab lands.

Juden raus (Ger. Jews, get out) One of the most offensive throwbacks to the days of NAZI persecution of the Jews, when the slogan was daubed by officially-inspired ANTI-SEMITES on the fronts of Jewish homes, shops and synagogues. Its use, regrettably, persists to this day.

judicial review (1) In America, the power of the courts to rule on whether legislation is CONSTITUTIONAL, and to refuse to enforce legislation that in their view fails that test. No provision was made for it in the Constitution, but Alexander HAMILTON argued for it in the FEDERALIST and in 1803 it was established by Chief Justice John Marshall in the case of Marbury v. Madison; he ruled that as special guardians of the Constitution, the courts must prefer it to any other law whenever there was a conflict. (2) In England and Wales, judicial review of decisions by Ministers and public authorities, to determine whether they have operated within the law, has become increasingly common since the 1970s.

judicial supremacy The power of America's courts, and ultimately of the SUPREME COURT, to be the final interpreters of the CONSTITUTION. The court adopted this power in the light of the Constitution's position as America's supreme law.

> The maxim that the Constitution is what the Supreme Court says it is. HUGH BROGAN.

> There is hardly a political question in the United States which does not sooner or later turn into a judicial one.
> ALEXIS DE TOCQUEVILLE (1805–59).

Judiciary, the A nation's courts, one of the three components of government with the EXECUTIVE and the LEGISLATURE. In America the Judiciary is supreme (*see above*); in Britain it will rule on whether the actions of the Executive are in accord with the law, but will not go against the stated decisions of Parliament.

> The subtle corps of sappers and miners constantly working under ground to undermine the foundations of our confederated fabric. THOMAS JEFFERSON, 1820.

> For heaven's sake discard the monstrous wig which makes the English judges look like rats peeping through branches of oakum. JEFFERSON.

July Measures The steps taken on 20 July 1966 by Harold WILSON's Labour government to support STERLING as estimates of the year's BALANCE OF PAYMENTS deficit rose from £100 to £350 million. They included tighter hire purchase controls, higher drink, tobacco and petrol duties and purchase TAX, a 10% surcharge on military and civil spending overseas – and a six-month FREEZE on prices and wages. Despite these measures, the pound had to be DEVALUED 16 months later.

junket An excursion or lavish meal for politicians which has only the thinnest pretence of being connected with their duties, but which costs either the taxpayer or some benefactor a great deal. *See* BOONDOGGLE; FREEBIE.

junta A government formed by a small group, frequently of military men, after a COUP D'ÉTAT.

> I will be perfectly calm when I personally command the firing squad that shoots those junta bastards.
> General KONSTANTIN KOBETS, Russian defence minister, after the failed KREMLIN COUP of August 1991.

The name is the Spanish for a council of state, but also has origins in the **Junto**, who from 1692 to 1710 exercised critical influence in Britain's House of Commons and for a time held office. It was made up of WHIGs whose main unifying factor was their desperation for power, among them Charles Montagu, later Earl of Halifax; Admiral Edward Russell, Earl of Orford; Sir John (later Baron) Somers; and Thomas Wharton. The junto was eventually broken by Robert Harley (1661–1724), the nearest to a Prime Minister prior to WALPOLE, and Sarah Churchill, Duchess of Marlborough (1660–1744), lost her influence with Queen Anne.

juste retour (Fr. fair returns) The argument which Britain has pursued over the EUROPEAN COMMUNITY Budget: that the amount a nation pays in should be reflected in what it gets back. The principle was for many years hotly resisted by France, which stood to gain heavily from the Common Agricultural Policy (CAP) which took up 70% of the Budget. Successive British Prime Ministers pressed for a formula limiting Britain's liability for the CAP, and Margaret Thatcher, after lengthy and acrimonious negotiations, eventually secured a system of rebates.

K

K Shorthand for a KNIGHTHOOD used by British civil servants and (especially Conservative) politicians. As in "I hope he gets a K."

Kalashnikov The Soviet-made (and much-copied) AK47 automatic or semi-automatic assault rifle that has become the hallmark of guerrilla and terrorist movements throughout the world. Capable of firing 600 rounds a minute, it is named after its inventor, Mikhail Timofeyevich Kalashnikov (1919–).

kamikaze tactics Reckless political action bordering on the self-destructive, named after the Japanese kamikaze ("divine wind") suicide pilots of WORLD WAR II.

Kangaroo group A cross-party grouping in the EUROPEAN PARLIAMENT which campaigns for the breaking-down of frontier barriers to individual movement and trade.

Kansas. Kansas Coolidge or Kansas Sunflower Nicknames for **Alf** (Alfred Mossman) **Landon** (1887–1987), Governor of Kansas 1933–37 and the Republican Presidential nominee routed by Franklin D. Roosevelt in 1936; he carried only Maine and Vermont, but as a consolation lived to be 100. Democrats presciently declared in a campaign bumper sticker: "Sunflowers wilt in November."

Kansas-Nebraska Act The measure, devised by Sen. Stephen Douglas and signed by President Pierce in 1854, which helped draw the battle-lines for the CIVIL WAR. Ostensibly designed to facilitate a northern transcontinental railroad, it carved two jurisdictions out of the Nebraska territory, nominally opening the region to slavery but in practice – because of its population of Northerners – excluding it. To appease the South, the Act also repealed the MISSOURI COMPROMISE, causing bitter Northern protests, splitting the WHIGs and leading directly to the foundation of the REPUBLICAN party.

> Part and parcel of an atrocious plot to exclude from a vast unoccupied region immigrants from the Old World and free laborers from our own States, and convert it into a dreary region of despotism, inhabited by masters and slaves. Sen. SALMON P. CHASE (1808–73).

bleeding Kansas The minor civil war that broke out in Kansas following the election of 1855 in which thousands of slave-owning "border ruffians" crossed from Missouri to vote to make the territory a slave state. An army of northern ABOLITIONISTS, John Brown among them, moved in to contest the fraudulent vote, and before long the two factions were capturing towns and taking prisoners. The pro-slavery government of Kansas remained in office, but was effectively neutered. However excesses of propaganda by both sides did much to raise the temperature in advance of the actual Civil War. It emerged later that while President Buchanan had been elected in 1856 because of his neutrality on "bleeding Kansas", some of his appointees had paid out heavy bribes to ensure it became a slave state.

crime against Kansas The speech which sparked one of the most shameful acts of violence in the history of the US Congress. It was delivered on 20 May 1856 by the ABOLITIONIST Sen. Charles Sumner of Massachusetts, and consisted of two hours of vituperation and sexual allusion. Sumner's speech caused a furore, splitting the Senate down the middle. He described supporters of slavery as "hirelings picked from the drunken spew and vomit of civilization", and abused Sen. Andrew Pickens Butler of South Carolina as "one of the maddest zealots" who had chosen a Black mistress who, "though polluted in the eyes of the world, is chaste in his sight – I mean the harlot Slavery." Butler was not in the Chamber to hear the attack, but three days later his nephew Rep. Preston Brooks entered the Senate chamber and beat Sumner close to death with his cane. Messages of sympathy to Sumner poured in from the North, while Brooks was inundated with new canes from well-wishing Southerners inscribed "Hit him again!". Lengthy House hearings established the severity of the attack, and with expulsion on the cards, Brooks resigned and won re-election – only to die of drink five months later. It was two years before Sumner could walk, read or write again; his empty chair became a potent symbol to the anti-slavery campaign.

KANU Kenya African National Union. The ruling (and for most of its existence the only) party in independent Kenya. Founded in 1960 by Jomo Kenyatta (1891–1978) as a pan-tribal independence movement and successor to the Kenya African Union (established by Kenyatta 1944), itself the successor of the Kikuyu Central Association, founded 1908 but banned by the British in 1940. KANU won the pre-independence elections in 1963, Kenyatta becoming Prime Minister. After independence Kenyatta became Kenya's first President and turned the country into a one-party state.

Kapital, Das *See* DAS KAPITAL.

Kapp putsch An armed rising by the Erhardt FREIKORPS Brigade, which marched into Berlin in protest at the German government's acceptance of the Treaty of VERSAILLES which required the Brigade's dissolution. The WEIMAR REPUBLIC was overthrown and a right-wing journalist, Wolfgang Kapp (1888–1922) declared Chancellor. The putsch collapsed after five days in the face of a GENERAL STRIKE by Berlin workers and the regular army's refusal to back the Freikorps. Kapp fled to Sweden.

Katie Graham's going to get her fat tit caught in the wringer One of the most celebrated sayings of WATERGATE. The comment, accompanied by a number of threats to the *Washington Post*, was made by former Attorney-General John Mitchell (1913–88) to Carl Bernstein of the *Post*, when the reporter woke him for reaction to the first Watergate story that directly incriminated him; Mitchell's target was Mrs. Katherine Graham, the paper's publisher. Mitchell subsequently served 19 months for conspiracy, obstruction of justice and perjury.

Katyn massacre The mass execution of 5000 Polish officers in April–May 1940 by Soviet secret service officers in a wood near Smolensk. The officers belonged to a Polish force of 15,000 captured and imprisoned by the Soviets after their occupation of eastern Poland under the 1939 HITLER-STALIN PACT. The Germans discovered the graves in 1943 and the Soviet Union refused to co-operate in a Red Cross investigation, blaming the atrocity on the Nazis. The dispute caused the wartime Polish government-in-exile to break off relations with its Soviet "ally". The Soviet Union finally admitted responsibility in 1989, but the whereabouts of the remaining 10,000 Poles remains a mystery.

Keating Five The five US Senators questioned by the Ethics Committee over their receipt of over $1.3 million in campaign contributions from Charles Keating, Arizona property developer and owner of the Lincoln Thrift of Irvine, California, which collapsed owing the taxpayer $2 billion. Keating had sought the senators' help in 1986 when sued by the Federal Government for fraud and racketeering. The five were Senators Alan Cranston, John Glenn, Donald Riegle, Dennis deConcini and John McCain; the committee found a case only against Cranston, saying there was "substantial credible evidence" of improper conduct.

kebab To confront a politician suddenly with a hostile question on an unexpected subject during a supposedly friendly interview. The term was coined by Neil KINNOCK in 1987 when interviewed by James Naughtie on BBC radio's *The World at One*. When Naughtie raised an unexpected issue, Kinnock told him: "I'm not going to be bloody kebabbed." The exchange was not broadcast, but a tape of it reached the newspapers. Some time later Naughtie and his wife took the Kinnocks to a Lebanese restaurant to put the episode behind them, and the speciality of the house turned out to be – an enormous kebab.

keep. Keep Left *See* LEFT.

keep the faith, baby Slogan adopted in America by 1960s Black activists, urging their race to carry on the struggle for CIVIL RIGHTS regardless of setbacks. It had been popularized by Rep. Adam Clayton POWELL when he was expelled from Congress.

Keep Sunday Special The campaign backed by English evangelical churches and the shopworkers' union USDAW which brought the defeat in 1987 of Government legislation to repeal laws against Sunday trading, and blocked reform for several years after. Late in 1991 the supermarkets decided to open anyway and John Major's government infuriated Keep Sunday Special by not intervening.

Kefauver hearings The first televised US Congressional hearings, in May 1950, which held the nation spellbound. Sen. Estes Kefauver (1903–63), was chairing a special Senate committee to investigate "Organized Crime in Interstate Commerce". The advertising agency Young and Rubicam took out newspaper advertisements saying the hearings had shown "a broader picture of the sordid intermingling of crime and politics, of dishonor in public life".

Kellogg pact The high-water mark of the international community's desire to avoid a repetition of WORLD WAR I, signed in Paris in 1928 by every eventual major participant in the next war except the Soviet Union and eventually by 48 nations. Popularly named after US Secretary of State Frank B. Kellogg (1856–1937), it renounced conflict without enabling isolationists to claim America was entering any alliance. After some minor successes in Latin America, it proved unable to halt the Japanese invasion of Manchuria in 1931 and the expansionism of Mussolini and Hitler. Also known as the Kellogg–Briand pact (after French Prime Minister Aristide Briand) and the Pact of Paris.

An international kiss. FRANK B. KELLOGG.

Kennebunkport The seaside vacation home in Maine, on Walker's Point, 90 miles north of Boston, of President George BUSH. When Bush had an announcement to make or a VIP visitor to greet, he would be filmed in front of the wooden porch to a small cottage. His actual home was a hundred yards behind the cottage; when the cameras beckoned, he would drive to the back door of the cottage in a golf cart and come out of his modest LOG CABIN to greet the White House media.

Kennedy dynasty The charismatic but tragic political family descended from and motivated by **Joseph Kennedy** (1888–1969), Boston-Irish stock market speculator, Securities and Exchange Commission chairman and US ambassador to Britain. Their glamour and torment captivated America and the world for three decades. Kennedy, described by Harry S Truman as "as big a crook as we've got anywhere in this country", was ambitious for his sons. The eldest, **Joe Jr.**, was blown up in World War II by 11 tons of high explosive he had volunteered to fly despite being ordered home on furlough; the mantle then fell on **John Fitzgerald Kennedy** (1917–63). JFK had according to his mother been "rocked to political lullabies". Joseph Kennedy said: "I told him Joe was dead and it was his responsibility to run for Congress. He didn't want to. But I told him he had to." A wartime torpedo boat commander (*see* PT-109), he was elected to the House as a Democrat in 1947 and the Senate in 1952, and won a Pulitzer prize with his 1956 book PROFILES IN COURAGE. In Hedrick Smith's words he was "no great shakes as a Congressman or Senator, but he won a mass following". In 1960, to the amusement of party regulars, he sought the Presidential nomination; LBJ remarked: "Have you heard the news? Jack's pediatricians have given him a clean bill of health", but ended as vice-presidential candidate on the Kennedy ticket. The party welcomed the boyish but assertive JFK as "a Truman with a Harvard accent"; one Southern senator observed:

He seems to combine the best qualities of Elvis Presley and Franklin D. Roosevelt.

Pitted against Richard Nixon in a campaign which included the first televised Presidential DEBATES, Kennedy scraped home (*see* COOK COUNTY) to become the 35th (and youngest) President – and the first Roman Catholic in the White House. He had defused this issue by declaring: "I am not the Catholic candidate for President. I am the Democratic party's candidate for President who happens to be Catholic. I do not speak for my Church on public matters – and the Church does not speak for me." Pope John XXIII joked to American bishops: "Do not expect me to run a country with a language as difficult as yours."

Kennedy struck a visionary and dynamic note, contrasting with the torpor of the Eisenhower years. After his election he declared: "Courage, judgment, integrity, dedication – these are the historic qualities which, with God's help, will characterize our Government's conduct in the four stormy years that lie ahead." And his inaugural address in January 1961 set a challenge for the NEW FRONTIER, with its enjoinder: "Ask not what your COUNTRY can do for you – ask what you can do for your country." Quoting George Bernard Shaw, he said: "Some men see things as they are and say: 'Why?' I see things that never were and say: 'Why not?'".

The notion that a new era had dawned was felt on a social and cultural as well as a political level, as a dour executive mansion was transformed into CAMELOT. Kennedy threw the White House open to the greatest names in the arts, leading John Steinbeck to write: "What a joy that literacy is no longer prima facie evidence of treason, that syntax is no longer subversive at the White House." And the visiting Harold Macmillan observed: "There is something very 18th-century about this young man. He is always on his toes during our discussion. But in the evening there will be music and wine and pretty women." And one pretty woman in particular, Kennedy's chic wife Jacqueline (*see* JACKIE O). She had proved a great asset in the 1960 campaign, Kennedy remarking: "As usual, Jackie's drawing more people than we are." As First Lady, Jackie Kennedy not only exuded style in the White House but charmed the world. JFK described himself as "the man who accompanied Jackie Kennedy to Paris", and the visit was worth it, President DE GAULLE hailing Kennedy as "a European". Their marriage was not easy. They suffered personal tragedy, a baby son dying just before Kennedy's own assassination. Jackie was extravagant; Kennedy in his will left her income "to enable her to maintain the standard of living to which she has been accustomed". And JFK himself had a prodigious reputation, carefully concealed by a loyal press, as a womanizer. When he took office, one aide gleefully remarked: "This administration is going to do for sex what the last one did for golf," and it did. Once Jackie, finding a female undergarment under a pillow, told her husband: "They're not even my size." Theodore H. White concluded: "Kennedy loved his wife, but Kennedy the politician exuded that musk odor which acts as an aphrodisiac to many women."

JFK's optimism was soon dented by the Bay of PIGS fiasco, and tested by a series of COLD WAR confrontations including the construction of the BERLIN WALL (*see* ICH BIN EIN BERLINER) and, finally, the CUBAN MISSILE CRISIS. Kennedy had prepared himself for this ultimate exercise in BRINKMANSHIP: "In the long history of the world, only a few generations have been granted the role of defending freedom in its hour of maximum danger. I do not shrink from this responsibility – I welcome it." His demeanour when the superpowers stared EYEBALL TO EYEBALL alarmed some. Robert Ruark saw him as "practically cold all the way, with a hard blue eye on Valhalla", and Norman Mailer wrote: "It is true that we have a President with a face. And it is the face of a potential hero. But he embodies nothing, he personifies nothing, he is power, rather a quizzical power, without light or principle." Yet Khruschev, the Soviet leader, appreciated JFK's firmness, saying: "I had no cause for regret once Kennedy became President." And Nixon later wrote: "Contrary to myth, Kennedy did not relish confrontation. Prudence was one of his favorite words." In private Kennedy could be caustic. When steel bosses went against his wishes to impose a price hike (*see* JAWBONING), he observed: "My father always told me that all businessmen were sons of bitches, but I never believed it until now." Later he added: "They are a bunch of bastards – and I'm saying this on my own now, not because my father told it to me." (*see also* DIEF THE CHIEF.)

Kennedy's domestic record was mixed. Early on he remarked: "When we got into office, the thing that surprised me most was that things were just as bad as we had been saying they were," and before long he was saying bemusedly: "The worse I do, the more popular I get." His initiatives made little headway in Congress, Sen. Everett Dirksen saying they had "about as much impact as a snowflake on the bosom of the Potomac". And in the fall of 1963 James Reston wrote: "There is a vague feeling of doubt and disappointment in the country about President Kennedy's first term".

JFK prepared a vigorous re-election campaign – but it ended at DALLAS on 22 November 1963 when he was assassinated, supposedly by Lee Harvey Oswald. Before his election Kennedy had told staff: "I'm 43 years old, and I'm the healthiest candidate for the Presidency of the United States. You have traveled with me enough to know that I'm not going to die in office." But in office he became philosophical. Just before the end, he remarked: "If someone is going to kill me, they will kill me".

> I should have known that he was magic all along . . . I should have guessed that it would be too much to ask to grow old with him and see our children grow up together . . . Now he is a legend when he would have preferred to be a man. JACQUELINE KENNEDY.

> Since 1963 the world has seemed a bleaker place, and for me and I suspect millions of my contemporaries he remains the lost leader – NEVER GLAD CONFIDENT MORNING AGAIN. Lord HARLECH.

The Presidency passed to Lyndon Johnson, and the Kennedy torch to JFK's younger brother, **Robert Fitzgerald Kennedy** (1925–68). Bobby Kennedy had, against Jack's advice, worked as an investigator for Joseph McCARTHY; he later made his mark prosecuting union racketeers. He ran his brother's Presidential campaign, then was controversially appointed Attorney-General, JFK remarking: "I can't see that it's wrong to give him a little legal experience before he goes out to practice law." Bobby Kennedy made an impact with a vigorous line on civil rights, but also made enemies; according to Henry Brandon, "people feared his quick temper and his adherence to one of the less attractive Kennedy traits: 'If you are not for us, you are against us'". In 1968, after breaking with LBJ on Vietnam, Bobby, by now a Senator for New York, reignited the Kennedy magic by entering the Presidential race. But his candidacy was not a return to Camelot; when Jackie Kennedy remarked: "Won't it be wonderful when we get back into the White House again", Bobby's wife Ethel tartly replied: "What do you mean, we?" Then tragedy struck again; Bobby Kennedy's campaign looked in sight of success when, straight after winning the California primary, he was shot at a Los Angeles hotel by the Jordanian-born Sirhan Sirhan.

> My thanks to you all. And now it's on to Chicago . . . and let's win there! RFK's last public remark.

On Bobby's death, the youngest Kennedy brother, **Edward Moore (Teddy)** (1932–) became head of the clan. He said:

> Like my three brothers before me, I pick up a fallen standard and sustained by their memory of our priceless

> years together, I shall try to carry forward that special commitment to justice, to excellence, to courage that distinguished their lives.

Teddy Kennedy had succeeded to JFK's Senate seat in 1962, his opponent dismissively saying: "If his name wasn't Kennedy he wouldn't even be in the race", and in 1969 became the youngest-ever majority WHIP. But as uncle of numerous orphaned children, he was reluctant to tempt fate. His cousin and longtime associate Joe Gargan said: "You can pick up the standard without picking up the Presidency. The standard is the cause – the work, the poor, the Blacks."

CHAPPAQUIDDICK left him tainted goods despite an outstanding record as a legislator, and persistent tussles with sex and alcohol maintained the image. Nevertheless he knew, as Sen. Ed Muskie put it, that "power is constantly enhanced when people perceive that you could be President someday"; and to George F. Will he was "the Democrats' heavy hitter". He also remained the best hope of liberal Democrats, in Hedrick Smith's words "the 1970s cult figure of the left", and in 1980 he went for the nomination against Jimmy CARTER. He failed, but fatally weakened Carter's bid for re-election against Ronald Reagan. Teddy Kennedy summed up his ambitions when he said:

> I don't mind not being President. I just mind that somebody else is.

The curse did not end with Teddy Kennedy. Drug problems, accidents and traumatic illness have plagued the next generation, overshadowing those eager to take up the standard in their turn.

Kennedy Center The John F. Kennedy Center for the Performing Arts, erected in his memory in Washington beside the Potomac.

> A national tragedy – a cross between a concrete candy box and a marble sarcophagus in which the art of architecture lies buried. ADA LOUISE HUXTABLE.

Kennedy round The round of GATT talks to lower world trade barriers between 1964–67, instigated by Kennedy through his US Trade Expansion Act. They secured average tariff cuts of 35%.

Cape Kennedy The space centre at Cape Canaveral, Florida, which was renamed Cape Kennedy in the assassinated President's memory, but has since reverted to its original title.

Kent State The fatal shooting by Ohio national guardsmen of four protesting students – nine more were wounded – at Kent State University on 4 May 1970 at the height of protests against the VIETNAM WAR. The guardsmen were provoked by coeds calling them "shit-heels, motherfuckers and half-ass pigs". The deaths brought to a head campus opposition to US involvement in Indo-China, and caused widespread revulsion among America's parents.

Kerensky A moderate politician whose accession to power is the prelude for a takeover by extremists whom he proves unable to control or resist. **Alexander Kerensky** (1881–1970) was the moderate socialist who headed the second Provisional GOVERNMENT of Russia between July and November 1917. After a series of disastrous setbacks in the war with Germany and a wave of revolutionary agitation, the BOLSHEVIKS under LENIN forced him from power.

Kerner Commission The BIPARTISAN Advisory Commission on Civil Disorders set up by President Johnson under former Illinois Governor Otto Kerner to investigate the causes of INNER CITY riots. The panel's unanimous report, issued in 1968, blamed the intolerable economic, social and psychological conditions of urban Blacks. "White racism is essentially responsible for the explosive mixture", it said. The Republican Presidential nominee Richard Nixon accused the commission of blaming "everybody except the perpetrators of the riots" and demanded retaliation against them.

Kerr sacking The most controversial episode in Australia's political history, revolving around the dismissal of the Labor Prime Minister Gough WHITLAM on 11 November 1975 by the GOVERNOR-GENERAL, Sir John Kerr (1914–91). Whitlam's ministry had been in increasing difficulties through the refusal of the Opposition majority in the Senate to vote SUPPLY, but refused to contemplate an election. Kerr was worried about the government's plans to borrow the money instead; he came to feel that he was being treated like a RUBBER STAMP and had "no wish for the vice-regal position to be diminished". As tension rose, Whitlam joked to Kerr: "It would be a question of whether I got to the Queen first for your recall, or you got in first with my dismissal", but Whitlam never imagined he would be removed. On the day, Kerr summoned Whitlam to YARRALUMLA and, without informing the Queen, sacked him. Kerr wrote:

> On 11 November 1975, time having in practical terms run out, I acted to end the deadlock. In exercise of the Governor General's reserve powers I withdrew the commission of the Prime Minister of Australia, Mr. Whitlam, and his colleagues, appointed the leader of the opposition, Mr. [Malcolm] Fraser, as caretaker Prime Minister, and swore in a CARETAKER GOVERNMENT. I obtained immediate passage through the Senate of the blocked Supply Bills, and dissolved the House of Representatives and the Senate.

Whitlam was outraged. He felt Kerr should have discussed the options with him first, and believed (correctly) that the Goveror-General had handed the initiative to Fraser's Liberals, who won the ensuing election. Kerr ignored a no-CONFIDENCE motion in Fraser from the House of Representatives, and had the proclamation read which dissolved both Houses. It ended with the words "GOD SAVE THE QUEEN", whereupon Whitlam commented:

> Well may we say God Save the Queen, because nothing will save the Governor-General.

To the end, Kerr defended his decision as right and proper, but Labor's outrage was unabated and Kerr was frequently booed in public. The episode did much to stir up REPUBLICAN feeling within the ALP.

key. keynote speech The speech, usually from the leader of a government, party or other organization, setting the tone and key themes for a conference, convention or campaign. It is usually, though not always, delivered at or near the beginning.
key indicator *See* INDICATOR.

Key Biscayne President Nixon's vacation retreat, on the Florida Keys 20 miles south of Miami.

Keynesianism The economic doctrine of **John Maynard Keynes**, 1st Baron Keynes (1883–1946) that a stagnant economy can be revived, and unemployment reduced, by the injection of funds raised by the State for public investment projects, in short to "spend their way back to prosperity". Keynes' *A Treatise on Money* (1930) and *General Theory of Employment, Interest and Money* (1936) countered the orthodox view that unemployment was unavoidable, and were influential in formulating the NEW DEAL. THATCHERISM was to take precisely the opposite view.

KGB (Russ. *Komitet Gosudarstvennoi Bezopasnosti*, Security Committee) The agency in the former Soviet Union, and in some of its successor states, responsible for internal security, intelligence gathering, foreign operations and border control. Set up in 1954, it developed into the largest and most powerful secret service in the world, with a highly sinister reputation. At its height it employed an estimated 90,000 officers supported by 150,000 technicians and clerical staff, with 250,000 border guards and 25,000 agents abroad. Its budget was estimated at between $6 and $12 billion.

Khaki election The UK general election of 1900, fought against the background of the BOER WAR. It took its name from the olive-green colour of the new uniforms worn by troops in South Africa. Public enthusiasm for the war was running high, with the opposition LIBERAL PARTY split on the issue. Lord SALISBURY's Conservatives won only a slight increase in seats despite claiming that "a vote for the Liberals is a vote for the Boers". Lord ROSEBERY, a Liberal supporter of the war, termed it "a wanton election". The term has come to be used for any election fought in an atmosphere of euphoria over war or victory.

Khmer Rouge (Fr. Red Cambodians) The Chinese-backed Communist political and military movement led by Pol Pot which in the late 1970s won international notoriety for GENOCIDE in Cambodia, allegedly killing more than 3 million people in its drive to stamp out urban and all other forms of civilization. The Khmer Rouge took power in 1974 after a lengthy GUERRILLA struggle, but were ousted after five years by the Vietnamese, who condemned Pol Pot to death in his absence. After Vietnam agreed to withdraw in 1988, the Khmer Rouge became active again, but when its leaders arrived in Phnom Penh in 1991 to join a UN-sponsored coalition, angry crowds forced them to flee.

khozraschot (Russ. *khozyaistvenny raschot*, self-supporting running) Economic ACCOUNTABILITY, with state-owned businesses responsible for their own financial state instead of relying on government subsidies. One of the chief aims of Mikhail Gorbachev in his efforts to reconstruct and revitalize the Soviet economy. *See* PERESTROIKA.

kibbutz (plural **kibbutzim** Heb. *qibbutz*, a gathering) The collective agricultural (or sometimes industrial) settlements that became the ideological backbone of the Israeli state and the Labour Party which ruled the new nation for almost 30 years. The pioneer settlements were established by the Jewish Colonization Association, formed by Edmond de Rothschild and Maurice de Hirsch in 1899. The kibbutzim, in which children are collectively reared, prospered despite violent opposition from Palestinian Arabs and after Israel was born in 1948 played a key role in its defence. More recently many young kibbutzniks have given up the austere rural life for the cities.

kick upstairs To promote a politician to an apparently-senior but less influential post – in Britain frequently by giving them a seat in the House of Lords. The phrase was coined by George Savile, Marquis of Halifax (1633–95), who said: "I had known many kicked downstairs, but I never knew any kicked upstairs before." In 1900 BOSS PLATT of New York decided to "kick upstairs" Theodore Roosevelt (*see* TEDDY), who had uncomfortably turned out to be a reforming Governor, to be the Republican Vice-Presidential nominee. The move backfired; within a year Roosevelt had succeeded the assassinated McKINLEY as President.

kill. killer rabbit One of a series of mishaps that afflicted Jimmy CARTER during 1979 and injected ridicule into media coverage of his Presidency. Shortly after he had collapsed while taking part in a "fun run", he suffered minor injuries when bitten by a rabbit near his home in PLAINS, Georgia. After his press secretary Jody Powell had briefed on the incident, the media, intrigued by its sheer improbability, depicted the offending creature as a "killer rabbit".

killer spot A key element of negative campaigning in American elections; the brief television commercial by one candidate intended to wreck a rival's chances.

killing fields The name given to the sinister countryside around Phnom Penh, dotted with the mass graves of Cambodians killed by the KHMER ROUGE during the Pol Pot regime (1975–79). After taking power the Khmer Rouge proclaimed YEAR ZERO, forced the entire population into agricultural labour camps and embarked on a horrifying social experiment including the extermination of all professionals and intellectuals. In four years over a quarter of the population died through starvation, disease, overwork or execution. These brutal and genocidal events were harrowingly told in *The Killing Fields* (1984), a film based on the true story of one man's struggle to survive this monstrous regime.

Kilmainham Treaty The agreement reached between Gladstone's government and Charles Stewart PARNELL to defuse the agitation for Irish land reform and against COERCION by releasing him from prison in Dublin on 2 May 1882. Parnell had been imprisoned the previous October on a warrant accusing him and others of intimidating people from paying just rents. It was while Parnell was in prison that he was christened the UNCROWNED KING OF IRELAND; the outcry was such that the Government had to negotiate through Captain O'Shea, husband of Parnell's mistress, for him to come out. FORSTER, the architect of coercion, resigned from the Cabinet and there was a flicker of hope for peace. But four days later the PHOENIX PARK MURDERS revived the tension.

Kincora A boys' home in Belfast whose inmates were subjected to sexual assaults for eight years from the early 1970s by men including at least one leading LOYALIST. Colin Wallace, a former Ministry of Defence press officer in Northern Ireland sacked for unauthorized leaks and later jailed for a manslaughter he has always denied, alleged that the intelligence organization MI5 had covered up the abuses. Ministers consistently denied this, but Wallace's campaign continued; he did win an admission of his related charge that elements in the security community waged a Black PROPAGANDA campaign in the 1970s against politicians on both sides of the SECTARIAN divide.

Kinder, Kirche, Küche (Ger. children, church, kitchen) The motto of conservative German nationalists, embraced by the NAZIS, which allocated a purely domestic role to women in order to maintain traditional values. It was partly responsible for Germany's defeat in WORLD WAR II, as Hitler flatly refused to permit the conscription of women for even civilian duties. In Britain, by contrast, almost the entire female population was mobilized for the war effort.

king. King and Country debate The debate at the Oxford University Union on 9 February 1933 on the motion "This House will under no circumstances fight for King and Country". The motion was carried by 275 votes to 153; although most of the students gave it little further thought, its passage was later widely blamed for NAZI Germany's mistaken belief as WORLD WAR II approached that Britain would not fight.

> We have all seen with a sense of nausea the abject, squalid, shameless avowal made in the Oxford Union . . . one can almost feel the curl of contempt upon the lips of the manhood of Germany, Italy and France when they read the message sent out by the Oxford Union in the name of Young England. CHURCHILL.

King Andrew the First The nickname accorded President Andrew Jackson (*see* OLD HICKORY) by his enemies as they formed the WHIG party. It was intended to equate Jackson's allegedly-dictatorial style – particularly in vetoing the Bill chartering the Second Bank of the United States – with the high-handedness of George III.

King Arthur The not entirely sympathetic nickname bestowed on **Arthur Scargill** (1938–), the militant President of Britain's National Union of Mineworkers from 1981, who sought confrontation with successive Conservative governments, culminating in the MINERS' STRIKE of 1984–85 which came close to wrecking the industry but failed to shift his greatest adversary, Margaret Thatcher.

King David Hotel bombing The greatest atrocity by the Jewish terrorist organization IRGUN ZVAI LEUMI against British rule in Palestine. On 22 July 1946 an Irgun gang led by Yisrael Levy (1926–90) planted a bomb at the hotel in Jerusalem, headquarters of the British administration, which claimed 91 lives. In the short term the bombing delayed the foundation of the state of Israel, heightening the ATTLEE government's reluctance to pull out and leave Jews and Arabs to fight a civil war. But within two years Israel was born.

King Dick The nickname given to Richard John Seddon, Liberal Prime Minister of New Zealand 1893–1906, by critics who felt his style despotic.

Kingfish The populist **Huey Pierce Long** (1893–1935) earned this nickname as his demagogic style ("always be sincere, even if you don't mean it") earned him near-total control over the state of Louisiana as well as a seat in the US Senate. The social and economic reforms Long championed as state governor (1928–31) and as Senator from 1931, with a nominee running the state, echoed the CORPORATISM of Mussolini and outstripped the NEW DEAL, which he scorned as feeble; taxes on large corporations financed spending to relieve unemployment and improve health and education standards. Long built a powerful political machine, aimed at winning the presidency with a "Share Our Wealth" programme. But he was assassinated on 8 September 1935 in the state Capitol at Baton Rouge by Dr. Carl Austin Weiss, who nursed a family grudge. Long's last words were:

> I wonder why he shot me.

An investigation in 1992 rejected the Weiss family's claim that Long had been shot by a bodyguard's bullet. *See also* HALITOSIS OF THE INTELLECT.

kingmaker A power-broker who can make or break a candidate; from Warwick the Kingmaker, an all-powerful English baron in the late Middle Ages.

King of Ulster *See* ULSTER.

King over the water Originally the term used by JACOBITES for their pretender to the English crown, in exile on the continent of Europe. Now any politician out of favour or power whose followers hope he can make a comeback, usually by ousting the present party leader.

King Street Shorthand for the leadership of Britain's COMMUNIST PARTY, from the address of its London headquarters from its foundation in 1920 until the 1980s. The building on the fringe of Covent Garden was ironically within a stone's throw of Moss Bros, London's grandest formal dress-hire shop.

King, Leslie The name at birth (Leslie Lynch King Jr.) of Gerald FORD, 38th President of the United States. When he was two years old his parents were divorced; his mother soon after married a paint salesman named Gerald Rudolph Ford, who adopted the young boy. The facts about his birth and adoption were kept from young Gerald (known as Junior) until he was 16, and he only saw his father twice; both meetings were unfriendly and Ford ruled out further contacts.

Dr. Martin Luther King Jr. (1929–68) Black America's pre-eminent campaigner for CIVIL RIGHTS, who as a young Baptist minister began campaigns of CIVIL DISOBEDIENCE that eventually shamed the political establishment into action. A follower of Gandhi's doctrine of NON-VIOLENCE, King was at the height of his influence in the early 1960s when his activities in BIRMINGHAM and SELMA, his campaign to make Chicago an "open city" (he said: "I have never seen such hate as in Chicago"), his massive MARCH ON WASHINGTON and his oratory (*see* I HAVE A DREAM) spurred the Kennedy and Johnson administrations to outlaw SEGREGATION and racial discrimination. Throughout his campaigns he suffered imprisonment, threats and actual violence (his house was dynamited), false allegations of graft and tax evasion, and harassment by FBI director J. Edgar Hoover (*see* COINTELPRO). Hoover was convinced King was a Communist and was also intrigued by his sexual adventures, repeatedly bugging his bedroom; Hoover branded him "the most notorious liar in the country". By 1967 King was being outflanked by militant advocates of violence and BLACK POWER, but before he could lose control of mass Black opinion he was assassinated in a Memphis motel (*see* I HAVE BEEN TO THE TOP OF THE MOUNTAIN) by James Earl Ray, a White drifter.

> What has violence ever accomplished? What has it ever created? No martyr's cause has ever been stilled by his assassin's bullet. No wrongs have ever been righted by riots and civil disorders. A sniper is only a coward, not a hero. And an uncontrollable mob is only the voice of madness and not the voice of the people . . . What we need in the United States is not division. What we need in the United States is not hatred. What we need in the United States is not violence or lawlessness, but love and wisdom and compassion toward one another, and a feeling of justice toward those who still suffer in our country whether they be White or they be Black. Let us dedicate ourselves . . . to tame the savageness of man and make gentle the life of this world. Let us dedicate ourselves to that and say a prayer for our country and our people.
>
> ROBERT F. KENNEDY on King's assassination, shortly before his own.

Rodney King riots The anarchy that broke out in southern Los Angeles on 28 April 1992, leaving 58 people dead and 2000 hurt, and causing $1 billion in damage, much of it to Korean-owned stores. The riots, California's worst, followed the acquittal by an all-White jury in suburban Simi Valley of four Los Angeles police officers who had beaten senseless Rodney King, a young Black man whom they had ordered from his car. Video film of the incident ashamed the nation when shown on television, but did not impress the jury. Such was the public outcry that President BUSH, facing re-election, ordered a Federal investigation of the case. He said:

> None of this is what we wish to think of as American. It is as if we were looking in a mirror that distorted our better selves and turned us ugly.

The King can do no wrong The dictum of the English judge Sir James Blackstone (1723–80), said by him to be "a necessary and fundamental principle of the Constitution". The claim could only be made once the GLORIOUS REVOLUTION had established the notion of the CROWN IN PARLIAMENT as sovereign; WATERGATE proved that the doctrine has no parallel in the United States.

The King is dead – long live the king The declaration, first made in 1461 on the death of Charles VII of France, which emphasizes the continuity of government despite the demise of its head. It is now used to reflect a smooth transition of power of any sort.

The King reigns, but does not govern The basis of Constitutional MONARCHY, laid down in the Polish Parliament by Grand Chancellor Jan Zamoyski (1541–1605). The French democrat Louis Adolphe Thiers (1797–1877) adapted it in 1830 to **The King reigns, and the people govern themselves**.

Kinnock – the movie The campaign film – shown twice on all Britain's TV channels – which created a devastating impact at the start of the 1987 election campaign by putting the LABOUR PARTY leader **Neil Gordon Kinnock** (1942–) firmly on the map. The video, which showed Kinnock the family man, Kinnock the visionary campaigner and Kinnock the ruthless cleanser of his own party, was directed by Hugh Hudson, who had made the Oscar-winning *Chariots of Fire* and whom Labour had just recruited back from the SDP. It had an even greater effect across the Atlantic: Sen. Joseph Biden pirated part of Kinnock's text in a TV spot of his own for the 1988 Presidential race, and dropped out when the plagiarism was spotted by a Labour activist helping in a rival campaign.

Kinnock, a working-class grammar school boy from South Wales, transformed Labour's fortunes during almost nine years as party leader (1983–92), but stood down after failing to win the 1992 General Election. Elected to Parliament in 1970 as a red-haired firebrand who modelled himself on Aneurin BEVAN, he took over the leadership when the party was on the point of disintegration after the founding of the SDP and Labour's near-annihilation in the 1983 election. Just two years before he had said: "As for being leader, I can't see it happening and I'm not particularly keen on it happening." Denis Healey felt that "he is politically intelligent, has character and courage, but has never been a Minister, lacks experience, and people know it". Yet Kinnock proved himself a leader of unprecedented organizational rigour, able to drive dissident groups out of the party (*see* MILITANT TENDENCY), abandon unpopular policies he himself had espoused such as UNILATERALISM, modernize the party machine and make it ELECTABLE. He was blessed in his wife Glenys with a highly intelligent, supportive and effective partner. And above all he had ambition, Edward Pearce writing: "To get to Downing Street he'd boil his granny down for glue."

Kinnock had a withering tongue. He once said of the Conservatives: "You cannot fashion a wit out of two half-wits." When the Tory MP Robert Adley asked: "Can you name one thing on which you haven't changed your mind?" Kinnock replied: "You and I came into the House on the same day. I formed the opinion that you were a jerk, and I haven't changed my mind." Of the Thatcher Cabinet he observed: "Norman Fowler looks as though he is suffering from famine, and Nigel Lawson looks as though he caused it," and when Sir Geoffrey HOWE, then Chancellor, lost his trousers on a train he remarked: "I never knew until now what the Tories meant when they said inflation was bottomless." He described Norman Tebbit (*see* CHINGFORD SKINHEAD) as "a boil on a verucca" and Sir Keith Joseph as "a mind without any visible means of support". But he was sometimes hard to pin down. New York's Mayor Ed Koch once told him: "Sure, we all want peace in Ireland. But what's your POSITION?" and the electricians' leader Frank Chapple said: "He reminds me of those beauty queen competitors who always smile and say they want to work with children and travel a lot." Kinnock was an emotional and effective campaigner, though one commentator wrote in 1987 that "he looks like a tortoise having an orgasm". But at critical moments at Westminster such as the WESTLAND crisis he proved unable to press home Labour's advantage, and two election defeats (one by Margaret Thatcher, one against the odds by John MAJOR) were enough for him. He gave up the leadership at 50, the age at which 12 years earlier he had said he would like to retire to play "cricket in the summer and geriatric football in the winter". Later in 1992 his successor John Smith proposed Kinnock as a European

COMMISSIONER, but Major passed him over because of Tory objections.

kiss. kissing babies The archetypal way in which candidates at election time are supposed to demean themselves in the search for votes. The tradition goes back a long way – in 1832 Andrew Jackson, confronted with a filthy baby, praised it as "a beautiful specimen of American childhood", then got his friend John Eaton to kiss it. And in 1960 John F. KENNEDY refused to pose for a campaign photo, saying: "Kissing babies gives me asthma".

kissing hands The formality with which a new British Prime Minister takes office, receiving the SEALS OF OFFICE from the Sovereign. No actual kiss takes place.

Give us a kiss, love Three Westminster MPs, two Conservative and one Labour, found themselves *c.* 1979 in a New Zealand guest house with only one single room. The Conservatives decided to share a double and leave the single to Walter Harrison, a bluff Yorkshire Labour whip. Next morning one Tory complained his colleague's snoring had kept him awake, so Harrison volunteered to take his place. The second morning, Harrison came down to breakfast fresh and cheerful, and the offending Tory with bags under his eyes. "What did you do?" asked the now-rested first Tory. "I turned out the light and said: 'Give us a kiss, love' ", said Harrison. "He didn't sleep a wink all night."

You can kiss my ass Senator George McGovern's exasperated remark to an airport heckler at Battle Creek, Michigan, on 2 November 1972, just before his LANDSLIDE defeat for the Presidency by Richard Nixon. McGovern apologized profusely when the remark was made public, but "KMA" badges started to appear at his rallies and Sen. James Eastland of Mississippi, on the other extreme of the Democratic party, told him:

> That was the best line in the campaign!

Kissinger. Henry Alfred (1923–) The German-born Harvard professor who became NATIONAL SECURITY ADVISER to President Nixon, with greater influence than Secretary of State William Rogers, who termed him "Machiavellian, deceitful, egotistical, arrogant and insulting". His efforts to negotiate an end to the VIETNAM WAR brought him the NOBEL PEACE PRIZE in 1973 (one South Vietnamese official described his joint nomination with Le Duc Tho as "like nominating a whore as honorary chairman of the PTA"), and his SHUTTLE DIPLOMACY eased East-West tensions and the dangers in the Middle East after the YOM KIPPUR WAR. But his commitment to DÉTENTE earned him the hatred of the Republican Right. Hugh Brogan rated him "the most remarkable diplomatist to emerge in America since 1945", and Kissinger traded on his public image, once remarking: "There cannot be a crisis next week. My diary is already full." He appeared regularly in the society pages, declaring that "power is the ultimate aphrodisiac", but Barbara Howar reported: "Henry's idea of sex is to slow the car down to 30 miles an hour when he drops you off at the door". He once remarked: "The nice thing about being a celebrity is that when you bore people, they think it's their fault." Eventually serving as Secretary of State – to Presidents Nixon and FORD – Kissinger held no public office after 1977 but remained a figure of great influence in the world of diplomacy.

kitchen cabinet *See* CABINET.

kitchen debate The impromptu debate on the merits of Communism and capitalism conducted by Vice-President Nixon and the Soviet leader Nikita S. Khruschev in the model kitchen of a US exhibition in Moscow on 3 August 1959. Nixon had only gained State Department clearance to make the visit provided it was purely "ceremonial", but in the kitchen, in front of television cameras and the travelling US press, he cut loose. While voices were raised, Khruschev was at his most expansive, throwing his arm round a Soviet worker and asking: "Does this man look like a slave labourer?" The reporters present scored a Nixon victory.

kite-flying The unofficial floating of an idea before it has become established policy to see how the electorate or the political community will react, or its premature release so as to condition opinion for the inevitable. *See* HAWARDEN KITE.

kith and kin The rallying-cry of supporters in Britain of Ian Smith's regime in Rhodesia following its declaration of UDI in 1965. They argued that Britain could not take any action against a people who were essentially its own – the 5% of Whites who controlled the country and had acted to head off MAJORITY RULE. Left-wingers ridiculed the notion with their own slogan:

> Kith my arse!

kleptocracy Government by thieves, from the Greek *kleptes*, thief. The term was first applied to Zaire under the leadership of President Mobutu Sese Seko Kuku Ngbendu Wa Za Banga (1930–), who with his officials systematically looted the country of billions of dollars for almost three decades from 1965 as its economy and infrastructure returned to jungle.

KMT Kuomintang/Guomindang. China's National People's Party, founded by Sun Yat-Sen (1866–1925) in 1905; it took power in a REVOLUTION in 1911 but was persecuted by President General Yuan Shikai, who had forced the resignation of the last Emperor. Sun, acknowledged founder of modern China, went into exile after leading a failed coup, returning in 1923 as president of the Canton-based southern republic. Only in 1926 was China united under KMT rule; the party subsequently passed under the control of GENERALISSIMO Chiang Kai-Shek (1887–1975). Before long the KMT was having to vie for power with Mao Tse-Tung's Communists and Japanese forces of occupation, who each seized Chinese territory. Chiang saw off the Japanese, but in 1949 was driven out by the victorious Communists. The Kuomintang still governs Taiwan, claiming with ever-decreasing conviction to be the true government of China.

knee. kneecapping The classic punishment administered from the early 1970s by extremist PARAMILITARY groups in NORTHERN IRELAND to alleged petty criminals, troublemakers and informers. It consists of boring through the miscreant's kneecap with a Black and Decker electric drill, or blasting it with a shotgun. Victims of kneecapping eventually recover, but generally refuse to tell the police who gave them their injuries or why. The term has come more generally to signify a severe punishment administered by one's peers.

knee-jerk A reflex action to an opinion or event, *i.e.* one that is automatic and requires no thought. It is derived from the patellar reflex, the involuntary jerk of the leg caused by tapping just below the knee. The term became popular in 1970s America, often in combination, *e.g.* a knee-jerk liberal is one whose liberal response to any situation is automatic rather than considered.

Kneel! One of the oldest jokes at Westminster, describing how in the Central LOBBY one MP calls out "Neil!" to another and a visiting tourist drops to his or her knees, imagining a general command has been given. The story has been told of a fellow-member greeting Neil KINNOCK, before him of the Conservative Minister Neil Marten, and before him of Niall MacDermot QC (1916–), a Labour MP 1957–59 and 1962–70 and a Minister in the first Wilson government. No doubt it goes back even further.

Knesset (Heb. Assembly) The Israeli parliament, a single chamber consisting of 120 members elected every four years by PROPORTIONAL REPRESENTATION. The first Knesset opened in Jerusalem on 16 February 1949, electing Chaim Weizmann (1874–1952) as the nation's first President.

knight. Knights of Labor A pioneering US labour union, founded in 1869 by Uriah S. Stephens, a Philadelphia tailor. In 1878 Terence V. Powderly became Grand Master of this Noble Order and turned it from a secret society into a mass union, which at its peak reported over 700,000 members in 5892 chapters. The Knights, politically and industrially moderate, called for one single union for all workers, Black and White, under highly centralized control, and advocated an eight-hour day, EQUAL PAY for women, abolition of child and contract foreign labour, industrial safety, the encouragement of CO-OPERATIVES, and government ownership of railroads and telegraph lines. The union's fame spread when it wrung concessions from the hated railroad magnate Jay Gould in 1885, but decline set in after a number of unsuccessful strikes in 1886. A mistaken public belief after an anarchist riot in Chicago that the Knights advocated violence, and the alienation of skilled workers, hastened its end. The craft union dissidents were instrumental in founding the American Federation of Labor (*see* AFL-CIO).

Knights of the shires The long-serving farming and landowning MPs of generally right-wing views, coupled with sound common sense about the politically possible, who formed the bedrock of the CONSERVATIVE PARTY at Westminster until well into the 1970s.

Plumed Knight The accolade given Rep. James G. Blaine, popular favourite for the 1876 Republican Presidential nomination, by Robert G. Ingersoll (1833–99) in his nominating speech. Ingersoll orated:

> Like an armed warrior, like a plumed knight, James G. Blaine marched down the halls of the American Congress and threw his shining lance full and fair against the brazen forehead of every traitor to his country and every maligner of his fair reputation.

Mud thrown at Blaine over the favouritism he had shown certain railroads when Speaker of the House had stuck, and the Republicans nominated Rutherford Hayes instead. But Ingersoll's speech is still rated a classic.

Knighthood The award, short of a PEERAGE, bestowed by the Sovereign each year on a number of distinguished Britons, including several politicians. In the political world a knighthood, which carries the prefix "Sir" and enables a wife to style herself "Lady", usually goes to a BACKBENCH Conservative MP with some 20 years' service. Occasionally it goes to an ex-Minister who is staying in the House of Commons and thus could not take a peerage.

knocking-up The term used by party activists in Britain for getting out the vote on election day, and particularly in the evening as time starts to run out. It involves calling at the houses of known supporters who have not voted and offering, where necessary, to give them a lift to the polls. In America the word has a very different meaning. *See also* NCR; READING SYSTEM.

know. Know-how Fund The fund established by the Thatcher government in 1990, and expanded under John Major, to finance training for key personnel in the former Communist countries of eastern Europe. Under it, professional people such as bankers, broadcasters and lawyers have either travelled to Britain to gain experience of Western ways or have received training on the spot.

Know-nothings The popular name for the American Party, formed in 1845 on an anti-Catholic, anti-immigrant platform after its founders had polled strongly at state level. It gained its name because members were bound by an oath to say they knew nothing if questioned on its policies which were agreed at secret grand councils; how it managed to campaign or attract votes is a mystery. In 1851 they nominated Daniel Webster for President, but he did not take up the offer. The party's influence peaked in 1854 as the pre-Civil War tide of immigration reached its height, and horrified former WHIGS deserted to it; there were "Know-Nothing riots" in Washington and Know-Nothing governors or legislatures were elected in four New England states, Maryland, Kentucky and California. The party tried to ignore the slavery issue, but split as its leaders were forced to take positions on the KANSAS-NEBRASKA ACT. Northern Know-Nothings adopted an anti-slavery platform and were at once eclipsed by the newly-formed Republican Party. The American Party's LAST HURRAH was the 1856 Presidential campaign of former President Millard Fillmore (1800–74); by 1859 it was confined to the border states.

> Where is the true-hearted American whose cheek does not tingle with shame to see our highest and most courted foreign missions filled by men of foreign birth to the exclusion of the native-born? MILLARD FILLMORE, 1856.

> As a nation, we began by declaring that "all men are created equal". We now practically read it "All men are created equal, except Negroes". When the Know-Nothings get control, it will read: "All men are created equal, except Negroes, and foreigners, and Catholics." ABRAHAM LINCOLN.

Komsomol The youth wing of the Soviet COMMUNIST PARTY, formally known as the All-Union Leninist Young Communist League. It was formed in 1918 as a BOLSHEVIK youth organization for agitation and propaganda, and membership became essential for anyone wishing to make their mark in Soviet life. Its offshoots included the daily newspaper *Komsomolskaya Pravda.*

Königswinter The castle on the Rhine, 20 miles south-east of Cologne, which since World War II has had an influential role as a conference centre, both for Germany's CHRISTIAN DEMOCRATS and for bringing together Germans in key positions in politics, business and the media and their counterparts from other European countries and beyond. Such meetings played an important part in re-integrating post-war Germany into the democratic world. The term also applies to the regular Anglo-German meetings, at various levels from youth to senior politicians, which also take place in Cambridge and elsewhere.

Korea. Korea, Communism and Corruption The keywords of the 1952 Republican Presidential campaign, decrying the Truman administration for its handling of the Korean War, its alleged infiltration by Communists and the INFLUENCE-PEDDLING that tarnished its final years; it contained more than an echo of McCARTHYISM.

Koreagate The scandal that broke in Washington in 1977 over INFLUENCE-PEDDLING by Tongsun Park, a South Korean rice broker who claimed over nine years to have spent $850,000 in gifts and cash to 31 Democratic Congressmen. In 1978 a grand jury indicted him on 36 counts of conspiracy, bribery, mail fraud, racketeering, failure to register as a foreign agent and making illegal campaign contributions. Washington sat back for a juicy trial, especially as a glamorous political demimondaine, Tandy Dickenson, was at the heart of the case. But all charges against Park were dropped in return for his testimony. California Rep. Richard T. Hanna served a year in jail for conspiracy to defraud the government; he had attended a meeting in Seoul in 1968 with Park and the former director of South Korea's CIA which had agreed to have Park made Korea's exclusive rice purchasing agent. Part of the $9 million due to him in commission was spent to influence Congressmen, notably by inviting them to Korea on "goodwill trips" and giving their wives envelopes stuffed with cash. But Speaker TIP O'Neill was cleared by the House of wrongdoing in attending a birthday party Park staged for him, and only three Congressmen were reprimanded. The most serious charge proven by the House was that Rep. John McFall had failed to report a $4000 contribution and had spent the money on himself.

> Lobbying is built into the American system. Teachers and labor unions do it. Why shouldn't foreign countries?
> TONGSUN PARK.

Korean war The bitter, and ultimately inconclusive three-year conflict precipitated by Communist North Korea's surprise attack on the democratic South on 25 June 1950. At the end of WORLD WAR II Korea had been temporarily divided by the allies at the 38TH PARALLEL; attempts by the UNITED NATIONS to reunite the country had failed. The UN – with the Soviet Union critically leaving an empty CHAIR – raised an international force to combat the invasion, dominated by the US contingent and led by General Douglas MacArthur. President Truman declared:

> The attack upon Korea makes it plain beyond all doubt that Communism has passed beyond the use of subversion to conquer independent nations, and will now use armed invasion and war.

And he told Secretary of State Dean Acheson: "Dean, we've got to stop those sons of bitches, no matter what." MacArthur masterminded the Inchon landings in September 1950 which cut the Communists' supply lines, then drove them back to the Yalu River, the boundary between North Korea and China. China entered the war in November 1950, pushing the UN forces back beyond the 38th parallel and capturing Seoul, the southern capital. The UN forces turned the tide and Seoul was recaptured in April 1951. In the same month Truman fired MacArthur for publicly advocating taking the war into China after being told he would not be given such orders (*see* MACARTHUR SACKING) and gave the command to General Matthew Ridgway. Of MacArthur's plan, Gen. Omar Bradley said it would create "the wrong war, in the wrong place, at the wrong time, with the wrong enemy". Negotiations began on a Soviet initiative in July 1951, but the fighting dragged on until an ARMISTICE was signed at Panmunjom on 27 July 1953; the tension and intermittent border incidents continued for almost four decades. The war left 55,000 American personnel dead, 12,000 other UN troops (including British), compared with 260,000 South Korean and 1.5 million Communist fighters.

I shall go to Korea The dramatic pledge that clinched the Presidency for General Dwight D. Eisenhower. Speaking in Detroit on 24 October 1952, he described the war as "never inevitable – always inescapable", and announced he would go to Korea to end the war. "I shall make that trip", he promised. "Only in that way could I learn how best to serve the American people in the cause of peace." His opponent Adlai Stevenson had considered such a move, but to his regret rejected it; the headline "I shall go to Korea" made a huge impact on public opinion.

Kraft durch Freude (Ger. strength through joy) A popular NAZI scheme for cheap package holidays, which allowed thousands of Germans to visit remote areas of the country, or travel abroad, during the 1930s. Based on the Italian FASCIST organization Dopo Lavoro, it was initially funded from confiscated trade union funds but later became big business, generating considerable income for the Nazis. KdF also organized sports and artistic activities such as subsidized theatre visits and travelling cabaret shows. The scheme, which proved a valuable propaganda vehicle, was given its name by Robert Ley (1890–1945), head of the Nazis' Labour Front.

Kremlin (1) The 12th-century citadel at the heart of Moscow which epitomized the ruthless power of TSARIST and Soviet Russia. Looking out over the River Moskva and with a frontage on RED SQUARE, the Kremlin's walls contain the former Imperial palace, three cathedrals and a number of government offices; by STALIN's time real power lay elsewhere.

> Like a baby, it has an appetite at one end and no sense of responsibility at the other. RONALD REAGAN.

(2) The STRANGERS' BAR in the basement of the House of Commons, close to the TERRACE. It gets its name from its forbidding demeanour – equalled only by that of its barman, Ted – and the serried ranks of elderly trade union Labour MPs who used to occupy it. Only MPs and their guests are permitted to use it, and MPs alone may order drinks.

Kremlin coup The attempt in August 1991 by Communist hard-liners led by deputy President Gennady Yenayev to oust Mikhail Gorbachev and turn back the tide of reform. On 19 August the plotters put Gorbachev under house arrest at his Crimean holiday home, and announced:

> Fellow Countrymen! Citizens of the Soviet Union! In a dark and critical hour for the destiny of our country and of our peoples we address you! A mortal danger hangs over our homeland!

The plotters failed to arrest the Russian President Boris Yeltsin, who went to the WHITE HOUSE and organized resistance as the tanks moved in. Yeltsin rallied Western support and key military commanders refused to obey orders, and after three days Gorbachev was invited back. He had known from foreign radio broadcasts that the plotters had not met with the success they claimed. Gorbachev said:

The lads rigged up an aerial and we were able to catch some broadcasts and find out what was happening. We got the BBC best of all.

The coup, in which three demonstrators were killed, proved disastrously counter-productive; Yeltsin's resistance gave him the initiative, and by the end of the year the coup leaders were in jail, the Soviet Union had collapsed and Gorbachev had gone into retirement.

The democratic genie is out of the bottle in the Soviet Union, and I don't believe they are going to be able to get it back in again. JOHN MAJOR.

Kremlinology The science of ascertaining what the Soviet regime was doing and intended to do either on behalf of Western governments, academic institutions or the media. It consisted of monitoring the Soviet media and reading between the lines, and building up personal and academic contacts. Kremlinology, unlike espionage, was an entirely reputable science.

Kristallnacht (Ger. night of glass) The night of 9–10 November 1938 when mobs led by NAZI BROWNSHIRTS roamed towns and cities all over Germany and Austria, smashing the windows of shops and houses belonging to Jews (hence the name). The looting of their property and the burning of synagogues was for many German and Austrian Jews the last straw in the humiliating persecution they had suffered at the hands of Hitler, his Nazi party and many ordinary citizens who supported him. Those Jews who were able to fled to Britain, America or anywhere else that would accept them; among this exodus were many of the physicists who were to be key figures in the creation of the ATOMIC BOMB.

I could scarcely believe that such things could happen in a 20th-century civilization. FRANKLIN D. ROOSEVELT.

Krokodil (Russ. crocodile) The humorous magazine which for most of the lifetime of the SOVIET UNION provided the only officially-tolerated satire on the regime and on life under Communism. The paper, published by PRAVDA, normally went for "safe" targets, but nevertheless had an enthusiastic readership.

Kronstadt mutiny The highly-significant revolt against BOLSHEVIK rule in March 1921 by the elite sailors at the Soviet naval base in the Gulf of Finland. The privations of the Civil War, including inadequate food distribution and harsh labour regulations, created widespread discontent with the new regime, manifested in a series of strikes in the cities. The Kronstadt sailors formed a Provisional Revolutionary Committee in support of the strikers and demanded an end to the Communist Party dictatorship, full "power to the SOVIETS", the release of non-Bolshevik prisoners and greater political freedoms. Although the mutiny was crushed by TROTSKY and Marshal Tukachevsky, it prompted LENIN to implement the milder NEW ECONOMIC POLICY soon afterwards.

Kruger telegram The telegram of support from Kaiser Wilhelm I to President Kruger of the Transvaal (*see* OOM PAUL) congratulating him on tackling the JAMESON RAID. Its publication in London took considerable heat off Lord SALISBURY's government in the winter of 1885–66 when it was under heavy political fire for alleged complicity in the raid.

Ku Klux Klan The RACIST secret society, mainly active in America's deep South, whose initials KKK, "night riders" in hooded white robes, LYNCHINGS and cross-burnings have struck terror into Black people ever since it was formed in the aftermath of the CIVIL WAR. The name is a corruption of the Greek *kuklos*, a drinking-bowl; "Klan" reflected the Scotch-Irish roots of its native Pulaski, Tennessee. Founded in 1866 as a social club for ex-CONFEDERATES with a fanciful ritual, it soon developed into a vehicle for intimidating Blacks emancipated by RECONSTRUCTION; there were also numerous imitators. The Klan's terrorist activities led to laws being passed against it in 1870–71; despite its disbandment by the Grand Wizard in 1869, local activity continued for some time.

In 1915 a new organization, The Invisible Empire, Knights of the Ku Klux Klan, was founded in Atlanta, by an itinerant preacher, William Simmonds. He adopted much of the original ritual, adding further puerile ceremonial, titles, nomenclature, *etc.*, and turning it against Jews, Catholics and foreigners as well as Blacks. Klansmen held Klonvocations and their local Klaverns were ruled by an Exalted Cyclops, a Klaliff, *etc.* Advocating supremacy for native-born Protestant Whites, support for PROHIBITION and opposition to the theory of evolution, it grew rapidly after World War I, first among poor Whites in the South and then sweeping the Mid-West; at its peak it claimed 20 million supporters. It gained considerable political influence by unsavoury methods; at the 1924 Democratic Convention a resolution denouncing the Klan was defeated. But after a series of scandals it had shrunk back by 1930 to a hard core of support which exuded FASCIST sympathies as World War II approached. In 1944 it was again disbanded, but continued locally; in 1965 a Congressional committee was set up to investigate it after a resurgence of Klan activity against enforcement of

CIVIL RIGHTS legislation, and the murder of a White woman driving a Black man near Montgomery, Alabama, by four Klansmen. The Klan again re-emerged, on a broader front, in the early 1990s as many Americans experienced economic hardship.

> The Negro is not a menace to Americanism in the sense that the Jew or Roman Catholic is a menace. He is not actually hostile to it. He is simply racially incapable of understanding, sharing or contributing to Americanism.
> Imperial Wizard HIRAM W. EVANS, 1924.

kulaks (Russ. fists) Prosperous Russian peasants who owned land and livestock, and were capable of employing labour and leasing land. They were key figures in the economic, social and administrative structure of pre-revolutionary Russian agriculture. Under LENIN, the kulaks' position was gradually undermined, though their economic and political value was exploited to maintain production along quasi-capitalist lines. However the policy of rapid COLLECTIVIZATION pursued by STALIN after 1919 aimed at the destruction of the kulaks as a class; by 1934 most had been arrested, deported to remote areas or executed, and their property confiscated.

Kuomintang *See* KMT.

L

La Guardia New York City's domestic airport, named after Fiorello Henry La Guardia (1882–1947), US Congressman and three times Mayor of New York (1933–45) who campaigned for the airport's construction. A political PROGRESSIVE and habitual dissenter, he is remembered as the most honest and best loved occupant of GRACIE MANSION. *See* HIZZONER.

Labby Nickname for **Henry Labouchère** (1831–1912), Radical British Liberal MP and owner/editor of the weekly *Truth*. Queen Victoria refused to allow him in Gladstone's CABINET because of his REPUBLICAN views.

labour. Labor Day The first Monday in September, in America a public holiday marking the end of the summer vacation in Washington and, in election years, the start of campaigning.

labour law reform The US unions' campaign to relax the RIGHT TO WORK laws, defeated by employer interests in 1978.

Labor Party Australia's oldest party, dating from the FEDERATION of the colonies in 1901. It formed its first federal government under John Christian Watson from April to August 1904, since when ten Labor administrations have held power for over 25 years. The present ALP came into existence when William Melbourne Hughes split the informal Labor group; it split again in 1931 over policies for the GREAT DEPRESSION, but returned to power in 1941, guiding Australia from the darkest point of WORLD WAR II to the post-war period. Periodic splits between predominantly Catholic and extreme left elements kept it out of power from 1949 until 1972; Liberal Prime Minister Sir Robert Menzies (1894–1978) asked: "If Labor cannot govern itself, how could they govern Australia?" By 1972 leading academics were ready to declare that "if denied office any longer, the Labor Party is in danger of disintegrating as a force in political life". Gough WHITLAM brought Labor back to power, but his pioneering ministry was ousted in 1975 (*see* KERR SACKING) amid bitter controversy and financial scandal; prior to Labor's 1983 return to power under Robert Hawke (*see* SILVER BODGIE), Malcolm Fraser said: "If Labor win it'll be safer to put your money under the bed." A decade later, Labor, now led by Paul Keating (*see* LIZARD OF OZ) was still in power.

> In my experience of the Labor Party, the fact that someone is a bastard has never been a disqualification from leadership. Sen. JOHN BUTTON.

Big Labor Pejorative for the influence of America's major unions.

Farmer-Labor For much of the 20th century the main radical force in the US state of Minnesota.

organized labour Collective term for the trade union movement, personified in America by the AFL-CIO and in Britain by the TUC and the LABOUR PARTY. Arthur Henderson, leaving Asquith's coalition, said that "in consequence of the decision of organized labour to oppose the Military Service Bill, I have no alternative but to tender you my resignation".

> Capital organizes, and therefore labor must organize. THEODORE ROOSEVELT.

Labour movement In Britain, the Labour Party and the trade unions; the term is often used by union and left-wing activists for whichever political and union elements support them in a particular cause.

Labour Party (1) The democratic Socialist, predominantly working-class party, formed in 1906, which has provided Britain with its government or opposition continually since 1924; it has held power from January–November 1924, 1929–31, 1945–51, 1964–70 and 1974–79. Keir Hardie (1856–1915), one of its founders, declared: "The demand of the Labour Party is for economic freedom. It is the natural outcome of political enfranchisement." When it first took office, King George V wrote: "Today, 23 years ago, dear Grandmama [Queen Victoria] died. I wonder what she would have thought of a Labour government?" In the wilderness from 1931 (*see* GREAT BETRAYAL; RAMSAY MAC), Labour bounced back at the close of WORLD WAR II to win a LANDSLIDE victory in 1945 under Clement ATTLEE. At that election Aneurin BEVAN said:

> We have been the dreamers. We have been the sufferers. Now we are the builders. We want the complete political

> extinction of the Tory Party – and 25 years of Labour government, for we cannot do in five years what requires to be done.

Labour promised a "Socialist Commonwealth of Great Britain", but warned this could not be built overnight. Yet by 1951, when it lost office, Labour had created the WELFARE STATE, with the NHS its greatest lasting achievement. Labour's partial foundation in religious nonconformism led Harold WILSON who led the party back to power in 1964 to state on his government's re-election in 1966: "This party is a moral crusade, or it is nothing." He later added: "Britain with a Labour government is an exciting place." As a LEFT-wing party, Labour has always been beset with ideological arguments and splits. Harold Wilson said it was

> like a stage coach. If you rattle along at great speed everyone inside is too exhilarated or too seasick to cause any trouble. But if you stop, everybody gets out and argues about where to go next.

Most of the arguments have been over defence policy, with the PACIFIST (later the UNILATERALIST) wing occasionally capturing the party (*see* FIGHT, FIGHT AND FIGHT AGAIN). Disputes over how far Labour should honour its commitment to public ownership (*see* CLAUSE FOUR; NATIONALIZATION) have also helped render the party unelectable for long periods. Hugh GAITSKELL reminded Labour when leader in the 1950s that "we can never go farther than we can persuade at least half of the people to go". Richard CROSSMAN said: "The two most important emotions in the Labour Party are a doctrinaire faith in nationalisation, without knowing what it means, and a doctrinaire faith in pacifism, without facing its consequences." The great columnist Cassandra (Sir William Connor) wrote: "What a genius the Labour Party has for cutting itself in half and letting the two parts writhe in public." And Edward Heath once said: "I don't often attack the Labour Party – they do it so well themselves." The difference between party factions has sometimes been hard to judge. The Conservative Chancellor Nigel Lawson (1932–) suggested that "the difference between their moderates and their extremists is that the extremists want to abolish private education now, while the moderates want to wait until their own children have finished school". And Sir Norman Fowler, Conservative Party chairman, said in 1992:

> Those whom the gods would destroy they first make leader of the Labour Party.

Labour's history, in power and in opposition alike, has been accompanied by prophecies of doom. The Labour MP Austin Mitchell termed it "The Red *Titanic* on a ski-slope to disaster". Its opponents have naturally been eager to write it off. CHURCHILL pronounced it "not fit to govern" in 1920, and in 1945 "not fit to manage a whelk stall". And in 1992 the Conservative minister Malcolm Rifkind (1946–) said: "Scotland needs Labour like Sicily needs the Mafia." But Labour has remained one of Britain's two great parties despite chronic shortage of funds and what Harold Wilson termed a "penny-farthing organization". Indeed one voter told Austin Mitchell: "I don't belong to any organised party – I'm Labour."

Wilson brought Labour back to power in 1974, and from 1976 James Callaghan (*see* SUNNY JIM) governed without a majority (*see* LIB-LAB PACT) till defeated by Margaret Thatcher in 1979. In opposition, the Party had a tendency to turn in on itself. Labour's fortunes reached their nadir in 1983 after the split which created the SDP; Denis Healey said its crushing defeat that year was due to its "disunity, extremism, crankiness and general unfitness to govern". Neil KINNOCK defeated the BENNITE left, laboriously drove out MILITANT TENDENCY, pushed through more moderate policies, reorganized the party and persuaded it to broaden its appeal. He declared: "The idea that there is a model Labour voter, a blue-collar council house tenant who belongs to a union and has 2.4 children, a five-year-old car and a holiday in Blackpool, is patronizing and politically immature." Not everyone was impressed by the party that emerged from the Kinnock reforms. Dr. David OWEN called it "the party of verbal Elastoplast" and Norman Tebbit declared: "The voters are not daft. They can smell a rat, whether it is wrapped in a red flag or covered in roses." Labour's fortunes did not revive enough to bring victory in 1992, with voters remaining suspicious of its fitness to govern and its tax policies

The party has had memorable slogans of its own. **Let's Go With Labour**, with "thumbs-up" symbol, accompanied its resurgence under Wilson prior to the 1964 election. It was re-elected in 1966 with **You Know Labour Government Works**. Its 1992 slogan was **It's Time for Labour**. The most scurrilous anti-Labour slogan was **If you want a nigger for your neighbour, vote Labour**, used by Conservative canvassers in the West Midlands in the 1964 election. The most effective was **Labour Isn't Working**: a poster campaign on unemployment devised by the advertising agency Saatchi and Saatchi which created a major impact prior to the Conservatives' 1979 victory over James Callaghan's minority Labour government.

(2) In Israel the **Labour Party** (originally *Mapai*) was one of the guiding forces of the new state from its birth, and represented the political ESTABLISHMENT until 1977, when the right-wing LIKUD forced it into opposition. It returned to power in 1992 as dominant force in a coalition led by Yitzhak Rabin.

(3) Ireland's **Labour Party** has been the Republic's political third force for decades, joining a coalition with FINE GAEL in the 1980s and in 1993, under Dick Spring, forming a coalition with FIANNA FAIL after registering heavy gains.

(4) New Zealand's **Labour Party**, founded in 1916, has held power sporadically since 1935.

Labour and Co-op Labout MPs at Westminister who are also sponsored by the CO-OPERATIVE PARTY.

Labour Research Department A left-wing body financed by trade unions – and not connected with the party – which provides authoritative data on political and employment issues, including a tally of corporate donations to the Conservative Party and bodies connected to it.

National Labour The Labour MPs who followed Ramsay MacDonald into supporting the NATIONAL GOVERNMENT.

Labourism The sometimes ruthless pursuit of cautious policies beneficial to right-wing trade union leaders and other vested interests in the party.

Lacey Act The pioneering US Congressional measure on wildlife conservation. Promoted by Rep. John Fletcher Lacey (1841–1913) and passed in 1900, it forbade the interstate transportation of illegally killed game.

lady. Ladies in a Bathtub Nickname for the eight-ton marble memorial in the crypt beneath the Rotunda of the US CAPITOL, presented by women's organizations in 1921 to honour the pioneer SUFFRAGETTES Susan B. Anthony, Lucretia Mott and Elizabeth Cody Stanton.

Lady Bird The usual name for President Lyndon Johnson's wife Claudia, giving her, too, the initials LBJ. It was given her not by LBJ but by her childhood nurse who said she was "purty as a ladybird".

Lady Bird Act The 1965 Highway Beautification Act which curbed billboards on highways, passed by Congress at Lady Bird's urging.

Lady Forkbender Nickname for Lady Falkender (1932–), formerly **Marcia Williams**, UK Prime Minister Harold WILSON's long-serving political secretary and reputed *eminence grise*. Its likely origin is PRIVATE EYE (MRS. WILSON'S DIARY, 1975): "So we set off, on a lovely May morning, with Mr. Haines at the wheel of his Mini, and myself, Harold and Lady Forkbender in the back." *See also* LAVENDER LIST.

the lady's not for turning. Margaret Thatcher's strident assertion to the 1980 Conservative Party conference, rejecting any suggestion of a U-TURN. It was an adaptation by her speechwriter Sir Ronald Millar of Christopher Fry's 1948 play title, *The Lady's Not For Burning*.

Lafayette Square The open park in WASHINGTON DC across Pennsylvania Avenue from the WHITE HOUSE. It was named after Marie Joseph, Marquis de Lafayette (1757–1834), French soldier, reformer and diplomat and one of the greatest friends of the American revolution. It is customarily the scene of DEMONSTRATIONS and at times of depression the home of down-and-outs emphasizing their plight.

Laffer curve In ECONOMICS, the tabulation of the theory that under certain conditions cutting tax rates can increase government tax revenues by increasing the incentive to work. Devised by Arthur Laffer of the University of Southern California, the curve became a fundamental of SUPPLY-SIDE economics. It showed that if taxes were set either at 0% or 100%, the Government would receive nothing, and that somewhere between these two points lay the optimal tax rate.

> Less a breakthrough in economic thought than a public relations miracle.
>
> E. J. DIONNE Jr, *Why Americans Hate Politics*.

laissez-faire Especially in ECONOMICS, non-intervention by the state, with the MARKET left totally free to operate. Its origin is either the mediaeval French jousting phrase *laissez faire–laissez passer* ("leave alone, let pass"), or finance minister Colbert in 1751 (as *laissez faire*, "let us get on with it"). First described as such by François Quesnoy in 1765, *laissez-faire* became the byword for classic LIBERALISM.

Lambeg drum An outsize bass drum whose booming rhythm drives the pipe bands that are an essential of ORANGE and LOYALIST parades in Northern Ireland. It is named after the village of Lambeg, on Lough Neagh west of Belfast. *See* MARCHING SEASON.

Lambton affair The scandal in Britain in 1973 when Lord Lambton (1922–) was forced to resign as Under-Secretary for the RAF after photos of him with Hanora (Norma) Levy, an Irish prostitute, were offered to the Press. "I have behaved with credulous stupidity," he said, resigning his Commons seat. When

Prime Minister Edward Heath asked his Ministers if any more of them had something to hide, Trade Minister Earl Jellicoe also resigned, citing "casual affairs" with call-girls.

lame. lame duck (1) Mainly US term for an INCUMBENT president, other elected official or administration in his/its final term, barred from re-election and enjoying waning power and influence. Its origin is in an 18th-century London stock market term for jobbers who defaulted on their obligations, went bankrupt and limped out of Exchange Alley with much quacking.

Lame Duck amendment The 20th amendment to the US Constitution, ratified in 1933, which ended the situation in which members of an outgoing Congress returned to Washington for a three-month "lame-duck" session after the next Congress had been elected, but before its members could take office.

(2) UK Prime Minister Edward Heath's term for businesses which had come to rely on State subsidies because of their inability to "stand on their own two feet". His government began by withdrawing such aid, but after its U-TURN increased aid to industry and actually nationalized the troubled Rolls-Royce aero engine company.

Lancaster House The UK government's official conference and hospitality centre, midway between Buckingham Palace and Whitehall, which has housed European and G7 Summit meetings.

Lancaster House agreement The agreement on the future of Zimbabwe/Rhodesia brokered by UK Foreign Secretary Lord Carrington in December 1979 after months of tense talks with former premier Ian Smith, then-premier Bishop Abel Muzorewa and the GUERRILLA movements led by Robert Mugabe (*see* ZANU-PF) and Joshua Nkomo. Under it the country ended 14 years of illegal independence (*see* UDI) and RETURNED TO LEGALITY under the Crown as a prelude to independence.

Lance. Bert Lance affair The controversy that broke out in Washington in 1977 after President CARTER nominated Thomas Bertram Lance (1931–), Chairman of the Calhoun First National Bank in his home state of Georgia, to head the Office of Management and Budget (OMB). Senators raised doubts over his nomination after alleged irregularities in his past banking practice were reported, and after long and gruelling hearings Lance eventually resigned. He was tried in 1980 on 33 counts ranging from conspiracy to falsifying statements and misapplying bank funds; 14 counts were dismissed and the jury acquitted Lance and three associates on a further 13; a retrial on the remaining six charges was avoided when Lance agreed in 1986 to pay a $50,000 fine and was barred from involvement with any Federally-insured bank. In the meantime Walter Mondale had hurriedly withdrawn an invitation to Lance to chair his 1984 campaign after adverse public reaction.

land. land fit for heroes to live in, a The historic promise made by Lloyd George in the 1918 COUPON ELECTION, and directed at men returning from WORLD WAR I. Speaking at Wolverhampton on 24 November, Lloyd George said:

> What is our task? To make Britain a fit country for heroes to live in.

land for peace The concept that peace between Israel, the PALESTINIANS and neighbouring Arab states can be achieved by Israel giving up some of the OCCUPIED TERRITORIES. The bitter opposition of Yitzhak Shamir's LIKUD government to any such deal was one factor in its defeat at the 1992 election and its replacement by a LABOUR-led government under Yitzhak Rabin.

Land of hope and glory The patriotic hymn written by A. C. Benson (1862–1925) at the height of IMPERIALIST fervour to the tune of Elgar's *Pomp and Circumstance March No. 1*. First sung by Dame Clara Butt in 1902 and traditionally sung at the last night of the Proms, it became an unofficial English national anthem – and also of the CONSERVATIVE Party. Its sentiments and Tory connections make it anathema to those who do not share them.

> Land of hope and glory, Mother of the Free,
> How shall we extol thee, who are born of thee?
> Wider still and wider shall thy bounds be set;
> God who made thee mighty, make thee mightier yet!

Länder The semi-autonomous provinces into which modern Germany is divided, each being called a *Land*.

landslide An overwhelming election victory in which the losing party is virtually swept away. Campbell-Bannerman's LIBERALS in 1906 won 400 seats (512 with their allies, the largest working majority since the 1832 REFORM ACT); F. E. Smith said that they "came floating into Parliament like corks on the top of a dirty wave". In 1983 Mrs. Thatcher dropped Francis Pym (1922–) from her Cabinet after he suggested a landslide victory might prove harmful in the long term. In America, says the scholar James Sundquist, "the system only works really well right after a landslide election". But Bryce Harlow wrote:

"The President who wins real big will blow himself up." Joseph Tumulty declared that Warren HARDING's Presidential victory in 1920 "wasn't a landslide – it was an earthquake". And during his 1952 Senate election, John F. KENNEDY joked of receiving a note from his wealthy father reading:

> Dear Jack, Don't buy a single vote more than necessary. I'm damned if I'm going to pay for a landslide.

Landslide Lyndon Not a reference to LBJ's swamping of Barry Goldwater in 1964, but to his narrow victory in his 1948 Senate race. His enemies claimed Johnson supporters had stuffed the ballot boxes. The story was told of a little Mexican boy found sobbing for his father in a San Antonio street. When reminded his father was long dead, the boy blubbed: "But he came back to vote for Lyndon Johnson and he didn't come to see me."

Lansdowne letter A letter sent by the Irish peer Henry Charles Petty-Fitzmaurice (1845–1927), fifth Marquess of Lansdowne, to the *Daily Telegraph* on 29 November 1917. It advocated a compromise peace with Germany to end WORLD WAR I – including guarantees of Germany's continuance as a political, commercial and territorial power. Despite evidence that many MPs and even some members of Lloyd George's COALITION Government shared his views, the letter was violently repudiated by the Government and the press as an act of disloyalty which weakened the Allied resolve to defeat Germany. As a result Lansdowne was expelled from the Tory party.

last. Last Call speech President Franklin D. Roosevelt's speech on 27 May 1941 appealing to nations throughout the Americas to join in a common defence of democracy as the danger grew of war with the AXIS powers. The phrase means a final opportunity, as in the "last call for dinner".

Last Chance Saloon In 1989 the then Home Office Minister David Mellor (1949–) warned Britain's tabloid press that repeated breaches of individuals' privacy had left it "drinking in the Last Chance Saloon"; one more abuse, and there might have to be legal curbs. When, in July 1992, Mellor was found by one of those tabloids to have been carrying on an extra-marital affair with out-of-work actress Antonia de Sancha, the *Sun* editorialized:

> It certainly was rich of Mellor to warn the press it was drinking in the Last Chance Saloon, while all the time he was playing the piano in the bordello next door.

last hurrah A politician's final moment of glory, often in a brave but unsuccessful re-election campaign. From the US film of the same name (1958), starring Spencer Tracy as a New England POL undertaking the last campaign of his life.

Last Lady Rep. Adam Clayton POWELL's derogatory nickname for Bess Truman (1885–1982), wife of US President Harry S Truman. Powell was contrasting Mrs. Truman's low profile with the hyperactivity of Eleanor Roosevelt, her predecessor (*see* FIRST LADY OF THE WORLD). Mrs. Truman had the last laugh; she went on to become the longest-lived First Lady in history, while Powell was ousted from Congress.

Lateran Treaty The CONCORDAT concluded between the Holy See and the Kingdom of Italy in 1929, with Italy confirming the SOVEREIGNTY of the 109-acre Vatican City and Pope Pius XI graciously recognizing the existence of the Italian state. It ended the **Roman Question** dating from 1870 when Italian unification (*see* RISORGIMENTO) finally abrogated the wider temporal power of the papacy and Rome became the capital of the kingdom.

laundering The circulation of money between numerous concealed accounts to disguise its true origin, or its relation between that origin and the purpose for which it is ultimately used. Used to describe the illicit collection of CAMPAIGN funds and their use for illegal purposes by backers of President Nixon in 1972, which was exposed in the WATERGATE scandal. Also the diversion of the profits of organized crime and drug trafficking through a chain of bank accounts into apparently-respectable hands.

Lausanne Treaty The peace settlement signed on 24 July 1923 which ended the conflict between Greece and Turkey after WORLD WAR I, but could not end the bitterness. It replaced the **Treaty of Sèvres,** imposed on the Turks in 1920 by the allied powers after the defeat of the pro-German Ottoman Empire. The Turks agreed to surrender non-Turkish sections of the former Empire, Greece returned Smyrna (Izmir) to Turkey, which also regained Thrace, Adrianople and the Dodecanese, and the Bosphorus and Dardanelles were demilitarized and opened to international shipping. The Treaty also provided for a forced exchange of national minorities between Greece and Turkey which has left powerful resentments, especially among Greeks.

Lavender list The controversial resignation HONOURS LIST drawn up by Harold Wilson in 1976 to reward prominent supporters of himself and the Labour Party, which earned him lasting discredit. The list included worthy and popular choices, but the number of financiers in it surprised the party, and a couple were subsequently disgraced – one, Lord Kagan, manufacturer of the Gannex raincoat which was Wilson's trademark, being imprisoned for evading excise duties. The list, rumoured to have been even more controversial at the outset, got its name because the final draft was typed on lavender-coloured paper by Wilson's political secretary Marcia Williams, ennobled as Lady Falkender (*see* LADY FORKBENDER). Mrs. Williams was seen by Wilson's enemies as his *eminence grise* and they alleged that the choice of names was hers rather than the Prime Minister's.

Law, Andrew Bonar *See* UNKNOWN PRIME MINISTER.

law. law and order A key domestic issue in many elections, which at times of fear over rising crime can be whipped into an election-winner by populists and DEMAGOGUES. Gore Vidal concluded that "to the right wing law and order is often just a code phrase, meaning 'get the niggers'. To the left wing it often means political oppression." Central to it is the assertion that more visible or aggressive policing and tougher sentencing will make the community safer; as J. Edgar Hoover pointed out, "justice is incidental to law and order". In the 1968 US Presidential election all three candidates – Richard Nixon, George Wallace and Hubert Humphrey – played the law-and-order card, leading San Francisco Mayor Joseph Alioto to comment:

> None of the candidates is running for President. They're all running for sheriff.

Though the issue strikes a chord with every social class, Herbert Marcuse observed that "law and order are always and everywhere the law and order which protects the established hierarchy". Uganda's tyrant Idi Amin took this argument to an extreme, saying: "I have to keep law and order, and it means that I have to kill my enemies before they kill me."

Law Commission A regulatory body, established in 1965 by the Labour LORD CHANCELLOR Lord Gardiner, to monitor the law of England on a continual basis with a view to its systematic development and reform. It has a permanent staff headed by five commissioners – two academics, two lawyers and a judge – and considers the need for CODIFICATION of the law, the elimination of anomalies, the repeal of obsolete measures, and general simplification and modernization. Its reports are often accompanied by draft legislation for the government to introduce into Parliament – which it frequently does.

slip law The first official publication of a statute enacted by the US Congress and the President (or passed without his agreement). Published as an unbound pamphlet but having full legal force, it contains a guide to the history of the measure and gives the President's view, if he has expressed one. Copies of slip laws are delivered to the document rooms of both Houses where they become available to officials and the public; they can be purchased from the Government Printing Office.

sunshine laws Laws which became the vogue in early 1970s America, requiring Congress and the Federal and state bureaucracies to carry out more of their functions in the public gaze instead of behind closed doors.

If the government becomes a lawbreaker, it breeds contempt for the law The dictum of Justice Louis Brandeis, dissenting, in the Supreme Court ruling on *Olmstead et al. v. United States* in 1928, which became a central principle of journalists, lawyers and politicians combating the WATERGATE cover-up. When applied to the President, the Supreme Court had long held that "No man is so high that he is above the law". In England Lord Denning enunciated a similar principle – **"no man, be he ever so high"** – in the Court of Appeal in the late 1970s in striking down a series of decisions by the Labour government which he held to conflict with individual freedom.

Sometimes you have to go above the written law The argument advanced in defence of wrongdoing in the IRAN-CONTRA affair by Fawn Hall, secretary to Colonel Oliver North.

The best way to get a bad law repealed is to enforce it strictly Abraham LINCOLN's dictum which was amply proved in America during PROHIBITION when the EIGHTEENTH AMENDMENT and the VOLSTEAD ACT eventually alienated most voters, and in England and Wales from the late 1980s in the shambles over Sunday trading.

The less people know about how laws and sausages are made, the better they will sleep at night The comment attributed to Bismarck which both reflects the unscientific nature of the legislative process and the IRON CHANCELLOR's contempt for democratic institutions.

LBJ The initials, and nickname, of **Lyndon Baines Johnson** (1908–73), 36th President of the United States (Democrat, 1963–69). A self-made Texan of questionable business and electoral propriety who became the ultimate political technician, he was elected Senate majority leader at 44 in his first term, drove himself to a heart attack at 47 but won the Vice-Presidential nomination five years later. His techniques were not always subtle; he once remarked: "I never trust a man unless I have his pecker in my pocket." But they were effective. "Not since James F. Byrnes had

Congress seen a man so skilled in modifying a measure to enlist the widest possible support, so adept at the arts of wheedling, trading and arm twisting, so persistent and so persuasive," wrote Arthur Schlesinger.

A larger-than-life and elemental figure who picked up his dogs by the ears (*see* HIM AND HER), he was ridiculed as gauche and naïve by Washington society. But he had the last laugh on them after being pitchforked into the presidency on the assassination of John F. KENNEDY. Addressing Congress for the first time, he said: "All I have, I would gladly have given not to be standing here today." But he added: "I am going to build the kind of nation that President Roosevelt hoped for, President Truman worked for and President Kennedy died for."

LBJ manoeuvred JFK's stalled NEW FRONTIER programme through Congress and took a tougher stance on CIVIL RIGHTS than any previous President. Ralph Ellison termed him "the greatest American President for the poor and for the Negroes". And Schlesinger simply stated: "Kennedy promised. Johnson delivered." Johnson won a landslide victory in his own right over Barry Goldwater in 1964, piling up a record majority of 15 million. He saw this as a mandate for a GREAT SOCIETY, but his domestic achievements were overshadowed by the torture of the VIETNAM WAR. LBJ steadily ESCALATED Kennedy's limited US involvement in Vietnam in the face of lack of results on the ground, declaring: "I am not going to lose Vietnam. I am not going to be the President who saw South-east Asia go the way China went." And to US troops he said: "I salute you. Come home with that coonskin on the wall." But Johnson developed a persecution complex; "I wake up at 5 a.m. some mornings and hear the planes coming in at National Airport and I think they are bombing me," he told one aide. And adverse press coverage provoked him to say: "If one morning I walked on the water across the Potomac, the headlines that afternoon would read: 'President can't swim.'" He once asked the veteran diplomat Dean Acheson why he was unpopular; Acheson replied:

> Let's face it, Mr President, you're not a very likeable man.

Against this background, the ridicule resumed. Hugh Sidey saw LBJ as "a great raw man of immense girth, wandering as a stranger in the Pepsi generation. Coarse, earthy – a brutal intrusion into the misty Kennedy renaissance that still clung to the land". His close aide Jack Valenti said: "He doesn't like cold intellectuals around him. He wants people who will cry when an old lady falls down in the street." But his demeanour is best summed up by an episode when a young Marine officer directed him to his helicopter. "Son," LBJ told him, "these are ALL my helicopters."

LBJ's home life was basically happy, despite his habit of turning up in the rooms of female house guests and saying: "Move over – this is your President." He once said: "I'm the luckiest man alive. None of my girls drinks or smokes or takes dope and they both married fine men." He and his wife LADY BIRD made a good team, she explaining: "Lyndon stretches you. He always expects more of you than you're mentally or physically capable of putting out. Somehow that makes you try a little bit harder, and it makes you produce a little more." With Johnson preparing to run again in 1968 the shock of the VIET CONG's TET OFFENSIVE split the Democratic Party, and when the anti-war Sen. Eugene McCarthy defeated him in early primaries, he stood down (*see* I SHALL NOT SEEK). LBJ secured a BOMBING HALT just before the November election, but it was too late to save his Vice-President Hubert Humphrey from defeat. He handed over the White House to Richard Nixon early in 1969 and went home to Texas.

All the way with LBJ The Democrats' slogan in his triumphal 1964 Presidential campaign.

Hey, hey, LBJ, how many kids did you kill today? Perhaps the cruellest slogan of the ANTI-WAR movement as it campaigned against LBJ's enthusiastic support, after initial reservations, for the US commitment in Vietnam.

LCC (1) London County Council. The elected body, led by giants such as John Burns and Herbert Morrison, which made the government of what is now Inner London a model between its foundation under the London Government Act of 1888, and 1965, when it was replaced by the GLC, which covered a larger geographic area to reflect suburban growth. It inherited the powers of the Metropolitan Board of Works, founded in 1855, and from 1903 ran the capital's schools; until 1933 it also operated most of London's tramways. Its most visible symbol was its headquarters, COUNTY HALL. (2) Labour Co-ordinating Committee. A hard LEFT group and an irritant to the Labour leadership when founded in 1979, it became in the late 1980s a moderate but active force for non-ideological party reform and revival.

LDCs Less-Developed Countries. A term widely used by politicians discussing the THIRD WORLD to avoid describing the world's poorest nations as "underdeveloped". *See also* ACP; LOMÉ CONVENTION.

LEA Local Education Authority. Those local authorities in England and Wales – county councils and metropolitan districts – which were responsible for all State schools until the advent of OPTING OUT. They were formed in 1902 to replace the previous system of School Boards; their numbers were reduced and their duties clarified by the 1944 BUTLER ACT, which also introduced a Minister of Education. LEAs have been responsible for the provision of local primary and secondary education, further education (now transferred to a separate Funding Council) and the recruitment and payment of teachers; the 1992 Education White Paper proposed further reductions in their powers.

leader. Leader of the Council In Britain, the political head of a local authority, being leader of the governing party group; the office of MAYOR or chairman/woman is purely ceremonial.

Leader of the House At Westminster, the Cabinet Minister responsible for the BUSINESS of the Commons; while getting the Government's legislation on to the STATUTE BOOK is the Leader's top priority, traditionally he or she also has a responsibility to members of all parties.

I must follow the people. Am I not their leader? This cynical remark, attributed to a range of figures from Disraeli to Gandhi, probably originated with Alexander Ledru-Rollin (1807–74), one of the leaders of the French revolution of February 1848.

Leaderene, the One of many nicknames for Margaret Thatcher (*see* IRON LADY); this one which originated early in her Premiership connects the idea of the all-powerful leader with the Biblical tale of the Gadarene swine, who rushed into the sea after Christ instilled in them an evil spirit he had cast out of a man.

Leadership contest The process of electing a leader in one of Britain's political parties. The Conservatives, whose leader traditionally EMERGED, now rely on a ballot of the party's MPs; Labour has moved on from such a system to an ELECTORAL COLLEGE; and the Liberal Democrats hold a ballot of all their members.

League of Nations The world organization set up by the Treaty of VERSAILLES to ensure that the global conflict of WORLD WAR I could never be repeated, and to police the new order of NATION STATES pioneered by Woodrow WILSON. He had called for

> an organization of peace which shall make it certain that the combined power of free nations will check every invasion of right and serve to make peace and justice more secure by affording a definite tribunal of opinion to which all must submit.

The League, based in Geneva, was formed on 10 January 1920, but the US SENATE inflicted a crippling blow by refusing to back it. The ISOLATIONIST Sen. Henry Cabot Lodge (1850–1924) denounced it as "the evil thing with a holy name", saying: "I have loved but one flag and I cannot share that devotion and give affection for the mongrel banner invented for a League". Franklin D. Roosevelt, running for Vice-President in 1920, said: "It may not end wars, but the nations demand the experiment;" by the time he took office in 1932 he was terming it "nothing more than a debating society, and a poor one at that". Yet despite the absence of America, and the Soviet Union which was excluded, the League for over a decade offered the then independent states of the world – 60 at its peak – a useful vehicle for co-operation and expressing their views. As late as November 1929 RAMSAY MACDonald could assert: "The League of Nations grows in moral courage. Its frown will soon be even more dreaded than a nation's arms, and when that happens, you and I shall have security and peace." But the withdrawal of NAZI Germany in 1933 and Italy's invasion of Abyssinia two years later, when the League tried in vain to impose SANCTIONS, sealed its fate. It lingered on after the outbreak of WORLD WAR II, its final meeting on 18 April 1946 by which time the UNITED NATIONS had supplanted it.

> What was everybody's business in the end proved to be nobody's business. Each one looked to the other to take the lead, and the aggressors got away with it.
>
> JAN CHRISTIAAN SMUTS (1870–1950), 1943.

leak The unauthorized disclosure of generally-embarrassing information from within government, particularly to the Press. The term goes back at least to Lord Chancellor Francis Bacon, Viscount St. Albans (1561–1626), who wrote:

> As for Cabinet Councils, it may be their motto, "*plenus rimarum sum*" (I am full of leaks). One futile person, that maketh it his glory to tell, will do more hurt than many that know it their duty to conceal.

There were leaks galore in the early days of the United States. HAMILTON's aides leaked to Jefferson's associates the rumour that the Treasury Secretary was going to put the new nation under British hegemony, and Jefferson himself was to write: "The abuse of confidence by publishing my letters has cost me more than all other pains." But it was with the explosion of the Washington media from World War II that leaks came into their own. Even in an era of FREEDOM OF INFORMATION, they have provided the best news stories. President Truman fumed that "95 per cent of our secret information has been leaked in newspapers and slick magazines". LBJ complained: "This goddam town leaks like a worn-out boot." Richard Nixon, at the height of WATERGATE, stormed:

"I don't give a damn how it's done. Do whatever has to be done to stop these leaks." And Jimmy CARTER said in exasperation: "If there is another outbreak of misinformation, distortion or self-serving leaks, I will direct the Secretary of State to discharge the officials responsible . . . even if some innocent people might be punished." Ronald Reagan had two views on leaks. On the one hand he complained that "sometimes I read memos in the paper I haven't even gotten yet", and declared: "I've had it up to my keister with leaks." But former Secretary of State Alexander Haig noted:

> In the Reagan administration, leaks were not a problem – they were a way of life. Leaks constituted policy, they were the authentic voice of government.

In Britain, the climate of official secrecy has made leaks rarer and more appreciated by the press. In 1873 Sir Ralph Lingen wrote: "The unauthorised use of official information is the worst fault a civil servant can commit. It is on the same footing as cowardice by a soldier." And Sir Robert Armstrong, CABINET SECRETARY for most of the Thatcher years, commented ironically of a letter he wrote to Whitehall MANDARINS against leaks: "I was very sad it took as long as six weaks to leak."

There are numerous reasons for leaking. Richard Darman, Reagan's budget director, said: "Winners leak out of pride in what they have won. Losers leak to try and change policies." And PENTAGON spokesman Henry Catto declared: "We object to the expression of minority opinion via leaks to the news media designed to influence the cause of events." Four generic kinds of leak have been identified: the

grudge leak when an official whose advice has been rejected, who has been passed over for promotion or feels hard done by in some way goes public. Such leaks are the staple of many Washington COLUMNISTS; the

pre-emptive leak designed to expose a course of action prematurely so that public opinion will stop it; the

trial-balloon leak a form of KITE-FLYING to test whether the public or the political community will wear some policy or action; and the

whistle-blower leak carried out to expose some activity which the leaker considers disgraceful.

leak inquiry The investigation customarily carried out within any bureaucracy once a leak with major implications has taken place. In WHITEHALL it is almost axiomatic that the inquiry will fail; sometimes, as with WESTLAND, ensuring that the culprit is not identified requires considerable skill. In Washington under the Reagan administration, lie-detector tests were introduced to track down leakers.

leap-frogging The process by which a nation which sees a competitor gaining more devastating armaments than it possesses will equip itself with an even more formidable arsenal, and the other nation may in turn acquire yet greater weaponry. Neil KINNOCK's use of the phrase in a discussion with French socialists in 1984 caused a brief misunderstanding, when Lionel Jospin, secretary of the French party, only caught the word "frog". Jospin was eventually persuaded that the Labour leader had not uttered an insult.

lease-lend *See* LEND-LEASE.

Lebensraum (Ger. room for living) Territory coveted by a state for expansion, to meet economic and population pressures or simply for national aggrandizement. Hitler seized on the concept to justify NAZI Germany's designs on a swathe of territory in central and eastern Europe, and beyond. The Nazi interpretation of the word included the forcible removal or murder of the existing non-German inhabitants, a policy that underlaid some of the worst atrocities of the period before and during World War II.

left, or **left-wing** The umbrella term for Socialist or radical political tendencies of every kind. It originated just before the French Revolution in the Estates-General, where supporters of the *status quo* sat on the right and opponents of the King's policies sat on the left. Within left-wing movements themselves, the term is used to define the most radical elements; Richard CROSSMAN described the Left in Britain's LABOUR PARTY as "a group of people who will never be happy unless they can convince themselves that they are about to be betrayed by their leaders". To those on the right, the term has sinister connotations; Michael Heseltine (*see* TARZAN) once brought a Conservative conference to its feet by exclaiming: "I hear the trade unions tramping towards us – Left; Left; Left, Left, Left!" Being on the left involves a political philosophy (or rather one of many) as well as organization; George Orwell wrote that "so much left-wing thought is . . . playing with fire by people who don't even know that fire is hot".

Left Book Club The imprint founded by the publisher Victor Gollancz in the late 1930s which, through the books it published such as GUILTY MEN, did much to rally the British non-Communist left prior to and during World War II, and contributed to the programme and ethos of the 1945 Labour government.

broad left The (usually non-Communist) coalition of left-wing elements which exerted considerable influence in Britain's trade and student unions during the 1980s.

hard Left In Britain, a range of groups spearheaded by the CAMPAIGN FOR LABOUR PARTY DEMOCRACY which came within a hair's breadth of securing the election of Tony BENN as Labour's deputy leader in 1981. It was instrumental in securing the RESELECTION of Labour MPs and the ELECTORAL COLLEGE to choose the party leader, previously elected by Labour MPs. It exerted great influence in local government, particularly in London, in the early 1980s, and gave rise to the CAMPAIGN GROUP of Labour MPs, but went into decline after Neil KINNOCK was elected Labour leader.

Keep Left A group of left-wing Labour MPs critical of the policy toward Soviet Russia of the foreign secretary Ernest BEVIN in 1946–47. Launched in November 1946, the group produced a pamphlet of the same name in April 1947 written by Richard CROSSMAN, Michael Foot (*see* WURZEL GUMMIDGE) and Ian MIKARDO, and signed by 12 other Labour MPs; the name was taken from Britain's most common traffic sign. The group, which met regularly at the Commons, opposed Bevin's COLD WAR stance and advocated a "third force", a European socialist alliance based on the UK and France, to hold the middle ground between the US and the Soviet Union, heal the widening breach between East and West and lessen Britain's dependence on America.

loony left A derogatory 1980s term for the more extreme elements of Labour's hard LEFT, particularly in London. It encompassed militant feminism, support for gay rights, positive DISCRIMINATION for ethnic minorities and frantic support for the single ISSUE of the moment. The former Labour, by then Tory, Minister Lord Marsh (1928–) categorized the loony left as "one-legged black Lambeth lesbians against foxhunting".

New Left *See* NEW.

soft Left A term produced as the hard LEFT reached its greatest influence to describe the traditional democratic Left in the Labour Party, focused on the TRIBUNE GROUP of MPs. The division became institutionalized when the Tribune Group split in 1982, with a minority of its members forming a hard left CAMPAIGN GROUP.

left can speak to left The argument used for the wartime Churchill coalition's despatch of the far-left Sir Stafford Cripps as British ambassador to Moscow. STALIN was less appreciative, scorning the faddish Cripps as "CHRIST AND CARROTS". The phrase also epitomized the initial hopes of Ernest BEVIN that as a Socialist Foreign Secretary he could deal with the Russians when America was hitting a brick wall; he very soon changed his mind.

We're going to have to move left and right at the same time The strategy offered by former California Governor Edmund G. (Jerry) Brown (1938–) in his campaign to develop a "new politics" in America.

Legion of Honour The sole mark of distinction awarded in Republican France, first instituted by Napoleon in 1802. Members can be identified by a red flash worn in their lapel.

legislation (1) Laws as enacted by the LEGISLATURE and approved, if necessary, by the EXECUTIVE.

> Foolish legislation is a rope of sand which perishes in the twisting. RALPH WALDO EMERSON (1803–82).

> The quality of legislation passed to deal with a problem is inversely proportional to the volume of media clamor that brought it on. G. RAY FUNKHOUSER, US researcher.

(2) The process of enacting laws, embodying the decision that such measures are necessary.

> You cannot legislate for virtue. Cardinal JAMES GIBBONS (1834–1921).

> In legislation we all do a lot of "swapping tobacco across the lines". Speaker JOSEPH CANNON (1836–1926).

portmanteau legislation A Bill or Act which incorporates a range of unrelated items instead of concentrating on addressing a particular problem. The name is a Victorian reference to the sizable suitcase required for disparate items of luggage.

primary legislation At Westminster, a measure which makes a significant change in the body of law in a particular area. Frequently a Minister can be heard to say: "We can't do that, it requires primary legislation." The objection is generally not one due to principle but to the lack of Parliamentary time for an extra Bill to be put through all its stages.

Legislative branch The term used in America to refer to CONGRESS by comparison with the EXECUTIVE BRANCH of government (the White House) and the JUDICIARY. James Madison wrote in the FEDERALIST: "In republican government the legislative authority necessarily predominates," and this is broadly true despite the dignity of the Presidency and the ability of the Supreme Court to determine what is or is not CONSTITUTIONAL.

Legislative Assembly The lower house of legislature in New South Wales, Victoria and Western Australia and the sole chamber in the Capital Territory, Northern Territory and Queensland. In South Australia and Tasmania it is known as the House of Assembly.

Legislative Calendar *See* CALENDAR.

legislative call system The system of lights and bells or buzzers in the US CAPITOL and its office buildings that alert Members to votes and other occurrences – with a special combination of the two for the onset of nuclear war.

Legislative Council (1) The upper house of legislature in every Australian state except for the CAPITAL TERRITORY, Northern Territory and Queensland, which have a UNICAMERAL system. (2) *See* HOUSE OF KEYS.

legislative day The period from when the US SENATE adjourns to when it next adjourns. Because the Senate frequently RECESSes rather than adjourns at the end of a working day, a legislative day can last weeks or even months. Only at the beginning of a legislative day is the CALENDAR called for consideration.

legislative hold In the US SENATE, a courtesy under which consideration of a Presidential appointment is delayed if a single member has personal objections. Most use it rarely, for instance when they want to meet the nominee prior to CONFIRMATION, but a handful of mavericks, notably Sen. Jesse Helms of South Carolina, have used it frequently to stress a political point.

legislator A member of a LEGISLATURE, not necessarily a politician whose principal interest is legislation.

> The best legislator is the one who votes for all appropriations and against all taxes.
> Rep. WALTER P. BROWNLOW (1851–1910, *attr.*).

> Legislators represent people, not trees or acres. Legislators are elected by voters, not farms or cities or economic interests.
> Chief Justice EARL WARREN (1891–1974).

legislature The body in a democracy which is elected to enact laws and provide a check on the EXECUTIVE. The term also covers America's state legislatures.

> The great virtue of a strong legislature is not what it can do but what it can prevent.
> Sen. J. WILLIAM FULBRIGHT (1905–).

the Legislature A formal description for the US CONGRESS.

> The tyranny of the legislature is really the danger most to be feared. THOMAS JEFFERSON.

> No man's life, liberty or property are safe while the legislature is in session. GIDEON J. TUCKER (1826–99).

> The legislature, like the executive, has ceased to be even the creature of the people; it is the creature of pressure groups and most of them, it must be manifest, are of dubious wisdom and even more dubious honesty.
> H. L. MENCKEN, 1930.

legitimacy The status of a government that has been lawfully and democratically elected.

> A government isn't legitimate just because it exists.
> JEANE KIRKPATRICK (1926–).

> Of course the Government has no legitimacy – they're a bunch of bastards.
> GEORGE GALLOWAY MP (Lab.) (1954–).

Leinster House The building in central Dublin, between the National Library and National Museum of Ireland, where DAIL EIREANN and the SEANAD meet. It was built between 1745 and 1748 at the east end of Molesworth Street by the Earl of Kildare, and known as Kildare House until he was granted the earldom of Leinster.

Lemonade Lucy The nickname earned by Lucy Webb Hayes (1831–89), the highly-religious wife of President Rutherford Hayes, because of her ban on alcoholic beverages in the White House.

Lend-lease (sometimes known as **Lease-lend**) The critical assistance given to Britain and her allies by President Franklin Roosevelt prior to America's entry into WORLD WAR II. Based on a precedent set in 1892, it involved "lending" guns, ships and other equipment to "any country whose defense the President deems vital to the defense of the United States" on the understanding that they would be "returned in kind" after the war. Roosevelt knew this was unlikely, but had to overcome opposition in Congress for his **Lend-Lease Act**, passed in March 1941, while making clear to Britain it would not be saddled with crippling post-war debt if victorious. The policy began with 50 superannuated destroyers sent to Britain in return for the US being granted bases in Britain and its Empire. By the time Lend-lease ended in 1945 America had received back less than one-sixth of the $50 billion worth of *matériel* it had "lent"; 60% went to Commonwealth countries, but 35 other nations including Soviet Russia also benefited.

> Suppose my neighbor's house catches on fire, and I have a length of garden hose four or five hundred feet away. If he can take my garden hose and connect it up with his hydrant, I may help him to put out his fire. Now what do I do? I don't say to him before that operation: "Neighbor, my garden hose cost me fifteen dollars. You have to pay me fifteen dollars for it." . . . I don't want fifteen dollars. I want my hose back after the fire is over.
> FRANKLIN D. ROOSEVELT, 17 December 1940.

Lenin The adopted name of **Vladimir Ilyich Ulyanov** (1870–1924), Russian REVOLUTIONARY and founder of the SOVIET UNION; the word has no obvious meaning in Russian. Lenin was deeply scarred by the execution of his elder brother, Alexander, by police in 1887, after he had attempted to assassinate the TSAR; after being expelled from two universities (the second time being exiled to Siberia for three years) he became a professional revolutionary. In 1900 he joined other MARXISTs in exile in Europe, waiting and preparing for the ideal moment to launch the revolution in Russia; he also mixed with democratic Socialists, describing one, George

Bernard Shaw, as "a good man fallen among FABIANS". In his 1902 book *What Is To Be Done?* he placed his faith in the idea of the Party as the engine of revolutionary CLASS CONSCIOUSNESS and the "vanguard of the PROLETARIAT". Maxim Gorky wrote: "The working class is for Lenin what ore is for a metal worker." At a conference of the Russian Social Democratic Workers' Party in London in 1903, the majority (BOLSHEVIKS) supported Lenin's proposals for the organization and revolutionary role of the party. After the collapse of the Tsarist government in March 1917, Lenin returned to Russia in a SEALED TRAIN with the connivance of Germany (*see* FINLAND STATION).

> The Germans turned upon Russia the most grisly of all weapons. They transported Lenin in a sealed truck, like a plague bacillus, from Switzerland into Russia.
> WINSTON CHURCHILL, 1929.

With the aid of the Bolshevik-organized Red Guard, Lenin overthrew the provisional government in the OCTOBER REVOLUTION, seizing power in the name of the people. For five years he wrestled to transform Russia's society and economy, while fighting a CIVIL WAR exacerbated by Western intervention. He suffered a stroke in 1922, by which time he had moderated his initially ruthless economic policy (*see* NEW ECONOMIC POLICY), and died on 21 January 1924, leaving in his writings a legacy of applied Marxism (*see* LENINISM) and a final *Testament*, warning colleagues against choosing STALIN as his successor and urging his removal as general secretary of the party. The party CENTRAL COMMITTEE failed to act on the Testament and Stalin suppressed it; in 1956 Khruschev caused a sensation by reading it to the 20th Party Congress. Lenin's body was embalmed and installed in a MAUSOLEUM in RED SQUARE, which became a place of pilgrimage for millions of Russians; Moscow's newly-weds frequently call there to pay their respects and receive his "blessing". With the collapse of the Soviet Union at the end of 1991 the future of the mausoleum and its occupant were put in doubt.

> The Russian people's worst misfortune was his birth, their next worst . . . his death.
> CHURCHILL.

> The dominant streak in his character and political practice was a ruthless will to coerce, dictate and subjugate. Stalin's terror and Stalin's tyranny are unmistakably foreshadowed by Leninism.
> MILOVAN DJILAS (1911–).

Lenin Prize An award granted for outstanding scientific, technical and cultural achievements, established in 1950 as the Soviet counterpart to the NOBEL prizes. The winner is announced on 1 May each year.

Order of Lenin The highest decoration in the former Soviet Union, established by the Presidium of the Supreme Soviet in 1930. It is conferred for outstanding service in fields including medicine, science and technology, defence, agriculture, education, fine arts, music, film, theatre and literature. The recipient was presented with a gold medal and enjoyed income tax exemption, pension rights, transport privileges and a monthly honorarium.

Leningrad The name given in 1924 after Lenin's death to Petrograd which, until 1914, was known as **St. Petersburg**; it reverted to this title in 1991 after a city referendum. The former Tsarist capital founded by Peter the Great in 1703, it was best known as Leningrad for its heroic resistance to a German siege in WORLD WAR II which lasted over two years.

Leningrad purge *See* PURGE.

Leninism Lenin's elaboration of MARXIST political and economic thought, and the adaptation to contemporary conditions of industrially underdeveloped and mainly agricultural societies, such as Russia in the early 20th century. In *What Is To Be Done* (1902) he stressed the indispensable role of a disciplined professional communist party.

> Lenin's method leads to this: the party organisation at first substitutes itself for the party as a whole, then one central committee substitutes itself for the party organisation, and finally a single dictator substitutes himself for the central committee.
> TROTSKY.

In *Imperialism – The Highest Stage of Capitalism* (1916) Lenin differed from Marx in stressing the revolutionary potential of pre-capitalist societies and the importance of a worker–peasant alliance in achieving revolution. *Left-wing Communism* (1920), written with experience of power, emphasized the importance of flexibility and PRAGMATISM in achieving revolutions and then sustaining Communist authority. This last book marked a clear divergence from the economic and historical determination of orthodox Marxism.

> A combination of two things which Europeans have kept for some centuries in different compartments of the soul – religion and business.
> JOHN MAYNARD KEYNES.

> Leninism is Marxism of the era of imperialism and the proletarian revolution.
> STALIN, 1917.

Let. Let Harold and Bob finish the job The slogan on which Robert Maxwell (1923–91), the larger-than-life and ultimately crooked Czech-born Socialist tycoon, stood for re-election as Labour MP for Buckingham in 1966. Maxwell, first elected in 1964, held the seat until 1970; the Harold with whom Maxwell modestly associated himself was Harold WILSON.

Let our children grow tall, and some taller than others if they have it in them to do so The statement with which Margaret

Thatcher established herself with American conservatives, made on her first US tour as Tory leader in 1975.

Let's call for a hatchet Richard Nixon's blast during the 1952 Presidential campaign against alleged communism in the Truman administration. He declared:

> If the dry rot of corruption and communism, which has eaten deep into our body politic during the past seven years, can only be chopped out with a hatchet – then let's call for a hatchet.

Let's do it The last words of Gary GILMORE prior to his execution by a Utah firing squad on 17 January 1977.

Let sleeping dogs lie The epitome of the doctrine of LAISSEZ-FAIRE, said to be the watchword of Robert WALPOLE, Britain's first PRIME MINISTER to be acknowledged as such.

Let the word go forth from this time and place, to friend and foe alike, that the torch has been passed to a new generation of Americans – born in this century, tempered by war, disciplined by a hard and bitter peace The central message of John F. KENNEDY'S INAUGURAL address, delivered on 20 January 1961.

Let us go forward together and put these grave matters to the proof The challenge which Winston CHURCHILL, as a member of Asquith's Liberal government, threw down to militant ULSTER UNIONISTS on 14 March 1914 as they threatened to use force to obstruct HOME RULE. Churchill said:

> If Ulster is to become a tool in party calculations, if the civil and parliamentary systems under which we have dwelt for so long, and our fathers before us, are to be brought to the rude challenge of force; if the Government and Parliament of this great country and greater Empire are to be exposed to menace and brutality; if all the loose, wanton and reckless chatter we have been forced to listen to these many months is, in the end, to disclose a sinister and revolutionary purpose, then I can only say to you: "Let us go forward and put these grave matters to the proof."

Let them eat cake (Fr. *Qu'ils mangent de la brioche*) Reputedly the comment of Queen Marie-Antoinette (1755–93) when told that the mob were protesting that they had no bread during the shortage of 1789. It was cited to justify the FRENCH REVOLUTION and the execution of Louis XVI and his queen. In fact the saying is much older, dating back at least to Queen Marie-Thérèse (1638–83), wife of Louis XIV, who was said to have asked: "Why don't they eat pastry?"

level. Levellers An ultra-republican group of Puritans active only for a few years during the English Civil War, but whose views were to form one of the bases of radical and Socialist demands two centuries later. Led by John Swinburne (1614–57) the Levellers, who mainly comprised soldiers in the Parliamentary army, were an influential force between 1647 and 1649; their demands which included universal male suffrage and an end to all class distinctions, ultimately proved too much for Cromwell and his Parliamentary/military governing group to take.

level playing field A situation in which all proponents of differing arguments, or all contenders for a contract, enjoy an equal chance of success, instead of the odds being stacked in favour of one of them.

Leviathan The landmark work of political theory written by Thomas Hobbes (1588–1679) and published in 1651 in the early years of the English COMMONWEALTH. Hobbes maintained that mankind advanced from the state of nature to the political state by way of a contract, giving up its right to act as individuals to a "sovereign" which could be an individual or an assembly, and by transferring those rights the people became part of a great commonwealth or "Leviathan" (a Biblical name for a great sea creature). Hobbes argued that rebellion against a sovereign was never justified, but that if one succeeded, this proved that the sovereign was incapable of ruling. Absolute obedience to the sovereign was essential, for

> How could a state be governed . . . if every individual remained free to obey or not to obey the law according to his private opinion?

L.G. The most neutral and dignified nickname for **David** (later Earl) **Lloyd George** (1863–1945), Britain's Liberal Prime Minister from 1916 till 1923. Other epithets for the Celtic spellbinder ranged from "the Goat" to "the WELSH WIZARD". He was inspirational as "the man who won the war", and a compelling orator; Arnold Bennett cynically reported: "Mr. Lloyd George spoke for a hundred and seventeen minutes, in which period he was detected only once in the use of an argument", and Harold Macmillan recalled:

> I can see, above all, the beautiful hands, an actor's or an artist's hands, by the smallest movement of which he could make you see the picture he was trying to paint.

Regardless of these gifts, he was regarded as PRAGMATIC to the point of duplicity. Churchill termed him "the vehement, contriving, resourceful, nimble-leaping Lloyd George", and A. J. P. Taylor saw him as "a master of improvised speech and improvised policies". F. S. Oliver wrote: "He is without malice of any kind, without prejudices, without morals. He has many enemies and no friends. He does not understand what friendship means . . . and yet he is the best man we have got." And Stanley Baldwin said: "He spent his whole life plastering together the true and the false, and therefrom manufacturing the implausible." Lloyd George himself confessed: "Poor Bonar [Law] can't bear being called a liar; now I don't mind." He was also a confirmed womanizer, and also led a double life with his secretary Frances Stevenson for 30 years before marrying her on the death of his wife. Miss Stevenson said of him:

> He is incapable of achieving anything without reducing all around him to nervous wrecks.

Lloyd George's power of invective was considerable, Margot Asquith saying: "He could not see a belt without hitting below it." Of the defeated Tories in 1906, he observed: "They died with their drawn salaries in their hands;" Lord Derby was "a harpooned walrus" who "like a cushion, always bore the imprint of the last man who sat on him"; and of Sir Herbert Samuel he remarked: "When they circumcised him, they threw away the wrong bit." Once when he called on Lord Beaverbrook and was told: "The Lord is out walking", he replied to the butler: "Ah, on the water, I suppose."

Elected MP for Caernarvon in 1890, he represented the seat for almost 55 years. He made his name leading the left wing of the Liberal Party against the BOER WAR, was appointed president of the Board of Trade by Campbell-Bannerman in 1906 and Chancellor of the Exchequer by ASQUITH in 1908. He laid the foundations of the WELFARE STATE with old age pensions and National Insurance, and his 1909 PEOPLE'S BUDGET prompted a constitutional clash with the HOUSE OF LORDS which led to curbs on its powers under the PARLIAMENT ACT of 1911. When war broke out, Lloyd George overcame his pacifist leanings, and in 1915 became Minister for Munitions and the next year Minister for War. His intrigues with the Conservatives at the close of that year brought the ousting of Asquith and a COALITION led by Lloyd George himself. This prosecuted the war with greater vigour but only ended it, with American help, after almost two more years of fighting. Lloyd George played a major role in the peace talks at VERSAILLES and at home won the COUPON ELECTION, but the Liberals lost ground and from now on he was dependent on Tory votes to stay in office. Then, with the CARLTON CLUB REVOLT of 1922, the Conservatives left the Coalition and won the ensuing election; the Liberals never held power again. Lloyd George, still involved in a feud with Asquith and under a shadow from the HONOURS SCANDAL, made several efforts to reunite and revive his party, most notably with the YELLOW BOOK of 1929. But like Churchill he became a voice in the wilderness; Harold Nicolson depicted him as "an old Rolls-Royce, backfiring and spluttering". At first receptive to Hitler's wiles, he later came out strongly against APPEASEMENT and gave Churchill critical support in the worst days of World War II.

> Of the three parties I find Labour least painful. My objection to the Tories is temperamental, and my objection to the Liberals is Lloyd George.
>
> BERTRAND RUSSELL.

> Lloyd George was greater than Churchill, and the greatest tribute to Churchill is that he recognized it.
>
> Sir WALTER ELLIOTT.

> He did not care in which direction the car was travelling, so long as he remained in the driver's seat.
>
> Lord BEAVERBROOK.

> He would have had a better rating in British mythology if he had shared the fate of Abraham Lincoln.
>
> JOHN GRIGG (Lord Altrincham).

liar A term which is UNPARLIAMENTARY in any legislature, but is nevertheless uttered both in debate and outside. The 18th-century playwright Richard Brinsley Sheridan tried to get round the prohibition with this apology:

> Mr. Speaker, I said the honourable gentleman was a liar it is true and I am sorry for it. The honourable member may place the punctuation where he pleases.

In the US Senate on 14 March 1925 Sen. Richard Ernst tried another tack, saying: "I wish to know if there be any way under the rules of the Senate whereby I can, without breaking those rules and without offending the senators about me, call a fellow member a wilful, malicious, wicked liar?" But Sen. Kenneth McKellar slipped the leash to describe the COLUMNIST Drew Pearson as

> An infamous liar, a revolting liar, a pusillanimous liar, a lying ass, a natural born liar, a liar by profession, a liar of living, a liar in the daytime, a liar in the night time, a dishonest, ignorant, corrupt and groveling crook.

Big Bill Thompson (1869–1944), Mayor of Chicago, had the ultimate answer to accusations of this kind. He once advised:

> If your opponent calls you a liar, call him a thief.

See also LIES.

Lib-Lab pact (1) A secret arrangement reached in 1903 by Herbert Gladstone for the LIBERALS and RAMSAY MACDonald for the infant Labour Representation Committee, to give LABOUR candidates a clear run in a limited number of seats provided the Liberals faced no Labour opposition in a far larger number. (2) The arrangement in 1977–78 under which James Callaghan's Labour government, which had lost its majority, remained in power through the support of David Steel's Liberals, who were consulted on major issues. Labour remained in power for several months after the Liberals terminated the pact, before being defeated on a no-CONFIDENCE vote.

Lib-Labs Labour representatives elected to Parliament on a Liberal platform before the foundation of the Labour Party in 1906. The Lib-Labs were dominant in working-class politics between 1860 and 1880. But economic instability and unemployment, growing CLASS CONSCIOUSNESS, the enfranchisement of manual workers in 1867 and 1884 and the failure of the Liberals to meet workers' aspirations led to the foundation of the Labour Representation Committee in February 1900. This officially became the Labour Party after the 1906 election; the last Lib-Lab MPs, together with the Miners' Federation which sponsored them, joined the Labour Party in 1909.

liberal (1) A person to the LEFT of centre who approves of state intervention in the economy, but opposes it on moral issues; also a pejorative for someone with a sentimental, charitable view of human nature, and even (as when used by George BUSH against Michael Dukakis in the 1988 Presidential election) a term of abuse. Ronald Reagan called liberalism "the L-word", and his Interior Secretary James Watt declared: "I never use the words Republican and Democrat. It's liberals and Americans." Definitions of a liberal include: "a man too broadminded to take his own side in a quarrel" – Robert Frost; "a man who is constantly being kicked in the teeth by the COMMIES and in the pants by the National Association of Manufacturers" – Anon.; "a conservative who's been mugged by reality" – Anon.; "a man who will give away everything he doesn't own" – Frank Dane.

> What the liberal really wants to bring about is change which will not in any way endanger his position.
>
> STOKELY CARMICHAEL (1941–).

> It is Hamlet-like torture to be truly liberal.
>
> LEONARD BERNSTEIN (1918–92).

> Liberals think that goats are just sheep from broken homes. MALCOLM BRADBURY and CHRISTOPHER BIGSBY.

> If God had been a liberal there would have been ten suggestions. *Ditto.*

> If optimism were a disease, they'd be immune for life.
>
> RONALD REAGAN.

> A liberal is a person who believes that water can be made to run uphill. A conservative is someone who believes everybody should pay for his water.
>
> THEODORE H. WHITE.

(2) Traditionally, a supporter of LAISSEZ-FAIRE, Free MARKET economic policies, now paradoxically on the Right of politics and generally opposed to political liberals.

liberal democracy The combination of representative democracy and the observance of fundamental human and civil rights which most Western nations would reckon to practise.

Liberal Democratic Party The party that has ruled Japan continuously since the country's political reconstruction after World War II. It is arguable whether it is either; it is an essentially conservative party, enmeshed with the country's business community, divided between a number of factions in which often-corrupt bosses exert PATRONAGE (*see* LOCKHEED SCANDAL; RECRUIT SCANDAL).

Liberal Democrats In Britain, the party formed from the merger in 1988 of most of the former LIBERAL PARTY and a majority of the SDP; for its first year it was known as the Social and Liberal Democrats (SLD). Under the leadership of Paddy Ashdown it recovered from abject poll ratings and humiliation by the GREEN Party in the 1989 Euro-elections to take 20 seats in 1992.

> Electoral support for them would be impressive only if it was measured on the Richter scale.
>
> NICHOLAS BENNETT MP (Con.).

> Labour is the music of dire straits. The Tories are the music of simple minds. But we are the new kids on the block.
>
> Liberal Democrat President CHARLES KENNEDY, 1991.

Liberal imperialists The Liberal MPs who in the late 19th century supported Britain's imperial expansion, without going so far as Joseph Chamberlain and realigning themselves with the Conservatives. Asquith, Edward Grey and R. B. Haldane were prominent in the late 1880s, but the most consistent Liberal Imperialist was Lord ROSEBERY, whose enthusiasm strained the party for over a decade after he resigned the leadership in 1896.

Liberal International The body representing Liberal parties from Britain, continental Europe, Canada and other nations where political liberalism is an organized force.

Liberal Party (1) The left-of-centre party which for almost a century from 1835 formed either Britain's government or the principal OPPOSITION. The party was born from the declining WHIGS and non-aligned MPs from a campaign (successful) to oust Manners Sutton, Tory Speaker of the Commons; the following year Liberal candidates made heavy gains in the first council elections since the reform of local government. But the division of loyalties into Liberal and Conservative only came about after PEEL split the Tory party in 1846, triggering a wholesale REALIGNMENT which took until 1859 to complete. Melbourne, Lord John (later Earl) Russell, Palmerston and Rosebery led the party before its great days under Gladstone, who served four times as Prime Minister between 1868 and 1894. Disraeli's Conservatives frequently outflanked the

Liberals as reformers, and the party became best known for Gladstone's enthusiasm for HOME RULE and its embodiment of the NONCONFORMIST CONSCIENCE. However after Lord Rosebery's failure as Prime Minister and the Liberals' split over Imperialism, Ulster and the BOER WAR, the party returned to power in 1905 under Campbell-Bannerman (*see* C-B) to begin a burst of reform unprecedented until ATTLEE's Labour government of 1945. Although ASQUITH, Prime Minister from 1908, stood firm against VOTES FOR WOMEN, he led the struggle to curb the powers of the HOUSE OF LORDS while Lloyd George (*see* L.G.) laid the foundations of the WELFARE STATE. Asquith continued in office with a makeshift coalition for the first two years of WORLD WAR I before Tory discontent with the conduct of the war installed Lloyd George in Downing Street – though Asquith continued as leader of the party. The struggle between the two weakened the Liberals before and after the break-up of the coalition in 1922, and with Labour breaking through to form a minority government in 1924 the Liberals slumped to third place – a position from which they never recovered. The party was reduced to just five MPs early in the 1950s, when the party was rumoured to hold its meetings in a telephone kiosk and Sir Gerald Nabarro (*see* NAB) called them "the shadow of a splinter". Revivals in the early 1960s (*see* ORPINGTON MAN), the early 1970s and (in conjunction with the SDP) the early 1980s gave fleeting hopes of a return to power; indeed from 1978 until 1979 the Liberals did have a stake in power through the LIB-LAB PACT. But after the collapse of the ALLIANCE in 1987 David Steel forced the amalgamation of the party with the SDP – leading to desertions from both before the LIBERAL DEMOCRATS emerged as a serious third force.

Every boy and every girl
That's born into this world alive
Is either a little Liberal
Or else a little Conservative. W. S. GILBERT, *Iolanthe*.

Liberalism has ever been a devotee of Mammon.
KEIR HARDIE.

There is nothing to be got by being a Liberal today. It is not a profitable or a remunerative career.
ASQUITH, 1920.

I am an English Liberal – I hate the Tory party – their men, their words and their methods.
WINSTON CHURCHILL, *c.* 1910.

So few and so futile. CHURCHILL, *c.* 1950.

The popularity of the Liberal Party is so low that they are considering employing Jacques Cousteau to see if anything can be done to resuscitate it.
AUSTIN MITCHELL MP (Lab.), *c.* 1976.

Dr. Barnardo's home for orphan voters.
GERRY NEALE MP (Con.).

Liberal Party (2) Australia's principal centre-right party, formed in 1944 by Sir Robert Menzies (*see* MING) in 1944 and the direct successor of the Liberal Party (1909–17), the Nationalist Party (1917–31) and the United Australia Party (1931–44). For more than half of its history it was led by two men: Menzies (until 1966) and Malcolm Fraser (1975–83). The Liberals have held power at COMMONWEALTH level from 1949 to 1967 (Menzies and Harold Holt), 1968–72 (John Gorton and William McMahon), and 1975–83 (Fraser) as well as frequently in the States. The party's Federal president Jim Forbes called it "a loose confederation of autonomous divisions"; the Labor Prime Minister Paul Keating was blunter, terming the Liberals "perfumed gigolos" and saying:

They wouldn't know a fiscal policy if it got up and bit them on the arse.

Liberal Party (3) One of Canada's two great parties, slightly left of centre though at times more radical. It began to emerge *c.* 1849 and coalesced as GRITS, ROUGES and Reformers amalgamated into a national movement in time for Alexander Mackenzie to lead it to power from 1873 to 1878. (Sir) Wilfrid Laurier led a Liberal government 1896–1911 before being defeated over RECIPROCITY with the United States. After Laurier's death in 1919 William Mackenzie King took charge, serving three times as Prime Minister between 1921 and 1948; the Statute of WESTMINSTER determining the future shape of the COMMONWEALTH was largely his work, and his contacts with President Roosevelt proved crucial to the Allied effort in World War II. Louis St.-Laurent took over from King, serving nine years as Prime Minister before the Liberals' defeat in 1957. The experienced diplomatist Lester Pearson (1963–8) came to power without a majority just as Quebec SEPARATISM was starting to stir, and the status and restlessness of French Canada dogged Pierre TRUDEAU, the Liberals' most charismatic leader, throughout his Premiership from 1968 until 1979; he held out for "One Canada" and faced down the separatists. Trudeau announced his resignation after his electoral defeat, then came back and ousted the Tories in 1980 after only a few months; he finally retired from politics in 1984, shortly after which the Liberals under John Turner were ousted.

The flying saucers of politics. No one can make head or tail of them and they are never twice seen in the same place. JOHN DIEFENBAKER.

The Liberals talk about a stable government, but we don't know how bad the stable is going to smell.

NDP leader TOMMY DOUGLAS, 1965.

Liberal Party (4) In New York City and state, a grouping which normally sides with the Democrats but occasionally endorses liberal Republican candidates, giving a critical boost if the contest is tight.

Liberal Unionists The 93 Liberal MPs at Westminster who, led by Joseph Chamberlain, voted against Gladstone's first HOME RULE Bill in June 1886, confirming the split in the party over Ireland. Many eventually moved over to sit with the Conservatives, who have officially been known ever since as the Conservative and UNIONIST Party.

National Liberals *See* NATIONAL.

White liberal In America and South Africa, a white person who strongly opposes racial discrimination – sometimes also lamenting that cheap Black domestic help is hard to find. The term is often used as a pejorative – both by right-wingers who feel many White liberals can afford to take such a stance because they live in comfortable all-White surroundings, and by Black militants who doubt their commitment and sincerity.

A man who tosses worms into the river – all the fish who take him for a friend, and think that worm's got no hooks in it, usually end up in the frying pan. MALCOLM X.

The strange death of Liberal England The title of a book (1923) by George Dangerfield which examined how the party which provided a reforming government with a large Parliamentary majority up to 1910 could within 13 years be in terminal decline. The phrase has stuck in the vocabulary of British politics; Roy Jenkins (*see* WOY) reminded Liberals and Social Democrats of it during the euphoric days of the ALLIANCE.

Liberalism A term variously used for the philosophy of both political and economic liberals, and of the various liberal parties. Gladstone described it as "trust of the people tempered by prudence", the poet Stephen Spender as "politics without ideology", and Harry Roskolenko as "the first refuge of political indifference and the last refuge of leftists".

Ultraliberalism today translates into a whimpering isolationism in foreign policy, a mulish obstructionism in domestic policy, and a pusillanimous pussyfooting on the crucial issue of law and order.

Vice-President SPIRO G. AGNEW.

New Liberalism The reforming, CORPORATIST and WELFARIST creed adopted by leading Liberals, especially Lloyd George, during the party's final period of governing alone, from 1905 to 1914.

liberation The freeing of any country or people from enemy occupation, and specifically the ousting of German forces from occupied France by the Allies (including the FREE FRENCH) in 1944.

liberation theology The religious teaching of radical Catholic clergy in Latin America, with its emphasis on social reform through Christ's commitment to liberate the oppressed. It is seen by right-wing military regimes as synonymous with support for Marxist guerrillas; the idea that the way they are governing is morally indefensible frequently does not occur to them.

Liberator, the The newspaper published by William Lloyd Garrison in Boston from 1831 which gave a powerful voice to the campaign for the abolition of slavery. Garrison's message, welcomed enthusiastically by his largely Black readership, was that only extirpation of the sin of slavery would be acceptable to God. But his insistence on campaigning for every kind of reform and his refusal to compromise caused friction with many who could have advanced his basic cause.

libertarianism Devotion to both personal and economic freedom, with no interference by the state in either personal life or the MARKET. Libertarianism was an influential force in the 1980s, especially on the Reagan administration which was open to radical ultra-conservative ideas; Margaret Thatcher's strong opposition to moral freedoms limited its impact within her Conservative Party, though a small faction did press for decriminalization of most drugs.

liberty. Liberty AND union, now and forever, one and inseparable! The peroration of the speech by Daniel Webster (1782–1852) to the US Senate on 26 January 1830, endeavouring to defuse the permanent conflict between advocates of a strong UNION and campaigners for STATES' RIGHTS. It was delivered over two days as the climax to debate on a proposal from Samuel Foote of Massachusetts to keep Western lands vacant until those nearer the East Coast had been fully occupied. This was seen as a YANKEE centralist ploy against the independence of the States. Robert Y. Hayne denounced Foote, with the slogan **Liberty first and Union afterwards**. But Webster's speech hitting back was immediately recognised as a classic.

Liberty! Equality! Fraternity! (Fr. *Liberté! Egalité! Fraternité!*) The motto of the FRENCH REVOLUTION and subsequently of France's Republican state. It goes back at least to a resolution passed by the *Club des Cordeliers* (Ropemakers' Club) on 30 June 1793, which concluded: "Unity, the indivisibility of the Republic, Liberty, Equality, Fraternity or death!" The words "or death" were dropped in 1795.

> At its birth the Republic gave voice to three words: Liberty! Equality! Fraternity! If Europe is wise and just, each of these words signifies peace.
>
> ALPHONSE DE LAMARTINE (1790–1869).

Liberty Bell The bell commissioned by Pennsylvania to mark the 50th anniversary in 1751 of William Penn's Charter of Privileges, which became the fundamental law of the colony until Independence. It was rung on 8 July 1776, along with many others, to announce the Declaration of INDEPENDENCE, and has been known as the Liberty Bell since about 1839. The name comes from the Biblical inscription it carries: **"Proclaim liberty throughout the land unto all the inhabitants thereof"** (Leviticus XXV, 10). The bell, now with a sizable crack in one side, is housed in a pavilion close to Philadelphia's Independence Hall. When Queen Elizabeth II paid her Bicentennial visit to the cradle of American Independence, the greatest talking-point was whether or not she actually touched the bell; the author was present and did not see. The Queen also presented a replica bell whose inscription "Let freedom ring" drew complaints from Fundamentalists who claimed the Bible was being slighted.

Liberty Bill The name given by supporters to William Lemke, a Republican Congressman from North Dakota who ran for the Presidency in 1932 for the right-wing agrarian populist Union Party. The play on words was unfortunate, as critics pointed out that the Liberty Bell was also cracked. Upstaged on the stump by the RADIO PRIEST Fr. Charles E. Coughlin and the Louisiana populist Rev. Gerald L. K. Smith, Lemke nevertheless polled 882,479 votes.

Liberty Lobby One of the most vocal and influential ultra-conservative pressure groups in Washington, founded by Curtis B. Dall in 1955; it has campaigned against higher taxes, CIVIL RIGHTS legislation, public housing, farm subsidies, FOREIGN AID, US participation in the UNITED NATIONS, and cancellation of ARMS CONTROL agreements.

Liberty's in every blow/Let us do or die The stirring call to arms penned by Robert Burns (1759–1796) in his verse *Scots, Wha Hae* (Robert Bruce's March to Bannockburn). Though the battle in question was fought by the Scots against the English, Burns's slogan has come to represent his passionate belief in the dignity and equality of mankind.

Eternal vigilance is the price of liberty These exact words were uttered by Wendell Phillips in 1852 and have been attributed to Thomas JEFFERSON. But in 1790 the Irish politician John Philpot Curran told the PRIVY COUNCIL:

> The condition upon which God hath given liberty to man is eternal vigilance.

Give me liberty or give me death! The phrase with which Patrick Henry (1736–99) is said to have ended his speech to the Virginia Convention in Richmond on 23 March 1775. Urging Virginians to reject compromise and take up arms in the revolutionary war, Henry is supposed to have said:

> Why stand we here idle? What is it that gentlemen wish? What would they have? Is life so dear, or peace so sweet, as to be purchased at the price of chains and slavery? Forbid it, Almighty God! – I know not what course others may take; but as for me, give me liberty, or give me death!

No note of the speech was taken, and the text as now quoted was reconstructed 42 years after the event by Henry's biographer William Wirt. Henry's speech was certainly dramatic but, tellingly, "Give me liberty or give me death!" did not become a household phrase until after Wirt's book was published in 1817.

Let every nation know, whether it wishes us well or ill, that we shall pay any price, bear any burden, meet any hardship, support any friend, oppose any foe to assure the survival and success of liberty One of the key phrases from the INAUGURAL address of President KENNEDY, on 20 January 1961, and one of the seven inscriptions carved on the walls by his grave in ARLINGTON NATIONAL CEMETERY.

life, liberty and the pursuit of happiness The "inalienable rights" of human beings spelt out in America's Declaration of INDEPENDENCE by Thomas JEFFERSON and others.

Oh Liberty! Oh Liberty! What crimes are committed in thy name! (Fr. *O liberté! O liberté! Que de crimes on commet en ton nom!*) The last words of the French revolutionary Mme. Marie Roland (1754–93) as she mounted the steps of the guillotine for her own execution during the Reign of TERROR.

The tree of liberty must be refreshed from time to time with the blood of patriots and tyrants. It is natural manure An unexpectedly bloodthirsty declaration from Thomas JEFFERSON, in a letter to W. S. Smith on 13 November 1787.

Sons of Liberty The society formed by Massachusetts tradesmen which led the protest through Britain's American colonies against the STAMP ACT of 1764, and became one of the moving forces of the AMERICAN REVOLUTION. As well as encouraging political action, the Sons of Liberty egged on the mob, partly for, partly to forestall smuggling charges faced by some of the "Loyal Nine" who founded the movement.

> They are of the opinion that no-one is entitled to riot but themselves. ANON. British officer, *c.* 1766.

The movement spread from colony to colony until it held power in 11 out of 13, but with Massachusetts under Samuel Adams firmly in the lead. Once independence was declared, the name became synonymous with the patriotic movement as a whole; the Sons of Liberty were later cited as the inspiration for America's WHIG party.

Libyan bombing The bombing raid on 14 April 1986 by American aircraft against the Libyan capital of Tripoli, in reprisal for alleged Libyan involvement in the bombing of a West Berlin disco used by US troops. The raid, carried out by planes from Upper Heyford near Oxford, caused widespread damage and killed a number of people including one of Colonel Gaddafi's children; President Reagan denied that Gaddafi himself was the target but US officials privately insisted he was. The planes flew from Britain by a circuitous route because other Western countries, notably France, refused to allow their facilities or air space to be used; it provoked a political storm in London – where it was seen as Margaret Thatcher's "thank you" to Reagan for help during the FALKLANDS war – as well as in Washington.

lie. lies As with LIAR above, the term is UNPARLIAMENTARY. In 1867 Rep. John Hunter was censured by the House of Representatives for saying of another's comments: "So far as I am concerned, it is a base lie." Winston CHURCHILL was more clever, getting away in the Commons with a rejoinder to one of Aneurin BEVAN's speeches that "I should think it hardly possible to state the opposite of the truth with more precision". *See also* TERMINOLOGICAL INEXACTITUDE.

> *Pitt the Younger:* If I cannot speak standing, I will speak sitting. And if I cannot speak sitting, I will speak lying.
> *Lord North:* Which he will do in whatever position he speaks.

lie detector *See* SCREENING.

Big Lie The basis, on his own admission, of the appeal of Hitler and his NAZI party to large sections of the German public. In MEIN KAMPF he wrote:

> In the big lie, there is always a certain force of credibility. In the primitive simplicity of their minds, the great masses of the people will more easily fall victim to a big lie than to a small one.

A lie can be halfway round the world before the truth has got its boots on A phrase widely credited to James Callaghan (*see* SUNNY JIM) after he used it in a speech on 1 November 1976, but in fact originated by the 19th-century Baptist preacher the Rev. C. H. Spurgeon.

I'll never tell a lie The promise made to the American people by the born-again Baptist Jimmy CARTER during his 1976 campaign for the Presidency. Though his single term was widely rated a failure at the time, it was a promise he came close to keeping.

If they stop telling lies about me, I'll stop telling the truth about them Perhaps the best one-liner in politics, it is the reversal of a statement by Sen. Chauncey Depew (1834–1928):

> If you will refrain from telling any lies about the Republican Party, I'll promise not to tell the truth about the Democrats.

It was refined by the Democratic Presidential nominee Adlai Stevenson, who said in Fresno, California, on 10 September 1952:

> I offer my opponents a bargain. If they will stop telling falsehoods about us, I will stop telling the truth about them.

In time of war truth is so precious, it must be attended by a bodyguard of lies Winston Churchill's justification for the conduct of BLACK PROPAGANDA during wartime.

The rulers of states are the only ones who should have the privilege of lying, either at home or abroad; they may be allowed to lie for the good of the state Plato's assertion, in Book II of *The Republic*, of what is now termed the RIGHT TO LIE.

There are lies, damned lies and statistics The dismissive assessment of statistics, now applied even more so to UK Treasury forecasts, which Mark Twain put forward in his autobiography, attributing it to Disraeli.

Lieutenant-Governor (1) In America, the deputy to the GOVERNOR of a state. (2) In Canada, the appointed representative of the Federal government in each PROVINCE.

life wasn't meant to be easy A cliché widely heard in the late 1970s after its use by the Australian Prime Minister Malcolm Fraser, in reference to his government's situation. What Fraser actually told his LIBERAL PARTY in 1977 was:

> It occurred to me that there are times when life is a little easier than it's meant to be.

light. light at the end of the tunnel A widely-used phrase in the early 1980s for the first indications of economic recovery (*see also* GREEN SHOOTS). By the end of the decade cynics were pointing out that the light might turn out to be another train heading straight for the watcher.

light on the hill The oft-quoted objective of the Australian LABOR PARTY, introduced in a speech by J. B. Chifley in 1949. It is synonymous with "light at the end of the tunnel", but also echoed Ronald Reagan's subsequent CITY ON THE HILL. In Australia at least, it acquired a particular relevance to Socialism, and became a standard phrase in the repertory of the movement's leaders. It represents the ideal that no person should be deprived of the hope of improving his or her lot.

Likud The right-wing and aggressively nationalist movement which, under first Menachem Begin and then Itzhak Shamir, governed Israel outright from 1977 until 1984, and in coalition until 1992. Formed in 1973, its main component was the *Gahal* bloc, comprising the *Herut* (Freedom) Party, which formally emerged in Israel's independence year of 1948, and the Liberal Party, a 1961 amalgamation of the former general ZIONIST and Progressive parties.

Limehouse Declaration The statement of aims issued on 25 January 1981 by the GANG OF FOUR who were soon to found Britain's SDP, after a meeting at Dr. David OWEN's home in Limehouse, on the north bank of the Thames in London's Docklands. They said:

> The calamitous outcome of the Labour Party's Wembley conference [entrusting the choice of a party leader to an electoral college] demands a new start in British politics. . . . We propose to set up a Council for Social Democracy. . . . We believe that the need for a realignment of British politics must now be faced. . . .

Limehousing A once-common term for violent abuse of one's political opponents; from a speech by Lloyd George at Limehouse on 30 July 1909 when he poured scorn and abuse on dukes, landlords, financial magnates, *etc.*

limousine liberal A derogatory term for a person with liberal leanings but an opulent lifestyle. The implication is that it is easy to have soft, humane views when one is being driven in comfort by a chauffeur. The phrase was invented by Mario Proccacino, the conservative Democrat defeated in 1969 by New York's liberal Republican Mayor John Lindsay. Its UK counterpart is **champagne socialist**.

Lincoln, Abraham (1809–65), 16th President of the United States (Republican, 1861–65). Perhaps America's greatest President, who led the UNION through the CIVIL WAR to victory over the CONFEDERACY, EMANCIPATING the slaves, and was assassinated before he could settle the peace. Born in Kentucky of poor frontier stock (*see* LOG CABIN TO WHITE HOUSE; RAIL-SPLITTER), he was raised in Illinois; his cousin Dennis Hanks said: "If you heard him fellin' trees in a clearing you would say that there was three men at work by the way the trees fell." As a young man he combined practising law with politics, starting his very first campaign speech: "Fellow-citizens, I believe you all know who I am." His law partner William Herndon recalled: "Politics were his life, newspapers his food and his great ambition his motive power." He became a WHIG Congressman in 1846, opposing the MEXICAN WAR; returning all but 75¢ of $200 given by the party for the campaign, he said:

> I did not need the money. I made the canvass on my own horse, my entertainment being at the houses of friends cost me nothing, and my only outlay was 75c for a barrel of cider, which some farmhands insisted I should TREAT them to.

Lincoln quit after one term when his ambitions were thwarted, but returned to politics as an opponent of slavery and the KANSAS-NEBRASKA ACT; he lost narrowly in an 1855 Senate race, and again in 1858 when he challenged Sen. Stephen Douglas, author of the Act. Lincoln characterized Douglas as "as thin as the homeopathic soup that was made by boiling the shadow of a pigeon that had been starved to death". Despite his defeat, his craggy looks and the drama of his DEBATES with Douglas up and down the state made him a national figure. Lincoln said:

> Nobody ever expected me to be President. In my poor, lean, lank face nobody has ever seen any cabbages sprouting.

Indeed he was christened the ILLINOIS BABOON, and the Republicans who nominated him in 1860 said: "We know old Abe does not look very handsome, but if all the ugly men in the US vote for him, he will surely be elected." He was also taciturn, his campaign manager David Davis reckoning him "the most reticent, secretive man I ever saw or expect to see". But he already had the command of words he showed in the GETTYSBURG ADDRESS, reputedly saying:

> I know there is a God, and he hates injustice and slavery. I see the storm coming, and I know that His hand is in it. If he has a place and work for me – and I think he has – I am ready.

In the campaign, dominated by Southern threats to secede from the Union, Lincoln carried all Northern states to be elected with just under 40% of the vote; his old foe Douglas was well behind. He told his hometown voters:

> My friends, I now leave, not knowing when, or whether, I may return, with a task before me greater than that

which rested upon Washington. Without the assistance of that Divine Being, who ever attended him, I cannot succeed. With its assistance, I cannot fail.

As soon as Lincoln was confirmed by the ELECTORAL COLLEGE, South Carolina seceded and the Civil War began. The new President declared: "I believe in the providence of the most men, the largest purse and the longest cannon." Lincoln manoeuvred the South into firing the first shots at FORT SUMTER, then welded together a credible war machine while leaving options open for reconciliation in the future. His slowness in acting against slavery upset many ABOLITIONISTS, Frederick Douglass terming him "the slow coach at Washington". To Wendell Phillips he was "a huckster in politics – a first-rate second-rate man", while Richard Henry Dana noted: "In Washington, the most striking thing is the absence of personal loyalty to the President. It does not exist. He has no admirers, no enthusiastic supporters, none to bet on his head." The following January Maryland's Sen. Willard Saulsbury declared:

I never did see or converse with so weak and imbecile a man as Abraham Lincoln, President of the United States.

The war was a long haul and the combination of reverses and heavy casualties – and his wife Mary's extravagance – brought Lincoln plenty of criticism; the *New York Herald* called him "a joke incarnate". He admitted to setbacks, saying: "I claim not to have controlled events, but confess plainly that events have controlled me." But he told supporters in 1863: "It is my ambition and desire to so administer the affairs of the government while I remain President that if at the end I have lost every other friend on earth, I shall at least have one friend remaining and that one shall be down inside me." But he also confessed: "All my life I have been a fatalist."

By the time he sought re-election in 1864 the war was nearing its end, but war fatigue in the North prompted a COPPERHEAD campaign from the Democrats, who fielded General George McClellan, to whom Lincoln had once written: "If you don't want to use the army, I should like to borrow it for a while." He won re-election as Union forces moved in for the kill, and six weeks after Lincoln's second inauguration the war was over; in his last speech on 11 April 1865 after Lee's surrender, he said: "We meet this evening not in sorrow, but in gladness of heart." Three days later he was shot at FORD'S THEATRE in Washington, where he had gone to celebrate the end of the war; his assassin, John Wilkes Booth, declared:

Our country owes all her troubles to him, and God simply made me the instrument of His punishment.

Lincoln's assassination stunned the world. Thomas d'Arcy McGee declared: "Never yet did the assassin's knife reach the core of a cause or the heart of a principle," while George P. A. Healey noted of its political consequences: "With his death the possibility of peace with magnanimity died." In the 1950s the episode coined the sick question: "Apart from that, Mrs. Lincoln, how did you enjoy the play?"

Now he belongs to the ages.
Secretary of War EDWIN STANTON at Lincoln's bedside.

He was the greatest character since Christ.
Lincoln's personal secretary JOHN HAY.

Not so often in the story of mankind does a man arrive on earth who is both steel and velvet, as hard as rock and soft as drifting fog, who holds in his heart and mind the paradox of terrible storm and peace unspeakable and perfect. CARL SANDBURG (1878–1967).

The cruellest thing to happen to Lincoln since being shot has been to fall into the hands of Carl Sandburg.
EDMUND WILSON.

Here we have the overall philosophy of Lincoln: in all things which deal with people, be liberal, be human. In all those things which deal with the people's money or their economy, be conservative – and don't be afraid to use the word. DWIGHT D. EISENHOWER, 1954.

In this temple
as in the hearts of the people
for whom he saved the Union
The memory of Abraham Lincoln
is enshrined forever.

ROYAL CORTISSOZ (1869–1948), inscription above the statute on the Lincoln Memorial, Washington DC.

Lincoln's ten points A list of rules for living attributed to Lincoln but not traced back before the 1940s. The first is: "You cannot bring about prosperity by discouraging thrift."

Lincoln Room and Bed The former Cabinet Room on the second floor of the WHITE HOUSE which President Truman fitted out with bedroom furniture from Lincoln's time. The imposing rosewood bed was bought by Mrs. Lincoln in 1861. The room is now used as a guest room for friends of the President's family; Sir Winston Churchill and Queen Juliana of the Netherlands both reckoned to have seen Lincoln's ghost when staying there.

Abraham Lincoln Brigade The band of American volunteers, frequently but not always correctly branded as Communists, who fought on the Republican side against Franco in the SPANISH CIVIL WAR.

line. line by line The Westminster term for the consideration a Bill receives during its COMMITTEE STAGE, with detailed, exhaustive and sometimes excessive discussion of the text.

line of route The course followed by parties shown round the Palace of WESTMINSTER by official guides.

linkage A compromise in which progress in solving one problem is made dependent on comparable progress over another. It was much relied on by Henry KISSINGER during international negotiations in the 1970s. One recent example was Saddam Hussein's effort during the GULF WAR to make his withdrawal from Kuwait conditional on the establishment of an independent Palestinian state.

> The two countries [America and the Soviet Union] also offered to work together for peace between Arabs and Israelis after the war ends. Mr. Bessmertnykh [Soviet foreign minister] denied that there was "linkage" between the two issues. *The Times*, 30 January 1991.

lion. Lion of Judah The title of Haile Selassie (1892–1975), emperor of Ethiopia from 1930 to 1974 except for the years of the Italian occupation (1936–41) during which he lived in exile in the UK. In 1974 he was opposed by a military coup and Ethiopia was declared a Socialist republic (*see* DERGUE). Rastafarians regard him as the Messiah, the incarnation of God; the name "Rastafarian" comes from his real name, *Ras Tafari Mekonnen*. He assumed the title *Haile Selassie*, meaning "Might of the Trinity", on becoming emperor. The lion is the emblem of the tribe of Judah, Christ sometimes being referred to as "the lion of the tribe of Judah".

I was not the lion. But I supplied the roar CHURCHILL's characterization of his role in rallying the British people in World War II. His actual words, from his speech at Westminster on his 80th birthday (30 November 1954), were:

> It was the nation and the race dwelling all round the globe that had the lion's heart. I had the luck to be called on to give the roar.

liquidation A euphemism used by Communist and other TOTALITARIAN regimes for the execution or murder of their political opponents – frequently members of the governing party who are considered a threat.

liquorice allsorts Clement ATTLEE's nickname for Conservatives and Liberals who joined forces, standing down for each other in certain constituencies in 1950 to keep Labour out. In both Bolton and Huddersfield, the arrangement led to one Liberal and one Tory MP being elected; the Liberals repudiated it before the 1964 election and lost both seats.

list system A system of election in which each party produces a national or regional list of candidates, and SEATS are allocated from the top downwards according to the share of votes the parties receive. Some supporters of PROPORTIONAL REPRESENTATION commend it as reflecting the overall wishes of the electorate; others, and supporters of FIRST PAST THE POST, reject it because there is no link between the elected member and a CONSTITUENCY.

little. little Ben One of the nicknames of Benjamin Harrison (1833–1901), 23rd President of the United States (Republican, 1889–93). The cigar-chewing, deeply religious former Civil War general stood only 5 ft. 6 ins. (*See also* WHITE HOUSE KEBERG).

Little Black Banda The derogatory nickname for Dr. Hastings Banda (1905–), Prime Minister of Malawi from 1963 and President from 1966, bestowed by David Frost in THAT WAS THE WEEK THAS WAS. It was patterned on *Little Black Sambo*, a character in a children's story now considered racially offensive.

Little Englanders Originally those late Victorian Liberals opposed to the IMPERIALISM of Lord ROSEBERY, the term has come to apply to anyone who considers that Britain has no international role. Margaret Thatcher was accused of being a "Little Englander" by Tories and others who resented her lack of enthusiasm for the EUROPEAN COMMUNITY.

Little Entente The political alliance formed between Czechoslovakia, Yugoslavia and Romania in 1920–22 to prevent the restoration of Habsburg power, which later became broader in scope.

Little Giant The nickname of Sen. Stephen Douglas (1813–61), author of the KANSAS-NEBRASKA ACT, who in 1858 defeated Abraham LINCOLN to retain his Illinois seat in the Senate after an epic series of DEBATES; Lincoln in fact polled a larger popular vote. Two years later Douglas ran against Lincoln for the Presidency, but pro-slavery Southern Democrats ensured his defeat by nominating Vice-President John C. Breckinridge to split the anti-Republican vote.

> Douglas can never be President, Sir. His legs are too short, Sir. His coat, like a cow's tail, hangs too near the ground, Sir. Sen. THOMAS HART BENTON (1782–1851).

little local difficulty The phrase used by Harold Macmillan (*see* SUPERMAC) on 7 January 1958 to describe the resignation of the entire team of Treasury Ministers – Peter Thorneycroft, Chancellor of the Exchequer, Enoch POWELL and Nigel Birch – in protest against increases in public spending they considered imprudent; it was often cited as an instance of his unflappability. They resigned as Macmillan was about to start a six-week Commonealth tour; instead of cancelling to restore his government's equilibrium, he went ahead with the trip, saying at Heathrow Airport:

> I thought the best thing to do was to settle up these little

local difficulties, and then turn to the wider vision of the Commonwealth.

Little Magician One of many nicknames for President Martin van Buren (*see* OLD KINDERHOOK). He earned it from the skill with which he organized the Republican Party in New York State during the ALBANY REGENCY.

Little Red Book The collected Quotations of CHAIRMAN MAO Tse-Tung, which was originally produced in 1964 for the INDOCTRINATION of China's RED ARMY, then appeared in a regular edition in 1965. The pocket-sized book, bound in bright red plastic, contained a collection of political quotations, homilies and aphorisms collected from Mao's writings over the years and designed to stimulate revolutionary awareness. It became a familiar sight during the upheavals of the CULTURAL REVOLUTION, when it was brandished aloft by zealous RED GUARDS and workers as they heeded Mao's call to root out REVISIONISTS among the bureaucratic and intellectual elite. It also enjoyed a vogue among student radicals and the NEW LEFT in Europe and America. *See* Political POWER grows from the barrel of a gun.

Little Rock State Capital of Arkansas, and scene in September 1957 of a confrontation between 500 paratroops sent in by President Eisenhower and the SEGREGATIONIST Governor Orval Faubus, who had used the NATIONAL GUARD to prevent nine Black students attending the previously all-White Central High School. Faubus withdrew the National Guard in response to a court order, but a mob of taunting Whites kept the Black children out until Eisenhower reluctantly ordered in the troops. For the entire academic year the eight students who continued to attend were guarded by troops – then the school was closed. The incident was decisive in speeding school desegregation in the Deep South and changing White attitudes; 35 years later another Governor of Arkansas, Bill Clinton, (*see* COMEBACK KID) was elected President with the backing of most Black voters.

Lizard of Oz The nickname bestowed by the *Sun* on **Paul Keating** (1944–), Prime Minister of Australia (Labor) from 1991, in February 1992 after one of a series of attacks on the country's British connections. It is a play on the old film title *Wizard of Oz*; ironically the *Sun*'s Australian-born owner, Rupert Murdoch, shared Keating's republican views. Keating, descended from rebel Irish stock, had told the Parliamentary Opposition:

> I learned about self-respect and self-regard for Australia, not about some cultural cringe to a country which decided not to defend the Malaysian peninsula, not to give us our troops back to keep ourselves free from Japanese domination. This was the country that you wedded yourselves to. Even as they walked out on you and joined the COMMON MARKET, you were looking for your MBEs and your knighthoods.

Keating, who succeeded Robert Hawke (*see* SILVER BODGIE) after eight years as Federal Treasurer (deputy prime minister from 1990), raised eyebrows by pressing for Australia to become a republic and through his sometimes UNPARLIAMENTARY language; Robert Hill, Opposition leader in the Senate, termed him "the most offensive prime minister in Australia's history". On 4 November 1992 a Senate majority CENSUREd him for "references to individuals as scumbags, scum, suckers, thugs, dimwits, swill, a pigsty, fools and incompetents, perfumed gigolos and stupid foul-mouthed grubs". Keating described the censure as the act of "pansies". Keating, a cultured man able to deliver a passable university lecture on the history of art, said of himself:

> I am the Placido Domingo of Australian politics.

In March 1993 Keating retained power in his own right, leading Labor to a decisive victory over the Liberals under John Hewson.

Lloyd George Fund The controversial fund established and personally controlled by **David Lloyd George** (*see* L.G.) as Prime Minister (1916–22) to finance a Liberal Party organization loyal to him after his split with Asquith, who remained party leader. His blatant use of the honours system to reward wealthy contributors to the fund without regard to their personal reputations or philanthropic credentials in other spheres of public life provoked the HONOURS SCANDAL of 1922. A commission of inquiry was set up to investigate the propriety of Lloyd George's administration of the fund; his refusal to relinquish control of it contributed to the downfall of his coalition government.

Lloyd George knew my father Every Welshman's facetious claim to fame, and an Englishman's self-deprecating hint at a murky past; also one of the best-known (and cleanest) songs sung by rugby clubs. The saying was heard even during the lifetime of the Welsh ex-Premier, who died in 1945. Its reputed originator was Tommy Rhys Roberts QC (1910–75), of whom it was literally true as his father, Arthur Rhys Roberts, had set up a solicitor's practice with Lloyd George in London in 1897. Tommy Rhys Roberts used to sing the lines "Lloyd George knew my father, father knew Lloyd George" to the hymn tune *Onward Christian Soldiers* at the close of speeches at circuit dinners, and Welsh rugby clubs and Liberal assemblies took it up.

The phrase also became the name of a play by William Douglas Home, first performed in London in 1972.

Loans scandal The political storm surrounding Gough WHITLAM's Australian government in 1975 which gave the Opposition a pretext to block SUPPLY and bring it down. It concerned two attempts to borrow in the Middle East to bolster Australia's fragile economic position. The first loan, for up to US$4 billion, was to have been negotiated by the Minerals and Energy Minister Francis X. Connor; Treasury officials objected and it apparently was not proceeded with. Then, on 6 March 1975 the Executive Council authorized Jim Cairns, the Federal Treasurer, to borrow US$500 million overseas; Cairns gave George Harris, a Melbourne businessman, power to act as an intermediary in return for a commission. Cairns denied to Parliament that a letter in these terms existed, and when Whitlam found that it did, he sacked Cairns. It then emerged that Connor, three days after his authority to negotiate had been revoked, had received and responded to a telex from Tirath Khemlani, a "fixer" with Mafia connections in the US, on progress in arranging the original loan. Amid immense unfavourable press coverage, Whitlam concluded that Connor had also misled Parliament by stating that the negotiations were at an end, and asked him too to resign. Within a month Whitlam himself had gone, with the KERR SACKING.

> Inspired by the purest and most benevolent motives, but executed secretly, deviously and with astonishing incompetence. BLANCHE D'ALPUGET.

lobby (1) The entrance-hall through which members of a legislature must pass to enter the Chamber. (2) A pressure group for a particular policy, tax break or course of action. To lobby means to press one's case with legislators by whatever means one can; when the evangelist Billy Graham set up an office in Washington, he declared: "I just want to lobby for God." *See also* LOBBYIST *below*.

> The most effective lobbies on Capitol Hill have always been the ones that played most skilfully to the Congressmen's egos. WILLIAM GREIDER.

(3) **The lobby** The informal and semi-secret organization of journalists at WESTMINSTER – now some 130 strong – which since 1884 has held regular meetings with Downing Street spokesmen, Ministers and Opposition leaders at which they are given information on a non-attributable basis. Criticized by some as a means of NEWS MANAGEMENT, its success hinges on a combination of mutual trust and a readiness by members to ask tough questions and get them answered. At one point in Harold WILSON's last premiership NUMBER TEN halted the briefings, claiming the Lobby could not be trusted; its members had in fact seen through a deliberate attempt to mislead them. In the late 1980s the *Guardian*, the *Independent* and the *Scotsman* boycotted lobby meetings for a time in protest at only being permitted to quote "Downing Street sources". The group's name is taken from the Members' LOBBY, where members of it are permitted to stand except when a DIVISION is in progress to talk with politicians – on the understanding nothing is said for quotation.

> An extremely secret organization that everyone at Westminster knows about. GERALD KAUFMAN.

> Representatives of the Press accredited by the Speaker to patrol the corridors of power. STEPHEN KOSS.

> The golden thread in Britain's Parliamentary democracy. HAROLD WILSON.

lobby fodder A derogatory term at Westminster for MPs who show no individualism, and can automatically be relied on to vote for their party no matter how misguided the policy.

lobby room The room, in a turret atop the Palace of Westminster, where the Lobby meets daily with the Prime Minister's press secretary when Parliament is sitting to run through the day's political timetable and ascertain new twists in Government policy and thinking. On four days a week, there is also a morning meeting in the front parlour of NUMBER TEN. On Friday afternoon there is a special session for Sunday newspapermen, at which tea is served.

central lobby The *Rialto* of the Palace of Westminster, the crossroads midway between the Commons' and Lords' chambers where members of the public gather, and wait to meet their MPs. On one side of the ornately-decorated hall is a post office; on another the entrance to the STRANGERS' GALLERY.

clear the lobbies! At Westminster, the cry of the Speaker on calling a DIVISION in the House of Commons.

division lobbies The corridors on either side of both Chambers at Westminster, and in many other legislatures, through which members pass during a DIVISION to have their votes recorded by the TELLERS.

Liberty Lobby *See* LIBERTY.

mass lobby At Westminster, an organized visit by hundreds or even thousands of people exercising their democratic right to see their member of Parliament, as a means of pressing a particular case – for example, for Third World development. The mass lobby has evolved as a weapon because it provides contact with individual MPs – and because demonstrations as such are banned from the PRECINCTS OF THE HOUSE.

Members' Lobby The lobby at the entrance to the House of Commons chamber at Westminster; members pass through the CHURCHILL ARCH to enter it. It is dominated by life-size bronze statues of Churchill, Lloyd George (L.G.) and ATTLEE, MPs of their respective parties touching their toe-caps for luck, Churchill's being the shiniest. Doors from it lead to all three WHIPS' OFFICES, and the VOTE OFFICE is next to the arch. The lobby, to which only MPs, lobby journalists and officers of the House are admitted, is guarded by two police officers at the "public" end and two BADGE MESSENGERS beneath the arch. The lobby is at its most animated just after a DIVISION, when MPs who have come in for the vote catch up with each other, or buttonhole Ministers they have been trying to reach.

> Benign and yet menacing, she would stalk through the lobby, one arm weighted with the heavy satchel which contained the papers on family allowances, another arm dragging the even heavier satchel in which were stored the more recent papers about refugees. Recalcitrant ministers would quail before the fire of her magnificent eyes.
>
> HAROLD NICOLSON on the Independent MP Eleanor Rathbone, the *Spectator*, 1946.

on lobby terms A conversation conducted under the rules of the Lobby; most lunches between political journalists and senior Westminster figures take place on this basis, with information freely imparted provided the source is not divulged.

lobbyist A person who attempts to influence legislators to pursue courses of action more favourable to either a single business or interest, or a range of clients. The term originated in New York State politics under the ALBANY REGENCY, when men eager to extract favours from legislators waited for them in the lobby of the State Capitol as they were not allowed on to the Floor. As early as 1819 Dennis Lynch could write:

> Corruption has erected her court on the heights of the Hudson, in the avenues of Albany, in the lobbies of the legislature. . . . Her throne was the lobby.

Lobbyists were evident in the US Capitol by 1832, and throughout the 19th century were seen by those not in receipt of their favours as the vanguard of corruption. Isaac Bassett, first a Senate PAGE and then assistant doorkeeper 1831–95, wrote: "Most of them are blackmailers. They are so crafty and treacherous that public men, men of reputation and means, are always on the alert against them." And President Buchanan denounced "the host of contractors, speculators, stockjobbers and lobby members who haunt the halls of Congress all desirous . . . on any and every pretext to get their arms into the public treasury, and sufficient to alarm every friend of the country". As the Federal Government and regulation grew, so did the scope and number of lobbyists; Sen. James Reed of Missouri was moved to declare: "A lobbyist is anyone who opposes legislation I want," and Harry S Truman said: "The President is the only lobbyist 150 million Americans have. The other 20 million are able to employ people to represent them." The practice of lobbying, and with it the great lobbying firms, has spread to all the world's major legislatures. Since 1946 all lobbyists in Washington have been required to register; that has not eliminated blatant INFLUENCE-PEDDLING, but it has enabled reputable lobbyists to maintain professional ethics. They had a friend in John F. KENNEDY, who wrote in 1956:

> Lobbyists are in many cases expert technicians and capable of explaining complex and difficult subjects in a clear, understandable fashion. Because our congressional representation is based on geographical boundaries, the lobbyists who speak for the various economic, commercial and other factional interests of this country serve a very useful purpose and have assumed an important role in the legislative process.

These technical skills make it hard for members of Congress to out-argue them. Rep. Allard Lowenstein said: "They have people who are able to spend out their time collating data on why pollution is good for River X. What Congressman can match that?"

> Lobbyists are men of revolutionary background – they are careful to see that no one who is taxed is unrepresented.
>
> Sen. EUGENE McCARTHY.

> They protect a Congressman with small favours, while the rest of the world beats him up. WILLIAM GREIDER.

Locarno Pacts A series of NON-AGGRESSION PACTS formulated at Locarno, Switzerland, on 16 October 1925 and signed in London on 1 December. They guaranteed the post-VERSAILLES TREATY frontiers between Germany and France, and Germany and Belgium. This settlement of Franco-German differences and the implied British and Italian guarantee of French territory appeared to herald a new era of international peace and security (the Locarno spirit), and Germany was admitted to the LEAGUE OF NATIONS shortly afterwards (September 1926); ten years later, in March 1936, Germany renounced Locarno and marched into the Rhineland.

lock A hold exercised by a party on a particular organ of government. The term was invented by the US political commentator Horace Busby, who concluded that the Republicans had between the 1968 and 1984 elections secured a "lock" on the Presidency, winning 77% of ELECTORAL COLLEGE votes. Correspondingly the Democrats have a "lock" on the House of Representatives, where they have had a majority since 1954, even in years of a Republican LANDSLIDE in elections for the White House and the Senate.

lock-out The exclusion of workers taking or threatening INDUSTRIAL ACTION from their workplace by their employers in order to pressure them into abandoning their action, negotiating or accepting terms imposed on them. A lock-in is a form of action that originated in America in the late 1960s, where workers lock themselves into their workplace to win concessions from management or attempt to prevent its closure.

Lockerbie disaster The UK's worst air disaster, and the cause of the international community's continued virtual ostracism of Colonel Gaddafi's Libya. On 21 December 1988 a bomb made of SEMTEX exploded in the hold of a Pan American Boeing 747 en route from Frankfurt and London to New York, as it flew over the small Scottish town of Lockerbie. All 259 passengers, and 11 people on the ground, were killed. Great public concern was aroused by the discovery that airport checks had been inadequate, despite warnings of terrorist attack received by the authorities weeks before. Two Libyan security agents were eventually accused of complicity in the bombing, and when Gaddafi refused to hand them over for trial in America or Scotland, the UNITED NATIONS imposed SANCTIONS. Some politicians and commentators claimed that there was as much evidence against Syrian agents, but that the West would not move against them as it needed Syria's help in the GULF WAR.

Lockheed scandal The furore arising from the discovery that America's Lockheed Aircraft Corporation, desperate to secure overseas orders, had paid out $24.5 million in bribes. The former Japanese Prime Minister Kakuei Tanaka was arrested for receiving 500 million yen to ensure that All Nippon Airways bought Lockheed aircraft; Prince Bernhard of the Netherlands, the consort of Queen Juliana, was disgraced for receiving $1.1 million; the Queen abdicated not long after. And in Italy eight arrests were made and two former defence ministers implicated over the purchase of Lockheed plans for the Air Force. The episode led Congress to push through laws against overseas bribery by US corporations, with limited success.

locofocos The New York-based radical branch of the DEMOCRATIC PARTY in the mid to late 1830s who opposed banks, paper money and all monopolies, and demanded equal rights for all men. They got their name, which was not intended as a compliment, because the conservatives who controlled TAMMANY HALL found themselves outnumbered at a meeting on 29 October 1835 and tried to end it by turning out the gas lights. The radicals lit candles, using the newly-invented "Loco-foco" friction matches, and continued the session. The next day the *New York Courier and Enquirer* christened them "Locofocos", and the name stuck.

locomotive for growth A country whose economic strength is such that, if it chose, it could REFLATE its economy and drag the rest of the industrialized world out of recession. The term has most frequently been used of Germany, in the late 1970s when Britain and America each urged Bonn in vain to adopt a more expansionist policy, and again in 1992 when Britain and other European states pressed for the BUNDESBANK to reduce its cripplingly high interest rates.

Lodge, the The official residence in Canberra of the Prime Minister of Australia.

Lodge Reservations The fourteen objections to the VERSAILLES TREATY proposed in September 1919 by the US Senate's Committee on Foreign Relations, and aimed at limiting the scope of the LEAGUE OF NATIONS and America's involvement in it. They were named after the committee's chairman, Sen. Henry Cabot Lodge senior. President WILSON asserted that the reservations nullified the Treaty and urged his supporters to oppose the Treaty itself if they were added to it. In the event the Senate rejected the Treaty – with or without the reservations.

log. log cabin and hard cider A WHIG slogan in America's 1840 Presidential election, praising the supposedly simple ways of General William Harrison (*see* TIPPECANOE AND TYLER TOO) compared with the foppish extravagances of President van Buren (*see* OLD KINDERHOOK). In fact Harrison was anything but a cider-swilling frontiersman, his lavish lifestyle putting him heavily in debt until he found two lucrative sinecures. The origin of the slogan was a comment by one of Henry Clay's friends at the nominating convention in December 1839:

> Give him a barrel of hard cider and a pension of two thousand a year and, my word for it, he will sit the remainder of his days in a log cabin, by the side of a sea-coal fire and study moral philosophy.

The phrase caught on so much that Daniel Webster felt he had to apologize for not having been brought up in a log cabin.

Log Cabin Bill An early 1840s forerunner of America's HOMESTEAD ACT, signed by President Tyler, under which settlers moving westward could claim 160 acres of land before it was offered publicly for sale, later paying $1.25 an acre.

log cabin to White House An essential of the American Dream, the ability of a humble boy from the backwoods to become President. The phrase, striking echoes of "Log cabin and hard cider", was the title of the 1881 biography of President Garfield (*see* BOATMAN JIM) by W. M. Thayer, but has since become linked with Abraham LINCOLN (*see* RAIL-SPLITTER).

> It is harder for a leader to be born in a palace than in a cabin.
>
> WOODROW WILSON campaigning in Denver, 7 October 1912.

logrolling In the US CONGRESS, the deals through which individual members get their own Bills through, from the phrase "help me roll my log, and I'll roll yours". For instance, in the 1930s urban legislators backed farm Bills, and those from farm states voted for urban reforms. It also covers the concessions a President will make in order to get his own programmes enacted.

> A game of trading favours, in which the President gives Congressmen bonbons and pastries to make them give away steak and potatoes.
>
> MARK GREEN, *Who Runs Congress?*

Lok Sabha (Hindi. House of the People) The directly-elected lower house of India's federal Parliament, the majority in which governs the world's largest democracy under a constitution approved in 1950. The upper house, elected from state legislatures, is the Council of States (*Rajya Sabha*).

Lombard Leagues The ground-breaking political movement, centred on Milan, which made widespread electoral gains across northern Italy from the late 1980s. Its twin targets were corruption in government and the debilitating influence of the crime- and poverty-ridden South on the national economy. Though not a specifically SEPARATIST party, the implications of its rising support were obvious to Rome.

Lomé Convention The agreements between the EUROPEAN COMMUNITY and 68 developing nations in Africa, the Caribbean and the Pacific (*see* ACP) that have provided for development assistance and preferential trade terms for some, but not all, of the world's poorest countries. The original agreement, signed in the capital of Togo in 1975, benefited 46 countries, mainly former French colonies; it has since been greatly expanded.

London. London Conference The conference at the end of August 1992 at which John MAJOR, as president of the EC COUNCIL OF MINISTERS, tried to open a peace process in Bosnia Herzegovina, to end the civil war between the largely Muslim government, insurgent Serbs, and Croats. It led to the imposition of a NO-FLY ZONE, and a peace conference in Geneva, with Dr. David OWEN and the former US Secretary of State Cyrus Vance as envoys to try to bring the factions together.

London effect The damage reckoned to have been done to the LABOUR PARTY in London and the south-east of England in the 1987 general election by the activities of the "Loony LEFT" in the party and local councils in the capital. While the party registered modest gains elsewhere, it actually lost several seats in and around London.

London Gazette The official daily publication in which the UK government issues public announcements. Hardly any members of the public ever see it.

London Naval Conference A meeting between the UK, America, France, Italy and Japan between 21 January and 22 April 1930, which enlarged the scope of the WASHINGTON NAVAL TREATY and agreed various new measures of disarmament. These included the regulation of submarine warfare, a five-year moratorium on construction of capital ships, and the limitation of US, British and Japanese battleship tonnage to a ratio of 10:10:7 respectively.

Declaration of London The international agreement reached in 1909 that codified the rights of belligerents and NEUTRAL countries during war. Its interpretation led to difficulties between Britain and America after the outbreak of WORLD WAR I over whether the Royal Navy could intercept US merchant ships and seize cargos bound for neutral destinations. The dispute was overshadowed before long by Germany's warning in February 1915 that its submarines would sink any neutral (including American) ship trading with Britain, and that citizens of neutral countries should stay off Allied ships.

Secret Treaty of London A secret alliance concluded on 26 April 1915 between the Triple ENTENTE of the UK, France and Russia, and Italy. It agreed terms for Italy's entry into WORLD WAR I against Germany and Austria, which had also been courting her since August 1914. Italy committed its forces to the *Entente* in return for promises of territory – South Tyrol, Trentino, Trieste and portions of Dalmatia. The Allies also promised to recognize Italian sovereignty over the Dodecanese, and to let Italy expand its holdings in Libya, Somalia and Eritrea. The text of the treaty was LEAKed by the BOLSHEVIKS in 1917 and later published by a Swedish newspaper, causing embarrassment at the 1919 Paris peace conference where Woodrow WILSON was pledged to stamp out secret diplomacy.

Lone Ranger The nickname awarded by fellow US Senators to their Democratic colleague **Wayne Morse** (1900–74) of Oregon, because he was so frequently left voting in a minority. The original Lone Ranger, in a radio series that became a TV classic, was the fictitious sole survivor of six Texas Rangers ambushed by the "Hole-in-the-Wall" Butch Cavendish gang, who became a masked crusader against injustice in the old West with his trusty Indian companion Tonto. He was created in 1933 by the radio scriptwriter Fran Striker and producer George W. Trendle; the first Lone Ranger movie was made in 1938, starring Lee Powell and Chief Thundercloud; the TV series of over 200 episodes, starring Clayton Moore and Jay Silverheels, ran from 1949 to 1957.

long. long hot summer The climate in which INNER CITY tensions boil over into riots. Originally used of the sticky summer climate in the GHETTO areas of America's big cities, the term has crossed the Atlantic to cover violence on summer nights in Britain's inner cities and run-down housing estates. The phrase emerged during July/August 1964, when looters ran riot in the ghettos of New York, Rochester, Philadelphia, Chicago and three New Jersey cities. The wave of violence began in 18 July when an off-duty New York policeman shot a Black youth; in the ensuing riot one person was killed, 114 injured, 185 arrests were made and 112 businesses attacked. The WATTS riots the next year, and the three summers' widespread disorder that followed, gave the phrase universal currency.

Long March The epic migration in 1934–35 of 100,000 Chinese communists from Kiangsi Soviet in Southeast China to a new base in Yenan in the Northwest. The KMT army under Chiank Kai-Shek had launched a series of offensives against Kiangsi after 1931; in October 1934 Mao Tse-Tung, Chu Teh and Lin Piao led a breakout through Nationalist lines and marched north. They arrived in October 1935, but after a trek of 6000 miles through rugged terrain, subject to near starvation, freezing cold and Nationalist attacks, only 30,000 of the Red Army survived. In Yenan, Mao consolidated his leadership of the Communist Party and prepared the military, economic and political foundations for the eventual communist victory, in 1949.

Long Tom A contemporary nickname for Thomas JEFFERSON, who stood 6ft 2½ in. tall.

the longest suicide note in history The damning verdict passed on the UK Labour Party's 1983 election manifesto, on which the party went down to its worst defeat since 1935, by Gerald Kaufman (1930–), who as a moderate member of the SHADOW CABINET was poles apart from its trenchantly left-wing content.

Longworth building The second of the huge office buildings erected on CAPITOL HILL since 1908 to accommodate Congressmen's offices, committee rooms and other facilities; being less lavish than more recent additions, its rooms are allocated to junior members of the House. It is named after Nicholas Longworth (1869–1931), Speaker of the House 1924–30. Longworth had a reputation as a womanizer. Once a Congressman rashly ran his hand over Longworth's bald pate and said: "It feels just like my wife's backside." Longworth felt it himself and replied: "So it does!"

loop, the A Washington term for the tight circle within which important decisions are taken and sensitive information circulated. Those "in the loop" in and close to the WHITE HOUSE receive essential digests of information, including the FTPO digest, have their own secure telephone network and have ACCESS to the President. The term is used more generally in Washington of those involved in any particular decision-making process.

loose cannon An uncontrollable ally, someone who although determinedly on one's side is prone to counterproductive actions and comments. Used by Washington officials and journalists since the 1980s – during the IRAN-CONTRA revelations, Lt.-Col. Oliver North was referred to as a loose cannon in the Reagan administration – the term now has global application. The expression dates from the days of sail, when a cannon not properly secured to a warship's deck was a danger to the crew when the ship pitched and rolled.

Lord The blanket colloquial title for any British PEER save for a DUKE. The custom is to refer to Viscount X on the first occasion or Lord X thereafter, but frequently "Lord" is used throughout.

Lord Advocate The politico-legal head of Scotland's legal system. The Lord Advocate, who customarily receives a PEERAGE, is a member of the UK Government, but the post more often goes to a distinguished lawyer who supports the party in power than to an active politician.

Lord Chancellor The senior UK Cabinet member who is both the head of the English legal system and Speaker of the HOUSE OF LORDS. At the State Opening of Parliament, the Lord Chancellor has to present the Sovereign with the text of the GRACIOUS

SPEECH, then walk backwards down the steps of the Throne to avoid turning his back on the monarch. Queen Elizabeth II eventually granted an exemption to the octogenarian Lord Hailsham because he had an arthritic knee.

Lord Cupid The nickname bestowed on Viscount Palmerston (*see* PAM) in the 1830s by *The Times*. It referred to his devastating reputation with women.

Lord Haw-Haw Possibly the best known nickname to come from WORLD WAR II, that of **William Joyce** (1906–46), who broadcast Nazi PROPAGANDA to the British people from Germany. The name, coined by Jonah Barrington, radio correspondent of the *Daily Express*, alluded to his drawling, exaggerated Oxbridge accent. Joyce's broadcasts, intended to threaten and demoralize, made him a figure of derision and loathing in Britain, but their tone and remarkably well-informed material attracted hundreds of thousands of listeners; this greatly worried the Government, even though the broadcasts probably stiffened British determination rather than weakening it. Joyce was hanged for treason after the war, despite the fact that he was of Irish descent and insisted he was not a British subject.

Lord High Everything Else An all-purpose politician, generally invaluable to his or her leader or loyal to the point of subservience, who may be appointed or volunteer to take on almost any task. The title originally belonged to POOH-BAH, in Gilbert and Sullivan's *The Mikado*.

Lord Lieutenant The title of the Queen's official representative in each UK county or region; the position is largely ceremonial and has no political significance, but conveys considerable prestige.

Lord Love-a-duck of Limehouse The title which the Labour Prime Minister Clement ATTLEE once said he would take if forced to accept a PEERAGE, "lord love-a-duck" being a Cockney expression for "come off it". In his old age he relented, and accepted an EARLdom.

Lord Mayor *See* MAYOR.

Lord Porn The tabloids' nickname for Frank Pakenham, 7th Earl of Longford (1905–), a champion of moral causes, who in 1972 held an unofficial inquiry into pornography in Britain and on the Continent, and the state of the nation's morality. He campaigned for a ban on school sex education without parental consent, stiffer penalties for breaches of the obscenity laws, and a higher moral tone for films, television and the Press. He earned his nickname leading a fact-finding mission to the sex parlours of Scandinavia, accompanied by a throng of Fleet Street journalists who couldn't believe their luck. Longford had previously been a Minister in two Labour governments, resigning as LORD PRIVY SEAL in 1968 in protest at Harold WILSON's deferment of an increase in the schoool leaving age. Wilson described him to the *Daily Mirror* publisher Cecil King as:

> Quite hopeless. Frank has a mental age of twelve.

Lord President of the Council Traditionally the member of the UK Cabinet who heads the PRIVY COUNCIL in its meetings with the Sovereign. The post is often combined with that of Leader of the Commons or the Lords.

Lord Privy Seal Traditionally the title of the keeper of the Great SEAL of England, and now of a member of the Cabinet, sometimes a second Minister in a department (such as the Foreign Office), sometimes a Minister without PORTFOLIO. Confusingly, the Lord Privy Seal is usually not a member of the House of Lords.

> Neither a lord, nor a privy, nor a seal.
> S. D. BAILEY, *British Parliamentary Democracy*.

Lord Suit The nickname bestowed by PRIVATE EYE on Lord Young of Graffham (1932–), the close associate of Margaret Thatcher who was brought in from the PRIVATE SECTOR in 1982 to chair the Manpower Services Commission, was appointed to the Cabinet in 1984 and went on to serve as Employment Secretary and Trade and Industry Secretary. He was anxious to become Conservative Party chairman after the 1987 election, but was blocked by the Tory establishment, headed by Viscount Whitelaw (*see* WILLIE). Lord Young earned his nickname because he was seen as the epitome of the MEN IN SUITS with successful business careers who lionized Mrs. Thatcher and were rewarded with high positions; he eventually became chairman of Cable and Wireless, which had been PRIVATIZED some years before.

> Other Ministers bring me problems; David brings me solutions. MARGARET THATCHER.

Lords, House of *See* HOUSE.

Lords and Commons The title of a number of sports teams comprising MPs, peers and their friends which play friendly matches against teams mainly in the London area. The cricket team is a particular institution; a sample eleven it fielded included Peter Brooke (*see* O MY DARLING CLEMENTINE), Michael Morris, later Deputy Speaker, the future Northern Ireland Minister Robert Atkins, two Tory backbenchers, a LOBBY correspondent and a recent Oxford Blue.

Louisiana purchase America's acquisition from France of the 828,000 sq. miles

(1,332,000 sq. km.) of territory between the Mississippi and the Rockies, which doubled the young country's size. Though they included New Orleans, the lands involved stretched well north and west of Louisiana. They were unexpectedly offered by Napoleon, who had just recovered them from Spain, for a bargain $11.5 million, plus $3.75 million to settle claims against France by US citizens. Talleyrand told emissaries from President JEFFERSON who signed the transfer on 30 April 1803 without the prior authority of Congress:

I suppose you will make the most of it.

Louvre accord An agreement between the G6 countries, reached in Paris in February 1987, to halt the slide of the dollar on world currency markets and establish a better balance of trade, and encourage non-INFLATIONARY world economic growth. It stabilized the dollar in the short term by boosting confidence in the US currency and attracting funds to New York, but has been blamed by some for the Stock Market crash on BLACK MONDAY the following autumn.

loyal. Loyal Address The formal reply sent by the House of Commons to the GRACIOUS SPEECH (*see also* QUEEN'S SPEECH), which provides the peg for the debate of four or five days which takes place immediately after the Sovereign has delivered it.

Loyalists (1) The supporters during the AMERICAN REVOLUTION of continued links with the British Crown, tens of thousands of whom sailed for Canada when the cause was lost. *See also* EMPIRE LOYALISTS. (2) In NORTHERN IRELAND, vociferous, usually working-class, supporters of an enduring UNION with Britain. The term came into its own in the early 1970s with the formation of Loyalist PARAMILITARY groups, and the GENERAL STRIKE by Loyalist workers in 1974 that brought down the POWER-SHARING Executive.

loyalty boards The panels set up by President Truman under an EXECUTIVE ORDER of 22 March 1947 to investigate the loyalty (freedom from Communist links) of over 3 million Federal employees. Two thousand resigned, 212 were fired as SECURITY RISKS and just one, Judith Coplon, was twice convicted of spying, but freed because of illegal FBI BUGGING. Truman's initiative helped create the climate of anti-Communist hysteria that enabled McCARTHYISM to flourish, but did not prevent the Republicans branding him as "soft on Communism".

LSE London School of Economics (and Political Science). The unspectacular complex of buildings in Houghton Street, off the Aldwych, which since 1895 has turned out many of the English-speaking world's political leaders and thinkers. Most but by no means all have been on the Left, influenced by such mentors as the School's founder Sidney Webb (1858–1947), and the controversial Labour Party chairman Harold Laski (1893–1950). LSE, part of London University since 1900, was the scene of bitter student unrest in 1968. In 1991 a proposal for it to move to the vacant COUNTY HALL attracted widespread support, but the School was outbid by a Japanese hotel chain.

Lublin committee Polish Committee of National Liberation. A group of left-wing Poles sponsored by the Soviets during WORLD WAR II as a pliant alternative to the Polish government-in-exile in London. After the RED ARMY's liberation of East Poland in July 1944, and after the Germans had been cynically left to put down the WARSAW UPRISING, the committee was installed in Lublin and recognized by Moscow as the legitimate authority. A Provisional GOVERNMENT was proclaimed in December 1944; of its 25 members 15 had been in the Lublin Committee. It was recognized by Britain and America on 5 July 1945, two months after the end of the war in Europe.

Lubyanka One of Moscow's notorious prisons under Soviet rule, reserved for political prisoners only. Thousands of NKVD victims were imprisoned, interrogated, tortured and executed here. The Lubyanka, in Dzerzhinsky Square, was originally the headquarters of an insurance company; it was taken over by the CHEKA in the 1920s. The NKVD offices occupied the outer section and the prison cells were located within an inner courtyard in a nine-storey building once used by the insurance company as a boarding house. There are around 110 small cells holding up to 200 prisoners; executions were carried out in the basement.

Lucy The name given by the Labour Cabinet Minister Barbara (later Lady) Castle (1910–) to the vivid red wig that superseded the equally fiery locks of her youth. In her *Diaries*, she recorded how when visiting an old people's home near Nottingham destroyed by fire in 1974, "Lucy" had been caught by a wire trailing from the ceiling. The TV cameras were on Mrs. Castle, then Social Services Secretary, and she "froze in embarrassment". Fortunately for her, no one appeared to notice.

Luddite An intransigent, even violent, opponent of industrial progress; a term much used about UK TRADE UNIONS in the 1960s and 1970s, and applied in America to any stubbornly backward-looking person.

> I voted for Mario Cuomo for Governor of New York in 1982 because I like what he was saying and because I thought his opponent, Lewis E. Lehrman, was a social Luddite and a moral troglodyte.
>
> WILLIAM E. KENNEDY, *New York Times Book Review*, 13 May 1984.

The original Luddites were workmen discontented by mechanization who, from 1811 to 1816, toured factories (especially in the Nottingham area) breaking the new machines they believed were putting men out of work. They were named after Ned Ludd, a simple boy from Leicestershire, who chased boys who were baiting him into a house and broke two stocking-frames there; the fictitious leader of the protesters was called General Ludd.

Lukens case The scandal surrounding Rep. Donald (Buzz) Lukens, a Republican Congressman from Ohio, who was jailed for 30 days in 1989 for a sexual act with a minor, a Capitol lift operator. Lukens was defeated in the 1990 elections while appealing against his conviction.

lust in my heart The key phrase of an extraordinary interview Jimmy CARTER gave to *Playboy* magazine at the height of the 1976 Presidential campaign which staggered Americans with its frankness, even naïveté, and disconcerted some of his fellow "born again" Christians. At the end of the interview with Robert Scheer, Carter made one last attempt to show that he was by no means a narrow-minded fundamentalist; his remarks about sex certainly did that when Playboy appeared on 20 September, to headlines like "Carter on Sin and Lust . . . I'm Human, I'm Tempted". Referring to Christ's teaching that "anyone who looks on a woman with lust in his heart has already committed ADULTERY", Carter said:

> I've looked on a lot of women with lust. I've committed adultery in my heart many times. This is something that God recognizes I will do – and I have done it – and God forgives me for it. But that doesn't mean that I condemn someone who not only looks on a woman with lust but leaves his wife and shacks up with somebody out of wedlock. . . . Christ says, Don't consider yourself better than someone else because one guy screws a whole bunch of women while the other guy is loyal to his wife. The guy who's loyal to his wife ought not to be condescending or proud because of the relative degree of sinfulness.

Carter offered up a politically embarrassing hostage to fortune in the same interview, bracketing LBJ with Richard Nixon for "lying, cheating and distorting the truth"; on this, he rapidly backtracked, but LADY BIRD Johnson made clear her frosty disapproval.

> Jimmy talks too much, but at least people know he's honest and doesn't mind answering questions.
>
> ROSALYNN CARTER.

Luxembourg compromise The informal arrangement within the EC's COUNCIL OF MINISTERS under which a member state can claim the right to VETO a decision if its "very important interests" are at stake, instead of the issue being decided by a Qualified MAJORITY. The Compromise, which has no legal status, stems from a statement by France when ending a 6-month boycott of the Council (*see* Empty CHAIR) in Luxembourg in 1966. The other five members at the time accepted it, and it has been invoked from time to time since, mainly over farm legislation; Britain tried and failed to do so in a bid to block the Community's SOCIAL CHARTER. It was expected to lapse when the MAASTRICHT TREATY took effect.

lying in state A nation's penultimate tribute to an exceptional leader, when the coffin containing his or her body stands, prior to a State funeral, in a revered public place so that the people may pass by it. In Britain, WESTMINSTER HALL has seen the lying-in-state of Kings and Queens, and statesmen from Gladstone to CHURCHILL; in Washington, the coffins of 26 Americans: Presidents (four of them assassinated), distinguished Senators and the Unknown Serviceman from the VIETNAM WAR, have lain in the ROTUNDA of the Capitol.

lynching The ugliest feature of American life in the near past (though it has occurred elsewhere): the "execution" by a mob of a person believed to have escaped punishment, or simply of the "wrong" colour, which became common in the Deep South after the CIVIL WAR, but also occurred more widely. Up to 5000 Americans have been lynched since records were first kept in 1885; most were Blacks, though Jews, Catholics and Italians were also killed. Leaders of lynch mobs, often members of the KU KLUX KLAN, were seldom punished locally, and in 1900 a Black North Carolina Congressman, G. H. White, brought in a Bill to make lynching a federal crime; in that year 105 Black Americans were lynched. The number declined as economic revival made Southern Whites less interested in finding scapegoats, but revived during World War I to a point where President WILSON was moved to compare the mobs with the German enemy. Between 1918 and 1927 454 people were lynched, 416 of them Black; 42 were burned to death. President Truman proposed an anti-lynching law as part of his FAIR DEAL, but conservative Southerners in Congress ensured that it was stillborn. Occasional lynchings continued into the 1950s, but they virtually ended with the advances of the CIVIL RIGHTS movement, though racial tensions have not entirely disappeared. The word stems from Captain William Lynch

(1742–1820), a Virginia magistrate who on 22 September 1780 formed a band to clear Pittsylvania County of "unlawful and abandoned wretches" by such punishment; the "lynch-men" were sworn to secrecy. The diary of the surveyor Andrew Ellicott records that under Lynch's form of justice,

> the person who it was supposed ought to suffer death was placed on a horse with his hands tied behind him and a rope about his neck which was fastened to the limb of a tree over his head. In this situation the person was left, and when the horse in pursuit of food or any other cause moved from his position the unfortunate person was left suspended by the neck – this was called "aiding the civil authority".

> It may be true that the law cannot make a man love me, but it can keep him from lynching me, and I think that's pretty important. MARTIN LUTHER KING.

lynching Northern-style *See* Adam Clayton POWELL.

judicial lynching *See* Clarence THOMAS CASE.

Lynskey tribunal The tribunal set up by Clement ATTLEE in 1948 under Mr. Justice Lynskey to investigate allegations in the Board of Trade that Ministers and officials had been taking bribes. The key witness at the tribunal's hearings was Sydney Stanley, a Polish-born confidence trickster who had made money by trading on supposed links with people in power. Stanley was exposed as a liar, but some Ministers had been slow to see through him. No successful bribery on any scale was detected, but misjudgments and unwise acceptance of gifts were; John Belcher, a junior trade minister, was forced out of politics, and George Gibson, a trade union-nominated director of the Bank of England, reprimanded. The affair also damaged Hugh Dalton (*see* BUDGET LEAK), who had been offered a directorship by Stanley while out of office (he had just returned as Chancellor of the DUCHY OF LANCASTER) and had written him a "Dear Stan" letter.

Lysenkoism The bogus science, based on the maverick ideas of the Soviet geneticist **Trofim Denisovich Lysenko** (1898–1976) and the horticulturist I. V. Michurin (1855–1935), that caused an ideological and political upheaval in Soviet academic circles from the 1930s and convinced Western scientists of the lunacy of STALINISM. Lysenko claimed to have proof that environmentally-induced changes in cereal seed to improve germination could be inherited by successive generations of the plant. This contradicted prevailing scientific orthodoxy, notably the genetic theories of Mendel and others. Stalin, untroubled by lack of corroboration, threw his weight behind the young Lysenko, and Soviet IDEOLOGUES entwined his ideas with orthodox MARXISM to denounce the theories of orthodox geneticists as BOURGEOIS. Nicolai Vavilov, a notable critic of Lysenko, was in 1938 replaced by him as president of the V. I. Lenin All-Union Academy of Agricultural Sciences; Vavilov was exiled to Siberia along with other respected Soviet geneticists, and died in 1943. Lysenko became director of the Genetic Institute of the Soviet Union in 1940, and in 1948 reached the high point of his influence with a report – backed by the CENTRAL COMMITTEE of the Communist Party – entitled *The Position in Biological Science*; all textbooks were rewritten to accommodate his theories. Lysenkoism kept its influence under Khruschev, and only after his fall in 1964 was it exposed as a fraud that had made Soviet genetics a laughing-stock for over three decades.

M

M0 One of seven definitions for MONEY SUPPLY used at various times from 1979 by successive UK CHANCELLORS; they choose the measure or measures they consider the most accurate and/or politically advantageous. M0 covers the notes and coins in circulation plus banks' till money and balances with the Bank of England. **M1** is the money in circulation plus private-sector current accounts and transferable deposit accounts. **M3** (formerly Sterling M3) is M1 plus all other private-sector bank deposits plus certificates of deposit. When Nigel Lawson embraced M3, Labour MPs branded him the **"M3 rapist"**, after a criminal who preyed on the M3 motorway. **M4** is the notes and coins in circulation plus private-sector current accounts and most private-sector bank deposits, plus holdings of money-market instruments. Norman Lamont adopted this measure after the DEVALUATION of 1992.

Ma, Ma, Where's my pa? A Republican chant at the expense of the 1884 Democratic Presidential nominee Grover Cleveland (*see* BEAST OF BUFFALO), when it was disclosed that he had improbably fathered a child out of wedlock by a 36-year-old Buffalo widow, Maria Halpin. Cleveland took the issue on the chin, telling aides: "Above all, tell the truth." With the Republicans attacking Cleveland as a "moral leper" and the Democrats denouncing his rival James G. Blaine as corrupt, Lord Bryce wrote that the contest seemed to be over "the copulative habits of one and the prevaricative habits of the other". The Democrats had the last laugh; when Cleveland was elected, they completed the couplet:

> Gone to the White House, Ha, Ha, Ha!

Maastricht Treaty The treaty on closer European economic and political union agreed by leaders of the twelve EUROPEAN COMMUNITY states at Maastricht in southern Holland in December 1991. The EC's greatest milestone since the Treaty of ROME, it involved a tighter European Union, the exercise of more SOVEREIGNTY by the EC itself, closer intergovernmental co-operation, and a SINGLE CURRENCY in 1997. Britain opted out of the Treaty's SOCIAL CHAPTER and secured the right to put the question of whether to join the single currency to Parliament at a later stage. Denmark's "No" vote in a REFERENDUM on 2 June 1992 put the Treaty in jeopardy, critics led by Margaret Thatcher and Norman Tebbit creating strong pressures in Britain's Conservative Party for John MAJOR to renounce it. These were heightened when France approved the Treaty by a margin of just 2%. Major saw off rebels led by Tebbit at the party conference in October, but only scrambled a 3-vote majority with Liberal Democrat support when he sought Commons approval for a prompt start on the Treaty Bill's COMMITTEE STAGE. The Bill became law in July 1993, but only after a late government defeat on the SOCIAL CHAPTER, with a vote of CONFIDENCE needed to secure ratification.

MacArthur sacking President Truman's dismissal of General Douglas MacArthur (1880–1964), American commander-in-chief in Korea, for campaigning to extend the KOREAN WAR by bombing and invading China, against Truman's stated policy. MacArthur's removal on 11 April 1951 caused a sensation, the young Sen. Richard Nixon saying:

> The happiest people in this country will be the Communists and their stooges.

The hero of America's Pacific victory and architect of post-war Japan was given ticker-tape parades in the great cities and received enthusiastically by a JOINT SESSION of Congress (*see* OLD SOLDIERS NEVER DIE). Commentators hailed his speech as one of the most memorable heard in the Capitol; Truman dismissed it as "a bunch of damn bullshit". MacArthur's political impact tailed off, leaving Truman largely vindicated. He reminisced:

> I fired MacArthur because he wouldn't respect the authority of the President. I didn't fire him because he was a dumb son of a bitch, although he was, but that's not against the law for generals. If it was, half to three-quarters of them would be in jail.

MacBird A satirical play staged in California *c.* 1967 in protest at the VIETNAM WAR. Based on Shakespeare's *Macbeth*, it equated President Lyndon B. Johnson with the murderous Lady Macbeth.

MacBride principles The agenda for AFFIRMATIVE ACTION to secure jobs for the Catholic minority in Northern Ireland created in 1976 by Dr. Sean MacBride (1904–88), the former IRA chief of staff who renounced violence to become a distinguished international jurist. Its main thrust is the need for US companies to use the threat of disinvestment in the province to secure more high-level jobs for Catholics. Supporters of the Principles say Northern Ireland's Fair Employment legislation, while outlawing discrimination against Catholics, does not do enough to break the Protestant grip on what is left of the province's heavy industry. In America, the Principles are used by supporters of militant Republicanism to discourage corporate investment in Ulster and as a stick to beat the UK government. Few if any US corporations have signed up to them, and SINN FEIN is the only Northern Ireland party to have fully endorsed them.

McCarran Act The Internal Security Act passed by Congress in September 1950, over President Truman's VETO. It provided for a Subversive Activists Control Board to register members of "Communist-action or Communist-FRONT" groups, made compassing the establishment of a TOTALITARIAN state a criminal conspiracy, and allowed for establishment of "emergency" CONCENTRATION CAMPS. The Act paved the way for McCARTHYISM; Dean Acheson described its sponsor, Sen. Pat McCarran (1876–1954), as "not a man who in the 18th century would have been considered a man of sensibility". A second measure, the **McCarran-Walter Act** of 1952, again passed over Truman's veto, codified the immigration law, retaining the quota system but cutting numbers from eastern Europe while allowing a trickle from Pacific nations including Japan, which was allowed 185 migrants a year. The Act also gave the Attorney-General power to deport any "subversive" and any Communist or member of a Communist front.

McCarthyism The anti-Communist WITCH-HUNT conducted in America between 1950 and 1954 by Sen. Joseph McCarthy (1909–57). McCarthy pilloried prominent people from film stars to senior officials of the Truman administration as traitors, Communists and FELLOW-TRAVELLERS. His campaign lost many citizens their livelihoods, sent ten Hollywood scriptwriters to jail, ended several political careers and led one Senator to commit suicide; he even accused General George Marshall and Secretary of State Dean Acheson of treason. Communists were indeed active in America, but McCarthy's central charge was never proved. McCarthy, a Wisconsin Democrat, took his seat in 1946 despite a Supreme Court ruling against him after fabricating a heroic war career, running on the slogan **"Congress needs a tail-gunner"**. He was facing defeat for re-election when the FBI leaked highly suspect documents to him; at that point, said his assistant Roy Cohn, he "bought Communism in much the same way as other people purchase a new automobile". On 9 February 1950, in a speech at Wheeling, West Virginia, McCarthy claimed to have a list of 205 Communists "known to the Secretary of State" working in the State Department; the next day the number was down to 57. The Republican establishment embraced him, Sen. Robert Taft telling him: "If one case doesn't work, try another". Richard Nixon was one of McCarthy's most vocal supporters, asserting that

> 96 per cent of 6,926 Communists, fellow travellers, sex perverts, people with criminal records, dope addicts, drunks and other security risks removed under the Eisenhower security programme were hired by the Truman administration. Mr. Truman, Dean Acheson and other administration officials covered up this Communist conspiracy and attempted to halt its exposure.

The campaign, promoted by McCarthy as **Americanism with its sleeves rolled up** continued relentlessly with the Republican Eisenhower in office – he found it distasteful but shied away from confrontation. But in 1954 McCarthy overreached himself in the Army-McCarthy hearings (*see below*), was accused of taking bribes, hit back with an attack on Eisenhower that finally alienated his party and was "condemned" by the Senate; he died of drink three years later.

To the Right McCarthy was a patriot unveiling a dastardly plot, to liberals he was an obsessive who threatened them personally. Joseph Alsop termed him "the only major politician in the country who can be labelled 'liar' without fear of libel". General Marshall said McCarthy "would sell his grandmother for any advantage". The veteran Washington hostess Alice Roosevelt Longworth cut him dead: "The policeman and the trashman may call me Alice. You may not." And Truman fumed: "When even one American who has done nothing wrong is forced by fear to shut his mind and close his mouth, then all Americans are in trouble. It is the job of all of us to rise up and put a stop to this terrible business."

> As squalid an episode as any in American history.
> HUGH BROGAN.

Army-McCarthy hearings The episode that killed McCarthyism. On 22 April 1954 Senate hearings began into McCarthy's charge that the Secretary of the Army was thwarting his investigation of "spying" at the Fort Monmouth, New Jersey, signal facility; the Army claimed McCarthy had started the probe because it refused one of his aides preferential treatment. Thirty-six days of testimony destroyed McCarthy's credibility. Under skilful cross-examination from Army counsel Joseph B. Welch, the Senator was exposed as a bully. At the critical moment before 20 million viewers, Welch told him:

> Until this moment, Senator, I think I never really gauged your cruelty or your ruthlessness. Let us not assassinate this lad further. Senator, have you no sense of decency, sir, at long last? Have you left no sense of decency?

MacDonald, Ramsay *See* RAMSAY MAC.

mace (1) Throughout the English-speaking world, the visible symbol of the LEGISLATURE in session, removed when the SPEAKER vacates the CHAIR. At Westminster, a silver-gilt ornamental club carried by the SERJEANT-AT-ARMS to attend the Speaker (the LORD CHANCELLOR in the Lords). A mace has been used since at least 1415; the present one, with a head in the form of a closed crown, dates from 1660. Oliver Cromwell removed a previous mace to terminate the RUMP with the words: "What shall we do with this bauble? Here, take it away." Michael Heseltine (*see* TARZAN) seized the mace and brandished it in 1976 in protest at the passage of legislation to nationalize aircraft and shipbuilding. His fellow Conservative MP Julian Critchley wrote: "If it is necessary in politics to demonstrate that one has passion and vulgarity, Michael demonstrated that he had both." And in 1989 Labour's Ron Brown (*see* AFGHAN RON) was suspended for removing the mace and dropping it, causing minor damage. In Washington, the first House mace was destroyed when the British burned the Capitol. The present one is a silver and ebony copy of the original, made in 1841. Slim, elegant and 46 inches long, it comprises an eagle on a globe surmounting bound rods representing the first 13 states.
(2) A form of riot gas, causing a burning sensation in the eyes, nose and throat and temporarily incapacitating the recipient. It was used by police in America in the late 1960s and early 1970s, particularly against anti-VIETNAM WAR demonstrations. The name is probably taken from the spice obtained from nutmeg.

Machiavellian Referring to the ruthless and cynical exercise of power for self-seeking purposes, so that the end justifies the means. From the doctrines of the Florentine diplomat and political theorist Niccolò Machiavelli (1469–1527), whose best-known work is *The Prince*. Some examples of his advice were benign, such as that "a man who is made prince by the people should work to retain that friendship". But he also wrote:

> A man who wishes to act virtuously necessarily comes to grief among so many who are not virtuous. Therefore if a prince wishes to maintain his rule he must learn how not to be virtuous.
>
> If an injury has to be done to a man, it should be so severe that his vengeance need not be feared.
>
> A wise prince sees to it that never, in order to attack someone, does he become the ally of a prince more powerful than himself. If you win, you are the powerful king's prisoner.

One of the most ringing denunciations of *The Prince* came from John Wesley (1703–91), the founder of Methodism, who wrote:

> If all the other doctrines of devils which have been committed to writing since letters were in the world were collected together in one volume, it would fall short of this; and that, should a Prince form himself by this book, so calmly recommending hypocrisy, treachery, lying, robbery, oppression, adultery, whoredom, and murder of all kinds, Domitian or Nero would be an angel of light compared to that man.

machine politics In America, the interweaving of patronage and political organization to create a self-perpetuating, normally Democratic, city or state government under powerful BOSSes, dedicated to serving its own but on occasion fulfilling genuine public needs. Strongly rooted by the 1820s in East coast Irish communities, it spread westward and across ethnic barriers. New York (TAMMANY HALL), Chicago (the DALEY MACHINE) and Boston have been prime examples. Rep. John Kluczynski explained to President Truman that in Chicago "the Poles get the votes and the Irish get the jobs". Since the 1960s this style of government has virtually disappeared, largely because of WHITE FLIGHT to the suburbs.

McKenna duties An import tax introduced in Britain during World War I by the Liberal Chancellor Reginald McKenna (1863–1943). Abolished in 1924, the duties were intended to restrict the import of luxury items, such as cars and watches.

McKinley tariff The PROTECTIONIST tariff imposed by the US Congress in 1890 which raised duties to their highest level, averaging 50%; the President was authorized to impose duties on those items still untaxed. The author was Rep. William McKinley (1843–1901), who was to be elected 25th President of the United States (Republican) in 1896. McKinley, a lawyer, 6-term Congressman and former Governor of Ohio, described himself as "a tariff man on a tariff platform". When the Republicans were seeking a nominee for 1896, Speaker Thomas Reed, asked about his own chances, said: "They might do worse, and they probably will"; when McKinley won on the first ballot, Reed commented:

> He has about as much backbone as a chocolate eclair.

Short, stout, always wearing a red carnation and devoted to his invalid wife, McKinley overcame William Jennings Bryan's first POPULIST campaign to enter the White House. In office he became the symbol of US IMPERIALISM; when the Philippines were captured he confessed: "I could not have told where those damned islands were within 2000 miles". The anti-war party denounced him as "a white-livered cur", but popular feeling for expansionism helped McKinley defeat Bryan more decisively in 1900; his slogan was **Stand pat with McKinley**. His running-mate was Theodore Roosevelt, whom the Republican establishment deeply distrusted; on his re-election McKinley's campaign manager Mark Hanna told him: "Your duty to the country is to live for four years from next March." But only months into his second term he was shot in Buffalo by a young anarchist, Leon Czolgosz. As he fell, McKinley saw security guards beating his assailant and told them: "Be easy with him, boys." Then he added: "My wife – be careful about her – she's sleeping, break the news gently to her".

> That kind, gentle, fatherly way of McKinley's made all comers feel that he was their friend, but left doubt in their minds as to the substantial result they had come to accomplish. White House usher IKE HOOVER.

> He would never consent to be photographed in a negligent pose and always took the most meticulous care about every detail of his appearance and his posture. He enbalmed himself, so far as posterity is concerned.
> C. W. THOMSON, *Presidents I Have Known.*

Macmillan, Harold *See* SUPERMAC.

McSharry plan The plan for reform of the EC's Common Agricultural Policy (CAP) put forward in 1990 by Agriculture Commissioner Ray McSharry (1938–). The aim of the former Irish TANAISTE was to check rapid increases in the Community's farm budget, and to head off retaliation by America that threatened the URUGUAY ROUND of GATT talks. McSharry proposed a cut in subsidies of up to 30%, less than half of what Washington was pressing for and twice the amount the EC's Council of Ministers eventually agreed to – spread over several years.

MAD *See* MUTUALLY ASSURED DESTRUCTION.

mad monk Originally used to describe **Rasputin** (1871–1916), the sinister cleric at the court of Tsar Nicholas II; more recently the nickname of the intellectually self-torturing **Sir Keith Joseph** (1918–), Margaret Thatcher's free-market ideological GURU and a member of the Heath and Thatcher Cabinets.

madam. Madam Speaker The form of address chosen by **Betty Boothroyd** (1929–) following her election in 1992 as the first woman SPEAKER of the House of Commons. Yorkshire-born Miss Boothroyd, once a high-kicking Tiller Girl, served a long political apprenticeship, entering Parliament (for West Bromwich in 1973) at the fifth attempt.

Madame Ecosse Nickname at the EUROPEAN PARLIAMENT for the Scottish Nationalist MEP Mrs. **Winifred Ewing** (1929–), the former Westminster MP who since 1979 has been the SNP's only member at Strasbourg.

Madison Group A powerful group of conservative Senate STAFFERs, allied to Sen. Jesse Helms, which was instrumental in keeping up right-wing pressure on President Reagan. It took its name from **James Madison** (1751–1836), fourth President of the United States 1809–17. Too frail for the Continental Army, he was a leading figure in drafting the US CONSTITUTION, co-author of The FEDERALIST, architect of the BILL OF RIGHTS and Jefferson's Secretary of State. Rep. Fisher Ames hailed him as "a man of sense, reading, address and integrity. He is our first man." But Madison, a "withered little apple-John", as Washington Irving described him, did not exude power. John C. Calhoun commented: "Our President, though a man of amiable manners and great talents, has not I fear those commanding talents which are necessary to control those about him". Indeed **"Jemmy"** was probably less popular than his lively wife Dolley; Charles C. Pinckney whom Madison defeated in 1808 said: "I was beaten by Mr. and Mrs. Madison. I might have had a better chance had I faced Mr. Madison alone." Dolley Madison went on to distinguish herself by her calm disdain when the British sacked Washington in 1814 after her husband had gone to war with Britain. Madison justified his action with the statement: "I flung forward the flag of the country, sure that the people would press onward and defend it." But it revived the Federalist opposition, and Madison only narrowly won a second term.

Madrid conditions The terms set by Margaret Thatcher at the Madrid EC summit in July 1988 for Britain's participation in the exchange rate mechanism (ERM). They were that the UK would join (1) when it had reduced inflation close to the EC average; (2)

when the European SINGLE MARKET was close to completion; and 3) when all EC countries had abolished exchange controls and freed capital movements. She set the conditions when Chancellor Nigel Lawson and Foreign Secretary Sir Geoffrey Howe threatened to resign unless she made a commitment to join. John MAJOR, as Chancellor, eventually secured Mrs. Thatcher's agreement to join the ERM in October 1990, with the conditions not fully met.

Mae West factor Pollsters' term for the tendency of some uncommitted voters to opt for the challenger on the ground that he/she could not be worse than the incumbent. From the Hollywood star's attributed claim:

> Whenever I'm caught between two evils, I take the one I've never tried.

MAFF Initials of the UK Ministry of Agriculture, Fisheries and Food, always pronounced as a word; coincidentally it rhymes with "naff".

mafficking Extravagant and boisterous celebration of a natural sporting or military triumph. From the uproarious scenes and unrestrained exultation in the centre of London on the night of 18 May 1900, when news arrived that the South African town of Mafeking had been relieved after a 217-day siege by the BOERS. The town had been defended by Colonel Robert Baden-Powell, who subsequently founded the Boy Scouts.

Magellan, Ferdinand President Franklin D. Roosevelt's private railway carriage. Built by the Association of American Railroads and sold to the White House for one dollar, it was equipped with two lifts to get his wheelchair on and off, an office, a lounge, a bedroom and a galley. The floor was of foot-thick steel-lined concrete to guard against explosions on the trackbed. There were three underwater escape hatches from Navy submarines in case the train toppled into a river. Engine drivers said the carriage was so heavy that pulling it was like pulling a fishing line with a lead sinker at the end.

Maggie, Maggie, Maggie – Out, Out, Out! The standard cry of anti-Tory demonstrators throughout the years of Margaret Thatcher's UK government. With the exception of "the IRON LADY", "Maggie" was one of the very few nicknames used by her supporters rather than her opponents; Mrs. Thatcher herself appreciated and used it.

magic. magic asterisk The accounting device invented early in the Reagan administration by David Stockman's budget team to make it appear that targets would be met. Stockman said:

> We invented the magic asterisk. If we couldn't find the savings in time – and we couldn't – we would issue an IOU. We would call it "Future savings to be identified". It was marvellously creative. A magic asterisk item would cost negative $30 billion . . . $40 billion . . . whatever it took to get a balanced budget.

magic circle In British politics, the term coined by Iain Macleod in 1963 for the milieu in which a new Tory leader "emerged", prior to the adoption in 1965 of a system of election. It was used specifically to describe the senior party figures who, on Macmillan's resignation, ensured that Lord Home (*see* SIR ALEC) was chosen ahead of RAB Butler and Lord Hailsham. Macleod wrote:

> It is some measure of the tightness of the magic circle on this occasion that neither the Chancellor of the Exchequer nor the Leader of the House of Commons had any inkling of what was happening.

Announcing his resignation, Macmillan had said: "I hope that it will soon be possible for the customary processes of consultation to be carried out within the party about its future leadership." The thinking behind the "emergence" of the Tory leader was summed up in 1921:

> Great leaders of parties are not elected, they are evolved. It will be a bad day for this or any party to have solemnly to meet to elect a leader. The leader is there, and we all know it when he is there.
>
> ERNEST PRETYMAN (1860–1931).

Maginot Line The 195-mile defensive fortification built by France along its eastern border from Belgium to Switzerland after World War I to prevent Germany ever again invading. Named after its promoter, Minister of Defence André Maginot (1877–1932), the Line lulled the French into a false sense of security, proving useless when, in 1940, German forces turned the Line's northern flank and invaded France through Belgium.

Maginot mentality A false sense of security in politics, based on outdated views and tactics.

Magna Carta The charter of rights forced on King John by his barons in 1215 which became one of the basics of English common law, and of the liberties of America and other English-speaking nations. The charter, agreed at Runnymede near Windsor, was intended to reinforce the barons' position rather than enshrine general human rights. But such provisions as that requiring no one to be tried except by their equals paved the way for trial by jury, due process of law and no taxation without representation.

> An insult to the Holy See, a serious weakening of the royal

> power, a disgrace to the English nation, a danger to all Christendom. Pope INNOCENT III (1160/1–1216).

Mahatma The title (Sanskrit. great soul) accorded by his followers to **Mohandas Karamchand Gandhi** (1869–1948), a champion of the poor and advocate of self-denial whose pursuit of CIVIL DISOBEDIENCE and advocacy of NON-VIOLENCE did much to bring about Indian independence and earned him world-wide respect. Gandhi's moral authority in India grew each time he was imprisoned by the British, who found his campaigning an increasing threat to the established order. The British could not get to grips with his moral authority or his twinkling humour; asked by an interviewer what he thought of Western civilization, Gandhi replied: "I think it would be a good idea." He was assassinated just after the end of British rule by Hindu fanatics who resented his fasting to bring about co-operation between Hindus and Muslims after fighting broke out between newly-partitioned India and Pakistan.

> I do not know how to tell you and how to say it. Our beloved leader is no more.
> JAWAHARLAL NEHRU, announcing Gandhi's death.

maiden speech The first speech a member makes after taking his or her seat in a LEGISLATURE. In Britain's HOUSE OF COMMONS the speech, by tradition, includes a tribute to the previous member for the same constituency, regardless of their politics. Similarly, the next member to speak is supposed to offer congratulations. Making a maiden speech is an ordeal, and so can hearing them; in Australia's HOUSE OF REPRESENTATIVES, wrote Blanche d'Alpuget, "listening to maiden speeches is one of the tiresome duties of a new Parliament, from which members usually excuse themselves". Few maiden speeches are classics; Disraeli (*see* DIZZY) had such a rough ride that he blustered: "The time will come when you shall hear me!" He glossed over this when writing in one of his novels of "an MP so inaudible that it was doubtful whether, after all, the young orator really did lose his virginity". The 18th-century Joseph Addison was so nervous that he paused three times on "I conceive" before giving up; the next speaker cruelly commented that he had "conceived three times and brought forth nothing". But occasional gems stand out, such as the first Commons speech by F. E. Smith, later Lord Birkenhead (1872–1930) on 12 May 1906. The editor J. L. Garvin recorded:

> He spoke for an hour, and put the House in his pocket.

Major, John (1943–). Prime Minister of the UK (Conservative) from 1990. Born in south London to elderly parents (his father had once been a trapeze artist) who fell on hard times, he enjoyed a meteoric rise based on personal charm and acute political skills. He left school early to support his family making garden gnomes, spent a time unemployed, then joined a bank, rising rapidly after a spell in Nigeria where he lost a kneecap in a road accident, ending a promising cricket career. Major got his first political experience as chairman of Lambeth housing committee; RED KEN Livingstone, who sat opposite him, said: "All Tories are monsters. John Major is charming. Therefore John Major isn't a Tory." He was elected an MP in 1979, and in 1987 entered the Cabinet as Chief Secretary to the Treasury. Margaret Thatcher admired his ability, loyalty and readiness to stand up to her, and she promoted him for an uncomfortable two months as Foreign Secretary in 1989 before making him Chancellor on Nigel Lawson's resignation. When Michael Heseltine toppled her in November 1990, Major came through to win as her favoured successor. "He is another ONE OF US", she told her supporters. Major was genuinely surprised to become Prime Minister. His wife Norma, asked about his chances, had said: "Things like that don't happen to people like us." And Major himself told his first Cabinet meeting: "Well, who would have thought it?" One Minister described that Cabinet, after Mrs. Thatcher's, as "like the released slaves' chorus from Fidelio". He soon got used to the job, telling the 1991 Conservative conference: "I've got it, I like it and with your help I'm going to keep it."

Major was immediately confronted with the GULF WAR, leading the nation through the brief conflict to free Kuwait. At home he was dogged by the twin problems of recession and regular Thatcher-inspired backbench rebellions over Europe. Major negotiated the MAASTRICHT TREATY, repealed the POLL TAX, then called an election at almost the last possible moment. For most of the campaign he looked sure to lose; but on 9 April 1992 he pulled off a shock victory over Neil KINNOCK, winning an overall majority of 21; he himself had the largest majority of any Conservative MP. Yet Europe and the economy re-emerged to dog him in a record fourth Tory term; Lady Thatcher ominously remarked: "I don't accept that all of a sudden Major is his own man," and when the Danes rejected Maastricht and the French almost followed suit, the party was at war again. Then, on BLACK WEDNESDAY in September 1992, his government was forced by a run on the pound to leave the ERM and DEVALUE; he faced down critics of Maastricht at his party's conference, but the economy continued in a tailspin. Major's authority was further dented by the furore over the announcement in October 1992 – hastily-shelved – of the closure of more than half Britain's remaining coal mines, a scrambled three-vote Commons majority over Maastricht and the outbreak of the MATRIX-CHURCHILL AFFAIR. But a successful outcome to the December 1992 EC SUMMIT in Edinburgh stabilized his position.

Major's banking background and lack of rolling phrases led commentators to brand him as "grey". When also accused of arrogance, he complained: "I can't be grey *and* arrogant." Edward Pearce described him as "the man who ran away from the circus to become an accountant". An airport worker told Neil Kinnock: "He always goes through the green channel. After a year he's still got nothing to declare." And Jackie Mason won easy laughs by saying: "He makes George Bush seem like a personality." But William Waldegrave remarked: "No man ever double crosses John twice." And a senior Irish official praised him as "one of the very few senior British politicians I have encountered who is in no way patronizing in his dealings with us". He also had to rein in his considerable wit. When a young MP, he heard Teddy Taylor (a former Glasgow MP who had moved to Southend and had learned of a vacancy in Glasgow) say: "I've had hundreds of letters asking me to stand." Major riposted: "How many were from Southend, Teddy?" At other times he was on the receiving end. When Tory candidate for St. Pancras, he was reputed to have had the following exchange:

> *Voice*: Who is it?
> *Major*: I am John Major, your Conservative candidate.
> *Voice*: Who is it?
> *Major*: I am John Major, your Conservative candidate.
> *Voice*: Who is it?.
> (Major opens the letter-box and sees . . . a parrot.)

majority. majority leader The head of the larger party group in the US SENATE, and in the House the most powerful figure after the Speaker. Former Senate majority leader Howard Baker said: "There are two roles for a majority leader in the Senate. One is the President's spear carrier, and the other is an independent force. I chose to be a spear-carrier." And in the House, as Rep. Jim Wright put it, the majority leader "has a hunting licence to persuade".

majority rule 1960s code for African, rather than White minority, rule in British COLONIES approaching INDEPENDENCE. At the height of the controversy over UDI, Rhodesian Prime Minister Ian Smith declared:

> I don't believe in black majority rule ever in Rhodesia – not in a thousand years.

absolute majority More than 50% of the seats available or votes cast, giving the victorious party or candidate more support than all the others put together.

moral majority An American right-wing evangelical movement, founded by the Rev. Jerry Falwell, which claims the authority to impose its views on the political community in such areas as prayer in schools, in parallel with the campaign against abortion.

overall majority In a legislature where one party has the numbers to govern alone, the difference between the number of seats it holds and the total of all other parties.

qualified majority The weighted formula for voting by nation in the EC COUNCIL OF MINISTERS to settle those issues that do not require unanimity under the LUXEMBOURG COMPROMISE. A "qualified majority" is 54 votes out of 76, with Britain, France, Germany and Italy having 10 votes each, Spain 8, Belgium, Greece, the Netherlands and Portugal 5 each, Denmark and Ireland 3, and Luxembourg 2.

silent majority The term popularized – though not coined – by President Nixon for the uncounted millions of ordinary people who can be relied on to give support to a conservative regime, undetected by opinion-formers. Liberals categorized the silent majority as "unyoung, unpoor and unblack". Nixon took up the phrase on 3 November 1969, in a speech credited with rallying support for the VIETNAM WAR, saying:

> And so tonight, to you – the great silent majority of my fellow Americans – I ask for your support.

working majority A majority of more than a handful, large enough for a ruling party in a legislature to govern without having to take regular precautions against defeat when votes are called.

a majority can do anything The attributed doctrine of Joe Cannon (1836–1926), SPEAKER of the US HOUSE OF REPRESENTATIVES. Winston CHURCHILL supported him, reckoning that "one is enough". But a later Speaker, Sam Rayburn, said: "When you get too big a majority, you're immediately in trouble." And in the earliest days of American democracy, Thomas Jefferson advised: "Great innovations should not be forced on slender majorities."

a majority of one is still a majority John F. Kennedy's comment after his election to the Presidency in 1960. He said:

> The majority is narrow, but the responsibility is clear. There may be difficulties with the Congress, but a majority of one is still a majority.

one man with courage makes a majority A saying of President Andrew Jackson, much modified by US politicians and commentators. Wendell Phillips (1811–84) wrote that "one on God's side is a majority"; House Speaker Thomas Reed (1839–1902) in turn qualified this by noting: "One, with God, is always a majority, but many a martyr has been burned at the stake while the votes were being counted." And Calvin Coolidge, accepting the Republican Vice-Presidential nomination in 1920, said that "one, with the law, is a majority".

putting a majority together is like a one-armed man wrapping cranberries The verdict of Sen. Robert Dole, himself with only one arm, on the difficulties of putting together a winning coalition for a Bill in the US Congress.

the majority are always wrong It has often been claimed that CONSENSUS politics produces disastrous results, and the American Socialist Eugene Debs (1855–1926) observed:

> When great changes occur in history, when great principles are concerned, as a rule the majority are wrong.

See also PLURALITY.

malice. with malice toward none, with charity for all The keynote of Abraham LINCOLN's second INAUGURAL ADDRESS on 4 March 1865, marking the start of what he hoped would be four years of reconciliation between North and South following the CIVIL WAR. Exactly two months later, Lincoln's hopes having been dashed with his assassination, the same words were read over his grave. He said:

> With malice toward none; with charity for all; with firmness in the right, as God gives us to see the right, let us strive on to finish the work we are in; to bind up the nation's wounds; to care for him who shall have borne the battle, and for his widow, and his orphan – to do all which may achieve and cherish a just, and a lasting peace, among ourselves, and with all nations.

Mall, the In WASHINGTON DC, the flat expanse, nearly a mile long, overlooked by the WEST FRONT of the Capitol and stretching to the Washington Monument. Originally bounded by Constitution Avenue to the north and Independence Avenue to the south, the Smithsonian Institution, the National Gallery, Air and Space Museum and other public buildings have encroached on it.

Malthusianism The doctrine of Thomas **Malthus** (1766–1834), historian and economist, that "population, when unchecked, increases in a geometrical ratio" while food supplies increase only arithmetically. He aimed to solve "the perpetual struggle for room and food" by postponing the age of marriage and requiring strict continence.

Malvinas, las Islas The Argentine name for the FALKLANDS, from the French Les Malouines (the people of St. Malo, an apparent reference to the first settlers). It is also used by those UK politicians who accept Argentina's claim to SOVEREIGNTY over the islands.

man. Man from Missouri One of many nicknames for President Harry S Truman (*see* GIVE 'EM HELL HARRY).

Man of Steel The English rendering of the Russian name STALIN, adopted by the Soviet dictator Joseph Vissarionovich Dzughashvili. The name coincidentally reflected both his hardline political beliefs and the ruthlessness with which he dealt with his enemies.

Man on Horseback A larger-than-life, capable and by inference authoritarian figure who will appear from outside the political world and solve a nation's problems. The term was first used in the 19th century of General Georges Boulanger (1837–91), who briefly saw himself as a potential dictator of France and, when a widely-expected COUP failed to materialize, was accused of treason. In 1961 John F. KENNEDY, attacking the last vestiges of McCARTHYISM, denounced "those who call for a 'man on horseback' because they do not trust the people." And former California Governor Edmund G. "Jerry" Brown (*see* SPACE CADET) said:

> Politics is a jungle and it's getting worse. People want a DICTATOR these days, a man on a white horse, to ride in and tell them what to do.

man on the Clapham omnibus A term for the view of the average member of the public which became popular in late 19th-century Britain, and has stuck.

Man on the Wedding Cake An unflattering nickname for Thomas E. DEWEY which was held partly responsible for his unexpected defeat by Harry S. Truman in the 1948 Presidential election. The phrase, with its overtones of ridicule, stiffness and lack of character, was bestowed on Dewey by Grace Hodgson Flandreau, and given maximum circulation in Washington by Alice Roosevelt Longworth.

management of decline The phrase summing up the defeatist atmosphere in WHITEHALL during the 1970s, with Britain seen as inevitably on the slide. It was used by William Armstrong, Head of the Civil Service, to appalled members of Edward Heath's Cabinet in 1973; he told them the business of his administrative corps was "the orderly (some members recall 'peaceful') management of decline".

manager The combined chief executive

and principal administrative officer of an American city, appointed as the alternative to a political mayor who exercises a leadership role. The manager is appointed by and responsible to the municipal council. The first municipality to adopt the system was Sumter, South Carolina, in 1912; about one-third of communities with over 5000 population now operate the system.

managers The appointees of both Houses of the US Congress who take part in a House-Senate conference on a disputed Bill. The name is also reserved for the House appointees who would prosecute an accused President in an IMPEACHMENT trial before the Senate.

Manchester school The grouping of Liberal MPs and their followers in the booming Northern city, headed by Richard Cobden (1804–65) and John Bright (1811–89), who from the early 1840s championed the cause of the working man, of wider democracy and – above all – of FREE TRADE. As a movement their impact on Westminster lasted barely a decade, but the name has stuck. The term was invented by Disraeli – who did not intend it as a compliment.

mandarins The occupants of the highest level of Britain's CIVIL SERVICE – PERMANENT SECRETARIES and the officials who work in closest proximity to them. The term reflects the widespread belief among politicians and political journalists that WHITEHALL has a subtly aristocratic culture of its own, whose leaders are able to manipulate the workings of government while using a language of suave opacity but deadly effect.

mandate (1) The legitimacy given to a government or an individual and their policies by having won an election. In 1984 after Ronald Reagan's 49-state victory, James BAKER said:

> We're going to play down the mandate. We need to be gracious winners.

(2) The authority under which the LEAGUE OF NATIONS delegated the administration of certain territories after World War I to member governments. The most controversial was Britain's mandate over Palestine, the longest-running was South Africa's over South-West Africa, which it refused to relinquish until Namibian independence in 1990. In 1945 mandates were formally superseded by the UN's TRUSTEESHIP system.

doctor's mandate *See* DOCTOR.

dual mandate The situation of a member simultaneously of both of the Westminster Parliament and the EUROPEAN PARLIAMENT at Strasbourg. Initially several MPs were members of both assemblies, but now only those who have served in one and are switching to the other, plus Northern Ireland members, maintain it.

Manhattan project The codename given to the US project which resulted in the development of the first ATOMIC BOMB. Franklin D. Roosevelt ordered action after PEARL HARBOR, having resisted a proposal from Einstein as early as 1938 for a fission bomb of unparalleled destructive power. Great secrecy and great haste were required to construct such a bomb before the Germans, who were thought to be working on a similar project. The project began at Columbia University, New York, in 1942, and the next year an international team of scientists under the physicist J. Robert Oppenheimer was brought together at Los Alamos, New Mexico, to develop the bomb; as early as February 1944 some were concerned that it would bring post-war tension between the SUPERPOWERS. Uraniam-235 was produced at Oak Ridge, Tennessee, and plutonium at Hanford, Washington State. The Manhattan Project culminated in the testing of the first atomic bomb on 16 July 1945, and its first use in war at HIROSHIMA on 6 August. Total expenditure on the project was around $2 billion.

> We knew the world would not be the same.
>
> J. ROBERT OPPENHEIMER, 1945.

Manifest Destiny The doctrine that America should put westward expansion at the top of its priorities, and that it had a historic mission to stretch to the Pacific and occupy all and more of its present coastline – and much of Canada. First put forward under other names in the late 18th century, it became a political catchphrase just prior to the MEXICAN WAR when America was absorbing Texas. The phrase was created in 1845 by the Democratic journalist John L. O'Sullivan; he argued that it was America's "manifest destiny to overspread the continent allotted by providence for the free development of our yearly multiplying millions" (*see also* FIFTY-FOUR FORTY OR FIGHT).

manifesto A document issued by a political party at or in advance of an election setting out its programme for government, and making pledges that will be held against it if it does not keep them.

Manifesto Group A centre-right grouping of Labour MPs, counterbalancing the TRIBUNE GROUP, which enjoyed considerable support in the late 1970s. The name reflected a desire to defend Labour's 1974 election manifesto against the Left's calls for more radical policies. The defection of a number of members to the SDP in 1981 marked the end of the group's effectiveness.

Tamworth Manifesto *See* TAMWORTH.

Manila Pact The treaty signed in Manila on 8 September 1954 on the creation of SEATO; the signatories were America, Australia, Britain, France, New Zealand, Pakistan, the Philippines and Thailand. It came into force on 19 February 1955 and was formally ended in 1977.

Mann Act The Act passed by the US Congress in 1910 to curb prostitution and "white slavery". It made it an offence to transport women across State lines, or bring them into the country, for immoral purposes. The Act closed red-light districts in 30 American cities, but New Orleans survived it.

Mann-Elkins Act Also passed in 1910, this measure finally made government regulation of America's railroads effective by empowering the Interstate Commerce Commission to suspend freight rates it felt excessive without first having to argue the case in the courts.

Manny Nickname for **Emmanuel** (later Lord) **Shinwell** (1884–1986), who started as a Glasgow street boxer and ended as Britain's longest-lived peer. Jailed in 1921 for inciting a workers' riot, he won a Parliamentary seat in 1923 and the next year served in RAMSAY MACDonald's first Labour government. He made his name in 1935 when he unseated MacDonald, now Prime Minister of the NATIONAL GOVERNMENT, at Seaham. He helped ATTLEE draft the manifesto for Labour's landslide victory in 1945, and as Minister of Fuel and Power NATIONALIZED the coal industry. The FUEL CRISIS of 1947 dented his reputation, and despite impressing as Minister of Defence he never held higher office. After a spell in the 1960s as chairman of the PLP, he retired from the Commons in 1970 with a Life PEERAGE. In his old age Shinwell, who in his day had threatened to punch opponents on the nose, gained new repute as an avuncular raconteur.

Manor of Northstead The position of steward of the manor is one an MP can apply for when he or she wishes to take the CHILTERN HUNDREDS. Northstead is a place of little consequence, but the stewardship, which has no practical purpose, is technically an OFFICE OF PROFIT UNDER THE CROWN and therefore renders the holder ineligible to sit in the Commons.

Mansfield judgment The ruling by Lord Mansfield (1705–93), Lord Chief Justice, in 1772 which established that slavery was illegal in England and Wales. Ruling on a claim by the owner of James Somersett, a runaway slave, to recover him, Mansfield said:

> The exercise of the power of a master over his slave must be supported by the laws of particular countries; but no foreigner in England can claim such a right over a man: such a claim is not known to the laws of England.

Mansion House speech The speech made each year, in June or October, by Britain's CHANCELLOR OF THE EXCHEQUER at the Mansion House, headquarters of the City of London, in which he sets out his view of the domestic and world economy. Lloyd George's speech in July 1911 attracted particular attention, as he departed from the habitual subject to warn Germany that Britain would support France in any conflict that arose from the AGADIR CRISIS.

Maoists Adherents of the highly-disciplined, revolutionary brand of Communism advocated by Mao Tse-Tung (*see* CHAIRMAN MAO). Maoist elements appeared in a number of Communist parties after the break between Moscow and Beijing in the early 1960s; the SHINING PATH movement in Peru achieved its greatest strength almost two decades after Mao's death.

Maquis A name for the French RESISTANCE in World War II, taken from the thick scrubland of the Mediterranean coast to which bandits formerly retreated to avoid capture.

march A form of DEMONSTRATION in which those making their point parade with banners between two points, usually with a RALLY at the start and always with one at the end. *See* ALDERMASTON; SELMA.

march my troops toward the sound of gunfire The rallying-call issued to the conference of Britain's LIBERAL PARTY on 15 September 1963 by its leader, Jo (later Lord) Grimond (1913–). With the 1964 election in prospect, Grimond told his party:

> And in bygone days, commanders were taught that, when in doubt, they should march their troops towards the sound of gunfire. I intend to march my troops towards the sound of gunfire.

March on Rome The arrival in Rome of Mussolini and thousands of his BLACKSHIRTS on 28 October 1922, shortly before the establishment of a FASCIST state in Italy. They travelled to Rome by various means – largely by rail – and entered the city with little or no opposition from military or civil authorities. The head of the Cabinet resigned and King Victor Emmanuel III invited Mussolini to form a new government.

March on Washington for Jobs and Freedom The largest ever demonstration in Washington, staged in August 1963 to support President Kennedy's landmark CIVIL RIGHTS Bill, then being debated by Congress. Marchers who had reached the capital on foot from the South were joined on the final leg from the Washington Monument to the

Lincoln Memorial by 200,000 people, some 60,000 of them White. They were addressed from the Memorial by Black and White civil rights leaders, among them Dr. Martin Luther KING who delivered his historic I HAVE A DREAM oration.

hunger march *See* JARROW CRUSADE.

marching season The period during the summer when the ORANGE Lodges and other LOYALIST groups in Northern Ireland take to the streets with drum-and-flute bands to commemorate William of Orange's victory at the Battle of the BOYNE in 1689, the resistance of the APPRENTICE BOYS OF DERRY and other past triumphs over the Catholics. The marches are occasionally routed through Catholic areas in order to provoke the inhabitants. In 1980 the then Northern Ireland Secretary Humphrey Atkins (later Lord Colnbrook) asked a police inspector the difference between the Temperance Lodges and the Total Abstinence Lodges who had joined one parade. The officer replied:

> It's simple. By the end of the day the Temperance will be well away, and the total abstainers will be fucking paralytic.

However regular marchers insist they never touch alcohol until the parades are over.

Marconi affair A financial scandal which tarnished Lloyd George when Chancellor of the Exchequer, but did not halt his rise. In 1912 he bought shares worth £2000 in the US Marconi company, at a preferential rate through its managing director Godfrey Isaacs, brother of the Attorney-General Rufus Isaacs (later Lord Reading). Meanwhile British Marconi shares rose sharply as a result of a government contract to build radio stations. While the two companies were separate, there were inevitably rumours of corruption. The SELECT COMMITTEE set up to investigate the matter cleared Lloyd George and Isaacs of corruption, though the transaction was described as imprudent; when pressed in the House on their Marconi holdings, neither had volunteered that they had speculated in the US company's stock. Lloyd George, who at one stage showed a paper profit but eventually made a loss on the deal, offered to resign; ASQUITH stood by him but wrote:

> I think the idol's wings are clipped.

marginal seat In British politics, a Parliamentary seat held by one party with a narrow majority over another and always liable to change hands between them; the UK equivalent of a SWING DISTRICT.

key marginal A party organizers' phrase for a seat the capture of which is essential to take power in a closely-fought election.

three-way marginal A seat where three parties all finished close together at the previous election, and where each has a strong chance of victory next time.

marginalization The tactic of manoeuvring a party or grouping into a position where it loses influence and support and becomes irrelevant. The word originated in America, but was widely used in Britain by the late 1980s.

margin of error The term used by pollsters for the allowance for SAMPLING ERROR that should be left in interpretation of their results. For example a margin of error of 3% would mean that a poll putting Party A on 51% and party B on 49% could reflect a 54–46% lead for Party A – or a 52–48% lead for Party B.

Marine One The name given to the first-choice helicopter of the President of the United States (*see* LBJ: "Son, these are all my helicopters"). It is a reminder to the American people, and the other armed forces, that of all the services with helicopters, the Marine Corps has been chosen to supply the Presidential chopper.

market, the A situation in which economic or other forces compete freely, without being distorted for good or ill by outside agencies.

> The best test of truth is the power of the thought to get itself accepted in the competition of the market.
>
> Justice OLIVER WENDELL HOLMES (1841–1935).

> You cannot buck the market. MARGARET THATCHER.

market economy An economy which operates subject to the disciplines of market forces of supply and demand, without any interference from or regulation by government. It is also known as the free market. When REAGANOMICS proved a less than runaway success, Ronald Reagan said:

> The system has never failed us once. But we have failed the system every time we lose faith in the magic of the marketplace.

> The trouble about a free market economy is that it requires so many policemen to make it work.
>
> NEAL ASCHERSON, *the Observer*, 1985.

Single Market *See* SINGLE.

social market An economic policy concept combining development of a relatively free market with a high level of social provision. It originated in Germany (Ger. *Soziale Marktswirtschaft*), and was taken up in the mid-1970s by Sir Keith Joseph (*see* MAD MONK) and other right-wing UK Conservatives, and in the early 1980s by Dr. David OWEN and the muscular wing of the SDP (*see* CARING BUT DARING). To left-wingers it is "THATCHERISM with a human face", to right-wingers like Nicholas (later Lord) Ridley the notion that "the main point of the free market is to provide the resources for the social services, and lavish provision of those services for all is the main purpose of political life".

markup session In the US Congress, the often-private sessions at which the draft of a proposed Bill is reviewed by the relevant committee.

> It is here that outside interests can slip in a loophole with the help of a committee STAFFER.
> MARK GREEN (1945–), *Who Runs Congress?*.

Marples must go *See* BALFOUR MUST GO.

Marseillaise, la The stirring battle-song of the FRENCH REVOLUTION which became the national anthem of Republican France. It was written in April 1792 by Claude Rouget de Lisle (1760–1836), a captain in the French garrison at Strasbourg and ironically a Royalist, for the mayor who wanted a marching song. He entitled it "War song for the Rhône Army", but it was renamed after revolutionary soldiers from Marseilles sang it on their march to the Tuileries on 10 August 1792. The opening lines of the *Marseillaise*, which ends with a call to citizens to take up arms, are:

> Allons, enfants de la patrie,
> Le jour de gloire est arrivé.
>
> (Let's go, children of our country,
> The day of glory has arrived.)

Marshall Aid or **Plan** The popular name for the programme devised by US Secretary of State General George C. Marshall (1880–1959) and announced by him in a speech at Harvard on 5 June 1947, to bring economic aid to stricken Europe after World War II. The plan, fleshed out at a conference with potential recipients in Paris, was intended both to end Europe's suffering and act as a bulwark against Communism; the Soviet Union refused, and her SATELLITES were ordered, not to participate, greatly easing Truman's task in getting the plan through Congress. $13 billion in aid – food, raw materials and machinery – was gratefully accepted between 1948 and 1951 by 16 non-Communist European countries, including Britain.

> General, I want the plan to go down in history with your name on it. And don't give me any arguments – I'm your COMMANDER-IN-CHIEF.
> President TRUMAN.

> The most unsordid act in history. CHURCHILL.

martial law The imposition of arbitrary power under military discipline by a government threatened by war or internal unrest. The most notorious instance in recent time was the martial law imposed in Poland by General Jaruzelski to halt the spread of the SOLIDARITY trade union.

Marxism The ideology formulated by Karl Marx (1818–83) as the basis of COMMUNISM, which has three main strands: that economic forces control political and social conditions; that private property must be abolished to ensure equality and an end to exploitation; and that Communism can only come about through the PROLETARIAT or its leaders gaining revolutionary consciousness and taking power. Mao Tse-Tung asserted: "There may be thousands of principles of Marxism, but . . . they can all be summed up in one sentence: Rebellion is justified"; Fidel Castro testified that for him "discovering Marxism was like finding a map in a forest". George Bernard Shaw, a FABIAN, wrote off Marxism as "not only useless, but disastrous as a guide to the practice of government". But Harold Macmillan is said to have observed in the 1950s: "We are all Marxists now".

Marx himself was the father of Communism. He fled to Brussels when his activities in Germany put him at risk, and in exile teamed up with Friedrich Engels (1820–95) to write the basic works of the movement, the COMMUNIST MANIFESTO (1848) and DAS KAPITAL (1867–94). Marx moved to London, where he worked in the British Museum reading room, spent a quiet but seldom dull life dogged by real or imagined ill-health, and was buried in Highgate Cemetery.

> All I know is I am not a Marxist. MARX.

> Karl Marx wasn't a Marxist all the time. He got drunk in the Tottenham Court Road. MICHAEL FOOT.

> Marx sought to replace national antagonisms by class antagonisms. H. G. WELLS.

> The world would not be in such a snarl
> Had Marx been Groucho instead of Karl.
> IRVING BERLIN.

Marxism-Leninism LENIN's elaboration of Marxist political and economic thought, and the stated credo of all disciplined Communists from the mid-1920s to the mid-1980s. Communist regimes who were at each other's throats (*i.e.* Moscow and Peking) each stressed their own Marxist-Leninist credentials, and their position as custodians of the true faith. In this respect Marxism-Leninism certainly did take the place of religion for millions of believers.

Mason-Dixon Line The boundary between Pennsylvania and Maryland drawn in 1767 to end half a century of argument and litigation. Its significance is that it marked the border between SLAVE STATES and those where slavery was illegal, and consequently the fault-line in the UNION.

mass. mass meeting In Britain a meeting of all the members of a trade union at a plant, called usually in the open to vote on the outcome of negotiations with management and whether to take strike or other action. Voting was done on a show of hands, and abuses of the process were one factor behind the Thatcher government's imposition of strike and other BALLOTS on trade unions in the early 1980s. Such meetings are now a rarity, save for the imparting of information.

Mass Observation The social monitoring organization whose surveys throughout WORLD WAR II gave the British government an unprecedented, and at times unwelcome, view of the state of public morale and opinion.

Massachusetts miracle The technology-based boom in Massachusetts which the state's Democratic governor Michael Dukakis (1933–) made much of in his unsuccessful Presidential campaign in 1988. The "miracle" collapsed not long after the inauguration of his Republican rival George BUSH.

massive retaliation The words of US Secretary of State John Foster Dulles in 1953 which were meant to signal a slight but important variation of the policy of immediate and devastating response to any nuclear attack which dominated Western strategic thinking, and the policy of DETERRENCE, at the start of the COLD WAR. Dulles spoke of "massive retaliation at a time and place of our own choosing", but only his first two words attracted attention and were taken as reinforcing previous policy. Even the policy Dulles meant to outline was a far cry from the doctrine of FLEXIBLE RESPONSE with which NATO replaced it in 1968.

masterly inactivity A now-common phrase first used, of France's THIRD ESTATE when it convened in 1789, by the Scottish lawyer and politician Sir James Mackintosh (1765–1832). He wrote:

> The commons, faithful to their system, remained in a wise and masterly inactivity.

It has been often used since in UK and American politics, most notably by Vice-President John C. Calhoun in the NULLIFICATION crisis, telling the South Carolina legislature in 1831:

> If the Government should be taught thereby, that the highest wisdom of a State is a "wise and masterly inactivity", an invaluable blessing will be conferred.

matching funds The Federal subsidy for Presidential campaigns, introduced by the Election Campaign Act of 1974, in response to the abuses thrown up by WATERGATE. The funds are offered to Presidential candidates (including candidates in the PRIMARY process), provided they have reached certain fund-raising thresholds themselves. The Act also imposed spending limits on all candidates taking up the subsidy, and tightened reporting requirements on candidates' fund-raising.

Matricides The term used by die-hard THATCHERITES for the Conservative Ministers and MPs who they believe plotted her removal in November 1990. (*see also* CATHERINE PLACE MEETING). It stems from their own description of the then Prime Minister as MOTHER.

Matrix-Churchill affair The scandal that broke at Westminster in November 1992 after the collapse of the trial of three executives of the Coventry machine tool firm Matrix-Churchill on charges of illegally trading with Iraq prior to the second GULF WAR. It emerged that the three – one an agent for British intelligence – had been acting with the encouragement of Ministers, who had loosened the arms embargo on Iraq imposed during the first Gulf War without telling Parliament. The trial was halted after former Trade and Defence Minister Alan Clark (*see* BONGO-BONGO LAND) retracted evidence he had given to the Customs and Excise, and the judge found that four documents ruled confidential by Ministers proved the defendants had had government backing. MPs were incensed that Ministers had apparently been ready both to deceive them about this change of policy and to let three men go to prison rather than reveal it. John MAJOR announced a judicial inquiry under Lord Justice Scott, but damaging questions continued to surface about the probity of government.

Matteotti murder The assassination by the FASCISTS of the Italian Socialist politician Giacomo Matteotti (1885–1924). On 30 May 1924 Matteotti spoke out against the Fascists in the Chamber of Deputies; several days later he was abducted and murdered by six assassins allegedly hired by Fascist Party officials. The discovery of Matteotti's body on 16 August was a damaging blow for Mussolini's government. The assassins were brought to trial; three were acquitted and the others give light sentences which were subsequently remitted. A retrial in 1947 resulted in sentences of 30 years' penal servitude for the three previously found guilty.

Mau Mau The secret political society among Kenya's Kikuyu people which developed into a violent rebellion in the early 1950s against White settlers, and Africans who refused to join. Formed in the 1940s as a breakaway from the Kenya African Union, Mau Mau's main aim was to drive the Europeans out of Africa by terrorism (the word *mau* means "get out!"); its members were bound by oaths and dire threats if they were broken. It remained secret until 1952 when the rebellion against the British colonial government broke out with a series of terrible atrocities, each member of a Mau Mau band sharing in every killing. Between 1952 and 1956 Mau Mau killed over 100 Europeans and 200 Africans, but suffered 11,000 losses in conflict with British and African troops. In 1953 Jomo Kenyatta, later the first post-independence President of Kenya, was sentenced to seven years' imprisonment as a suspected leader of Mau Mau; tough security subdued the rebellion, but it lingered until 1959. For a time, "to mau-mau" became US slang for harass or bully.

Maurice letter The episode which did more than any other to wreck Britain's LIBERAL PARTY, making irreparable the split between ASQUITH and Lloyd George just as LABOUR was preparing its decisive challenge. The letter was sent to the press in May 1918 by Maj.-Gen. Sir Frederick Maurice, who had just been removed as Director of Military Operations at the War Office, contradicting Lloyd George's claim that the British Army in France was "considerably stronger" at the start of the year than 12 months before. Maurice admitted it was a breach of military discipline, but Lloyd George also saw it a plot against him by the Prime Minister he had ousted; Asquith was a friend of Maurice, but only heard of the letter when the papers did. Asquith moved for a SELECT COMMITTEE into the facts of the case in an uncertain speech, Lloyd George made a barnstorming appeal for instant vindication; Asquith divided the House and Lloyd George won, with the Liberals split: 100 for Asquith's motion, 71 for Lloyd George.

> *Asquith*: What is the alternative to a Select Committee?
> *Charles Stanton MP* (Lab.): Get on with the war.

mausoleum A building which houses the preserved remains of a political leader. The most celebrated is LENIN's in RED SQUARE, cutsomarily visited by all Communist newlyweds, which has survived the collapse of the Soviet system. Lenin's enbalmed body is in near-perfect condition, being regularly checked by a special team of scientists and removed for a thorough overhaul every 18 months; originally dressed in military uniform, he has since the 1950s won a jacket, shirt and tie in 1920s style.

maverick An unpredictable, independent-minded loner who cannot be relied upon to follow the party line. The name originated in Texas where the rancher Samuel A. Maverick (1803–70) neglected to brand many of his calves; before long any beast running free was known as a maverick and by the 1880s the term was current in US politics.

maximum. max out In US politics, to allocate the maximum amount a party may legally contribute to a candidate.

maximalist A person or party that insists that all their demands be met and all their goals be achieved in full, rejecting all thought of COMPROMISE.

Maximum John The nickname of US District Judge John Sirica (1904–92), who in 1973 blew open the WATERGATE scandal. He did so by imposing punitive sentences of up to 40 years on the burglars, on the correct assumption that they would break their silence about who was behind the raid, and by ruling that the court, not the President, would decide whether the Watergate Tapes were evidence. Sirica earned his reputation as a tough sentencer well before Watergate, but the crisis gave him comparable status as a jurist; all his rulings were upheld by the SUPREME COURT.

Maxwell-Fyfe rules The archetypal guidance on when a Minister should take responsibility for actions by his or her civil servants and resign, laid down by the Home Secretary Sir David Maxwell-Fyfe (later Lord Kilmuir), in 1954 after the CRICHEL DOWN affair.

> There is nothing more like death in life
> Than Sir David Maxwell-Fyfe.
>
> Quoted by DENIS HEALEY in the Commons, 22 November 1990.

May Day The public holiday observed in many countries, on 1 May or the first Monday in the month, to celebrate international workers' SOLIDARITY; in many cases it is a festival of SOCIALISM. In Moscow May Day has traditionally seen a massive parade through RED SQUARE, with the nation's leaders reviewing its military might from a rostrum on the KREMLIN wall above Lenin's MAUSOLEUM; since the mid-1980s the occasion has been festive rather than military. In Communist days, there was much speculation as to who would appear among the leadership, and in what order.

Mayaguez A US container ship seized by Cambodia in the Gulf of Siam on 12 May 1975. She was released after President FORD, anxious not to appear weak after America's retreat from VIETNAM, ordered air strikes against KHMER ROUGE gunboats and the bombing of mainland Cambodia. On 14 May, US Marines landed on the Tang Islands, claimed by the Khmers, and boarded the deserted ship. Thirty-nine crew members of the *Mayaguez* were freed – at a cost of 38 US lives.

Mayflower The yacht based on the POTOMAC which was used by US Presidents from McKinley to Coolidge. It was named, of course, after the ship in which the Pilgrim Fathers sailed.

Mayor The civic head of a town or city. In America, France and some other countries the Mayor heads the city government and wields considerable power; in England and Wales the position is ceremonial, though the Mayor holds the CASTING VOTE during his or her year of office. English and Welsh cities – the title is bestowed by Royal charter on communities with over 250,000 inhabitants – have a **Lord Mayor**.

Maze prison The high-security prison built just south-west of Belfast in the early 1970s to hold suspected or convicted terrorists. REPUBLICANs in Ulster still refer to it by its original name of Long Kesh or simply as **the Kesh**. Both LOYALIST and Republican prisoners were at first housed in Nissen huts; after a Republican hunger strike in 1972 for prisoner-of-war status, convicted prisoners were granted "special status". This decision was reversed in 1976, from when new inmates were housed – segregated on SECTARIAN lines – in eight single-storey H-BLOCKS; each with 25 cells, dining room, exercise yard and recreation room. The complex, said at the time to be the most modern in Europe, included a sports hall, workshops, hospital and two all-weather sports pitches. Soon after the H-blocks were opened, Republican prisoners began a campaign for reinstatement of special status, refusing to wear prison uniform and from 1978 staging the BLANKET PROTEST and DIRTY PROTEST when they stayed in their cells and smeared excrement on the walls. The campaign culminated in the HUNGER STRIKE of 1981 in which Bobby Sands, elected to Parliament while in the Maze, starved himself to death on 5 May. The British Government refused to concede, despite a wave of rioting in the province; after nine further deaths the Republicans abandoned their campaign. However a mass breakout by 38 Republican terrorists, in which one prison officer was killed, soon after the end of the hunger strikes further embarrassed the authorities. The prison, and particularly the H-blocks, remained a potent propaganda symbol for SINN FEIN and militant Loyalists throughout the 1980s.

MCAs Monetary Compensatory Amounts. In the Common Agricultural Policy (CAP), the differential between GREEN currencies and the real foreign exchange values of the various EC currencies. Calculated each week, MCAs serve as export subsidies for countries with weak currencies, yet make their farm exports more expensive. Correspondingly, they keep down the export prices of countries with strong currencies, while ensuring that farm incomes do not fall.

me-tooism A state of mind in which a political party or candidate tries to win votes by offering policies very similar to those of their opponents. The term, used by those who believe elections can only be won by offering the voters a fundamental choice, has been common in US politics since the late 1940s.

means test The principle that evidence of need must be supplied to qualify for support from public funds; *i.e.* a test of one's means. Such tests were introduced by the UK's NATIONAL GOVERNMENT in 1931 for those whose unemployment benefit was exhausted, and the resulting inquisition was much resented by those concerned – leading the LABOUR PARTY to adopt a rigid opposition to means testing that lasted half a century. The test involved listing any earnings by members of the household and all monetary assets, and penalized the provident. The regulations governing public assistance were modified after World War II, but some non-contributory social security benefits are still means-tested.

Mebyon Kernow (Sons of Cornwall) The society of Cornish nationalists, established in 1951, which has contested a number of Parliamentary elections though with minimal success. They advocate the cultivation of the extinct but revived Cornish language, from which their name is taken, and a degree of self-government in concert with other Celtic peoples such as the Bretons, the Welsh, the Irish and the Gaelic-speaking Scots. Their flag is the emblem of St. Piran, a 5th- or 6th-century saint who is reputed to have discovered tin in Cornwall. It consists of a white cross, which symbolizes tin, on a black field, representing the ground rock from which it is extracted.

meddle and muddle The colourful phrase first used by the Earl of Derby (1799–1869) to describe the foreign policy of the Liberal leader Earl (formerly Lord John) Russell. Derby told the House of Lords on 4 February 1864:

> The foreign policy of the noble Earl may be summed up in two short, homely but expressive words: "meddle and muddle".

media The press, radio and television (electronic media), a powerful force (*see* FOURTH ESTATE) capable of exposing scandals like

WATERGATE, or hounding or misrepresenting a party or its leaders; consequently a whipping-horse for every politician who dislikes criticism. Enoch POWELL remarked philosophically that "politicians who complain about the media are like ships' captains who complain about the sea", but Ronald Reagan, who had a better press than Powell, complained:

> People in the media say they must look at the President through a microscope. But boy, when they use a proctoscope, that's going too far.

John F. KENNEDY, for whom the media covered up again and again, was moved to tell the press: "I have always said that when we don't have to go through you bastards, we can really get our story over to the American people", while RED KEN Livingstone, a target of Fleet Street in the early 1980s, observed: "If I blew my nose they would say I was trying to spread germ warfare."

> To hell with them. When history is written they will be the sons of bitches, not I. HARRY S TRUMAN.

media event An event of no real political significance, arranged by public relations personnel specifically to attract media coverage; it generally includes a PHOTO OPPORTUNITY.

mediation The role of a third nation or independent figure in bringing together two parties to an international, political or industrial dispute in an effort to generate agreement between them.

Medicaid The US public-health programme to provide hospital and medical care for those who cannot afford it. It was established by Congress in 1965 as a joint plan in which the Federal government funds 50 to 80% of a state's costs, depending on its citizens' average income. Each state must meet federal standards, but may choose the services it wishes to provide. Any indigent person qualifies for Medicaid, and some states stretch this to the "medically indigent" who are unable to pay medical bills incompatible with their earnings.

Medicare The insurance programme to provide hospital and medical care to Americans aged 65 or over, and some disabled persons. First proposed by President KENNEDY and approved by Congress in 1965, it is funded by a tax added to social security payments. It covers treatment in hospitals, in nursing homes and at home (after a deductible sum of over $500 is paid each year), and meets 80% of physician and medical costs not covered by the hospital insurance. In 1988 Congress passed the Medicare Catastrophic Coverage Act to expand coverage, but so many elderly Americans objected to the surtax to fund its cost (more than $32 billion over five years) that the Act was repealed the next year.

medium term financial strategy (MTFS) The name adopted by Margaret Thatcher and her first Chancellor Sir Geoffrey HOWE, at the suggestion of Nigel Lawson, for the MONETARIST strategy adopted by them from 1979, with monetary targets published several years ahead. Known to sceptics as **"Mrs. Thatcher's Final Solution"**, the MTFS was adhered to seriously for a couple of years, but the name and targets lived on for several more.

> Intended to set a reliable framework of government policy within which the markets could form "rational expectations", it simply demonstrated that no one should take seriously anything a Conservative Chancellor said.
>
> DENIS HEALEY.

Meech Lake The agreement negotiated between the Canadian provinces in 1987 by Brian Mulroney which attempted to resolve the deadlock over amending the Federal constitution by granting Quebec **distinct society** status. The accord was always fragile, and collapsed in 1990 when Manitoba and Newfoundland failed to ratify it. A constitutional crisis ensued, which the equally-abortive CHARLOTTETOWN ACCORD of 1992 was designed to resolve.

Meet the challenge. Make the change The slogan with which the LABOUR PARTY under Neil KINNOCK relaunched itself after its POLICY REVIEW, and went into the 1992 election campaign with high hopes – only to suffer its fourth successive defeat. Labour's updated image and its jettisoning of controversial policies like UNILATERALISM enabled it to slash the Tory majority, but left the voters uneasy as to what "the change" would actually be.

Mein Kampf (Ger. my struggle) The book in which Adolf Hitler (1889–1945) set out his political and racial theories and misreadings of history; the combination of autobiography, anti-Semitic rantings and an alarmingly accurate prediction of how he would transform central Europe became the NAZI "Bible". It was published in two parts in 1925 and 1927; the first was written in prison after the abortive MUNICH BEER HALL PUTSCH of 1923. The original title was *Four and a Half Years of Struggle against Lies, Stupidity and Cowardice*, but the author was persuaded to think of something snappier. The outbreak of WORLD WAR II and the revelation of the HOLOCAUST left many educated people in Germany and beyond claiming to be surprised, but anyone who read *Mein Kampf* and took it literally would have known what to expect.

Mellon fiscal policy The policies pursued at the US Treasury Department from 1921 to 1932 by the oil and commodities magnate Andrew Mellon (1855–1937). Reckoned the second richest man in America, Mellon served three Presidents – Harding, Coolidge and Hoover – and was allowed ever greater latitude until the GREAT DEPRESSION struck. He set up the Bureau of the Budget in 1921, and pressed for lower taxes on corporations and the wealthy, meeting resistance in Congress which eased when prosperity became widespread after 1924. Hailed by Republicans as the greatest Treasury Secretary since HAMILTON, he was an unashamed supporter of the business community and of the MARKET. Though he conspicuously failed to foresee the GREAT CRASH, few of his peers did, either.

melt. melting-pot The image of America as a society capable of absorbing members of disparate races and cultures and rendering them into a single and unified whole with opportunities for all, relied on heavily by those who oppose limits on immigration. The phrase was the title of a popular play by the English Jew Israel Zangwill (1864–1926), staged in New York in 1909. In its first scene a character says:

> America is God's Crucible, the great Melting-Pot where all the races of Europe are melting and re-forming.

Within two years the concept was rebutted by the DILLINGHAM REPORT which paved the way for tight controls on immigration; while a rainbow of ethnic groups continues to swell America's population, many would agree with the Rev. Jesse Jackson:

> I hear that melting pot stuff a lot, and all I can say is that we haven't melted.

Some commentators have said that America's ethnic mix is more of a tossed salad, with each legume remaining identifiable. But native American singer Buffy Ste. Marie put it more starkly:

> Here the melting-pot stands open – if you're ready to get bleached first.

meltdown The spectacularly sudden collapse of a political campaign which has appeared to be going well. The term is taken from the nuclear power industry, meltdown being the point at which the rise in a reactor's temperature becomes irreversible, making disaster inevitable (*see* CHERNOBYL)

men. men in grey suits The silent power-brokers of Britain's CONSERVATIVE PARTY, who at the critical moment will call on its leader and tell him or her that they no longer enjoy the confidence of the party and should resign. In practice such advice has seldom been offered, and never been taken. **Men in suits** was a dismissive term for the clone-like and slightly flashy middle-aged businessmen who surrounded Margaret Thatcher and were frequently appointed by her to high office (*see* LORD SUIT; PARKINSON AFFAIR).

men in white coats An old US term for the male nurses who would lead away those of unsound mind to detention in a mental hospital. In politics anyone felt by colleagues to be uttering suitably eccentric views is said to be liable to a visit from them.

men or measures The argument over whether the composition or policies of a government were more important, and whether a party offering one rather than the other was the more worthy of election. Though it has never subsided, it was at its height in England in the late 18th and early 19th centuries.

> The cant of "not men, but measures", a sort of charm by which many people get loose from every honourable engagement.
>
> EDMUND BURKE, *Thoughts on the Cause of the Present Discontent*, 1770.

> If the comparison must be made . . . men are everything, measures comparatively nothing.
>
> GEORGE CANNING, House of Commons, 9 December 1802.

Mensheviks (Russ. minority) The moderate wing of the Russian SOCIAL DEMOCRATIC Workers' Party who initially worked alongside the BOLSHEVIKS to overthrow the Tsarist political system, then opposed the OCTOBER REVOLUTION of 1917. They believed that gradual reform would lead to a Socialist state and the primacy of the working class, and were deeply divided over co-operating with the Bolsheviks and KERENSKY's provisional government after the February 1917 revolution. As the Bolsheviks seized power, TROTSKY told their former allies:

> You are miserable isolated individuals. You are bankrupt. You have played out your role. Go where you belong – to the dustheap of history.

The Mensheviks tried to continue as a legitimate opposition party, but by 1922 their leaders had been killed by the Bolsheviks or had fled into exile.

Menzies, Sir Robert *See* MING.

MEOW Abbreviation of MORAL EQUIVALENT OF WAR.

MEP Member of the EUROPEAN PARLIAMENT. The official abbreviation and designation for members of the Strasbourg assembly.

merger The issue that destroyed the SDP/Liberal ALLIANCE following the 1987 UK General Election. Less than 48 hours after the parties' poor showing (22 seats between them) the LIBERAL leader David Steel called for immediate moves for them to merge. Many SDP members had anticipated a merger, but others including the party leader Dr. David OWEN felt Steel was "bouncing" them. When a majority of SDP members showed themselves ready to negotiate a merger, Dr. Owen resigned as leader in August 1987, and Robert Maclennan took his place. The first attempt that winter to produce a blueprint for a merged party pleased no one (*see* DEAD PARROT), but eventually a deal was struck and on 3 March 1988 the two parties merged. Steel and Maclennan stood down, and in July the Liberal MP Paddy Ashdown defeated Alan Beith for the leadership of what were at first called the Social and Liberal Democrats. Dr. Owen persevered with his separate SDP with three MPs, coming close to winning a by-election at Richmond, Yorkshire, in February 1989. But as the Liberal Democrats picked up speed the SDP faded away.

merit system The system for civil service recruitment and promotion which largely replaced PATRONAGE in Britain and America in the third quarter of the 19th century. In Whitehall the principle of recruitment by competitive examination was established after bitter resistance through the NORTHCOTE-TREVELYAN REFORMS; in America Rep. Thomas Jenckes introduced a Bill for similar reforms in 1865, President Hayes (*see* OLD 8 TO 7) struck several blows against patronage, but it took the assassination of President Garfield to introduce merit selection for all but the highest posts, which remain open to POLITICAL APPOINTEES.

meritocracy Rule by those of superior intellect and talents. The term was popularized by Michael Young (later Lord Young of Dartington) in his book The *Rise of the Meritocracy* (1958), in which he argued that educational achievements had replaced noble birth and inherited wealth as the route to power in society.

Messina conference The conference held in Sicily in June 1955 which began serious planning for the creation two years later of the EUROPEAN (Economic) COMMUNITY, by the Treaty of ROME. Anthony EDEN turned down an invitation for Britain to participate, and the six nations whose foreign ministers and technical experts attended went on to found the Community in their own image and paved the way for the creation of the European COMMON MARKET: the European Economic Community and EURATOM.

Mexican stand-off Ronald Reagan's comparison of SUPERPOWER tension with a confrontation between two gunslingers, America and the Soviet Union each with nuclear pistols drawn "and if one man's finger flinches, you're going to get your brains blown out".

Mexican War The war between the United States and Mexico provoked by the admission of Texas to the Union at the end of 1845. It resulted in total American victory, but lasted almost two years and has hardened Mexican attitudes ever since. Mexico refused to recognize the Rio Grande boundary of its former province of Texas, and after several months of manoeuvring, its troops crossed the river on 30 April 1846. The battle of Palo Alto followed, after which Congress declared war on 13 May. The following February, General Zachary Taylor with 5500 troopers took on a Mexican force almost four times as large at Monterrey and beat them. Battles followed at Resaca de la Palma and Buena Vista, and General Winfield Scott captured Mexico City. The war ended on 2 February 1848 with the Treaty of GUADALUPE HIDALGO, under which Mexico conceded California and what are now the states of Arizona, Colorado, Nevada, New Mexico and Utah.

MHR Member of the House of Representatives. The abbreviation used to describe a member of the lower and more influential house of Australia's Federal parliament.

MIA's The more than 2400 American service personnel still Missing in Action when the final US forces were withdrawn from South-East Asia in 1975. The families of many refused to believe they were dead, as the North Vietnamese and other former enemies claimed and as Washington seemed to want to believe. Several freelance expeditions were mounted with support from ultra-conservative groups to bring back men who had reputedly been seen alive, but none succeeded. Public eagerness to locate and REPATRIATE any MIAs who had survived became an issue in several election campaigns, and also triggered a series of inconclusive Congressional investigations. As relations improved, a number of bodies were returned, but into the 1990s stories were still coming to light of men held in remote areas beyond the end of the war, who might still be there.

MI5 The popular name for Britain's Security Service, which is charged with the detection and surveillance of those known or suspected to be engaged in espionage, or subversion, in the UK. In 1992 MI5, which is answerable first to the HOME SECRETARY and ultimately to the Prime Minister, was made responsible for thwarting IRA terrorism on the British mainland, as the police struggled to cope. The same year it gained its first woman director,

Mrs. Stella Rimington; her appointment was the first to be publicly announced, following legislation by John MAJOR's government to bring MI5 out of the shadows and put it on a statutory basis. MI5 (Military Intelligence, section five) was the agency's original title when established in 1916.

MI6 Again a title long since dropped but still a household phrase, this time for the **Secret Intelligence Service** (SIS), Britain's, senior, equivalent of the CIA. Its members are engaged on espionage and other intelligence activities abroad, using British agents and disaffected nationals of the countries in which they operate; its focus has changed markedly since the end of the COLD WAR. The SIS was formed as MI6 (Military Intelligence, section six) in 1921; it is responsible to the FOREIGN SECRETARY, and ultimately to the Prime Minister.

middle. Middle America A social and geographical term for the "Silent MAJORITY" of Americans, who believe in traditional values and reject extreme views or tastes. They believe their views are seldom represented in the MEDIA based largely on the East and West Coasts, hence their concentration in America's heartlands. The term was coined in 1968 by the Washington commentator Joseph Kraft, with reference to the people to whom Richard Nixon pitched his electoral appeal. It came into prominence again in 1990 when many mothers of Middle America protested against the likely involvement of their sons in a GULF WAR.

middle class A term both for the social grouping which takes pride in having differentiated itself from the WORKING CLASS "beneath" it, and on having more refined if narrower attitudes. Traditionally the smooth operation of democracy is supposed to be dependent on a strong middle class. A survey in America during the 1992 election showed that 92% of the population regarded themselves as middle-class. In Britain this group in the 1960s and 1970s felt itself being unfairly squeezed by taxation; Margaret Thatcher saw herself as the embodiment of middle-class values. This was a mixed blessing; as her government went down to a crushing defeat in the HOUSE OF LORDS *c.* 1980 on a plan to charge rural and Roman Catholic parents for their children's use of school buses, an Earl from the BACKWOODS turned to the hereditary Labour peer Lord Ponsonby in the DIVISION LOBBY and observed:

> Trouble with the middle classes – never did understand the people!

Labour voters in this grouping have customarily felt a touch of guilt and social obligation, Hugh GAITSKELL remarking: "Middle-class Socialists have got to have a profound humility."

> The British people, being subject to fogs and possessing a powerful middle class, require grave statesmen.
>
> DISRAELI.

middle ground The body of voters in the political CENTRE, who can be captured by a party ready to renounce EXTREMISM and offer moderate policies. This group is generally considered vital to electoral victory, Margaret Thatcher's LANDSLIDE victories in 1983 and 1987 being the result of an equally divided opposition rather than a readiness of voters in the middle ground to support her brand of radicalism.

middle of the road A voter or politician who sticks obdurately in the centre, refusing to make concessions to the extremes of Right or Left. Dwight D. Eisenhower, the ultimate middle-of-the-roader having been wooed for the Presidency by both parties, commended it as "all the usable surface. The extremes, right and left, are the gutters". But Aneurin BEVAN said in 1953:

> We all know what happens to people who stay in the middle of the road. They get run over.

The Middle Way The book published by Harold Macmillan (*see* SUPERMAC) in 1938 which set out in full the KEYNESIAN philosophy he had been developing over the previous six years, out of conviction that LAISSEZ-FAIRE and deliberate avoidance of planning could not solve the problems of the GREAT DEPRESSION. Among his most radical proposals were the replacement of the Stock Exchange by a National Investment Board and the introduction of a minimum wage – something Labour only advocated half a century later. He saw these views, first put forward in 1932 in his pamphlet *The Next Step*, as a middle course between hands-off capitalism and egalitarian socialism. *The Middle Way* was not liked by the Tory leadership, and Macmillan's old nanny said of it:

> Mr. Harold is a dangerous PINK.

But it was welcomed by Labour thinkers, and by liberal Tories at Oxford including Edward Heath and Hugh Fraser. At various times after, notably as the WETS regrouped in the early days of THATCHERISM, the phrase *The Middle Way* was to become a rallying-cry for the Left of the party.

Midlothian Campaign The barnstorming radical campaign with which the supposedly retired Gladstone returned to politics at the start of 1880 at the age of 71. Adopted as candidate for Midlothian, the area of Scotland just west of Edinburgh, in the election that was looming, Gladstone embarked on an aggressive "stump" campaign, peppered with public meetings at which the GRAND OLD MAN poured scorn on Disraeli's foreign policies, which he said had failed from the Balkans to South Africa. It set the tone for a vigorous election campaign that saw the Liberals returned to power that April with a paper majority of 176 – but heavily dependent on the CELTIC FRINGE and the Irish nationalists.

Mik The Westminster nickname for **Ian Mikardo** (1908–93), the Labour MP for READING from 1945 to 1959 and for Poplar from 1964 to 1987 who was a pillar of the TRIBUNE GROUP for many years and was a key left-wing member of Labour's national executive (NEC). The beetling Mikardo, described by one Labour leader as "not as nice as he looks", was a leading BEVANITE in the 1950s. He hit the headlines in 1975 when, at Tribune's party conference FRINGE MEETING, he launched an attack on the Wilson government's PRICES AND INCOMES POLICY which provoked the T&GWU leader Jack Jones to storm off the platform, grab the microphone from Mikardo and shout: "I detest these attacks on the trade union movement." Yet Mikardo was voted off the NEC in 1978 for his greatest service to the party: the **Mikardo Compromise** to resolve the conflict between hard LEFT advocates of mandatory RESELECTION of MPs and the leadership who wanted the *status quo*. The compromise scraped through for the moment, and Mikardo's supporters ditched him, claiming betrayal. The subsequent abandonment of the compromise triggered the warfare that led to the formation of the SDP and Labour's disastrous performance in the 1983 election.

milch-cow An easily tappable source of funds, especially for Congressmen seeking PORK BARREL projects. Originally a word for a cow kept for milking, this essentially American term incidentally reflects the role of the Federal government as provider for the FARM BELT.

militancy The pursuit of one's political aims by vigorous argument, campaigning and action; because of the energy with which the views are promoted, the assumption will be that they are extreme. The term is an old one, a reference to the "Church militant" stemming from 1413. In 1905 the SUFFRAGETTES officially adopted "Militancy" as their watchword – its first manifestation was the breaking-up by Christabel Pankhurst and Annie Kenney of a meeting in Manchester addressed by the Liberal statesman Sir Edward Grey – ironically a strong supporter of VOTES FOR WOMEN.

Militant Tendency The TROTSKYIST movement in the UK founded by the South African-born ideologist Ted Grant, whose ENTRYIST tactics reduced parts of the LABOUR PARTY to near-paralysis in the early 1980s, until Neil KINNOCK took decisive (though slow-working) action against it. Originally the Revolutionary Socialist League, the Tendency began burrowing into the Labour Party in 1964, when the weekly newspaper *Militant* was founded under the editorship of Peter Taaffe. Though its prophecies of the imminent collapse of capitalism and its call for "NATIONALIZATION of the 250 major maonopolies, the banks and the insurance companies under WORKERS' CONTROL" remained unchanged for almost three decades, its sellers varied their appeal. Bob Edwards, a member of Militant's Central Committee, once sold it to homeward-bound commuters with the slogan:

> All the winners! All the winners! Marx! Lenin! Engels! Trotsky!

Organizing as a PARTY WITHIN A PARTY, it built up a national organization while recruiting Labour Party members in the constituencies. Its influence grew steadily, despite repeated warnings to the National Executive, culminating in the UNDERHILL REPORT; at its height *Militant's* annual rally could fill the Royal Albert Hall and there was talk of making the paper a daily. By late 1982 even the Executive had run out of patience as tales of mayhem poured in from constituency parties; *Militant* was declared ineligible for affiliation to the Party and expulsion proceedings begun against the paper's five-strong editorial board; it took months of court challenges before they were ousted. In 1983 two Militant supporters, Terry Fields and Dave Nellist, were elected to Parliament, and Militant captured control of the Labour group on Liverpool city council, and thus the council itself. Militant had always avoided confrontation with the Labour leadership, but the activites of the council's deputy leader Derek Hatton in confronting the Government in breach of Party policy, accompanied by rumours of thuggery and corruption, provoked Neil Kinnock into a bitter attack at Labour's 1985 Conference. An inquiry led to organizational changes and around a dozen expulsions from the Party, and a National Constitutional Committee was set up to deal solely with expulsions, to prevent the NEC hearing demanded by each Militant turning into a media circus. Militant's march was checked despite the election of two more MPs in 1987, but the expulsions went at a snail's pace and it took another provocation in Liverpool to break it. When the veteran left-wing MP Eric Heffer (*see* I, TOO, WAS A CARPENTER) died in 1990, Militant fielded a candidate against Labour in the ensuing BY-ELECTION, suffering a humiliating defeat and rendering all its campaigners liable to expulsion from the Party. Militant split between advocates of continued entryism and proponents of a separate Party; only in Scotland, where a Scottish Militant Labour faction won a string of council seats in 1992, did it remain a serious force.

militarism A national policy based on pressures for war and domination by an army or military class anxious for battle. The term is most commonly used of Prussia's aggressive policies, both before and after its creation of the German state in 1870.

> A fever for conquest, with peace as a shield, using music and brass buttons to dazzle and divert the populace.
>
> ELBERT HUBBARD.

> We want to get rid of the militarist not simply because he hurts and kills, but because he is an intolerable thick-voiced blockhead who stands hectoring and blustering in our way to achievement.
>
> H. G. WELLS, 1920.

> The day that militarism is undermined, capitalism will fail. HELEN KELLER, *The Story of My Life*.

military-industrial complex The network of defence contractors and PENTAGON officials and generals who, in the view of their critics, have a vested interest in arming America beyond its needs and, ultimately, in war. Intriguingly, the phrase was coined by the former supreme Allied commander President Eisenhower (*see* IKE), who said on 17 January 1961 in his farewell address:

> In the councils of government, we must guard against the acquisition of unwarranted influence, whether sought or unsought, by the military-industrial complex. The potential for the disastrous rise of misplaced powers exists and will persist . . . Only an alert and knowledgeable citizenry can compel the proper meshing of the huge industrial and military machinery of defence with our peaceful methods and goals, so that security and liberty may prosper together.

However Sen. Barry Goldwater later remarked: "Thank heaven for the military-industrial complex. Its ultimate aim is peace for our time."

military wing *See* POLITICAL WING.

militia A citizen force kept in reserve and able to be raised to combat any threat or emergency. The RIGHT TO KEEP AND BEAR ARMS clause of the US Constitution specifies the need for a militia – hence the NATIONAL GUARD. In wartime France the *milice* were the COLLABORATIONIST reserve police of the VICHY regime. In Lebanon during the 1980s each Christian and Muslim faction had its own so-called "militia" whose nominal duty was to protect its community; they ranged from the private armies of rival warlords to pro-Iranian terrorist groups.

> The citizens of America from 18 to 50 Years of Age should be borne on the Militia Rolls, provided with uniform arms, and so far accustomed to the use of them that the Total strength of the country might be called forth at a Short Notice on any very interesting emergency.
>
> GEORGE WASHINGTON to Alexander HAMILTON, 2 May 1783.

milk. milk-snatcher The nickname bestowed on Margaret Thatcher (*see* IRON LADY) when as Education Secretary in Edward Heath's government she ended the supply of free milk daily to all children in State schools.

Milk Street Meeting A meeting of influential Tories at the height of the party leadership campaign in late January 1975, which concluded that Edward Heath would not be re-elected. It was convened by Edward du Cann, chairman of the 1922 COMMITTEE, who had himself considered standing, and held at his flat in Milk Street in the City of London. When du Cann, renowned at Westminster as an arch-plotter, was asked shortly afterwards if he was still loyal to Heath, he replied:

> I think I'm the only one who is.

Margaret Thatcher was duly elected leader, and du Cann chaired the '22 for a further nine years.

Millie The dog who provided the lighter moments of George and Barbara BUSH's tenure of the White House. In May 1991 she was suspected of having passed auto-immune disease to her master and mistress, and in a campaign speech on 29 October 1992 Bush said of his Democratic challengers Bill Clinton and Al Gore:

> My dog Millie knows more about foreign policy than these two bozos.

Milner's kindergarten The notable group of young men gathered together by Sir Alfred (Viscount) Milner, High Commissioner for South Africa, for the work of reconstruction after the BOER WAR. They were Robert Brand, Lionel Curtis, John Dove, Patrick Duncan, Richard Feetham, Lionel Hitchens, Philip Kerr, Douglas Malcolm, J. F. Perry, Geoffrey Robinson and Hugh Wyndham. Others associated with them included L. S. Amery (*see* YOU HAVE SAT HERE LONG ENOUGH), Basil Blackwood, John Buchan and Basil Williams. They went on to become an important propagandist group for closer Imperial ties, both political and economic, in the years prior to World War I. The name was probably invented by the lawyer Sir William Marriott.

minder An experienced political operator, usually an MP, who is drafted into a BY-ELECTION campaign to keep a close eye on a party's candidate and guide him or her through potentially embarrassing moments. The parties began to appoint minders in the mid-1980s after a series of catastrophic performances by inexperienced candidates who suddenly found themselves subjected to a probing and hostile media. The term *minder* comes from Fleet Street where papers that had "bought" members of the public at the heart of sensitive stories would give them a rugged companion to keep them out of the hands of the competition; *Minder* was also the title of a highly successful TV series as the parties first deployed such handlers in by-elections.

Mine eyes have seen the glory of the coming of the Lord The opening line of the Battle Hymn of the Republic, the most stirring of America's patriotic anthems. It was written at the height of the CIVIL WAR by the feminist and peace worker Julia Ward Howe (1819–1910) after seeing President Lincoln review over 50,000 UNION troops at Bailey's Crossroads outside Washington on 20 November 1861. She felt they should have something more suitable to sing than JOHN BROWN'S BODY and composed these words to the tune; they were published in the *Atlantic Monthly* the next February. When Lincoln heard the song, he asked to hear it again and gave it his personal endorsement.

miners' strike The term used at the time for each of a series of confrontations between Britain's National Union of Mineworkers and Conservative governments, in 1972 and 1974 over pay and in 1984–85 over pit closures; the miners won the first two, winning pay increases and in the second bringing down Edward Heath's government. The phrase is now used solely for the third and bitterest strike, when the NUM president Arthur Scargill (*see* KING ARTHUR) took on Margaret Thatcher's government over pit closures he claimed were imminent. There was widespread support in the union for a strike, but Scargill refused to allow a BALLOT and the Nottinghamshire miners, joined by an increasing number of others, defied Flying PICKETS to stay at work. The strike lasted over a year, with union members and their families suffering great hardship, before the combination of large coal stocks at the powe stations, the output of the WORKING MINERS and the impact of Tory union legislation outlawing secondary action (*see* PICKETING) broke the dispute. The strike harmed the Labour Party, which traditionally supported the miners but was split over Scargill's tactics. Neil KINNOCK, who was endeavouring to shed Labour's extremist image, did his best to distance himself from Scargill while sympathizing with the miners' personal plight. But it did even greater damage to the NUM, as the working miners split away to form the Union of Democratic Mineworkers and the collapse of the strike was followed by a closure programme as severe as Scargill had predicted in more prosperous times. *See also* ENEMY WITHIN; Battle of ORGREAVE)

the miners, united, will never be defeated! The chant, to a Marxist-originated Latin American rhythm, of supporters of the NUM in the strike of 1984–85.

Ming The nickname of the Australian Liberal Prime Minister Sir **Robert Menzies** (1894–1978), coined by analogy with Ming the Merciless, a character in the Flash Gordon cartoon strip series. The long period of Menzies' premiership (1939–41 and 1949–66) inevitably came to be known as the "**Ming dynasty**". At Westminster the name was later given to the former Olympic athlete Menzies Campbell QC (1941–), Liberal Democrat MP for North-East Fife from 1987.

Miniature for Sport The nickname given at Westminster to the diminutive Conservative MP Colin Moynihan (1955–) in 1987 when he became Minister for Sport in Margaret Thatcher's government. Moynihan, who in 1980 won an Olympic silver medal as coxwain to the UK rowing eight, subsequently served as an energy minister under John MAJOR before losing his Parliamentary seat in 1992.

mini-budget *See* BUDGET.

minimum lending rate (MLR) Between 1971 and 1981, the rate at which the Bank of England would lend to discount houses, and thus the rate of interest that determined those charged and paid by banks and building societies throughout the economy. Before 1971 this was known as **Bank Rate**; after 1981 as **Base Rate**. When the Government suspended the MLR as a measure of policy in 1981, it reserved the right to reintroduce it at any time if needed; it did so for one day in January 1985.

MINIS The management information system launched at the UK Department of the Environment in 1980 by Michael Heseltine (*see* TARZAN) which became a model – after initial resistance by Cabinet colleagues and MANDARINS who dismissed it as "nonsense" – for similar techniques in other parts of WHITEHALL. Designed to instil what Heseltine called a "private sector management ethos", it involved asking the heads of the DoE's 66 directorates to define their tasks, explain the reason for doing them, and state the cost. Heseltine concluded that nine of them were unnecessary; a restructuring was carried out, which his supporters reckon saved a considerable amount of money, and a series of charts were drawn up setting out the department's new management and functional structure.

Minister A term used widely (except in the United States) for a member of a government or Cabinet. It should not technically be used individually of the most senior British Ministers, as the entire Cabinet except for the Minister of Agriculture and the Ministers without PORTFOLIO have the rank of SECRETARY OF STATE. The rank of **Minister of State**, the sub-Cabinet deputy to each Departmental Minister (sometimes he or she may have two) dates back only to the 1940s, when the burden of work became too great for a Secretary of State and Parliamentary Under-Secretaries alone to handle. The term **junior Minister** should correctly apply only to Parliamentary Secretaries and Under-Secretaries.

> Very shining Ministers, like the sun, are apt to scorch when they shine their brightest; in our constitution I prefer the milder light of a less glaring Minister.
> EARL OF CHESTERFIELD, letter to his son, 1754.

> God help the Minister that meddles with art.
> Viscount MELBOURNE (1779–1848).

> The first concern of a Minister should be the health of the people.
> DISRAELI, Speech in Manchester, 3 April 1872.

> Ministers exist to tell the civil servant what the public will not stand. Sir WILLIAM HARCOURT (1827–1904).

> If you are not careful as a Minister, you find yourself the titular head of a bureaucratic structure.
> MICHAEL HESELTINE.

"Minister" was also, traditionally, the title of a senior diplomatic representative, for instance the British Minister in St. Petersburg. Henry Clay, in his "EMANCIPATION of South America" speech in the House of Representatives on 28 March 1818, said:

> Yes, Sir, from Constantinople, or from the Brazils; from Turk or Christian; from Black or White; from the Dey of Algiers or the Bey of Tunis; from the devil himself, if he wore a crown, we should receive a Minister.

Minister of Fun The title unofficially given to David Mellor (1949–) on his appointment by John MAJOR in April 1992 as Britain's first Secretary of State for the Nationai Heritage, with responsibilities including sport and the arts. Mellor took the title somewhat too literally; that summer the tabloids revealed that he had had a toe-sucking affair with Antonia de Sancha, a small-time actress, and when it also transpired that September that he had accepted a family holiday from Mona Bauwens, daughter of a senior figure in the PLO, he reluctantly resigned.

Ministerial broadcast *See* BROADCAST.

Ministerial responsibility The doctrine that a Minister in charge of a UK government department takes absolute responsibility for any errors or wrongdoing (other than in personal matters) by his officials, and that if a sufficiently grave injustice comes to light, he or she should resign. It was most strictly observed in the CRICHEL DOWN affair, when the Minister of Agriculture resigned over actions of which he had no knowledge; but in recent years it has been honoured in the breach.

Ministry (1) A UK Government Department, headed by a member of the CABINET. (2) In Australia, the government of the day, as in "the Keating Ministry". The term was formerly used in Britain, as when Walter Bagehot wrote in *The English Constitution*: "*The Times* has made many ministries".

Ministry of All the Talents The name given, a touch ironically, to William Grenville's UK COALITION government of 1806–07, because followers of both PITT THE YOUNGER and Charles James Fox agreed to serve in it. Its contemporary equivalent would be Dream TICKET.

Ministry of Truth The all-pervading organ of State propaganda in George Orwell's novel *1984*. *See also* BIG BROTHER.

minority Any element of the population which, by race, religion, culture, sexual orientation or political opinion, is outnumbered by those of a different background or persuasion. Many political ESTABLISHMENTS see articulate minorities as a threat, no matter how small their numbers. Justice Oliver Wendell Holmes once said of America: "If a man is in a minority of one, we lock him up," and Al Smith (*see* HAPPY WARRIOR) observed: "The thing we have to fear in this country is the influence of organized minorities;" the Norwegian dramatist Henrik Ibsen showed the reason for such concern when he asserted: "The minority is always right."

In the US CONGRESS it is the formal term for the party with the smaller number of seats in either House. Speaker Thomas Reed declared:

> The right of the Minority is to draw its salaries, and its function is to make a QUORUM.

> So long as a minority conforms to the majority, it is not even a minority. They must throw their whole weight in the opposite direction. Mahatma GANDHI, 1907.

> The White race is in the minority, the Free-ENTERPRISE system is in the minority, and the majority are looking at us harder and longer than they ever looked before.
> JOHN F. KENNEDY.

minority government A government that lacks an overall majority in the legislature from which it is drawn, *e.g.* Harold WILSON's UK Labour government of March–October 1974. During that HUNG PARLIAMENT, the Liberal leader Jeremy THORPE observed:

> Looking around the House, one realizes that we are all minorities now – indeed, some more than others.

minorities Specifically, ethnic groups who form less than 50% of a nation's population, often being concentrated in a particular area. Shortly after the OCTOBER REVOLUTION when the BOLSHEVIKS briefly granted a degree of autonomy to non-Russian communities, LENIN assumed the post of Commissar for Minorities.

Minority Leader The leader of the party with the smaller number of seats in the US SENATE or HOUSE OF REPRESENTATIVES. *See also* RANKING MEMBER.

minority mentality The mind-set that comes from permanently being in a minority; in the mid-1980s Rep. Newt Gingrich claimed that the House Republican leadership had "as a culture, a defeatist, minority mentality".

minority President A President of the United States elected with less than 50% of the popular vote; examples include Presidents Clinton, Nixon (1968), Kennedy, Eisenhower (1956), Truman, Wilson (twice) – and Lincoln.

minority report A separate report issued by one or more members of a committee who cannot agree findings or recommendations with the rest.

minute A WHITEHALL term for a memorandum from a Minister or senior official.

minutes The record of a meeting, which is written down contemporaneously and put to the next meeting of the same body for approval. In UK local government, the monthly meeting of a council consists largely in going through the Minutes of its previous meeting and those of all its committees, with the opportunity for questions, amendments and observations, before going on to deal with other business.

Minutemen A small, armed and ultra-right wing US organization formed during the COLD WAR to conduct GUERRILLA warfare in the event of a Communist invasion. The name was inspired by the American militiamen of the same name who, at the onset of the War of Independence, promised to take arms at a minute's notice; the war began when 75 Minutemen intercepted 700 British troops at Lexington, Massachusetts, on 18 April 1775 (*see* THE BRITISH ARE COMING!). Minuteman is also the name of a US ICBM.

Miranda decision The landmark decision of the US SUPREME COURT in 1966 that requires police to explain, when arresting a suspect, that they have the right to remain silent during questioning and be represented by a lawyer, and that anything they do say may be used against them. This protection is found in the FIFTH and Sixth AMENDMENTs to the Constitution, but until then the decision did not have to be spelt out to anyone being arrested. The Court laid down the rule in reversing an Arizona court's conviction of Ernesto A. Miranda, who had confessed to kidnapping and rape but had not been advised of his rights.

MIRV Multiple Independently Targeted Re-entry Vehicles. The multiple warheads fitted from 1968 to US (and later Soviet) strategic missiles, so that warheads from one rocket could hit a number of different targets. The deployment of such weapons first destabilized the ARMS RACE in America's favour, then accelerated it as the Soviet Union caught up with SS-18s each carrying 10 warheads. The MIRV warheads were highly accurate and designed to knock out enemy missile silos; Sen. Albert Gore (*see* OZONE MAN) and others believed this greatly increased the risk of a FIRST STRIKE. MIRVs were eventually outlawed by the START II agreement between the US and Russia at the close of 1992.

misery index The yardstick, combining the rates of INFLATION and unemployment, developed by Jimmy CARTER's 1976 Presidential campaign to demonstrate how the FORD administration had failed the American worker. Carter successfully exploited the index's reading of 15.3 – but the index boomeranged on him in 1980 when Ronald Reagan reported that under Carter it had shot up to 21.3.

mislead the House A phrase used at Westminster which is almost, but not quite, a euphemism for telling a LIE. A member accusing another of misleading the House will generally be asked to WITHDRAW, but will have got the point across. ASQUITH pointed up the inference of trickery when he took the War Office to task for producing three sets of figures,

> one to mislead the public, another to mislead the Cabinet and the third to mislead itself.

misquote Legislators who make comments and then come in for criticism when they are reported by the media frequently claim that they have been misquoted: that what was printed was not what they said. At times their complaints are justified, but at others the tactic is a means of evading responsibility (*see also*

DENIABILITY). The UK Labour politician Gerald Kaufman once achieved a crushing put-down of a self-justifying speech from former Chancellor Nigel Lawson by saying:

> Not only has the Right Honourable Gentleman made an idiot of himself, but he has achieved the remarkable feat of misquoting himself.

Missile gap The issue raised by John F. KENNEDY during the 1960 US Presidential election, with Kennedy claiming that the Eisenhower/Nixon administration had allowed the Soviet Union to build up a more powerful strategic nuclear arsenal. When the Democrats came to power, they found that America was in fact considerably stronger.

unguided missile A more deadly version of a LOOSE CANNON, a politician who not only may go off in any direction but may do so with thermonuclear force. The term was most notably used of Dr. Jeane Kirkpatrick, Ronald Reagan's hard-line ambassador to the UN, by the liberal Republican Sen. Charles Percy. Earlier, in the mid-1960s, Dr. Martin Luther KING had said:

> We have guided missiles and misguided men.

Missouri compromise (1) The series of Bills passed by the US Congress in 1820 to resolve the dilemma over whether to admit Missouri to the Union as a SLAVE STATE. The compromise, engineered by Henry Clay, prohibited slavery from all parts of the LOUISIANA PURCHASE north of latitude 36° 30′ except in Missouri; Maine was admitted simultaneously as a free state. It kept the peace for a time, but at the price of exacerbating feeling for and against slavery in the longer term; Thomas JEFFERSON regarded it as a FIREBELL IN THE NIGHT. The Compromise was effectively repealed in 1854; three years later the Supreme Court, in the Dred SCOTT case, declared it UNCONSTITUTIONAL, enraging Northerners and stoking up the fires for the CIVIL WAR. (2) The phrase was used again in 1944 to describe the process under which Sen. Harry S Truman of Missouri (*see* GIVE 'EM HELL HARRY) emerged as Franklin D. Roosevelt's Vice-Presidential choice at that year's Democratic CONVENTION. FDR wanted Henry Wallace, but party regulars deemed him too liberal; his second choice, James F. Byrnes, was unacceptable to liberals because of his views on race and labour unions. Truman trailed Wallace on the first ballot, but was nominated on the second.

Missy LeHand The willowy private secretary to Franklin D. Roosevelt who from the early 1920s (after he had been struck by polio) until her retirement through illness in 1940 was FDR's mistress, apparently with Eleanor Roosevelt's tacit consent. The public knew nothing of it until FDR's son Elliott detailed it in a book of reminiscences. Margaret LeHand, whom Roosevelt met in the 1920 election campaign, was not his only lover; the most serious was Lucy Mercer (later Rutherfurd), then Eleanor's social secretary, whom FDR fell for in 1918. He might have divorced Eleanor for her, had not his mother threatened to cut off his inheritance. After Missy's death in 1943 Roosevelt resumed contact with Lucy, travelling to her New Jersey home; she was with him at WARM SPRINGS when he died the following year.

> Missy LeHand had her own suite in the White House consisting of a living room, a bedroom and bath. It was not uncommon to see Missy in the President's suite at night in a nightgown, or in the OVAL OFFICE on his lap. The extent of Missy's discretion . . . was in not remaining in the President's bedroom when his breakfast tray was served. SHELLEY ROSS, *Fall From Grace*.

mistake. A man who believes the 20th century is a mistake The verdict of the Westminster SKETCH WRITER Frank Johnson on (Sir) John Stokes (1917–), an UNRECONSTRUCTED Conservative who had been MP for Halesowen from 1970 to 1983.

I beseech you in the bowels of Christ, think it possible you may be mistaken Oliver Cromwell's despairing plea to the General Assembly of the Church of Scotland, in a letter sent in 1650 as his exasperation with inflexible Puritan divines was reaching its height.

Most mistakes in politics arise from flat and inexcusable disregard of the plain maxim that it is not possible for the same thing to be and not to be The conclusion reached, at the end of a long political career, by the British Liberal statesman John (later Viscount) MORLEY (1828–1923).

The politician who didn't make a mistake is never a politician; and the politician who admitted them to you wouldn't be a politician John MAJOR's standard reply to reporters when asked if a particular Government policy had proved a mistake.

We made our mistake when we sent him to college where he learned to read The comment made by Frances McCoy McGee, the Republican mother of Gale McGee (1915–), on his election as a Democratic Senator for Wyoming.

When I make a mistake, it's a beaut One of the candid sayings of New York's Mayor Fiorello LA GUARDIA (1882–1947).

mister. Mr. Chamberlain's pocket handkerchief Lloyd George's description of a UNION JACK waved by a HECKLER at a Liberal meeting during the KHAKI ELECTION of 1900. His reference to the UNIONIST Colonial

Secretary Joseph Chamberlain (*see* JAMESON RAID) was seized on by the Tories as confirmation that Lloyd George was a PRO-BOER. When the heckler shouted and waved the flag, L.G. said:

> I didn't realize it had become Mr. Chamberlain's pocket handkerchief.

Mr. Clean (1) A generic term for anyone in politics who has a reputation for being incorruptible. (2) A congratulatory name from ENVIRONMENTALISTS for a politician who has promoted anti-pollution legislation; an early recipient was Sen. Edmund Muskie.

Mr. Cube The sugar lump in human form devised by the sugar refiners Tate and Lyle in 1950 to fight the threat of NATIONALIZATION by Clement ATTLEE's UK Labour government. Prior to the election at the end of the year, the company plastered hoardings with pictures of Mr. Cube and the slogan **Tate, not State**; Labour won the election, but with a majority too small to press ahead with much more nationalization. Mr. Cube stayed on the sugar packets for years after the original reason for him had been forgotten.

Mr. President The way in which the PRESIDENT of the United States is formally addressed.

Mr. Republican The nickname for the conservative Republican Sen. Robert TAFT, son of America's 26th President and Senate MAJORITY LEADER. An ISOLATIONIST in foreign policy, he was co-author of the TAFT-HARTLEY ACT and an initial supporter of Sen. Joseph McCARTHY, telling him of his drive against supposed Communists in high places: "If one case doesn't work, try another." Taft fought Dwight D. Eisenhower for the 1952 Presidential nomination, and died of cancer the following year. He fought to the end; weeks before he died he was seen in the Senate chamber filling in an order form for a new refrigerator.

Mr. Sam The affectionate nickname in the US House of Representatives for Sam Taliaferro Rayburn (1882–1961), the Texan who served as SPEAKER with eight Presidents from FDR to Kennedy.

Mr. Speaker The title of every male SPEAKER of the House of Commons, and the form of address used by Members when speaking; all their comments have to be addressed to the CHAIR and not to other members.

Mrs. Wilson's Diary The column that appeared in PRIVATE EYE throughout Harold WILSON's two spells of government (1964–70, 1974–76) giving a plausible caricature of life at NUMBER TEN. Purporting to be the diary of Wilson's wife Mary, who was known not to enjoy the political life, it brought to life vividly the world of Wilson, LADY FORKBENDER and Boris the handyman, who had a peculiar foreign accent and knew a surprising amount about electronics.

Mrs. Wilson's Stewardship The period from October 1919 until well into the following year during which Edith Galt Wilson, second wife of President WOODROW WILSON, effectively ran the United States while her husband was recovering from a stroke; some historians believe she retained control until he left office in March 1921. *See also* Petticoat GOVERNMENT; PRESIDENTRESS.

MITI Japan's Ministry for International Trade and Industry, the organ of government which since World War II has spearheaded the country's development into an industrial superpower by assisting new industries and technology, while facilitating an orderly rundown of outdated industries. In 1969 it took the critical decision to lift restrictions on Japanese investment overseas.

Miz Lillian The family nickname of Lillian Carter (1898–1983), mother of President Jimmy CARTER, whom he sent on a number of international goodwill and charitable missions. A tough Southern lady who lent unspoken support to her son, she did much to underpin his administration's humanitarian credentials. The President's brother was another matter (*see* BILLYGATE). Miz Lillian was quoted in 1977 as saying:

> Sometimes when I look at my children I say to myself: "Lillian, you should have stayed a virgin."

MLA Member of the Legislative Assembly. A member of the legislative house of that name (the lower or the only one) in each Australian state except South Australia and Tasmania.

MLC Member of the Legislative Council. A member of the upper house of the legislature in every Australian state with a BICAMERAL system.

MLF Multilateral Force. The proposal emanating from the 1962 Nassau meeting between President Kennedy and Harold Macmillan for a force to which all NATO navies would contribute, with Britain including its POLARIS submarines. France opposed the idea on principle, Germany only supported it to make its *rapprochement* with France acceptable to Washington, and the force was stillborn though it took until the end of 1964 for the Johnson administration to admit it.

> A Heath Robinson contraption whose only purpose was political; it was designed to control the British and French strategic nuclear weapons and to give the non-nuclear

> Europeans the impression that somehow they would share in the decision to use America's nuclear deterrent.
> DENIS HEALEY.

M'Lords The formal term used by members of the HOUSE OF LORDS in the Chamber to address those present.

MLR *See* MINIMUM LENDING RATE

moaning minnies Margaret Thatcher's dismissive term for critics of her economic policies, which caused considerable offence when she uttered it on a visit to Tyneside, where several unemployment blackspots remained even in the boom of 1988.

mob, the In political terms, not the Mafia but the mass of the urban population who at critical moments can take to the streets and change the course of history. Jefferson wrote: "The mobs of great cities add just so much to the support of pure government as sores do to the strength of the human body." And Calvin Coolidge pointed out that "the only difference between a mob and a trained army is organization".

moderate One who avoids extremes in politics, and takes a more cautious line than other members of a party. Moderation is frequently seen as a sign of weakness, and the term is also misapplied; the *Daily Telegraph* once carried a report about "bomb-throwing moderates" in the Lebanon. Thomas Paine took the view that "moderation in temper is always a virtue, but moderation in principle is always a vice", and Metternich cautioned: "Any plan conceived in moderation must fail when the circumstances are set in extremes." More passionately, William Lloyd Garrison wrote of slavery: "Tell a man whose house is on fire to give a moderate alarm; tell him to moderately rescue his wife from the hands of the ravisher; tell the mother to gradually extricate her babe from the fire into which it has fallen; but urge me not to use moderation in a case like the present."

> The hardest job today is to have the courage to be a moderate. HUBERT HUMPHREY.

I stand astounded at my own moderation The response of Lord Clive (1725–1774) during Parliamentary cross-examination in 1773 on his conduct in India, which had given rise to allegations of corruption and self-enrichment.

moderator An impartial person appointed to chair a partisan debate or discussion.

modified, limited hangout One of the stratagems prepared in the Nixon White House for surviving WATERGATE. Revealed when the Watergate tapes were made public, it involved forming a defensive position behind a highly limited and selective disclosure of facts.

Mogadon man An uncomplimentary nickname given by newspapers to Sir Geoffrey (later Lord) Howe (1926–), Chancellor, Foreign Secretary and deputy Prime Minister to Margaret Thatcher between 1979 and 1990. It reflected his sleep-inducing speaking style, Mogadon being a tranquillizing drug; this widely-held view of his debating style made the impact of the dramatic HOWE RESIGNATION, which set in motion Mrs. Thatcher's fall from power, even more devastating.

mole A word popularized by the novels of John le Carré for a spy or traitor who obtains a position of trust, especially in a government or intelligence organization, and uses it to serve his or her true masters. The name reflects the hidden undermining activities of such agents. The most notorious mole unmasked since the term caught on in the early 1980s was Sir Anthony BLUNT, who spied for Russia when a wartime member of MI5 and went on to become Surveyor of the Queen's Pictures – a post he was allowed to keep even after his treachery was proven.

Molotov cocktail A home-made anti-tank bomb, invented and first used by the Finns against the Soviets in 1940 and adopted in the UK as one of the weapons of the Home Guard. It consisted of a bottle filled with petrol or a thicker liquid, with a slow match or cloth protruding from the top. When thrown at a tank the bottle burst, the liquid igniting, spreading over the plating of the tank or (with luck) setting fire to it. It was named after the Soviet Prime Minister and Foreign Affairs COMMISSAR Vyacheslav Molotov (*see* NIET!), real name Skriabin, either because the Finns saw his hand in the Soviet invasion or because such bombs became a weapon of pro-Communist guerrillas and rioters the world over.

monarchy A system of government where the ultimate SOVEREIGNTY is vested in a King or Queen, almost always hereditary rather than elective. The poet Percy Bysshe Shelley denounced monarchy as "the string which ties the robbers' bundle".

> A monarchy is a merchantman which sails well but will sometimes strike a rock and go to the bottom; a republic is a raft which will never sink, but then your feet are always in the water. Rep. FISHER AMES (1758–1808).

> The best reason why a monarchy is a strong government is that it is an intelligible government. The mass of mankind understand it, and they hardly anywhere in the world understand any other.
> WALTER BAGEHOT (1826–77).

It is termed a **constitutional monarchy** when it operates in a largely ceremonial capacity with a democratically-elected legislature enjoying comprehensive powers, as in Britain, Scandinavia, Spain and the BENELUX countries. Harold WILSON described the contemporary British monarchy as "a labour-intensive industry".

> When a monarchy gradually transforms itself into a republic, the executive power there preserves titles, honours, respect and even money long after it has lost the reality of power. ALEXIS DE TOCQUEVILLE (1805–59).

absolute monarchy *See* ABSOLUTISM.

Dual Monarchy The twin crowns of Austria and Hungary between 1867, when the Hungarian kingdom was given a separate existence within the Austrian Empire, though with the same Monarch, and 1919 when that empire collapsed.

Fifth Monarchy Men A fanatical Puritan sect, aligned to the LEVELLERS, who maintained during the English CIVIL WAR that Christ was about to return and establish the fifth universal monarchy. The four preceding monarchies had been the Assyrian, the Persian, the Macedonian and the Roman. As with other such sects, their existence and assurance that they alone were right hampered Oliver Cromwell's efforts to establish a stable and enlightened Republican government.

monarchist In countries where the rival claims of a republic or a crowned head are debated, the faction that supports the maintenance of royal rule. The term is also used for US conservatives who attach almost royal respect to the presidency.

Monday Club A stridently right-wing group of UK Conservatives, founded in 1961 by the Marquess of Salisbury, Julian Amery and others. It originally met for lunch on Mondays, hence its title. In its early years the Monday Club championed Rhodesia's UDI, and endorsed POWELLITE views on race and Europe; more recently it has taken a strongly pro-UNIONIST line on Northern Ireland. During the 1970s it was shunned by mainstream Conservatives; however in recent years its activities have been less controversial and Ministers have been readier to speak at its meetings.

Monday morning quarterback A US phrase for a political observer gifted with extraordinary powers of hindsight. It was originally, and remains, a sporting term, for the "expert" who arrives for work at the start of a new week able to explain exactly how his favourite football team could have won.

monetarism The economic doctrine that sees the MONEY SUPPLY as the centre of macro-economic policy. First formulated by David Hume (1711–76), it was revived in the late 1970s, especially by Margaret Thatcher and Sir Keith Joseph, as the panacea for breaking with failed variants of KEYNESIANISM. They took the view that an expansion of the money supply would create INFLATION rather than jobs, and from 1979 until *c.* 1985 Chancellors Geoffrey Howe and Nigel Lawson stuck rigidly to the policy, creating the foundations for an economic BOOM which subsequent relaxation of money policy sent out of control.

punk monetarism The condemnatory phrase of Denis Healey (*see* GROMYKO OF THE LABOUR PARTY) for the more ruthless and ideological varieties of economic policy pursued in the mid-1980s by some of Mrs Thatcher's most committed Ministers.

money. Money Bill At Westminster, legislation of a fiscal nature which, since the PARLIAMENT ACT of 1911, cannot be blocked by the House of Lords. In the US Congress, Money Bills can under the Constitution only be introduced in the HOUSE OF REPRESENTATIVES.

money resolution A resolution put to the House of Commons immediately after the SECOND READING of a Bill, authorizing money to be spent in connection with it; for major measures there is an opportunity for further debate.

money supply The amount of money available to the economy of a nation. Since the mid-1970s most western nations have accepted the central tenet of MONETARISM, that an increase in the money supply leads directly to INFLATION. There are at least seven different ways of defining the money supply (*see* M0), with M1 the tightest, covering only cash in circulation and bank deposits.

a billion here, a billion there, and pretty soon you're talking about real money A dictum of Sen. Everett DIRKSEN, said OFF THE CUFF while campaigning in Illinois, according to his confidant John Kriegsman.

I want my money back Margaret Thatcher's blunt statement to fellow EC heads of government when pressing for Britain to be given a rebate on its payments to the Community budget, to reflect its situation as the largest net contributor after Germany. Mrs. Thatcher first made the demand at the 1979 Dublin summit, and reiterated it at all further meetings until it was conceded at FONTAINEBLEAU five years later.

politics has got so expensive, it takes a lot of money even to get beat with One of the most celebrated sayings of the US comedian Will Rogers, who up to his death in a plane crash in 1935 was both unofficial court jester to Congress and a highly respected visitor to Capitol Hill. Here Rogers was taking a dig at the spiralling cost of getting elected – without venturing too far into what the money was spent on.

Monkey Business The yacht that sank the Presidential ambitions of the democratic front-runner Sen. Gary Hart early in 1987. With Hart on its cruise to Bimini were Donna Rice, the 29-year-old from Miami with whom he was having an affair, her friend Lynn Armadt and Hart fundraiser William Broadhurst; Hart and Broadhurst claimed they had been on a separate boat to the girls, but Armadt told the *National Enquirer* that Hart and Rice shared the master bedroom. The story of the cruise on the *Monkey Business* broke in May 1987 after intense media scrutiny of Hart's private life, which he at first encouraged (*see* ADULTERY). On 3 May the *Miami Herald* broke the news of Hart's affair with Rice, and then the *National Enquirer* told of the cruise just as Hart and his wife were pulling out of the Presidential race; he tried a comeback in the winter of 1987–88 but flopped. Hart's womanizing was notorious; Rice's other amours allegedly included Prince Albert of Monaco, the Arab arms dealer Adnan Khashoggi and a convicted drugs dealer, James Bradley Parks.

Monopolies and Mergers Commission (MMC) A commission established by the UK government in 1948 as the Monopolies and Restrictive Practices Commission; it took its present title in 1973. It investigates questions referred to it on the existence of monopolies in the supply of goods within the UK, mergers requiring investigation under the 1973 Fair Trading Act, and any uncompetitive or restrictive-labour practices covered by the 1980 COMPETITION Act.

> Why is there only one Monopolies Commission?
>
> OFFICIAL MONSTER RAVING LOONY PARTY Manifesto, 1987.

Monroe doctrine America's resolution not to countenance any further colonization of the Western Hemisphere by Europe's colonial powers, and in return not to interfere in purely European affairs, or in existing colonies. It was set out by James Monroe (1758–1831), 5th President of the United States (1817–25), who said in his annual message to Congress on 2 December 1823:

> The American continents . . . are henceforth not to be considered as subjects for future colonization by any European powers.

Monroe, the third successive Virginian President after Jefferson and Madison, presided over the ERA OF GOOD FEELINGS when party politics ceased to exist; he was re-elected in 1820 with only one vote against in the ELECTORAL COLLEGE. Jefferson praised him as "a man whose soul might be turned wrong side outwards without discovering a blemish to the world"; his biographer Arthur Styron wrote:

> His virtue was not in flying high but in walking orderly, his talents were exercised not in grandeur but in mediocrity.

The doctrine, only named after Monroe 30 years later, was actually created by Secretary of State John Quincy ADAMS in response to a suggestion from UK Foreign Secretary George Canning that Britain and the US jointly warn the Holy Alliance of Russia, Austria, Spain and France against a restoration of Spanish rule in the newly-independent republics of Latin America. The most serious challenge to the Monroe Doctrine came in 1864 when Emperor Napoleon III attempted to instal Archduke Maximilian of Austria on the Mexican throne; US protests were ignored, but with war looming with America, France had to withdraw its troops because of trouble in Europe, and Maximilian was executed by his "subjects".

> The Government of the United States is not entitled to affirm as a universal proposition that its interests are necessarily concerned in whatever may befall . . . states simply because they are situated in the Western Hemisphere.
>
> LORD SALISBURY on the boundary dispute over VENEZUELA, 26 November 1895.

> In the Western Hemisphere, adherence . . . to the Monroe Doctrine may force the United States, however reluctantly, in flagrant cases of wrongdoing or impotence, to the exercise of an international police power.
>
> THEODORE ROOSEVELT, message to Congress, 6 December 1904.

> Nations should with one accord adopt the doctrine of President Monroe as the doctrine of the world: that every people should be left free to determine its own policy, its own way of development, unhindered, unthreatened, unafraid – the little along with the great and powerful.
>
> WOODROW WILSON, speech to the Senate, 22 January 1917.

Montgomery bus boycott A peaceful BOYCOTT of BUS services in Montgomery, Alabama, from December 1955 by Blacks protesting against racial SEGREGATION. Organized by Martin Luther KING, it was reputedly sparked off by a White bus driver's offensive treatment of Mrs. Rosa Parks, who refused to sit at the back of the bus where Blacks were supposed to travel. After an 11-month boycott the SUPREME COURT gave victory to the protesters by declaring racially segregated seating in local transportation UNCONSTITUTIONAL. The protest achieved more than the desegregation of Montgomery's buses; it brought the CIVIL RIGHTS movement to the attention of the nation and encouraged Dr. King to take his place at the head of the campaign.

Monticello The graceful and sophisticated home atop a 500 ft. hill near Charlottesville, Virginia, which Thomas JEFFERSON designed for himself and built in the 1770s. Owing much to the influence of the Italian architect Palladio, it is modest in size by Virginia planters' standards, but includes many of his inventions, in marked contrast to Washington's strictly traditional home of MOUNT VERNON. Jefferson retired to Monticello and died there; in 1926 the ladies of Virginia purchased it as a national shrine, which it remains.

> Mr. Jefferson is the first American who has consulted the Fine Arts to know how he should shelter himself from the weather. Marquis de CHASTELLUX, 1780.

Montoneros The militant wing of the PERONIST youth movement which waged a terrorist campaign against the military JUNTA under, in turn, Generals Videla and Galtieri, which ruled Argentina from the overthrow of Isabel Perón in 1975 until the armed forces' defeat in the FALKLANDS WAR. The military acted against all actual or suspected Montoneros with total ruthlessness, many joining the DISAPPEARED.

Montreal protocol The international agreement in 1988 to protect the ozone layer by phasing out damaging **CFCs** (chlorofluorocarbons), widely used in aerosol sprays and in refrigeration, by the year 2000. It was the first world-wide initiative to halt destruction of the layer; a further meeting in Copenhagen in November 1992 tightened the deadline.

moral. moral equivalent of war The phrase popularized by President CARTER in 1977 to describe America's energy dilemmas. Its originator was William James (1842-1910), who in an essay in 1910 criticized "anti-militarists" for having found "no substitute for war's disciplinary function, no moral equivalent of war". On 18 April 1977, Carter said in a broadcast to the nation:

> Our decision about energy will test the character of the American people and the ability of the President and the Congress to govern this nation. This difficult effort will be the "moral equivalent of war", except that we will be uniting our efforts to build and not to destroy.

See MEOW.

Moral Majority *See* MAJORITY.

Moral Rearmament *See* REARMAMENT.

we know of no spectacle so ridiculous as the British public in one of its periodic fits of morality A truism attributed to many, in particular Oscar Wilde, but actually coined by Thomas Babington (Lord) Macaulay in his *Moore's Life of Byron*, published in 1830.

morganatic marriage A marriage contracted by a crowned head or heir to the throne, generally with a commoner, in which it is accepted that any children will be excluded from the succession. The most celebrated morganatic marriage was that between Archduke Franz Ferdinand, whose assassination at SARAJEVO triggered World War I, and Sophie Chotek. Such a marriage was also suggested at the time of Britain's ABDICATION CRISIS as a means of enabling Edward VIII to keep his throne, yet still marry Mrs. Wallis Simpson.

Morgenthau Plan A project for the "pastoralization" of Germany after World War II, drawn up by US Treasury Secretary Henry Morgenthau (1891–1967) and Secretary for War Henry Stimson and presented to Roosevelt and Churchill at the 1944 QUEBEC CONFERENCE. It proposed "eliminating the war-making industries in the Ruhr and in the Saar", and "converting Germany into a country primarily agricultural and pastoral in its character". Churchill reluctantly accepted the proposal, but Roosevelt and Truman did not pursue it.

Morley-Minto reforms The administrative and representative reforms to the British Raj pursued between 1905 and 1910 by the VICEROY the **Earl of Minto** (1845–1914) in consultation with **John** (Viscount) **Morley** (1838–1923), Secretary for India, which gave a voice to the Indian people. An Indian was appointed to the Viceroy's executive council for the first time, and others brought into the legislative and consultative organs of government. Born of the confidence given the Campbell-Bannerman/ASQUITH government by its large majority, the reforms were pursued even when civil disorder broke out and Lord and Lady Minto narrowly escaped assassination.

morning. Morning Cloud The name given by Edward Heath (*see* GROCER) to a series of five ocean-going yachts which he owned, skippering most of them in the Admirals' Cup and other major races. Yacht-racing and music, up to and including conducting a symphony orchestra, were Heath's main ways of releasing the tensions of politics. The third *Morning Cloud* had a tragic end, being wrecked off the Sussex coast in September 1974 with the loss of the two crewmen who were ferrying it between berths; the most recent was launched in 1977.

Morning Star The name given in 1966 by the Communist Party of Great Britain to the relaunched DAILY WORKER; the aim was to produce a tabloid daily that would broaden the appeal of contemporary Communism. In fact the paper became far more hard-line than the party, and with the collapse of Soviet Communism in 1991 it lost the guaranteed overseas market that had provided most of its 30,000-odd sales. Though chronically short of money, it has however struggled on.

Morosi affair The furore in Australia over the appointment in 1974 by Dr. Jim Cairns, deputy LABOR Prime Minister and federal Treasurer, of the glamorous 41-year-old Juni Morosi to run his private office. The Opposition claimed Mrs. Morosi had been allocated a Government apartment out of turn, and that she and her husband were involved in shady business deals; their company was bankrupt, but the couple were cleared of illegality. Once Prime Minister Gough WHITLAM was satisfied there was no financial impropriety, he treated the appointment as a matter for Cairns. But some Labor parliamentarians thought the presence of Morosi, described as "a stunning cross between Jackie Kennedy, Elizabeth Taylor and Brigitte Bardot", was harming the party, and persuaded her to resign. Then, on 29 December 1974, Cairns reappointed her. The following February, during the ALP's conference at Terrigal, they gave an interview that knocked the conference out of the news; the *Sydney Sun* headlined the story "My Love for Juni". Tensions grew between Cairns and the rest of his staff, which proved damaging when the LOANS SCANDAL broke, forcing his resignation as Treasurer that June. The Morosi affair could also indirectly have caused the KERR SACKING in November 1975. The publicity led Whitlam in December 1974 to delay appointing Sen. Lionel Murphy to a vacancy in the High Court; by the time he did so the political climate in New South Wales had changed and Murphy was replaced by an Independent, not a Labor, Senator, thus depriving Whitlam of a critical vote to break the deadlock over SUPPLY.

> Either Cairns was being extraordinarily naïve or he enjoyed the notoriety. Whatever it was said little for his political acumen.
>
> LAURIE OAKES, *Crash Through or Crash.*

> When everything has been said on the Morosi controversy the inescapable conclusion remains: in the final analysis, it was sexist. She was that most disturbing thing – a woman with influence.
>
> GRAHAM FREUDENBERG, *A Certain Grandeur.*

Moscow Conference A meeting between CHURCHILL, STALIN and the US ambassador Averell Harriman in Moscow from 9 to 20 October 1944. The purpose was to discuss the partition of Southeast Europe at the end of WORLD WAR II. The Soviet Union was given a controlling interest in Romania, Bulgaria and Hungary; the UK was given a controlling interest in Greece; Yugoslavia was to be a zone of counterbalanced Soviet and British influence. The last of these decisions proved academic with the rise of TITO.

Moscow line The line of policy set by the KREMLIN and dictated to Communist parties throughout the world, who were expected to follow it unquestioningly. In those parties and movements where there was genuine debate over tactics and policy, the Moscow-liners were those who advocated the Soviet position.

Mosley. Mosleyites The supporters of Sir Oswald Mosley (1896–1980) after his break with the LABOUR PARTY in 1930 following its refusal to accept his NEW DEAL-type plan for tackling mass unemployment. Mosley, originally elected a Conservative MP in 1918, CROSSED THE FLOOR to Labour in 1924, broke with RAMSAY MACDonald and founded first the NEW PARTY and then, in 1932, the British Union of FASCISTS. The BUF, also known as BLACKSHIRTS, staged mass rallies at which Mosley styled himself after Hitler, and ANTI-SEMITIC demonstrations in the East End of London which inevitably led to violence (*see* Battle of CABLE STREET). The Public Order Act, 1936, restricted the activities of the Mosleyites, who are thought to have been 20,000 strong. The BUF was banned in 1940, and Mosley was INTERNED 1940–43. His second wife was Diana Mitford, whose sister Unity was besotted with Hitler and shot herself in Germany during World War II, lingering on until 1948.

> I am not, and never have been, a man of the right. My position was on the left and is now in the centre of politics.
>
> Sir OSWALD MOSLEY, 1968.

> He stinks of money and insincerity. HUGH DALTON.

Mossad Israel's ruthless secret intelligence service, which has become a byword for harassment of the country's opponents overseas and for the cloak-and-dagger murder or abduction of individuals whose existence or published comments are inconvenient to Jerusalem. The Committee for Illegal Immigration – *Mossad le Aliyeh Beth* – was formed in 1937 as part of the Jewish defence force, HAGANAH, to arrange the immigration of Jews into Palestine as part of the campaign to establish a Jewish homeland. It was revived after World War II to organize – through a network of agents directed from Paris – the illicit migration of Jews displaced by the horrors of the HOLOCAUST, first to Allied refugee camps and thence to Palestine, where they were landed secretly in defiance of the British authorities. By 1948 Mossad members were also engaged in GUN-RUNNING and other covert activities; with the foundation of the Israeli state it formed the basis of the new country's intelligence service. It has played a crucial role in the conflict with surrounding Arab states, and above all in Israel's struggle against the PLO and its offshoot guerrilla organizations, both in the Middle East and throughout the world.

mossback A US term for an extreme conservative. Southerners who fled to the woods and swamps to avoid conscription to the Confederate Army were known as "mossybacks" and the term reappeared in the 1880s to describe western farmers in general, and conservative Ohio Democrats in particular.

Mother One of many nicknames for Margaret Thatcher, this one originated and mainly used by reasonably-devoted supporters. *See also* MATRICIDES.

motherhood and apple pie Vacuous utterances by politicians combining sentimental patriotism with appeals to traditional values, coupled with a total absence of positive or original content. Though the phrase originated in America where such speeches trip lightly from the tongue and find willing audiences, its use, and relevance, has crossed the Atlantic.

mother of all resolutions The resolution (no. 687) passed by the UN SECURITY COUNCIL in March 1991 which governed the ceasefire in the second GULF WAR, and maintained tough sanctions against Saddam Hussein's régime. It echoed Saddam's defiant warning that any move by the UN-backed COALITION to retake Kuwait after his invasion the previous August would trigger the "mother of all battles".

Mother of Parliaments A now-traditional term for Britain's HOUSE OF COMMONS, and its ethos which has been replicated in legislatures across the English-speaking world – even if some have failed to take root. The phrase was first used by the English radical John Bright (1811–89) when, in a speech at Birmingham on 18 January 1865, he declared:

> England is the mother of Parliaments.

motion A proposal formally put forward to be debated and voted on, and often capable of AMENDMENT.

Early Day Motion *See* EDM.

motor. motorcade A procession of cars in support of, or escorting, a visiting politician or candidate for office; in the case of a dignitary in office or a Presidential candidate, it will be accompanied by motorcycle outriders. The most celebrated motorcade was that taking President KENNEDY through DALLAS at the moment of his assassination.

Motorman The codename of the security operation in NORTHERN IRELAND in July 1972 when the British army moved in strength into the NO-GO AREAS which had been established by the PROVISIONAL IRA. Motorman re-established control by the SECURITY FORCES, especially over West Belfast and parts of Londonderry, and for a time blunted the terrorist campaign, but at the price of heightened resentment by Republican supporters.

motormouth A politician who is unable to stop talking. Before the internal combustion engine caught on, the phrase was "automatic mouth". In the 1890s Rep. Marriott Brosius of Pennsylvania told a fellow Congressman who kept interrupting him:

> You love your automatic mouth;
> You love its giddy whirl;
> You love its fluent flow;
> You love to wind your mouth up;
> You love to hear it go!

Mount Rushmore A mountain in the Black Hills of Dakota, the side of which bears the epic sculpture by Gutzon Borglum (1876–1941) of the heads of four Presidents: WASHINGTON, JEFFERSON, Theodore Roosevelt (*see* TEDDY) and Abraham LINCOLN, each measuring 60 ft. from the chin to the top of the forehead. Borglum began work in the 1920s; when the work was finished it soon became one of America's most popular tourist attractions. It was also the scene of the memorable final confrontation of Cary Grant and Eva Marie Saint with the villainous James Mason in Alfred Hitchcock's 1959 thriller *North by Northwest*. Borglum worked on another massive carving – of General Robert E. Lee, Stonewall Jackson, Jefferson Davis and 1200 Confederate soldiers – on Stone Mountain, but the project was plagued by disagreements and Borglum died before it could be completed.

Mount Vernon The genteel but not lavish Virginia plantation home of George WASHINGTON, on the bank of the POTOMAC just south of the city named after him, which is preserved in its 18th-century condition as a national memorial to the leader of the Revolutionary army and the United States' first President. Visitors find the slave quarters of particular interest.

mountain. beef mountain, butter mountain Derogatory terms for the surpluses of farm produce run up by the EC's Common Agricultural Policy (*see* CAP). At times there have been a million tons of beef in cold stores, which cannot be sold within the community without lowering prices; much of the butter mountain was sold at knockdown prices to the former Soviet Union, though some – and some beef – was made available to the EC's needy old folk.

I have been to the top of the mountain *See* I.

move. we shall not be moved One of the best known PROTEST SONGS of the 1960s, first heard in a political context at the Civil Rights SIT-INs a decade earlier when demonstrators refused to budge. It was originally a Negro spiritual:

> We shall not, we shall not be moved.
> We shall not, we shall not be moved.
> Just like the tree that's standing by the waterside.
> We shall not be moved.

Football spectators in Britain will have heard the same verse sung with the third line rendered as "Just like the team that's going to win the Football League (or F. A. Cup)".

modern movements A euphemism for FASCIST and NAZI parties used in the 1930s by Sir Oswald MOSLEY and other British supporters of Mussolini and Hitler.

this great movement of ours *See* THIGMOO.

mover The person who leads the sponsors of a MOTION or RESOLUTION, and opens debate on it.

moving the goalposts Sneakily changing the terms of debate midway, so that a person arguing a particular point finds it dismissed as irrelevant. The phrase is often used by contractors who have tendered for a project only to find the specifications have changed. The term comes from informal games of soccer or hockey where the goalposts at either end are portable, and a player who thought he was shooting for goal finds he has been tricked into missing the target.

Let's get America moving again The slogan used by John F. KENNEDY in his successful 1960 campaign for the US Presidency; it harnessed his youth and vigour to the notion, not now accepted, that the American economy had stagnated under Eisenhower. It has since been used, in suitably amended form, by challengers to the INCUMBENT government in many countries.

Moynihan. Moynihan report An internal paper written for the Johnson administration in 1965 by **Daniel Patrick Moynihan** (1927–), then assistant secretary for Labour and later a prominent Senator, which drew attention to the emergence of a Black UNDERCLASS, though the word did not yet exist. It argued that while middle- and working-class Blacks were making progress, a lower-class group frequently composed of single-parent families was falling behind; borrowing a phrase from the Black sociologist Kenneth Clark, he maintained that "at the center of the tangle of pathology is the weakness of the Negro family". Moynihan argued that White America had broken the will of Black American families through slavery, and that forcing Black men to take submissive jobs "worked against the emergence of a strong father figure". Moynihan was immediately accused of RACISM, and of diverting attention from the need for government to act against poverty, and it was many years before the plight of the Underclass was addressed again.

MP Member of Parliament. The universally-used abbreviation for members of the HOUSE OF COMMONS at Westminster.

muck-rakers The name given by Theodore Roosevelt to US investigative journalists at the turn of the 20th century, whom he branded as "irresponsible" and sensationalist. Sensationalism was indeed used to boost circulations, notably by William Randolph Hearst's papers whose IMPERIALISM had catapulted TEDDY to fame and office. But many reforms were brought about as a result of articles in magazines such as *Colliers* and *McClure's*, and in newspapers led by Hearst's *New York Journal* and Joseph Pulitzer's *New York World*. Two effective muckrakers were Ida M. Tarbell (1857–1944), whose 1904 exposé of Standard Oil encouraged new ANTI-TRUST legislation, and Lincoln Steffens (1866-1936), who exposed municipal corruption in 1904 (*see also* I Have Seen The FUTURE). Upton Sinclair's book *The Jungle* (1906) describing insanitary practices in the meat industry led directly to the Food and Drugs Act that same year. Roosevelt coined the word when he laid the stone of the first House office building on 14 April 1906; borrowing a passage from John Bunyan's *Pilgrim's Progress*, he compared them to

> the Man with the Muckrake . . . who when offered the Celestial crown could look no way but downward . . . [and continue] to rake the filth on the floor.

He added:

> The men with the muck-rakes are often indespensable to the well-being of society; but only if they know when to stop raking the muck.

mudslinging The practice of attempting to secure political advantage or win an election by revealing (or inventing) unsavoury facts about one's opponent; by 1992 its practitioners were terming it NEGATIVE RESEARCH (*see also* NERD SQUAD).

> He who slings mud usually loses ground.
>
> ADLAI STEVENSON.

mugwump A US term for a political INDEPENDENT, or more specifically, a REPUBLICAN who will not support the TICKET or, even worse, has gone over to the Democrats. It also covers active Republicans or Democrats who remain officially "unaffiliated", often because their employment prevents them "going public". The word, originally the Algonquin for "chief" and later applied to the self-important, was being used for Independents by 1872; in the 1884 Presidential election it was applied by their opponents to idealistic, liberal Republicans who switched from the party's nominee James G. Blaine to the more attractive Grover Cleveland (*see* BEAST OF BUFFALO).

> A mugwump always has his mug on one side of the political FENCE and his wump on the other.
>
> *Attr.* both to HAROLD WILLIS DODDS, president of Princeton University 1933–37, and the jurist ALBERT J. ENGEL (1904–).

mujaheddin (Arab. fighters) The loose coalition of rebel groups formed in Afghanistan to oppose the Soviet-backed government that came to power after a military coup in 1979; ruggedly independent and often ready to fight each other, they conducted a successful 10-year GUERRILLA campaign against Soviet forces, who finally left in 1989. Three years later the government of Najibullah Ahmadzi finally fell and the *mujaheddin* – who had formed a provisional Islamic government in exile – took over, only for fighting to break out immediately between rival groups. They comprise a wide range of political and ethnic factions, including Sunni and Shi'ite Muslims, Islamic traditionalists and fundamentalists, fiercely anti-Western elements and others that welcomed US assistance. Most factions were led from across the border in Pakistan, and received arms from China, Iran, Saudi Arabia and Egypt as well as the West; they also relied heavily on weaponry captured from the Soviets.

Muldergate *See* INFORMATION SCANDAL.

multi-. multiculturalism The educational, social and political view that has gained ground in America, Britain and other Western countries since the 1970s, that it is wrong to impose a stereotyped national culture on those arriving from other lands. It has led to keen public argument over whether, for example, children should be taught in their mother tongue or the language of their new country, and whether the former will lead to "cultural ghettoes" and make it harder for second-generation immigrants to integrate.

multi-fibre agreement (MFA) An agreement concluded in 1973 by more than 50 countries providing a framework for international trade in products made of wool, cotton or man-made fibres. By establishing a QUOTA system it enabled THIRD WORLD countries to export to the developed world without fear of prohibitive TARIFFS, yet without killing established textile industries. It was due to be superseded under the URUGUAY ROUND of GATT talks.

multilateralist Someone who believes that nations should disarm step by step with each other, unlike a UNILATERALIST who believes that for moral as well as economic reasons their own country should abandon nuclear weapons without any commitment from others to do so.

multinational force A force consisting of troops from several nations serving alongside each other with some degree of joint command; the term was particularly used of US, UK, French and other troops who made a vain attempt to keep the peace in the Lebanon in the early 1980s (*see* BEIRUT AIRPORT BOMBING).

multinationals Large global corporations with more power than many governments, who have the ability to boost or wreck the economy of a country or region by establishing a plant or closing it.

Munich agreement The agreement concluded by Hitler, Neville CHAMBERLAIN and the French premier Edouard Daladier (with the Italians also present) in Munich on 30 September 1938 for the transfer of the SUDETENLAND to Germany in return for assurances that the rest of Czechoslovakia would not be touched. The high point of Chamberlain's policy of APPEASEMENT was widely hailed in Britain as bringing PEACE IN OUR TIME and PEACE WITH HONOUR, and its critics were in a small minority. CHURCHILL branded it "a defeat without a war", and Christopher Mayhew "*reculer pour mieux reculer*"; Clement ATTLEE declared:

> We have today seen a gallant, democratic and civilized people betrayed and handed over to a ruthless despotism.

Chamberlain was cheered by Tory MPs, but Harold Macmillan recalled:

> I saw one man silent and seated – his head sunk on his shoulders, his whole demeanour depicting something between anger and despair. It was Churchill.

One Minister, the First Lord of the Admiralty Duff Cooper, resigned, saying that he could not have stayed in the Government with his head erect. The pro-appeasement editor of *The Times*, Geoffrey Dawson, inserted into his LOBBY correspondent's account of Cooper's speech the words "damp squib"; the reporter, Antony Winn, also resigned.

The agreement was discredited six months later when Hitler invaded Bohemia and Moravia; by the outbreak of WORLD WAR II less than a year after Munich, it was seen as a shameful act and the **Men of Munich** were vilified. Chamberlain's supporters argue that it was essential to give Britain a year to prepare for war; his critics that it merely encouraged Hitler, who was rearming faster, to grab more territory. The word "Munich" is now shorthand for an act of betrayal, and when Margaret Thatcher visited Prague in 1990 she made a public apology to the Czechoslovak Parliament.

> This morning I had another talk with the German Chancellor, Herr Hitler, and here is the paper that bears his name upon it as well as mine. We regard the agreement signed last night and the Anglo-German naval agreement as symptomatic of the desire of our two peoples never to go to war with one another again.
> CHAMBERLAIN, Heston Airport, 30 September 1938.

Munich beer hall putsch The abortive attempt by Adolf Hitler on 12 November 1923 to take control of Bavaria. It took place in Munich's largest beer hall, the *Bürgerbraukeller*, where Gustav von Kahr, the state commissioner, was speaking. Hitler and his BROWNSHIRTS burst in and took the floor, claiming the support of the war hero Field Marshal von Ludendorff (1865–1937). Hitler, Ludendorff and others including Rudolf HESS were arrested, Hitler being sent to prison where he wrote MEIN KAMPF.

Munich Olympics massacre The terrorist atrocity on 5 September 1972 when Palestinian terrorists from BLACK SEPTEMBER attacked the Israeli team quarters in the Olympic village, killing two Israelis and taking nine hostage. A bungled effort to rescue them led to all the hostages being killed, together with five terrorists, the rest being flown to Libya.

Murchison letter A Republican hoax in the 1888 US Presidential campaign which damaged Grover Cleveland's chances of re-election and gravely embarrassed the British government. Charles Osgoodby, a California Republican, wrote to Sir Lionel Sackville-West, the British Minister in Washington, claiming to be an American of English origin who favoured Cleveland over Benjamin Harrison, a high-tariff man who was "a believer in the American side in all questions" and "an enemy to British interests", and asking how he should vote. Sir Lionel was stupid enough to tell him, saying that the Democrats were "still desirable of maintaining friendly relations with Great Britain" and that Cleveland would "manifest a spirit of conciliation". Osgoodby released his letter and the reply to the press, and waited for the bang. Faced with a barrage of embarrassing headlines, Cleveland asked the British government to recall Sackville-West, and when they refused, dismissed him. But the dirt stuck, and although Cleveland finished narrowly ahead in the popular vote he was handsomely beaten in the ELECTORAL COLLEGE.

Murder, Inc President Reagan's name for Iran under the AYATOLLAH, bestowed because of Teheran's involvement in terrorist activity against US citizens and interests. It made the involvement of senior subordinates in the IRAN-CONTRA affair all the harder for Americans to credit.

Murphy Brown *See* FAMILY VALUES.

mushroom cloud The terrifying symbol of nuclear war, from the characteristic shape of a nuclear explosion, especially one near ground level. The massive energy release of the explosion creates a shock wave and fireball which render the air luminous. Such a cloud was first witnessed by scientists of the US MANHATTAN PROJECT who detonated a prototype ATOMIC BOMB at the Alamogordo test site, New Mexico, on 16 July 1945. The physicist Enrico Fermi described it:

> After a few seconds the rising flames lost their brightness and appeared as a huge pillar of smoke whith an expanded head like a gigantic mushroom that rose rapidly beyond the clouds, probably to a height of the order of 30,000 feet.

The next month America exploded nuclear weapons over the Japanese cities of HIROSHIMA and NAGASAKI, and the mushroom cloud claimed its first victims.

Mussolini, Benito *See* DUCE.

mutual aid The practice within Britain's CONSERVATIVE PARTY under which safe constituencies are linked to those the party might win (or avoid losing) with enough help, party workers being ferried there at election times.

mutually assured destruction Appropriately abbreviated to **MAD**. The ultimate form of nuclear DETERRENCE, the likelihood that if NUCLEAR WAR broke out both SUPERPOWERS would be obliterated because of the sheer size of their nuclear arsenals. Pursued by America and the Soviet Union from the 1960s, MAD maintained the BALANCE OF TERROR through the knowledge that enough of the nuclear firepower of each would survive a FIRST STRIKE to set off devastating retaliation.

MVD (Russ. *Ministerstvo Vnutrennikh Del*, Ministry of Internal Affairs) The Soviet police organization which replaced the NKVD in 1946. The official duties of its uniformed members included general police work, the control of labour camps, the supervision of border troops, the issue of passports and visas, *etc.* The MVD is also believed to have been involved in the secret trial and punishment of STALIN's opponents. In 1960 the MVD was replaced by the KVD.

MX Missile Experimental (Missile X). A sophisticated "silo-busting" ICBM developed during the 1970s as part of a drive to modernize the ageing US arsenal of Titan and Minuteman III missiles. The MX was designed to carry 10 MIRVed warheads and deliver them with pinpoint accuracy, using the latest inertial guidance technology. It was also planned for delivery from mobile launchers to survive a first attack, but a successful and cost-effective method of concealing and moving the missiles underground could not be found. In 1983 Congress refused further funding for mobile launch (**Racetrack**) development; Defense Secretary Caspar Weinberger (*see* CAP THE KNIFE) briefly suggested the alternative of **Densepack** under which they would be based so close together that Soviet missiles targeted at them would blow each other up as they approached. Development proceeded on the understanding that a limited number would be deployed in old Minuteman silos, but the START II agremeent's ban on MIRVs made anything more than a single-warhead MX highly unlikely.

my. My distinguished colleague The way in which US SENATORS refer to colleagues from their own party.

My honourable friend *See* FRIEND.

My last appeal to reason Hitler's speech to the REICHSTAG on 19 July 1940, following the fall of France and with invasion of Britain imminent, in which the FÜHRER held out a final offer of peace to Britain. Hitler – still perhaps influenced by Chamberlain's policy of APPEASEMENT – imagined the British people had no desire to fight, but were being led by the nose by the warlike CHURCHILL. He appealed to them directly, and several days later the *Luftwaffe* dropped copies of the speech over southern England; a cinema newsreel showing a copy being cut up and hung on a lavatory wall won huge applause. Hitler was greatly annoyed when the Foreign Secretary, Lord Halifax, rejected the overture.

My lips are sealed The gist of Stanley BALDWIN's comments to the Commons on 10 December 1935, when his government was under attack at the height of the crisis over Italy's invasion of Abyssinia. Attempting to convince Tory backbenchers that he could not give a full explanation because promising initiatives were under way, he told them:

> I shall be but a short time tonight. I have seldom spoken with greater regret, for my lips are not as yet unsealed. Were these troubles over I would make a case, and I guarantee that not a man would go into the LOBBY against us.

What was under way was the conclusion of the ignominious HOARE-LAVAL PACT, which eight days later forced Samuel Hoare to resign as Foreign Secretary after details were LEAKed in Paris; the 38-year-old Anthony EDEN succeeded him.

My Lai massacre For many Americans, including firm supporters of US intervention, the most shameful episode of the VIETNAM WAR: the machine-gunning of over 300 old men, women and children by US soldiers at the village of My Lai (also known as Song My) in Quang Ngai province; some of the women were also raped. The massacre was carried out on 16 March 1968 by Charlie company of 1st Battalion 20th Infantry, led by Lieutenant William Calley; they had been led to expect a head-on battle with a VIET CONG battalion. Army officers conspired to conceal the truth, but a year later Ronald Ridenhour, a soldier serving in Vietnam who had heard of the incident, wrote an open letter to the Army Departmnent and members of Congress calling for an investigation. Later in 1969 photographs of the massacred villagers, taken by Army photographer Ron Haeberle, appeared in a newspaper alongside Haeberle's eyewitness account. In November 1970 Calley and 24 other men went on trial for murder at Fort Benning, Georgia. Four months later all but Calley, who at one point said of the massacre "It was no big deal, Sir", were acquitted; Calley was dismissed from the service and sentenced to life imprisonment, but President Nixon ordered a review and he was released on parole after three years. Calley's defence rested on the claim that he was "following orders" and that the guilt lay with his superiors, and ultimately the US people. For many Americans the incident confirmed their worst fears; others regarded Calley as the dupe of an incompetent and indisciplined command structure – or even a martyr.

N

NAACP National Association for the Advancement of Colored People. America's most respected organization pressing for equal Black RIGHTS. Founded in 1908 at the National Negro Congress in New York by W. E. B. DuBois, Jane Addams, William Dean Howells and others as a bi-racial group demanding civil, constitutional and educational rights, much of its early work was against LYNCHING. For decades the leading campaigning vehicle against racial DISCRIMINATION, it was treated by successive administrations as the voice of Black Americans. Its legal challenges to discrimination brought gains as early as the 1920s and particularly in post-war years, and in the 1940s was using SIT-IN tactics to force DESEGREGATION. It supported the 1955 MONTGOMERY BUS BOYCOTT led by Dr. Martin Luther KING and his 1963 MARCH ON WASHINGTON. But by then, despite wise leadership from Roy Wilkins, it was losing the initiative to Black radicals who scorned its relative conservatism, and with the emergence also of a strong Black middle class its influence has continued to decline.

Nab Nickname for Sir **Gerald Nabarro** (1913–73), flamboyant and eccentric Conservative MP, first for Kidderminster and then for S. Worcestershire. He campaigned against anomalies in the purchase (sales) tax which preceded VAT, saying: "Why is there this invidious distinction between doorknocking nutcrackers and nutcracking doorknockers?" He named his autobiography *Nab 1* after the registration number of his favourite Rolls-Royce; he had six cars altogether, registered NAB 1 to 6.

nabobs All-powerful figures in the US CONGRESS, and the political or media establishment outside. The origin of the word is the Hindi *nawab*, a wealthy provincial administrator of the Moghul empire. The phrase "rich as a nawab", corrupted to "nabob", was applied to British merchants who became wealthy in the Indies and returned home; the word crossed the Atlantic to apply to Southern plantation owners, and later persons of power and influence generally.

> In the United States today, we have more than our share of nattering nabobs of negativism.
>
> SPIRO T. AGNEW (1918–).

Nader's raiders The team of consumer-affairs lobbying researchers built up in Washington by **Ralph Nader** (1934–) from the mid-1960s to press CONGRESS for tighter legislation on consumer protection, pollution and FREEDOM OF INFORMATION. Nader's organization Public Citizen Inc. has kept up the campaigning on a more formal basis. *See* UNSAFE AT ANY SPEED.

NAFTA North American FREE TRADE Area. The common market comprising 360 million inhabitants of the United States, Canada and Mexico agreed in August 1992. Subject to ratification, NAFTA would eliminate all TARIFFS and other barriers between the three countries over 15 years from 1994, create international haulage routes across America, enable US financial institutions to open up in Mexico, and prevent European and Far Eastern firms using Mexico to penetrate US markets by the back door.

Nagasaki The port city in West Kyushu, Japan, largely destroyed on 9 August 1945 by the dropping of the second ATOMIC BOMB. Damage was less severe than at HIROSHIMA, but nonetheless 75,000 people were killed or wounded, hastening Japan's surrender and the end of WORLD WAR II. The city was rapidly rebuilt after the war, but its destruction continues to serve as an awful warning to the world.

naked into the conference chamber Aneurin Bevan's warning to fellow UK Labour left-wingers at the 1957 party conference that he could not embrace unilateral nuclear disarmament. Many former BEVANITES could not understand what they saw as a SELL-OUT, pleading with him: "Come back NYE, unilaterally." But Bevan told them:

> If you carry this resolution and follow out all its implications, you will send a Foreign Secretary . . . whoever he may be, naked into the conference chamber. . . . You call that statesmanship – I call it emotional spasm.

naming The action taken by Britain's House of Commons against a member for grossly disorderly conduct, disregarding the authority of the CHAIR or persistently disrupting business. The SPEAKER first names the member, and a motion for suspension is then put. If this is carried, the offending member must leave the Chamber at once and remain outside the PRECINCTS OF THE HOUSE for 5 sitting days for a first offence, 20 for a second.

Nansen passport A passport introduced in 1922 as a travel document for "stateless" persons. It was named after the Norwegian explorer Fridjof Nansen (1861–1930), who received the NOBEL PEACE PRIZE in 1922 for his humanitarian work on behalf of the LEAGUE OF NATIONS. Nansen had suggested such a passport to relieve the plight of refugees.

napalm An explosive jelly formed from a petroleum compound – *na*pthenic acid and *palm*itic acid – which causes severe burns. Used in bombs and flame-throwers in WORLD WAR II and KOREA, it became to anti-war groups one of the most abhorrent of weapons because of its indiscriminate use, causing horrific civilian casualties. The sight on US television of napalm casualties in VIETNAM intensified demands for withdrawal from the war.

NASA The government agency that, since 1958, has co-ordinated America's space programme (excluding military projects). After the Challenger disaster on 28 January 1986, the agency was completely reshaped to counter charges of bureaucratic atrophy and inadequate safety checks. At the time the initials were said to stand for "Need Another Seven Astronauts". *See* SPACE RACE; TOUCH THE FACE OF GOD.

Nassau conference A meeting in the Bahamas in 1962 between President John F. KENNEDY and British Prime Minister Harold Macmillan (*see* SUPERMAC). Macmillan's decision during the conference to opt for the US POLARIS missile system rather than an Anglo-French alternative greatly angered President DE GAULLE and contributed to his determination to keep Britain out of a united Europe (*see* NON!).

nation. Nation of shopkeepers A term of abuse for Britain, popularly attributed to Napoleon but first used in 1776 by Samuel Adams on British reaction to the Declaration of INDEPENDENCE – and by Adam Smith in his WEALTH OF NATIONS. Smith wrote:

> To found a great empire for the sole purpose of raising up a people of customers . . . is extremely fit for a nation governed by shopkeepers.

Nation shall speak peace unto nation The motto of the BBC, devised by a schoolmaster, Montague John Rendall (1862–1950), in 1927 as the winning entry in a competition.

nation state An independent nation with a clear ethnic or cultural identity, contrasted with loose empires or with city-states. It was the basis, at Woodrow WILSON's insistence, for the post-1918 world order. I. F. STONE wrote:

> The nation state system that enables one or two men to decide life or death for the planet is the common enemy – not Russians, not Americans, capitalists or Communists.

most favoured nation Status granted by the US under the provisions of GATT, bestowing certain trading advantages on deserving countries. Withholding it is a means of exercising pressure or showing disapproval (*see* JACKSON-VANIK AMENDMENT).

One Nation A group of liberal Conservative MPs formed at Westminster in 1950 to press for a greater commitment by the party to the social services. The pamphlet, *One Nation* (in homage to Disraeli's paternalistic conservatism) was published that October; after the Conservatives under CHURCHILL returned to power a year later, it strongly influenced government social policy.

Two Nations The situation in England that Disraeli (*see* DIZZY) exposed and was eager to remedy. In his *Sybil, or the Two Nations* (1845), Egremont said: "I was told that an impossible gulf divided the Rich from the Poor; I was told that the Privileged and the people formed two Nations, governed by different laws, influenced by different manners, with no thoughts or sympathies in common; with an innate inability of mutual comprehension".

national. National Assembly The legislature of the French republic.

National Committee The bodies which represent and administer America's political parties on a permanent basis, regardless of whether the party is in government.

> We made no progress at all, and we didn't intend to. That is the function of a National Committee.
>
> RONALD REAGAN.

national debt The debt that a state has built up through borrowing to finance its activities, most frequently war and development of the economy. JEFFERSON was "for a government vigorously frugal and simple, applying all the possible savings of the public revenue to the discharge of the national debt". And Alexander HAMILTON said: "A national debt, if it is not excessive, will be to us a national blessing"; but MADISON was convinced that "a public debt is a public curse, and in a republican government a greater than any other". This was a reversal of PITT THE YOUNGER's declaration that "a public debt is a public blessing". The radical

William Cobbett (1762–1835) took a more THATCHERITE view: "Nothing is so calculated to produce a death-like torpor in a country as an extended system of taxation and a great national debt." But Franklin D. Roosevelt, elected to balance the budget, soon reversed his position to say: "Our national debt is after all an internal debt owed not only by the nation but to the nation. If our children have to pay interest on it, they will pay that interest to themselves."

A crazy aunt we keep down in the basement.
H. ROSS PEROT, 1992.

National Front A far-right UK RACIST party that attracted some working-class support in the mid-1970s but never made an electoral breakthrough.

National Government The UK administration formed with largely Conservative support by RAMSAY MACDonald in 1931 when his minority Labour government split over an economy package (*see* GREAT BETRAYAL). Chancellor Philip Snowden expected the grouping to be purely temporary, saying later: "The Tories have got the power, and they mean to use it." It remained nominally in existence under the Conservatives BALDWIN and CHAMBERLAIN until the outbreak of World War II.

National Guard America's part-time MILITIA organized on a state-by-state basis which can be mobilized by a GOVERNOR in support of the civil power, or activated in wartime to reinforce the regular US armed forces.

National Health Service *See* NHS.

national interest, the The cause in which political leaders claim to be acting when pursuing a policy unpopular with the electorate or with other states – or especially when pursuing their own interests.

National Labour Those Labour MPs who supported the NATIONAL GOVERNMENT in 1931 while the bulk of their party went into opposition. Twenty made the break – including Philip Snowden, Sir John Sankey and J. H. Thomas – and 13 survived that autumn's general election. RAMSAY MACDonald had hoped they would form the core of a new movement, but they became a rump in an overwhelmingly Tory administration.

National Liberals The 25 LIBERAL MPs led by Sir John Simon (1873–1954) who broke with their party over FREE TRADE in what they saw as an emergency requiring PROTECTIONIST measures and backed the NATIONAL GOVERNMENT. They outlasted their NATIONAL LABOUR colleagues; their Liberal National Group survived until 1948, being renamed the National Liberal Party but being steadily integrated with the Conservatives. Its last four MPs joined the CONSERVATIVE PARTY in 1966.

National Military Establishment The forerunner of America's unified Department of Defense, set up in 1947 under the National Security Act. Until then each service had its own entirely separate bureaucracy.

National Origins Plan The regulations introduced by the US government in 1929 under the QUOTA Act of 1924, which set the number of immigrants from outside the Western Hemisphere at approximately 150,000 a year. Each country was given a quota based on the proportion of that "national origin" in the total US population for 1920. Each European country was allowed at least 100 people a year, but all immigration from Asia was prohibited. The quota system lasted until 1965. *See also* DILLINGHAM REPORT.

National Party (1) A centre-right party in Australia (changing its name from *National Country Party* in 1982), where in government it shares power with the Liberals; and the leading such party in New Zealand. (2) In South Africa the largely Afrikaner party which pioneered APARTHEID, governing continuously from 1948 to the ending of that system by F. W. de Klerk.

National Plan The blueprint for five years' economic development in the UK issued in 1965 by the newly-established Department of Economic Affairs headed by George BROWN (1914–85). Aiming for a 25% increase in national output by 1970, it was the first and only attempt by Harold WILSON's first Labour government to assert control over the entire economy. It was "blown off course" in Wilson's words by periodic BALANCE OF PAYMENTS difficulties culminating in the JULY MEASURES of 1966.

national question, the Shorthand in the Irish Republic for the argument over the continued existence of NORTHERN IRELAND as a separate entity and the claim asserted in the Irish Constitution to sovereignty over all 32 counties. *See* IRA.

National Policy The policy on which Sir John Macdonald's Conservatives swept the country in the 1878 Canadian election: PROTECTIONISM, completion of the Pacific railway, a new drive for immigrants to fill the prairies, and incentives for investors.

National Recovery Administration *See* NRA.

National Review The magazine founded by William F. Buckley Jr. in 1955 whose right-wing RADICALISM paved the way for the revival of CONSERVATISM in US politics, for the unsuccessful Goldwater campaign in 1964 and eventually for the triumph of Ronald Reagan.

National Rifle Association *See* NRA.
national security A largely US term for the protection of the state against external, and sometimes internal, threat.
national security adviser The US President's principal adviser on foreign policy and related matters, sometimes, as with Henry KISSINGER, overshadowing the SECRETARY OF STATE.
National Security Agency The organization co-ordinating the US Government's communications systems. Established under the Defense Department in 1952, it embraces the communications, code-breaking and electronic intelligence-gathering operations of the armed services, CIA, FBI and other agencies. Its activities, notably its signals monitoring arm at Fort Meade, Maryland, are even more secret than those of the CIA.
National Security Council (NSC) The Cabinet-level advisory group that advises the President on national security matters, and its highly-professional staff. Established in 1947 on a plan devised by Navy Secretary James F. Forrestal to co-ordinate policy and the activities of the various government agencies, and strengthened in 1963, it developed from a civil-service neuter into a body exercising clout over those agencies through the NATIONAL SECURITY ADVISER, who is nominally secretary of the committee. The council's other members are the VICE-PRESIDENT, Secretaries of State, Defense and Treasury, Attorney-General, director of the CIA and the chairman of the JOINT CHIEFS OF STAFF.
National Socialism The ideology behind Germany's NAZI party, based on Hitler's MEIN KAMPF. Its essentials were the superiority of the German race and its expansionist destiny, and hatred of the Jews. CHURCHILL termed it "a perverted science". But Hermann Goering (1893–1946) revelled in it:

> Our movement took a grip on cowardly Marxism, and from it extracted the meaning of socialism. It also took from the cowardly, middle-class parties their nationalism. Throwing both into the cauldron of our national way of life there emerged, as clear as crystal, the synthesis – National Socialism.

National Union The voluntary organizational wing of the UK CONSERVATIVE PARTY, its executive committee being the party's governing body, though with, in theory, no say over party policy. Its annual meeting is the CENTRAL COUNCIL in March.
National Unity The banner under which the former Republican Rep. John Anderson of Illinois (with former Democratic Governor Patrick Lucey of Wisconsin) sought the Presidency in 1980. Their platform was fiscally conservative but liberal on social issues. Anderson finished third to Ronald Reagan, with 5,719,000 votes and none in the electoral college.
National Urban League Formed in 1910 as a biracial group to help Black migrants from the rural South adjust to city life, it has been, along with the NAACP, a leading voice of America's Black communities. In the 1960s it developed a programme of vigorous but NON-VIOLENT community action under A. Whitney Young, taking a firm stand against BLACK POWER.
nationalization The transfer of sectors of industry and commerce from the PRIVATE SECTOR to state control, with or without compensation to the owners. In the UK, the keystone of LABOUR's economic policies, implemented from 1945 (the Bank of England) to 1977 (aircraft and shipbuilding) (*see* CLAUSE FOUR). The Conservatives strongly contested most instances of nationalization, reversing them where they were not too firmly entrenched (steel was nationalized and denationalized twice). The reverse process came to be known under Margaret Thatcher as PRIVATIZATION. CHURCHILL is reputed to have taunted ATTLEE in the "Gents" of the House of Commons: "Anything that's large and successful, you want to nationalize it". Hugh Dalton (1887–1962) once dreamed he was chairing a Labour Party Conference where a proposal to nationalize the Solar System was going through smoothly until an AMENDMENT was moved to add the words "and the Milky Way". In Egypt, the nationalization of the Suez Canal by President Nasser (1918–70) precipitated the SUEZ crisis.
Morrisonian nationalization The formula followed by Herbert Morrison (1888–1965) (later Lord Morrison of Lambeth), the ATTLEE government's nationalization supremo, of a rigid centralized hierarchy for newly-acquired industries and no role for worker representatives.

nationalism Devotion to the cause of a nation and its independence. Albert Einstein (1879–1955) termed it "an infantile disease; the measles of mankind".
New nationalism The policy of radical economic regulation and intervention set out by Theodore Roosevelt in 1910, with the explanation: "The citizens of the United States must effectively control her mighty commercial forces which they have themselves called into being."
nationalist An adherent or practitioner of nationalism. In the early days of American independence, the opposite of FEDERALIST, advocating a more unitary state.
Irish Nationalist An advocate, peaceful or

otherwise, of the reunion of NORTHERN IRELAND with the Republic (formerly, of HOME RULE).

Nationalist China The state established on Taiwan by Chiang Kai-Shek (*see* GENERALISSIMO) following the Communist capture of power on the mainland. *See* CHINA CARD; CHINA LOBBY; KMT; QUEMOY AND MATSU; Who Lost CHINA?.

nationalities question The issue of how the many diverse peoples of the former Soviet Union could be controlled from the Kremlin, and how much power, if any, should be devolved to them.

NATO North Atlantic Treaty Organization. The ATLANTIC ALLIANCE of 12, eventually 16, nations formed with the signature of the North Atlantic Treaty on 4 April 1949 as a conventional and nuclear DETERRENT to Soviet aggression against any member. Its headquarters, SHAPE, is at Chièvres, Belgium, and its first supreme commander was General Dwight D. Eisenhower. Lord Ismay (1887–1965) confessed that NATO had been set up "to keep the Russians out, the Americans in and the Germans down". President KENNEDY stressed the Atlantic dimension: "I want two strong towers in NATO, one American and one European." But despite this France withdrew in 1966 because President DE GAULLE saw the alliance as unacceptably dominated by the US. Harold Macmillan had dismissed this notion, saying: "There might be one finger on the trigger, but there are 15 fingers on the safety catch." But its nuclear deterrent role was played down by supreme Allied Commander general Bernard Rogers, who said: "the last thing we want to do is make Europe safe for a conventional war". Pierre Trudeau was dismissive of its political dimension: "NATO heads of state and governments meet only to go through the tedious motions of reading speeches drafted by others, with the principal objective not rocking the boat." And the UK Labour MP Ken Livingstone said of Gerald Kaufman, the party's Shadow Foreign Secretary, during the debate over UNILATERALISM: "He has crawled so far up the backside of NATO that you can't see the soles of his feet." With the end of the COLD WAR, its forces have been reduced and its role is now in question.

Naught for your Comfort One of the classic texts against APARTHEID, written in South Africa in 1956 by the Anglican priest Fr. Trevor Huddleston (1913–), later president of Britain's Anti-Apartheid Movement.

naval. naval estimates crisis The cause of the fall of Gladstone's last UK government. All his Ministers became convinced during 1893 of the need for higher naval spending; Gladstone accused them of falling to a "monstrous conspiracy" by the admirals. The crisis came to a head in early 1894; Gladstone finally retired at the "blubbering CABINET" of 1 March 1894.

naval holiday The ten-year pause in the construction of warships over 10,000 tons agreed at the WASHINGTON CONFERENCE in February 1922 by America, Britain, Japan, France and Italy; Germany, having been forcibly disarmed after WORLD WAR I, was thought not to pose a threat.

Naval Observatory The official Washington home of the VICE-PRESIDENT, within the Observatory Circle between Massachusetts and Wisconsin Avenues, NW.

Navigation Acts The 17th-century British mercantilist legislation which confined many cargoes to specifically British ships. It thus barred Britain's colonies, notably in America, from trading with other powers, so was a major factor in provoking American Independence. Subsequently an irritant also to Canada, the Acts were finally repealed in 1849.

Nazi German abbreviation for Hitler's NATIONAL SOCIALIST German Workers' Party (*Nationalsozialistische Deutscher Arbeiterpartei*), which became worldwide shorthand not just for the party but its adherents and its ideology.

Nazi-Soviet pact *See* HITLER-STALIN PACT.

NCR system No carbon required. The UK Conservative equivalent of Labour's READING SYSTEM for monitoring TURNOUT on POLLING DAY. Supporters who have voted are crossed off the uppermost sheet of a pad at intervals, with the impression of the crossings-off being reproduced on sheets below. KNOCKERS-UP are sent out with these sheets at intervals to persuade those yet to vote to do so.

NDP New Democratic Party. Canada's democratic Socialist party, founded in 1961 by the CCF, in consultation with the Canadian Labour Congress. It has formed several provincial governments, but has yet to gain power nationally.

Neanderthal A stone-age CONSERVATIVE, from the hominid remains found near Düsseldorf in 1856. The term was probably first used by Judge Samuel Rosenman in a 1948 memo to President Truman: "the Neanderthal men of the Republican Party".

Neave assassination The murder by an INLA car bomb on 30 March 1979 of Airey Neave (1916–79), the former Army intelligence officer and Colditz escaper who masterminded

Margaret Thatcher's election as Tory leader in 1975, was her hard-line Shadow NORTHERN IRELAND Secretary and would have given her crucial support and advice in government. He died the day after the defeat of the Labour government on a motion of no-CONFIDENCE made an election certain and a Tory victory highly likely. Neave was the first MP to be killed by Irish terrorists in the present troubles, and the first for over 150 years to be murdered in the precincts of the House. He was picked as a target because of his tough line on Ulster and his closeness to Mrs. Thatcher; the bomb was attached to his car outside his flat, and went off on the ramp leading to the Commons' underground car park.

NEC The National Executive Committee of the UK LABOUR PARTY, its guiding body and the heart of its policymaking – often in opposition to the leadership – until emasculated by Neil KINNOCK in the mid-1980s.

necessary and proper clause Also known as the **elastic clause**, the provision in the US CONSTITUTION (Section 8, clause 18) empowering CONGRESS to "make all laws which shall be necessary and proper" for carrying out the functions vested in it. It does not give Congress *carte blanche* to enact whatever laws it wishes.

necessity knows no law The words used by the German chancellor Bethmann-Hollweg in the REICHSTAG on 4 August 1914 as a justification for the infringement of Belgian neutrality.

> Gentlemen, we are now in a state of necessity, and necessity knows no law. Our troops have occupied Luxembourg and perhaps have already entered Belgian territory.

necklace killings The particularly vicious method used by extremists in South Africa's Black townships to "execute" their political opponents: fixing a rubber tyre round their neck, filling it with petrol, then setting fire to it. When Nelson Mandela announced that he and his militant wife Winnie were separating, a columnist in *The Scotsman* wrote: "Nelson's getting the Mercedes and Winnie will keep the tyres." In Haiti the petrol-filled tyre is known as "Père Lebrun".

Neddy Britain's National Economic Development Council, set up by Harold Macmillan in 1962 as a forum for communication and economic assessment involving all sides of industry; it fell into virtual disuse under Margaret Thatcher, who saw it as CORPORATIST, and was wound up by Chancellor Norman Lamont in 1992. **Little Neddies** were the mini-versions of Neddy which concentrated on particular sectors of the economy. **NEDO** was the National Economic Development Office, whose staff submitted forecasts and economic assessments to Neddy.

negative income tax A form of UNIFIED TAX AND BENEFIT SYSTEM under which a person whose income does not merit taxation receives social benefits through the same system of assessment.

negative research A polite term, rife in the 1992 US Presidential campaign, for the unearthing of sleazy facts or rumours about the opposing candidate and their planting on the media. *See also* NERD SQUAD.

Nehru dynasty The domination of Indian politics for more than 40 years by the family of the statesman **Jawaharlal Nehru** (1889–1964). A disciple of MAHATMA Gandhi, Nehru became president of the Indian National CONGRESS Party in 1929 and was imprisoned nine times for his opposition to British rule. He became Prime Minister of independent India in 1947 and remained in the post until his death, providing much-needed political stability.

He groomed his daughter **Indira Gandhi** (1917–84) as his successor. Although no relation to Mahatma Gandhi and at times ruthless in pursuit of her chosen policies, the name gave added strength to her claim to power and undoubtedly helped her become Prime Minister from 1966 until 1977 and again 1980–84. She in turn prepared her son **Sanjay Gandhi** (1946–80) as her successor, and when he was killed in a plane crash she brought her other son **Rajiv** (1942–91), previously an airline pilot, into the political limelight.

When Indira Gandhi's suppression of Sikh unrest led to her assassination by Sikh members of her bodyguard, Rajiv immediately succeeded her as Prime Minister. As leader of his mother's Congress (I) party, he continued Nehru's balancing act between differing political and religious traditions, but lost office in 1989. In the third tragedy to strike the family, Rajiv was killed during the election campaign of 1991 by a terrorist bomb.

Nenni telegram The telegram sent by 37 LABOUR MPs to the pro-Communist Italian socialist Pietro Nenni and his supporters at the time of the 1948 Italian general election, in defiance of the Labour leadership which backed the more independent Italian Socialist Party. Two of the MPs, John Platts-Mills and Konni Zilliacus, were EXPELLED from the party as a result, though Zilliacus was later readmitted.

neo-. neo-colonialism The exercise of influence by a nation over a former colony in such a way as to perpetuate its dependency.

neo-communism or fascism or Nazism A philosophy, programme or movement similar in many respects to the original, but not so close as to be identical. For instance, most neo-Nazi groups, especially in reunified Germany, are so scruffy that Hitler would instantly have had them imprisoned.

neo-conservative The term invented by the socialist Democrat Rep. Michael Harrington for Democrats who took a harder line against liberal positions than many Republicans. The ideological core of neo-conservatism was the magazine *The Public Interest*, founded in 1965; in their later years Senators Henry SCOOP Jackson and Daniel Patrick MOYNIHAN, both liberals at the outset, were widely regarded as neo-conservatives in the fields of defence and welfare respectively.

NEP *See* NEW ECONOMIC POLICY.

nerd squad A "dirty tricks" unit of Republicans in the 1992 Presidential campaign planting derogatory tales about potential Democratic candidates – notably Governor Bill Clinton – with the media. Similar Democratic units spreading BLACK PROPAGANDA about President Bush were known as **propeller-heads**. Not to be outdone, H. Ross PEROT traded charges with the Bush campaign that each had engaged in subversive activities against the other.

nervous nellies President Lyndon Johnson's term for opponents of the VIETNAM WAR as Congressional criticism grew in May 1966. He was particularly outraged by a charge from Sen. William Fulbright (1905–) that America was "succumbing to the arrogance of power".

neutrality The status of a nation which chooses not to take sides in a conflict between others, rendering it free from attack by either. It must not help the warlike purposes of any of the combatants, but in other respects may continue trading with them. George WASHINGTON issued a Proclamation of Neutrality in April 1793, just after commencing his second term. In 1914 President Woodrow WILSON said that America "must be neutral in fact as well as in name during these days that are to try men's souls. We must be impartial in thought as well as in action." Seen by its adherents either as a noble moral position or a way of avoiding suicidal entanglements (*see* ISOLATIONISM), it has been much criticized as a token of weakness or a means of evading responsibilities. President KENNEDY quoted Dante (1265–1321) as saying that "the hottest places in Hell are reserved for those who in a period of moral crisis maintain their neutrality". The Hungarian patriot Kossuth (1802–94) declared that "neutrality as a lasting principle is an evidence of weakness", and Mussolini (*see* DUCE) said: "Neutrals have never dominated events. They have always gone under." At the height of the COLD WAR, John Foster Dulles described neutrality as "an obsolete conception, and except under very exceptional circumstances an immoral and short-sighted conception". And the radical Indian foreign minister Krishna Menon declared:

> Positive neutrality is a contradiction in terms. There can no more be positive neutrality than there can be a vegetarian tiger.

Neutrality Acts The Acts passed by the ISOLATIONIST majority in the US Congress in 1935, 1936 and 1937 to take foreign policy powers to itself in an attempt to thwart any attempt by Franklin D. Roosevelt to involve the country in the coming World War. Their provisions, notably a requirement on the President to ban the export of war materials to belligerents, severely tied Roosevelt's hands, but Congress slightly eased them after the outbreak of war in 1939 and FDR was able to sidestep those remaining through such provisions as LEND-LEASE until PEARL HARBOR changed the mood in Congress overnight.

armed neutrality A position designed to stay out of conflict through strength rather than weakness, pioneered by the Russian Empress Catherine the Great in response to England's high-handedness during the Seven Years' War in the late 18th century. Declaring war on Germany in April 1917, President WILSON stated sadly:

> Armed neutrality, it now appears, is impracticable.

neutron bomb A type of tactical nuclear weapon developed by America and publicized in the mid-1970s. Hailed as a "clean" bomb that destroyed "people but not buildings", President CARTER urged its deployment by NATO forces in Europe as a deterrent to Soviet tank attacks. Vocal public opposition in Europe – though not from the British and German governments – led Carter to drop the plan. Delivered by missiles or artillery shells, the bomb created a blast over only a few hundred yards but threw off intense neutron and gamma-ray radiation over a large area. This could penetrate defences including tank armour, killing attacking troops outright or causing their death in a few days.

never. Never again! The slogan used by advocates of lasting world peace after WORLD WAR I, the horrific war that was supposed to end all wars. In the 1960s it was adopted by the JEWISH DEFENCE LEAGUE to recall the HOLOCAUST and justify militant action against Arabs.

Never complain, never explain Disraeli's advice to fellow-politicians, cited by Lord BALDWIN in 1943 at the height of the press campaign against him for allegedly having brought about WORLD WAR II by hesitating to rearm. *See* APPALLING FRANKNESS.

Never forget, rarely forgive The more robust political motto of Edward Koch (1924–), Democratic Mayor of New York City from 1978 to 1989.

Never glad confident morning again The payoff line from Robert Browning's poem *The Lost Leader*, in which he complained that Wordsworth had lost the revolutionary zeal of his youth. It was employed to deadly effect in the House of Commons on 17 June 1963, at the height of the PROFUMO AFFAIR, against Harold Macmillan (*see* SUPERMAC) and his government by the former Conservative Minister Nigel Birch. He told Macmillan: "I myself feel that the time will come very soon when my Rt. Hon. Friend ought to make way for a much younger colleague.... I certainly will not quote at him the savage words of Cromwell (*see* YOU HAVE SAT HERE LONG ENOUGH), but perhaps some words of Browning might be appropriate in his poem on *The Lost Leader* . . . :

> Let him never come back to us!
> There would be doubt, hesitation and pain.
> Forced praise on our part – the glimmer of twilight,
> Never glad confident morning again!"

Never in the field of human conflict was so much owed by so many to so few Winston CHURCHILL's tribute at the height of the Battle of Britain to the fighter pilots of the Royal Air Force, in a House of Commons speech on 20 August 1940. The format has frequently been copied; for instance John MAJOR said of press inquiries about his school examination results:

> Never has so much been written about so little.

Never lose your temper with the Press or public According to the SUFFRAGETTE Christabel Pankhurst (1880–1958) this was "a magic rule of political life". She did not extend her magic rule to relations with the police; she was once arrested for assaulting an officer who removed her from an election meeting.

Never murder a man who is committing suicide Woodrow WILSON's reason for not countering the attacks on his administration from his Republican opponent Charles Evans Hughes during his 1916 campaign for re-election.

Never trust a man whose eyes are too close to his nose One of the more printable homespun dicta uttered by Lyndon B. Johnson (*see* LBJ) during his career in Washington.

new. New Covenant The programme put forward by Bill Clinton (*see* COMEBACK KID) in 1992 which helped secure him the Presidency. It embodied improved incentives for enterprise, guaranteed health care, skills training for young people not bound for college and a drive to cure the problems of the INNER CITIES.

New Deal President Franklin D. Roosevelt's policy of KEYNESIAN economic reconstruction, announced on 2 July 1932 at the start of his campaign for the presidency. The announcement came in typically dramatic form; FDR broke with tradition by flying to Chicago to accept the Democratic nomination in person, and declared:

> I pledge you, I pledge myself, to a new deal for the American people.

The phrase had its origin in a book by Stuart Chase, published that same year. FDR's programme of action to end America's economic tailspin after the GREAT CRASH of 1929, which was throwing millions into poverty, contrasted starkly with the self-imposed near paralysis of the HOOVER administration. When a friend told him: "If the New Deal is a success, you will be remembered as the greatest American president", FDR replied:

> If I fail, I will be remembered as the last one.

On taking office (*see* HUNDRED DAYS), Roosevelt immediately closed the banks while plans were drawn up to regulate them, introduced currency controls, underpinned farm prices and stimulated industrial recovery to curb mass unemployment. He explained: "These unhappy times call for plans that build from the bottom up, and not from the top down, that put their faith once more in the forgotten man at the bottom of the economic pyramid." Richard Hofstadter wrote that the essence of the New Deal was "Roosevelt's confidence that even when he was operating in unfamiliar territory he could do no wrong, commit no serious mistakes". It also led to accusations against him of Socialism and FASCISM; Sen. Daniel Hastings said the New Deal gave the President "more power than any good man should want, and more power than any other kind of man ought to have".

Eventually the New Deal had three phases: a First New Deal from March 1933 which concentrated on economic relief and recovery from the depths of the DEPRESSION, a Second New Deal concerned with social reform – collective bargaining, unemployment benefits, old age pensions – from January 1935, and a Third New Deal in 1938 to maintain the momentum as the economy again faltered. It was the onset of war that finally put America fully back to work.

New Dealer A supporter of or participant in the New Deal programmes, and subsequently any Democratic politician who continued to advocate INTERVENTIONIST, Keynesian prescriptions for poverty and a sluggish economy.

New Economic Policy (NEP) A series of economic reforms introduced by LENIN in March 1921 to quell widespread discontent with the BOLSHEVIK regime. The policy was announced at the Tenth Party Congress in the wake of urban riots, strikes and the KRONSTADT MUTINY. It amounted to a complete reversal of the previous economic strategy; rigid centralized planning was replaced by a mixed ECONOMY, heavy industry and banking remained in state control but agriculture and production of consumer goods were returned to the private sector, cash wages were reinstated for industrial workers and the profit motive encouraged to promote growth. The NEP was successful in reviving the economy and restoring popular support for the regime; its early years (1921–28) also brought a flowering of Soviet art and culture. But STALIN's seizure of power after Lenin's death in 1924 signalled the end of the NEP. In 1928 he announced the first FIVE-YEAR PLAN, which enforced a return to centralized planning, outlawed private enterprise and began the COLLECTIVIZATION of agriculture.

New Frontier President John F. KENNEDY's vision of a more challenging and outward-looking agenda for America after the torpor of the Eisenhower years. Accepting the Democratic Presidential nomination on 15 July 1960, the youthful JFK said:

> We stand today on the edge of a new frontier. But the new frontier of which I speak is not a set of promises. It is a set of challenges. It sums up not what I intend to offer the American people, but what I intend to ask of them. It appeals to their pride, not their pocketbook – it holds out the prospect of more sacrifice instead of more security.

In terms of social reform, the New Frontier was not a great success; the narrowness of Kennedy's majority and lack of a Congressional MANDATE stalled a legislative programme which was never over-adventurous. On the world stage, the revival of the COLD WAR limited its scope. But in terms of the SPACE RACE, America's relationship with the developing world and, above all, the intellectual ferment of the BEST AND THE BRIGHTEST in the Kennedy White House gave an impression of dynamic change.

New Hampshire primary The first major event of a US Presidential election year, the chance to establish the BIG MO and a graveyard for many hopes. Held in late winter, this opening PRIMARY in a small state attracts blanket attention from Presidential hopefuls and the media alike; one woman questioned by a reporter said of a candidate: "Oh, no, I couldn't possibly vote for him, I've only met him four times." For decades the primary was overshadowed by the viciously right-wing campaigning of William Loeb, publisher of the *Manchester Union-Leader*; his obituary recalled that "he called President Eisenhower a dope and Senator Eugene McCarthy a skunk". McCarthy's moral defeat of President Lyndon Johnson in 1968 led LBJ to quit the race; four years later Loeb's promotion of the CANUCK LETTER caused Sen. Ed Muskie to self-destruct. In 1992 President George Bush was given a fright by the ultra-conservative Pat Buchanan; Bush campaigner Bill Bennett said:

> New Hampshire wasn't a wake-up call. It was BIG BEN falling on your head.

New Jewel Movement The radical, but democratic, movement led by Maurice Bishop which governed GRENADA until overthrown in October 1983 with great brutality by ultra-leftists. The coup triggered the controversial US invasion of Grenada six days later.

New Left In America, the grouping which emerged from the PROTEST movement of the 1960s to challenge traditional Liberalism. Its stated aim was to win for individuals power over the decisions that affected their own lives. The New Left gained its impetus from opposition to the VIETNAM WAR; though largely anti-Communist, this led to its being widely perceived as UN-AMERICAN. New Left activism overlapped into the DEMOCRATIC PARTY, having a considerable say in the platform on which Sen. George McGovern lost heavily in 1972.

New Order The reshaping of Europe under the domination of Germany as envisaged by Hitler. In Berlin on 30 January 1941, the FÜHRER said:

> I am convinced that 1941 will be the crucial year of a great New Order in Europe. The world will open up for everyone.

After the collapse of Communism in eastern Europe and the Soviet Union, George BUSH spoke of a **New World Order** in which the former SUPERPOWERS would generate an atmosphere of co-operation. His hopes reached their height when the Kremlin in 1990 accepted US-led military action under the auspices of the UNITED NATIONS to oust Iraqi forces from Kuwait.

New Palace Yard At Westminster, the courtyard facing PARLIAMENT SQUARE through whose gates Ministers and MPs arrive at the HOUSE OF COMMONS. It is lined with catalpa trees and adorned by a fountain. Below ground is a four-level car park, in whose exit the

Conservative Northern Ireland spokesman Airey Neave was assassinated by an Irish National Liberation Army (*see* INLA) bomb in March 1979.

New Party The party established by Sir Oswald MOSLEY on his resignation from the Labour government after the 1930 party conference had refused to adopt his radical KEYNESIAN programme to tackle the economic crisis and reduce unemployment. Mosley's memorandum enlarging on these policies was published on 6 December and signed by 17 Labour MPs, six of whom joined Mosley when he formed the New Party in February 1931. The party failed to win any seats in the 1931 General Election, only Mosley of its sitting MPs saving his DEPOSIT. In 1932 the New Party was renamed the British Union of FASCISTs. Setting out the movement's aims, Mosley said:

> The only actions we shall employ will be English ones. We shall rely on the good old English fist.

new realism In the British trade union movement, the readiness in the mid to late 1980s to accept the new climate of enterprise and industrial relations created by THATCHERISM, with class conflict replaced by worker share ownership and a common interest in generating wealth. Its advocates, especially in the electrical and engineering unions, were much scorned by class-warriors who felt these unions were serving the interests of the employers, not the workforce.

New Republic The weekly which, since its foundation by Herbert David Croly in 1914, has given America's liberals a serious forum for their views. Backed financially from the outset by the Standard Oil heiress Dorothy Whitney Straight, the *New Republic* was seen by Croly as a vehicle for "starting little insurrections", but its tone soon moderated. It backed Woodrow WILSON, opposed the Treaty of VERSAILLES, opposed the RED SCARE, opposed Franklin D. Roosevelt but rallied to the NEW DEAL. Former Vice-President Henry Wallace took over as editor in 1946 but moved it so far to the left that Michael Straight forced him to resign. Today it reflects a range of views, being seen overall as neo-liberal.

New Statesman The weekly magazine with a moderate but not complacent Socialist tone, which for most of the 20th century has been the intellectual companion to the Fabian end of Britain's Labour Party – save for a brief and disastrous venture into AGITPROP in the early 1980s. Founded in 1913 by Sidney and Beatrice Webb, its great days were under the editorship of Kingsley Martin (1897–1969) from 1930–60. The *New Statesman* was relaunched early in 1993 under the editorship of Steve Platt, but the celebration issue contained an article discounting rumours of an alleged affair between John MAJOR and Clare Latimer, head of a London catering firm, which prompted writs for libel from both parties and the prospect of having to pay crippling damages. Platt argued that the magazine had merely been showing how an unjustified rumour could spread; Major was not impressed. The magazine settled out of court that summer.

Newcastle programme The first comprehensive range of policies adopted by a British political party, following on from the UNAUTHORIZED PROGRAMME of 1885. Hammered out for Gladstone's Liberals by the National Liberal Federation in September 1891, it included HOME RULE for Ireland, DISESTABLISHMENT of the Scottish and Welsh churches, employers' liability to compensate workers injured in accidents, local options on selling liquor, payment of MPs, universal male suffrage and three-year Parliaments.

> It held everything or nothing like a bottomless net; almost no one believed in all these things.
>
> MICHAEL BENTLEY, Politics Without Democracy.

news management The art of ensuring that events are presented in the best possible light for a government, a politician or a political party, and that disagreeable news attracts little attention. Timing is crucial, with good news scheduled for days when little else is happening and potentially harmful announcements timed to coincide with even bigger stories that will keep them out of the headlines. Harold WILSON in Britain, and the Reagan White House in America, were supreme practitioners of the art.

Next Steps agencies Sections of the UK CIVIL SERVICE hived off into free-standing agencies operating as businesses, each headed by their own chief executive and only responsible through him or her to a Minister. They were first proposed to Margaret Thatcher (*see* IRON LADY) just before the 1987 General Election by Sir Robin Ibbs, head of the Downing Street efficiency unit 1983–88. Early candidates for "next steps" status included the Driver and Vehicle Licensing Directorate and the Civil Service College. Labour MPs have complained that the separation of the agencies from the centralized Government machine means they can no longer table Parliamentary QUESTIONS on their activities.

NGOs Non-Governmental Organizations. A term applied particularly to the role of charities and other private-sector groups in providing development aid for the THIRD WORLD.

NHS National Health Service. Founded by Aneurin Bevan (*see* NYE) in 1948, Britain's free medical service for all was the centrepiece of the WELFARE STATE and the "jewel in the Crown" of Labour's post-war achievements. Resisted fiercely by the medical profession, it pulled a patchwork of private, local authority and charitable hospitals and practices into a single organization, eventually Europe's largest employer after the RED ARMY. Bevan said soon after its foundation:

> The NHS and the Welfare State have come to be used as interchangeable terms, and in the mouths of some people as a reproach.

His fellow Labour Minister Douglas Houghton declared: "The NHS has emancipated the sick." Bevan imagined the NHS would reduce demands for health care, but within a year the service came under pressure to economize – as ever since – and Bevan, Harold WILSON and John Freeman resigned from the Cabinet in 1951 when charges for spectacles and false teeth were imposed. Bevan said:

> The Government's abandonment of the principle of a free and comprehensive health service would be a shock to our supporters in the country and a grave disappointment of Socialist opinion throughout the world.

In the 1980s Margaret Thatcher's assurance that **the NHS is safe in our hands** was not accepted by the public as her government opened it up to the disciplines of the MARKET, and the NHS remains Labour's electoral trump card (*see* WAR OF JENNIFER'S EAR).

NIBMAR No Independence Before Majority African Rule. The principle followed by Harold WILSON's government in its efforts during 1964–65 to prevent Ian Smith's administratiuon in Southern Rhodesia declaring UDI.

Niet! (Russ. No!) The trademark of Vyacheslav Mikhailovich Molotov (1890–1986), Soviet Ambassador to the United Nations from 1945 to 1953, the most critical years of the COLD WAR. Molotov's regular use of the Soviet VETO paralysed the world organization and earned him notoriety throughout the West. He had already attracted considerable odium in 1939 as the joint signatory with Ribbentrop of the HITLER-STALIN PACT.

Night of the Long Knives (1) In Germany, the night of 30 June 1934 when the leaders of the BROWNSHIRTS (SA), homosexuals occupying key positions in the NAZI party and some Catholic leaders were murdered by the GESTAPO on Hitler's orders. The shootings, mainly in Munich and Berlin, actually began on the Friday night of 29 June and continued into the Sunday; between 60 and 400 people were killed in a PURGE whose main aim was to break the influence of the SA and its chief of staff Ernst Röhm. Himmler presented the assassins with daggers of honour inscribed with their names. (2) The sacking of seven Cabinet Ministers by Harold Macmillan (*see* SUPERMAC) on 12 July 1962, a deed which earned him the nickname **"Mac the Knife"**. The principal casualty was Chancellor Selwyn Lloyd. Macmillan acted to remodel his government as its popularity slumped, but worse lay ahead in the shape of the PROFUMO AFFAIR.

> Greater love hath no man than he who lays down his friends for his life. JEREMY THORPE MP (Lib., 1929–).

nightmare scenario A combination or sequence of events too ghastly to contemplate, but which nevertheless could well become reality. A classic example was the scenario in which the UN-backed coalition won the GULF WAR while leaving Saddam Hussein's war machine largely intact – as eventually happened.

our long national nightmare is over Gerald FORD's remarks which closed the door on WATERGATE, made when he took the oath of office on 9 August 1974. Despite the controversy over his subsequent PARDON of Richard Nixon, Ford proved right. He said:

> My fellow Americans, our long national nightmare is over. Our Constitution works; our great Republic is a government of laws and not of men. Here the people rule. But there is a higher Power, by whatever name we honour Him, who ordains not only righteousness but love, not only justice but mercy.

Nihilism (Lat. *nihil*, nothing) The ultimate in negative political tendencies, which enjoyed a vogue in Tsarist Russia in the late 19th century. From it grew a TERRORIST movement which aimed to wipe out all existing institutions of society in order to start anew.

Nimbyism An acronym for Not In My Back Yard, coined in Britain *c.* 1986 to describe people who are vociferously in favour of progress, and especially new construction, unless it directly affects them. Initially it referred to supporters of nuclear power or the storage of nuclear waste, whose attitude suddenly changed in the face of a proposal to site such activities locally. Nicholas Ridley, when Environment Secretary, was accused of Nimbyism when he objected to plans for new homes in his own village after overriding objections to new rural housing projects elsewhere.

Ninepence for fourpence The slogan with which Lloyd George launched Britain's first National Insurance scheme in 1911. By requiring a contribution from employers as well as employees, Lloyd George was able to offer a sickness insurance scheme where workers who had paid 4*d*. a week into the scheme would receive 9*d*. when unable to work. Many Liberals, including ASQUITH, questioned whether the proposal was attractive enough and feared it would be an electoral ALBATROSS; however WORLD WAR I prevented an election being held until 1918, by which time other issues predominated.

nineteen. Nineteenth Amendment The amendment to the US CONSTITUTION, otherwise known as the ANTHONY AMENDMENT after the suffragist Susan B. Anthony, which gave all American women the vote. It read:

> The right of citizens of the United States to vote shall not be denied or abridged by the United States or by any state on account of sex.

It was passed by the House on 10 January 1918, but the conservative Senate held out for 18 months; it was eventually ratified by the states on 18 August 1920.

1922 Committee The group embracing all BACKBENCH Conservative MPs at Westminster, which meets every Thursday evening when Parliament is in session. It takes its name from the CARLTON CLUB REVOLT of that year when Tory MPs forced the break-up of the Lloyd George COALITION. The '22, through its meetings, its chairman and its executive, enjoys immense influence with the party leadership; any initiative or policy that falls foul of it will be hastily withdrawn.

> The first three people to speak at the 1922 Committee on any subject are invariably mad.
> DAVID WALDER MP (Con., 1928–78).

> Too frequent attendance can result in what religious people call "doubts".
> JULIAN CRITCHLEY MP (Con., 1930–).

Nineteen Eighty-four The nightmarish vision of a TOTALITARIAN future, conjured up by George Orwell (Eric Arthur Blair, 1903–50) in his final novel of that name. Published in 1949, it depicted a state in which history has been destroyed, truth replaced by propaganda and surveillance on behalf of BIG BROTHER is all-pervasive. The novel, based partly on Orwell's experiences in Britain's wartime Ministry of Information, was a warning against authoritarian tendencies present in Communist and Western societies after World War II. Orwell chose the date by transposing the final digits of 1948, the year he wrote the book; until the actual year was reached 1984 was a "doomsday" date.

1992 The year in which the SINGLE MARKET was due for completion, and thus shorthand for the achievement of an important phase of European unity. In fact the package of 265 (originally 301) legislative changes took effect over a period, not being completed until early 1993.

1997 The date set by Britain and China for the reversion of Hong Kong to Chinese sovereignty, and thus shorthand for the point at which the colony would become a capitalist enclave within a Communist state. Under a treaty of 1898, the New Territories were to revert to China in 1997; Britain concluded in the early 1980s that it would be impractical for the far smaller Crown COLONY of Hong Kong, with its teeming population and limited water supplies, to survive beyond then as a separate entity.

ninety. Ninety-two Group A right-wing pressure group of CONSERVATIVE MPs which had considerable effect in the late 1980s in keeping up the RADICAL thrust of Margaret Thatcher's government; it grew out of a dining club of the same name which until the early 1980s did not admit women. The group was widely imagined to have taken its title from the claimed size of its membership; it actually referred to 92 Cheyne Walk, one of the locations where its members dined.

> One of the earlier, less hidebound, utterly snob-free groups.
> NORMAN (later Lord) TEBBIT.

Ninety-two Resolutions The document in which Louis-Joseph Papineau in 1834 listed the political grievances of the French-speaking population in British-ruled Quebec. Papineau, speaker of the House of Assembly, put forward a radical programme for autonomy which the British government rejected; in 1837 his supporters rebelled and Papineau fled to the United States.

Ninety-eight, the The rebellion against British rule in Ireland which broke out around Dublin in late May 1798, brought sporadic uprisings from Wexford to Sligo, and ended in the Wexford rebels' defeat at Vinegar Hill on 21 June. Two months later a French force landed at Killala in the hope of broadening the struggle; after defeating Government troops on 27 August at the "Races of Castlebar" it surrendered at Ballinamuck on 8 September. The exiled patriot Wolfe Tone landed on Lough Swilly with a further French force on 3 November; Tone was captured and committed suicide in prison on 19 November. The '98 was followed by the abolition of the Irish Parliament and by greatly heightened sectarian feeling; it came to take pride of place in Irish NATIONALIST mythology.

Nixon. Nixon doctrine The policy enunciated by President Nixon (*see* TRICKY DICK) in July 1969 that America would in future expect her overseas allies to provide for their own defence, so that conflicts like the VIETNAM WAR could be avoided. The statement, made informally to reporters on Guam, was intended to clarify his policy of VIETNAMIZATION, but the White House subsequently elevated it into a general doctrine of US foreign policy.

Nixonland The scathing term devised by Democratic nominee Adlai Stevenson (1900–65) during the 1956 Presidential campaign for the twilight world of McCARTHYISM and Vice-President Richard Nixon's links to it. Stevenson said:

> Our nation stands at a fork in the political road. In one direction lies a land of slander and scare; the land of sly innuendo, the poison pen, the anonymous phone call and hustling, pushing, shoving; the land of smash and grab and anything to win. This is Nixonland. But I say to you that it is not America.

Mundt-Nixon Bill Richard Nixon's first legislative attempt, after his election to Congress in 1946, to crack down on "subversives". Even fellow-Republicans considered the measure excessively severe, Thomas DEWEY denouncing it as a move "to beat down ideas with clubs", and Congress refused to pass it.

New Nixon The US media's categorization of the Richard Nixon who campaigned for the Presidency in 1968, showing a mellow statesmanship instead of the grudging partisanship with which he had "retired" from politics six years before.

You don't have Nixon to kick around any more Nixon's farewell remarks in November 1962 after failing to win the governorship of California. When told the press wanted a statement from him, Nixon responded: "screw them", then, looking nervous and dishevelled before the cameras, launched into this tirade:

> Now that all the members of the press are so delighted that I have lost . . . I have no hard feelings against anybody, against any opponent and least of all the people of California. . . . And as I leave the press, all I can say is this. For 16 years, ever since the HISS CASE, you've had a lot of fun – a lot of fun – that you've had an opportunity to attack me. . . . Just think about how much you're going to be missing. You won't have Nixon to kick around any more, because, gentlemen, this is my LAST PRESS CONFERENCE.

NIXXON *Mad* magazine's comment when the Esso petroleum company changed its name to EXXON. (It had earlier opted for "enco" before discovering that this was Japanese for a broken-down car.) *Mad* carried a cartoon of the Nixon White House flying a flag bearing the word "Nixxon"; the caption read: "It's the same old gas."

Nkosi sikelele Afrika (God bless Africa) The unofficial anthem of the African National Congress (*see* ANC) and many other movements campaigning for freedom and equal rights in southern Africa.

NKVD (Russ. *Narodniy Kommissariat Vnutrennykh Dyel*, People's Commissariat for Internal Affairs) The Soviet agency responsible for state security from 1934 to 1943. Succeeding the OGPU (*see* GPU), it was notorious for carrying out Stalin's PURGES. In 1943 its state security function was taken over by another agency, the NKGB, but it continued to manage internal affairs, becoming a ministry – the MVD – in 1946.

no. No, No, No! Margaret Thatcher's ringing denunciation of Jacques DELORS's vision of European union in the House of Commons on 30 October 1990. The strength of her language when she departed from a carefully-crafted statement on the Rome EC summit was one factor behind Sir Geoffrey HOWE's resignation as Deputy Prime Minister, which contributed to her removal a month later from the Conservative leadership. She said:

> The President of the Commission, Mr. Delors, said at a press conference the other day that he wanted the EUROPEAN PARLIAMENT to be the democratic body of the Community. He wanted the Commission to be the EXECUTIVE, and he wanted the Council of Ministers to be the Senate. No, no, no!

No, not a sixpence! The terms in which Charles Cotesworth Pinckney, US Minister to France, reported on 27 October 1797 his country's response to a French request for a bribe before it would discuss the release of captured American ships. He gave this verdict on the X, Y AND Z affair in a letter to Timothy Pickering.

no first use One of the formulae put forward by peace campaigners and others in the 1980s to ease tension between the SUPERPOWERS. Had it been adopted, both America and the Soviet Union would have agreed not to unleash any of their nuclear weapons unless the other had already done so.

no-fly zone An area from which all military (and sometimes civil) aircraft are barred, on pain of being shot down. The first such zone was agreed in August 1992 by the GULF WAR coalition in response to Iraq's bombing, strafing and NAPALMing of Shi'ites in its southern marshlands in violation of UN resolutions. America, Britain, France and Russia told Iraq that if any of its planes flew south of the 32nd parallel, it would be attacked. The following month, the LONDON CONFERENCE on former Yugoslavia proposed a no-fly zone barring (Serbian) military aircraft from the skies over Bosnia.

no-go area Originally an area barred to unauthorized persons for security reasons, the term achieved notoriety when PARA-

MILITARY groups in NORTHERN IRELAND sealed off parts of Belfast and (London)Derry to prevent troops and police patrolling them. Certain deprived and crime-ridden INNER-CITY areas are also described as no-go areas, implying that the police enter at their own risk, and only in substantial numbers.

No more Mr. Nice Guy The most picturesque way for politicians to say that the gloves are off, and that whatever scruples they have previously possessed will now be abandoned. In 1972 aides of the Democratic Presidential hopeful Sen. Ed Muskie (*see* CANUCK LETTER) said it as their candidate tried to shed his virtuous image. In the mid-1950s a joke surfaced that Hitler had decided on a comeback "but this time – no more Mr. Nice Guy".

no overall control In UK local government, another term for a HUNG COUNCIL where no one party has an outright MAJORITY.

No Popery! The slogan against Roman Catholic influence in British (specifically Northern Irish) public life which dates back to at least the 18th century, when it sparked the GORDON RIOTS. It is still the regular cry of the PAISLEYITES.

No taxation without representation! The slogan which is widely believed to have triggered the AMERICAN REVOLUTION, stemming from the imposition of the STAMP ACT on Britain's American colonies. It stems from the declaration of James Otis (1725–83) that "taxation without representation is tyranny". In 1947 the historian Arnold Toynbee, pressing for greater UK representation at the UNITED NATIONS, devised the slogan: **No annihilation without representation!**.

No Turning Back The most die-hard group of THATCHERITE MPs, mainly from the 1983 intake, who were firmly wedded to the IRON LADY's radical free-market policies. On the night of 21 November 1990, leaders of the group made a dramatic last-minute appeal to Mrs. Thatcher not to stand down as Prime Minister and party leader after being forced to a second leadership ballot by Michael Heseltine.

Nobel Peace Prize One of the six international awards established under the will of Alfred Nobel (1833–96), the Swedish chemist who invented dynamite. Winners have included Dr. Albert Schweitzer (1875–1965), Chief Albert Luthuli (1899–1967), Dr. Martin Luther KING, and most controversially Le Duc Tho (1911–90) and Dr. Henry KISSINGER for supposedly bringing peace to VIETNAM; two of the prize committee resigned in protest. First made in 1901 it is awarded by the Norwegian Parliament (Sweden and Norway were then united) and presented at Stockholm. The winner receives an average of $185,000, a gold medal and a diploma. As well as for services to peace, Nobel prizes are awarded for distinction in Chemistry, Physics, Medicine, Literature and Economics.

nodding through The procedure at Westminster under which an MP who is well enough to get to the House of Commons but not well enough to pass through the DIVISION LOBBIES can have his or her vote recorded; in the last months of the 1945–51 and 1974–79 Labour governments when every division was critical, MPs were even nodded through in oxygen tents. Labour forfeited power in the CONFIDENCE vote of 28 March 1979 because Ministers and whips refused to summon Dr. Alfred Broughton to vote, knowing he was dying; had he voted the result would have been a tie and the Government would have survived.

Nomenklatura In the Soviet Union and across the Communist world, those selected by the PARTY and its leadership for advancement and privileges and to perform key tasks; often they did not know they had been singled out in this way.

nomination The process by which a candidate is entered for an election. In most forms of election, nomination is achieved by the lodging of papers bearing the signature of the candidate and a certain number of supporters with the relevant authorities. In a US Presidential election the placing of a **nominee**'s name on the BALLOT is overshadowed by the CONVENTION at which the decision to nominate is taken. Margaret Taylor, wife of the future President Zachary Taylor, described his nomination by the WHIGS in 1848 as "a plot to deprive me of his society, and shorten his life by unnecessary care and responsibility"; it turned out to be just that. General William Tecumseh Sherman (1820–91) is said to have told Republicans who wanted to nominate him: "I will not accept if nominated, and will not serve if elected". And in 1980 the former Democratic Presidential hopeful Rep. Morris Udall joked: "If nominated I will run to Mexico. If elected I will fight extradition."

nominating speech The convention speech which formally proposes a candidate for nomination; if no candidate has established a clear lead, several such speeches will be made. The making of a dramatic enough nominating speech, such as Franklin D. Roosevelt's for Al Smith in 1924, can be the first step in a subsequent Presidential campaign.

Non! UK media and political shorthand for President DE GAULLE's effective veto on

British membership of the EC, delivered at an ELYSÉE press conference on 14 January 1963. It took France another two weeks to force the other five member states to reject the application. Harold WILSON said of the snub administered to Edward Heath who had headed the negotiating team:

> No British Minister must ever again be put in the position of waiting outside in the cold while others decide our fate.

non-. non-aggression pact A treaty under which two countries agree not to attack each other. It can form the basis of friendship or improved relations – but equally, as with the HITLER-STALIN PACT of 1939, can be the prelude to grand betrayal.

non-aligned movement The "third force" of states linked to neither SUPERPOWER, which was founded at the BANDUNG CONFERENCE in 1955; its prime movers included Jawaharlal NEHRU of India and Yugoslavia's President TITO. Britain, and even more so America, harboured doubts about the movement's genuine independence because of its denunciations of COLONIALISM, but it has offered for the most part a genuinely independent, if inconvenient, voice.

Nonconformist Conscience One of the driving forces of 19th-century LIBERAL politics in Britain, and to a lesser extent of the developing LABOUR PARTY. The phrase originated *c.* 1870 to describe the POLITICIZATION of many Methodists, Congregationalists, Baptists and others in opposition to the FORSTER EDUCATION ACT and relaxation of the liquor licensing laws, and in favour of DISESTABLISHMENT. Nonconformists had been barred from Parliament until the early 19th century, but by 1880 they comprised a quarter of all Liberal MPs and their influence became out of proportion to their numbers. The "Nonconformist Conscience" probably exerted its greatest impact at the 1906 election when the BALFOUR government was rejected partly because it had permitted the import of indentured Chinese labourers to the Transvaal, a process Campbell-Bannerman castigated as "slavery".

non-implementation The stand taken against the Heath Government's 1972 Housing Finance Act by CLAY CROSS and other left-wing Labour councils which felt that they were being compelled to make a profit from their tenants instead of providing housing as a social service. Several major councils, among them Sheffield, initially backed the campaign but split and reversed their position as the consequences of illegality became clear.

Non-intervention Committee An international committee formed in 1936 to prevent other countries becoming involved in the SPANISH CIVIL WAR. As Germany and Italy stepped up their participation in the conflict, the committee and its proceedings became increasingly irrelevant; Britain interpreted non-intervention as doing nothing to assist Spain's Republican government even in non-military matters.

non-person The status to which anyone who fell foul of the COMMUNIST hierarchy in the Soviet Union or one of its eastern European SATELLITES would be reduced. It involved the deletion of any reference to their past achievements, or even their existence, from the country's history or media.

Non-proliferation Treaty The treaty signed in 1968 by America, Britain and the Soviet Union, undertaking not to provide the technology for making nuclear weapons to countries that had not already acquired it; France and China refused to sign. The treaty, under which dozens of states have since renounced nuclear weaponry, was based on the belief that with the SUPERPOWERS in nuclear deadlock, the greatest threat to world peace would be the development of nuclear weapons by some unstable and fanatical regime outside their control. The treaty has not prevented Algeria, Argentina, Brazil, Egypt, Iraq, Israel, Pakistan, Taiwan and South Africa all reputedly developing a nuclear capability, but has been a moral force against even greater proliferation.

non-violence The principle of winning political arguments by moral force which was pioneered by MAHATMA Gandhi and developed by Dr. Martin Luther KING. Gandhi, who organized non-violent protests in South Africa and India, wrote: "Non-violence is the first article of my faith. It is also the last article of my creed;" he also said: "Non-violence is the law of our species as violence is the law of the brute." Dr. King first advocated non-violence in 1955 when he led the year-long MONTGOMERY BUS BOYCOTT, declaring: "The negro all over the South must come to the point where he can say to his White brother: 'We will soon wear you down by our sheer capacity to suffer.'" He said of his philosophy: "The ultimate weakness of violence is that it is a descending spiral, begetting the very thing it seeks to destroy." By the mid-1960s Black militants were challenging the notion that non-violence could bring real change, George Jackson (*see* SOLEDAD BROTHERS) saying: "In a non-violent movement there must be a latent threat of eruption, a dormant possibility of sudden and violent action, if concessions are to be won."

> Organized love. JOAN BAEZ (1941–).

none of the above The phrase sometimes written on BALLOT Papers by voters who are dissatisfied with the choice offered to them, or as a protest against the entire political system.

noose. a halo only has to slip nine inches to become a noose A telling summary of the suddenness with which a political career can be ended by scandal; the nine inches may have a phallic significance or represent the distance from the top of a man's head to his Adam's apple. The phrase is said to have been coined by Iain Macleod, the Conservatives' most devastating wordsmith in opposition from 1964 to 1970.

no noose is bad noose Ostensibly an argument for the retention or return of hanging, this slogan was probably coined by anti-hangers; **no** NUKES **is bad nukes** is a variant, making the same statement about nuclear weapons.

NORAD North American Air Defence. The joint command protecting the United States and Canada from Soviet air attack from the Arctic, set up in 1957; until 1981 it covered only aircraft because of Canadian sensibilities over linkage with US ballistic missile systems. To America NORAD secures the northern flank and is sound common sense. Canada's LIBERALS objected to the agreement when the Diefenbaker government signed it, but later broadened its scope; the NDP has gone into some elections pledged to withdraw if elected.

NORAID Irish Northern Aid. The Irish Republican fund-raising organization in the United States (and to an extent in Canada) which has channelled millions of dollars to the IRA since the early 1970s. Its officials insist the money, much of it collected openly at charity events in New York and other cities, is for the welfare of prisoners' families and other non-military purposes, but the British and US authorities have always doubted this.

Norder, Laura Not a person, but a derisive term for LAW AND ORDER. She could be a cousin of BINDING, SOLOMON.

normalcy The reassuring offer made to the American people by Warren G. HARDING in the 1920 Presidential election. Before his nomination, Harding declared:

> America's present need is not heroics, but healing; not nostrums, but normalcy; not revolution, but restoration; not agitation, but adjustment; not surgery, but serenity; not the dramatic, but the dispassionate; not experiment, but equipoise; not submergence in internationality, but sustainment in triumphant nationality. . . .

He returned to the theme of "normalcy" throughout the Presidential campaign, but once he was in the White House the word turned out to be shorthand for an unprecedented orgy of graft and corruption by Harding's cronies (*see* TEAPOT DOME).

normalization The process of re-establishing relations with a country with whom one has had no formal diplomatic contacts. The term was used by Richard Nixon and the Chinese leaders Mao Tse-Tung and Chou En-Lai in 1972 to describe the process of establishing contacts, broken 23 years before when the Communists finally defeated the NATIONALIST CHINESE. Contacts were gradually developed and formalized, and full diplomatic relations were restored by the CARTER administration in 1979.

north. North Briton The paper in which John Wilkes (1725–97) ridiculed Lord Bute, Prime Minister 1762–63, to such an extent that, coupled with blistering polemics from Wilkes in the House of Commons, it brought about Bute's downfall. The title was a reference to Bute's Scottish origins; the *Dictionary of National Biography* says of him:

> The details of his administration are peculiarly disgraceful, and for corruption and financial incapacity it is not likely to be surpassed.

In issue 45 of the *North Briton*, Wilkes turned his guns on King George III, charging that Ministers had put lies into his mouth in the King's Speech at the opening of Parliament; his vitriolic attack landed him in the Tower of London, but he was acquitted of libel on grounds of Parliamentary PRIVILEGE. Exiled to France, he returned in 1768 to serve a two-year sentence for obscenity in his *Essay on Woman*; a mob of his supporters demonstrated outside the prison and was dispersed with heavy loss of life. The number 45 was daubed on doors throughout England, and one nobleman was dragged from his carriage and had the number chalked on the soles of his feet. *See also* WILKES AND LIBERTY.

north of Watford The phrase used in British politics to explain and condemn the parochiality of the southern English and the Westminster/WHITEHALL Establishment, who are felt to regard all events as centred on London and everything beyond the capital's northern fringe as an irrelevance.

North-South Shorthand for the problems of the developing world (the South) and the interest the prosperous industrialised nations (the North) have in finding a solution to them. It was taken from *North-South: A Programme for Survival*, the title of the BRANDT COMMISSION's first report published in 1980. The term came to apply to any dialogue between the two blocs, and indeed to the time-bomb which the lack of THIRD WORLD development threatened for more prosperous states.

North-South divide The apparently unclosable gap between the prosperous South of England and the unemployment-stricken North and Scotland; efforts to close it by pumping in money and diverting industry to the North have achieved fractional success in times of prosperity, but only in the RECESSION starting in 1991 did it seriously narrow, through the South falling back to the North's less happy situation.

> There is a growing division in our comparatively prosperous society between the South and the North and Midlands, which are ailing, that cannot be allowed to continue.
>
> Maiden speech of the Earl of Stockton (HAROLD MACMILLAN), 13 November 1984.

Northcote-Trevelyan reforms The radical changes made in Britain's CIVIL SERVICE in the mid-19th century at the urging of Sir Charles Trevelyan (1807–86) and Sir Stafford Northcote, later Earl of Iddesleigh (1818–87). A Whitehall high-flier and a civil servant turned politician, they outraged Ministers by proposing that civil service posts be filled by competitive examination. It took the exposures of ineptitude by officials who owed their places to PATRONAGE, resulting from the Crimean War, to bring action; a Civil Service Commission was set up in 1855, and Trevelyan and Northcote finally got their way in 1870.

> In future the Board of Examiners will be in place of the Queen. Our institutions will become as harshly republican as possible, and the new spirit of public offices will not be loyalty, but republicanism.
>
> Lord JOHN RUSSELL to Gladstone.

Northern Ireland The portion of Ireland left in the United Kingdom by the PARTITION of 1921, which became a political entity in its own right. Comprising SIX COUNTIES of the province of ULSTER, it was governed from STORMONT by the Protestant, LOYALIST majority until the imposition of DIRECT RULE in 1972 as 300-year-old SECTARIAN conflicts reopened. William Whitelaw, the first Northern Ireland Secretary, said on his arrival: "I do not intend to prejudge the past." Conflict has continued between Republican and Loyalist terrorists, with the IRA posing a constant threat to the SECURITY FORCES. Initially after 1972 strenuous efforts were made to set up a POWER-SHARING administration, but an elected Executive and Assembly both collapsed. The 1985 ANGLO-IRISH AGREEMENT gave Dublin an advisory role in the North, as the Nationalist/Catholic community had urged, but it provoked Loyalist outrage without stemming the Republican violence. However, while the death toll has continued to mount, talks have been under way since 1991 involving Britain, the Irish republic and all the Northern Ireland parties except Provisional SINN FEIN, who were not invited.

> Britain stands towards peace in Northern Ireland today where America stood in South East Asia during the early 1960s. Sen. EDWARD KENNEDY, 1971.

Northwest Ordinance The measure promulgated in 1787 by America's new government which laid down that no more than five states could be carved from the area between the Appalachians and the Mississippi, north of the Ohio River. It outlined a system of transitional governments, and provided that when 60,000 people had settled in each embryo state, it would be admitted to the Union "on an equal footing with the original states in all respects whatever". The new states promised the older ones that they would guarantee civil and religious rights and prohibit slavery.

Norwegian Wood The nickname former Vice-President Walter Mondale (1928–) attracted during his campaign for the Presidency in 1984. He earned the tag, originally the title of a song by the Beatles, through his Scandinavian descent and his deadpan delivery on the STUMP. One campaign aide said after one of his television appearances:

> The speech was typed better than it was read.

Not a penny off the pay, not a minute on the day The slogan of Britain's striking miners and their leader, A. J. Cook, in the dispute over cuts in wages and longer hours which culminated in the 1926 GENERAL STRIKE.

Not Contents In the HOUSE OF LORDS, the name given to those who vote against a proposition; those voting for are described as CONTENTS.

not for attribution In political, especially LOBBY, journalism, the phrase used for information divulged by a SOURCE on the condition that he or she is not identified.

note-taker A senior official, often a diplomat, who sits in on BILATERAL meetings between HEADS OF GOVERNMENT to ensure that a record is kept, and to remind the participants of what was discussed and agreed.

nothing for nothing The warning that "there is nothing for nothing any longer", quoted by President CARTER in his 1980 State of the UNION message, made a particular impact. It was originally given by the COLUMNIST Walter Lippmann in his speech on 18 June 1940 to the 30th reunion of the Harvard class of 1910. Lippmann told them:

> You have lived the easy way; henceforth you will have the hard way. . . . You came into a great heritage made by the insight and the sweat and the blood of inspired and devoted and courageous men; thoughtlessly and in

utmost self-indulgence you have all but squandered this inheritance. Now only by the heroic virtues which made this inheritance can you restore it again. . . . You took the good things for granted. Now you must earn them again. For every right that you cherish, you have a duty which you must fulfil. For every hope that you entertain, you have a task that you must perform. For every good that you wish to preserve, you must sacrifice your comfort and your ease. There is nothing for nothing any longer.

The phrase also has a resonance outside US politics; Mussolini, at the height of his power, declared: "My foreign policy is 'nothing for nothing'."

Novus Ordo Seclorum (Lat. the new order of things) The motto of the United States of America. One of several Masonic phrases adopted by the newly-formed nation, it appears on the Great SEAL, and has become a fixture on the reverse of the dollar bill.

NOW National Organization of Women. The largest and most influential organization behind the women's movement in America, which since 1966 has taken legal and political action to end sex discrimination. Founded largely on the initiative of Betty Friedan, author of *The Feminine Mystique*, it played a leading role in getting the Equal Rights amendment (ERA) through Congress, but just failed to secure RATIFICATION.

NRA (1) National Recovery Administration. One of the lead agencies for Franklin D. Roosevelt's NEW DEAL, set up during the first HUNDRED DAYS of his administration. Its initial role was as a confidence-booster: its first head, General Hugh Johnson (who had served in Wilson's wartime administration) chose a blue eagle as its motif and staged huge parades of NRA participants, the largest of which brought almost 2 million people on to the streets of New York on 13 September 1933. But its purpose was to promote industrial recovery through a series of nationwide regulatory codes to limit unfair competition, improve working conditions, establish a minimum wage and guarantee the right to collective bargaining. Employers subscribing to the codes (eventually there were 557 basic and 208 supplementary codes) were allowed to display a Blue Eagle emblem. Despite its bureaucracy, it did register successes including an end to child labour in US cotton mills, but although it created two million jobs it became a scapegoat for disillusion with the New Deal, and was widely criticized for giving large firms advantages over small businesses. It was declared UNCONSTITUTIONAL by the SUPREME COURT on 27 May 1935 (BLACK MONDAY), but many of its provisions were incorporated into later legislation. Sen. Huey KINGFISH Long branded the NRA the "National Racketeers' Arrangement", "Nuts Running America" and "Never Roosevelt Again".

For two dizzy years, America had a fling at NATIONAL SOCIALISM.
ALISTAIR COOKE.

(2) National Rifle Association. One of the most formidable LOBBIES in US politics, through its ability to mobilize millions of hunters and persuade them that any move toward GUN CONTROL to curb inner-city crime would be a violation of their constitutional RIGHT TO KEEP AND BEAR ARMS. With a million members and a 250-strong staff in Washington, it has been successful in blocking the BRADY BILL and other measures to restrict the sale, ownership and use of firearms.

nuclear. nuclear freeze *See* FREEZE.

nuclear-free zone A territory or community from which all nuclear weapons are banned, and often all nuclear activity including reactors for peaceful uses and the transport of nuclear waste. The concept attracted some world leaders who saw the exclusion of nuclear weapons from, say, central Europe as a way of limiting the spread of a war between the SUPERPOWERS. It was taken up by nuclear disarmers in various European countries, and particularly by left-wing Labour councils in the UK who designated communities under their control as "nuclear-free zones". Conservatives denounced the concept as fatuous in the extreme. The editor of this dictionary lived in a block of flats through which ran the boundary between a nuclear-free council and one that was not; in the event of nuclear war the residents agreed they would shelter in one of the "nuclear-free" apartments.

nuclear proliferation *See* NON-PROLIFERATION TREATY.

nuclear sword of Damocles John F. KENNEDY's vivid characterization of the threat of nuclear annihilation which hung over the world throughout the COLD WAR. In ancient mythology, the tyrant Damocles awoke to find a sword suspended over his head by a thread.

nuclear umbrella The term given to the role of America's nuclear arsenal in protecting the non-nuclear nations of the democratic West against the threat of invasion or extermination by the Soviet Union. Americans charge that the umbrella has been sheltered under by states with much-publicized moral quirks about possessing nuclear weapons themselves.

We are not bent on conquest or on threatening others. But we do have a nuclear umbrella that can protect others, above all the states to which we are allied or in which we have a great national interest.
President NIXON, *New York Times* interview, 8 March 1971.

nuclear war The most devastating conflict mankind has yet devised, and if it ever breaks out, probably its last. Nikita S. Khruschev is reputed to have said that if such a war did break out, "the survivors would envy the dead", and few would disagree. One who did was Sen. Richard Russell, a supporter of strong US nuclear defences, who told the Senate on 2 October 1968: "If we are to start again with another Adam and Eve, then I want them to be Americans and not Russians, and I want them on this continent and not in Europe." Seven years before, General Douglas MACARTHUR told the Congress of the Philippines that nuclear war was "a Frankenstein to destroy both sides", adding: "This very thought of scientific annihilation has destroyed the possibility of war's being a medium for the practical settlement of international differences." And another veteran of World War II, General Omar Bradley, said bluntly:

> The way to stop an atomic war is to make sure it never starts.

nuclear weapons Types of weapon in which an explosion is produced by a nuclear reaction, rather than by a chemical reaction as in so-called CONVENTIONAL explosives. Their vastly increased destructive power, first witnessed at HIROSHIMA, has transformed world politics and the exercise of power as well as placing the human race at risk of annihilation. Nuclear weapons are of two types: fission weapons such as the original ATOMIC BOMB, and fusion weapons like the later and even more destructive H-BOMB.

> It's like having a cobra in the nursery with your grandchildren. You get rid of the cobra or you won't have any grandchildren.
>
> THEODORE M. HESBURGH, President, Notre Dame University 1952–87.

> If the third world war is fought with nuclear weapons, the fourth will be fought with bows and arrows.
>
> Earl MOUNTBATTEN of Burma (1900–79).

nuclear winter *See* WINTER.

nukes Slang for nuclear weapons or for to attack using them. Originally an Americanism of the 1970s, its use has spread throughout the English-speaking world. The nuclear disarmers' slogan **No nukes is good nukes** (*see also* NOOSE) is an example of its first application, the cry of **nuke the bastards!** by protesters against any troublesome regime an example of the second.

nullification The strategy devised by Jackson's Vice-President John C. Calhoun (1782–1850) as an alternative to secession of the Southern States from the UNION. It came to a head when South Carolina flexed its sovereignty by "nullifying" a heavy TARIFF imposed by Congress in 1828 on English imports which Calhoun feared would bring British retaliation that would endanger cotton production, and the system of slavery that it sustained. Jackson denounced as treasonable South Carolina's refusal to let US customs officials enforce the tariff and, with no other state following suit, prepared forces to march on Charleston; meanwhile Henry Clay persuaded Congress to accept a less draconian tariff. The narrowness with which conflict had been averted killed nullification, and Calhoun's hopes of the Presidency.

Number. Number Ten The colloquial name for 10 DOWNING STREET, the home and office of PRIME MINISTERS since WALPOLE and nerve-centre of the British Government; also shorthand for the power of the Prime Minister. It is a modest and much-extended 17th-century town house halfway up Downing Street, facing the rear of the FOREIGN OFFICE; at one time the crowds could gather freely outside and small boys, including the young Harold WILSON, could be photographed outside its famous front door. Access has been restricted since the assassination of Earl Mountbatten in 1979, but in February 1991 the IRA came close to wiping out John MAJOR's Cabinet in a mortar attack on No. 10 from the other side of Whitehall. No. 10 itself has 60 rooms, ranging from the ground-floor CABINET ROOM and working and ceremonial rooms to the offices of the GARDEN GIRLS and the FLAT where the Prime Minister actually lives; 130 people work there and the building is linked to the Cabinet office and to NUMBER ELEVEN next door. No. 10 has been heavily restored since Campbell-Bannerman, who died there, branded it "this rotten old barracks of a house" and Margot ASQUITH termed it "an inconvenient house with three poor staircases". But several premiers, including James Callaghan, have only slept there when business required.

> More of a monastery than a power house.
>
> MARCIA WILLIAMS (*see* LADY FORKBENDER).

> From the street outside it is a classic example of British understatement. Today it harbours only Britain's crises, but once it was the eye of the storms that shook the world.
>
> JOE HAINES, Harold Wilson's press secretary.

beer and sandwiches at Number Ten *See* BEER.

measuring the curtains for Number Ten The interest shown by the wife of a prospective Prime Minister in the prospect of her spouse's early arrival in Downing Street.

Number Eleven The official residence in Downing Street, next door to NUMBER TEN, of the CHANCELLOR OF THE EXCHEQUER. The front halls of the two houses are connected by a corridor, so that the Chancellor can visit the Prime Minister without their consultations becoming public knowledge.

Number Twelve 12 Downing Street, the office of the Government CHIEF WHIP and his team, at the head of the street looking toward Whitehall.

Number –, Sir or **Madam** The formal way in which an MP introduces an oral QUESTION in the House of Commons. The Speaker calls the name of the next member with a question on the ORDER PAPER, that member rises to give the number of the question instead of asking it in full, and the Minister responsible gives an answer. The way is then clear for the member to ask a SUPPLEMENTARY before the question is thrown open to the House.

Nuremberg laws The NAZI decrees announced by Hitler at the close of the 1935 NUREMBERG RALLY, and unanimously ratified by the REICHSTAG, which made all Jews second-class CITIZENS, closed the professions to them and forbade marriage or sexual relations between Jews and ARYANS; this last was said to be for "the protection of German blood and honour".

Nuremberg rallies The mass gatherings and parades organized by the NAZI Party for propaganda purposes, first held in January and August 1923 and then annually from 1926, first in July and later in September until 1938. Organized by Goebbels to generate nationalistic hysteria and intimidate the Nazis' opponents, they took an increasingly elaborate form with massed torchlight parades and the use of anti-aircraft searchlights to surround the assembly with vertical columns of light, always culminating in a speech from the FÜHRER. The 1934 rally lasted a full week and was the subject of Leni Riefenstahl's *The Triumph of the Will*, perhaps the most powerful PROPAGANDA film ever made. The same year Hitler's architect Albert SPEER was commissioned to design a massive permanent auditorium for the rallies; its grandiose structure was never completed and it remains a bleak memorial to the evil of the THIRD REICH. The term "Nuremberg rally" has come to be used derogatorily for any STAGE-MANAGED event involving unthinking adulation for a political leader; it was frequently applied by critics to the closing speeches Margaret Thatcher delivered at Conservative party conferences.

Nuremberg trials Primarily the trial for WAR CRIMES and GENOCIDE of 23 surviving NAZI leaders conducted at Nuremberg from September 1945 to May 1946 by an International Military Tribunal of eight US, British, French and Soviet judges. Goering, Ribbentrop and nine others were sentenced to death, three were acquitted and the rest sentenced to terms of imprisonment. Goering and GAULEITER Robert Ley committed suicide before they could be executed; Rudolf HESS remained in Spandau prison until his death in 1987. The Nuremberg tribunal established in international law that it is no defence for the accused to say that they were simply following orders. In the full series of Nuremberg trials of 177 Germans and Austrians over two years, 25 were sentenced to death, 117 imprisoned (20 for life) and 35 acquitted.

> Now is the time for BOLSHEVISM's Nuremberg.
>
> VYTAUTIS LANDSBERGIS, President of Lithuania, after the abortive 1991 KREMLIN COUP.

Nye The usually-affectionate nickname for Aneurin Bevan (1897–1960), the Welsh firebrand who galvanized left-wing politics in Britain after WORLD WAR II, splitting the LABOUR PARTY, and is best remembered as the founder of the NHS in 1948; "Nye" is a corruption of his Christian name. In 1955, at the height of the split between the left-wing BEVANITES and the party leadership, Attlee told Labour's National Executive in a Biblical pun:

> If thy Nye offend thee, pluck it out.

And in the 1959 election, Labour supporters in Northampton hoisted a poster reading:

> Repent, for the kingdom of Bevan is Nye!

One of 13 children, Bevan followed his father down the mines of South Wales at 13, but soon showed powers of oratory and leadership and at 29 was one of the Welsh miners' leaders in the GENERAL STRIKE. Elected to Parliament for the ILP in 1929 and Labour in 1931, he soon took over Lloyd George's mantle as the most brilliant, emotional and fiery orator of his day; his biographer Michael Foot wrote: "Bevan would be possessed by Lloyd George's terrible urge to claw down the enemy." He was a thorn in CHURCHILL's side throughout World War II, though the Great Man confessed: "He is one of the few people I would sit still and listen to"; when Labour took power in 1945 Churchill commented: "He will be just as great a curse to this country in peace as he was a squalid nuisance in time of war." Yet his most constructive period was as Minister of Health in ATTLEE's Cabinet, when he created the NHS despite the obstructiveness of most of the medical profession; in 1951 he resigned, with Harold WILSON and John Freeman, over the imposition of charges for spectacles and false teeth. After Labour lost power later that year, the Bevanites tried Attlee to the limit by pressing a radical left-wing agenda and ignoring party discipline, Bevan narrowly escaping expulsion from the party. A furious Attlee told Labour MPs: "Just when we were beginning to win the match, our outside-left has scored against his own side." Bevan's ally Richard CROSSMAN said of him: "Nye wasn't cut out to be a leader; he was cut out to be a prophet," and he himself said: "If the Labour Party is not going to be a Socialist party, I don't want to lead it." Yet Bevan was not just an embarrassment to the Labour leadership; he was a devastating critic of the Tories (*see* ALBATROSS; ORGAN GRINDER); Harold Macmillan once remarked: "He keeps prophesying the end of the capitalist system, and is prepared to play any part in its burial except that of mute." He also had the readiest wit; when Churchill upbraided him for not "taking the trouble to dress properly" for the Queen's Coronation dinner by wearing formal dress, Bevan replied: "Prime Minister, your fly buttons are undone!" When Hugh GAITSKELL replaced Attlee as Labour leader, he found Bevan ranged against him; but Bevan did not join his fellow left-wingers in embracing UNILATERALISM, and after SUEZ he was reconciled with Gaitskell, becoming Shadow Foreign Secretary and, a year before his death, deputy Labour leader. His wife Jennie Lee, herself a Labour MP and a future Arts Minister, wrote: "Nye was born old and died young."

> The greatest Parliamentary orator since Charles James Fox.
>
> R. A. BUTLER.

See also his own worst ENEMY.

O

O. O God, this sea is so great, and my boat is so small An old Breton prayer which President KENNEDY kept on his desk. It was given by Admiral Hyman Rickover to each nuclear submarine commander.

O My Darling Clementine The song, sung on a late-night Dublin television show by Northern Ireland Secretary **Peter Brooke** (1934–) in 1991, which nearly brought his political career to an end. Brooke was coaxed into song by the talk-show host Gay Byrne, unaware of the strength of reaction to the terrorist shooting of seven construction workers near the border earlier that evening. There was an outcry from Northern Ireland politicians; Brooke dramatically told the House of Commons that he was ready to resign, but John Major insisted that he stay on.

OAS (1) Secret Army Organization (*Organisation de l'Armée Secrète*) Far-right French terrorist organization, based in the military, which conducted a bombing campaign and plotted the assassination of President DE GAULLE because of his "betrayal" of Algeria. The incident in which it came closest to success, in September 1961, prompted Frederick Forsyth's novel *The Day of the* JACKAL. The OAS collapsed after the capture in 1962 of its leader General Raoul Salan (1899–). *See* ALGÉRIE FRANÇAISE. (2) Organization of American States. Founded in 1948 but based on earlier pan-American groups, the OAS was designed to bind together free governments for a common purpose. Canada has never joined, and Cuba was expelled at America's insistence in 1962. With headquarters in Washington, the OAS has tended to side with the US on crucial issues, making it vulnerable to left-wing and nationalist criticism in Latin America. It has also been weakened over time by dictatorship and internal conflict in member states.

> They couldn't pour piss out of a shoe if the instructions were printed on the heel. LYNDON B. JOHNSON.

oath. oath of Allegiance At Westminster, the oath a newly-elected or re-elected MP (and peers at the start of each PARLIAMENT) must swear or affirm before he or she can sit or vote:

> I swear by Almighty God that I will be faithful and bear true allegiance to Her Majesty Queen Elizabeth, her heirs and successors according to law, so help me God.

oath of office In America, the oath all elected and appointed officials below the rank of President must take:

> I, AB, do solemnly swear [or affirm] that I will support and defend the Constitution of the United States against all enemies, foreign and domestic; that I will bear true faith and allegiance to the same; that I take this obligation freely, without any mental reservation or purpose of evasion; and that I will well and faithfully discharge the duties of the office on which I am about to enter. So help me God.

Presidential oath *See* I DO SOLEMNLY SWEAR.

Tennis Court Oath The oath sworn in 1789 in a tennis court at VERSAILLES by representatives of the locked-out THIRD ESTATE. They declared themselves a NATIONAL ASSEMBLY, and vowed not to disband until a constitution was established for France; they got rather more than they bargained for in the form of the FRENCH REVOLUTION.

OAU Organization of African Unity. A supranational organization, similar to the UNITED NATIONS in its structure, founded in 1963 to promote a common purpose among independent and mainly ex-colonial African states and based in Addis Ababa. The struggle against COLONIALISM and APARTHEID has provided a negative cohesive force for almost all of its life, but it has been dogged by disputes and warfare between and within member states; several national leaders have been deposed while at OAU summit meetings.

Object! At Westminster, when uttered by one (usually Government) whip or backbencher, this word is enough to block a Private Member's BILL by preventing it being passed ON THE NOD in the Commons. In the US HOUSE OF REPRESENTATIVES, this cry from any member when the Clerk is reading the Consent CALENDAR will result in the relevant Bill being carried over until the Calendar is next called. If three or more members object, the Bill is stricken from the Calendar for the rest of that session.

occupied territories Widely-used term for the GAZA STRIP, GOLAN HEIGHTS and WEST BANK, captured by Israel from Egyptian control, Syria and Jordan respectively in the war of 1967. *See* INTIFADA; PEACE PROCESS.

October. October Manifesto The proclamation by TSAR Nicholas II, following the abortive REVOLUTION of 1905, that he would allow the establishment of an elected DUMA.

October Revolution The BOLSHEVIK revolution in October 1917 (November in the Western calendar) in which LENIN came to power, overthrowing KERENSKY and the MENSHEVIKS. It ushered in 74 years of COMMUNIST rule.

October Surprise Originally the coup the Republicans feared during the closing days of the 1980 US Presidential election, in the form of a last-minute breakthrough that would enable the CARTER administration to take credit for the release of the Teheran HOSTAGES. In fact Iran only agreed to free them on the last full day of Carter's presidency – and then held back till Ronald Reagan had taken office. The term boomeranged on the BUSH administration in 1991 when Gary Sick published a book alleging that during the 1980 campaign Bush, as Republican vice-presidential nominee, and future CIA director William J. Casey collaborated with the US hostages' captors to ensure that they were not released until the Reagan/Bush ticket had defeated Carter. Bush strongly denied the charges, and an investigation appeared to clear him.

Octobrists A constitutional CENTRE party in Russia supported by the landlords and wealthy mercantile interests, which was prominent in the DUMA between 1907 and 1914. It took its name from the OCTOBER MANIFESTO.

Ode to Joy The hymn to freedom by the German poet Schiller which Beethoven set to music as the final movement of his *Ninth (Choral) Symphony*. With its message that "all peoples will be brothers" (*alle Menschen werden Brüder*) it has become the anthem of the EUROPEAN COMMUNITY.

Oder-Neisse line The German-Polish border imposed under Soviet pressure after WORLD WAR II which follows the rivers Oder and Neisse, leaving a large slice of pre-war Germany in Poland; in a parallel action, Stalin incorporated a similar belt of Polish territory in the Soviet Union. Poland and East Germany recognized it in 1950, but Western powers did not. In West Germany right-wingers and exiles from the lost territories pressed for their recovery, but after reunification in 1990 Helmut Kohl's government formally accepted the border.

> A frontier of peace. NIKITA S. KHRUSCHEV (1894–1971).

OECD Organization for Economic Cooperation and Development. An international body to expand world trade and encourage economic growth. Founded by Western European nations after World War II as the Organization for European Economic Cooperation, it was relaunched as OECD in 1961. Based in Paris, its 24 members include all EC and EFTA countries, America, Canada, Japan, Australia, New Zealand and Turkey.

off. off the cuff Extempore or impromptu comments, originally from the practice by waiters of taking down orders in restaurants by jotting them down on their shirt cuffs. President Nixon once said that "no television performance takes such careful preparation as an off the cuff attack". Sometimes confused with the following.

off the record Comments made and information given to a reporter to give background, but not for specific use and certainly not for attribution to the SOURCE providing them. Those which may be used and quoted are said to be **on the record**.

off-year In America, an even-numbered year when there are elections for the House of Representatives and for a number of places in the Senate – but not for the Presidency.

office. office of honour or profit in the civil or uniformed services A position requiring the holder to take the US OATH OF OFFICE. Under the CONSTITUTION "no person holding any office under the United States" can be a member of either House of CONGRESS.

office of profit under the Crown A UK civil service or other PUBLIC-SECTOR position whose holder is consequently disqualified from sitting in Parliament.

seals of office The insignia a senior UK Minister receives of the monarch on taking office, and surrenders on relinquishing it.

Tenure of Office Act An Act passed in 1867 by the Republican-controlled US Congress in an attempt to prevent President Andrew Johnson dismissing Secretary of War Edwin Stanton, who was secretly reporting Johnson's plans to Republican radicals. Making any dismissal by the President subject to Senate approval, it was eventually ruled UNCONSTITUTIONAL. Johnson fired Stanton anyway, triggering IMPEACHMENT proceedings which almost succeeded.

outer office The office which controls ACCESS to a head of government or senior member of an administration. Sir Les Patterson (the impressionist Barry Humphries) said of Australia's WHITLAM ministry:

> You can pick up your money from the Arab in the outer office.

private office In the UK and other commonwealth countries, a MINISTER's personal civil service nerve-centre.

official. Official IRA *See* IRA.

Official Monster Raving Loony Party In Britain, a deliberately facetious political party which contested BY-ELECTIONS as a joke from the early 1980s. One of its candidates was the former rock singer Screamin' Lord Sutch, who has fought dozens of by-elections and in the general election of 1987 opposed Margaret Thatcher; though he usually polled only a couple of hundred votes, he did deliver the death-blow to the SDP by outpolling it at the Bootle by-election in 1990.

Official Report At Westminster, the formal name for HANSARD.

Official Secrets Act The legislation which has enabled Britain to be governed with almost total secrecy for much of the 20th century. An Official Secrets Act was first passed in 1889, but the most notorious was enacted in a single afternoon in 1911 to counter a German spy scare. It not only imposed sanctions on the passing of information to a potential enemy, but through its CATCH-ALL Section 2 an almost total blackout on the publication of facts concerned with the functions of government. After a series of controversial trials of civil servants for LEAKing information to MPs and the media brought the Act into disrepute and the SPYCATCHER affair showed its limitations, it was relaxed in 1989, notably through repeal of Section 2.

> The acme of clumsy and illibertarian legislation conceived in panic and passed in haste. PETER HENNESSY

Official Unionists *See* UNIONIST.

official visit A visit to another country with full honours by a HEAD OF GOVERNMENT who is not the HEAD OF STATE.

officialdom The culture of government and BUREAUCRACY.

officialese A pejorative term for the jargon of civil servants.

OGPU *See* GPU.

Ohio gang The friends and cronies of President Warren G. HARDING whose corruption, most spectacularly through the TEAPOT DOME affair, cast a cloud over his presidency; growing worry as he discovered the extent of their wrongdoing may have contributed to his death. Charles R. Forbes milked the Veterans Bureau of nearly $250 million for friendly contractors and suppliers. Colonel Thomas W. Miller as Alien Property Custodian allowed his office to distribute captured industrial patents at bargain prices. The Department of Justice under Harry Daugherty dispensed liquor permits and pardons to criminals for hard cash. And Interior Secretary Albert B. Fall became the first Cabinet officer to be sent to jail for his role in Teapot Dome.

Ohio idea A keystone of the unsuccessful 1868 Democratic election campaign, headed by Presidential nominee Horatio Seymour. The brainchild of Congressman George H. Pendleton, it involved easing the post-Civil War financial burden, especially on farmers, by paying off the NATIONAL DEBT in GREENBACKS.

OH(B)MS On Her (Britannic) Majesty's Service. The initials on every item of Government mail in Britain and some Commonwealth countries, and on official bags.

old. Old Bullion Nickname for **Thomas Hart Benton** (1782–1858), one of the first US Senators for Missouri, who after seeing the misery caused by the crash of the Second Bank of the United States in 1819, campaigned throughout his political life against an all-powerful national bank and for "hard money".

Old 8 to 7 One of the many derogatory nicknames accorded to **Rutherford Hayes** (1822–93), 19th President of the United States (Democrat, 1877–81), because of the circumstances in which he took office. In the 1876 election he lost in the popular vote to Samuel Tilden, who seemed certain of victory with 184 votes in the ELECTORAL COLLEGE to Hayes's 165. Twenty votes (in Florida, Louisiana and South Carolina, plus one in Oregon) were disputed, but just one would give Tilden victory. The Republican National Committee, and subsequently the party's majority in Congress, colluded with massive fraud to hand the results in all states to Hayes. The crowning event was the 8–7 vote by an Electoral Commission of both Houses of Congress, on straight party lines in favour of Hayes. Tilden retired from politics, saying: "I shall receive from posterity the credit of having been elected to the highest position in the gift of the people, without any of the cares and responsibilities of the office." Prior to his election, Hayes had a reputation as a man of duty. While serving in the Army he had refused to campaign for his House seat, saying: "An officer fit for duty who at this crisis would abandon his post to electioneer ought to be scalped." In office he proved, according to Sen. John Sherman, "a very modest man, but a very able one", and Hayes felt he had done well, saying: "No one ever left the Presidency with less regret, less disappointment, fewer heartburnings, or general content with the result of his term (in his own heart, I mean)." But the popular verdict was inevitably harsh:

> Mr. Hayes came in by a majority of one, and goes out by unanimous consent. ANON.

Old EOB The Old Executive Office Building next to the WHITE HOUSE in Washington, which originally housed the STATE DEPARTMENT. An office there is not as prestigious as one in the West Wing of the White House; Mike Deaver said that people would work in closets in the White House rather than be banished to "Death Row" in the EOB where there was no ACCESS to the President. Francis X. Clines called the building "a mass of Victorian tiles and granite that resembles a battleship in the rain and a wedding cake in the sun"; President Truman simply termed it "the greatest monstrosity in America".

Old Glory Affectionate term for the STARS AND STRIPES, devised in 1831 by the Salem, New England, seaman William Driver. Saluting the flag as it was unfurled at the start of a voyage to Asia, he said: "I name thee Old Glory." The phrase caught on among troops in the UNION army during the CIVIL WAR.

Old Guard In Australia, the 25,000-man right-wing organization of armed volunteers, mainly ex-service small farmers, which formed up in the New South Wales countryside to confront the inter-war Labor premier Jack Lang. In 1932 one of its most dashing figures, Captain Francis de Groot, galloped ahead of Lang to slice the tape and open Sydney Harbour Bridge.

Old Hickory The affectionate nickname of **Andrew Jackson** (1767–1845), 17th President of the United States (Democrat, 1829–37). A frontier lawyer born in poverty and a Revolutionary volunteer at 14, he won national fame as the hero of a campaign against the Creek Indians and as victorious general of the Battle of New Orleans. His troops named him after hickory, the toughest wood they knew. In 1827 Thomas D. Arnold, an anti-Jackson Congressional candidate, said of Jackson: "He spent the prime of his life in gambling, in cock-fighting, in horse-racing, and to cap it all tore from a husband the wife of his bosom." Jackson was combatively loyal to his pipe-smoking wife Rachel, whom he had rescued from a previous unhappy marriage, wedding her when he mistakenly believed her divorce was through. He once killed a man in a duel for casting a slur on her. When any man referred to her, Jackson would exclaim: "Great God! Do you mention *her* sacred name?" And Sen. Thomas Hart Benton (*see* OLD BULLION) reminisced:

> Yes, I had a fight with Jackson. A fellow was hardly in the fashion who hadn't. But mine was different from his other fights – it wasn't about Rachel.

Jackson was thus a far cry from the gentlemen who preceded him in the White House, but rose through the House and the Senate and a narrow defeat by John Quincy Adams in 1824 (*see* CORRUPT BARGAIN) to gain his revenge in 1828 and become the first President to be the "people's choice" of the new nation. In 1824 he said of himself: "I can command a body of men in a rough way, but I am not fit to be President." And JEFFERSON warned: "I feel much alarmed at the thought of seeing General Jackson President. He is one of the most unfit men I know for such a place." His fears seemed borne out when frontiersmen flooded into Washington to celebrate his inauguration in hillbilly fashion, an event the capital has still not forgotten. Daniel Webster noted: "I never saw such a crowd here before. Persons have come 500 miles to see General Jackson, and they really seem to think that the country is rescued from some dreadful danger." Jackson's presidency, though his methods were rough and ready, was a success. It was marred by his wife's death soon after he entered the White House, an assassination attempt (the first on a President) in 1835 and ferocious clashes with the backers of the second Bank of the United States, whose monopoly he tried to break. "The bank is trying to kill me , but I will try to kill it," Jackson declared. He declared war on the Senate after it rejected his nomination of Martin van Buren as Minister to Britain, exclaiming: "By the Eternal, I'll smash them." Nor was he afraid of the Supreme Court. When Chief Justice Marshall urged him to secure the release, ordered by the Supreme Court, of two missionaries imprisoned in Georgia for living among the Cherokee Indians, Jackson stood firm, saying: "John Marshall has made his decision. Now let *him* enforce it!" On leaving office, Jackson declared: "I have only two regrets – that I have not shot Henry Clay or hanged John C. Calhoun."

> Haughty and sterile intellectualism opposed him. Musty reaction disapproved of him. Hollow and outworn traditionalism shook a trembling finger at him – all but the people of the United States. FRANKLIN D. ROOSEVELT.

Old Kinderhook The nickname of **Martin van Buren** (1782–1862), 8th President of the United States (Democrat, 1837–41), taken from his home in New York state. The first President born under the US flag, van Buren was a lawyer and, as organizer of the ALBANY REGENCY, one of the earliest MACHINE politicians. He served in the Senate, as Governor of New York, Secretary of State and Jackson's Vice-President before defeating four different Whig opponents in 1836 for the Presidency. Jackson hailed him as "a true man with no guile", but his subdued style was in marked contrast to his rumbustious predecessor. John Randolph wrote that van Buren "rowed to his object with muffled oars", while John C.

Calhoun declared: "He is not of the race of the lion or the tiger; he belongs to the lower order – the fox." In the early stages of his presidency he was hailed as "Matty van" and "The LITTLE MAGICIAN", but as the DEPRESSION of 1837 took hold the Whigs branded him "Martin van Ruin" and "Van, Van, the used-up man". Van Buren was said to live in "oriental splendour" – which gave an easy target to the LOG CABIN AND HARD CIDER campaign of William Henry Harrison and John Tyler which swept van Buren from office in 1840. Unusually, he made two attempts at a comeback – seeking the Vice-Presidential nomination in 1844 and standing as FREE SOIL candidate in 1848.

The Old Man, the Old Flag and the Old Policy The slogan on which the Canadian Premier John Macdonald's Conservatives fought his last election, in 1891; Macdonald's majority was sharply reduced and he died, exhausted, only months later.

Old Man Eloquent The nickname won by John Quincy ADAMS during his lengthy career (1830–48) as a Congressman after losing the Presidency. He was a greater success in the House than as President, and himself said: "No election or appointment conferred on me ever gave me so much pleasure." He earned the nickname during his nine-year campaign to repeal the GAG RULE against the discussion of anti-slavery petitions. When the House finally backed him, in 1844, he exclaimed: "Blessed, forever blessed, be the name of God!" He died in the Capitol in 1848.

Old Oil-Jug The nickname of Felix Walker, an 1820s US Congressman from North Carolina, earned by his flowing speeches in praise of his native Buncombe County (*see* BUNKUM).

Old Red Socks Derogatory term for the Pope among hard-line Protestants in ULSTER.

Old Rough and Ready The nickname of **Zachary Taylor** (1784–1850), 12th President of the United States (1849–50). An Indian fighter who became a national hero as a Brigadier-General in the MEXICAN WAR, he was thus named by his soldiers for his sloppy uniform, his cursing and his habit of tobacco-chewing. Daniel Webster described him as "an illiterate frontier colonel"; Taylor himself had never voted in a Presidential campaign until the WHIGS nominated him in 1848. He classed himself "a Whig, but not an ultra-Whig", and once said: "The idea that I should become President seems to me too visionary to require serious answer. It has never entered my head, nor is it likely to enter the head of any sane person." His wife Margaret regretted his nomination as "a plot to deprive me of his society and to shorten his life by unnecessary care and responsibility". Taylor was elected to the White House after the rival Democrats split, and began robustly. When asked how he would treat SECESSIONists, he replied: "Persons taken in rebellion against the Union I would hang, with less reluctance than I hanged deserters and spies in Mexico." But he died after 15 months in office, through eating too much in blazing heat during the Fourth of July celebrations.

Old soldiers never die; they just fade away A much-quoted phrase from Gen Douglas MACARTHUR's historic address to a joint session of the US Congress on 19 April 1951 after his dismissal by President Truman. MacArthur probably heard it first at West Point, from which he graduated in 1903; it is a soldiers' parody of a 19th-century gospel hymn "Kind words can never die", known by then on both sides of the Atlantic.

Old Veto The title conferred by his Democrat opponents on **John Tyler** (1790–1862), 10th President of the United States. A lawyer who served in both Houses of Congress and as governor of Virginia, Tyler was elected Vice-President in 1840 as junior partner on the TIPPECANOE AND TYLER TOO ticket. The first Vice-President to assume the function of the Presidency when Harrison died (some argued he was not actually President), he earned his nickname by VETOing a then-record nine Bills in less than four days of office. He survived the first serious attempt to impeach a President, for "gross usurpation of powers"; Charles Dickens commented that he "looked somewhat worn and anxious, and well he might be, being at war with everybody". Widowed in the White House, he caused a sensation by marrying the 23-year-old Julia Gardiner, a Washington beauty 29 years younger than himself; she bore him seven children.

Ole Miss An affectionate nickname for the University of Mississippi, scene in 1962 of an episode that gained worldwide notoriety. When James Meredith became the first Black student to qualify for admission, the university refused him and the SEGREGATIONIST Governor Ross Barnett intervened to bar him, despite Meredith's obtaining a court order. Four times Meredith failed to register, blocked by Barnett personally (the last time with State troopers and a crowd of 2500 Whites). The fifth time Meredith, now escorted by US marshals, succeeded – but the ensuing riot by White students left two people dead and 375 injured, including 166 marshals. It took 3000 Federal troops and National Guardsmen to restore order. Meredith was shot and wounded in 1966 while leading a march encouraging Blacks in Mississippi to register to vote; the university is now fully integrated.

oligarchy In Greek, government by the best, or an elite. In common usage, a clique which keeps power in its own hands, regarding others as incapable of exercising it or as a threat.

Olympia rallies The mass rallies of BLACK-SHIRTS in the mid-1930s at Olympia, the exhibition centre in West London, at which Sir Oswald MOSLEY attempted to emulate Hitler's feats of mesmerism and DEMAGOGY. The British public found them partly threatening, partly ridiculous.

OMB In the US Federal government, the Office of Management and Budget which prepares the BUDGET and controls the administration's legislative agenda. For any Bill with financial implications put forward by the EXECUTIVE branch to proceed, OMB's endorsement is essential, and its director normally wields great influence in the WHITE HOUSE. It was established by President HARDING in 1921 as the Bureau of the Budget, and given its present name in 1970.

> The real switchboard of the Executive Branch.
>
> DAVID STOCKMAN.

Ombudsman (Swed. commissioner) An official who takes up complaints from the public to protect the rights of the individual against infringement by the state. The post originated in Sweden, which has had an ombudsman since 1809; Denmark followed in 1955, Norway and New Zealand in 1962 and the UK in 1967 with a Parliamentary Commissioner for Administration, commonly known as the Ombudsman. Since then Ombudsmen have also been appointed in Britain for local government and the National Health Service. The British Ombudsman can only act on complaints fed to him through a member of Parliament. In Washington, no such post has been created, largely because members of Congress see it as a threat.

OMOV The abbreviation for "one member, one VOTE" used by activists in Britain's LABOUR PARTY and Trade Union movement as pressure for balloting of individual members grew from the mid-1980s.

on. on his bike The remark by which Norman Tebbit (*see* CHINGFORD SKINHEAD) will, to his regret, be most remembered. At the 1982 Conservative Party conference Tebbit, then Employment Secretary, responded to public unrest over high unemployment by saying:

> My father did not wait around. He didn't riot. He got on his bike and looked for work, and he kept looking till he found it.

This angered trade union leaders, the Left and militant youth groups. But many voters felt it logical and justified.

on the bell A house, flat, office or restaurant within DIVISION-BELL range of the Palace of Westminster, *i.e.* where a Division bell is fitted and from which, when it rings, an MP can be sure of getting to the Commons in time to vote. In practice this means just under twelve minutes' walk. MPs with money often look for a home "on the bell" – a factor which inflates property prices in Westminster.

on the knocker A British, mainly Labour, term for door-to-door campaigning, covering both CANVASSING and KNOCKING UP. It harks back to the time when every door had a knocker but few had a bell.

on the nod The passage of an item of legislation without either discussion or a vote. At Westminster the nod in question is either one of approval from the Speaker, or of disinterest from Government WHIPS who frequently block Private Members' BILLS which look like getting a clear run.

on the record *See* OFF THE RECORD.

oncer A mainly Australian term for an elected representative who wins a seat that he or she is unlikely to retain or who, from the moment of election, looks incapable of winning a second term.

one. 1-800 The format of a broadcast public discussion between a US Presidential candidate and individual voters who CALL IN on a toll-free (1-800) telephone line. First used by former California Governor Jerry Brown (*see* SPACE CADET) during his abortive quest for the 1992 Democratic nomination, it was used that summer to great effect by H. Ross PEROT when campaigning as an UNDECLARED CANDIDATE.

one-club golfer The implementer of an economic policy which relies entirely on one element of control. The phrase was coined by the former UK Prime Minister Edward Heath *c.* 1985 to describe Chancellor Nigel Lawson's total reliance on interest rate policy.

one-hour rule The rule passed in 1841 by the US HOUSE OF REPRESENTATIVES to end filibusters by imposing a one-hour limit on members' speeches. It was criticized for hastening the end of true oratory in the House, Sen. Thomas Hart Benton declaring it "an eminent instance of permanent injury done to free institutions".

one-liner (1) The throw-away line in a politician's speech which is designed to elicit immediate laughter and then stick in the public memory. (2) At Westminster, a one-line WHIP, in practice an indication to legislators by the party machine that they need not be present.

one man's wage increase is another man's price increase Harold Wilson's dictum on the inflationary effects of wage increases, uttered in January 1970 at a time when his Labour government was trying to curb pay claims after a period of WAGE RESTRAINT.

One Nation *See* NATION.

one of us Margaret Thatcher's ultimate term of approval for a colleague or subordinate, denoting a fellow true believer in her own set of free-market economic theories. Hugo Young chose it as the title of his highly-acclaimed Thatcher biography, first published in 1989. Mrs. Thatcher's use of the term in its rigidly exclusive sense may have been new, but the phrase was not; when the BEVERIDGE REPORT was published in 1943, Labour's Hugh Dalton wrote that Beveridge, a Liberal, had produced a "fine, stimulating document" even though "he is not one of us".

Oom Paul The Afrikaner nickname for Stephanus Johannes **Paulus Kruger** (1825–1904), who led the revolt against Britain's annexation of the Transvaal in 1877, and as the territory's President in 1883 resisted the incursion of *Uitlander* gold prospectors and settlers. His rout of the JAMESON RAID in 1896 and the KRUGER TELEGRAM in which Kaiser Wilhelm II congratulated him stoked IMPERIALIST feeling in Britain, paving the way for the BOER WAR. When war broke out, Kruger was eclipsed and moved to Switzerland.

OPA The Office of Price Administration, established by Franklin D. Roosevelt in April 1941, to prepare American industry for a total war effort. The OPA, headed at first by "Czar" Leon Henderson, set production priorities and maximum prices, held back supplies from plants refusing to co-operate, and rationed items in the civilian market – starting, just after PEARL HARBOR, with rubber tyres. While not totally successful, its impact was considerable; Roosevelt termed Henderson "the toughest bastard in town".

OPD WHITEHALL and Ministerial shorthand for the Overseas Policy and Defence committee of the British CABINET, the group of Ministers which meets regularly to deal with the most important issues in these fields.

OPEC The Organization of Petroleum Exporting Countries. An international cartel of (mainly Middle Eastern) oil producers formed in 1960 to combat exploitation by Western companies, largely through NATIONALIZING member states' production. Based in Vienna, it sets prices and production levels for roughly 30% of world output – and can thus dictate world oil prices. OPEC became a household word in 1973 when, after acquiescing for years in the low producer prices, it quadrupled them, triggering world inflation and economic slowdown. OPEC's pricing policy has caused a significant transfer of wealth from industrialized nations to developing countries with oil deposits. Its members include Algeria, Ecuador, Gabon, Indonesia, Iraq, Iran, Kuwait, Nigeria, Qatar, Saudi Arabia, the United Arab Emirates and Venezuela. Britain, the United States and the former Soviet republics have never belonged.

open. open convention In US politics, a party's nominating CONVENTION at which all DELEGATES are released from the candidates they were sent to support so that they can make an independent choice. In 1980 Sen. Edward Kennedy sought to frustrate Jimmy Carter's renomination by calling for an open Democratic convention; when he was voted down he withdrew from the race, but Carter had to make concessions on the PLATFORM.

open diplomacy The first demand made by Woodrow WILSON in his Fourteen Points for a peace settlement and new order in Europe at the end of World War I: "**Open covenants of peace openly arrived at**, after which there shall be no private international understandings of any kind". It was an attempt to stamp out the practice of secret treaties, under which nations agreed to carve up third parties' territory or give each other a free hand to make territorial gains. But it is also the case that the VERSAILLES Treaty, though its terms were made public, was negotiated in secret, mainly by Wilson himself, Clemenceau and Lloyd George. With the rise of the dictators and the onset of WORLD WAR II, Wilson's first point, like most of the other thirteen, proved a dead letter.

open door policy The China policy devised in 1899 by John Hay, US Secretary of State, and reluctantly agreed to – though only after the shock of the BOXER REBELLION – by Britain, Germany, Russia, France, Italy and Japan. Its essence was that none of these nations claiming a sphere of influence in China should interfere with the trade of other nations – thus ensuring American traders equal access. The Open Door policy checked the scramble for Chinese trade and territory – largely because of generous payments to the countries concerned, including America, from the Chinese treasury.

open government The doctrine and practice of the workings of government being conducted in the public eye, rather than behind a cloak of secrecy. In Washington, the

FREEDOM OF INFORMATION Act has for two decades given an insight into decision-making – though not the whole picture, most major scandals still being revealed through leaks to the Press. In Britain the Thatcher government embarked on a limited "open government" initiative in the early 1980s, but with few practical effects on WHITEHALL's traditional climate of obsessive secrecy. The eventual repeal of Section 2 of the OFFICIAL SECRETS ACT and the publication by John Major's government in 1992 of documents including QUESTIONS OF PROCEDURE FOR MINISTERS have since brought some change.

> The Government being the people's business, it necessarily follows that its operations should be at all times open to the public view. Publicity is therefore as essential to honest administration as freedom of speech is to representative government.
>
> WILLIAM JENNINGS BRYAN, US Secretary of State, 1915.

open housing The popular US term for the ending of racial DISCRIMINATION in housing, notably against Blacks. The Senate's blocking in 1966 of an Administration Bill for open housing was one of the few reverses for President Johnson's CIVIL RIGHTS programme. But a similar law was passed two years later, forbidding discrimination in the rental or sale of housing on the basis of race, colour, religion or ethnic origin. LBJ's last great legislative victory brought an end to major abuses, but discrimination continues in subtle forms.

open letter Ostensibly a letter sent by a politician to another person (in Britain, frequently by a Minister or MP to his or her constituency chairman), but in practice purely a vehicle for its contents to be released to the Press.

open mike One of the greatest pitfalls of modern politics: the radio microphone left switched on which catches a politician's unguarded comments. Ronald Reagan's "Bomb Russia" GAFFE was a prime example, as was his statement during a sound test heard by reporters in November 1982:

> My fellow Americans, I've talked to you on a number of occasions about the economic problems and opportunities our nation faces. And I'm prepared to tell you, it's a hell of a mess . . . We're not connected to the press now yet, are we?

In 1991 George BUSH, in conversation with Arnold Schwarzenegger, said of microphones generally:

> These, they're dangerous. They trap you, especially those furry ones . . . it's the furry guys that get you into real trouble.

an open mind is like an open sewer A typical dictum of Ernest BEVIN (1881–1951), the blunt former trade union leader who from 1945 to 1951 was one of Britain's most respected Foreign Secretaries.

open selection A bone of contention during the brief lifetime of the Liberal–SDP ALLIANCE. One faction wanted the parties centrally to decide which party's candidate should stand in each constituency; another, which eventually prevailed, wanted the choice made locally through "open selection" by all members of both parties.

open skies policy The policy of airline DEREGULATION pushed through in America by the Carter administration, and advocated for Europe by the Thatcher and Major governments.

opening to the Left or Right A move by a party or leader on to the territory of another, either by shifting its own ground or through some kind of arrangement with the other party. It embodies an element of outflanking or of STEALING AN OPPONENT'S CLOTHES.

opera. The opera ain't over till the fat lady sings The phrase coined by the San Antonio sportswriter Dan Cook *c.*1976 to emphasize the importance of playing on till the very last moment; it echoed an old Texas phrase "the rodeo ain't over till the bull riders ride". Washington Bullets' basketball coach Dick Motta used "the opera ain't over . . ." as his motto in the 1978 NBA playoffs; it was taken up by US politicians, and especially Presidential contenders, to stress that no candidate is defeated until all the votes have been counted.

Operation Candour The campaign conducted by President Nixon to clear himself of allegations of complicity in the WATERGATE burglary and cover-up. In it, during the second half of 1973, he professed to be open and frank, particularly about the zeal with which he claimed to be trying to seek out the truth, while concealing his true involvement.

Operation Push The drive to wean inner-city Black children away from drugs and toward a future of achievement, spearheaded in Chicago in the mid-1970s by the Rev. Jesse JACKSON. Jackson's slogan was:

> It's not the dope in your veins – it's the hope in your brains.

opinion. opinion-formers A term used in the political community for editors, television PUNDITS and others who can shape public opinion, and thus need to be cultivated.

opinion polls The surveys of national and local voting intentions, and of public attitudes on key issues, which have come to dominate political life, especially during election campaigns. The first such polling, on a sociological basis, was carried out by George S. Gallup in America just before World War II. Australia's first polls were conducted in 1941 by the Roy Morgan Research Centre; they were first used for a British election in 1945, though Mass Observation had given the wartime government invaluable insight into public attitudes and the level of morale. Rosalynn Carter gave the definitive politician's attitude to polls during her husband's presidency, saying: "Don't worry about polls – but if you do, don't admit it." *France-Soir* once editorialized that "there is as much difference between an opinion poll and an election as between shooting blank cartridges and live ones". And Margaret Thatcher declared: "If you are guided by opinion polls, you are not practising leadership – you are practising followship."

Opium wars The 19th-century conflicts during which Britain established influence over much of China. The first was fought over the right of British merchants to sell opium to the Chinese; it ended in the 1842 Treaty of Nanking which ceded Hong Kong to Britain.

> A war more unjust in its origins, a war more calculated to cover this country with permanent disgrace, I do not know, and I have not read of. GLADSTONE.

The second broke out after the CRIMEAN WAR. Britain's influence was confirmed in 1858 with the Treaty of Tientsin, but the fighting continued for several years.

opportunist A politician who seizes chances for self-advancement rather than following the course of principle. The word originated in 19th-century French politics and was adopted with enthusiasm by Communists Around 1900 LENIN wrote: "Axelrod and Martov have dropped into the opportunist wing of our Party . . . They have to repeat opportunist phrases to seek some kind of justification for their position." Since World War II it has had a more general application, there being no shortage of candidates.

opposition The task of opposing the government of the day within the confines of democracy, a position institutionalized in the WESTMINSTER system into **His or Her Majesty's Loyal Opposition**. The phrase, minus the "loyal", was first applied to the principal opposition party in 1826 by the English radical politician John Cam (later Baron) Hobhouse (1786–1869); it is usually shortened to **The Opposition**. It is said that **"the duty of the Opposition is to oppose"**, or more fully, as put by an early 19th-century English Whig named Tierney: "The duty of an opposition is very simple: to oppose everything and propose nothing". Lord Hailsham in the mid-20th century took the same view, saying of a Labour measure: "The Conservatives do not believe it necessary, and even if it were necessary we would oppose it." Yet in practice the Parliamentary system hinges on the Opposition allowing the elected Government to get its BUSINESS through, provided that Government behaves reasonably. Campbell-Bannerman struck the balance right when he wrote: "The duty of an opposition, if it has no ambition to be permanently on the left-hand side of the Speaker, is not just to oppose for opposition's sake, but to oppose selectively." Gladstone went a stage further, arguing: "it is, when strictly judged, an act of public immorality to lead an opposition on a certain plea, to succeed, and then in office to abandon it". The concept of a loyal opposition is not universal; STALIN once exclaimed: "My real opposition is myself." But the notion of a coalition of political forces essentially opposed to the Administration, yet not contemplating its overthrow is a given in US politics. As long ago as 1865 Thaddeus Stevens told Charles Sumner: "While we hardly approve of all the acts of government, we must try to keep out of the ranks of the opposition."

Opposition days *See* SUPPLY.

in Opposition The situation of the principal party which is out of power. Anthony Trollope (1815–82) reckoned that "the delight of political life is altogether in opposition – the very inaccuracy which is permitted to opposition is in itself a charm". But Margaret Thatcher took the contrary view: "When you are in government, five years is a very short time. When you are in opposition, it is a hell of a long time." And one of her advisers, Sir Adam Ridley, warned that "parties come to power with silly, irresponsible policies because they have spent their whole period in opposition destroying the lessons they learned in government".

Leader of the Opposition The formal position allotted in Britain's unwritten CONSTITUTION to the leader of the principal opposition party. He or she receives a Ministerial salary, has the right to grill the Prime Minister at QUESTION TIME twice weekly and is briefed by the Prime Minister on PRIVY COUNCIL TERMS on sensitive matters. Despite this status the position does not appeal to outgoing Prime Ministers. In 1945 CHURCHILL heard that a Yugoslav woman had written in alarm of his election defeat: "That poor Mr. Churchill. I suppose he will now be shot." Churchill observed: "They have reserved a far worse fate for me than that." The Leader of the Opposition holds that position at the pleasure of the party. When Sir William Harcourt resigned as Liberal leader in 1898 after being pilloried for his handling of the FASHODA crisis, he wrote:

> The leader of opposition who finds his whips speaking and voting against him cannot maintain that respect which is due to his position, still less when he finds the organization of the party working against him in the country.

oppositionism A state of mind in which members of a party are not only used to being in opposition but prefer it, because they would have to show repsonsibility and think positively were they to find themselves in power.

opting out The doctrine first advanced by Margaret Thatcher's Conservatives in their 1987 election MANIFESTO under which individual undertakings in the PUBLIC SECTOR could become self-governing. It was tried first with schools, which could opt out of local authority control if the parents voted for **grant-maintained status**; by 1993 several hundred had done so. More controversially, hospitals were from 1992 encouraged to detach themselves from the NHS bureaucracy and turn themselves into free-standing trusts, competing for business within the Health Service. Labour bitterly opposed opted-out hospitals as a backdoor means of dismantling and PRIVATIZING the NHS, something John Major strongly disputed.

Options for Change The strategy for drastic reductions in the size of Britain's armed forces following the end of the COLD WAR and the conclusion of INF and other ARMS CONTROL agreements, set out by Tom King, Defence Secretary under Margaret Thatcher and John Major, and developed by his successor Malcolm Rifkind. Central to it was the halving of British forces in Germany and the disbandment and amalgamation of historic regiments and RAF squadrons.

Orange The Royal House of the Netherlands which assumed the British crown in 1689 when the Protestant **William of Orange** (King William III) and his wife Mary were invited by Parliament to take the throne jointly. The concurrent defeat in the Battle of the BOYNE of Catholic forces loyal to the ousted King James II ensured the Protestant ascendancy in ULSTER; the **Orange Order**, founded in 1795 to maintain the Protestant constitution, champions that ascendancy to this day (*see* MARCHING SEASON).

Orange card, playing the The whipping-up of LOYALIST sentiment in Ulster in order to frustrate first HOME RULE and, since the PARTITION of Ireland, any accommodation between London and Dublin or the imposition of POWER SHARING in the province. The term dates back at least to Lord Randolph Churchill (1849–94) who wrote of Gladstone *c.* 1886:

> I decided some time ago that if the G.O.M. went for Home Rule the Orange Card would be the one to play. Please God it may turn out the ace of trumps and not the two.

oratory. The art of delivering not just a political speech but a *tour de force*, which has been pronounced dead at regular intervals since the mid-19th century. The American socialist Norman Thomas declared it "the harlot of the arts, so subject is it to abuse and degradation", and the Italian statesman Vittorio Emanuele Orlando conceded this, saying: "Oratory is like prostitution – you must have little tricks". In the late 18th century Benjamin FRANKLIN scathingly observed: "Here comes the orator, with his flood of words and his drop of reason"; by the mid-19th such criticism had struck home with Wendell Phillips declaring: "If you want to be an orator, first find your great CAUSE". Memorable oratory has been most common among POPULISTS of the Right and firebrands of the Left; Julian Critchley, leaving Churchill to one side, has observed:

> Oratory has rarely been a Tory failing.

Boy Orator of the Platte *See* BOY.

order. Order, Order! The words with which the SPEAKER calls the HOUSE OF COMMONS into session and prefaces new items of business. When radio broadcasting of the Commons began in the late 1970s, Speaker George Thomas (1909–), became an instant national celebrity for his rich Welsh delivery of the phrase. The single word **Order**! is shouted from the CHAIR if the conduct of the House is becoming unruly.

Order Paper The paper produced each day by each House of Parliament at Westminster which lists the BUSINESS for that day. The Commons Order Paper lists, in turn, Private BILLS to be considered, oral QUESTIONS, TEN-MINUTE RULE BILLS, the remaining ORDERS OF THE DAY (*see below*), Committees sitting that day, written questions, and important matters pending.

Order in Council In Britain, measures subordinate to primary LEGISLATION, which are enacted in the name of the SOVEREIGN by a committee of the PRIVY COUNCIL acting with the authority of the CABINET.

Order of Merit The award made personally by the SOVEREIGN to individuals who have excelled in the arts, public life or other fields, when a KNIGHTHOOD is not appropriate. It was instituted in 1902 by King Edward VII, and limited to 24 members; there is a military and a civil class.

Orders of the Day The business down for discussion in the HOUSE OF COMMONS on a particular day, once QUESTION TIME has been completed and any STATEMENTS, Private Notice QUESTIONS or requests for EMERGENCY DEBATES have been dealt with.

call to order The formal opening by the CHAIR of proceedings in a legislature. In both Houses of the US CONGRESS, the call to order is usually at 12 noon.

out of order Conduct or statements when a legislature is in session which violate its STANDING ORDERS or Rules of order.

point of order The pretext under which a member of an elected body may interrupt business, and even a DIVISION or speech by another member, to complain that the rules of the House have been violated. It is often used as a device for raising a political point before the CHAIR has a chance to rule that the point of order is bogus.

special orders In the US HOUSE OF REPRESENTATIVES, the point around 7 p.m. when the regular order of business is completed and members can make long speeches about points of interest to them or their constituents. Since the advent of C-SPAN this part of the legislative day has taken on new importance as up to 250,000 Americans may be watching, unaware that the Chamber is almost empty.

Oregon question The long-unresolved dispute between Britain and America over the western border between the US and Canada, and the status of the Oregon Territory which stretched from California to Russian Alaska. It caused severe tension in the early 1840s before the adoption of the FORTY-NINTH PARALLEL as the dividing line. *See* FIFTY-FOUR FORTY OR FIGHT.

Oreo A Black person considered by others to act like a White one. The term, in use since at least 1968, comes from the cookie of the same name which is black on the outside and white inside.

organ grinder and monkey One of the most devastating put-downs in the 20th-century House of Commons, uttered by Aneurin Bevan (*see* NYE) in the wake of the SUEZ crisis. When Selwyn Lloyd, the Foreign Secretary, rose to answer him instead of Prime Minister Harold Macmillan, Bevan said:

> I am not going to spend any time whatsoever attacking the Foreign Secretary. Quite honestly, I am beginning to feel extremely sorry for him. If we complain about the tune, there is no reason to attack the monkey when the organ grinder is present.

organic change Gradual and natural, yet still fundamental change to a political movement or system; the opposite is change imposed by legislation or some other concrete act. Roy Hattersley, in a slip of the tongue, once told the author that

> The Labour Party is going through a period of orgasmic change.

Orgreave, battle of One of the pivotal confrontations of the 1984–85 MINERS' STRIKE, when a mass picket of several thousand of Arthur Scargill's Yorkshire miners tried to shut down British Steel's coking plant outside Sheffield; there were in fact several confrontations, on 29 and 30 May, 1 June and 18 June 1984. A pitched battle between miners and mounted police ended with a number of arrests, and the miners complaining that undue force had been used against them. A year later the charges against 14 miners charged with riot and unlawful assembly were dropped.

Orpington man The phrase coined, after the stunning Liberal victory in the 1962 Orpington BY-ELECTION, for a disenchanted Tory commuter in Southeast England who kicks over the traces and votes Liberal. Eric Lubbock (later Lord Avebury, 1928–), who won the seat from the Conservatives, triggering a brief Liberal revival, and held it until 1970, was himself a commuter in Orpington, on London's Kentish fringe. He later shrugged off the connection with the average man by announcing that he would leave his body to the inmates of Battersea Dogs' Home.

Osborne judgment The HOUSE OF LORDS ruling in 1909 outlawing the POLITICAL LEVY which Britain's trade unions raised from members for their own campaigning and to finance the infant LABOUR PARTY. W. V. Osborne, a member of the Amalgamated Society of Railway servants (later NUR, now RMT), contended that the union had no right to use its own funds to support the Labour Party or to impose a levy. The legality of the political levy, provided members were allowed to contract out of it, was restored in the 1913 Trade Union Act. The Osborne judgment also hastened the introduction in 1911 of salaries for MPs, Labour members usually having no other source of income.

O'Shea case A landmark case in Australian trade unionism, stemming from the refusal of Clarrie O'Shea, Communist secretary of the Victorian Tramways Employees' Union, to yield up the union's books to allow the recovery of fines imposed on it. Justice John KERR of the Commonwealth Industrial Court jailed O'Shea for contempt on 15 May 1969, and half a million workers went on strike. It took the intervention of an anonymous citizen who had won $200,000 in a lottery to get O'Shea out of jail after five days and end the strike. The penal provisions that Kerr had exercised were never used again. The judge went on to become Sir John and Governor-

General of Australia, and cause Australia's biggest-ever political furore by sacking Prime Minister Gough WHITLAM in 1975.

OSS Office for Strategic Services. The US espionage and sabotage organization which was the forerunner of the CIA and the equivalent of Britain's wartime SOE (Special Operations Executive). It was established by President Roosevelt in June 1942 and put under the direction of his intelligence adviser General "Wild Bill" Donovan (1883–1959). Its role combined information-gathering and analysis with covert operations including GUERRILLA warfare, the rescue of Allied servicemen, and support for underground resistance movements.

Ossewa-Brandwag (Afrik. ox wagon sentinel) A South African pro-NAZI PARAMILITARY organization that emerged in 1938 after the symbolic re-enactment of the Great Trek, achieving popular support in the wake of German victories in the early years of World War II. An elite inner unit, the *stormjaers* (storm-troopers), was dedicated to sabotaging South Africa's war effort. Led by Hans van Renseberg, the OB included numerous prominent Afrikaners such as John Vorster, later Prime Minister (1966–78), and Hendrik van den Bergh, who became head of BOSS. With the defeat of Germany the OB disintegrated and its remnants were incorporated in the National Party as it came in sight of power.

Ossi The nickname given to residents of former East Germany when Germany was reunified in 1990. A Westerner is known as a WESSI.

Ostpolitik (Ger. eastern policy) The dramatic West German policy departure of NORMALIZING relations with East Germany and other East European Communist countries, pioneered by Willy BRANDT (1913–92), the country's SPD Chancellor from 1969 until 1974. Previously West German foreign policy had been constrained by the HALLSTEIN DOCTRINE, prohibiting diplomatic relations with any country that recognized East Germany; Brandt's initiative did much to ease the tension over BERLIN and hasten the end of the COLD WAR. The term OSTPOLITIK was also used before the collapse of Communism in 1989 to signify any conciliatory policy by a Western nation toward the East.

other. the other body The way in which members of each House of the US CONGRESS refer to members of the other in debate.

other place, the or **another place** The similar courtesy which members of the HOUSE OF LORDS and HOUSE OF COMMONS extend to each other. Soon after losing his Commons seat in 1970 and accepting a PEERAGE, Lord George-Brown told an interrupter in the Lords who objected to his abrasive style:

> I could never be shouted down in the other place, and I am not going to be shouted down here.

Other Club, the A dining club founded in 1911 by Winston CHURCHILL and F. E. Smith (later Lord Birkenhead); it was said to be so called because the two rumbustious politicians were not wanted at an existing fraternity known as The Club. The Other Club is still discreetly in existence.

Ottawa agreements The PROTECTIONIST measures agreed at the Imperial Economic Conference in the Canadian capital from 21 July to 20 August 1932, at the height of the GREAT DEPRESSION. They were series of bilateral agreements which established a system of IMPERIAL PREFERENCE, by which Britain and her colonies and dominions exchanged TARIFF preferences to promote trade within the Empire and exclude certain classes of goods from outside it.

our. Our Country Cousin The play which Abraham LINCOLN and his wife were watching at FORD'S THEATRE, Washington, on 14 April 1865 when John Wilkes Booth opened the door of the Presidential box and shot him. The play, first staged in England in 1851, starred Laura Keene.

Our language, our institutions, our laws The motto of the newspaper *Le Canadien*, founded at the end of the 18th century by radicals in Quebec, which became the first focus of French-Canadian nationalism and was suppressed by Sir James Craig, governor of Lower Canada 1807–11. Its owners were sent to prison, but the political movement it had fostered lived on.

out. out of area capability The ability of a nation or alliance – especially NATO – to take military or PEACEKEEPING action outside its accepted sphere of operations.

Outer Seven The original members of the European Free Trade Association (EFTA) on its formation in 1959: Denmark, Norway, Sweden, Austria, Portugal, Switzerland and Britain. "Outer" was a contrast with the "inner" six founder-members of the EUROPEAN COMMUNITY: France, Germany, Italy and the BENELUX countries.

outing A public declaration by militant homosexuals that a prominent person whose sexual orientation has not been a matter of record is in fact "gay". It originates in "out of the closet", the phrase used to describe the open acknowledgment by an individual that they are homosexual. Militant gays reckon that those who conceal their homosexuality are perpetuating the climate of shame that traditionally put everyone thus orientated at a disadvantage.

outnigger, to The phrase used by SEGREGATIONIST politicians in America's Deep South for the adoption of even more RACIST positions than their rivals in order to win White votes. As in "I'm not going to let myself be outniggered by George Wallace".

Oval Office The WHITE HOUSE office of the President of the United States and as such the heart of the government of America, sited since 1934 in the south-east corner of the WEST WING overlooking the ROSE GARDEN. Built for President Theodore Roosevelt and then moved from the centre of the building, its elliptic design was copied from the White House's Blue Room. Its bullet-proof windows have a purplish tinge.

> You know, every day, many important papers come across the desk in that marvellous Oval office, and very few items remain there for long. Got to keep that paper moving or you get inundated. Your snorkel will fill up and there will be no justice. GEORGE BUSH.

The oval office is also the presidency personified. When chief of staff James BAKER rebuked Budget Director David Stockman for giving a damagingly frank interview about REAGANOMICS, he told him: "When you go through the Oval Office door, I want to see that sorry ass of yours dragging on the carpet." And George Bush invoked the sanctity of the room when pressed by a television reporter during the 1992 campaign about an alleged extra-marital affair:

> I'm not going to take any SLEAZE questions. You're perpetuating the sleaze by asking the question, to say nothing of asking it in the Oval office.

over. overflow meeting A gathering in an adjacent hall or in the open comprising members of the public unable to get into a political meeting because the hall is full. Sometimes the speaker at the main meeting will give a further, impromptu address to those outside; on other occasions a loudspeaker link may be arranged.

overheating The situation in an economy which has expanded too fast, so that there is too much money chasing too little capacity and prices and borrowing rise sharply. Demand and interest rates have to be managed to cool the economy down; corrective measures have to be firm enough to have the required effect, but if too severe can precipitate a HARD LANDING and RECESSION.

overkill Originally this was a term from the nightmare vocabulary of nuclear warfare, popularized during the KENNEDY administration, reflecting the ability of the SUPERPOWERS' nuclear arsenals to wipe out the population of the world several times over.

> Why make the rubble bounce? CHURCHILL.

> There is a limit. How many times do you have to hit the target with nuclear weapons? JOHN F. KENNEDY.

It has since come to apply to an excessive response or over-reaction of any kind.

override The ability of the US Congress to force through legislation despite the imposition of a Presidential VETO. It can do this on a vote of two-thirds of both the Senate and the House.

oversight The role of the US Congress in supervising the operations of government, and above all of the spending of Federal funds APPROPRIATED by it. Cynics argue that the word is fortuitously ambiguous, reflecting both the responsibility incumbent on Congress and its frequent "oversights" in omitting to exercise the requisite degree of control.

Ovra The Italian FASCIST secret political police established in 1927 by Arturo Bocchini, Mussolini's chief of security 1926–40. The actual meaning of the word is a mystery; it may have been coined by Il DUCE as a vaguely sinister term to frighten his opponents. Ovra was used to spy on both anti-Fascists and many of the dictator's supporters. Though it used torture to terrorize its victims, its activities were never on the same scale as those of the GESTAPO; at most it employed under 1000 informers.

> To govern you need only two things: policemen, and bands playing in the streets.
> MUSSOLINI, on governing the Italians.

Owen. Owenites (1) The followers of **Robert Owen** (1771–1858), the Welsh-born pioneer of Socialism and the CO-OPERATIVE movement, who in *A New View of Society* (1813) maintained that an individual's character is moulded by his or her social environment. Humbly born, Owen became the manager of a cotton mill at 19 and bought his own at 29, soon becoming a millionaire. He offered model conditions to workers at his mill at New Lanark, Scotland, including a co-operative shop, day nursery, infant school and adult education classes in the village attached to it. An attempt to promote similar ideals in the US, through a manufacturing community in Indiana, lost him most of his fortune; New Lanark was restored to much of its former glory in the 1970s. (2) The followers of the former Labour Foreign Secretary and GANG OF FOUR member **Dr. David** (now Lord) **Owen** (1938–), who in 1987 as leader of the SDP resisted the Liberal leader David Steel's post-election call for a MERGER of the two parties. With most Social Democrats opting to join a merged party (*see* LIBERAL DEMOCRATS), Owen kept a separate SDP going with the support of two fellow-MPs, John Cartwright and Rosie Barnes, and in February 1989 nearly won a by-election at Richmond, Yorkshire. However the party failed to establish itself, and Owen wound it up the following summer after it was outpolled in the Bootle by-election by the OFFICIAL MONSTER RAVING LOONY PARTY. In 1992 John Major appointed him as the EC's co-chairman of the Geneva peace talks on the Bosnian civil war, alongside former US Secretary of State Cyrus Vance. Owen's mission, which continued well into 1993, involved extensive SHUTTLE DIPLOMACY to prepare the constructive but doomed Vance–Owen plan, and frequent visits to the war zone.

Dr. Owen was seen by his supporters as a man of principle, by his allies as infuriating; Steel said:

> I am reminded of Dame Sybil Thorndike's comment on her long marriage. She considered divorce never, murder frequently. With Dr. Owen it is murder, occasionally.

Labour simply regarded him as a traitor. Neil KINNOCK accused him of having "an ego fat on arrogance and drunk on ambition", or being "orthopaedically arrogant in every corpuscle" and of "purveying retread Thatcherism"; Dennis Skinner (*see* BEAST OF BOLSOVER) termed him more simply "a pompous git" (when the Speaker protested, he withdrew the word "pompous").

own. own goal A terrorist attack, usually a bombing, in which the would-be perpetrator is killed by his or her own weapon. The term comes from soccer, where an own goal is one scored by a player against his own team. It acquired its political connotation in the British Army in NORTHERN IRELAND in the early 1970s for the at first numerous occasions when IRA terrorists blew themselves up.

own resources A EUROPEAN COMMUNITY term for the amount which the EC can budget to spend each year, which has been received from member states as a fixed share of their GDP. The phrase specifically refers to the size of that share: historically it has been 1.2%, but Jacques DELORS lobbied hard for a more ambitious budget requiring an increase, and the 1992 Edinburgh summit agreed a compromise under which own resources would initially be pegged, but would rise to 1.27% by 1999.

Oxford by-election The notorious electoral test of the MUNICH agreement in the autumn of 1938, when A. D. Lindsay, Master of Balliol College, stood as an anti-APPEASEMENT candidate against the official Conservative nominee, Quintin Hogg (later Lord Hailsham) in a contest that POLARIZED the city, the University and the country. Harold Macmillan, who had resigned the Tory whip, and the young Edward Heath campaigned for Lindsay, but Hogg ran out the winner to begin a Parliamentary career that included 42 years on the Conservative Front BENCH and the dramatic renunciation of his title in a vain bid for the Tory leadership.

Oxford group *See* Moral REARMAMENT.

oxygen of publicity Respectability or glamour conferred on an organization or activity that is illegal, dangerous or unacceptable as a result of undue attention from the media. Margaret Thatcher gave currency to the phrase when she protested against the publicity, especially on television, given to terrorists and the IRA in particular; it was actually coined by Britain's then Chief Rabbi Lord Jakobovits. Mrs. Thatcher told the American Bar Association's London meeting on 15 July 1985:

> Democracies must try to find ways to starve the terrorist and the hijackers of the oxygen of publicity on which they depend.

Ozone Man George BUSH's scornful nickname for Sen. Albert Gore (1948–), conferred in the closing days of the 1992 Presidential campaign. Bush intended to link the Tennessee senator with cranky environmentalists by playing up the fact that the Democratic Vice-Presidential nominee had written a book, *Earth in the Balance*, drawing attention to the threat to the ozone layer (*see* MONTREAL PROTOCOL) and the risks of global warming. Gore had the last laugh when the Democratic ticket ousted Bush and Vice-President Dan QUAYLE from office.

P

P2 The Masonic lodge headed by the shadowy, ruthless and corrupt Licio Gelli (1926–), which in the late 1970s gained a stranglehold on the Italian political ESTABLISHMENT, bringing down the CHRISTIAN DEMOCRAT government when its activities were exposed in 1981. In its prime the lodge, said to have links with the Naples-based *Camorra* crime syndicates, had four Cabinet ministers, 38 Parliamentary deputies and 195 military officers as members. Gelli, a former FASCIST who once gave Pope Paul VI a gold-plated bed as an attempted bribe, became head of the lodge in 1976. He was tried for complicity in a string of right-wing terrorist outrages, and convicted of acting as paymaster to the bombers who killed 86 people at Bologna station. Gelli fled to Switzerland, and was EXTRADITED in 1987 to face further, minor charges; in 1992 he was reported to be rebuilding the lodge's influence as its former 16-strong "board of directors", including generals and five high-ranking secret service officers, went on trial on charges up to plotting to overthrow the constitution.

PAC (1) Political Action Committee. In the US, a body set up by business, labor or single-interest groups (pro-Israel, PRO-LIFE, *etc.*) to lobby Congress and raise campaign funds for candidates who support the cause or can be won over, or to defeat its opponents. They have thrived since the early 1970s when Congress imposed legal curbs on funding presidential, but not congressional, campaigns, and now dispense twice as much money as the parties themselves; Bill Clinton was elected President in 1992 on a pledge to curb spending by PACs. They have had the advantage of being relatively impervious to political criticism, NCPAC (National Conservative PAC) chairman John T. Dolan observing:

> A group like ours could lie through its teeth and the candidate it helps stays clean.

The benefits offered by support from a PAC are not lost on the politicians themselves. Business and Industry PAC manager Bernadette Budde confessed: "I called this place the doctor's office because we had [politicians] lined up waiting to come in." Those seeing the impact of lobbying by PACs on the governmental process question their place in a democratic system:

> One step away from bribery.
>
> LLOYD CUTLER, Carter White House counsel.

(2) Public Accounts Committee. At Westminster, the most influential SELECT COMMITTEE of the Commons, with an effective record as a watchdog of public spending and the application of funds. (3) Pan Africanist Congress. The only rival to (though much smaller than) the African National Congress as a Black freedom movement in South Africa. More militant than the ANC with a MAOIST slant and the slogan "one settler, one bullet", it has 125,000 members; its military wing, the **Azanian People's Liberation Army**, claims 750 cadres trained in Libya, and in Tanzania by Chinese instructors. The PAC was founded in 1959 with Robert Sobukwe as its president after a split with MOSCOW-LINERS in the Transvaal ANC. Sobukwe explained:

> To us the struggle is a national struggle; to the ANC it is a class struggle. We claim Africa for the Africans; the ANC claims South Africa for all.

Like the ANC, the PAC was banned in 1960; the ban was lifted in 1990, but the PAC refused to join the CODESA talks on a democratic constitution unless One Man, One VOTE elections were held first.

Pacific rim Collective term for the economically powerful nations of East Asia, notably Japan and South Korea, and their strategically-important non-Communist neighbours. It was increasingly used under the Reagan administration, with its roots in California, to embrace both those Asian powers and America's western states, and as shorthand for a Pacific-orientated range of policies.

Pacific scandal The Canadian scandal which brought about the fall of Sir John Macdonald's Conservative government in 1873. Macdonald had won re-election in 1872 on funds secretly solicited from Sir Hugh Allen's consortium for building a trans-Canadian railway, in return for which Macdonald awarded him the contract. The affair was dubbed "the Thermopylae of Canadian virtue" by the *Toronto Globe*.

> By the base betrayal of private communications, the names of certain members of the Government, including myself, were mixed up in the obtaining of these subscriptions. Sir JOHN MACDONALD.

pacification The process, usually military, of subduing or eliminating enemy or terrorist activity by rendering the affected area inhospitable or unusable. Unlike PEACEKEEPING, it is carried out during hostilities to win peace, typically by securing the co-operation of the local population or removing them from the area. Buildings, food supplies, crops, animals and ground cover that could offer support or protection to the enemy may be destroyed. During the VIETNAM WAR US forces engaged in a policy of pacification to lower the morale of the VIET CONG and recapture rural areas.

Pacifico, Don David Pacifico, a Spanish Jew born in Gibraltar and thus claiming to be a British subject despite having been naturalized by the Portuguese. At Easter 1846, an anti-Semitic mob burst into Pacifico's house in Athens, manhandled his wife and child, stole jewellery and set fire to the building. The authorities refused to compensate Pacifico, who had been the Portuguese consul, and he appealed to Britain. In 1847 Palmerston (*see* PAM) threatened force if Pacifico were not compensated and also given £27,000 he claimed to be owed by the Portuguese government. Two years later British ships blockaded Piraeus in pursuit of this and several other grievances, Palmerston declaring:

> It is our long forbearance, and not our precipitation, that deserves remark.

Greece paid Pacifico £8500; his claim against the Portuguese was found by arbitrators to be essentially fraudulent and he was awarded just £150. Palmerston (*see* CIVIS ROMANUS SUM) treated the episode as the height of British influence for good; the truth was rather murkier.

pacifism The belief that the use of violence under any circumstances is immoral: the basis for all specifically anti-war movements. With strong roots in the Society of Friends (Quakers), pacifism became an organized political force in the early 1930s, especially in the UK through the PEACE PLEDGE UNION, as a public horrified by World War I sought to avert a second conflict. Since 1945 pacifism has given rise to a loosely-organized "peace movement", has been a major influence on the anti-nuclear movement (*see* CND) and has been a factor in the opposition to conflicts from VIETNAM to the GULF WAR.

> My pacifism is not based on any intellectual theory but on deep antipathy to every form of cruelty and hatred.
> ALBERT EINSTEIN, on the outbreak of World War I.

packed meeting A phrase carelessly used to describe an overcrowded meeting, but intended for one which a faction has rigged by ensuring that enough of its members are present to distort any debate and win any vote that may be taken.

pact. Pact of Steel A formal ALLIANCE between Germany and Italy, concluded in May 1939, which cemented the AXIS by committing Italy to support Germany in the event of war. Mussolini coined the term after wisely abandoning his first choice, "Pact of Blood".

non-aggression pact An agreement between two potential adversaries not to attack each other, sometimes concluded by the stronger power as an exercise in cynicism.

Paddy Pantsdown The nickname bestowed by the *Sun* on the British politician Paddy (Jeremy John Dunham) Ashdown, (1941–), leader from 1988 of the LIBERAL DEMOCRATS, when in 1992 he disclosed a five-year-old affair with his former secretary. The publicity did Ashdown little harm after the immediate trauma to himself and his family; his party's poll rating rose by 6%, an increase of one half.

pages In the US CAPITOL, the corps of young people, chosen by the legislators themselves, who run errands for them. Used in the House since at least 1800 and the senate since 1829, they keep legislators' desks filled – and the Senate snuffboxes – and sit on the steps of the Senate rostrum and on benches in the House in case they are needed. Visitors frequently ask them for advice; one new page, asked why the bells kept ringing for a QUORUM, said:

> I don't know. But I think maybe one of them has escaped.

There are 66 pages aged 16 to 18 in the House, and 30 aged 14 to 16 in the Senate; until 1971 all were boys. Pages of both sexes have on occasion been subjected to sexual harassment by Congressmen. Before reporting for work they attend high school in the LIBRARY OF CONGRESS.

pair The arrangement under which a legislator may arange to miss important votes if another from the other side of the house does the same. At Westminster, pairs are made on a lasting basis, and registered with the relevant party WHIPS. The opponent with whom a member regularly makes such arrangements is known as his or her pair. When the governing party has a narrow majority, the Opposition may step up pressure by refusing to make pairing arrangements. In the US Congress, pairing was operating by the 1820s; pairs are announced by the CLERK OF THE HOUSE and listed in the CONGRESSIONAL RECORD after the names of members not voting.

breaking a pair The ultimate in Parliamentary sharp practice, turning up to vote when a pair has been made.
general pair In Congress, an arrangement to cover several votes on differing subjects over a period of days.
live pair A US legislator who is able to vote despite being paired, so withdraws his vote and declares himself "present" to protect the other member.
pairing whip *See* WHIP.
unpaired A member who lacks a pair on the other side, and thus is unable to get away (*see also* BISQUE).

Paisley. Paisleyite A supporter of the Rev. **Ian Paisley** (1926–), MP, MEP, Free Presbyterian minister and leader of the militantly Protestant and predominantly working-class Democratic UNIONIST party in NORTHERN IRELAND. From the 1960s into the 1980s he led LOYALIST opposition to all efforts to introduce POWER SHARING between the Protestant majority and the Catholic minority, and to any links with the Irish Republic, notably the ANGLO-IRISH AGREEMENT.

Palace, the Westminster shorthand for BUCKINGHAM PALACE, official London residence of the Sovereign, and for the political influence of the monarch and his or her advisers, *e.g.* "the Palace are very upset about this".
palace guard US term for the inner core of WHITE HOUSE aides who control ACCESS to the President. The term was first used of H. R. Haldeman and John Ehrlichman who, critics claimed, sealed off Richard Nixon.
Palace of Westminster *See* WESTMINSTER.
palace revolution A revolution within the clique or elite governing a country, power changing hands without the people being in any way involved. The term is said to date from an occasion in a Latin American republic when the ruling general was woken by a fellow-member of the junta to be told he was no longer President. The new President went downstairs to announce that he had taken power, only to be ousted by the head of the palace guard. The phrase has come to refer to any upheaval within a self-contained organization.

Palestinian An Arab inhabitant of, or refugee from, the WEST BANK and GAZA STRIP, occupied by ISRAEL following the SIX-DAY WAR of 1967. Though the West Bank was previously part of Jordan and Gaza was administered by Egypt, the Palestinians under Israeli rule have developed a strong desire for their own state, an aspiration promoted by the PLO which regards itself both as the legitimate representative of the Palestinians and their GOVERNMENT-IN-WAITING.

Pam Nickname of **Henry John Temple, Viscount Palmerston** (1784–1865), who was twice British Prime Minister (1855–58, 1859–65). A WHIG who flirted with Toryism, Palmerston held office for 48 years altogether, and as Foreign Secretary and Prime Minister during the CRIMEAN WAR and US CIVIL WAR was the embodiment of British world power. Metternich saw this coming; when Palmerston was denied the Foreign Office in 1845, Metternich observed: "We can sleep easier in our beds." Queen Victoria was not amused by his robust line toward other European rulers, most of them her relatives. She once wrote that "he will be a source of mischief to this country as long as he lives". And on his death she wrote:

> We had, God knows, terrible trouble with him about foreign affairs. Still, as Prime Minister, he managed affairs at home well, and behaved to me well, but I never liked him.

His relations with the Queen were not helped by his reputation – justified – as a roué. After Palmerston, at the age of 69, had displayed "temerity" in the bedroom of a female house guest at WINDSOR, the diarist Charles Greville recorded: "The Queen has not forgotten and will never forgive it." Of the same incident involving a Mrs. Brand, Prince Albert noted: "He had barricaded the door and would have consummated his fiendish scheme by violence had not the miraculous efforts of his victim and such assistance attracted by her screams saved her." Lady Stanley complained of the brusque way he courted married women well into his 80s: "Ha! Ha! I see it all – beautiful woman, neglected by her husband, allow me, *etc.* . . ." Palmerston was famed for his temperament and unpredictability. According to Princess Lieven, "Europe depended on which leg – the left or the right – he put out of bed first." Lord Lytton wrote: "Palmerston is Mama England's spoilt child and the more mischief he does, the more she admires him. 'What spirit he has!' cries Mama – and smash goes the crockery." And Greville observed: "His great fault is want of punctuality, and never keeping an engagement if it did not suit him, keeping everybody waiting for hours on his pleasure or caprice." Indeed it was a standard saying in London society that "Palmerston always misses the soup." His freewheeling attitude earned him the hostility of the rising Disraeli (*see* DIZZY), who sharply observed: "He will not give trouble about principles." On a personal level he was even more scathing, describing him as "at best ginger beer, not champagne", and "that great Apollo of aspiring understrappers, menacing Russia with a perfumed cane". Palmerston's last words were reputedly: "Die, my dear Doctor? That's the last thing I shall do."

> If the Devil has a son
> It is surely Palmerston.
> ANON.

Panama Canal treaties The treaties under which America undertook to hand control of the Panama canal to Panama by the year 2000 in return for its permanent neutralization and permanent rights of passage for US warships, and return the CANAL ZONE to Panama immediately. Concluded by the CARTER administration, they were ratified by the Senate in 1978 by the narrowest of margins after a conservative rearguard action.

> We built it, we paid for it, and we're going to keep it.
> RONALD REAGAN.

> The culmination of that pattern of surrender and APPEASEMENT that has cost us so much all over the world.
> Senator ORRIN HATCH.

Panama invasion The US intervention in December 1989 to overthrow Panama's strongman Manuel Noriega after disputed elections, and secure his prosecution in America for drug-running. US troops swiftly broke resistance from the Panamanian military and Guillermo Endora, apparent winner of the elections, was sworn in as president. Noriega held out for 11 days, eventually emerging from the Vatican embassy to give himself up. President BUSH was criticized in Latin America for sending in the troops, but his action came to be seen as justified. Noriega claimed that he had been put into the drugs trade by the CIA and that Bush must have known this; nevertheless a Florida court in July 1992 sentenced him to 40 years in jail.

Pandit (Hindi. a wise and learned man) The courtesy title accorded in India to Jawaharlal NEHRU (1889–1964), who led the nation to independence and was its first Prime Minister. *See also* PUNDIT.

panel (1) In the UK, a list of qualified persons compiled by a political party, from which candidates for local or Parliamentary election may be chosen. (2) In opinion polling, a group of individual voters who are repeatedly questioned during a campaign to detect shifts in opinion.

pan-Serbism The feeling for a greater Serbia, and for the rights of Serbs in neighbouring republics, traditionally with the sympathy of Russia. Such sentiment sparked off WORLD WAR I through the assassination of Archduke Franz Ferdinand in SARAJEVO in 1914 by a Bosnian Serb, Gavrilo Princip, and contributed to the bloodshed following Croatia's secession from Yugoslavia in 1991, and Bosnia's the following year.

Papa Doc Nickname for François Duvalier (1907–71), President-for-Life of Haiti, who was sustained in office by a reign of terror conducted by the TONTONS MACOUTE. His son Jean-Claude Duvalier (1951–), who succeeded him and ruled for 15 years before being overthrown, was known as Baby Doc.

Papa Dop The unflattering nickname given by left-wingers to Georgios Papadopoulos (1919–), leader of the Right-wing dictatorship imposed by the Greek COLONELS in 1967. The comparison with the Haitian leader was intentional, signifying the savagery with which the Colonels treated their opponents.

papabile Suitable for the highest office, from the Ital. *papabile* (fit to be Pope).

paper candidate *See* CANDIDATE.

paper tiger An apparent threat posing no danger. The term originated in 19th-century China (in Chinese *tsuh lao fu*) and was popularized by Mao Tse-Tung (*see* CHAIRMAN MAO).

> The atomic bomb is a paper tiger which the US reactionaries use to scare people. It looks terrible, but in fact it isn't. All reactionaries are paper tigers.
> MAO TSE-TUNG, 1946.

Papists Hostile term for Roman Catholics, first used in 16th-century England and subsequently by anti-Catholic political groups into Victorian times (and more recently in NORTHERN IRELAND). *See also* GORDON RIOTS.

para-. paramilitary (1) A semi-official or secret political organization which takes on the trappings of a military force, frequently also having an outright terrorist wing to press home its aims. Also an individual member of such a body. A typical paramilitary group is the UDA (Ulster Defence Association), whose members drill and wear uniforms, yet which operated within the law for over 20 years; its murkier activities are carried on by nominally-separate groups. A well-known US example was the BLACK PANTHERS. (2) Civil forces or organizations that legitimately support military forces.

parastatal Especially in Africa, a state-owned concern engaged in commercial activity, frequently on a monopoly basis.

pardon The exemption of an individual from the rigours of the law for an action which either threatens them with criminal charges or has already led to a conviction. The most controversial has been President Gerald FORD's pardon of Richard Nixon (*see* TRICKY DICK) for his role in WATERGATE. Just one month after Nixon's resignation in August 1974, Ford caused a political storm by announcing a "full, complete and absolute pardon" for his predecessor. This freed Nixon from any threat of prosecution, though many of those involved in the conspiracy subsequently went to jail. Had Nixon been IMPEACHED, Ford would have been barred by the Constitution from pardoning him. Ford justified his action by saying:

> I do believe that the buck stops here, that I cannot rely upon public opinion polls to tell me what is right. I do believe . . . that I, not as President but as a humble servant of God, will receive justice without mercy if I fail to show mercy.

The furore died down, and Ford's action – if premature – is now widely seen as having helped the healing process. A further furore broke out at Christmas 1992 when President BUSH, just before leaving office, pardoned President Reagan's Defence Secretary Caspar Weinberger who was about to stand trial on charges of lying to Congress over the IRAN-CONTRA affair. Shortly before the 1992 election, leaked testimony from Weinberger not only indicated that he had known more of the affair than he had admitted, but that Bush, despite his denials, was in the LOOP. Weinberger claimed the charges against him were a political stunt; Democrats that Bush had pardoned him to avoid being himself called to testify under oath.

Parfumée. la Parfumée (Fr. the perfumed one) Nickname for Edith Cresson (1934–), the French SOCIALIST politician who was President Mitterrand's highly-controversial Prime Minister for a brief period in 1991–92.

Paris. Paris Club Also known as the **Group of Ten**, an informal forum under the auspices of the French Treasury that provides a channel between Western officials in overseeing government-to-government loans, especially to assist the THIRD WORLD. The nations first met in Paris in 1962, agreeing to lend money to the International Monetary Fund (*see* IMF) and inaugurated the concept of SPECIAL DRAWING RIGHTS as a standard unit of account. The ten are Belgium, Canada, France, Italy, Japan, the Netherlands, Sweden, West Germany, the UK and America.

Paris Commune The working-class revolution in Paris in 1871 after France's defeat in the FRANCO-PRUSSIAN WAR. The Commune, backed by the National Guard, abolished CONSCRIPTION, separated Church and State, reduced officials' salaries to those of skilled workmen, brought women into government and planned to transfer empty factories to workers' control. On 21 May, the regular army of the new VERSAILLES-based French Republic under Thiers entered Paris, executed 20,000 COMMUNARDS, arrested 36,000 citizens and jailed or deported 15,000. Engels hailed the Commune as "the dictatorship of the proletariat"; Marx more realistically termed it "a heroic self-holocaust".

Paris Peace talks The long-running talks aimed at ending the VIETNAM WAR which opened in May 1968, finally producing an **Agreement** in January 1973 that America would end direct military aid to its southern ally. The final talks, between a US delegation led by Henry KISSINGER and North Vietnamese officials headed by Le Duc Tho were hailed as having brought peace, and earned both men the NOBEL PEACE PRIZE. But the American withdrawal led to a North Vietnamese takeover (*see* DECENT INTERVAL).

Paris summit A pioneering SUMMIT meeting between Dwight D. Eisenhower (*see* IKE), Nikita Khruschev, Harold Macmillan (*see* SUPERMAC) and Charles DE GAULLE, which was scheduled for 16 May 1960. All four leaders arrived in Paris, but the summit was abandoned at the last minute when Eisenhower refused Khruschev's demand that he apologize for the U2 incident.

Charter of Paris The agreement reached by the CSCE countries in Paris in November 1990 to monitor threats to peace throughout Europe and endeavour to prevent conflicts breaking out in and between the countries experiencing their first freedom after the collapse of Communism. CSCE proved impotent when war broke out in former Yugoslavia the following year; the meeting was most memorable as Margaret Thatcher's final appearance on the international stage, the crucial vote denying her re-election as Conservative leader on the first ballot taking place while she was in Paris.

Treaty of Paris (1) The treaty concluded on 3 September 1783 that ended the American WAR OF INDEPENDENCE. Britain recognized American independence and made peace, and the new republic gained generous boundaries and the right to fish in Canadian waters. (2) The treaty of 30 March 1856 which embodied the settlement of the CRIMEAN WAR, an ARMISTICE having been agreed in Paris a month before. The key point was the demilitarization of the Black Sea, a major gain for Britain and setback for Russia. (3) The treaty signed on 10 December 1898 which disposed of Spain's empire after its defeat in the SPANISH-AMERICAN WAR. The treaty gave Cuba its independence, ceded the Philippines to the US for $20 million and also gave America Guam and Puerto Rico. (4) The treaty of 27 May 1952 between France, West Germany, Italy and BENELUX which agreed to form a European Defence Community. The community was still-born because the French NATIONAL ASSEMBLY refused to ratify the treaty, largely because it was seen as a back-door means of German REARMAMENT. However the Western European Union (*see* WEU), serving many of the same purposes, was agreed on soon after.

parish (1) In rural England, the smallest unit of local government based on the area originally served by a village's parish church. The parish council or parish meeting is the governing body.

parish pump politics Politics of an extremely parochial nature; indeed the word parochial is derived from parish.

(2) In Louisiana, the unit of government corresponding to a COUNTY in the rest of the United States.

parity The situation in an elected body, especially at local level, when two parties enjoy the same level of representation. At election times parity is gained by the party making ground, lost by the party falling back.

Parkinson affair The scandal which curtailed, and seemed for a time to have ruined, the political career of **Cecil** (later Lord) **Parkinson** (1932–), one of Mrs. Thatcher's favourite Ministers. In May 1983 Parkinson, who had just chaired the Conservative party to a landslide victory, told Mrs. Thatcher his former secretary Sara Keays, with whom he had had a long affair, was expecting his baby. Parkinson decided to stay with his wife and daughters. That October, the week before the Tory party conference, *The Times* broke the story and other papers gave it banner headlines. The Labour Party conference was in session, one delegate exclaiming from the rostrum:

> Is there nothing the Tories won't do to keep us off the front page?

Parkinson, by now Trade and Industry Secretary, stood his ground, with Downing Street declaring:

> The question of Cecil Parkinson's resignation does not, and will not, arise.

The embattled Minister won a warm but not euphoric reception when he appeared with his wife at the Tories' Blackpool gathering. But after further revelations from Miss Keays he resigned on the final night of the assembly. The spurned Miss Keays duly had a daughter, and an embittered Parkinson went into the wilderness. He came back in 1987 as Energy Secretary and later as Transport Secretary, but when Mrs. Thatcher was ousted in 1989 he was out of the running for the Tory leadership, and left the Government.

> Had Cecil been a Minister of the THIRD REPUBLIC, the Parkinson Affair would have made him President.
>
> JULIAN CRITCHLEY MP (Con.).

> Q: Why is Cecil Parkinson like MFI?
> A: One loose screw, and the whole Cabinet falls apart.
>
> ANON.

Parliament (Fr. *parlement*, a meeting to exchange views) (1) In Britain and COMMONWEALTH countries, the Houses that make up the LEGISLATURE and (as the House of Lords tends to be overlooked) the embodiment of democracy. Cromwell's victory in the English Civil War created an image of Parliament as all-powerful; in 1648 the Earl of Pembroke declared:

> A Parliament can do anything but make a man a woman, and a woman a man.

Edmund BURKE told the electors of Bristol that "Parliament is a deliberative assembly of one nation. You choose a Member indeed, but when you have chosen him, he is not the Member for Bristol, but he is a Member of Parliament." And Anthony Trollope, just as loftily, wrote: "I have often thought that to sit in the British Parliament should be the highest object of ambition to every educated Englishman".

Parliament does not always inspire such noble thoughts. Prior to the Union of 1707, a popular Scottish prayer was: "God bless the Houses of Parliament, and overrule their deliberations to the benefit of the common people." Thomas Carlyle advised that "Parliament will train you to talk; and above all things to hear, with patience, unlimited quantities of foolish talk". He also argued that "a Parliament with newspaper reporters firmly established in it is an entity which by its very nature cannot do work, but talk only". And the Russian jurist Konstantin Podednostsev (1827–1907) maintained that

> Parliaments are the great lie of our time.

Charles II described Parliament, despite what it had done to his father, as "better than a play". In Victorian times Robert Louis Stevenson observed: "We all know what Parliament is – and we are all ashamed of it." Sir Cyril Smith (*see* BIG CYRIL) termed it "the longest-running farce in the West End". And former Beatle George Harrison, backing the Natural Law Party in the 1992 election, told an Albert Hall rally:

> All we need now is to get rid of those stiffs in Parliament and we'd be laughing.

(2) A Parliament. The duration of a Parliamentary term, in Britain a maximum of five years and frequently less. Radicals have traditionally advocated shorter, fixed-term Parliaments – in the CHARTISTS' case with elections every year to increase ACCOUNTABILITY. Henry Labouchère (*see* LABBY) wrote at the turn of the century: "Long Parliaments are as fatal to sound business as long credits are to sound trade."

Parliament Acts The legislation passed in 1911 and 1949 under which the House of Lords lost its right to kill Bills passed by the Commons (it retains a DELAYING POWER, reduced from two years to one in 1949), and any say in the passage of the Budget and other MONEY BILLS. The first Act, which also reduced the maximum life of a Parliament from seven years to five, was pushed through by ASQUITH's Liberal government, after two general elections in 1910 had given it a MANDATE, following the Lords' rejection of the PEOPLE'S BUDGET. Only the threat to create hundreds of Liberal peers broke the Lords' resistance; they approved it finally on 10 August 1911 (*see* HEDGERS AND DITCHERS) by just 131 votes to 114 with George V writing: "I am spared any further humiliation." The second stemmed from the Lords' rejection of the ATTLEE government's plans for steel NATIONALIZATION. It is now up to the Government to decide whether to override the Lords if it defeats a Bill. In 1991 the WAR CRIMES ACT was pushed through by the MAJOR government despite bitter opposition from the upper house.

Parliament Square The square at the heart of Britain's government quarter, whose non-descript grassy and paved centre with the odd tree is graced by CHURCHILL's statue. The TREASURY abuts part of its north side, which faces up Parliament Street to WHITEHALL and the CENOTAPH. To the east lie the way to Westminster Bridge, NEW PALACE YARD and WESTMINSTER HALL, to the south St. Margaret's church, Parliament's own, and to the west Victoria Street and the Middlesex Guildhall.

High Court of Parliament One of the British Parliament's official titles, reflecting both its function as the ultimate arbiter on behalf of the people and, more specifically, the judicial functions of the HOUSE OF LORDS as the ultimate court of appeal.

hung Parliament *See* HUNG.

Imperial Parliament A term popular in the early 20th century for Westminster's predominance among the Parliaments of the British Empire, and also for its role as the legislature for the entire United Kingdom.

Parliamentarian (1) At Westminster, a politician who demonstrates outstanding commitment to, and grasp of, the ways of the House of Commons. Such a figure frequently infuriates his own party and makes common cause with rebels on the other side of the House who feel their rights are being threatened. Three outstanding Parliamentarians of recent times have been Tony BENN, Michael Foot (*see* WURZEL GUMMIDGE) and Enoch POWELL. (2) In the US Congress, the senior official of the House of Representatives who advises the SPEAKER on procedure and on what is or is not permitted.

Parliamentary agents The specialized legal firms operating in the Westminster area who will present Private BILLS to Parliament and lodge objections to them.

Parliamentary Commissioner In Britain, the official title of the OMBUDSMAN.

Parliamentary draftsmen The legal technicians in WHITEHALL who draft Government legislation and make sure that amendments and Private Members' BILLS are worded in watertight fashion.

Parliamentary leper Harold WILSON's electrifying description when Parliament opened on 5 November 1964 of Peter Griffiths (1928–), who had won Smethwick from Labour at the previous month's election with a campaign widely perceived as RACIST. This campaign, though not Griffiths himself, was said to have spawned the slogan: "If you want a nigger for your neighbour, vote Labour." Wilson told the Commons:

> Smethwick Conservatives can have the satisfaction of having topped the poll, of having sent a Member who, until another election returns him to oblivion, will serve his time here as a Parliamentary leper.

Griffiths lost his seat in 1966, but made a non-controversial return in 1979 as MP for Portsmouth North.

Parliamentary occasion An event at Westminster considered memorable by those present, for instance the Saturday emergency debate on 3 April 1982 that followed the Argentine invasion of the FALKLANDS.

Parliamentary Private Secretary (PPS) At Westminster, an MP probably bound for Ministerial office who serves as the unsalaried "eyes and ears" of a Minister, sitting behind him or her at QUESTION TIME. A PPS is regarded as part of the PAYROLL VOTE, and is expected to resign if he or she fails to vote with the Government on a controversial matter.

Parliamentary Secretary or Under-Secretary The most junior Ministerial rank in the British government. Most Departments have two or more, carrying out duties delegated to them by the more senior members of the team.

Parliamentary system The system in which the head of government is based in the LEGISLATURE, as opposed to the PRESIDENTIAL system, as in France or the United States, where the leader of the nation is elected separately and doubles as the HEAD OF STATE.

Manual of Parliamentary Practice The document drawn up by Thomas JEFFERSON in 1800 which set out the first rules of ORDER and procedure for the US CONGRESS. They still form part of the rules of the HOUSE OF

REPRESENTATIVES, which Jefferson reckoned needed them more than the Senate.

Parnell. Parnellites The supporters of **Charles Stewart Parnell** (1846–91), the UNCROWNED KING OF IRELAND, who during the 1880s led a militant campaign at Westminster for HOME RULE. From a Protestant landowning family in Co. Wicklow, Parnell entered the Commons in 1875 and was soon manipulating Parliamentary procedure to obstruct Government business. This attribute, and his Presidency of the Irish National Land League which raised £70,000 in America to revive agriculture after the IRISH POTATO FAMINE, led Irish MPs to elect him their chairman in 1880. Parnell's advocacy of BOYCOTTs against absentee landowners led to violence and his imprisonment with 34 other Irish MPs. But he was freed under the KILMAINHAM TREATY after undertaking to denounce Nationalist excesses in return for a Government promise to soft-pedal on rent arrears. In 1885 the 86 Parnellite MPs threw their weight behind Gladstone's first Home Rule Bill. They brought down Lord SALISBURY's government, but the Bill failed because of defections by Liberal MPs. When the Unionists won the ensuing election, Parnell, described by T. P. O'Connor as "a madman of genius", was thrown into an alliance with Gladstone. This was only a marriage of convenience for Parnell, the Liberal G. W. E. Russell observing:

> He hated England, he condemned the House of Commons, he despised the Liberals much more profoundly than the Tories, and he regarded his followers as merely voters, or at best fit for work too dirty for a gentleman to undertake.

In 1889 Parnell was cleared by a Commission of Enquiry of complicity in the PHOENIX PARK and other outrages, in which he had been implicated by a forged letter reproduced in *The Times*. Richard Piggott, the forger, fled to Madrid and shot himself. But his character was only briefly rehabilitated; the following year Captain O'Shea, husband of Parnell's mistress Kitty, cited him in the divorce court and costs were awarded against the Irish leader. The Irish party first re-elected him as leader, then rescinded their decision after pressure from Gladstone; Campbell-Bannerman declared: "He has shown by his acts that he is unfit to be the leader of a political party." The following year Parnell died suddenly in Brighton, five months after his marriage to Mrs. O'Shea, and in the 1892 election all but nine of his party lost their seats.

> The fall of Parnell left Ireland with a dead god instead of a leader. G. M. YOUNG.

> As a Protestant he was probably the only man who might eventually have conciliated Ulster. CHURCHILL.

partisan (1) A guerrilla fighter for independence, notably a member of Communist units in Nazi-occupied Yugoslavia (*see* TITO), Italy and Russia during WORLD WAR II. (2) A participant in the political process who puts his or her party or faction above all other considerations.

> In the hour of danger there is no partisanship. In that hour we shall all stand as one people in support of America.
> House Minority Leader
> JOSEPH W. MARTIN, after Pearl Harbor.

partition The division of a territory, usually along ethnic or religious lines, in an effort to create homogenous communities. Notable 20th-century examples are Ireland (by Treaty between Britain and the newly-formed IRISH FREE STATE), India (by Britain in creating independent states of India and Pakistan, after Muslims made it clear they would not accept a single Hindu-majority Indian state), Germany (through the creation of separate western and Communist states in the great powers' respective zones), Korea (in settlement of the KOREAN WAR, creating Communist and free states), Vietnam (under the GENEVA AGREEMENT following the French defeat at DIEN BIEN PHU) and Cyprus (after Turkey's occupation of northern Cyprus in 1974 (not internationally recognized)). None has entirely solved the problem it was set up to remedy, and Pakistan has itself split in two. But only Vietnam and Germany have been reunited.

party The basic unit of political organization, bringing together people of supposedly like mind. The American scholar James Sundquist defines party as "the tie that binds, the glue that fastens, the bridge that unites the disparate institutions that make up the government". It was not always so. In the 17th and 18th centuries parties were regarded as inherently harmful to the process, Alexander Pope describing them as "the madness of many, for the gains of the few" and George Savile, Earl of Halifax, asserting: "The best party is but a kind of conspiracy against the nation. Ignorance maketh most men go into a party, and shame keepeth them from getting out of it."

The FOUNDING FATHERS of the United States were deeply divided over whether there should be political parties. George WASHINGTON, in his Farewell Address, said: "Let me . . . warn you in the most solemn manner against the baneful effects of the spirit of party generally". And John ADAMS confessed: "There is nothing I dread so much as the division of the Republic into two great parties." But James MADISON argued that "No free country has ever been without parties, which are a natural offspring of freedom", and eventually his view prevailed.

The mood changed in England, too. In the 1790s Edmund Burke could commend a party as "a body of men united for promoting by their joint endeavours the national interest, upon some particular principle in which they are all agreed". Parties, he said, "must ever exist in a free country". And by Disraeli's time the argument was almost over. Applauding the party system as "organized opinion", he said: "You cannot choose between party government and Parliamentary government. I say you can have no Parliamentary government if you have no party government." And he reminded the great statesmen of the day: "It is not becoming in any Minister to decry party who has risen by party. If we were not PARTISANS we should not be Ministers." Yet in more cynical mood, Disraeli once exclaimed:

> Damn your principles! Stick to your party!

Nevertheless the uniformity imposed by the party system continued to cause amusement and concern. Ralph Waldo Emerson described party as "an elegant incognito designed to save a man from the vexation of thinking". And in *HMS Pinafore*, W. S. Gilbert had Sir Joseph Porter, First Lord of the Admiralty, declare:

> I always voted at my party's call
> And I never thought of voting for myself at all.

Abraham LINCOLN once said that "the party lash and the fear of ridicule will overrule justice and liberty". But later Presidents disagreed. Rutherford Hayes observed: "He serves his party best who serves his country best." James Garfield asserted that "all free governments are party governments". And Calvin Coolidge later insisted: "It is necessary to have party organization if we are to have effective and efficient government."

Lord SALISBURY, one of the last great reactionaries, felt that "parties are formed more with reference to controversies that are gone by than to the controversies which these parties have actually to decide". And Woodrow WILSON also reckoned they could be hollow vessels, saying: "The success of a party means little unless it is being used by the nation for a great purpose." The FASCIST movements of the 1920s and 1930s took the argument further, the Portuguese dicator Antonio Salazar asserting:

> We have arrived at the stage in which a political party founded upon the individual rights of citizens or electors has no longer the right to exist.

In America the party system underwent a friendlier onslaught from Will Rogers, who at various times declared: "I am for the party which is out of power, no matter which one it is"; "No party is as bad as its leaders"; and "The more you read about politics, you've got to admit that each party is worse than the other." Stanley BALDWIN echoed this last remark, declaring: "No party is on the whole better than another." But A. P. Herbert, one of Britain's last Independent MPs, defended the system as "right and necessary", saying: "All cannot be fly-halves – there must be a scrum."

But is it a case of "my party, right or wrong"? The Canadian poet John Bengough asserted that "you cannot influence a political party to do right if you stick to it when it does wrong". John F. KENNEDY once declared that "sometimes party loyalty asks too much". But Harold WILSON believed that "no one should be in a political party unless he believes that party represents his own highest religious and moral ideas".

Party, the The term used by COMMUNISTs to describe the all-embracing control, unique and totalitarian nature of their own party.

> The Party in the last instance is always right, because it is the single historic instrument which the working class possesses for the solution of its historic problems.
> TROTSKY.

party line Again originally a Communist term, the position set out by a party's leadership or decision-making body to which members are expected to adhere. The Yugoslav Communist dissident Milovan Djilas once observed of TITO's rule: "The Party Line is that there is no Party Line."

party managers The shadowy figures who manipulate power behind the scenes, frequently ACCOUNTABLE to no one.

> When I came into power, I found that the party managers had taken it all to themselves. I could not even name my own Cabinet. They had sold out every place to pay the election expenses. President BENJAMIN HARRISON.

party political broadcast In Britain, a statement from a political party, carried free of charge on all television (and BBC radio) channels, with time allocated in ratio to the votes polled by each party at the last election and (during a campaign) the number of candidates it is fielding. Often treated by voters as an oppportunity to put the kettle on, occasional broadcasts like the KINNOCK video or the Labour broadcast in 1992 that sparked the WAR OF JENNIFER'S EAR have made a sensational impact.

party room An Australian term for a Parliamentary CAUCUS meeting.

party within a party The Labour leadership's characterization of the MILITANT TENDENCY at the height of its influence; also the constitutional grounds for the expulsion of Militant's adherents from the party as belonging to an organization with its own separate and identifiable programme and membership.

multi-party system A democratic society in which the voters have a choice between three or more serious parties.

one party state Pioneered by Fascists and Communists, a state in which only one party is permitted as both a means of enforcing uniformity, also of governing a country with limited reserves of talent without half of it being "wasted" in opposition. This last pretext was used by many rulers in post-colonial Africa for imposing an effective dictatorship; however Zimbabwe has stopped just short of imposing such rule, and Kenya and Zambia have backed away from it.

the party's over The warning to Britain's local authorities in 1974 from the Labour Environment Secretary Anthony Crosland (1918–77) that they could not carry on with spending plans seen by WHITEHALL as lavish, at a time when the economy was in crisis.

two-party system A system in which the electors permanently have a choice between just two parties, whose policy stances are supposed to fluctuate to reflect changing times and moods. The United States from 1828, and Britain from the mid-1930s to the mid-1970s, and maybe since 1987, have been two-party systems. In 1858 Sen. Stephen Douglas asserted: "There can be but two great political parties in this country." And in England his contemporary John Stuart Mill wrote: "A party of order or stability, and a party of progress or reform, are both necessary elements of a healthy state of political life." More cynically Ralph Waldo Emerson observed: "The two parties which divide the State, the party of Conservatism and that of innovation, are very old, and have disputed the possession of the world ever since it was made." And in 1891 Charlie Glyde, leader of a strike in Bradford that helped create the LABOUR PARTY, said:

> We have had two parties in the past; the can't and the won't; and it's time we had a party that will.

In America, Speaker Tom Reed (*see* CZAR) once said: "The best system is to have one party govern and the other party watch." But the Russian revolutionary Nikolai Bukhanin took the idea one stage further: "We might have a two-party system, but one of the two parties would be in office and the other in prison".

Now is the time for all good men to come to the aid of the party The sentence devised to test the speed of the first typewriter in Milwaukee, Wisconsin, in 1867. Charles E. Weller, historian of the typewriter, may have been the author; he did not claim credit himself, merely saying that the sentence was appropriate because the machine was tested during "an exciting political campaign".

Pasionaria. la Pasionaria (Sp. The passionate one) The Communist Dolores Ibarruri (1895–1989), who was an inspirational leader during the SPANISH CIVIL WAR with her cries of ¡*No pasaran*! (*see* THEY SHALL NOT PASS *below*) and "It is better to die on your feet than to live on your knees!" Revered in exile during the Franco years, she returned when democracy was restored and was re-elected a Communist member of the CORTÈS.

PASOK The Pan-Hellenic Socialist Party, founded by Andreas Papandreou (1919–) in 1974 as the regime of the Greek COLONELS collapsed. Shrilly left-wing and anti-American in opposition, it won power in 1981 and governed in more pragmatic vein. Pasok and its leader were forced from office by the voters in 1989; Papandreou had suffered a heart attack and attracted ridicule over his association with a young air hostess whom he divorced his wife to marry, and his party was tarnished by the looting of the Bank of Crete, which Pasok ministers did not prevent and may have been been assisting.

pass. Pass Laws The laws regulating the movement of Black labour which were a keystone of the APARTHEID system in South Africa. Introduced in 1948, they barred rural Africans from visiting towns for longer than 72 hours without a special permit, on pain of arrest or deportation. Such measures had been sporadically applied in some Afrikaner areas since the 18th century, but the all-embracing nature of the laws and their clear political thrust provoked bitter resentment, and protest campaigns from the African National Congress (ANC) and later the PAC. Arrests for violating the Pass Laws peaked at 381,858 in 1976. In 1986 the South African government announced the scrapping of the hated laws as part of the move toward dismantling *apartheid*.

they shall not pass! (Fr. *ils ne passeront pas*) The famous rallying cry associated with Marshal Pétain during the fighting between the French and German armies at Verdun in WORLD WAR I. In fact, it was uttered by his subordinate General Robert Georges Nivelle (1856–1924) in an Order of the Day in June 1916. As ¡*No Pasaran*! the cry was taken up by the Communist leader LA PASIONARIA (Dolores Ibarruri) in the SPANISH CIVIL WAR.

Passkey The US SECRET SERVICE code word for President Gerald FORD.

passive resistance A form of protest combining NON-VIOLENCE with CIVIL DISOBEDIENCE, in which those staging the protest refuse to co-operate with the authorities but commit no positive acts of obstruction. It was pioneered by MAHATMA Gandhi, who said: "The sword of passive resistance does not require a scabbard and one cannot be forcibly dispossessed of it." Gandhi confessed: "I do not like the term. Still, I adopt the phrase because it is well known and easily understood." Zambia's President Kenneth Kaunda (1924–) did not consider passive resistance an effective political weapon; he dismissed it as "a sport for gentlemen – or ladies".

paternalism (Lat. *pater*, father) The provision of welfare and other services in a way that implies that the mass of the people are unable to decide for themselves and need government to resolve basic issues for them. The intention is often honourable, but there is an element of self-interest – paternalism was at the heart of British TORYism in the first half of the 19th century, of Disraeli's social reforms which aimed to benefit the working class while keeping it out of the political process.

patriality The concept introduced into UK law by James Callaghan's controversially restrictive 1968 Immigration Act. It confined the basic right to enter and settle in Britain to "patrials" – those intending immigrants who could claim a parent (or in some cases a grandparent) born in the country.

patriation The term used in Canada for the transfer of the country's constitution from British to Canadian law. For over a century Canada was governed under the BRITISH NORTH AMERICA ACT passed by Westminster in 1867; efforts to patriate the constitution from the mid-1970s were held up by political and legal wrangles over what degree of consent between the provinces short of unanimity would enable its subsequent amendment. Finally, in 1982, the UK Parliament passed the **Canada Act** which handed all responsibility for the Canadian constitution to Ottawa and the provinces.

patriotism One of the most basic forces in politics the world over, stemming from the conviction, in George Bernard Shaw's words, that "this country is superior to all other countries because you were born in it". Calvin Coolidge injected a further note of self-interest, declaring that "patriotism means looking out for yourself by looking out for your country". Lord ROSEBERY reckoned: "There is no word so prostituted as patriotism. Every government fails in it, and every opposition glows with it." But many statesmen have been less cynical, echoing the words of the British author Tobias Smollett (1721–71) that "true patriotism is of no party".

Patriotism, and its exploitation by politicians, has always aroused deep cynicism. William Randolph Hearst asserted that "a politician will do anything to keep his job – even become a patriot". Dr. Samuel Johnson wrote that "patriotism is the last refuge of a scoundrel", while Bertrand Russell observed that "patriots always talk of dying for their country, and never of killing for their country". Moreover August Bebel, co-founder of Germany's SPD, declared in 1870: "In time of war the loudest patriots are the greatest profiteers."

The American nation was founded on an open and assertive patriotism. Benjamin FRANKLIN claimed at the outset that the English "believe that threepence in a pound of tea is sufficient to overcome the patriotism of an American". And in his farewell message, George WASHINGTON told the people: "Citizens by birth or choice, of a common country, that country has a right to concentrate your affections. The name of American, which belongs to you, in your national capacity, must always exalt the just pride of Patriotism, more than any appellation derived from local discriminations." The founders of the Soviet Union looked for something less noble, TROTSKY declaring: "Patriotism to the Soviet state is a revolutionary duty; whereas patriotism to a bourgeois state is treachery."

Patriotism is not enough The final words of Edith Cavell (1865–1915), before being shot by a German firing squad in Brussels on 12 October 1915. Nurse Cavell, who had tended wounded Britons and was alleged to have spied on the Germans, told the chaplain who attended her:

> Standing, as I do, in the view of God and eternity, I realize that patriotism is not enough. I must have no hatred or bitterness towards anyone.

The shooting of Edith Cavell caused outrage in Britain and did much to sustain support for the prosecution of WORLD WAR I.

No money – no patriotism The blunt assessment of the English "Friends of Liberty" made by the statesman and diplomat Charles Maurice de Talleyrand (1754–1838) at the height of the FRENCH REVOLUTION. The "Friends" had angered him by wanting French support while offering the Revolution no financial help.

patronage The use of political power to allocate jobs to supporters and relatives, frequently in return for political loyalty or hard cash. Practised over the centuries, patronage reached its height in England during the ministry of WALPOLE, who once declared: "There is enough pasture for all the sheep" and is wrongly alleged to have said: "Every man has his price", and in America in the era of MACHINE POLITICS. In the early days of the new nation, Thomas JEFFERSON wrote: "We are endeavouring to reduce the government to the practice of a rigorous economy, to avoid burdening the people and arming the magistrate with a patronage of money which might be used to corrupt and undermine the principles of our government." And at the height of the CIVIL WAR, Secretary for War Edwin Stanton wrote to Mary Todd LINCOLN explaining his refusal to appoint a man she had put forward:

> If I should make such appointments, I should strike at the very root of all confidence of the people in the government, in your husband and you and me.

patronage secretary At Westminster, one of the unofficial titles of the Government Chief WHIP.

> No one knows better than a former patronage secretary the limitations of the human mind and the human spirit.
> EDWARD HEATH.

pavement politics *See* POLITICS.

Paving Bill In the UK political system, a Bill preparing the way for PRIVATIZATION of a State industry or some other event where authority is needed in advance of the definitive legislation; the Paving Bill for the eventual legislation to abolish the GLC was a case in point. Moreover, in November 1992 John MAJOR's government took the unprecedented step of staging a **Paving Debate** before the European Communities (Amendment) Bill incorporating the MAASTRICHT TREATY went into committee. It had already been given a Second Reading by a majority of 244, but after the Danish and French referenda and a hard-fought party conference debate, Major wanted clear authority to continue; he got it by a majority of just three, with 26 Tories voting with Labour and only the votes of 19 Liberal Democrats seeing him home.

Pax Americana (Lat. American peace) The notion of a world order imposed by the United States, canvassed by non-ISOLATIONISTS at various junctures, particularly the close of WORLD WAR II before it was clear there would be a lasting challenge from the Soviet Union. It derived from **Pax Britannica** (British peace), the phrase coined in Palmerston's day to give a benevolent edge to Britain's world role, which Joseph Chamberlain later used to categorize British authority in India. *See also* WORLD POLICEMAN.

pay. pay freeze *See* FREEZE.

pay pause The initiative to restrain wage increases taken in 1961 by Chancellor (later Lord) Selwyn Lloyd (1904–78) as prosperity under the Macmillan government began to wane. Lloyd's drive for voluntary WAGE RESTRAINT and general economic belt-tightening after a period of near boom led Labour to coin the term STOP-GO for Tory policies.

payroll vote The term used at Westminster for the support the Government can mobilize in a critical DIVISION, comprising both Ministers and unsalaried PARLIAMENTARY PRIVATE SECRETARIES who are expected to toe the line. The use of this patronage to defeat Private Member's BILLS which the Government finds inconvenient is a regular source of controversy.

PC (1) The formal abbreviation for PRIVY COUNCILLOR. (2) Popular shorthand for POLITICAL CORRECTNESS. (3) PCs. Canada's PROGRESSIVE Conservatives.

PDs The Progressive Democrats, the new-look Irish party launched on 21 December 1985 by the former FIANNA FAIL Minister Desmond O'Malley (1939–). Seen by some as a parallel "mould-breaking" (*see* BREAK) force to Britain's SDP, the PDs showed greater staying power; they won 14 seats in the DAIL in 1987, and in 1989, though cut back to just six TDs, they went into COALITION with Fianna Fail, O'Malley becoming Minister for Industry and Commerce, a post he had twice held for his old party. The coalition broke up in November 1992 when the TAOISEACH, Albert Reynolds, accused O'Malley of giving dishonest evidence to a judicial inquiry into the collapse of the Goodman beef empire, which had received vast state aid under the HAUGHEY government. O'Malley quit and Reynolds called a SNAP ELECTION, in which Fianna Fail suffered heavy losses but survived in office – ditching the PDs as coalition partners and aligning themselves with Labour instead.

peace. Peace at any price The slogan on which the KNOW-NOTHINGS fought the 1856 US Presidential election. The full wording, "Peace at any price; peace and union", referred to the party's readiness to live with slavery if that would avoid a CIVIL WAR. The phrase was used earlier in the 19th century by the French foreign minister Alphonse de Lamartine, but it has been traced back to the Earl of Clarendon's *History of the Rebellion*, written in 1647.

Peace Ballot The national ballot organized in Britain for 27 June 1935 by the National Declaration Committee, chaired by Lord David Cecil and closely linked to the LEAGUE OF NATIONS Union. Over 11.5 million votes were cast in favour of adherence to the League and its policy of COLLECTIVE SECURITY, and over 10 million for a reduction in armaments. The ballot discouraged the NATIONAL GOVERNMENT under Stanley BALDWIN from rearming (*see* appalling FRANKNESS), and was interpreted by the AXIS powers as a sign of British weakness.

Peace Corps The organization founded by President KENNEDY to assist THIRD-WORLD and other countries by supplying young volunteers to perform skilled tasks, living "at the same level as the citizens of the countries they are sent to". Kennedy also hoped the arrival of idealistic Americans sharing the burdens of others would break down suspicion of the West in developing countries. The Corps was announced by Kennedy in March 1961 and ratified by Congress in the Peace Corps Act that September; it is operated by the STATE DEPARTMENT. The first project was for engineers to help in road construction in Tanganyika (now Tanzania). Peace Corps volunteers work for subsistence wages, usually on a two-year tour with a brief training session beforehand. About half are teachers; the rest include agricultural experts, health workers, engineers and community development workers. For the most part, the Peace Corps has proved a conspicuous success.

peace dividend The boost to the economies of the West that was supposed to follow the end of the COLD WAR, through the relaxation of tension and the reduction in forces and weaponry – and military spending – that could follow. The GULF WAR, the conflict in former Yugoslavia and instability in the former Soviet Union have meant that the full forecast benefit has not been felt.

peace in our time The highly unfortunate phrase attributed to Prime Minister Neville CHAMBERLAIN on 30 September 1938 at the high point of his APPEASEMENT policy, after flying back from meeting Hitler in MUNICH. The optimism was short-lived; in less than a year Hitler had gone back on his assurances and Britain and Germany were at war. The words come from the versicle in Church of England morning prayer: "Give peace in our time, O Lord." What Chamberlain actually said to the cheering crowd in Downing Street was: "My good friends, this is the second time in our history that there has come back from Germany PEACE WITH HONOUR. I believe that it is *peace for our time*. Go home and have a nice, quiet sleep." Lord Home (*see* SIR ALEC), who as Lord Dunglass was Chamberlain's PPS, said forty years later:

> Chamberlain regretted these words the moment he had spoken them.

peace is indivisible The phrase coined by Maxim Litvinov (1876–1951), Soviet COMMISSAR for Foreign Affairs, in a speech in February 1920. It means that nations cannot claim peace exists in one theatre when they are engaged in conflict elsewhere – a rebuke to Britain and other World War I allies who were using force against the Soviet regime while claiming to have negotiated a post-war peace.

Peace, Jobs, Freedom The slogan on which the LABOUR PARTY fought, and went down to a humiliating defeat, in Britain's 1983 General Election. It was taken from the title of the party's encyclopaedic campaign document (*see* LONGEST SUICIDE NOTE IN HISTORY).

peace offensive An active and co-ordinated programme of DIPLOMACY designed to secure peace. Winston Churchill, in his book *The Gathering Storm*, attributed the phrase to Neville CHAMBERLAIN; it has been frequently used by political leaders since World War II.

Peace People The movement founded in 1976 by Mairead Corrigan and Betty Williams to campaign for an end to SECTARIAN violence in Northern Ireland. Mrs. Corrigan's sister had seen her three children killed when a car ran out of control after the gunman at the wheel had been hit by shots from a British Army patrol. There were mass demonstrations against all terrorism, by Republican and Loyalist factions alike, and in 1977 the Peace People won the NOBEL PEACE PRIZE. However the movement faded away amid much-publicized splits and persistent denigration from the IRA.

Peace Pledge Union Britain's leading PACIFIST organization, founded in 1936 by Canon Dick Sheppard of St. Martin's in the Fields. Its influence was greatest prior to World War II; since the late 1950s it has been overshadowed by CND.

peace process The US-sponsored search for peace between Israel, its Arab neighbours and the Palestinians in the Middle East, since at least the 1978 CAMP DAVID AGREEMENT. At times America has seemed the only party interested in peace, despite the assertions of the others; however the pace accelerated after Israel's 1992 election when a LABOUR-led coalition under Yitzhak Rabin ousted Yitzhak Shamir's LIKUD ministry, until the kidnap and murder of an Israeli sergeant by HAMAS halted the talks.

Peace, Retrenchment and Reform The personal platform of the MANCHESTER SCHOOL Liberal John Bright (1811–89), and the slogan of Britain's embryonic Liberals a generation before. On 28 April 1859 Bright told a meeting in Birmingham:

> I am for "Peace, Retrenchment and Reform", the watchword of the great Liberal party 30 years ago.

Peace Ship *See* FORD.
peace sign *See* V.
peace through strength Ronald Reagan's words for the stated aim of almost every American president, starting with George Washington, who said in his first address to Congress in 1790:

> To be prepared for war is one of the most effectual means of preserving peace.

peace with honour The phrase used by Disraeli (*see* DIZZY) after the Congress of BERLIN in 1878, which Neville CHAMBERLAIN unfortunately revived 60 years later (*see* PEACE IN OUR TIME *above*). It has an earlier origin; on 19 September 1853 Lord John (Earl) Russell (1792–1878) said at Greenock of the growing crisis in the CRIMEA:

> If peace cannot be maintained with honour, it is no longer peace.

In the House of Lords on 16 July 1878 after signing the Berlin treaty, Disraeli said:

> Lord SALISBURY and myself have brought you back peace – but a peace, I hope, with honour.

And Salisbury himself had written in 1864:

> Peace without honour is not only a disgrace, but, except as a temporary respite, it is a chimera.

peace without victory A formula for ending WORLD WAR I which President Woodrow WILSON put to the combatants in an address to the US Senate in January 1917. His initiative was ignored, and within three months America had been sucked into the conflict.
a just and lasting peace The theme of Abraham LINCOLN's second INAUGURAL ADDRESS on 4 March 1865, which also pledged "malice toward none, and charity for all". The end of the CIVIL WAR was just six weeks away – as was Lincoln's assassination.
All we are saying is give peace a chance The first line of the song written by John Lennon and performed by his *Plastic Ono Band* which in 1969 became almost the mantra of the movement against the VIETNAM WAR, and campaigners for peace generally.
an extra mile for peace The phrase conjured up by President BUSH after Iraq's invasion of Kuwait in August 1990 to indicate his desire to go as far as was necessary to secure a peaceful settlement and avoid a bloody end to the GULF WAR, if Saddam Hussein would respond.
Every night, whisper "peace" in your husband's ear The appeal of Soviet Foreign Minister Andrei GROMYKO (1909–89) to Nancy Reagan at a White House reception in 1984. It was almost the last throw of the old-timers in the KREMLIN before the advent of Mikhail Gorbachev and the end of the COLD WAR.
Land for Peace *See* LAND.
Open covenants of peace, openly arrived at The first of WILSON'S FOURTEEN POINTS, as spelt out by the President to Congress on 8 January 1918.
Since wars begin in the minds of men, it is in the minds of men that the defences of peace must be constructed The preamble to the constitution of UNESCO, adopted in London on 16 November 1945. It has been attributed to Prime Minister Clement ATTLEE and, more recently, to Archibald MacLeish, chairman of the US delegation to the London conference.
Uniting for Peace resolution The motion carried by the United Nations GENERAL ASSEMBLY late in 1950 at the urging of America, providing that if the SECURITY COUNCIL failed to act on "important questions" the Assembly itself would recommend to members collective action to preserve world peace. It was under this resolution that the UN interposed an Emergency Force between Israel and Egypt at the end of the SUEZ crisis.
We are going to have peace, even if we have to fight for it A comment attributed to President Eisenhower, who on other occasions, despite his military pedigree, spoke of the overwhelming desire of the peoples of the world for peace. Eisenhower must have been speaking at the height of the COLD WAR, when I. F. STONE condemned US policy as:

> We Smiths want peace so bad we're prepared to kill every one of the Joneses to get it.

We prepare for war like ferocious giants, and for peace like retarded pygmies A scathing comment at the height of Cold War tension and sabre-rattling from the Canadian Liberal Prime Minister Lester Pearson (1897–1972).
Where the peace has been broken anywhere, the peace of all countries everywhere is in danger Franklin D. Roosevelt's warning to the American people on 3 September 1939, as WORLD WAR II broke out in Europe.
winning the peace Many politicians have used this phrase, but the French prime Minister Georges Clemenceau (*see* TIGER) may have been the first. He is reputed to have said at the close of World War I:

> We have won the war. Now we have to win the peace – and that may be very difficult.

Clemenceau certainly did say, in a speech at Verdun on 14 July 1919: "It is far easier to make war than to make peace."
peaceful co-existence The doctrine put forward after STALIN's death in 1953 by Georgi Malenkov, who had won the first of a

series of power struggles in the KREMLIN. Responding to the Republicans' "New Look" in foreign policy, he talked of "peaceful co-existence" with capitalist countries and a switch at home from defence equipment to consumer goods, and began releasing political prisoners. The policy collapsed when East Germans, encouraged by his message, rose up against their Stalinist rulers and were brutally suppressed by Soviet troops. But Khruschev, the ultimate winner of the struggle to succeed Stalin, frequently used the term himself.

peacekeeping The use of military forces to preserve a truce, or police or separate two or more hostile armies or communities. It has become the most visible function of the UNITED NATIONS.

peaceniks A term of abuse for America's ANTI-WAR campaigners, and others who objected to US policy during the COLD WAR. Much loved by the political Right, it bore overtones of PEACE AT ANY PRICE and of fanatical detachment from reality; the "nik" conveyed an accusation of beatnik scruffiness, and of pro-Sovietism.

peak too soon To achieve a party or candidate's highest level of popularity well before election day, the inference being that it will slip back. When Labour's opinion poll rating reached the mid 30s at the start of Britain's 1983 election campaign, party wags warned their leader, Michael Foot (*see* WURZEL GUMMIDGE), that Labour was in danger of peaking too soon; it finished on 27%, its worst showing since 1935.

Pearce Commission The commission set up in November 1971 by SIR ALEC Douglas-Home, Foreign Secretary in Edward Heath's government, to determine whether proposals for a settlement of Rhodesia's UDI were acceptable to its people as a whole. Headed by Lord Pearce, a retired Lord of Appeal, opponents of UDI saw it as a WHITEWASH until it reported on 23 May 1972 that the African majority strongly opposed the scheme agreed by Sir Alec and Rhodesia's breakaway Premier Ian Smith. This involved a steadily increasing African stake in the colony's Parliament as Rhodesia's indigenous people achieved the same qualifications as Whites. The commission arrived in Salisbury (now Harare) on 11 January to an upsurge of demonstrations for MAJORITY RULE, with some violence. A week later the Smith regime arrested Garfield Todd, a former Premier of Southern Rhodesia, and his daughter Judith for campaigning against UDI; Pearce considered cancelling his mission, but took evidence from the Todds in jail.

Pearl Harbor The surprise Japanese air attack on the Hawaiian base of the US Pacific fleet on 7 December 1941 that brought America into WORLD WAR II; President Franklin D. Roosevelt declared war on Japan on 9 December and on Germany and Italy two days later. When told of the attack, FDR exclaimed: "This means war!" and CHURCHILL declared: "So we have won after all!" For almost two hours 350 Japanese carrier-borne aircraft strafed, bombed and torpedoed the fleet at anchor; eight battleships and 16 other vessels were sunk or seriously damaged, and 175 aircraft destroyed on the ground. The attack cost 2335 American lives and left a further 1178 wounded. On the same day the Japanese attacked the Philippines, Guam, Hong Kong and the Malay peninsula. The failure of the Pearl Harbor command to act on intelligence of Japanese movements was severely criticized by a government inquiry; some sceptics wondered if FDR had allowed the attack to happen, as Pearl Harbor unified all but the most ISOLATIONIST politicians behind a war which the President had been preparing for against strong domestic opposition. Indeed Sen. Gerald Nye of North Dakota complained:

> This is just what Great Britain planned for us. We have been maneuvred into this by the President.

Pearl Harbor, the base constructed on Oahu under an 1887 treaty with then-independent Hawaii, became a byword for unpreparedness and the ruthless deviousness of an enemy, as did its anniversary, which Roosevelt instantly termed a DATE THAT WILL LIVE IN INFAMY. This did not stop George BUSH telling an American Legion convention on 7 *September* 1988: "Today, you remember – I wonder how many Americans remember – today is Pearl Harbor Day."

> I fear all we have done is awaken a sleeping giant and fill him with a terrible resolve.
>
> Admiral ISOKURU YAMAMOTO (1884–1943, *attr.*).

Peasants' Revolt The name given by the Conservative MP Julian Critchley to the BACKBENCH upsurge that installed Margaret Thatcher as leader in February 1975. Edward Heath's supporters did not imagine the former Education Secretary with increasingly right-wing views and little obvious support could oust the incumbent leader. But discontent with Heath (*see* GROCER) was greater than they realized, and Mrs. Thatcher (*see* IRON LADY) won votes because she had the courage to stand when more obvious challengers held back; her campaign was shrewdly organized by the one-time Colditz escaper Airey NEAVE. In the first ballot on 4 February she polled 130, against 119 for Heath and 16 for Hugh Fraser.

Heath dropped out and challengers previously loyal to him came forward, headed by William Whitelaw (*see* WILLIE). But in the second ballot a week later Mrs. Thatcher won outright with 146, against 79 for Whitelaw, 19 for Sir Geoffrey HOWE, 19 for James Prior and 11 for John Peyton. It was over 15 years before Mrs. Thatcher was herself ousted in a similar revolt.

Pecora Committee The Congressional committee, named after its special attorney Ferdinand Pecora (1885–1971), which at the time of President Franklin D. Roosevelt's inauguration in 1933 was investigating corruption in the world of high finance. The probe was conducted with such insight and ruthlessness that it unnerved America's bankers a great deal more than did FDR's initiative in closing the banks to restore economic stability. The Pecora probe also gave Roosevelt the ammunition he needed to introduce a Bill making the issue of a misleading company prospectus a criminal offence. Pecora himself was one of the first members of the Securities and Exchange Commission (SEC) until becoming a New York Supreme Court justice; he served 15 years until resigning in an unsuccessful bid to become Mayor of New York.

Peel. Peelites The 110 Tory MPs, headed by **Sir Robert Peel** (1788–1850) who had up to then been Prime Minister, who broke away in 1846 over the FREE TRADE issue after Peel had split the party by repealing the CORN LAWS. Peel's secession, taking with him most of the Cabinet and the organs of the Tory party, marks the effective start of the CONSERVATIVE PARTY from the ranks of Tory MPs who were left behind by their leader and had to start a new movement from scratch. Initially the Peelites held the BALANCE OF POWER; after the following year's election which gave the WHIG Lord John Russell a paper majority over the Tories in whom Disraeli was the strongest force, they still numbered over 70 but were handicapped by the uninterest of their nominal leader, who wrote:

> I will take care not again to burn my fingers by organizing a party.

A leading Peelite and future Liberal, Edward Cardwell (1813–86) complained:

> Sir Robert Peel's party saved England from confusion and has been rewarded by its own annihilation.

The Peelites survived their leader's death from a riding accident in 1850, and in 1852, still 52 strong, joined forces with the Whigs under Peel's former foreign secretary, the Earl of Aberdeen. Gladstone (*see* GRAND OLD MAN), himself a Peelite, brought down that government in 1857; in the subsequent election only 26 Peelites kept their seats. After the deaths of several senior Peelites in 1860–61, the rump of the group joined the Whigs in the new Liberal Party.

Peel, best known for founding the Metropolitan Police in 1829 and for splitting the Tory party by repealing the Corn Laws, was one of the great enigmas of British politics. He was groomed for power, his father, also an MP, telling him:

> Bob, you dog, if you are not Prime Minister one day I shall disinherit you.

Elected an MP in 1809, he was a junior minister by 1812 but had to resign in 1818 because of his strong opposition to Catholic EMANCIPATION; the same issue led him to resign as Home Secretary in 1827, but he reluctantly reversed his stand in 1829. His inability to toe a party line was already evident; in 1830 he told a friend: "I feel a want of many essential qualifications which are requisite in party leaders." Peel would have become Prime Minister in July 1834, but was in Rome and the job went to Wellington who was easier to reach; he finally got the job that December, surviving only four months. The BEDCHAMBER CRISIS over the young Queen Victoria's refusal to part with her Whig ladies when the government fell prevented Peel's Tories taking power in 1839, but he took office again in 1841 after a convincing win at the polls. He told the House:

> No considerations of mere political support should induce me to hold such an office as that which I fill by a servile tenure, which would compel me to be the instrument of carrying other men's opinions into effect.

In his second ministry, Peel blocked Whig moves for Free Trade and countered dissent in Ireland, having Daniel O'Connell (1775–1847) tried for sedition. But the IRISH POTATO FAMINE convinced him "cheap corn" was essential, and in a dramatic U-TURN he moved to repeal the Corn Laws, destroying the old Tory Party. Hearing Richard Cobden (1804–65) speaking out against the laws, he turned to Sidney Herbert and said:

> You must answer this, for I cannot.

As a man, Peel aroused mixed feelings. Walter Bagehot (1826–77) ascribed to him "common opinions and uncommon abilities", adding: "No man has come so near to our definition of a constitutional statesman: the powers of a first-rate man and the creed of a second-rate man." O'Connell memorably described Peel's smile as "like the silver plate on a coffin", and Disraeli underlined the impression of a cold fish, saying: "He is reminiscent of a poker. The only difference is that a poker occasionally gives off signs of warmth." Disraeli wrote later: "When he attempted to touch the tender passions it was painful. His face became distorted, like that of a woman who wants to cry but cannot succeed." Resigning from the Government on 29 June 1846, he told the House:

> In relinquishing power I shall leave a name severely censured, I fear, by many who on public grounds deeply regret the severance of party ties . . . but it may be that I shall leave a name sometimes remembered with expressions of goodwill in the abodes of those whose lot it is to labour.

Disraeli put the betrayed Tory view, declaring:

> He is so vain that he wants to figure in history as the settler of all the great questions, but . . . things must be done by parties, not by persons using parties as tools.

Harold Macmillan (*see* SUPERMAC) commended Peel as "the first of the modern Conservatives", but BALFOUR bitterly observed:

> He smashed his party, and no man has the right to destroy the property of which he is trustee.

Lord ROSEBERY wrote of his reversals on Catholic emancipation and the Corn Laws: "Granted that he was right in the first transition, he should not have repeated it; the character of public men cannot stand such shocks." But the most eloquent verdict came from an anonymous Tory who compared Peel with

> the Turkish admiral who steered his fleet into the enemy's port.

peer A member of Britain's aristocracy qualified to sit in the HOUSE OF LORDS: a Duke, EARL, Countess, Marquess, VISCOUNT, BARON or Baroness. Peers, whose titles and privileges are traditionally passed down from father to son or to the nearest male relative (very few women have succeeded to peerages in their own right), can vote in the Upper House, but not in Parliamentary elections – in common with "lunatics and convicted felons".

> The layer of blubber which encases an English peer, the sediment of permanent aduiation.
>
> CYRIL CONNOLLY (1903–74).

> I don't have a vote because I'm a peer. If I did, I'd vote Labour. But I think my butler's a Conservative.
>
> Earl MOUNTBATTEN OF BURMA (1900–79, *attr.*).

life peer A member of the HOUSE OF LORDS appointed to serve during his or her lifetime, without the heirs having any claim on a seat. The idea was first mooted by Lord SALISBURY in 1888, but it was 1958 before Harold Macmillan recommended the first life peers to Queen Elizabeth II. Life peers now contribute up to one-third of the membership of the House. Since 1964 only three hereditary peers have been created; only the Earl of Stockton (Macmillan himself) had male heirs who would perpetuate the title and sit in the Lords.

spiritual peers The two Archbishops of the Church of England and the 24 senior diocesan bishops (including London, Durham and Winchester) who are eligible to sit in the House of Lords as long as they remain in their post.

temporal peers All peers who are not bishops.

working peers Life peers well below retirement age, created on the nomination of the political parties to strengthen their teams of spokesmen in the upper house. The LABOUR PARTY relies heavily on such creations, because it has few hereditary peers and is required to draw on slim resources of ageing retired politicians in the Lords to match the Government's ministerial team.

The peers against the people Lloyd George's slogan as he rallied the public in support of his 1909 PEOPLE'S BUDGET and against the efforts of the House of Lords to defeat it. For the first time in 250 years, the Lords threw out his Budget, but in two General Elections in 1910 the Liberals kept power after making great use of the slogan. The Lords passed the Budget a year late, and after a threat by ASQUITH to create hundreds of Liberal peers to force the Government's legislation through, the Lords (*see* HEDGERS AND DITCHERS) accepted limitation of their powers under the PARLIAMENT ACT, 1911.

peerage The rank or dignity of a peer, as conferred on those newly created. Not everyone regards the offer of a peerage as a compliment. The newspaper magnate who eventually became Lord Northcliffe reputedly said: "When I want a peerage, I shall buy one like an honest man." And when Clement ATTLEE offered R. H. Tawney a peerage, the political scientist wrote back:

> Thank you for your letter. What harm have I ever done the Labour Party?

disclaim a peerage To give up the right to one's title and to one's seat in the Lords, without affecting the position of one's heirs. It is done because (1) someone succeeding to a peerage would prefer to stand for the House of Commons, (2) the son of an eminent peer feels his father has made the title unique, or (3) the inheritor of the title does not believe in the House of Lords or hereditary titles. Winston CHURCHILL first proposed to Asquith in 1911 that peers be permitted to disclaim, but it was only after Tony BENN had twice been elected an MP and denied his seat after inheriting his father's title of Lord Stansgate that the law was changed in 1963. Fortuitously, the change took place just in time for Lords Home and Hailsham to disclaim their titles and compete for the Tory leadership that autumn, with Home (*see* SIR ALEC) emerging the winner and Hailsham hamstrung by his pledge to return to the Commons.

elevation to the peerage The creation of a peer, comprising the Sovereign's declaration, normally announced from Downing Street but sometimes from Buckingham Palace, that the honour is being awarded, and their subsequent introduction to the House of Lords once they have chosen the title by which they wish to be known.

hereditary peerage A place in the House of Lords that is inherited, rather than awarded for life.

> I have not sought and do not seek a hereditary peerage.
> MARGARET THATCHER, 1991 (she was created a life peer the following year).

Pendleton Act The legislation passed by the US Congress in 1883 that freed much of the CIVIL SERVICE from political patronage. Named after its sponsor, Sen. George H. Pendleton, it stemmed from public outrage at the corruption revealed in the trial of President Garfield's assassin, himself denied a civil service post. Backed by President Arthur (*see* ELEGANT ARTHUR), the Act set up a three-member commission to draft and administer competitive examinations to establish applicants' merit, banned the collection of campaign funds from Federal officeholders and established a list of positions (10% at first) to be filled by merit. Ironically Arthur had been removed as Collector of Customs for the port of New York by President Hayes (*see* OLD 8 TO 7) because his efforts to establish a MERIT SYSTEM there had not been vigorous enough.

pendulum The apparently inevitable historic swing of support in a two-PARTY system from one to another and back again. When the social and economic system continues to develop in the same direction despite such swings the RATCHET EFFECT is said to apply. The argument that "the pendulum will swing back", put forward by Speaker Joe Cannon (*see* UNCLE JOE), emphasized that ideas out of fashion one day may become accepted wisdom again the next.

pendulum arbitration *See* ARBITRATION.

Pentagon The massive headquarters of the US Department of Defence across the Potomac from Washington; the concrete building, with three times the office space of the Empire State Building, takes its name from its five-sided shape. The term "Pentagon" has also come to personify America's military BUREAUCRACY and US defence policies; one Russian commentator observed: "The Pentagon has five sides on every issue." The Pentagon was planned in 1941 when 41,000 civilian employees of the military were spilling out of 23 buildings in and around the capital. Congress jibbed at the $35 million cost (it eventually rose to $87 million) and questioned its necessity, Sen. Everett DIRKSEN saying: "We may not need all that space when the war comes to an end." President Roosevelt was unhappy with the site close to ARLINGTON NATIONAL CEMETERY and the windowless design; he was still objecting when the War Department sent in the contractors, who finished the building in just a year. When they finished, 40,000 administrators moved in – but it was already too small. The Pentagon is now part of the Washington landscape.

> That immense monument to modern man's subservience to the desk.
> British Ambassador OLIVER (later Lord) FRANKS, 1952.

> A place where costs are rounded to the nearest tenth of a billion dollars. C. MERTON TYRRELL, 1970.

> Bombing can end the war – bomb the Pentagon now!
> Anti-Vietnam War slogan.

Pentagon papers An official, secret and brutally frank history of US involvement in VIETNAM which was LEAKed to the *New York Times* in 1971 by Daniel Ellsberg, a former Pentagon employee who had become convinced the war was immoral. It revealed that the American public had been systematically lied to, and told of miscalculations, unauthorized offensives and policy clashes at the heart of the Johnson administration. When the first instalment hit the news stands the Nixon administration tried to halt publication, but the Supreme Court ruled by 6 to 3 that such a ban would violate the FIRST AMENDMENT. The leak gravely embarrassed Nixon and the shapers of US policy in Indo-China and infuriated supporters of the war. An outraged President set up the PLUMBERS' unit to get even with Ellsberg and combat what he saw as a campaign of subversion; WATERGATE, and Nixon's own fall, were the result.

> The greatest representative democracy the world has known, the nation of Jefferson and Lincoln, has let its nose be rubbed in the swamp by petty war lords, jealous Vietnamese generals and grand-scale dope pushers.
> Sen. MIKE GRAVEL on the message of the Papers.

Pentagonese A style of language characterized by euphemisms, circumlocutions and vagueness, frequently attributed to US military bureaucrats, especially in their dealings with the Congress.

Pentonville Five The five dockers sent to Pentonville Prison for contempt of court in July 1972 for picketing an East London cold store in defiance of an order from the National

Industrial Relations Court. The episode finally discredited the Heath government's INDUSTRIAL RELATIONS ACT, introduced not long before, and through the subsequent absence of any legislation against Secondary PICKETING paved the way for the WINTER OF DISCONTENT seven years later. The jailing of the men brought widespread sympathy action, the withdrawal of the TUC from talks with Ministers on the economy, and the threat of the first GENERAL STRIKE since 1926. With constant mass demonstrations outside the prison, the Government was rescued by a House of Lords decision in another case that enabled the NIRC to release the men without their purging their contempt. As the dockers were led away to Pentonville, one shouted:

> How can they arrest me? The UNION JACK grows out of my bloody head.

people. people bath In US politics, a welcoming crowd on the campaign trail which swamps a candidate. The term sounds contemporary, but was first used by Abraham LINCOLN.

people power The NON-VIOLENT popular SOLIDARITY which brought Mrs. Corazon Aquino (1933–) to power as President of the Philippines in 1986 after the incumbent President Ferdinand Marcos had rigged the outcome of elections she had clearly won. When the Church, the Army and (belatedly) the Reagan administration withdrew support from Marcos in the face of massive demonstrations, Marcos was forced to concede defeat and flee the country. *See also* POWER TO THE PEOPLE.

People's Budget The Budget introduced in April 1909 by David Lloyd George (*see* L.G.), so-called because it proposed to raise money for old age pensions (and rearmament) by increasing the tax burden on the landed classes. Death duties were doubled, taxes on land and unearned income raised to unprecedented levels, and a new supertax levied on all income over £5,000 p.a. The Budget provoked a violent outcry from Tory landowners, who denounced it as legalized robbery. Until then the Budget had been purely an exercise in balancing the books; now for the first time it was used as a direct instrument of social policy. So radical did it seem to the aristocracy that the House of Lords refused to pass it (*see* PEERS AGAINST THE PEOPLE) until threatened with the loss of their powers.

> We are placing the burdens on the broadest shoulders. I made up my mind that in forming my Budget, no cupboard should be barer, no lot should be harder to bear.
> LLOYD GEORGE, 30 July 1909.

people's courts The infamous tribunals that tried political offences in NAZI Germany, and most notoriously the conspirators against Hitler in the STAUFFENBERG PLOT. Altogether some 7000 people were brought before the "people's courts" during the THIRD REICH and some 2000 sentenced to death; no evidence for the defence was permitted. On Hitler's orders, several of the 20 July conspirators were sentenced to be hanged "like carcasses of meat", suspended from nooses of piano wire from meathooks at the Plotzensee barracks; the FÜHRER had home movies shot of this revolting scene.

people's democracies The self-justifying and blatantly false description of their regimes adopted by the Communist leaders of the Soviet Union's eastern European SATELLITES after World War II.

The people's flag is deepest red The first line of the RED FLAG.

the people's President One of the nicknames accorded Andrew Jackson (*see* OLD HICKORY) during his successful campaign for the Presidency in 1828; it reflected his undoubted popularity with the mass of the American people and their desire to reverse the CORRUPT BARGAIN with which John Quincy ADAMS was reckoned to have captured the White House four years previously.

People's Republic The title chosen by Mao Tse-Tung (*see* CHAIRMAN MAO) for the Communist state established in mainland China after Chiang Kai-Shek's Nationalists were finally driven out in 1949.

the People's War The name bestowed by Woodrow WILSON on WORLD WAR I on 14 June 1917, not long after he had belatedly bowed to the inevitable and declared war on Germany. In his Flag Day address, Wilson anticipated his Fourteen Points when he said:

> This is the People's War, a war for freedom and justice and self-government amongst all the nations of the world, a war to make the world safe for the peoples who live upon it . . . the German peoples themselves included.

God gave the land to the people The stirring anthem of radicals in Britain's LIBERAL PARTY, led by Lloyd George, in the years prior to World War I. It was sung to the tune of *Marching Through Georgia*.

religion is the opium of the people The best-known saying of Karl MARX, who wrote in his *Criticism of the Hegelian Philosophy of Right*: "Religion is the sigh of the oppressed creature, the heart of a heartless world, and the soul of soulless conditions. It is the opium of the people."

Set the people free The title of the MANIFESTO on which Winston CHURCHILL and his Conservatives fought and won Britain's 1951 General Election.

Trust the people The axiom of TORY DEMOCRACY credited by Winston Churchill to his father Lord Randolph Churchill (1849–95). He said: "I was brought up in my father's house to believe in democracy. Trust the people: that was his message." The phrase was taken up in 1956 by the Democratic Presidential nominee Adlai Stevenson, who said: "If I was to attempt to put my political philosophy into a single phrase, it would be this: Trust the people."

We the people The opening words of the United States CONSTITUTION. The first paragraph reads:

> We the people of the United States, in order to form a more perfect union, establish justice, insure domestic tranquillity, provide for the common defence, promote the general welfare, and secure the blessings of liberty to ourselves and our posterity, do ordain and establish this Constitution for the United States of America.

People of the same trade seldom meet together, even for merriment and diversion, but the conversation ends in a conspiracy against the public, or in some contrivance to raise prices The cynical but regrettably often true axiom on the proliferation of MONOPOLIES and cartels which Adam Smith (1723–90) put forward in his WEALTH OF NATIONS.

I do not know a method of drawing up an indictment against a whole people The warning of Edmund BURKE to his Bristol constituents in 1777 on the futility of Britain's conflict to retain its American colonies.

My plan cannot fail if the people are with us, and we ought not to succeed unless we do have the people with us The words with which the POPULIST William Jennings Bryan in 1899 rejected the steel magnate Andrew Carnegie's appeal to join him in working to defeat the peace treaty concluded at the end of the SPANISH-AMERICAN WAR; he was anxious not to compromise the purity of his own campaign. Bryan told him:

> I can not wish you success in your effort to reject the treaty because while it may win the fight it may destroy our cause.

No-one ever went broke underestimating the intelligence of the American people The ultimate cynical view of the inhabitants of the United States, taken by H. L. Mencken.

One third of the people of the world are asleep at any given moment, the other two-thirds are awake and probably stirring up trouble somewhere US SECRETARY OF STATE Dean Rusk voicing the deepest thoughts of all those in high office, 1966.

One fifth of the people are against everything all the time A remark made by Robert F. KENNEDY in 1964 which is borne out by study of the way public opinion behaves. RFK was arguing that no politician should let predictable opposition from a small and easily-defined section of the electorate prevent the adoption of policies which would be supported by the rest.

The American people are slow to wrath, but when their wrath is once kindled, it burns like a consuming flame Franklin D. Roosevelt's description of the outraged response of American opinion to PEARL HARBOR, quoted by Ronald Reagan in 1981 in a televised warning to Congress that public patience was running out with its failure to tackle the crisis facing the economy.

There is no cause half so sacred as the cause of the people Woodrow WILSON's declaration to a campaign rally of over 12,000 people at Madison Square Garden on 31 October 1912. The future President was so overwhelmed at the hour-long ovation he received that he forgot his prepared speech and delivered these lines instead. He added: "There is no idea so uplifting as the idea of the service of humanity." Not all great Americans have regarded the people in this light; Alexander HAMILTON once told JEFFERSON:

> Your people, Sir, is nothing but a great beast!

To make a people great, it is necessary to send them to battle, even if you have to kick them in the pants A typical dictum of Mussolini (*see* DUCE), speaking volumes both about the philosophy of the founder of FASCISM and his view of the Italian people he led.

Would it not be easier for the government to dissolve the people and elect another? The apt if savagely ironic comment of Bertolt Brecht (1898–1956) after the Communist government of East Germany had called in Soviet troops to put down the popular uprising of 17 June 1953. Brecht also remarked that

> The people had lost the confidence of the government and could only win it back by renewed efforts.

You may fool all the people some of the time; you can even fool some of the people all the time. But you can't fool all the people all the time A saying attributed to Abraham LINCOLN, who is supposed to have uttered it in a speech at Clinton, Illinois, on 2 September 1858. However there is no evidence that he ever said it, and it has been attributed with equal conviction to the showman Phineas T. Barnum.

Peoria To Presidents and presidential hopefuls, the heart of MIDDLE AMERICA and the the embodiment of the electorate their policies must satisfy. Peoria is a town in Illinois with a population around 130,000; its name comes from an Indian word meaning "place of fat beasts". It has been a cultural yardstick at least since the late 19th century when Ambrose Bierce noted in the "dullard" entry for his *Devil's Dictionary* that "the intellectual centre of the race is somewhere about Peoria, Illinois". The term was bandied about for decades before becoming a catchword in the Nixon White House, where the test of anything planned was **Will it play in Peoria?** John D. Ehrlichman, who made the phrase his own, explained to the political lexicographer William Safire:

> Onomatopoeia was the only reason for Peoria, I suppose. And it personified – exemplified – a place, remote from the media centers on the coasts, where the national verdict is cast, according to the Nixon doctrine.

percentage poll *See* TURNOUT

perestroika (Russ. restructuring) A policy, linked with GLASNOST, much publicized since 1986 when Mikhail GORBACHEV set out to transform the Soviet Union by introducing economic and political reform and allowing greater freedom of expression. Gorbachev, who became Communist Party leader in 1985 and president in 1988, saw perestroika as a means of renewing the Soviet state, but instead it hastened its collapse. His reform programme met with stiff resistance inside the POLITBURO, but he nevertheless said in May 1988: "Every member of our leadership is deeply committed to the cause of perestroika."

> If the Russian word *perestroika* has easily entered the international lexicon, it is due to more than just interest in what is going on in the Soviet Union. Now the whole world needs restructuring; that is, progressive development, a fundamental change.
>
> GORBACHEV, in his book, *Perestroika*.

> *Perestroika* has transformed and deformed society – but it is not the Soviet Union that is falling apart but the system – and Gorbachev started the process.
>
> Russian President BORIS YELTSIN addressing Euro-MPs in Strasbourg, 15 April 1991.

Perfidious Albion (Fr. *L'Albion* (*Angleterre*) *perfide*) The phrase which embodies one strand of French attitudes toward England: the conviction that, deep down, it can never be trusted. It is revived by the media in one country or other whenever the two are at loggerheads, which happens frequently despite (or because of) their mutual membership of the EUROPEAN COMMUNITY. The phrase was coined by the cleric Jacques-Bénigne Bossuet (1627–1704) who wrote:

> England, ah, faithless England, which the rampart of whose seas made inaccessible to the Romans, the faith of the Saviour spread even there.

It was refined into its popular form by the poet Augustin, Marquis of Ximénez (1726–1817), who in a revolutionary poem written in 1793 included the phrase:

> Let us attack in her own waters
> Perfidious Albion!

permanent. permanent members Also known as the **permanent five**. The five nations – former World War II allies – who sit on the SECURITY COUNCIL of the United Nations as of right and alone possess the power of VETO. They are the US, UK, Russia, China and France. Pressure has been growing in recent years for Germany, Japan and at least one THIRD WORLD representative to have permanent status instead of taking one of the less prestigious seats when its turn comes along.

permanent revolution The doctrine promulgated by TROTSKY that the Bolshevik revolution, once begun, would spread to engulf the entire world. He set it out most fully in his 1930 book *The Permanent Revolution*, in refutation of Stalin's programme for SOCIALISM IN ONE COUNTRY:

> The democratic revolution grows directly into the socialist revolution and thereby becomes a permanent revolution. . . . The completion of the socialist revolution within national limits is unthinkable. . . . The socialist revolution begins in the national arena, it unfolds in the international arena, and is completed in the world arena.

Permanent Secretary The Whitehall MANDARIN occupying the highest Civil Service position in each UK Government department; very occasionally a department such as the Treasury will have a Second Permanent Secretary to reflect its status, workload or breadth of responsibilities.

Peronism The nationalist, largely working-class movement in Argentina which **Juan Perón** (1895–1974) used as the mass base for his two spells as dictator, from 1946 to 1955 and 1973 until his death. Perón wooed Argentina's powerful unions through his fixing of a minimum wage as a member of the military JUNTA that ruled from 1943, and his equally charismatic wife Eva (*see* EVITA) secured the fanatical backing of the DESCAMISADOS of the lower classes. He did not take kindly to opposition, declaring: "The order of the day for every Peronist is to answer a violent action with a still more violent action." Perón's fellow officers jailed him in 1945 as his influence soared, but were forced to release him and the next year he was elected President. He set out to establish a CORPORATIST dictatorship, but while his expropriation of British-owned firms was popular, the increasing brutality and incompetence of his regime was not; even the cult of Evita which he promoted after her death in 1952 could not save him, and he was exiled to Spain in 1955. However his party outlived him, and when the military eventually allowed a free Presidential election the victorious candidate stood down for him and he returned in triumph with his new wife

Isabel, a Madrid nightclub singer. Isabelita, as the Peronists called her, succeeded Perón on his death, but showed little flair for government and was ousted by the military in 1976. Nevertheless the movement continues, and at any time could supply Argentina with a government, democratic or otherwise.

> If I had not been Perón, I would have liked to be Perón.
> JUAN PERÓN, 1960.

> Without me there will be chaos. ISABEL PERÓN.

peroration The final portion of a political speech, in which the speaker tries to rouse his or her audience to a climax of enthusiasm for the message being put across, frequently employing repetition or flowery phrases that would sound overblown in the main body of the speech.

Perot. Perotnistas Supporters of **H. Ross Perot**, the maverick Texas billionaire who won 19% of the popular vote in the 1992 Presidential election, despite pulling out of the race from July to September. The word, a play on "Peronistas", was invented by the novelist Peter Tauber. George Bush's speechwriter Peggy Noonan described Perot as resembling "a hand grenade with a bad haircut". But millions warmed to his message that America could do better without the politicians, despite his amateurish and bizarre campaigning style almost entirely based on TV commercials, and persistent media suggestions that he had a persecution complex and had put both his own staff and his opponents under surveillance.

perquisites The side benefits of being a US CONGRESSMAN, over and above the official salary. These include cheap meals and haircuts on the premises, free plants from the botanical garden, a free photography service, free ice, 33 free trips to their home district each year and free travel abroad if an official pretext can be found. However, by contrast with UK Members of Parliament who can earn what they like outside unless they hold Ministerial office, and who enjoy most of these same privileges, members of Congress are only supposed to earn 15% on top of their official salaries.

Pershing missile A US intermediate-range ballistic missile which first became operational in 1962; the Pershing II, developed in the late 1970s, had a range of 425 miles (680 km.) and was ten times more accurate than its predecessor. They were deployed in Western Europe in 1983 alongside CRUISE missiles to counter the threat from the Soviet medium-range SS20 which had been based throughout East Europe from the mid-1970s. Together with Cruise, the Pershing IIs were removed from Europe under the US-Soviet INF Treaty of December 1987, and for the most part destroyed. They were named after General John J. Pershing (1860–1948) who commanded US forces in World War I.

persona non grata The Latin term used in the world of diplomacy and foreign affairs for an official of one country who is no longer welcome in another, usually because of espionage or some personal lapse. Sometimes country A orders the expulsion of diplomats from country B whose conduct has been faultless, as a "tit for tat" reprisal for the action of country B in expelling country A's representatives.

personal statement At Westminster, the statement that a Minister who has resigned or an MP facing a personal crisis is entitled to make to the House of Commons on application to the Speaker. By convention such statements cannot be interrupted or questioned. John PROFUMO owed his downfall to his lying to the House in a personal statement in which he denied any sexual relationship with Christine Keeler; the most celebrated personal statement in recent years was that of Sir Geoffrey HOWE in October 1990 which triggered the fall of Margaret Thatcher.

personality cult The raising of the leader of a TOTALITARIAN regime to an almost Godlike pre-eminence, completely subordinating both the ideology of the regime and the other members of the government. It came into use in the early 1950s as a codeword for STALINISM, which had raised such excesses to an art form.

> The cult of the individual acquired such monstrous size because Stalin himself, using all conceivable methods, supported the glorification of his own person. Comrades! We must abolish the cult of the individual decisively, once and for all.
> NIKITA S. KHRUSCHEV to the Secret Session of the 20th Party Congress, 25 February 1956.

personation Under UK election law, the act of an individual in gaining an extra vote by claiming to be someone else. Personation is very rare in mainland Britain, though it sometimes occurs in Asian communities, but is a regular feature of Northern Ireland elections.

Peruvian peace plan A proposal for settling the dispute over the FALKLANDS, put forward by President Belaunde of Peru at approximately the time that the Royal Navy sank the BELGRANO. When Britain showed interest in the plan, Argentina flatly rejected it in the wake of the sinking. Opponents of the war and CONSPIRACY THEORISTS in Britain have claimed ever since that Margaret Thatcher ordered the sinking specifically to frustrate the peace plan and ensure that Britain could fight a victorious war to recapture the islands. The plan, like several others carried between London and Buenos Aires by US Secretary of State Alexander Haig, involved Argentine withdrawal, the halting of the approaching British task force, joint UK/Argentine control of the islands under US supervision and negotiations over SOVEREIGNTY which protected the islanders' position for a period.

PESC Public Expenditure Scrutiny. The spending round, conducted by the CHIEF SECRETARY to the Treasury each autumn to determine the level of UK public spending for the financial year commencing the following April. The exercise, which involves the Chief Secretary saying "No" to the pet schemes of more senior Cabinet colleagues, is designed to produce a spending programme for announcement in the Chancellor's Autumn STATEMENT in early November. The process includes BILATERALS between the Chief Secretary and spending Ministers as the total of "bids" is squeezed down to the overall spending level fixed by Cabinet. Up to 1991 the final say rested with a "STAR CHAMBER" to which individual Ministers could appeal; from then the Cabinet set departmental totals and left the Ministers responsible to work out how to live within them.

PEST *See* TORY REFORM GROUP.

Peter the Painter *See* SIDNEY STREET SIEGE.

Peterloo The bloody scene on 16 August 1819 when cavalry attacked a peaceful crowd of 60,000 that had assembled in St. Peter's Fields, Manchester, to hear "Orator" Hunt speak on Parliamentary reform. Eleven people were killed, 140 others run through by sabres and a further 400 injured. The atrocity caused public anger and increased the pressure for reform, but it made little immediate impression on Lord Liverpool's government. The name was a bitterly ironic comparison with the British Army's triumph at Waterloo four years before under Wellington, who had just entered the Cabinet. But much of the opprobrium fell on Foreign Secretary Castlereagh, who had certainly not been party to a decision taken by local magistrates.

> I met murder on the way –
> He had a mask like Castlereagh.
>
> SHELLEY, *The Mask of Anarchy* (1819).

petition A request to a government or legislature for action, or redress of grievances, made directly by members of the public. In the House of Commons petitions ranging from a prisoner's request for parole that has been denied to a call for legislation to protect hedgehogs can be introduced by individual MPs after the main business of the day.

Petrov case The espionage case in 1954 which raised suspicions of links between FELLOW-TRAVELLERS in Australia and Soviet agents, further weakening the already-divided LABOR PARTY. On 13 April, the Liberal Prime Minister Sir Robert Menzies announced that Vladimir Petrov, a junior diplomat at the Soviet embassy in Canberra and an organizer of the MVD's espionage service, had sought and been granted POLITICAL ASYLUM. Petrov's wife was recalled to Moscow, but after her escort was disarmed at Darwin she spoke to Petrov and also sought asylum. It also emerged that ASIO had been working on Petrov, who was paid £A5000 when he handed over papers. The Russians alleged Petrov had broken Soviet law and that his wife had been forcibly detained, and on 23 April broke off relations with Australia. A ROYAL COMMISSION into the security implications of the case was immediately set up, and the parties agreed not to make it an issue in the pending Federal elections. The Labor leader, Dr. H. V. Evatt, twice appeared before the Commission to defend two of his staff mentioned as possible sources of an Australian Communist journalist; Evatt claimed the affair was a plot to discredit Labor, alleging that some party documents had been forged for this purpose. Labor failed to regain power in the elections, and split while the commission was sitting, seven anti-Communist MHRs and one Senator breaking away. In 1955 the Commission confirmed that the Soviet embassy had been used as cover for espionage, but that no Australian had committed an offence. A further election in December 1955 strengthened Menzies' hand; the breakaway group lost seats, but split the anti-Liberal vote.

PFLP Popular Front for the Liberation of Palestine. One of the most militant and active Palestinian terrorist groups, led by Ahmed Jibril. It has been responsible for a number of spectacular atrocities, including the 1972 Lod Airport massacre, when 25 people were machine-gunned to death. *See also* JACKAL.

Phalange A right-wing Christian MILITIA in the Lebanon, founded in 1936 on the basis of Spain's fascist FALANGIST movement.

PHARE The European Community's major economic aid programme for central and East Europe after the collapse of Communism. The acronym stands for Poland Hungary Assistance Reconstruction Economy, and replicates the French *phare*, lighthouse. It was quickly extended beyond Poland and Hungary to East Germany, Czechoslovakia and the

Baltic states. Much of the aid has gone to the Black Triangle, an area of high unemployment and environmental devastation from lignite mining and air pollution centred on Görlitz in Saxony, and spilling into Poland and Bohemia.

Philadelphia convention The gathering in Philadelphia from May to September 1787, presided over by George WASHINGTON, at which the US CONSTITUTION was framed. Convened to amend the Articles of CONFEDERATION, it went considerably further. All 13 states bar Rhode Island were represented, and most of the Revolutionary leadership; Thomas JEFFERSON was away in Paris, Tom Paine refused to go, saying: "I smell a rat." The structure of the new nation was agreed on the basis of the VIRGINIA PLAN, and the balance between large and small states at Federal level on the CONNECTICUT COMPROMISE; arguments over slavery were pushed to one side with their fissile potential recognized. By ten states to none, delegates also voted against adding a BILL OF RIGHTS – a decision reversed within four years. The Constitution itself, which they termed "the supreme law of the land", was approved with 16 delegates dissenting and put to the states for ratification. As the convention broke up, a woman asked the ageing Benjamin FRANKLIN: "Well, doctor, what have we got? A republic or a monarchy?" Franklin replied: "A republic, if you can keep it."

> An assembly of demi-gods. THOMAS JEFFERSON.

Phoenix Park murders The killings in Dublin on 6 May 1882 of Lord Frederick Cavendish, who had arrived in Ireland that day as Cabinet-level chief secretary, and of permanent under-secretary, Thomas Henry Burke. The outrage horrified Westminster and led Gladstone's government to introduce a Crimes Act to check FENIAN outrages; it proved ineffective. PARNELL sensed that the outrage weakened the Irish party at Westminster and asserted that the murders had been "committed by men who absolutely detest us".

phone-bank A highly-organized telephone CANVASSING operation mounted from a central point. A regular feature of US political and election campaigning.

phone-in A radio (or less frequently, television) programme where a political leader or candidate is exposed to telephone questioning from the public. It is known in America as a **call-in** (*see also* 1-800). The callers are sometimes more effective at drawing blood than highly-paid professional interviewers: one example was Mrs. Diana Gould's highly-effective and damaging questioning of Margaret Thatcher over the sinking of the BELGRANO in the 1983 election campaign.

phone-tapping scandal The episode in early 1992 that finally ended Charles HAUGHEY's dominance of Irish politics. It stemmed from the commitment by his FIANNA FAIL/PD government to bring in a Bill to regulate phone tapping. This outraged Sean Doherty, speaker of the SEANAD, whose career had been seriously damaged in 1982 when he carried the can for the BUGGING of political reporters. On 21 January 1992 Doherty called a press conference at a Dublin hotel at which he said:

> I am confirming tonight that the TAOISEACH, Mr. Haughey, was fully aware in 1982 that two journalists' phones were being tapped, and that he at no stage expressed a reservation about this action.

Within two days, Haughey had resigned as *Taoiseach* and as leader of Fianna Fail.

photo opportunity A MEDIA EVENT where a politician is made available for photographs but not for questioning by reporters. The ploy is not always successful; in 1982 the White House barred television networks from sending reporters with their camera crews to such occasions because ABC's stentorian Sam Donaldson had made a practice of shouting questions to President Reagan – who had insisted on answering them.

picketing The practice of stationing supporters of or participants in an industrial dispute outside a workplace that may or may not be relevant to it to encourage, persuade or force those employed there to stop work or otherwise show sympathy. Its origins lie in the military practice of posting pickets or sentries. Seen by TRADE UNIONS as essential to the prosecution of an effective STRIKE, the right to picket and the laws governing the practice have been subject to reversal and political strife throughout the past century in most democratic countries.

picket line The point where workers arriving at a plant or hauliers delivering goods to it are confronted by pickets. Refusal to cross a picket line has traditionally been a fundamental of working-class SOLIDARITY, crossing one the ultimate betrayal.

don't picket, it'll bleed A flippant parody in the late 1970s labour movement of politicians' condemnation of industrial militancy. From the old parental advice to children not to pick their spots: "Don't pick it; it'll bleed."

flying picket A group of pickets who travel from one plant to another attempting to halt operations, with surprise an important factor. The tactic was pioneered in Britain during a series of miners' strikes in the 1970s by Arthur Scargill (*see* KING ARTHUR).

mass picket A concentration of pickets so great as to hamper the operation of a plant through sheer weight of numbers, even if the workers show no interest in joining the dispute. Pioneered again by Scargill (*see* SALTLEY), it was harnessed at GRUNWICK by a combination of trade-union, left-wing and ethnic groups and reached its peak, in violent clashes with the police at ORGREAVE, during the 1984–85 MINERS' STRIKE. Even before then, a government code of practice supported in theory by the TUC had set a limit of six pickets per plant.

secondary picketing The practice, common during the WINTER OF DISCONTENT, of picketing a plant with little or no connection with a dispute in order to bring its employees out on strike, increasing disruption and pressure for a settlement.

Pierce, Franklin *See* HANDSOME FRANK.

pigs The derogatory term for the police, the use of which became the hallmark of the PROTEST MOVEMENT during the VIETNAM WAR. Its origins go back to 1800, but it came into its own when used against the police by demonstrators at the CHICAGO CONVENTION and thereafter. Faced with student protestors in 1967, the Californian conservative academic (and later Senator) S. I. Hayakawa said:

> When you've got a problem with swine, you have to call in the pigs.

Pigs, Bay of The abortive invasion of Cuba by CIA-backed *émigrés* which was the first military adventure, and the greatest catastrophe, of the KENNEDY presidency. Kennedy reluctantly approved plans inherited from the Eisenhower administration for the CIA to train secretly and equip 1400 Cuban refugees to land on the island and start a popular rising to overthrow Fidel Castro. On 17 April 1961 they landed at the *Bahia de Cochinos* (Bay of Pigs) on Cuba's southern coast. Without air support and with minimal US reinforcements, they were routed and the 1100 survivors soon rounded up; they were later "ransomed" for $53 million worth of aid to the Marxist regime. The adventure was denounced throughout Latin America, and its approval and failure harmed Kennedy's standing at home. But he recovered ground by taking full responsibility and promising to learn the lessons of the affair.

> All my life I've known better than to depend on the experts. How could I have been so stupid, to let them go ahead? JFK.

living proof that a pig's bladder on a stick can be elected as a member of Parliament One of a string of insults in the House of Commons directed against Terry Dicks (1937–), Conservative MP for Hayes and Harlington, by Tony Banks (1943–), former Labour chairman of the GLC Arts Committee. The taunts were provoked by Dicks's opposition to what he deemed frivolous and unnecessary spending on arts projects.

pink A pejorative term used by both the Left and the Right for mildly left-wing people, the colour being a watered-down version of the red associated with Socialism or Communism. Most fashionable at the height of the COLD WAR, it dates back at least to 1837 when Thomas de Quincy wrote:

> Amusing it is to look back upon any political work of Mr. Shepherd's . . . and to know that the pale pink of his Radicalism was then accounted deep, deep scarlet.

Behind its use by right-wingers was the inference that "pinks" might be dupes of Communism.

Pink Lady Richard Nixon's denunciatory name for Rep. Helen Gahagan Douglas, the liberal former film actress whom he defeated in 1950 to become Senator for California at the age of 38. In a "pink sheet" circulated throughout the state, Nixon (*see* TRICKY DICK) claimed that on 354 occasions she had voted the same way as a "notorious Communist-line congressman". It failed to mention that Mrs. Douglas had frequently voted against him, or that on 112 occasions Nixon had actually voted with him.

pinko A more insulting derivative of "pink", used against liberals and other "UN-AMERICAN" types by Vice-President Spiro T. AGNEW (1918–) and other US conservatives.

pink triangle The symbol that the Nazis required homosexuals to wear in the CONCENTRATION CAMPS, singling them out for attention and for ridicule by implying effeminacy.

parlour pink The predecessor of RADICAL CHIC, a derogatory term from Cold War America for affluent supporters of the cause of world workers' solidarity and other liberal causes.

Pioneers The youth movement of the Soviet Communist Party, emulated in Eastern European countries during the Cold War and itself modelled on the Boy Scouts. LENIN replaced God as the object of their reverence. Lucky members of the Russian Pioneers could even operate their own scaled-down railway system.

Pitchfork Ben The nickname of South Carolina's Sen. Benjamin Tillman (1847–1918), a wealthy plantation owner and former state governor. He gained it during the 1894 campaign that won him his seat by saying of Grover Cleveland:

> If I go to the Senate I promise that I will use a pitchfork in the President's fat old ribs.

Tillman was re-elected three times despite being censured for manhandling his fellow South Carolina senator in the chamber. President Theodore Roosevelt was so affronted by Tillman's behaviour that he withdrew an invitation for him to meet Prince Henry of Germany at the White House. Tillman was also an unashamed WHITE SUPREMACIST. The Indiana Republican Congressman James Watson assured his own re-election by paying Tillman $250 a time to address open meetings in his district; Black voters who attended the meetings were so outraged by Tillman that they rallied to the Republican ticket.

Pitt. Pitt the Elder The posthumous nickname of **William Pitt**, 1st Earl of Chatham (1708–78), thrice Prime Minister and the most forceful critic of Britain's treatment of its American colonies. Entering Parliament in 1735 as a violent opponent of WALPOLE, he quickly made his mark as a forceful speaker; Walpole declared: "We must muzzle this terrible cornet of horse," but Pitt was unrepentant, telling the Commons: "The atrocious crime of being a young man . . . I shall neither attempt to palliate nor deny." As war loomed with France in 1756 he declared: "I know that I can save the country and that no one else can." That December he became Prime Minister, but George II dismissed him after four months. The King had to reinstate him 11 weeks later, nominally under Newcastle. Pitt's mastery of the Commons was complete, largely because of his opposition to the growth of party. George III plotted with Bute against him; he resigned in October 1761, refusing the Governorship of Canada. He told the Cabinet:

> I was called by my Sovereign and the Voice of the People to assist the State when others had abdicated the service of it. That being so, no one can be surprised that I will go on no longer since my advice is not taken.

He returned to power in July 1766, taking the title Earl of Chatham. The GREAT COMMONER's elevation was unpopular with the people. Lord Chesterfield noting: "The joke here is that he has had a fall upstairs." In 1767 he was struck by mental illness, resigning in October 1768; David Hume commented: "He is not mad – that is, no madder than usual." Gout soon relieved the disorder, and in 1774 Pitt began his campaign for a "more gentle way of governing America". He spoke brilliantly in the crisis years of 1776–77, warning: "You may ravage, but you cannot conquer", but died in 1778.

Pitt the Younger. William Pitt (1759–1806), second son of Pitt the Elder. Britain's youngest Prime Minister (1784–1800, 1804–06), with the most meteoric career of any holder of the office. His gained early advantage from his father's reputation, but before long Edmund BURKE was hailing him as "not merely a chip of the old block, but the old block himself". Entering Parliament when barely 22 as a member of Lord North's opposition, he became Chancellor of the Exchequer and Leader of the Commons at 23, declining the Premiership when Lord Shelburne resigned. In 1784, aged only 24, he became Prime Minister. Though ridiculed for his inexperience by Charles James Fox, he stayed in office 17 years through one of the most turbulent periods in Britain's history. He healed wounds opened by the loss of the American colonies, reduced the NATIONAL DEBT, ended public hangings at Tyburn and allowed Roman Catholics into the army and the legal profession. But his greatest success was in insulating Britain from the FRENCH REVOLUTION; Ralph Creyke wrote:

> I shall ever revere his memory for standing between the dead and the living, and staying the plague which in the French revolution had infected the continent, and might have spread and desolated this island.

Georgiana, Duchess of Devonshire, detected one reason for his survival: "His eloquence was so great he could explain even every disaster into almost the contrary." And Samuel Rogers wrote: "Pitt's voice sounded as if he had worsted in his mouth."

In 1800 Pitt, by now a declining 41 and scorned by William Cobbett as "the great snorting bawler", resigned in protest at George III's opposition to Catholic EMANCIPATION and his merging of Ireland's government with that of Britain. He returned to meet the threat of Napoleon, but was broken by the French victory at Austerlitz; he died aged 46 shortly after hearing of Nelson's victory at Trafalgar. His last words were: "I think that I could eat one of Bellamy's veal pies." His death brought a moving epitaph from Sir Walter Scott:

> Now is the stately column broke,
> The beacon-light is quench'd in smoke;
> The trumpet's silver sound is still,
> The warden silent on the hill.

But Byron was more cynical:

> With death doomed to grapple
> Beneath this cold slab, he
> Who lied in the Chapel
> Now lies in the Abbey.

(The Chapel is St. Stephen's Chapel where the Commons then met.)

place. place in the sun Germany's demand for COLONIES, on a par with Britain, France and other European nations. Realizing that the newly-united state had been left behind at the height of the Scramble for AFRICA and other IMPERIALIST adventures, the future Chancellor Bernhard von Bülow told the REICHSTAG on 6 December 1897:

> In a word, we desire to throw no one into the shade [in East Asia], but we also demand our own place in the sun.

Less than four years later, after the AGADIR CRISIS and German muscle-flexing in China, Kaiser Wilheim II declared: "We have fought for our place in the sun and won it. Our future is on the water."

placeman Someone who owes his office purely to PATRONAGE, generally having paid the patron or entered into some other corrupt commitment to obtain it.

> Patriot: a candidate for place. Politics: the art of getting one. HENRY FIELDING (1707–54).

Plaid The Welsh term for any political party, and shorthand for **Plaid Cymru** (Party of Wales), the party set up in 1925 to secure self-government. The Plaid won its first Parliamentary seat in 1966, and survived an overwhelming "No" vote in the 1979 DEVOLUTION referendum; in 1992 it made its strongest showing, taking four seats in the Welsh-speaking north-west of the principality.

Plains The tiny home town in southwest Georgia, near Americus, of President Jimmy CARTER. It became the focus of intense media attention during his campaign for the Presidency and term of office; for a brief period the Carter peanut farm and the town depot where brother Billy Carter (*see* BILLYGATE) held court became household names.

plan. Five-year plan *See* FIVE.

National Plan *See* NATIONAL.

planning agreements The concept arrived at by Britain's LABOUR PARTY in 1972–73 for agreements between government and individual companies on their future production and development. They were a key feature of Labour's economic programme in the two 1974 general elections, but the Wilson and Callaghan governments never put the idea into practice, except where firms were forced to go to the State for financial assistance.

planning blight The dead hand that falls over a property or a neighbourhood which is the site of a proposed new development, such as a road. Such blight makes homes and other property unsaleable and leads to the deterioration of the area; in Britain compensation is sometimes offered to relieve the problem.

Plant commission The group set up by Britain's LABOUR PARTY in 1991 under Raymond Plant, Professor of Politics at Southampton University, to consider the case for PROPORTIONAL REPRESENTATION. Neil KINNOCK hoped that it would resolve divisions in the party between those, such as Robin Cook and Arthur Scargill, who were anxious to see PR adopted, and trenchant opponents of an end to FIRST PAST THE POST led by Roy Hattersley. Its interim report suggested PR for European elections and elections to a Scottish Parliament, but not for the House of Commons. The commission became an issue in the 1992 election when, with the LIBERAL DEMOCRATS gaining ground, Kinnock invited them to join it. The move blunted the Liberal challenge, but also helped turn the tide against Labour. The commission's report in 1993 tentatively opted for the supplementary vote, and John Smith promised a PR referendum when Labour returned to power.

platform (1) The programme on which a party fights an election. In America, a party's platform is hammered out in drafting sessions immediately before its nominating CONVENTION.

> The political platform is just a breach of promise. ARNOLD GLASGOW.

(2) A mainly UK term for the dignitaries who sit behind the party leader or other keynote speaker at conferences or mass meetings.

Platt amendment The notorious measure which gave America the right to intervene at will in Cuba. It was forced through Congress in 1901 as a RIDER to an APPROPRIATIONS Bill by Sen. Orville H. Platt of Connecticut, as the condition for withdrawing US forces. The amendment stipulated that Cuba would sign no treaty affecting its SOVEREIGNTY without US permission, that the US could intervene to protect its independence or political stability, and that Cuba would give it land for naval bases; one was established at Guantanamo. Cuba was prevented from incurring international debt, and obliged to include the terms of the amendment in its constitution. Franklin D. Roosevelt had it repealed in 1934 under his GOOD NEIGHBOUR policy toward Latin America; the Guantanamo base survives.

Plaza agreement An agreement reached in New York in September 1985 by the Group of Five nations – America, Britain, France, Japan and West Germany – to maintain world currency stability by lowering the value of the US dollar. Finance ministers agreed to use "co-ordinated intervention" in the markets to bring this about, and did so well into 1986.

Please accept, (your) excellency, the assurances of my highest consideration The standard sign-off for a formal letter between high-ranking diplomats of different countries.

plebiscite A vote by the entire people of a nation or region. The term is interchangeable with REFERENDUM but tends to be used of a ballot to determine which nation a disputed region would prefer to become part of. The name comes from ancient Rome, being a vote taken by the representatives of the *plebs*, the common people.

Pledge of allegiance Now a cornerstone of American life, the Pledge of allegiance to the flag is not steeped in antiquity but was first published in the *Youth's Companion* of 8 September 1892 and recited at the dedication of the Chicago World's Fair grounds on 21 October that year. Its author is believed to have been Francis Bellamy, chairman of the executive committee for the first Columbus Day celebrations. The full text is:

> I pledge allegiance to the Flag of the United States of America, and to the Republic for which it stands, one Nation under God, indivisible, with liberty and justice for all.

The words "under God" were added in the 1950s. The Pledge became an issue in the 1988 Presidential election when the Bush camp accused Michael Dukakis of having "vetoed the Pledge". What the Democratic nominee had in fact done was vote for a Bill that would not force the children of Jehovah's Witnesses to recite the pledge in school.

PLO Palestine Liberation Organization. A politico-military organization founded in 1964 to represent PALESTINIAN Arab refugees and re-establish a Palestinian state. These aims have pitted it against Israel, as the Palestinians lay claim to most of the OCCUPIED TERRITORIES, but it has also crossed swords with Jordan (*see* BLACK SEPTEMBER) and hastened civil war in the Lebanon. Since 1967 the PLO has been dominated by the AL-FATAH group headed by Yassir Arafat (1929–), and since 1974 has been recognized by the United Nations. However it has been plagued by splits; in 1983 Arafat and 5000 supporters were forced to quit the Lebanon for Tunis. The PLO has conducted terrorist campaigns against Israel, including the murder of 11 Israeli athletes at the 1972 MUNICH Olympic Games. But in 1988 the leadership declared the existence of a Palestinian state, renounced terrorism and recognized Israel's right to exist within secure borders. It has continued to encourage the INTIFADA against Israeli occupation of the WEST BANK, the home of 1.7 million Palestinians, and has failed to check terrorist activity by some of its more militant offshoots. Arafat lost some Western credibility by supporting Saddam Hussein in the GULF WAR, but the PLO subsequently took a conciliatory role in the Arab-Israeli PEACE PROCESS.

> A humanitarian organization, entirely devoted to helping elderly, disabled Americans off the decks of cruise liners.
> PRIVATE EYE.

> The PLO never pass up an opportunity to pass up an opportunity. ABBA EBAN (1915–).

PLP Parliamentary Labour Party. The body comprising all Labour MPs at Westminster, which until 1981 elected the party leader. It meets twice weekly: on Wednesday to discuss policy and party matters, and on Thursday briefly to consider the following week's BUSINESS.

Plum Book The book listing the 7000-odd jobs in Washington that are filled by POLITICAL APPOINTEES and change hands with a new President. It is the "Bible" of an incoming administration's TRANSITION team.

Plumbers The "dirty tricks department" of the Nixon White House, which was embarrassingly exposed as the WATERGATE scandal broke. Its true name was the "special investigations unit", and Nixon formed it in June 1971 to "stop security leaks and investigate other sensitive matters". On 3 September that year the Plumbers, led by the ex-CIA agent E. Howard Hunt, broke into the office of Lewis J. Fielding, the psychiatrist who was counselling Daniel Ellsberg, the former deputy Secretary of Defence who had confessed to leaking the PENTAGON PAPERS. For this operation, intended to recover incriminating information, the CIA lent Hunt a red wig, a special camera and a "speech-altering device". The Plumbers got away undetected, but came to grief a year later when they were caught red-handed in the Watergate building.

> *John Dean*: These people are going to cost $1 million over the next two years.
> *Richard Nixon*: You could get a million dollars. You could get it in cash. I know where it could be gotten.
> *Watergate Tapes*, 21 March 1973.

pluralism A political system which provides for diversity between different views and traditions, and consequently for competing parties and ideologies.

plurality A MAJORITY by a winner over the nearest challenger; in America the word majority applies to the winner's absolute majority over all others combined.

plutocracy A democracy dominated by wealth; a **plutocrat** is one who is powerful because of his or her riches. The word comes from *Plutus*, the Greek god of wealth.

PM The abbreviation for PRIME MINISTER which frequently occurs in WHITEHALL conversation; as in "He's been asked to go in and brief the PM."

PMC In Australia's Federal government, the Department of Prime Minister and Cabinet.

It sets public servant against public servant.
ANDREW PEACOCK (1939– , Liberal leader 1983–5, 1989–90).

PNQ Private Notice Question. At Westminster, a question on a matter of urgency tabled either by an Opposition front-bencher or by a member on either side of the House with a direct interest, *e.g.* by a member whose constituents have been lost in a fishing disaster. If the SPEAKER grants the application, the member rises after QUESTION TIME to elicit a reply from the Minister responsible, who makes a statement on the matter in hand. A period of questioning by MPs on both sides then follows.

a PNQ running The phrase for the period when an application for a PNQ has been lodged, and it is not yet known whether or not the Speaker will agree to it.

Pocatello "You can't go back to Pocatello" has come to signify the reluctance or inability of some home-town politicians to make their way back from Washington once their Congressional career in Washington is over – Pocatello, Idaho, being the example. The inference that the attraction of home palls when compared to the fleshpots of the capital is similar to

How you gonna keep 'em down on the farm
After they've seen Paree?

The phrase was coined in 1943–44 by Richard Neuberger, later a Senator for Oregon (it is not recorded if he went back there) and Jonathan Daniels, one of FDR's White House aides.

pogrom (Russ. destruction or riot). A drive to massacre or terrorize an ethnic minority, specifically the Jewish rural population of Russian-governed eastern Europe in the decades prior to World War I. Pogroms were for a time an unofficial arm of Tsarist policy, particularly in Poland, the Ukraine and western Russia.

point. Point Four programme The foreign policy initiative President Truman announced in his INAUGURAL address in January 1949 after his surprise victory over Thomas Dewey. Its aim was to counter Soviet bids for influence in what is now the THIRD WORLD by offering practical assistance to its people. Over the next three years America spent nearly $40 million on medical and technological aid, despite Congressional objections that "charity begins at home" and elements in some recipient countries who denounced it as IMPERIALISM".

point man A person appointed to spearhead a US political campaign, either for a party or candidate or against a policy pursued by others. When President Reagan needed support in 1976 for his STAR WARS policy, he sent Vice-President Bush to Europe as a point man to allay the gathering doubts. This term, in use since the early 1970s, grew out of its World War II usage, for the front soldier in a military patrol.

point of order *See* ORDER.

pointy-heads A term for intellectuals in use in America since World War II, the inference being that their pointed heads would fit neatly into dunces' caps. It was popularized by Governor George Wallace of Alabama during his campaigns for the Presidency; he applied it particularly to eastern LIBERALS and opponents of the VIETNAM WAR.

As an aide to Gov. Wallace and his national campaign director in 1970–71, I helped the Gov'nuh blame it all on those "integrating, scallywagging, race-mixing, pointy headed liberals who can't even park their bicycles straight".
TOM TURNIPSEED, *New York Times*, 30 August 1984.

pol An American abbreviation, the equivalent of "cop" for policeman but less complimentary; it refers not so much to a politician as to one of the fatted patrons of MACHINE POLITICS. Hugh Rawson, in his *Dictionary of Invective*, notes:

The short form reeks of SMOKE-FILLED ROOMS and is almost always used pejoratively.

Polaris A submarine-launched ballistic nuclear missile which formed one leg of the US nuclear TRIAD from the 1960s, and provided Britain's sole naval nuclear deterrent throughout the 1970s and 1980s. It was developed by America in the late 1950s to help bridge the perceived MISSILE GAP between the SUPERPOWERS. The first Polaris-equipped nuclear submarine, USS *George Washington*, was launched on 15 November 1960. In 1962 President KENNEDY offered Polaris technology to Britain, enabling it to cancel its own missile programme; the first British Polaris submarine, HMS *Renown*, was completed in 1968. The US Navy replaced its Polaris with Poseidon missiles from 1969, but Britain updated its missiles with MIRV warheads under the CHEVALINE programme, completed in 1982; these weapons are in turn being replaced by TRIDENT, which has a far greater THROW-WEIGHT but is again dependent on US facilities.

polarisation A situation in which each of the parties in a two-PARTY system adopts a steadily more extreme position, with the gulf between them steadily increasing. Such a process, as witnessed in Britain in the early 1980s, increases social tension and unrest, and can also lead to a stampede by voters towards a moderate third party until the established parties veer back towards the middle ground.

policy The course of action a government intends and endeavours to pursue, overall or in respect of a particular subject or issue. Politicians have long argued over whether policy is dictated by events or can be used to determine them. The 19th-century Austrian statesman Metternich declared that "policy is like a play in so many acts, which unfolds inevitably once the curtain is raised. [For] intelligent people the problem lies in the decision whether the curtain is to be raised at all." Lord SALISBURY reckoned there could be "no such thing as a fixed policy, because policy, like all organic entities, is always in the making"; and MAHATMA Gandhi described a policy as "a temporary creed liable to be changed, but while it holds good it has got to be pursued with apostolic zeal". And Richard Nixon observed of the art of governing in the age of the electronic media:

> What makes good television makes bad politics.

policy review The wholesale reassessment of its policies conducted by Britain's LABOUR PARTY after sustaining its third successive election defeat in 1987. The principal casualties of the review were Labour's commitments to UNILATERALISM and NATIONALIZATION; when Labour narrowly lost a further election in 1992, the review was seen as having helped narrow the gap with the Conservatives – but also as having left the party with no obvious beliefs.

> A sort of BOSTON TEA PARTY with Labour jettisoning electoral liabilities wherever they are discovered.
>
> ANON. Conservative MP.

policy unit The small group of civil servants and secondees from the PRIVATE SECTOR, based in 10 DOWNING STREET, who advise Britain's Prime Minister on the merits of policies that might be adopted and assess those being implemented.

policy wonk Someone with an interest, bordering on obsession, in the policy options open to government. Originally a Harvard term, it was given wider currency when President Clinton (*see* COMEBACK KID) self-deprecatingly used it to describe himself.

Centre for Policy Studies The pioneer Thatcherite THINK-TANK, founded in 1974 by Sir Keith Joseph (*see* MAD MONK), which under the direction of Alfred Sherman eclipsed the official Conservative Research Department and originated many of the radical economic and other policies carried out by the party in office after 1979. It was set up with Edward Heath's permission on condition that it did not compete for funds with the party's traditional backers; the promise was not kept and Heath regarded the founding of the CPS as one element of the 'treachery' which installed Mrs. Thatcher as Tory leader in his place.

My policy is to have no policy A semi-serious statement made by Abraham LINCOLN, but not originated by him; in 1826 Metternich had written: "The only good policy is to pursue no policy."

Polisario Front (*PO*pular front for the *LI*beration of *SA*guira hamra and *RIO* de oro) The movement of Saharwi tribesmen which has been fighting for the independence of the Western Sahara since the withdrawal of the Spanish colonial authorities after Morocco's GREEN MARCH in 1975. Backed by Algeria, Polisario formed a government-in-exile, the Saharwi Arab Democratic Republic (**SADR**), in 1976. Some 70 countries now recognize it and in 1989 it was accepted at the OAU – a step which led Morocco to withdraw. Morocco and Mauritania divided the territory between them in 1975, and when Mauritania dropped its claim in 1979 Morocco tried to annex the entire territory. Twenty thousand Polisario guerrillas armed by and operating from Algeria drove King Hassan's troops back, since when Morocco has controlled part of the Western Sahara from behind a defensive wall and minefields. The UN has voted Western Sahara the right of self-determination, but repeated efforts to stage a PLEBISCITE in the territory have broken down.

Polish corridor The strip of former German territory given to Poland by the 1919 VERSAILLES Treaty to ensure the new state access to the Baltic. The corridor, roughly along the line of the river Vistula, broke through to the sea west of Danzig (which became a free city), cutting East Prussia off from the rest of Germany. The loss of the corridor, inhabited largely by Germans, was a cause of friction between Germany and Poland from the outset and gave Hitler an additional pretext for invading Poland in 1939, the offensive which finally triggered WORLD WAR II.

Politburo The chief policy-making body of the COMMUNIST PARTY of the Soviet Union, first formed in 1917. The five-member committee reviewed decisions to be taken before they were submitted to the government. The Politburo was replicated in Communist regimes throughout eastern Europe and Asia; in 1952 it was superseded in the Soviet Union by the Presidium of the Communist Party's CENTRAL COMMITTEE, but that body was renamed the Politburo in 1966. Even before the collapse of Communism, "politburo" had become a derogatory term in the West for any group of decision-makers who displayed arrogance and lacked ACCOUNTABILITY. Ronald Reagan's budget director David Stockman once referred to the House Democratic committee chairmen as "the Politburo of the WELFARE STATE".

political. political adviser Also known as a **special adviser**. At Westminster a person, often a young member of the party's research department, appointed by a Minister to advise on the political dimension of decisions to be taken. A political adviser holds temporary civil service rank.

political animal Someone with an instinctive interest or flair for politics. Aristotle reckoned that "man is by nature a political animal", but he meant by this that participation in society is a natural human activity.

political appointee Someone appointed to a post, not necessarily one with any political connotations, by virtue of their political allegiance or the PATRONAGE of a politician or party. Such appointments are much more widespread in America than in Britain.

political asylum The right of a person persecuted for his or her political beliefs or activity in his or her own country to seek refuge in another. The granting of asylum to those under threat, with criteria set by the UNITED NATIONS, has been a hallmark of a Western democracy. But in Germany the automatic right of anyone to asylum under the country's BASIC LAW was waived in 1993 after a tidal wave of immigration from Eastern Europe, and John Major's government has legislated to curb the seeking of asylum in Britain by so-called "economic refugees".

political co-operation The EUROPEAN COMMUNITY term for agreement by member states to pursue joint FOREIGN POLICY initiatives.

political correctness The doctrine widely held and enforced by radical US academics that the only acceptable terminology is that which accords with their beliefs; it is most frequently and rigidly applied in cases of race and gender. The basis for it is a desire to avoid causing offence to particular groups, but in practice it has escalated from insisting that "Black" people be referred to as "African-Americans" to demanding, at the extreme, that the dead be described as "terminally-challenged". Advocates of political correctness regard it as assertion of basic human dignity; critics condemn its most extreme manifestations as a form of FASCISM. Some US newspapers employ computers to make sure that their language is politically correct, but they have their limitations; the financial pages of one California paper reported that a previously loss-making corporation had now "moved into the African–American".

political football An issue which is seized on and exploited by one or more political factions for their own ends, with eventual disregard for the real interests of those affected.

political levy The levy raised from their members by Britain's TRADE UNIONS for political ends, primarily to support and finance the LABOUR PARTY. It was established after the OSBORNE JUDGMENT barred the unions from contributing to the party from their general funds; an argument has raged ever since over whether the onus should be on members who do not want to pay to contract out, or on active Labour supporters to contract in. Under legislation passed by the Thatcher government, contracting-out continues, provided a ballot of union members agree.

political prisoner Someone detained in prison purely or primarily because of his or her political beliefs, not having committed any crime under the civil law. Notorious régimes the world over have always imprisoned their opponents rather than submit to rational argument and the judgment of the people; the political inmates of Hitler's CONCENTRATION CAMPS and the occupants of the Soviet GULAG have been among many 20th-century victims. The **Unknown Political Prisoner** was commemorated in a UNITED NATIONS-backed competition for a commemorative sculpture after World War II, won by the UK sculptor Reg Butler.

> Nothing can be more abhorrent to democracy than to imprison a person or keep him in prison because he is unpopular. That is the real test of civilization.
>
> CHURCHILL, 21 November 1943.

political science The science or study of government, and the interaction of political forces, with reference to its principles, aims, methods and conduct.

political status The special status accorded to suspected terrorists INTERNED in Northern Ireland in the early 1970s, which convicted Republican and LOYALIST prisoners subsequently sought for themselves. The demand for political status was pursued in the H-BLOCKS through the BLANKET and DIRTY PROTESTs, and ultimately through a traumatic HUNGER STRIKE in which Bobby Sands and nine other IRA prisoners died before the goal was abandoned.

political union One of the twin aims of the MAASTRICHT TREATY, the binding together more closely of the member states of the EUROPEAN COMMUNITY and the development of common political institutions.

political wing In a PARAMILITARY organization, the part which acts as a legitimate party or movement, as opposed to the **military wing** which engages in terrorism. In the case of the Provisional IRA, SINN FEIN forms its political wing.

politician A practitioner of the art of POLITICS, essential to the working of human society but frequently despised by those outside the political arena; indeed the word is sometimes a term of abuse. In ancient Greece Aristophanes wrote that "under every stone lurks a politician", Shakespeare 2000 years later wrote in *King Lear*:

> Get thee glass eyes
> And like a scurvy politician, seem
> To see the things thou dost not.

Every humorist, and many non-humorists, have put forward their own definition of a politician: "Like the bones of a horse's shoulder. Not a straight one in sight" – Wendell Phillips; "An eel in the fundamental mud upon which the superstructure of organized society is reared. When he wiggles, he mistakes the agitation of his tail for the trembling of the edifice. As compared with the statesman, he suffers the disadvantage of being alive" – Ambrose Bierce; "An animal who can sit on the fence and yet keep both ears to the ground" – H. L. Mencken; "an ass on which everyone has sat except a man" – e e cummings; "a statesman who approaches every question with an open mouth" – Adlai Stevenson; "that insidious and crafty animal whose councils are directed by momentary fluctuations of affairs" – Adam Smith; "little tin gods on wheels" – Rudyard Kipling; "a number of anxious dwarfs trying to grill a whale" – J. B. Priestley; "dangerous lunatics to be avoided when possible, and carefully humoured; people, above all, to whom we must never tell the truth" – W. H. Auden; "An acrobat. He keeps his balance by saying the opposite of what he does" – Maurice Barrès; "someone who divides his time between running for office and running for cover" – Anon.

Shakespeare's *doppelgänger* Francis Bacon observed: "It is as hard and severe a thing to be a true politician as it is to be truly moral." H. L. Mencken reckoned that "a good politician is quite as unthinkable as an honest burglar"; Walter Lippmann stated that "successful democratic politicians are insecure and intimidated men. They advance politically only as they placate, appease, bribe, seduce, bamboozle or otherwise manage to manipulate the demanding and threatening elements in their constituencies"; Simon Cameron said more sharply: "An honest politician is one who, when he is bought, stays bought." Frank Kent declared: "The only way a reporter should look at a politician is down"; Sam Shaffer that "the effectiveness of a politician varies in inverse proportion to his commitment to principle", while Brendan Francis noted: "Politicians, like prostitutes, are held in contempt. But what man does not run to them when he needs their services?" Lucille Ball announced: "Just say the word 'politician' and I think of chicanery"; while the veteran election-watcher Theodore H. White confided: "The best time to listen to a politician is when he is on a street corner, in the rain, late at night, when he's exhausted. Then he doesn't lie."

The politician's stock in trade is words. Theodore Roosevelt reckoned that "the most successful politician is he who says what everyone is thinking, more often in the loudest voice"; Enoch POWELL went a stage further, saying: "A politician crystallizes what most people mean – even if they don't know it." Paul Harwitz wrote: "The reason politicians make strange bedfellows is because they all use the same bunk", but Clare Boothe Luce drew comfort from her belief that "sooner or later all politicians die of swallowing their own words". Sen. Henry F. Ashurst asserted that "the politician must always tell the people what they want to hear", Ed Murrow that "the politician is trained in the art of inexactitude". G. K. Chesterton noted tartly that "every politician is emphatically a promising politician", the ICI chairman Sir Paul Chambers that "exhortation of other people to do something is the last resort of politicians who are at a loss to know what to do themselves", and Iain Macleod that "a politician's pronouncements have a news value in direct proportion to his prospects of power". DE GAULLE cynically observed that "since a politician never believes what he says, he is surprised when others believe him", and Khruschev that "politicians are the same all over. They promise to build a bridge even where there is no river."

There have been some equally picturesque views of the characteristics required by a politician: "A horrible voice, bad breath and a vulgar manner" – Aristophanes; "the ability to foretell what is going to happen tomorrow, next week, next month and next year – and the ability afterwards to explain why it didn't happen" – CHURCHILL; "One has to be a lowbrow, a bit of a murderer; ready and willing to see people sacrificed, slaughtered for the sake of an idea – whether a good one or a bad one" – Henry Miller; "three hats: one for throwing in the ring, one for talking through, and one for pulling rabbits out of if elected" – Carl Sandburg. Sen. Mike Mansfield once observed that "even a politician is human", but many people are not so sure. John F. KENNEDY confessed: "Mothers all want their sons to grow up to be President, but they don't want them to be politicians in the process", the *New Orleans Times* editorialized: "It is no wonder politicians get hard-boiled. They're always in hot water," and Richard Harris reckoned "selective cowardice" was an attribute of most. Edward Heath said: "If politicians lived on praise and thanks, they'd be forced into some other line of business", so Australia's Stanley Melbourne Bruce was at an advantage when he asserted: "My chief advantage as a politician is that I did not give a damn." Field-Marshal Montgomery reminisced: "I have spent most of my life fighting the Germans and fighting the politicians. It is much easier to fight the Germans." Harold Macmillan warned idealists: "If people want a sense of purpose they should get it from an archbishop. They should certainly not get it from their politicians," while Harold WILSON concluded that "the practised performance of latter-day politicians is the game of musical daggers – never be left holding the dagger when the music stops."

> Render any politician down and there's enough fat to fry an egg. SPIKE MILLIGAN.

> Your politicians will always be there when they need you.
> Carter Campaign T-shirt, 1980.

> We are not politicians. We made our revolution to get the politicians out. FIDEL CASTRO, 1961.

> It has been the great fault of our own politicians that they have all wanted to do something.
> ANTHONY TROLLOPE.

See also STATESMAN.

politicization The arousal of political consciousness and activism among a previously apathetic section of the population, either by positive campaigning from a motivated group or (more often) by some blunder or act of malice on the part of the authorities.

politics The conduct of government at all levels, and the interaction of political parties and movements within a social system, and of men and women within those movements. Also the views held by an individual, as in "What are her politics?" There is no shortage of definitions: "nothing more than a means of rising in the world" – Dr. Johnson; "the gizzard of society, full of guts and gravel" – Thoreau; "an ordeal path among red hot ploughshares" – John ADAMS; "the systematic organization of hatreds" – Henry Adams; "not a science, but an art" – Bismarck; "a deleterious profession, like some poisonous handicrafts" – Ralph Waldo Emerson; "the conduct of public affairs for private advantage; a means of livelihood affected by the more degraded portion of our criminal classes" – Ambrose Bierce; "the art of looking for trouble, finding it whether it exists or not, diagnosing it incorrectly and applying the wrong remedy" – Sir Ernest Benn; "a dog's life without the dog's decencies" – Rudyard Kipling; "the art of preventing people from busying themselves with their own business" – Paul Valéry; "all politics is apple sauce" – Will Rogers; "the gentle art of getting votes from the poor and campaign funds from the rich, by promising to protect each from the other" – Oscar Ameringer; "the science of who gets what, when and why" – Sidney Hillman; "war without bloodshed" – CHAIRMAN MAO; "the art of government" – Harry S. Truman; "a blood sport" – Aneurin Bevan; "who gets what, when, how" – Harold Lasswell; "the diversion of trivial men who, when they succeed in it, become important in the eyes of even more trivial men" – George Jean Nathan; "the skilled use of blunt objects" – Lester Pearson; "too serious a matter to be left to the politicians" – DE GAULLE; "politics is property" – Murray Kempton; "a form of astrology, and money is its sign" – John Leonard; "yesterday's answers to today's problems" – Marshall McLuhan; "a thing that only the unsophisticated go for" – Kingsley Amis; "like a Brahma's horns – a point here, a point there and a lot of bull in between" – Ruth Fountain; "like sex in a hula hoop" – Richard Reeves; "the art of acquiring, holding and wielding power" – Indira Gandhi.

> All politics is local. TIP O'NEILL.

Above all, politics is a rough and tumble. CHURCHILL wrote: "Politics are as exciting as war, and quite as dangerous. In war you can be killed only once, but in politics many times," and Lloyd George said: "Piracy, broadsides, blood on the decks – you'll find them all in politics." Konrad Adenauer reckoned that "the art of politics consists in knowing precisely when it is necessary to hit an opponent slightly below the belt", Kenneth Clarke observed that "the more caring the subject, the rougher the debate", while the Australian Fred Daley ruefully noted: "politics is a funny game. One day you're a rooster, the next a feather duster." Yet the US commentator James Reston identified the magic of politics when he described it as "like booze and women: dangerous but incomparably exciting", and Lord Hailsham warned: "The moment politics becomes dull, democracy is in danger."

> Until you've been in politics
> You've never really been alive
> It's rough and sometimes it's
> dirty and it's always hard
> work and tedious details
> But, it's the only sport for grownups – all other
> games are for kids.
> Quotation from *Heinlein* in US Sen. John Culver's private office.

The idea of politics as a game has produced numerous sporting comparisons. Sen. Eugene McCarthy asserted: "Being in politics is like being a football coach. You need to be smart enough to understand the game – and dumb enough to think it is important;" John F. KENNEDY reckoned that "politics is like football – if you see daylight, go for the hole", and Art Buchwald mischievously commented: "I always wanted to get into politics, but was never light enough to make the team." Sen. Henry Ashurst felt politics was more like roller skating: "You go partly where you want to go, and partly where the damn things take you." Julian Bond noted "a thin line between politics and theatricals", and Professor C. Northcote Parkinson observed of the British: "If they cannot be playing golf or tennis, they can at least pretend that politics is a game with very similar rules."

Opinions have differed on the personal qualities required for politics. Robert Louis Stevenson considered it "perhaps the only profession for which no preparation is thought necessary", and George Bernard Shaw wrote: "He knows nothing and thinks he knows everything. That points clearly to a political career." Napoleon declared that "in politics, absurdity is not a hardship", Thiers that "one must take nothing tragically and everything seriously", and Lord Carrington that "if you take yourself seriously in politics, you've had it". Barbara Castle was convinced that "in politics, guts is all", Henry Adams that "practical politics consists in ignoring facts", while James C. Wright lamented:

> A rhinoceros is an animal with a hide two feet thick, and no apparent interest in politics. What a waste.

Lyndon B. Johnson put the case for intuition, saying: "If you're in politics and you can't tell when you walk into a room who's for you and who's against you, you're in the wrong line of work." Woodrow WILSON ruled out tolerance as "an admirable intellectual gift, but of little use in politics. Politics is a war of causes, a joust of principles." John Kenneth Galbraith observed that "nothing is so admirable in politics as a short memory", echoing de Tocqueville's observation: "I have often noticed in politics how men are ruined by having too good a memory", and Chris Patten quickly discovered that "it rarely pays in politics to be wise before the event". As to what politics does to its practitioners, Ronald Reagan asserted: "The only experience you get in politics is how to be political", and Josef Goebbels revealingly stated: "Politics ruin the character. They develop the worst and meanest qualities."

> I am not made for politics because I am incapable of wishing for or accepting the death of my adversary.
> ALBERT CAMUS (1913–60).

> Men enter local politics largely as a result of being unhappily married.
> Professor C. NORTHCOTE PARKINSON (1919–93).

The morality of politics has been in question since Plato branded it as "nothing but corruption", though Aneurin BEVAN maintained: "I have never regarded politics as the arena of morals. It is the arena of interests." MACHIAVELLI, not surprisingly, reckoned that "politics have no relation to morals"; Rousseau that "those people who treat politics and morality separately will never understand either"; Disraeli that "in politics there is no honour", Lord ROSEBERY that "a gentleman may blithely do in politics what he would kick a man downstairs for doing in ordinary life", and LENIN that "there are no morals in politics, only expedience". Lord Bryce asserted that "a political career brings out the basest qualities in human nature", and FDR's close aide Louis Howe that "you cannot adopt politics as a profession and remain honest". Russell Long concluded that "the first rule of politics is not to lie to somebody unless it is absolutely necessary", while Ronald Reagan quipped: "I used to say that politics was the second oldest profession, and I have come to know that it bears a gross similarity to the first".

> Politics, it seems to me, for years, or all too long
> Has been concerned with right and left instead of right and wrong.
> RICHARD ARMOUR.

> The sad duty of politics is to establish justice in a sinful world.
> REINHOLD NIEBUHR.

> The cardinal rule of politics: never get caught in bed with a live man or a dead woman.
> Larry Hagman as J. R. Ewing in CBS television's *Dallas*.

Politics and money are inextricably connected; indeed Jesse Unruh termed money "the mother's milk of politics". This is even truer in America than in Britain, Will Rogers observing: "Over there politics is an obligation; over here it's a business." Harry S. Truman remarked: "The difficulty with businessmen entering politics, after they've had a successful business career, is that they want to go straight to the top." Politicians reckon they handle businessmen on their own terms; Jesse Unruh explained: "If you can't drink their booze, take their money, fool with their women and then vote against them, you don't deserve to be in politics." And Donald Rumsfeld, with one eye on the farm lobby, warned: "When anyone with a rural accent says: 'I don't know anything about politics', zip up your pocket."

The venal side of politics generates revulsion both within and outside the political community. President TAFT opined that "politics, when I am in it, makes me sick", and the Royalist French Minister Chamfort declared: "One would be disgusted if one saw politics, justice and one's dinner in the making." Yet the ultimate comment came from the anonymous American who wrote:

> Nothing can be said about our politics that hasn't already been said about haemorrhoids.

The nexus between politics and morality also embraces religion. Edmund BURKE argued that "politics and the pulpit are terms that have little agreement. The case of civil liberty and civil government gains as little as that of religion by [the] confusion of duties." Lord Hailsham reckoned that "the introduction of religious passion into politics is an end to honest politics, and the introduction of politics into religion is a prostitution of true religion", and declared: "The man who puts politics first is not fit to be called a civilized being, let alone a Christian." And the Beirut HOSTAGE Terry Waite stated with devastating simplicity:

> Politics come from man. Mercy, compassion and justice come from God.

Where does the ordinary citizen fit in? Harry S. Truman reckoned that "a man who is not interested in politics is not doing his patriotic duty towards maintaining the constitution of the United States", and Dwight Eisenhower that "politics ought to be the part-time profession of every citizen who would protect the rights and privileges of free people and who would preserve what is good and fruitful in our national heritage." Yet H. L. Mencken considered that "the whole aim of practical politics is to keep the populace alarmed (and hence clamorous to be led to safety) by menacing it with an endless series of hobgoblins, all of them imaginary", and James Reston concluded that "all politics are based on the indifference of the majority". Dolley Madison saw politics as "the business of men", but Hermione Gingold observed: "There are too many men in politics, and not enough elsewhere."

> The end move in politics is always to pick up a gun.
> R. BUCKMINSTER FULLER (1895–1987).

> There is life after politics.
> BOB HAWKE, on his resignation as Australian Prime Minister, 1991.

politics of envy The exploitation of envy of the possessions and lifestyle of the rich or better-off to mobilize the poor and less prosperous to support a party or leader.

> Envy is capable of . . . making the rich moderate their habits for fear of arousing it. It is because of the existence of envy that one does not drive Rolls-Royces through the slums of Naples.
> Sir KEITH (later Lord) JOSEPH (1918–).

community politics *See* COMMUNITY.

gesture politics The cultivation of electoral support by associating oneself dramatically with a cause or the resolution of a crisis in a way which achieves little practical good.

kerbstone or pavement politics The building of a power-base, especially at local level, by concentrating on small issues of immediate importance to electors, such as broken paving-stones, rather than on national issues or matters of high principle. *See also* COMMUNITY POLITICS.

machine politics *See* MACHINE.

porcupine politics In US politics, the achievement of power and results, especially in Congress, by prickly MAVERICKS who can make life awkward or painful for the majority.

politics is the art of the possible The ultimate statement in PRAGMATISM used by R. A. Butler (*see* RAB) as the title for his autobiography, but originally coined by Bismarck (*see* IRON CHANCELLOR) in 1867 in a conversation with Meyer von Waldeck. John Kenneth Galbraith has since ventured to disagree, writing: "Politics is not the art of the possible. It consists in choosing between the disastrous and the unpalatable."

politics ooze from his every orifice The vivid description of the attributes of the Scottish Labour MP George Foulkes (1942–) given to the *Glasgow Herald* by his Liberal Democrat contemporary Archy Kirkwood.

a week is a long time in politics The most celebrated dictum of Harold WILSON, taken by critics as a sign of the deepest pragmato-cynicism. Wilson probably said it first at a meeting with LOBBY correspondents during the sterling crisis soon after Labour took office in 1964; he repeated it a number of times in 1965–66. There was a precedent; in 1886 Joseph Chamberlain said to BALFOUR: "In politics there is no use looking beyond the next fortnight."

confound their politics A controversial phrase from the seldom-sung second verse of the United Kingdom's national anthem (*see* GOD SAVE THE KING). It forms part of an appeal to the Almighty to scatter the sovereign's enemies, and all those who intrigue against the throne.

The Triumph of Politics The controversially frank account by David Stockman, President Reagan's first budget director, of the illusory and almost fraudulent nature of REAGANOMICS, which caused the administration considerable embarrassment when published in 1986.

poll (1) An ELECTION, as in "the only poll that counts is on the day".

eve of poll The night before voting takes place in a UK election, when each Parliamentary candidate customarily suspends CANVASSING to hold an eve of poll meeting or rally in their constituency.

percentage poll *See* TURNOUT.

polling booth In UK elections, the wooden cubicle to which the voter takes his or her BALLOT paper and where they mark their X with a pencil before folding the paper and putting it in the BALLOT BOX.

polling day The day on which voting takes place in an election.

polling district Again in UK politics, the area whose electors use a single POLLING STATION; it is usually a subdivision of a local government WARD, with anything from half a dozen to 4000 on the ELECTORAL REGISTER.

polling station The premises where electors turn out to vote; it may be anything from a school or church hall to a caravan or even the front room of a house. Staffed by local government officials who check names against the ELECTORAL REGISTER and hand out BALLOT papers, it contains POLLING BOOTHS and one or more BALLOT BOXES. Outside there are usually TELLERS from the various political parties to check on how many of their supporters have actually voted, and periodically a policeman.

(2) A test of public attitudes or voting intentions (*see* OPINION POLLS).

exit poll A survey of how electors have voted, taken as they leave the polling stations. If they are truthful, it should give an accurate PROJECTION of the result well before it is officially declared; however in the UK elections of 1987 and 1992 a reluctance of voters to admit they had supported the Conservatives led to exit polls suggesting Labour had done much better than was actually the case. The BBC's continued reliance on this suspect instrument has cast shadows over its election coverage.

Gallup poll The best known of the OPINION POLLS, instituted by Dr. George Gallup (1901–84) of the American Institute of Public Opinion in 1935. Trained interviewers interrogate a carefully selected but small (usually around 1000) cross-section of the population. For the British election of 1945, 1809 out of 25 million voters were interviewed and the poll forecast was within 1%; however the Gallup forecast – like everyone else's – was wrong for the US Presidential election of 1948. Despite the increasing sophistication of other polls, Gallup has remained in the forefront of such research on both sides of the Atlantic.

> Polling is merely an instrument for gauging public opinion. When a president or other leader pays attention to polling results, he is in effect paying attention to the views of the people. Any other interpretation is nonsense.
> GEORGE GALLUP.

poll of polls A device much loved by newspapers and television stations which lack the resources to conduct polls of their own. In it, the expressions of opinion from all the opinion polls conducted within the previous few days are grossed up and averaged out to produce a single, and supposedly more reliable, forecast of voting intentions.

private polls The polls conducted privately for a political party to give it instant and confidential information on how its campaign is going and what issues are gaining and losing it votes.

rogue poll An opinion poll way out of line with all others taken at the time, and thus assumed to be wrong. On rare occasions the poll denounced as a "rogue" has turned out to be the only one accurately pointing to the result of an election.

straw poll An informal test of opinion, such as a reporter arriving in a town may conduct among the first few people he or she meets.

> A straw vote shows only which way the hot air is blowing.
> O. HENRY.

tracking poll One of a series of polls conducted for a party or candidate which shows underlying and longer-term trends, rather than giving a snap verdict.

pollster A colloquial term, common since the 1970s, for the political scientists who initiate and conduct opinion polls, then interpret them to the public.

poll tax (1) The mediaeval tax on the King of England's subjects which provoked the PEASANTS' REVOLT of 1381 and other upheavals. (2) The tax imposed in America's Deep South on those registering to vote, which in the late 19th and early 20th century disenfranchised many Blacks and poor Whites. Ten states adopted a poll tax between 1889 and 1902; as late as 1937 the Supreme Court ruled Georgia's constitutional. Poll taxes for Federal elections, still in force in five states, were finally outlawed in 1964 by the 24th Amendment. Such taxes pre-dated the Civil War; in 1846 Henry David Thoreau refused to pay his $1 Massachusetts poll tax as a protest against slavery and was jailed until his aunt paid the next morning. (3) The controversial flat-rate local tax, officially termed the COMMUNITY CHARGE, brought in by Margaret Thatcher's government to replace the RATES. Introduced in Scotland in 1989 and in England and Wales in 1990, it proved so unpopular (with riots in the streets of London) that John MAJOR moved to abolish it as soon as Mrs. Thatcher left office. It was hated because the less well-off paid as much per head as the wealthy, because some Labour councils pushed up the tax to make the government unpopular, and because the 25% of the people who had never paid local taxes disliked the idea of doing so. When the COUNCIL TAX replaced it in 1993, it was denounced as unfair by many householders who had paid less under the poll tax.

pollution. polluter pays The principle under which the cost of remedying damage to the environment is met by the industry responsible. It has been taken up enthusiastically by environmental groups, and in America by some States.

> It actually means the customers of the polluter.
> NICHOLAS RIDLEY.

Eighty per cent of pollution comes from plants and trees Ronald Reagan's remark allegedly showing a breathtaking incomprehension of the crisis facing the environment. What the GREAT COMMUNICATOR actually said, towards the close of the 1980 Presidential campaign, was: "Approximately 80% of our air pollution stems from hydrocarbons released by vegetation, so let's not go overboard in setting and enforcing tough emission standards from man-made sources." When attacked by Sen. Edward Kennedy, he retorted: "I didn't say 80%, I said 92%, 93%, pardon me. And I didn't say air pollution, I said oxides of nitrogen. And I am right. Growing and decaying vegetation in this land are responsible for 93% of the oxides of nitrogen."

> Put the President of the SIERRA CLUB in a sealed garage with a tree. Put Ronald Reagan in a sealed garage with a running automobile, and wait to see which of them yells to get out first. *San José Mercury-News.*

Ponting affair The case which finally destroyed the credibility of the CATCH-ALL Section 2 of Britain's 1911 OFFICIAL SECRETS ACT, severely embarrassing Margaret Thatcher's government. Clive Ponting, a senior official in the Ministry of Defence, was acquitted by an Old Bailey jury in March 1985 on charges of breaching the Act after LEAKing the previous summer classified information suggesting that Ministers had lied to the Commons for two years over the circumstances of the sinking of the General BELGRANO in 1982. Ponting acted when the incoming Defence Secretary Michael Heseltine (*see* TARZAN) and his officials decided to stick to the previous line that the Belgrano had been sunk because it posed an immediate threat to the British fleet. Ponting passed the papers to the Labour MP Tam Dalyell, in the hope that Parliament would learn the true facts. His acquittal torpedoed the doctrine advanced by the prosecution, that the interests of the state are identical with those of the government of the day.

Pooh-bahs Highly influential and slightly stuffy politicians whose writ extends over a number of varying fields of legislation and patronage. A term often used on CAPITOL HILL, it arises from the characterization of Pooh Bah, the "Lord High Everything Else", in W.S Gilbert and Sir Arthur Sullivan's 1885 comic opera *The Mikado*.

pool report In political journalism, a report written by one reporter or a small group, for circulation to the media as a whole. Pool reporting is frequent during election campaigns or on Presidential or Royal visits when the personage being reported on is meeting people or seeing artefacts in a confined space, and there is only room for a few reporters.

poor. Poor Bastards Bill The Bill introduced by the Democratic Congressman Morris Udall in the early 1960s to ensure that the illegitimate children of civil servants qualified for benefits. President Kennedy signed the Bill and the next weekend Udall, back in his Arizona district, was confronted by a member of the John BIRCH Society who asked him: "You guys are throwing our money away in Africa, Europe and everywhere else. When are you going to do something for the poor bastards in this country?" Udall replied:

> I'm glad you asked that question. Why, just last week . . . .

Poor Law The laws governing the support, management or confinement of the poor in England from 1601 until the BEVERIDGE REPORT. Originally they were based on parish relief, to assist the aged and settled sick and prevent the poor moving from one parish to another. After 1834 a system of workhouses was set up, to house the poor and give them tasks – often including labour on a treadmill; from 1890 the system was humanized, toys and books and tobacco being allowed to the inmates. The Poor Law system broke up after further reforms in 1919–20 reduced the number of authorities by three-quarters, and the post-war DEPRESSION was the final straw, the Poplar guardians being SURCHARGED for paying higher benefits in 1922 than the Government would approve.

the poorest he that is in England hath a life to live, as the greatest he The argument for democracy put by Colonel Rainborough, in disputation with Oliver Cromwell, at the PUTNEY DEBATES of 1647. Cromwell retorted that there was not sufficient ground to argue that "by a man's being born here, he shall have a share in that power that shall dispose of the lands here".

Pope. The Pope, how many divisions has he got? STALIN's dismissive response to the

French Foreign Minister Pierre Laval, who urged him on 13 May 1935 to encourage Catholicism in Russia so as to placate the Pope.

No Popery! *See* NO.

Popish Plot The alleged Jesuit conspiracy to murder King Charles II and enthrone his Catholic brother the Duke of York (later James II), which was "exposed" by WHIGS in 1679, largely through the perjured evidence of Titus Oates (1649–1705). What the Whigs really feared, but could not allege, was a joint conspiracy by the King and his brother against the Protestant religion. The unveiling of the "plot" created public hysteria in London, followed by a number of blatantly-rigged trials following which 35 innocent Catholics, including the Primate of Ireland, were put to death. When James came to power in 1685, Oates was pilloried, whipped and imprisoned.

poppycock A word for nonsense, deriving from the Dutch *pappekak*, soft dung. Its use in a political context dates back at least to 1865 when Charles Farrar Browne wrote: "You won't be able to find another pack of poppycock gabblers as this present Congress of the United States." In February 1973 Sen. Sam ERVIN, confronted with the Nixon Administration's insistence that senior officials testify to the Senate WATERGATE committee in secret on grounds of EXECUTIVE PRIVILEGE, responded: "Executive poppycock!"

Popular Front An alliance of left-wing parties (Communists, Socialists, Liberals, Radicals, *etc.*) against a reactionary government or the threat from powerful DICTATORS abroad. The idea of an anti-FASCIST Popular Front was proposed by the Communist International in 1935; such a government was set up in Madrid in 1935, but was unable to avert the SPANISH CIVIL WAR. France did enjoy a Popular Front government from 1936 to 1938 under Léon Blum, but apart from enabling the French Communist Party to strengthen its power base it could not achieve long-term unity on the Left or pose an effective counterweight to Fascism and NAZISM in neighbouring states.

Population Registration Act The legislation passed by South Africa's NATIONAL PARTY government in 1950 which became a cornerstone of APARTHEID. Under it, everyone in South Africa had to be registered according to their assessed racial origin: White, Coloured or Bantu. A category for Asians was added later.

populism A political philosophy or movement appealing to voters' visceral feelings, with a touch of DEMAGOGY from its leaders. Frequently populism manifests itself in a SINGLE-ISSUE campaign, against abortion, against high taxes (*see* POUJADISTS), against a particular ethnic group (*see* RACISM). In America it has had a special meaning, representing the successive Populist or PROGRESSIVE movements based in the Mid-Western Farm Belt that have combined religious fundamentalism with demands for a fairer economic deal (or preferential treatment) from the Federal government.

Populist Party The party formed in 1892 by discontented Mid-Western and Southern US farmers under the slogan "We do not ask for sympathy or pity: We ask for justice". They advocated FREE SILVER, tax cuts, government ownership of the railroads and help with farm marketing, and as a pitch to industrial workers, an end to the use of the Pinkerton agency to break strikes and a curb on immigration. The Populists nominated James Baird Weaver, a former Union General and former GREENBACK Presidential candidate, for President, and James C. Field, a former Confederate General, for Vice-President; this ultimate Balanced TICKET polled over a million votes. The Populists managed to elect four State governors (Colorado, Kansas, North Dakota, Wyoming), two Senators, 11 Congressmen and 354 State legislators, and held their ground in the 1894 mid-term elections. The party joined with the Democrats in 1896 to nominate the BOY ORATOR William Jennings Bryan, but the economic slump which gave Bryan his head of steam, and a ferocious counter-attack by Republican big business, saw McKINLEY elected.

> A taste for charming and cultivated friends, and a tendency to bathe frequently, causes in them the deepest suspicion. THEODORE ROOSEVELT.

pork barrel One of the greatest American political institutions, despite the efforts of successive Presidents to curb its excesses; the practice of members of Congress of obtaining large-scale funding for marginally necessary or completely pointless projects at home for electoral purposes. The building of canals and waterways, the siting of military bases and the awarding of military aircraft projects in order to shore up politicians' power-bases have all been subjects of controversy. The phrase dates from old plantation days, when slaves assembled at the pork barrel to receive their allowance of the meat. "Pork" has come to be shorthand for the Federal projects won by the champion pork-barrellers.

> During the American revolution, George Washington used to call for "beef, beef, beef"; but the Continental Congress called out for "pork, pork, pork".
> ANON., quoted by Rep. CLARENCE CANNON (1879–1964).

> Pork Barrel spelt backwards is infrastructure.
> Rep. JAMES HOWARD (1928–88).

King of Pork The nickname of Sen. Quentin Burdick (1908–92), a Republican-turned-Democrat who during 32 years as a Senator lived by the motto "I'll get everything North Dakota is entitled to – now." He finally overreached himself in 1990 when he persuaded Congress to appropriate millions of dollars for a museum to honour the bandleader Lawrence Welk. With the Federal budget careering out of control, Burdick's plan attracted ridicule as the ultimate in pork-barrelling, and the following year Congress cancelled the appropriation.

> I'm all for Lawrence Welk. Lawrence Welk is a wonderful man. He used to be, or what, or . . . wherever he is now, God bless him.
>
> GEORGE BUSH in the NEW HAMPSHIRE PRIMARY, 16 February 1992.

Port Huron statement The definitive policy statement prior to the VIETNAM WAR of America's NEW LEFT, drawn up at Port Huron, Michigan, in 1962 by the leaders of Students for a Democratic Society (SDS); it was largely written by Tom Hayden. It demanded a share for every individual in decisions affecting their lives, and the organization of society to encourage personal independence and participation.

portfolio The area and weight of responsibilities allocated to a Cabinet member, Minister or EC COMMISSIONER. A **Minister without Portfolio** is one with no specific departmental responsibilities, who is able to take on special projects and chair committees as the need arises. When William Deedes (*see* DEAR BILL) was Minister without Portfolio in the Macmillan government to present its case, David Frost commented:

> The reason that he is without portfolio is because the Government has got no case.

porthole to porthole A Washington term for the way in which senior Administration officials are always chauffeured by limousine from building to building, air-conditioned all the way and with no contact with the general public. Such a service is provided for Cabinet secretaries, the JOINT CHIEFS OF STAFF and half a dozen other key figures.

position The stance adopted by a politician on any particular issue; a candidate running for office will have a position paper on every conceivable subject, written by a horde of STAFFERS. Adlai Stevenson maintained that "all progress has resulted from people who took unpopular positions", but Robert Fuoss wrote:

> When a politician changes his position, it's sometimes hard to tell whether he has seen the light or felt the heat.

consider your position The phrase intended to make the person it is delivered to sit down and write out their letter of resignation forthwith. In UK politics, it will be delivered by the Prime Minister to a member of the Government who has committed an act or omission that makes it, in the PM's judgment, impossible for them to remain in office; similarly, it is used by a Minister to an appointee he or she feels should resign. For instance the Transport Secretary Paul Channon told the chairmen of London Transport and London Undergound, Sir Keith Bright and Dr. Tony Ridley, to consider their positions after the Kings Cross disaster; the former did instantly, the latter after hesitating.

positioning The art of aligning oneself so as to capitalize on an upsurge of public interest or concern over a particular issue, for instance an upsurge in crime. Shrewd positioning, combined with luck, can enable a party to appear ahead of the game or make its opponents look curmudgeonly or over-reactive, while in an election campaign it can prevent an opponent carving out the space to present distinctive policies of their own.

positive discrimination *see* DISCRIMINATION.

positive vetting The method of screening those in line for promotion or transfer to sensitive positions in the UK civil service, to weed out SECURITY RISKS. The system, under which all candidates had to complete a questionnaire, was introduced by the Macmillan government; when Macmillan's own private secretary, John Wyndham was required to answer the question: "Are you in debt?", he replied: "Yes, about £1 million."

post-Fordism The idea promulgated by liberal Marxists in the 1980s that industrial society had advanced from the mass production methods of Henry FORD, dependent on vast workforces which became heavily unionized, to smaller units within which workers had greater freedom. The implicit message was that left-wing parties could no longer claim to represent the workforce without offering them something in return.

post office parties Political party organizations in certain American states which conducted no serious campaigning, existing largely to receive patronage – such as appointments to postmasterships – when that party was in power in Washington. The term was applied particularly to the Republican Party in the South during the first half of the 20th century. In 1952 backers of Dwight D. Eisenhower successfully challenged the right of delegates from "post office parties" in Texas, Louisiana, Florida and Georgia to vote at the Republican

CONVENTION; Eisenhower's move was dictated by self-interest, as the delegates were pledged to his rival Sen. Robert Taft. But it sparked a revival of genuine Republican organization in the South, followed by a recovery in its electoral fortunes.

potatoe The final great GAFFE of Dan QUAYLE's Vice-Presidency, when on 15 June 1992 he looked into a school classroom in Trenton, New Jersey, and saw 12-year-old William Figueroa write the word "potato" on the blackboard. Quayle immediately told the boy he had spelt the word wrong – and added a final "e". Figueroa was subsequently paid $4000 by a California computer company to endorse its new spelling game. Prior to the Vice-Presidential DEBATE, Quayle asked if his Democratic challenger, Sen. Albert Gore (*see* OZONE MAN) minded his bringing a copy of Gore's book *Earth In The Balance*; Gore said he had no objection, provided Quayle would let him bring a potato.

Potemkin village A situation created to mislead the voters into believing that things are much better than they really are. The term originates from Catherine the Great's minister and former lover Count Grigory Potemkin (1735–91), who had plywood "villages" erected along the river Volga in 1787 to give Catherine the illusion that the peasants in her newly-acquired southern dominions were well cared for.

Potomac Washington's broad river, running between the District of Columbia and the Virginia suburbs where the PENTAGON and the CIA are sited. Abraham LINCOLN once declared in desperation:

> I could as easily bail out the Potomac river with a teaspoon as attend to all the details of the Army.

Potomac fever The addiction to political power and inside information that comes from working in Washington: as a member of Congress or the Administration, a LOBBYIST or political journalist. It is also used specifically for a politician's determination to become President, regardless of the odds.

> [Sen. George] McGovern did not become a peace advocate intil 1968 when he contracted Potomac Fever. And he is still infected. RONALD REAGAN, 1972.

Potsdam conference The last Allied wartime conference, held from 17 July to 2 August 1945, at the old Prussian and Imperial capital of Potsdam, just west of Berlin. It was attended by STALIN, Truman (*see* GIVE'EM HELL HARRY), CHURCHILL and ATTLEE (who became Prime Minister when Labour won the general election and took over from Churchill during the second round of discussions). In a declaration on 26 July they demanded the unconditional SURRENDER of Japan; from Potsdam Truman ordered the preparations for dropping the atomic bomb on HIROSHIMA, but did not tell Stalin. The conference went on to agree the basis of the post-war settlement in Germany, involving the division of the country and of Berlin into four zones administered by the occupying powers – the UK, America, the Soviet Union and France. The Soviet delegation gave the first signs that it would be less co-operative now the war in Europe was over, and the KREMLIN's subsequent imposition of Communism on East Germany made many of the Potsdam arrangements unenforceable, hastening the COLD WAR.

POTUS President of the United States. The code word which Franklin D. Roosevelt used in his secret correspondence and conversations with CHURCHILL in 1940–41, before America entered World War II (*see* FORMER NAVAL PERSON).

Potus phones Direct telephone lines to the President which are the ultimate status symbol for senior WHITE HOUSE officials.

Poujadists A short-lived French political party founded in 1953 by the right-wing grocer-demagogue Pierre Poujade (1920–), with opposition to taxes its main platform. His *Union de la Défense des Commerçants et Artisans* was born out of a tax revolt by small shopkeepers and farmers in the Lot, who also felt threatened by the end of food rationing and the post-war growth of big retail chains. His vitriolic attacks on the tax inspectorate and parliamentary government, his support for ALGÉRIE FRANÇAISE, and the quixotic demand for the calling of the Estates General to represent the voice of the little man briefly attracted mass support. In France's 1956 elections the Poujadists won 2.5 million votes, a surprising 11.6% of the poll, and 50 seats in the NATIONAL ASSEMBLY. Among those elected was Jean-Marie Le Pen, future leader of France's NATIONAL FRONT.

Poulson affair The corruption scandal that shook British politics, civil service and local government at the same time as WATERGATE. Brought to light in 1972 during bankruptcy hearings over the architect John Poulson, it involved the large-scale bribery of national and local politicians and officials over a period of 22 years in the hope of securing design contracts and other favours. Poulson, who eventually went to prison, brought down with him the Conservative Home Secretary Reginald Maudling, who resigned over gifts Poulson made to a theatre supported by Mrs. Maudling;

T. Dan Smith, the Labour former city BOSS of Newcastle, who went to prison; George Pottinger, Secretary of the Scottish Department of Agriculture, convicted of corruption; senior councillors and officials of councils, British Rail and health authorities; and the Conservative MP John Cordle who resigned from the House of Commons in 1977 when facing expulsion. The deputy Labour leader Ted Short (later Lord Glenamara) found himself explaining the receipt of a $250 consultancy fee 12 years before.

> Over the years Mr. Poulson had succeeded in corruptly penetrating high levels of the Civil Service, the National Health Service, two nationalized industries and a number of local authorities.
>
> *Royal Commission on Standards of Conduct in Public Life*, 1976.

pound. the pound in your pocket The phrase used by Harold WILSON in his broadcast on 19 November 1967 to explain the DEVALUATION of the pound which, in the words of his biographer Ben Pimlott, "ricocheted through the rest of his career" as an instance of his supposed deviousness. Wilson aimed to avoid a repetition of the 1949 devaluation when the public thronged the banks fearing that for every pound invested, they would only get back 17 shillings. But the words he used were turned against him, the accusation being that he kidded the public that devaluation would have no effect at all. Wilson said:

> From now on the pound abroad is worth 14 per cent or so less in terms of other currencies. It does not mean, of course, that the pound here in Britain in your pocket or in your purse or in your bank has been devalued.

green pound *See* GREEN.

run on the pound A situation in the currency markets when dealers sell sterling on a large scale, forcing down the value of the currency.

poverty line The level of income below which a family or individual is officially classified as being poor, and thus "below the poverty line".

poverty trap An invidious situation in which low earners who manage to increase their income find themselves worse off through the loss of welfare benefits or because they fall into a higher tax bracket, and which thus deters those on benefit from finding work. Ending the trap is the aim of many politicians, but the only foolproof solution is a UNIFIED TAX AND BENEFIT SYSTEM.

Powell. Adam Clayton Powell case The repeated scandals surrounding the hedonistic Black Harlem Congressman Adam Clayton Powell, who remained a hero to his constituents despite (or perhaps because of) his flagrant disregard for the mores the House tried to force on him. He was known as **the Congressman from Bimini** or **the Harlem globetrotter** because of his frequent vacations, often with attractive women and always at Government expense. His one achievement was to end racial segregation in the Capitol. He put his wife on the Congressional payroll although she was living in Puerto Rico, and in 1958 was indicted for tax evasion, but by 1961 he had enough SENIORITY (22 years) to become chairman of the Education and Labour Committee, a job he treated as a sinecure. By 1966 he could not return to his district because of the threat of arrest, and in January 1967 the Democratic Caucus stripped him of his chairmanship and the House voted 365–65 to deprive him of his seat – the first time a member had been excluded for 46 years. With the Justice Department threatening an indictment for falsifying expense claims, the seat was declared vacant and a SPECIAL ELECTION held; Powell was re-elected and won a declaration from the Supreme Court that he should never have been excluded, but in 1970 was defeated in the Democratic primary.

> You are looking at the first black man who has ever been lynched by Congress. ADAM CLAYTON POWELL, 1967.

Powellite A follower of the maverick UK politician **J. Enoch Powell** (1912–), who attracted mass support from the late 1960s because of his views on RACE and immigration and from the early 1970s through his opposition to membership of the EUROPEAN COMMUNITY; he was also an early advocate of MONETARISM and a foe of the ANGLO-IRISH AGREEMENT. Powell, a Black Countryman, became a Cambridge don and was Professor of Greek at Sydney University when World War II broke out, returning to become the British Army's youngest Brigadier. After the war he caught the attention of CHURCHILL, who wrote to R. A. (RAB) Butler:

> I have had a letter from a man called Powell who says we could reconquer India with four divisions. Is he all right?

Elected to Parliament in 1950, he served as a junior Minister under EDEN and Macmillan, resigning in 1957 over the relaxation of spending curbs (*see* LITTLE LOCAL DIFFICULTY). Macmillan brought him back as Minister of Health; when Macmillan retired, he urged Butler to press for the Tory leadership. When SIR ALEC Douglas-Home emerged as Prime Minister, Powell refused to serve under him; he never held office again. He served in Edward Heath's Shadow Cabinet, but was sacked after the RIVERS OF BLOOD speech in April 1968 – his subsequent campaign for the REPATRIATION of immigrants earning him ethusiastic racist support. *The Times* commented:

In dismissing Mr. Powell, Mr. Heath takes the known risk of having Mr. Powell as an enemy; that fortunately is less grave than the risk of having Mr. Powell as a colleague.

Despite his dismissal, Powell's views probably helped the Tories in the 1970 campaign; Tony BENN caused a furore by saying:

The flag of racialism which has been hoisted in Wolverhampton is beginning to look like the one which fluttered 25 years ago over Dachau and Belsen.

When Heath took Britain into the EC, Powell bitterly opposed him, and in February 1974 gave up his seat, urging his supporters to vote Labour as the only way of keeping Britain out of Europe (*see* ENOCH FACTOR). That autumn he came back as an ULSTER UNIONIST MP, and until his defeat in 1987 spoke out strongly against any accommodation with the Irish Republic. Margaret Thatcher admired his economic views and referred to him early on as "that golden-hearted Enoch", but they drifted apart, particularly after his bitter attacks on the Anglo-Irish Agreement.

A POPULIST is a politician who says things because he believes them to be popular. I have never been that. My worst enemies wouldn't say that. ENOCH POWELL, 1981.

He suffers from an excess of logic. IAIN MACLEOD.

Disembowel Enoch Powell! One of the favourite slogans of left-wing and ANTI-RACIST groups in the early 1970s, who linked opposition to Powell's views on immigration with the campaign against APARTHEID in South Africa – a régime which Powell never publicly supported.

power The elusive elemental force of politics and government, described as "a dangerous thing to leave lying about" – Edmund BURKE; "the simple indestructible will of the people" – Fidel Castro; "the ultimate aphrodisiac" – Henry KISSINGER; "like a seafront; when you achieve it, there's nothing there" – Harold Macmillan; "merely the organized power of one class for oppressing another" – Marx and Engels; "like a woman you want to stay in bed with forever" – Patrick Anderson; "the ability to make something happen and keep it happening" – Hedrick Smith. So where does power lie? Bismarck said that "he who has his thumb on the purse has the power"; Theodore H. White that "power in America today is control of the means of communication". Jimmy Breslin doubted that it exists at all, writing: "All political power is primarily an illusion: mirrors and blue smoke"; Sen. Wyche Fowler that "people have power when other people think they have power". Tacitus declared that "the lust for power, for dominating others, influences the heart more than any other passion"; BOSS TWEED that "the way to have power is to take it". Once achieved, Burke wrote, "the greater the power, the more dangerous the abuse", but Aneurin BEVAN believed that "the purpose of getting power is to be able to give it away".

An honest man can feel no pleasure in the exercise of power over his fellow citizens. THOMAS JEFFERSON.

Men of power have no time to read, yet the men who do not read are unfit for power. MICHAEL FOOT.

Being powerful is like being a lady. If you have to tell people you are, you ain't. JESSE CARR.

power base The geographical area, community or group of fellow politicians that provides a political figure with his or her fundamental support.

power broker *See* BROKER.

power corrupts; absolute power corrupts absolutely One of the classic dicta about politics which was never said in precisely those words. What Lord Acton (1834–1902) actually said in a letter to Bishop Mandell Creighton in April 1887 was:

Power tends to corrupt, and absolute power corrupts absolutely.

Nor was the remark entirely original, PITT THE ELDER having said: "Unlimited power is apt to corrupt the minds of those who possess it." Adlai Stevenson had a different view, declaring:

Power corrupts – but lack of power corrupts absolutely.

power dance US Black slang for resistance to oppression, usually expressed in RIOTs and looting.

power-sharing A political system in which a community's ethnic or political minority has an institutionalized stake in power. The creation of a stable system of power-sharing in NORTHERN IRELAND has been an aim of UK governments since the abolition of STORMONT in 1972. In 1973 the Northern Ireland Secretary William Whitelaw (*see* WILLIE) announced that Protestant and Catholic leaders had agreed to serve together in an assembly responsible for all domestic matters, except security; the SUNNINGDALE AGREEMENT soon afterwards provided for a Council of All Ireland including members from Westminster, the DAIL and the Assembly. The assembly was duly elected, and opened in January 1974 under the leadership of a power-sharing **Executive** headed by Brian Faulkner (1921–77). From the start it faced a campaign of organized disruption by Protestant extremists led by the Rev. Ian PAISLEY. In May 1974 it was finally brought down by a GENERAL STRIKE of LOYALIST workers, backed by widespread intimidation, which reduced the province to chaos. DIRECT RULE was resumed, and the UNIONIST parties have been reluctant ever since to repeat the power-sharing experiment.

power to the people The slogan of the BLACK PANTHERS *c.* 1969, turned into a best-selling single by John Lennon and Yoko Ono.

Power to the Soviets! *See* SOVIET.

power without responsibility, the prerogative of the harlot throughout the ages The devastating phrase with which Stanley BALDWIN torpedoed the campaign of the PRESS BARONS for EMPIRE FREE TRADE in a BY-ELECTION speech at the Queen's Hall, London on 17 March 1931. Baldwin's cousin Rudyard Kipling had supplied him with it; the Conservative leader's actual words were:

> The papers conducted by Lord Rothermere and Lord Beaverbrook are not newspapers in the ordinary acceptance of the term. They are engines of propaganda for the constantly changing policies, desires, personal wishes, personal dislikes of two men. What are their methods? Their methods are direct falsehood, misrepresentation, half-truths, the alteration of the speaker's meaning by publishing a sentence apart from the context. . . . What the proprietorship of these papers is aiming at is power, and power without responsibility – the prerogative of the harlot throughout the ages.

Lady Diana Cooper, who was in the audience, wrote: "I saw blasé reporters, scribbling semi-consciously, jump out of their skins to a man." And the Duke of Devonshire turned to his son-in-law Harold Macmillan and observed:

> Good God, that's done it. He's lost us the tarts' vote!

balance of power *See* BALANCE.

concentration of power A situation in which all effective power in a nation or community has gravitated into the hands of a few, generally unACCOUNTABLE, people. Woodrow WILSON described it as "what always precedes the destruction of human initiative, and therefore of human energy".

corridors of power The heart of WHITEHALL where Britain is effectively governed by a class anonymous to the outside world. The phrase was coined by C. P. Snow (1905–80) in his book *Homecomings* (1956), where he wrote:

> The official world, the corridors of power, the dilemmas of conscience and egotism – she disliked them all.

It immediately caught on among political commentators – Sir Douglas Corridor being invented as the ultimate Whitehall MANDARIN – and Snow used the phrase again as the title of a further, highly successful, novel in 1964.

in power Holding political office and exercising power, by contrast with the impotence of being out of office. In his 1931 novel *Maid in Waiting*, John Galsworthy (1867–1933) had a character advise:

> Don't say in power what you say in opposition. If you do, you only have to carry out what the other fellows have found impossible.

political power grows from the barrel of a gun One of the most celebrated sayings of CHAIRMAN MAO, extolling the virtues of GUERRILLA war. He first used it in *Problems of War and Strategy*, published on 6 November 1938.

protecting power The nation whose EMBASSY protects the interests of another's nationals in a foreign capital after DIPLOMATIC RELATIONS have been broken off.

transfer of power The process under which a COLONY ceases to be dependent on the power that has controlled it, and becomes INDEPENDENT.

concurrent powers One of many types of authority derived from the US CONSTITUTION, being one which both Federal and State governments can exercise at the same time – *i.e.* through levying taxes. **Enumerated powers** are those specifically set out; **exclusive powers** those possessed entirely by the national government (only Congress can declare war); **expressed powers** are those covered by the NECESSARY AND PROPER CLAUSE; **implied powers** are those that stem from powers given without being spelt out (the power to incorporate the FED stemming from that to issue coinage); **national police powers** are those covering public safety, health and morality; **resulting powers** are those possessed by the Federal government which stem from a combination of expressed powers in the constitution, such as the powers to wage war, make treaties or acquire territory.

reserve powers The phrase which caused Australia's greatest political controversy, the KERR SACKING of 11 November 1975. The GOVERNOR-GENERAL, Sir John Kerr, considered that he possessed reserve powers under the constitution to dismiss a Prime Minister despite his having a majority in the House of Representatives; the ousted Labor government fervently disagreed.

PPB In Britain, politicians' abbreviation for PARTY POLITICAL BROADCAST.

ppc Prospective parliamentary CANDIDATE; an abbreviation used by all major UK parties.

PPS At Westminster, shorthand for PARLIAMENTARY PRIVATE SECRETARY.

PQ (1) In Canada, abbreviation for *Parti Québecois*, the Quebec separatist party. (2) At Westminster, abbreviation for Parliamentary QUESTION, as in "put down a PQ".

PR Abbreviation for PROPORTIONAL REPRESENTATION.

pragmatism Government on the merits of each issue (or the needs of the moment) rather than by ideology. Harold WILSON made a virtue of being a pragmatist; his critics used the term against him. More recently Chris Patten said of Margaret Thatcher's administration:

> The government has a heroic commitment to hard-nosed pragmatism.

Prague Spring The blossoming of freedom in Czechoslovakia during 1968 under the leadership of Alexander Dubcek (1921–92) who advocated "COMMUNISM WITH A HUMAN FACE" (*see under* SOCIALISM). It was snuffed out by the Soviet invasion that August in pursuit of the BREZHNEV DOCTRINE. *See also* VELVET REVOLUTION.

Prairie Avenger The nickname of **William Jennings Bryan** (1860–1925), the POPULIST Nebraska lawyer and former Congressman who three times contested the Presidency for the Democrats, being defeated by McKINLEY in 1896 and 1900, and TAFT in 1908. Bryan's impact in 1896 was devastating, rousing the Democratic convention with a speech for FREE SILVER that concluded:

> You shall not press down upon the brow of labour this crown of thorns, you shall not crucify mankind upon a cross of gold!

Handsome and with a riveting oratorical style, Bryan conjured up in Western farm states what one observer described as "the fanaticism of the crusades", but a powerful Republican counter-attack based on the FULL DINNER PAIL ensured his defeat. In 1900 he fought on the issue of McKinley's EXPANSIONIST policy after the SPANISH-AMERICAN WAR, and lost by a wider margin. Not all the eloquence was on one side, McKinley's Secretary of State John Hay describing Bryan as "a half-baked glib little briefless jackleg lawyer . . . grasping with anxiety to collar that $50,000 salary, promising the millennium to everybody with a hole in his pants and destruction to everybody with a clean shirt". Theodore Roosevelt observed sourly that Bryan "represents only that type of farmer whose gate hangs on a hinge, whose old hat supplies the place of the missing window pane, and who is more likely to be found out at the crossroads grocery store than behind the plow". In 1908 Bryan, mellowing but still evangelistic, failed to rouse America with his slogan "Shall the people rule?" against Taft, polling fewer votes than in 1896. Bryan's LAST HURRAH came in the final year of his life when he successfully led the prosecution in the infamous SCOPES CASE – a hollow victory for the forces of religious fundamentalism.

> His mind was like a soup dish, wide and shallow; it could hold a small amount of nearly everything, but the slightest jarring spilt the soup into somebody's lap.
>
> IRVING STONE.

Pravda (Russ. truth) The mass-circulation daily paper which was the mouthpiece of the SOVIET state for over 70 years. Founded underground in St. Petersburg in 1912 by LENIN and others, it moved to Moscow with the BOLSHEVIK revolution; its editors included STALIN, Beria and Molotov. With GLASNOST in the late 1980s *Pravda*'s hard line softened; with the banning of the Communist party in 1991 it struck out as an independent paper.

prawn cocktail offensive Shadow Chancellor John Smith's heavy programme of lunches in the City of London prior to the 1992 UK election to convince the financial community that Labour's policies would be good for the economy.

> Never have so many crustaceans died in vain.
>
> MICHAEL HESELTINE.

prayer At Westminster, a motion tabled against the passage of an ORDER IN COUNCIL, to ensure that it is debated in the Commons.

Prayers Said as the prelude to the day's proceedings in most legislatures. In Britain's House of Commons, press and public are excluded from the galleries while they are said. In the Lords, they are said by a bishop. In the US Congress, the rules of the House prevent a member raising "no QUORUM" during the daily prayer.

prayer room A room in the US CAPITOL set aside for prayer. A stained glass window bears the motto: "Preserve me, O God, for in thee do I put my trust."

prayer groups In the US Congress, informal pressure groups of like-minded Democrats or Republicans in both the House and the Senate. Some are *ad hoc*, others have a continuing existence.

preamble The text at the start of a BILL which sets out its purpose or the ill it is designed to redress.

precedence The order in which the mighty of the nation should appear at a state engagement. In America the President, Vice-President and Speaker of the House take the first places. In Britain, the Royal family headed by the Sovereign, the Archbishop of Canterbury and the Lord Chancellor head any procession.

precedent An event, decision or action which becomes a guideline for future conduct. "The precedent, Mr. Prime Minister, is accomplished fact," Henri Bourassa said to Sir Wilfrid Laurier on Canada's participation in the BOER WAR.

precedents In the US Congress, the customs of the House and the Senate, based on previous practice and decisions of the CHAIR and running into many volumes.

Hinds' precedents The 7346 House precedents put together and published in 1907 by Asher Hinds (1863–1919), clerk at the Speaker's table and subsequently a member of the House, and added to since. It is augmented by **Cannon's Precedents,** to 1935, and **Deschler's Precedents,** from 1936.

precept In UK local government, a set amount creamed off from local taxes by a body other than that which immediately collects the money, *e.g.* a police or transport authority.

precinct In America, the subdivision which comprises the basic unit of voting and political organization. President Coolidge said:

> If you can't carry your own precinct you're in trouble.

precincts of the House At Westminster, the area immediately adjoining the HOUSES OF PARLIAMENT, over which the Commons exercise a degree of authority, *e.g.* through a ban on demonstrations.

prefect Originally a Roman commander or magistrate, now the administrative head of a French DÉPARTEMENT (the post was created by Napoleon in 1800), a province of Italy and jurisdictions in some other countries.

Premier From the French *Premier Ministre*, PRIME MINISTER, a colloquialism for a national Prime Minister but also, correctly, the head of government of a Canadian PROVINCE or an Australian STATE. In Australia John Carrick, Malcolm Fraser's federal affairs minister, observed:

> The Premiers don't believe in federalism; they believe in STATES' RIGHTS.

Prendergast machine The corrupt Democratic political organization in Kansas City built up by "Big Tom" Prendergast in the early 20th century. Its one conspicuously honest member, whom Prendergast in consequence only reluctantly promoted, was Jackson County judge – and later President – Harry S. Truman. Prendergast's backing was crucial in Truman's unexpected 1934 Senate victory.

prepare three envelopes President Jimmy CARTER's story of the advice left him by his predecessor, Gerald FORD. Carter joked that on stepping down as President, Ford handed him three envelopes, to be opened when times got tough. After a year, with his administration in trouble, Carter opened the first, to find the message: "Blame your predecessor." He made a speech attacking Ford and his fortunes for a time improved. A year later and in trouble again, he opened the second and found the message: "Blame the Congress." He made a speech attacking the Congress and won a further remission. A year later and in even deeper trouble, Carter said he opened the third envelope to find the message:

> Prepare three envelopes.

prerogative The scope a ruler or government has to take decisions and make appointments without reference to the legislature and free of challenge from the courts. In Britain, the government of the day enjoys wide powers under the Royal prerogative, starting with the Prime Minister's right to appoint his or her Cabinet. Governments throughout the world are also able to exercise a prerogative of mercy to reprieve or free those sentenced to death or imprisonment.

preselection In Australia, the process by which a constituency party chooses its candidate to contest an election.

presidency (1) In the EUROPEAN COMMUNITY, the institution under which member states take it in turn to preside for six-month periods over the COUNCIL OF MINISTERS and hence over the political workings of the Community, *e.g.* the Luxembourg Presidency. (2) The office of President of the UNITED STATES. According to Hedrick Smith, it "combines the functions of chief of state and Prime Minister"; Anthony Burgess saw it as "a Tudor monarchy plus telephones". Theodore Roosevelt used it as a "bully pulpit" and Franklin D. Roosevelt "a position of moral leadership". But the presidency is not all-powerful. Harry S Truman said: "People think I sit here and push buttons and get things done. Well, I spent today kissing behinds." He also warned: "When you get to be President, there are the honours, the 21-gun salute, all those things. You have to remember it isn't for you – it's for the Presidency." And when making way for Eisenhower, he cautioned: "He will sit here and he'll say: 'Do this', 'Do that'. And nothing will happen. Poor IKE – it won't be a bit like the Army. He'll find it very frustrating."

Some incumbents have revelled in the office, notably the Roosevelts and Ronald Reagan; others have hated it. WASHINGTON, the first occupant, was the first to have forebodings, saying: "My movements to the chair of government will be accompanied by feelings not unlike those of a culprit who is going to the place of execution." His successor John ADAMS declared that "no one who has ever held the office of President would congratulate a friend on obtaining it". Thomas JEFFERSON warned that "no one will ever bring out of the presidency the reputation he carries into it". He also called it "a splendid misery", compared with which the office of VICE-PRESIDENT was "honourable and easy". Van Buren declared: "The two happiest days of my life were those of entrance upon the office and my surrender of it." Garfield, prophetically, exclaimed: "My God! What is there in this place that a man should ever want to get into it?" And John F. Kennedy was blunter:

> What a lousy, fucked-up job this turned out to be.

Seekers for the presidency are distrusted. Wendell Phillips wrote: "You can always get the truth from an American statesman after he has turned seventy or given up hope of the presidency," and Sen. Eugene McCarthy said: "You really must be careful of politicians who say they have no further ambitions: they may run for the presidency." David Broder was even more cynical: "Anybody that wants the presidency so much that he will spend two years organizing and campaigning for it is not to be trusted with the office."

Imperial Presidency The criticism, prior to WATERGATE, that the Nixon presidency was taking on more trappings than befitted the leader of a democracy. The charge was not original: at the PHILADELPHIA CONVENTION Edmund Jennings Randolph denounced the proposed office of President as "the foetus of monarchy". Yet in 1980 Gerald FORD was declaring: "We have not an imperial presidency but an imperilled presidency".

storybook presidency Hedrick Smith's term for the image created by President Reagan's video managers, "using the pageantry of presidential travel to hook the networks and capture the popular imagination. . . . The more Reagan wrapped himself in the flag, the harder it became for mere mortal politicians to challenge him". Smith also coined the phrase **video presidency** for the priority given by Reagan's White House staff to playing to the requirements and appetite of the television networks to get their message across. *See* SOUND-BITE; PHOTO OPPORTUNITY; VIDEO FEED.

a cancer within, close to the presidency John Dean's warning to Nixon on 21 March 1973 as the WATERGATE scandal began to grow. In a taped conversation, he said:

> We have a cancer within, close to the Presidency, that is growing. It is growing daily. It's compounded, growing geometrically now, because it compounds itself.

a heartbeat away from the presidency Since the 1950s, shorthand for the position of the VICE-PRESIDENT, who at any moment might have to take over the reins of power. After George BUSH was elected with Dan QUAYLE as his Vice-President, the story went round Washington that Quayle was accompanied everywhere by two armed CIA men – with orders to shoot Quayle if anything happened to Bush.

President Under the US CONSTITUTION, "the Executive power shall be vested in a President of the United States of America". He or she must be a natural-born US citizen, at least 35 years old, and have resided in the US for at least 14 years. The President is also COMMANDER-IN-CHIEF of its armed forces. Americans often refuse to believe their system throws up the best candidate. Ambrose Bierce defined the President as "the leading figure in a small group of men of whom – and of whom only – it is positively known that immense numbers of their countrymen did not want any of them for president". The view goes back some way; in 1840 John Stuart Mill wrote: "He is now always an unknown mediocrity, or a person whose reputation has been acquired in some field other than politics." Such sentiments led Treasury Secretary Salmon Chase to say: "I would rather that people should wonder why I wasn't President than why I am." Henry Clay declared: "I had rather be right than President," but the Socialist Norman Thomas was more flexible:

> While I'd rather be right than President, at any time I'm ready to be both.

Becoming President is the ultimate American dream. Clarence Darrow wrote: "When I was a boy I was told anybody could become president; I'm beginning to believe it." Adlai Stevenson was as cynical: "In America, any boy may become President. I suppose that's just one of the risks he takes." Sen. Barry Goldwater sadly noted after his 1964 defeat: "It's a great country where anyone can grow up to be president – except me." And Averell Harriman doubted if the effort was worthwhile, saying: "Anyone who wants to be President should have his head examined." Or, as Gore Vidal put it,

> Any American who is prepared to run for President should automatically be disqualified from ever doing so.

The President is not just a partisan figure but, in Edwin Corwin's words, "the American people's one authentic trumpet". Harry S Truman put it differently: "All the President is is a glorified public relations man who spends his time flattering, kissing and kicking people to get them to do what they are supposed to do anyway." He also said: "Being President is like riding a tiger. A man has to keep on riding, or be swallowed." Ronald Reagan's philosophy of government was more relaxed: "Surround yourself with the best people you can find, delegate authority and don't interfere."

The President, under the Constitution, does not govern alone. Abraham LINCOLN, when in Congress, asked: "He is the representative of the people . . . elected by them, as well as Congress is. But can he, in the nature [of] things, know the hearts of the people as well as 300 other men, coming from all the various localities of the nation? If so, where is the propriety of having a Congress?" It is a question many Americans have asked since. Yet a President does have awesome power and responsibilities. Woodrow WILSON felt that "no one but the President seems to be expected to look out for the general interests of the country", adding: "Let him rightly interpret the national thought and he is irresistible." According to Coolidge, "the first lesson a President has to learn is that every word he says weighs a ton". And Eisenhower told the incoming KENNEDY: "There are no easy matters that will come to you as President. If they are easy they will be settled at a lower level." Kennedy himself came to feel that a President "must wield extraordinary powers under extraordinary limitations". He might have cited TAFT's opinion that "the President can exercise no power which cannot be fairly and reasonably traced to some specific grant of power . . . in the Federal Constitution or an Act of Congress. . . . There is no undefined residuum of power which he can exercise because it seems to him to be in the public interest." But Richard Nixon stood the argument on its head when he declared:

> When the President does it, that means it is not illegal.

Being President can encourage remoteness and self-importance. John Eisenhower reckoned that "the longer a President is in office, the more headstrong he becomes". And Truman said: "The President has a hundred voices telling him that he's the greatest man in the world. He must listen carefully indeed to hear the one voice that tells him he is not." Such advice may come from world-weary confidants like Henry KISSINGER, who once said: "If you've seen one President, you've seen them all." Yet George Reedy cautioned:

> Nobody is strong-minded around a President. It is always "Yes, Sir", "No, Sir". The "No, Sir" comes when he asks whether you're dissatisfied.

Eisenhower found one compensation in being President: "There is one thing about being President. Nobody can tell you when to sit down." And to the outsider David Frye, "being President is never having to say you're sorry".

President-elect A President whose election has been confirmed by the ELECTORAL COLLEGE but who has yet to be inaugurated.

President of the European Commission The head of the Brussels administration of the EC, and often a powerful political figure in his own right. He is appointed by member states for a four-year term, which is generally renewed.

President of the Senate In the US CONGRESS, the post held in the first instance by the Vice-President, or in his absence by a **President pro tem**, short for *pro tempore* (Lat. for the time being), from among the members of the Senate.

President's Commission A body set up by the President and reporting to him, generally concerning some controversial event (*see* WALKER Commission into the CHICAGO CONVENTION riots), national calamity (*see* WARREN COMMISSION), or a disquieting social trend.

acting President Under the 25th Amendment, ratified in 1967, the President may in the event of his incapacity hand over his powers to the VICE-PRESIDENT who becomes "acting President". If the President is incapable of taking this step or will not do so, the Vice-President and CABINET can take it for him. Until 1967 there was no machinery to cover the event of a President being in office but incapacitated; when Woodrow WILSON was unfit to govern, his wife simply took care of matters.

assistant President The nickname bestowed on former Senator and Supreme Court Justice James Byrnes, who as head of FDR's Office of War Mobilization acquired immense influence in Washington.

former President The official position of anyone still living who has held the office. Henry Watterston, for 50 years editor of the *Louisville Courier-Journal*, had a simple answer for the problem of finding a role for them:

> Take them out and shoot them.

one-day President The unique position of Sen. David Rice Aitchison, who took office for a day in March 1849 between the expiry of President Polk's term and the INAUGURATION of Zachary Taylor. Aitchison, PRESIDENT PRO TEM of the Senate, took over because Taylor would not take the Presidential OATH on a Sunday. Aitchison later claimed he had slept right through his term.

one-term President A President who serves only one of the permitted two TERMs in the White House. The term is applied especially to one, such as Jimmy CARTER or George BUSH, who sought a second term and was defeated; the voters' refusal to re-elect them is taken as proof that their Presidency has been a failure, whatever the eventual judgment of history.

State President The head of STATE in South Africa, since the separate office of Prime Minister was abolished by P. W. Botha.

All the President's Men The title of Bob Woodward and Carl Bernstein's best-selling book on their role in uncovering the WATERGATE scandal and of a subsequent film. The phrase, symbolizing unquestioning loyalty to the President, originated with Henry KISSINGER who had said when discussing the Nixon administration's policy on Cambodia in 1970: "We are all the President's men."

Making of the President, the The classic series of books on successive Presidential election campaigns by Theodore H. White; the first, closely analysing KENNEDY's win in 1960 in superb narrative style, revolutionized the way campaigns are covered. "Everything was sitting around waiting to be reported," said White. The books spawned imitations and so did the title, notably *The Selling of the President*, in which Joe McGinniss catalogued the role of advertising men in getting Nixon elected in 1968, and *The Breaking of the President*, a 1969 *Washington Post* column in which David Broder condemned anti-VIETNAM WAR activists for their attacks on the Nixon administration.

the President is dead, but the Government lives and God omnipotent reigns The moving statement of then-Congressman James Garfield (*see* BOATMAN JIM) on the assassination of LINCOLN; Garfield was to meet the same fate 16 years later.

Tell him he's no longer President The comment made to the butler of Charles Evans Hughes, who went to bed thinking he had defeated Woodrow WILSON in 1916 and woke to be told he had lost.

Presidential action The action a President must take within 10 days to sign or VETO any piece of legislation sent to him by Congress.

Presidential debates *See* DEBATE.

Presidential medal of freedom The highest award an American civilian may receive in peacetime. Instituted by President KENNEDY in 1963, it is given for achievement in a wide range of fields, including the arts.

Presidential-style campaign In UK politics, a campaign which concentrates on the personality of a party leader, to the exclusion of the party's other leading figures and generally of its policies. The term has been used in a derogatory sense about many political leaders, starting with Lloyd George.

Presidential succession Prior to 1947 there was no provision for governing the United States if both the President and Vice-President were dead or incapacitated. In that year an Act was passed under which the SPEAKER of the House of Representatives would take over as President in such circumstances (*but see* ACTING PRESIDENT *above*).

Presidential system The system under which a country, like the US, France or South Africa, is governed by a strong chief executive, with or without a subordinate Prime Minister. George BUSH said in 1991:

> I count my blessings that we have a Presidential system and not a PARLIAMENTARY SYSTEM.

Presidentress The nickname bestowed on Edith Bolling Wilson (1872–1961) who for up to 17 months from September 1919 effectively ran the Federal government in place of her ailing husband Woodrow WILSON, even decoding secret telegrams. Mrs. Wilson insisted:

> I myself never made a single decision regarding the disposition of public affairs.

presiding officer (1) The VICE-PRESIDENT of the United States in his role of presiding over the SENATE, or, when he cannot attend, the Senator who performs the task.

> I have seen a Presiding Officer of the US Senate amusing himself, while a Senator was speaking, catching flies on the Vice-President's desk.
>
> Assistant Doorkeeper ISAAC BASSETT (1819–95).

(2) In British elections, the local authority official in charge at each POLLING STATION.

press. press barons Newspaper proprietors in Britain who have been raised to the PEERAGE during the 20th century, either out of gratitude by a government they have helped elect or in the misguided hope that they will become less critical (*see* POWER WITHOUT RESPONSIBILITY).

press conference A formal occasion at which a politician responds to questions put to him by journalists who have gathered for the purpose. Presidents of the United States and of the French Republic regularly stage such events; British Prime Ministers seldom, except when overseas. Herbert HOOVER refused to hold them at all, saying: "The President of the United States will not stand and be questioned like a chicken thief by men whose names he doesn't even know." But since WORLD WAR II regular Presidential press conferences have been a constant of Washington life.

Last press conference The occasion on 7 November 1962, thus christened by Richard Nixon, when the defeated Republican candidate for the governorship of California announced his retirement from public life. As well as announcing that "YOU DON'T HAVE NIXON TO KICK AROUND ANY MORE", he also declared:

> The media have a right and a responsibility, if they're against a candidate – give him the shaft, but also

recognize, if they give him the shaft, put one lonely reporter on the campaign who will report what the candidate says now and then.

press corps The accredited pack of journalists who cover the activities, both ceremonial and political, of the President of the United States from their base in the Press Room of the WHITE HOUSE. When the President travels, the entire operation travels with him. Richard Nixon earned particular popularity from the press corps (who steered clear of WATERGATE) by ferrying reporters' girl friends and spouses to his holiday homes in Florida and California for as little as $25 when there was room on the plane. One reporter dumped his girl friend at one such destination – only to encounter her as a hotel clerk when the Nixon entourage hit Rome a few months later. He was not given one of the best rooms.

Press Gallery (1) At Westminster, the balcony overhanging the Speaker's chair in the House of Commons where reporters from the media and HANSARD take notes of Parliamentary debates; a gallery reporter is one who produces news items based purely on speeches and events in the CHAMBER, ignoring the LOBBY. The Press Gallery is also the complex of facilities behind it where the parliamentary media operate. There are over a dozen offices shared by various publications and broadcasting organizations, a library, a bar, a café, a restaurant and numerous telephone boxes. The House of Lords has a small reporters' gallery and a single workroom. In the US Capitol each House has a reporters' gallery, other press facilities being concentrated on the House of Representatives; they are far less spacious and comprehensive than at Westminster. (2) The organization to which all reporters at Westminster are accredited, its total membership (including the foreign press) being over 300.

pressing the flesh The ritual of endless handshaking by any candidate running for office or hoping for re-election. The phrase was first heard *c.* 1910, and soon acquired a political connotation in America.

pressure group A group that tries to exert pressure on legislators, government officials, the media and public opinion to promote its own special interests or causes. Such groups' campaigns – conducted through letter-writing, demonstrations, LOBBYING or advertising – are often aimed at promoting, killing or amending new legislation.

price. prices and incomes policy A Government policy that attempts to restrict rises in both the price of goods and individual earnings in order to control INFLATION. It can be based on either voluntary restraint, negotiated with unions and employers, or statutory controls. In Britain, the first such policy was tried with a degree of short-term success by Harold Wilson's Labour government in the late 1960s. Both main parties tried it in the 1970s, but with the advent of THATCHERISM the whole idea of Government interference with market forces – save for the MONEY SUPPLY – became anathema.

a price worth paying Chancellor Norman Lamont's comment on unemployment which became a millstone around the neck of John MAJOR's government in the run-up to Britain's 1992 general election. In the Commons on 16 May 1991, Lamont said:

Rising unemployment and the recession have been the price we have had to pay to get inflation down. That price is well worth paying.

the price of petrol has gone up by a penny The wartime *Daily Mirror* cartoon by Zec which so enraged Winston CHURCHILL that he tried to have the paper closed down. It showed a sailor from a torpedoed oil tanker adrift on a raft in mid-Atlantic, and was intended to show the sacrifices being made to keep ungrateful motorists supplied, but Churchill took it differently. On 19 March 1942 Sir John Anderson, Home Secretary, told the Commons that the *Mirror* had been warned that if it published anything else "calculated to foster opposition to the successful prosecution of the war", it would be shut down.

primary A ballot held in an American state in the opening months of a Presidential election year to choose delegates to the parties' nominating CONVENTIONs. In most recent elections, a candidate has emerged from the primaries with enough delegates, or enough momentum, to make sure of their party's presidential NOMINATION. Not all states hold primaries, but they have become steadily more widespread; the first primary was held by Democrats in Crawford County, Pennsylvania, in 1842, the first state to require them was Wisconsin in 1903.

closed primary A primary in which only party members may participate; this applies to the majority of such contests.

White primary Primaries held in the Deep South in which only White voters could participate. Because the Democratic Party was a voluntary organization, it was able to operate such primaries legally until the Supreme Court outlawed them in 1944, in the Smith v. Allwright case brought by the NAACP.

Prime Minister The HEAD OF GOVERNMENT in Britain and most other countries, either the effective source of power under a CONSTI-

TUTIONAL MONARCHY or ceremonial PRESIDENT, or as in France firmly subordinate to the President. The name originated as a term of abuse in 17th-century Britain, and was being used in government circles by 1710 when the Whig White Kennett was asking:

> Who is, or ought to be, prime minister, the Earl of Rochester or Mr. Harley [Robert Harley, later Earl of Oxford]?

At first the term was applied to the Minister most in the monarch's favour, but under the supremacy of Robert WALPOLE from 1721 to 1742, the term acquired its present meaning – not least through Walpole's spectacular use of PATRONAGE. Officially, however, the head of government was known as First Lord of the TREASURY or Leader of the Commons; the first Prime Minister actually to bear the title was Campbell-Bannerman (*see* C-B) on his appointment in 1905. The post of Prime Minister is, as Disraeli put it, "the top of the greasy pole". Yet Enoch POWELL rightly remarked that on the evidence of history, "more than any other position of eminence, that of Prime Minister is filled by fluke". And on the same evidence James Callaghan concluded: "Prime Ministers tend either to be bookmakers or bishops, and they take it in turn." Stanley BALDWIN said in a gloomy moment that "the work of a Prime Minister is the loneliest job in the world". And Harold Macmillan elaborated:

> On the whole nobody comes to see you when you are Prime Minister. The nice people don't come because they don't want to be thought courtiers, and the tiresome people – you don't want to see *them*.

Under the doctrine of CABINET GOVERNMENT the Prime Minister is supposed to be FIRST AMONG EQUALS. ROSEBERY, a sound observer if a spectacular failure at NUMBER TEN, wrote that "a First Minister has only the influence with the Cabinet which is given him by his personal argument, his personal qualities, his personal weight". James Callaghan claimed that being Prime Minister was "the easiest job in the world. Everyone else has an instrument to play – you just stand there and conduct." And Harold WILSON reckoned that "the main essentials of a successful Prime Minister are sleep and a sense of history". The potential power a Prime Minister can exercise is awesome; according to Tony BENN "no mediaeval monarch in the whole of British history ever had such power as every modern British Prime Minister has in his or her hands. Nor does any American President have power approaching this." Yet the Australian writer Patrick Weller was correct to observe: "Prime Ministers need help. They cannot do everything." And CHURCHILL woefully reminisced: "Headmasters have powers at their discretion with which Prime Ministers have never yet been invested." A secretary could persuade Melbourne to take the job by arguing that it was "a position no Roman or Greek could ever aspire to". And Gladstone could console Lord Aberdeen when he lost office: "You have now been Prime Minister of England. You are one of a lofty line." Yet except during exceptional tenures like Margaret Thatcher's, the post reflects Britain's influence in the world. And in the mid-1970s at the trough of national self-confidence Bernard Levin wrote:

> Once when a British Prime Minister sneezed, men half a world away would blow their noses. Now when a British Prime Minister sneezes, nobody else will even say "bless you".

prime minister designate The somewhat clumsy title accorded to Roy Jenkins (*see* WOY) when he headed the ALLIANCE's campaign in Britain's 1983 general election. It was designed to quell any confusion among voters over who would lead a LIBERAL/SDP government if the parties between them won a Parliamentary majority. As it was, the arrangement barely held until POLLING DAY, David Steel and other key Liberals reducing Jenkins's authority in the ETTRICK BRIDGE COUP.

Prime Minister's Office A uniquely Canadian institution, giving the Prime Minister a department of his own with far-reaching influence. It achieved its greatest power under Pierre TRUDEAU.

Prime Minister, think again Harold Wilson's broadcast plea to the Southern Rhodesian Premier Ian Smith in November 1965, on the eve of Smith's declaration of UDI.

Next Prime Minister but three A semi-serious term for a political prodigy, maybe with the implication that he or she will fall by the wayside without reaching the highest office. In his *Cautionary Tales*, Hilaire Belloc (1870–1953) has the youthful Lord Lundy told after some harmless peccadillo:

> We had intended you to be
> The next Prime Minister but three:
> The stocks were sold; the Press was squared;
> The Middle Class was quite prepared;
> But as it is! . . . My language fails!
> Go out and govern New South Wales!

The best Prime Minister we have The remark quoted most often as a sign of R. A. (RAB) Butler's deviousness. It was in fact a reporter who asked Butler when he landed at Heathrow in December 1955: "Mr. Butler, would you say that he [EDEN] is the best Prime Minister we have?" All Butler did was reply: "Yes."

prime time The peak viewing hours for television – generally from 7 to 11 p.m. –

which command the highest advertising rates. Politicians naturally wish to command the largest audience for positive messages about themselves and negative propaganda about their opponents. In the eyes of the American public and political community, the most damning sign of the amateurism of the 1972 Democratic Convention was that George McGovern delivered his ACCEPTANCE speech (*see* COME HOME, AMERICA) well after prime time, when few viewers were still at their sets.

primrose The primrose was Disraeli's favourite flower and the **Primrose League** survives as a Conservative organization loyal to his memory. Tim Renton, later Tory chief whip and arts minister, found a different view of the flower when CANVASSING a Sheffield steelworker in a hopeless seat in 1970:

> *Renton:* Did you know primroses were Disraeli's favourite flower?
> *Steelworker:* Is that so? I'll dig the buggers up tomorrow.

Prince, the *See* MACHIAVELLIAN.

Prince of Darkness The nickname accorded in Washington to Richard Perle (1941–), Ronald Reagan's hardline Assistant Secretary of Defence for International Security. A former aide of Sen. Henry "SCOOP" Jackson, Perle was for most of the Reagan years an inveterate foe of ARMS CONTROL negotiations with the Soviet Union. The phrase comes from Shakespeare's *King Lear*.

Prince of Piffle One of the many derogatory nicknames earned by Sen. Huey "KINGFISH" Long.

Prince of Wales The principal title of the heir to the throne of the UNITED KINGDOM, when that heir is the monarch's first-born son.

principles Fundamental moral beliefs, which for a politician are often challenged by opportunities to earn easy popularity. The Australian Labor leader Arthur Calwell put the noble view: "It is better to be defeated on principle than to win on lies," and America's Sen. Henry F. Ashurst the cynical: "You must learn that there are times when a man in public life is compelled to rise above his principles." The British union leader Ron Todd cautioned: "You don't have power if you surrender all your principles – you have office," but Lord Melbourne noted long before: "Nobody did anything very foolish except from some strong principle." Some politicians feel they have no choice; Eric Williams, premier of Trinidad, confessed:

> A small country like ours has only principles.

in principle A phrase accepting that it is right for something to be done, with the implication that there are obstacles to doing it at present. Bismarck brazenly admitted:

> When you say that you agree to something in principle, you mean that you have not the slightest intention of carrying it out in practice.

man of principle One of the highest accolades a politician (often an unsuccessful one) can receive. Sen. Everett DIRKSEN self-deprecatingly sought to have it both ways, declaring: "I am a man of firm and unbending principle, the first of which is to be flexible at all times."

Damn your principles! Stick to your party! *See* PARTY.

private. private enterprise The system on which CAPITALISM and MARKET economics is based, in which business enterprise by individual entrepreneurs and companies creates economic activity, jobs and wealth.

> The sole function of government is to bring about a condition of affairs favourable to the beneficial development of private enterprise. HERBERT HOOVER.

Private Eye The UK satirical fortnightly founded by Richard Ingrams, Christopher Booker, William Rushton and Peter Cook in October 1961, which has been an irritant to governments of all parties ever since. In its early days its satirical impact was reinforced by the parallel television programme THAT WAS THE WEEK THAT WAS. As well as providing a diet of gossip, some of it true, it has exposed humbug and scandal in government from the PROFUMO and POULSON affairs to the Iraqi SUPERGUN. *Private Eye*, whose future has frequently been jeopardized by massive libel damages awarded against it, has been edited since 1988 by Ian Hislop.

Private John The nickname of Congressman **John M. Allen** of Mississippi, coined at an election meeting in 1884 which he shared with his opponent, former Confederate General Tucker. Tucker recalled how "after a hard fought battle on yonder hill, I bivouacked under yonder clump of trees." Allen followed him to the podium and said: "I was a vedette picket and stood guard over the general while he slept. Now then, fellow citizens, all of you who were generals vote for General Tucker, and all of you who were privates and stood guard over the generals while they slept, vote for Private John Allen!" Allen, who always signed himself "Private John Allen, Tupelo, USA", won the election.

Private Notice Question *See* PNQ.

private office The team of civil servants who service a Cabinet or junior Minister. In Australia Prime Ministers, starting with Gough Whitlam, have used their private office as a political powerhouse.

private sector The sector of the economy actuated by private enterprise, consisting of companies owned by their shareholders and small businesses. In a mixed ECONOMY, it co-exists with the PUBLIC SECTOR.

private visit A visit to another country by a head of state, head of government or other senior figure which includes no formal, official or public engagements.

private opulence and public squalor The emotive phrase coined by Professor John Kenneth Galbraith (1908–) to describe the situation in some affluent Western countries where individual wealth co-exists with ill-financed and inadequate public services for the masses.

privatization The process of transferring state-owned enterprises to the PRIVATE SECTOR by selling off their shares to the public. Margaret Thatcher was not the first British Prime Minister to sell off NATIONALIZED industries, but it was her supporters who coined the term. Privatization was bitterly opposed by the LABOUR PARTY and the trade unions, and questioned by some Conservatives (*See* SELLING OFF THE FAMILY SILVER). But the initiative was copied all over the world, particularly behind the former IRON CURTAIN. In 1991 the Soviet Prime Minister Valentin Pavlov declared:

> Privatization must come from the liberalization of prices.

privilege The special rights enjoyed by a legislature and its members in terms of freedom from arrest except on a criminal charge, and freedom to speak one's mind in debate without fear of legal action.

breach of privilege The offence with which the House of Commons, advised by its **Select Committee on Privileges,** may charge whoever tries to impede its work. Such charges have been brought against editors of newspapers that have indulged in malicious criticism of Parliament as such, and trade unions who have sought to compel their SPONSORED MPs to vote in a particular way. An alleged offender may be called to the BAR OF THE HOUSE to be admonished; in theory they could, as in times past, be imprisoned on the premises.

executive privilege *See* EXECUTIVE.

motion of the highest privilege In the US HOUSE OF REPRESENTATIVES, a procedural motion of the utmost importance. One occasion for such a motion is when, after 20 calendar days, House-Senate CONFEREES have failed to report agreement.

personal privilege motion Again in the US Congress, a motion enabling a member to raise a controversial matter relating to his or her own personal affairs.

under the cloak of privilege The Westminster term for comments made in the Commons chamber by an MP which would have been actionable for libel had they been said outside. The procedure is used from time to time to unmask criminal wrongdoing; sometimes a private citizen who feels he or she has been the subject of an unjustified personal attack in the Commons will challenge the member to repeat the allegations outside.

privilege to revise and extend The latitude accorded by the CONGRESSIONAL RECORD for members of Congress to edit or clarify their spoken remarks before they appear in print. Without it, one Congressman has said, the *Record* would be "really sad reading next day – the best comic you ever saw." The danger in the procedure is that it could make it harder for the courts subsequently to ascertain the true intent of Congress in passing a particular item of legislation.

Privy Council The pool of UK and COMMONWEALTH statesmen, judges and others who have been admitted to the councils of the SOVEREIGN. In practice the council, which advises the Monarch and transacts some official business, comprises a handful of current UK Cabinet Ministers, with the Sovereign (or designated representative) and the LORD PRESIDENT OF THE COUNCIL always present. The Privy Council as an institution predates the CABINET, having its roots in the Middle Ages. Its Judicial Committee is the final court of appeal for a number of Commonwealth countries.

privy council terms The basis of total confidentiality on which a Prime Minister briefs and consults Opposition leaders at Westminster. To enable this to take place, the leaders of the Labour and Liberal Democrat parties are by convention admitted to the Privy Council, membership of which carries with it a strict oath of secrecy.

pro-. pro-Boer The name given to opponents and critics of the BOER WAR and its conduct by Britain's IMPERIALISTS, during the war itself and the KHAKI ELECTION campaign.

pro-choice The label assumed for themselves in the mid-1980s by advocates of more liberal abortion laws, especially in America. It was devised as a counter to the following.

pro-life The highly effective name chosen in the 1970s by American opponents of abortion, and taken up by their allies throughout the West. Supporters of the RIGHT TO LIFE regard the destruction of any unborn foetus as murder, and thus seek to outlaw abortion and ban experiments on embryos. In 1989 President BUSH supported pro-lifers who organized large marches immediately before the Supreme Court put new restraints on abortion, limiting the landmark ROE v. WADE ruling.

pro-marketeers Supporters of UK membership of the EUROPEAN COMMUNITY (EC). The term had particular force in the 1960s and early 1970s when it was an open question whether Britain would join.

procedural manoeuvres The use of the rules of a legislature to frustrate the passage of business or to ensure that a particular subject is raised against the wishes of those in charge of the agenda.

procurement The commissioning or purchase of items needed by a governmment department or agency, especially the process of developing and obtaining military hardware of all kinds from the defence industries.

Prod In NORTHERN IRELAND, a mildly offensive term for a Protestant. It is considerably less abusive than TAIG, used by some Protestants of Catholics.

Profiles in Courage The best-selling book, published in 1956, with which then-Senator John F. KENNEDY won a Pulitzer Prize. It described Senators who had stood bravely against public opinion, and established the link between "Kennedy" and "courage" in the public mind. Kennedy wrote the book while convalescing from a second spinal operation to ease the pain from his war wounds (*see* PT-109). His recovery kept him away from the Senate during the crucial debates on whether to censure Sen. Joseph McCARTHY; Kennedy's eagerness to be associated with courage did not prompt him to voice an opinion on the matter.

Profumo affair The sex-and-security scandal which riveted the British public for months in 1963, forced the resignation of a Cabinet Minister and contributed to the end of the Conservative government first elected in 1951. **John Profumo** (1915–), Secretary for War in Harold Macmillan's government, resigned in June 1963 after admitting lying to the House when he denied having a liaison with the call-girl Christine Keeler (1942–). She had also been sleeping with Lt.-Cdr. Yevgeny Ivanov, an assistant Soviet naval attaché, suspected of being a spy, who had pumped her for information. Profumo first met Keeler in July 1961, naked in a swimming pool at CLIVEDEN, the country estate of Lord Astor; also at the party was Dr. Stephen Ward with whom Keeler lived. Ward, an artist/osteopath with famous patients to whom he occasionally supplied "popsies", had already introduced Keeler to Ivanov. MI5 learned of Profumo's association with Keeler through Ward, who was also informing them on Ivanov's activities. Warned by a colleague of MI5's concern at the implications of having a Secretary for War sharing a mistress with a Soviet agent, Profumo broke off the relationship. But after a shooting incident at Ward's flat in December 1962 aimed at her even-younger friend Mandy Rice-Davis, the press latched on to Keeler's activities and rumours of Profumo's relationship with her became rife; they were hinted at in PRIVATE EYE and the BBC's newly-launched satirical programme THAT WAS THE WEEK THAT WAS. On 22 March 1963 Profumo told MPs in a PERSONAL STATEMENT:

> There was no impropriety whatsoever in my acquaintanceship with Miss Keeler.... I shall not hesitate to issue writs for libel and slander if scandalous allegations are made or repeated outside the House.

Though subsequent pressure from the Opposition on the security angle forced his resignation, it was his lie to the Commons, soon revealed as such, that lost him his own party's support; he had even lied to Cabinet colleagues when they pressed him. Macmillan had been kept in ignorance by MI5, and his apparent unworldliness led a Tory ex-Minister, Nigel Birch, to ask: "What does the Prime Minister think whores are for?" *The Times* summed up the ESTABLISHMENT's feeling of grubbiness and betrayal with a leader headed "It *is* a moral issue", and the new Labour leader Harold WILSON moved in for the kill, declaring:

> There is something nauseous about a system of society which pays a harlot 25 times as much as a Prime Minister, 250 times as much as it pays its members of Parliament and 500 times as much as it pays its ministers of religion.

The left-winger Michael Foot said in scorn: "The members of our secret service have apparently spent so much time looking under the bed for Communists that they haven't had time to look in the bed." MI5 and Macmillan both declared themselves satisfied that there had been no breach of security, and the subsequent DENNING REPORT broadly agreed. Yet the political furore at times made the government seem on the verge of collapse, though Macmillan said afterward:

> I was determined that no British Government should be brought down by the action of two tarts.

This echoed Lord Hailsham's words that "a great party is not to be brought down by a scandal by a woman of easy virtue and a proven liar". Hailsham's moralizing earned from the fox-hunting Labour MP Sir Reginald Paget one of the most stinging denunciations heard in the Commons:

> From Lord Hailsham we have had a virtuoso performance in the art of kicking a fallen friend in the guts.... When

self-indulgence has reduced a man to the shape of the Right Honourable and Noble Gentleman, sexual continence requires no more than a sense of the ridiculous.

Stephen Ward was tried in July 1963 on charges ranging from running a brothel to arranging then-illegal abortions. The trial turned into a farrago of two-way mirrors, whips, and a masked man in a FREEMASON'S APRON whose identity was too sensitive to be revealed. When Lord Astor repudiated the evidence of Mandy Rice-Davies, who was Ward's mistress, she retorted: "HE WOULD, WOULDN'T HE". Ward killed himself on 3 August with an overdose of Nembutal. Profumo devoted himself to charity work at Toynbee Hall in London's East End, and in 1975 was REHABILITATED with the award of a CBE. Keeler achieved lifelong notoriety and was jailed for nine months for perjury; the *News of the World* paid £23,000 for her story but the scandal brought her neither wealth nor happiness. Mandy Rice-Davis declared: "I am notorious. I may go down in history as another Lady Hamilton", and lived into prosperous and respectable middle age. Ivanov was recalled to Moscow as the scandal broke and spent some time in a mental institution. Macmillan resigned that autumn while in hospital for prostate surgery; his government, now headed by SIR ALEC Douglas-Home, narrowly lost the 1964 General Election.

The Tory party ran screaming from side to side of the sinking ship before tossing Harold Macmillan over the side as an act of propitiation. JULIAN CRITCHLEY.

"What have you done?" cried Christine.
"You've wrecked the whole party machine!
To lie in the nude
May be rude
But to lie in the House is obscene." ANON.

progressive In general terms, a person or movement who advocates progress or reform. Hugh Brogan has called it "a curiously empty word", but from time to time a party (usually a POPULIST one) has taken the word for its title. America has had three Progressive Parties. The first was founded in a rebellion in 1910 by Congressional Republicans against the Speakership of Rep. Joe Cannon (*see* UNCLE JOE; FOUL-MOUTHED JOE). In 1911 Sen. Robert La Follette of Wisconsin (1855–1925) formed the **National Progressive Republican League**, and ex-President Theodore Roosevelt stepped forward to head it; the Progressives backed his BULL MOOSE candidacy in 1912 before fading away. A second **Progressive Party** was launched in 1924 by malcontents in Wisconsin and other farm states, with La Follette as its Presidential nominee. It proposed a "housecleaning" in Washington, public control of natural resources, public ownership of railroads and cuts in taxes. La Follette polled nearly 5 million votes, but carried only his home state. Finally, in 1947, former Vice-President Henry Wallace launched a leftist **Progressive Party** to protest at the Truman administration's deteriorating relations with Soviet Russia, and demand an end to the MARSHALL PLAN. Truman loyalists feared Wallace's intervention might ensure a Republican win, but the ticket polled a disappointing 1,156,103 votes and won no electoral seats.

In Canada a farmer-backed **Progressive Party** took power in Ontario in 1919, and in the 1921 general election won 65 Parliamentary seats, many in the west and 15 more than the Conservatives. Mackenzie King manoeuvred the Progressives under T. A. Crerar into backing his minority government; they were reduced to 24 MPs in the 1925 election and in the further poll following the 1926 CONSTITUTIONAL CRISIS they were almost wiped out. But they turned Canada into a multi-party democracy, which it has remained for most of the time since. In 1942, the **Conservatives** added **"Progressive"** to their title to underline an accentuated commitment to reform and social provision.

In Britain the term has had less significance, though in the early 20th century the non-Labour group on the London County Council (*see* LCC) termed themselves **Progressives**.

progressive taxation *See* TAX.

Prohibition The ban on the sale or consumption of intoxicating liquor introduced in America in 1920 following by the passage of the VOLSTEAD ACT and ratification in 1919 of the 18TH AMENDMENT. The introduction of the "noble EXPERIMENT" was the result of decades of pressure from temperance and church groups; Maine had banned alcohol as long ago as 1856, a **Prohibition Party** was formed in 1869 and has contested Presidential elections ever since, and Prohibition was a key element of the PROGRESSIVE platform. By 1906, 18 states had introduced some sort of restriction or ban on the sale of alcohol and many counties and cities were also DRY by virtue of a "local option" offered them by state legislatures; when grain ran short during World War I and drinking by servicemen was seen as a problem, the pressure intensified. Prohibition, however, proved unenforceable; the supply of illicit liquor to a thirsty population by bootleggers spawned organized crime and widespread corruption among police and politicians. It was repealed in December 1933, though eight states stayed "dry".

There is as much chance of repealing the 18th Amendment as there is for a humming bird to fly to the planet

Mars with the Washington Monument tied to its tail. This country is for temperance and prohibition, and it is going to continue to elect members to Congress who believe in that.
Sen. MORRIS SHEPPARD (1875–1941), 24 September 1930.

projection A computerized estimate of the outcome of an election, based on analysis of a limited number of results.

proletariat The poorest labouring class; the ancient Roman word for those so poor that they could only breed children for military service, taken up by MARXISTs to represent the elements in society who should rightfully capture power. Marx and Engels wrote in the COMMUNIST MANIFESTO of 1848: "The proletariat alone is a truly revolutionary class", and LENIN in *One Step Forward, Two Steps Back* declared:

In the struggle for power the proletariat has no other weapon but organization.

dictatorship of the proletariat The penultimate stage in social progress as envisioned by MARX and his spiritual heirs. In the COMMUNIST MANIFESTO Marx stated: "The class struggle necessarily leads to the dictatorship of the proletariat, and that dictatorship itself only constitutes the transition to the abolition of all classes and to a CLASSLESS SOCIETY."
lumpenproletariat Marx's term, coined in 1850, for the very poorest of the working class. The word combines the Ger. *lump*, ragamuffin and *proletariat*. Although not intended as a term of denigration, it has widely become such.

prompt cards Cards on which key phrases are written, for a politician to carry to remind him- or herself of key phrases to utter before an audience or the cameras. Much use was made of them by Ronald Reagan's advisers, in an effort to keep up the flow of apparently-spontaneous ONE-LINERS and to offset his ability to forget or alter basic facts.

propaganda (Lat. to be spread) The spreading of information favourable to the regime or organisation disseminating it, often with little regard to its veracity. Originally a term from the 17th-century Roman Catholic church, it was taken over and perfected by the COMMUNIST and FASCIST regimes of the inter-war period and their spiritual successors; Hitler's Propaganda Minister Josef Goebbels claimed: "We have made the *Reich* by propaganda." Powerful groups in the democracies are also skilled in its use; President Truman once observed that "the US Marine Corps have a propaganda machine that is almost equal to Stalin's". **Black propaganda** is information circulated in the knowledge that it is false, in order to discredit an enemy or opponent.

The art of persuading others of what one does not believe oneself. Israeli Foreign Minister ABBA EBAN (1915–).

The propagandist's purpose is to make one set of people forget that certain other sets of people are human.
ALDOUS HUXLEY (1894–1963).

propeller heads *See* NERD SQUAD.

property. property-owning democracy The principle and the appeal of Britain's CONSERVATIVE PARTY from the 1950s, based on the belief that home ownership would give individuals a greater stake in society – and make them more likely to vote Conservative. The phrase, much used by generations of senior Tories, was coined by the Scottish Conservative MP Noel Skelton (1880–1935), whose promising Ministerial career was cut short by his early death.
Property is theft One of the classic slogans of communism and anarchism, devised in 1840 by Pierre-Joseph Proudhon (1809–65).
Government has no other end but the preservation of property A typically minimalist statement from the English philosopher John Locke (1632–1704), made in his *Second Treatise on Government* (1690).
Next to the right of liberty, the right of property is the most important individual right guaranteed by the Constitution and the one which . . . has contributed more to the growth of civilization than any other. The philosophy of President TAFT, set out in his book *Popular Government* (1913).
Our civilization is built up on private property, and can only be defended by private property Winston CHURCHILL's rejoinder in 1947 to proposals by the ATTLEE government to take sweeping "transitional powers", including the right to direct labour, to hasten post-war reconstruction and the rebuilding of the economy. Churchill saw the plan as TOTALITARIAN and a threat to basic human rights; it was not fully implemented.
There is something that Governments care for far more than human life, and that is the security of property The rationale set out by Emmeline Pankhurst (1858–1928) for SUFFRAGETTES to take MILITANT and destructive action. In a speech at London's Royal Albert Hall on 17 October 1912, she continued:

So it is through property that we shall strike the enemy. . . . Be militant each in your own way . . . I incite this meeting to rebellion.

proportional representation A system of electing a legislature or other body which directly reflects the overall vote cast for each party; the opposite is the FIRST PAST THE POST system under which the winner in each constituency is elected and parties which cannot reach that threshold are not represented. A system of PR was recommended for Britain by a SPEAKER'S CONFERENCE after World War I but never implemented; since the early 1970s the issue has again been the subject of controversy. Traditionally the third-party Liberals/LIBERAL DEMOCRATS have been the greatest advocates of PR, but LABOUR has switched since the mid-1980s from total opposition to wary interest (*see* PLANT COMMISSION). Opponents of PR argue that as no party ever gains 50% of the total vote, their own party would never achieve an outright Parliamentary majority; advocates of it see it as a way of preventing other parties exercising absolute power with 40% or less of the vote. Critics also point to the continual instability of governments in some countries with PR, notably Italy, and argue that the system gives small parties excessive power. There are numerous forms of PR including the ADDITIONAL MEMBER, Alternative VOTE and Single Transferable VOTE.

After the anti-H-BLOCK candidate Owen Carron won the Fermanagh and South Tyrone by-election in 1981, the Liberal MP Stephen (later Lord) Ross asked Margaret Thatcher in the Commons if the result didn't prove the case for PR. "As there were only two candidates, I don't see what difference it would have made", she replied.

> PR is fundamentally undemocratic.
>
> NEIL KINNOCK, 1983.

Proposition 13 The revolutionary INITIATIVE approved by California voters in 1978 which slashed property taxes in half. The taxes, pegged to soaring real estate values, had been rising far more sharply than incomes, and home owners led by the conservative businessman Howard Jarvis rebelled. It took Jarvis years to get the proposition on to the ballot, but it was carried by a 2–1 majority. Dire warnings about the collapse of government if tax revenues were pegged were not borne out, and Proposition 13 became a precedent for the application of REAGANOMICS three years later.

> The WATTS RIOT of the White middle class.
>
> Letter to the *Los Angeles Herald-Examiner*.

prorogation In Britain, the act of terminating a PARLIAMENT so that new elections may be held. Prorogation is ordered by the Sovereign, and takes the form of a brief ceremony in both Houses.

prospective candidate *See* CANDIDATE.

protectionism The policy of protecting a nation's industries by erecting a TARIFF barrier to make imports uncompetitive, thereby risking retaliation against one's own exports. In America the tradition runs deep; Thomas JEFFERSON, in a letter in 1815, wrote:

> I have come to a resolution myself, as I hope any good citizen will, never again to purchase any article of foreign manufacture which can be had of American make, be the difference of price what it may.

Protectionism reached its height in late 19th-century America, with Senators imposing rigorous tariffs even when the White House wanted cuts. And in a campaign speech in 1923, Herbert HOOVER warned:

> The grass will grow in the streets of a hundred cities, a thousand towns; the weeds will overrun the fields of millions of farms if [protection] is taken away.

Protectionism has been less of a force in Britain, though IMPERIAL PREFERENCE was as much a form of co-ordinated protectionism by a number of countries as a move toward FREE TRADE. When Joseph Chamberlain began his campaign for such preference in 1903, Margot Asquith wrote:

> This caught on like wildfire with the semi-clever, moderately educated, the Imperialists, Dukes, journalists and Fighting Forces.

protectorate (1) The formal title of the COMMONWEALTH, the republican form of government in England over which Oliver Cromwell (1599–1658) presided as Lord Protector between 1653 until his death. (2) A territory in the British Empire administered by Britain without ANNEXATION and without its inhabitants being granted British citizenship.

protest. protest and survive The slogan launched by Britain's CND in the early 1980s in response to a government CIVIL DEFENCE leaflet entitled *Protect and Survive*, which suggested that elementary precautions could enable a considerable number of people to survive a nuclear war.

protest movement The initially student movement which from *c.* 1967 staged frequent outrageous protests against the basics of American society, with SIT-INs and takeovers in many universities. It was given a moral edge by the depth and sincerity of opposition to the escalating VIETNAM WAR, but some of its adherents flirted with MARXISM. The movement, which emphasized peace and NON-VIOLENCE despite some excesses, caught the imagination of many young people as the cultures of rock music, drugs and Flower Power shattered many taboos. It gave birth to the NEW LEFT, and enraged conservatives including the Nixon administration. Vice-President Spiro G. AGNEW waged a counter-offensive against extremists in the movement who were silencing all opposition, and in 1969 set out Ten Commandments of Protest:

Thou shalt not allow thy opponent to speak.
Thou shalt not set forth a program of thy own.
Thou shalt not trust anybody over thirty.
Thou shalt not honor thy father or thy mother.
Thou shalt not heed the lessons of history.
Thou shalt not write anything longer than a slogan.
Thou shalt not present a negotiable demand.
Thou shalt not accept any ESTABLISHMENT idea.
Thou shalt not revere any but totalitarian heroes.
Thou shalt not ask forgiveness for thy transgressions, rather thou shalt demand amnesty for them.

protest songs The canon of popular songs against war, poverty and injustice and the policies that cause them, pioneered by Bob Dylan in the early 1960s and taken up by Joan Baez and many other singers and songwriters.

protest vote *See* VOTE.

protocol (1) The draft of a TREATY, or an agreement appended to a treaty, or an international agreement of less moment than a treaty. (2) In diplomacy, the body of etiquette which determines both the conduct of relations between states and their representatives and, specifically, the ceremonial involved in OFFICIAL, STATE and other VISITS.

province In Canada, the ten units which make up the CONFEDERATION (plus the Yukon and the North-West Territories). The provinces have jealously guarded their rights in respect of the Federal government in Ottawa and each other; efforts to put them on an agreed and durable basis have consistently broken down because of disagreements between Quebec and the western provinces (*see* CHARLOTTETOWN ACCORD; MEECH LAKE).

Provisionals (*also* **Provos** and (to the British military) **PIRA**. The Provisional IRA, formed in 1969 when the Irish Republican Army split into the OFFICIAL IRA, who preferred mainly political action to secure a united Ireland, and the belligerently high-profile Provisionals and their POLITICAL WING, Provisional SINN FEIN. Ever since, the Provisionals have carried out a terrorist campaign against British rule in NORTHERN IRELAND; over 3000 people have died there in the ensuing violence, some 2000 killed by the Provisionals. They have also killed over 50 in attacks on the British mainland (the worst being the 1974 Birmingham pub bombings, *see* BIRMINGHAM SIX), and a number of UK service personnel in continental Europe. The movement is financed through robberies, protection rackets, fund-raising from well-wishers at home and Irish romantics abroad (including through NORAID in America) and apparently legitimate businesses; their fighters have been trained in eastern Europe and throughout the Middle East, and much of their arsenal, including large supplies of SEMTEX, has come from Libya. Much of the Provisionals' manpower is in prison and their goal is as far away from fulfilment as ever. But their campaign of violence has posed severe strains on the UK and the Irish Republic, and their ACTIVE SERVICE UNITS can still call on a pool of up to 300 dedicated fighters.

Provost In Scottish local government, the ceremonial head of the authority, the equivalent of a MAYOR in England. In the great cities of Scotland, he or she takes the title of **Lord Provost**.

proximity talks In delicate international or industrial negotiations, talks when the conflicting parties are in adjacent rooms and mediators shuttle between them.

proxy. proxy bomb A bomb delivered under duress by someone other than the terrorists who intend it to explode. A car, taxi or truck is HIJACKED, a bomb placed on board and the driver ordered at gunpoint to take it to a sensitive security target. The PROVISIONAL IRA has used this technique both in Northern Ireland and in London.

proxy vote A vote cast by one person on behalf of another who is unable to be present, for reason of illness, business or removal, and has given their authority.

PSBR PUBLIC SECTOR Borrowing Requirement. The amount the UK government has to borrow in any financial year, to cover the gap between receipts (from taxes, PRIVATIZATION proceeds, *etc.*) and the total of budgeted public spending.

psephology The study of electoral behaviour as reflected in elections and OPINION POLLS. The word was invented in 1948 by the Cambridge classical scholar Frank Hardie. It comes from the Greek *psephos*, a pebble; the Athenians in classical times voted by putting pebbles in one of two jars.

PSOE (Sp. *Partido Socialista Obrero Español*, Spanish Socialist Workers' Party) The Democratic SOCIALIST party that emerged after the death of General Franco as the principal force on the Left. Under the leadership of Felipe González, it was elected to power in 1982, and was re-elected in 1986, 1989 and (just) in 1993. It is the successor of the Socialist Party founded by Pablo Iglesias in the late 19th century which was part of the POPULAR FRONT government against which Franco launched the SPANISH CIVIL WAR.

PT-109 The torpedo boat which John F. KENNEDY commanded in the Pacific during World War II, and the title of a 1962 movie about his naval exploits. In 1943 the boat was rammed and sunk by a Japanese destroyer; Kennedy was thrown against the cockpit bulkhead, aggravating an old injury to his back, but rounded up the 10 survivors and swam with them to a nearby island, holding with his teeth for several hours the life preserver of one too badly wounded to swim. He was awarded the Navy Medal and a Purple Heart, but his back was to trouble him for the rest of his life; when Kennedy embarked on a political career, his father went to great pains to publicize and amplify his heroism.

public. Public Against Violence The Slovak counterpart to the Czech lands' CIVIC FORUM; between them they took power from the Communists in the VELVET REVOLUTION of 1989. The former liberal Communist hero Alexander Dubček (*see* PRAGUE SPRING) was among its leaders.

Public Energy Number One One of the many nicknames for Eleanor Roosevelt (*see* FIRST LADY OF THE WORLD); she gained it for her boundless energy on her own account and as her husband's ambassador during his presidency. It is a play on the FBI's "Public Enemy Number One".

public inquiry In UK environmental politics, the hearing held by a Department of the Environment inspector to determine whether a new road or building scheme should go ahead.

public interest, the A phrase which means very different things to different people. To campaigners for greater information and ACCOUNTABILITY, it implies the interest of the people as a whole; to those in power it too often means the interest of the governing clique, to which excessive public involvement is anathema.

public opinion The view of the community as a whole, and a voice which many politicians aim to reflect and to which all must ultimately listen. Abraham LINCOLN declared: "Public opinion in this country is everything," Bulwer Lytton that "when people have no other tyrant, then public opinion becomes one", and Franklin D. Roosevelt observed: "A government can be no better than the public opinion which sustains it." John C. Calhoun described public opinion as "nothing more than the opinion or voice of the strongest interest or combination of interests"; Sir Robert PEEL as "a compound of folly, weakness, prejudice, wrong feeling, right feeling, obstinacy and newspaper paragraphs"; Clarence Darrow as "the greatest enemy that ever confronted man"; Mark Bonham-Carter as "the last refuge of a politician without any opinion".

> No Minister ever stood, or could stand, against public opinion. JOHN WILSON CROKER, 1835.

Public Order Act *See* CABLE STREET.

public ownership Another word for NATIONALIZATION, though lacking the overtone of rigid centralized control associated with that term.

> It is inconceivable that we could transform this country without a major extension of public ownership. NEIL KINNOCK, 1983.

public sector The portion of a nation's economic activity conducted and financed by organs of central and local government. With the PRIVATE SECTOR, it makes up the totality of the economy. *See also* PSBR.

public speaking The art of making SPEECHES, often but not always in a political context. The phrase "unaccustomed as I am to public speaking" has become a caricature of how not to begin a speech.

> The human brain starts working the moment you are born, and never stops until you stand up to speak in public. GEORGE JESSEL.

public spending review In the UK, the annual exercise (*see* PESC) in which the CHIEF SECRETARY TO THE TREASURY reconciles "bids" from spending departments with the amount the Cabinet has agreed can be spent. Public spending was described by the early US Congressman John Randolph as "the most delicious of all privileges: spending other people's money", but Thomas JEFFERSON put a more responsible view: "The same prudence which in private life would forbid our paying our own money for unexplained projects, forbids it in the dispensation of the public moneys". Coolidge (*see* SILENT CAL) was equally firm, stating: "The appropriation of public money always is perfectly lovely until someone is asked to pay the bill", and the subsequent big spender Franklin D. Roosevelt, before his election in 1932, said in a broadcast:

> Any government, like any family, can for a year spend a little more than it earns. But you and I know that continuation of that habit means the poorhouse.

publicist A mildly derogatory term for a person who conducts a vigorous campaign, often by writing articles and leaflets, in support of a particular party, campaign or course of action.

Publish and be damned! The classic response to a blackmailer, delivered by the Duke of Wellington to Joseph Stockdale who was threatening to publish the memoirs of the IRON DUKE's former mistress Harriette Wilson. Stockdale had written to Wellington: "I have stopped the Press for a moment; but as the publication will take place next week, little delay can necessarily take place". Wellington wrote his response across the letter and posted it back to him.

Publius The anonymous author of the FEDERALIST Papers, the pamphlets putting the case for RATIFICATION of the US CONSTITUTION, which were produced in New York between October 1787 and the following August. They were in fact written by Alexander HAMILTON, James MADISON and, to a lesser extent, John JAY.

Pugin room A sedate tea-room and bar in the Palace of WESTMINSTER, above the riverside TERRACE, where MPs may entertain their guests. It was named in the early 1980s after Augustus Welby Pugin (1814–52), the workaholic prodigy who was responsible for the richly Gothic style of the new Palace's internal decoration.

Pugwash A series of annual conferences held to promote the constructive and peaceful uses of scientific knowledge. The first was held in July 1957 at the home of the Canadian philanthropist Cyrus Eaton in Pugwash, Nova Scotia. It was inspired by the Einstein-Russell memorandum, a document describing the appalling consequences for humanity of nuclear conflict, and called for a conference of scientists from both sides of the IRON CURTAIN. Subsequent meetings have been held in many different countries; subjects for discussion have included nuclear disarmament, environmental problems and the problems of the developing world. The Pugwash movement, co-ordinated by an International Co-ordinating Committee, has produced various reports on ARMS CONTROL, contributing to the course of disarmament since the 1970s. The name Pugwash brings a smile to British faces, as Captain Pugwash was a faintly ridiculous pirate in a BBC children's cartoon.

pump priming The direction of relatively small amounts of state investment or tax revenue to reviving key sectors of the economy, in particular those whose own expansion could speed a general economic recovery and hasten overall growth.

pundit Hindi for a person learned in the Sanskrit disciplines. In English the word is used for someone who is an eminent authority on a particular subject. Pundits can be seen, for example, on television giving their expert ideas on such subjects as the political or economic situation or the best strategy to be followed in wartime. *See also* PANDIT.

purdah The isolation into which a CHANCELLOR OF THE EXCHEQUER traditionally retreated for two months or so while devising his BUDGET. During that time he would answer questions in the House of Commons, and would receive deputations pressing him to take one course of action or another, but would not comment on the package he was working on. The practice ws abolished by Kenneth Clarke when he became Chancellor in 1993. The word was the Urdu and Persian term for the curtain which separates the women's apartments in a Muslim household, and thus describes the state of seclusion in which strict Islamic men maintain that women should live.

purge The removal from office, disgrace and often execution of apparently loyal colleagues by a TOTALITARIAN leader; while Hitler and other extreme rightist leaders indulged in purges, they were turned into a grotesque art form by STALIN and his Puppets (*see* puppet GOVERNMENT) in post-war East Europe. The first and greatest purge was the orgy of arrests, SHOW TRIALS and executions between 1934 and 1938 by which an increasingly paranoid Stalin eliminated the BOLSHEVIK old guard, most of the command of the RED ARMY, and thousands of Communist Party members and ordinary Soviet citizens. The era of purges was triggered by the Law of 1 December 1934 issued on Stalin's orders after the murder of his aide Sergei Kirov by a deranged gunman; they were resumed after World War II when national unity against a common enemy was no longer necessary. One of the grisliest post-war purges was carried out in the Leningrad party organization after the death of the city's party boss Andrei Zhdanov in 1948. It was conducted by Abukamov, the ruthless head of SMERSH during World War II, and was probably initiated by Georgy Malenkov and Paul Beria to eliminate supporters of Zhdanov, who had been Malenkov's chief rival for Stalin's favour. Over 2000 party functionaries were executed, including A. A. Kuznetsov, a CENTRAL COMMITTEE member, and Nikolay Voznesensky, a member of the POLITBURO.

Putney debates The debates in Putney church in Southwest London in 1647 in which LEVELLERS and other radical members of the Cromwellian army argued with their leaders for the establishment of a genuinely democratic and tolerant society. They were held to argue out the principles under which England should be governed after the CIVIL WAR; the outcome was inconclusive and no new or democratic framework was ever agreed or established. *See also* the POOREST HE THAT IS IN ENGLAND).

putsch The sudden and violent overthrow of a government or political system, from the Swiss German word for a revolution. *See also* KAPP PUTSCH; MUNICH BEER HALL PUTSCH.

Q

quadriad In America, the four bodies – the TREASURY, Office of Management and Budget (OMB), COUNCIL OF ECONOMIC ADVISERS and the FED – which dominate economic policy and keep it under review.

Quai d'Orsay The home beside the Seine in Paris of the French foreign ministry, and of a ruggedly independent and self-interested foreign policy pursued by governments regardless of political shade. *See* la GLOIRE.

quango Acronym for "quasi-autonomous national (or non-) government organization". A body independent from the department that created it, save for the appointment of its members from the ranks of the GREAT AND THE GOOD, and nominally under the control of its Minister, though not fully accountable to Parliament. Proliferation of quangos, especially in Britain, became a political issue in the late 1970s. But the initial Thatcherite drive to "cull" unnecessary quangos has not been sustained. *Compare* AGENCY.

quarantine Action, preferably international, to isolate an offending nation both economically and politically. In 1937 Franklin D. Roosevelt, in a speech that outraged ISOLATIONISTS, called on the world to "Quarantine the aggressors". He said:

> It seems to be unfortunately true that the epidemic of world lawlessness is spreading. When an epidemic of physical disease is about to spread, the community approves and joins in a quarantine of the patients in order to protect the health of the community against the spread of the disease.

President Kennedy, citing the charter of the OAS, imposed a naval quarantine on ships carrying military hardware for CUBA during the missile crisis.

quasi-judicial The role, especially in British government, of a Minister or official charged with making decisions from which an appeal might lie to the courts, and which consequently inhibits him or her from comment during the decision-making process.

Quayle Quarterly An ostensibly learned magazine chronicling the performance and dicta of **J. Danforth "Dan" Quayle** (1947–), US VICE-PRESIDENT from 1989 to 1993; its closure was announced the moment Bush/Quayle were defeated in 1992. Its editors had a rich vein to mine, but conservatives never appreciated their efforts. The Rev. Thomas Naismith of Bad Ass, Texas, wrote: "It's a crying shame you anarchist liberals have nothing productive to do, like reading the Bible, and must whittle away the time God has given you attacking our Vice-President, a God-fearing man." And Bush media adviser Roger Ailes termed the Quarterly "an attempt by a couple of Democrats to denigrate the vice president through the selective use of unchecked newspaper reports and allegations". But they did check, disappointingly finding that Quayle never made the comment most often attributed to him:

> I had no problem communicating with Latin American heads of state – though now I do wish I had paid more attention to Latin when I was in school.

Quayle's nomination after serving as a Congressman and Senator for Indiana brought questioning of his ability, and criticism of the man who chose him. William Watson of Morton Grove, Illinois, observed: "The real proof that George Bush might be a dangerous person is the fact that he selected this privileged airhead as his RUNNING-MATE". Quayle's ultra-conservatism also sat oddly with his record of having joined the National Guard rather than serve in VIETNAM. He said: "While I have not apologized for my National Guard service, and never will, I recognize that the members of my generation who served in Vietnam made a sacrifice that was far greater than mine." Later Quayle observed: "Vietnam is a jungle . . . Kuwait, Iraq, Saudi Arabia you have sand." He was also criticized for not releasing his school grades, and having entered college on a disadvantaged students' programme despite his family's wealth. But Democratic efforts to embroil him in a sex scandal failed, not least because his wife Marilyn said: "Anyone who knows Dan Quayle knows he would rather play golf than have sex any day." An exchange with Sen. Lloyd Bentsen in the 1988 Vice-Presidential DEBATE finally put him on the map. When

Quayle said: "I have as much experience in the Congress as Jack Kennedy did when he sought the Presidency", Bentsen replied:

> Senator, I served with Jack Kennedy. I knew Jack Kennedy. Jack Kennedy was a friend of mine. Senator, you're no Jack Kennedy.

In the campaign, one television critic wrote that he performed "like Bambi on ice", and *Time* observed: "Quayle, who often seems as lost as an actor missing half the pages of his script, struggled to overcome his own THROTTLEBOTTOM image – and lost." Art Buchwald reckoned: "Viewers like watching Quayle for the same reason they enjoy watching a train wreck." And Maureen Dowd commented: "He treats language like a Lego set, taking a phrase, repeating and building on it, often without regard to meaningful content." At the close the *Buffalo News* editorialized:

> Dan Quayle is still justly regarded as unfit for presidential duty by a large majority of Americans.

In office, Quayle kept his infelicity with words, with unfortunate results. He termed the HOLOCAUST "an obscene period in our nation's history", said that America expected El Salvador to "work toward the elimination of human rights", and said of Alexander Dubček, hero of the PRAGUE SPRING, "who would have predicted that Dubček, who brought in the tanks in 1968, is now being proclaimed a hero in Czechoslovakia?" Quayle told Western Samoans: "You all look like happy campers to me. Happy campers you are, happy campers you have been, and as far as I am concerned, happy campers you always will be." Of the rise of the former Klansman (*see* KU KLUX KLAN David Duke, he observed: "Unfortunately the people of Louisiana are not racists." And he told one interviewer that "Republicans understand the importance of bondage between parent and child". Passing mourners at a funeral, he urged them to "Have a nice day." He told one Republican meeting: "My friends, we can and we will never, never, never surrender to what is right." On TERM-LIMITATION, Quayle declared: "I support efforts to limit the terms of members of Congress, especially members of the House and members of the Senate." Seeing the effects of the fatal San Francisco freeway earthquake, he observed: "Well, it looks as if the top part fell on the bottom part." And to him the GULF WAR was "a stirring victory for the forces of aggression against lawlessness". *See also* POTATOE.

Some of Quayle's remarks were downright incomprehensible. He baffled the United Negro College Fund by converting its slogan "A mind is a terrible thing to waste" into "What a waste it is to lose one's mind, or not to have a mind is being very wasteful". On another occasion he said: "Every once in a while, you let a word or phrase out and you want to catch it and bring it back. You can't do that – it's gone forever." And trying to explain his remarks on the Holocaust, he declared: "We all lived in this century – I didn't live in this century."

Some opponents underrated him. Sen. Birch Bayh of Indiana, whom Quayle ousted, told his handlers prior to the contest: "The boy's retarded." And Quayle also had self-confidence, Roger Simon noting that "the inability to see your own inadequacies can be a tremendous plus in politics". Halfway through his term Adam Myerson was reporting: "In conservative circles there is a feeling that Dan Quayle has been an outstanding vice-president." And Kevin Phillips wrote: "On the chicken-dinner circuit he has a very strong core of support. Among grassroots conservatives he is more popular than Bush." Yet there was widespread disquiet that Quayle was "a heartbeat away from the PRESIDENCY". The *Chicago Tribune* editorialized that "A heart flutters, a nation shudders", while Washingtonians joked: "The six words the world fears most are: 'Dan, I don't feel very well.'" Arsenio Hall said dismissively that Quayle had "the IQ of lunch meat".

Quayle attracted his fair share of jokes. A writer to the *Los Angeles Times* said of his "Overlord" role in the space programme: "NASA got where it is by putting monkeys in high places." One story was that "he was asked to become a Jehovah's Witness, but said he hadn't seen the accident". One anonymous gagster said: "Quizzed about the SOVIET BLOC, Dan said it wasn't as good as Lego." In California, *Mother Jones* magazine organized a "pin the tail on J. Dan Quayle" competition.

He was aware of his reputation, frankly saying: "I stand by all the misstatements that I've made." He told reporters: "I'm my own handler. There's not going to be any more handler stories because I'm the handler . . . I'm Doctor Spin." Yet a handler was still needed. Campaigning in a shopping mall in 1992 he said to a woman: "I'm Dan Quayle, who are you?" She replied: "I'm your Secret service agent."

Quebec Act One of the measures passed by the Westminster Parliament which precipitated American INDEPENDENCE. The Act, passed in 1774 at the urging of Governor Sir Guy Carleton, strengthened the hand of the French-Canadian upper class, restored Catholic liberties – thus upsetting Protestant New

England – and, more explosively, extended Quebec's boundaries to include the region between the Ohio and the Mississippi. Though Montreal fur traders were still the dominant economic force in this region, its assignment to Quebec was seen as a provocation and a long-term threat to westward expansion by the 13 American colonies, four of whom already had claims in the area.

Quebec conference The conference, code-named Quadrant, held at the Citadel in Quebec from 11 to 24 August 1943 between FDR, Churchill and other Allied leaders. Its aim was to discuss preparations for the Allied invasion of Europe, and to review strategy and command.

Quebec Resolutions The 72 resolutions agreed at Quebec in 1864 by provincial leaders, which formed the basis of the BRITISH NORTH AMERICA ACT and paved the way for Canada's CONFEDERATION.

Vive le Québec libre! (Fr. long live free Quebec!) The slogan of the SEPARATIST movement seeking independence for French-speaking Quebec from Canada (*see* FLQ; PQ). It was notoriously recited by President DE GAULLE in a speech in Montreal in 1967; the ensuing furore led to the cancellation of the rest of his Canadian tour. De Gaulle explained his outburst as "an opportunity to make up for France's cowardice" during World War II.

Queen. Queen Lil Liliuokalani, the last native ruler of Hawaii, who came to the throne in 1891 but was overthrown two years later by a committee of American businessmen headed by Sanford B. Dole when she insisted on "Hawaii for the Hawaiians". President Cleveland demanded her restoration and refused to submit a Treaty of ANNEXATION drafted by Dole to the Senate, but Dole proclaimed himself President of Hawaii in 1894. America annexed Hawaii in 1898 and it achieved STATEHOOD in 1959.

Queen's or **King's commission** In Britain, the invitation from the SOVEREIGN to the victor of an election, or the chosen successor to an outgoing PRIME MINISTER, to form a government.

Queen's or **King's Speech** In the UK and many COMMONWEALTH Parliaments, the address delivered at the opening of a new Parliamentary session detailing the government's legislative programme. It is written for the sovereign by Ministers. When the Sovereign cannot be present, it is delivered by a representative, at Westminster a senior member of the Royal family and in Commonwealth countries where he or she is Head of STATE by the GOVERNOR-GENERAL. *See* the CROWN IN PARLIAMENT; GRACIOUS SPEECH.

Queer Hardie Nickname for the British Labour pioneer (James) **Keir Hardie** (1856–1915). A former Scots miner and active trade unionist, he was a co-founder and chairman of the Independent Labour Party (see ILP) and Labour Representation Committee, which became the LABOUR PARTY in 1906. His nickname relates to his eccentricity; on his first day in Parliament he arrived in the cloth cap that became his trademark. For the last 15 years of his life Hardie was MP for Merthyr Tydfil. An ardent pacifist, he died disillusioned with Labour's support for World War I.

Quemoy and Matsu Two islets off the Chinese coast which remained in NATIONALIST hands after the Communist victory on the mainland in 1949. In 1954 the Communist Chinese Premier, Chou En-Lai, pledged himself to oust the Nationalists from the islands, and from September 1954 they were shelled repeatedly. The islands became a flashpoint of the COLD WAR, but despite a renewed bombardment of Quemoy in 1958 the Communists never attempted to invade. The Nationalist build-up prompted US objections and finally brought an end to America's commitment to the FREE WORLD "recovering" China. As symbols of Communist ambitions, Quemoy and Matsu played a major part in the 1960 Kennedy-Nixon DEBATES.

question A central feature of British Parliamentary life, both in writing and, more theatrically, to Ministers at **Question Time** on the floor of the Commons. Question Time is held from 2.30 to 3.30 p.m. every Monday to Thursday, with questions to the Prime Minister for 15 minutes every Tuesday and Thursday, which have become a ritualized exchange, conducted since 1990 before a live television audience. The Conservative MP Michael Fallon described Question Time as "like setting pet mice to work on a toy treadmill". And after watching it President Bush said: "I count my blessings for the fact that I don't have to go into that pit that John Major stands in, nose-to-nose with the Opposition, all yelling at each other." However Tennessee Congressman Jim Cooper asked: "Why can't *we* do this?" Question Time is also a feature of many COMMONWEALTH Parliaments and, in a limited way, the EUROPEAN PARLIAMENT.

Question! Shouted to a questioner by unsympathetic legislators or members of an audience to get him or her to come to the point.

Questions of Procedure for Ministers The 44-page "Bible" on the conduct of government which is given to all newly-appointed Ministers in Britain. Drawn up by the CABINET SECRETARY, it was treated as highly confidential until May 1992, when the Major government made it public. While an invaluable guide to the functions of government and WHITEHALL etiquette, it leaves the distinct impression that Ministers are there for the benefit of the Civil Service MANDARINS.

business questions The session after Prime Minister's Questions every Thursday when the LEADER OF THE HOUSE takes questions on the following week's business, allowing MPs to raise almost any matter of their choice.

open question The standard backbencher's question to the Prime Minister asking him to list his engagements for the day. This enables any member to ask "whether in the course of an otherwise busy day" he will address any issue they care to raise.

oral question Any question asked on the floor of the House, whether printed in the ORDER PAPER to give the Minister warning or put as a supplementary (*see below*).

planted question A question which Ministers arrange to have asked so that they can place a particular item of information on the record or score a political point.

private notice question *See* PNQ.

putting the question The act of the CHAIR in calling a vote.

supplementary question Any unscripted question raised on the floor of the House once the initial questioner has had his or her say.

the question is . . . At Westminster, the way the Speaker puts a motion to the vote.

written question Any question submitted to the TABLE OFFICE for a Minister to answer in writing.

quiet. Quiet, calm deliberation/Disentangles every knot The couplet from a song by W. S. Gilbert which Harold Macmillan (see SUPERMAC) hung as a motto in his private office.

Quiet Revolution The transformation wrought in Quebec from 1960 by the provincial LIBERAL government of Jean Lesage, which both curbed Anglophone cultural domination and tackled the corruption and archaism of traditional Francophone politics and society. The party held office until 1966, when it was ousted by the Union Nationale; after its defeat René Levesque, having failed to move it to a more nationalist position, resigned and founded the PQ.

Quinquennial Act In Britain, the popular term for the provision of the 1911 PARLIAMENT ACT that reduced the life of a Parliament (the TERM of a government) from a maximum of seven years to five.

quisling A traitor or puppet COLLABORATOR. Named after **Vidkun Quisling** (1887–1945) the former Norwegian Defence Minister who founded a tiny NAZI party and declared himself Prime Minister when the Germans invaded. Berlin recognized him and he sent over 1000 Jews to CONCENTRATION CAMPS. He was shot for treason, theft and murder after liberated Norway specially reinstituted the death penalty. The term became current within days of Quisling seizing power, Ed Murrow saying on CBS radio: "I don't think there were many quislings in the Norwegian Army or Navy." In December 1941 Churchill spoke of "a vile race of quislings – to use the new word which will carry the scorn of mankind down the centuries".

quorum The number of members of a legislature or committee who must be present for its proceedings to be valid. At Westminster, the quorum for the House of Commons is 40 – but 100 are needed for the CLOSURE if a vote is to be taken. The quorum in the US House of Representatives, for the COMMITTEE OF THE WHOLE, is 100.

quorum call In the US CONGRESS, the summons to legislators – by bell – to raise a quorum or ascertain if one is present.

> *Guest:* I thought I heard a quorum call.
> *Anon. Senator:* No doubt you did. This is their mating season.

quorum count In the US CONGRESS, the process of confirming whether a quorum is present.

disappearing quorum A delaying tactic used by CONGRESSMEN from the 1860s; though present, they would avoid voting. The practice was stamped out by the newly-elected Speaker Thomas REED in 1890.

quota A numerical or proportional limit imposed in trade, immigration, employment, *etc.*, to a particular competing nation or ethnic group strengthening its position or becoming over-represented (*see* POSITIVE DISCRIMINATION). Also, the shares subscribed by individual member nations to the IMF.

R

R In Britain and COMMONWEALTH countries acknowledging the MONARCHY, the signature of the sovereign, an abbreviation of the Latin *Rex* (King) or *Regina* (Queen). As in "Elizabeth R". Also, the monarch's legal person as representing the civil power; *R v. Smith* is the equivalent of *The People v. John Doe*.

R-word The polite word for RECESSION, used ironically by politicians in both Britain and America in the late 1980s when the economy was heading into recession and neither the BUSH administration nor the THATCHER government was prepared to admit it.

Rab The nickname of the British Conservative politician **R(ichard A(usten) Butler** (1902–82), later Lord Butler of Saffron Walden, formed from his initials. Harold WILSON is said to have described him as "the best Prime Minister we never had". He served before and into World War II as a Foreign Office minister; Harold Macmillan branded him "the most clinging of the MUNICHites", CHURCHILL praised his "delicate manner of answering Parliamentary questions without giving anything away". He masterminded the BUTLER EDUCATION ACT, then after the Tory rout of 1945 brought together **Rab's Boys,** bright young Tories who reshaped Conservative social and economic policy. They were mostly, like Iain Macleod, Reginald Maudling and Enoch POWELL, members of the Conservative Research Department or the party's industrial policy committee; Butler headed both. They are credited with changing Tory attitudes to the WELFARE STATE, NATIONALIZATION and unemployment, and instituting the CONSENSUS Politics which lasted until Margaret Thatcher became leader. In 1962 David Frost said of Butler:

> Let us never forget that after the last war it was Mr. Butler who transformed the Conservative Party into the fresh, liberal, lively, progressive, radical force it was after the last war.

As Chancellor from 1951, Butler pursued the middle way known as BUTSKELLISM; he went on to hold a wide range of senior posts until 1963, from Churchill's retirement in 1955 being seen as heir to the leadership. Yet he fell short, lacking the killer touch when first EDEN (*see* WAB OR HAWOLD?) and then Macmillan retired. When Macmillan succeeded Eden, Butler said: "I couldn't understand why, when I had done a most wonderful job picking up the pieces after SUEZ, they then chose Harold." Nigel Nicolson felt Butler had lost out by having no clear view on Suez, appearing a "reluctant apologist", and Alistair Horne wrote: "As the absent Eden's deputy he was in the unhappy position of having to answer, officially, to all the accumulated anger in the party in the aftermath of Suez." Butler consoled himself with the thought that "it's not every man who nearly becomes Prime Minister of England", and that

> if you're not made Pope, you can still be a perfectly good Cardinal Archbishop of Milan.

When Macmillan was taken ill in 1963 Butler was again wrong-footed, with the MAGIC CIRCLE choosing Lord Home (*see* SIR ALEC). Their colleague Anthony Head remarked: "If Rab had been more forceful he could have been Prime Minister, but there was an ambivalence in him all the way." Macmillan observed: "He had the ambition but not the will, a sort of vague ambition, like saying it would be nice to be Archbishop of Canterbury." And Chris Patten, looking back, wrote: "He lacked the dash, the vulgarity, the smoking-room popularity. . . . Like oysters and gulls' eggs, he was an acquired taste."

> I think the Prime Minister has to be a butcher, and know the joints. That is perhaps where I have not been quite competent in knowing the ways that you can cut up a carcass.
>
> BUTLER.

Rab's Law Butler's one consistent rule was "Never resign". He had seen too many Ministers do it as a mark of protest in the hope of winning their point, then sink without trace.

race (1) Colloquial, mainly US, term for an electoral contest, *i.e.* "the race for the White House", "the gubernatorial race". (2) The biological, tribal or (to a lesser extent) national groups into which humankind is divided, thus the most obvious determinant between people, a cause of prejudice and an explosive issue in politics.

> I am in favour of the race to which I belong having the superior position. ABRAHAM LINCOLN.

> All those who are not racially pure are mere chaff. ADOLF HITLER.

race relations industry Pejorative for the network of committees, QUANGOS and agencies set up to assure ethnic minorities of their rights, which critics see as provocative, wasteful and self-perpetuating.

race riot A RIOT by a disaffected racial group, or against one seen as a scapegoat.

Race track *See* MX.

playing the race card Injecting race as an issue into an election, often by subliminal or indirect means.

racialism A mainly British term, dating from the eary 20th century, for the support for, or practice of DISCRIMINATION and SEGREGATION between the races, instigated by the dominant group.

racism Belief in the genetic superiority of a particular race (invariably one's own), and the display or exercise of prejudice against another or all other racial groups. Although that prejudice has always existed, it was elevated in the late 19th century into a pseudoscience, based on the writings of the Comte de Gobineau, whose *Essay on the Inequality of the Human Races* was published in 1853. Racism was a driving force of the NAZIs, then in the 1950s and 1960s the term was widely used in US policies before becoming universally applied. **Anti-racism** has become a rallying point not just for the hard LEFT but for a broad spread of political groups. *See* ANTI-SEMITISM; APARTHEID; BLACK; COLOUR BAR; KU KLUX KLAN; LYNCHING; POWELLITE; RIVERS OF BLOOD.

> I am not going to promise a Cabinet post or any other post to any racial or ethnic group. That would be racism in reverse at its worst. JFK.

Rachmanism Bullying and extortionate behaviour toward tenants by a private landlord. From the activities of Peter Rachman (1920–62), a Polish immigrant to Britain whose undesirable activities in the Paddington area came to light during the PROFUMO AFFAIR and prompted political pressure for new safeguards for private tenants. Despite those safeguards, some landlords continue to prosper by terrorizing those who rent from them.

radical, radicalism An adherent of, or the pursuit of, bold and fundamental policies for change within the democratic system. From the Latin *radix*, root. It originated in Britain with the late 18th-century radical reform movement within the WHIG party, before long becoming a pejorative; in 1819 Sir Walter Scott wrote: "Radicalism is a word in very bad odour here, being used to denote a set of blackguards." One group in America who gained the name were those Republicans who opposed President Andrew Johnson over RECONSTRUCTION. The term is customarily applied to the LEFT ("a person whose left hand doesn't know what the other left hand is doing" – Bernard Rosenberg); and in the US to UN-AMERICANISM ("There is a foreign atmosphere about him, the stamp of an alien radical, a strong resemblance to the type ANARCHIST as portrayed, bomb in hand, in newspaper cartoons" – Eugene O'Neill). Radicals were seen by critics as woolly-minded ("a radical is a man with both feet planted firmly in the air" – FDR) and fractious ("two deputies, one of whom is a radical, have more in common than two radicals, one of whom is a DEPUTY" – Robert de Jouvenel). From the mid-1970s radicalism has been captured by the Right (*see* THATCHERISM; REAGANOMICS), with the term Radical RIGHT describing a range of Free-MARKET, LIBERTARIAN proposals.

radicalize To encourage or provoke a body of people into adopting a radical course of action that would not otherwise have occurred to them.

radical chic Trendiness in adoption of good causes, literature and fashion dictated by (left-wing) radicalism (*see* POLITICAL CORRECTNESS). The expression was coined by the US journalist and writer Tom Wolfe (1931–) to describe the late-1960s fad among members of high society for socialism and sympathy with revolutionaries.

Radical Jack Nickname for John Lambton, first Earl of Durham (1792–1840), who played a leading part in the passage of the 1832 REFORM ACT and subsequently produced the DURHAM REPORT on the future of Canada.

Radio Doctor Dr. Charles Hill, later Lord Hill of Luton (1904–89), who in World War II became a celebrity in Britain by broadcasting as the BBC's "Radio Doctor". His common touch gave him an audience of over 14 million, making him "the doctor with the greatest number of patients in the world". He was secretary of the British Medical Association 1944–50, spanning the introduction of the NHS, which it opposed, and then a key figure in the Conservatives' near-successful 1950 campaign. He became Minister of Health, and chairman successively of the Independent Television Authority and the BBC.

Radio Priest Fr. Charles E. Coughlin, a broadcast sermonizer from Michigan who originally supported the NEW DEAL but broke with FDR to become a virulent opponent of his "communistic" administration and of Wall Street. In 1936 his Society for Social Justice backed the Union Party challenge of the

Republican Rep. William Lemke. In a speech at Cleveland that July, Coughlin ripped off his clerical collar and denounced "Franklin Double-Crossing Roosevelt" as a liar and a "betrayer". The Union Party polled fewer than 900,000 votes as FDR won a LANDSLIDE.

Ragged Trousered Philanthropists, The Title of a novel by Robert Tressell, written *c.* 1906, which became one of the basic texts of the UK LABOUR and trade union movement. It described evocatively the hard lives of a group of tradesmen renovating a house for its rich absentee owner.

rail-splitter The ultimate accolade for a US politician as a homespun outdoor type, originating in Abraham LINCOLN's successful campaign for the 1860 Republican nomination. His cousin John Hanks brought to a meeting in Illinois "two rails from a lot made by Abraham Lincoln and John Hanks in the Sangamon Bottom in the year 1830." Lincoln said he could not remember splitting those rails, but was sure he had split rails every bit as good. Soon his son Tad could say: "Everybody in this world knows Pa used to split rails." Lincoln's opponent Stephen Douglas argued that "we want a statesman, not a rail-splitter, for president", but battalions of rail-splitters were marching for Lincoln. Candidates ever since have been pictured with an axe and timber to make the connection, but Eisenhower said of his Democratic opponent Adlai Stevenson: "He's no rail-splitter – just a hair-splitter." *See* LOG CABIN TO WHITE HOUSE.

Rainbow Coalition The coalition of ethnic and liberal forces, and the socially disadvantaged, put together by the Rev. Jesse JACKSON in pursuit of his campaign for the Democratic presidential nomination in 1984 and 1988.

> Our flag is red, white and blue, but our nation is a rainbow – red, yellow, brown, black and white – and we are all precious in God's sight. . . . America is not like a blanket – one piece of unbroken cloth, the same colour, the same texture, the same size. America is more like a quilt – many patches, many pieces, many colours, many sizes; all woven and held together by a common thread.
>
> JESSE JACKSON.

Rainbow Warrior The flagship of the GREENPEACE environmentalist group, sailed by activists to impede whalers and marine dumpers, and into nuclear test zones. It became the subject of a diplomatic incident and world-wide protests in 1985 when French agents sank it in Auckland harbour, New Zealand, with the loss of one life, to prevent Greenpeace protesting against French (underground) nuclear tests at Mururoa atoll in the South Pacific. The agents, Alain Mafart and Dominique Prieur, were arrested in New Zealand and imprisoned, but soon handed over to the French authorities after pressure from Paris. An undertaking thet they would be kept in detention was not adhered to.

raison d'état (Fr. reason of state). The justification for any action, no matter how unethical, on the ground that the interests of the state require it.

rally A large set-piece political meeting to which the like-minded are brought from a distance to hail their leaders.

Ramsay Mac Nickname for **James Ramsay MacDonald** (1866–1937), the first, and most controversial, UK Labour Prime Minister. A founding activist in the LABOUR PARTY, he served as its leader 1911–14, resigning over the party's support for World War I, and 1922–31. He led Labour to power at the start of 1924, only to lose it at the close of the year after the ZINOVIEV LETTER affair. As party leader during the GENERAL STRIKE, he advised caution, saying:

> With the discussion of general strikes and Bolshevism and all that kind of thing, I have nothing to do at all. I respect the Constitution.

Labour returned to power in 1929, again as a minority government, but two years later economic crisis split the MacDonald Cabinet and he and a minority of Labour Ministers and MPs formed the NATIONAL GOVERNMENT in alliance with Baldwin's Conservatives. MacDonald's action became known to the majority who stayed with Labour as the GREAT BETRAYAL. But he felt he had to do it, writing: "I commit suicide to save the crisis. If there is no other way I shall do it as cheerfully as an ancient Jap." But breaking with his origins as the illegitimate son of a Scots servant girl had its attractions. As he made the break, he said: "Tomorrow every duchess in London will be wanting to kiss me." And MacDonald once observed: "If God were to come to me and say: 'Ramsay, would you rather be a country gentleman or Prime Minister?' I should say: 'Please, God, a country gentleman.'" But Henry Channon (*see* CHIPS), commented cruelly: "Fatuous old snob, he is hated by all parties." MacDonald's political somersaults led CHURCHILL to call him the BONELESS WONDER. Lloyd George declared that "he has sufficient conscience to bother him, but not enough to keep him straight", while to Beatrice Webb he was "a super-autocrat". Philip Snowden, who as Chancellor had seen the National Government as a temporary expedient, warned: "He will be used by the Tories for the same purpose as the reformed drunkard is used at the temperance meeting."

And as the Tory grip over his government increased, ATTLEE described him as

> a melancholy traveller in the Conservative ship.

MacDonald handed over to Baldwin prior to the 1935 election, when he was unseated by Emmanuel (MANNY) Shinwell. He found another seat and stayed in the Cabinet, but was going to pieces. He had never been good with words, Churchill once remarking: "He has, more than any other man, the gift of compressing the largest amount of words into the smallest amount of thought." But by the end he was telling the Commons: "Society goes on and on and on. It is much the same with ideas." During one of his last speeches the Labour MP James Maxton called out: "Sit down, man. You're a bloody tragedy." He died on an ocean cruise, leading an anonymous obituarist to write: "He died as he lived, at sea."

> We'll hang Ramsay Mac on a sour apple tree,
> We'll hang Snowden and Thomas to keep him company,
> For that's the place where traitors ought to be.
>
> ANON., 1931.

Ramseyer rule In the US CONGRESS, the requirement that a Committee of the House REPORTING a Bill must list all changes it would require in the existing law, and the text of laws being repealed. The Senate equivalent is the CORDON RULE.

RAND Corporation The first scientific THINK-TANK which, though mainly composed of economists, became the leading source of advice on COLD WAR strategy to the PENTAGON. It was set up at the end of World War II as the US Air Force's propaganda agency under the guise of a scientific institute, initially as an adjunct to the Douglas Aircraft Company in Santa Monica, California. The name was a composite of "R and D" (research and development). Its ability to THINK THE UNTHINKABLE gave birth to such chilling concepts as MUTUALLY ASSURED DESTRUCTION. RAND specialized in computerized war games; when asked in 1968 when America would win in VIETNAM, the computer answered: 1964.

rank and file The ordinary membership of a movement or organization, as opposed to its leaders. Leaders of militant minority groups usually claim to represent it.

ranking member The senior member of a Congressional committee from the minority party. The word "ranking" dates back at least to the Civil War, when it was used for the most senior member of a military unit.

Rapacki plan A proposal put forward in 1957 by Adam Rapacki, Poland's Communist foreign minister, for nuclear disengagement in central Europe and cuts in conventional forces by both NATO and the WARSAW PACT.

Rapallo treaties Two treaties signed after World War I at Rapallo, a coastal resort in Northwest Italy. Under the first, in November 1920, Italy renounced its claim to Dalmatia, the independence of Fiume (Rijeka) was acknowledged, and the rights of Italians and Yugoslavs in each other's countries were established. The second, signed on 16 August 1922 by the German and Soviet foreign ministers, brought the immediate resumption of DIPLOMATIC RELATIONS between the two countries and enabled Germany to develop secretly on Soviet territory weapons banned under the Treaty of VERSAILLES.

rapid. rapid deployment force The small, lightly-serviced and easily transportable force designed for emergencies in the Middle East which America developed after the CAMP DAVID agreement and the failed attempt to rescue the US HOSTAGES from Teheran in 1980.

rapid reaction force The force created by the European members of NATO after the end of the Cold War to deal primarily with OUT-OF-AREA threats.

rapporteur In committees of the EUROPEAN PARLIAMENT, a member chosen to analyse the proposal under discussion and prepare a draft report on it for the committee to consider. If approved by the committee, the draft becomes a public document and the rapporteur joins in negotiations within the Parliament on its ultimate adoption.

rat As an insult, US Interior Secretary Harold Ickes described Governor Eugene Talmadge of Georgia (*see* HIS CHAIN-GANG EXCELLENCY) as looking "more like a rat than any other human being I know; [with] all the mean, poisonous and treacherous characteristics of that rodent".

to rat To desert one's party like a rat leaving a sinking ship. The phrase was first used by the Earl of Malmesbury in 1792, and is recorded in America in 1800. CHURCHILL, who left the Conservatives for the Liberals, then rejoined the Tories, said on making his second move: "Anyone can rat, but it takes a certain amount of ingenuity to re-rat." This did not deter him from saying when a celebrated war hero joined the LIBERALS in 1948 to contest a seat for them: "It's the first time I've heard of a rat swimming out to join a sinking ship."

ratfucking Distasteful stunts to sabotage an opponent's campaign, such as bugging offices, forging and stealing correspondence, cancelling or disrupting rallies, or ordering delivery of vast quantities of unwanted food, ready-mixed concrete or manure. Popularized in the late 1950s as a student prank in California's universities, it became a household word as the WATERGATE scandal unfolded. Donald H. Segretti had from the White House organized the collapse of Democratic challengers' campaigns prior to the 1972 election so that Richard Nixon would face the least electable Democrat, Sen. George McGovern. His actions ranged from sending unordered pizzas to Muskie headquarters to circulating letters falsely asserting that Sen. Henry (SCOOP) Jackson was a homosexual and that Sen. Hubert Humphrey had been involved with a call-girl. Segretti admitted that he and his associates had refined their ratfucking techniques when at the University of California.

ratchet effect The gradual but relentless shifting of political and economic assumptions from left to right or vice versa despite successive changes of government.

> Britain is no longer in the politics of the pendulum, but of the ratchet. MARGARET THATCHER, 1977.

rates The form of local taxation in Britain, based on notional rental values of property, which aroused widespread discontent among householders and businessmen until replaced by the POLL TAX. Each local authority fixed its own rate at so much in the pound. The even greater controversy aroused by the Poll Tax led Labour to promise a return to a system of "fair rates" if it won the 1992 election. Businesses continue to pay a modified but standardized version of the rates, the **Uniform Business Rate**.

ratepayers Those liable for payment of rates – less than half the electorate – who, particularly under LABOUR councils, considered they were subsidizing extravagance toward voters who made no contribution. In some towns and cities they organized to contest local elections and serve on the council, usually as an alternative to or in alliance with the Conservatives.

Rate Support Grant The block grant paid by central government to local authorities towards the cost of local services, to keep down the level of domestic rates. With the end of the Rates it was renamed the **Revenue Support Grant**.

ratification The process under which the legislature or electorate of a state endorses the action of its government in concluding a TREATY with another power or powers. In America, treaties negotiated by the President require a two-thirds majority of the Senate; the PANAMA CANAL TREATIES just overcame the hurdle, the Treaty of VERSAILLES and the SALT II treaty could not. The term also applies to the role of the STATES in approving AMENDMENTs to the CONSTITUTION; three-quarters of states have to ratify an amendment for it to take effect. In Britain, major Treaties are confirmed by Act of Parliament, as with the MAASTRICHT TREATY. And in the Irish Republic, the nation itself ratifies treaties affecting the Constitution in a REFERENDUM.

rattlesnake A common term of US political abuse, with undertones of guile and readiness to strike back. In 1975 the Missouri Democrat Rep. Richard Bolling said of the 81-year-old Texas Democrat Rep. Wright Patman:

> The old man has always been a rattlesnake, and now he's senile.

Ravenscraig The steelworks at Motherwell, south of Glasgow, the forlorn fight against closure of which became a rallying-point for advocates of a self-contained Scottish economy and opponents of the steady decline in its traditional industries. Steelmaking at the plant finally ceased in June 1992 after a battle lasting more than six years. British Steel chairman Sir Robert "Black Bob" Scholey and the Conservative government were cast as the villains of the piece; Ministers were privately dismayed with the way the company brought the closure about, but argued that with the evaporation of the markets which Ravenscraig had been built with grants from the Macmillan government to serve, its retention could not be justified despite record productivity.

Rawhide The codename allocated by the US SECRET SERVICE to President Reagan, reflecting his desire to be seen as a latter-day Wild West figure.

Rayburn Building The second office building to be built for the US HOUSE OF REPRESENTATIVES as space in the Capitol was exhausted. Opened in 1965, it was named after **Samuel** Taliaferro **Rayburn** (1882–1961) (*see* MR SAM), longest serving Speaker of the House (21 years). Costing $122 million even at 1960s prices and built in a style known as "Mussolini Modern" or "Texas Penitentiary", it measures 720 feet by 450. It contains 25 elevators, 23 escalators, garage space for 1600 cars, a swimming pool, a gymnasium and several overnight rooms.

> A national disaster. Its defects range from a profligate mishandling of 50 acres of space to elephantine aesthetic brutality at record costs. It is quite possible that this is the worst building for the most money in the history of the construction art. It stuns by sheer mass and boring bulk.
> ADA LOUISE HUXTABLE.

Rayner scrutiny The detailed efficiency reviews conducted on selected programmes throughout WHITEHALL by Sir Derek (later

Lord) Rayner, Margaret Thatcher's efficiency adviser 1979–83. Rayner, a senior executive at Marks and Spencer who had worked on defence procurement for Edward Heath, was a committed THATCHERITE who aimed to "travel light and dig deep" in searching for economies. He told his scrutineers to "look for bad news only" and come up with a solution within 90 days. By the time he left, five waves of scrutinies involving 155 agencies, programmes and tasks had identified potential savings of £421 million a year – about half of which were made. Although the reviews tailed off after Rayner returned to Marks, he left a legacy in the FINANCIAL MANAGEMENT INITIATIVE and, eventually, the NEXT STEPS agencies.

reactionary A CONSERVATIVE who not only opposes progress but longs for, and is anxious to return to, the ways of the past. The word is also an adjective; TITO wrote:

> Any movement in history which attempts to perpetuate itself becomes reactionary.

read. read into the record In the US Congress, to seek to have written into the CONGRESSIONAL RECORD a speech, article or other text of which a member strongly approves, or whose publication will boost his or her prospects of re-election.

Read my lips. No new taxes The phrase used by George BUSH in his ACCEPTANCE SPEECH on 19 August 1988 which played a major part in his defeat of Michael Dukakis, but came back to haunt him two years later when taxes were indeed raised. Bush made his statement in the context of promising to resist Congressional pressure to raise taxes, saying:

> I'll say no, and they'll push, and I'll say no, and they'll push again, and I'll say to them: "Read my lips. No new taxes."

The expression "read my lips" dates back at least to 1978, when the British rock artist Tim Curry used it as an album title. It carries the inference that the speaker thinks the listener to be stupid, and unable to grasp the meaning of simple words. Bush amended it to "read my hips" when asked major political questions while out jogging.

Reading system The basis for the KNOCKING-UP system used by Britain's LABOUR PARTY, its name taken from the Berkshire constituency of the MP Ian Mikardo (*see* MIK) where it was pioneered. It involves a pad of lined sheets on which party supporters are listed, similar to the Conservatives' NCR system except that carbon paper was initially used; the Liberal Democrats' pads are known as Shuttleworths. As each team of helpers is sent out on election night, it is given a sheet from the pad, with the names of those who have already voted crossed out.

Reagan. Reaganauts The devoted right-wing coterie who set the agenda for Ronald Reagan (*see* GREAT COMMUNICATOR) on his election to the Presidency in 1988 and throughout his first term.

Reaganomics The policy which Reagan claimed would balance the US Budget through a combination of massive tax cuts, cuts in WELFARE programmes and a huge increase in defence spending. The term is credited to Speaker TIP O'Neill. Reaganomics were denounced by Democrats and sceptical Republicans ("VOODOO ECONOMICS" – George BUSH; "a riverboat gamble" – Sen. Howard Baker; "the only way you can do that is with mirrors" – Rep. John Anderson), but Reagan pursued it in office. He secured most of the tax cuts, using the SUPPLY-SIDE argument that resulting economic growth would boost federal revenues. But the spending cuts proved hard to achieve, and the budget deficit soared. The days of Reaganomics were numbered when one of its progenitors, budget director David Stockman, confessed in a December 1981 *Atlantic Monthly* interview with William Greider:

> None of us really understands what's going on with all these numbers.

In his book *The Triumph of Politics*, Stockman later confessed:

> We insisted that we had found the economic Rosetta Stone. But our Rosetta Stone was a fake.

Reagan Democrats Traditional Democratic voters (mainly BLUE-COLLAR), who switched to the Republican ticket out of conservatism in 1980 to elect Ronald Reagan, stayed with him in 1984 and gave George BUSH their support in 1988; in 1992 many swung back to the Democrats to elect Bill Clinton.

real. Real Lives A BBC television documentary on the life of Republican and LOYALIST activists in NORTHERN IRELAND which was pulled from the schedule in August 1985 at the urging of the Home Secretary, Leon Brittan. The programme included interviews with Martin McGuinness, a leading spokesman for the PROVISIONAL IRA, and a high-ranking member of the UDA. Brittan's intervention, apparently anticipating anger from Mrs. Thatcher if a programme "advocating terrorism" were transmitted, provoked a strike by BBC staff – including those of the WORLD SERVICE – who felt management had been spineless in the face of Government interference. Brittan was widely felt to have acted heavy-handedly; he was moved to the Department of Trade and Industry soon after. And when the programme was eventually screened, few objections to it were raised.

real wages The level of wages after allowance has been made for INFLATION.

Realpolitik A German word meaning practical politics, but generally construed as involving a streak of ruthlessness and the triumph of PRAGMATISM over PRINCIPLE in pursuit of national, material or self-seeking interests.

realignment (1) A fundamental change in the party structure of a country, with the balance changing between competing parties on either the left or the right, maybe with parties merging. In Britain the term has long been used for a scenario in which LABOUR and the Liberals (LIBERAL DEMOCRATS) join forces, possibly with the left of the Labour Party forming a new, firmly Socialist party. (2) Within the European Exchange Rate Mechanism (ERM), a process whereby the values of all member currencies are reassessed, with some being revalued or DEVALUED against the others.

reapportionment A US term for the revision of electoral boundaries within a jurisdiction so as to allocate elected representatives on a fairer basis. *See* REDISTRICTING.

rearmament The process of halting the run-down of a nation's armed forces after one war and re-equipping them so as to lessen the chances of another, or to fight it if it becomes unavoidable.

> I do not hold that we should rearm in order to fight. I hold that we should rearm in order to parley.
>
> CHURCHILL, 8 October 1951.

German rearmament The issue which caused divisions in most West European countries in the early 1950s, when Britain, America and other NATO members decided to end the post-WORLD WAR II prohibition on West Germany having significant armed forces, so that it could take a front-line (but non-nuclear) role in defending the West against Communist attack from behind the IRON CURTAIN.

Moral Rearmament A movement founded at Oxford in 1938 by Frank Buchman (1878–1961) to promote strict Christian values in every walk of life. It grew out of the **Oxford Group**, as Buchman's evangelical followers at Oxford in the 1920s called themselves. Its influence spread to a number of countries, and after World War II it played an important part in right-wing resistance to Communism in several major trade unions.

rebellion Originally an armed uprising against a government, the term has come to embrace resistance by dissident BACKBENCHERS to their own party leadership, and acts of dissent by rugged individualists. Benjamin FRANKLIN, at the time of the AMERICAN REVOLUTION, declared that "Rebellion against tyrants is obedience to God"; after the new nation had been founded, Thomas JEFFERSON confessed that "a little rebellion now and then is a medicine necessary for the sound health of government".

recall (1) The process, adopted by many of the United States and local communities within them, under which elected officials may be deprived of office by a majority in a ballot if enough voters petition for one. The idea was borrowed from Switzerland by US POPULISTS; the city of Los Angeles in 1903 was the first jurisdiction to adopt it. The existence of recall has acted as a check on bad government and as a safety-valve; a rare example of a successful initiative was in 1921 when North Dakota's governor, attorney-general and agriculture commissioner were all ousted. In a few states, such as Arizona, judges too may be recalled. (2) At WESTMINSTER, the reconvening of Parliament during a RECESS to debate some matter of urgency that has arisen. The SPEAKER will generally recall Parliament if the Prime Minister agrees to a request from the Leader of the Opposition.

recess A period when a legislature is not in session. At Westminster it applies solely to the holidays taken in the summer, at Christmas, Easter and Whitsun. In the US Congress it covers any time when a recess is called from the Chair; when on 1 March 1954 Puerto Rican nationalists shot five Congressmen from the House gallery, Rep. Joe Martin, presiding, shouted: "The House stands recessed", then ran for his life.

recession A cyclical downturn in the economy, which officially comes into existence when national product has declined for two or more successive quarters. In times of economic difficulty, those in power go to enormous lengths to argue that a recession is not on the way or has not arrived (*see* R-WORD). Harry S. Truman once said: "It's a recession when your neighbour loses his job, it's a DEPRESSION when you lose your own"; Ronald Reagan in 1980 expanded this to:

> It's a recession when your neighbour loses his job, it's a depression when you lose your own – and it's a recovery when Jimmy CARTER loses his!

Two weeks before the 1992 Presidential election George BUSH, in a telling slip of the tongue, thanked Republican workers in New Jersey for "your lovely recession".

Reciprocity Treaty The US-Canadian treaty concluded in 1854 which lifted TARIFFS from non-manufactured goods traded between the two countries, and authorized reciprocal use of Atlantic fisheries and the St. Lawrence-Great Lakes waterways. The Canadian negotiators "floated it through on a sea of champagne", allied with Southern legislators who saw it as a first step toward Canada being absorbed by the United States. America refused to renew the treaty in 1866 because of irritation over Canada's allegedly unsupportive role for the North in the Civil War. Canada continued to seek FREE TRADE with its southern neighbour; "Unrestricted Reciprocity" was a Liberal slogan in the 1891 election. But it was almost a century later before a comprehensive Free Trade agreement was negotiated.

recision The power of a President to notify Congress that he will not spend certain funds that have been APPROPRIATED. Until 1974 the President could act unilaterally; in that year the law was changed to make recision subject to a majority in both Houses. *See also* IMPOUNDMENT.

recognition (1) In the US Congress, the act of the Chair in calling a member who wishes to speak. A member hoping to be called – or with the right to be called under rule – is said to be seeking recognition. (2) Refusal to recognize Britain's criminal courts by entering a plea has at times been the practice of IRA men charged with terrorist offences. (3) The act of one nation in agreeing to open diplomatic contacts with another. Recognition can be *de facto*, where it is accepted that a regime is in control, or *de jure*, where a government takes power by constitutional means.

> If you recognise anyone, it does not mean that you like him. We all, for instance, recognise the Rt. Hon. Member for Ebbw Vale [Aneurin BEVAN].
>
> Winston CHURCHILL on UK recognition of Communist China, 1952.

recommit To send a Bill back to a committee that has considered it at an earlier stage. The term is particularly used in the US House of Representatives after the previous question has been ordered on the passage of a Bill or joint resolution.

reconciliation In the US Congress, the procedure under which APPROPRIATIONS, TAX-WRITING and other committees are directed to determine and recommend changes in laws or Bills to bring about the tax and spending levels set by a BUDGET resolution. The committees are instructed what total amounts must be changed, but are free to decide how and in what areas the adjustments should be made. Reconciliation is normally resorted to only if the committees have twice failed to recommend the necessary changes without targets being set for them.

Reconstruction The process of bringing the defeated South back into the political system of the United States after The CIVIL WAR. Some Northerners saw it as an opportunity for vengeance and self-enrichment, but the 1867 Military Reconstruction Act also brought for a time widespread Black suffrage and some representation. The Act divided the ten UNRECONSTRUCTED states into five military districts; for each to be restored to the Union a constitutional convention of Blacks and loyal Whites had to pass a state constitution guaranteeing suffrage for all, qualified voters were to elect a state legislature to ratify the FOURTEENTH AMENDMENT, and after ratification the state could apply for representation in Congress. The political argument over how to restore the South began before Lincoln's assassination and intensified as Andrew Johnson took a moderate line. Sen. Charles Sumner accused Johnson of "throwing away the fruits of the victory of the Union Army", and in December 1865 Congress set up a joint committee which wrested control of Reconstruction from the President and produced an aggressive programme of its own. Tales of a reign of terror against freed slaves based on the BLACK CODES whipped up public support; the future Interior Secretary Carl Schurz (1829–1906), nicknamed **Carl Squirt** by Southerners, reported:

> The lash and murder is resorted to to intimidate those whom fear for an awful death alone causes to remain, while patrols, negro dogs, and spies disguised as YANKEES, keep constant guard over those unfortunate people.

Johnson's continued opposition to Reconstruction even after the Act was passed led to the almost-successful move to IMPEACH him in 1868. The effective period of Reconstruction lasted from 1865 until 1877, the period during which Federal troops were stationed in the former CONFEDERATE states. By the end, Northern profiteers had pocketed hundreds of millions in fixed assets and funds for post-war development, White supremacists had regained control of the South, and Congress had largely lost interest.

> We have the right to treat them as we would any other province that we might conquer.
>
> Rep. THADDEUS STEVENS, 1863.

recount The counting of votes a second or further time because of claims that a mistake has been made or because of the narrowness of the result. In British Parliamentary elections a recount can normally be sought by the losing party if the margin is less than 1000 votes, sometimes a little more; one may also be sought by a candidate who has narrowly lost his or her DEPOSIT.

Recruit scandal The scandal concerning the Recruit Cosmos real estate company which brought down the Japanese government of Noburu Takeshita in 1989. In November 1988 some 16 politicians were accused of insider trading in the company's shares and one, the Socialist Takumi Veda, resigned from the DIET. Five days later an official of the company was arrested on charges of trying to bribe investigators. In December the Justice and Finance Ministers were forced to resign because of their involvement – and eventually the scandal reached the Prime Minister.

red(s) A derogatory term for COMMUNISTS, revolutionary leftists and Socialists in general. The colour red has been associated with revolution since at least 1848, when the workers of Paris manned the BARRICADES under red banners. "Reds" became a general journalistic term for communists with the Russian Civil War of 1918–22, in which Trotsky's RED ARMY ultimately triumphed. Its use was especially prevalent during the McCarthy WITCH-HUNTS in America, when it was applied to alleged subversives of every kind.

Red Army The highly-disciplined and immense army of the Soviet Union, originating in the forces organized by Trotsky to defend the infant BOLSHEVIK regime. Eventually victorious in the Civil War of 1918–22 against the conservative WHITES, the Red Army was weakened in the late 1930s by a series of PURGES which stripped it of most of its commanders, leaving it weakened and prone when Hitler invaded in 1941. It took four years of the most bitter fighting the world has known, at times in atrocious weather, for the invaders to be repelled and crushed; Stalingrad lives on as its greatest triumph even now much of the Red Army has fragmented into a series of national forces.

> The hopes of civilization rest on the worthy banners of the courageous Red Army.
>
> General DOUGLAS MACARTHUR, 1942.

Red Army Faction (RAF; Ger. *Rote Armee Faktion*) The preferred name of West Germany's BAADER-MEINHOF GANG, normally used for the terrorist splinter group that survived its founders and continued with sporadic acts of violence into the 1980s. By 1985 it was down to an estimated 20 hardcore activists, 200 militants willing to help in guerrilla attacks, and about 2000 supporters who would protect other members if required; the numbers are since reckoned to have fallen even further.

> Don't argue – destroy.
>
> Slogan of the Red Army Faction.

Red Brigades (Ital. *Brigade Rosse*) The Italian left-wing terrorist group that was responsible for the kidnap and murder in March 1977 of Aldo Moro, ex-prime minister and president of the Christian Democratic Party. The organization was formed in 1969 with the aim of attacking the heads of large corporations, such as Fiat and Pirelli, who were regarded as "enemies of the working class". They subsequently conducted a campaign of kidnappings, bombings and murders of police chiefs, judges and government officials as well as business leaders with the aim of undermining the Italian state and initiating a MARXIST revolution. The body of Moro, their most notable victim, was found in the boot of a car in May 1977; he had been shot after the government refused to release 13 Brigade leaders. The Brigades were linked to other terrorist groups including the RED ARMY FACTION. In January 1982 the Italian police scored a major success in freeing the US Brigadier-General James Dozier, a deputy NATO commander, who had been abducted in Verona in December 1981. Leading Brigade ideologues, such as Renato Curcio (1948–) and Alberto Frascechini, as well as those responsible for the Moro and Dozier kidnappings, were captured and tried, the last of the Moro kidnappers being sentenced in 1983. Since then the authorities have had increasing success in penetrating and neutralizing the Brigades' CELLS throughout the country.

Red China The colloquial term used in America for the PEOPLE'S DEMOCRACY established in Peking by Mao Tse-Tung in 1949 following the final Communist victory over Chiang Kai-Shek's Nationalists.

Red Clydeside The term used to describe the upsurge of revolutionary Socialism and civil unrest in and around Glasgow at and just after the close of World War I. During the war several left-wingers who called on workers to strike were imprisoned, including the pacifist John Maxton (1885–1946). In January 1919 the Cabinet sent in English troops to quell what the Lord PROVOST feared was an imminent Bolshevik rising; Scots troops were confined to barracks, and tanks, machine gunners and artillery were put in position – but no uprising came. The wartime agitation was led by the schoolmaster John Maclean, who to Tory alarm had been elected an honorary president of the First All-Russian Congress of SOVIETS; from 1922 Red Clydeside had a democratic voice with the election of a strong

Labour/ILP contingent to Westminster, led by Maxton. The bulk of the ILP eventually merged with Labour, but Maxton left the party in 1932, claiming that it had betrayed Socialism. Some historians argue that Labour's breakthrough in the West of Scotland in fact came because the PARTITION of Ireland enabled Catholic voters to switch from Irish Nationalist to Labour.

> No government is going to take from me my right to speak, my right to protest against wrong, my right to do everything that is for the benefit of mankind. I am not here, then, as the accused; I am here as the accuser of capitalism dripping with blood from head to foot.
>
> JOHN MACLEAN addressing a Glasgow court, 1918.

> If I had to live in conditions like that, I would be a revolutionary myself. King GEORGE V to John Wheatley.

Red Dean The nickname of Dr. Hewlett Johnson (1874–1966), Anglican Dean of Canterbury from 1931 and former Dean of Manchester. He attracted controversy for his belief, in the face of all the evidence, that STALIN's Soviet Union was a model of the practical application of Christian ethics.

Red Flag, the The anthem of Britain's LABOUR PARTY and of democratic Socialists throughout the English-speaking world. It is sung to the German tune O TANNENBAUM ("O Christmas Tree"). Labour MPs sang it in the House of Commons when they took their seats after their 1945 LANDSLIDE; Tories present were horrified. It is also sung at the close of Labour's annual CONFERENCE. The words were written in 1889 by James Connell (1852–1929):

> The people's flag is deepest red;
> It shrouded oft our martyred dead,
> And ere their limbs grew stiff and cold
> Their heart's blood dyed its every fold.
> Then raise the scarlet standard high!
> Within its shade we'll live or die.
> Tho' cowards flinch and traitors sneer,
> We'll keep the red flag flying here.

In 1939 the Labour leader Clement ATTLEE, eager to discourage talk of a POPULAR FRONT or any alliance with other parties, had this verse anonymously printed in the *Daily Herald*:

> The people's flag is deepest pink,
> It is not red blood but only ink.
> It is supported now by [the FABIAN] Douglas Cole,
> Who plays each year a different role.
> Now raise our Palace standard high,
> Wash out each trace of purple dye,
> Let Liberals join and Tories too,
> And Socialists of any hue.

A more irreverent version lampooning working-class SOLIDARITY and definitely not written by Attlee begins:

> The working class can kiss my arse,
> I've got the foreman's job at last.
> And now that he is on the dole
> You can stuff the red flag up your hole.

Red Guards The young, fanatical supporters of CHAIRMAN MAO during China's CULTURAL REVOLUTION. The mobilization of the Red Guards began at a rally in Peking's TIANANMEN SQUARE on 18 August 1966. These unruly mobs consisted chiefly of students from secondary schools, colleges and universities; their task was to rampage the streets and countryside, harassing and attacking Mao's supposed enemies and opponents, and destroying private and public property – anything that represented "old" ideas, culture, customs or habits. They wore red armbands and carried copies of Mao's LITTLE RED BOOK.

Red Hunt The anti-Communist crusade begun on New Year's Day 1920 by the "fighting Quaker", US Attorney-General A. Mitchell Palmer. In an act of overkill even for the height of the RED SCARE and despite President Wilson's appeals for caution, he ordered simultaneous raids on every alleged BOLSHEVIK cell in the country. In a week over 6000 people had been arrested, their property confiscated, their friends detained for aiding revolutionaries; the raids on these supposed insurgents yielded just three pistols. Palmer was actuated partly by an attempt on his own life, but rather more by Presidential ambitions.

> Palmer, do not let this country see red.
>
> WOODROW WILSON.

Red Ken The popular nickname for **Ken Livingstone** (1945–), a former cancer lab technician who became the hard LEFT leader of the Greater London Council (GLC) from 1981 until its abolition in 1986, and a more moderate though unpredictable MP for Brent East from 1987. The putsch against group leader Andrew Mackintosh the day after the 1981 elections that gave him power, and his outspoken views, at first made him a bogeyman of the right-wing tabloids, one of which termed him "The Most Odious Man in Britain". But Livingstone countered this onslaught by presenting himself as a self-deprecating type whose great love was his tank of newts and salamanders. His policies at COUNTY HALL, ranging from highly unpopular fringe groups to a popular fare-cutting programme on London Transport, were increasingly seen as a provocation to Margaret Thatcher's government; her decision to abolish the GLC, announced in October 1983, turned Red Ken into a folk hero with Londoners, many of whom had previously detested him. However his switch to Westminster did not give him equal status in national politics.

> The Minister has asked to see me again. I think he wants me for my body.
>
> KEN LIVINGSTONE after a meeting with Transport secretary Norman Fowler, *c.* 1981.

Red Letter *See* ZINOVIEV LETTER.

Red Robbo The media nickname for **Derek Robinson** (1937–), the militant shop stewards' convenor at British Leyland's Longbridge, Birmingham, plant who was sacked by company chairman Sir Michael Edwardes in 1976. Edwardes claimed that unofficial strikes and other disputes fomented by Robinson had cost the plant £200 million.

red rose The emblem of Britain's LABOUR PARTY in the 1987 and 1992 elections, and of Continental Socialists, especially in France and Spain, for some time before; Labour's rose stands alone, its Spanish counterpart is held in a clenched fist.

> The voters are not daft. They can smell a rat, whether it is wrapped in a red flag or covered in roses.
>
> NORMAN TEBBIT.

Red Scare The phobia about an imminent Communist takeover that swept America following the RUSSIAN REVOLUTION. As revolution spread in Europe, the conviction grew that aliens and subversives were plotting the overthrow of the US government and its institutions; the foundation of the US COMMUNIST PARTY in 1919 and that year's BOSTON POLICE STRIKE added to the alarm. At the end of 1919 almost 250 foreigners whose views were regarded as dangerously radical were deported to the Soviet Union. Attorney General A. Mitchell Palmer's RED HUNT was given a tragic boost when, on 16 November 1920, a bomb exploded on Wall Street killing 38 people; Palmer declared that the Reds were ready to "destroy the government at one fell swoop". It was in this climate that the Italian anarchists SACCO AND VANZETTI were sentenced to death in 1921 for a murder they insisted they did not commit. The Red Scare triggered a revival of the KU KLUX KLAN, but the anti-Communist hysteria subsided as it became clear that the world revolution would not materialize.

Red Square The square at the heart of Moscow beside the KREMLIN, which contains LENIN's mausoleum. Throughout the Soviet era, it witnessed massive demonstrations of military power on MAY DAY and the anniversary of the OCTOBER REVOLUTION, overlooked by members of the POLITBURO; in 1941 the troops marched straight off the square into the front line. The word "red" has nothing to do with Communism and predates Lenin by several centuries; the Russian word also means "beautiful".

red star Like the HAMMER AND SICKLE, a symbol of international Communism; it also appears as a gold star on a plain red banner.

Red Wedge A collective of rock musicians committed to the UK LABOUR PARTY, headed by Billy Bragg, who before and after the 1987 election campaigned and staged concerts to woo young voters.

red, white and blue The patriotic and national colours of numerous countries including Britain, the United States, France, Russia and the Netherlands.

> White is for purity, red for valour, blue for justice.
>
> Sen. CHARLES SUMNER (1811–74).

> The politicians were talking themselves red, white and blue.
>
> CLARE BOOTHE LUCE (1903–87).

reds under the bed A derogatory phrase for an excessive preoccupation with Communists and a belief that they are behind anything one disapproves of. The phrase dates from the McCarthyite WITCH-HUNT, when supposed Communists were said to have been found in the most unlikely and dangerous places, hence "reds under the bed". *See also* PROFUMO AFFAIR.

better dead than red or **better red than dead** The double-sided phrases that summed up the positions of COLD WARRIORS and nuclear disarmers respectively in the late 1950s. One would rather perish in nuclear war than see Communism prevail, the other opposed such conflict even if the price was subservience to Moscow. It is arguable which came first; *Time* magazine in 1961 claimed (wrongly) that the "better Red" version had been taken up by CND as its slogan. However Bertrand Russell (*see* COMMITTEE OF 100) did write:

> If no alternative remains except communist domination or the extinction of the human race, the former alternative is the less of two evils.

Danny the Red Nickname for Daniel Cohn-Bendit (1945–), a French student born of German-Jewish refugee parents who led a student revolt at Paris' Nanterre campus during the ÉVÈNEMENTS of 1968. He was later deported to West Germany, where as a GREEN politician he became deputy mayor of Frankfurt in the late 1980s.

The East is Red One of the great anthems of MAOIST rule in China; its simple message included an implied dig at the Khruschev regime in Moscow for alleged backsliding from true Communist principles.

redlining In America, the practice of systematically denying loans, mortgages and insurance to property owners or prospective purchasers in the poorest sections of a city. Although banks and other institutions argue that redlining is used purely to minimize financial risk, there is considerable evidence that it has been used to practise racial discrimination because the areas in question frequently have large Black or Hispanic populations.

Redlining originated in the late 1960s as America's INNER CITY problems first surfaced; it takes its name from the supposed practice of outlining such areas in red on a map.

redneck A derogatory and patronizing US term for a country person who is poorly educated, narrow-minded and instinctively right-wing. It was originally used to describe White Southern farmers (the backs of whose necks would be red from working in the fields under the hot sun), but its use spread in the late 1960s to describe anyone with uneducated right-wing views – not just a rural Southerner with a baseball cap and a pickup truck. The phrase spread to Britain in the 1980s.

Redshirts (1) The volunteer force of Italian patriots raised by Giuseppe Garibaldi in the 1860s for his successful campaign to free the country of Austrian influence and unite it under a single crown (*see* RISORGIMENTO). (2) The private army formed in South Carolina in the 1870s by former Confederate General Wade Hampton against the Republican state government elected under RECONSTRUCTION. It was formed consciously in the image of Garibaldi's crusade.

Redeemers The Southerners who organized in the dying days of RECONSTRUCTION to redeem the states of the former CONFEDERACY for self-rule under the Democratic Party. In the South they campaigned with skill and vigour, making promises they often intended to keep to give freed slaves a better deal than they had received from swindling Northern CARPETBAGGERS. They increased their influence by forming an alliance with liberal Republicans in an unsuccessful challenge to the corruption of the GRANT administration. The Redeemers took over in the state capitols of the South after President Hayes withdrew Federal troops in 1877, but were soon outflanked by arch-conservative WHITE SUPREMACISTS.

redistribution (1) The use of taxation and other measures to transfer wealth from the richest to the poorest members of society, and sometimes *vice versa*. Redistributive policies are those consciously designed to bring about such a shift.

> It is less important to redistribute wealth than to redistribute opportunity.
>
> Sen. ARTHUR H. VANDENBERG (1884–1951).

(2) In the UK, the redrawing of boundaries for Parliamentary CONSTITUENCIES to keep their ELECTORATES of approximately equal size. Such redistributions are carried out by the independent BOUNDARY COMMISSION roughly every 15 years; they generally involve a reduction of seats in INNER-CITY areas and an increase in representation for commuter areas further out. The process has tended to benefit the Conservatives at the expense of Labour. In 1969 Home Secretary James Callaghan presented orders for a redistribution to Parliament, as required by law, then got Labour MPs to vote them down so that the 1970 election could be fought on less unfavourable boundaries; Labour lost the election.

redistricting In America, the reallocation of Congressional DISTRICTs within a State, with the ostensible purpose of creating more even representation. However because the process is overseen by State legislatures, there have been frequent allegations of GERRYMANDERING; the party in control aims to give itself as many districts as possible, and confine its opponents to a minimum number where their support is solid.

Reed rules The rules for the conduct of the US HOUSE OF REPRESENTATIVES pushed through in 1890 by the Republican SPEAKER Thomas Reed (1839–1902) (*see* CZAR), and still in force today. Strongly resisted by the minority Democrats, they greatly reduced the scope for FILIBUSTERS and other forms of obstruction, and marked the emergence of the Speaker as a dominant force in the legislature. When he had finally forced the rules through, Reed said:

> Thank God! The House is no longer the greatest deliberative body in the world.

reference back A decision by a legislative or executive body to refer a recommendation about which it is unhappy back to the COMMITTEE that proposed it, for further consideration.

referendum (Lat. something that must be referred) A BALLOT in which the voters of a nation or region give a binding decision on a particular aspect of policy which their government feels unable to determine itself, or which under law it must refer to the people. In some countries (Switzerland, France, the Irish Republic) referendums are a regular feature of national life. In Britain there has been strong resistance to them by traditionalists who fear it would hand the initiative over issues like Europe and the death penalty to populists, and undermine the sovereignty of Parliament; in 1945 ATTLEE told CHURCHILL:

> I could not consent to the introduction into our national life of a device so alien to all our traditions as the referendum, which has only too often been the instrument of Nazism and Fascism.

In 1992–93 John MAJOR's government strongly resisted calls for a referendum on the MAASTRICHT TREATY, despite Margaret

Thatcher's call to "let the people speak". There have, however, been two referendums on constitutional issues: in 1979 over DEVOLUTION for Scotland and Wales, and in 1975 over Britain's continued membership of the EC. The left-wing journalist James Cameron described that referendum, which gave a resounding "Yes", as:

> Like asking a patient: "Would you like your appendix back?"

reflation The taking of steps to stimulate an ECONOMY that has had demand taken out of it to the point where it has become deflated and RECESSION looms. Reflation will give rise to INFLATION if too great a stimulus is administered.

reform The achievement of substantial change in the political and social system while still preserving its essentials, brought about through the process itself. REVOLUTIONARIES both scorn reformers and feel threatened by them; TROTSKY wrote: "A reformist party considers unshakeable the foundations of that which it tends to reform."

> Cautious, careful people, always casting about to preserve their reputation and social standing, can never bring about a reform. SUSAN B. ANTHONY (1820–1906).

> A reformer is a guy who rides through a sewer in a glass bottomed boat.
> New York Mayor JAMES J. WALKER, 1928.

> We have not got democratic government today. We never have had it and I venture to suggest . . . that we shall never have it. What we have done in all the process of reform and revolution is to broaden the basis of the oligarchy. ANTHONY EDEN.

Reform Acts The landmark legislation from 1832 which converted Britain's HOUSE OF COMMONS from (largely) a body of PLACEMEN supposedly representing tiny and even non-existent electorates (*see* pocket BOROUGH; rotten BOROUGH) to a legislature democratically elected, though by limited male SUFFRAGE. The original battle was by far the fiercest, as the Commons of 1831 was elected on boundaries and a franchise that had been barely democratic three centuries before, and change was fiercely opposed both by REACTIONARIES in the HOUSE OF LORDS, and by those MPs who felt it would destroy the qualities of the House of Commons. There was vast support for the 1831–32 Bill from the urban working and middle class, even though it did nothing for them; it merely killed off the most discredited anomalies and gave a handful of seats to the new industrial cities. As tensions rose, Lord Brougham campaigned in the 1831 election for "The Bill, the whole Bill and nothing but the Bill", and Macaulay declared: "The voice of great events is proclaiming to us: 'Reform, that you may preserve.'" However the Duke of Wellington (*see* IRON DUKE), a leader of the diehards, insisted that "beginning reform is beginning revolution", and as the Bill finally went through Lord Melbourne commented:

> If it was not absolutely necessary, it was the foolishest thing ever done.

The process was taken much further in 1867, when Disraeli's Tory government shifted the balance further towards the industrial cities, though still with a very limited franchise. Lord Salisbury termed this Act as:

> A political betrayal that has no parallel in our annals.

A third Reform Act in 1887 not only gave the vote to much of the male working class, but also accelerated the arrival in Parliament first of working men to represent it, then of LIB-LABs, and finally the birth of the Labour Party.

Reform Party In Canada, a moderate reforming party formed in the 1840s which was a forerunner of the LIBERAL PARTY. Led by the Quebec lawyer Louis H. Lafontaine, the Toronto lawyer Robert Baldwin and the editor and banker Francis Hincks, the Reformers did much in the wake of the DURHAM REPORT to develop the case for Responsible GOVERNMENT.

To hell with reform! Perhaps the best-known slogan of TAMMANY HALL.

refusenik A citizen of the Soviet Union who had been refused an exit visa to another country – most refuseniks were Jews wishing to emigrate to America or Israel. Under Soviet law emigration was a state-granted privilege, though the HELSINKI ACCORD of 1975, to which the USSR was a signatory, guarantees emigration as a basic human right. During the 1970s many Soviet Jews were granted visas, partly in response to pressure from the West (*see* JACKSON-VANIK AMENDMENT). But many were refused, branded as DISSIDENTS and persecuted by the authorities. One of the most prominent refusenik campaigners was Anatoly Shcharansky, imprisoned in 1978 for treason but eventually released and allowed to settle in Israel in 1986. Under Mikhail Gorbachev's policy of GLASNOST restrictions on the emigration of Soviet citizens were gradually removed; 72,500 Jews left in 1989 and some 200,000 in 1990. But the wholesale abolition of exit visas, dreaded by some Western countries who feared an unwanted influx of economic immigrants, was still being processed by Boris Yeltsin's Russian government late in 1992.

regency A situation in which a MONARCH, through youth, insanity or other incapacity, cannot govern or is not allowed to, and an individual or council governs on his or her behalf. Sometimes, as with Admiral Horthy in Hungary between the wars, a regent may rule when the monarchy has effectively been abolished, using the title to conceal his personal power. The term also has connotations of grandeur deriving from the upsurge in culture and foppishness which accompanied the regency of the future King George IV in early 19th-century Britain during the madness of George III; America's ALBANY REGENCY may have owed its title to this trait.

régime The persons and ideology governing a country, the somewhat derogatory term implying a degree of AUTHORITARIANISM and lack of LEGITIMACY; as in "the Pinochet régime in Chile", "Rhodesia's Smith régime" or "the repressive régime in Pyongyang".

> In judging a régime it is very important to know what it finds amusing.
>
> PALMIRO TOGLIATTI (1893–1964), founder of the Italian Communist Party, 1924.

register of electors The list of all those in the United Kingdom entitled to vote, compiled by local authorities from forms which everyone eligible is required to return and from door-to-door CANVASSING. The list, carried over from year to year, is supposed to be comprehensive but, especially in INNER CITY areas, it is frequently only 75% accurate. The introduction of the POLL TAX led some voters to remove themselves from the register in an effort to avoid payment.

registration In America, the process involved in registering one's eligibilty to vote; in some states its complexity – for instance a need to drive 50 miles to register – deters many of those entitled to vote from doing so. The hurdles were erected largely to prevent Blacks and poor Whites from voting, but many survive as a general inhibitor. In the mid-1970s there were strong demands from liberal groups for **postcard registration**, under which anyone could obtain the vote simply by writing in, but there was resistance from more conservative States. Registration usually involves not only gaining the qualification to vote, but declaring oneself a REPUBLICAN or DEMOCRAT to gain the right to vote in PRIMARIES, or (in a few states) an INDEPENDENT. *See also* ELECTORAL REGISTER.

regulation The moderation by government of the trading policies of commercial concerns in the PRIVATE SECTOR.

> It is hardly lack of due process for the government to regulate that which it subsidizes.
>
> Justice ROBERT H. JACKSON, US Supreme Court, 1943.

Regulation 18b A provision of Britain's Emergency Powers (Defence) Acts of 1939, amended by Parliament in 1940 to give the HOME SECRETARY the power to detain without trial members of any organization sympathetic to an enemy power. Defence regulation 18b(1A) was specifically targeted at the British Union of FASCISTS and its leader, the former Labour Minister Sir Oswald MOSLEY, who was arrested and imprisoned in Brixton from 23 May 1940 until November 1943, when he was released for health reasons. Altogether 763 BUF members were rounded up, including Mosley's wife Diana, who was sent to Holloway; 1769 British subjects suspected of being pro-German and pro-Italian were INTERNED during the war, most of them in Peel Camp on the Isle of Man.

regulator, the (1) The power available to a CHANCELLOR OF THE EXCHEQUER to vary rates of INDIRECT TAX without requiring a separate Budget and FINANCE BILL. (2) The arbiter appointed by the UK government to regulate a specific sector of industry, normally a former State-owned concern that has been PRIVATIZED, such as British Gas, Telecom or the electricity companies.

regulatory agencies The plethora of agencies of the US Government that perform regulatory functions over industry and commerce. In some cases they involve a greater BUREAUCRACY than if the Federal government actually owned the industry in question.

> There are a thousand agencies that can regulate, restrain or control [the great corporations], but there is a corporation we may all well dread. That corporation is the Federal Government.
>
> Sen. BENJAMIN H. HILL, US Senate, 27 March 1878.

rehabilitation The reinstatement in official esteem of a previously-disgraced public figure. A frequent practice in COMMUNIST countries, especially after the death of STALIN, rehabilitation would occasionally mean the return to a position of responsibility of the person previously denounced as a traitor or REVISIONIST; more often it involved the withdrawal of unfavourable obituaries and the reinterment of the body in a more prominent plot.

Reich (Ger. empire or realm) *Deutsches Reich* was the official title of the German state from its creation in 1871 to the surrender of the NAZI leadership in 1945. The **First Reich** was the mediaeval Holy Roman Empire, which lapsed in 1806; the **Second Reich** the state established in 1871 when Wilhelm I was proclaimed Kaiser, which ended with the abdication of Wilhelm II (*see* HANG THE KAISER!) in 1918, and the **Third Reich** the regime established by Hitler in January 1933, which he claimed would last a thousand years but which perished in flames just over 12 years later.

Reichstag The Parliament, first of the loose German confederation, then of Imperial Germany, and finally of the WEIMAR REPUBLIC. Its building in central Berlin, completed in 1894, was restored after World War II as a shrine to democracy; it housed the first meeting of the BUNDESTAG after re-UNIFICATION in 1990 and will become its seat when Germany's capital moves back from Bonn. Hitler described the election of Nazi deputies to the *Reichstag* as "merely a means to an end", and in 1933 proved his point when on 27 February the building was gutted by a fire almost certainly started by the Nazis. The fire was critical to Hitler's seizure of absolute power, enabling him to blame the Communists, who with the rest of the left had blocked total Nazi supremacy. A 24-year-old Dutchman, Marius van der Lubbe, was identified as the communist who had started the blaze, tried and executed on 10 January 1934; and in the four days after the fire, 5000 Communists were rounded up. During the post-war NUREMBERG TRIALS, the German Chief of General Staff recalled hearing Goering boast: "The only one who really knows about the *Reichstag* is me, because I set it on fire." Sefton Delmer, Berlin correspondent of Britain's *Daily Express*, recalled a phone call from Goering before the fire was public knowledge telling him the *Reichstag* was ablaze; he filed the exclusive story, only to be told that the paper could not use it unless he could say how many fire engines attended the blaze.

rejectionists Militant PALESTINIANS and other Arabs who reject any Middle East peace settlement and advocate the total destruction of Israel.

Rejoice! Rejoice! Margaret Thatcher's euphoric pronouncement on the steps of 10 DOWNING STREET after British forces recaptured South Georgia from its Argentine occupiers on 25 April 1982. It was the first good news for Britain since Argentina's capture of the Falklands three weeks earlier; Mrs. Thatcher's injunction to the nation to "Rejoice, just rejoice" showed her at her most buoyant. South Georgia had been a pretext for the FALKLANDS WAR; Argentine scrap merchants arrived in the British dependency without permission on 19 March to remove material from an old whaling station at Grytviken, and less than two weeks later Argentine forces evicted a tiny Royal Marine garrison – but not before the lieutenant in charge had holed the approaching ship with an anti-tank missile.

relocation camps The camps in Wyoming, Arkansas, Colorado and the California desert where over 100,000 Japanese-Americans were INTERNED by the Federal authorities after being rounded up following PEARL HARBOR in a reaction now seen as almost as infamous as the Japanese surprise attack itself. President Franklin D. Roosevelt championed the plan, even referring to the camps as CONCENTRATION CAMPS, despite being warned by his Attorney-General that it was both objectionable and UNCONSTITUTIONAL; the Supreme Court took until 1944 to strike it down. It was the 1980s before Congress passed legislation to compensate survivors of the anti-Japanese hysteria who had been branded as potential traitors and torn away from their homes and jobs, some for almost five years.

Relugas compact The abortive agreement by senior LIBERAL IMPERIALISTS to reduce the party's leader, Sir Henry Campbell-Bannerman (*see* C-B), to a cipher after its LANDSLIDE election victory in 1905. Sir Edward Grey, Herbert ASQUITH and R. B. Haldane, the instigator, met that September at Grey's fishing lodge at Relugas in North-east Scotland and agreed that Campbell-Bannerman should be persuaded to go to the HOUSE OF LORDS, with Asquith effectively leading the Government as CHANCELLOR OF THE EXCHEQUER; unless this was done, they would not join the government. Edward VII sounded out Campbell-Bannerman about a PEERAGE, but he dug in his heels; once in office three months later, C-B according to his own account called in each of the plotters and told them:

> Now look here, I have been playing up till now. . . . But now let me just say – that it is I who am the head of this Government; it is I who have the King's Command; I am on horseback, and you will all be pleased to understand that I will not go to the House of Lords; that I will not have any condition of the kind imposed on me.

All three took senior posts in Campbell-Bannerman's government, Asquith as Chancellor, and worked harmoniously until C-B's death early in 1908, when Asquith succeeded him.

Remember the Maine! The cry of the Hearst newspapers which precipitated the SPANISH-AMERICAN WAR. The battleship USS *Maine* blew up on 15 February 1898 in Havana harbour with the loss of 260 lives while on a goodwill visit to Spanish-ruled Cuba. The cause of the explosion was never traced, but IMPERIALISTS led by William Randolph Hearst pointed the finger at Spain – which had no reason to stage such a provocation – and with Congressional elections due, the unwarlike President McKINLEY bowed to pressure and declared war two months later. The phrase is thought to have first appeared under a front-page cartoon by Clifford Berryman in the *Washington Post* of 3 April; the caption read:

> Stout hearts, my laddies! If the row comes, *remember the Maine*, and show the world how American sailors can fight.

remilitarization The reintroduction of armed forces into a region from which they have been removed under the terms of a peace agreement or other international accord, by the nation which had been required to withdraw them. The word is most often used of Hitler's despatch of German troops into the Rhineland in March 1936 in breach of the LOCARNO PACTS. Hitler had feared Britain and France would call his bluff and order him to remove them; their acquiescence encouraged Hitler in the view – justified during the era of APPEASEMENT but ultimately mistaken – that he could expand Germany's borders at will.

remit (1) With the emphasis on the first syllable, the terms of reference set for a committee or inquiry, within which it has *carte blanche*, but beyond which it is not supposed to investigate. (2) With the second syllable emphasized, the action taken by a LABOUR PARTY conference in referring back to the NEC a proposal about which it has doubts, when it is unwilling to embarrass the leadership by inflicting an outright defeat. The platform will often ask the MOVERs of a critical resolution to remit it rather than force a vote; if they feel strongly enough, they will insist that it be put to the conference.

RENAMO (National Resistance of Mozambique) The movement which has fought a ruthless GUERRILLA campaign against Mozambique's FRELIMO government since the establishment of a Marxist PEOPLE'S REPUBLIC on independence from Portugal in 1975. Initially a small organization backed by Bavarian and exiled Portuguese businessmen and with some help from South Africa, it developed – ironically as FRELIMO became less Marxist – into a force ready to stage bloody raids on government bases and civilian farms alike, and to wage a civil war leading to mass starvation. After MEDIATION by the Presidents of Kenya and Zimbabwe, President Joaquim Chissano and the RENAMO leader Alfonso Dhlakama met in December 1989; formal peace negotiations have taken place sporadically in Rome.

rentacrowd A crowd specially organized or paid to swell the numbers or show appropriate emotions at a DEMONSTRATION or RALLY. Such a group may be organized by a candidate's campaign manager to mob him or her to convince television viewers that the candidate is in with a real chance. The word was coined in 1962 by the *Daily Telegraph* columnist Peter Simple (Michael Wharton), who wrote of

> Rentacrowd Ltd – the enterprising firm that supplies crowds for all occasions, and has done so much to keep progressive causes in the public eye.

rentamob A term that has taken over the original meaning of RENTACROWD as a travelling collection of extremists who can be turned out to demonstrate for or against almost anything.

rentaquote A nickname applied to a number of UK politicians – mainly BACKBENCH MPs with no serious prospects – whose views are splashed all over the media, especially on quiet weekends and during Parliamentary recesses. For some unfathomable reason, most Rentaquote MPs have been Conservatives – starting with Nicholas Winterton, MP for Macclesfield since 1970. They have gained their fame through the diligence of Chris Moncrieff, for many years chief political correspondent of the *Press Association* news agency, who has the ability to talk MPs into uttering crass statements that will generate a story, not that some of them require much encouragement. During one recess, two Cabinet Ministers asked a LOBBY correspondent why, after a week, no one had demanded the RECALL of Parliament. "Moncrieff's on holiday," they were told.

Rep The formal abbreviation for REPRESENTATIVE, the name by which a US CONGRESSMAN is formally known.

Rep. by Pop Representation by Population. The slogan of the GRITS in the mid-1850s in what was soon to become Ontario, who wanted seats in Canada's legislature to be allocated by population instead of the main provinces being equally represented. This would have put Quebec and other French-speaking regions at a disadvantage; it led to many French Canadians breaking with the Reform Alliance and siding with the Conservatives, who thus became a second national party after the Grit/Liberals.

reparations The transfer of money, industrial machinery, ships, railway equipment and other goods essential to a productive economy from the loser of a war to the victors, as compensation for the loser's perceived responsibility for damage done during the conflict. Reparations on a massive scale were prised from Germany by France under the Treaty of VERSAILLES; the DAWES PLAN and YOUNG PLAN scaled them down because of Germany's inability to pay in full and avoid penury, but large sums were still owing when Hitler repudiated them in 1935.

repartee One of the joys of politics, the swift and devastating capping of one well-turned phrase with another. Examples of repartee are scattered throughout this dictionary (*see*, particularly, HECKLING), but a selection is given here. Two involve Horatio Bottomley (1860–1933), the larger-than-life UK Liberal MP who ended in prison for fraud. When Bottomley heard that F. E. Smith had been appointed Lord Chancellor, he told him: "I shouldn't have been surprised to hear you'd also been made Archbishop of Canterbury." "If I had," said Smith, "I should have asked you to my installation. I should have needed a crook." While Bottomley was in jail, a visitor found him sewing mailbags. "Ah, Bottomley, sewing?" asked the visitor. "No, reaping," he replied. The Labour actor-MP Andrew Faulds, easily angered by Tory laughter, once said: "This is a serious matter, even for the Girl Guides opposite." When a woman Conservative replied: "There's nothing wrong with Girl Guides," Faulds hit back: "Perhaps I have known more Girl Guides than the honourable lady." In the mid-1980s Labour's John Maxton was asking if vasectomy operations at a Scottish hospital were at risk, when the Conservative Jerry Hayes broke in: "I didn't know they went in for micro-surgery." And when, after the release of the ANC leader Nelson Mandela from prison in 1990, the Labour front-bencher Dr. Jack Cunningham asked Sir Geoffrey HOWE to ensure "proper accommodation for Mr. Mandela to address members when he comes here next week", the boisterous Tory Nicholas Soames interjected:

> How about the rifle range?

Tristan Garel-Jones, the Old Etonian deputy Tory Chief WHIP and Euro-Minister, once told the Yorkshire miners' MP Mick Welsh: "We public schoolboys and you miners have one thing in common. We're both used to communal showers." Welsh replied: "Aye, lad. But we didn't have to watch out when we bent down for the soap." Politicians can also be on the receiving end of withering put-downs. One of the best came from a cowman working for the left-wing Labour Minister Richard CROSSMAN, who had patronizingly invited the cockney Chief Whip Bob Mellish to his farm for a glimpse of country life. When Mellish asked why a cow was lying in a peculiar posture, Crossman told him: "They often do that" – only for the cowman to interrupt:

> That one be dead, zur.

The Labour MP Dr. Edith Summerskill was floored when she went on television to argue the case against boxing with the British and Commonwealth heavyweight champion Henry Cooper. Getting nowhere, she turned to the boxer and asked: "Mr. Cooper, have you ever looked in the mirror and seen the state of your nose?" Cooper counterpunched:

> Madam, have you looked in the mirror and seen the state of your nose? I done it boxing – what's your excuse?

The US Congress has always offered a rich vein in repartee. In the early 19th century John Randolph of Roanoake met Henry Clay in a narrow alley, and told him: "I never GIVE WAY for a scoundrel." Clay gallantly stepped aside, saying: "I always do." Clay also had the last word when Alexander Smith, during a lengthy speech, grandly told him: "You, sir, speak for the present generation, but I speak for posterity." Clay retorted to Smith: "Yes, and you seem resolved to speak until the arrival of your audience."

A few decades later, a Congressman said to Georgia's Alexander Hamilton Stephens: "You little shrimp! Why, I could swallow you whole." Stephens replied: "If you did, you'd have more brains in your belly than ever you had in your head."

Sen. Chauncey Depew (1834–1928) once said of Joseph Choate: "All you need to get a speech out of Mr. Choate is to open his mouth, drop in a dinner and up comes a speech." Choate retorted: "If you open your mouth and drop in one of Mr. Depew's speeches, up will come your dinner."

More recently, Rep. William Jenner, an Indiana Republican, brought the House to a standstill during a wordy and sentimental speech from Idaho's Rep. Glen Taylor. When Taylor told how "my father was an itinerant Baptist preacher. He baptized 15,000 people in the great West. Why, he baptized me five times", Jenner shouted: "Son-of-a-gun's waterlogged!"

One day in a Senate elevator, Sen. Edward KENNEDY told Sen. Thomas Eagleton: "I've got a new Polish joke." When the Polish-descended Sen. Ed Muskie pointed out: "I'm in this elevator too, Ted," Kennedy told him: "All right, Ed, I'll tell it slowly."

Adlai Stevenson was a master of the art, but was sometimes content not to have the last word. He once met a woman who gushed: "Oh, Mr. Stevenson, your speech was superfluous!" Stevenson, deadpan, replied: "Thank you, Madam, I'm thinking of having it published posthumously." The woman came back: "Won't that be nice! The sooner the better."

Tony BENN tells of a reputed meeting between Nikita Khruschev and Chou En-Lai when China's Communist rulers were starting to chafe at the Kremlin's HEGEMONY. Khruschev said: "Isn't it remarkable that you, a member of the middle class, and I, from the working class, should control the two greatest Socialist nations that have ever existed?" "Yes," replied Chou, "and more remarkable still, each of us has betrayed the class from which he came."

repatriation The return to their country of origin of prisoners of war, illegal immigrants or convicted criminals. Enoch POWELL opened bitter divisions in Britain from the time of his RIVERS OF BLOOD speech in 1969 by advocating the repatriation of legal Commonwealth immigrants; this became a rallying call for extreme right-wing groups throughout the 1970s. In the late 1980s America objected strongly to Britain repatriating Vietnamese BOAT PEOPLE who had fled to Hong Kong but were held not to be genuine refugees.

repeal The abolition by a legislature of legislation previously passed, because it is reckoned to be inappropriate, unnecessary or obsolete. This may be done by promoting a new measure to repeal a particular law, or including the repeal in a broader measure; this latter is usually done with obsolete laws whose abolition will cause no controversy. Celebrated repeals include that of the CORN LAWS in 1846, which split the old TORY party, and the repeal of PROHIBITION in America by the Twenty-first amendment to the Constitution, ratified in December 1933.

Report. Report Stage At Westminster, the step in the legislative process between COMMITTEE STAGE and THIRD READING. After LINE-BY-LINE consideration by a STANDING COMMITTEE, a Bill comes back to the FLOOR of the House for the principal AMENDMENTS (including those from the Opposition that have been rejected in Committee) to be fully debated and voted on. Except for the most wide-ranging and controversial of Bills, the Report Stage takes less than a day of Parliamentary time before the formal debate and vote on the Third Reading.

reporting a Bill In the US House of Representatives, the action of a committee in approving a Bill for further consideration. One of the members of the committee is designated to write a report stating the purposes and scope of the measure and the reasons for approving it. Under the RAMSEYER RULE, the report must set out all changes the Bill would make to existing law, and the text of all laws being repealed. Committee amendments must be set out, and explained, and executive communications regarding the Bill quoted in full. The committee report, after which the Bill is reprinted with its report number, is of particular use to the courts and executive departments in explaining the purpose and meaning of a law once passed.

representation The role of a legislator or other person elected to a public body in acting on behalf of the people in whose name they hold office. The Libyan leader Colonel Gaddafi declared that "representation is fraud"; the British Labour MP Bill Stones went to the other extreme when he said: "There's a lot of bleeding idiots in this country, and they deserve some representation." For a similar American comment see Sen. Roman Hruska on the CARSWELL NOMINATION.

Representation of the People Acts The body of legislation passed during the 20th century under which UK Parliamentary elections are held and regulated, and seats in the House of Commons are distributed.

no taxation without representation *See* NO TAX.

proportional representation *See* PROPORTIONAL.

representative (1) An individual elected to represent a community or a number of people. Daniel Webster declaimed in 1834: "We have been taught to regard a representative of the people as a sentinel on the watch tower of liberty," but Alphonse de Lamartine, confronted with the shambles of mid-19th century French politics, confessed:

> The more I see of the representatives of the people, the more I admire my dogs.

A strict distinction is drawn between a representative who acts as he or she thinks best on behalf of those represented, and a DELEGATE who is under instruction to act or vote in a particular way. In 1774 Edmund BURKE told the electors of Bristol:

> Your representative owes you, not his industry only, but also his judgment.

(2) The official title of a US CONGRESSMAN. A Representative must be at least 25 years old, have been a US citizen for at least seven years, and reside in the State for a district of which he or she has been elected to Congress. (3) A participant in a UK CONSERVATIVE PARTY conference; those attending on behalf of constituency ASSOCIATIONS are never known as delegates.

representative democracy or government Those systems of government in which decisions are taken by elected representatives, on behalf of the population as a whole.

reprieve The suspension of a legal penalty, notably the death penalty, and substitution of a lesser punishment. In America the decision generally rests with the GOVERNOR of a State (or with the President for Federal offences); in Britain it has been a matter for the HOME SECRETARY. The difference between a reprieve and a PARDON is that a person pardoned incurs no legal process or penalty, while one reprieved still has a sentence to serve.

reprimand One of the forms of disciplinary action available to both Houses of the US Congress against erring members. Under it, the member is rebuked for his or her conduct in terms less severe than a CENSURE, and continues to serve. The KOREAGATE scandal led to the House voting to reprimand three members; a recent reprimand was administered to Barney Frank of Massachusetts in 1990. Frank (1940–), a gifted legislator and openly gay, had allegedly allowed a former assistant/male friend to use his apartment for prostitution; the House Ethics Committee did not accept this, but did recommend a reprimand because of a letter Frank had written to the man's probation officer and his fixing of 33 parking tickets. The reprimand was voted by 408–18.

republic (Lat. the public concern) A non-MONARCHical state, in which the supreme power is vested in the people and their elected representatives; its head of state, or PRESIDENT, will often be the HEAD OF GOVERNMENT as well. Thomas JEFFERSON reckoned it "the only form of government which is not eternally at war with the rights of mankind", but Palmerston asserted that "large republics seem to be essentially and inherently aggressive".

> The republican form of government is the highest form of government, but because of this it requires the highest type of human nature – a type nowhere at present existing. ROBERT SPENCER (1820–1903), *The Americans*.

> The republic is a dream;
> Nothing happens unless first a dream.
> CARL SANDBURG, *Washington Monument by Night*.

> *Lady:* Well, doctor, what have we got? A republic or a monarchy?
> *Benjamin Franklin* (leaving the PHILADELPHIA CONVENTION, 1787): A republic, if you can keep it.

Battle Hymn of the Republic *See* MINE EYES HAVE SEEN THE GLORY OF THE COMING OF THE LORD.

Plato's Republic The blueprint for an ideal state set forward *c.* 370 B.C. by the Greek philosopher Plato (427?–347 B.C.). He set its population at 5040, the most he felt could be addressed by an orator, and divided them into guardians (rulers), auxiliaries (warriors), farmers and artisans, and slaves. The top two tiers were to hold property, meals and children in common, with only the "best" permitted to breed.

Republican (1) An advocate of a republican form of government in place of the monarchy, notably in Britain or Australia. (2) In newly-independent America, the supporters of Thomas JEFFERSON and James MADISON who by 1792 were accusing George WASHINGTON and Alexander HAMILTON of being "monarchists", both because of the first President's love of pomp and his Treasury Secretary's ambitious tax schemes. (3) In Ireland, an advocate of revolutionary action to reunite the island as a 32-county republic.

Republican cloth coat The phrase used by Richard Nixon (*see* TRICKY DICK) about his wife Pat in his 1952 CHECKERS speech, which convinced most viewers that he had not enriched himself from a $18,000 secret fund set up by supporters. His assertion that his wife wore such a plain garment was a dig at INFLUENCE-PEDDLING under the Truman administration; E. Merl Young, a former examiner for the Reconstruction Finance Corporation, had accepted a mink coat for his wife, a White House secretary, from a lawyer who had applied for an RFC loan. Nixon declared:

> It isn't very much, but Pat and I have the satisfaction that every dime we've got is honestly ours. I should say this – Pat doesn't have a mink coat. But she does have a respectable Republican cloth coat. And I always tell her that she'd look good in anything.

Republican Party The party of Abraham LINCOLN and Ronald Reagan, which has occupied the White House for over 80 years since its foundation in 1854, but has controlled either House of Congress for relatively short periods. Originally a radical party, it moved to the right in the late 19th century but retains a liberal element. Harry S. Truman remarked that "the Republican Party either corrupts its liberals or expels them", Adlai Stevenson that "every four years the Republican programme is interrupted by the liberal hour", while Sen. Eugene McCarthy declared: "The function of liberal Republicans is to shoot the wounded after the battle." The party's emblem is an ELEPHANT; which Adlai Stevenson considered appropriate:

> The elephant has a thick skin, a head full of ivory and proceeds best by grasping the tail of his predecessor.

The party was formed by Democrats who broke away from the party after Sen. Stephen Douglas introduced the KANSAS-NEBRASKA ACT in January 1854. The name Republican was proposed by Alan Bovay, an attorney from RIPON, Wisconsin, and adopted by a meeting at Jackson, Michigan on 6 July 1854. Appealing to national rather than sectional interests, it absorbed the remaining WHIGs and KNOW-NOTHINGS, and won control of the House in elections that November. Its first national CONVENTION was held in Philadelphia on 17 June 1856, John C. Fremont being nominated for President. Four years later the Republicans nominated Abraham Lincoln, a former Whig Congressman, and carried the election. Lincoln said that the Republicans were

> For both the man and the dollar, but in case of conflict the man before the dollar.

The CIVIL WAR installed them as the party of the UNION and of ABOLITIONISM, Frederick Douglass (*see* LIBERATOR) declaring:

> I recognize the Republican Party as the sheet anchor of the coloured man's political hopes and the ark of his safety.

With Lincoln's assassination at the close of the war triumphant northern Republicans adopted an aggressive programme of RECONSTRUCTION. For the rest of the 19th century, save for the presidencies of Grover Cleveland, they were the dominant power in federal politics, becoming steadily more identified with big business and correspondingly less radical. The TARIFF, the GOLD STANDARD and IMPERIALISM gave them a new lease of life under Theodore (TEDDY) Roosevelt and TAFT; but the BULL MOOSE split of 1912 let in Woodrow WILSON. Post-war prosperity brought the election of HARDING, Coolidge (*see* SILENT CAL) and HOOVER, after which the GREAT DEPRESSION put them into the wilderness, even though Will Rogers insisted:

> I don't want to blame the Republicans for the depression. They aren't smart enough.

For a generation the Republicans were seen as WASPs with pince-nez, but they fought back to win control of Congress just after World War II, and capture the White House with Eisenhower (*see* IKE) in 1952. The prosperous inertia of his administration gave John F. Kennedy a strong suit to defeat Richard Nixon in 1960, and a flirtation with Barry Goldwater's ultra-conservatism brought a landslide defeat in 1964. However a "new Nixon" won election in 1968, partly because the Democrats were in disarray over VIETNAM but also because the Republicans were making inroads in the South. The coalition held in 1972, and the Republicans overcame the trauma of WATERGATE for Gerald FORD to run Jimmy Carter close in 1976. Then came the Reagan years, when a revival of conservatism plus the FEELGOOD FACTOR gave the Republicans three terms in the White House, the last under George BUSH; yet only for the first years could Reagan put together a majority in Congress, and even then he was dependent on conservative Democrats in the House.

> The Republicans have their splits right after an election – Democrats have theirs just before. WILL ROGERS.

> They've been peddling eyewash about themselves and hogwash about the Democrats. What they need is a good mouthwash. LYNDON B. JOHNSON.

> We have to decide whether we're going to be a business party or a people's party. Rep. JACK KEMP.

> We're the party that wants to see an America in which people can still get rich. RONALD REAGAN, 1982.

> The one thing we're able to do is raise money. DAN QUAYLE.

Mr. Republican *See* MISTER.

research assistant At Westminster, the only member of staff an MP is likely to have apart from a secretary. Advertisements for research assistance usually stress the low pay offered, and many just out of university do the job for almost nothing.

reselection The process by which one of Britain's constituency Labour Parties with a sitting MP determines whether he or she should continue as its candidate. Until 1980 the reselection of a member wishing to stand again was almost automatic, but then the party gave way to BENNITE pressure for "mandatory reselection". This obliged each constituency to hold a full candidate selection process prior to every election regardless of whether there was a sitting member. Some parties tried to get round this by approving a SHORT-LIST of one, so that the MP was unopposed at the final selection stage. The hard LEFT saw mandatory reselection as a means of ousting right-wingers and installing hard-liners through manipulation of the electoral process, where the decision rested with the constituency management committee and not with all party members. In the event no more than half a dozen sitting members were ousted prior to each of the 1983 and 1987 elections, but a number of others gave up in exasperation and at least one who fought off the challenge was harried to an early grave. By 1992 mandatory reselection was on the way out, with most constituency parties balloting their entire membership.

reserve currency An internationally-traded currency that CENTRAL BANKS will keep as part of their reserves, along with gold, and will use when necessary to meet their foreign commitments.

reshuffle A UK Prime Minister's reconstruction of the Cabinet, with Ministers being moved between jobs and usually some new appointments to replace Ministers who have retired, resigned or been sacked. Anthony EDEN confided that "the worst of being sacked is that you can never find your car"; the public-sector trade-union leader Rodney Bickerstaffe described the impact of one of Margaret Thatcher's reshuffles as "like being cured of diarrhoea and then finding that you have dysentery", while Reginald Maudling, dropped from her SHADOW CABINET, remarked bitterly: "There comes a moment in every man's life when he must make way for an older man."

> It does no harm to throw the occasional man overboard, but it does not do much good if you are steering full speed ahead for the rocks.
>
> Sir IAN GILMOUR (1926–) after being sacked by Mrs. Thatcher.

Resident Commissioner The title given to Puerto Rico's elected delegate to the US HOUSE OF REPRESENTATIVES. In common with the DELEGATES from the District of Columbia and America's island Territories, he or she has most of the privileges of a Congressman, including the right to speak, but may not vote.

Resignation Honours *See* HONOURS LIST.

Resistance The underground organization in German-occupied and VICHY France during WORLD WAR II that continued the struggle after the country's leaders surrendered. It sabotaged enemy operations, passed information about enemy movements to the Allies by clandestine radio communication, hid members of the Allied forces (such as airmen who had been shot down) and helped them escape. From May 1943 the various Resistance groups – including former army officers, Communists and supporters of DE GAULLE – were co-ordinated as the *Conseil National de la Résistance*, led by Jean Moulin (and after his arrest in June 1943 by Georges Bidault). In February 1944 the *Maquis*, provincial guerrilla groups operating in the countryside, became part of the newly formed *Forces Françaises de l'Intérieur* (*FFI*), which played a vital role in the LIBERATION of France (*see also* FREE FRENCH). During World War II there were also active resistance groups in Belgium, Holland, Denmark, Norway, Poland, Yugoslavia (*see* PARTISANS), Greece, Italy and elsewhere.

Resolute desk The desk used by the President of the United States in the OVAL OFFICE of the White House. Made of timbers from HMS *Resolute*, a Royal Navy ship saved by American whalers in the Arctic in 1854, it was presented by Queen Victoria to President Hayes. It has been variously sited in the Yellow Oval Room, where Presidents Benjamin Harrison, Cleveland, Franklin D. Roosevelt and Truman used it, and in the Oval Office proper, by most recent Presidents.

resolution. Resolution 242 The UN SECURITY COUNCIL resolution that has governed peacemaking efforts in the Middle East since shortly after the SIX DAY WAR of 1967. Approved on 22 November 1967, it states that conquest is inadmissible; just and lasting peace must be established, belligerency ended and Demilitarized zones established; Israeli troops should withdraw from occupied territories; refugee problems be solved; and acknowledgment made of the sovereignty and territorial integrity of all states in the region and their right to live in peace within secure and recognized boundaries.

affirmative resolution In the UK legislative process, the specific approval required from the Commons (in some cases both Houses) before an Order can take effect.

Budget resolution(s) *See* BUDGET.

concurrent resolution A Washington term for resolutions put to both Houses, not necessarily simultaneously, concerning their operations. They are not legislative in nature and are a vehicle purely for expressing facts, principles, opinions and the purposes of the Houses.

joint resolution In the US Congress, a piece of legislation virtually indistinguishable from a BILL, except that a joint resolution is the instrument for proposing an AMENDMENT to the Constitution. Despite its name, a joint resolution does not have to be considered simultaneously by the House and Senate.

money resolution *See* MONEY.

mother of all resolutions *See* MOTHER.

simple resolution A resolution concerning the operation of one House only of the US Congress, which is considered by it alone, without reference to any other authority.

Restricted One of the lowest levels of sensitivity of official documents which a government or military service wishes to keep secret. Although care is taken to limit a Restricted document's circulation, it is less vital to security than one marked CLASSIFIED, and far less sensitive than one marked Top SECRET.

retreads A Westminster term for MPs who come back to the Commons to resume a political career interrupted by the loss of their previous seat. *Compare* VIRGINS.

return. Returning Officer In UK Parliamentary elections, the official of the relevant local authority in charge of conducting the election in a given CONSTITUENCY, ensuring that the law is observed, conducting the COUNT and announcing the result.

duplicate return The document listing the outcome of any US Congressional election which is sent direct to the relevant House of Congress by the authorities of the State where it was held.

unopposed return (1) The outcome of an election where only one candidate is put forward to fill a vacancy, and the result can be notified without the need to conduct a poll. (2) The procedure under which a report or other document is lodged with Parliament with no provision for it to be debated.

return to legality The phrase used throughout the 14-year Rhodesian crisis for the process of ending UDI by the Smith regime and the setting up of an internationally-recognized government. A return to legality was said by successive British governments to be a prerequisite for the lifting of SANCTIONS.

revaluation The opposite of DEVALUATION, and thus a word of which the British have no direct experience. It involves a country's CENTRAL BANK unilaterally increasing the value of its currency against others in the world, because pressures in the currency markets make it impossible to hold it down. At a number of points since the collapse of the BRETTON WOODS system in 1971, there has been pressure from other countries for the revaluation of either the German mark or the Japanese yen.

revenue. revenue-neutral A budgetary package which is constructed so as neither to raise nor to lower the overall level of taxation that will have to be imposed, extra spending in one area being offset by cuts in others and minor tax adjustments cancelling each other out.

revenue-sharing The scheme devised by the Republican RIPON SOCIETY and implemented by President Nixon, under which a proportion of Federal tax revenues is passed back to State, city and county governments. The original aim was both to decentralize spending and decision making and to lower property taxes; revenue-sharing also gave a powerful boost to social programmes at State and local level. The Reagan administration, immediately after taking office in 1981, sought to scrap it as a means of saving billions of tax dollars; an alliance of Congress and the US Conference of Mayors defeated that proposal, but revenue-sharing was cut back later in the decade.

Revenue Support Grant *See* RATE SUPPORT GRANT.

reverse discrimination *See* AFFIRMATIVE ACTION.

revising chamber A subordinate chamber in a legislature which lacks the power to determine policy, but performs a valuable role in ensuring that legislation passed by or to be submitted to the more powerful house is sound in detail, watertight and workable. The term is frequently used of the HOUSE OF LORDS.

revisionism An abusive Communist term for any sign of original thought, and of deviation from the Party's set ideological path into dangerous heresies. It was originally a moderate, non-revolutionary form of socialism first advocated in Germany in 1899 by Eduard Bernstein, who felt the socialist movement should include all classes and not be restricted to workers.

> There is only one answer to revisionism: smash its face in.
>
> LENIN, 1904.

revisit A euphemism for the discarding by a victorious candidate of a promise or commitment made during the election campaign. Shortly before his INAUGURATION in January 1992, Bill Clinton (*see* COMEBACK KID) said that after studying Budget projections, he would have to "revisit" his promise to cut taxes on the middle class.

Revolt of 1910 The coup mounted in the US House of Representatives by Republican INSURGENTS to oust Speaker Joe Cannon (*see* FOUL-MOUTHED JOE) from the RULES COMMITTEE and thus break his near-total influence. Cannon, by selecting the committee and sitting on it himself, had been able to halt the progress of any Bill of which he disapproved. Exasperated by what they saw as his dictatorial conduct, a minority of Republicans led by George W. Norris of Nebraska joined with Democrats in March 1910 to force through a rule-change depriving the Speaker of the power to appoint members to the Rules Committee or serve on it himself. The Democrats, after winning a majority in the 1910 elections, went on the following year to bar the Speaker from appointing members of STANDING COMMITTEES.

revolution A sudden and complete change in a country's system of government brought about by radical opponents of the previous regime; Napoleon termed revolution "an opinion backed by bayonets", Germaine Greer "the festival of the oppressed", Ambrose Bierce more dubiously "an abrupt change in the form of misgovernment".

Some revolutions take place within the ESTABLISHMENT (*see* PALACE REVOLUTION). PLATO wrote: "In any form of government, revolution always starts from an outbreak of dissension in the ruling class." Others involve the overthrow of democracies: Richard CROSSMAN considered that "a revolutionary party is a contradiction in terms"; G. K.

Chesterton that "You can never have a revolution in order to establish a democracy. You must have democracy in order to have a revolution." Aristotle identified a more general factor: "Revolutions are not about trifles, but they spring from trifles." Some are planned for years by highly-motivated groups determined on change; LENIN maintained an element of patience and surprise, saying: "It is impossible to predict the time and progress of revolution. It is governed by its own more or less mysterious laws"; TROTSKY's view was that "the revolution does not choose its paths. It made its first steps toward victory under the belly of a Cossack's horse." Those committed to revolution generally feel that there is no other course for them. Pierre Joseph Proudhon asserted: "There is no middle way between REACTION and revolution," Alexander Herzen that it is "better to perish with the revolution than to seek refuge in the almshouse of reaction", but Heinrich Heine was realistic enough to argue that "a revolution is a misfortune – but an unsuccessful revolution is an even greater misfortune". However CHE Guevara proclaimed that "in a revolution one wins or dies", and Mao Tse-Tung that "to die for the reactionary is as light as a feather, but to die for the revolution is heavier than Mount Tai".

The Italian patriot Mazzini proudly asserted that "great revolutions are the work rather of principles than of bayonets", but the bayonets come in useful, particularly when the revolution is spearheaded by a minority of zealots; indeed Robespierre, just before the Reign of TERROR, asked: "Citizens, do you want a revolution without revolution?" Lenin insisted: "The substitution of the proletarian for the bourgeois state is impossible without a violent revolution." CHAIRMAN MAO wrote: "A revolution is not the same as inviting people to dinner, or writing an essay, or painting a picture. . . . A revolution is an insurrection, an act of violence by which one class overthrows another;" and Malcolm X told Black Americans: "Revolutions are never waged singing 'We shall overcome'. Revolutions are based upon bloodshed."

The ruthlessness may continue once the revolutionaries have taken power. STALIN in 1917 declared: "The revolution is incapable either of regretting or burying its dead," and the Algerian revolutionary leader Ahmed Ben Bella: "It is an illusion to think that you can have a revolution without prisons." What revolutions achieve for the people is a matter of opinion. Many are born of idealism, and Abraham LINCOLN said in apparent approval that "revolutions do not go backward"; but Shirley Williams lamented: "The saddest illusion of revolutionary socialists is that revolution itself will change the nature of human beings." The Czech statesman Jan Masaryk considered that "revolution or dictatorship can sometimes abolish bad things, but they can never create good or lasting ones"; George Bernard Shaw that "revolutions have never lightened the burden of tyranny; they have only shifted it on to another shoulder". Revolutions do not end with the seizure of power. Metternich wrote that "in revolutions those who want everything always get the better of those who only want a certain amount"; Che Guevara that "a revolution that does not continue to grow deeper is a revolution that is retreating"; and on a lighter note Indonesia's President Sukarno declared: "We must be on guard lest our revolution die out. Therefore give it romanticism."

> Revolution is the pod
> Systems rattle from
> when the Winds of Will are stirred.
>
> EMILY DICKINSON (1830–86).

> One revolution is just like one cocktail: it just gets you organized for the next. WILL ROGERS.

> The word revolution is a word for which you kill, for which you die, for which you send the labouring classes to their death, but which does not possess any content.
> SIMONE WEIL (1909–43), *Oppression and Liberty*.

> If you want to know the taste of a pear, you must taste the pear by eating it yourself. If you want to know the theory and methods of revolution, you must take part in revolution. MAO TSE-TUNG, 1937.

American Revolution *See* AMERICA.
French Revolution *See* FRENCH.
Glorious Revolution *See* GLORIOUS.
October Revolution *See* OCTOBER.
Permanent Revolution *See* PERMANENT.
Quiet Revolution *See* QUIET.
Russian Revolution *See* RUSSIA.

Revolution of 1800 Thomas JEFFERSON's own words for his election as President and the changes in American government that followed. With Jefferson and Aaron BURR tied on 75 electoral votes each, and John ADAMS and Charles Pinckney just behind, the election went to the House of Representatives, and after six deadlocked ballots Jefferson was elected with ten states to Burr's four. Some ultra-FEDERALISTS threatened a new election or even a military COUP, but Jefferson was sworn in and the TWELFTH AMENDMENT was passed to require separate voting in future for the President and Vice-President; the role of parties was thus acknowledged in the CONSTITUTION. Jefferson's Republicans also regarded the Federalist-appointed Supreme and Federal courts with suspicion; they repealed the Judiciary Act of 1801 under which the outgoing John Adams had manned an expanded court system with Federalist appointees, and sought unsuccessfully to IMPEACH Chief Justice Samuel Chase.

As real a revolution in the principles of our government as that of 1776 was in its form.
Chief Justice OLIVER ELLSWORTH.

Revolution of 1905 The combination of a successful GENERAL STRIKE by urban workers and rural unrest peaking in uprisings by various ethnic minorities that led Tsar Nicholas II to concede modest reforms, including the convening of an elected DUMA. Russia's recent humiliating defeat by Japan, and the impact of atrocities committed against demonstrators by Tsarist troops, weakened Nicholas's hand.

revolution of rising expectations The phrase coined in 1953 by Adlai Stevenson for the upsurge of political awareness and desire for progress in the developing world, transcending the COLD WAR, that has since profoundly changed the horizons of Western politicians. Stevenson wrote in *Look* magazine of 22 September 1953:

Many of the world's troubles are not just due to Russia or communism. They would be with us in any event because we live in an era of revolution – the revolution of rising expectations. In Asia, the masses now count for something. Tomorrow, they will count for more. And, for better or worse, the future belongs to those who understand the hopes and fears of masses in ferment. The new nations want independence, including the inalienable right to make their own mistakes. The people want respect – and something to eat every day. And they want something better for their children.

revolutionary A person who makes a career of revolution, or puts his or her commitment to revolution above everything else. Fidel Castro stated the obvious, that "the duty of every revolutionary is to make a revolution", but disciplined Marxists are divided from others over whether the revolution should be planned for. Castro, with the benefit of experience, declared that "it does not matter how small you are as long as you have faith and a plan of action", but Daniel Cohn-Bendit (Danny the RED) argued anarchistically that "the moment you have a plan you cease to be a revolutionary". The revolutionary needs an indomitable spirit, the BLACK PANTHER Bobby Seale saying: "You can jail a revolutionary, but you cannot jail the revolution", but his YIPPIE contemporary Abbie Hoffman said more realistically: "The first duty of a revolutionary is to get away with it." Albert Camus declared sourly that "every revolutionary ends by becoming either an oppressor or a heretic", but Castro disagreed: "A man who does not believe in human beings is not a revolutionary."

If today I stand here as a revolutionary, it is as a revolutionary against the revolution.
HITLER at his trial after the MUNICH BEER HALL PUTSCH, 26 February 1924.

The revolutionary wants to change the world; the rebel is careful to preserve the abuses from which he suffers so that he can go on rebelling against them.
JEAN-PAUL SARTRE (1905–80), *Baudelaire*.

Revolution allows the revolutionary to sublimate his sado-masochistic, neurotic, anal tendencies into a concern for the working class.
ANON. graffiti.

revolving door The Washington term for the situation in which Government officials leave their jobs and immediately start work for a corporation with which they have been dealing or which they have been regulating. At the highest level, immediate moves are ruled out by the Ethics in Government Act, but concern is frequently voiced about the traffic between the Pentagon and defence contractors. Exactly the same phenomenon occurs in Whitehall, with Ministry of Defence officials the most frequent leavers for the companies with which they have been dealing.

He wouldn't go two rounds with a revolving door The memorable description of Billy Snedden, leader of Australia's Liberal Party 1972–75, by the DLP Senator Vince Gair.

Rexists A Belgian Catholic political party advocating FASCIST methods, formed by Léon Degrelle in 1936. Markedly COLLABORATIONIST during the German occupation, it was suppressed when they were driven out in 1944. The name is an adaptation of *Christus Rex*, Christ the King, the watchword of a Catholic Young People's Action Society founded in 1925.

Reykjavik summit A meeting between Ronald Reagan and Mikhail Gorbachev in the Icelandic capital in October 1986, at which the Soviet leader offered to reduce his nation's stockpile of medium-range and strategic nuclear missiles if Reagan agreed to a 10-year moratorium on aspects of the STAR WARS programme. Reagan refused, and the summit came to a sudden end. However the next time he and Gorbachev met, in Washington in December 1987, they signed the INF treaty.

Reyne. la Reyne le veult (Norman Fr. the Queen wishes it) The phrase uttered by the Queen or her representative which constitutes the ROYAL ASSENT for legislation passed by the UK Parliament.

RFK The initials of Robert Fitzgerald ("Bobby") KENNEDY, almost as often used as those of his brother John (JFK); Washington's football stadium has them as its title.

rhetoric The showy and hectoring over-use of language in political speeches, from the Greek *rhetor*, a professional orator. At a White House meeting on combating hunger on 17 March

1969, Richard Nixon told members of his Administration:

> Use all the rhetoric – as long as it doesn't cost money.

rhetorical question A question asked by a political speaker to make a point, rather than because he or she wishes to hear the answer. It poses the hazard that as the speaker pauses for effect before continuing, someone in the audience may give a highly inappropriate answer. At a feminist FRINGE MEETING at the 1983 Labour Party conference, a speaker asked: "What do women in the Labour Party really want?" Before she could continue, a voice shouted: "Cut Neil Kinnock's balls off!"

rich. Don't make the rich poorer, make the poor richer A quotation from Abraham LINCOLN that Margaret Thatcher, not surprisingly, carried with her in her handbag. Lincoln also said: "I don't believe in a law to prevent a man getting rich; it would do more harm than good," and "That some should be rich shows that others may become rich, and hence is just encouragement to industry and enterprise."

eat the rich! A slogan used in the 1980s by militant UK ANARCHISTS.

soak the rich! An aim imputed to the UK LABOUR PARTY by their Conservative opponents when it was committed to a WEALTH TAX; it was not, however, a slogan the party ever used, though many left-wingers would have applauded it.

squeeze the rich until the pips squeak A phrase once used by Lloyd George to describe property speculators, which was later attributed to Denis Healey (*see* GROMYKO OF THE LABOUR PARTY). Healey insisted he had never said it, though he had quoted his Cabinet colleague Anthony Crosland as repeating it. However Healey did say at Labour's 1973 conference:

> But before you cheer too loudly, let me warn you that a lot of you will pay extra taxes, too. That will go for every Member of Parliament in this hall, including me. . . . There are going to be howls of anguish from the 80,000 people who are rich enough to pay over 75% on their last slice of income. But how much do we hear from them today of the 85,000 families at the bottom of the earnings scale who have to pay over 75% on the last slice of *their* income?

rider In the US SENATE, an unrelated proposal tacked on to an APPROPRIATION Bill; in the House AMENDMENTs to a Bill must be germane to its purpose. In 1943 Senators tacked on a rider withholding the salaries of three Federal officials; President Roosevelt was opposed to it, but let the Bill go through unsigned because it authorized essential funds for the operation of government. A rider may only be attached if a day's written notice is given and there is a two-thirds vote for it to be considered.

riding The Canadian term for a member of Parliament's CONSTITUENCY.

Ridley, Nicholas *See* GERMAN RACKET.

right (1) The right wing, a political tendency that is almost invariably NATIONALIST and usually CONSERVATIVE; its adherents usually want a lean but strong government that does not interfere with them. The term derives from France's pre-revolutionary Estates-General, in which those who were neither aristocratic nor clerical, and were thus more likely to be radical, sat on the left and the others on the right. THATCHERISM marked the triumph of the right wing of Britain's Conservative Party, challenging Harold Macmillan's judgment that:

> A successful party of the right must continue to recruit from the centre and even from the left centre. Once it begins to shrink into itself like a snail, it will be doomed.

Of Mrs. Thatcher's initial impact, Sir Ian Gilmour warned: "A sharp right turn is likely to be followed by an even sharper left turn." It has yet to happen. (2) Virtue and justice in politics, and particularly in international relations. Woodrow WILSON judged that "right is more precious than peace", but Theodore Roosevelt maintained that "aggressive fighting for the right is the noblest sport the world affords"; Hitler went one further, declaring:

> There is only one right in the world, and that is one's own strength.

The word is also used in connection with the morality of politicians in office. Harry S. Truman used to quote Mark Twain's adage: "Always do right. This will gratify some people, and astonish the rest," and Daniel O'Connell is reputed to have said: "Nothing is politically right which is morally wrong." Abraham LINCOLN acknowledged that the right course was not always obvious, saying:

> I know that the Lord is always on the side of the right. But it is my constant anxiety and prayer that I and this nation should always be on the Lord's side.

Lyndon B. Johnson put it his own way: "Doing what's right isn't the problem. It's knowing what's right."

> The best way I know to win an argument is to start by being in the right. Lord HAILSHAM.

> There are times in politics when you must be on the right side and lose.
> Professor JOHN KENNETH GALBRAITH, 1968.

The Right Approach The first of two policy documents that started to develop the THATCHERITE bent of Britain's Conservative Party. It appeared in 1976, the year after

Mrs. Thatcher's election as leader. The following year a more detailed paper, *The Right Approach to the Economy*, was produced; put together by Sir Keith Joseph (*see* MAD MONK), Sir Geoffrey HOWE, David Howell and the Heathite James Prior, it advocated control of the money supply, lower direct taxation and "firm management of government expenditure". Some right-wingers thought it too timid, particularly towards the unions, and more forceful policies were subsequently adopted. But it discarded much of the Heath legacy, including any thought of an INCOMES POLICY.

Right Honourable Gentleman The way in which a PRIVY COUNCILLOR must be referred to in the House of Commons at Westminster, with "and learned" added for a Queen's Counsel (university professors are not described as "learned") and "gallant" for a former senior military officer.

The Right Road for Britain The first comprehensive policy statement from Britain's CONSERVATIVE PARTY after World War II and its defeat in the 1945 election, drafted by R. A. (RAB) Butler and launched by CHURCHILL on 23 July 1949; marking a clear break from the negativism of pre-war years, it sold 2.2 million copies in the first three months. Its proposals foreshadowed the BUTSKELLITE line taken in government from 1951; it advocated the reform and modification of the WELFARE STATE created by Labour, and added a commitment to EQUAL PAY.

the Right Stuff The 1930s US Army slang phrase adopted by the author Tom Wolfe (1931–) to describe the special quality of steadiness and courage, going beyond routine bravery and excluding all those without it, required by America's fraternity of test pilots. Wolfe chose it as the title for his book (1979) on the trials and tribulations of the first US astronauts. It later attached itself to John Glenn, one of those astronauts, who had become a US Senator for Ohio and challenged for the Democratic Presidential nomination in 1984, just after the film of *The Right Stuff* went on release. However it soon emerged that Glenn lacked the right stuff to become President. Wolfe wrote:

> The idea was to prove at every foot of the way up . . . that you were one of the elected and anointed ones who had the right stuff and could move higher and higher and even – ultimately, God willing, one day – that you might be able to join that special few at the very top, that elite who had the capacity to bring tears to men's eyes, the very Brotherhood of the Right Stuff itself.

the right to be consulted, the right to encourage and the right to warn The three powers attributed to the SOVEREIGN in a Constitutional MONARCHY by Walter Bagehot in his *The English Constitution* (1867).

Right to Buy The trump card of the MANIFESTO on which Margaret Thatcher's Conservative Party fought and won the 1979 General Election: the granting to millions of families renting houses and flats from local authorities the right to buy them on easy terms. Many Labour councils resisted the "Right to Buy" drive, but it caught the imagination of over 2 million council tenants who not only bought their homes but, in many cases, switched their votes to the Tories in the next three elections.

right to keep and bear arms The right campaigned for by the NRA and other US gun-owners' groups whenever GUN CONTROL legislation is before Congress. It stems from the Second amendment to the Constitution, contained in the BILL OF RIGHTS:

> A well regulated militia being necessary to the security of a free state, the right of the people to keep and bear arms shall not be infringed.

The NRA has long argued that the Amendment does not simply refer to the maintenance of the NATIONAL GUARD, but to a right to keep guns for any purpose; however Congress was able to pass in 1934 an anti-gangsterism law regulating the sale and distribution of shotguns less than 18 inches long without its being ruled UNCONSTITUTIONAL.

right to kidnap The term used by critics for the June 1992 SUPREME COURT decision authorizing US agents to kidnap suspects abroad and bring them back for trial in the absence of a bilateral extradition treaty. The case arose from a 1990 kidnapping in Mexico, and was denounced by three dissenting justices and most Latin American leaders as a "judicial monstrosity".

> When we wake one day to learn that the director of the Federal Bureau of Investigation languishes in some Teheran prison after being abducted from his Washington home, we shall know that our Supreme Court, the custodian of our law-based state, has brought this outlaw code upon our heads. Sen. DANIEL PATRICK MOYNIHAN.

right to lie The notion, advanced by Assistant Secretary for Defence Arthur Sylvester after the CUBAN MISSILE CRISIS, that a Government has a "right to lie" in moments of national emergency. Sylvester's assertion that "the inherent right of the Government to lie to save itself when faced with nuclear disaster is basic" had some jurisdiction despite the furore it caused, but gave later generations of political leaders a cast-iron excuse for telling falsehoods to the American people.

Right to Life The demand of PRO-LIFE groups for the tightest possible restrictions on abortion, and if possible its total prohibition. The phrase dates back at least to the formation of the US National Right to Life Committee in 1970, and was soon in use on both sides of the

Atlantic. In Britain the lobby has had limited success, partly because David Steel's Bill broadly legalizing abortion was passed before the Right to Life lobby had fully mobilized in the late 1960s, and partly because it has refused to compromise when legislation such as the ALTON BILL and CORRIE BILL has been promoted to tighten it; when a more stringent time-limit on pregnancies was set, it was despite as much as because of the anti-abortion campaign. In America the pro-life campaign has been far more bitter, with picketing and even fire-bombing of birth control and abortion clinics. The Supreme Court did eventually, in 1992, tighten its earlier liberal ruling in ROE v. WADE, and George Bush signed more restrictive regulations just before leaving office, only for Bill Clinton to revoke them as one of his first executive acts.

Right to Work laws The laws passed by many Southern US states to limit the ability of labour unions to organize, and thus to encourage corporations to move their plants to the SUNBELT from more unionized States. They have had considerable success, though with the advent of the North American Free Trade Area (NAFTA) companies eager to cut costs were starting to move straight to Mexico.

New Right The combination of the moral MAJORITY, religious fundamentalists and LIBERTARIAN right-wingers who were galvanized into political action by such apparent liberal triumphs as the Supreme Court decision on abortion in ROE v. WADE and the PANAMA CANAL TREATIES, and eventually gave crucial support to Ronald Reagan's campaign for the Presidency.

to the right of Genghis Khan A widely-used phrase in 1980s Britain for someone with UNRECONSTRUCTED or alarmingly extreme right-wing views; it was frequently applied to the most fanatical THATCHERITES.

rights Those inalienable essentials to which humanity is supposedly entitled; the US Declaration of INDEPENDENCE lists them as "Life, LIBERTY AND THE PURSUIT OF HAPPINESS". Harry Weinberger, in a letter to the *New York Post* after America's declaration of war in 1917, asserted that "the greatest right in the world is the right to be wrong".

> The public good is in nothing more essentially interested, than in the protection of every individual's private rights.
> Sir WILLIAM BLACKSTONE, *Commentaries on the Laws of England* (1783).

> I am not interested in picking up crumbs of compassion thrown from the table of someone who considers himself to be my master. I want the full menu of rights.
> Archbishop DESMOND TUTU, 1985.

Rights of Man Thomas Paine's treatise on government that started as an inflammatory reply to Edmund BURKE, forced him to flee from England in 1792 when facing prosecution for treason, and earned him an honoured place as one of the theoreticians of the FRENCH REVOLUTION, despite his difficult nature. Paine's ideas struck a chord in Britain, where his demand for a WELFARE STATE created a sensation, in France where his defence of the Revolution was appreciated by its prime movers, and in America where his *Common Sense* had been a runaway best-seller.

Bill of Rights *See* BILL.

civil rights *See* CIVIL.

human rights *See* HUMAN.

women's rights *See* WOMEN.

ring-fencing In the budgetary process, the allocation of money to a particular programme on the understanding that it cannot be diverted to any other purpose, and that if the project is cancelled the cash must be returned.

Rinka The name of the dog belonging to the male model Norman Scott which was shot on Exmoor by Andrew Gino Newton in October 1975 to frighten Scott out of publicizing his past affair with the UK Liberal leader Jeremy THORPE. The attempt failed, and Thorpe was eventually disgraced, though acquitted of a charge of conspiring to murder Scott, who had been blackmailing him.

Riom trials The trials of a number of French politicians and military men, held from February 1942 before a supreme court set up by the VICHY government at Riom, just north of Clermont-Ferrand. Opponents of the COLLABORATIONIST regime of Marshal Pétain, including Edouard Daladier, Léon Blum, Paul Reynaud and Maurice Gamelin, were blamed for the fall of France in 1940. The trials were suspended indefinitely after two months and the accused spent the rest of World War II in prisons and CONCENTRATION CAMPS.

riot An act of mass violence against symbols of authority that either has begun as a political protest or has from the start been an expression of frustration. Martin Luther KING, urging the redressing of injustices before the patience of Black Americans finally ran out, said: "A riot is at bottom the language of the unheard."

> Black people have never rioted. A riot is what White people think Blacks are involved in when they burn down stores.
> JULIUS LESTER (1939–).

> A rioter with a Molotov cocktail in his hand is no more fighting for CIVIL RIGHTS than a Klansman with a sheet on his back and a mask over his face.
> President JOHNSON, speech in Washington, 20 August 1965.

Riot Act The Act of 1714 which gave magistrates in Britain the power to order rioters to disperse in the Sovereign's name, on pain of life imprisonment (originally death) if they persisted. The magistrate's action, which could not take place until twelve or more people had been rioting for an hour, was known as "reading the Riot Act". The Act was repealed as an archaism early in the 1980s – since when there have been numerous occasions when, according to some Conservative MPs, it would have come in handy.

communal riots Mass violence in the cities of the Indian sub-continent by Hindus against Muslims, and *vice versa*.

Gordon Riots *See* GORDON.

Rodney King riot *See* KING.

It took a riot The title of a MINUTE prepared for Margaret Thatcher in the late summer of 1981 by the then Environment Secretary Michael Heseltine (*see* TARZAN), which called for a major programme of investment in Britain's INNER CITIES and the giving of responsibility for a particular city each to Cabinet colleagues. It stemmed from the riots in Brixton (south London), Toxteth (Liverpool) and elsewhere that June. Officials were impressed, but Mrs. Thatcher believed spending extra on the inner cities would make it look as though rioting paid off, and stacked the decisive Ministerial committee against Heseltine. He was, however, allowed to develop a modest programme for Merseyside.

race riot *See* RACE.

Ripon Society A liberal, intellectual grouping in the US REPUBLICAN PARTY founded in 1962 and modelled on Britain's BOW GROUP. Named after the home city in Wisconsin of the party's founder, Alan Bovay, the society had strong Harvard connections. It put forward a number of radical policy ideas, including an all-volunteer army and a NEGATIVE INCOME TAX, but lacked the persuasive power to prevent the party moving right for a quarter of a century from Barry Goldwater's 1964 campaign.

rise In the US House of Representatives, the COMMITTEE OF THE WHOLE "rises" to report a Bill to the House with amendments that have been adopted; the House itself comes back into session, with the SPEAKER replacing the chairman of the relevant committee in the Chair.

Rise and Fall of the Great Powers *See* GREAT.

Rise of the House A Westminster term for the point at which either House ADJOURNS. The House is said to be UP.

rise to the occasion The classic *double-entendre* delivered in 1990 by the UK Armed Forces Minister Archie Hamilton (1941–) when asked how previously all-male crews of Royal Navy ships would react to the presence of servicewomen (Wrens) on board. Hamilton told them:

> I am sure they will rise to the occasion.

Risorgimento (Ital. rebirth, awakening) Italy's great national revival of the mid-19th century when Garibaldi and other patriots, and the diplomacy of Foreign Minister Cavour of Piedmont, reunited the country under a single crown. It involved the expulsion (with help from France) of the Habsburgs from Lombardy and Venetia, the overthrow of the BOURBON kingdom of Naples and Sicily, and the eclipse of the temporal power of the Vatican.

river. River Companies Shadowy commercial organizations, named after the rivers of England, through which the CONSERVATIVE PARTY has channelled much of its income from business and other sources for more than two decades. Their existence was unknown even to many in the party until the *Independent* tracked them down in 1989.

rivers of blood The speech on the consequences of coloured immigration delivered by Enoch POWELL in Birmingham on 20 April 1968 that led Edward Heath (*see* GROCER) to sack him from the SHADOW CABINET for exacerbating racial tensions – and made Powell the hero (unwitting or otherwise) of Britain's RACISTS, receiving 100,000 letters of support. Powell said:

> Those whom the gods wish to destroy, they first make mad. We must be mad, literally mad, as a nation to be permitting the annual inflow of some 50,000 dependants, who are for the most part the material of the future growth of the immigrant-descended population. It is like watching a nation busily engaged in heaping up its own funeral pyre. . . . As I look ahead, I am filled with foreboding. Like the Roman, I seem to see "the river Tiber foaming with much blood".

Powell, a former professor of classics, was quoting from Virgil, who in Book VI of the *Aeneid* had the Sybil prophesy to Aeneas of his return to Italy:

> I see wars, horrible wars, and the Tiber foaming with much blood.

He later said that he had been evoking a prophecy of doom, and not forecasting an actual bloodbath, but by then the damage was done. CHURCHILL had used a similar phrase in 1948 when, speaking in a less inflammatory context on European unity, he said:

> We are asking the nations of Europe between whom rivers of blood have flowed to forget the feuds of a thousand years.

Rivonia trial The year-long trial on "sabotage" charges of ANC activists in South Africa which culminated in Nelson Mandela and seven others being sentenced to life imprisonment on

12 June 1964. Mandela (who had been on the run for 17 months) and four others admitted sabotage, but argued that they had been driven to it because all legitimate forms of protest were barred to them. As the trial neared its close the UN SECURITY COUNCIL urged its abandonment, but Prime Minister Henrik Verwoerd said South Africa would not give in to any pressure even if the death penalty were imposed.

Robben island An island in Table Bay, 10 miles from Cape Town, which once housed a mental hospital and leper colony and became a secure prison for opponents of South Africa's APARTHEID government, including for many years the ANC leader Nelson Mandela.

Rochdale pioneers The founders of Britain's CO-OPERATIVE movement, who in 1844 opened their first shop in Toad Lane in the Lancashire mill town of Rochdale. Their basic principles were: membership open to all; democratic control with one member, one vote; limited interest on capital invested; and the distribution of the trading surplus in proportion to the amount spent. The Rochdale experiment was widely copied, and in 1869 the Co-operative Union was formed.

Rocky The nickname of **Nelson Rockefeller** (1908–79), four-term Governor of New York (Republican, 1966–73) and VICE-PRESIDENT of the United States from 1974 to 1977; he was nominated by Gerald FORD on his own succession to the Presidency in place of Richard Nixon. Rockefeller, who for years had formed a close team with his second wife HAPPY, died suddenly of a heart attack while working on an art book with his 25-year-old special assistant Megan Marshak; his press secretary unfortunately stated that the former Vice-President had been "having a ball" at the time.

Roe v. Wade The landmark judgment of the US SUPREME COURT on 23 January 1973 that struck down State laws imposing a total ban on abortion and in the eyes of its critics, virtually permitted abortion on demand. (The Roe in the case was a fictitious "Jane Roe", whose real name was Norma McCorvey). The decision enraged the PRO-LIFE movement, and paved the way for a 20-year campaign for tighter abortion laws and even a Constitutional ban on the practice, which gained the support of Presidents Reagan and Bush. In 1989 the Court, with a more conservative membership, voted 5 to 4 to uphold a Missouri law that restricted a woman's access to an abortion, and in 1992, in *Planned Parenthood v. Casey*, further tightened the regime – though not enough for hard-line anti-abortionists.

roll, to Washington slang for putting together a coalition to outvote someone who appears to have a majority, *e.g.* a Republican President pushing a programme through the House against the wishes of a Democratic Speaker.

roll call (1) In the US Congress, a vote where each member has to answer by name; in the House, with 435 voting members, the process can take 25 minutes. In the Senate asking for a roll call is a means of delaying business, but a Senator making the request loses the FLOOR. In the 1890s one Senator whose mind was on other things is supposed to have called out: "Not guilty!" when the clerk read out his name. (2) The weekly newspaper of Congress, which keeps inhabitants of the Capitol village, legislators and STAFF alike, in touch with events of common interest.

rolling programme A programme of spending on capital projects which lasts for a number of years, new schemes being budgeted for as others finish.

roll up that map; it will not be wanted these ten years The exclamation made by PITT THE YOUNGER in December 1805 on hearing the news of Napoleon's victory at Austerlitz. He was correct almost to the month; Bonaparte's sway over the continent only ended in 1815.

Rome. Treaty of Rome The basic legal text governing the establishment, structure, powers and development of the EUROPEAN COMMUNITY. It was in fact concluded in Brussels on 17 April 1957, and signed by the six founder members of the EC: France, Germany, Italy and the BENELUX countries. The Treaty has been substantially amended since, notably by the ENLARGEMENT of the Community, the SINGLE EUROPEAN ACT and the MAASTRICHT TREATY.

Roman Question *See* LATERAN TREATY.

Rooker-Wise amendment The UK legislation under which the annual BUDGET and FINANCE BILL provides for the automatic indexation of tax allowance thresholds in line with INFLATION unless the Commons specifically decides otherwise. It was the brainchild of the Labour MPs Jeff Rooker (1941–) and Audrey Wise (1935–), who in June 1977 pushed through their amendment with Conservative support, against the wishes of the Labour Government which desperately needed the £40 million it cost in tax revenue.

> It has created a great panic and it looks as if the Government is falling apart at the seams.
>
> TONY BENN, *Diaries*, 14 June 1977.

Roosevelt corollary The expansion of the MONROE DOCTRINE by President Theodore Roosevelt (*see* TEDDY) to provide for active US intervention in unstable central American nations. In his State of the UNION message to Congress in December 1901, Roosevelt announced:

> Chronic wrongdoing, or an impotence which results in a general loosening of the ties of civilized society, may [compel the United States] to the exercise of an international police power.

His initiative was spurred by threats of force from France, Italy and Belgium against the Dominican Republic for non-payment of its debts. Roosevelt and subsequent Presidents went on to intervene in the Dominican Republic, Haiti and Nicaragua.

Roosevelt's four freedoms The vision and parameters for the future of a secure world (implicitly after the defeat of Nazi Germany) set out by Franklin D. Roosevelt in his State of the UNION message on 6 January 1941, eleven months before America entered WORLD WAR II. FDR said:

> In the future days, which we seek to make secure, we look forward to a world founded upon four essential freedoms. The first is FREEDOM OF SPEECH and expression - everywhere in the world. The second is the freedom of every person to worship God in his own way - everywhere in the world. The third is freedom from want - which, translated into world terms, means economic understandings which will secure to every nation a healthy peacetime life for its inhabitants - everywhere in the world. The fourth is freedom from fear - which, translated into world terms, means a world-wide reduction of armaments to such a point and in such a thorough fashion that no nation will be in a position to commit an act of physical aggression against any neighbour - anywhere in the world.

Rosebery, Archibald Philip Primrose, 5th Earl of Rosebery (1847–1929). The IMPERIALIST Liberal aristocrat who was Gladstone's successor as Prime Minister for a brief but disastrous spell. Twice Foreign Secretary - managing to combine the post with the chair of the LCC, he appeared the obvious heir to the GRAND OLD MAN and succeeded him in 1894 after the "Blubbering CABINET". He had always shown a marked lack of enthusiasm, saying "So be it" to Gladstone when first offered the Foreign Office, and once confiding:

> The secret of my life, which seems to me sufficently obvious, is that I have always detested politics.

And when Gladstone retired, Sir William Harcourt told Rosebery: "Without you the government would have been ridiculous. With you, it is only impossible." As Prime Minister he showed from the start the languor and lack of consistent interest that was to mark the rest of his political life, ASQUITH soon writing: "The leadership of the Liberal party, so far as I am concerned, is vacant." The next year his Government was mercifully defeated in the CORDITE VOTE and lost the ensuing election, Rosebery characteristically commenting:

> There are two pleasures in life. One is ideal, the other real. The ideal is when a man receives the seals of office from his sovereign. The real pleasure comes when he hands them back.

Rosebery remained, uneasily, as party leader until 1896, when he roused himself from his inertia and resigned - Harcourt accusing him of "funking the future he saw before him" - then began a decade of sporadic activity which raised repeated and tantalizing suspicions of a comeback. This was heightened by his active support for the BOER WAR. On 19 July 1901 Rosebery said in London:

> For the present, at any rate . . . I must plough my own furrow alone. That is my fate, agreeable or the reverse. But before I get to the end of that furrow it is possible that I may find myself not alone.

Asquith, near the end of his patience, accused him of "ploughing the sands". Rosebery's political interest continued to splutter, to the frustration of the party leadership, throughout the Edwardian era. But he concentrated increasingly on writing political biographies, and on his real love - horse racing; he owned three Derby winners.

> He sought the palm without the dust.
>
> Rosebery's tutor at Eton.

> When he tries to roar like a lion, he only brays like an ass.
>
> General Sir GARNET WOLSELEY.

> He never missed an occasion to let slip an opportunity.
>
> GEORGE BERNARD SHAW (*compare* PLO).

> By marrying a young Rothschild, becoming Prime Minister and winning the Derby he demonstrated that it was possible to improve one's financial status and run the Empire without neglecting the study of form.
>
> CLAUD COCKBURN.

Rose Garden At the WHITE HOUSE, the garden outside the French doors of the OVAL OFFICE, where the President traditionally receives foreign dignitaries and recipients of the CONGRESSIONAL MEDAL OF HONOR. Occasionally it is used for Press conferences or State dinners. The first roses were planted by President WILSON's first wife Ellen in 1913; the garden was redesigned in 1962 by Mrs. Paul Mellon at John F. KENNEDY's request. In 1976 Gerald FORD updated the FRONT PORCH CAMPAIGN by adopting what became known as a **Rose Garden Strategy** - spending much of the PRIMARY campaign firmly rooted in the White House appearing Presidential. He abandoned it when it was clear Ronald Reagan was mounting a serious challenge for the Republican nomination; Reagan described Ford's campaigning style as "a sure winner if all you want is the horticulture vote". In 1981, at the height of controversy about Interior Secretary James Watt, Reagan told a dinner in New York:

He would be here, but he's working on a lease for strip-mining the Rose Garden.

Rosenberg spy case The case of the US couple Julius (1918–53) and Ethel Rosenberg (1915–53), who were arrested in 1950 on suspicion of supplying the Soviet Union with atom bomb secrets, and were executed three years later. The episode, at the height of the COLD WAR and McCARTHYISM, was an uncanny echo of the SACCO AND VANZETTI case during the RED SCARE after World War I. The case was based largely on the evidence of Harry Gold, a Soviet agent, and David Greenglass, Ethel Rosenberg's brother, who worked at the Los Alamos research base (*see* MANHATTAN PROJECT); both had been exposed by the arrest of Klaus FUCHS. Greenglass – one of three others convicted – claimed that his own spying, which he admitted in return for leniency, was instigated by the Rosenbergs, both of whom protested their innocence throughout. The main physical evidence was two halves of a *Jell-o* box said to have been used by the spies to identify each other. The political climate of the time and the outbreak of the KOREAN WAR – of which the trial judge accused them – gave the Rosenbergs little chance of acquittal. They were sentenced to death in March 1951, but a series of appeals and stays of execution (coupled with worldwide pleas for mercy and demonstrations) prolonged the agony until 19 June 1953, when they were electrocuted in Sing Sing prison. The Rosenbergs would have been REPRIEVED if they had confessed, but they steadfastly refused. The question of their guilt or innocence has yet to be resolved, and may never be; however latest research suggests that Julius Rosenberg was indeed guilty, but that his wife was framed by the FBI in a vain attempt to pressure her husband into revealing his full espionage activities.

I can only say that, by immensely increasing the chance of an atomic war, the Rosenbergs may have condemned to death tens of millions of innocent people all over the world. President EISENHOWER.

Ethel wants it made known that we are the first victims of American fascism.
JULIUS ROSENBERG, on the day of their execution.

Fascism is not defined by the number of its victims, but by the way it kills them. JEAN-PAUL SARTRE.

rostrum (Lat. a beak) A platform for an individual public speaker; the original *Rostra* in the Forum of ancient Rome were adorned with the prows, or beaks, of captured ships.

rosy scenario The nickname given by White House aides and economists to the forecasts for the impact of REAGANOMICS prepared in 1981 by Budget director David Stockman. Their author had realised at the time that the predictions, including a balanced Budget by 1984, were wildly out of line. *See also* the Triumph of POLITICS.

rottweiler A UK term for a ruthless political fighter who savages his or her opponents; it became current in the late 1980s when the rottweiler became first a popular pet and guard dog, and then notorious for savaging young children.

Rotunda The 180ft-high circular hall at the centre of the US CAPITOL, beneath the Dome, where 25 of the most famous Americans including Presidents LINCOLN, Garfield, McKINLEY and KENNEDY and the Unknown Soldiers have lain in state. One cynic remarked that it was "built so the statesmen will find it easier to run round in circles". Completed in 1824 in time to welcome the visiting LAFAYETTE, its walls are adorned with oil paintings, four by John Trumbull depicting scenes from the AMERICAN REVOLUTION, and four depicting colonial events; one by John Chapman on *The Baptism of Pocahontas* includes a six-toed Indian. The Rotunda's fresco, started by Constantino Brumidi, also shows scenes from early America; the bronze doors by Randolph Rogers, depicting events in the life of Columbus, were cast in Germany and hung in 1871. The Rotunda was the scene of the first attempted assassination of a President, Andrew Jackson in 1835, and in 1852 Henry Clay was the first politician to lie in state there. It was converted into a 1500-bed military hospital during the CIVIL WAR, and in 1985 staged President Reagan's second INAUGURATION because of severe weather.

Rouges (Fr. reds) The Radicals in 19th-century QUEBEC who were a powerful force in the formation of Canada's LIBERAL PARTY.

Rough Riders The 1st regiment of the US Cavalry Volunteers in the SPANISH-AMERICAN WAR, which was organized by Theodore Roosevelt and gave critical impetus to his political career; it got its nickname from the cowboys of Buffalo Bill's Wild West show. Roosevelt was not in fact their commander – that task fell to Leonard Wood who had military experience – and the Rough Riders actually fought on foot in Cuba, having left their horses in Florida. TEDDY feared after the chaotic engagement of San Juan Hill on 1 July 1898 in which the victorious but inexpert US forces lost one-tenth of their men that they would in the end be defeated, but the Spanish defenders proved even more inept and he returned a hero.

round. round robin Originally a joint letter of mildly subversive nature with all the signatures in a circle so that none would appear the ringleader; now any proposal collectively signed by several people and sent to higher authority.

Round Table conference A conference between nations or disputing parties at which a point is made of giving all the participants equal status, with none monopolizing the CHAIR. The idea comes from the legendary Round Table of CAMELOT round which all King Arthur's knights were seated to make sure none predominated. One significant Round Table conference was that initiated by RAMSAY MACDonald's Labour government in London in 1930 on the future of India, to which all interested parties including MAHATMA Gandhi were invited.

round-tabling A Washington term for submitting a proposal to open discussion by all the members of the CABINET or other responsible body before a final decision is taken on it.

Who is Mr. Round and why does he object? *See* WHO.

royal. Royal Assent The point at which an ACT of Parliament in any of the countries of which the British Sovereign is Head of State becomes law. It is signified at Westminster by a brief ceremony in the HOUSE OF LORDS (*see also* la REYNE LE VEULT).

Royal Brute of England The abusive nickname for King George III popularized during the AMERICAN REVOLUTION by the radical English migrant Thomas Paine (*see* COMMON SENSE; RIGHTS OF MAN).

Royal Commission In Britain, a vehicle for conducting the most thorough investigation into some area of public policy where a new direction is needed. Normally composed of the GREAT AND THE GOOD, such Commissions take a couple of years to report, and the Government is not bound to accept their recommendations. Margaret Thatcher refused to set any up, preferring to put her theories into practice in the certainty that they would work; in 1991, after a series of miscarriages of justice had come to light, John Major reactivated the process by setting up a Royal Commission on Criminal Justice. In Australia Royal Commissions are more frequently set up, often to enquire into a highly specific matter, such as the deaths of Aboriginal suspects in police custody.

> A broody hen sitting on a china egg. MICHAEL FOOT.
>
> They take Minutes and waste years. HAROLD WILSON.

Royal family The collective term for the House of WINDSOR: the Sovereign and their immediate family, and those less closely related who nevertheless carry out official engagements and whose activities can give rise to embarrassing headlines in the tabloids. The Royal family, like the institution of MONARCHY, has gone through phases of public reverence, indifference and hostility. In 1894 Keir Hardie (*see* QUEER HARDIE) wrote in the *Labour Leader*:

> The life of one Welsh miner is of greater commercial and moral value to the British people than the whole Royal crowd put together, from the Royal great-grandmama down to the puling Royal great-grandchild [the future King Edward VIII].

Royal prerogative The provision of Britain's unwritten CONSTITUTION under which the Government of the day may act without reference to Parliament. In February 1993 a heated but largely academic row broke out over whether John MAJOR's government could sign the MAASTRICHT TREATY under the Royal prerogative if Parliament failed to RATIFY it. The general view was that it might technically be free to do so, but that such a course of action would be politically suicidal.

Royal We The use by a reigning monarch of the plural in talking about themselves, as in "we are not amused", Queen Victoria's reaction to an off-colour joke. Margaret Thatcher incurred public ridicule by declaring of a new addition to her family: "We are a grandmother".

RSG (1) Regional Seats of Government. The subterranean headquarters built during the COLD WAR so that each region of Britain would have its own government in the event of nuclear war. A CND offshoot **Spies for Peace**, published the locations of the RSGs early in 1963, and embarrassed the Government even more by revealing which bureaucrats would be whisked to safety when the FOUR-MINUTE WARNING went. (2) RATE/REVENUE SUPPORT GRANT. The principal instrument by which central government in Britain channels funds to local authorities to supplement taxes raised locally.

rubber. Rubber bullets *See* BULLET.

Rubber chicken *See* CHICKEN.

rubber stamp A legislature which has been so denuded of real power that it merely confirms the actions of the EXECUTIVE.

> The Senate is not meant to be a rubber stamp and is not going to be a rubber stamp.
>
> Majority Leader Sen. ROBERT BYRD, 1976.

ruffles and flourishes The brief musical introduction played just before the PRESIDENT of the United States makes his appearance at many official engagements. The ruffles were customarily drumbeats, the flourishes the tune picked out by the brass.

rule (1) To govern a nation. Louis de St. Just, advocating the trial of Louis XVI in the French National Assembly on 13 November

1792, put forward the ANARCHIST argument that "no one can rule guiltlessly". The leftist James Connolly, one of the leaders of Ireland's EASTER RISING, was convinced that "those who rule industrially will rule politically", and H. L. Mencken cautioned:

> The urge to save humanity is almost always a false face for the urge to rule it.

Rule, Britannia The boisterously defiant national song originating in Britain's maritime tradition, which is sung irreverently at the Last Night of the Proms but still has a patriotic expression. It was woundingly sung by a number of Tory BACKBENCHERS when CHAMBERLAIN fell in May 1940 (*see* YOU HAVE SAT HERE LONG ENOUGH). *Rule, Britannia* was written just 200 years before by the Scottish poet James Thomson (1700–48) as part of the libretto for Thomas Arne's masque *Alfred*; the first stanza runs:

> When Britain first, at Heaven's command
> Arose from out the azure main,
> Arose, arose, arose from out the azure main,
> This was the charter, the charter of the land
> And guardian angels sang this strain:
> "Rule, Britannia! Britannia, rule the waves!
> Britons, never, never, never will be slaves!"

Rule of Law The vital concept behind a truly democratic state, that principles of justice, fairness and due process are applied automatically and indiscriminately to all by every organ of the State and the legal and law-enforcement system.

> If you are a murderer or a rapist you will still have the protection of the rule of law. But if you are a political danger to rulers, you will have none.
> ALAN PATON, on South Africa, 1976.

(2) A regulation: In the US Congress the rules (the equivalent of STANDING ORDERS at Westminster) govern the conduct of business. Speaker Thomas Reed (*see* CZAR) once asserted:

> The only way to do business inside the rules is to suspend the rules.

Rules Committee The fulcrum of the HOUSE OF REPRESENTATIVES, which through its power to set the agenda for debate can accelerate or block the progress of any Bill. Its history has thus been marked by struggles between its members and the House as a whole for control. Speaker Joe Cannon (*see* FOUL-MOUTHED JOE) made himself chairman of the Rules Committee in 1903 and appointed every member, thus gaining a personal VETO on all legislation; Republican INSURGENTS removed him from the committee in 1910, making it responsible to the House. From the 1930s to the early 1960s it was dominated by a coalition of southern Democrats and conservative Republicans who frustrated progressive legislation; a reforming move in 1949 to force any Bill out of the committee after 21 days was reversed two years later. The Committee even refused to send on an Eisenhower administration Bill authorizing Federal funding for school construction to a House-Senate CONFERENCE after both Houses had passed it. This dictatorial regime was broken in 1961 when the House expanded the committee to ensure that its chairman, Rep. "Judge" Howard Smith of Virginia, could be outvoted. It still flexes its muscles occasionally; when in 1974 it blocked legislation that would have safeguarded North Carolina farmers and wildlife against a new dam, the columnist Colman McCarthy branded it:

> A government within a government, a mediaeval court of magnificos and viziers that holds terrifying power over people's lives and uses that power without fear of accountability.

> The Rules Committee has an almost complete power to determine in important issues whether the rest of us can vote at all.
> Rep. MORRIS UDALL.

> Counted on to keep off the FLOOR bills that would embarrass too many members.
> TOM WICKER.

rules of engagement The parameters set for those ordered to carry out a military operation by their political masters. In the case of the FALKLANDS they aroused particular interest because of the controversy over whether the torpedoing of the General BELGRANO fell within the Rules of Engagement.

Manual of Rules The "Bible" that determines how the US SENATE conducts its business.

ruling class *See* CLASS.

rum. rum, Romanism and rebellion The anti-Catholic crack which probably cost James G. Blaine the Presidency in 1884. It was uttered on 29 October by the Rev. Samuel Burchard as he welcomed the Republican nominee to a meeting of supportive Protestant clergy in New York. Burchard, quoting a remark made about the Democrats by Garfield in 1876, ended:

> We are Republicans, and don't propose to leave our party and identify ourselves with the party whose antecedents have been Rum, Romanism and Rebellion.

Blaine and most of the audience missed the punchline, but a reporter contacted the Democrats, who were stunned that he had not disowned it; the Cleveland campaign immediately flooded Irish-American neighbourhoods with FLIERS carrying the remark. The day got even worse for Blaine; he went on to a banquet at Delmonico's with some of America's wealthiest men which lowered his credibility still further. On election day, he lost New York by 1149 votes – and with it the election.

rum, sodomy and the lash Winston CHURCHILL's devastating response when a Naval officer objected that a wartime operation the Prime Minister was supporting ran against the traditions of the Royal Navy. Churchill responded:

> Don't talk to me about Naval tradition! After all, what is it? Rum, sodomy and the lash!

The phrase was popularized in the mid-1980s as the title of an album by the Irish folk-rock group the Pogues.

rumour factory A tightly-knit, almost incestuous community where the atmosphere creates unlikely rumours which are often taken seriously. Washington and its various political and bureaucratic forcing houses is regarded as such, but it is not in the same league as the City of London, where political rumours have an effect on the market in inverse proportion to their credibility.

Rump The nickname given to the remnant of England's Long Parliament that was ejected by Oliver Cromwell in April 1653 (*see* YOU HAVE SAT HERE LONG ENOUGH); also to the later remnant of that same Parliament that was restored in May 1659 after Cromwell's death, and dissolved by General Monk the following February prior to the Restoration of King Charles II, which its members strongly opposed.

run The US word for contesting a vacancy for elective office, the UK equivalent being to STAND. The British historian Hugh Brogan explained:

> In England, of course, we stand for election; in more dynamic America they run.

Colorado state senator Martin Hatcher (1927–) tried to put running for office into context: "Running for the third Congressional district is my second priority. My first is swimming naked through a pool of piranhas."

I do not choose to run for President in 1928 The deadpan words, despatched by telegram, with which President Coolidge (*see* SILENT CAL) opted out of running for a second full Presidential term.

You can run, but you can't hide A phrase associated with the US world heavyweight champion Joe Louis (1914–81); he used it before his victory over Billy Conn in 1946, but probably did not invent it. President Reagan used it in 1985 as a warning to all international terrorists after the hijacking by Palestinian extremists of a TWA airliner to Beirut; Neil KINNOCK taunted John MAJOR with it in 1991 when the Tories fought shy of calling a General Election they might well have lost.

run-off A decisive electoral contest between two candidates after a first poll involving a larger number, none of whom has obtained a clear majority.

running against Washington *See* WASHINGTON.

running-dogs *See* DOG.

running-mate The candidate for VICE-PRESIDENT running on the same ticket as a particular Presidential nominee, or *vice versa*.

Russell building The first and most easterly, of the three huge office buildings erected for the US Senate on Capitol Hill. Named after Sen. Richard B. Russell of Georgia (1897–1971), it was authorized in 1904 and opened in 1909; it stands at the corner of Constitution and Delaware Avenues, and is the terminal of the SENATE SUBWAY.

Russia. Russia has two generals on whom she can rely – Generals Janvier and Février The axiom of Tsar Nicholas I (1796–1855), delivered in respect of the role of the terrible winter of 1812 in driving Napoleon from Moscow but whose reality was borne home even more horribly to the invading Germans as they froze on the Russian front from 1941 to 1944.

A riddle wrapped inside a mystery inside an enigma CHURCHILL's words on the ambiguities of Soviet policy in the early weeks of WORLD WAR II, delivered in a radio broadcast on 1 October 1939. They were prompted by the Soviet occupation of East Poland on 18 September, in league with the Germans. At the time Britain had little idea whether the HITLER-STALIN PACT would stick, or whether Stalin realized that Germany would inevitably turn against him and was simply being opportunistic. Churchill's phrase has often been used out of historical context, as if it were a general reflection on the Russian national character. He said:

> I cannot forecast to you the action of Russia. It is a riddle wrapped in a mystery inside an enigma.

Nothing has changed Russia's policy. Her methods, her tactics, her manoeuvres may change, but the pole star – world domination – is immutable Not an astonishingly frank admission by one of Soviet Russia's Communist leaders or even an expansionist TSAR, but the assessment of Karl MARX, made in a speech in London on 22 January 1867.

Russian revolution The process of ferment and, eventually, violence beginning with the overthrow of TSAR Nicholas II early in March 1917, the establishment of a provisional government under KERENSKY, the mobilization of LENIN's BOLSHEVIKS to seize power in the OCTOBER REVOLUTION, the introduction of COMMUNISM and the ruthless crushing of all opposition, and eventual victory for the RED ARMY in a bitter CIVIL WAR. Lenin, on returning to the FINLAND STATION in Petrograd on 16 April 1917, told his supporters:

> I greet you as the advance guard of the world proletarian army. The hour is not far off when . . . the German people will turn their weapons against their capitalist exploiters. The sun of the socialist revolution has already risen.

CHURCHILL, as a member of a government which had had to finish the war against Germany without support from Russia, said in April 1919:

> Every British and French soldier killed last year was really done to death by Lenin and Trotsky – not in fair war, but by the treacherous desertion of an ally without parallel in the history of the world.

Sixty years later, before the collapse of the Soviet state was widely foreseen, the DISSIDENT Roy Medvedev declared:

> The Russian people have moved forward, not by way of religious uplift but through revolution, and despite all their disappointments . . . they will leave our descendants not a religious heritage but socialism and democracy.

Russo-Japanese War The conflict in 1904–05 in which the Japanese inflicted a crushing defeat on the Russians, establishing themselves on the world stage with shattering force. The Japanese were determined to crush all Russian power in Korea and Manchuria and to establish their own HEGEMONY in the area. In February 1904 they launched a pre-emptive strike against Port Arthur on the tip of Manchuria's Liaotung Peninsula, which inflicted serious damage on the Russian fleet at anchor there. Port Arthur was then besieged by Japanese land forces, surrendering in January 1905. The conflict between the opposing armies in central Manchuria was less decisive. However in May 1905, in the Battle of Tsushima, the Japanese fleet under Admiral Togo inflicted severe losses which brought the Russians to the conference table. By the Treaty of Portsmouth in September 1905, the Russians surrendered Port Arthur and half of Sakhalin to Japan as well as evacuating Manchuria. Japan's victory dramatically torpedoed the myth of the superiority of White Europeans over Orientals, but its effect on Russia was immediate and traumatic: loss of confidence in the TSARIST system leading within months to the REVOLUTION OF 1905, and a switch of interest by the KREMLIN from Asia to expansion in Europe, stoking up the fires in the Balkans that generated WORLD WAR I. *See also* DOGGER BANK INCIDENT.

> I have today seen the most stupendous spectacle it is possible for the mortal brain to conceive – Asia advancing, Europe falling back, the wall of mist and the writing thereon.
>
> Lt.-Gen. SIR IAN HAMILTON on the Battle of Liaoyang (*A Staff officer's Scrap Book during the Russo-Japanese War*, 1907).

Rustbelt The opposite of SUNBELT, the traditional "smokestack" industrial areas of the North-eastern United States, from which production and jobs have been shifted to the less unionized and lower-cost South, or even abroad.

Ryrie rules The rules in WHITEHALL governing the circumstances under which NATIONALIZED industries could borrow on the open market to fund investment, which essentially stated that they could not do so without appearing as a charge on the PSBR. A classic of orthodoxy, they were blamed by Labour, and some of the industries concerned, for hampering the development of those industries, and encouraged their managements to welcome Tory PRIVATIZATION plans from the early 1980s. The rules were devised by and called after William Ryrie (1928–), when Under-Secretary at the Treasury's Public Sector Group in the early 1970s; he was later UK representative at the IMF, and Second Permanent Secretary in turn at the Treasury and the Overseas Development Administration.

S

S The complete middle name of US President Harry S Truman (*see* GIVE'EM HELL HARRY). It was a compromise by his parents who could not decide between Shippe (his paternal grandfather's middle name) and Solomon (his maternal grandmother's Christian name).

S&L scandal The crisis that broke in 1989, at the start of the BUSH administration, with the collapse of a number of savings and loan institutions, which had taken advantage of lack of regulation in the Reagan years and made excessive payments to their own executives and imprudent loans and investments. In 1982 Congress, most of whose members had received campaign contributions from S&Ls, had passed legislation removing the restriction limiting their investment activity to home mortgages. The ensuing bonanza led to 15% out of over 3000 S&Ls becoming insolvent or close to it; of the hundreds taken over by the federal government at an initial cost to the taxpayer of $166 billion, 60% were riddled with fraud. The ramifications of the scandal reached into the US Senate (*see* KEATING FIVE).

Sacco and Vanzetti The electrocution of the Italian ANARCHIST immigrants Nicola Sacco and Bartolomeo Vanzetti on 23 August 1927 for killing two men in a payroll robbery at a South Braintree, Mass., shoe factory on 15 April 1920 became a *cause célèbre*. Their trial and conviction in a Massachusetts court in July 1921 passed largely unnoticed by the US public, but news of the case aroused radical indignation in Europe, provoking demonstrations and attacks against US property in Europe and South Africa. Publicity about these events divided opinion in America between those who believed they had been convicted because of their political beliefs and those who felt that those beliefs compounded their guilt. Evidence that the two men were victims of mistaken identity was strengthened by the dignified demeanour of the defendants themselves, but an independent commission appointed by the Governor of Massachusetts upheld their conviction. They were refused clemency and executed, prompting a silent demonstration by 250,000 in Boston, bomb explosions in New York and Philadelphia and protests throughout the world.

> Never in our full life could we hope to do such work for tolerance, for justice, for man's understanding of man as we now do by accident. VANZETTI's last letter.

SACEUR Supreme Allied Commander Europe, the Brussels-based head of all NATO forces in Europe.

sachem An office-holder of TAMMANY HALL, the term coming from an Indian word for leader.

sacred cow A programme or institution that cannot be interfered with because of popular sentiment. From the Hindu reverence for the cow and its consequent immunity from slaughter in India.

Saddam Hussein still has a job. Do you? Democrats' bumper sticker in the 1992 US presidential campaign contrasting George BUSH's failure to oust the Iraqi leader with the effects of the domestic recession.

safety. Safety First The slogan of Britain's governing Conservatives under Stanley BALDWIN in the 1929 election. Taken from a road safety campaign, it implied a risk in voting for radical Labour or Liberal policies; a minority Labour government under RAMSAY MACDonald was elected, only to collapse two years later.

> My unhappy constituents did not want "safety". Safety meant the dole. They wanted work. So they very properly voted me out. HAROLD MACMILLAN.

safety net Limited social provision by the State, concentrated on protecting those suffering greatest hardship or disadvantage, as opposed to a comprehensive WELFARE STATE. In his successful 1992 campaign for the Presidency, Bill Clinton (*see* COMEBACK KID) argued instead for a "springboard", to provide the disadvantaged with opportunities.

Sailing the seas depends on the helmsman One of the great propaganda anthems of Communist China in the 1960s, dedicated to CHAIRMAN MAO Tse-Tung.

Saint. St. Stephen's entrance The public entrance to the Palace of WESTMINSTER, halfway along the building. It leads up through an ante-chamber on the site of **St. Stephen's Chapel**, where the Commons sat from 1547 until the fire of 1834, and up again to the Central LOBBY.

Salads Pejorative term for Britain's Social and Liberal Democrats (abbreviated to SLD), formed in 1988 by the merger of most of the Liberal Party and a majority of the Social Democrats. The name was refined the next year to "LIBERAL DEMOCRATS", but the original and the abbreviation remained in use.

salami tactics The post-war Hungarian Communist leader Matyas Rakosi's term for his successful operation in repeatedly slicing off the most moderate remaining sections of the non-Communist left until a hard-line rump remained which could be merged with the Communist Party.

salary grab The 50% pay increase, retroactive for two years, which US Senators and Congressmen voted themselves – along with the President (whose salary was doubled) and the judiciary – in 1873. The millionaire Massachusetts Congressman Ben Butler thought less affluent members needed the money – and said any legislator not worth it should resign. Public anger was such that Congress was forced to repeal the rises the following year, though a Constitutional technicality meant that Supreme Court justices kept their back pay. Butler lost his seat.

Salisbury, Robert Arthur Talbot Gascoyne-Cecil, 3rd Marquess of (1830–1903). Leader of the Conservative Party 1881–1902 (jointly with Sir Stafford Northcote until 1885) and three times Prime Minister, 1885–86, 1886–92, 1895–1902. The last great Victorian political leader, and probably the most REACTIONARY since Wellington. He took an Olympian but low-key and detached view of affairs, though haunted by the fear of social revolution. Joseph Chamberlain told a meeting that Salisbury "constitutes himself the spokesman of a class, of the class to which he himself belongs, who 'toil not, neither do they spin'". And Lord Curzon termed him "that strange, powerful, inscrutable and brilliant obstructive deadweight at the top". Yet he could be a forceful speaker; Disraeli described him as "a great master of jibes and sneers" and G. W. E Russell wrote: "The combination of such genuine amiability in private with such calculated brutality in public utterance is a psychological phenomenon." Lord Randolph Churchill was a particular target; asked after Churchill's resignation as Chancellor whether he would have him back, Salisbury replied: "Have you ever heard of a man who, having had a boil on his neck, wanted another?" He had earlier observed: "I have four departments: the Prime Minister's, the Foreign Office, the Queen and Randolph Churchill; the burden of them increases in that order." On Sir Michael Hicks Beach, he observed: "He would make a very good Home Secretary, and hang everybody." Salisbury said of himself: "I rank myself no higher in the scheme of things than a policeman, whose utility would disappear if there were no criminals." Though his foreign policy was consistent and he presided over peace in Europe and expansion of the EMPIRE, Bismarck described him as "lath painted to look like iron".

Salisbury convention The doctrine formulated by the 6th Marquess (*see* BOBBETY) as Leader of the Opposition in the HOUSE OF LORDS to ATTLEE's Labour government. It lays down that the Tory peers may use their inbuilt majority to amend, but not defeat, legislation for which the electorate has clearly voted. Successive leaders of Tory opposition peers have had to strike a balance between avoiding a constitutional crisis and mounting an effective attack on legislation the party sees as damaging or misguided.

Salo Republic The puppet FASCIST government established by Mussolini on Lake Garda in October 1943 after German paratroopers under Otto Skorzeny had rescued him from Allied custody. Firmly under Hitler's thumb, the Salo Republic nominally controlled the portion of Italy still under Nazi occupation until early 1945, when the DUCE tried to flee the country and was captured and shot by Communist PARTISANS.

SALT Strategic Arms Limitation Talks. The SUPERPOWER negotiations on reducing ballistic missiles (ICBMs), begun by Presidents Johnson and Brezhnev in 1969, which led to a **SALT 1** treaty signed by Presidents Nixon and Brezhnev in 1972 and **SALT II** concluded by Presidents Carter and Brezhnev in 1979. SALT I was RATIFIED by the Senate and took full effect, technically expiring in 1977 but continuing to be observed. SALT II was never ratified because the Soviet invasion of Afghanistan intervened, but was observed by the US until 1986.

Saltire The cross of St. Andrew, diagonal white on dark blue, the national flag of Scotland.

Saltley, "battle of" The mass picket of a Birmingham coke depot in support of the 1972 British MINERS' STRIKE which established Arthur Scargill as a national figure and virtually settled the dispute in the National Union of Mineworkers' favour.

samizdat Unauthorized, and therefore "underground", literature published and circulated by dissidents in Soviet Russia – some directly political, much simply out of step with the cultural tone permitted by the regime. An abbreviation of the Russian *samizdatelstvo*, self-publishing house, it was first used in English in the mid-1960s.

sample In opinion polling, a group selected as representative of the electorate as a whole.

sampling error Faulty selection of a sample which produces a rogue POLL.

Samuel Commission The Government inquiry under Sir Herbert Samuel set up early in 1926 to settle a coal strike caused by mineowners cutting wages and extending working hours. Its report did not achieve its purpose; the TUC subsequently called the GENERAL STRIKE in an unsuccessful effort to win the dispute for the miners.

San. San Clemente The compound on the California coast, midway between Los Angeles and San Diego, to which Richard Nixon retired after his resignation over WATERGATE in 1974.

San Francisco conference The meeting of 46 nations which settled the UNITED NATIONS charter, signed on 25 June 1945, and created the structure for the world organization. Though a momentous occasion, it was overshadowed by President Roosevelt's death shortly before, CHURCHILL's absence as his government sought (and failed to win) re-election, and STALIN's refusal until the last minute to let Foreign Minister Molotov attend.

sanctions Steps taken by one nation, or a concert of nations, against a state that has transgressed against international law or basic morality – or is claimed to have done so. They were first used as a form of law-enforcement by the LEAGUE OF NATIONS against Italy in the 1930s after its invasion of Abyssinia – also setting the precedent that sanctions are seldom effective. When America was advocating them against Japan before World War II, Anthony EDEN observed: "There were two kinds of sanctions, effective and ineffective. To apply the latter was provocative and useless. If we were to apply the former, we ran the risk of war." More recently they were imposed against Rhodesia after UDI; when Zimbabwe's President Robert Mugabe wanted them tightened, Margaret Thatcher told him: "If you want to cut your throat, don't come to me for a bandage." There was also a long-running campaign, partially successful, for international sanctions against South Africa in protest against APARTHEID. And as F. W. de Klerk began his reform programme, Nelson Mandela insisted: "Sanctions must remain until apartheid is eradicated." The UNITED NATIONS imposed sanctions against Iraq following Saddam Hussein's invasion of Kuwait, and these were continued after the end of the GULF WAR.

sanctions-busting The use of subterfuge or sheer brazenness by the nation being isolated and by its suppliers to evade sanctions (*see* BINGHAM REPORT).

Sandinistas The leftish Sandinist National Liberation Front which took power in Nicaragua after the overthrow of the dictatorial President Anastasio Somoza-Debayle and which ruled until defeated in elections in 1990. Named after August Cesar Sandino, an insurgent leader murdered in 1934, the movement was founded in 1962 as an anti-Somoza guerrilla group – finally ousting him 17 years later in an offensive launched from Costa Rica and Honduras. Once in power under President Daniel Ortega Saavedra, the Sandinistas came under attack from the CONTRAS, guerrillas who included right-wing Somoza supporters but came to include some former Sandinistas. Washington saw the Sandinistas as Communists and a threat to regional peace; the backing the Contras received from the US during the Reagan administration gave rise to the IRAN-CONTRA affair. Ceasefire talks in 1988 led to free elections, which Sandinista supporters throughout the world expected them to win. In conceding defeat to the National Opposition Union's Violetta Barrios de Chamorro, Ortega declared:

> We, the Sandinistas, have given Nicaragua this democracy and peace.

SANROC The South African Non-racial Olympic Committee, one of the bodies that led the sporting boycott of South Africa in protest against APARTHEID which was almost totally effective for a quarter of a century.

sans-culotte (Fr. without breeches) Originally derisive term for a radical or REVOLUTIONARY, dating back to the French Revolution. The poor people of Paris wore trousers (pantaloons) instead of the knee-breeches worn by the upper classes. In cartoons lampooning the revolutionaries, the sans-culottes were depicted completely unclothed below the waist. It has come to represent the lowest class in any revolutionary or anarchic movement.

Sarajevo The capital of Bosnia and flashpoint of 20th-century Europe, from the assassination that started WORLD WAR I to the bloody siege in 1992–93 as Serb forces tried to oust Croats and Muslims through ETHNIC CLEANSING. Sarajevo first gained infamy on 28 June 1914 when the Archduke Franz Ferdinand, heir to the Habsburg throne, was shot by 19-year-old Gavrilo Princip (1895–1918), a Bosnian Serb and member of the violently nationalist BLACK HAND GANG. The shot fired in the name of Serb independence from Austria reverberated round the world. Austria despatched a humiliating ULTIMATUM to Serbia, which was only partly accepted. Austria then declared war on Serbia on 28 July. This in turn prompted the mobilization of Russia in solidarity with Serbia, which provoked Germany to declare war on Russia (1 August) and France (3 August). Germany then invaded Belgium in accordance with the SCHLIEFFEN PLAN, prompting Britain to declare war on Germany (4 August) in defence of Belgian NEUTRALITY. The spot where Princip fired the fatal shot is marked by two footprints in the pavement. The football manager Brian Clough, shown them when in Sarajevo with his Derby County team, observed:

> If I'd just shot an Archduke I wouldn't stand around with my feet in wet cement.

Sarajevo returned to the headlines in 1992 when, after Croatia's secession from Yugoslavia, Bosnia declared itself independent and a three-way battle for territory broke out, with the Serbs best armed. A UNITED NATIONS operation to fly in relief supplies to Sarajevo was only possible after France's President Mitterrand braved the threat of artillery and snipers' bullets to visit the city, much of it reduced to rubble.

satellite countries Small nations adjacent to and firmly under the control of a larger one – specifically the Communist nations of Eastern Europe, under rigid Soviet control during the COLD WAR. The implication is that the satellites have no will of their own. The word was first used in a political sense in 1776 by Thomas Paine, in denying such a connection between America and Britain.

Saturday Night Massacre One of the pivotal events of the WATERGATE crisis, which led directly to the House of Representatives empowering its Judiciary Committee to consider IMPEACHMENT proceedings against President Nixon. On 20 October 1973 Nixon ordered Attorney-General Elliot Richardson to fire the Watergate SPECIAL PROSECUTOR Archibald Cox, because Cox was seeking key tapes of Nixon's conversations in the White House. Richardson refused, and resigned. Deputy Attorney-General William Ruckelshaus also refused, and was fired. Nixon then promoted Robert Bork, Solicitor-General, to acting Attorney General; he fired Cox and abolished the office of special prosecutor. All the resignations were announced by the White House that Saturday night. The Congressional and public reaction was so hostile that three days later Nixon offered to release the tapes Cox had sought, and re-establish the special prosecutor's office. But he never recovered his position.

sausage. custodians of the national sausage Harold WILSON's scornful description of the Heath government in terms of its failure to get INFLATION under control. It came in a speech during the February 1974 election campaign in which Wilson reeled off a series of price increases in stable foods, culminating with the rise in the price of sausages.

threat to the British sausage The phrase used by EURO-SCEPTICS to characterize the propensity of Brussels to interfere in everyday aspects of British life. There has indeed been an effort by the European Commission to determine what sausages in member states must contain. But it was a case of life following art, as the words were first used in an episode of YES, MINISTER when the fictional Minister Jim Hacker was able to redeem his reputation by detecting a plot in Brussels to "standardize" the British sausage out of existence.

SAVAK The notorious secret police of the Shah's regime in Iran, prior to his overthrow in 1979. With over 60,000 agents, SAVAK was active in monitoring and curbing dissent in Iranian communities throughout the world as well as at home.

Save, Save the Argylls The slogan of the successful campaign waged in the late 1960s for the exemption of the Argyll and Sutherland Highlanders from merger with another regiment of the British Army under the Labour government's defence cuts.

Save the Whales The most emotive, and best-known, slogan of ecological campaigners from the mid-1970s. It became a global term not only for the battle to keep traditional whaling nations like Japan and Norway from resuming the slaughter, but generally GREEN campaigning.

Say it loud, I'm Black (gay) and I'm proud Originaly the title of a song by James Brown, the phrase was taken up as a slogan of self-belief in the late 1960s by Black activists in America. Before long, GAY RIGHTS activists were chanting their own version.

scab The greatest insult in Britain's labour and trade-union movement. Directed (and frequently chanted) against workers brought in to break a strike. *See* BLACKLEG.

scapegoating The practice of singling out an individual or group and blaming them for the failure of a policy or a situation of acute political or economic difficulty.

> The [1990] elections raised the prospect that one of the most dismal traditions of American political life might be revived: that of scapegoating racial minorities in times of trouble. E. J. DIONNE Jr., *Why Americans Hate Politics*.

schedule An appendix to a BILL or an ACT of Parliament, listing specific matters to which the measure applies.

Schengen group The group of European Community countries – not including Britain – which moved to co-ordinate their police and immigration functions in advance of the MAASTRICHT TREATY. From 1 January 1993 Germany, France, the BENELUX countries, Italy, Spain and Portugal agreed to remove border controls and institute complete freedom of movement between them; however to make "Schengenland" work, they had to tighten frontier controls with the rest of the EC.

Schicklgruber The surname of Adolf Hitler's father, Alois Schicklgruber (1837–1903), an official in the Austrian Imperial customs, whose mother, Maria Anna Schicklgruber, conceived him by Johann Georg Heidler, whom she married in 1842. Alois kept his mother's surname until he was nearly 40, when he adopted the name Hitler, based on a local priest's misspelling. The FÜHRER went to considerable lengths to conceal his ancestry, though details were dredged up by opponents of the NAZIs in the early 1930s. And when CHURCHILL wanted to make his contempt for Hitler most evident, he would describe him as "Herr Schicklgruber". No firm evidence has ever substantiated Hans Frank's claim at the NUREMBERG TRIALS that Hitler's father was the child of a Jew from Graz, named Frankenberger, in whose household Maria Anna became pregnant while working as a maid.

> HEIL SCHICKLGRUBER!
> Headline in an Austrian newspaper during the July 1931 German elections.

Schleswig-Holstein question The dispute between Denmark and Prussia, which flared sporadically between 1848 and 1866, over two duchies lying between them; they were eventually incorporated into Prussia.

> There are only three men who have ever understood it; one was Prince Albert, and he is dead; the second was a German professor who became mad; I am the third and I have forgotten all about it. PALMERSTON.

Schlieffen Plan The plan on which Germany eventually fought WORLD WAR I, devised by Count von Schlieffen (1833–1913), chief of staff 1890–1906. It envisaged a war on two fronts, against France to the west and Russia to the east. Schlieffen's strategy for a quick victory was to hold off Russia with minimal forces, then overwhelm the French armies by a massive flanking movement through neutral Belgium, thus avoiding the formidable barriers along France's eastern border. Germany's main forces would then be free to confront the Russians who, it was assumed, would be slow to mobilize. The plan was initially successful when implemented in August 1914 by Schiieffen's successor, Helmuth von Moltke. But Moltke had modified the blueprint by weakening the crucial right wing of the German advance from 90% to 60% of the total forces. At the Battle of the Marne in September, the Allies halted the advance of the German First Army under General Alexander von Kluck. The subsequent trench warfare marked the failure of the modified strategy, and on 14 September the hapless Moltke was replaced by the German Minister of War, Erich von Falkenhayn.

> When you march into France, let the last man on the right brush the Channel with his sleeve.
> Count von SCHLIEFFEN.

schools you can walk to A phrase used by candidates in US elections as shorthand for "no Blacks", usually when competing for blue-collar ethnic votes. It stems from the advent of BUSING *c.* 1970, when some school districts began transporting White children to schools in overwhelmingly Black areas to create a racial mix. To promise "schools you can walk to" quickly became the code for a commitment to fight busing of white children out – and of Black children in – to previously all-White schools. Even liberal candidates would use the phrase, as it looked harmless out of context and was often essential to their chances of getting elected.

Schuman Plan The plan put forward in 1950 by the French Prime Minister **Robert Schuman** (1886–1963) which was the genesis of first the EUROPEAN COAL AND STEEL COMMUNITY, and eventually of the EC itself. Ostensibly a proposal to pool French and German coal and steel production, it was designed to go much further and tie the two countries so closely together that another war between them would be impossible. Britain's Labour government refused to join in, a decision Dean Acheson termed "the greatest mistake of the post-war period". And while Churchill praised it from opposition, he stayed out on his return to power the following year.

> Not just a piece of convenient machinery. It is a revolutionary, and almost mystical conception.
> HAROLD MACMILLAN, Strasbourg, 15 August 1950.

SCLC Southern Christian Leadership Conference. The organization headed by Dr. Martin

Luther KING which assumed the leadership of the CIVIL RIGHTS movement in the late 1950s. It brought about many of the gains of the following decade, and outlived its founder. Formed in Atlanta in January 1957, the SCLC was from the outset committed to non-violent Direct ACTION to back up the campaigning of the NAACP which was falling foul of racist violence; its initial title 'The Southern Christian Leaders Conference on Transportation and Integration' reflected the bus boycotts (*see* MONTGOMERY) being waged at the time. The SCLC's Crusade for Citizenship began with 22 simultaneous mass meetings across the South on 12 February 1958; from 1961 it attacked the literacy problem with "citizenship schools". The Student Non-Violent Co-ordinating Committee (SNCC) was an offshoot of the SCLC.

> There has been nothing in the annals of American social struggle to equal this phenomenon, and there probably never will be again. BAYARD RUSTIN (1912–87).

Scoop The nickname of Sen. Henry Jackson (1912–87), the heavyweight Democrat who combined strong support for liberal domestic policies with a HAWKISH line toward defence and the Soviet Union. Co-author of the JACKSON-VANIK AMENDMENT and a strong opponent of the SALT agreements, he made an unsuccessful bid for the Presidency in 1976. The nickname "Scoop" was given him at the age of four by his sister; when a young man he was known as **Soda Pop Jackson** because of his crusade as a moralistic district attorney against prostitution and bootlegging. A Washington state Congressman from 1940 and Senator after 1952, he was responsible for the pioneering National Environmental Policy Act.

Scopes case The trial in July 1925 of a Dayton, Tennessee, schoolmaster for teaching the theory of evolution to his high school biology class. John Scopes had challenged a newly-passed State law prohibiting the teaching in its schools of "any theory that denies the story of the divine creation of man as taught in the Bible . . . and that man has descended from a lower order of animals". The case, headlined as the "monkey trial", turned into a *cause célèbre*; Clarence Darrow led for the defence, while William Jennings Bryan (*see* PRAIRIE AVENGER), making his final contribution to American history, was one of the prosecution team. Scopes was found guilty and fined $100, but the Fundamentalist case attracted world-wide ridicule and it was six decades before Creationism, as it is now known, regained serious political adherents.

> There is no more reason to believe that man descended from some inferior animal than there is to believe that a stately mansion has descended from a small cottage. WILLIAM JENNINGS BRYAN.

Scorecard The US SECRET SERVICE's codename for Vice-President Dan QUAYLE.

Scotland Bill The measure introduced by James Callaghan's Labour government which offered DEVOLUTION to Scotland, subject to a REFERENDUM. It succeeded a combined measure for Scotland and Wales, which ran out of Parliamentary time. The Bill passed in 1978, but only after anti-devolutionist Labour MPs had hitched on the CUNNINGHAM AMENDMENT which contained the seeds of the proposal's defeat.

Scotland free in '93 The slogan on which the Scottish National Party (SNP) fought the 1992 General Election, substantially increasing its vote but emerging with just three seats, the same as in 1987. It reflected the party's target of winning 37 Scottish seats – a majority – which they would then treat as a MANDATE to negotiate independence from the UK. The SNP leader Alex Salmond had the slogan sprung on him, and would have preferred something more cautious. The Conservative Minister Lord James Douglas-Hamilton capped it with **"on the floor in '94"** if the SNP did achieve its aims.

Scotland United The militant HOME RULE movement formed after the setback of the 1992 General Election, when the SNP and the pro-DEVOLUTION parties all lost seats. Its founders included Labour and Nationalist MPs; contacts between them angered the Labour leadership which saw the group as a STALKING HORSE for the SNP. Scotland United's leaders insisted that their aim was to force the REFERENDUM to which Labour, after the 1992 election was committed. Their first initiatives included rallies in Glasgow and Edinburgh, disrupting the House of Commons and threatening to paralyse South-east England by abandoning cars on the M25; more effectively they rallied 25,000 supporters outside the Edinburgh EC Summit in December 1992.

Scott. Dred Scott case The explosive US Supreme Court decision in March 1857 which ruled the MISSOURI COMPROMISE unconstitutional and made the CIVIL WAR almost inevitable. It concerned an illiterate slave, originally from Virginia, who had drifted away from his owner and was freed in Missouri by the son of his first master. The court proceedings to give Scott that freedom ended with first the Missouri Supreme Court and then the Supreme Court itself ruling that he was still a slave. By seven to two, the justices ruled that slaves could not become US citizens, and so could not sue in the nation's courts – and that slavery was valid in Missouri despite the painful compromise reached by Congress 37 years before.

scramble. scramble for Africa *See* AFRICA.

scrambler A telephone used by political leaders, the senior military and others in sensitive positions. Calls to and from it are "scrambled" electronically, so that anyone tapping the line will not be able to decipher what is being said.

Scrap of Paper The description of the 1839 Treaty of LONDON made in August 1914 by the German Chancellor Theobald von Bethmann-Hollweg (1856–1921). Under the Treaty the UK was committed to defending Belgian NEUTRALITY, which was violated by Germany's invasion (in accordance with the SCHLIEFFEN PLAN) on 4 August, following its declaration of war on France and Russia. On 3 August Britain informed Germany that it would stand by the treaty; this prompted Bethmann-Hollweg's contemptuous reply to the British ambassador Sir Edward Goschen:

> Just for a word – "neutrality", a word which in wartime has so often been disregarded – just for a scrap of paper, Great Britain is going to make war on a kindred nation which desires nothing better than to be friends with her.

screening The process under which a country's security authorities check the background of present or potential public servants to ascertain their "trustworthiness, patriotism and integrity". In Washington the word also covers lie-detector tests on Federal officials in sensitive posts. In 1983 President Reagan sought to make such tests compulsory for thousands of bureaucrats; he dropped the plan after a furore in Congress but in 1985, 4863 non-intelligence officials in the PENTAGON alone took lie-detector tests. Secretary of State George Shultz said of the move to introduce the tests:

> The moment in this government I am told I am not trusted is the day I leave.

scrutineers In many forms of ballot, particularly in political parties and trade unions, the functionaries who supervise the voting process and announce the result. In Britain's LABOUR PARTY their role was critical until the adoption of a computerized recorded VOTE in the mid-1980s, with union leaders and others regularly claiming – often for tactical reasons – that their votes had been miscounted. After one such dispute, the blind Labour MP David Blunkett declared:

> Next time the scrutineers will be me and my dog.

scuttle The withdrawal of a colonial power from its overseas possessions with indecent haste, without any warning, or creation of a governmental structure to take over. On 20 December 1946 Winston CHURCHILL told the Commons on negotiations for the independence of Burma:

> The British Empire seems to be running out almost as fast as the American loan. The steady and remorseless process of divesting ourselves of what has been gained by so many generations of toil, administration and sacrifice continues. . . . This haste is appalling. "Scuttle" is the only word that can be applied.

SDECE (Fr. *Service de Documentation et Contre Espionnage Extérieur*, Service for documentation and external counter-espionage) The highly-effective external arm of France's security and intelligence services, which is backed up by a formidable team of analysts in Paris.

SDI Strategic Defence Initiative. *See* STAR WARS.

SDLP Social Democratic and Labour Party. The mainly Roman Catholic party in NORTHERN IRELAND which takes a moderate NATIONALIST position, favouring POWER-SHARING and closer links with the Irish Republic. Founded in 1973, it has competed from the start for Catholic votes with SINN FEIN, which advocates all-out support for the IRA's campaign of terrorism. In the 1992 General Election under John Hume's leadership it won four of the province's 17 seats at Westminster, ousting Sinn Fein president Gerry Adams from his party's only seat.

SDP Social Democratic Party. The party launched on 16 March 1981 by the GANG OF FOUR defectors from the Labour Party, which for brief moments in the early to mid-1980s looked as if it might achieve its aim of BREAKING THE MOULD of British politics. The SDP gained its impetus from the strife in the Labour Party as the BENNITE left came close to taking control, and from widespread initial support from voters who had never previously taken an interest in politics; Roy Jenkins (*see* WOY) had anticipated it in his EXPERIMENTAL AIRCRAFT speech the previous year. It soon attracted 30 MPs – 29 from Labour, one from the Conservatives – and briefly topped 50% in the opinion polls; under Jenkins it began negotiating an ALLIANCE with David Steel's LIBERAL PARTY. The SDP's middle-class image and moderate policies which led to them being known as "soggy Dems" attracted ridicule from Labour and the Tories alike. Roy Hattersley accused them of "trying to build a land fit for credit-card holders", Norman Tebbit described them as "like a bunch of bananas – green round the edges, soft in the middle and not quite straight", while the political journalist Walter

Terry simply termed them "the bland leading the bland". Many of the jokes revolved around Jenkins's love of good claret; the Conservative Party chairman Lord Thorneycroft remarked:

> I had rather thought of joining myself. After all it isn't a party, it hasn't a programme and I'm told the claret is good.

And Francis Pym, the Conservative Defence Secretary, dismissed their policies as "stale claret in new bottles – a confidence trick not to be mistaken for the elixir of life".

The SDP won spectacular BY-ELECTION victories at Crosby (Shirley Williams) and Glasgow Hillhead (Jenkins) but was squeezed hard by the FALKLANDS FACTOR and won only six seats in the 1983 election. Under David Owen it developed a sharper edge with such slogans as "Caring but Daring" and "Tough but Tender", but tension with the Liberals weakened its appeal, and despite a further breakthrough at Greenwich in 1987 it lost further ground in the 1987 election. Warfare immediately broke out in the SDP over Steel's efforts to force a merger with the Liberals, and it split, a majority under Robert Maclennan eventually merging to form the LIBERAL DEMOCRATS and a rump SDP under Dr. Owen continuing until 1990, when it collapsed after finishing behind the OFFICIAL MONSTER RAVING LOONY PARTY in the Bootle by-election.

> A social democratic party without deep roots in the WORKING-CLASS movement would quickly fade into an unrepresentative intellectual sect. ROY JENKINS, 1972.

> The heterosexual wing of the Liberal Party.
> SHIRLEY WILLIAMS.

> *Speaker at the SDP's 1986 conference:* What have the Liberals got that we haven't got?
> *Voice:* MPs.

SDS Students for a Democratic Society. One of the seminal groups of America's NEW LEFT, founded in 1959 at the University of Michigan by Al Haber and Tom Hayden. By 1962 it was protesting on campus against research which might embroil America in a VIETNAM WAR, against the chemical firm producing NAPALM and against the presence of the ROTC (Reserve Officers' Training Corps). It set out a range of liberal and idealistic principles in the 1962 PORT HURON STATEMENT, but was gradually hijacked by extremist militants set on violence, and was eclipsed as the ANTI-WAR movement got under way; nevertheless a number of its activists matured into the mainstream of a Democratic Party which itself had become more radical.

seal (1) The ultimate symbol of approval by the SOVEREIGN POWER dating back at least 1200 years, a wax seal applied to a document bearing the emblem of that power (in the UK the monarch), the seal generally being kept by the LORD CHANCELLOR, and in America the President. (2) Seals of office. In the UK, the emblems of authority granted by the CROWN to SECRETARIES OF STATE, and surrendered by them on their resignation or dismissal.

sealed train The train in which the German authorities despatched Lenin and his closest associates from exile in Switzerland to Russia in 1917, lighting the fuse for the RUSSIAN REVOLUTION. The train was sealed to prevent the revolutionaries contaminating the people with their ideology as they passed through German-held territory.

Seanad (Ir. Senate) The upper house of the Parliament of the Irish Republic; it does not have a power of VETO over decisions taken by the DAIL.

Searchlight (1) The US SECRET SERVICE codename for President Nixon. (2) In Britain, a trenchantly anti-FASCIST paper produced by the crusading journalist Gerry Gable, which for a generation has exposed extreme right-wing groups and highlighted what he sees as instances of their infiltration into mainstream British life.

seasonally adjusted Referring to economic statistics published monthly or quarterly, which are adjusted to eliminate seasonal fluctuations, caused for instance by fine summer weather boosting tourism, winter snows shutting down the construction industry or the pre-Christmas shopping boom.

> With seasonally adjusted temperatures you could eliminate winter in Canada.
> ROBERT STANFIELD (1914–), Progressive Conservative leader.

seat The place a legislator occupies in the CHAMBER, and thus the thing he or she acquired by being elected. The strength of parties in any legislature is tallied in terms of seats, not of individuals.

> Timid and interested politicians think much more about the security of their seats than about the security of their country. THOMAS BABINGTON MACAULAY (1800–59).

seat of government The building, complex of buildings or city from which a government exercises its authority.

marginal seat *See* MARGINAL.

open seat In US elections, a seat where there is no INCUMBENT running for re-election.

safe seat A seat traditionally held by one party, which is considered highly unlikely to change hands.

target seats *See* TARGET.

seated and covered In the UK HOUSE OF COMMONS, the formal term for the condition in which a member may raise a Point of

ORDER during a DIVISION. The Speaker will not acknowledge members raising such a point unless they are sitting in their place, and wearing the top hat kept for such contingencies.

SEATO South East Asia Treaty Organization. An organization for mutual defence against "Communist aggression" and for economic co-operation, formed on the model of NATO. The treaty was concluded in Manila on 8 September 1954 by Australia, the UK, France, New Zealand, Pakistan, the Philippines, Thailand and America; Laos, Cambodia and non-Communist Vietnam were given "protection". China saw it as a threat and immediately began shelling QUEMOY AND MATSU; India, Burma, Ceylon and Indonesia felt it an unnecessary provocation and refused to join. But SEATO proved toothless, and after 1964 the UK, France and Pakistan reduced their commitment to avoid becoming involved in the VIETNAM WAR. In 1975, with Vietnam, Laos and Cambodia under Communist control the treaty was ended, the remaining non-Communist Asian nations forming the non-military ASEAN for mutual economic aid.

secession The term used in the years preceding America's CIVIL WAR for the threatened withdrawal of certain slave states from the UNION. It recalled the secession of the plebs in ancient Rome, when the representatives of the lower orders of free citizenry pulled out of the Republic's government. After Abraham LINCOLN's election in 1860 South Carolina led the first states out of the Union; by his inauguration in March 1861 seven states had gone and war was inevitable.

> The constitution of the United States forms a government, not a league . . . secession does not break a league, but destroys the unit of a nation.
>
> ANDREW JACKSON, anti-NULLIFICATION proclamation, 1832.

On 7 January 1861 Sen. Robert Toombs said of the secessionists:

> They appealed to the Constitution, they appealed to justice, they appealed to fraternity, until the constitution, justice and fraternity were no longer listened to in the legislative halls of their country, and then they prepared for the arbitrament of the sword; and now you see the glittering bayonet, and you hear the tramp of armed men from your capital to the Rio Grande.

Second Front Now! The slogan pushed by the UK (and after PEARL HARBOR, the US) Communist Parties between the Nazi invasion of the Soviet Union in 1941 and the D-Day landings three years later. Its purpose was to pressure Britain, the US and their allies to invade occupied France at the earliest possible moment so as to divert Nazi forces from the Russian Front. Establishing a Second Front was a matter of urgency for STALIN, who feared his Western allies would let the Soviet Union and Germany fight each other to extinction. In May 1942 Molotov, the Soviet Foreign Minister (*see* NIET!), was promised in Washington and London that a second front would open soon to relieve the pressure; the next month CHURCHILL told Roosevelt that US plans to invade France in 1942 were unrealistic, and in August he explained this to Stalin. However in October 1942 Allied landings (Operation Torch) did take place in North Africa. Churchill was determined there should be no invasion until success was assured and sufficient UK forces were available; at CASABLANCA in January 1943 it was again postponed, and a British plan for invading Sicily adopted. With domestic political pressure growing, Churchill agreed at the QUEBEC Conference of August 1943 that France should be invaded on 1 May 1944; **D-Day** eventually took place on 6 June. Though German forces mounted stiff resistance to the invaders, they were by now retreating in the east; the time taken to open the Second Front meant that instead of the West rescuing Stalin, the Soviet leader was able to dictate the post-war shape of central Europe.

> There is no doubt that the absence of a second front in Europe considerably relieves the position of the German Army, nor can there be any doubt that the appearance of a second front on the Continent of Europe – and this undoubtedly will appear in the near future – will essentially relieve the position of our armies to the detriment of the German Army.
>
> STALIN, radio broadcast, 6 November 1941.

Second Reading Despite its title, the first consideration of a Bill by either House at WESTMINSTER. The First Reading is a formality; the Second generally involves a full day's debate on the principle of the measure (sometimes less, occasionally two days), culminating in a DIVISION; if passed, the Bill goes to a STANDING COMMITTEE for LINE-BY-LINE consideration. In the US HOUSE OF REPRESENTATIVES, the term applies to the procedure in the COMMITTEE OF THE WHOLE when a Bill is read section by section, with members having the right to offer amendments to each section in turn, and speak on them for up to five minutes.

seconder Where two sponsors are required for a MOTION or an AMENDMENT in any political forum, the proposer must find a seconder to give public support to the proposal before a vote can be taken.

secondary action *See* PICKETING.

Secret. Secret Intelligence Service *See* MI6.

secret police In all TOTALITARIAN states and

some others, a shadowy body whose purposes are to gather intelligence about opponents of the regime, arrest them or worse (*see* DEATH SQUADS) and instil fear into the population, ensuring that they acknowledge resistance to be useless. Some secret police forces, like Hitler's GESTAPO or the Soviet KGB, had a high profile on occasions and a clearly-known structure; others like East Germany's STASI concentrated on undercover work, often clandestinely inducing members of suspected DISSIDENT families to inform on each other.

Secret Service The body, operating under the auspices of the US TREASURY, which affords protection to the President and other public figures who might be at risk – alongside their original role of protecting the currency. The Secret Service were purely Treasury investigators until 1901 when agents were drafted to protect President Theodore Roosevelt in the wake of McKINLEY's assassination; the VICE-PRESIDENT has only been protected since 1951, and the Presidential family, President-elect and former Presidents more recently still. Members of the Secret Service detail accompanying the President are clearly recognizable, as they are continually scrutinizing the crowds. Out of the spotlight their duties remain the protection of the person they guard from attack. When the secret serviceman assigned to protect President Ford's teenage daughter Susan was asked what he would do if one of her dates became unexpectedly amorous, he replied:

> I'm there to protect her from other people, not from herself.

secret session A session of a legislature from which the Press and public are excluded, generally on grounds of national security. The HOUSE OF COMMONS regularly met in secret session throughout World War II, and nothing of substance ever LEAKed from the debates.

secret treaty or **protocol** An agreement concluded between countries who desire all or part of it to remain confidential; it may involve plans to attack or dismember another state, or might prove fatal in terms of domestic politics. The renunciation of secret treaties was one of WILSON'S FOURTEEN POINTS.

> All there is to do is publish the secret treaties, then close the shop.
>
> TROTSKY, after becoming Soviet COMMISSAR for Foreign Relations in 1917.

Official Secrets Act *See* OFFICIAL.

Top Secret Services or governmental information about which the greatest secrecy is observed. There is a hierarchy of epithets for information that is CLASSIFIED; "top secret" is for the eyes and ears of only a very few, **secret** may be shared a little more widely, and "restricted" is available to a somewhat larger number.

secretary. secretary-general The chief executive officer of the UNITED NATIONS, responsible for implementing the decisions of the SECURITY COUNCIL and GENERAL ASSEMBLY.

Secretary of State (1) The Presidential appointee who conducts America's FOREIGN POLICY; as well as being head of the STATE DEPARTMENT and consequently of the foreign service, the Secretary of State is the senior member of the Cabinet and the principal member of the Administration after the President. The most dramatic confirmation of this was the addressing to Secretary of State Henry KISSINGER of Richard Nixon's letter resigning the Presidency. President KENNEDY observed that "everybody wants to be Secretary of State", and the post is indeed highly sought after for the influence and ACCESS that it generally commands; however in the early Nixon years it was overshadowed by that of NATIONAL SECURITY ADVISER.

sectarianism (1) In NORTHERN IRELAND and elsewhere where religion is a determining factor in politics, the pursuit of policies supposedly designed to further one religious faction at the expense of another. (2) In especially left-wing politics, the fragmentation of a movement as proponents of slightly varying ideologies or strategies pursue them with quasi-religious zeal and intolerance.

Securitate The hated SECRET POLICE of the Romanian dictator Nicolae Ceauşescu (1918–89). They remained loyal to the Communist autocrat after his capture, trial and execution in December 1989, fighting running gun battles with the army (who had joined in the popular uprising) and firing at random into crowded streets. They were supposedly eliminated after a week of fighting believed to have left more dead than any other European conflict since World War II and the civil wars in Yugoslavia; however a number secretly regrouped after the advent of democracy and continued campaigns of terror against ethnic Hungarians, gypsies and advocates of a break with the past.

security The degree of protection afforded to a nation by a combination of a sound defence, often in alliance with others, and an unambiguous foreign policy, which is considered adequate to remove the threat of attack.

> There is no security on this earth; there is only opportunity. General DOUGLAS MACARTHUR (*attr.*).

> If all that Americans want is security, they can go to prison.
>
> DWIGHT D. EISENHOWER, Speech at Galveston, 8 December 1949.

The difference between defence and security is much the same as the difference between sex and love.
ALAIN LAMASSOURE, French MEP, 1991.

security clearance The confirmation required from a security or intelligence agency that a certain person is loyal and trustworthy enough to handle sensitive information.

Security Council The main executive organ of the UNITED NATIONS, with the primary responsibility for the maintenance of international peace and security. The UK, America, France, Russia and China sit on it as of right (*see* PERMANENT MEMBERS), and ten other nations (originally six) serve for two years by rotation. The Council has proved more effective than the LEAGUE OF NATIONS in maintaining COLLECTIVE SECURITY because of its range of military, economic and diplomatic sanctions for use against member states, yet these powers have been only intermittently successful. During the COLD WAR effective action was often blocked by use of the VETO by the two SUPERPOWERS to prevent action against their own interests. The UN intervention in the KOREAN WAR, for instance, was only possible because of the Soviet Union's absence from the Council. The first test of the Council's effectiveness since the Cold War was its successful mobilization of forces from enough member states to expel the Iraqis from Kuwait in March 1991 (*see* GULF WAR); however the strife after the disintegration of Yugoslavia has proved a much tougher nut to crack.

security forces A frequently used umbrella term for the forces of law and order in a society afflicted by terrorism, embracing the police, the military and sometimes more sinister organs of the State.

security risk A person of doubtful loyalty, whose background and associations make their employment in state service inadvisable, especially in posts that involve access to confidential information likely to be useful to a hostile government. Unfortunately officialdom's idea of a security risk did not always accord with the facts; throughout the COLD WAR innocuous individuals suffered through unjustified suspicions, while committed Communist agents sometimes operated with impunity for years.

national security *See* NATIONAL.

SED (Ger. *Sozialistiche Einheitspartei Deutschlands*, German Socialist Unity Party) The party which ruled East Germany throughout the state's existence, under a series of mainly colourless and always unprepossessing leaders subservient to the KREMLIN. It was formed prior to the creation of the "German Democratic Republic" through a forced absorption of Social Democrats in the Soviet zone of occupation into the Communist Party. Many members of the SPD refused to co-operate, and either fled to the West or were forced out of politics.

sedentary position The term used in the HOUSE OF COMMONS to describe the situation of a member in his or her seat, especially when they interrupt without rising to catch the SPEAKER's eye. The Labour Shadow Minister Gwyneth Dunwoody claimed that only Mrs. Thatcher's Cabinet favourite Nicholas Ridley (*see* GERMAN RACKET) was able to "strut from a sedentary position"; the accusation had earlier been levelled against Thomas DEWEY.

sedition A political action held or alleged to be directed at the undermining of the state; any act against the state short of TREASON. As a criminal charge, it is most often brought against the publishers of provocative or inflammatory articles.

segregation The separation of the races, notably as practised in the American South and beyond until the 1960s as a means of DISCRIMINATING against the Black population. Well-meaning White politicians long accepted segregation as legitimate, Woodrow WILSON telling Black leaders in 1913 that it was "not a humiliation but a benefit", and Eisenhower saying in 1948: "If we attempt to force someone to like someone else, we are fast going to get into trouble." **Segregationists** were those Southerners who held out for RACIST policies and practices as CIVIL RIGHTS legislation began to bite, under George Wallace's slogan of "Segregation now, segregation tomorrow and segregation forever". Martin Luther KING condemned the practice as

The offspring of an illicit intercourse between injustice and immorality.

Sejm The UNICAMERAL Parliament of Poland, both under Communist rule and under democracy.

Select Committee A body set up by a legislature to investigate or monitor a particular topic or range of activities. In the US Congress the system is highly developed; at Westminster, apart from the PAC, the Select Committees enjoyed limited power and prestige until a system directly linking a specific committee to the work of most individual government departments took effect in 1979–80. Brought about by the then Leader of the House Norman St. John-Stevas (later Lord St. John of Fawsley), the new system has been patchily effective, but showed its mettle during the WESTLAND and SUPERGUN affairs.

selection conference Under the system used by the UK LABOUR PARTY until the mid-1980s for selecting Parliamentary candidates, a meeting of a constituency party's General Management Committee before which SHORT-LISTed applicants would appear and which would select the Prospective CANDIDATE by ballot. Such meetings were criticized by advocates of OMOV because party members as a whole had no direct say, and such a committee could be hijacked by an ENTRYIST or extremist group out to DESELECT the sitting member in a Labour-held seat.

selectmen The annually-elected administrators, whose origins date back to the 17th century, who provide local government in some New England townships.

self. self-basting The devastating adjective, normally applied to oven-ready turkeys, which the columnist Edward Pearce directed against Kenneth Baker (1934–), Education Secretary and Conservative Party chairman under Margaret Thatcher, and John Major's first Home Secretary. One Conservative MP elaborated: "I don't think he has his hair cut – just an oil change."

Self-defence Forces The official name for Japan's armed forces in the period since World War II, when the country's constitution has specifically ruled out their use for aggressive purposes. It was not until 1992 that they served overseas, Japanese troops taking part in UN PEACEKEEPING operations in Cambodia.

self-determination The right of a people to decide whether it should have the independence and attributes of a NATION STATE, or to form part of a nation of its choice. At Woodrow WILSON's insistence self-determination for the peoples of Europe – especially of the former Austro-Hungarian Empire – became a key feature of the peace settlement after WORLD WAR I. Wilson declared:

> Self-determination is not a mere phrase. It is an imperative principle of action, which statesmen will henceforth ignore at their peril.

self-government The right of a people or community to govern itself, either as a separate nation or within a national framework. After Spain's colonies in South America won their independence, Thomas JEFFERSON wrote:

> The qualities of self-government in society are not innate. They are the result of habit and long training, and for these they will require time and much suffering.

self-immolation The grisly but highly-effective protest against the authorities of the day perfected by Buddhist monks in South Vietnam in the early 1960s; it involved soaking themselves in petrol, assuming a prayerful posture and then being set on fire. Images of the monks meeting their death were flashed around the world and did much to undermine support for the US-backed Diem regime; they also inspired the Czech student Jan Palach to carry out a similar protest in WENCESLAS SQUARE in 1969 in protest at the Soviet occupation of his country. Palach's funeral became a national day of mourning for the PRAGUE SPRING, and the square to this day contains an informal shrine to his sacrifice.

self-regulation The notion that financial institutions can most effectively be cleansed of abuses, irregularities and corruption by monitoring them themselves, rather than through the imposition of an outside investigatory and disciplinary body. Long the practice in the City of London, the doctrine reached its apotheosis in the 1986 Financial Services Act, under which UK financial institutions, following the Big Bang, were placed under the supervision of five self-regulatory organizations answerable to a Securities and Investment Board (SIB). Some of the five have proved effective; the competence of others has been questioned, notably after the ease with which Robert Maxwell was able to defraud his pension funds, unbeknown to the Investment Management Regulatory Organization (IMRO) whose existence was supposed to prevent infinitely smaller frauds.

sell. selling off the family silver The withering denunciation of PRIVATIZATION delivered by the former Harold Macmillan (*see* SUPERMAC) after his ennoblement as Earl of Stockton to a meeting of the TORY REFORM GROUP in 1984. He said:

> First of all the Georgian silver goes, then all that nice furniture that used to be in the salon. Then the Canalettos go.

sell-out One of the most wounding accusations in politics, that a politician has betrayed the principles on which he or she was elected. Specifically it involves abandoning a principled course of action for a cosier one, abandoning in the process the interests of the people the person was supposed to be representing.

Sellafield The nuclear installation on the Cumbrian coast of Northwest England, which has been a source of lasting political and diplomatic controversy since an accident at the site (then known as Windscale) in 1957 released radioactive substances into the air and contaminated milk over an area of 500 sq. km. Plutonium has been manufactured there since 1942 and nuclear fuel reprocessed since 1952; in 1956 the world's first nuclear power station at Calder Hall came on stream within the complex. The level of radioactive discharge into the Irish Sea, greatly reduced since the early 1970s, has aroused persistent protests from GREENPEACE and from politicians in the Irish Republic across the water; there have also been repeated claims from health campaigners that the plant has induced a cluster of leukaemia cases in the local community. However the State-owned British Nuclear Fuels Ltd. is adamant that after an initial period when the industry's safety standards were not strict enough, it is operating one of the safest plants of its kind in the world.

Selma The seat of Dallas County, Alabama, which in 1965 became the centre of the battle over CIVIL RIGHTS when Dr. Martin Luther KING chose it to dramatize the bars to Black voting in many Southern states; at the time only 335 of Selma's 13,115 voting-age Blacks were registered to vote, despite the passage of the 1964 Civil Rights Act. The peaceful protest – begun on 18 January after four years of court orders had proved fruitless – was bitterly resisted by local Whites; two protesters were killed and 2000 arrested. On 7 March 200 state police attacked the demonstrators with TEAR GAS, whips and nightsticks; Governer George Wallace refused to protect a second march from Selma to Montgomery, and President Johnson mobilized the NATIONAL GUARD. He went on to introduce the VOTING RIGHTS ACT, enforcing the FIFTEENTH AMENDMENT to guarantee the vote to all US citizens.

Selsdon Man The name, with primitive anthropological echoes, with which Harold WILSON branded Edward Heath's Conservatives as ruthless and unfeeling in the run-up to the 1970 General Election. It stemmed from a meeting Heath (*see* GROCER) convened with his SHADOW CABINET on 31 January 1970 at the Selsdon Park Hotel, near Croydon, to review party strategy. Publicity accompanying the meeting gave the impression that Heath was adopting harder-line, more right-wing policies. Except in the field of industrial policy (*see* LAME DUCKS) that impression was not borne out once he won the election, but Wilson seized on it, telling a meeting in Birmingham on 21 February:

> Selsdon Man is not just a lurch to the Right, it is an atavistic desire to reverse the course of 25 years of social revolution. What they are planning is a wanton, calculated and deliberate return to greater inequality. Selsdon Man is designing a system of society for the ruthless and the pushing, the uncaring. His message to the British people would be simple and brutal. It would say: "You're out on your own."

semi. semi-detached The phrase used by Bernard Ingham (*see* YORKSHIRE RASPUTIN) to describe **John Biffen** at a meeting with LOBBY journalists *c.* 1986. Biffen, then Leader of the Commons, had been a loyal THATCHERITE but had started to campaign for CONSOLIDATION of gains already made instead of embarking on fresh radical initiatives. Ingham's description of Biffen as a "semi-detached member of the Cabinet" was assumed to have been made on Mrs. Thatcher's authority, and was thus seen as a way of undermining him. Once the Conservatives had won the following year's election, Biffen was duly sacked from the Cabinet.

semi-housetrained polecat Probably the rudest thing ever said by one member of the House of Commons about another without being ruled UNPARLIAMENTARY by the Speaker. The description was used *c.* 1977 by the then Employment Secretary Michael Foot (*see* WURZEL GUMMIDGE) about Norman Tebbit (*see* CHINGFORD SKINHEAD), after Tebbit had provoked him by asking: "Does Mr. Foot know he is a FASCIST?"

Semtex The devastating nitrogen-based plastic explosive manufactured in Czechoslovakia which became a favourite of terrorists in the early 1980s because it is also odourless and thus very hard to detect. Large quantities were supplied to Libya, which passed it on to militant Palestinian groups and the IRA, to whom it was shipped with conventional arms on the motor vessel *Eksund*, until the French customs seized the ship. The Provisionals have used Semtex to deadly effect in Northern Ireland and on the British mainland, and are believed to have enough for their next 150 years of terrorist operations. When the playwright Václav Havel became Czech president in 1990, he curbed exports of Semtex, but reported to Western governments that 150 years' supply was already in the hands of terrorists throughout the world.

Senate (1) The senior house of the United States CONGRESS, presided over by the VICE-PRESIDENT when he is available and comprising two members from every State of the Union, popularly elected every six years; currently there are 100 members. Until the passage of the SEVENTEENTH AMENDMENT (ratified in 1913), Senators were elected by State legislatures. The Senate was designed as a restraint on both the HOUSE and on the PRESIDENCY; when Thomas JEFFERSON asked why it was necessary, George WASHINGTON replied:

> Why do I pour coffee in a cup? To cool it.

James MADISON put it less obliquely, writing: "The ends to be served by it: first, to protect the people against their rulers, secondly to protect the people against the transient impressions into which they might be led." The Senate was also supposed to be an elite; Gouverneur Morris declared: "It must have great personal property; it must have the aristocratic spirit; it must love to lord it through pride", and John ADAMS stated: "The rich, the well-born and the able acquire an influence among the people that will be too much for the simple honesty of a House of Representatives. The most illustrious must be separated from the mass and placed by themselves in a Senate." It took time for the Senate to acquire augustness; in 1826 Anne Royall noted: "I attended a few times to hear the debate but was unable to hear, owing to the noise made in the galleries, lobbies and that made by the slamming of the doors. I was greatly surprised that so little order was maintained," and Charles Dickens wrote in 1842:

> The state to which the carpets are reduced by universal disregard of the spittoon do not admit of being described.

The Senate has traditionally been more conservative than the HOUSE, though this has been less the case as the SENIORITY system has eased. It is generally what Woodrow WILSON termed "a body of individual critics" rather than an assembly divided by party. It was long the home of special INTERESTS, Theodore Roosevelt observing:

> When they call the roll, Senators do not know whether to answer "present" or "not guilty".

In the early 1970s Sen. Robert Kerr said: "If everyone ABSTAINED on grounds of personal interest, I doubt if you could get a QUORUM on any subject." And in 1990 Rep. Pat Schroeder, a former Senator, declared: "It's a never-never land, a genteel millionaires' club."

The Senate is also the home of the FILIBUSTER, the great weapon used by conservative Southern senators to resist what they see as harmful progress. As late as the mid-1980s Sen. Tim Wirth of Colorado could say: "In the House you learn how to get something done by putting together a coalition. But in the Senate, people's power arises from their ability to say no, their power to block anything." Vice-President Dan QUAYLE, a former Indiana Senator, made a different distinction:

> In the House you get a bunch of guys and go down to the gym and play basketball. You can't do that in the Senate.

Gladstone hailed the Senate as "the most remarkable of all the inventions of modern politics". Yet Sen. John Spooner (1843–1919) felt moved to remind those making such claims that the Senate was "not the greatest legislative body in the world; [but] one of the branches of perhaps the greatest legislative body in the world". And its members have differed sharply over whether the prestige is merited. John F. KENNEDY scorned it as "the iron lung of politics", South Dakota's Sen. James Abourezk, retiring early, said: "I can't wait to get out of this chickenshit outfit", and Sen. John Sharp Williams declared after the Senate's rejection of the LEAGUE OF NATIONS: "I'd rather be a hound dog and bay at the moon from my Mississippi plantation than remain in the United States Senate." As for what the Senate actually does, Sen. J. William Fulbright said: "We have the power to do any damn fool thing," and Kennedy, once President, opined: "I never realized how powerful the Senate is until I left it and came up to this end of Pennsylvania Avenue." Yet Sen. Robert Dole once confessed: "We spend a lot of time doing very little, and that may be an understatement." Sen. David Pryor of Arkansas declared in a moment of frustration that "being in the Senate is like getting stuck in an airport and having all your flights cancelled", and Sen. Philip Hart of Michigan admitted: "There's a terrible tendency here to think that everything we do and say, or omit to do, is of world consequence. But you know full well that you can go across the street and the bus driver couldn't care less." Most of the Senate's real work takes place in committee, and as for its status as a debating forum, Sen. William Proxmire claimed: "The so-called greatest deliberative body in the world hasn't had even a third-class debate in years. And even if we had it no one would be on the FLOOR to hear it." Eventually the MAJORITY LEADER Sen. Mike Mansfield had to remind colleagues: "None of us was DRAFTED for this job. With the position goes a duty to attendance on the floor of the Senate."

> *Lost visitor:* How do I get out of the Senate?
> *Sen. Harry New of Indiana (just defeated):* Madam, I advise you to run in an Indiana primary.

> A place filled with goodwill and good intentions, and if the road to hell is paved with them, the Senate is a pretty good detour. Sen. HUBERT HUMPHREY, 1978.

> A club of prima donnas intensely self-orientated – 99 kings and one queen dedicated to their own personal accommodation. Sen. MARGARET CHASE SMITH (1898–).

> The windows need washing.
> Arkansas Sen. HATTIE CARAWAY arriving to take her seat, 1931.

(2) The less powerful upper house of many other legislatures, including most in the COMMONWEALTH. In Australia the Senate, with 76 members elected by PROPORTIONAL REPRESENTATION and with the influence of the smaller states weighted; it has no powers over administration or foreign affairs, but as in 1975 can bring a Ministry to its knees by failing to vote SUPPLY. Canada's Senate is nominated and has few powers, constitutional

amendments to add to its powers having fallen because of continued deadlock over the status of QUEBEC. Kenneth McNaught described the Canadian Senate as "even less successful than the HOUSE OF LORDS in opposing the full development of democratic politics centred in the Commons".

half-senate election In Australia, an election for half the seats in the Senate which may be called by the Ministry to break a deadlock between the two Houses by ensuring it – if victorious – of a majority in both.

Senator A member of the United States SENATE. In 1886 Sen. George Hearst declared that Senators were "the survivors of the fittest", and in terms of the political process they are, having overcome every hurdle except those of a Presidential campaign. Henry Adams wrote in 1906: "No man, however strong, can serve ten years as schoolmaster, priest or senator and remain fit for anything else," but most have taken to the life and served far more, the voters permitting. As for their duties, Sen. Henry Ashurst admitted: "I am not in Washington as a statesman. I am there as a very well paid message boy doing your errands. My chief occupation is going around with a forked stick picking up little fragments of patronage for my constituents." Keeping an eye on the Administration takes other forms; Dean Acheson as Secretary of State found that "Senators are a prolific source of advice and most of it is bad".

> I look at the Senators and pray for the country.
> Senate chaplain EDWARD EVERETT HALE (1822–1909).

> If we introduced the Lord's Prayer here, Senators would propose a large number of amendments to it.
> Sen. HENRY WILSON (1812–75).

> Senators prey on women as if they were groupies.
> HARRIET WOODS, National Women's Political Caucus.

the distinguished Senator from – A courtesy by which members of the US Senate refer to their colleagues. Sen. Alben Barkley warned FRESHMEN that

> If he refers to you as "the able and distinguished Senator from Ohio", be on your guard, for the knife is going in sharper. If he refers to you as "the able and distinguished Senator from Ohio and my good friend", then duck fast because he's trying to see if the jugular vein is exposed. And should he refer to you as "my very good friend, the able, distinguished and outstanding Senator", run for your life.

junior Senator The Senator from a particular State who has most recently been elected; the longer-serving of the two is correspondingly referred to as the "senior Senator from –".

shadow senator The individual elected by the DISTRICT OF COLUMBIA, which is unrepresented in the Senate, to represent its interests as if he or she were a Senator. *See* HIS SHADOWSHIP.

Senatorial courtesy The custom under which a Senator of a particular party may object to a Federal appointment proposed for his or her State. The rest of the Senate will go along with the objection by refusing to approve the appointment.

send. send for papers The technicality on which a member of the HOUSE OF LORDS raises a subject in debate; when a peer once asked for the papers, no one knew what they actually were, and a bundle had to be hastily put together and tied with red ribbon.

Send them a message! The slogan on which Governor George Wallace campaigned for the Presidency in 1972, the inference being that the Washington ESTABLISHMENT had no idea what ordinary Americans were thinking. In 1976 Jimmy CARTER, tapping the same vein though with vastly different views on race, said:

> Don't send them a message. Send them a president.

send to Coventry The action of ostracizing someone by refusing to speak to them. The practice was frequently used by UK trade unionists in the 1950s against workmates they felt had been over-co-operative with management, but it goes back much further than that. In his speech on 19 September 1880 that began Ireland's BOYCOTTing campaign, Charles Stewart PARNELL said:

> When a man takes a farm from which another has been evicted, you must show him . . . by outing him into a moral Coventry, by isolating him from his kind as if he were a leper of old. You must show him your detestation of the crimes that he has committed.

seniority The US Congressional term for years of service beyond the first two, and from *c.* 1910 until the early 1970s the sole factor in determining the allocation of committee chairmanships. Described by Jack Anderson as the "Senility System", it ensured that most chairmanships were in the hands of elderly members of the majority party, who tended to be conservative Southern Democrats. More importantly, it enshrined enormous power in the hands of a self-selected group. Newly-elected Democrats broke the system in 1975 by rebelling and ousting four committee chairmen, since when such posts have been filled by election. In the Senate the seniority system has largely survived, but committee chairmen have become more responsive to the public mood.

> The committee member who has served 20 years is not just 5 per cent more powerful than the member who has served 19 years. If he is chairman he is 1000 per cent more powerful. Rep. MORRIS UDALL.

separate. separate but equal The guiding principle for racial SEGREGATION in America's South, set by the Supreme Court in 1896 in the case of *Plessy v. Ferguson*, which endured for almost half a century. The ruling, one of the court's most invidious and taken with only one dissenting opinion, justified separate carriages for Black passengers on Louisiana's railroads, and volunteered that "separate but equal" schools would also be lawful. Only in 1938 did the Court rule that for separate facilities to be constitutional, they had to be truly equal – not inferior as was almost always the case. Not until the landmark case of BROWN v. TOPEKA BOARD OF EDUCATION was the principle overthrown, paving the way for true CIVIL RIGHTS for Blacks. However in 1968 the KERNER COMMISSION on riots in America's cities warned that urban Blacks were becoming "separate and unequal".

separate development One of several euphemisms for APARTHEID used by South Africa's NATIONAL PARTY government, notably after it began to coerce its Black population into taking the citizenship of nominally-independent BANTUSTANS to prevent them acquiring rights in White urban society.

separation of Church and State One of the fundamentals of the US Constitution, the FIRST AMENDMENT specifying that "Congress shall make no law respecting an establishment of religion". Those who advocate a similar division in England are said to favour DISESTABLISHMENT of the Anglican church. When John F. KENNEDY was seeking the Presidency, extreme Protestants claimed that he would be under the influence of the Catholic chuch, and that the separation would not be observed. But Kennedy told them:

> I believe in an America where the separation of church and state is absolute, where no Catholic prelate should tell the President (should he be a Catholic) how to act.

separation of powers An even more critical basic of the American state, and of many other democracies. It depends on the complete separation of the EXECUTIVE, the LEGISLATURE and the JUDICIARY, with none of the three able to exercise supreme authority; explaining it, James MADISON said: "Ambition must be made to counter ambition", and John ADAMS explained:

> The judicial power ought to be distinct from both the legislature and the executive, and independent of both, so that it may be a check upon both, as both should be checks upon that.

In Britain and other PARLIAMENTARY systems, the separation is not total, as Ministers (the Executive) are drawn from, and accountable to, the Legislature.

separatism A movement for the separation of a region or community from the nation of which it is a part. The term, the opposite of IRREDENTISM, has been most frequently used of the Quebec separatists (*see* PQ), but also applies to a number of other movements throughout the world. The Canadian Prime Minister Brian Mulroney, himself a Quebecker, once told a separatist HECKLER:

> To hell with you! You can't be a part-time Canadian.

Sequoia The Presidential yacht used on the Potomac by LBJ, Richard Nixon and Gerald FORD, before being pensioned off by Jimmy CARTER as an extravagant hangover from the Imperial PRESIDENCY. At the time it was costing nearly $800,000 a year to run. Nixon used to hold dinners on the *Sequoia*, ostentatiously having the wine waiter serve him with the finest Margaux, his guests receiving cheap wine with the waiter's napkin obscuring the label.

Seretse Khama affair The joint action in 1949 by Britain's Labour government and South Africa's newly-elected SEGREGATIONIST National Party to exile the Bamangwato tribal leader Seretse Khama (1921–80) from the British protectorate of Bechuanaland (now Botswana) for marrying a White Englishwoman. Seretse, chief-designate of the tribe, took his new wife, Ruth Williams, a 24-year-old typist, home after qualifying as a barrister in London. The marriage outraged the South Africans, who wanted to ANNEX Bechuanaland, perturbed the British and flouted the wishes of Seretse's uncle and regent, Tshekedi Khama. Despite support for Seretse from the tribe generally, it was decided that he should be exiled for six years; he returned in 1956 after renouncing the chieftainship. In 1965 he was elected head of government, and on Botswana's independence in 1966, he became its first president; the same year the Queen made up for his past treatment by KNIGHTing him. Sir Seretse ruled over Botswana until his death 14 years later.

Sergeant at Arms The official in each House of the US Congress who carries out a range of ceremonial and practical functions, and generally ensures the smooth and safe running of the legislature. Sergeant at Arms in the House, for instance, carries the MACE, used to round up members for a QUORUM and, until abuses by members forced its closure in 1992 (*see* HOUSE BANK SCANDAL), operated a bank for members in his office. It was the Senate Sergeant at Arms of the day who delivered the IMPEACHMENT summons to President Andrew Johnson. In happier times, he greets the President when he arrives to deliver the

State of the UNION Message; Nordy Hoffman, who held the post from 1975 until 1981, had played on Knut Rockne's legendary Notre Dame football team, and was thus entitled to greet Ronald Reagan with: "Hiya, GIPPER!". Hoffman said of his Senatorial charges:

> We've got more egos up there on the Hill than we've got any place else in the world. And if you can handle those, you can handle anybody.

Serjeant-at-Arms The functionary, ACCOUNTABLE only to the Royal Household, though always ready to accommodate the SPEAKER, who exercises supreme power through a large staff over the ceremonial, administration and good order of the HOUSE OF COMMONS at Westminster. (There is also a Serjeant-at-Arms in the Lords, but his powers are strictly limited, the real authority resting with BLACK ROD.) Over the years the House has gained some control over its own affairs, but the Serjeant-at-Arms, usually a retired military officer, has ultimate control over who enters the Commons' end of the Palace of Westminster and its surrounding office buildings and what they can do there; he even has the power, occasionally exercised, to have MPs' cars towed away if they are parked in the wrong space. The office dates back to the days of King Richard II; its holder wears a uniform of cocked hat (seldom worn), cutaway coat, lace ruffle at the throat, knee breeches, black silk stockings and silver-buckled shoes.

Sermon on the Mound Margaret Thatcher's address to the General Assembly of the Church of Scotland in Edinburgh on 21 May 1988 which was intended to prove to Scots Calvinists that THATCHERISM was in line with their thinking. In fact it convinced most Scots that she was on another planet; one of the clergy present described it as "a disgraceful travesty of the Gospel". Her theme was that the creation of wealth was not unchristian:

> How could we invest for the future or support the wonderful artists and craftsmen whose work also glorifies God, unless we had first worked hard and used our talents to create the necessary wealth?

SERPS State Earnings-Related Pension Scheme. A UK government scheme pioneered by the Labour Social Services Secretary Barbara Castle and introduced in 1978, which aimed to provide every employed person with an earnings-related pension in addition to the basic flat-rate pension. Contributions came from contributors' National Insurance payments and the pension, payable at 65 for men and 60 for women, is calculated using a formula based on a person's earnings. When the cost of SERPS was found to be spiralling in the late 1980s, Margaret Thatcher's government began offering contributors incentives to contract out and join a personal or occupational pension scheme instead.

session The cycle of SITTINGS by a legislature, lasting approximately a year. The US Congress is required by the Constitution to convene on 3 January each year unless an exception is made; it generally sits until late the same year. In Britain, the Parliamentary session begins with the STATE OPENING, usually in November. It lasts just under a year except when a General Election intervenes; if so, the session will be truncated and the first session of the new Parliament may last as much as 18 months, *e.g.* from May or June until late October the following year, as in 1992–93.

closed session A session of a legislature or other gathering that is closed to Press and public. Such sessions (*see* SECRET SESSION) were frequently held at Westminster to debate the conduct of World War II, only one significant LEAK of information (in 1942) ever coming out. In 1953 the LABOUR PARTY conference at Margate went into closed session to debate a proposal to expel Aneurin Bevan (*see* NYE); however no one thought to switch off the public address system on the roof of the hall, and reporters simply gathered round the loudspeaker to report the proceedings.

joint session *See* JOINT.

Sessional Orders The resolutions formally passed by Britain's HOUSE OF COMMONS at the start of each session, to reassert its rights and privileges. They include the outlawing of double election returns, excluding PEERs from voting and forbidding bribery at elections, and authorizing the publication of the House's proceedings.

Seventh of March speech The speech delivered in the US Senate on 7 March 1850 by Daniel Webster (1782–1852) which proved crucial to the passage of the COMPROMISE OF 1850. By repudiating his FREE SOIL followers and also compromising his previous opposition to any extension of slavery, it also cost him his last chance of the Presidency.

Seventeen. Seventeenth Amendment The amendment to the US Constitution, RATIFIED on 31 May 1913, that provided for the popular election of SENATORS; up to then, they had been elected by state legislatures, a system that denied the voters a choice and was open to abuse. The change reduced the power of the States, and increased popular control over Congress.

Seventeenth Parallel The CEASEFIRE line dividing North and South Vietnam, set by the GENEVA AGREEMENT signed by the French and the VIET MINH on 21 July 1954. The agreements stressed that it "should not in any way be interpreted as constituting a political boundary", but should be a temporary division pending FREE ELECTIONS in July 1956. It separated the North, under *Viet Minh* control, from the South, under the French-supported Emperor Bao Dai. America, which had not signed the Agreement, vetoed the elections and pressed ahead with creating a non-communist state south of the Seventeenth Parallel, ensuring the formal division of Vietnam. US policy thus guaranteed continuing instability in the region and the eventual recurrence of hostilities between HO CHI MINH's Communist government in the North and the US-backed regime in the south that became the VIETNAM WAR.

Sèvres meeting The secret meeting between French and Israeli leaders on 22–24 October 1956 at Sèvres, 10 miles Southwest of Paris, which agreed that an Israeli invasion should give Britain and France the pretext to intervene in SUEZ and overthrow Egypt's President Nasser. Those present were the French prime minister Guy Mollet, with Christian Pineau and Maurice Bourges-Manoury, and the Israeli premier David Ben Gurion with Shimon Peres, Moshe Dayan and Mordechai Bar-On. Under the plan drawn up by General Maurice Challe, Israel would attack Egypt, Britain and France would issue an ULTIMATUM to both to withdraw, and when Egypt refused they would attack. Ben Gurion was unenthusiastic, the more so after a brief visit from UK Foreign Secretary Selwyn Lloyd who seemed equally lukewarm towards a plan enthusiastically backed by Anthony EDEN, but Dayan talked him round and on 24 October the agreement was signed, Britain being represented by officials. When Eden heard that a written agreement existed, he sent the officials back to Paris to urge its destruction; the request was refused but Britain's copy, sent to Eden, has disappeared. Anthony Nutting, who resigned as a Foreign Office minister shortly afterward over Suez, described Sèvres as a "sordid conspiracy". On October 29 Israel attacked, and the Suez fiasco began.

Seward's folly The contemporary reaction to America's purchase of Alaska in 1867 for $7.2 million, or just under 2 cents an acre. The deal was negotiated in the small hours of 30 March by Secretary of State William H. Seward and the Russian Minister Baron de Stoeckl, who had called on him at home, interrupting a game of whist. The Senate RATIFIED the treaty of cession in June, but the House did not appropriate the money until July 27 because money was tight after the CIVIL WAR. In 1959 Alaska achieved STATEHOOD. The 49th State was, as now, the largest by area and the smallest by population; its oil reserves were still undetected.

sexism The practice of DISCRIMINATION on grounds of sex, generally against women. The word is thought to have been coined by Pauline M. Leet, director of special programmes at Franklin and Marshall College, Lancaster, Pennsylvania, in a talk she gave on 18 November 1956 on "*Women and the Undergraduate*". The word, and its derivative **sexist**, were given currency in the late 1960s by the feminist author Caroline Bird.

> Sex prejudice is so ingrained in our society that many who practice it are simply unaware that they are hurting women. It is the last socially acceptable prejudice.

sexual politics The role of gender in political, business and social institutions. Traditionally women have been discriminated against in most churches, the armed forces, law, medicine and banking in relation to advancement, and often even to employment. The US feminist Kate Millet introduced the phrase in her book *Sexual Politics* (1970); the Women's Movement maintains that the sociocultural role of gender differs from the biological gap of sex, and that sexual equality will change political and social structures for the better. *See also* WOMEN'S RIGHTS.

shadow. Shadow Cabinet At Westminster, the chief spokesmen of the principal OPPOSITION party who "shadow" the activities of government. Headed by the Leader of the OPPOSITION, it includes the Shadow Chancellor and a team of other senior Front BENCHers responsible for areas of policy broadly matching those of the Cabinet, and who lead the attack on their opposite numbers at each departmental QUESTION TIME. A Conservative Shadow Cabinet is appointed by the party leader; the bulk of a Labour Shadow Cabinet is elected by Labour MPs as the **Parliamentary Committee.**

shadow senator *See* SENATOR.

shadowing the Deutschmark The policy of keeping the value of the pound in line with the German currency which Nigel (later Lord) Lawson followed as CHANCELLOR OF THE EXCHEQUER in 1987–88, and which produced increasing disagreements between himself and Margaret Thatcher. The effect of Lawson's strategy was the same as if Britain had joined the ERM; when the economy headed into RECESSION at the end of the decade, this management of sterling was felt by many to have contributed to it.

Shakes The nickname of William Shepherd Morrison (later Lord Dunrossil, 1893–1961), who was a wartime Minister, then became SPEAKER of the Commons 1951–59, earning tributes for his handling of the House at the time of SUEZ, and GOVERNOR-GENERAL of Australia from 1960 until his death the following year.

Shankill, the The heart of Ulster LOYALISM, a street of terraced houses that runs due west from the centre of Belfast, just north of and almost parallel to the equally strongly Nationalist FALLS.

SHAPE Supreme Headquarters of the Allied Powers, Europe; the military headquarters of NATO at Chièvres, Belgium.

Share-our-Wealth movement The rival to Franklin D. Roosevelt's NEW DEAL put forward by Sen. Huey (KINGFISH) Long of Louisiana. Long wanted the Federal government to guarantee every American family a homestead worth $5000 and a minimum annual income of $2000. The appeal of this and other simplistic and extremist plans to counter the GREAT DEPRESSION heightened FDR's sense of urgency in pressing ahead with practical measures of his own.

Sharpeville The mass shooting on 21 March 1960 of demonstrators against South Africa's PASS LAWS in the Black TOWNSHIP of Sharpeville, 40 miles south of Johannesburg. Sixty-nine were killed (many shot in the back), and 180 injured after Transvaal police panicked when 20,000 protesters without passes offered themselves for arrest at the local police station. The killings provoked worldwide condemnation, and anger in South Africa led the government to declare a STATE OF EMERGENCY. In the aftermath of the massacre both the Pan-Africanist Congress (PAC), which had called for the demonstration, and the African National Congress (ANC) were banned. Eighteen thousand people were arrested and draconian powers introduced to suppress dissent, effectively transforming the country into a Police STATE. Sharpeville precipitated South Africa's expulsion from the COMMONWEALTH and the campaign for international SANCTIONS to force an end to APARTHEID.

Shaw. Norman Shaw Building The two Victorian buildings at Westminster, formerly New Scotland Yard, headquarters of the Metropolitan Police, which the HOUSE OF COMMONS took over for members' offices when the police moved to Victoria. Standing beside the Embankment just north of Westminster Bridge, they are known after their architect as Norman Shaw North and Norman Shaw South; the South building is occupied mainly by Conservative MPs, the North largely by other parties.

sheep in sheep's clothing Someone who is totally weak, by contrast with a sheep in wolf's clothing which looks formidable but is not. The phrase is often attributed to CHURCHILL, who is supposed to have used it of his successor Clement ATTLEE. However Churchill never underestimated Attlee, especially after losing an election to him in 1945, and the phrase is known to have a much older origin: the British writer and critic Edmund Gosse (1849–1928), used it of his contemporary T. Sturge Moore.

dead sheep *See* DEAD.

Sheffield rally The extravaganza staged by Britain's LABOUR PARTY a week before the April 1992 General Election, whose triumphalist tone was widely blamed for the party's shock defeat. Almost the entire SHADOW CABINET gathered under a montage of rippling flags before 12,000 party faithful bused in from all over northern England and beyond, to demonstrate that Labour was confident of victory and ready to govern. With one opinion poll putting Labour 7 points ahead that evening, the atmosphere was euphoric and Neil KINNOCK jarringly fervent. Those in the hall rated the event a success, but the juxtaposition on television of Kinnock shouting: "Well . . . all Right!" and Labour's growing poll lead frightened many FLOATING VOTERS into switching from Labour or the Liberal Democrats to John MAJOR's Conservatives.

> The political equivalent of the launch party for *Eldorado*.
> Sir NORMAN FOWLER.

> A mixture of *Götterdämmerung* and the Eurovision song contest.
> NORMAN LAMONT.

> You don't belch before you've had the meal.
> DEREK FULLICK, head of the train drivers' union ASLEF.

shenanigan An originally Irish word for any kind of devious and dishonest behaviour aimed at preventing the obvious from happening; in politics its applications are numerous.

Sherman Act The pioneer ANTI-TRUST legislation passed by the US Congress in 1890 in the face of widespread anger at the strength and ruthless defiance of the public interest of the great trusts, controlling the supply of essentials like steel and oil. Although the Act is linked in history with the Republican Sen. John Sherman of Ohio, the Bill was proposed by President Benjamin Harrison, and all Sherman did was agree to introduce it in the Senate. The aims of the Act were "to protect trade and commerce against unlawful restraints and monopolies" by outlawing "every contract, combination in the form of trust or otherwise, or conspiracy, in restraint of trade and commerce among the several States, or with foreign nations". Although more effective than the Interstate Commerce Act passed three years before had been in curbing the excesses of the railroads, its impact on the trusts was limited; indeed until 1902 when President Theodore Roosevelt used it against a deal negotiated by the banker J.P. Morgan to end competition between North-western railroad magnates, it had only been invoked to restrain labour unions. One of the Act's framers, Sen. Orville Platt of Connecticut, had admitted when President Benjamin Harrison signed the Act:

> The conduct of the Senate . . . has not been in the line of honest preparation of a Bill to prohibit and punish trusts. It has been in the line of getting some Bill with that title that we might go to the country with.

sherpas The senior officials, one from each participating country, who prepare the ground for SUMMIT meetings, especially the annual gatherings of the G7 heads of government, and fill in the details of agreements reached there for the final COMMUNIQUÉ. The original sherpas are the Nepalese mountain guides who accompany climbers attempting Everest and the other great Himalayan peaks.

Shin Bet The internal security arm of the Israeli state, MOSSAD handling external security. Its name is taken from its Hebrew initials, which stand for General Security Services. Shin Bet is an investigative agency with a special interest in potential sabotage, Arab terrorism, and security matters with a strong political flavour.

Shining Path (Sp. *Sendero Luminoso*) The MAOIST guerrilla group led by Abimael Guzman (1935–) which between 1980 and 1992 killed 23,000 people in an attempt to destroy Peru's political fabric. The name originated in the doctrine of José Carlos Mariátegui, a Peruvian leftist of the 1920s, who advocated a "shining path" return to the co-operative agricultural system of the Incas. Guzman, a former philosophy professor, split the Peruvian Communist Party to found Shining Path *c.* 1970; it went underground in 1979 and on 17 May 1980 declared war on the Peruvian State. Shining Path has been noted for its Messianic PERSONALITY CULT (Guzman was praised as Chairman Gonzalo) and the fanatical barbarism of its campaign; at one point its cadres hanged dogs from traffic lights in Lima, their mouths stuffed with dynamite and placards round their necks denouncing the Chinese leader Deng Xiaoping. They also cut off Lima's electricity supply during a Papal visit, then illuminated the capital with HAMMER-AND-SICKLE bonfires. Guzman was arrested in Lima in September 1992 amid surprise that the security forces had been able, and had wanted, to take him alive; the next month he was jailed for life.

shoo-in A US term for a candidate who is considered a certainty for election.

shoot to kill The alleged policy pursued by the security forces in Northern Ireland toward IRA suspects, which led to the controversy over the STALKER REPORT. Critics of the Army and, especially, the Royal Ulster Constabulary claimed that suspects were being shot in cold blood at roadblocks and in ambushes without any effort being made to challenge or detain them. The charges were strongly disputed by the RUC, but the evidence suggested some breaches of procedure, in one case involving the death of an innocent civilian, did occur. LOYALIST politicians countered that the IRA had always followed a "shoot to kill" policy, never giving its victims a chance.

short. short-list The list from which the final choice of a party's electoral candidate, or an appointed official, is made after less promising aspirants have been eliminated.

Short money The financial assistance given by the State for the functioning of Opposition parties at WESTMINSTER. It is named after the Labour Leader of the House Edward Short (later Lord Glenamara, 1912–), who first agreed to it in 1975. The money, intended for paying staff in the party leaders' offices, is paid according to the number of MPs a party has and the number of votes it received at the previous election. In the 1987–92 Parliament Labour received £839,000 a year towards the running of Neil KINNOCK's office and staff for members of the SHADOW CABINET; early in 1993 discussions opened on an increase to reflect Labour's extra number of seats, with the party hoping for an extra £400,000.

short, sharp shock The tough regime introduced at certain young offenders' institutions from 1979 by the Conservative Home Secretary William Whitelaw (*see* WILLIE) in response to pressure from party hard-liners on LAW AND ORDER. Whitelaw himself first used the phrase in a party conference speech on 10 October that year. The regime involved near-military drill, discipline, haircuts and dress, and an emphasis on obeying orders. It was not a conspicuous success, one London magistrate observing:

> At least now when they re-offend they stand straight up in the dock and call me "Sir".

short-termism A preference for finding instant answers to problems rather than more productive and durable long-term solutions. The term is used particularly of financial institutions which demand immediate high rates of return from a business rather than allowing it to secure its long-term future through investment.

Shortly-Floorcross, Sir *See* CROSSING THE FLOOR.

show of hands A vote in which participants show their assent or disapproval by raising their hands, which are then counted. Democratic in small groups, the system has been widely abused when larger numbers are voting, especially at union MASS MEETINGS; indeed such votes were outlawed in Britain by the Thatcher government after evidence that workers opposed to the line taken by their local leadership were being intimidated, and that majorities against strike action were being ignored by leaders bent on confrontation.

show trial One of the most potent weapons of STALINISM and other ruthless totalitarian states: the trial of former members of the regime for alleged TREASON against its leader. A key feature would be a grovelling apology by the defendants for crimes they had almost certainly not committed, accompanied by glorification of the man who was sending them to almost certain death. Such trials were a feature of the great PURGES in the Soviet Union just before World War II, and of Soviet SATELLITE states in East Europe in the years after it. Occasionally the offence had genuinely been committed, sometimes there had been a policy difference with the losing faction paying the price; more often personality clashes or simply the egotism and insecurity of the great leader were responsible.

shroud-waving In UK politics, the practice of campaigning for greater government spending on the National Health Service (NHS) by claiming that patients are suffering or even dying through underfunding. First used *c.* 1980 to describe hospital consultants who were using such tactics to demand more money for their own specialities, it was taken up by John MAJOR in the 1992 election to denounce the tenor of Labour's campaigning over the NHS, culminating in the WAR OF JENNIFER'S EAR. (*Compare also* WAVING THE BLOODY SHIRT.)

shuffle The random process at Westminster by which oral QUESTIONS that have been tabled are placed numerically on the ORDER PAPER. Until 1989 the Speaker presided over a draw conducted by his staff; since then the shuffle has been conducted by computer.

shuttle diplomacy *See* DIPLOMACY.

Siberian pipeline The greatest irritant to US-European relations in the early 1980s: the efforts of the Reagan administration to kill plans for a pipeline to supply Siberian natural gas to West Germany. Washington argued that completing the pipeline would boost the Soviet economy and amount to endorsement of the BREZHNEV regime following its invasion of Afghanistan. European nations, including Britain, argued that the pipeline meant much-needed work for construction and petrochemical companies, and that without it Europe would face damaging energy shortages; more bluntly they asserted that the pipeline, from which US firms had been barred by their own government, was none of America's business. On 13 November 1982 President Reagan announced that the EMBARGO was being lifted after the "industrialized democracies reached substantial agreement"; Britain and France both insisted there had in fact been a climb-down by Washington.

sic semper tyrannis! (Lat. thus always to tyrants!) The motto of the State of Virginia, but also the cry of John Wilkes Booth after he shot Abraham LINCOLN at FORD'S THEATRE in Washington on 14 April 1865. Lincoln's bodyguard was so entranced by the play, *Our Country Cousin*, that he left his post and Booth stepped into the President's box. After shooting him, Booth jumped down to the stage, but one of the spurs he was inexplicably wearing caught in a drape of bunting and he fell, breaking his left leg. He managed to stand up and shout "Sic semper tyrannis – the South is avenged!" before escaping through the wings.

sick chicken case *See* CHICKEN.

Sidney Street siege The dramatic siege by the police, Scots Guards and Horse Artillery of a house (100 Sidney Street) at Stepney, in London's East End, on 3 January 1911. It was witnessed by Winston CHURCHILL, Home Secretary in Asquith's government, who had sent in the troops to flush out the "Houndsditch Gang", three Latvian ANARCHISTS led by **Peter the Painter**, a signwriter from Riga; they had killed three policemen three weeks before following an abortive raid on a jewellery shop in Houndsditch. Two of the anarchists died when the troops stormed the house; Peter the Painter escaped.

Sierra Club One of America's most active and prestigious environmental pressure groups, based in San Francisco and taking its name from California's High Sierras, whose preservation is one of its highest priorities. Founded in 1892, it has 600,000 members across the United States and campaigns on the complete range of North American environmental issues as well as such matters as global warming, world population growth and rain-forest preservation.

silent. Silent Cal The nickname of **Calvin Coolidge** (1872–1933), the monosyllabic 30th President of the United States (Republican, 1923–29). The Governor of Massachusetts who made a national reputation by breaking the BOSTON POLICE STRIKE, Coolidge won the Vice-Presidential nomination in 1920 and on 3 August 1923 assumed the Presidency on the death of Warren HARDING. He avoided association with TEAPOT DOME and other scandals of the Harding administration, and with post-war prosperity apparently here to stay, won re-election in 1924 by a LANDSLIDE over John W. Davis with the slogan: KEEP COOL AND KEEP COOLIDGE. Four years later he decided he had had enough, and announced: "I Do Not Choose To Run"; asked why he had not sought a further TERM, he replied: "No prospect of advancement." He went home to Massachusetts, dying there four years later. When word of his death reached Dorothy Parker, she asked:

> How could they tell?

Coolidge was essentially a dour man; he once said: "My hobby is holding office." Alice Roosevelt Longworth was blunter, observing: "He looks as if he has been weaned on a pickle."

Coolidge's economy with words – though not with the truth – was legendary. One Washington hostess declared: "He is so silent he is always worth listening to," and another, "every time he opens his mouth, a moth flies out". Indeed he revelled in his reputation; once at a dinner, a young woman guest told him: "I've made a bet with a friend that I can get you to say at least three words this evening." Coolidge replied: "You lose", then sat silent for the rest of the evening. Another time, he was asked on leaving Church what the sermon had been about. Coolidge said: "Sin," and when asked what the preacher had actually said, added: "He said he was against it." He said of himself: "I have never been hurt by anything I didn't say." And he explained: "Many times I say 'Yes' or 'No' to people. Even that is too much: it winds them up for 20 minutes more." To Will Rogers this put him at an advantage over his contemporaries; after the SCOPES CASE Rogers proclaimed Coolidge

> A better example of evolution than either Bryan or Darrow, for he knows when not to talk, which is the biggest asset the monkey possesses over the human.

Coolidge had little to say, either, to his wife Grace, who remarked when asked about their early romance: "Have you ever *MET* my husband?" Yet he did have a sense of humour with her; once when she complained that she had nothing red to wear to offset the colour of their white dog, he told her: "If it's contrast you want, why not wear white and paint the dog red?" Mrs. Coolidge was very much a FIRST LADY of her time, once observing:

> I am rather proud of the fact that after nearly a quarter of a century of marriage, my husband feels free to take his decisions and act on them without consulting me.

> I always figured the American public wanted a solemn ass for President, so I went along with them. COOLIDGE.

> An economic fatalist with a God-given inertia. He knew nothing and refused to learn. WILLIAM ALLEN WHITE.

> Distinguished for character rather than for heroic achievement. His great task was to restore the dignity and prestige of the Presidency when it had reached the lowest ebb in our history. AL SMITH.

> Nobody has worked harder at inactivity with such a force of character, with such unremitting attention to detail, with such conscientious devotion to the task.
> WALTER LIPPMANN, Obituary.

> He had no ideas, but was not a nuisance.
> H. L. MENCKEN, Obituary.

silent majority *See* MAJORITY.

Silent Spring, The The book written by Rachel Carson and published in America in 1962 which did as much as any to create the ENVIRONMENTALIST movement, by creating public concern over the destruction of wildlife and danger to the food chain caused by the use of dangerous pesticides.

silver. Silver Bodgie The nickname of **Robert Hawke** (1929–), President of the Australian Council of Trade Unions 1970–80 and Prime Minister (Labor) 1983–91. Hawke, an ebullient former Rhodes Scholar who overcame a serious drink problem, gained the name from his mane of silver hair (Bodgie is Australian for a 1950s teddy boy). Patrick White wrote:

> From underneath his cockatoo hairdo, the platitudes he has got by heart.

A son of the Manse and ardent supporter of Zionism who once said: "If I were to be born again, I would want to be born a Jew," Hawke ably made the transition from backroom union technocrat to leader of the movement, to Labor BACKBENCHER, party leader and, one month later, Prime Minister. Hawke knew he would have to go into politics at the top, saying: "It would not be sensible for me to put my bum on a backbench seat," and just before he did enter politics, Peter Blazey wrote:

> He's the most popular politician in Australia without really being one.

Once in the House of Representatives, he had a devastating effect on the morale of Malcolm

Fraser's Liberal government, Lionel Bowen observing: "It appears that whenever the Hon. Member for Wills decides to do anything in this House, the government takes fright." With Bill Hayden making heavy weather as Labor leader and the 1983 election imminent, Hawke was an obvious replacement. Hayden – whom Hawke had branded "a lying cunt with a limited future" – complained: "I can't stand down for a bastard like Bob Hawke," but did so just before the election which Labor duly won under Hawke's leadership. Hawke's Ministry started shakily; after a few months the *Observer* reflected:

> The former grog-artist, womanizer and Rhodes scholar has made himself in his first year the most unpopular Australian since *Pharlap*, the freak wonder horse of the 1930s.

But he went on to lead an eight-year ministry, taking Labor to election victories unprecedented for half a century. Pursuing economic policies that at times echoed THATCHERISM, he toned down Labor's strident anti-Americanism and also held back the tide of REPUBLICAN feeling. Several challenges were mounted to his leadership, but his end when it came was sudden, Paul Keating (*see* LIZARD OF OZ) succeeding him. As he left the LODGE, he observed: "Eleven years ago I'd have been getting thoroughly drunk." Out of office, Hawke took up a new career as a TV interviewer; his debut, interviewing political leaders he knew well in Britain's 1992 election, was surprisingly shaky.

> People, like china ornaments, bewilderingly came apart in his hands. BLANCHE D'ALPUGET.

free silver *See* FREE.

Silverman Bill The Private Member's BILL to abolish the death penalty in Britain, sponsored by the left-wing Labour MP Sidney Silverman, which passed the Commons in March 1955 after the Ruth ELLIS case but was rejected by the Lords. With the Commons clearly in favour of change the EDEN government, after a counterproductive delay, brought in a Homicide Bill of its own that limited the death penalty to specific forms of murder. Silverman kept up his campaign for abolition, and was eventually to succeed in 1965.

Simonstown agreement The long-standing agreement under which Britain had the use of the Simonstown naval base near Cape Town, greatly increasing the Royal Navy's ability to operate in the South Atlantic and Indian Oceans. The deal, which also involved joint manoeuvres with South Africa, was bitterly criticized by the left in Britain as APARTHEID became more repressive, and was terminated by the Labour government in the late 1970s – a decade too late as far as most of the party was concerned. As late as 1974 Tony BENN was rebuked by Harold WILSON for speaking out against the agreement in Labour's National Executive.

simultaneous translation A burgeoning feature of international relations since World War II, with the growth of world and regional organizations whose proceedings have to be instantly translated from an infinite number of languages into as many others, for the benefit of the participants. A translator's work is difficult and thankless; he or she has to cope with regional accents, poor grammar and syntax and sheer waffle. The EUROPEAN PARLIAMENT has provided some spectacular mistranslations. One Frenchman congratulating a colleague on "*sa prudence Normande*" was baffled by howls of laughter from British MEPs who had heard the man apparently compared with the comedian Norman Wisdom, a professional idiot. And in an agricultural committee a British member speaking about the use of frozen semen to inseminate cattle met a hysterical French reaction when the phrase was translated as "*matelots congelés*" (frozen sailors). The editor of this dictionary heard an otherwise excellent translator in Berlin speak of an "Anglo-Dutch amphibian force", conjuring up visions of newts and frogs storming ashore. And President Jimmy CARTER, arriving in Warsaw on a much-heralded visit, had the effect completely destroyed when the translator hired by the State Department converted his protestations of respect for the Poles into the shattering news that he desired them carnally.

single. Single European Act The amendment to the Treaty of ROME in 1987 which paved the way for the SINGLE MARKET (*see also* 1992). Constitutionally it substituted the Qualified MAJORITY, in most cases, for the requirement that decisions of the COUNCIL OF MINISTERS must be unanimous.

single currency The ultimate aim of European economic and monetary union (EMU), the creation by 1997 of a single currency for the EUROPEAN COMMUNITY to replace all those of its member states. Britain agreed the treaty subject to an opt-out leaving a final decision on participation to the Parliament of the day. Since the treaty was concluded in December 1991 the prospects for a single currency have looked steadily bleaker, but elements in France and Germany are eager to proceed in the belief that only by taking the step can the problems be eliminated; the BENELUX countries whose currency is already tied to the German mark are enthusiastic supporters.

Single Market The umbrella term for a wide range of measures to generate completely FREE TRADE within the European Community that were to take effect by the start of 1993. Of 301 DIRECTIVES originally put forward for eliminating Non-TARIFF Barriers, over 270 were agreed, but several – notably on the elimination of border controls between member states – were not fully implemented. In the end the success of the single market, advocated at length in the CECCHINI REPORT and supported enthusiastically in principle by all EC governments, depended on the initiative of individual businesses and the readiness of governments to eliminate red tape; Britain's Customs and Excise responded to the final removal of all barriers by demanding a 650-page report in quadruplicate each month from companies engaged in external trade.

Sinn Fein (Ir. ourselves alone) The Irish nationalist movement founded by Arthur Griffith in 1907, which in its present incarnation is the POLITICAL WING of the Provisional IRA. After the EASTER RISING Sinn Fein organized as the party of independence, winning a string of BY-ELECTION victories starting with Count Plunkett at Roscommon in February 1917. In the 1918 COUPON ELECTION under de Valera (*see* DEV) it almost swept the board, winning 73 seats at Westminster whose holders (including Countess Markiewicz, the first woman elected to the Commons) stayed away to form the first DAIL EIREANN. The party split in 1922 over the IRISH TREATY, the pro-treaty faction winning a large majority in the *Dail.* The anti-treaty faction was marginalized by FIANNA FAIL, but retained some support north and south of the Border and became identified with the continuing faction of the IRA; in 1957 it got four TDs elected to the Dublin Parliament. At the start of the renewed TROUBLES in 1969, Sinn Fein split again. The Marxist Officials (*see* IRA) evolved into first the WORKERS' PARTY and then the DEMOCRATIC LEFT; Provisional Sinn Fein remained the visible symbol of support for Republican terrorism and opposition to British rule. Sinn Fein, through a combination of sound COMMUNITY POLITICS and intimidation, benefited greatly from the hunger STRIKES of 1981, and won local government seats in many Nationalist areas of Ulster. In 1983 the party's articulate leader Gerry Adams captured the West Belfast Parliamentary seat from the SDLP veteran Gerry Fitt. Adams refused to take his seat then and after re-election in 1987 and the voters eventually tired, unseating him in 1992. Sinn Fein never ousted the SDLP as Ulster's principal Catholic party, but did well enough to prevent the SDLP speaking for the entire Nationalist community – and to give LOYALIST paramilitaries an excuse to organize. The UK government controversially gagged Sinn Fein by preventing its spokesmen being heard on radio and television except during elections. In the Republic, where tight controls had always applied, the movement registered consistent electoral failure throughout the 1980s and into the 1990s.

> A vote for Sinn Fein is a vote for peace. GERRY ADAMS.

Sir The prefix to the name of anyone in Britain who has been accorded a KNIGHTHOOD, in place of Mr., Dr. or whatever. A male recipient becomes *Sir* Bernard, a woman thus honoured becomes *Dame* Bernadette.

Sir Alec The affectionate nickname earned by the former and future **Lord Home** (1903–) during his seven years in the House of Commons (1963–70), first as Prime Minister, then as Tory leader and finally as Shadow Foreign Secretary. (A less flattering soubriquet was BAILIE VASS.) A Scottish landowner of immense tact and charm, Home overcame the image Harold WILSON painted of him as a chinless and probably brainless aristocrat to be a competent Premier, a successful Foreign Secretary and, in old age, a revered Tory elder statesman. His childhood was sheltered, his nurse Florence Hill recalling: "I had to see that master Alec didn't talk to the servants and that he didn't leave our part of the house." He also suffered a withering illness that left him with almost skeletal looks; one Tory MP was to comment: "I have seen better-looking faces on a pirate flag," and Christopher Booker observed: "His bleak, deathly smile is the smile not of the victor but of the victim." In later life when a TV make-up girl told him: "You have a head like a skull," Home replied: "Doesn't everybody?"

As Lord Dunglass he was a Conservative MP from 1931 until 1951, serving as PPS to Neville CHAMBERLAIN at the time of MUNICH. In 1951 he succeeded his father as 14th EARL of Home, and as a PEER held a number of Ministerial posts including Commonwealth Secretary and Leader of the Lords. In 1960 Macmillan made him Foreign Secretary; when SUPERMAC resigned through ill-health in October 1963 Lord Hailsham renounced his peerage in the hope of defeating R. A. (RAB) Butler for the succession, but Home was Macmillan's choice, to the astonishment of many politicians and the incredulity of the MEDIA. Harold Wilson, as Labour leader, could not believe his luck and trumpeted:

> After half a century of democratic advance, the whole process has ground to a halt with a 14th Earl.

Home shrewdly retorted that he imagined

his rival was the FOURTEENTH MR. WILSON, but even the pro-Tory Sunday Express commented:

> The only real and distinctive achievement of the 14th earl was to have been heir of the 13th.

Home became Prime Minister in October 1963, remarking laconically: "The doctor unfortunately said I was fit." He renounced his title to become plain Sir Alec Douglas-Home (he was a KNIGHT of the Thistle in his own right). A seat was found for him at Kinross and West Perthshire and he won a BY-ELECTION to re-enter the Commons. Home had once said that he would never become Prime Minister "because I do my sums with matchsticks", but despite his matchstick ECONOMICS he was successful. He only had ten months at NUMBER TEN before going down to electoral defeat, but restored shattered Tory fortunes and came close to denying Labour a majority. In opposition he harried the first WILSON government for a year before standing down as leader, Edward Heath (*see* GROCER) succeeding him. He remained in the Shadow Cabinet and from 1970–74 served as Foreign Secretary again before returning to the Lords as a LIFE PEER.

> There are two problems in my life. The political ones are insoluble and the economic ones are incomprehensible.
> SIR ALEC when Prime Minister.

> He is used to dealing with estate workers. I cannot see how anyone can say he is out of touch.
> His daughter-in-law Lady CAROLINE DOUGLAS-HOME.

> In the 18th century he would have been Prime Minister before he was thirty; as it is he appeared honourably ineligible for the struggle of life.
> CYRIL CONNOLLY, *Enemies of Promise* (1938).

> Alec Douglas-Home, floating on the lethargic sea of his own simplicity, could not for a moment compete with Wilson.
> BERNARD LEVIN.

Sir Humphrey A 1980s term for a Whitehall MANDARIN, stemming from the silken and duplicitous CABINET SECRETARY Sir Humphrey Appleby (played by Nigel Hawthorne) in the BBC television series YES, MINISTER.

SIS Secret Intelligence Service. The formal name for the UK government's external intelligence agency better known as MI6.

sisters The term used by FEMINISTS in politics to refer to each other, in much the same way as left-wingers used to refer to each other as COMRADES. However the term is essentially collective rather than individual. Anti-feminists use it as a term of contempt.

sit At Westminster, each MP is said to sit for whichever CONSTITUENCY they represent.

sit-down A widely-practised form of protest, frequently involving CIVIL DISOBEDIENCE, when demonstrators for or against a particular policy or practice sit down in a place where they will attract maximum attention or cause the most disruption, and refuse to move until their demands are met.

> I want every American free to stand up for his rights, even if he has to sit down for them.
> JOHN F. KENNEDY.

sit-in The US derivative of the SIT-DOWN which became a highly effective part of the CIVIL RIGHTS campaign and was taken up by student protesters against the VIETNAM WAR and other perceived wrongs of society. It was born on 1 February 1960 when four Black students from the Agricultural and Technical College of North Carolina occupied a "Whites only" lunch counter at Woolworth's in Charlotte and refused to leave unless served. The idea, which accorded perfectly with the NON-VIOLENT teaching of Dr. Martin Luther KING, caught on like wildfire: the first victory was won in San Antonio on 21 March, and by the end of 1961 eating facilities in 108 cities across the South had been DESEGREGATED, after sit-ins involving an estimated 75,000 young people – 3600 of whom had been arrested and 245 been expelled from their colleges. Their success prompted kneel-ins to desegregate churches, read-ins to integrate libraries, and wade-ins to end "Whites-only" beaches.

sitting At Westminster, the daily cycle of business in either House from PRAYERS until the House is ADJOURNED. An all-night sitting, if it goes on long enough, can lead to the next day's BUSINESS being "lost".

sittings motion The first item considered by a STANDING COMMITTEE of the House of Commons that is handling the COMMITTEE STAGE of a Bill. The motion sets out how often each week, and at what times, the committee shall sit. Occasionally, when the Government wishes to make indecent haste or members feel the Bill should not immediately be considered, it becomes a matter of controversy. Debate on the sittings motion will also be prolonged if the Opposition wishes to FILIBUSTER against a Bill it particularly objects to.

situation room The room in the basement of the WHITE HOUSE where NATIONAL SECURITY COUNCIL staff and others handle (mainly international) crises, with the President in attendance at critical stages.

the situation has not developed entirely to our advantage The explanation of the state of World War II given by Emperor Hirohito to the Japanese people, most of whom had never previously heard his voice, after the bombing of HIROSHIMA.

Six, the The six nations – France, West Germany, Italy and the BENELUX countries – who were the original participants in the three constituent parts of the EUROPEAN COMMUNITY: the European Coal and Steel Community (1951), the European Economic Community (1957), and EURATOM.

Six Counties The counties – Armagh, Antrim, (London)Derry, Down, Fermanagh and Tyrone – which, at the PARTITION of Ireland in 1921, became part of NORTHERN IRELAND instead of being included in the IRISH FREE STATE. The term came to be shorthand, particularly in the South and among Northern Catholics, for the British enclave in the North.

> The Six Counties have, towards the rest of Ireland, a status and a relationship which no Act of Parliament can change. They are part of Ireland. They always have been part of Ireland, and their people, Catholic and Protestant, are our people. DE VALERA to Churchill, 26 May 1941.

Six Day War The short but bloody conflict between Israel and its Arab neighbours in 1967 in which Israel conquered East Jerusalem and the WEST BANK from Jordan, the GAZA STRIP from Egypt and the Golan Heights from Syria, giving the country defensible borders, inflicting a shattering blow to Arab morale and creating the plight of the Palestinians. The suddenness of Israel's onslaught, which pre-empted an expected Arab attack, led *Time* to term it "the **Blintzkrieg**". In May, Egypt's President Nasser secured the removal of UN PEACEKEEPING troops from his border with Israel, closed the Gulf of Aqaba to Israeli shipping and signed a security pact with King Hussein of Jordan. On 5 June Israel struck against Egypt, destroying over 400 jets on the ground, then poured tanks into Sinai, reaching the SUEZ CANAL in four days. Meanwhile Israeli forces repulsed an attack by Jordan, occupying the old city of Jerusalem and the West Bank; they also defeated Syrian attacks to secure the Golan Heights. A UN-arranged ceasefire came into effect on 11 June. A quarter of a century later, diplomatic deadlock remained over the scope for Palestinians in the lands captured then (*see* OCCUPIED TERRITORIES) to govern themselves. *See* INTIFADA; LAND FOR PEACE.

> If we lose this war, I'll start another in my wife's name. General MOSHE DAYAN (*attr.*).

600-ship navy The goal set by the Reagan administration in its early months, reflecting its determination to boost America's naval strength after a period of decline. Reagan inherited 479 ships (fifty of them started under the Carter administration); Navy Secretary John Lehman made an increase to 600 his top priority and did his best to further it by persuading Secretary of Defence Caspar Weinberger (*see* CAP THE KNIFE) to authorize not one, but two new aircraft carriers – which meant two new carrier groups. The impetus toward such a large fleet had dissipated by the end of the COLD WAR in 1989.

sixteen. Sixteenth Amendment The amendment to the US CONSTITUTION, proposed in February 1909 and RATIFIED four years later, which specifically authorized the Congress to levy a Federal income tax. Such a tax was imposed during the CIVIL WAR, but when it was revived in 1894 the SUPREME COURT ruled it a DIRECT TAX and therefore UNCONSTITUTIONAL. The importance of allowing Congress to impose an income tax to meet extraordinary expenses, as in wartime, was widely acknowledged, but the amendment was only approved after heated debate.

1600 Pennsylvania Avenue The postal address of the WHITE HOUSE; the zip code is Washington, DC 20004.

sketch-writers The select band of journalists at Westminster who, since the 1930s, have reported the proceedings of the Commons (and occasionally the Lords) in the form of a theatrical review rather than as a news report. The format enables a wordsmith to be exceptionally rude about a politician supported by the paper employing them, or to compliment one whose politics their paper's leader columns abhor. Norman Shrapnel of the then *Manchester Guardian* was a pioneer of the art-form; other gifted sketch-writers have included Colin Welch of the *Daily Mail*, Frank Johnson of the *Daily Telegraph*, Andrew Rawnsley of the *Guardian* and the freelance Edward Pearce.

Skinner, Dennis *See* BEAST OF BOLSOVER.

skunk A classic US term of political abuse, from the stripy creature that squirts evil-smelling liquid over anyone or anything that annoys it. An insult by 1840, it was considered so offensive by politicians that in this historic clash on 19 May 1856 between Senators Charles SUMNER and Stephen Douglas (*see* STEAM ENGINE IN BRITCHES) the animal could not be named:

> *Sumner*: No person with the upright form of a man can be allowed, without violation of all human decency, to switch out from his tongue the perpetual stench of offensive personality. . . . The noisome, squat and nameless animal to which I now refer is not a proper model for an American senator. Will the Senator from Illinois take notice?
> *Douglas*: I will, and therefore will not imitate you, Sir.
> *Sumner*: Mr. President, again the Senator has switched his tongue, and again he fills the Senate with an offensive odour.
> *Douglas*: . . . I will only say that a man who has been branded by me in the Senate, and convicted by the Senate

of falsehood, cannot use language requiring reply, and therefore I have nothing to say.

Later generations were less bashful. In the 1968 NEW HAMPSHIRE PRIMARY William Loeb, publisher of the *Manchester Union-Leader*, castigated Sen. Eugene McCarthy as "a skunk's skunk's skunk". And in the early 1970s an anonymous Congressman said of Rep. Wayne HAYS:

Getting into a debate with him is like wrestling with a skunk. The skunk doesn't care – he likes the smell.

Skybolt The air-delivered nuclear missile with which America agreed to supply Britain in 1960 when the UK abandoned its own BLUE STREAK ground-launched system; it was to be delivered from RAF V-bombers. Two years later the Kennedy administration cancelled the project without consulting Britain, but at Nassau in December 1962 Harold Macmillan pursuaded JFK to provide POLARIS instead.

slagheap affair One of a series of supposed scandals with which Harold WILSON's opponents, backed by much of Britain's press, attempted to smear him between the two 1974 general elections when Labour was governing without a majority. It involved property deals by Tony Field, brother of Wilson's political secretary Marcia Williams (LADY FORKBENDER), and a letter on House of Commons notepaper to Ronald Milhench, a Wolverhampton insurance broker who had discussed with Field the sale of a slagheap and quarry at Ince-in-Makerfield, Lancashire. The letter bore Wilson's signature, which Milhench was later convicted of forging. Field bought the land in 1967 and made Mrs. Williams co-director of the quarry company; it lost money, but property prices took off and Field – who had by now been working in Wilson's private office – sold it at a profit of nearly £200,000. Field became involved in a further deal with Milhench, which fell through when the affair became public. Wilson was in no way involved and Field had done nothing illegal, but Wilson, who admitted having known about the deals, defended him with counter-productive stridency. The Conservatives and the press made much of the fact that Wilson, who had always condemned speculation, defended it when it could be described as "reclamation".

If you buy land on which is a slagheap 120 ft. high and it costs £100,000 to remove it, that is not land speculation in the sense we condemned it, but reclamation.

HAROLD WILSON, House of Commons, 4 April 1974.

slate A list of candidates for a multi-member body (often the executive of a political party or trade union) put forward semi-formally by a particular faction.

slavery The institution under which one group of human beings keep others in servitude, exerting total and generally brutal control over every aspect of their lives and treating them as chattels to be bought, sold and exploited. The MANSFIELD JUDGMENT of 1772 confirmed that slavery was illegal in England, but it thrived in the Caribbean and American colonies as slave-traders shipped in half-dead Africans to till the plantations. In America's South it became the staple of the economy, and revolutionaries such as George WASHINGTON (*see* MOUNT VERNON) and Thomas JEFFERSON saw no inconsistency between their belief in equality and the ownership of slaves; however some in the new nation were affronted by the practice, Dr. Benjamin Rush saying in 1773:

The plant of liberty is of so tender a nature that it cannot thrive long in the neighbourhood of slavery.

Britain abolished the slave trade to its remaining colonies in 1809, and the institution of slavery in 1833, three days before the death of the ABOLITIONIST William Wilberforce who declared:

Thank God, that I should have lived to witness a day in which England is willing to give twenty millions sterling for the abolition of slavery.

From the MISSOURI COMPROMISE of 1820 through the KANSAS-NEBRASKA ACT slavery became an ever more divisive issue for the expanding America, with ABOLITIONIST fervour growing in the North and the South opposing any attempt to limit the number of **slave states**, let alone any move to emancipate slaves. President Buchanan warned:

There are portions of the Union where if you emancipate your slaves they will become your masters. Is there any man who would for a moment indulge the horrible idea of abolishing slavery by the massacre of the chivalrous race of men in the south?

Abraham LINCOLN believed slavery could be strangled, saying:

Let us draw a cordon around the slave states and the hateful institution, like a reptile poisoning itself, will perish by its own infamy.

Then came the CIVIL WAR; though it was strictly fought over the right of the CONFEDERATE states to SECEDE from the Union, it was slavery that drew the moral battle-lines and moved Lincoln to sign the EMANCIPATION PROCLAMATION. Lincoln had told Stephen Douglas in one of their DEBATES in 1858: "I have no purpose, either directly or indirectly, to interfere with the institution of slavery in states where it exists", but with the war under way, he could take the high ground. Lincoln declared that "If slavery is not wrong, nothing is wrong," and maintained:

I can clearly foresee nothing but the rooting out of slavery can perpetuate the existence of our union by consolidating it in a common bond of principle.

He confessed: "Whenever I hear anyone arguing for slavery, I feel a strong impulse to see it tried on him personally." And to those who claimed that he was advocating forcible integration of the races, Lincoln replied:

I protest, now and forever, against the counterfeit logic which presumes that because I do not want a negro woman for a slave I do necessarily want her for a wife. My understanding is that I do not have to have her for either.

Slavery duly ended with the defeat of the Confederacy, though it was a century before Black Southerners began to be truly free. The institution lives on in some Middle Eastern countries and parts of India, where the revulsion of the rest of the world makes no impression.

half slave, half free *See* HOUSE DIVIDED.

SLD Social and Liberal Democrats. The original name of the party created in 1988 by the merger of Britain's LIBERAL PARTY and SDP, which the next year took the shortened title of LIBERAL DEMOCRATS.

sleaze factor The phrase that became current in Washington *c.* 1984 to describe the large number of members of the Reagan administration accused of breaches of ethics or the criminal law – 225 when the House Civil Service Subcommittee last counted. The word "sleaze" (from the original "sleazy") apparently stems from the name of Silesia, on the German–Polish border, whose products were regarded in the 17th century as inferior; it conveys a whiff not only of corruption but of tackiness.

White House pollster Richard Wirthlin said Wednesday the resignation of Attorney-General Edward Meese III doesn't erase the "sleaze factor" for Vice-President George Bush in the fall presidential campaign, but makes it easier for him to deal with.

Associated Press report, 7 June 1988.

Our administration has been the victim of individuals who haven't had the judgment or integrity to put the public's interest above their own selfish interest.

Vice-President GEORGE BUSH.

sleep Something much needed by persons in public life who frequently work long and unsocial hours and have exhausting travel schedules. It is also a political trap for politicians who are unable to stay awake. The UK Defence Secretary Fred (later Lord) Mulley (1918–) attracted front-page headlines in 1977 when he fell asleep while sitting next to the Queen at an air display; the American media were more tolerant of President Reagan who frequently nodded off in Cabinet meetings and once quipped: "Remember when I fell asleep during my audience with the Pope?" Margaret Thatcher deplored such tendencies, saying of her husband Denis: "I can trust him not to fall asleep on a public platform and he usually claps in the right places." But Ernest Brown, a member of Stanley BALDWIN's government (*see* TELEPHONE), stated bluntly:

I like a nap. A man who cannot sleep ought not to be in the Cabinet.

A lot depends on the kind of sleep. Henry (CHIPS) Channon experienced the right kind, writing:

I slept for five hours this afternoon in the library of the House of Commons. A deep House of Commons sleep. There is no sleep to compare with it – rich, deep and guilty.

But Norman Willis, general secretary of the TUC, was less fortunate:

I've no problems. I sleep like a baby, one hour sleeping and one hour crying.

Sleep can be a blessed release when someone else is making a bad speech. A fellow-peer once said to Lord North during an interminable speech: "My Lord, I fear you have been asleep"; North replied: "I wish I had."

He had one really valuable talent. He slept more than any other President whether by day or by night. Nero fiddled – but Coolidge only snored.

H. L. MENCKEN on Calvin Coolidge.

sleeper A terrorist who "goes to ground" as an apparently normal member of the community for many years, waiting for eventual instructions to start shooting or bombing.

slogan Originally the war-cry of a Scottish clan, a slogan is now a brief phrase which sets the key for a political campaign or (closer to its origins) a chant raised during a DEMONSTRATION. Sloganizing is the conduct of politics through the exchange of such phrases, rather than through a meaningful dialogue.

If you feed the people with revolutionary slogans they will listen today, they will listen tomorrow, they will listen the day after tomorrow, but on the fourth day they will say: "To Hell with you!"

NIKITA S. KHRUSCHEV (1894–1971, *attr.*).

slump Another word for a DEPRESSION, involving a nosedive in economic activity of all forms.

slush fund An undisclosed fund used by well-heeled supporters of a politician to give him or her some invisible means of support; such a fund may well consist of corrupt or illegal payments and be used for same. The term was well established when Richard Nixon (*see* TRICKY DICK) went on television to give his CHECKERS speech in 1952; it was Nixon again whose career was ruined by the uses to which the secret fund administered by CREEP was put prior to and after the WATERGATE break-in. The phrase is of US nautical origin: the money accumulated by sailors from selling slush, the waste fat from the galley (from *slusk*, the Norwegian for slops).

small is beautiful Originally the title of a book (1973) by the German-born UK economist E. F. Schumacher (1911–77), this has become the slogan of those who oppose huge industrial conglomerates and centralization in government. The phrase was originated not by Schumacher, who wanted to call his book *The Homecomers*, but by his publishers Anthony Blond and Desmond Briggs. One of the doctrine's keenest advocates has been Edmund G. (Jerry) Brown (*see* SPACE CADET), former governor of California and a contender for the presidency in 1976 and 1992.

SMERSH (Russ. *Smert' Spionam*, death to spies) The Section for Terror and Diversion of the KGB that specialized in eliminating enemies outside the Soviet Union. An organization with the same function had existed since the OCTOBER REVOLUTION, and it was a SMERSH agent who murdered TROTSKY in 1940 on STALIN's direct orders. During the COLD WAR, SMERSH became notorious (after the Russians had stopped using the name themselves) for disposing of Western agents and other opponents of the regime by murder, blackmailing or kidnapping, using a variety of ingenious and lethal gadgets. They had less success in their encounter with the fictional British agent James Bond in Ian Fleming's 1957 novel *From Russia With Love.*

Smith. Smith Act The Alien Registration Act drafted by Rep. Howard W. Smith of Virginia and passed by Congress on 28 June 1940. With fears of Communist and Fascist subversion heightened since the outbreak of war in Europe, the Act required that all aliens be registered and their fingerprints taken. The Act also made it illegal to belong to any organization advocating the overthrow of the US government. The Act was revived as McCARTHYISM took hold, with a dozen leaders of the US Communist Party indicted under it in 1949; the Supreme Court declared its use in such circumstances CONSTITUTIONAL in 1951.

Smith-Connally Act The wartime Act pushed through Congress by conservatives in reaction to the miners' strike called by John L. Lewis in June 1943, which went ahead despite President Roosevelt having seized the mines. The Act, the first of a series of attempted curbs on the right to strike, authorized the Federal government to operate strike-hit plants and made strikes in plants under government control a criminal offence.

Smith Square The quiet square 600 yards west of the Palace of Westminster, which has customarily been the heart of British party politics. Conservative CENTRAL OFFICE is there, across the road from TRANSPORT HOUSE, which the Labour Party used at the 1983 and 1987 elections even though it had moved its headquarters to WALWORTH ROAD. The LIBERAL DEMOCRATS' headquarters is in Cowley Street, a stone's throw away.

Adam Smith Institute One of the RADICAL right-wing THINK TANKs that flourished in Britain in the 1980s under the patronage of Margaret Thatcher, and urged her on to even more adventurous policies under the direction of Dr. Madsen Pirie, a Scot like Adam Smith (*see* WEALTH OF NATIONS), after whom the Institute was named. When John MAJOR came under heavy attack from Thatcherites in 1992–93 for "abandoning" her policies, Dr. Pirie rallied to his defence, arguing that in pursuing policies such as rail privatization which Mrs. Thatcher had shied away from, Major was proving himself at least as radical.

Sir Cyril Smith *See* BIG CYRIL.

smoke-filled room The selection of a candidate or adoption of a policy by a group of shadowy but powerful figures striking a deal away from the public gaze and in their own interests. The CAUCUS CLUB that ran colonial Boston in the 18th century has been called the original smoke-filled room, but the name was apparently first bestowed in 1920 by the Ohio politician Harry Daugherty on the process that led to Warren HARDING receiving the Republican nomination:

> The convention will be deadlocked, and after the other candidates have gone their limit, some 12 or 15 men, worn out and bleary-eyed for lack of sleep, will sit down about 2 o'clock in the morning in a smoke-filled room in some hotel and decide the nomination. When that time comes, Harding will be selected.

The room in question was Suite 404-6 on the 13th floor of the Blackstone Hotel in Chicago, where Harding was summoned by fifteen Republican power brokers and asked to swear that there were no skeletons in his cupboard. After retiring for ten minutes to ring one or both of his mistresses, Harding returned to assure them there were not, and was handed the nomination. There followed the most corrupt administration in America's history.

smoking bimbo An attractive and probably air-headed young girl who is waiting for a critical moment in an election campaign to "kiss and tell" about an affair – real or alleged – with one of the candidates. The phrase, coined after the exposure of Gary Hart in 1988 (*see*

MONKEY BUSINESS), gained wider currency after the charges levelled by Gennifer Flowers against Bill Clinton (*see* COMEBACK KID) at the start of the 1992 campaign. It was a derivation of the following.

smoking gun One of many graphic phrases given to the political vocabulary by the WATERGATE affair. The "smoking gun" was the transcript of a tape of three conversations between Richard Nixon (*see* TRICKY DICK) and his CHIEF OF STAFF H. R. Haldeman which proved that Nixon had ordered the Watergate COVER-UP six days after the break-in. It took a unanimous ruling by the SUPREME COURT before the White House would hand over the tapes; within hours of the transcript's release, previously pro-Nixon members of the House Judiciary Committee threw their weight behind a first article of IMPEACHMENT.

smoking room The inner sanctum close to the Chamber of the HOUSE OF COMMONS, beyond the TEA ROOM, where MPs – customarily mainly Conservatives – may relax away from the pressures imposed by staff, visiting constituents and the Press.

> The toffs' bar. RICHARD NEEDHAM MP (Con.).

Smoot-Hawley tariff The PROTECTIONIST measure passed by the US Congress in 1930 that raised TARIFFs to their highest levels ever – the average duty rising from the already-high FORDNEY-McCUMBER levels to 60% – and was widely blamed for the severity of the GREAT DEPRESSION. The world economy was already tottering, not least because of the GREAT CRASH on Wall Street, but Smoot-Hawley was seen as the final shove. A thousand economists petitioned President HOOVER to VETO the Bill, but he ignored their warnings. By the end of the year, 33 countries had taken retaliatory action and world trade was spiralling into SLUMP. Sen. Reed Smoot, the Bill's co-sponsor, was the first Mormon Senator when he took his seat in 1903 (*see* ADULTERY).

> It gave protectionism, with which Congress had been preoccupied for most of a century, a bad name and dethroned the tariff as a dominant issue in American politics.
>
> JAMES H. HUTSON, *To Make All Laws*.

snake. snake in the tunnel The forerunner of the Exchange Rate Mechanism (ERM) of the European Monetary System. Although the phrase recalls the "one-eyed trouser snake" of the Australian entertainer Barry Humphries, it actually applies to a graph of how the values of the currencies of the EC's founder members should perform against each other. If a currency rose above or fell below the "tunnel" of permitted relative values it would either have to take remedial economic measures or make a formal DEVALUATION or REVALUATION.

snake-oil salesman A political trickster, trading false promises for votes. The term originated in 19th-century rural America, where hucksters offered bogus cures and medicines (snake oil being one of them) at country fairs.

snap election In a system (like Britain's and those of many Commonwealth countries) where the head of government is free to determine the date when an election can be called, the sudden announcement of an election at a time when the political community is not expecting it. Such elections are usually called well before the last appointed date, at a moment when a government with a slim majority or none at all believes it can capture the initiative and tighten its grip on power.

SNCC Student Non-violent Co-ordinating Committee. A CIVIL RIGHTS organization founded by Black and White student activists in Raleigh, North Carolina, in April 1960. In the early 1960s the SNCC joined other groups, such as CORE and Martin Luther KING's Southern Christian Leadership Conference, to organize SIT-INs to desegregate lunch counters and other facilities in the South; it also campaigned to encourage Black voter registration. The SNCC originally espoused King's NON-VIOLENT integrationism, but by 1966, under Stokely Carmichael, it had abandoned this for the militant CHAUVINISM of BLACK POWER, and supporting the revolutionary tactics of the BLACK PANTHERS, whose emblem it had adopted in 1965. The organization collapsed in 1969 when Carmichael's successor, Hubert "Rap" Brown, was convicted of armed robbery.

> The only position for women in the SNCC is prone.
>
> STOKELY CARMICHAEL, 1965.

snouts in the trough The graphic phrase for trade unions' determination to get at least their share out of the UK economy, popularized in the late 1970s by Sid (later Lord) Weighell (1922–), general secretary of the National Union of Railwaymen. He told the Labour Party conference on 6 October 1978:

> If you want it to go out . . . that you now believe in the philosophy of the pig trough – that those with the biggest snouts should get the largest share – I reject it.

But during the election campaign the following April, he said:

> I don't see how we can talk with Mrs. Thatcher . . . I will say to the lads: "Come on, get your snouts in the trough."

SNP Scottish National Party. The party that since 1928 has campaigned for independence for Scotland as a sovereign nation, and can now count on support from around a quarter of the country's voters. It was founded as the National Party of Scotland by a combination of disaffected ILP members, journalists, intellectuals and nationalist activists, and retains both the intellectual and the propaganda high ground. The party, which merged with others in 1934 to take its present form, won its first Parliamentary seat (briefly) at Motherwell in 1945, but had to wait until the late 1960s for lasting success. Disenchantment with the established UK parties, the decline of the Scottish economy and the discovery of North Sea oil off Aberdeen and Shetland gave the SNP a head of steam, and in 1967 Winifred Ewing (*see* MADAME ÉCOSSE) won the Hamilton BY-ELECTION from Labour. In 1970 the SNP doubled their vote at any previous election and won one Parliamentary seat (Mrs. Ewing losing hers). In February 1974 the party captured seven seats and that October won 30% of the vote in Scotland, taking 11 seats and panicking Labour into embracing DEVOLUTION. When Labour eventually held a Home Rule referendum in March 1979, the SNP pressed for a "Yes" vote while hinting that rejection of the plan would mean a General Election and the end of the unpopular Callaghan government. This duly happened, but the SNP were as heavy losers (*see* TURKEYS VOTING FOR AN EARLY CHRISTMAS). From 1979 the SNP slipped back as Labour, now in opposition, reasserted itself as Scotland's dominant party; in 1987 it won three seats and 14% of the vote. The party suffered strains and splits between its Socialist wing and those anxious for gains outside the central belt (*see* tartan TORIES). The party's fortunes revived in the closing years of the Thatcher government, and under the aggressive leadership of Alex Salmond as the 1992 election approached. A sudden upsurge of media support for independence gave the SNP a new impetus, but although the party – which had refused to co-operate with the Home Rule Constitutional Convention – almost doubled its vote, it still took only three seats.

> They dream of the politics of Brigadoon.
>
> DONALD DEWAR, Labour's Shadow Scottish Secretary 1983–92.

> The day the SNP's problems began was the day it took on its second member. FERGUS EWING.

> Political maggots. DENNIS CANAVAN MP (Lab.).

so little done, so much to do The last words of Cecil Rhodes (1853–1902), financier, Prime Minister of Cape Colony 1890–96 and founder of Rhodesia (*see* CAPE TO CAIRO). His words have often been misquoted as "So much to do, so little time." Rhodes looked in his will to the "ultimate recovery [by Britain] of the United States of America". Some sources claim his actual last words were

> Turn me over, Jack.

S.O.20 Standing Order 20. The rule under which MPs at Westminster may seek an EMERGENCY DEBATE. It entitles any member, at the end of QUESTION TIME, to apply to the SPEAKER for the suspension of STANDING ORDERS for a debate on a matter of urgency; it is up to the Chair to decide whether the issue is so important that it should be given precedence over scheduled business. On the rare occasions that such a request is granted, the debate takes place either that evening or the following day. Until the mid-1980s the procedure was governed by Standing Order 9.

Soames. l'affaire Soames The furore in 1969 caused by the leaking of uncomplimentary remarks about President DE GAULLE by Sir Christopher (later Lord) Soames (1920–87), British Ambassador in Paris and Winston Churchill's son-in-law.

soapbox campaign An election campaign featuring informal street-corner speeches, delivered standing on a wooden box. John MAJOR, who had started his political life making such speeches as a teenager in Brixton, did it to great effect during his come-from-behind election campaign in 1992. Many Tory voters who turned out for his early WALKABOUTs complained that he did not speak; when the soapbox was produced from his campaign bus, all that changed. Neil KINNOCK observed scornfully: "What's at issue in this election is not soap boxes that Prime Ministers stand on. It's cardboard boxes that people live in." But Major had the last laugh by winning the election.

Social. Social Chapter The section of the MAASTRICHT TREATY which advanced Europe's SOCIAL DIMENSION; it was only to apply to eleven of the twelve signatories as Britain insisted on being exempted. In July 1993 a vote on the Chapter came within a whisker of bringing down John MAJOR's government. It only survived after demanding a vote of CONFIDENCE.

Social Charter The package of social measures devised and largely implemented by the EC in advance of Maastricht. It dealt with such areas as maternity leave, night work and maximum hours. Britain under Margaret Thatcher (*see* IRON LADY) refused to accept it, but UK Ministers then opted back into two-thirds of its provisions.

Social Contract Originally the blueprint for DEMOCRACY advocated in 1762 by the French philosopher Jean-Jacques Rousseau. It was based on the concept of the general will. Rousseau wrote:

> In order that the social compact may not be an empty formula, it tacitly includes the undertaking . . . that whoever refuses to obey the general will shall be compelled to do so by the whole body. This means nothing less than he will be forced to be free.

The idea terrified generations of conservatives, Metternich writing to Tsar Alexander I: "You only have to mention a social contract and the revolution is made."

In 1973 Harold WILSON adopted it as the title for the agreement reached between his LABOUR PARTY and the TUC. Labour agreed to pursue economic and social policies that would benefit union members; in return the unions promised to hold down wage increases. But Labour was elected the following year with the economy deteriorating and in autumn 1975 the unions were obliged to accept a voluntary PRICES AND INCOMES POLICY. Later pacts between Labour and the Unions were known as the **Social Compact** – a term Rousseau also used.

> You might as well try to control a rutting elephant with a pea-shooter. LORD HAILSHAM.

Social Credit An economic doctrine based on the ideas of an English engineer, Clifford Douglas (1879–1952), which spawned a political movement in Canada after 1930. Douglas believed that money, or "social credit", should be distributed to give people access to the goods and services produced by a capitalist economy, and that lack of that credit provoked economic instability. During the GREAT DEPRESSION a Social Credit party came to power in Alberta in 1935 under the radio evangelist William Aberhart (1878–1943); backed by hard-pressed ranchers with heavy mortgages, it won nine successive elections, staying in power until 1971 but becoming increasingly conservative. British Columbia elected a Social Credit government in 1952. The federal party held seats in the Ottawa Parliament until 1980; since then the movement has declined and the Alberta party has been disbanded. *See also* CRÉDITISTES.

social democracy In the late 20th century a term for a socially-concerned and left-of-centre political stance, firmly anti-Communist, but originally a term commensurate with Marxism. The term **Social Democrat** was adopted by Wilhelm Liebknecht and August Bebel when they founded Germany's MARXIST Social Democratic Labour Party in 1869. Britain's first Marxist party was the Social Democratic Federation, founded by H. M. Hyndman in 1881; it amalgamated with other groups to create the British Socialist Party in 1911 and the COMMUNIST PARTY of Great Britain in 1920. The rump of the SDF was dissolved in 1958.

> The main characteristics of the tactics of social democracy are not "invented" but are the result of a continuous series of great creative acts of the elementary class struggle. ROSA LUXEMBURG (1871–1919).

As social democracy moved towards the centre, STALIN denounced it as "the moderate wing of fascism". In Britain, it reached its apotheosis in the SDP.

social dimension The functions and competency of the EUROPEAN COMMUNITY in the field of social affairs, which most member states (though in most respects not Britain) have been eager to embrace in the 1990s.

> There can be no Europe without a social dimension. JACQUES DELORS.

Social Fund The fund devised by Margaret Thatcher's government, and implemented by John MAJOR as social security minister, to make loans – instead of the previous grants – to the needy poor. The grants were paid whenever there was proven need; the Social Fund is CASH-LIMITED.

social market *See* MARKET.

social ownership Ownership of industries or enterprises by the community. The term embraces NATIONALIZATION but covers a number of other ways in which the public can take a stake.

social security The system of payments made by modern states to cushion the effects of poverty, unemployment, disability and other forms of disadvantage on members of the community. In America the 1935 Social Security Act was a central feature of the NEW DEAL; but the decision to finance the scheme totally from employee's contributions slowed the economy. The British system, pioneered by Lloyd George and made comprehensive in Attlee's WELFARE STATE, has always required contributions from employee *and* employer.

socialism The most durable and broadly-based of the political doctrines to have emerged from the Industrial Revolution. Its essence is common provision for those with less by those with more, with common ownership of the economy (or elements of it) and an ultimate goal of equality. One of its early champions, Keir Hardie, declared: "Defeat is not in the Socialist dictionary" – a theme taken up by the RED FLAG. It has also traditionally had a strong visionary and romantic element (*see* JERUSALEM). COMMUNISTS have seen socialism as an ultimate objective, but have been unwilling or unable to achieve it. Indeed LENIN wrote:

> We cannot outline socialism. What socialism will look like when it takes on its final form we do not know and cannot say.

Despite its intellectual adherents, socialism is inherently a mass movement. First advocated in coherent form by the Frenchman Louis Blanc (1811–82) at much the same time as MARX and Engels were developing Communism, it developed differently country by country – with varying degrees of militancy. In Britain it became the ideology of the LABOUR PARTY; it drew inspiration from Marxism, OWENISM, religious nonconformism and trade unionism, and its heart has been CLAUSE FOUR. Socialism in the US has never been able to shrug off connotations of UN-AMERICANISM. But Eugene Debs and Norman Thomas polled up to 2 million votes as Presidential candidates, and one Socialist was elected to Congress in 1990.

To George Bernard Shaw socialism meant "equality of income or nothing", to H. G. Wells it was "no more and no less a criticism of the idea of property in the light of public good". In the ATTLEE years "equality of opportunity" was the watchword, while Harold WILSON asserted: "If there is one word I would use to identify modern socialism, it is 'science.'" In America Earl WARREN scored a bull's eye when he said: "Many people consider the things which government does for them to be social progress, but they consider the things government does for others as socialism."

The deepest division between socialists has been over how far to go in achieving their aims. Georges Sorel (1847–1992) maintained that "socialism would not continue to exist without an apology for violence", and Rosa Luxemburg declared: "The victory of socialism will not descend like rain from heaven." The American trade unionist William HAYWOOD (*see also* WOBBLIES), insisted that "no socialist can be a law-abiding citizen". But Claude-Frédéric Bastiat (1801–50), argued: "You would oppose law to socialism. But it is the law that socialism invokes. It aspires to legal, not extra-legal plunder." Socialism has had its fair share of critics. John Maynard KEYNES, in the 1920s, termed it "a dusty survival of a plan to meet the problems of 50 years ago, based on a misunderstanding of what someone said 100 years ago"; the *Detroit Journal* tagged it "Bolshevism with a shave". To CHURCHILL socialism was "the philosophy of failure, the creed of ignorance and the gospel of envy"; the rumbustious Tory Lord Hailsham saw it as "an excellent way of sharing misery, but not a good way of creating abundance". And the Conservative MP Sir Gilbert Longden argued that "since excellence is the first casualty of equality, socialism is the standard-bearer of the second rate". More recently Norman Tebbit declared socialism "not dead but brain-dead". Cecil Palmer reckoned that "socialism is workable only in heaven, where it isn't needed, and in hell where they've got it". Margaret Thatcher denounced Socialism as "an alien creed". And Frank Dobson told a Labour SELECTION CONFERENCE: "The two greatest obstacles to socialism are Margaret Thatcher and Camden housing department"; he gave the credit for the one-liner to his colleague Jack Straw.

As to socialists themselves, George Orwell, after his bitter experiences in Spain, declared: "As with the Christian religion, the worst advertisement for socialism is its adherents." And the playwright Tom Stoppard wrote: "Socialists treat their servants with respect and then wonder why they vote Conservative." Britain's CONSERVATIVE PARTY for many years insisted on always referring to LABOUR as "the Socialists", and Tory-controlled newspapers followed suit, making the study of election results mildly confusing.

socialism by the back door Margaret Thatcher's characterization of the plans of Jacques DELORS for the European Community, especially in the social field.

socialism in one country The doctrine was at first scorned by LENIN and STALIN; subsequently adopted for Soviet Russia by Stalin in opposition to TROTSKY's doctrine of PERMANENT REVOLUTION.

Socialism in Our Time The policy statement issued by the Independent Labour Party (ILP) in 1927. Its main proposal, based on the views of the KEYNESIAN economist J. A. Hobson, was that a future Labour government should introduce a "living wage" to keep up demand and create full employment. For two years RAMSAY MACDonald was pressed to adopt this policy, but he opted for a less radical approach.

socialism is the language of priorities The watchword for realistic Socialist progress sounded by Aneurin BEVAN, speaking for Attlee's government, at Labour's 1950 party conference; his actual words were:

> The language of priorities is the language of socialism.

Within months, Bevan had resigned over the Attlee government's decision to impose charges for NHS false teeth and spectacles.

Save America from Socialism The Republicans' campaign slogan in 1936 when they put forward Alf Landon (*see* KANSAS COOLIDGE) to defeat Franklin D. Roosevelt and his NEW DEAL policies.

socialism with a human face Also quoted as "Communism with a human face", this was the aim of Alexander Dubček (1921–92), Czech Communist leader during the PRAGUE SPRING. It involved freedom of expression and an opening of links with the West, without taking Czechoslovakia out of the Communist bloc; it was not a doctrine the Soviet Union under Leonid BREZHNEV (1906–82) would tolerate. The phrase was suggested to Dubček by his colleague Radovan Richta.

African socialism The doctrine and style of government evolved in post-colonial Africa by Julius Nyerere (1922–), President of Tanzania for a quarter of a century from 1962, and others. To its supporters it is a vigorous and appropriate means of caring for the people, to many Westerners a byword for stagnation and decline.

creeping socialism President Eisenhower's term for the NEW DEAL policies of Franklin D. Roosevelt and Harry S. Truman. Opposing continued expansion of the TVA, Ike said on 11 June 1953:

> I believe that for the past 20 years there has been a creeping socialism spreading in the United States.

Christian Socialism The catch-all name for a variety of movements and tendencies which have promoted Socialism as the Kingdom of God on earth, or regarded it as identical with the social teachings of Christ. MARX and Engels scorned it as "the holy water with which the priest consecrates the heart-burnings of the aristocrat". And Pope Pius IX scathingly dismissed it as "a contradiction in terms".

democratic socialism The ethos of Britain's LABOUR PARTY for most of its history, and of most European socialist parties since World War II. The term emphasizes a contrast with the centralist nature of Communism, and with SOCIAL DEMOCRACY which lacks the cutting edge of a concrete ideology. Yet according to the Australian Russell Prowse: "The term Democratic Socialism makes as much sense as pregnant virginity."

designer socialism Not quite the same as RADICAL CHIC, designer socialism is a 1980s term suggesting a watered-down ideology composed of trendy off-the-peg notions with immediate, glitzy appeal.

Future of Socialism, The The seminal book, published in 1956, by the British Labour politician Anthony Crosland (1918–77), which argued that socialist parties would increasingly have to veer away from ideology to concentrate on provision for the disadvantaged. It was attacked by the left as a GAITSKELLITE heresy, but since the mid-1980s Labour has adopted a very similar stance.

gas and water socialism In Britain, the powerful strain in the LABOUR PARTY before and after World War II involved in the provision of ever-improving public services through municipal SOCIALISM or under NATIONALIZATION. The powerful base Labour established between the wars in the government of London and other major cities heightened this emphasis on the community as provider, through its elected representatives. After Labour took office in 1945 most of the municipal services were transferred to the state (*see* Morrisonian NATIONALIZATION); ironically Morrison as leader of the LCC had done much to perfect the system at local government level.

guild socialism A movement, prominent in early 20th-century Britain, that sought to reorganize each industry under workers' guilds, creating a form of WORKERS' CONTROL. Its ideological impetus came from A. J. Penty's *The Restoration of the Guild System* (1906). His arguments for reviving the mediaeval guilds were taken up by A. R. Orage and S. G. Hobson, who delevoped them into a comprehensive blueprint for modern guilds based on existing trade unions, with a strongly SYNDICALIST tinge. Orage and Hobson argued that the guild structure would avoid the BUREAUCRACY inherent in a centralized SOCIALIST state. The National Guilds League, formed in 1915, promoted the idea within the trade unions and at first made a considerable impact. But its influence dwindled as the unions became firmly politicized at the end of World War I. A National Building Guild briefly enjoyed some success building low-cost houses, but petered out when its Government contract ended.

municipal socialism The doctrine and practice under which elected local authorities create as much of a CRADLE TO GRAVE support system for their people as central government will permit. Some Labour councils in Britain have diversified beyond transport systems and comprehensive social services to back – and even attempt to own – new local industries.

scientific socialism The term used for COMMUNISM by the founders of the movement, and made much of in the 1970s and 1980s by the Soviet leadership and leaders of Communist regimes in eastern Europe.

> These two great discoveries, the materialistic conception of history and the revelation of the secret of capitalistic production through surplus-value, we owe to Marx. With these discoveries, socialism becomes a science.
>
> FRIEDRICH ENGELS (1820–95).

Socialist International The body comprising mainly Western European parties which brings together the world's principal Democratic SOCIALIST movements. Its affiliates in Eastern Europe turned out to be *émigré* groups, and have made little impact since the collapse of Communism.

Socialist Organizer A far-left group, based like MILITANT on a magazine, which has caused the leadership of Britain's Labour Party considerable embarrassment, leading to the expulsion of a number of its activists from the party. It is strongest in London.

socialist realism The approved – and only permitted – method of artistic composition in the Soviet Union from the 1930s, devoted to building and glorifying the socialist achievement. Though it produced some interesting results at first, *e.g.* in the work of Andrei Goncharov (1903–), the style later degenerated into idealistic representations of the alleged heroic successes of the Soviet economy and society, devoid of artistic or literary merit. Its mirror-image was a rigid censorship of the arts.

Socialist Workers' Party (SWP) Together with its rival the WORKERS' REVOLUTIONARY PARTY, Britain's most active party to the left of Labour from the mid-1970s. It grew from *International Socialism*, a sect originally within the Labour Party founded by Tony Cliff *c.* 1960. It places particular emphasis on ANTI-RACISM and opposition to immigration controls.

> We don't pretend we believe in the Parliamentary system. We bloody well don't believe in it.
>
> SWP spokesman DUNCAN HALLAS, 1982.

> The SWP are the worst kind of racists – liberal racists. They are the ones who believe they have to help blacks. They don't believe blacks can help themselves.
>
> LINTON KWEZI JOHNSON, poet.

We are all socialists nowadays A remark attributed both to King Edward VII when Prince of Wales, and to Sir William Harcourt (1827–1904), Liberal Chancellor of the Exchequer. It was made in 1895, when many in the political community felt – and some regretted – that a lasting and progressive CONSENSUS had been reached on social and economic issues.

socialized medicine A generally hostile US term for a system of free medical care supervised by the state, with doctors paid by the agency running the system rather than by their patients. Used habitually to denigrate such systems in Britain and Canada, it is also turned by conservatives against any scheme to improve health care for America's less fortunate – starting with MEDICAID and MEDICARE.

society. Great Society *See* GREAT.

there is no such thing as society A remark frequently attributed to Margaret Thatcher, and seen by her opponents as the benchmark of an ideology which they believe caused severe strains within a community whose existence she would not acknowledge.

Socks The black and white cat who moved into the White House with the Clinton family in January 1993. Chelsea Clinton's parents had bought Socks in 1990 to help her over the death of her dog Zeke. The close media attention Socks attracted after her master's election led to pet psychiatrists offering to help her adjust to the high profile she would have in Washington after the quiet home life in Little Rock. Within a month of Socks moving into the White House, the ROSE GARDEN corridor smelt of cat.

Soda One of the family terriers (the other one is called Whisky) of Chris Patten, former chairman of the Conservative Party and Governor of Hong Kong, which went missing in the colony in November 1992. Australia's Foreign Minister Gareth Evans (*see* DRAFT), who was visiting Hong Kong, suggested Soda might have been served up as a delicacy by the Hong Kong Chinese; he was swiftly forced to apologize, and the dog turned up safe and sound.

soft A party's potential vote if its supporters are less than enthusiastic, and probable support for it which cannot be relied on to turn out, and which could be won over by a rival. As in "the Tory vote in Yorkshire is rather soft".

soft landing The term used by financial and political commentators *c.* 1989 for the hoped-for stabilization of the British economy after the BOOM of 1987–88 and the imposition of high interest rates by Chancellor Nigel Lawson (1932–) when it was evident the economy was dangerously OVERHEATING. John MAJOR, who succeeded Lawson in October 1989, wondered at first if there would be a landing at all, as the record 15% base rate took time to bite. But by the time he became Prime Minister late in 1990 it was clear there would be a very HARD LANDING.

soft left A pejorative comparison first made in the early 1980s between Britain's committed, BENNITE, hard LEFT and the more moderate, Tribunite (*see* TRIBUNE) left of the Labour Party who instinctively backed Michael Foot. The term lost much of its sting as the hard left lost its influence under Neil KINNOCK's leadership of the party.

soldier. A Soldier's Song (Irish *Amhran na bhFiann*) The national anthem since 1926 of the IRISH REPUBLIC. It was written in English and Irish in 1907 by Patrick Kearney, the music jointly with Patrick Heeney. Until the mid-1980s it was an offence to play the tune in NORTHERN IRELAND lest it inflame SECTARIAN feeling. The first stanza is:

> Soldiers are we, whose lives are pledged to Ireland;
> Some have come from a land beyond the wave,

Sworn to be free, no more our ancient sireland
Shall shelter the despot or the slave.
Tonight we man the *bearna baoil* (gap of danger);
In Erin's cause, come well or weal;
'Mid cannon's roar and rifle's peal,
We'll chant a soldier's song.

Soledad brothers A *cause célèbre* for US liberal activists and Black revolutionaries, arising from the shooting of the BLACK POWER activist George Jackson on 28 August 1971 as he tried to escape from San Quentin prison in California. The belief persisted in the radical community that Jackson had been encouraged to escape to give a pretext for the shooting. George Jackson (1942–) had become a hero to opponents of Martin Luther KING's creed of NON-VIOLENCE through his book *The Soledad Brothers*, written in the prison of that name. His parents were less understanding, Jackson writing to his mother on 26 March 1967:

You don't want us to resist and defeat our enemies. What is wrong with you, Mama?

Solidarity (1) The principle of "one for all and all for one", particularly among trade unionists and between left-wing international movements. (2) In EUROPEAN COMMUNITY jargon, the assurance by nations or the EC itself of the means to provide each family with its basic needs. (3) The free, strongly Catholic trade-union movement in Poland, which challenged the COMMUNIST system and survived persecution to take power. Solidarity was born of the 1979 Gdansk shipyard strike over the sacking of the workers' leader Lech Walesa (1943–) from his job as an electrician. In 1980 he was re-employed, and that August founded Solidarity (*Solidarność*). In November 1980 Solidarity forced the authorities to register it as a trade union, with rights of free association and COLLECTIVE BARGAINING. But its rising popularity (it soon gained 10 million members) and the effectiveness of the strikes it organized for better conditions alarmed the government of General Jaruzelski, and in 1981 it was banned and martial law declared. Walesa was imprisoned, but was released the next year, though Communist efforts to smear his reputation continued. With the Kremlin in retreat under Mikhail Gorbachev, Solidarity stood its ground and in 1989 took a stake in power in Eastern Europe's first non-Communist government for four decades. In 1990 Walesa was elected President in Poland's first free elections for 45 years.

He who once became aware of the power of Solidarity and who breathed the air of freedom will not be crushed.
LECH WALESA.

something must be done The verdict of King Edward VIII (1874–1972) on the GREAT DEPRESSION, given on a visit to a closed-down steelworks in South Wales during his brief reign in 1936. His remarks embarrassed the BALDWIN government, but gave him lasting popularity in the Welsh valleys. The King said:

These works brought all these people here. Something must be done to find them work.

Sonnenfeldt doctrine America's acceptance during the FORD administration that encouraging resistance to Communism by citizens of Europe's Soviet SATELLITES would bring a brutal crackdown, not freedom. The doctrine was proposed in 1976 by Helmut Sonnenfeldt, a senior member of the NATIONAL SECURITY COUNCIL. After the brutal Soviet suppression of the HUNGARIAN UPRISING in 1956 with the loss of 7000 lives, Congressional hearings blamed the US-sponsored Radio Free Europe for inciting the people to rebel. The intervention by WARSAW PACT countries to end the PRAGUE SPRING of 1968 reinforced the West's impotence in the face of the BREZHNEV DOCTRINE. The Sonnenfeldt doctrine also reflected the Nixon/Ford administration's belief that a less hawkish line towards Communism would aid DETENTE; the Carter administration abandoned the policy in reaction to the Soviet invasion of Afghanistan at the end of 1978.

sound. sound bite A term first used by American TV and radio journalists *c.* 1968, and seized on by political managers, for a brief quote making the maximum political impact. The proliferation of the sound bite stems from research showing that most viewers and listeners can absorb information for at most 30 seconds. In 1968 a Presidential candidate could speak uninterrupted during the average interview for 43 seconds; by 1988 it was down to 9 seconds. In 1992 some networks refused to let sound bites set the agenda and insisted that any statement broadcast must last at least 20 seconds.

When Nixon went out to make a statement in the White House briefing room, he insisted that he be given one hundred words – and we had to count 'em.
DAVID GERGEN (1942–), later Communications Director in the Reagan and Clinton White House.

sound on A mainly British term for a legislator's reliability on a particular issue, *i.e.* "sound on Europe".

Most MPs are not clever – it is just enough that they are sound. JULIAN CRITCHLEY MP (Con.).

source. sources close to the Prime Minister The phrase frequently used by Westminster journalists to describe the Downing Street press secretary, who under LOBBY convention cannot be named unless he chooses to speak "on the record" (*see* OFF).

informed source, an A term common to political journalists in Washington, at Westminster and elsewhere for an insider who provides information but does not wish to be named.

> Nobody believes the official spokesman, but everybody trusts an unidentified source.
>
> Gerald FORD's press secretary, RON NESSEN.

South, the The states of the CONFEDERACY, also the losing side in America's CIVIL WAR. The northern position, as the conflict approached, was put by Rep. David Wilmot of Pennsylvania, who said in 1846:

> I am jealous of the power of the South. The South holds no prerogative under the Constitution which entitles her to wield forever the scepter of power in this Republic, to fix by her own arbitrary edict the principles and policy of this government and to build up and tear down at pleasure.

During the war Rep. Benjamin Harris of Maryland was censured by Congress for telling supporters of the UNION: "The South asked you to let them live in peace. But no; you said you would bring them into subjection. I hope that you will never subjugate the South."

South Lawn The expanse of grass beneath the south portico of the WHITE HOUSE, facing toward the ELLIPSE, on which WELCOMING CEREMONIES are held when world leaders arrive to meet the President.

> Someone asked why we didn't put a stop to Sam [Donaldson] shouting out questions at us when we're out on the South Lawn. We can't. If we did, the starlings would come back.
>
> RONALD REAGAN.

Solid South The power-base of Conservative DEMOCRATS in the century following the CIVIL WAR, with the Republicans discredited among White voters as the party of Blacks, CARPETBAGGERS and RECONSTRUCTION. Between 1876 and 1920, the Republicans failed to carry a single Southern state in Presidential elections. The almost-automatic re-election of INCUMBENTS, combined with the SENIORITY system, gave its representatives a stranglehold on Congressional committee chairmanships until the 1970s, when the posts were opened to election. The term became current in the 1880 election, when after the withdrawal of Federal troops southern Whites were free to "vote as they shot" in the Civil War, and Republicans warned that the old Confederacy could, with a few Northern allies, win control of the Federal government.

Southern strategy The strategy followed by REPUBLICAN Presidential candidates from Barry Goldwater onwards, to capture the White House with a conservative platform that would win key Southern states from the Democrats, giving it critical votes in the ELECTORAL COLLEGE. At the heart of the strategy was an emphasis on STATES' RIGHTS and a reluctance to expand CIVIL RIGHTS legislation.

sovereign A supreme ruler or head; specifically the Monarch of the United Kingdom and those Commonwealth countries which acknowledge the CROWN. King Charles I held that "a subject and a sovereign are clear different things", and paid for his belief with his head.

> Obedience to the laws and to the Sovereign is obedience to a higher Power, divinely instituted for the good of the people, not of the Sovereign, who has equally duties and obligations.
>
> Queen VICTORIA.

sovereignty The "absolute and perpetual" power of a nation to control its own affairs. In the United Kingdom that power is customarily vested in the CROWN IN PARLIAMENT, though some of that sovereignty has since 1973 been, controversially, "pooled" within the EUROPEAN COMMUNITY. CHURCHILL anticipated this development, saying in 1950: "National sovereignty is not inviolable, and it may be resolutely diminished for the sake of all the men in all the lands finding their way home together." Shortly afterward, Anthony EDEN observed: "Every successive scientific discovery makes greater nonsense of the old-time conceptions of sovereignty." Margaret Thatcher, especially in her anti-MAASTRICHT mode after losing office, did not agree. In America the concept of sovereignty relates both to Federal and state jurisdictions. Henry Clay declared in 1850: "I owe allegiance to two sovereignties: one is to the sovereignty of this Union and the other is to the sovereignty of the state of Kentucky."

sovereignty association The formula for a looser relationship between Quebec and Canada, amounting to political but not economic independence, which the SEPARATIST *Parti Québecois* Premier René Levesque put to a referendum on 20 May 1980. After a strong campaign against the proposal by Federal Prime Minister Pierre TRUDEAU, 59.2% of electors voted "Non", including 52% of French speakers.

popular sovereignty The theory, embodied in the US CONSTITUTION, that sovereignty rests in the people and not in a crowned head. In 1795 George III removed Charles James Fox from the PRIVY COUNCIL for giving the toast: "Our sovereign, the people!" The Austrian statesman Metternich later dismissed the concept because "the sovereignty of the people must be delegated by them to an authority other than the sovereign".

Soviet A local council or workplace body elected by workers, peasants or soldiers, and a fundamental of the BOLSHEVIK state established by LENIN in Russia from 1917. The system came to cover the entire Union of Soviet Socialist republics (Soviet Union), with the higher tiers containing representatives of those below.

Soviet bloc The term which gained currency after WORLD WAR II for the voting bloc of Communist states at the UNITED NATIONS headed by the Society Union, and the geographical entity they comprised.

Soviet Union The state founded by Lenin in 1917, and presided over with varying degrees of brutality by STALIN, Khruschev and Brezhnev, which collapsed in the autumn of 1991 after the unsuccessful Communist coup against President Gorbachev.

> Judged by every standard which history has applied to governments, the Soviet government of Russia is one of the most tyrannical that has ever existed in the world. It accords no political rights. It rules by terror. It punishes political opinions. It suppresses free speech. It tolerates no newspaper but its own. It persecuted Christianity with a zeal and a cunning unmatched since the times of the Roman emperors. It is engaged at this moment in trampling down the peoples of Georgia and exterminating their leaders by hundreds. CHURCHILL, 1924.

As the Soviet Union ossified but remained threatening under Brezhnev, President Carter's NATIONAL SECURITY ADVISER Dr. Zbigniew Brzezinski termed it "the only nation entirely surrounded by hostile Communist countries", and Denis Healey (*see* GROMYKO OF THE LABOUR PARTY) as "Upper Volta with rockets". After the brief interregna of Yuri Andropov and Konstantin Chernenko, Mikhail Gorbachev from 1985 abandoned key aspects of Soviet policy and ideology, bringing an end to the COLD WAR. But his inability to reform the economy prompted the reactionary KREMLIN COUP of 19 August 1991.

Supreme Soviet The ultimate executive authority in the Soviet Union, the peak of the pyramid of the system of Soviets.

All power to the Soviets! A slogan adopted by BOLSHEVIK forces during the OCTOBER REVOLUTION of 1917, and taken up officially by the new Soviet state.

space. Space Cadet The nickname accorded to **Jerry** (Edmund G.) **Brown** (1938–) as he developed from an environmentally-sensitive Governor of California who as the spiritual heir of Robert F. KENNEDY made a strong pitch for the Presidency in 1976, into a long-shot candidate in 1992 with an almost New Age philosophy and a yen for direct public ACCOUNTABILITY (*see* 1–800).

> Edward G. (Jerry) Brown Jr., the former Governor of California who has been alternately labeled a visionary and a "space cadet", was elected chairman of the state Democratic Party late Sunday. *New York Times*, 13 February 1989.

Space Race The defence-related rivalry between America and the Soviet Union to get a man into space, a man to the Moon and then onward to interplanetary travel. The Soviets' launch of the first *Sputnik* in 1957 began the race, and John F. KENNEDY accelerated it when he told a JOINT SESSION of Congress on 25 May 1961:

> I believe that this nation should commit itself to achieving the goal, before this decade is out, of landing a man on the moon and returning him safely to earth.

And on 20 July 1969, when America won the race to the Moon, Richard Nixon declared:

> For years politicians have promised the moon. I'm the first one to be able to deliver it.

Spaceship Earth The concept of our planet as a spacecraft that carries its inhabitants as passengers. The implication is that we are travelling through space alone, with our survival depending on a fragile ecology with limited natural resources and threatened by a polluted environment. The idea dates back at least to 1965 when Adlai Stevenson, in his last speech to UNESCO, said:

> We travel together, passengers on a little space ship, dependent on its vulnerable reserves of air and soil.

It was popularized by the *Operating Manual for Spaceship Earth* (1969), written by R. Buckminster Fuller (1895–1983), the US architect who developed the geodesic dome, and was influential in creating the GREEN movement.

> The most important thing about Spaceship Earth: an instruction book didn't come with it. R. BUCKMINSTER FULLER.

> There are no passengers on Spaceship Earth. Only crew. MARSHALL McLUHAN (1911–81).

Spanish. Spanish-American War The five-month conflict in 1898, triggered by sensationalist reports of Spanish atrocities in Cuba, which resulted in America gaining the Philippines, Guam and Puerto Rico as colonies under the Treaty of PARIS, and Cuba securing nominal independence. President McKINLEY declared America's first foreign war for 50 years under pressure from the Hearst newspapers after the USS *Maine* blew up in Havana harbour on 15 February 1898. It brought Theodore Roosevelt to prominence through the feats of his ROUGH RIDERS, gave McKinley the popular support he needed to defeat William Jennings Bryan (*see* PRAIRIE AVENGER) a second time in 1900, and gave the US interests in the Pacific which were eventually to bring it into conflict with Japan.

> The most absolutely righteous foreign war. THEODORE ROOSEVELT.

Spanish Civil War The bitter conflict (1936–39) between Spain's Republican government and Nationalist insurgents, which for many contemporaries represented a classic struggle between good and evil, though they differed over which was which, and drew ideological battle lines for WORLD WAR II. The democratically-elected POPULAR FRONT government supported by urban workers, farm labourers, ANARCHISTS, Communists and much of the INTELLIGENTSIA was pitted against a reactionary coalition of the Army, Catholic Church, monarchists, industrialists and wealthy landowners. Support for the rebels from Hitler and Mussolini, and more limited backing for the Republicans from the Soviet Union, and left-wing volunteers from Europe and America in the INTERNATIONAL BRIGADES, broadened the struggle into a foretaste of the world struggle to come. Up to a million people were killed, many of them in massacres committed by both sides.

A military coup in July 1936, led by the Generals Franco and Mola, gave the rebels control of much of the south and north-west, but Barcelona and Madrid – where Soviet aid and the International Brigades proved crucial – were saved for the government by workers' militias. There followed a war of attrition, in which the Republican forces succumbed over three years to the Nationalists' superior economic and military resources. The Republicans were starved of support from the European democracies by the Anglo-French formation of a NON-INTERVENTION COMMITTEE. Openly contemptuous, Hitler sent the fighters and bombers of the Condor Legion, and Mussolini 100,000 Italian troops, to fight for Franco; both dictators used Spain as a testing ground for their latest weaponry. By 1937 Bilbao and the Basque country had been bombed into submission (*see* GUERNICA); the Nationalists then drove eastward to the Mediterranean, splitting the republic in two in April 1938. Catalonia was overrun by February 1939; fighting then erupted in Madrid between rival Communist factions and on 28 March the city surrendered to the Nationalists. The war established Franco as unchallenged CAUDILLO of Spain for 36 years (*see also* FALANGE).

Spartacists An extreme socialist group in Germany that flourished between 1916 and 1919. It was founded by Karl Liebknecht who, with Rosa Luxemburg, led the attempted GERMAN REVOLUTION in January 1919; it was crushed by the government of Karl Ebert, with both being killed. The movement took its name from the Thracian gladiator Spartacus, who in 73 B.C. led a slave rebellion against Rome.

Spartist A professional leftist agitator with comically infantile and KNEE-JERK views. The term was coined in Britain *c.* 1970 by PRIVATE EYE, which carried a sporadic column of militant but incoherent ramblings from "Dave Spart", which satirized the pitch made by many of the PROTEST MOVEMENT. Dave Spart was matched in the late 1970s by Deirdre Spart, a FEMINIST with equally predictable and ludicrous opinions; the pair figured regularly in lampoons of the hard LEFT.

speak. Speak for England! The resounding cry of the anguished Conservative backbencher Leo Amery (1873–1955) at Neville CHAMBERLAIN's failure to give a lead on the eve of WORLD WAR II. At 7.30 p.m. on 2 September 1939, Chamberlain disappointed the Commons by stating that further negotiations were in progress to persuade Hitler to withdraw his troops from Poland. What both sides of the House wanted was an ULTIMATUM. As Chamberlain sat down to a dismayed silence, Arthur Greenwood, the acting Labour leader (Attlee was ill) rose to speak and Amery called out: "Speak for England, Arthur!" Greenwood's declaration that "every minute's delay now means the loss of life, imperilling our national interests . . . imperilling the very foundations of our national honour" was probably the push Chamberlain needed to send the ultimatum the next morning. The absence of a German reply (*see* I HAVE TO TELL YOU THAT NO SUCH UNDERTAKING HAS BEEN RECEIVED) led Britain and France to declare war on Germany on 3 September.

Speak softly and carry a big stick – you will go far One of the most celebrated sayings of Theodore Roosevelt; in a speech at the Minnesota State Fair on 2 September 1901: TEDDY said:

> There is a homely old adage which runs: "Speak softly and carry a big stick; you will go far." If the American nation will speak softly, and yet build and keep at a pitch of the highest training a thoroughly efficient navy, the MONROE DOCTRINE will go far.

speaker (1) A person who engages in public speaking, or is delivering a speech at a particular time.

> A speaker who doesn't strike oil in ten minutes should stop boring. LORD MANCROFT (1917–).

(2) The officer who since 1376 has presided over Britain's HOUSE OF COMMONS and defended its liberties and privileges, most notably against King Charles I. The Speaker is elected from the membership of the House to represent the House to the Lords and the Crown, and to keep order in an impartial fashion; on election, it is customary to put up

a show of resistance before taking the CHAIR. The Chair is normally the last stopping-place in a political career; Lord ROSEBERY wrote: "I hate to see a man of real ability embedded in that pompous tomb." In 1992 Betty Boothroyd was elected the 186th Speaker, and the first woman (*see* MADAM SPEAKER). Her predecessor, Bernard (later Lord) Weatherill, was the first Speaker to be regularly televised at work.

> The Speaker is their mouth, and trusted by them, and so necessary as the House of Commons cannot sit without him. Sir EDWARD COKE (1552–1634).

> One of the jobs that, if you want it, you will never get it – and if you're seen to want it, you will certainly never get it. BERNARD WEATHERILL.

> I am not here to save Hon. members from themselves. GEORGE THOMAS (Viscount Tonypandy, 1909–).

(3) The most powerful figure in the US HOUSE OF REPRESENTATIVES, combining the roles of Chairman, intermediary with the President and leader of the House, outranking the MAJORITY LEADER. This role was not spelt out in the Constitution, but built up by Henry Clay (1777–1852) between 1812 and 1825. Clay not only enforced order; he also ensured that committees were dominated by his supporters, that legislation he favoured made progress and that the President took his views into account. The prestige of the Speaker sagged, but was revived during the 21-year tenure of Sam RAYBURN (1882–1961), and was more recently maintained by TIP O'Neill.

> As Speaker, a constitutional officer of this House, I must be more charitable and responsible toward my colleagues than they sometimes are towards me. TIP O'NEILL.

Speaker's Conference At Westminster, an all-party discussion convened under the Speaker to consider potential reforms to the structure of the House or the electoral system. In the late 1970s such a conference was convened to discuss how many MPs Northern Ireland should have; it agreed to raise the number from an arbitrary 12 to the 17 the province's population would require.

Speakers' Corner A paved area of London's Hyde Park, close to Marble Arch, where any citizen may exercise their right of FREEDOM OF SPEECH and try to catch the attention of passers-by. The makeshift rostrums used by some of the speakers have also earned it the name of SOAPBOX Corner.

Speaker's House The portion of the Palace of WESTMINSTER, facing the river by Westminster Bridge, which forms the official residence of the SPEAKER.

Speaker's Lobby The panelled corridor behind the Speaker's chair, with anterooms through arched doorways, which is an informal meeting-place for members of the US HOUSE OF REPRESENTATIVES. It is lined with portraits of former Speakers.

Speaker's Panel The roster of senior backbench members of the House of Commons who may be selected to chair STANDING COMMITTEES.

Speaker's procession The ritual which precedes the start of a day's business in the HOUSE OF COMMONS, when the Speaker processes with mace-bearer, chaplain and attendants from the SPEAKER'S HOUSE (*see above*) through the Central and Members' LOBBIES to the CHAMBER.

catching the Speaker's eye The Westminster phrase for being called to speak. Stanley BALDWIN, sharing the frustration of generations of MPs at not being called as often as they felt they might, described the Speaker's eye as

> That most elusive organ that nature has ever yet created.

Mr. Speaker *See* MISTER.

special. special adviser *See* POLITICAL ADVISER.

Special Drawing Rights An international unit of reserve currency created by the IMF in 1969; since 1981 it has comprised a "basket" of the five most widely-traded currencies: the US dollar, the mark, sterling, the French franc ansd the yen. In recent years it has been somewhat overshadowed by the ECU, which is traded to a far greater extent.

special election In America, an election to fill a vacancy in Congress or a State legislature caused by death or resignation. The Governor of a state is empowered to set in motion the machinery for a special election to the House or Senate, except where the state legislature has provided for the vacancy to be filled by a nominee of the governor.

special interests *See* INTEREST.

special prosecutor In particularly sensitive cases of alleged wrongdoing in high places in America, a lawyer with the highest credentials may be appointed special prosecutor in order to ascertain what charges, if any, should be brought. The most celebrated use of a special prosecutor was over WATERGATE; the IRAN-CONTRA affair is just one of many other episodes that one has been appointed to investigate.

special relationship The relationship that is supposed to exist between Britain and America, to Britain's political advantage, by virtue of their common language and historical ties. The phrase had been used before World War II, but it was CHURCHILL who promoted it as he sought to draw America into the war, then build the ATLANTIC ALLIANCE. While Churchill clearly enjoyed a "special relationship" with Roosevelt, he wanted the concept to last; in the Commons on 7 November 1945, he said:

> We should not abandon our special relationship with the United States and Canada about the atomic bomb.

And in his 1946 FULTON SPEECH, he asked:

> Would a special relationship between the United States and the British Commonwealth be inconsistent with our overriding loyalties to the World Organisation [UN]?

The special relationship has been strained by a number of crises, starting with SUEZ, when one of the partners took independent action. It has also been warped by America's ever-greater relative strength. The closeness between President Reagan and Margaret Thatcher and the extent of US aid for Britain during the FALKLANDS conflict, made the special relationship look artificially strong; but the incoming President Clinton in 1993 made plain his personal commitment, having lived in Britain.

> The dependence of London on Washington for the supply of our so-called independent nuclear weapons is all that remains of the "special relationship". It is really a ball and chain limiting our capacity to play a more positive role in the world. TONY BENN.

speech (1) The process and art of public speaking; Hitler wrote: "The broad mass of the people will only be moved by the power of speech." (2) An address to an audience or legislature, scripted or otherwise but comprising more than a question or interjection. CHURCHILL described speech-making as "the art of making deep sounds from the stomach sound like important messages from the brain". Gerald FORD stated the obvious when he said: "When a man is asked to make a speech, the first thing he has to decide is what to say," but the English statesman John Morley reckoned otherwise: "Three things matter in a speech – who says it, how he says it and what he says – and of the three, the last matters the least." And Sen. Henry Ashurst maintained that "a speech is entertaining only when serenely detached from all information". Perhaps the crispest advice to would-be speakers has come from the Duke of Wellington ("Don't quote Latin. Say what you have to say, then sit down"), Franklin D. Roosevelt ("Be sincere, be brief, be seated") and the Scottish Labour MP Jimmy Maxton ("Dinna put too much meat in your pie").

To legislators and members of the public alike, lengthy speeches have always been a trial. Samuel Pepys wrote in 1668 after speaking in the House of Commons: "We were in hopes to have a vote this day in our favour, and so the generality of the House was; but my speech being so long, many had gone out to dinner and come in again half-drunk." Thomas Jefferson observed that "speeches measured by the hour die with the hour", and Benjamin Disraeli is reputed to have said: "It is better, when a member resumes his seat after he has made a speech, for the House to have the feeling that they wish he had gone on longer instead of wondering why he did not stop sooner." Lord Brabazon of Tara advised that "if you cannot say what you have to say in 20 minutes, you should go away and write a book about it", and Lord Mancroft noted: "A speech is like a love affair. Any fool can start it, but to end it requires considerable skill." In 1984 a House of Commons motion advocating time limits stated: "This House recognizes that for a speech to be immortal it does not have to be eternal." Making a brief speech requires particular skill; Woodrow Wilson once said: "If I am to speak ten minutes, I need a week for preparation; if fifteen minutes, three days; if half an hour, two days; if an hour, I am ready now." Sometimes speeches are prolonged because the speaker inadvertently reads part of it twice; when William Whitelaw had this pointed out to him by gleeful Labour MPs, he told them: "Don't you realise that this is the most important page of my speech?" Some speeches are tedious and some downright dreadful; in 1974 Michael Foot said of a speech by the Tory front-bencher John Davies: "I have been in this House for 30 years. I thought that when I heard the Right Honourable member for Mitcham [Robert Carr] I had heard the worst speech ever delivered in the Commons. I was to be proved wrong." When Will Rogers addressed Congressmen in 1933, he told them: "You should stay awake tonight. This is one speech you haven't heard a dozen times." And Winston Churchill was moved to tell a woman who congratulated him on the turnout for one of his speeches: "If instead of making a speech I was being hanged, the crowd would be twice as big."

Perhaps the most remarkable speech ever heard in an English-speaking legislature was made by Davy Crockett (1786–1836), who alongside his other achievements served three terms in Congress. He once rose and said:

> Who-Who-Whoop-Bow-Bow-Wow-Yough! I say, Mr. Speaker, I've had a speech on soak this six months, and it has swelled me like a drowned horse; if I don't deliver it I shall burst and smash the windows. . . . I'm a screamer, and have got the roughest racking horse, the prettiest sister, the surest rifle and the ugliest dog in the district. . . . My father can whip any man in Kentucky, and I can lick my father. I can outspeak any man on this floor, and give him two hours' start. I can run faster, dive deeper, stay longer under, and come out dryer, than any chap this side the big swamp. I can outlook a panther and outstare a flash of lightning, tote a steamboat on my back and play at rough and tumble with a lion, and an

occasional kick from a zebra. To sum it all up in one word, I'm a horse. Goliath was a pretty hard colt, but I could choke him. . . . I can walk like an ox, run like a fox, swim like an eel, yell like an Indian, spout like an earthquake, make love like a mad bull, and swallow a nigger whole without choking if you butter his head and pull his ears back.

Speech! The cry that goes up when a celebrity is not due to speak, and those present want to hear them. Sometimes the shout is ironically delivered at the close of a particularly poor speech.

Speer? The question-mark that saved the life of Albert Speer (1905–81), the architect who became Hitler's Armaments Minister, after the failure of the STAUFFENBERG PLOT on 20 July 1944. The conspirators had drawn up a post-Hitler Cabinet, but had left a query against Speer's name as they could not reach him to find if he would serve. Speer survived the war, was imprisoned at NUREMBERG as a war criminal, and after his release in 1966 wrote *Inside the Third Reich*, in which he gave a revealing account of the functioning of the NAZI system and maintained that he had done his best from the inside to offset its most evil effects.

SPGB Socialist Party of Great Britain. A small, dedicated and purist but not militantly left-wing party that has operated on the margins of British politics throughout most of the 20th century. Though it has occasionally contested elections, its adherents generally write the word "Socialism" on the ballot paper, thus SPOILing it.

Spiegel affair The scandal in October 1962 which forced the resignation of the West German defence minister Franz Josef Strauss (1915–88), and was probably decisive in denying him the CHANCELLORship. The editors of the news weekly *Der Spiegel* (Mirror) were arrested and office files seized on suspicion of treason for publishing details of a NATO exercise. The ensuing furore was so great that the ultra-conservative Strauss, leader of Bavaria's CSU, had to resign; he returned to the cabinet in 1966 but his reputation was permanently damaged.

spillover The period each year, usually for three weeks or so from mid-October, when Parliament reconvenes at Westminster after the long summer RECESS to clear up outstanding business before the session is concluded. Frequently it involves the Lords returning for longer than the Commons, as most legislation completes its progress in the Upper House.

spin doctor A campaign official or public relations expert attached to a party or a candidate whose task is to channel facts to the media which put the best possible construction on events in an effort to build momentum (*see* BIG MO). The word "spin" is also used on its own, as in "If we can get people to call the show today, it will help with spin", a message faxed to all Lawyers for BUSH-QUAYLE Leadership in October 1992 by the group's executive director, Nancy Nord. The term, relating to the spin given to a ball in flight to fool the recipient, originated in America in the 1980s and has spread rapidly throughout the English-speaking political community.

Spitting Image The satirical puppet programme broadcast from 1986 by Britain's Central TV which made its name by bitter and Rabelaisian lampoons on Margaret Thatcher's Cabinet. It was devised by the cartoonists Luck and Flaw.

split A division within a party, movement or Cabinet over an issue or series of issues that weakens it in the eyes of the voters and can, on rare occasions, develop into a permanent break. Splits are much sought by political journalists, and most frequently been found in left-of-centre parties.

The Republicans have their splits right after the election, and Democrats have theirs just before an election.

WILL ROGERS (1879–1935).

splitting the anti-X vote The accusation levelled by the second-placed candidate in an election against a third who has intervened and weakened the challenge to the front-runner, *e.g.* in Britain a Labour candidate trying to narrow a Tory majority may accuse a third-placed Liberal Democrat of "splitting the anti-Tory vote".

splitting the ticket *See* TICKET.

spoil. spoiled paper A BALLOT PAPER rejected by officials conducting the COUNT because it contains marks or comments other than the simple "X" or other symbol required by law.

spoiler A candidate who intervenes in an election with no interest in victory, but purely to weaken the chances of another. They may have a similar name to the candidate they wish to harm, or a similar range of policies, or simply compel the person targeted to increase their campaign spending.

spoils system The system of PATRONAGE, originating in the ALBANY REGENCY of the 1820s and 1830s, which became the basis of US MACHINE POLITICS and even, for a time, of the Presidency. Under it, a change of political control at Federal, State or local level brought the dismissal of all office-holders assumed to belong to the defeated faction, and their replacement by supporters of the new administration at even the humblest levels; inevitably this was a recipe for graft and corruption. The scramble for the trough every four years was a feature of Washington life throughout much of the 19th century, and only slackened when the shooting of President Garfield in 1881 by a disappointed office-seeker brought the extent of corruption to light. At national level the system survives only in the uppermost reaches of the government (*see* HOLDOVER; TRANSITION), but it is alive and well in some cities.

to the victor, the spoils The principle behind the spoils system, again stemming from the Albany Regency. Sen. William Learned Marcy told the Senate on 25 January 1832:

> It may be, sir, that the politicians of New York are not so fastidious as some gentlemen are, as to disclosing the principles on which they act. They boldly preach what they practise. When they are contending for victory, they avow their intentions of enjoying the fruits of it. If they are defeated, they expect to retire from office. If they are successful, they claim, as a matter of right, the advantages of success. They see nothing wrong in the rule that to the victor belong the spoils of the enemy.

spokesman (1) A legislator nominated or elected by his or her party to put across its policies and question and challenge opposing parties on theirs. In the Westminster system where the Opposition SHADOWs the Government, spokesmen not in the Shadow Cabinet have a formal place. (2) A person who, officially and "on the record" (*see* OFF), represents the policies and activities of a government or other organization to the media.

> *David Frost:* You are a spokesman?
> *William Rushton:* Yes, I've just been promoted from being an informed SOURCE.
> THAT WAS THE WEEK THAT WAS, BBC television, 1962.

sponsor A legislator who places his or her name on a BILL at the start of its progress. In the US CONGRESS any member may sponsor almost any category of Bill; at Westminster Ministers alone sponsor Government Bills and backbenchers only Private Members' BILLS.

sponsored candidate In Britain, a Parliamentary candidate who receives ENDORSEMENT and funding from a body other than his or her own party; the practice applies mainly to trade unions sponsoring Labour candidates who belong to their organization.

Spycatcher The political storm in Britain in 1985–88 caused by the attempts of the former MI5 operative Peter Wright (1917–) to publish his autobiography of that name. It purported to expose a catalogue of abuses by the agency, which he said had "BUGGED and burgled our way across London"; his principal charge was that there had been a conspiracy within MI5 to undermine and overthrow Harold Wilson as Prime Minister in the mid-1970s. Although books saying much the same had already appeared, Margaret Thatcher decided *Spycatcher* had to be stopped, and a series of legal actions to prevent publication were started throughout the world. The critical action was fought out in Australia, where Wright now lived. The CABINET SECRETARY, Sir Robert Armstrong, was despatched to defend the decision in the Supreme Court of New South Wales, arguing that publication would breach security and the national interest. Armstrong received a gruelling cross-examination, at one point rashly conceding that he had been "economical with the TRUTH". Efforts to ban it in Britain continued for some years, ending in total defeat for the Government; at this point Mrs. Thatcher promoted legislation imposing an "obligation of confidentiality" on retired members of the security services.

Square Deal The ambitious, pioneering programme of social and political reform followed from 1901 to 1909 by Theodore Roosevelt (*see* TEDDY) on behalf of the poorer sections of US society. The programme involved an attack on the power of MONOPOLIES, conservation of America's natural resources, and a new relationship with labour unions that brought improvements in working conditions.

> A man who is good enough to shed his blood for the country is good enough to be given a square deal afterwards. More than that no man is entitled to, and less than that no man shall have.
> THEODORE ROOSEVELT, speech at the Lincoln Monument, Springfield, Illinois, 4 June 1903.

squeaker A mainly US term for a desperately close election victory; the winning candidate is said to have "squeaked in".

squeeze The pressure exerted on a party during an election campaign as the voters perceive that its candidates have little chance of election and POLARIZE between those perceived to have a better chance. In Britain the squeeze always threatens to damage the LIBERAL DEMOCRATS during general elections, but may hit one of the two main parties at a BY-ELECTION if the Liberal Democrats look like posing the major threat.

squeeze until the the pips squeak The threat made by successive generations of POPULISTs against supposedly privileged or undeserving groups in society. It was made first by Lloyd George against property speculators, then against the Germans on post-war REPARATIONS by Sir Eric Geddes (1875–1937), and finally by Denis Healey in 1973 – who insisted he was not advocating such a course but quoting Lloyd George to warn how Labour's tax policies would affect the better-off, including MPs. Geddes' use of the phrase was the most notorious. On 10 December 1918 he told an election meeting in Cambridge:

> The Germans, if this Government is re-elected, are going to pay every penny; they are going to be squeezed, as a lemon is squeezed – until the pips squeak. My only doubt is not whether we can squeeze hard enough, but whether there is enough juice.

Squiffites The Asquithian Liberals, who followed their leader into opposition after his overthrow by Lloyd George in December 1916, and remained a separate faction under the party's titular leader for a further ten years. They were called after ASQUITH's nickname of "Squiffy"; the great man's heavy drinking may explain why "squiffy" remains a synonym for "tipsy". Asquith and many of his supporters refused to serve under Lloyd George in the reshaped COALITION government; while they stopped short of condemning the handling of the war, L.G. was convinced they were plotting against him and the breach became irreparable with the MAURICE LETTER debate in May 1918. In the 1918 COUPON ELECTION the Squiffites won 26 seats against 136 for the Lloyd George faction, with Asquith himself losing his seat. Asquith returned at a BY-ELECTION, and with the party nominally reunited after the Tories' CARLTON CLUB REVOLT of 1922 his faction co-existed uneasily with Lloyd George's dominant force until Asquith belatedly stood down as party leader in October 1926.

stab in the back The legend that Germany had not been on the point of military collapse in November 1918 when its new civilian leaders ordered its troops to surrender, and that a military capable of fighting on had been betrayed by unpatriotic and treacherous politicians. Spread with vigour both by arch-conservative generals such as Ludendorff and by political nationalists including the newly-demobilized Adolf Hitler, the "stab in the back" became a cornerstone of NAZI doctrine and motivation. The fervour with which the belief was held was one reason for the Allies' demand for unconditional SURRENDER in World War II; they could not risk again a resurgent Germany which asserted that it had not suffered military defeat.

staff In WASHINGTON, the functionaries who make the wheels of power go round and do the detailed work for politicians, both in the WHITE HOUSE and on the HILL. Some staffers, especially for Congressional committees, exercise more influence than the elected members; according to the pioneer consumer campaigner Ralph NADER

> Special interests long ago learned that gifts, free trips, cash and women lavished on key committee or other Congressional staffers can result in the desired behavior by the boss without much risk of exposure.

Ken McLean, staff director of the Senate Banking, Housing and Urban Affairs Committee, took a less sinister view, saying: "To be a politician you have to go out and shake a lot of hands. It's much more fun to be a staffer," while Sen. Eugene McCarthy said of his staff: "You need them for protection, to go to lunch for you." Of White House staffers, John Eisenhower noted:

> The staffer sometimes takes the President more seriously than the Great Man himself.

Chief of Staff *See* CHIEF.

stage-management The art of turning a potentially unwieldy political gathering which may give off a negative image into a vehicle for the presentation of the most favourable aspects of a party or candidate. The term has been used with greatest justice of the formal meetings in the KREMLIN of the Communist Party of the Soviet Union and the annual CONFERENCEs of Britain's CONSERVATIVE PARTY. The Soviets proved marginally more successful in ensuring prolonged ovations for the leadership, and in preventing any criticism of the leadership from the rostrum; to this day resolutions selected for debate at the Conservative conference are almost totally anodyne. A senior Soviet diplomat observing a Tory conference in Brighton *c.* 1983 told the author:

> It's very similar. We don't invite 6000 people to the Kremlin to find out what they think.

Stage-management reached a high point under Margaret Thatcher, through techniques introduced by Harvey Thomas, who had also worked on Billy Graham's evangelistic crusades; under John MAJOR greater openness has been encouraged, at the price of sometimes embarrassing dissent.

stagflation An economic situation in which INFLATION coincides with stagnant output and employment. The word was coined by the Conservative front-bencher Iain Macleod (1913–70) in November 1965, when he told the Commons:

> We now have the worst of both worlds – not just inflation on one side or stagnation on the other, but both of them together. We have a sort of stagflation situation.

Stakhanovite A fanatically hard worker, originally a follower of the Soviet system of encouraging higher productivity among all workers by making heroes of those with spectacular achievements. It was named after Alexei Stakhanov (1906–77), a Donetz coal miner who was credited with an astonishing daily output. In 1935 STALIN held a conference of Stakhanovites in which he extolled the working man.

Stalin (Russ. man of steel) The name chosen by Joseph Vissarionovich Dzugashvili (1879–1953), the Communist who for almost 30 years governed the Soviet Union with the utmost ruthlessness. Originally a candidate for the priesthood in his native Georgia, he became a BOLSHEVIK in 1903, and was frequently imprisoned and exiled prior to the OCTOBER REVOLUTION of 1917. By 1922 he was general secretary of the COMMUNIST PARTY under LENIN, who did not trust him and left a Testament urging the Party not to make him its leader; Lenin said: "This cook will give us nothing but spicy dishes." Stalin seized control anyway after Lenin's death in 1924, breaking with TROTSKY, who observed: "It was the supreme expression of the mediocrity of the apparatus that Stalin himself rose to his position," and eventually having him murdered. By 1929 he wielded absolute power and embarked both on the FIVE-YEAR PLANS and a reign of terror that made his assumed name synonymous with brutality and repression. Enforced COLLECTIVIZATION cost the lives of 10 million peasants, who starved to death or were executed, and mass PURGES and SHOW TRIALS not only stripped the Soviet hierarchy of all potential rivals, but left the RED ARMY almost leaderless when Hitler launched his surprise attack in 1941. Before then Stalin had shown a cynicism matching his paranoia by concluding the 1939 HITLER-STALIN PACT which divided Poland with Germany and left Hitler free to launch his BLITZKRIEG to the West; in 1941 he refused to heed Western warnings that a Nazi attack on the Soviet Union was imminent. Stalin, despite periods of alcoholic depression, remained in the KREMLIN as the Germans advanced to within 12 miles of Moscow, and achieved new status as a national leader fighting a GREAT PATRIOTIC WAR. Yet he himself said of the Russian people: "We are under no illusion that they are fighting for us. They are fighting for Mother Russia."

His western allies did their best to show loyal support, Roosevelt declaring: "UNCLE JOE is my man." Yet he showed by allowing the non-Communist Warsaw Uprising to fail that he would be as ruthless as ever once the fighting was over. And in the late 1940s he presided over still greater repression at home, and after YALTA took and kept an iron grip over eastern Europe. Even then, with the IRON CURTAIN descending, President Truman said: "I like old Joe Stalin. He's a good fellow but he's a prisoner of the POLITBURO." Before long he revised that opinion to "a lying son of a bitch". ATTLEE, more circumspect, foreshadowed Margaret Thatcher's view of Mikhail Gorbachev when he termed Stalin "a man you could do business with; he was obviously the man who could take decisions, and he was obviously going to be difficult". Stalin died in 1953, suspecting his intimates to the last of plotting against him and not hesitating to have them shot.

> Stalin, that great lover of peace, a man of giant stature who moulded, as few others have done, the destinies of his age. PANDIT NEHRU, obituary speech, 9 March 1953.

> I, like everyone else, called him "The Boss"; in the same way the Jews of the past never pronounced the name of God. ILYA EHRENBURG (1891–1967).

> Every great leader is a reflection of the nation he leads and Stalin, in this sense, was Russia. I. F. STONE.

> My father died a difficult and terrible death. God grants an easy death only to the just.
> SVETLANA ALLILUYEVA, *Twenty Letters to a Friend.*

Stalinism The ruthless personalized form of MARXISM-LENINISM forced on the Soviet Union by Stalin, and which outlived him both in his home country and throughout Eastern Europe. It involved unthinking obedience to a centralized party that might change its position at any moment, a PERSONALITY CULT for frequently uncharismatic and often sinister leaders, ruthless control from the KREMLIN of SATELLITE states through Puppet GOVERNMENTS, harsh suppression of dissidents and rivals in PURGES, and general political terror centred on a system of GULAG forced-labour camps.

> He turned Marxism on its head by making it fit his own theories. GEORGE LUKACS.

destalinization The reversal of Stalin's policies and reputation following his death in 1953. A campaign to discredit Stalin's memory was begun by his successor, Nikita Khruschev (1894–1971), in a bitter speech at a closed SESSION of the 20th Party Congress in March 1956. He denounced Stalin as a despot and brutal mass-murderer interested only in "the glorification of his own person". It has been said that Khruschev's speech was interrupted by a shout from the audience of "Why didn't you stop him?" Khruschev glared at the delegates and shouted: "Who said that?" Nobody spoke, and Khruschev continued: "Now you know why!" Khruschev also told the Congress:

> What could we do? There was a reign of terror. You just had to look at him wrongly and the next day you lost your head.

Stalin's body was removed from Lenin's MAUSOLEUM the following year, but destalinization was not a smooth or irreversible process; the suppression of the HUNGARIAN UPRISING in 1956 and the PRAGUE SPRING of 1968, the continued persecution of DISSIDENTS and the brutal maintenance of the BERLIN WALL all showed that Stalinism was alive and well until the final collapse of communism between 1989 and 1991.

> Many people thought we had changed cars at the 20th Congress. Quite wrong: we threw out some luggage, but we are still travelling in the same car.
>
> ALEXANDER SURKOV, First Secretary of the Soviet Writers' Union 1953–60.

Stalker report The interim report completed in 1985 by John Stalker, deputy chief constable of Greater Manchester, on his investigation of an alleged SHOOT TO KILL policy against suspected IRA terrorists by members of the Royal Ulster Constabulary. The circumstances surrounding delays by the RUC in forwarding it to Ulster's Director of Public Prosecutions gave CONSPIRACY THEORISTS a field day. Mr. Stalker was convinced that five men – all but one of them IRA suspects – had been unlawfully killed, and was believed to have uncovered irregularities implicating senior officers. He had compiled the report despite resistance within the RUC, which had refused him access to a tape of the shooting of one victim. Then in May 1986, while still pursuing his inquiries, he was accused of misconduct in dealing with Kevin Taylor, a suspected criminal in Manchester. His investigation in Ulster was completed by Colin Sampson, chief constable of West Yorkshire, who also led inquiries into Stalker's own conduct; Sampson was handed the vital tape within days. Stalker was exonerated, but resigned from the force; Taylor was cleared of all charges. The Sampson report, when published in 1988, was dismissed by some as a WHITEWASH; it recommended disciplinary action against a number of junior RUC officers; and 20 were punished that July.

stalking horse A candidate who enters an election with little hope of victory, in order to establish support for a challenge by a more serious contender. The term was particularly used of the backbench Tory WET Sir Anthony Meyer, who in 1989 challenged Margaret Thatcher for the party leadership. It was widely perceived that Meyer, who polled just 31 votes, had only stood to test the water for Michael Heseltine (*see* TARZAN), whose challenge the following year ousted the IRON LADY without winning him the Premiership. A stalking horse was one trained to conceal a hunter stalking wild fowl, but as early as 1612 it had come to mean a person acting as a decoy, John Webster in his play *The White Devil* writing:

> You . . . were made his engine and his stalking horse to undo my sister.

Staller, Ilona *See* CICCIOLINA.

Stalwarts Conservative Republicans during the Hayes administration who had supported President Grant and looked to Sen. Roscoe Conkling of New York as their leader. The stalwarts, who included Senators Benjamin Butler and John Logan and ex-Senator Zachariah Chandler, were ranged against the HALF-BREEDS, led by Sen. James G. Blaine, who backed Hayes's Southern policy and civil service reform. When in 1881 Charles Guiteau shot President Garfield – a Half-Breed – he was heard to shout:

> I am a stalwart, and Arthur is President now.

Stamp Act The Act passed at Westminster in 1765 which taxed documents and newspapers in the American colonies to help pay for their defence. It sparked non-compliance and bitter opposition from educated men who were fast becoming revolutionaries. It was a light tax, but in Americans' eyes broke new ground by taxing them without their consent, provoking the cry of "NO TAXATION WITHOUT REPRESENTATION". That October representatives of nine colonies met in New York for a Stamp Act Congress, which set out moderate statements of the American case. When word of resistance reached London, PITT THE ELDER, who wanted justice for the colonies, not their independence, declared:

> I rejoice that America has resisted. Three millions of people so dead to all the feelings of liberty as voluntarily to submit to be slaves, would have been fitting instruments to make slaves of the rest.

stand To put oneself forward for election; a UK term whose US equivalent is RUN. One speaks both of standing for office, the council, Parliament, *etc.*, and of a candidate standing at Barnsley, Torquay or wherever.

Standing Committee (1) In the US CONGRESS, the 38 committees of the House and the Senate which each oversee a particular area of government and which write, amend and consider and review the functioning of legislation relevant to them. (2) At Westminster, the eight or so committees of the House of Commons empanelled each session to conduct the COMMITTEE STAGEs of Bills (other than purely private legislation) that have received a SECOND READING. One standing committee customarily handles most Private Members' BILLS, one or two each deal purely with Scottish legislation or Europe, and the rest, known by letter as "Standing Committee A" and so on, deal in turn with Government legislation.

standing orders The basic rules for the conduct of meetings of a UK elected body or political party. The US equivalent is RULES OF ORDER.

standing ovation An enthusiastic display of support for a politician shown by standing to applaud, usually at the end of a major speech and occasionally at the beginning. SPIN-DOCTORS and STAGE-MANAGERS try to ensure such displays when there is particular media attention, notably when the leader of the UK CONSERVATIVE PARTY delivers the closing CONFERENCE speech; as a result, journalists time the ovation with stop-watches and look for signs of flagging and lack of spontaneity.

Standards, Battle of the The popular name for the US election campaign of 1896, when the Republicans under McKINLEY championed the GOLD STANDARD and William Jennings Bryan (*see* BOY ORATOR; PRAIRIE AVENGER) led a coalition of Democrats, POPULISTS and breakaway Republicans to press for FREE SILVER.

star. Star Chamber The Cabinet committee established by Margaret Thatcher as the ultimate arbiter of disputes between the TREASURY and spending Ministers during the annual autumn public spending negotiations (*see* PESC). Initially chaired by Mrs. Thatcher's deputy William Whitelaw (*see* WILLIE), it was seldom convened as Ministers were anxious to resolve such arguments without having judgment passed on them by colleagues. The system was scrapped in 1992 when John MAJOR's Cabinet began to set global targets for departments, within which each had to set its own priorities. The original Star Chamber was a civil and criminal court, abolished in 1641, which met without a jury and was empowered to use torture. The term, derived from the blue ceiling of the old Council chamber at Westminster where it met, came to stand for any organ of the state which denied those at its mercy a fair hearing.

Star Spangled Banner The patriotic song written in 1814 by Francis Scott Key (1779–1843) during the British bombardment of Fort McHenry to commemorate the resolution shown by the young nation's troops, which was formally adopted as America's national anthem by EXECUTIVE ORDER in 1916 and by Act of Congress in 1931; the tune is taken from an English drinking song by J. S. Smith, *Anacreon in Heaven*. The first verse is:

> O say! Can you see by the dawn's early light
> What so proudly we hailed at the twilight's last gleaming,
> Whose broad stripes and bright stars through the perilous fight
> O'er the ramparts we watched were so gallantly streaming?
> And the rockets' red glare, the bombs bursting in air
> Gave proof through the night that our flag was still there.
> O say, does that star spangled banner yet wave
> O'er the land of the free and the home of the brave?

Star Wars The UN nickname for the Strategic Defence Initiative (SDI), the system backed by President Reagan in 1983 for defending America against nuclear attack by using laser-beam weapons orbiting in space to shoot down Soviet missiles with nuclear-generated blasts. His support was given to a general concept, and the reliability, cost and technical details of the scheme were still being researched and argued when the COLD WAR ended; President Clinton effectively cancelled it in May 1993. The name was taken from the cult 1977 film *Star Wars*, and reflected the surreal sci-fi aspect of the project.

> That great PORK BARREL in the sky. PAUL WARNKE.

> The notion of a defense that will protect American cities is one that will not be achieved, but it is that goal that supplies the political magic in the President's vision.
> Former Defence Secretary JAMES SCHLESINGER, 1987.

Stars and Bars The flag of the eleven CONFEDERATE States that SECEDED from the United States in 1861 at the start of the CIVIL WAR. It consisted at first of two horizontal red bars with a narrow white bar between them; in the top left was a blue union bearing eleven white stars in a circle. The term is more popularly applied to the later Confederate flag of a 13-starred blue diagonal cross with white fringe on a red background; the two extra stars represented Kentucky and Missouri, who were claimed for the Confederacy but were not part of it.

Stars and Stripes The familiar name for the flag of the United States, which has flown – with the addition of extra stars for newly-admitted States – since 1777. This name for OLD GLORY gained world-wide currency with John Philip Sousa's march, *Stars and Stripes Forever* (1897); it was also the name of the US Army newspaper in both World Wars. Originally there was one stripe per State, and the stars (again one per State) formed a circle on a blue ground, but they were squared up in 1818; while the number of stars equals the number of States, no star represents a particular State. The number of stripes at first increased with the number of States, but in 1815 they were reduced to 13. The Stars and Stripes in its present form, with 50 stars, was first flown in 1960, after the admission of Alaska and Hawaii to the Union.

stark raving bonkers The denunciatory phrase popularized in the late 1950s by the pugnacious Tory party chairman Lord Hailsham, when he said of Labour's programme: "If the British public falls for this it'll be stark raving bonkers." The term – which caused a stir at that comparatively genteel time – has nothing to do with the later slang word "bonk" (to have sexual relations); it was originally 1920s British slang for being tipsy or tight-headed, and came to mean downright crazy. In 1983 Sen. Gaylord Nelson said of Interior Secretary James Watt: "The Secretary has gone bonkers. It's time the white-coat people took him away."

Starr. Blaze Starr affair The political scandal in the 1950s arising from the relationship between Louisiana's Governor Earl Long and Blaze Starr, a New Orleans stripper. Governor Long, who served 1948–52 and 1956–60, inherited the Louisiana MACHINE from his brother, Sen. Huey (KINGFISH) Long, and ran it for 25 years. In his second term his increasingly erratic behaviour, including his public dalliance with Ms. Starr, led to his being committed to a mental hospital. According to Ms. Starr, who wrote a book on their affair that was later turned into a film, *Blaze*, the governor had a penchant for sex with his boots on. Long won election to Congress in 1960, but died before he could take his seat.

START agreements Strategic Arms Reduction Talks. The two ARMS CONTROL agreements between the SUPERPOWERS, concluded respectively by America and the Soviet Union in 1991 and America and Russia at the close of 1992, which brought the ARMS RACE to an end and for the first time imposed major cuts in strategic nuclear arsenals. The first START agreement, signed by George BUSH and Mikhail Gorbachev in Moscow on 31 July 1991 after nine years of talks, called for 30% cuts in strategic nuclear missiles, with America retaining its slight edge. The second, signed by Bush and Boris Yeltsin in Moscow on 3 January 1993, involved a two-thirds reduction in strategic nuclear arsenals over ten years, with an end to ground-launched MIRVed missiles. It was not to take effect until the Soviet Union's other nuclear successor states – Ukraine, Belarus and Kazakhstan – ratified START I; there were also doubts over whether Russia's increasingly nationalistic CONGRESS OF PEOPLE'S DEPUTIES would ratify START II.

Stasi The popular name for the hated and pervasive former State Security Police (*Staatssicherheitsdienst*) in East Germany. Responsible for espionage, counter-espionage and the suppression of political dissent, they were notorious for their minute surveillance of every citizen's life – often by suborning other family members. The *Stasi* were disbanded in December 1989, a few months after the breaching of the BERLIN WALL. Several prominent Germans – East and West – were later accused of having been *Stasi* informers, a number having to quit politics regardless of the veracity of the charges.

Stassen candidacy A hope that starts off as real and becomes increasingly forlorn, from the pursuit of the US Presidency by Harold Stassen (1907–), who became Minnesota's youngest-ever Senator at 31 and then State Governor, and at the 1948 Republican convention forced Thomas DEWEY and Sen. Robert Taft to a third ballot. Stassen staged an abortive challenge in 1952; while he became a special ambassador for Eisenhower, he never gave up hope of the Presidency, trying again with little support in 1964 and 1968, and as late as 1976 received one single delegate.

state (1) The State, the body politic and core of a nation, and its power personified. To INTERVENTIONISTS and WELFARISTS it is a weapon for good, to DEMAGOGUES and TOTALITARIANS it is a means of power to be captured, to REVOLUTIONARIES it is anathema – until they have won control. Hegel termed the State "the divine idea as it exists on earth"; the pioneer Socialist saw it as "the poor man's bank", the ANARCHIST Bakunin as "the State is the most flagrant negation, the most cynical and complete negation of humanity", Engels as "an instrument of oppression of our class by another – no less so in a democratic republic than in a monarchy". Kropotkin declared that "the word 'state' is identical with the word 'war'", and LENIN asserted that "so long as the State exists there is no freedom. When there is freedom there will be no State," but Goebbels cynically reckoned: "Whoever can conquer the street can one day conquer the State." Edmund BURKE wrote: "A state without the means of some change is without the means of its conservation," and Paul Valéry observed: "If the State is strong, it crushes us. If it is weak, we perish." Lord BEVERIDGE maintained: "The State is, or can be, master of money. But in a free society it is master of very little else."

Of the relationship between the state and the individual, Montesquieu wrote: "The state owes to every citizen an assured subsistence, proper nourishment, suitable clothing and a mode of life not incompatible with health." Macaulay tartly observed that "no particular man is necessary to the state", and J. S. Mill considered that "the worth of a state, in the long run, is the worth of the individuals comprising it".

> The State exists for the sake of society, not society for the sake of the State. WOODROW WILSON.

> The State has no business in the bedrooms of the nation. PIERRE TRUDEAU, 1967.

(2) A nation whose existence and borders are

recognized by others. Bakunin argued that "every state must conquer or be conquered", Treitschke that "no state can pledge its future to another". And Oliver Wendell Holmes, in a Supreme Court opinion in 1911, said:

> A state cannot be expected to move with the celerity of a private businessman; it is enough if it proceeds, in the language of the English Chancery, with all deliberate speed.

(3) One of the 50 component and in many ways SOVEREIGN jurisdictions of the United States. Friction between the States and the Federal power go back to the earliest days of the UNION, when George WASHINGTON wrote: "The primary cause of all our disorder lies in the different state governments, and in the tenacity of that power which pervades the whole of their system". Yet in 1819 Chief Justice John Marshall declared: "No political dreamer was ever wild enough to think of breaking down the lines which separate the states, and of compounding the American people into one common mass."

> I do not think the United States would come to an end if we lost our power to declare an Act of Congress void. I do think that the Union would be imperiled if we could not make that declaration as to the laws of the several states. OLIVER WENDELL HOLMES, 1913.

> It is one of the happiest incidents of the federal system that a single courageous state may, if its citizens choose, serve as a laboratory; and try novel social and economic experiments without risk to the rest of the country.
> Justice LOUIS BRANDEIS, dissenting in *New State Ice Co. v. Liebmann*, 1932.

(4) The six British colonies which came together in 1901 to form the Commonwealth of Australia.

(5) Washington and diplomatic shorthand for the STATE DEPARTMENT (*see* below).

state capitalism A phrase coined by LENIN and briefly used by him to describe BOLSHEVIK economic policy between the OCTOBER REVOLUTION and the launching of the NEW ECONOMIC POLICY. He meant that Russia had not yet experienced the complete transformation from feudalism to capitalism; moderate Leftists argued that, if so, progress to Socialism should wait until bourgeois capitalism broke down, but Lenin responded that the State could hasten the progress by developing a full infrastructure under PROLETARIAN control. The phrase has more recently been used by TROTSKYISTS and other critics to scorn the undemocratic and unimaginative nature of Soviet Communism.

State Department The section of the US Government which since 1789 has conducted its relations with other countries (*see* FOGGY BOTTOM; SECRETARY OF STATE). Despite the professionalism of its career diplomats, it has been the subject of as much scathing criticism from right-wing politicians as has the FOREIGN OFFICE in London.

> Full of weaklings, sissies and people with mush for brains.
> Sen. GORDON HUMPHREY, 1982.

state funeral The funeral, with all the pomp of a state occasion and accompanying military honours, accorded to a pre-eminent statesman by a grateful nation. Often, as with Winston CHURCHILL's spectacular obsequies in 1965, the details have been arranged by the departing figure well in advance; Harry S Truman planned "a damn fine show – I just hate that I'm not going to be around to see it", but when he died in 1972, his widow Bess ignored the plans and ordered the simplest of ceremonies instead. A state funeral will generally be preceded by a LYING IN STATE.

state of emergency The suspension of normal constitutional procedures, declared by a government to enable it to take speedy action to tackle a civil emergency, keep services moving despite a disruptive industrial dispute, or maintain order at a time of war or civil unrest.

state of the parties In UK politics, the tabulation of the number of seats held by the respective parties in the HOUSE OF COMMONS; it also covers the up-to-the minute tally of results as the votes are counted after a GENERAL ELECTION.

State of the Union *See* UNION.

state of war A phrase used in a declaration of WAR, asserting that "a state of war now exists" between the two countries in question.

State opening The glittering occasion at which the Sovereign opens a new SESSION of Parliament at Westminster, travelling in pomp from Buckingham Palace with available members of the Royal family in a procession of horse-drawn coaches and donning the Crown to deliver the GRACIOUS SPEECH from the THRONE in the HOUSE OF LORDS. When the Sovereign cannot attend – sometimes because she is in a Commonwealth country where she may be opening Parliament with rather less splendour – a senior member of the Royal family takes her place and delivers the Speech, which is in any case written by Ministers. The State opening generally takes place in early November, unless a General Election has produced a break in the Parliamentary timetable at another time of year.

State visit A visit made by a HEAD OF STATE to another country, where his or her counterpart receives them with full honours; customarily the streets of the host capital are decked with the flag of the visitor, and host and guest hold lavish official banquets for each other.

enabling state The phrase used by the UK

LIBERAL DEMOCRAT leader Paddy Ashdown in the run-up to the 1992 election, to describe a state in which the citizen is encouraged and assisted to maximize his or her potential.
home state For a US politician, the State whose voters have elected them to the House or the Senate, and which provides a base for a Presidential campaign.

> If you can't raise money in your home state, you're in trouble. LYNDON B. JOHNSON.

nanny state The derogatory term given by THATCHERITES in the 1980s for a central government which indulged in what they saw as unnecessary and even harmful supervision of the public at large, protecting it from the normal adverse forces present in society.
nation state *See* NATION.
Offences against the State Act The legislation that forms the backbone of the Irish Republic's legal machinery for dealing with the IRA, whose aims encompass not only the freeing of NORTHERN IRELAND from British rule but the replacement of the Dublin government by a Marxist state. A key element is the provision that a person may be imprisoned if a senior police officer testifies that, in his or her belief, they are a member of an illegal organization. The Act was first passed in 1939 and has been strengthened several times since, most recently in 1985 when provision was made for the confiscation of terrorists' assets.
police state A political and social system in which the SECRET POLICE detect and crush any opposition to those in power.
Welfare state *See* WELFARE.
withering away of the state In the eyes of MARXIST revolutionaries, the ultimate achievement of COMMUNISM, the point at which central authority becomes unnecessary. The concept was advanced in 1878 by Friedrich Engels (1820–95), who wrote in his *Anti-Dühring*:

> The first act by which the state really constitutes itself the representative of the whole of society – the taking possession of the means of production in the name of society – is at the same time its last independent act of the state. The state is not abolished; it withers away.

statecraft The art of conducting government and managing state affairs.
statehood In America, the achievement by a TERRITORY of full membership of the United States; Alaska and Hawaii in 1959 were proclaimed the 49th and 50th States of the Union. The people of Puerto Rico, now a COMMONWEALTH, have long been divided over whether statehood would benefit them; a Statehood Party enjoys considerable, but not majority, support.
States of . . . the legislatures that govern the Channel Islands of Jersey and Guernsey (including Alderney), which though under British sovereignty are not fully part of the United Kingdom, being unrepresented at Westminster and outside the EUROPEAN COMMUNITY.
States' Rights The doctrine dating back to the foundation of the United States that the individual states should have more freedom to act, compared with the Federal government. The argument over states' rights became embroiled with that over slavery, Abraham LINCOLN declaring: "Each community, as a state, has a right to do exactly as it pleases with all the concerns within that state that interfere with no other state, and the general government, upon principle, has no right to interfere with anything other than that general class of things that does concern the whole." After the CIVIL WAR States' Rights increasingly became shorthand for the ability of the SEGREGATIONIST South to defy federal CIVIL RIGHTS legislation. In 1948 the DIXIECRAT Strom Thurmond ran for the Presidency under the banner of a States' Rights Party.

> I say the time has come to walk out of the shadow of states' rights and into the sunlight of human rights.
> HUBERT HUMPHREY to the 1948 Democratic Convention.

statement At Westminster, a formal announcement made to either House by a Minister. He or she delivers the statement, the appropriate Opposition spokesman asks a lengthy and comprehensive question which is responded to, and questions are then taken from each side of the House in turn until the Speaker ends the exchanges. The SPEAKER gives permission for the statement to be made, but the scheduling is a matter for the Minister and for BUSINESS MANAGERS. Occasionally a Minister blunders. On 9 May 1969 Richard Crossman, Secretary for Health and Social Security, announced an increase in National Health charges on the day of local elections; he was widely blamed for Labour's disastrous showing. Crossman, who prided himself on his mastery of government, wrote laconically in his diary:

> When I got to the office I found waiting for me a statement on teeth and spectacles. I knew this was a bit unpleasant.

Autumn Statement At Westminster from the early 1980s until 1992, the statement made by the CHANCELLOR OF THE EXCHEQUER each November in which he set out public spending plans for the coming year, and gave an overview of the performance of the economy. Sir Geoffrey HOWE, Chancellor 1979–83, institutionalized the Autumn Statement, which had previously been little more than a recital of the INDUSTRY ACT FORECASTS, but insisted it would never supersede the BUDGET, traditionally delivered in March. However in 1992

Norman Lamont announced that from November 1993 the Budget and the Autumn Statement would be merged.

business statement *See* BUSINESS.

personal statement *See* PERSONAL.

statesman A complimentary term for a politician, implying wisdom, vision, dignity and a lifetime of experience. Once in common use, the word has acquired *gravitas* to the point where it is used of relatively few senior figures. Originally the word had connotations of cunning, Davy Crockett saying in 1835:

> Statesmen are gamesters, and the people are the cards they play with . . . the way they cut and shuffle is a surprise to all young beginners.

Before long the term became a positive one, the 19th century French premier Gustave Thiers remarking:

> A statesman should be possessed of good sense, a primary political quality; and its fortunate possessor needs a second quality: the courage to show that he has it.

Next a hint of stuffiness crept in. The British Liberal G. W. E. Russell wrote in 1912:

> The perfection of parliamentary style is to utter platitudes with a grave and informing air; and if a little pomposity may be superadded, the House will recognise the speaker as a statesman.

Dean Acheson took the process one stage further, saying: "The first requirement of a statesman is that he be dull. This is not always easy to achieve." However DE GAULLE restored the balance by declaring that "the true statesman is the one who is willing to take risks"; Henry KISSINGER added that "the statesman's duty is to bridge the gap between his nation's experience and his vision".

The comparison between a statesman and a politician has produced many definitions. Benjamin Disraeli declared that "the world is weary of statesmen whom democracy has degraded into politicians", Lloyd George that "when you're abroad you're a statesman; when you're at home you're a politician"; the WELSH WIZARD also said: "A politician is a person with whose policies you do not agree. If you agree with him, he's a statesman." The US humorist Austin O'Malley reckoned that "the statesman shears sheep – the politician skins 'em", Harry S Truman that "a statesman is a politician who's been dead from 10 to 15 years," Adlai Stevenson that "a politician is a statesman who approaches every question with an open mouth", and Governor John Connally that "when you're out of office, you can be a statesman". Sen. Margaret Chase Smith put it the other way round, saying: "Before you can become a statesman you have to get elected. And to get elected you have to be a politician, pledging support for what the voters want." President Georges Pompidou declared that "a statesman is a politician who places himself at the head of the nation. A politician is a statesman who places the nation at his service"; Richard CROSSMAN that "a statesman imposes his will and his ideas on his environment; a politician adapts himself to it".

> My father was a statesman. I am a political woman. My father was a saint. I am not.
>
> INDIRA GANDHI on Pandit Nehru.

elder statesman A political figure who is in retirement after a lifetime of valued service and whose advice and support is valued. When a reporter once referred to Harry S Truman as an elder statesman, he replied:

> I'm not an elder statesman. I hate elder statesmen. I'm a Democrat and a politician and I'm proud of it.

act of statesmanship. A step – generally an unpopular one – which requires wisdom and apparent sacrifice to achieve an outcome benefiting the community as a whole.

statism Control by the state of social and economic affairs, and the belief that such control should be exercised.

> We are going down the road to statism. . . . If some of the new programs seriously proposed should be adopted, there is the danger that the individual – whether farmer, worker, manufacturer, lawyer or doctor – will soon be an economic slave pulling on oar in the galley of the state.
>
> JAMES F. BYRNES (1879–1972), former head of FDR's Office of War Mobilization, speech at Lexington, Virginia, 18 June 1949.

Statuary Hall of the House The semi-circular chamber with deep rose hangings in which the US HOUSE OF REPRESENTATIVES met from 1806 to 1857; gutted by the British in 1814, it was rebuilt for the 16th Congress, partly rectifying what a Congressional committee had termed "its only defect – difficulty of hearing and speaking in it". It was the scene of six Presidential inaugurations, and also witnessed John Quincy ADAMS's fatal stroke in 1848. In 1864 Congress invited each State to place in the now empty hall the statues of two distinguished citizens; to date 94 have been donated, ranging from Ethan Allen, the hero of Ticonderoga, to Dr. John Gorrie, the Floridan who invented the world's first ice machine, and Jeannette Rankin, the Montana Congresswoman who voted alone against the declaration of World War I – and 25 years later against the declaration of World War II. The Hall cannot accommodate them all, so many now line corridors elsewhere in the Capitol.

> Handsome, and fit for anything but the use intended.
>
> Rep. JOHN RANDOLPH (1773–1833).

Statute of Westminster *See* WESTMINSTER.

Statutes at Large The totality of the laws passed by the US Congress; after each SESSION a new volume is published containing the measures enacted during it.

on the statute book A UK term for a law currently in force; Parliament's passing of an Act is known as putting it on the statute book. No one such book exists; all new Acts of Parliament are bound into volumes, SESSION by session.

statutory instruments At Westminster, regulations, ORDERS and other items of delegated legislation made by Ministers which may or may not be subject to approval by Parliament. A special committee of MPs determine whether or not such approval is necessary.

statutory woman A pre-feminist term for the frequent appointment of a sole woman to UK official bodies, because convention required it rather than out of any interest in hearing her views.

Stauffenberg plot The unsuccessful attempt by idealistic members of the German officer corps to assassinate Hitler with a bomb on 20 July 1944. A briefcase containing the bomb was left by Colonel Count Claus von Stauffenberg under the conference table at the FÜHRER's headquarters (Wolf's Lair) at Rastenberg, East Prussia. In a parallel plan, known as "Operation Valkyrie", the conspirators were supposed to seize key government installations in Berlin after Hitler's death, and a few officers went ahead and arrested leading Nazis. However Hitler, shielded by the heavy oak table, escaped with only shock and minor injuries, commenting:

> Who says I am not under the special protection of God?

He was well enough to meet Mussolini two hours later. Not unexpectedly, Hitler took immediate and savage revenge. Stauffenberg and three others were immediately shot, Rommel was forced to take poison, and 7000 other suspects were arrested and in many cases tortured and tried by PEOPLE'S COURTS; 4000 were executed. A number were hanged with piano wire, Hitler then watching a film of the executions. *See also* SPEER?

Stavisky affair The financial scandal surrounding the affairs of Serge Alexandre Stavisky (*c.*1886–1934), a Russian-born French swindler, which came to a head in 1933–34, threatening the survival of the FOURTH REPUBLIC. Stavisky, an adept at establishing fraudulent businesses, led an extravagant lifestyle, mixing with influential society in Cannes and Deauville until in December 1933 he was exposed in a Fr. 500 million bond swindle involving the Bayonne municipal pawnshop. He fled to the resort of Chamonix, where he was found dead the next month, supposedly by his own hand; many suspected he had been killed by the police to protect his influential patrons in government, the judiciary and the Sûreté itself. In February 1934 widespread suspicion of government corruption prompted violent anti-government and anti-parliamentary demonstrations in Paris led by the right-wing ACTION FRANÇAISE and *Croix de Feu*, which brought down the government and momentarily threatened Parliamentary democracy.

steady as she goes! The nautical phrase with which UK Chancellor James Callaghan (*see* STOKER JIM) characterized his 1967 BUDGET. He ended his speech by saying:

> I sum up the prospects for 1967 in three short sentences. We are back on course [after the JULY MEASURES of 1966]. The ship is picking up speed. The economy is moving ahead. Every seaman knows the command at such a moment: "Steady as she goes!"

Callaghan's hopes were not borne out. Three months later the SIX DAY WAR produced a run on the POUND, and the blockage of the Suez Canal damaged Britain's BALANCE OF PAYMENTS. That November, Callaghan DEVALUED and resigned from the Treasury. He wrote of his Budget phrase:

> This was a hostage to fortune which rapidly returned to haunt me. But I feel no remorse, for I know of no one who foretold . . . that by November both sterling and I would be shipwrecked.

stealing an opponent's clothes The adoption by one party of another's distinctive policies, leaving them without a worthwhile programme to campaign on. The phrase was coined by Disraeli (*see* DIZZY), when on 28 February 1845 he said of PEEL:

> The Rt. Honourable Gentleman caught the WHIGS bathing, and walked away with their clothes.

In the 1936 Presidential election Al Smith (*see* HAPPY WARRIOR), once a supporter of FDR but now concerned at the leftist tone of the NEW DEAL, appropriated the phrase, saying:

> The young BRAIN-TRUSTERS caught the Socialists in swimming and they ran away with their clothes.

Stealth candidate A phrase first heard in America's 1992 Congressional campaign: a candidate dialling for dollars behind closed doors instead of getting out meeting the voters. It was a reference to the USAF's highly-successful Stealth bomber, which was developed to attack without showing up on enemy radar screens. A **Stealth issue** is one that suddenly emerges as crucial, having been carefully fostered by one candidate.

steam engine in britches The nickname accorded the US statesman Sen. Daniel Webster (1782–1852) by the English writer, cleric and philosopher Sydney Smith (1771–1845). He wrote of the great orator: "Daniel Webster struck me much like a steam-engine in trousers", and Americans soon took up the phrase. The nickname was also applied to Sen. Stephen Douglas (*see* LITTLE GIANT), who narrowly defeated Abraham LINCOLN in Illinois in 1858 after a memorable series of DEBATES, but lost the Presidency to him two years later.

Steel, David *See* BOY DAVID.

Steel Magnolia Washington's nickname for Rosalynn Carter, wife and close collaborator of President Jimmy CARTER; it reflected both her determined temperament (steel) and her Southern origins (magnolia).

Steiger amendment The reduction in capital gains taxes brought about in 1978 when a rebellion led by Rep. William Steiger, a Wisconsin Republican, overturned a key element of President CARTER's tax programme. Together with the defeat of a Bill for common site PICKETING the year before, it demonstrated to business that shrewd LOBBYING could bring it results even in a Democratic Congress – and was followed by a massive influx of trade associations and lobbying firms anxious to press their own agendas.

Stem van Suid-Afrika (Afrik. The voice of South Africa) The National Anthem of White-ruled South Africa, introduced in 1936 which replaced GOD SAVE THE QUEEN in 1957. To non-Afrikaners *Die Stem* is the symbol of Boer supremacy and APARTHEID; when it was played at a Rugby international in Johannesburg in August 1992, the African National Congress (ANC) threatened to reactivate the world sporting BOYCOTT of South Africa.

step by step The description given by James (later Lord) Prior (1927–), Employment Secretary 1979–81, to his gradualist approach to the introduction of laws to curb the powers of Britain's trade unions. First in opposition and then in government, Prior resisted strong right-wing pressure (not least from Margaret Thatcher, *see* JIM IS VERY, VERY SORRY) for instant and draconian measures in favour of a series of Bills outlawing one set of abuses at a time. His successors, including Norman Tebbit (*see* CHINGFORD SKINHEAD) continued the "step by step" approach.

sterling The British pound, whose erratic performance on world currency markets since the 1960s became what Enoch POWELL, with tongue in cheek, once called "an index of our national turpitude". At the height of the 1966 election campaign Harold WILSON told a BBC interviewer:

> I hope no-one is going to bring sterling into this election. Sterling should be above politics.

But it was a pious hope. That summer a sterling crisis led to the JULY MEASURES to maintain the parity of the pound at $2.80, and in November 1967 Wilson's government was forced to DEVALUE. Wilson had barely retired from politics when a further sterling crisis in the autumn of 1976 obliged Chancellor Denis Healey (*see* GROMYKO OF THE LABOUR PARTY) to obtain a stanby credit from the IMF.

sterling area An association (also called the sterling bloc, or scheduled territories) formed after Britain left the GOLD STANDARD in 1931, when a large number of countries agreed to stabilize their currencies in terms of the pound and hold sterling balances as part of their reserves. It included the independent members of the British COMMONWEALTH (except Canada), Eire, Jordan, Iraq, Libya, Burma and Iceland. The sterling area declined in importance after 1949, as the progressive devaluation of sterling made it less attractive as a reserve currency, and the need to maintain the value of the sterling balances became a millstone around the neck of successive UK governments in the 1960s and 1970s. Few countries, except for some present and former members of the Commonwealth, now hold sterling on a large scale, preferring more stable currencies such as the mark and the yen.

Stern gang A small Jewish terrorist organization, founded in Palestine in 1940, which concentrated on assassinating British personnel. It was named after an early leader, Abraham Stern (1907–42), who was killed in a gunfight with British police. On 6 November 1944 the gang murdered Lord Moyne, Minister of State for Middle East Affairs, in Cairo. From 1945 it collaborated with two other groups, the IRGUN ZVAI LEUMI and HAGANAH, in a guerrilla campaign to force the establishment of a Jewish state in Palestine. Although denounced by the official ZIONIST leadership, the activities of the Stern Gang and other groups were effective in helping to secure the British withdrawal from Palestine, which eventually led to the founding of ISRAEL in May 1948. A former leading member of the Stern Gang, Yitzhak Shamir, served as the LIKUD Prime Minister of Israel 1983–84 and 1986–92.

Stockholm appeal A petition to ban the ATOMIC BOMB, allegedly signed by 500 million people in over 70 countries, which was launched at the Communist-organized World Peace Congress in Stockholm in March 1950. The Congress was to have been held in Sheffield, but Britain's Labour government refused visas to a number of the participants.

Stoker Jim One of several nicknames for the UK Prime Minister James Callaghan (*see* SUNNY JIM), reflecting his wartime service in the Royal Navy; he was not, in fact, a stoker but a Sub-Lieutenant who served in home waters and the Far East, as well as writing the Naval Manual on Japan.

Stone. I. F. Stone's weekly The one-man newsletter circulated from Washington by the liberal journalist Isidore F. Stone (1907–82). Stone published this irritant to the governmental and military ESTABLISHMENT between 1952 and 1971, achieving influence well beyond its 74,000 subscribers.

Stonehouse affair The bizarre circumstances surrounding the disappearance of the former Labour Cabinet Minister John Stonehouse in November 1974 when his clothes were found on a beach in Florida, and his discovery in Melbourne not long after. An early supporter of Harold WILSON, Stonehouse had been a rising star in the 1964–70 Labour government as Postmaster-General and Minister of Aviation, but MI5 marked his card as a SECURITY RISK – something apparently confirmed in 1971 by a Czech DEFECTOR – and colleagues increasingly saw him as a shallow OPPORTUNIST; when Labour returned to power in 1974 Stonehouse, who now had interests in property and banking, though he was not a wealthy man, stayed a BACKBENCH MP. He had hoped to fake his death to convince his wife and family and, with a false passport obtained in the name of a dead constituent in Walsall, start a new life with his Commons secretary Sheila Buckley. He left behind large queries about his activities as chairman of a Bangladeshi bank, and was eventually EXTRADITED from Australia. He continued to sit in the Commons as an Independent, ostracized by former colleagues, while insisting that he was the victim of a plot. On 5 August 1976 Stonehouse, who had conducted his own defence, was convicted on 18 out of 19 charges of theft, fraud, forgery and conspiracy; he was imprisoned for seven years. Miss Buckley was found guilty on five counts out of six, receiving a two-year suspended sentence. Later that month Stonehouse applied for the CHILTERN HUNDREDS; Labour's defeat in the subsequent BY-ELECTION eventually contributed to the fall of the Callaghan government. On his release he married Ms. Buckley and started a business, but died in 1989.

stop-go A pejorative term coined *c.* 1960 for government economic policies that seek to REFLATE the economy when there is high unemployment, then slam on the brakes at the first signs of OVERHEATING. It implies that a government, incapable of long-term planning, can only control the economy by short-term KNEE-JERK reflexes. In 1963 the new Labour leader Harold WILSON ridiculed Harold Macmillan and his Chancellor Selwyn Lloyd as "Stop-go and Son" – a play on the then-new BBC television series *Steptoe and Son* about the irascible old rag-and-bone man and his frustratedly ambitious son.

Stop the '70 tour! The slogan under which opponents of APARTHEID in Britain prevented the 1970 cricket tour by an official South Africa team from taking place. Cricket in South Africa was then SEGREGATED, and in 1968 Pretoria had refused to accept an MCC team because the Coloured player Basil D'Oliveira was included. With civil disorder looming and security costs rising even for a truncated tour, the Cricket Council on 19 May 1970 ruled that there would be no further tours until South Africa selected its team on a non-racial basis.

Blackmail has become respectable. Sir ROBERT MENZIES.

stopping the clock The technique used in EUROPEAN COMMUNITY Ministerial meetings to avoid a breakdown of negotiations when a deadline for agreement expires, under which a decision is made to "stop the clock" just before the deadline but keep talking.

storm. the gathering storm The phrase about the imminence of WORLD WAR II that Anthony EDEN used in November 1938 in a speech to the National Association of Manufacturers in New York. It was later taken up by CHURCHILL for the title of one of his own books of reminiscence.

Stormont The seat of the DEVOLVED government under which NORTHERN IRELAND was administered from 1921 to 1972, and of the UNIONIST supremacy that prevailed. The centrepiece of the 300 miles of parkland 6 miles east of Belfast is the Parliament House, designed in the "Official Classical" style by Sir Arnold Thornley and opened in 1932 by King George V. Nearby stands Stormont Castle, formerly the official residence of Viscount Craigavon, Northern Ireland's first prime minister; since 1972 it has housed the offices of the Secretary of State and other Northern Ireland ministers. The other main administrative building is Dundonald House, designed by Gibson and Taylor and opened in 1963. The last Stormont government resigned in 1972 in protest at the British government's assumption of responsibility for law and order, since when the province has been governed by DIRECT RULE from Westminster, a series of POWER-SHARING experiments having broken down. The Parliament Chambers are tended as if sittings might resume, giving the impression of a time-warp.

straight fight In UK politics, an election fought out between just two candidates.

Strangelove A fanatic or insane MILITARIST who advocates large-scale pre-emptive nuclear strikes; more generally, a Washington term for anyone in the PENTAGON who THINKS THE UNTHINKABLE. The name comes from Stanley Kubrick's 1963 black-comedy film, *Dr. Strangelove*, in which the title role and two other parts were played by the British comedian Peter Sellers. An insane USAF general, played by George C. Scott, comments:

> I don't say we wouldn't get our hair mussed, but I do say no more than 10 to 20 million people killed.

strangers At Westminster, HOUSE OF COMMONS jargon for members of the public, as in the **Strangers' Gallery** (the gallery where the public can watch proceedings in the CHAMBER) and the **Strangers' Bar** (*see* KREMLIN). **Strangers Withdraw** is a procedural motion aimed at delaying or disrupting Commons BUSINESS. When a member calls **"I see strangers"**, a DIVISION has to be held on the technicality of whether the public and press should be ejected from the galleries, thus consuming some 15 minutes of time.

Strength through Joy *See* KRAFT DURCH FREUDE.

Stresa Front An agreement signed in April 1935 by Britain, France and Italy at Stresa in Italian Piedmont, in response to German REARMAMENT which Hitler had declared the month before. They agreed to uphold the *status quo* imposed by the Treaty of VERSAILLES and other post-World War I settlements, and defend Austria's independence from the threat of a forced ANSCHLUSS with Germany. The Front presented no serious threat to German ambitions in Europe and collapsed within six months when Mussolini invaded Abyssinia.

strike (1) In industrial relations, the organized withdrawal of labour by workers in pursuit of improved pay or conditions or to force redress of a grievance. In many countries it has also been a political weapon, but has seldom been used as such in America and never in Britain save for the GENERAL STRIKE of 1926. The right to strike is much prized by organized labour, and, subject to some curbs on its abuse, notably in Britain by Margaret Thatcher's government (*see* STEP BY STEP) is a hallmark of a free society; indeed Abraham LINCOLN remarked:

> I am glad to know that there is a system of labor where the laborer can strike if he wants to! I would to God that such a system prevailed all over the world.

Other Presidents were less charitable. Grover Cleveland, ordering in troops to break a rail strike in Chicago, declared:

> If it takes the entire army and navy of the United States to deliver a postcard in Chicago, that card will be delivered.

And during the BOSTON POLICE STRIKE Calvin Coolidge stated as trenchantly:

> There is no right to strike against the public safety by anybody, anywhere, any time.

The right to strike has also been seen by generations of revolutionaries as a means to an end. Engels wrote:

> If trade unionists failed to register their protest by striking, their silence would be regarded as an admission that they acquiesced in the pre-eminence of economic forces over human welfare.

And Rosa Luxemburg declared:

> Mass strikes appear as the natural method to mobilize the broadest proletarian layers into action, to revolutionize and organize them.

See also Industrial ACTION; PICKETING.

(2) A form of extortion practised by Senators and Congressmen in late 19th-century Washington; it involved promoting legislation aimed at inconveniencing big business, in the expectation that the interests involved would offer handsome bribes to withdraw it.

First Strike *See* FIRST.

hunger strike A time-honoured form of political protest by the most committed and self-sacrificing adherents of a cause, generally when imprisoned. It was practised prior to World War I by Britain's SUFFRAGETTES (*see* CAT AND MOUSE ACT), and after it by Terence McSwiney, Lord Mayor of Cork, who perished after 74 days in 1920 in an effort to precipitate Irish independence. The most concentrated, and fatal, use of the hunger strike as a weapon was in 1981 by convicted PROVISIONAL IRA prisoners in the H-BLOCKS, in support of their campaign for "political status" which had already included BLANKET and DIRTY PROTESTS. They hoped to force concessions from Margaret Thatcher by confronting her with horrendous deaths, leading to civil unrest in Ulster and world-wide pressure to capitulate. Yet the hunger-strikers had met their match. Mrs. Thatcher stood firm when the first, Bobby Sands, died on 5

May after fasting for 66 days, telling the Commons:

> Mr. Sands was a convicted criminal. He chose to take his own life. It was a choice that his organization did not allow to many of its victims.

Nine more hunger strikers died that summer before the Provisionals abandoned their campaign.

Miners' strike *See* MINERS'.

stroke. at a stroke The phrase that haunted Edward Heath (*see* GROCER) as INFLATION began to take hold during his administration, earning him many taunts from Harold WILSON and other opponents. During the 1970 election campaign Heath was supposed to have said: "We will reduce the rise in prices at a stroke." The words were not actually said by him but stemmed from a handout distributed at one of Heath's election PRESS CONFERENCES:

> This [tax cuts and a freeze on nationalized industry prices] would, at a stroke, reduce the rise in prices, increase productivity and reduce unemployment.

with a stroke of a pen The flourish with which John F. KENNEDY promised as a Presidential candidate in 1960 to end racial discrimination in Federal housing. CIVIL RIGHTS groups lamented that it took JFK almost two years to carry out his pledge, not picking up the pen until November 1962.

strong man A euphemism for a DICTATOR, usually pro-Western in orientation and generally with a military power base. The term is most often used in a Latin American context, sometimes describing an officer who wields the real power in a state while not being its titular head; an example was General Omar Torrijos of Panama. It was also used to describe Ngo Dinh Diem, South Vietnam's prime minister in the early stages of the VIETNAM WAR, and successive rulers of Thailand and South Korea.

structural funds Special funds allocated by the EUROPEAN COMMUNITY for projects in member states, especially those whose economies are less advanced and who are eager for assistance to enable them to catch up (*see* COHESION). A substantial increase in such funds was agreed at the Edinburgh EC summit in December 1992 after determined advocacy by Jacques DELORS and Spain's prime minister Felipe González.

STUC Scottish Trades Union Congress. Scotland's equivalent of the TUC, which covers the whole of Britain, but a body with far more status and political muscle, reflecting the more concentrated and pervasive nature of trade unionism north of the Border. Andrew Marr, in *The Battle for Scotland*, wrote that for many years the STUC could almost be regarded as "the political wing of the Labour Party in Scotland".

stump. on the stump A mainly US term for the form of campaigning in which a candidate gets out and makes often-impromptu speeches, instead of concentrating on large-scale set-piece appearances. The phrase dates back to the early 19th or even the late 18th century, when candidates campaigning in the BACKWOODS to the West harangued crowds from the stumps of newly-felled trees. The phrase **stumping the country** has the same origin.

STV Single Transferable Vote. One of the most popular forms of PROPORTIONAL REPRESENTATION. Under it each elector lists the candidates in order of preference; if their first choice finishes bottom of the poll, the second preferences are distributed among the other candidates and the process continues until one candidate receives over 50% of the total.

style versus substance The late 20th-century counterpart of MEN OR MEASURES, the comparison between a candidate or leader with strong personal CHARISMA and one with greater governmental skills or intellectual weight.

sub-committee A formally- or informally-constituted body composed of members of a COMMITTEE and reporting to it; generally it deals with a portion of the full committee's remit, or matters deemed too routine for the entire panel to consider in detail. In Britain, sub-committees are primarily found in local government. In the US Congress, they came into their own in 1974 when the House of Representatives devolved much of the power of its 22 STANDING COMMITTEES to 172 sub-committees; at a stroke, this broke the power of the BARONS who had controlled the main committees through their SENIORITY, and catapulted relatively junior members into positions of some influence.

sub judice (Lat. under a judge) The convention that matters which are currently the subject of legal proceedings may not be commented on in Parliamentary debate, lest anything said prove prejudicial.

Sublime Porte (Fr. lofty gate) The central government in Istanbul of the Ottoman Empire, which was eclipsed during World War I. It took its name from a building near one of the city's twelve gates called *Bab-i-Humajun*, which itself had a tall gate. It was both the official residence of the vizier, and the offices of all chief ministers of state from which Imperial edicts were issued.

subliminal influence The influencing of voters without their being aware of it, for instance by the repeated transmission of a slogan on television for too brief an instant for viewers to realize that they have seen it. Subliminal techniques first appeared in the world of advertising in 1957, when James Vicary demonstrated a "tachistoscope" which would flash a message lasting 0.03 second on to a cinema screen every five seconds. The political applications of such a technique are obvious, but though subliminal propaganda is widely seen as unethical, few concrete measures have been taken to prevent it.

subsidiarity One of the catchwords of the debate in Europe over the MAASTRICHT TREATY, the doctrine that BRUSSELS should only undertake those activities that national governments could not perform as effectively, and that whatever national governments could handle best should be left to them. It was advanced by John MAJOR as a brake on greater centralization of power in the hands of the the EC COMMISSION, but was seen by some Continental leaders as at best meaningless and at worst a deliberate attempt to hamper the functioning of the Community. Nevertheless the 1992 Birmingham and Edinburgh summits agreed that subsidiarity – together with TRANSPARENCY – should be applied to the EC's activities. Advocates of HOME RULE for Scotland argued on the fringes of the Edinburgh summit that under true subsidiarity, Scotland and other component parts of member states should have power DEVOLVED to them where they could exercise it more effectively, but Major strongly resisted this interpretation.

subterranean campaign A vigorous campaign by a party to maximize its support at election times, conducted without its opponents realizing the scale of activity. The term was widely used in 1992 to explain the Conservatives' unexpected UK election victory; the party held many key MARGINAL SEATS through intensive CANVASSING, mainly by telephone, of voters who had supported it in the past, rather than by trying to win converts.

subversion The undermining of a state from within, without the public as a whole being aware of the existence or nature of the threat (*see also* DESTABILIZATION; FIFTH COLUMNIST). By contrast, in the days of McCARTHYISM, the belief that every aspect of life was at risk from **subversives** led to the BLACKLISTING of many law-abiding Americans. In 1981 the newspaper publisher Jacobo Timerman (1923–), arguing against the use of unlawful methods by Argentina's military dictatorship to combat subversion (*see* DISAPPEARED), wrote:

> The political defeat of subversion is as important as its military defeat. Applying legal methods to repression eliminates one of the major elements exploited by subversion: the illegal nature of repression.

succession The chain of individuals who, in turn, would stand to fill a particular post if the occupant were to die or otherwise leave it. In Britain the line of succession to the THRONE is established on a basis laid down by law; it passes first to the Sovereign's eldest son, if there is one, and to first his sons and then his daughters. Next in line come the Sovereign's other sons and their heirs, or the daughters of the monarch and their families if there are no sons. The line of succession to the US PRESIDENCY starts with the VICE-PRESIDENT, but the question of how to proceed if neither was able to serve has posed problems. Under an Act of 1886 the succession passed to members of the CABINET by order of precedence, starting with the SECRETARY OF STATE. In 1947 this was modified to put the SPEAKER of the House of Representatives and the President pro tem (*see* PRESIDENT OF THE SENATE) of the Senate ahead of the Cabinet members. Neither of these provisions was ever used, and in 1967 the TWENTY-FIFTH AMENDMENT provided for the President to nominate a new Vice-President, subject to Congressional approval. Richard Nixon invoked the amendment to appoint Gerald FORD after Spiro AGNEW's resignation, and Ford in turn appointed Nelson Rockefeller (*see* ROCKY) after his own elevation to the Presidency on Nixon's resignation.

Sudeten crisis The war scare provoked by Hitler's claim to the German-speaking Sudetenland in Czechoslovakia which was eventually conceded by British, French and Italian leaders at MUNICH in September 1938. The Sudeten Germans had been placed in Czechoslovakia in 1919 by the Treaty of St. Germain. In the 1930s, the NAZIS fomented agitation for regional autonomy and the redress of economic grievances; the demands were met by the Czech government in April 1938 but the agitation continued. Hitler seized his opportunity, and at Munich the Prague government was ordered to cede the Sudetenland to Germany by 10 October 1938; within months Hitler was in Prague, and within a year Europe was at war. When peace returned in 1945, the Sudetenland was restored to Czechoslovakia, which expelled most of its German population.

> Before us stands the last problem that must be solved, and will be solved. It is the last territorial claim I have to make in Europe, but it is the claim from which I will not recede

and which, God willing, I will make good. With regard to the problem of the Sudeten Germans, my patience is now at an end.

HITLER, speech at the Berlin *Sportpalast*, 26 September 1938.

Sudeten Scots The scathing term for Conservative MPs unseated in Scotland who returned to Westminster representing English constituencies, which was coined in the late 1960s by the Labour Scottish Secretary William Ross (later Lord Ross of Marnock).

Suez. Suez Canal purchase Benjamin Disraeli's purchase for the British government in 1875 of 177,000 shares in the Suez Canal – 44% of the ordinary shares – from the near-bankrupt Khedive Ismail of Egypt, just five years after the canal's completion. The price DIZZY paid was £4 million, borrowed from the banker Lionel de Rothschild until Parliamentary approval could be secured. The deal gave Britain a degree of control over the waterway for which it provided 80% of the traffic, and which was becoming the umbilical cord between Britain and its new Indian empire.

Suez crisis The botched military adventure by Britain and France in 1956 to retake the Suez Canal after its NATIONALIZATION by the Egyptian leader Colonel Gamel Abdel Nasser. It finally destroyed British illusions of Empire, strained the US–UK SPECIAL RELATIONSHIP to breaking point, gravely damaged British influence in the Arab world and made Nasser an instant hero, enabled Russia to crush the HUNGARIAN UPRISING unchallenged by the West, split UK public opinion, and ended the political career of Anthony EDEN. Nasser nationalized the canal on 26 July in the wake of America's refusal – brought about by ever closer links between Cairo and Moscow – to finance the ASWAN HIGH DAM as previously promised. This incensed the British and French, who had been the canal's main owners and feared for the safety of their oil supplies. While making overt diplomatic moves to resolve the crisis, they prepared secret plans for the conquest of the canal zone and the overthrow of Nasser, whom Eden perceived as a latter-day Hitler. Eden was backed by most of his own party; he was egged on particularly by his Chancellor, Harold Macmillan, who said:

If Nasser gets away with it, we are done for.

But Walter Monckton, who was about to retire as Minister for War, enquired: "How do we actually start this war?" and Dick White, Director of MI6, described the invasion plan as "a pretty tall order". The Labour leadership was initially supportive, Hugh GAITSKELL saying on 2 August:

It is all very familiar. It is exactly the same that we encountered from Mussolini and Hitler.

But the Labour Party, spurred by GRASS-ROOTS opinion, soon turned against a military adventure, and a small but vocal group of Tory rebels, including the Foreign Office Minister Anthony Nutting who resigned in protest at "this sordid conspiracy", also warned that the exercise would end in tears; when it did, the party turned against them, one, Nigel Nicolson, being rejected by his constituency.

An agreement was reached at SÈVRES under which ISRAEL, threatened by Egypt since its foundation in 1948, invaded on 29 October and Anglo-French forces landed at Port Said and Port Fuad on the pretext of enforcing a call from the UNITED NATIONS to separate the combatants. Macmillan had told Eden: "IKE's not going to make any real trouble if we have to do anything drastic", but the duplicity of this action enraged President Eisenhower, who was facing a re-election ballot within days, and Secretary of State John Foster Dulles, who told him: "The French and the British are deliberately keeping us in the dark." Eisenhower, and Dulles who had been ambivalent over whether US support would be forthcoming, threatened to back a call from the UN GENERAL ASSEMBLY for economic SANCTIONS against Britain and France. In the process America triggered a run on the POUND and the franc that forced the invaders to withdraw: the British and French on 22 December, the Israelis the following March. By then Eden had resigned through ill-health. *See also* ARMED CONFLICT.

I want Nasser destroyed – not removed, destroyed.

EDEN.

God damn it, we're going to apply sanctions, we're going to the United Nations, we're going to do everything that there is so we can stop this thing.

EISENHOWER to Dulles, 29 October 1956.

During the past few weeks I felt sometimes that the Suez Canal was flowing through my room.

Eden's wife Lady CLARISSA EDEN, November 1956.

Like going through the preliminaries without having an orgasm.

ANTHONY HEAD, Monckton's successor as UK Minister for War.

Suez group The hard core of right-wing Conservative MPs who gave enthusiastic support for the Suez venture, but despaired of Eden's handling of it. Led by Julian Amery and Hugh Fraser, they pressed for the military operation to continue in the face of US and UN objections until the Canal was under Anglo-French control.

East of Suez The world, rather than regional role for Britain's armed forces, and specifically its commitment to Singapore and the Gulf. The maintenance of a presence east of Suez was an emotive political issue in the late 1960s, with Harold WILSON's Labour government reluctantly taking the decision to pull out and Edward Heath's Conservatives completing its implementation. The phrase originated with Rudyard Kipling (1865–1936), who wrote in his poem *Mandalay*:

> Ship me somewheres east of Suez, where the best is like the worst,
> Where there aren't no Ten Commandments, an' a man can raise a thirst:
> For the temple bells are callin', an' it's there that I would be –
> By the old Moulmein Pagoda, looking lazy at the sea.

suffrage. universal [manhood] **suffrage** The possession of the right to vote by all. At first it implied only votes for all adult men; VOTES FOR WOMEN came later, though in America a convention at Seneca Falls, New York, demanded votes for all as early as 1848.

> Universal suffrage exists in the United States, without producing any very frightful consequences.
>
> THOMAS BABINGTON MACAULAY in the House of Commons, 2 March 1831.

> Universal suffrage is counter-revolution.
>
> PIERRE-JOSEPH PROUDHON (1809–65).

Women's suffrage *See* WOMEN.

Suffragettes Members of the Women's Social and Political Union, founded in 1903 by Emmeline Pankhurst (1858–1928), who conducted a campaign of increasing MILITANCY in Edwardian Britain to secure the vote. Some sought VOTES FOR WOMEN on the same property qualification as then applied to men; others wanted universal adult suffrage. The militants, led by Mrs. Pankhurst and her daughter Christabel (1880–1958), chained themselves to railings, attacked property, refused to pay taxes, staged DEMONSTRATIONS and disrupted meetings addressed by male politicians. Thwarted in their aims by the attitude of ASQUITH, their tactics also alienated many of his Cabinet, Lloyd George saying when one group interrupted him:

> I see some rats have got in; let them squeal, it doesn't matter.

The suffragettes were repeatedly imprisoned (*see* CAT AND MOUSE ACT), and endangered their lives by hunger STRIKES which the authorities tried to break with brutal FORCE-FEEDING. On the outbreak of World War I the suffragettes suspended their campaign and supported the war effort; in 1918 Lloyd George recognized the important role played by women in achieving victory by granting the vote to women over 30, subject to property qualifications. In 1928 these last restrictions were removed and the vote extended to all women over 21 (*see* flapper VOTE).

> We have taken this action, because as women . . . it is our duty even to break the law in order to call attention to the reasons why we do so . . . We are here, not because we are law-breakers, we are here in our efforts to become law-makers.
>
> EMMELINE PANKHURST, speaking in court, 21 October 1908.

summit A meeting between the most influential of world leaders; a word much devalued since CHURCHILL used it in the early 1950s for his ambition of a "parley at the summit" between President Eisenhower, himself and the successors of STALIN to ease the ARMS RACE and the COLD WAR. True summit meetings should really cover few more than the periodic meetings of the Presidents of the United States and of Russia (*see also* GENEVA; HELSINKI; PARIS; REYKJAVIK), but the term is stretched a little to cover the annual "economic summit" of the leaders of the G7 countries, and further to include the 6-monthly meetings of the leaders of the EUROPEAN COMMUNITY. More loosely it is also applied to the regular talks between the French President and German Chancellor. The practice and art of conducting summit meetings is known as **summitry**. *See also* SHERPAS.

> The only summit meeting that can succeed is the one that does not take place. Sen. BARRY GOLDWATER.

Seasick Summit The term given by US officials to the meeting between George BUSH and Mikhail Gorbachev off Malta in December 1989, the month after the breaching of the BERLIN WALL and with Communism collapsing throughout Eastern Europe. The meeting gained its name from the appalling seas in which the leaders were ferried between warships belonging to their respective countries.

Shamrock Summit The meeting of President Reagan and the Canadian Prime Minister Brian Mulroney in QUEBEC City on 17 March 1985. It earned its name through the capital both leaders made of their common Irish origin, culminating in them joining in a chorus of *When Irish eyes are smiling*. On a more serious note, the meeting paved the way for talks on RECIPROCITY in trade, which in turn led ultimately to the North American FREE TRADE Area (*see* NAFTA).

sun. Sunbelt strategy In US politics, a strategy for winning the Presidency (or control of Congress) by picking up votes in what has since the late 1960s been known as the Sunbelt: the chain of states running west from Florida, which with their RIGHT TO WORK LAWS have attracted jobs and prosperity from the "rustbelt" of the North-East. The term was first used to describe Richard Nixon's breakthrough in traditionally Democratic Southern states in 1972, and again for Ronald

Reagan's defeat of Jimmy Carter on his home ground in 1980.

sunset legislation Legislation to which a fixed term is set, so that the programme or agency created under it automatically lapses after that period unless there is a specific vote to continue it. Such laws were pioneered by US state governments in the mid-1970s in a bid both to curb BUREAUCRACY and curb spending.

sunshine laws Laws to guarantee the public information about the process of government, guaranteeing admission to meetings, the availability of documents and knowledge. *See also* FREEDOM OF INFORMATION ACT; TRANSPARENCY.

place in the sun *See* PLACE.

Sunningdale agreement The high-point of hopes for POWER-SHARING in Ulster: the agreement brokered in the summer of 1973 by Edward Heath at Sunningdale, Berkshire, to reinforce the newly-elected Assembly at Stormont with a **Council of All Ireland**, drawing members from both the Assembly and the DAIL; there was also to be an **All-Ireland Court**. It was agreed to by Heath, his Northern Ireland Secretary Francis Pym, Liam Cosgrave, TAOISEACH of a FINE GAEL–Labour coalition, and members of the Executive that was due to take power in Ulster. However the deal meant different things to each of the participants, and soon fell apart. First the ULSTER UNIONISTS rejected it, then the Irish government temporized when challenged in the courts by Kevin Boland (*see* ARMS CRISIS) over Sunningdale's legality. Then Heath called a General Election for February 1974; in Britain it was a referendum on the MINERS' STRIKE, in Ulster it was a referendum on Sunningdale. Pro-Executive candidates were routed by the hard-line slogan **Dublin is only a Sunningdale away**, and when a minority Labour government took office it was forced by a GENERAL STRIKE of Loyalist workers to scrap the entire power-sharing experiment.

> It was very typical of Ted Heath that he thought he achieved something by dragooning people at Sunningdale into accepting something they not only didn't mean, but which those upon whom they depended, the electors upon whom they depended, couldn't possibly mean.
>
> ENOCH POWELL.

Sunny Jim One of the nicknames of **(Leonard) James** (later Lord) **Callaghan** (1912–), the Labour politician who held all three great offices of State – CHANCELLOR, HOME SECRETARY and FOREIGN SECRETARY – before serving as Prime Minister from 1976 until 1979. The original Sunny Jim was the character used to advertise Force breakfast cereal, invented *c.* 1902 by Minny Maud Hanff and Edward Ellsworth. The son of a Naval petty officer, Callaghan left school to join the Inland Revenue and became assistant secretary of the tax officers' trade union before joining the Navy himself in World War II (*see* STOKER JIM). He was elected an MP for Cardiff in 1945, serving until 1987 when he took a Life PEERAGE. A junior Minister under ATTLEE, he made his mark in opposition as a tough Centrist with a trade unionist's eye for creating beneficial alliances. On Hugh GAITSKELL's death he stood for the leadership, finishing third behind Harold WILSON and George BROWN. When Labour returned to power in 1964 he became CHANCELLOR, a series of STERLING crises (*see* JULY MEASURES) and periods of relative stability (*see* STEADY AS SHE GOES!) alternating until the trauma of DEVALUATION in November 1967. Callaghan resigned, but took the Home Office, where he gained a reputation on the left for illiberality for his efforts to tighten the immigration laws (*see* PATRIALITY). However his most notable and controversial act in the closing phase of the first Wilson government was his ruthless torpedoing of the trade union reform proposals IN PLACE OF STRIFE. After four years in opposition, he became Foreign Secretary in 1974 just as the crisis in Cyprus provoked by the Greek COLONELS came to a head; he was criticized because Britain, as one of Cyprus's three guarantors, failed to prevent the Turkish invasion and the island's subsequent partition. When Wilson suddenly resigned in 1976, Callaghan beat Michael Foot (*see* WURZEL GUMMIDGE to succeed him. As Prime Minister he had to cope almost at once with the economic crisis which led to the IMF being brought in. He also had to supervise an ambitious legislative programme, including the NATIONALIZATION of aircraft and shipbuilding and DEVOLUTION for Scotland and Wales, with Labour's majority having evaporated. In 1977 he staved off defeat for a year by concluding the LIB-LAB PACT with David Steel; the economy began to revive and in 1978 Labour's re-election began to look thinkable, but the WINTER OF DISCONTENT undermined Callaghan's credibility (*see* CRISIS, WHAT CRISIS?) and after the abortive Scottish REFERENDUM the Opposition parties united in a no-CONFIDENCE vote on 28 March 1979 and brought the Government down amid electrifying scenes by 311 votes to 310. Callaghan did his best in the ensuing election campaign, but the tide was with Margaret Thatcher and Labour went back into opposition to begin the process of tearing itself to pieces which culminated in the formation of the SDP two years later. Callaghan stayed on for 18 months;

he had promised Denis Healey he would "take the shine off the ball" for him, but it was Foot - just - who won the vote to succeed him.

Until he showed himself a competent and fair Prime Minister, Callaghan did not always inspire confidence or admiration. Hugh Dalton branded him as "too stupid by three-quarters", Michael Foot as "PC Callaghan" (reflecting his work at Westminster for the Police Federation); Woodrow Wyatt as "skilful in debate, persuasive in speeches and disastrous at his job"; Edward Heath called him "the man of indecision" and John Lennon, playing on words, "Mr. Caravans". It was his alleged duplicity that aroused most comment from colleagues. Richard Crossman complained: "He talks to me in the friendliest way and fights me ruthlessly behind my back"; Wilson condemned him as "individually ambitious and inordinately weak - so weak that as Chancellor of the Exchequer he used to weep on my shoulder and then go away and intrigue against me"; and Roy Jenkins (see WOY) lamented: "There is no case I can think of in history where a man combined such a powerful political personality with so little intelligence." Callaghan's then son-in-law Peter Jay caused amusement when, after his appointment as Ambassador to Washington, he revealed:

> As the Prime Minister put it to me, he saw his role as being Moses leading Britain to the Promised Land.

The Labour MP Austin Mitchell responded: "As Moses, he would have mistimed his arrival at the parting of the waves". In somewhat the same vein, Callaghan once himself confided: "When I am shaving in the morning I say to myself I would like to emigrate, and then I wonder: 'Where would I go?'"

Yet Callaghan ended his career having lived down his reputation as a bruiser who could not always be trusted - and in his final years on the BACK BENCHES earned plaudits from all sides for his patriotism, his common sense and his use of graceful but basic English, echoing another non-graduate, Winston CHURCHILL.

> He suffers from what you might regard as a fatal defect in a Chancellor. He is always wrong. IAIN MACLEOD.

> If Hugh Gaitskell's motto was "FIGHT, FIGHT AND FIGHT AGAIN", Callaghan's is "manoeuvre, manoeuvre and manoeuvre again". IAN BRADLEY, *The Times*.

> Living proof that the short-term schemer and the frustrated bully can be made manifest in one man. HUGO YOUNG.

> Wrong on devaluation, East of Suez, immigration policy, most libertarian issues at the Home Office, trade union reform and Europe, but sound on the Atlantic alliance, no dogmatic supporter of nationalisation and with a built-in respect for the rule of law. ROY JENKINS.

> A lot of people say I'm not clever at all - but I became Prime Minister and they didn't. Lord CALLAGHAN, 1992.

super. Supergun The scandal that broke in early 1991 about the supply of components by UK firms to Saddam Hussein's regime (*see* BUTCHER OF BAGHDAD) for a massive artillery piece, capable of firing projectiles against Israel or beyond. What was most scandalous, as came to light in hearings of the Commons Trade and Industry Committee, was that organs of the British government had circumvented their own EMBARGO on the export of military hardware to combatants in the first GULF WAR. However the guilty parties contrived to muddy the waters, only for the issue to resurface more damningly in the MATRIX-CHURCHILL AFFAIR late in 1992.

Supermac The nickname that stuck to the UK Conservative Prime Minister **Harold Macmillan** (later Earl of Stockton, 1894–1986) after the *Evening Standard* cartoonist *Vicky* (Victor Weisz) (1913-66) depicted him on 6 November 1958 as the US comic-strip hero Superman. Macmillan said of his public image: "I am Macwonder one moment, and Macblunder the next".

An active member of the Macmillan publishing family who made much of being the grandson of a Scottish crofter, he was wounded three times in World War I, then served as ADC to the GOVERNOR-GENERAL of Canada. He was MP for the North-Eastern town of Stockton 1924–29 and 1931–45, identifying strongly with the misery of its workers during the GREAT DEPRESSION; he wrote: "The memory of massive unemployment began to haunt me then [in the 1920s] and for many years to come." As he pioneered the social doctrine of the MIDDLE WAY, he was at serious odds with the Tories over social policy when World War II broke out; his biographer Alistair Horne wrote:

> It is difficult to believe that he could have stood as an orthodox Conservative candidate if a general election had been held in 1939 or 1940.

CHURCHILL made him a junior Minister, then in 1942 sent him to North Africa as Resident Minister at Allied HQ where, according to his private secretary John Wyndham, he became "VICEROY of the Mediterranean by stealth"; in 1944 he correctly estimated: "If I do become Prime Minister, it will be in about 12 years."

From 1945 as MP for Bromley, he helped mould the party's BUTSKELLITE post-war line in opposition. In 1951 he returned as Minister of Housing, setting an apparently unreachable total of 300,000 homes a year and reaching it; Churchill told him on his appointment:

It is a gamble – make or mar your political career. But every humble home will bless your name if you succeed.

Macmillan was briefly Defence Minister and then Foreign Secretary, but for most of the foreshortened EDEN government he was CHANCELLOR; though a strong supporter of intervention at SUEZ, it was he whom the MAGIC CIRCLE wanted to succeed Eden (*see* WAB OR HAWOLD?). Of Suez Macmillan was soon saying: "I was all for going in, but I know now I should never have agreed." As the operation collapsed, Brendan Bracken cruelly observed:

Until about a week ago Macmillan, whose bellicosity was beyond description, was wanting to tear Nasser's scalp off with his own fingernails. Today he might be described as the leader of the bolters.

Harold WILSON branded him as "first in, first out", and even more cuttingly remarked:

He had an expensive education – Eton and Suez.

Taking office in January 1957, Macmillan restored Tory morale, presided over unprecedented prosperity (*see* YOU'VE NEVER HAD IT SO GOOD) and won a LANDSLIDE victory over Labour in October 1959. In the field of transatlantic affairs, where he acted as "wise uncle" to John F. KENNEDY during the CUBAN MISSILE CRISIS and concluded the TEST BAN TREATY, his winning streak continued; the outgoing Eisenhower told JFK that Macmillan was "a good friend whose counsel you should listen to". But at home things went sour: the economy began slipping (*see* PAY PAUSE), his urbanity slipped with the NIGHT OF THE LONG KNIVES when he sacked seven Ministers in 1962, DE GAULLE vetoed his effort to take Britain into the COMMON MARKET (*see* NON!), and the PROFUMO AFFAIR left his government teetering. Before he had a chance to weather Profumo, Macmillan had prostate trouble diagnosed in October 1963, and believing it worse than it was, he resigned, declaring:

I will not be able to carry the physical burden of leading the Party into the next General Election. I hope it will soon be possible for the customary processes of consultation to be carried on within the party about its future leadership.

Of the scene when the Queen came to accept his resignation, he wrote:

The bed covers were down, and concealed underneath the bed was a pail, with a tube full of bile coming out of me. I made my resignation to the Queen of England for an hour, in great discomfort.

His immediate legacy was dynamite: the choice of Lord Home (*see* SIR ALEC) as his successor rather than the more obvious R. A. (RAB) Butler or Quintin Hogg (Lord Hailsham). Macmillan left the Commons in 1964 and returned to writing and publishing – only to make a devastating return to politics in 1984 when Margaret Thatcher, no friend to what he stood for, gave him an EARLDOM. Until his death two years later, the Earl of Stockton, as he had become, pilloried her government from the House of Lords (*see* SELLING OFF THE FAMILY SILVER). Roy Jenkins observed: "His brief Parliamentary resurrection as Earl of Stockton was theatre with high box-office appeal," but Frank Johnson opined: "One can never escape the suspicion that all his life was a preparation for elder statesmanship."

With his Edwardian manner, lugubrious voice, drooping moustache and ability to conjure up tears, Macmillan was varyingly praised as a brilliant political actor and condemned as a fraud. Lord WOOLTON once complained:

A public man has to be something of an actor. I wonder whether it is really necessary for him to be a showman as well.

And Bernard Levin wrote: "It was almost impossible to believe he was anything but a down-at-heel actor resting between engagements." There was a widespread view that one seldom saw the real Macmillan. Pamela, Lady Egremont said: "One moment you had a salmon in your hand, the next it was a horse." The Labour MP David Marquand once asked: "What is he trying to hide? The obvious answer is, himself." But to Malcolm Muggeridge he was simply "a parody of a Conservative politician in a novel by Trollope".

Quintin Hogg rightly called him "unflappable"; to Henry (CHIPS) Channon he was "that very nice ass"; to the Young Conservative Harry Phibbs, who in Macmillan's final year accused him of betraying fleeing Cossacks in 1945, he was "a war criminal". His concern for the jobless earned him a mixed press from Labour. ATTLEE regarded him as "by far the most radical man I've met in politics", MANNY Shinwell as "not a true Socialist, but compassionate"; however Maurice Edelman noted:

His sympathy was undoubted; his manner was all wrong. His forays were like those of a public school missionary to the East End.

Michael Foot thought him "unctuous and grandiloquent" and Aneurin BEVAN declared: "He and all his middle-of-the-roaders are the parasites of politics." Macmillan also epitomized the GROUSE-MOOR IMAGE, his supposed humble beginnings betrayed by the fact that his wife, Lady Dorothy, was a daughter of the Duke of Devonshire. Lady Dorothy had a long-running affair with Macmillan's Parliamentary colleague Lord

Boothby, who was the actual father of one of "his" children. His son Maurice observed:

What he minded most was being dishonoured.

In dignity, voice, manners, dress and personality almost the American popular image of an English gentleman.
Ambassador ROBERT MURPHY.

He has inherited the streak of charlatanry in Disraeli without his vision, and the self-righteousness of Gladstone without his dedication to principle.
HAROLD WILSON.

He held his party together by not allowing his left wing to see what his right wing was doing.
Lady VIOLET BONHAM-CARTER.

He seems, in his very person, to embody the national decay he supposed himself to be confuting. He exuded a flavour of mothballs. MALCOLM MUGGERIDGE.

The eyes were hooded, they seemed to hover always on the verge of a wink at his fantastic good fortune at being set down in the country of the blind, where none could see through him. BERNARD LEVIN.

superpowers The term used during the later part of the COLD WAR for the United States and the Soviet Union, as they confronted each other with their massive nuclear arsenals. Its origin was a book of the same name written in 1944 by the US strategic expert William Fox, which forecast much of the post-war pattern in world affairs. Such a pattern – without the name – had actually been predicted in the late 1830s by Alexis de Tocqueville, who in his *Democracy in America* wrote:

There are now two great nations in the world which, starting from different points, seem to be advancing toward the same great goal: the Russians and the Anglo-Americans.

The Superpowers often behave like two heavily-armed blind men feeling their way around a room, each believing himself in mortal peril from the other whom he assumes to have perfect vision. HENRY KISSINGER.

Super Tuesday The Tuesday in April or May of a US Presidential election year when the largest number of PRIMARIES are held, their combined results having a heavy and often decisive effect on the nominating process. The phrase, which first stuck during the 1976 campaign, was borrowed from the vocabulary of American football.

Supper Club A secret DINING CLUB of left-wing and other Labour MPs dissatisfied with the thrust of party policy under Neil KINNOCK whose existence embarrassingly came to light at the height of the GULF WAR, which they opposed. The group, including several Shadow Ministers, was rash enough to circulate an AGENDA for its discussions, and a copy left in a Commons photocopier swiftly found its way to the media.

supplementary At QUESTION TIME in the UK House of Commons, the point put to follow up the initial question set out on the ORDER PAPER. When a member's turn comes, he or she calls out the number of the question, the Minister replies and the member then comes back with the supplementary to seek further information or make a political point. The term also applies to subsequent questions asked by other members on the same point before the Speaker moves on to the next one.
supplementary estimates In Whitehall and UK local government, extra APPROPRIATIONS for spending over and above the sums originally voted for the year. They have to be put to Parliament or the council for approval.

supply The financial life-blood that has to be voted by a Parliament for the operations of government to continue. The clash between the House of Lords and Asquith's government over the PEOPLE'S BUDGET amounted to a refusal to vote supply. In Australia both Jack Lang's New South Wales Labor government in 1932, and Gough WHITLAM's Commonwealth Labor ministry in 1975, were removed from office because they could not guarantee supply.
supply day Until the late 1980s, the term at Westminster for days when the OPPOSITION could choose the subject for debate. They were then named **Opposition days**.
supply side economics The approach to macro-economics popular on the right of politics in the late 1970s and 1980s; it was pioneered by the US economist Jude Wanniski in *The Way The World Works*, a tract based on the theories of the 18th-century French economist Jean-Baptiste Say. Wanniski argued that the KEYNESIAN idea of fighting recession by boosting demand had merely created INFLATION, and that a better way would be to boost production and supply, with demand bound to rise as the MARKET came into play. A key element in supply-side economics, and one on which REAGANOMICS and THATCHERISM were based, was the doctrine that cutting taxes would stimulate the economy and thus more than offset the initial loss in revenues.

On the side of the people who are well supplied.
HERBLOCK.

The good news is that a busload of supply-side economists has plunged over a cliff. The bad news is that three seats were unoccupied at the time. Rep. MORRIS UDALL.

supreme. Supreme Court In America, the nine Justices, appointed in most cases by previous Presidents, who are the ultimate arbiters of whether the actions of the Administration, the Congress, the States, corporations and individuals accord with the CONSTITUTION. At times (*see* BLACK MONDAY) it has been a conservative brake on a reforming President; at others (*see* WARREN COURT) a liberal irritant to an Administration committed to the *status quo*. The resulting strains date back at least to the days of Abraham LINCOLN, who cautioned:

> If the policy of the government upon vital issues affecting the whole people is to be increasingly fixed by decisions of the Supreme Court, the people will have ceased to be their own rulers.

Franklin D. Roosevelt (*see* FDR) attempted to limit the justices' power by COURT-PACKING, but was thwarted by Congress; since then it has been accepted that only through filling CASUAL VACANCIES will the balance of the court be changed. As Sen. George W. Norris (1861–1944) put it, "the people can change Congress, but only God can change the Supreme Court."

> An institution of political judgment masquerading as a council of priests. THEODORE H. WHITE.

> The Constitution is not a panacea for any blot upon the general welfare, nor should this Court, ordained as a judicial body, be thought of as a general haven for reform movements. Justice JOHN M. HARLAN (dissenting), 1964.

> However the court may interpret the provisions of the Constitution, it is still the Constitution which is the law and not the decision of the court.
> CHARLES WARREN (1868–1954).

> The Supreme Court follows th'illiction returns.
> Mr. Dooley (FINLEY PETER DUNNE) (1867–1936).

Supreme Head of the Church The title borne by the Kings and Queens of England since Elizabeth I, reflecting their status as temporal head of the Church of England. North of the Border in Scotland, Sovereigns become Presbyterians through their status in the Church of Scotland.

Supreme Soviet *See* SOVIET.

surcharge A sum which a member of a the UK local authority may be ordered to pay if the DISTRICT AUDITOR concludes that they have improperly authorized expenditure by the authority.

surgery The word used by MPs in Britain for the advice bureaux they conduct in their CONSTITUENCIES. Most hold a surgery every weekend or at least once a fortnight; MPs with urban seats may always hold them in the same place, those representing more scattered or rural constituencies will rotate between a number of locations: party or local council offices, public libraries, village halls and the like.

surrender. No surrender! The rallying cry of Ulster LOYALISTS in the face of any Nationalist or Catholic challenge to the Protestant supremacy, or any moves toward a united Ireland.

we shall never surrender *See* WE SHALL FIGHT.

we surrender The message, in Russian, attached to a telephone answering machine that the MAVERICK Danish politician Mogens Glistrup proposed in the late 1970s should replace the country's armed forces. It won his party, which also opposed taxes, a substantial number of Parliamentary seats.

unconditional surrender The war aim agreed by CHURCHILL and FDR at CASABLANCA in January 1943, requiring that the conflict against all the Allies' enemies be pressed home until they laid down their arms. Some critics believed the commitment prolonged German resistance, but it did something to ease STALIN's paranoia that the Atlantic partners might conclude a separate peace. At POTSDAM on 27 July 1945 the war leaders sent Japan a warning of "utter devastation" unless they surrendered; it was ignored and the holocaust of HIROSHIMA followed. The phrase had been used at least as early as 1862, when General Ulysses GRANT told Simon Bolivar Buckner, CONFEDERATE commander at Fort Donelson:

> No terms except unconditional and immediate surrender can be accepted. I propose to move immediately upon your works.

suspend (1) To compel a legislator to stay away for a period following a breach of discipline. (2) The action of the CHAIR in halting a session for a time because of disorder or some other emergency. (3) Suspension of STANDING ORDERS, in a UK elected body, or of the RULES in America, which enables urgent business to be dealt with; in the US House of Representatives a motion to suspend the rules may be put every Monday or Tuesday or in the last six days of a SESSION for an individual member to put forward a Bill or resolution.

Sussex Drive The official residence in Ottawa – at no. 24 – of Canada's PRIME MINISTER.

Sussex pledge Germany's promise to America in March 1916 that its submarines would not sink merchant vessels "without warning and without saving lives". It followed the sinking of the French steamer *Sussex* in the English Channel, in which two Americans were among the injured. President Wilson gave Germany an ULTIMATUM that America would break off diplomatic relations unless it ended indiscriminate submarine warfare; the threat worked until 31 January 1917, when Germany announced that it was resuming. The following month America did break off relations with Germany and began arming merchant ships.

sustainable development The central theme of the BRUNDTLAND REPORT, that all nations should be helped to achieve as much economic growth as is consistent with maintaining their environments. It was designed to strike a constructive balance between poor countries who argued that they had to develop their economies regardless of the environmental cost, and wealthy ones who insisted that the environment in the THIRD WORLD remained inviolate, even at the cost of preventing economic growth.

swamping The phrase used about immigration to Britain by Margaret Thatcher in January 1978, which led non-White Britons to fear the Conservatives in power would indulge in RACISM. Though deeply offensive to many Tories, it did have the effect of neutralizing truly racist parties such as the NATIONAL FRONT for a considerable time, the far right believing Mrs. Thatcher was "one of them". What she said in a television interview, having not consulted colleagues on the subject, was that there was a legitimate fear among White Britons of being "swamped by people with a different culture". There would be four million Black people in Britain by the end of the century, and "we are not in politics to ignore people's worries, but to deal with them". Under pressure from her Home Affairs spokesman William Whitelaw (*see* WILLIE), she never repeated her remarks, but they had in her view served their purpose.

swastika The symbol of Hitler's NAZI movement and of the evil state it created. It was the reverse of a cross-shaped design with arms, also known as a *gammadion* or *fylfot*, which had long been used in India and the Near East as a charm to ward off evil and bring good luck (the word is derived from the Sanskrit *svasti*, good fortune). It was adopted by Hitler about 1920, probably from the German Baltic Corps, who wore it on their helmets after service in Finland, on whose aircraft it was a distinguishing mark. Described by CHURCHILL as the "crooked cross", it was to become feared throughout Europe.

swear in To induct an elected head of state or office-holder, or an appointee, to office through the administration of an OATH.

sweetbreads President Franklin D. Roosevelt's least favourite food, which was repeatedly served to FDR at the White House until he told his wife Eleanor (*see* FIRST LADY OF THE WORLD):

> I am getting to the point where my stomach rebels, and this does not help my relations with foreign powers. I bit two of them today.

swing (1) The statistical measure by which the switch of voters from one party to another on a national or constituency basis can be judged. It is calculated by adding the rise in one party's vote to the fall of the other, and dividing by two. Thus if the vote of party A rises between elections or opinion polls by 3% and that of party B falls by 2%, there is a 2.5% swing from party B to party A. The calculation of swing becomes more complex, and ultimately meaningless, in a multi-party system, though it can still work on a local basis if comparisons are needed. (2) A US term for a burst of activity by a politician, usually a candidate, involving a series of appearances in rapid succession in a chain of cities, each within easy reach of the next; in a Presidential campaign such a swing will take the candidate to three or four states. The term dates back at least to September 1866 when President Andrew Johnson tried to rally the people behind him with a **swing round the circle** through Northern and Western states. The tour proved disastrous; Johnson was shouted down in city after city and trailed back to Washington, having lost the initiative and with a narrow escape from IMPEACHMENT ahead of him.

swing district In US politics, a Congressional district held by one party that is seen as potentially winnable by the other, and is likely to be TARGETED for extra effort by both prior to the two-yearly elections.

swing voters The US equivalent of Britain's FLOATING VOTERS: the critical groups in the electorate whose loyalties are not set in concrete and who might be persuaded to change party allegiance, determining the fate of key seats.

swingometer The device that has formed the centrepiece of the BBC's television coverage of UK General Elections since its invention by the Oxford PSEPHOLOGIST David Butler in 1955. In its crude form, it consisted of a cardboard arrow, pointing downward, against a sundial-like background showing the number of seats that would fall to a swing to either main party of 1%, 2%, *etc.*, with particular reference to the swing needed for a change of government. Though gradually refined, it remained essentially the same up to 1979. The swingometer was retired for the elections of 1983 and 1987, when a three-way split in the electorate reduced the relevance of a straightforward calculation of swing between the Conservatives and Labour, but was resurrected in high-tech form for the 1992 election by the presenter Peter Snow.

variable swing The degree to which the swing between parties may differ from one region or electoral district to another.

Sybil The novel completed by Benjamin Disraeli (*see* DIZZY) in 1845 in which he set out the condition of the Two NATIONS; indeed that was its alternative title. While Sybil, like CONINGSBY, was a satire on PEEL, it also dwelt on the condition of the poor in early Victorian England. Indeed Disraeli, in his preface, had to warn genteel readers:

> So little do we know of the state of our own country, that the air of improbability which the whole truth would inevitably throw over these pages, might deter some from their perusal.

Sykes-Picot agreement A secret pact, negotiated by Sir Mark Sykes of the UK and François Georges-Picot for France, for dividing up the Ottoman Empire after WORLD WAR I. France was given control of coastal Syria, the Lebanon, and Mosul, while Britain would control southern Mesopotamia, including Baghdad, and the ports of Haifa and Akka. Palestine was to be placed under international control, and a number of independent Arab states were to be created. The agreement was conditional on the approval of Russia, which was given in May 1916 in return for control over Turkish Armenia; the Italians, also promised Ottoman territory by the Treaty of LONDON, assented in August 1917 in return for portions of Anatolia. The treaty was made public by Russia's BOLSHEVIK government after the OCTOBER REVOLUTION, causing the allies considerable embarrassment as it contradicted the BALFOUR DECLARATION of 2 November 1917 which had just promised the Jews a national home in Palestine, and made pledges to Hussein, the Sherif of Mecca.

sympathetic action *See* ACTION.

syndicalism (Fr. *syndicalisme*, trade unionism) The overthrow of the political and industrial system by STRIKES and other forms of Industrial ACTION, with the aim of securing a takeover of the means of production by the TRADE UNIONS and the installation of a government comprising a federation of union bodies. It originated *c.* 1890 in France, where it was known as *syndicalisme révolutionnaire*, and gained currency through Georges Sorel's *Réflexions sur la Violence* (1906). Syndicalism played an important part in the GREAT UNREST in the UK just before World War I and in the development of the WOBBLIES in America; and the Syndicalists were also a prominent faction in the SPANISH CIVIL WAR. *See also* ANARCHO-SYNDICALISM; WORKERS' CONTROL.

T

table (1) The point for settling disputes, also the status inherent in being allowed to participate.

> If we can't sit at the table, let's saw the fucking legs off.
> JAMES FORMAN at Selma.

(2) To lodge a formal proposal for discussion. In Britain, specifically to put down an AMENDMENT to a Bill or motion. In America, confusingly, also to shelve a proposal that has been under discussion but which lacks the support to make further progress.

shape of the table The cause of bitter arguments before international conferences aimed at resolving intractable disputes. "Arguing about the shape of the table" has become shorthand for the reluctance of participants in talks to get down to the issues.

Table Office In the HOUSE OF COMMONS, the office which receives questions, *etc.*, from members for insertion into the ORDER PAPER.

Taff Vale judgment The HOUSE OF LORDS ruling in July 1901 that a TRADE UNION is liable in law for the acts of its agents, which severely limited the unions' ability to take industrial action. It arose from a suit by the Taff Vale Railway against the Amalgamated Society of Railway Servants (now RMT) for breach of contract under the Conspiracy and Protection of Property Act (1875) by picketing its Cardiff station. The ruling was followed in December 1902 by an award of £23,000 plus costs against the union. The decision, backed by the Conservative government, was a major factor in the birth of the LABOUR PARTY. It convinced trade unionists that direct Parliamentary representation for Labour was essential; union affiliation to the embryo party increased dramatically and its representation in Parliament rose from 2 in 1900 to 29 in 1906. The unions' IMMUNITY against legal action for prosecuting a dispute was reinstated by the Liberal government's Trade Disputes Act 1906, but partly removed again by the Thatcher government in the 1980s.

> Trade unionism is being assailed, not by what the law says of it, but of what judges think the law ought to say of it. That being so, it becomes necessary for the unions to place men in the House of Commons, to challenge the decisions which I have no doubt will follow.
> RAMSAY MACDONALD.

Taft, William Howard (1857–1930) 27th President of the United States (Republican, 1909–13). The son of a US Attorney-General, he was a career lawyer whose ambition of becoming CHIEF JUSTICE was derailed for a time by his wife's insistence that he seek the Presidency. His own view was that "politics, when I am in it, makes me sick". When Theodore Roosevelt (*see* TEDDY) first offered Taft a justiceship when he was Governor of the Philippines, he declined. Roosevelt telegraphed him:

> Taft, Manila. All right stay where you are. I shall appoint someone else to the Supreme Court. Roosevelt.

Taft went on to serve as Roosevelt's Secretary for War, and was elected President in 1908 as his hand-picked successor; his supporters' slogan was:

> Roosevelt has cut enough hay. Taft is the man to put it into the barn.

In the White House Taft gained a reputation for aloofness, Ring Lardner Jr. once writing: "He looked at me as if I was a side dish he had ordered." But he had a sense of humour, as shown by this exchange with Sen. Chauncey Depew about the size of Depew's pregnant-looking stomach:

> *Depew*: I hope if it is a girl, Mr Taft will name it for his charming wife.
> *Taft*: If, as I suspect, it is only a bag of wind, I shall name it Chauncey Depew.

Taft described his administration as "very humdrum", but Roosevelt despaired, saying: "Taft meant well, but he meant well feebly." Taft's frostiness and conservatism led Roosevelt to mount a comeback; splitting the Republican Party with his 1912 BULL MOOSE campaign which pushed Taft into third place. Taft commented: "No candidate was ever elected ex-President by such a large majority," and in later years he insisted: "I don't remember that I ever was President." He went on to be Professor of Law at Yale, and eventually was appointed Chief Justice in 1921, serving till 1930.

> It's very difficult to understand how a man who is so good a Chief Justice could have been so bad a President.
> JUSTICE LOUIS BRANDEIS (1856–1941).

Taft-Hartley Act Landmark legislation passed by the Republican-controlled US Congress in 1947 which limited LABOUR's ability to pursue industrial disputes and broader aims. It outlawed STRIKES by government employees, banned the CLOSED SHOP, made unions liable for breach of contract, barred them from financing political campaigns and gave the President power to impose an 80-day "COOLING-OFF PERIOD". Union leaders also had to swear they were not Communists before they could approach the National Labor Relations Board. Promoted by Sen. Robert Taft (*see* MR. REPUBLICAN) and Rep. Fred Hartley, President Truman termed the Act "a slave labor law", but Congress overrode his VETO.

Taig A derogatory term for a Roman Catholic in NORTHERN IRELAND, especially Belfast, used by working-class Protestants. It originated in the Irish Christian name *Tadhg* and its 17th-century corruption *Teague*, an Irishman. More abusive than PROD, used in the other direction.

take. take down In the US HOUSE OF REPRESENTATIVES, a call for the clerk to "take down" what has been said requires the member in question to repeat the words, with the PARLIAMENTARIAN deciding whether the House rule forbidding personal attacks and insults has been violated.

take note In the UK HOUSE OF COMMONS, a "take note" resolution records the passing of an event or the publication of a document without forming a view on it. This can avoid an embarrassing DIVISION for one party or other.

take stock John MAJOR's promise in Glasgow prior to Britain's 1992 General Election that if re-elected he would "take stock" of arrangements for governing Scotland. Intense speculation ensued over whether Major might soften his opposition to DEVOLUTION and accept some measure of Scots self-government. But after the Conservatives gained seats in Scotland on their firmly UNIONIST programme, the package, unveiled in 1993, built largely on existing arrangements.

take-up A percentage figure indicating what proportion of people eligible for a particular welfare benefit have applied for it.

talk out To continue debate on a Bill in the UK HOUSE OF COMMONS to the point where its supporters have run out of time to put it to the vote. *See* FILIBUSTER.

talk up Of one party or politician, to boost the fortunes of another for its own purposes. As in: "George BUSH's supporters are talking up Ross PEROT in the hope that Democrats will switch to him and let their man in."

talks about talks Tentative exploration of the scope for negotiations, ascertaining whether there is a chance of progress or if the talks would break down, making matters worse.

tall poppy syndrome Australian term for the national characteristic of cutting the rich, prominent or self-important down to size. It has been current since 1931, when Jack Lang (1876–1975), LABOR Premier of New South Wales, described his egalitarian policies as "cutting the heads off the tall poppies". It derives from the legend that Tarquin, king of Rome, showed his intentions for the captured city of the *Gabii* by decapitating the tallest poppies in his garden; accordingly, the leading citizens were executed. Margaret Thatcher (*see* IRON LADY) may not have known this when, prior to becoming Prime Minister, she defined her philosophy to a US audience by saying: "Let your poppies grow tall."

Tallaght strategy The initiative taken in September 1987 by Ireland's FINE GAEL leader Alan Dukes which wrongfooted Charles HAUGHEY'S FIANNA FAIL minority government by pledging to support it, provided it pursued "responsible" economic policies. The decision was taken at a meeting in Tallaght, a south-western suburb of Dublin.

Tammany Hall A derogatory term for MACHINE POLITICS and political graft. From the Democratic organization in New York city and state, which throughout the 19th century and into the 20th was a byword for graft, patronage and manipulation of the voters, especially recent immigrants. Founded in 1786 as a social and patriotic body, the "Society of St. Tammany" took its name from the Delaware chief Tamanend who reputedly welcomed William Penn to America in 1682 and became the unofficial patron saint of the revolutionary army. Tammany's corruption was evident by 1807, but it reached its greatest notoriety during the reign of BOSS TWEED later in the century.

> Look at the bosses of Tammany Hall in the last 20 years. What magnificent men! To them New York owes pretty much all it is today. John Kelly, Richard Croker and Charles F. Murphy – what names in American history compares with them, except Washington and Lincoln?
>
> Of course we aren't all bookworms and professors. If we were, Tammany might win an election once in 4000 years.
>
> GEORGE WASHINGTON PLUNKITT (1842–1924), interviewed in 1905.

Tamworth manifesto Sir Robert PEEL's election address to his constituents in 1834, regarded as one of the foundations of pragmatic TORYism. It committed the Tories to accept the 1832 REFORM ACT and to a "careful review of institutions" without further widening the suffrage. Disraeli called it "an attempt to construct a party without principles".

Tanaiste (Ir. 'Heir-apparent') Official title of the deputy Prime Minister of the Irish Republic.

Tanaka memorial A Japanese blueprint for aggressive expansion in China, said to have been presented to the Emperor in 1927 by the Prime Minister, General Tanaka Giichi (1864–1929). The memorial, widely circulated in China in the late 1920s, supposedly stemmed from a conference of top military officials called by Tanaka on taking office. Its authenticity has yet to be proved, but subsequent Japanese aggression in China followed a strategy similar to that recommended.

Tankies 1980s term for hard-line STALINISTS who believed the Soviet Union was entitled to maintain its control over Eastern Europe by sending in the tanks.

tanks. don't mess with me I got tanks The warning issued to a rival by Kim Campbell (1947–) when Canada's Defence Minister. In 1993 the combative, twice-divorced Mrs Campbell succeeded Brian Mulroney as PROGRESSIVE CONSERVATIVE leader and Prime Minister. She was previously best known for being photographed apparently (but not) naked, apart from the legal trappings of her appointment as Attorney-General.

get your tanks off my lawn. *See* GET.

Tante Yvonne (Fr. Aunt Yvonne) Nickname for Yvonne Charlotte Anne Marie, *née* Vendroux (1900–79), wife of President DE GAULLE, who was renowned for her preference for domesticity and her prudishness. Ironically she is best remembered in England for an apparently risqué answer she gave an interviewer on the de Gaulles' visit to London in 1959. Asked what she would most like in life, her audience thought she said "a penis". Her husband hurriedly interjected to correct her pronunciation to "'appiness".

Taoiseach (Ir. Chieftain, pronounced *tee-shuk*) The official title of the Prime Minister of the Irish Republic.

targeting (1) The concentration of campaigning activity on seats which look the most winnable, instead of spreading effort indiscriminately. (2) Ensuring that the neediest groups receive social security payments.

target seats Seats held by one party on which another concentrates its greatest effort, in the hope of capturing them. While all MARGINAL SEATS are keenly fought, special effort is made in some, and occasionally seats that look safe on paper fall to well-planned targeting.

tariff A PROTECTIONIST tax on imports which shields domestic producers while depressing world trade and inviting retaliation. The issue of whether to impose tariffs to protect home industry and agriculture, while forcing up prices to the consumer, was a burning issue in politics throughout the English-speaking world in the late 19th and early 20th centuries, splitting parties and bringing down governments. *See* FORDNEY-McCUMBER; FREE TRADE; GATT; McKINLEY; SMOOT-HAWLEY; UNDERWOOD.

> No more than a means of casting feudal interests in capitalist form. ROSA LUXEMBURG (1871–1919).

Tariff Reform The campaign launched in Britain by Joseph Chamberlain (1836–1914) which tore apart BALFOUR's Unionist coalition and paved the way for the LANDSLIDE Liberal victory of 1905. Chamberlain unilaterally launched the campaign, aimed at strengthening the bonds of the British Empire through IMPERIAL PREFERENCE, on 15 May 1903 in a speech in Birmingham, alienating FREE TRADE supporters of the Government. It was 1932, after further disasters over the issue for the Conservative party, before PROTECTION was re-introduced.

A tariff man on a tariff platform The slogan on which William McKINLEY won the US Presidency in 1896.

non-tariff barriers Obstructionist measures to discourage imports without recourse to a tariff; excessive paperwork, changes in specification and delays at frontiers all fall into this category. In the early 1980s France sought to check imports of Japanese video recorders by insisting that all be checked through a tiny customs post at Poitiers. France's attitude to Japanese imports generally became known as the "spirit of Poitiers".

Tarzan Nickname for **Michael** (Ray Dibdin) **Heseltine** (1933–), the Swansea-born magazine publishing millionaire who was a junior Minister throughout the Heath government, and held senior posts under Margaret Thatcher until WESTLAND, returning to the Cabinet after bringing about her downfall. She described the INTERVENTIONIST Heseltine as "not ONE OF US", but he always insisted: "I never was a WET in the 'soft' sense." His high profile, as Environment Secretary trying to revive Merseyside and as Defence Secretary, earned him mixed reviews; the Lebanese Druze militia leader Walid Jumblatt described him to Neil KINNOCK as: "How do you say it? A pryke?" But he turned back the tide against UNILATERALISM before dramatically resigning in 1986 over Westland. His biographer Julian Critchley wrote:

> The Celt had taken over from the calculator. Samson-like, he kicked out at the columns of the temple, bringing the roof down on the head of the Prime Minister and burying them both in the rubble.

Heseltine insisted in the autumn of 1989:

> I can foresee no circumstances in which I would allow my name to be put forward for the leadership of the Conservative Party.

But a year later, as controversy grew over Mrs. Thatcher's European policies following Sir Geoffrey HOWE's dramatic resignation speech, he announced:

> I am persuaded now that I have a better prospect than Mrs. Thatcher of leading the Conservatives to a fourth election victory and preventing the ultimate calamity of a Labour government.

His challenge forced her from office, but did not win him the leadership; he later said: "He who wields the dagger never wears the crown." He pledged his loyalty to John MAJOR and returned to the Cabinet as Environment Secretary and later President of the Board of Trade, where he seriously damaged his reputation by suddenly announcing in October 1992 the closure of more than half Britain's remaining coal mines. Heseltine had earned his nickname (after Edgar Rice Burroughs's film character) through high-profile acts of political daring (rashness, his critics would say), and his flowing mane which also won him the soubriquet GOLDILOCKS. His strength was a mesmeric hold over Conservative party conferences, and especially the women, which he exercised through his oratory. Simon Hoggart described him as "rabble-rouser to the gentry"; but a Cabinet colleague scathingly remarked: "He may have the looks of Adonis, but he has a mind like Hampstead Garden Suburb."

> He tends not to be able to see a parapet without ducking below it . . . doing his famous impression of Clint Eastwood playing Mussolini. JULIAN CRITCHLEY.

> He knows where to find the clitoris of the Conservative Party. NOEL PICARDA.

task force (1) A naval flotilla comprising various complementary types of ship sent to perform a specific task, ranging from recovery of the FALKLANDS to a visit to far-off parts to "show the flag". (2) A group of experts and/or officials set to work to sort out a particularly difficult area of policy.

TASS (1) In Britain, the Technical and Supervisory Staffs' union, originally known as ASSET and now part of MSF (Managerial, Scientific and Finance). (2) *Telegrafnoe Agentstvo Sovetskovo Soyuza*, the official news agency of Soviet Russia. Established in 1925 to replace the original Bolshevik agency *Rosta*, TASS was the main source of news for Soviet national newspapers, television and radio. With bureaux in over 100 countries – some a cover for espionage – it provided bulletins in a variety of major languages for clients overseas. Its pronouncements reflected the MOSCOW LINE on domestic and world affairs; since the collapse of the Soviet state it has been seeking to adapt to life as a straightforward purveyor of news.

> It's always a compliment to be denounced by TASS.
> New York Mayor ED KOCH.

tax. tax and spend Democrats A standard denunciation by US conservatives of Northeastern and liberal Democrats, with their penchant for expensive social programmes. It may originate from a 1938 statement attributed to Harry Hopkins (*see* HURRY UPKINS): "We shall tax and tax, and spend and spend, and elect and elect."

tax reform In Washington, the process of reconstructing the tax structure so as to make it simpler, fairer and more effective, supposedly without altering its thrust. House WAYS AND MEANS Committee chairman Rep. Dan Rostenkowski reckoned that "passing a tax reform Bill is like walking through an eggfield". And Sen. Russell Long summed up the principle behind it as:

> Don't tax you, don't tax me, tax that fellow behind the tree.

tax-writing The art of compiling a tax Bill for the US Congress, as practised by the House WAYS AND MEANS Committee, the Senate Finance Committee, their staffs and JOINT TAX.

purchase tax The predecessor in Britain to VAT, levied on a far narrower range of goods and not at all on services. It was targeted heavily on luxury goods, whose tax level actually fell when VAT was introduced in 1973.

wealth tax The tax on the total assets of the better-off which the UK LABOUR PARTY was pledged to introduce in the mid-1970s – but lacked the clear Parliamentary majority to push through. It was modelled on a similar tax, believed to have been widely evaded, in France.

direct taxation Taxes imposed directly on a person's means; income tax is the prime example.

double taxation The imposition of taxes on the same income or assets of an individual or company by two or more nations.

indirect taxation Taxes like VAT or sales taxes, levied on a person's purchases or consumption, rather than directly on their income or assets.

progressive taxation Taxes which bite most heavily on the best-off. Direct taxes normally work in this way.

regressive taxation Taxes which penalize the worst-off, or at the very least hit them as hard proportionately as those with more to pay.

unitary taxation The system, insisted on by the state of California despite world-wide protests, under which a multinational company based in another state or country is taxed in California on its global, rather than local, activities.

taxpayer "Someone who works for the Federal government but doesn't have to take a civil service examination." A dictionary definition coined by Ronald Reagan (*see* GREAT COMMUNICATOR).

no taxation without representation! *See* NO.

nothing is certain except death and taxes A statement that has become a proverb, but was in fact coined by Benjamin FRANKLIN. His actual words were: "In this world nothing can be certain except death and taxes".

the art of taxation consists in so plucking the goose as to obtain the largest amount of feathers with the smallest possible amount of hissing A dictum of the French finance minister Jean-Baptiste Colbert (1619–83), echoed by Chancellor Norman Lamont in his 1991 BUDGET speech.

the power to tax is the power to destroy This much-quoted phrase, delivered by 1819 by US Chief Justice John Marshall in the case of *McCulloch v. Maryland*, was a variant of Daniel Webster's words in the case: "An unlimited power to tax involves, necessarily, a power to destroy."

to tax and to please, no more than to love and be wise, is not given to men One of the best-known dicta of Edmund BURKE.

Taylor, Zachary *See* OLD ROUGH AND READY.

TD (Ir. *Teachta Daila*, Member of the Dail) The Irish Republic's equivalent of an MP.

tea. tea room In Britain's HOUSE OF COMMONS the tea room, together with the SMOKING ROOM, comprises the inner sanctum where MPs may relax and converse without any intrusion. The various groups – factional or regional within each party – have tables and clusters of chairs of their own. Anyone holding or seeking high office is well advised to mingle with backbenchers in the tea room to show themselves "in touch". After one particularly bad day in the Commons, Margaret Thatcher was said by shell-shocked Tory rebels to have conducted a "search and destroy mission in the tea room".

cold tea The beverage served on request to members of the US Congress during PROHIBITION, and at other times when CONSTITUENTS opposed to hard liquor were present. Despite the genteel cup and saucer, it was not, in fact, tea.

Teapot Dome One of the greatest scandals in American history, and one of a series which made the HARDING administration a byword for corruption. It stemmed from the discovery that Albert B. Fall, Secretary of the Interior, had secretly leased government oil fields, part of the Teapot Dome naval oil reserves in Wyoming, to a private company. Fall then negotiated drilling rights with Harry F. Sinclair of the Monmouth Oil Company and granted similar rights in reserves at Elk Hills and Buena Vista Hills, California, to an old friend, Edward F. Doheny. Fall quit the Cabinet in March 1923 as a Senate investigation found blatant evidence of corruption – his family had received $200,000 in bonds from an "unknown source". The inquiry led to a series of civil and criminal court actions, which kept the affair in the headlines for years and made "Teapot Dome" a byword for political corruption. Reading news reports of the case, the 11-year-old Richard Nixon (*see* TRICKY DICK) told his mother:

> When I get big, I'll be a lawyer who can't be bribed.

In November 1929 Fall was finally convicted of receiving at least $404,000 in bribes and sentenced to a one-year prison term – becoming the first US Cabinet secretary ever jailed for crimes committed in office.

Teapot Dome was the tip of the iceberg. Charlie Forbes, head of the Veterans' Administration, was caught bootlegging hospital drugs to narcotics dealers and profiteering on war surplus goods. Thomas Miller, the alien property custodian, was found to have looted the assets in his care. And Attorney-General Harry Daugherty, Harding's campaign manager, had taken kickbacks from violators of the PROHIBITION laws – and failed to prosecute Forbes despite clear evidence against him. Two years after being ousted by President Coolidge (*see* SILENT CAL), Daugherty was tried for conspiracy to defraud the government, but acquitted.

Harding died in office in August 1923, before the full extent of his appointees' crimes was known. He had had some clue that things were amiss, once asking Herbert HOOVER: "If you knew of a great scandal in your administration, would you for the good of the country and the party expose it publicly, or would you bury it?" But he had also declared:

> If Fall isn't an honest man, then I am not fit to be President.

It was left to his successor to clear up the mess; as the full extent of the scandal broke, Coolidge stated:

> If there has been any crime, it must be prosecuted. If there has been any property of the United States illegally transferred or leased, it must be recovered. . . . Every law will be enforced. And the right of the people and the Government will be protected.

Teamsters America's giant labour union – the International Brotherhood of Teamsters, Chauffeurs, Warehousemen and Helpers of America – which for two decades from the 1950s was a byword for racketeering and corruption. The union – a teamster is the handler of a team of horses or mules – was founded in 1899, and by 1940 had become America's largest, with over a million members. Persistent allegations of racketeering led to its expulsion from the AFL-CIO in 1957. That year Jimmy Hoffa was elected President of the Teamsters; under his leadership the union became synonymous with gangsterism and organized crime. Hoffa allowed his criminal friends to use the Teamsters as a front for their activities, and in return he and the union acquired great wealth, much of which they used to bribe politicians. Eventually, as a result of investigations led by Attorney-General Robert KENNEDY, Hoffa was imprisoned in 1967; the feud between Hoffa and Kennedy was a powerful sub-plot to mid-1960s US politics and there are even claims that the death of Marilyn Monroe was connected to Teamster efforts to blackmail RFK. Hoffa was paroled by President Nixon in 1971 and in 1975 disappeared, presumably murdered by fellow-gangsters. Two of Hoffa's three immediate successors as union President also fell foul of the law; in 1986 the PRESIDENT'S COMMISSION on organized crime dubbed the Teamsters the "most corrupt" union in America, and in 1988 the Justice Department indicted its entire 18-man executive and over 20 suspected gangsters for racketeering; 246 Congressmen protested. Federal appointees took over the running of the union, and in 1991 Ron Carey (1936–) was elected general president on a "get the bums out" platform. Taking office in 1992, he took speedy action to clean up the union and halt the membership slide from its peak of 2 million.

tear gas A worldwide instrument of RIOT control, and often of repression. When disorder breaks out, police or troops fire a gas (or dispersed liquid or powder) from gun-like canisters which reduces the rioters to tears, temporarily disables and generally breaks up the protest. Tear gas is a blanket term for various chemical compounds which in recent decades have included CS GAS and MACE. Sometimes the boot is on the other foot; when the Shah of Iran visited President Carter early in 1978, protesting Iranian students fired tear gas at police on the ELLIPSE and the wind blew it straight at the WELCOMING CEREMONY, gassing the official party on the White House lawn. As the choking cloud enveloped the attendant press, a photographer exclaimed:

> I was in the 'Nam, and you gotta be ready,

and slapped on a gas mask he had brought as a precaution.

Tebbit, Norman *See* CHINGFORD SKINHEAD.

technocracy A system of government by technical experts (**technocrats**). A radical US movement advocating the control of society and the economy by engineers and scientists adopted this name in the 1930s; it took its ideology from Thorstein Veblen's *The Engineers and the Price System* (1921), which sought to replace the irrationality of the free market by a PLANNED ECONOMY. The movement lost impetus with the improvement in social and economic conditions brought about by the NEW DEAL.

Teddy The affectionate nickname for **Theodore Roosevelt** (1858–1919), the rumbustious 26th President of the United States (Republican, 1901–9). The teddy bear was christened after him, following a bear hunt in 1903 whose organizers stunned a young bear and tied it to a tree to make sure the President made a kill. A law graduate and professional author from a wealthy old Dutch family, who became a cowboy to get over the death of his first wife, the fiercely patriotic and populist Roosevelt won his first election (in New York state) at 23; he resigned as assistant Secretary of the Navy when the SPANISH-AMERICAN WAR broke out, and became a national hero organizing the ROUGH RIDERS. Elected Governor of New York on his return in 1900, his reforming zeal unnerved BOSS PLATT who arranged to KICK him UPSTAIRS by nominating him as McKINLEY's Vice-President. Within months, McKinley was dead and Roosevelt was rampant in the White House. The Republican kingmaker Sen. Mark Hanna declared:

> I told McKinley that it was a mistake to nominate that man as Vice-President. Now that damned cowboy is President of the United States.

A "hands-on" President, Roosevelt said: "I did not usurp power, but I did greatly broaden the use of executive power." His techniques were not subtle, George Bernard Shaw maintaining: "His idea of getting hold of the right end of the stick is to snatch it from the hands of someone who is using it effectively ansd hit him over the head with it." His vigorous foreign policy, including the creation of the CANAL ZONE, and his attacks on monopolies won him easy re-election in 1904, enabling him to say: "I am no longer a political accident"; four years later he stood down after a happy Presidency in favour of TAFT. His successor's lack of charisma so appalled him that he made a come-back with the BULL MOOSE campaign of 1912, forcing Taft into third place but handing the Presidency to Woodrow WILSON. A big-game hunter and conservationist who was also the first White House jogger, Roosevelt remained immensely popular, and up to his sudden death was still a Presidential contender.

Roosevelt, in the words of Henry Adams, was "pure act". A relative said: "When Theodore attends a wedding he wants to be the bride and when he attends a funeral he wants to be the corpse." He insisted: "I am only an average man, but, by God, I work harder at it than an average man." And he revelled in challenges, declaring: "I wish to preach not the doctrine of ignoble ease, but the doctrine of the strenuous life. For us is the life of action, of strenuous performance of duty; let us live in the harness, striving mightily; let us rather run the risk of wearing out than rusting out." His opinions of others were pungent. He branded the revolutionary Tom Paine "that dirty little atheist", President Marroquin of Colombia "a pithecanthropoid", President Castro of Venezuela "an unspeakably villainous little monkey", Sen. William Alfred Peffer "a well-meaning, pin-headed, anarchistic crank, of hirsute and slabsided aspect", the writer Henry James "a very despicable creature, no matter how well equipped with the minor virtues and graces, literary, artistic and social – a miserable little snob"; and Charles Evans Hughes, the 1916 Republican nominee, "the bearded iceberg". As he ended an age of corruption, Roosevelt also set a high moral tone. He once fired a ranch hand who had branded one of his neighbour's cattle, telling him: "A man who will steal for me will steal from me".

Alistair Cooke wrote: "T. R. is affectionately remembered as a half-heroic, half-comic figure, a bespectacled barrel of a man, choking with teeth and happiness". But Hugh Brogan described him, beneath the bluster, as "the ablest man to sit in the White House since LINCOLN, the most vigorous since Jackson, the most bookish since John Quincy ADAMS". And Cooke noted that despite his love of the outdoors "he was the first influential man of his time to see clearly that the United States was no longer a rural nation but an industrial giant running amok".

In his later years he could justly claim:

> No man has had a happier life than I have led; a happier life in every way.

teenage scribblers The dismissive term for Britain's financial press coined by Nigel (later Lord) Lawson (1932–) during his initially successful period as Margaret Thatcher's CHANCELLOR OF THE EXCHEQUER. The hubristic Lawson, himself a former financial journalist, built on foundations laid by Sir Geoffrey Howe after succeeding him in 1983 to create a runaway boom, but resigned in 1989 after a clash with the Prime Minister with the economy heading for a HARD LANDING and recession. The "scribblers" ensured him a bad press in the years that followed.

Teflon presidency The ability of the Reagan presidency (*see* GREAT COMMUNICATOR) to dissociate itself from misdeeds (*see* SLEAZE FACTOR) and incompetence by those close to the seat of power. Teflon is the non-stick substance which by the 1980s was lining pans in every Western kitchen.

> He has achieved a breakthrough in political technology – the Teflon Presidency. He sees that nothing sticks to him.
>
> Rep. PAT SCHROEDER (1940–).

Teheran conference The meeting of the "Big Three" WORLD WAR II leaders in the Persian capital from 28 November to 1 December 1943; CHURCHILL and Roosevelt's first meeting with STALIN. The main decision was to launch a SECOND FRONT by invading France in May 1944, instead of staging the main offensive in the Mediterranean theatre as Churchill preferred. Stalin, who had pressed hard for a Second Front, promised a strong Soviet offensive to coincide. He also gained FDR's agreement to Soviet expansion into East Poland and Poland's acquisition of Danzig and East Prussia. There were inconclusive talks on the zoning of post-war Germany and the form the UNITED NATIONS should take, and commitments to Persia's postwar independence and greater aid for Tito's PARTISANS in Yugoslavia. Their closing declaration said:

> We leave here friends in fact, in spirit and in purpose.

telegram. the telegrams The term used by Britain's FOREIGN OFFICE for the daily communications from embassies and High Commissions throughout the world. They are seen by senior officials, the Foreign Secretary and other Ministers, and the Queen.

Ems telegram *See* EMS.

Kruger telegram *See* KRUGER.

telephone box The reputed meeting place of Britain's LIBERAL MPs in the early 1950s, when at one point they were reduced to just five seats in the House of Commons.

Why doesn't he use the telephone? The

exasperated comment of Stanley BALDWIN at the noisy conversation of Ernest Brown, his Minister of Labour. Hearing Brown bellowing (down the telephone) in the adjoining room, he asked what was going on and was told: "Mr. Brown is talking to Birmingham". Baldwin replied: "Why doesn't he use the telephone?" There was a sequel in Washington; when the House was considering installing a public address system, Franklin D. Roosevelt said from the White House: "Why? I can hear Florence Kahn's voice without it." The booming-voiced California Republican sat in the House from 1934 until 1936, when her constituents decided they had heard enough.

teleprompter The device used by television presenters to read a script; the text is scrolled-down on a screen built into the camera. A variant, involving a transparent reflective lectern attached to the ROSTRUM, was pioneered for major speeches by Ronald Reagan and Margaret Thatcher and is now widely used by politicians.

televangelists The fundamentalist and largely right-wing television preachers whose influence spilled over into American politics in the 1980s. Taking their cue from the election of the born-again Jimmy CARTER (a Democrat) as President in 1976, several Conservative televangelists threw their weight behind Ronald Reagan's 1980 campaign and the moral thrust of his Presidency. And in 1988 Pat Robertson, head of the Christian Broadcasting Network, made a bid for the White House himself, running a strong third in the Republican primaries to George BUSH and Sen. Robert Dole.

Teller amendment The portion of the Congressional resolution declaring war on Spain in 1898 which guaranteed Cuban autonomy. However IMPERIALIST feeling was strong; US forces occupied Cuba and in 1901 the PLATT AMENDMENT put it under Washington's effective control.

teller vote The unrecorded VOICE-VOTES, especially on amendments, which were taken in the US HOUSE OF REPRESENTATIVES until 1970; reformers believe their replacement by recorded votes has discouraged PORK BARREL projects because Congressmen can no longer support them anonymously.

tellers The individuals deputed to supervise a vote in a legislature or conference. At Westminster the tellers do not vote, and a teller from the winning side announces the result of each DIVISION. The term is also used for party representatives who oversee the COUNT at an election, to make sure the papers are properly counted.

ten. Ten days that shook the world The title of the epic book on the RUSSIAN REVOLUTION written in 1919 by the American socialist John Reed (1887–1920).

10 Downing Street *See* NUMBER TEN.

Ten minute rule Bill At Westminster, a measure a backbench MP can introduce after QUESTION TIME to make a point or obtain the sense of the House. The sponsor may speak for ten minutes, or allow an opponent half the time; those opposed are free to divide the House. In 1978–79 the Conservative opposition used such votes to gain majority support for their proposed industrial relations reforms; ten minute rule Bills do occasionally get enough backing to get on to the STATUTE BOOK through the Private Member's BILL procedure.

Ten per cent plan Abraham LINCOLN's plan for RECONSTRUCTION, proclaimed in December 1863 for Arkansas, Louisiana, Tennessee and Virginia. It pardoned all Southerners who would swear allegiance to the United States and accept anti-slavery legislation, except high Confederate officials and those who had deserted Federal posts. It also authorized the establishment of new governments, represented at national level, in any state where one-tenth of its qualified voters took the oath. It amounted to an invitation to rebuild the South's political structures without delay, then re-enter national life. It was bitterly resented by many in Congress, which retaliated with the WADE-DAVIS BILL, and was one of the first casualties after Lincoln's assassination.

Tenth amendment The last of the Constitutional amendments in the US BILL OF RIGHTS, ratified in December 1791. It specifically leaves to the STATES all power not granted by the Constitution to the Federal government.

term The length of time a representative of the people is elected to serve. A US Presidential term is four years, against six for a Senator and two for a Congressman. In Britain the maximum Parliamentary term is five years.

term-limitation The principle that no one should be allowed to serve indefinitely even if the voters are ready to re-elect them. Republican distaste at Franklin D. Roosevelt's unprecedented FOURTH TERM (*see below*) led to the TWENTY-SECOND AMENDMENT, limiting any President to two terms. In 1992 fourteen States approved legislation limiting their Senators to two terms, and Congressmen to from three to six terms.

> The United States ought to be able to choose for its President anybody that it wants, regardless of the number of terms he has served. President EISENHOWER, 1956.

one-term President *See* PRESIDENT.

second term The term during which, since the passage of the TWENTY-SECOND AMENDMENT, a President has become a LAME DUCK. Yet election for a second term is also proof that a first victory was no fluke.

> Anyone can be elected by accident. Beginning with a second term, it's worth paying attention.
>
> ABRAHAM LINCOLN.

third term Margaret Thatcher (*see* IRON LADY) introduced the phrase and the concept into British politics with her third successive General Election victory in 1987. In America, there was a tradition that no President would seek a consecutive third term until Franklin D. Roosevelt ran in 1940. When Republicans backing Wendell Willkie cried "foul", the Democrats replied:

> Better a third termer than a third-rater.

fourth term FDR's decision to seek a fourth term aroused less controversy than his third, although the result of the 1944 election was closer. The lack of protest was primarily due to America being immersed in World War II, and for a perceived need for continuity in leadership. In Britain, Margaret Thatcher failed in her ambition to win a fourth or even a fifth term, but the Conservative Party did secure a fourth term on 9 April 1992 under John MAJOR's leadership.

terminological inexactitude The classic euphemism for a lie, attributed to Winston Churchill since he said in the House of Commons on 22 February 1906:

> It cannot in the opinion of His Majesty's Government be classified as slavery in the extreme acceptance of the word without some risk of terminological inexactitude.

It is UNPARLIAMENTARY for one MP to call another a LIAR, or accuse them of telling a lie. Since Sir Robert Armstrong's unfortunate use of the phrase "economical with the TRUTH", that, like Churchill's phrase, has been an acceptable substitute. However Churchill's son Randolph insisted that his father never intended "terminological inexactitude" to mean an outright lie.

Terrace The paved terrace overlooking the river Thames which runs along almost the entire south-east frontage of the Palace of WESTMINSTER; it faces across the river to St. Thomas's Hospital. Since it was constructed in the 1850s, its level has had to be raised to prevent flood tides spilling over the parapet and inundating lower floors of the building; the Thames Barrier downstream at Woolwich has now removed the threat, which led to the Connaught Rooms, a Masonic suite in Holborn, being designated as an emergency Parliament building. On summer evenings, the terrace and its marquee containing a bar and reception rooms are crowded with MPs and their families and CONSTITUENTS, LOBBY correspondents, staff of the House and political groupies; the festive scene gets a mixed reception from trippers passing on river cruises. Before the barrier stabilized the flow of the river, MPs on the terrace could at times observe the flow of used contraceptives flushed from London's drainage system.

territory An area of land lacking full self-government and specifically the component parts of the United States before they achieved STATEHOOD.

territorial departments The Scottish Office, Welsh Office and Northern Ireland Office, the three government departments responsible, under a Cabinet Minister, for the outlying parts of the United Kingdom.

Incorporated Territories Areas lacking full statehood which are integral parts of the United States. Only the DISTRICT OF COLUMBIA now fits that category. Unincorporated Territories enjoy basic Constitutional rights without being fully part of the nation. The CANAL ZONE, Guam, Samoa, the Virgin Islands and the Pacific Trust areas fall into this category.

No Territory! The WHIG slogan in America's 1846 Congressional elections, opposing Southern moves to prosecute the MEXICAN WAR as a means of opening up new lands for slavery.

Occupied Territories The territory captured by Israel in the SIX DAY WAR of 1967 and governed by it ever since: East Jerusalem and the WEST BANK from Jordan, the GAZA STRIP from Eypt and the GOLAN HEIGHTS from Syria. Israel's determination to retain these territories for defensive purposes (and under LIKUD, reasons of Biblical precedent), its creation of Israeli settlements on the West Bank and Golan Heights and its reluctance to grant self-government to the Arab inhabitants have been a major obstacle to the PEACE PROCESS. However in 1992 the incoming Labour-led coalition offered to hand part of the Golan Heights back to Syria; the response from Damascus was not encouraging.

terror. Great Terror STALIN's grotesque and ruthless PURGES of the late 1930s, when at least 10 million people were executed or deported to labour camps on the flimsiest of pretexts to ease the Soviet leader's pathological feelings of insecurity. The persecution of supposed dissidents and opponents of the regime began in 1935, and from 1936 to 1938 its chief instigator was Nikolai Ivanovich Yezhov

(1884–1940), head of the NKVD. Yezhov, a brutal man of low intelligence and barely five feet tall, was described by one contemporary as "a bloodthirsty dwarf". He began by purging the NKVD itself, then cut a swathe through the RED ARMY's high command, and then staged SHOW TRIALS of Stalin's old comrades in the BOLSHEVIK leadership. Although these purges were orchestrated by Stalin, Yezhov became synonymous with the Great Terror; but in December 1938 he himself was arrested, and replaced as head of the NKVD by Beria. He was probably shot two years later, a convenient scapegoat for a campaign of state murder which exceeded even the HOLOCAUST, and which left the Soviet Union critically weak when Hitler invaded.

Reign of Terror The bloody 420 days during which the FRENCH REVOLUTION devoured its own children, and the GUILLOTINE reigned supreme in the hands of the JACOBINS. It began with the fall of the GIRONDISTS on 31 May 1793, four months after the execution of Louis XVI and Marie-Antoinette, and ended with the overthrow of Robespierre on 27 July 1794. The perpetrators of the Terror revelled in the title, Bernard Barère de Vieuzac, who outlived it, telling the National Convention: "Let us make terror the order of the day." And Robespierre proclaimed in February 1794:

> Terror is nothing but justice: prompt, secure and inflexible.

Robespierre would soon face the guillotine himself and discover just how inflexible it was.

terrorism The use of violence or intimidation to achieve political ends. Walter Laqueur termed it "propaganda by deed", and Richard E. Rubenstein "the violence of the intelligentsia". Most governments are pledged to resist it, but a few (including some Communist countries, Libya, Iran and Syria) have fomented and encouraged it, creating state-sponsored terrorism.

> We are not going to tolerate these attacks from outlaw states, run by the strangest collection of misfits, looney tunes and squalid criminals since the advent of the Third REICH. RONALD REAGAN.

All terrorists nurse the conviction that even if they personally fail, ultimately their cause will prevail and will bring down a regime they consider oppressive or win freedom for a people they consider downtrodden. Their belief is strengthened by a number of instances in which one day's so-called terrorist has become a respected hero of liberation.

> All terrorists at the invitation of the Government end up with drinks at the Dorchester. HUGH GAITSKELL.

Prevention of Terrorism Act The legislation first passed after the 1974 BIRMINGHAM pub bombings under which the authorities may bar anyone they consider a terrorist suspect from entering mainland Britain from NORTHERN IRELAND, and terrorist suspects in Britain can be held for questioning for longer than the standard 48 hours. Introduced by a Labour Government, it has stayed on the Statute Book in modified form; Labour now opposes it as a violation of civil liberties.

test. Test Act The Act passed in 1673 which barred Roman Catholics and Protestant dissenters from holding national or local office in England and Wales. It required anyone elected to take a "test" of loyalty to the sacraments of the Church of England. It was not repealed until 1829, and then only after a bitter struggle between supporters of Catholic EMANCIPATION and upholders of the *status quo*, who included King George IV.

Test Ban Treaty The treaty concluded by America, the Soviet Union and Britain in July 1963 which ended atmospheric – but not underground – testing of nuclear weapons. It was the first superpower agreement after the CUBAN MISSILE CRISIS, and a historic step in getting the ARMS RACE under control, but was as much a victory for environmentalists as for disarmers, given growing concerns about the level of nuclear fall-out. More than 110 nations have endorsed the treaty, France being a notable if predictable exception. Britain's Tory government, facing defeat in the imminent General Election, put out an advertisement showing an anti-nuclear campaigner with CND placard, with the caption: "Meanwhile the Conservatives have signed the Test Ban Treaty."

> A journey of a thousand miles must begin with a single step. President KENNEDY, quoting a Chinese proverb.

Tet offensive The co-ordinated surprise attack by the VIET CONG on more than 100 towns and cities, launched on 31 January 1968, which traumatically called in question America's ability to win the VIETNAM WAR. The month-long onslaught by 70,000 troops backed by North Vietnamese jets and tanks which broke the *Tet* (lunar New Year) truce came as a total shock to the US public; for the first time in the war they saw their troops fighting the Viet Cong not deep in the countryside but for their own bases at Da Nang and Khe Sanh, in the streets of Hué and Saigon – and even the US Embassy itself. Ever since ground troops were first committed in 1965, the military had assured politicians, the media and the people that the Communists were on the verge of collapse; though the *Tet* offensive was beaten back with very heavy Communist losses, it suggested the opposite and was thus an important psychological victory for the Viet Cong. The following month Walter Cronkite, the "most trusted face" on network TV, reported from Saigon: "It seems now more certain than ever that the bloody experience of Vietnam is to end in a stalemate." President Johnson, watching, commented that if he lost Cronkite he had lost America, and indeed the *Tet* offensive was the final nail in his presidency. Public support for the war, already starting to slip, fell more rapidly and with even his own staff starting to urge US disengagement, Johnson announced in March that he would not seek re-election and ordered a BOMBING HALT.

Texas School Book Depository The building in DALLAS from whose sixth-floor window Lee Harvey Oswald (1939–63) is supposed to have fired the shots that killed President KENNEDY. Oswald, a former US Marine who had married the daughter of a KGB colonel and lived for a time in Russia, had started work in the Depository a month before the shooting. A witness to the WARREN COMMISSION testified that the shots were fired from the fifth floor; those who believe someone else shot Kennedy reckon they came from the GRASSY KNOLL nearby.

Texas v. White The case on which the US SUPREME COURT ruled in 1869 that the UNION was constitutionally indestructible, and that the defeated South had thus never left it. *See also* HELL.

Thank you for your letter, contents of which have been noted The crushing response of Clement ATTLEE in May 1945 to a letter that he received from Professor Harold Laski, chairman of Britain's LABOUR PARTY, telling him that "the continuance of your leadership is a grave handicap to our hopes of victory in the coming election", and urging him to resign. Two months later the monosyllabic Attlee succeeded in leading Labour to its greatest victory, with a majority of 180 over Winston CHURCHILL's Conservatives. The whole episode speaks volumes about Laski's lack of political *nous* and judgment (*see also* VIOLENCE).

that. That these United Colonies are, and of right ought to be, free and independent States, that they are absolved from all allegiance to the British Crown, and that all political connection between them and the State of Great Britain is, and ought to be totally dissolved The first of three resolutions passed by the CONTINENTAL CONGRESS on 2 July 1776 which paved the way for the Declaration of INDEPENDENCE. They were drawn up in advance, and presented, by Richard Henry Lee on behalf of Virginia.

That this House has no confidence in Her Majesty's Government The standard wording of a no-CONFIDENCE motion in the House of Commons, defeat on which leads by custom to the resignation of the Government or the holding of an election.

That this House will in no circumstances fight for King and Country The motion whose passage by the Oxford Union in its KING AND COUNTRY debate on 9 February 1933 fostered the impression that Britain would not stand up to the DICTATORS.

That Was The Week That Was The pioneering satirical programme, transmitted live by BBC television from 24 November 1962, which shot David FROST to stardom and critically undermined Harold Macmillan's government, notably through its savage treatment of the PROFUMO AFFAIR. Produced by Ned Sherrin, it could also be serious; its spontaneous and moving tribute to President KENNEDY on his assassination gained it a transatlantic reputation. **TW3,** which ran intermittently for just over a year, was taken off as a looming general election made the BBC hierarchy nervous; Millicent Martin, William Rushton, Kenneth Cope and Lance Percival were among others to make their names in it.

Thatcherism The rigorous economic and political ideology, and the personal style of leadership, associated with Margaret Thatcher (*see* IRON LADY). She favoured the unhindered operation of the Free MARKET, the PRIVATIZATION of public utilities, the encouragement of share ownership and the sale of council houses to further the "ENTERPRISE culture" she stood for. MONETARISM replaced KEYNESIANISM, the individual ousted SOCIETY, and the power of the TRADE UNIONS was curtailed. In foreign affairs she was resolute in her opposition to Communism and her support for America, but despite endorsing the SINGLE EUROPEAN ACT she resisted any moves to greater union within the European Community that would weaken British sovereignty or independence. Since the collapse of the economic BOOM of 1988, Thatcherism seems likely to be remembered more for the stridency and divisiveness of its tone than for its considerable achievements.

> No obligation to the community, no sense of solidarity, no neighbourhood, no number other than one, no time other than now, no such thing as society – just me! and now!
>
> NEIL KINNOCK.

thaw The term used throughout the COLD WAR for periods when the hostility between East and West eased somewhat.

theocracy A state governed by priests or the religious elect, as opposed to a secular democracy or dictatorship. Iran under the AYATOLLAHs is a contemporary example.

theoretician In an ideologically-based party, state or movement, a person who develops the theory behind the practice of government or the programme to be followed.

there. There are no gains without pains An axiom of politics coined by the Democratic nominee Adlai Stevenson in a Presidential campaign speech in Chicago on 26 July 1952. What he actually said was:

> Let's talk sense to the American people. Let's tell them the truth, that there are no gains without pains.

Its linking of progress with sacrifice puts it in a long line of statements from Walter Lippmann's NOTHING FOR NOTHING to John Major's IF IT'S NOT HURTING, IT'S NOT WORKING.

There are three groups that one should never provoke: The Vatican, the Treasury and the miners A rule of thumb for British politics variously attributed to BALFOUR and BALDWIN, and much quoted during the MINERS' STRIKES of 1972, 1974 and 1984–85.

There is no alternative The assertion that formed the basis of THATCHERISM, which was uttered by the IRON LADY herself at the Conservative womens' conference on 21 May 1980. Justifying the harsh economic measures taken in her first year in office, she said:

> There is no easy popularity in that, but I believe people accept there is no alternative.

The phrase was seized on both by Mrs. Thatcher's supporters and critics as exemplifying her approach; Young Conservatives soon abbreviated it to **TINA**.

There is no Democratic or Republican way of cleaning the streets The argument put forward by New York's Mayor Fiorello La Guardia (1882–1947) to justify the adoption of good city government rather than the pursuit of old-style MACHINE POLITICS.

There is no free lunch A fundamental of the American Dream, variously attributed (by Alistair Cooke) to an Italian immigrant asked what 40 years of American life had taught him, and by others to the economist Milton Friedman (*see* MONETARISM) in a lecture in 1973.

There I was, waiting at the church The old music-hall song quoted by James Callaghan in his speech to the TUC on 5 September 1978, as he teased the Tory opposition over when he would call an election. The rhyme told of a woman left waiting at the church to marry a man who eventually sent a note reading:

> Can't get away to marry you today.
> My wife won't let me.

Union delegates loved it, but Callaghan's levity had a sting in the tail. Two days later, Callaghan enraged Margaret Thatcher and staggered his own party by going on television to announce that his minority government would carry on; he eventually called an election (which Labour lost) the following Spring after being defeated by one vote in a no-CONFIDENCE motion. *Compare* She didn't say YES, SHE DIDN'T SAY NO.

There you go again Ronald Reagan's dismissive comment to Jimmy CARTER in their PRESIDENTIAL DEBATE in Cleveland on 28 October 1980. Delivered when the President was pressing him on points of detail, the phrase implied that Reagan was in command of the evening; coupled with his question to voters, ARE YOU BETTER OFF THAN YOU WERE FOUR YEARS AGO?, it gave him the edge.

they. They have asked for my trousers, and I have given them; for my coat, I have given that also; now they want my life, and that I cannot give The defiant message toward the British of President Paulus Kruger of Transvaal (*see* OOM PAUL) on 7 September 1899 as the BOER WAR reached its height.

They may be sons of bitches, but they're our sons of bitches Franklin D. Roosevelt's retort to reform Democrats who asked him how he could do deals with big city BOSSES and SEGREGATIONIST Southern Senators. In the 1992 Presidential campaign one Indiana voter said of Vice-President Dan QUAYLE:

> He may be an idiot, but he's our idiot.

They now ring the bells, but they will soon wring their hands The apocalyptic warning of Britain's first recognized Prime Minister, Robert WALPOLE, as public enthusiasm greeted the outbreak of the WAR OF JENKINS' EAR. The war with Spain, and broader conflicts that ensued, not only led to the setbacks Walpole feared, but also brought the end of his 21 years in office.

They shall not pass! *See* PASS.

First they came for the Jews, but I didn't protest because I was not a Jew. Then they came for the Communists, but I didn't protest because I was not a communist. Then they came for the trade unionists, but I didn't protest because I was not a trade unionist. Then they came for me, and there was no one left to protest The chilling parable of the consequences of failing to stand up to the NAZIs in pre-war Germany, told by Martin Niemöller (1892–1984), the former U-boat commander who became an evangelical pastor and was sent to a CONCENTRATION CAMP in 1937; he survived to become a bishop. Three decades later the Black author James Baldwin echoed Niemöller in a message of support to the imprisoned militant Angela Davis, telling her:

> If they take you in the morning, they will come for us at night.

THIGMOO This Great Movement Of Ours. An affectionate but ironic shorthand term for the British TRADE UNION movement, popular from the early 1970s.

think tank A group of people with specialized knowledge and great intellectual ability, brought together to study particular problems (usually social, political and technological) and to provide possible solutions and new directions. America's RAND CORPORATION was among the first; in Washington the BROOKINGS INSTITUTION is perhaps the best known. Edward Heath in 1970 set up a think tank within 10 Downing Street, titled the **Central Policy Review Staff**. Headed by Lord Rothschild (1910–90), its function was to provide the Cabinet and individual Ministers with advice on strategy. It survived until 1983 when Margaret Thatcher, who had used it to torpedo policy initiatives she disliked, wound it up and handed its vestigial functions to the No. 10 POLICY UNIT. Mrs. Thatcher had in 1974 been involved in the launch of an independent right-wing think tank, the Centre for POLICY STUDIES.

thinking the unthinkable The process, indulged in especially in Washington during the COLD WAR, of considering the details and merits of particular types of NUCLEAR WAR, rationally and without thought for the consequences for the planet. Those involved in such discussions argued that they had to take place if a credible defence policy were to evolve; nuclear disarmers regarded them with horror. *See also* STRANGELOVE.

Third Estate (Fr. *Tiers État*) The commoners in France's pre-revolutionary parliament; the aristocracy and the bishops formed the first two estates. It was the Third Estate who met to demand reform and basic human rights at the onset of the revolution. *See* Tennis Court OATH.

> What is the Third Estate? Everything. What has it hitherto been in the political order? Nothing. What does it ask? To be something. Who will dare deny that the Third Estate contains within itself all that is needed to constitute a nation?
>
> Abbé EMMANUEL SIEYÈS (1748–1836), 1789.

Third Man The third Soviet agent suspected of being involved in the defection of the British diplomats BURGESS AND MACLEAN in 1951; there was widespread press speculation, and ironically he turned out to be a journalist, H. A. R. "Kim" Philby of the *Observer*. As early as 1955 Harold Macmillan, then Foreign Secretary, was asked point blank by the Labour MP Marcus Lipton whether Philby was a spy; as there was no conclusive proof, Macmillan was forced to clear him. In 1963 Philby, then working in Beirut, also defected to Moscow and the whole story came out. The name came from the title of the 1949 Graham Greene and Carol Reed film *The Third Man*, a tale of intrigue in post-war Vienna.

Third Reading At Westminster, the final stage through which a BILL passes in one House before going to the other. On major Bills it involves a full day after completion of the REPORT STAGE; on less controversial matters it follows on immediately and may only take a couple of hours. In the US Congress the Third Reading is a vote taken after debate on a Bill reported from the COMMITTEE OF THE WHOLE HOUSE.

Third Reich *See* REICH.

Third Republic The regime under which France was governed from the defeat of the Second Empire by Prussia in 1870 to the fall of France to the NAZIS in 1940 (*see* VICHY). The Third Republic was noted for its political instability, especially after 1918 when governments came and went with great rapidity before the advent of the POPULAR FRONT. The Republic was punctuated by a series of crises that threatened the French Parliamentary system itself; these included the machinations of General Boulanger (*see* MAN ON HORSEBACK), the DREYFUS CASE, and the STAVISKY AFFAIR of the 1930s. Yet the Third Republic proved the longest-lived system of governing France since the FRENCH REVOLUTION.

Third World The underdeveloped countries of the world, in Africa, Asia and Latin America, which are heavily dependent on mainly subsistence agriculture, and thus cannot develop industries of their own and a competitive economy without help from other nations. Prone to famine and population pressures, they are weighed down by heavy debt to western banks and government (*see* TRINIDAD TERMS); recognizing the resentments and potential for conflict posed by their poverty, many Western politicians have sought to mobilize help (*see* BRANDT COMMISSION; NORTH-SOUTH). The Third World was named by the French writer Georges Balandier in comparison with the capitalist western nations (First World) and the states of the former Communist bloc (Second World);

it is an echo of the pre-revolutionary THIRD ESTATE.

thirteen. Thirteen plots of 13 May The dramatic and secretive plotting and counter-plotting which returned General DE GAULLE to power in France in May 1958 after twelve years in the political wilderness, and which ended the FOURTH REPUBLIC. By 1958 a powerful body of secret GAULLISTS were plotting to secure his return to power; they consisted of malcontents in the Army and among White French settlers (*pieds-noirs*) in Algeria, angered by what they saw as inadequate backing from the mainland, and of right-wing opponents of the government in metropolitan France. On 13 May, as a new Prime Minister, Pierre Pfimlin, was about to be appointed, a large crowd took over the government offices in Algiers, establishing a Committee of Public Safety. The army generals supported the Committee's call for de Gaulle's return, and on 15 May he dramatically announced that he was willing to assume power if invited. Meanwhile the rebellion in Algeria escalated; on 24 May Algerian-based troops occupied Corsica and there were rumours that the generals were planning to occupy Paris on 27 May. Against this background of political crisis, heightened by fears of an imminent military coup and the threat of civil war, Pfimlin agreed to step down in favour of de Gaulle. On 1 June the NATIONAL ASSEMBLY confirmed de Gaulle's appointment as Premier, gave him full power for six months and left him to draw up a new constitution. De Gaulle was certainly aware of the plots to secure his return, but he wisely refused to commit himself until the collapse of the Fourth Republic was certain; he could then assume power on his own terms.

thirteen wasted years The emotive, and effective, theme of Labour's campaigning in the run-up to the 1964 UK general election, and during the election itself. Harold WILSON and his colleagues took every opportunity to depict SIR ALEC Douglas-Home's Conservative government, first elected under Churchill in 1951, as worn-out and bankrupt of ideas. In the event the Tories pegged Labour back to a majority of six – well short of the landslide Wilson had hoped for, and for which he had to wait a further 18 months.

> Thirteen wasted years; thirteen wasted years – fast taking on the look of a golden era. IAIN MACLEOD, 1969.

Thirteenth amendment The amendment to the US CONSTITUTION, ratified on 16 December 1865, that finally outlawed slavery.

thirty. thirty year rule The cornerstone of secrecy in WHITEHALL, the provision that the contents of no government document not intended for publication shall be made public for 30 years, if then. Slightly relaxed by John Major in 1992, the procedure is for all government papers to be sent to the Public Record Office; all but the most sensitive are released to researchers and the press at year's end 30 years on. In 1993 it was discovered that the Foreign Office had yet to deCLASSIFY files from 1782 relating to the WHIG politician Charles James Fox.

thirty-six faceless men The newspaper caption seized on by Robert Menzies's ruling Liberals which did Australia's LABOR Party immense damage in the 1963 Federal elections. The 36 faceless men were the 36 delegates to Labor's policy-making federal conference; the photo showed the ALP leader, Arthur Calwell, and his deputy Gough Whitlam standing under a lamp-post outside the meeting waiting to be given the PARTY LINE. The inference that Labor's leaders were puppets in the hands of anonymous and maybe sinister forces contributed to the party's heavy defeat.

thirty-eighth parallel The dividing line between North and South Korea, agreed by America and the Soviet Union in 1945 as a temporary device for accepting the surrender of Japanese forces in the region; it was hastily suggested by the US as Soviet forces moved into northern Korea in the final days of the war. Stalin surprisingly agreed, although the absence of US forces would have enabled him to move further south. The division left America in control of the capital, Seoul, two-thirds of the population and the main agricultural region, while the Soviets controlled the industrial north. COLD WAR tensions turned the 38th parallel into a rigid border between East and West; after the outbreak of the KOREAN WAR US troops crossed it on 7 October 1950 in their first advance. And when peace was restored, the 38th parallel was once again the frontier between North and South Korea. When President Eisenhower made a particularly banal remark at a White House press conference, one commentator remarked:

> Ike's just crossed the 38th platitude.

this was their finest hour Winston CHURCHILL's defiant speech to the House of Commons on 18 June 1940 after the collapse of France, when a German invasion seemed imminent; it was indeed only prevented by the Royal Air Force's defeat of the Luftwaffe in the Battle of Britain. Churchill said:

> What General Weygand called the Battle of France is over. I expect that the Battle of Britain is about to begin. Upon this battle depends the survival of Christian civilization. Upon it depends our own British life, and the long continuity of our institutions and our Empire. The

whole fury and might of the enemy must very soon be turned on us. Hitler knows that he will have to break us in this Island or lose the war. If we can stand up to him, all Europe may be free and the life of the world may move forward into broad, sunlit uplands. But if we fail, then the whole world, including the United States, including all that we have known and cared for, will sink into the abyss of a new Dark Age made more sinister, and perhaps more protracted, by the lights of perverted science. Let us therefore brace ourselves to our duties, and so bear ourselves that, if the British Empire and its Commonwealth last for a thousand years, men will still say: "This was their finest hour."

Thomas. Clarence Thomas case The Senate hearings in 1992 over George BUSH's nomination of the Black Judge Clarence Thomas to the SUPREME COURT, which turned into a televised trial of claims of sexual harassment by him from a former colleague, Professor Anita Hill. Both Judge Thomas and Professor Hill, who insisted: "I am not given to fantasy," fought their corners with passion and total conviction. Senators pitched in with sharp questioning, leading Sen. John Danforth to declare: "This is not ADVICE AND CONSENT. This is slash and burn." And his fellow-Republican Sen. Arlen Specter, Professor Hill's sharpest questioner, said: "The Senate is on trial." The hearings aroused intense feeling, especially among feminists who felt the Senate's eventual approval of Judge Thomas was an insult to women. The judge called his ordeal "a high-tech lynching for uppity Blacks", protesting:

This is not America. It is Kafkaeqsue. It has got to stop. It must stop for the benefit of future nominees and our country. Enough is enough. No job is worth what I've been through.

I would have preferred an assassin's bullet than this kind of living hell they have put me and my family through.
JUDGE THOMAS.

I know of no system of government where when you add the kerosene of sex, the heated flame of race and the incendiary nature of television lights, you're not going to have an explosion. Sen. JOSEPH BIDEN.

Thorpe case The astonishing farrago of homosexual intrigue, dog-shooting and murder plots which racked the UK LIBERAL PARTY in the late 1970s. It revolved around the debonair Jeremy Thorpe (1929–), party leader from 1967 until 1976. That March Andrew Gino Newton, an airline pilot, was jailed for two years for shooting Norman Scott's dog RINKA on Exmoor. During the trial Scott, a male model, claimed to be in fear for his life because he was writing a book about a homosexual relationship between himself and Thorpe; Newton said he shot the dog because Scott was blackmailing him. Thorpe denied the whole story, but over a period a highly incriminating correspondence, interspersed with tales of teeth marks in Thorpe's Commons desk, hit the media; he was forced to resign that summer as party leader. In 1978 he and three other men were charged with conspiracy to murder Scott, but after a lengthy trial they were acquitted; by then he had lost his North Devon seat in the 1979 election after a campaign in which the columnist Auberon Waugh intervened as a Dog Lovers' candidate. All the time that the scandal was emerging, Thorpe kept up his political activity; on one appearance in the Commons in 1976 Cyril Smith (*see* BIG CYRIL) called out:

Shot any good dogs lately?

those damned dots Lord Randolph Churchill's denunciation of decimal points, recorded by his son Sir Winston; from a CHANCELLOR OF THE EXCHEQUER (briefly in 1886), Lord Randolph's confession that "I could never make out what those damned dots meant" was mildly unnerving.

thousand days Arthur Schlesinger Jr.'s characterization of the dynamic, dazzling administration of John F. KENNEDY (*see* CAMELOT). From Kennedy's inauguration on 20 January 1961 until his assassination on 23 November 1963 was in fact 1036 days.

1000 per cent support The phrase that haunted George McGovern's 1972 campaign for the Presidency. McGovern used it when standing by vice-presidential nominee Sen. Thomas Eagleton of Missouri when it emerged that he had been treated several times for severe mental depression. Party and media pressure soon forced McGovern to ditch Eagleton and replace him with former PEACE CORPS director Sargent Shriver; despite Shriver's popularity and competence, the Eagleton episode told heavily against the Democratic ticket as Richard Nixon won a second term by a LANDSLIDE.

thousand points of light The inspirational phrase from George BUSH's ACCEPTANCE SPEECH at the 1988 Republican convention, conjured up by the Reagan/Bush speechwriter Peggy Noonan (*see* TOUCH THE FACE OF GOD); it was supposed to symbolize individual endeavour and voluntary charitable effort. On Bush's INAUGURATION the following January, 40,000 people in Washington were issued with torches to switch on and dramatize the point. Bush frequently garbled the phrase; once when he called it "1000 points of life", the *Washington Post* cartoonist Herblock drew a drunk pledging his vote to Bush because he had promised "1000 pints of Lite". What Bush originally said was:

I will keep America moving forward, always forward – for a better America, for an endless enduring dream and a thousand points of light.

thousand-year Reich *see* REICH.

three. three acres and a cow The slogan of the English radical Jesse Collings (1831–1920) for his land-reform scheme which was part of the Liberals' UNAUTHORIZED PROGRAMME, championed by Joseph Chamberlain prior to the 1885 general election. On 27 January 1886 Collings moved the proposal as an amendment to the LOYAL ADDRESS after the opening of the new Parliament; 16 Liberals voted with the Conservatives against it, but SALISBURY's government fell over Ireland soon after. John Stuart Mill (1806–73) originated the phrase, writing in his *Principles of Political Economy* (1848):

> When the land is cultivated entirely by the spade and no horses are kept, a cow is kept for every three acres of land.

three-cornered fight An electoral contest that takes place between three candidates or parties.

three-day week The tight régime for British industry ordered by the Heath government on 13 December 1973 in order to counter the Arab oil boycott and the National Union of Mineworkers' overtime ban, which later developed into a full-scale strike. The three-day week, which took effect from 31 December, was viewed at the time as devastating to the economy, but statistics later showed that industrial production actually increased. However the MINERS' STRIKE achieved its political objective; after a period of increasing privations (*see* CLEAN YOUR TEETH IN THE DARK), Heath decided to call an election on the question of WHO GOVERNS BRITAIN? – and lost.

Three-in-a-Bed The nickname of Sir Charles Dilke (1843–1911), the radical Liberal lawyer/politician whose alleged sexual antics scandalized English society, and Queen Victoria in particular. Appointed Gladstone's local government minister in 1882, he lost his seat in 1886 after being cited as co-respondent in a divorce case. Dilke's young sister-in-law Mrs. Donald Crawford accused him of seducing her, teaching her "every French vice", and persuading her to share a bed with Fanny, his servant-girl. Even before the case came to trial, Gladstone had marked Dilke as "unavailable" for his new government. At the first hearing the case against Dilke was dismissed, but Crawford was awarded a decree nisi. Dilke had the case reopened, and in the second trial Mrs. Crawford added the "odious details"; Dilke was publicly branded a perjurer and an adulterer, his credibility weakened by having cut holes in relevant pages of his diary. Dilke returned to the Commons in 1892 and served until his death, but lived under a permanent shadow.

> The victim of a conspiracy, the main lines of which are shrouded in mystery. ROY JENKINS.

three Is Ireland, Italy, Israel, the three ethnic and foreign-policy interests US presidential hopefuls (and especially Democrats) have traditionally taken up to gain critical community support.

three-liner At Westminster, a three-line WHIP, amounting to a summons to every MP or peer to attend for a crucial DIVISION. The three lines underline the request to be present – politely put, but carrying disciplinary pains if ignored.

Three Mile Island The site near Harrisburg, Pennsylvania, of America's most serious nuclear reactor accident, which gave an impetus to the anti-nuclear campaign and effectively brought the construction of US nuclear power stations to a halt. On 29 March 1979, due to human and technical failure, the fissile core, normally immersed in water, became exposed to the air and began to melt, releasing radioactive gases into the air. Complete MELTDOWN of the core was avoided, but the public realized it had had a narrow escape. President CARTER visited Three Mile Island; when Vice-President Walter Mondale was asked if the plant were safe once again, he replied:

> If it wasn't safe, they'd have sent the Vice-President.

300 Group The group which since the late 1970s has campaigned for more women in Britain's House of Commons. Led by the former Liberal candidate Lesley Abdela, it set 300 women members of the 651-member chamber as a target; by 1992 the number of women MPs had reached one-tenth of that number.

Threshergate The bizarre episode in November 1992 when Norman Lamont, UK CHANCELLOR OF THE EXCHEQUER, was reported to have bought a bottle of Bricout champagne and a pack of 20 Raffles cigarettes for £17.47 at Thresher's off-licence in Praed Street, Paddington. Two of the shop's staff confirmed to reporters that Mr. Lamont had been the customer. However the story was vehemently denied by the Treasury, which insisted Lamont had bought three bottles of wine at another branch of Thresher's the previous night; the staff first stuck to their story, then changed it when the chain's head office took an interest. The Chancellor's denials were fully accepted and a till receipt for the three bottles of wine eventually produced. The episode built on the bad press Lamont had received for not resigning after BLACK WEDNESDAY, breaching his credit card limit

22 times in eight years, and allowing the Treasury and an anonymous contributor to party funds to meet legal expenses for evicting a "sex therapist" from a house he owned and for answering Press queries about the eviction.

threshold agreements Pay agreements negotiated through COLLECTIVE BARGAINING under which workers receive a fixed increase, plus further automatic rises if the rate of INFLATION exceeds a set figure. Pioneered by the Heath government in the early 1970s, they proved counter-productive by ensuring that when prices were rising fastest, they automatically triggered pay increases which forced up the rate of inflation still further, triggering further increases. . . .

throne The ceremonial seat on which a MONARCH sits, and hence a word that personifies the monarchy itself, as in **heir to the throne**. King Charles X of France, who reigned from 1824 until forced into exile six years later, told Talleyrand: "There is no middle course between the throne and the scaffold"; Talleyrand replied presciently:

> You are forgetting the postchaise.

steps of the throne The edge of the podium in the HOUSE OF LORDS on which stands the throne from which the sovereign delivers the GRACIOUS SPEECH, otherwise known as the **speech from the throne**. Sons of PEERS, and members of the House of Commons, are permitted to squat on the steps of the throne to hear debates in the upper house.

throttlebottom A US term for a bumbling, incompetent politician; it originated in the 1931 musical *Of Thee I Sing*, in which Vice-President Alexander Throttlebottom was such a nonentity that White House guards did not recognize him and refused to let him in. By chance the stars of the show included the song-and-dance man George Murphy, who later became a Republican senator. Politicians against whom the epithet has been used include Harry S Truman and Dan QUAYLE.

throw. throw-weight The amount of destructive force delivered by a nuclear missile. It is normally given in megatons: the equivalent in millions of tons of TNT. However this measure takes no account of the radiation and nuclear fall-out generated.

throw money at a problem To try to eradicate an area of deprivation or solve some other policy conundrum by large-scale spending, rather than detailed appraisal of what might work. As long ago as 1834, Sir Robert PEEL told the House of Commons:

> Of all the vulgar acts of government, that of solving every difficulty which might arise by thrusting the hand into the public purse is the most delusory and contemptible.

throw to the wolves To sacrifice an unpopular politician to his or her critics in order to prevent that unpopularity attaching to the entire party or government to which they belong. When J. E. B. Seely offered to resign as Britain's Minister for War in March 1914 after his misjudgments had precipitated the tensions in the Army that led to the CURRAGH MUTINY, Bonar Law (*see* UNKNOWN PRIME MINISTER) told the Commons:

> We have heard of people being thrown to the wolves, but never before have we heard of a man being thrown to the wolves with a bargain on behalf of the wolves that they would not eat him.

thundering disgrace The comments by Ireland's Defence Minister Paddy Donegan in 1976 about President Cearbhall O'Dalaigh (1911–78) that prompted O'Dalaigh to resign, complaining that his office had been insulted. Donegan was angered by the President using his powers to delay legislation designed to thwart IRA terrorism; O'Dalaigh, a former Chief Justice of the Supreme Court, considered the measure UNCONSTITUTIONAL. Though Donegan, who was speaking to military personnel, was quoted by the reporter present as calling O'Dalaigh "a thundering disgrace", it was known that the Minister's actual words were "a fucking disgrace". O'Dalaigh was never an easy man; when he visited the European Parliament in Strasbourg he insisted on addressing reporters from Irish newspapers in Irish, which not all of them understood; they had to wait until he spoke to the British press, and then hide behind pillars to listen.

Tiananmen Square The site next to Peking's Forbidden City of the massacre in June 1989 of 2000 unarmed Chinese civilians by the People's Liberation Army during pro-democracy demonstrations led by university students. The protests started in late April during the funeral of the liberal Hu Yaobang, a deposed former general secretary of the Chinese Communist Party; by mid-May more than a million demonstrators, including some government officials, were staging the largest protest in Communist China's history. The protesters were encouraged by Hu's fellow-liberal, the party chief Zhao Ziyang, who aimed to "enhance democracy, expose corruption and expand openness", and took heart from a visit by the reforming Soviet leader Mikhail Gorbachev, who on 16 May interrupted his schedule to lay a wreath in the square. The students turned the protest into a permanent occupation and erected a Statue of Liberty.

Then, on 20 May, Communist hard-liners loyal to the veteran Deng Hsiao-Ping rallied and imposed martial law, and on 3 June some 10,000 troops entered the city; the next day tanks and armoured personnel carriers went in to kill the retreating students, one of whom had stood defiantly before them. The massacre, and the ensuing mass arrests and executions, provoked worldwide condemnation and trade reprisals. However Deng's regime continued to crush the "counter-revolutionary rebellion", and in 1992 made it clear it would not tolerate moves toward democracy in Hong Kong, either.

ticket The combination of candidates put forward by a party for election to different offices; in America it will be headed by the Presidential and Vice-Presidential candidates, candidates for the Senate and the House, for Governor and for the state legislature, and then for local offices. The term originated in America prior to the universal adoption of the Australian BALLOT in 1884; in those states where voting was by ballot, the parties prepared their own ballots and handed them out near voting stations. Such papers were known as the parties' tickets.

ticket-splitting To vote for some candidates on one party's ticket and some from another; *e.g.* a Republican for the Presidency and a Democrat for the Senate.

balanced ticket A SLATE of candidates representing sharply contrasting opinions within a party. Usually a US Presidential nominee chooses a RUNNING-MATE representing not only a different ideology from his own but coming from a different part of the country; the belief is that this will bring in votes that the nominee alone would not attract. In the 1987 UK general election, John Biffen (*see* SEMI-DETACHED) called for Margaret Thatcher to put forward a balanced ticket by giving a high profile to party moderates eager for CONSOLIDATION, as well as hard-line radicals in her own image; Mrs. Thatcher campaigned at full throttle, then sacked Biffen from her Cabinet.

dream ticket A combination of candidates of such obvious charm, appeal and ability to work together that their election is virtually assured. The term was used in 1980 by Republicans who hoped Ronald Reagan would name former President Gerald FORD as his running-mate. Neil KINNOCK and Roy Hattersley (*see* HATTERJI) were given this accolade by Labour SPIN-DOCTORS in 1983; their election as party leader and deputy leader was seen as ending Labour's nightmare of internal strife and electoral disaster. However Jeffrey Archer told the subsequent Conservative conference:

> It really doesn't matter, because *we* have the return ticket.

voting the ticket The action, frequently taken almost automatically, of voting for every one of a party's nominees.

tiger. Tiger, the The nickname of the French statesman and journalist **Georges Clemenceau** (1841–1929), who as Prime Minister negotiated the VERSAILLES Treaty of 1919 imposing draconian peace terms on Germany. A determined fighter, single-minded in achieving his objectives, he was an early campaigner over the DREYFUS CASE, and gained a reputation for destructive political power by bringing down one ministry after another, using his newspaper, *La Justice*, to carry his criticisms. Prime Minister 1906–09, he was recalled by President Poincaré as the carnage in WORLD WAR I reached its height, and led France to victory. Clemenceau pursued that aim single-mindedly, telling the NATIONAL ASSEMBLY in March 1918:

> My home policy? I wage war. My foreign policy? I wage war. Always, everywhere, I wage war.

He could be scathing of his generals' performance, remarking of Marshal Joffre: "The only time he ever put up a fight in his life was when we asked him for his resignation." He also told Winston Churchill: "I have no political system and I have abandoned all political principles. I am a man dealing with events as they come in the light of my experience." Clemenceau emerged from the war a popular hero, but in 1920 he was passed over for the Presidency by the NATIONAL ASSEMBLY, and left politics.

> He had only one illusion: France; and only one disillusion: mankind. JOHN MAYNARD KEYNES.

> There the old Tiger would be sitting, in his grey gloves and grey skull-cap, usually wearing grey slippers, looking like a grey cat. BERNARD BARUCH (1870–1965).

> Time and time again Monet, who was going blind, wrote that he could do no more. Whereupon Clemenceau would leave his Cabinet room and drive to Monet's studio and bid him take up his brush. Lord CLARK (1903–83).

Tiger talks The first of two negotiations aboard Royal Navy cruisers (the second were on HMS FEARLESS) at which Harold WILSON urged the Rhodesian leader Ian Smith to end UDI and RETURN TO LEGALITY. In the *Tiger* talks, off Gibraltar early in December 1966, Wilson offered Smith concessions to secure an agreement, and believed one had been reached; when the deal was rejected by hard-liners in Salisbury, he made his negotiating hand public, creating astonishment over how far he had been prepared to go. The former Rhodesian Prime Minister Sir Edgar Whitehead said the agreement would have postponed "the possible date of African MAJORITY RULE almost certainly beyond the end of the century".

tightly knit group of politically-motivated men The phrase rashly used by Harold WILSON to denounce the prime movers of the 1966 seamen's strike (*see* JULY MEASURES); it hinted at deliberate Communist wrecking tactics without saying so outright or naming those allegedly involved. Speaking in the Commons on 20 June 1966, Wilson said that "a few individuals" had pressured the executive of the National Union of Seamen to prolong the dispute over pay and hours by refusing to negotiate; those responsible were "a tightly-knit group of politically-motivated men who, as the last General Election showed, utterly failed to secure acceptance of their views by the British electorate" and were now determined to endanger the security of the industry and the welfare of the nation. According to Wilson's biographer Ben Pimlott "everything was wrong with this statement", which was based on innuendo from the security services; it told trade unionists their phones were being tapped and exaggerated the Communists' power to sway a group of evident individualists. Wilson's conspiracy theory was regarded by some colleagues as "completely bonkers" and did long-term damage to his contacts with trade union leaders. *See also* BEER AND SANDWICHES AT NUMBER TEN.

time The critical commodity in a Parliamentary system, its allocation determining whether a government can get its BUSINESS through. The one power an OPPOSITION has is to restrict the amount of time available; a government thus has to avoid causing needless irritation to parties which cannot defeat it but can frustrate its legislative intentions.

time agreement In the US SENATE, a "unanimous consent agreement" to bring forward a measure on the CALENDAR for consideration, generally with a time limit set for debate and a list of amendments to be considered. By tradition it is for the MAJORITY LEADER to propose such an agreement.

TINA THERE IS NO ALTERNATIVE. A nickname for Margaret Thatcher (*see* IRON LADY) stemming from her use of this phrase to justify her economic and social policies; it became current in 1980–81.

tinhorn A US phrase for a pretentious, shabby and worthless politician; it originates in the British "tinpot", current by the late 19th century, and the US "tinhorn gambler". The word was probably first applied to a politician by William Allen White in an editorial in the *Emporia* (Kansas) *Gazette* on 25 October 1901.

Tip The nickname of **Thomas P. O'Neill** (1912–), SPEAKER of the US House of Representatives 1976–86, formed from compressing his first two initials. An affable but tough Massachusetts-Irish pol, who termed himself "an old-hat FDR liberal Democrat", he presided over the Democrat-controlled House under Jimmy CARTER and throughout the REAGAN presidency, once declaring of the latter: "I am the Opposition." As youngest-ever Speaker of the Massachusetts House, he demanded absolute party loyalty, once locking out a maverick Democrat to prevent him abstaining on a key vote. He took over John F. KENNEDY's Congressional seat and became Speaker in 1977, guiding the novice President CARTER. Though known as "Jimmy Carter's best friend in Washington", Carter's distrust of Congress made the relationship difficult. As O'Neill could make or break the President's legislative programme, his influence was immense. When Reagan took office, the Speaker told him: "I'll give you your right, but, Jesus, don't push me"; but once, when angered by what he saw as White House meddling, he stormed: "Did you ever hear of the SEPARATION OF POWERS?" In the House, O'Neill, one of the FOUR HORSEMEN, commanded respect as a strong Speaker, declaring: "I set the agenda." But he shrugged off his native tradition of MACHINE POLITICS to become a considerable reformer.

> Everyone knew Tip O'Neill was an old shoe – a friendly, clubbable backroom man. But he became a modern politician who changed the ways of the House.
>
> HEDRICK SMITH, *The Power Game*.

Tippecanoe and Tyler too The slogan on which the WHIG ticket of General William Henry Harrison (1773–1841) and John Tyler (1790-1862) were elected US President and Vice-President in 1840. Harrison was **Old Tippecanoe**, after the victory to which he led his troops in the Indian Wars. Harrison was a nationalist and Tyler an advocate of STATES' RIGHTS; the New York Whig Philip Hone, who considered the ticket a mismatch, declared it to be "rhyme, but no reason".

Harrison had gone on from fighting the Indians and the British to serve in the House and Senate, serving as Minister to Colombia and a court clerk to pay off debts run up by high living. Despite this he was able to portray himself as the LOG CABIN AND HARD CIDER candidate, in contrast with the "oriental splendor" of Martin van Buren (*see* OLD KINDERHOOK), whom he defeated to become America's 9th President; privately he described himself as a "clerk and clodhopper". He served as President for just 31 days before dying of a cold caught while delivering his

INAUGURAL ADDRESS. Tyler (*see* OLD VETO) was the first Vice-President to take up the reins of office, and indeed was only confirmed as having actually been President in 1967. Theodore Roosevelt reckoned him "a politician of monumental littleness".

tired and emotional A euphemism for "drunk" that has proved useful to the UK media, which has to be mindful of the libel laws when reporting people's peccadillos. The expression was first used by a BBC press officer in November 1963 when explaining the overwrought condition in which George BROWN, then deputy leader of the Labour Party, had appeared on the night of President KENNEDY's assassination. It was immediately taken up by PRIVATE EYE to refer to anyone in a similar condition, and before long the phrase had general application, though it was frequently used of Brown during his colourful Cabinet career in the mid-1960s. *See also* DRINK.

tit for tat expulsion The expulsion of one or more of a country's DIPLOMATS by a foreign country, in retaliation for a similar number of expulsions by the other. Failure to respond in this way created a widespread presumption that the diplomats expelled in the first place were guilty of whatever they were accused of – usually espionage. Consequently the majority of expulsions are followed by tit-for-tat action, regardless of whether they were justified.

Tito. Titoism The pragmatic communism implemented in Yugoslavia after 1945 by **Josip Broz Tito** (1892–1980), the Croat former Austro-Hungarian soldier who joined the RED ARMY and helped form the Yugoslav Communist Party. Tito welded the wartime PARTISANS into a formidable and victorious force, then rejected the Soviet model of communist social and economic development imposed by STALIN on the eastern bloc countries, believing instead in "separate roads to socialism". His policies included decentralized profit-sharing workers' councils and a NON-ALIGNED stance in world affairs. But the greatest difference was that alone among East European Communist leaders, Tito stood up to Stalin, who thus regarded him as a dangerous threat to his authority, expelling Yugoslavia from the COMINFORM in 1948. A purge was then carried out of suspected Titoist heretics throughout East Europe's communist parties and governments; Tito carried out a less publicized but just as deadly purge of Stalinists in his own party. The partisans' war record probably persuaded Stalin not to crush his reformist movement, as the KREMLIN did later in East Germany, Hungary and Czechoslovakia. Tito's regime became stagnant in his old age, but his triumph in holding the country together only became evident in the early 1990s when it disintegrated in a bloody CIVIL WAR.

tokenism The practice of some companies, schools, sports teams – even political parties – of conforming to pressure for EQUAL OPPORTUNITIES by accepting or promoting a token member or members of a minority group, especially Blacks or women. This early-1960s Americanism spread to the UK in the following decade. A **showcase nigger** is Black slang for a token Black given high visibility in the company's front office.

Tokyo Round The round of GATT negotiations between 1974 and 1979 which built on the TARIFF reductions achieved by the KENNEDY ROUND, the resulting agreements surviving when the URUGUAY ROUND. was begun seven years later.

Tolpuddle Martyrs The six Dorset farm labourers sentenced at Dorchester Assizes in 1834 to transportation to Tasmania for seven years for setting up their own TRADE UNION, who are hailed as pioneers of British organized labour. They were charged with administering "illegal oaths" – declarations of loyalty to the ideals of organized labour – to members of their "friendly society". Public outrage at the sentence led to their being PARDONed two years later, but it was another two years before they were brought home. One of the six, George Loveless (1805–40) told the court:

> If we have violated any law it was not done intentionally. We have injured no man's reputation, character, person, or property. We were meeting together to preserve ourselves, our wives, and our children from utter degradation and starvation.

Tonton The nickname of François Mitterrand (1916–), Socialist President of France from 1981. It is nursery French for "uncle".

Tontons Macoute (Creole, Uncle Knapsack, a bogeyman who hunts naughty children and captures them in his sack) The fearsome private MILITIA and SECRET POLICE created in Haiti by President François PAPA DOC Duvalier (1907–71) who ruled the country from 1957. The Tontons Macoute were Duvalier loyalists (and often voodoo practitioners) who, in return for weapons and occasionally money, were licensed to terrorize, torture and murder those perceived as enemies of the regime. Many of the recruits (known after 1960 as the Volunteers for National security – VSN) were ex-soldiers, many were criminals; all could be easily identified by their unofficial uniform – smart suit, dark glasses and bulging hip holsters. When Duvalier died the tontons transferred their loyalty to the new president, his son Jean Claude "Baby Doc" Duvalier; when he was toppled by a revolution in 1986, they remained in existence to terrorize the voters during election campaigns and overthrow the governments that were elected.

Tonypandy The myth that Winston CHURCHILL, when Liberal Home Secretary in 1910, authorized troops to fire on striking South Wales miners, killing a number of them; in fact no miners died and Churchill was largely responsible for preventing bloodshed. The episode created a distrust of Churchill from the labour and trade-union movement that persisted even after his coalition with the Labour Party in World War II. On 10 November 1910 the Chief Constable of Glamorgan requested the local military commander to act to curb violent riots at Tonypandy, in the Rhondda Valley. When Churchill heard that a small force of troops was on its way, he insisted that it be held in reserve and extra unarmed police be sent instead; they managed to restrain the rioters without causing serious injury. The issue caused a flare-up in the Commons during the WINTER OF DISCONTENT, 1978–79, Prime Minister James Callaghan referring to Churchill's alleged use of troops against the strikers and his grandson, the Conservative MP Winston Churchill, furiously demanding that he WITHDRAW. The temperature was diplomatically lowered by Speaker George Thomas (later Viscount Tonypandy), a babe in arms at the time of the riots, who told the House:

> I never imagined a former pupil of Tonypandy Grammar School would have the last word on this.

too. too bad all the people who know how to run the country are busy driving cabs and cutting hair One of the classic complaints of politicians frustrated by repeated lectures from know-all taxi drivers and barbers, and heard on both sides of the Atlantic. Its originator seems to have been a non-politician, the veteran US comedian George Burns (1896–).

too much football without a helmet Lyndon B. Johnson's withering verdict on the cause of Gerald FORD's supposed intellectual limitations, delivered when he was House MINORITY LEADER. LBJ was referring to Ford's past as in Star College footballer in Michigan.

Tortilla Curtain Slang for the fences along the US-Mexican border that are meant, but fail, to keep illegal immigrants (WETBACKS) from central America out of the United States. An echo of the phrase IRON CURTAIN, it refers to the cornmeal pancake that is a staple of the Mexican diet.

Tory (1) At the time of the AMERICAN REVOLUTION, a term for a supporter of the Colonies remaining under the British crown; thousands of Tories sailed to Nova Scotia when Washington's forces emerged victorious. (2) A colloquial word for a supporter of Britain's CONSERVATIVE PARTY, the two words being interchangeable. The word is of 16th-century Irish origin; a corruption of *toraidhe,* the Gaelic word for "pursuer", it was first used as an abusive term for Catholic outlaws who attacked English soldiers and settlers. The original political Tories emerged as a force under Charles II, opposed the GLORIOUS REVOLUTION of 1688–89, became a governing force by 1710, and were tarred with being JACOBITES during the 18th century, the WHIG Horace Walpole writing:

> All the sensible Tories that I ever knew, were either Jacobites or became Whigs; those that remained Tories remained fools.

Despite a highly conservative CV, elements of the Tory party were often more radical than the Whigs, who in the 18th century were founded on a corrupt political ESTABLISHMENT sustained by PATRONAGE. Yet they were terrified by the FRENCH REVOLUTION (*see also* BURKE), and as consistent backers of lost causes opposed the REFORM ACT. When their government fell in September 1831 as a result, Macaulay wrote:

> Dark and terrible beyond any season within my remembrance of political affairs was the day of their flight. Far darker and far more terrible will be the day of their return.

That return was short-lived, the party splitting fatally in the 1840s over the repeal of the CORN LAWS, being rebuilt as the Conservative Party by PEEL and Disraeli (*see* DIZZY), who declared in 1872:

> The Tory party, unless it is a national party, is nothing.

Almost everything said about Tories and the Tory party has been said by its opponents. John Bright declared: "They have always been wrong, they will always be wrong; and when they cease to be wrong, they will cease to be the Tory party"; Sir William Harcourt that "it is not the *métier* of a Tory to have a policy, any more than it is that of a king to be a democrat"; Lloyd George: "a tired nation is a Tory nation"; the Canadian Premier Sir Wilfrid Laurier: "Toryism like the serpent sheds its skin, but ever remains the same reptile"; and the 1960s Boilermakers' Union leader Ted Hill: "I wouldn't trust the Tories any farther than I can throw them. And I'm an old man, and I can't throw very far."

> No amount of cajolery, and no attempts at ethical and social seduction, can eradicate from my heart a deep burning hatred for the Tory Party. . . . So far as I am concerned they are lower than vermin.
>
> ANEURIN BEVAN, speaking in Manchester, 4 July 1948.

> The Tories never panic, except at times of crisis.
>
> Sir JOHN HOSKYNS, first head of Margaret Thatcher's POLICY UNIT.

> The Tories have ceased to be gentlemen without becoming democrats. WILLIAM REES-MOGG, 1963.

Tory Democracy The aggressive Toryism that Lord Randolph Churchill (1849–95) attempted to promote from 1885 as a counter to Joseph Chamberlain's UNAUTHORIZED PROGRAMME, each causing considerable embarrassment to their parties' official leaders. Churchill seized on the BRADLAUGH CASE to build a popular base among Anglicans, also scorning the Toryism of the country squires. Lord Randolph told a meeting in Manchester on 6 November 1885:

> What is the Tory democracy that the Whigs should deride it and hold it up to the execration of the people? It has been called a contradiction in terms; it has been described as a nonsensical appellation. I believe it to be the most simple and most easily understood political denomination ever assumed. The Tory democracy is a democracy which has embraced the principles of the Tory Party.

Tory men and Whig measures The classic formula for government put forward by Taper in Disraeli's CONINGSBY:

> A sound Conservative government," said Taper, musingly. "I understand: Tory men and Whig measures."

See also MEN OR MEASURES.

Tory party at prayer *See* CONSERVATIVE.

Tory Reform Group (TRG) A pressure group for moderate Conservatism, seen by Margaret Thatcher as a nest of WETS. For a member of her Cabinet to speak at its meetings was seen as an act of rebellion, though Peter Walker, an acknowledged Wet, managed to combine being the TRG's patron with sitting at the Cabinet table with Mrs. Thatcher for a decade; John Major's appearance at a TRG reception within days of becoming Prime Minister was seen as evidence of a clean break with his predecessor. The group had its origins in the Tory Reform Committee, formed during World War II with members including Quintin Hogg (Lord Hailsham), and PEST (Pressure for Economic and Social Toryism), formed in the mid-1960s by Michael Spicer, later a MAASTRICHT rebel.

High Toryism The strongly PATERNALISTIC Toryism that thrived *c.* 1820–40, closely linked to the Anglican establishment and backed by the great aristocratic landowners; its adherents regarded PEEL as their greatest foe.

tartan Tories The pejorative term for the SNP (Scottish National Party) coined in the late 1960s by William Ross (later Lord Ross of Marnock), Labour's strongly anti-HOME RULE Secretary of State for Scotland.

totalitarianism A system of government in which the rulers not only control every aspect of political life, but deny the individual the right to make decisions in every other sphere of activity. The test of whether a DICTATORSHIP or AUTHORITARIAN government is totalitarian is not just the power it possesses, but how it uses it.

> This administration expects to be running some sort of totalitarian government either before or after the end of the war and is prudently getting ready for same.
>
> The *New York Daily News* on the proliferation of wartime agencies under the Roosevelt administration.

Touch the face of God Ronald Reagan's memorable remarks on 28 January 1986 (written by his speechwriter Peggy Noonan), in a TV broadcast after the Challenger disaster. He was quoting *High Flight*, a poem by the Royal Canadian Air Force pilot John Gillespie Magee, who was killed aged 19 on 11 December 1941 on a Spitfire training flight from RAF Scopwick, Lincolnshire. His poem, copies of which were circulated to all RCAF airfields and which became the sign-off for a Washington TV station, included the lines:

> Oh! I have slipped the surly bonds of earth
>
> And, while with silent lifting mind I've trod
> The high, untrespassed sanctity of space,
> Put out my hand and touched the face of God.

Tower Commission The three-member special review board set up by President Reagan in 1986 into the IRAN-CONTRA affair, which was headed by former Sen. John Tower of Texas. Its report, published in February 1987, attacked members of the President's staff for undertaking actions that Congress had expressly forbidden, and criticized Reagan for "lax management". It described the Administration's policies toward Iran and the Contras as being underpinned by deception and disregard for the laws of the nation, but argued that the exercise had been an "aberration".

town meeting The traditional form of community government in New England, with all the inhabitants who wish to attend deciding on actions to be taken. Its influence has spread further; the township form of government can be found as far west as Nebraska. Several Presidents and candidates have held "town meetings" in selected communities to keep in touch with public opinion; Bill Clinton caused some resentment in the Washington press corps by opting after his inauguration to hold televised "town meetings" with the public in preference to press conferences. Sen. Bill Bradley of New Jersey built up a reputation for holding **walking town meetings**, meeting the voters on the beaches of his State.

township A settlement in South Africa where Black or Coloured people who work in the cities have had to live because APARTHEID prevented them living in "White" areas near their work. The Government has provided the basics of a road grid and concrete sites for small houses with a water pipe, but the community has been to left to create its own facilities; where they are absent, frustration and political tension can spill over into violence. The townships have been strongholds of support for the African National Congress (ANC), with INKATHA drawing most of its strength from migrant hostel-dwellers; some townships, like Soweto outside Johannesburg, are the size of a largish city.

T. R. The initials of President Theodore Roosevelt (*see* TEDDY), commonly used in place of a nickname.

trade. Trade Expansion Act The US legislation, signed by President KENNEDY in 1962, which eased the TARIFF system to facilitate flexible dealings with the EUROPEAN COMMUNITY. It freed the market by permitting the President to lower tariff duties by as much as 50% over five years, and abolish tariffs on certain goods produced both by America and the six founder members of the EC. The Act was one of a range of US measures to stimulate world trade, the KENNEDY ROUND of GATT negotiations being another. Kennedy said:

> We must either trade or fade.

trade gap The difference between the value of what a nation imports and what it exports; the term implies that imports are the larger. The difference between a trade gap and a BALANCE OF PAYMENTS deficit is that the latter makes allowance for INVISIBLES such as shipping and insurance premiums.

trade union An organization of workers with similar employment and skills who combine together to improve their conditions through COLLECTIVE BARGAINING backed by the sanction of industrial ACTION, and to secure their employment. The former TUC general secretary Len (later Lord) Murray declared:

> Trade unions are about individuals, and the right of a man to answer back to his boss.

The term has become increasingly a British one, Americans normally saying "labor union" (*see* AFL-CIO); however the US union pioneer Samuel Gompers (1850–1924) did say:

> We will stand by our friends . . . to secure the election of intelligent, honest, earnest trade unionists, with clear, unblemished, paid-up union cards in their possession.

H. L. Mencken saw the unions as essentially a reactionary and negative force, writing:

> Unionism seldom if ever uses such power as it has to insure better work; almost always it devotes a large part of that power to safeguard bad work.

And when the TEAMSTERS – for decades out of the mainstream of American unionism though now trying to return – were repeatedly in the headlines for their leaders' links with organized crime, Robert Orben declared:

> Unions are getting such a bad name, it's no wonder they're called Brother Hoods.

At the peak of their influence in the 1970s, UK trade unions could claim almost 10 million members, proportionally a far greater degree of unionization thant has ever been achieved in the United States. With its roots in the 1830s (*see* TOLPUDDLE MARTYRS), the movement developed throughout the 19th century, the Trades Union Congress (TUC) being formed in 1868; the first trade union members of Parliament were elected (as Liberals) the same year, and in the 1870s suppressive laws against unions were repealed. The unions were instrumental in forming the LABOUR PARTY in 1906 and in funding it (*see* OSBORNE JUDGMENT), and most have remained closely linked to it – a fact that has benefited both on occasions but also created widespread public suspicion as to who is running whom (*see* BEER AND SANDWICHES AT NUMBER TEN; block VOTE; GET YOUR TANKS OFF MY LAWN). In 1947 Emmanuel Shinwell (*see* MANNY) told the electricians' union:

> We know that you, the organized workers of the country, are our friends. As for the rest, they do not matter a tinker's cuss.

Britain's trade unions have a culture all of their own, based on rigid adherence to their own procedures and rule books. Ernest BEVIN reckoned that "the most conservative man in the world is the British trade unionist when you want to change him", but Aneurin BEVAN, well to the left of him, termed the unions "islands of anarchy in a sea of chaos".

The unions – in Britain, America, Australia and elsewhere – have always been targeted by leftist groups, most notably the highly-disciplined Communist Party, either to build a vanguard of working-class support or to DESTABILIZE the established order. LENIN wrote shortly before his death in 1924:

> It is necessary to be able, if need be, to resort to all sorts of stratagems, manoeuvres and illegal methods, to evasion and subterfuge in order to penetrate trade unions, to

remain in them and carry out communist work in them at all costs.

The most cathartic moment in the British unions' history was in 1926 when they called a GENERAL STRIKE to support miners resisting a wage cut, and lost. John Maynard KEYNES wrote then of

the trade unionists, once the oppressed, now the tyrants, whose selfish, sectional pretensions need to be bravely opposed.

While individual unions have indulged in extremism and militancy, they have never again taken such concerted action. The movement has achieved many of its aims, though FULL EMPLOYMENT remains as far away as ever. But its perpetuation of outdated demarcation lines and working practices after World War II, the inability of its leaders to check unofficial strikes, the abuse of PICKETING and the final straw of the WINTER OF DISCONTENT gave the Thatcher government broad public support for putting them on a tight rein. Previous efforts – Labour's IN PLACE OF STRIFE in 1969 and the Conservatives' Industrial Relations Act (*see* PENTONVILLE FIVE) had ended in failure. The 1990s opened with a largely chastened trade union movement and a less stridently anti-union government under John MAJOR re-opening tentative contacts.

The trade union movement has become, with the hereditary peerage, an avenue to political power through which stupid untrained persons may pass up to the highest office. BEATRICE WEBB, 1917.

As a trade unionist, people often ask me why I vote Conservative. The answer is, because I am a stupid cunt. *Private Eye* election record, 1964.

Trades Union Congress *See* TUC.

Board of Trade The permanent committee of the PRIVY COUNCIL established by King William III in 1696 (stemming from one first founded in 1621) that was the direct ancestor of the present UK Department of Trade and Industry. Reformed in 1786 to become a conventional government department, it was in the thick of many Victorian reforms – notably the repeal of the CORN LAWS – and became the guinea-pig for the NORTHCOTE-TREVELYAN REFORMS of Whitehall itself. Until the formation of a separate Ministry of Labour it also collected employment and wage statistics and INTERVENED to resolve industrial disputes. It became the Department of Trade and Industry in 1970, but the title of **President of the Board of Trade** was revived by Michael Heseltine (*see* TARZAN) when he arrived at the DTI in April 1992.

Trafalgar Square The customary venue for great DEMONSTRATIONS in London, being the nearest point to the Palace of Westminster where it is permissible to hold a public meeting. It was the scene of BLOODY SUNDAY in 1887, the start and then the finish of the ALDERMASTON MARCHES, and the scene of riots against the POLL TAX in 1990.

Train of Shame The title given by travelling media and party officials to the train which the infant SDP used to ferry its leaders between Perth, Bradford and London for its "rolling conference" in September 1981. The experiment, which gave rise to its own songbook, was repeated the following year – then dropped because of the length of time the party leadership had been marooned when the train's locomotive broke down in the Fens *en route* for Great Yarmouth.

transition The period of ten to eleven weeks between the election that decides who the new President of the United States will be, and the day when that President is INAUGURATED. If there is a change of party as in 1976–77, 1980–81 and 1992–93, a new ADMINISTRATION has to be formed from scratch, so that it can take over the running of the country from 20 January. A victorious candidate will normally have been too busy campaigning to have thought whom they will want in their Administration; and a frantic search for a Cabinet balanced politically, geographically and in respect to gender and race then ensues. The process is slowed because of the need for the transition team to screen all the POLITICAL APPOINTEES who will require CONFIRMATION by the SENATE; the BAIRD NOMINATION early in 1993 highlights the pitfalls. No matter how energetically the incoming President's special transition team works, it will be months before all 3000 jobs in the PLUM BOOK are filled.

translation *See* SIMULTANEOUS.

I'd like that translated if I may The reaction of Harold Macmillan (*see* SUPERMAC) at the United Nations in 1960 when the Soviet leader Nikita Khruschev showed his anger at the U-2 AFFAIR, and alleged "colonialism" by the West, by taking off his shoe and banging it on the desk.

transparency The catchword for the openness of the operations of the EUROPEAN COMMUNITY to the public gaze that, along with SUBSIDIARITY, was pressed by John MAJOR and other EC leaders after the signature of the MAASTRICHT TREATY. At the Edinburgh Summit in December 1992, the COUNCIL OF MINISTERS agreed that more information be made available on what the Community was doing, with certain Ministerial sessions thrown open at least in part to the television cameras.

Transport House The headquarters in SMITH SQUARE, Westminster, of Britain's Transport and General Workers' Union (T&G), which from 1928 to 1980 also housed the LABOUR PARTY; the building, the brainchild of Ernest BEVIN, also housed the TUC headquarters until 1958. To RANK AND FILE members of the party "Transport House" came to symbolize the solidly right-wing party machine, which until well into the 1960s took a firm line against rebellion and dissent by even the humblest party member.

Travail, Famille (Patrie) (Work, Family, (Country)) The motto of the VICHY government which ruled unoccupied France, by the leave of the Germans, from 1941 to 1944. The traditional Republican slogan of LIBERTY! EQUALITY! FRATERNITY! was considered too explosive by Marshal Pétain's COLLABORATIONIST government, most of them arch-conservatives.

TRB The anonymous column in the NEW REPUBLIC, written from 1943 to 1983 by Richard L. Strout (1898–1990), which was required reading for anyone involved in US politics. The signature was the initials of the Brooklyn Rapid Transit in reverse, dating from when the *New Republic* was produced in New York and the then editor, Bruce Blevin, had to carry copy by subway. Strout, a New Yorker who began his journalistic career in England on the *Sheffield Independent*, joined the *Christian Science Monitor* in 1921 and in 1923 moved to Washington, going on to observe every President from HARDING to Reagan. He took on the already-running TRB in 1943, turning it into a revered institution; in 1955 he wrote of the new administration:

> Ike has picked a CABINET of eight millionaires and a plumber.

In his final column, Strout noted:

> You can measure the passage of time by counting things we knew wouldn't happen.

treason The compassing of the overthrow of the State (and in Britain, of the Sovereign). In the UK, treason is one of the very few offences for which one could be executed, though no charges have been brought in modern times. By definition, an act of treason is one that fails; Sir John Harington wrote in 1618:

> Treason doth never prosper, what's the reason?
> For if it prosper, none dare call it treason.

In 1765 Patrick Henry (1736–99), warned that his speeches against Britain's treatment of its American colonies were verging on the treasonable, told the Virginia Convention:

> Caesar had his Brutus – Charles the First, his Cromwell – and George III [Treason!, cried the Speaker] . . . may profit by their example. If this be treason, make the most of it.

Treason trial The four-year trial in Pretoria from 1957 to 1961 in which the South African government tried, and failed, to break resistance to APARTHEID. The process began in December 1956 with the arrest of 156 anti-government activists. The following year 91 were committed for trial by a special three-judge court in a former synagogue. The indictment was quashed by a higher court, but 30 of the accused, including Nelson Mandela, were subjected to a new trial. Eventually 28 were acquitted; one had died and one absconded. The trial provided opponents of Apartheid with a world-wide cause to rally round and raise funds for; the National Party government responded to its failure with new forms of repression as internal resistance, particularly from the African National Congress (ANC) increased.

Treasury The Government department that in Britain (and in Australia) exerts an unrelenting brake on public spending and on economic growth generally, and which effectively controls much of the agenda of government. It is small enough to be democratic, with members of staff at all levels expected to chip in with their views, but the Treasury view is nearly always cautious, something the CHANCELLOR and CHIEF SECRETARY have always to be aware of. Descended from the mediaeval Exchequer whose name the Chancellor still carries, it gained control over the rest of WHITEHALL in the late 17th century, and was also responsible for the CIVIL SERVICE until the late 1960s. Harold WILSON tried to break the Treasury's grip over economic policy in 1964 by forming a separate **Department of Economic Affairs**, but the experiment did not succeed. Justifying the attempt, Wilson wrote:

> I had spent over 20 years in Whitehall and Westminster watching, and whenever possible countering, the wily and dominating ways of the Treasury. I was determined that this department should be cut down to size.

> The Crown is, according to the saying, the "fountain of honour", but the Treasury is the spring of business.
> WALTER BAGEHOT, *The English Constitution* (1867).

> A bunch of bank clerks who think they are MANDARINS.
> Lord BELOFF (1913–).

> The engine-room of government.
> BRUCE ANDERSON, *John Major*.

> The Treasury never sleeps. MICHAEL HESELTINE.

In Washington the Treasury Department, founded in 1789, originally had as extensive powers, but the foundation of the Bureau of the Budget (now OMB) in 1939 greatly reduced its scope. The Secretary of the Treasury remains financial adviser to the President, and the Treasury administers the collection of most Federal taxes, the manufacture of the currency, and law-enforcement agencies such as the SECRET SERVICE and the Bureau of Alcohol, Tobacco and Firearms.

Treasury bench *See* BENCH.

Treasury model The computerized forecast of the UK economy which the Treasury was obliged to maintain under the 1975 INDUSTRY ACT, into which the impact of various future policies can be fed.

First Lord of the Treasury The official title of Britain's Prime Minister; although the title of Prime Minister gained legal recognition in 1905, the brass plate on the door at NUMBER TEN still reads: "First Lord of the Treasury".

treating The provision of liquor, food or other hospitality by a candidate for the voters. George Washington won a seat in the Virginia House of Burgesses in 1758 after providing 160 gallons of drink for just 391 voters and even HONEST ABE Lincoln admitted to spending 75 cents on a barrel of cider for supporting farmhands. In Britain, "treating" was an accepted feature of elections to the unreformed House of Commons, but has long been outlawed under the REPRESENTATION OF THE PEOPLE ACTS.

treaty A solemn agreement between two or more sovereign states to conclude or guarantee peace, to resolve differences, to establish and further peaceful mutual goals or to come to each other's help if attacked.

> The first object of a treaty of peace should be to make future war impossible. Lord SALISBURY, 1870.

> Treaties are like roses and young girls: they last while they last. CHARLES DE GAULLE.

Treaty Room The room in the WHITE HOUSE where the CABINET met from 1865 to 1902, when it became a sitting-room. President KENNEDY renamed it after restoration in 1961, since when it has served as a meeting room and the setting for the signature of important documents, such as the TEST-BAN TREATY on 7 October 1963 and the ABM TREATY on 30 September 1972. It is furnished in the Victorian style of the GRANT administration.

Trevi group The grouping of Interior Ministers from EUROPEAN COMMUNITY countries that meets regularly to co-ordinate national action against terrorism, drug trafficking and illegal immigration.

TRG *See* TORY REFORM GROUP.

triad A PENTAGON term for the three legs of America's nuclear DETERRENT: land-based missiles (*see* CRUISE; ICBM; MX), submarine-launched missiles (*see* POLARIS; TRIDENT) and air-delivered missiles and bombs.

Trianon Treaty The Treaty concluded at VERSAILLES in 1920 which set new national boundaries in Central Europe following the collapse of the Austro-Hungarian Empire. Its most notable and traumatic feature was the dismemberment of Hungary, large numbers of whose nationals found themselves as members of sizable minorities in surrounding states. The Grand Trianon and Petit Trianon are ornate pavilions in the grounds of the Palace of Versailles.

Tribunal of Inquiry The most powerful instrument of investigation available to a British government, but one which is seldom used. It comprises a panel chaired by a senior judge which has the power to compel witnesses to attend and to answer the questions put to them. Tribunals have been convened by the government of the day to inquire into alleged corruption in high places (*see* LYNSKEY TRIBUNAL) and security leaks (*see* VASSALL TRIBUNAL), but Ministers and senior civil servants consider them too weighty and majestic for most inquiries. There is concern that the setting-up of an inquiry may impede the operation of the criminal law – and also on occasions a fear that something embarrassing that has not yet come to light may be discovered.

Tribune The independent and perpetually financially-strapped weekly newspaper that has since 1936 given the left wing of Britain's LABOUR PARTY an articulate and often thoughtful voice. Most closely associated with its founder Aneurin BEVAN and its long-term editor Michael Foot (*see* WURZEL GUMMIDGE), it has harassed both Conservative governments and Labour leaderships. Ironically it was during Foot's leadership in the early 1980s that *Tribune*, under Chris Mullin, briefly went BENNITE; the relationship hit a low point when Mullin went to interview Foot and was asked to leave after accusing him of selling out the left. Following a bitter struggle for control of the paper, it settled down again as the at times prickly voice of the soft LEFT.

Tribune Group The group of Labour MPs, originally organized around the newspaper, which formed the heart of the BEVANITE opposition to Hugh GAITSKELL in the early 1950s. The Parliamentary party voted for its disbandment in 1952, but it was soon reconstituted and until the breakaway of the CAMPAIGN GROUP in 1982 was the only organized forum for the Labour left at Westminster. It has always enjoyed strong support within the constituency parties, reflected in the domination of the constituency section of the National Executive (NEC) until the late 1980s by Tribune Group members.

trickle-down The theory advanced by some conservative politicians and economist that the greater the prosperity of the better-off, the more chance there is of some of it filtering down to improve the lot of the UNDERCLASS. Its proponents use it as justifying the pursuit of tax cuts and incentives for the wealthy, as opposed to higher spending TARGETED on the poorest groups in society. The term is widely assumed to be a product of the Nixon administration, but it dates back at least to 1932, when Franklin D. Roosevelt scorned

> the theory that if we make the rich richer, somehow they will let a part of the prosperity trickle down to the rest of us.

Tricky Dick The nickname that haunted **Richard Milhous Nixon** (1913–), 37th President of the United States (Republican, 1969–74) throughout his political career, save for an accomplished first Presidential term before the disgrace of WATERGATE revived it in full force. He was first given the name in 1950 by Southern California's *Independent Review* as he fought Rep. Helen Gahagan Douglas, whom he branded the PINK LADY, in a campaign marked by innuendo about her supposed (and non-existent) Communist sympathies. But it stuck to him through the controversies over his CHECKERS speech, the HUGHES LOAN and other politico-financial dealings that tarnished him. In 1968, during his second bid for the Presidency, Nixon told his staff:

> All right. They still call me "Tricky Dick". It's a brutal thing to fight. The carefully cultivated impression is that Nixon is devious. I can overcome this impression in one way only: by absolute candor.

An embittered and insecure man even when at the height of his powers, Nixon fought his way to the White House without ever earning the affection of the American people. Denis Healey described him as "more lacking in self-confidence than any other leading politician I have known", and Nixon himself once said:

> If ever the time comes when the Republican Party are looking for an outwardly warm, easygoing, gregarious type, then they will not want the sort of man I am.

Had it not been for Watergate, he might have been remembered as an outstanding President for his achievements in foreign affairs – but his record made it more than likely that he would overreach himself. From a poor farming family, the hard-working and obsessive Nixon battled his way to law school and the California Bar, serving in the Navy during World War II despite being exempt as a Quaker. In 1946 he answered an advertisement from local Republicans for a Congressional candidate, was nominated as the best of an unpromising bunch and defeated the INCUMBENT Jerry Voorhis by branding him as a "friend of the Communists" despite his active work on the House UN-AMERICAN ACTIVITIES Committee – to which Nixon was promptly appointed. In Washington Nixon immediately made a name for himself by pursuing the HISS CASE, and in 1948 he won re-election with the backing of local Democrats as well as Republicans. Two years later, aged 38, he beat Mrs. Douglas to enter the Senate; he was helped by the extreme right-wing columnist Gerald L. K. Smith who wrote:

> The man who uncovered Alger Hiss is in California to do the same housecleaning here. Help Richard Nixon get rid of the Jew-Communists.

Back in Congress he championed General Douglas MACARTHUR against President Truman, and formed a close working alliance with Sen. Joseph McCARTHY. As the 1952 Presidential election neared, he ingratiated himself with Dwight D. Eisenhower by undermining the candidacies of Sen. Robert Taft (*see* MR. REPUBLICAN) and his fellow-Californian Governor Earl WARREN. Eisenhower picked Nixon as his RUNNING-MATE, one Republican pol recalling: "We took Dick Nixon not because he was right-wing or left-wing, but because he came from California and we were tired." The campaign went well until the Checkers affair broke, IKE being poised to drop him from the ticket until Nixon turned the situation round. At one point Nixon told the Presidential nominee: "General, there comes a time when you have to piss or get off the pot." The signs of menace were also evident on the campaign trail; at one point Nixon told a HECKLER:

> When we're elected we'll take care of people like you.

As Vice-President, Nixon at first took a low profile, and with McCarthy broken, Eisenhower would have dropped him in 1956 but for conservative pressure; asked what decisions his VEEP had participated in, Eisenhower told reporters: "If you give me a week, I might think of one." In his second term he was more active, braving anti-American demonstrators in Latin America and conducting his celebrated KITCHEN DEBATE with the Soviet leader Nikita Khruschev. In 1960 he was well-placed for a first run at the Presidency, but was wrong-footed after the inert Eisenhower years by the "youth" challenge of John F. KENNEDY, who in reality was little younger than Nixon. The Republican nominee fought a workmanlike campaign and "won" the DEBATES on radio – but his FIVE O'CLOCK SHADOW contributed to his "losing" them on television and he went down to a very narrow defeat. Two years later he took on "Pat" Brown for the governorship of California (*see* HUGHES LOAN), and on losing announced his retirement, telling reporters: "You won't have NIXON TO KICK AROUND ANY MORE."

For the next six years Nixon quietly and conscientiously built a network of support in the Republican Party, and in 1968 was the pre-eminent candidate to recover the White House from the split and demoralized Democrats. Nominating him at the Republican national convention, Spiro Agnew proclaimed:

> When a nation is in crisis and history speaks firmly to that nation, it needs a man to catch the time. You don't create such a man; you don't discover such a man – you recognize such a man.

And Nixon, in his ACCEPTANCE speech, declared: "Let us begin by committing ourselves to the truth." He went on to defeat Vice-President Hubert Humphrey (*see* HAPPY WARRIOR), though not by as much as expected.

In office Nixon assumed the trappings of the IMPERIAL PRESIDENCY, attracting some ridicule, but he set in place a workmanlike administration which initially pursued radical domestic policies before lapsing into BENIGN NEGLECT. On the world stage he was greatly helped by his National Security Adviser Henry KISSINGER as he first pursued and then wound down the VIETNAM WAR, established DÉTENTE with the Soviet Union, wielded unprecedented influence in the Middle East and – reversing his own deep commitments of two decades before – paved the way for normal relations with Communist China. With the Democrats in 1972 committed to a suicidally radical PLATFORM, Nixon massively won re-election, but sowed the seeds of his disgrace in the process. Kissinger was later to observe:

> Nixon had three goals: to win by the biggest electoral LANDSLIDE in history; to be remembered as a peacemaker; and to be accepted by the establishment as an equal. He achieved all these objectives – and he lost them all two months later.

The Watergate burglary never caught on as an election issue, but in the ensuing months the COVER-UP and related lawbreaking was traced ever closer to the White House, and the administration was not helped by the forced resignation of Vice-President AGNEW for accepting kickbacks. Nixon pursued his foreign-policy agenda faster and faster while fighting an increasingly desperate battle to convince Congress and the American people that Watergate was not his problem, and becoming ever more embattled, telling close aides: "Nobody is a friend of ours, let's face it." The disclosure of the Watergate tapes did him incalculable damage, as his statement on releasing them that "I am placing my trust in the basic fairness of the American people" was not reciprocated. Of this period Dan Rather commented:

> There were days when the entire White House seemed to be in the grip of a morbid obsession, not unlike the mood aboard the *Pequod* when Ahab was at the helm.

Kissinger more prosaically, but just as alarmingly, observed: "Sometimes I get worried. The President is like a madman." With the House of Representatives moving to IMPEACH him, he resigned the Presidency on 8 August 1974. Echoing his Checkers broadcast, he declared:

> I have never been a quitter. To leave office before my term is completed is abhorrent to every instinct in my body.

Nixon – PARDONed almost immediately by his successor Gerald FORD – flew in disgrace to his compound at SAN CLEMENTE with his loyal wife Pat. He said of her demeanour over Watergate: "She has always conducted herself with masterful poise and dignity. But, God, how she could have gone through what she does, I simply don't know." Nixon suffered serious illness (phlebitis) before beginning a gradual political rehabilitation. His FROST INTERVIEWS in 1977 were marked by self-justification and an unwillingness to concede the full scale of his wrongdoing, but he did admit:

> I let down my friends, I let down my country, I let down our system of government.

They also reminded Americans of his considerable abilities, and Nixon's subsequent autobiography, *RN*, further demonstrated the strengths that had made him in many ways a highly accomplished President. Disbarred in New York in 1976, he made a first political reappearance in Kentucky in 1978, and in 1981 returned to centre-stage at a FUND-RAISER in Ohio. In his old age he remained a figure of controversy, but no longer the pariah he had been after his resignation.

> He has no taste. JOHN F. KENNEDY.

> Wandering limply and wetly about the American heartland begging votes on the excuse that he had been too poor to have a pony when he was a boy.
> MURRAY KEMPTON, 1960.

> Nixon is a shifty-eyed goddam liar and everyone knows it. He is one of the few men in the history of this country to run for high office talking out of both sides of his mouth at the same time and lying out of both sides.
> HARRY S. TRUMAN, *Plain Speaking*.

> Nixon essentially impeached himself. He had done everything possible to show how guilty he was.
> Rep. JOHN CONYERS (Dem.).

> He had the morals of a private detective.
> WILLIAM S. BURROUGHS (1914–).

> His motto was, if two wrongs don't make a right, try three. NORMAN COUSINS (1915–).

> To have striven so hard, to have molded a public personality out of so amorphous an identity, to have sustained that superhuman effort only to end with every weakness disclosed and every error compounded: that was a fate of Biblical proportions. HENRY KISSINGER.

> I would have made a good Pope. NIXON.

See also I AM NOT A CROOK; last PRESS CONFERENCE; WOULD YOU BUY A USED CAR FROM THIS MAN?

tricolour Any national flag made up of equal bands of three colours. In the case of the French and the Irish flags the combination has had particular revolutionary connotations; indeed until the mid-1980s it was an offence to fly the Irish flag in NORTHERN IRELAND in some circumstances.

Trident (1) The codename of the US–UK conference held in Washington from 12 to 25 May 1943. At it Franklin D. Roosevelt pressed a British commitment to open a SECOND FRONT by a cross-Channel invasion of France; CHURCHILL argued for an attack on Sicily followed by an invasion of Italy. A compromise was reached, with FDR agreeing to preparations to invade Italy, and Churchill agreeing to landings in France on 1 May 1944; prior to it, there would be a combined bombing offensive to destroy German military, industrial and economic capacity. The US Pacific strategy was approved – and it was secretly agreed that the MANHATTAN PROJECT to develop the atomic bomb should be a joint enterprise. (2) The US submarine-launched ballistic missile (SLBM) system developed as a replacement for *Poseidon*, which Britain acquired as an infinitely deadlier successor to POLARIS. Deployed by America from the early 1980s, each missile carries eight 100-kiloton MIRVs with a range of up to 6900 miles (11,000 km.). Trident II, with greater accuracy and more powerful warheads, was developed for deployment by both America and Britain from the early 1990s. The political storm in Britain over Trident was less intense than over the deployment of CRUISE missiles, and by 1992 the only live questions were whether three or four submarines should be constructed, and whether a new generation of ARMS CONTROL agreements with Russia might jeopardize the entire undertaking.

Trilateral Commission A group of 325 highly influential current and retired political figures from Western industrial nations who meet regularly to discuss world problems and offer possible solutions. Founded in 1973 with backing from Rockefeller interests, and with an unlisted member in New York City, the Commission is regarded by some CONSPIRACY THEORISTS in America as a vehicle for bypassing and subverting elected governments in pursuit of an unstated grand design against the true interests of mankind; the truth is almost certainly far more prosaic and innocuous.

trimmer A PRAGMATIST who trims his or her sails to catch the prevailing political wind, changing tack instead of remaining true to fixed principles (*see also* VICAR OF BRAY). The term dates from the 1680s, when George Savile, 1st Marquess of Halifax (1633–95), gained the nickname "Halifax the Trimmer" because of his uncommitted position between WHIGs and TORIES and his willingness to compromise and shift his ground. Halifax treated it as a compliment, saying:

> True virtue hath ever been thought a Trimmer, and to have its dwelling in the middle of two extremes.

Trinidad terms A formula for forgiving the debts of the world's poorest countries that was proposed by John MAJOR when Chancellor of the Exchequer and agreed by Commonwealth finance ministers at a meeting in port of Spain, Trinidad, in September 1990 and subsequently largely accepted by the Paris Club and the main creditor nations. By early 1993 $3.5 billion in debt had been rescheduled or forgiven.

Tripartite pact The extension of the Rome-Berlin AXIS on 27 September 1940 to include Japan; it committed the signatories to a ten-year military alliance. Japan had initially refused Hitler's invitation to join the Axis powers in 1939 but reversed the decision after the outbreak of war, when German successes against France and Belgium left their Far Eastern colonies vulnerable to Japanese attack. Japan hoped that support from Germany and Italy would deter the Soviet Union and America from opposing her plans for southern expansion. In the event, there was no attempt to co-ordinate German and Japanese strategy after 1940, although in 1941 Hitler unwisely promised to support Japan if she attacked America. After PEARL HARBOR Germany duly declared war on America – effectively guaranteeing her own defeat. The Axis was later joined by Hungary, Bulgaria, Romania, Slovakia and Croatia.

Triple Alliance The pact between unions in Britain representing miners, dockers and railwaymen to threaten a national strike for improved conditions in the autumn of 1914. It built on the success of a wave of strikes two years previously, but was rendered abortive by the outbreak of World War I. The miners tried to revive the alliance in 1921, but only found co-ordinated support during the brief GENERAL STRIKE of 1926.

Triple Entente *See* ENTENTE.

troika A Russian word for a carriage pulled by three horses, which has a number of political and diplomatic applications. It is used for any three representatives of different governments working to achieve a particular end. Specifically it applies to the three EC Foreign Ministers who conduct diplomacy together to ensure continuity; they represent the state now holding the PRESIDENCY, the previous president nation and the one that will take over at the end of the next half-year. In Washington the term is applied to the combination of the Treasury, Office of Management and Budget (OMB) and Council of Economic Advisers when they stage a joint review of the economy.

Troika plan The demand, first made by Nikita Khruschev on 23 September 1962, for the replacement of the Secretary-General of the UNITED NATIONS with a three-man *troika*. Throughout the 1950s the Soviet Union regarded the UN as a tool of the capitalist West and its Secretary-General, Dag Hammarskjold, as a NATO puppet. Khruschev's attempt after Hammarskjold's death to replace the post with a *troika* of a Western representative, one from the Soviet bloc and one from the THIRD WORLD was rejected as an assault on the independence and capacity to act of the world body and a ploy to extend Soviet influence.

Trot A UK term for a **Trotskyist**, a supporter of the ideology of PERMANENT REVOLUTION promulgated by **Leon Trotsky** (Lev Davidovich Bronstein, 1879–1940). The word is applied not only to the MILITANT TENDENCY, who pride themselves on being Trotskyists, but loosely, incorrectly and as a term of abuse to the entire non-Communist revolutionary left. Trotsky himself was a Jew born in the Ukraine, who was exiled to Siberia for his revolutionary activities but escaped in 1902 to join LENIN in London. He returned to Russia in 1905 after that year's abortive revolution to head the first Soviet in St. Petersburg, but again went through the cycle of arrest, exile and escape. Expelled from Paris in 1916 for making PACIFIST propaganda, he returned to Russia with Lenin the next year to organize the OCTOBER REVOLUTION. As COMMISSAR for Foreign Affairs from 1917 to 1925, he negotiated the peace of Brest-Litovsk with Germany, but he is better remembered for creating the RED ARMY, a force of 5 million men to defend the Revolution. In Trotsky's view that Revolution could only survive if there were continual and parallel revolutions in the West, but as the prospect of this receded, so did his chances of succeeding Lenin. On Lenin's death in 1924 STALIN manoeuvred himself into power, and when Trotsky organised factions of his own, Stalin had him expelled from the party in 1927 and exiled two years later. From this point, Trotsky became a traitor in the eyes of Moscow-line Communists, and "Trotskyist" a term of abuse. After a time fomenting revolution in Turkey, Trotsky mobilized his supporters to fight in the SPANISH CIVIL WAR, then in 1937 settled in Mexico – where three years later he was murdered with an ICE-AXE by a Stalinist agent, Ramon Mercader.

> Our standard is, clearly, political, imperative and intolerant. TROTSKY, *Literature and Revolution* (1924).

> It is well to know the limitations of force; to know when to blend force with manoeuvre, assault with conciliation.
> TROTSKY, *What Now?* (1932).

> In a serious struggle there is no worse cruelty than to be magnanimous at an inopportune time.
> TROTSKY, *History of the Russian Revolution* (1933).

> The end may justify the means, as long as there is something that justifies the end.
> TROTSKY, *An Introduction to His Thought*.

Troubles, the The term originally applied to the vicious civil war in Ireland between January 1919, when the newly-formed IRA took up arms to drive out the British, and April 1923 when rival forces in the newly-independent IRISH FREE STATE laid down their arms. The initial conflict was bloody enough, especially after Britain introduced the BLACK AND TANS to coerce the population. But the civil strife south of the Border imposed in 1921 was more bitter still, with forces for and against the IRISH TREATY indulging in an orgy of terrorism and murder, which a few extreme Republicans continued after the majority accepted partition in 1922. The word is nowadays used also to describe the civil and sectarian strife in NORTHERN IRELAND since 1969, when Britain sent in regular troops to protect the Catholic minority against harassment; the Army soon became, and has remained, the target of a renewed terrorist campaign by the Provisional IRA, with LOYALIST terrorists responding in kind and both sides also indulging in racketeering and extortion; to date over 3000 people have died.

Truck Acts The Acts passed at Westminster in 1831, 1887 and 1896 to end the system under which some companies refused to pay their workers in cash, instead allowing them credit at a company store. The practice was not confined to Britain; Tennessee Ernie Ford, in his 1956 hit *16 Tons*, sang of having "pledged my soul to the company store". The Acts were repealed in 1985 as an anomaly preventing firms paying staff wages straight into their bank accounts, and by 1993 cases were being reported of garage workers being sacked for refusing to accept overtime payments in the form of department store vouchers.

Trudeau. Trudeau pilgrimage The mildly derogatory name given by Canadian Conservatives to the "peace initiative" undertaken in the autumn of 1983 by the country's LIBERAL Prime Minister **Pierre-Elliot Trudeau** (1919–). With East-West tension rising, Trudeau visited world leaders to propose a combined effort to cool US and Soviet tempers over nuclear arms, Nicaragua, Poland and other issues. Trudeau got a warm welcome in most COMMONWEALTH countries, but his mission upset the Reagan administration, one under-secretary of State comparing him with a leftist high on marijuana. Trudeau scornfully replied:

> The kind of third-rate, third-level pipsqueaks who say I'm not allowed to participate in the peace process because we don't contribute enough to NATO – that's BALONEY.

Trudeau, Prime Minister from 1968 to 1984 (apart from a short break in 1980–81), was Canada's most charismatic leader, and a world figure in his own right. A radical Francophone Montreal law professor and propagandist who had originally backed the NDP, he joined the Liberals and in 1966 was elected to the Commons, where he made an immediate impact. The next year he became Minister of Justice and Attorney-General, taking an uncompromisingly hard line with Quebec SEPARATISTS who quickly came to loathe him, and in 1968 succeeded Lester Pearson as Prime Minister. Trudeau, an open man with a trendy streak just right for young voters at the end of the "swinging sixties", immediately called and won an election – and was to be re-elected in 1974 and 1979. At home the integrity of the nation was his greatest headache as the separatist FLQ stepped up its campaign and he met force with toughness (*see* WAR MEASURES ACT; BLEEDING-HEARTS). After the violence subsided, the Parti Québecois (PQ) won power in the province but failed in a REFERENDUM to win approval for its SOVEREIGNTY-ASSOCIATION form of separatism. Trudeau commented of his handling of the situation:

> My driving forces were twofold. One was to make sure that Quebec would not leave Canada through separatism and the other was to make sure that Canada wouldn't shove Quebec out through narrow-mindedness.

Trudeau adopted an independent line toward the United States, renouncing nuclear weapons in 1977, but behind the scenes he was quietly co-operative. Trudeau gave Canada a strong voice in the COMMONWEALTH, and also made the country respected in the THIRD WORLD. His public image always attracted comment; his marriage to the young "flower child" student Margaret Sinclair attracted publicity, but nothing like as much as when she deserted him and their three young sons for a series of flings with celebrities – once leaving Trudeau to host alone a dinner for James Callaghan (*see* SUNNY JIM) – before finally walking out on him. At least one of Trudeau's election victories was attributed in part to his appearance on the STUMP as a lone parent with the boys alongside him. Yet Trudeau himself also had a deserved reputation as a *bon vivant*. In the House of Commons he could be mordant, saying of one critic: "The Honourable Gentleman disagrees. I hear him shaking his head." And when he was criticized for installing a new swimming pool at SUSSEX DRIVE, he told them: "You may come over any time to practice your diving – preferably before the water is in." (*See also* FUCK). Discontent over the economy, among other issues, brought him defeat in 1980 at the hands of Joe Clark (*see* JOE WHO?), but he was back in power again the following year and served until 1984 before finally stepping down. The main achievement of his final term was the PATRIATION of Canada's constitution, but he was unable to follow this up with agreement among the provinces on how to amend it.

> In Pierre-Elliott Trudeau, Canada at last has a political leader worthy of assassination.
> IRVING LAYTON (1912–), *The Whole Bloody Bird* (1969).

> For Socialists, getting into bed with him is like having oral sex with a shark. LARRY ZOFF (1934–).

Truman Committee The committee investigating graft and incompetence in the American military and war industries which made Harry S. Truman's national reputation, and saved the taxpayer an estimated $15 billion from its formation in 1941. Truman heard of waste and corruption at first hand in Missouri during his 1940 re-election campaign, and on his return made such a fuss that the Senate set up a special panel and put him in charge of it. Its effectiveness in unearthing scandals turned Truman (*see* GIVE 'EM HELL HARRY) from someone hardly known outside his home state into FDR's choice as his Vice-President in 1944.

Truman Doctrine The strategy set out by President Truman in March 1947 for the CONTAINMENT of the Soviet Union by granting US economic and military aid to the peoples of Europe to resist Soviet aggression and encroachment. The immediate occasion was Soviet pressure on Greece and Turkey and the inability of Britain, out of money and paralysed by the FUEL CRISIS, to resist the threat itself. Truman went before a JOINT SESSION of Congress to ask for $350 million in assistance for the two countries, and was granted it; but the principle was general and set the tone for US policy throughout the COLD WAR. Truman told the Congress:

> It must be the policy of the United States to support free peoples who are resisting attempted subjugation by armed minorities or by outside pressures.

to err is Truman One of the slogans from Thomas E. DEWEY's Republican Presidential campaign in 1948, which appeared victorious until the last votes were counted. It was a play on the old saying "to err is human".

trust. Anti-Trust legislation *See* ANTI.

blind trust A trust into which a politician taking salaried public office may put his or her assets in order to avoid a Conflict of INTEREST. The critical feature of the trust is that it is administered without the knowledge of the beneficiary.

we don't trust anybody over 30 One of the basic mottoes of late-1960s student radicals, coined in 1965 by the Free Speech movement at Berkeley University, California.

when a man assumes a public trust, he becomes public property Thomas JEFFERSON's dictum about the need for probity and transparency among public servants, said to Baron von Humboldt in 1807. On other occasions Jefferson voiced resentment at the loss of privacy he had suffered through public interest in his personal affairs.

trusteeship The procedure under which certain COLONIAL territories being prepared for independence were assigned by the UNITED NATIONS to a member state for administration. The lands in question were previously mandated to member states of the LEAGUE OF NATIONS, or were colonies taken from the AXIS powers at the end of WORLD WAR II. The last such land to receive independence was Namibia, a former mandated territory retained by South Africa in defiance of the UN.

truth A less controversial commodity in politics than LIES, though cynics would say this is because there is less of it around. It can also meet with greater suspicion: Benjamin Disraeli remarked that "something unpleasant is coming when men are anxious to speak the truth", Bismarck that "when you want to fool the world, tell the truth", and Adlai Stevenson that "the truth is often unpopular. We Americans are suckers for good news." Thomas JEFFERSON took the purist view that "It is error alone that needs the support of government. Truth can stand by itself." And Gerald FORD, after WATERGATE, asserted: "Truth is the glue that holds governments together". Yet Arthur BALFOUR insisted: "It has always been desirable to tell the truth, but seldom possible (if ever necessary) to tell the whole truth," and Speaker Sam RAYBURN warned colleagues: "You'll get mixed up if you simply tell the truth. Then you don't have to remember what you have said, and you never forget what you said." Will Rogers put it even more bluntly:

> If you ever injected truth into politics, you would have no politics.

truth is the first casualty The warning about the propensity of governments to tell lies to justify their conduct of a war, first given in that form either by Sen. Hiram Johnson (1866–1945) in a speech to the US Senate when America was entering WORLD WAR I, or in Britain by Arthur Ponsonby at much the same time. Johnson said:

> The first casualty when war comes is truth.

and Ponsonby: "When war is declared, truth is the first casualty." The sentiment was not original, however; in 1758 Dr. Samuel Johnson wrote in *The Idler*:

> Among the calamities of war, may be justly numbered the diminution of the love of truth, by the falsehood which interest dictates, as credulity encourages.

More recently Speaker TIP O'Neill broadened the saying's application, declaring with equal justification:

> Truth is the first casualty in the heat of a political campaign.

economical with the truth The words for which the SPYCATCHER affair is best remembered, and which demonstrated the cultural gulf between the Whitehall MANDARIN and the rest of humanity – particularly in Australia. They were uttered in the Supreme Court of New South Wales in November 1986 by the UK CABINET SECRETARY Sir Robert Armstrong (1927–), who was testifying in support of Margaret Thatcher's determination to prevent Peter Wright's book on wrongdoing in MI5 being published in Australia. The critical exchange ran:

> *Malcolm Turnbull* (counsel for Wright): What's a misleading impression? A kind of bent untruth?
> *Armstrong:* As one person said, it is perhaps being economical with the truth.

Armstrong was intending to deliver a silken *bon mot* about the use of language, but appeared to his down-to-earth observers to be trying to admit telling a lie without actually doing so; not surprisingly the UK government lost the case. The trip was a harrowing one for Armstrong, who on leaving Heathrow had taken an out-of-character swing at a press photographer. The words were not in fact a devious invention; the cultured Armstrong was repeating a phrase previously used by (among others) Arnold Bennett, Mark Twain, Edmund BURKE and Samuel Pepys. But it has since entered the political vocabulary as a euphemism for a lie.

pricking the bladder of falsehood with the poignard of truth One of the most elegant phrases used in Parliamentary oratory by Aneurin BEVAN (*see also* NYE), in an exchange with Winston CHURCHILL over the devaluation of the pound. When Churchill complained that he was being accused of telling lies, the SPEAKER replied: "Oh, I thought it was a quotation." MPs present marvelled, as on many other occasions, at Bevan's ability to bring to life with colourful language what others would have delivered as a routine and impactless insult.

We hold these truths to be self-evident: That all men are created equal, that they are endowed by their Creator with certain inalienable rights, that among these are life, liberty and the pursuit of happiness The majestic opening sentence of the second paragraph of the preamble to the Declaration of INDEPENDENCE, as finally drafted by Thomas JEFFERSON. It forms part of a longer extract inscribed on the Jefferson Memorial in WASHINGTON DC. Jefferson had not wanted to write the Declaration, but John ADAMS, another of the five-strong drafting committee, told him: "You write ten times better than I do". Jefferson's original draft in June 1776 began:

> We hold these truths to be sacred and undeniable: that all men are created equal and independent, that from that equal creation they derive rights inherent and inalienable, among which are the preservation of life, and liberty, and the pursuit of happiness.

Tsar The title of the former Emperors of Russia, the autocratic and frequently brutal system which they headed being known as the Tsarist state. The word is, like *Kaiser*, a corruption of the Latin *Caesar*. *See also* CZAR.

TSR2 The strike-reconnaissance aircraft cancelled by Britain's Labour government in April 1965 after hundreds of millions of pounds had been spent on its development. The aviation lobby dates the end of Britain as a major aircraft-building power from this date, but Defence Secretary Denis Healey argued that the cost of the programme, which had tripled to £750 million since 1960 with the first production plane still two years away, could not be justified when the cheaper US F111 could be bought "off the shelf". Three years later, the F111 purchase was also cancelled. Healey reckoned that a British solution could have been found at the outset by a variant of the Royal Navy's Buccaneer strike aircraft – but the RAF would not accept a Navy product.

Tube Alloys The codename of the committee set up in October 1941 to supervise UK research into nuclear fission during WORLD WAR II. It was formed as a division of the Department of Scientific and Industrial Research under Sir John Anderson, Lord President of the Council. The Tube Alloys committee itself was headed by Wallace Akers, Research Director of ICI, and his assistant Michael Perrin. At the TRIDENT Anglo-American conference in May 1943 it was secretly agreed that developing an atomic bomb should be a joint effort between Tube Alloys and the US MANHATTAN PROJECT.

TUC Trades Union Congress. The body founded in 1868 which represents and co-ordinates the activities of most of Britain's major TRADE UNIONS, and was memorably compared with a CARTHORSE by the left-wing cartoonist Low. Its Congress at the start of September each year is not only the annual showcase for the views of organized labour, but the start of the CONFERENCE SEASON; its executive body is the General Council. With an affiliated membership which has at times exceeded 8 million, the TUC in theory has enormous strength, but has seldom exercised it. Its most critical moment on the politico-industrial stage came in 1926 when it orchestrated the GENERAL STRIKE in support of the miners; in the early 1980s it did stage a series of markedly unsuccessful "days of ACTION" against trade union laws planned by the Thatcher government (*see* STEP BY STEP). For most of its history individual unions and their leaders have either been in the forefront, or have been so divided by personalities or ideology as to blunt the effectiveness of the movement. Few of the TUC's general secretaries have been heavyweights; an exception was Walter (later Lord) Citrine who, with Ernest BEVIN, chairman of the General Council, handled the General Strike and afterward developed a less confrontational stance that led CHURCHILL to include Bevin in his wartime government, with conspicuous success. The TUC has a close relationship with the LABOUR PARTY, but the membership and interests of the two are not identical; several "non-political" unions are not affiliated to the party. The TUC is able to influence Labour governments, and *vice versa* (*see* SOCIAL CONTRACT), but the relationship can fray if Labour tries to curb INFLATION or STRIKES without first wooing the unions. Traditionally the TUC and Tory governments have attacked each other in public but talked quietly behind the scenes, but Margaret Thatcher set a new style by ignoring both the TUC and the unions as a whole; the last tie was broken in 1991 with the abolition of NEDDY. The refusal of some unions to accept the NEW REALISM of the 1980s led the electricians to pull out of the TUC, the first major defection it had suffered; they were likely to return after merging in 1992 with the engineers, who had stayed in.

> If the TUC entered a javelin-throwing contest, they would elect to receive.
>
> NORMAN WILLIS, TUC General Secretary 1984–).

Tupamaros (MLN – *Movimiento de Liberacion Nacional*) The Uruguayan urban GUERRILLA group, most of them professional men and women, who in the early 1970s reduced the country to near chaos with kidnappings, bank robberies and daring escapes from prison – one in 1972 involving a breakout by 14 guerrillas through a 200 ft. tunnel. Well armed and equipped, they had not only a network of safe houses but laboratories capable of forging almost anything and a chain of emergency clinics. The Tupamaros, who took their name from the last great Inca leader Tupac Amaru who held out against the Spaniards, were formed *c.* 1963 out of a militant Socalist faction in a sugar workers' union. From 1973 they were ruthlessly suppressed by the military under President Juan Maria Bordaberry.

> Everybody dances, or nobody dances.
>
> Tupamaro slogan.

turf battle A dispute between two politicians or officials in which each claims responsbility for a certain programme, area of policy or set of staff.

turkeys voting for an early Christmas The memorable phrase used by James Callaghan (*see* SUNNY JIM) in the House of Commons on 28 March 1979 to describe Scottish Nationalist (SNP) MPs who had tabled a no-CONFIDENCE motion in the Government and now stood to lose their seats if the vote forced a General Election. He was also making the point that while the SNP might consider Labour over-cautious over DEVOLUTION, they had no chance of achieving any measure of HOME RULE if Margaret Thatcher's Conservatives came to power. Callaghan's forecast was accurate: Labour lost that night by one vote (311–310), the SNP lost nine of their eleven seats and Mrs. Thatcher went on to become the most unpopular Prime Minister in Scotland in living memory.

turn. turncoat Someone who deserts a political cause and goes over to its opponents. The word was reputedly first used of a Duke of Saxony whose coat was white (for France) on one side, and blue (for Spain) on the other; its use in a political sense dates back at least to 1557, but after four and a half centuries it is as cutting a term of abuse as ever.

turnout The percentage of registered voters who cast their ballots in an election, a figure ranging from 10% or less in some UK council by-elections to over 100% in a few areas where PERSONATION is rife. Turnout in US Presidential elections is customarily between 50 and 60%, and in UK General Elections around 75%; in Australia where voting is compulsory the figure is nearer 95%, deaths and unavoidable absences making up most of the difference. The term **percentage poll** is used as an alternative to turnout; in its 1989 Euro-election results coverage the *Guardian* programmed the word "poll" to appear as "turnout" throughout. This was unfortunate for a victorious Labour candidate whose name was Anita Pollack, and appeared both in the paper – and a subsequent attempted correction – as Anita Turnoutack.

TV affair The farcical scandal that broke in Australia in April 1982 over an alleged COVER-UP of the import of a television set the previous October by Michael Mackellar, Health Minister in Malcolm Fraser's Liberal government, and whose handling weakened Fraser's hold on power. Mackellar's customs declaration card, signed by one of his staff, had "No" written against the question of whether he had a TV set with him, even though he was carrying it under his arm. Colour sets were liable to duty, black-and-white sets not, and Mackellar and the customs officer who challenged him had different recollections of which he said it was; it was in fact colour. Customs Minister John Moore rang Mackellar to voice concern and told officials he wanted no more inaccurate statements; the matter was then regarded as closed. Mackellar wrote offering to pay any duty and received no reply, despite a 1976 circular stressing that Ministers must not receive preferential Customs treatment. When the story broke, Fraser demanded that Mackellar and Moore produce a statement of what had happened, and when they could not agree the wording, he and the media pressed them to resign, which they did. When told by other colleagues that he was setting excessively high standards, Fraser replied:

> Some of my colleagues would find it difficult to understand the distinction which a prime minister has to maintain between loyalty to values and loyalty to people. . . . If he is not loyal to the values that are important, who else is going to be?

TVA (1) Tennessee Valley Authority. The Federal corporation created by Franklin D. Roosevelt in 1933 as one of the first elements in his NEW DEAL, to develop the basin of the Tennessee River, mostly to build dams for flood control and provide cheap electric power. Its central feature was the Wilson Dam and accompanying electric plants and factories at Muscle Shoals, begun as a munitions complex in World War I but never completed owing to conservative opposition in Congress; the agency set up by FDR to supervise this and further tasks was "clothed with the power of government but possessed of the flexibility and initiative of private enterprise". Critics assailed this measure to combat the effects of the GREAT DEPRESSION on an already impoverished area as "creeping SOCIALISM", and the TVA's existence remained a source of political controversy for years, with private electric companies fuelling the opposition. However the TVA is now highly regarded: it has turned a once-backward area into a prosperous farming and industrial centre. Its 39 dams and about 160 non-profit-making power distributors provide electricity at one-third less than the US average cost to consumers in a 210,000 sq. km. (80,000 sq. mile) area. The river, which once flooded regularly, has been converted into a series of lakes. (2) In France, the abbreviation for VAT (*Taxe de Valeur Additionelle*).

Tweed ring The group of corrupt TAMMANY HALL politicians headed by William M. (BOSS) TWEED who defrauded residents of New York of up to $100 million before they were brought down in 1871. The ring's destruction was largely due to investigative reporting by the *New York Times* and the incisive cartoons of Thomas Nast.

Twelfth amendment The amendment to the US CONSTITUTION, proposed in December 1803 and RATIFIED the following September, which prevented anyone from seeking the offices of both President and Vice-President, and thus established the principle of PARTY and the TICKET. Until then the runner-up in the Presidential contest automatically became Vice-President, regardless of whether the two held compatible opinions or even wanted to work together. It stemmed from the outcome of the REVOLUTION OF 1800 when Thomas JEFFERSON and Aaron BURR, whose names were on the same ballot even though Burr was known to be Jefferson's choice as his deputy, tied and it took 36 ballots in the House of Representatives to decide between them.

twenty. Twenty-Two, the The colloquial name among Conservative MPs at Westminster for the 1922 COMMITTEE.

Twenty-second amendment The amendment to the US CONSTITUTION forced through by vindictive Republicans during the Truman administration to check the Democratic ascendancy by ensuring that no President ever again served more than two terms, as Franklin D. Roosevelt had done. It was to rebound on them, as the only two Presidents since who might have sought, and won, a third term, were Dwight D. Eisenhower and Ronald Reagan – both Republicans. Under the amendment, proposed in 1947 and ratified in March 1951, no President who has completed two terms, or has completed two or more years of another President's term and then served a term of their own, may run again. The maximum a President could thus serve would be ten years minus one day; Truman was exempt from this provision, but decided not to run again in 1952.

Twenty-fifth amendment The further amendment to the Constitution, proposed in 1965 and RATIFIED in February 1967, which sought after John F. KENNEDY's assassination to end confusion over the PRESIDENTIAL SUCCESSION. It established for the first time that a VICE-PRESIDENT taking over the office of President actually became President, thus validating the position of John Tyler, who on William Harrison's death in 1841 had to establish that he was President in name and fact. It also provided for the President to nominate a new Vice-President if a vacancy arose, subject to confirmation by a majority of both houses of Congress; this provision was exercised twice in 1973–74, with Gerald FORD, the first nominee, becoming President within months. The amendment also empowered the President to designate the Vice-President as acting President in the case of his own incapacity, and the Vice-President and Cabinet to do so if the President became "unable to discharge the powers and duties of his office". A two-thirds majority in each house of Congress would be necessary for such a Vice-Presidential declaration to take effect.

Twenty-Six Counties The term used by Irish Republicans for the IRISH FREE STATE and the fully-sovereign republic that succeeded it. There are 32 Irish counties, and reference to the Republic in this way is a statement of support for a united Ireland and the ending of PARTITION. By the same token, Nationalists refer to Northern Ireland as the SIX COUNTIES.

26th July movement The political group formed in Cuba by Fidel Castro at a meeting with close colleagues on 19 July 1955 to further his revolutionary goals, and support the trained guerrilla group he hoped to form in

Mexico (*see* GRANMA) to overthrow President Fulgencio Batista; it evolved into a guerrilla group itself. Many of its members were to be prominent in the Marxist government Castro eventually formed after toppling Batista in 1959. The movement's name was adopted in the weeks after its formation; it apparently refers to an inaugural meeting of its members after Castro had left for Mexico.

twin. twin pyramids of the Nile The alleged remark by President CARTER's chief of staff Hamilton Jordan at a Washington dinner in 1977 that delighted prurient gossip columnists in the capital, and enabled them to build on the myth that Carter's entourage even at the highest levels were gauche Georgia REDNECKS. Jordan, the astute political strategist who had played a large part in propelling the virtually-unknown Carter into the White House, was supposed to have used the phrase while staring down the cleavage of Mme. Ghorbal, wife of the Egyptian ambassador.

twin-track strategy A description of any policy combining two separate actions. It was heavily used by Western politicians to characterize NATO's dual policy on CRUISE MISSILES of deploying them to meet the threat from Soviet SS20s in Eastern Europe while negotiating for the removal of both. And at his first White House meeting with Bill Clinton in February 1993, John MAJOR used it to describe the relief programme for Bosnia, combining distribution of food by land by UK and other forces, and the US plan to drop supplies by air to Muslim communities behind Serb lines which the ground forces could not reach.

two-door system A way round the statute dating from 1863 which prevents members of the US CONGRESS who are lawyers from representing clients with claims against the Federal government. A Congressman's name will appear on his law firm's front door, through which the bulk of his or her clients enter; next to it is another door minus the legislator's name, through which those with cases in the restricted category are ushered. New York's Rep. Emmanuel Celler, a veteran of the House with almost 50 years' service, came under media criticism for the practice, Robert Sherrill terming it "one of the longest-standing and most notorious embarrassments to Congress". Celler replied:

> Your constituents are the final arbiter of any conflicts [of interest], and I'm always re-elected.

Shortly afterward, in 1972, he was unseated in a Democratic PRIMARY by Elizabeth Holtzman.

Two Camps doctrine The doctrine, first advanced by LENIN, that the communist and capitalist worlds are condemned to a struggle that must end in victory for one side or the other. In the Communist view the climactic event would probably be a war resorted to by the capitalists because they could not succeed in peaceful competition. As developed under STALIN, there was no such thing as a single world society, and thus no impartial and all-embracing role for a world body like the UNITED NATIONS. *See also* TROIKA PLAN.

two plus four talks The talks which hammered out the legal and constitutional small print of German re-UNIFICATION in 1990, and the end of the four-power status under which Berlin was still nominally under the control of the World War II Allies: the US, Soviet Union, Britain and France. The talks involved representatives from West and East Germany and the four "occupying" powers, but in practice it was the Germans who took the decisions, the others (despite stated misgivings from Margaret Thatcher) having no wish or ability to prevent the Germans reuniting.

two-way street A phrase often heard, but seldom honoured, in speeches about trans-atlantic arms procurement. It stems from repeated attempts by Britain and other West European countries to ensure that in return for their agreeing to purchase costly items of American hardware, the PENTAGON will purchase a corresponding value of equipment from them. Promises have frequently been made, especially in the late 1970s, and some items of UK and European equipment have entered service with the US military, but the traffic remains largely one way with UK spending on such items as TRIDENT and AWACS far from offset.

Tydings-McDuffie Act The Act passed by the US Congress in 1934, and unanimously ratified by the Philippine legislature, that established the then-US COLONY as a COMMONWEALTH, to become completely independent in 1946. Manuel Quezon became the Philippines' first president and prepared the way for independence, which came on schedule despite the Japanses occupation of the islands from 1941 until 1945.

Tyler, John *See* OLD VETO.

Tynwald The Parliament of the Isle of Man, whose principal House is the HOUSE OF KEYS. Until the summer of 1992 the PRESS GALLERY at Westminster boasted a collection of photographs and prints of *Parliament Houses of the Empire*, Tynwald being depicted by an open-sided marquee beside which its ceremonial opening was conducted.

tyranny The ruthless, absolute and by inference illegal exercise of power. John Locke (1632–1704) asserted that "wherever law ends, tyranny begins"; William Penn (1644–1718) is reputed to have said: "Men must be governed by God or they will be ruled by tyrants", and Thomas JEFFERSON declared that "resistance to tyrants is obedience to God". Jefferson's contemporary Thomas Paine, though a supposed atheist, also stressed the need for resistance, writing: "Tyranny, like hell, is not easily conquered . . . yet the harder the conflict, the more glorious the triumph." MAHATMA Gandhi took the high ground to argue: "The willing sacrifice of the innocents is the most powerful retort to insolent tyranny that has yet been conceived by god or man." Definitions of tyranny are highly subjective. De Tocqueville spoke of the "tyranny of the majority"; Dostoevsky asserted that "tyranny is a habit. It may develop, and does develop at last, into a disease"; Pierre Joseph Proudhon that "whoever puts his hand on me to govern me is a usurper and a tyrant; I declare him my enemy"; Louis de St. Just that "he who makes jokes as the head of a government has a tendency to tyranny".

> The only tyranny I accept in this world is the still voice within. GANDHI.

> Tyranny is the normal pattern of government. It is only by intense thought, by great effort, by burning idealism and unlimited sacrifice that freedom has prevailed. ADLAI STEVENSON.

U

U. U-turn A U-shaped reversal of direction by a ship or vehicle, used metaphorically of a fundamental change of POLICY or IDEOLOGY by a government or political leader. In November 1971 the term was widely used to describe the Heath (*see* GROCER) government's decision to abandon its previous policy of relying on MARKET Forces (*see* LAME DUCK) to curb inflation and revive the economy, and embark on an INTERVENTIONIST industrial policy with wage and price controls. In October 1980, Margaret Thatcher (*see* IRON LADY) scorned assertions by Tory WETS that she would be forced to perform a similar U-turn when she told the Conservative Party conference:

> U-turn if you want to. The lady's not for turning.

The phrase, inspired by the title of Christopher Fry's 1948 play *The Lady's Not for Burning*, was supplied by one of Mrs. Thatcher's speechwriters, the playwright Ronald Millar; he was knighted the same year. The term has also been used in a non-ideological sense. When John Biffen, a member of Mrs. Thatcher's Cabinet married well into middle age, the Labour front-bencher Denzil Davies said in the Commons:

> I congratulate the Rt. Hon. Gentleman on his own personal U-turn.

U-2 affair The incident that wrecked the much-heralded 1960 PARIS SUMMIT meeting, intensifying and prolonging the COLD WAR. On 1 May 1960, a fortnight before the Soviet leader Nikita Khruschev was due to meet his three Western counterparts, an American U-2 high-level reconnaissance aircraft was shot down by the Soviet Union; its pilot, Francis Gary Powers, was captured and confessed to spying. This was the first intimation of US spy missions over the Soviet Union, which President Eisenhower admitted had been under way for four years. Khruschev demanded an apology from Eisenhower and the punishment of those responsible for the flights. Eisenhower did halt the flights, but refused to apologize, calling espionage a "distasteful but vital necessity" brought about by the Soviets' "fetish of secrecy and concealment"; Khruschev cancelled the conference and Eisenhower's forthcoming visit to the Soviet Union. In 1962 the Soviets returned Powers in exchange for Colonel Rudolf Abel, a Soviet spy held in America; he became a helicopter pilot for a TV station in Los Angeles and was subsequently killed in a crash.

UDA Ulster Defence Association. The principal LOYALIST PARAMILITARY group in Northern Ireland, founded in 1971. It operated within the law with the Ulster Freedom Fighters acting as its terrorist wing, but in August 1992 was banned in Ulster – though not in mainland Britain. The UDA is strongest in East Belfast, but enjoys considerable support in western Scotland and even in Canada.

UDI Unilateral Declaration of INDEPENDENCE, specifically that by Southern Rhodesia (now Zimbabwe) on 11 November 1965. Southern Rhodesia was a self-governing British COLONY, and Ian Smith's government made the break, which had no legal validity, rather than accept Black MAJORITY RULE. UDI was ended by the LANCASTER HOUSE AGREEMENT of 1979, with British rule re-established prior to free elections and legitimate independence. *See* FEARLESS TALKS; NIBMAR; PRIME MINISTER, THINK AGAIN; RETURN TO LEGALITY; TIGER TALKS; WEEKS, RATHER THAN MONTHS.

> We have struck a blow for the preservation of justice, civilisation and Christianity; and in the spirit of this belief we have this day assumed our sovereign independence.
>
> IAN SMITH (1919–).

UDR Ulster Defence Regiment. The combined regular and part-time volunteer military force raised in Northern Ireland to support British forces and the Royal Ulster Constabulary (RUC). It was formed in 1970, following disbandment of the B SPECIALS, as a more professional and non-sectarian force; but partly because of threats against Catholic members from the IRA it became overwhelmingly Protestant, and some personnel were convicted of acts of LOYALIST terrorism. The UDR had a strength of just over 6000; more than 200 serving personnel plus a number of former members have been killed by the IRA. Under OPTIONS FOR CHANGE the UDR was amalgamated with the Royal Irish Rangers, and thus absorbed into the mainstream British Army.

Uhuru (Swahili, freedom) The slogan of many African independence movements of the 1950s and 1960s, but specifically that of Kenya under Jomo Kenyatta.

UK *See* UNITED KINGDOM.

UKREP The United Kingdom Permanent Representative – effectively its ambassador to the EC – in Brussels, and his or her staff.

Ulster Historically the province comprising the nine northern counties of Ireland; since partition the SIX COUNTIES of NORTHERN IRELAND (Ulster less Cavan, Donegal and Monaghan). To LOYALISTS Ulster is the Protestant heartland which owes loyalty to the Crown and defies attempts to subordinate it to Dublin.

> Ulster will never agree to send representatives to an Irish Parliament in Dublin, no matter what safeguards and guarantees you may provide. GEORGE V to Asquith.

Ulster Covenant The pledge by Protestant ULSTER UNIONISTS led by the lawyer and politician Sir Edward Carson (1854–1935) to resist the imposition of all-Ireland Home Rule, signed in Belfast City Hall on 28 September 1912. The "solemn covenant" echoed the anti-PAPIST Solemn League and Covenant signed by Scottish Presbyterians in the early 17th century. The queue of Protestants waiting to sign stretched for three-quarters of a mile, and the covenant eventually carried 471,414 signatures, many inscribed in the signers' own blood.

Ulster Unionists The main body of Protestant voting strength in Northern Ireland, which opposed HOME RULE, later provided the backbone of STORMONT, and maintains Ulster's commitment to the UNION with the rest of the UK. Until 1972 its MPs at Westminster took the Conservative whip. The movement is now divided into three: the Official Unionists under James Molyneaux, the heirs of traditional Unionism; the Democratic Unionists under the Rev. Ian PAISLEY, smaller but with concentrated, more militant support; and the tiny Popular Unionists, comprising the MP James Kilfedder and his supporters.

> We must be prepared, the morning Home Rule is passed, ourselves to become responsible for the government of the Protestant province of Ireland. Sir EDWARD CARSON.

Ulster says No The rallying-call of the LOYALIST protest campaign against the 1985 ANGLO-IRISH AGREEMENT.

Ulster Volunteers A private army founded by Carson (*see above*) in 1913 to resist HOME RULE. Within months the Ulster Volunteer Force had up to 100,000 members drilling publicly – a sight which, coupled with Carson's threats, the Volunteers' GUN-RUNNING and the CURRAGH MUTINY, convinced Asquith's government that special provision would have to be made for the Protestant North. The outbreak of war in 1914 led to the whole question being shelved. The present-day Ulster Volunteer Force (UVF) is a Protestant terrorist organization, illegal since 1966.

Ulster will fight, and Ulster will be right Lord Randolph Churchill's emotive slogan against Gladstone's HOME RULE initiatives of the 1880s, which did much to create militant Unionism.

King of Ulster Nickname for the Rev. Ian PAISLEY, bestowed by critics of his highly personal style and of alleged British ambitions to instal him in the early 1980s as leader of a devolved administration at STORMONT.

ultimatum A challenge issued by one government to another, requiring it to take certain action by a specified time. As in the British ultimatum to Germany to withdraw from Poland in September 1939. *See* I HAVE TO TELL YOU THAT NO SUCH UNDERTAKING HAS BEEN RECEIVED.

umbrella. umbrella group A body comprising adherents of different political parties brought together for a specific campaign, notably the "Yes" and "No" campaigns in Britain's 1975 REFERENDUM on EC membership.

nuclear umbrella *See* NUCLEAR.

Umkhonto we Sizwe (Zulu, spear of the nation) In South Africa, the military wing of the African National Congress (*see* ANC).

UN Initials of, and common abbreviation for, the UNITED NATIONS.

unacceptable face of capitalism The key phrase of the Lonrho affair, which shook the British establishment in 1973. The international mining and trading company Lonrho was accused of making large payoffs to business contacts, including the former Tory Cabinet minister Duncan Sandys, later Lord Duncan-Sandys (1904–87), a non-executive director of the company who accepted £130,000 from it for giving up a consultancy job. The money was to be paid into a tax-free account in the Cayman Islands. The transaction was not illegal, but provided evidence of the exploitation of tax loopholes by top people which was seized on by opponents of Edward Heath's Tory government. To the surprise of many, Heath made a scornful criticism of his own, saying on 15 May 1973 in reply to a Commons question from the Liberal Jo Grimond:

It is the unpleasant and unacceptable face of capitalism, but one should not suggest that the whole of British industry consists of practices of this kind.

Un-American activities The holding and propagation of views seen by MIDDLE AMERICA as subversive. To LIBERALS, the essence of McCARTHYISM. Specifically the activities investigated from 1938 to 1975 by the House Committee to Investigate Un-American Activities, set up at the instigation of the New York Republican Rep. Hamilton Fish and the American Federation of Labor to investigate neo-Fascists, but turned against "Communists" by the Texas Rep. Martin Dies. In 1947 alone the committee collected files on over a million known or suspected COMMUNISTS, FELLOW-TRAVELLERS, "dupes" and "BLEEDING-HEART liberals". The investigations petered out after the fall of McCarthy. President Truman called the committee "the most un-American activity in the whole Government", and its activities "simply a red herring". When committee members investigated Hollywood, Humphrey Bogart declared: "They will nail anyone who ever scratched his ass during the National Anthem." And Lillian Hellman told them: "I cannot and will not tailor my conscience to this year's fashions." The historian Hugh Brogan described the process as "a cause of shame for Americans ever since". *See also* FIFTH AMENDMENT; WITCH-HUNT.

unassailable The British equivalent of 1000 PER CENT, a declaration of confidence that turns out to be anything but. The word was used by Margaret Thatcher in the early autumn of 1989 to describe the position of Chancellor Nigel Lawson, whose policies had just started to turn sour. Within weeks he had resigned after accusing Mrs. Thatcher and her economic adviser, Professor Alan Walters, of making his position untenable. Since then, any Minister in trouble has been greeted with Opposition shouts of "Unassailable!"

Unauthorized Programme The POPULIST programme put forward by Joseph Chamberlain and Jesse Collings (THREE ACRES AND A COW) in the 1885 UK election campaign without the consent of the Liberal leadership.

uncle. Uncle Joe Nickname in the West for STALIN, widely if naïvely seen as a benign figure by his allies during World War II. Also, in Washington, for Rep. Joe Cannon (1836–1926), Speaker of the House 1903–11. Also known as "the hayseed Member from Illinois" and FOUL-MOUTHED JOE. President Taft warned Alice Roosevelt Longworth never to get between Cannon and his spittoon; at one poker evening where none was provided, Cannon said the umbrella stand would do just fine.

Uncle Sam An affectionate nickname for the United States, and its government personified. It is said to be based on Sam Wilson (1766–1854), an army meat inspector in New York State during the war of 1812, who stamped "U.S." on barrels of salt pork and beef for the troops. The term was in use by 1813, often by New Englanders disenchanted with the administration's handling of the war, and in 1816 *The Adventures of Uncle Sam* was published. He first appeared as a cartoon character in 1830, wearing a toga. He acquired his tall hat, goatee beard, Stars-and-Stripes trousers and swallowtail coat in Lincoln's time, reaching his apotheosis in the cartoons of Thomas Nast. His costume was based on that of the comic YANKEE character Maj. Jack Downing, created by the humorist Seba Smith. The World War I "I want You" recruiting poster confirmed him as a national institution; Congress recognized him as the national symbol in 1961.

Uncle Tom A Black American too ready to accept the limitations set by white prejudice and domination. The name was taken from Harriet Beecher Stowe's novel *Uncle Tom's Cabin*, published in 1852, which provoked a wave of hatred against slavery; when Abraham Lincoln met the author at the height of the CIVIL WAR, he greeted her with:

So this is the little lady who made this big war!

uncommitted delegates Delegates sent to a US political party's nominating CONVENTION from a PRIMARY or CAUCUS who are not committed to support any particular candidate.

unconstitutional Not in accordance with the spirit of the US CONSTITUTION. The grounds on which the SUPREME COURT will hold that an action or item of legislation cannot be permitted.

The illegal we do immediately. The unconstitutional takes a little longer. HENRY KISSINGER.

Uncrowned King of Ireland The title given to Charles Stuart PARNELL (1846–91) when, at the height of his powers, his imprisonment for the militancy of his campaign against Irish land reform caused unprecedented civil unrest. It was bestowed on him by a speaker at a Ladies' Land League meeting in Dublin on 2 January 1882, and the name stuck after Parnell's release under the KILMAINHAM TREATY.

undeclared candidate A politician campaigning hard for a particular office without actually admitting that he or she is in the race. A classic example was the US Presidential campaign of the billionaire H. Ross PEROT in the spring and early summer of 1992, before his sudden withdrawal. When he relaunched his campaign in September, it was as a declared candidate for the Presidency.

under. underclass Collective term for those individuals and families at the bottom of the social pile, poor, jobless, in poor housing, lacking education and often from ethnic minorities, whose lot continues to worsen whatever welfare provision is made. They are ALIENATED from the established political order and thus perceived as a threat to it.

underdog A candidate in an apparently losing position who gains popular sympathy, support and sometimes even the votes needed to win as a result.

Underground Railroad The escape routes set up from the 1790s to enable slaves from America's South to escape to the northern states and on to Canada. Secrecy was essential, as any escaped slave who was recaptured would be shipped back to his master without recourse to law. Fourteen Northern states were involved in the operation, which at its height *c.* 1840 was helping 500 to 1000 escapers a year. The term predated by at least two decades the first actual underground railway, which opened in London in 1863.

Underhill Report The document which first informed Labour's national executive in 1979 of the full scale of ENTRYISM being carried out by the MILITANT TENDENCY. It was prepared by Reg (later Lord) Underhill (1914–93), the party's national agent, and was pigeonholed by the national executive in February 1980 despite the urgings of Neil KINNOCK. The report was eventually leaked to the press, but although Michael Foot described Militant as a "pestilential nuisance" when leader from 1980-83, it was 1985 before the party, under Kinnock, dealt with the tendency head-on.

Underwood tariff One of the main accomplishments of Woodrow WILSON's first administration, the first tariff passed by Congress since the Civil War to lower appreciably the barriers erected to protect US manufacturers against foreign competition. Named after the conservative Rep. Oscar W. Underwood of Alabama, the tariff also imposed a graduated income tax to offset the anticipated loss of revenue.

UNESCO United Nations Educational, Scientific and Cultural Organization. An autonomous agency of the United Nations, based in Paris, with the remit of promoting learning worldwide, preserving the world's heritage, and the exchange of ideas and information between nations. UNESCO owes its origins to the founding assembly of the UN in 1945, and began operating the next year with Julian Huxley as its Director-General. It now has some 160 member states, but America left in 1984 and Britain the following year; they felt UNESCO had become tainted by nepotism, bureaucracy and anti-Western propaganda.

ungovernability The condition when a society has run out of control of the organs of government. Commentators used the term of Britain in the 1970s, when successive governments appeared unable to confront problems of economic decline, trade union militancy and growing political extremism.

unicameral system A political structure in which the LEGISLATURE comprises a single chamber, rather than two. From the Latin *uni-*, one; *camera*, chamber.

unify. unification West German politicians' preferred term for the reunification of the country achieved in 1990 after the removal of the BERLIN WALL.

unified tax and benefit system A system in which individuals' liability to pay income tax and eligibility for welfare benefits are assessed in the same process and a single demand or payment is issued. Such a system is supposed to be less bureaucratic than separate tax and benefit systems, with some people paying taxes and then getting the money back from other agencies. Proposals to introduce it in Britain have been strongly resisted by civil servants.

unilateralism (1) The doctrine of the complete renunciation by Britain of all nuclear weapons, championed from the mid-1950s by the Campaign for Nuclear Disarmament (*see* CND) and by most of the Left of the LABOUR PARTY. It was adopted as official party policy briefly in 1960 against the wishes of the leadership (*see* FIGHT, FIGHT AND FIGHT AGAIN), and again in the early 1980s, under the leadership of Michael Foot, a founder of CND. After Labour's 1987 defeat Neil KINNOCK, himself a unilateralist, concluded that the policy was keeping Labour from power and won its abandonment. (2) The conviction that America must remain a free agent, outside the entanglement of any foreign alliances. A cornerstone of ISOLATIONISM during the 1930s, it relied on the absence of such links since the infant state had ended its treaty with France during the Revolutionary War.

Union, the (1) The states forming the United States of America, from the time of its inception. As the PHILADELPHIA CONVENTION struggled with the shape of the new nation, Benjamin FRANKLIN observed:

> That a Union is necessary, all are agreed. But when it comes to the form and nature of such a Union, their weak noddles are perfectly distracted.

HAMILTON described the original thirteen states as "bound together in a strict and indissoluble union". But the division between believers in a single nation and advocates of STATES' RIGHTS who believed in something less was there from the outset. It came into the open at a White House banquet in 1830, when President Jackson gave the toast: "Our Union – it must be preserved," and a shocked Vice-President John C. Calhoun responded:

> The Union, next to our liberty, most dear. May we all remember that it can only be preserved by respecting the rights of the States and by distributing equally the benefits and burdens of the Union.

It was to defuse such tension that Daniel Webster delivered his celebrated LIBERTY AND UNION speech.

When the CONFEDERATE STATES seceded, it was natural that the North should fight the ensuing CIVIL WAR in the name of the Union, which Lincoln declared "the last, best hope of earth". In 1862 Lincoln wrote to Horace Greeley: "My paramount object in this struggle is to save the Union. . . . If I could save the Union without freeing any slave, I would do it; and if I could do it by freeing all the slaves, I would do it; and if I could save it by freeing some and leaving others alone, I would also do that." But Robert E. Lee retorted:

> A union that can only be maintained by swords and bayonets, and in which strife and civil war are to take the place of brotherly love and kindness, has no charm for me.

(2) The formal joining together of two nations to be governed as one. One example is the union between Great Britain and Northern Ireland which survived the PARTITION of Ireland in 1921, and which is regarded as sacrosanct by the ULSTER UNIONISTS, the ORANGE movement and other LOYALIST groups. Another is the union between England and Scotland, as enshrined in the ACT OF UNION of 1707. In contemporary politics only the SNP is opposed to continuance of the Union, but the Conservative Party has maintained that the DEVOLUTIONary policies of Labour and the Liberal Democrats would be a fatal first step to the break-up of the Union. A further example is the union between Britain and France, offered by Churchill in 1940 as German forces overran France; Marshal Pétain said of it:

> To make a union with Great Britain would be fusion with a corpse.

Union Jack Technically the Union Flag is the flag of the United Kingdom, and the Jack is the post from which it is flown. The flag comprises the cross of St. George (for England), red on white; the cross of St. Andrew (Scotland), white on blue (diagonal) and the cross of St. Patrick (Ireland), red on white (also diagonal), the crosses superimposed on each other. The same device appears as part of the flags of a number of nations including Australia and South Africa, three Canadian provinces and the State of Hawaii. The flag in its present form dates from Act of Union of 1801 when the Irish Parliament was abolished and that land governed from Westminster; from 1606 until then the old "Union Flag" bearing simply the crosses of St. George and St. Andrew had been flown. Only a trained observer can tell when the flag is being flown upside down, but flag-waving politicians, notably Dr. Ian PAISLEY, sometimes make the claim to embarrass the authorities.

Union Nationale The conservative Francophone party in Quebec. Founded by Maurice Duplessis from the remnants of the province's old Conservative party and reforming Liberals, it overthrew the corrupt Taschereau regime in 1936 but in office developed some of the same habits. Ousted when war broke out, the Union Nationale returned to power in 1946 and ruled for 14 years, all but one of them under Duplessis. It won a third spell of office in 1966 when Daniel Johnson was elected on a virtually SEPARATIST programme; this moderated after Johnson died in 1968, but the party lost to the Liberals two years later.

Union Treaty The framework for the survival of the SOVIET UNION as a loose confederation, which Mikhail Gorbachev was endeavouring to persuade the constituent republics to accept at the time of the coup against him in August 1991 and the collapse of the Union that autumn.

one big union for all the workers The slogan of the American Railroad Union, formed in 1894 by Eugene Debs. The union was immediately plunged into a strike in support of Pullman workers, and when 260,000 railroad workers stopped work Federal troops were sent into Chicago, the strike's main centre. The strike degenerated into violence, with 34 strikers killed and troops called out in seven states. Debs, who had opposed moves to promote a GENERAL STRIKE, was arrested and jailed for conspiracy and the men drifted back to work. One reason for the strike's failure was that despite its slogan, the union did not admit Blacks; it was thus easy to recruit them as strikebreakers.

state of the Union The message which the President of the United States delivers to the Congress at the start of each year. It is now a highlight of the political calendar, but only since Woodrow WILSON has the President delivered it in person.

Union of Democratic Control (UDC) An

ad hoc coalition of socialists, radicals and PACIFISTS formed in Britain in September 1914, just after the outbreak of WORLD WAR I. Its main aims were parliamentary control over foreign policy, a negotiated peace on reasonable terms to all, and more open diplomacy to prevent a repetition of the secret alliances and covenants that were widely blamed for the war. In an atmosphere of war hysteria the UDC, whose founding members included Ramsay MacDonald, Bertrand Russell and Joseph Rowntree, were widely regarded as traitors and their meetings broken up by soldiers on leave. E. D. Morel, its secretary, was imprisoned and Russell fined for a pamphlet in which he allegedly discouraged recruiting. Much of the UDC platform was adopted by the LABOUR PARTY after 1917; it remained active until World War II.

Unionist (1) The full title of Britain's CONSERVATIVE PARTY is the Conservative and Unionist Party. Historically this reflects mainly the merger between Tories and Liberal supporters of the Union with Ireland in the late 19th century, but the Union with Scotland has since become a factor. (2) During the US CIVIL WAR, supporters of the North were known as Unionists.

UNITA União Nacional para a Independencia Total de Angola (Port. National Union for the Total Independence of Angola). A Western-backed guerrilla organization in Angola led by Dr. Jonas Savimbi (1934–). It was in the forefront of the struggle against Portuguese rule, but after Portugal's withdrawal in 1975 it fought a civil war against the Marxist MPLA which took power the following year. UNITA's acceptance of South African backing discredited it in the eyes of many Black Africans, but Savimbi exuded great personal charisma and enjoyed strong regional support. UNITA refused to accept the terms of an agreement devised in Geneva in 1988 to end the conflict, but peace talks with the MPLA did bring an uneasy truce, and elections in October 1992. When the MPLA were declared the winners, UNITA having polled less than 40%, Dr. Savimbi refused to accept the result and threatened to restart the war.

unitary authority A structure of local and regional government in which all powers not exercised over an area by central government are in the hands of a single elected local body. Britain's metropolitan districts, and formerly county boroughs, are a case in point. The alternative is a two-tier system, such as exists in America (states and counties or cities), and in most of the United Kingdom (counties or regions and districts).

united. United Kingdom The nation which took shape as the crown of England gained sway over Wales, Scotland and Ireland. It acquired its present form on the PARTITION of Ireland in 1922, now comprising England and Wales, Scotland and NORTHERN IRELAND.

United Nations The world organization founded at the close of WORLD WAR II, as the successor to the failed LEAGUE OF NATIONS, to prevent another world conflict and keep peace. It had its origins in the ATLANTIC CHARTER agreed by Franklin D. Roosevelt and Churchill in 1941; the name was coined by Roosevelt to cement the World War II alliance without the need to refer a treaty to Congress. The organization itself sprang from the 1944 DUMBARTON OAKS conference between Anerica, the UK and the Soviet Union; its charter was drawn up at the SAN FRANCISCO CONFERENCE in May–June 1945, President Truman declaring: "We did much more than draft an international agreement among 50 nations. We set down on paper the only principles that will enable civilized human life to continue to survive on this globe."

The organization was inaugurated on 21 October 1945 with 51 founder-members; more than three times as many states now belong. The UN held its first formal session in London in January 1946; at its close Secretary-General Paul Henri Spaak (1899–1972) said: "Our agenda is now exhausted. The Secretary-General is exhausted. All of you are exhausted. I find it comforting that, beginning with our very first day, we find ourselves in such complete agreement." Temporarily housed at Lake Success, New York State, the UN moved into its skyscraper HQ in New York City in 1952. There have been frequent complaints from civic leaders about the anti-Americanism of many delegations and the activities of some "diplomats" accredited to it, Mayor Ed Koch terming the UN "a cesspool". But it has stayed there ever since.

John F. Kennedy termed the UN "the protector of the small and weak, and a safety valve for the strong". US Ambassador Henry Cabot Lodge was blunter: "This organization is created to prevent you from going to hell. It is not created to take you to heaven." And Dag Hammarskjold (1905–61), its greatest Secretary-General, wrote: "It is not the Soviet Union or indeed any other big powers who need the United Nations for their protection. It is all the others."

The UN has had a stormy career; during the COLD WAR its efforts to create a civilized world were hampered by frequent Soviet use of the VETO. With the break-up of the British and other Empires, it also became a cockpit for anti-Western propaganda by Communist countries and "non-aligned" former colonies. This led Enoch POWELL to describe it as "the very capital and the New Jerusalem of humbug", and South Africa's Prime Minister Henrik Verwoerd to declare: "The grand adventure of nations has become a sordid scramble for the microphone – the new toy for the exhibitionist and the agitator." The cost of the organization and the nepotism practised by some member governments prompted the Australian R. J. D. Turnbull to denounce it as "a temple to Parkinson's Law, where inefficiency and extravagance worship at its shrine and hypocrisy at its altars". Yet the US Ambassador Warren R. Austen had an answer to claims that the UN was just a talking-shop. He said: "It is better that aged diplomats be bored than for young men to die."

The UN's efforts to enforce SANCTIONS during a number of conflicts have seldom had much success. But it developed from its early days a technique of PEACEKEEPING which has quietly prevented conflict in numerous flash-points. Through its numerous agencies it has also carried out important humanitarian functions, for children, refugees and the starving. The UN Secretary-General has become a highly prestigious figure in efforts to resolve world crises. And, first in KOREA (after a Soviet walkout from the Security Council prevented the Kremlin exercising its veto) and more recently in the Gulf War, the authority of the UN has been carried into the battlefield. The UN's GENERAL ASSEMBLY, in which each member state has a seat, holds a highly-publicized plenary session every autumn. Matters of urgency are dealt with by a 15-member SECURITY COUNCIL, five of whose seats are held by PERMANENT MEMBERS – America, Britain, China, France and Russia.

United States of America The title given to Britain's rebelling American colonies by the CONTINENTAL CONGRESS of 1775; it came into use on 7 June that year. The name was devised by Thomas Paine (1737–1809). The nation grew to be the world's most powerful, CHURCHILL stating: "The United States is like a gigantic boiler. Once the fire is lighted under it, there is no limit to the power it can generate." That power could be overwhelming to a neighbour; Pierre TRUDEAU remarked: "Living next to it is like sleeping with an elephant. No matter how friendly and even-tempered is the beast, one is affected by every twitch and grunt." Yet American leaders (Ronald Reagan apart) have seen limits to it. John F. KENNEDY said in 1961: "We must face the fact that the United States is neither omnipotent nor omniscient – that we are only 6 per cent of the population, that we cannot impose our will upon the other 94 per cent of mankind – that we cannot right every wrong or reverse every adversity – and that therefore there cannot be an American solution to every problem." But whatever the limits to its power, George BUSH struck a chord when he described his country as

> The best and fairest and most decent nation on the face of the earth.

United States Code The entire body of law enacted by the US Congress, minus repetitive language in Acts of amendment, published under 50 title headings in largely alphabetical order. Prepared by the Law Revision Counsel of the House of Representatives, new editions are published every six years. So far 22 of the titles have been revised and re-enacted; two others have been merged with other parts of the text.

United States of Europe A dream of European FEDERALISTS and a nightmare for supporters of national SOVEREIGNTY. Each believes that one could develop from the European Community. The notion originated in the mid-19th century, the French radical premier Léon Gambetta (1838–82) declaring: "I absolutely reject this theory as fatal for France, false as a matter of general history, and dangerous for democracy and the freedom of the world." Its contemporary use began when Churchill said in Zurich on 19 September 1946:

> We must build a kind of United States of Europe.

United We Stand The political movement arising from Ross PEROT's third-force challenge for the Presidency in 1992, which he hoped would perpetuate the fresh approach that brought him 19% of the popular vote. **United we stand, divided we fall** is a much-used motto, taken from *The Liberty Song* (1768):

> Then join hand in hand, brave Americans all,-
> By uniting we stand, by dividing we fall.
>
> JOHN DICKINSON (1732–1808).

unity is strength An even older expression of common purpose, originating in Aesop's classical fable, *The Bundle of Sticks*. Aesop's words have been literally translated as "In Union there is strength", or "Union gives strength".

Unknown Prime Minister The epitaph bestowed by ASQUITH on **Andrew Bonar Law** (1858–1923), who held office as Conservative Prime Minister from October 1922 to May 1923, when cancer forced him to resign. At Law's funeral in Westminster Abbey that November, Asquith observed: "It is fitting that we should have buried the Unknown Prime Minister by the side of the Unknown

Warrior"; the Unknown Warrior from the dead of Flanders had been "buried among the Kings" three years before. Born in Canada, Bonar Law made his fortune as an iron merchant in Glasgow, became a UNIONIST MP in 1900 and after the Conservatives' two election defeats of 1910, succeeded BALFOUR the following year as party leader. Pushed forward by Lord Beaverbrook, Bonar Law told him: "If I am a great man, then a good many of the great men of history are frauds"; indeed Roy Jenkins wrote: "Simplicity was one of his few engaging characteristics." A bachelor, his only interest in life outside politics and business was bridge. Bonar Law was a model of Scots-Canadian dourness; Lord Birkenhead said of him: "He would sooner keep hot coals in his mouth than a witticism." Asquith considered that "he has not the brains of a Glasgow bailie", Austen Chamberlain termed him "an amateur who will always remain one", while Lloyd George reminisced: "Bonar would never make up his mind on anything, [though] once a question had been decided, he would stick with it and fight for it to a finish." He served in the wartime coalitions under Asquith and Lloyd George as Colonial Secretary, Chancellor of the Exchequer, Leader of the House and Lord Privy Seal before retiring in 1921. When the Conservatives withdrew from the coalition in 1922, forcing Lloyd George's resignation, he was recalled as Prime Minister but was almost immediately afflicted by illness.

Unlock! The cry of police and attendants at the House of Commons as they unlock the LOBBIES after a DIVISION.

unpaired A member of a legislature who does not possess a PAIR on the opposing side, and consequently cannot miss a vote without affecting the outcome.

unparliamentary A word or expression which is regarded as too profane, obscene, derogatory or uncouth to be uttered in a legislature. The use of such a word will prompt the CHAIR to intervene, and refusal to withdraw could lead to a member being ordered from the Chamber. At Westminster words regarded as unparliamentary include blackguard, cad, corrupt, coward, criminal, hypocrite, jackass, murderer, rat and traitor. The Labour MP Tam Dalyell, at the height of his campaign over the BELGRANO and WESTLAND, tacked most of them together to brand Margaret Thatcher "a bounder, a LIAR, a deceiver, a cheat and a crook". In the Australian Federal Parliament almost anything goes; in the US Congress better conduct is generally observed (*see* FUCK), but Speaker Sam Rayburn once declared:

If they're from the Bible they're not unparliamentary.

unreconstructed Originally those Southern States who emerged from RECONSTRUCTION under the same conservative, racist rule that the exercise had been intended to abolish. Now a term for anyone, not necessarily a right-winger, whose views on an issue have remained unchanged despite the passage of time, the course of events, or the facts.

Unsafe at Any Speed The celebrated (and to Detroit notorious) book by Ralph Nader (1934–) about the poor safety record of General Motors' Corvair and the company's indifference to it, which caused a sensation when published in 1965 and is widely credited with the birth of effective consumerism in America. GM reacted to the book by denying the charges and putting private investigators on to Nader, a young lawyer, and 50 of his friends and neighbours. This attempt to "dig up dirt" backfired on the company during Congressional hearings; it was subsequently ordered to pay Nader $300,000 damages for harassment.

up At Westminster, the House of Commons is said to be *up* when it has been adjourned for the night.

upset A surprise defeat for an INCUMBENT legislator or government who had appeared certain of re-election.

urban guerrilla *See* GUERRILLA.

Uruguay Round The round of GATT negotiations aimed at bringing down world trade barriers, begun at Punta del Este, Uruguay, in 1986 and which had yet to be completed as this dictionary went to press. The greatest difficulty was over farm subsidies; America refused to sign until the European Community (with France resisting most strongly) slashed them by more than envisaged in the McSHARRY PLAN, while stepping up its own support to the Farm Belt, and the CAIRNS GROUP pressed for fairer competition from the US and EC alike. EC and US negotiators finally settled their differences – over oilseed production – in November 1992 despite frenetic attempts by France, and EC President Jacques DELORS, to sabotage the talks; with militant French farmers rioting, the French government then tried to build a coalition within the EC to overturn the agreement.

US *See* UNITED STATES OF AMERICA.

Ustase The Croatian nationalist movement which conducted a terrorist campaign against Austro-Hungarian rule in the 19th century, revived it against Serb domination of Yugoslavia in the 1920s, produced a neo-

Fascist puppet regime (*see* puppet GOVERNMENT) during World War II and revived on the break-up of Yugoslavia from 1990. It was implicated in the murder of King Alexander I in 1934, and under the COLLABORATIONIST regime of Ante Pavelic from 1941 was accused by Serbs, PARTISANS and others of widespread atrocities. The Ustase conducted a sporadic terrorist campaign against TITO's unified Communist state in the 1960s and 1970s, and was seen by Serbs as a sinister influence behind the breakaway Croatian regime of Franjo Tudjman, established in 1991 with German support.

usual channels At Westminster, the means of contact between Government and Opposition BUSINESS MANAGERS and WHIPS, either directly or through staff of their respective offices. It is these contacts that defuse procedural emergencies, and determine the agenda for debate, the amount of time given to particular measures and the size and composition of committees.

The most polluted of waterways. TONY BENN.

Utopia (Gr. nowhere) The name of the ideal and imaginary state devised by Sir Thomas More (1478–1535) to set out his theories of government, and now applied to any concept of a perfect or better world. In his book *Utopia* written in 1516, More described a crescent-shaped island including 54 cities of roughly 100,000 people each, sited at least 24 miles apart. The (patriarchal) family was to be the basic political and industrial unit, with an elected hierarchy of magistrates topped by a prince, chosen yearly from four names submitted by the people. Everyone would have to do two years of agricultural labour before taking up a trade passed down in the family; there would be no private property. A high premium would be placed on cultivation of the mind.

A map of the world that does not include Utopia is not even worth glancing at. OSCAR WILDE.

The Socialist dream is no longer Utopia, but Queuetopia. WINSTON CHURCHILL on the post-war Labour government.

For other nations, Utopia is a blessed past never to be recovered; for Americans it is just beyond the horizon. HENRY KISSINGER.

Utrecht, Treaty of The basis for Britain's continuing rule of Gibraltar. Under the Treaty, concluded in 1713, Britain and France acknowledged Spain's sovereignty over its territories in the New World in return for her surrender of Gibraltar, Naples and Sicily, Milan and her final influence in the Netherlands. In Spain's view the treaty was one-sided and exacted under duress.

UVF *See* ULSTER VOLUNTEERS.

V

V The symbol of victory to the World War II Allies (especially Britain and the FREE FRENCH). It has based on the Morse code letter V (. . . –), the opening bar of Beethoven's Eroica Symphony, the French "*victoire*" and the Flemish "*vrijheid*". The letter as a sign of defiance was originated by Victor de Laveleye in a BBC broadcast to Belgium on 14 January 1941, the sound by "Colonel Britton" (Douglas Ritchie) on 31 July 1941. As a sign of defiance in occupied territory, it was painted on walls and stuck as a paper cut-out on German soldiers' backs. It was popularised by CHURCHILL as a sign made by the third and index fingers of the right hand, the other two and thumb crossed over a palm facing outwards. The same sign used in reverse with an upward movement of the hand is a gesture of obscene contempt first used by English archers at Agincourt, 1415.

> The PM will give the V sign with two fingers in spite of the representations repeatedly made to him that this gesture has quite another significance.
>
> Sir JOHN COLVILLE, Churchill's private secretary, 1941.

The symbol was subsequently taken over by the 1960s Peace Movement as its own, and known as the "peace sign".

Vacher's *Vacher's Parliamentary Companion*, a slim blue paperback published in Britain, updated quarterly, which gives a complete list of MPs, peers, Parliamentary and senior government officials.

vagueness. a little vagueness goes a long way in this business A law of political life invented by Edmund G. "Pat" Brown (1905–), Democratic governor of California.

values The moral instincts which define a politician, a party, a programme, a society or a voter.

> It is not our affluence, or our plumbing, or our clogged freeways, that grip the imagination of others. Rather, it is the values upon which our system was built.
>
> Sen. WILLIAM FULBRIGHT (1905–).

core values The essentials of a party's philosophy and programme.

Victorian values Term applied by Margaret Thatcher (*see* IRON LADY) in 1982 to the virtues of thrift, industry, self-reliance, provision for the family and personal charity which she saw her government as embodying – "the values when our country became great".

van Buren, Martin *See* OLD KINDERHOOK.

Vance–Owen plan *See* OWEN.

variable geometry The attribute of an organization, specifically of European nations, whose members would opt into or out of particular functions, *e.g.* political but not economic union, participation or non-participation in joint defence or a single currency. The term originated in the 1960s to describe "swing-wing" aircraft.

Vassall tribunal The Commission of Inquiry under Lord Radcliffe set up in 1962 by Britain's Macmillan government after William Vassall, a homosexual Admiralty clerk, was found to have been passing secrets to Moscow for seven years. It cleared Ministers – one, T. G. D. Galbraith, had resigned – of any impropriety. But the scandal left the government vulnerable when the PROFUMO AFFAIR broke the following year.

VAT Value Added Tax. An indirect tax on most goods and services levied at differing rates (currently 17.5% in the UK) by all member states of the EC, largely replacing national sales taxes (in Britain, purchase tax). Each trader has to remit the tax to the Customs and Excise after deducting the amount he or she has paid for goods and services (but not labour costs). The tax is thus borne not by traders but by consumers. A percentage of receipts pass as a PRECEPT to Brussels to finance the Community budget (*see* OWN RESOURCES).

Veep Shorthand term for the VICE-PRESIDENT of the United States, used especially in newspaper headlines. First applied to Alben Barkley, Vice-President 1948–52.

Velvet Revolution The peaceful uprising in Czechoslovakia at the close of 1989 that overthrew the hard-line Communist regime of Gustav Husák and installed a democracy under the presidency of the playwright Václav Havel, previously imprisoned as a DISSIDENT. It was triggered by a brutal police attack on protesting students – said to have been ordered by the KGB to prompt Husák's overthrow and let in more moderate Communists. Led by intellectuals, it was marked by mass rallies in Prague's WENCESLAS SQUARE at which the former Communist leader Alexander Dubček (*see* PRAGUE SPRING) re-emerged to adulation after 20 years as a NON-PERSON.

Venceremos! (Sp. we shall conquer!) A slogan of the defeated Republican forces in the SPANISH CIVIL WAR.

Venezuela boundary case The dispute which, after the US Civil War, brought the United States and Britain closest to conflict. The disputed boundary between Venezuela and British Guiana (now Guyana) became an explosive issue when gold was discovered there in the 1880s. America volunteered in 1886, 1890 and 1894 to act as MEDIATOR, but both countries rejected the offer. Then, in 1895, Secretary of State Richard Olney sent London a series of blunt notes in which he asserted America's interest under the MONROE DOCTRINE and argued that only ARBITRATION could settle the issue. When the Foreign Secretary, Lord SALISBURY, rejected both arguments, President Cleveland (*see* BEAST OF BUFFALO) sought Congressional approval to set up a commission to draw a boundary which the US would defend against Britain. This sparked an outbreak of war fever in America, but before long tempers on both sides of the Atlantic subsided; in 1897 Britain and Venezuela signed under US auspices a treaty providing for an international board of arbitration. It reported in 1899, upholding Britain's claim.

Vereeniging Treaty The treaty that ended the second BOER WAR, agreed at Vereeniging and signed in Pretoria on 31 May 1902. The South African Republic and Orange Free State were placed under British military administration, but promised eventual self-government. A general amnesty was declared, the civil population disarmed and £3 million allocated for payment of war debts and to provide for economic reconstruction of the Transvaal. The issue of native voting rights was left for settlement after the granting of self-government, which helped smooth the creation of a unified South Africa in 1910, but opened the way for Black and Coloured South Africans to be eventually stripped of their rights through APARTHEID.

verification The process under which nations bound by ARMS CONTROL agreements determine whether their co-signatories are observing them. The extent to which agreements might be verifiable has been a sticking point in negotiations on arms limitation.

verkrampte (Afrik. inflexible) The hard-line faction in South Africa's NATIONAL PARTY which opposed any erosion of APARTHEID; many broke away in the early 1980s to join the Herstigte National Partei and in the late 1980s to form the fractionally less extreme Conservatives. The opposite of *verkrampte* is *verligte* (enlightened), a term used for the more liberal Afrikaner, a few of whom exist.

Versailles The splendid palace just outside Paris of the former Kings of France, from Louis XIV onward, and briefly the French capital. It played host to the 1919 Peace Conference at which the "Big Four", US President WILSON, the French Prime Minister Clemenceau (*see* TIGER), Britain's Lloyd George and Orlando, the Italian Prime Minister, imposed a crippling settlement on Germany (which was not represented) after WORLD WAR I at French insistence. They took control of the conference after 9 weeks of shambolic deadlock in Paris; Lloyd George wanted to HANG THE KAISER, Clemenceau wanted territory as well as REPARATIONS. The **Treaty of Versailles**, agreed on 28 July 1919 with no German representatives present and imposed under threat of resuming the war, was one of a series of separate treaties with each of the former adversaries. It included the Covenant of the LEAGUE OF NATIONS, but also draconian peace terms. Germany lost one eighth of its European territory, including Alsace-Lorraine, the Rhineland (to be occupied by Allied troops) and the Saar, placed under League of Nations control for 15 years pending a PLEBISCITE. Germany also lost Eupen and Malmedy to Belgium and North Schleswig to Denmark. Poland was given access to the Baltic along a POLISH CORRIDOR, at the head of which was Danzig (now Gdansk), declared a free city under League control. Austrian independence was guaranteed following the dismemberment of the Austro-Hungarian Empire, and Germany forfeited all her colonies, which became MANDATES of the League. The military terms were also harsh. Germany was to disarm, abolish military service, maintain an army of not more than 100,000 men and reduce the size of her navy. In Article 231, the famous War Guilt clause, Germany had to accept responsibility for the war and pay reparations for damage caused to Allied nations. The treaty gave rise to German disaffection throughout the WEIMAR REPUBLIC, and was thus a major factor in the rise of Hitler and the NAZIS and – although Germany systematically violated it in the 1930s – in the eventual outbreak of WORLD WAR II. The refusal of the US Senate to ratify the treaty because it would commit

America to the League of Nations reflected an ISOLATIONISM which dominated US political life until PEARL HARBOR; Wilson's illness had prevented him completing his campaign for its adoption.

> Dare we reject it, and break the heart of the world?
> WOODROW WILSON.

vesting day In Britain, during the process of NATIONALIZATION, the date on which ownership of an industry formally passed from the private shareholders to be vested in the state.

veto (Lat. I forbid) A vote which will, when cast, prevent a majority decision taking effect. (1) Exercised by the President of the United States in dealings with the Congress (*see* OVERRIDE) or by a state governor. Franklin D. Roosevelt, (*see* FDR) determined that Congress should not be "uppity", vetoed a record 635 Bills; he was only overridden on nine. (2) At the UNITED NATIONS, the last resort available to any of the five PERMANENT MEMBERS of the SECURITY COUNCIL; most frequently cast by the Soviet Union during the COLD WAR. Article 27 of the UN Charter requires the "concurring votes of the permanent members" on all non-procedural decisions; America pressed for the right of veto but it was the outnumbered Soviets who used it to block decisive action and weaken the UN itself. However the veto did also prevent one SUPERPOWER attacking the other with UN sanction. (3) In the EC it can be exercised, in a decreasing range of circumstances, by a member state in the European Council (*see* LUXEMBOURG COMPROMISE; qualified MAJORITY).

Cat Bill veto Adlai Stevenson's refusal in 1949, as Governor of Illinois, to sign a bill promoted by bird-lovers to restrain cats. "The problem of cat versus bird is as old as time," he wrote in his veto message to the state legislature. The Bill was a precedent for intervention in "the age old problems of dog versus cat, bird versus bird, or even bird versus worm". The State of Illinois had "enough to do without trying to control feline delinquency".

double veto In the US CONGRESS, the ability of either House to frustrate the President's legislative plans.

legislative veto A device adopted by Congress to give it control over REGULATORY AGENCIES without infringing the SEPARATION OF POWERS. Achieved by writing into legislation establishing or empowering such agencies the right of Congress to pass resolutions forbidding them from following policies opposed by the legislature; such resolutions are not subject to Presidential veto. Despite a Supreme Court ruling in 1983 (*INS v. Chadha*) that once Congress delegates authority to an agency it cannot interfere in its actions, legislation containing such provisions continues to be passed.

line-item veto In Washington, the ability to kill individual items in a departmental budget, notably for defence. Denied by Congress to the President, but unofficially exercised by key staffers of the Congressional Budget Office. The governors of 43 states also possess this power.

loyalist veto A pejorative used by Irish nationalists and, at times, the Dublin government to describe the capacity of the two-thirds Protestant majority in NORTHERN IRELAND to thwart through the UK political system demands within the minority Roman Catholic community for union with the Irish Republic.

message veto A veto in which the President refuses to sign a Bill and sends it back to the House where it originated, with his reasons for disapproval.

pocket veto The procedure under which the President can prevent a Bill becoming law once Congress has passed it by failing to sign it before Congress ADJOURNs.

scorched earth veto strategy The term was used by Donald Regan, President Reagan's CHIEF OF STAFF, for regaining the political initiative early in his second term by confronting Congress on every issue.

vicar Representative, usually of God or the church but used in a political sense. Secretary of State Alexander Haig described himself as President Reagan's vicar on foreign policy.

Vicar of Bray A politician skilled at adapting himself to sudden shifts in the prevailing ideology (*see* TRIMMER). Its origin was the anonymous 18th-century English rhyme with the chorus:

> And this is law that I'll maintain
> Until my dying day, Sir.
> That whatsoever King may reign
> Still I'll be the Vicar of Bray, Sir.

vicar on earth A pejorative, taking the analogy of the Pope as Vicar of Christ, for the more accessible acolyte of a remote or lofty political figure. The British Labour politician Michael Meacher, stressing that he was his own man, once said: "I'm not [Tony] BENN's vicar on earth."

Vice-President Elected on the same TICKET as the President of the United States to serve as his deputy and succeed as chief executive in the event of his death or resignation; he acts as PRESIDING OFFICER of the Senate. His office is normally in the Old Executive Office Building (OLD EOB), though some Vice-Presidents have worked from the White House; since the 1970s the Naval Observatory off Massachusetts Avenue has been his official residence.

The vice-presidency has come in for criticism since its inception. John Adams termed it "the most insignificant office that ever the invention of man contrived", and said of his own tenure: "I am vice-president; in this I am nothing, but I am everything." Theodore Roosevelt (*see* TEDDY), who briefly held the office before being rescued by a Presidential assassination, scorned it as "a stepping-stone to oblivion". On becoming Vice-President he observed: "I have taken the veil." John Nance Garner (*see* CACTUS JACK) saw himself as "the spare tire of the constitution", but once declared: "It's not worth a pitcher of warm piss; it doesn't amount to a hill of beans." To Harry S Truman (*see* GIVE'EM HELL HARRY) the vice-presidency was "about as useful as a cow's fifth teat", and LBJ remarked: "All Hubert [Humphrey] needs over there is a girl to answer the phone and a pencil with an eraser in it"; Humphrey, under fire because of Johnson's VIETNAM policy, said: "The President has not made me his slave and I am not his humble servant." Ronald Reagan (*see* GREAT COMMUNICATOR) never was Vice-President; not surprisingly as he once said: "There is absolutely no circumstance whatever under which I would accept that spot. Even if they tied and gagged me, I would find a way to signal by wiggling my ears." But Dan QUAYLE inevitably saw it in a better light: "I used to be a Batman fan until I had this job. Now all of a sudden Robin looks good."

Commentators and political scientists have had a more sober view of a job whose holder is "a heartbeat away from the PRESIDENCY". A 20th Century Fund report described the Vice-President as "the presumptive front-runner for his party's nomination". Bill Vaughan said the office was "the last cookie on the plate. Everyone insists he won't take it, but somebody always does," while Sol Barzman observed:

> It was the cynical attitude of the politicians, and not the office itself, that gave us the near-disasters we have stoically endured in the vice-presidential chair.

viceroy A ruler, "vice-king", acting with Royal authority in a territory overseas. Under the British EMPIRE, ultimate power in India was vested in a viceroy responsible to the CROWN; Ireland for a time also had a viceroy, but his role was more limited. The GOVERNOR-GENERAL of a DOMINION is technically a viceroy.

Vichy (France) The half of the country not occupied by AXIS forces after the fall of France in 1940, and the régime that governed it from the spa town of Vichy, in the central department of Allier, under the COLLABORATIONIST régime of Marshal Pétain. The Vichy régime was later vilified for co-operation with Nazi atrocities and its key figures – Men of Vichy – were put on trial. But at the time it enjoyed broad public support, and its colonial troops put up strong resistance to the FREE FRENCH. *See* TRAVAIL, FAMILLE, PATRIE.

Vichy mentality A pejorative for alleged over-keenness by an organ of a state or political group to compromise or accept defeat. It was used of the UK Foreign Office by Brian Sedgemore in his 1977 minority report to the Select Committee on the Civil Service.

Victoria tower The crowning glory of Sir Charles Barry's Palace of WESTMINSTER, at 336 ft. taller than the clock tower of BIG BEN and topped by a 76 ft. flagpole with a UNION JACK the size of a tennis court. Constructed over a ceremonial arch ready for Queen Victoria to pass through in 1852, its interior was left incomplete because of the weight of the structure. From 1959 it was completely reconstructed after being found in imminent danger of collapse; it now houses historic manuscripts.

victory Election-winners have at times had surprising comments to make. Guy Barnett, on unexpectedly winning the South Dorset by-election for Labour in 1963, declared: "Frankly I'm amazed." And the Liberal Bill Pitt, victor at Croydon North-West in 1981, exclaimed: "Mind my suit!" when sprayed with champagne.

victory at all costs Sir Winston CHURCHILL's first speech in the House of Commons as Prime Minister, 13 May 1940, included the passage: "You ask: 'What is our aim?' I answer in one word: 'Victory'. Victory at all costs, victory in spite of all terror, victory however hard or long the road may be: for without victory there is no survival."

victory of the cradle The French-Canadian nationalist dream up to the late 19th century of taking political control through a higher birthrate than that of English-speakers.

Victory Special The campaign train of Thomas E. DEWEY in the 1948 US Presidential election.

to the victor the spoils *See* SPOILS SYSTEM. *See also* DEFEAT.

video feed From the 1980s in the US Congress, a means used by members of both parties to maximize their exposure to the voters by recording their own reactions to major events and beaming them straight to hometown and state television stations, bypassing the networks. *See also* video PRESIDENCY.

Vienna Convention The international agreement concluded in 1961 under which nations undertake to respect the rights, privileges and

IMMUNITIES of each other's diplomats and embassies.

Viet Cong (Short for *Viet Nam Cong Sam*, Vietnamese Communists) The Communist guerrilla force in South Vietnam which fought government, US, Australian and other forces from 1957 to 1975, ultimately bringing about union with the North. The Viet Cong was formed from some 10,000 VIET MINH insurgents who stayed behind after the GENEVA AGREEMENT of 1954 under which the French withdrew and the country was partitioned. Its political wing was the National Liberation Front, formed in 1960.

Viet Minh The Communist and nationalist guerrilla movement under Ho Chi Minh, formed in 1941, that resisted Japanese occupation of Indochina during WORLD WAR II and forced the French to leave in 1954 after a campaign of several years (*see* DIEN BIEN PHU). They became the ruling government of North Vietnam and three years later began military support for the VIET CONG.

Vietnam. Vietnam War America's most traumatic conflict since the CIVIL WAR, with repercussions that linger to this day. US troops were deployed in South Vietnam from 1961 to 1974, first as "advisers" and then in combat strength of up to 544,000 (1969) in an ultimately vain attempt to prevent the Viet Cong and North Vietnamese forces taking control of South Vietnam. Over 58,000 US personnel were killed in combat and 365,000 wounded. The war, though backed by the silent MAJORITY, prompted widespread and passionate opposition at home (*see* ANTI-WAR MOVEMENT), led to world-wide student riots and crystallized in Sen. Eugene McCarthy's challenge for the Democratic presidential nomination in 1968 and Lyndon B. Johnson's decision not to seek re-election (*see* I SHALL NOT SEEK, AND I WILL NOT ACCEPT). The war, which spilled over into Laos, Cambodia and North Vietnam, was supposedly ended by the PARIS PEACE AGREEMENT of 1973, but in 1975 after US troops had been withdrawn, Saigon finally fell to Viet Cong and North Vietnamese forces.

The last crusade. CHESTER COOPER.

The US build-up was slow and at first almost indiscernible, with Presidents insisting America was not fighting the war for its client. John F. Kennedy said: "We can help them, we can give them equipment, we can send our men out there as advisers, but they have to win it, the people of Vietnam, against the Communists." And Lyndon B. Johnson declared: "We are not about to send American boys nine or ten thousand miles away from home to do what Asian boys ought to be doing for themselves." But when the crunch came, Johnson declared: "Just like the Alamo, somebody damn well needed to go to their aid. Well, by God, I'm going to Vietnam's aid." His argument was that "if America's commitment is dishonored in Vietnam, it is dishonored in 40 other alliances we have made", and that "if we quit Vietnam, tomorrow we'll be fighting in Hawaii, and next week we'll have to fight in San Francisco". But he knew Vietnam could not have a high profile in US politics: "If you have a mother-in-law with only one eye and she has it in the centre of her forehead, you don't keep her in the living room" – LBJ explaining why he gave Vietnam a low political profile. Johnson was not only criticized by the DOVES; in 1965 Ronald Reagan said: "We should declare war on North Vietnam. We could pave the whole country, put parking stripes on it and still be home for Christmas." And former President Eisenhower also felt fatal half-measures were being undertaken: "I believe when you get in a war, [you] get everything you need and win it." Later in the build-up, IKE said: "With 450,000 troops now in Vietnam, it is time that Congress decided whether or not . . . a state of war exists with north Vietnam." Johnson was not alone, however, in his confidence that American might and values would prevail. Arthur Goldberg said: "We are confident that we can get the enemy to mend his ways," and before his election to the Presidency Richard Nixon insisted: "There is no substitute for victory in South Vietnam." But during his 1968 campaign he declared: "Never has so much military, economic and diplomatic power been used as ineffectively as in Vietnam." Once elected he took to the field and told US troops: "Out here in this dreary, difficult war, I think history will record that this may well have been one of America's finest hours, because we took on a difficult task and we succeeded." And in 1970 he said: "I would rather be a one-term President and do what is right than a two-term President, at the cost of seeing America become a second-rate power and see this nation accept the first defeat in its proud 190-year history." But by the next year Nixon was ruminating: "I seriously doubt if we will ever have another war. This is probably the very last one." With the war almost over, in 1975, Gerald FORD declared: "The Communist leaders in Moscow, Peking or Hanoi must fully understand that the United States considers the freedom of South Vietnam vital to our interests. And they must know that we are not bluffing in our determination to defend these interests." But Australia's Prime Minister John Gorton was more realistic: "I don't think we will have achieved our objectives, but it was fair enough for us to have attempted them." Throughout the war American leaders realized they were vulnerable on the home front. Nixon declared: "North Vietnam cannot defeat or humiliate the United States. Only Americans can do that." Dean Rusk, Johnson's Secretary of State, once asked reporters: "Which side are you on?" And Vice-President Spiro Agnew characteristically observed: "A spirit of national masochism prevails, encouraged by an effete corps of impudent snobs who characterize themselves as intellectuals."

The opponents used moral, legal and political arguments against the war. To Dean Acheson it was "worse than immoral – a mistake". Sen. William Fulbright asserted that "the United States is succumbing to the arrogance of power". And one of the leading anti-war campaigners, the child psychologist Dr. Benjamin Spock, maintained: "To win in Vietnam we will have to exterminate a nation." An emotional Sen. George McGovern told the Senate: "It doesn't take any courage at all for a Congressman or a Senator or a President to wrap himself in the flag and say we're staying in Vietnam. Because it isn't our blood that's being shed." At the world Council of Churches, Eugene Carson Blake declared: "We cannot remain silent on Vietnam. We should remember that whatever victory there may be possible, it will have a racial stigma . . . it will always be the case of a predominantly White power killing an Asian nation." And Lieutenant (later Sen.) John F. Kerry, spokesman for Vietnam Vets Against the War, termed it "the war the soldiers tried to stop". *See* CHICAGO CONVENTION; DRAFT DODGING; GROSVENOR SQUARE DEMONSTRATION; GULF OF TONKIN RESOLUTION; KENT STATE; MIAS; MY LAI MASSACRE; PENTAGON PAPERS; TET OFFENSIVE.

> Vietnam was lost in the living rooms of America, not on the battlefields of Vietnam.
> MARSHALL MCLUHAN on the impact of television coverage.

Vietnamization The policy adopted by President Nixon after taking office in 1969, for gradually removing US forces from Vietnam and transferring responsibility for the war to the South Vietnamese. *See* NIXON DOCTRINE.

Vietnam syndrome The impact of the loss of Vietnam on the US political community, manifested in a reluctance to engage in risky foreign commitments and a lack of confidence about America's role in the world.

> By God, we've kicked the Vietnam syndrome once and for all.
> GEORGE BUSH.

Vietnam Vets A vocal, largely unorganized lobby of disillusioned and often disabled men who had served in Vietnam and found America ungrateful and anxious to forget them. They were partly assuaged by Ronald Reagan's dedication of the Vietnam Memorial in Washington DC.

vigil A silent and static demonstration with an implied note of anguish, protest and often of prayer, usually continuing overnight or for several days. Religious in origin, and most often directed against perceived enormities such as an impending execution, the atomic bomb or apartheid (*see* BLACK SASH), and held at a location selected to embarrass those demonstrated against.

vigilantes Unauthorized – but sometimes officially encouraged – groups of armed men who patrol an area ready to take the law into their own hands, often with the aim of provoking or intimidating a particular ethnic, political or social group.

violence A frequently inevitable adjunct of politics, regarded by some of the most committed as an acceptable or even desirable means to an end, and by a few extremist groups as an end in itself (*see* GUERRILLA; INSURGENTS; REVOLUTION). To the BLACK POWER activist H. "Rap" Brown, "Violence is as American as cherry pie." The former Zambian president Kenneth Kaunda observed that "the power which establishes a state is violence, the power which maintains it is violence, the power which eventually overthrows it is violence". As America's PROTEST MOVEMENT reached its height in 1970 and the threat of INNER CITY riots lingered, the liberal Justice William O. Douglas wrote:

> Violence has no constitutional sanction, and every government from the beginning has moved against it. But where grievances pile high and most of the elected spokesmen represent the Establishment, violence may be the only effective response.

But at Drogheda in 1979 Pope John Paul II appealed to the IRA and other TERRORISTS in NORTHERN IRELAND:

> Violence is a lie, for it goes against the truth of our faith, the truth of humanity. Violence is against humanity, for it destroys the very fabric of society. On my knees I beg you to turn away from the paths of violence.

even if it means violence The phrase used by Professor Harold Laski (1893–1950), chairman of Britain's Labour Party, which brought about his eclipse. Laski uttered the words in an election speech at Newark in 1945; it was in the context of the party's determination to introduce Socialism. The *Daily Express* printed a scathing editorial and Laski sued for libel; after an erratic performance in the witness box, Laski lost his case and had to pay the Express £13,000 in costs. *See also* THANK YOU FOR YOUR LETTER.

Virginia Plan The blueprint for the US CONSTITUTION reflecting the ideas of James MADISON, which Governor Edmund Randolph of Virginia presented to the PHILADELPHIA CONVENTION in 1787.

virgins A term applied at Westminster to incoming MPs who have never served in Parliament before. *Compare* RETREADS.

Viscount In the British system of nobility, a hereditary PEER, senior to a BARON but junior to an EARL. Viscountcies are still occasionally awarded to retiring senior politicians, *i.e.* Speaker George Thomas (Viscount Tonypandy) and William Whitelaw, who kept his own name.

vision. the vision thing The concept of having the imagination to capture the heart of the electorate with a vision of a better future, which George BUSH attempted – and not surprisingly given his command of the English language, failed – to articulate prior to and during the 1992 Presidential campaign.

volatility The readiness of sections of the electorate to switch from one party to another instead of showing a consistent loyalty. A contrast with traditional voting patterns.

Völkischer Beobachter (Ger. observer of the race) The official daily newspaper of the NAZI party prior to and during the Third REICH.

Völstead Act The Act passed by the US Congress in 1919 over President Wilson's VETO which introduced PROHIBITION by implementing the 18th Amendment to the Constitution, prohibiting manufacture, transportation and sale of all alcoholic beverages. Unlike the amendment, it also banned their purchase and consumption, and defined an alcoholic drink as containing more than 0.5% of alcohol by volume. Its promoter was Rep. Andrew Volstead (1860–1947) of Minnesota. Prohibition was abolished by the 21st Amendment in 1933, but FDR amended the Act after his inauguration to allow production of beer and light wine.

vote, to To reach a decision by voting, or to cast one's vote when a decision is to be taken or choice made.

the vote (1) The point of decision. (2) The instrument available to each person in a democracy for choosing their rulers or taking collective decisions, or the right to exercise that choice by participating in elections.

> The right of voting for representatives is the primary right by which other rights are protected. To take away this right is to reduce a man to slavery. THOMAS PAINE.

> The vote is the most powerful instrument ever devised by man for breaking down injustice and destroying the terrible walls that imprison men because they are different from other men. LYNDON B. JOHNSON.

Thoreau reckoned that "all voting is a sort of gaming, like checkers or backgammon, with a slight moral tinge to it"; H. L. Mencken that "voting is simply a way of determining which side is the stronger without putting it to the test of fighting". Richard Nixon (*see* TRICKY DICK) took the high ground with critics of the system, saying: "One vote is worth a hundred obscene slogans". But Ronald Reagan (*see* GREAT COMMUNICATOR) was more down-to-earth: "I had an uncle who was a Democrat in Chicago. He received a silver cup from the party for never having missed voting in 15 elections. He'd been dead for 14 of them." On voting in the US Congress, John F. KENNEDY said: "You can milk a cow the wrong way and still be a farmer, but vote the wrong way on a water tower and you're in trouble." In Britain, G. D. H. Cole reckoned: "Voting is merely a handy device; it is not to be identified with democracy, which is a mental and moral relation of man to man." And the playwright Tom Stoppard claimed: "It's not the voting that's democracy, it's the counting." (3) At Westminster, the bundle of blue and white papers circulated to MPs each morning listing the proceedings of the previous evening and giving that day's agenda.

vote of confidence In a PARLIAMENTARY SYSTEM, a vote sought by or forced on an administration under pressure. If defeated, that administration is obliged to resign or, in Britain, submit to an election.

Vote Office At Westminster, the office at the House of Commons from which members obtain the Vote, HANSARD and other Parliamentary papers.

Vote of thanks At the end of a meeting or dinner of a political or non-political group, a motion put by a member of the audience to show appreciation of the guest speaker.

Alternative vote The system of PROPORTIONAL REPRESENTATION in which electors cast a second vote (and perhaps further votes) which comes into play if their first preference candidate finishes at the bottom of the poll.

block vote In Britain, the system under which trade unions dominate decision-making in the LABOUR PARTY by casting millions of votes which may or may not reflect the view of their membership.

card vote In many political and trade-union organizations, a BALLOT that is held on request from the floor if a SHOW OF HANDS is too close to call or if the issue is of importance.

compulsory voting The obligation to vote or pay a fine, imposed in a number of countries, notably Australia (since 1925 for the House, 1934 for the Senate).

deferred vote In the US HOUSE OF REPRESENTATIVES, votes held back to the end of the day, or a two-day period, by the Speaker to be decided in a batch before further business is begun.

electronic voting In the US House of Representatives, the process by which recorded and ROLL-CALL VOTES (*see below*) and QUORUM CALLS are usually taken; each member has a vote-ID card which can be used at vote stations throughout the Chamber, marked "yea", "nay", "present" and "open".

flapper vote The electoral impact of women aged 21 to 29, enfranchised for the first time under the Equal Franchise Act of 1928 for the 1929 general election, and known as "flappers" from the hairstyle of the day – a pigtail that "flapped" against a girl's back.

ghost voting In the US Congress, a trick, in violation of the rules, by which Congressmen can get their votes recorded while away from the CAPITOL.

informal vote In Australia, a vote on a ballot paper disallowed because it does not follow the instructions for preferential voting.

payroll vote *See* PAY.

personal vote The extra support a candidate (usually an INCUMBENT) receives from voters who do not share his or her politics but support them as an individual.

plural voting The ability of an elector to cast his or her vote in more than one electoral district, if REGISTERED there.

preferential voting Under PROPORTIONAL REPRESENTATION as in Australia, a system where an elector expresses a preference (usually in numerical order) on the ballot paper instead of making a single cross.

postal vote A ballot cast by post, normally available to the chronic sick and those away on business.

Present vote A vote cast in the US House of Representatives to register an ABSTENTION.

protest vote Votes cast individually or collectively for one candidate or party as a protest against another. In Britain, frequently blamed by ousted parties for by-election upsets.

recorded vote A vote in which the choice made by individual representatives, delegates or organizations is formally noted, and later made public.

roll-call vote The same as a yea-and-nay vote (*see below*).

Service vote The element in the electorate made up of serving military personnel; specifically the overwhelmingly pro-Labour vote cast by British servicemen in 1945 which sealed Clement ATTLEE's landslide victory.

Single transferable vote A form of PROPORTIONAL REPRESENTATION involving multi-member constituencies with the voter listing candidates in order of preference. Candidates receiving a set "quota" are automatically elected, and any votes above this minimum transferred to the voter's second choices.

Supplementary vote A system of PROPORTIONAL REPRESENTATION, tentatively recommended by the PLANT COMMISSION, under which voters take part in an essentially FIRST PAST THE POST election but list second preferences which are taken into acount only if no candidate gains an outright majority.

sympathy vote Votes cast for a candidate out of sympathy rather than through party or personal support, *e.g.* because of the death of a popular predecessor or some tragedy involving themselves.

tactical vote The practice in a FIRST-PAST-THE-POST system where more than two parties are competing, under which electors vote for a party they would not normally support in the hope of stopping the party they most dislike. In the UK, the readiness of traditional Labour or Conservative supporters to switch to the Liberal Democrats (or Scottish National Party) to deprive the other major party of a seat.

teller vote *See* TELLER.

Twilight Zone vote In America, a vote at a party CONVENTION which could fall just short enough of target to enable a candidacy to be derailed by procedural challenges to delegates. It originated in the vote between George McGovern and Hubert Humphrey at the 1972 Democratic convention.

voice-vote A US term for a vote in which Ayes and Nays are each registered collectively, with the Chair determining which were the more vocal.

Yea-and-Nay vote In the US House of Representatives, a roll-call vote taken if one-fifth of those present rise to demand it.

Vote early and vote often A slogan attributed to Irish ward activists in their home country and – by 1858 – in American MACHINE POLITICS. It was first quoted by Sen. William P. Miles.

Votes for Women The slogan of the SUFFRAGETTES.

Vote, Vote, Vote for Nigel Barton A humorous 1960s BBC television drama by Dennis Potter which laid bare the workings of Britain's constituency party organizations.

Don't vote – it only encourages them A 1960s ANARCHIST and PROTEST slogan.

One man, one vote The basis of democracy. In 1780 John Cartwright wrote: "One man shall have one vote." It has since 1964 been the US Supreme Court's basis for apportionment of Congressional seats, and was also the key

British demand which Ian Smith refused to countenance in Rhodesia before and after UDI.

one member, one vote The basis of organizational reforms in the Labour Party under Neil Kinnock's leadership, often abbreviated to OMOV, with individual members gaining power at the expense of both the trade unions and constituency caucuses. Before the process got under way, Kinnock joked:

> There is one man, one vote in this party, and I am the man.

John Smith took up OMOV after being elected leader in 1992, leading to clashes with union leaders in the summer of 1993 as he sought to abolish their block VOTE. The unions were accused of being the tail that wagged Labour's dog, but John MAJOR told the Commons:

> The unions are the dog, and Labour are the lamp-post.

voter An actual or potential participant in the elective process. The defeated Rep. Morris Udall declared: "The voters have spoken – the bastards". Bernard Epton, a Chicago mayoral candidate, said: "They are just slime." With the cynicism of office, Sen. Henry Ashurst reportedly said: "Voters never grow weary of illusory promises," and Richard Nixon observed: "Voters quickly forget what a man says." Nixon also said: "It doesn't matter whether they knock down the wall when they vote for you or hold their noses. It all counts the same." But Hedrick Smith had the last word: "The voters do not want their leader to appear too much smarter than they are." Generally they succeed.

absent voter A voter who cannot be present for the vote and who is permitted to vote by post or by proxy.

voter registration The process of recording the names of all those entitled to vote; exclusion or omission from the register deprives a person of the vote.

floating voter *See* FLOAT.

League of Women Voters In America, a respected non-party group best known for organizing televised presidential DEBATES.

voting intentions The basic information recorded by OPINION POLLS, recording which party the interviewee would support if an election were held that day.

voting machine A device used in many American states to record votes, particularly in elections with lengthy party TICKETS or large numbers of INITIATIVES on the BALLOT paper. Some are computerized, others make rapid and effective use of punch-cards.

voting record A tabulated voting performance on key issues by elected representatives, often kept by pressure groups (*see* ADA RATING).

Voting Rights Act 1965 One of a series of such Acts, the cornerstone of the CIVIL RIGHTS programme championed by President Lyndon B. Johnson, who said it would "strike away the last major shackle" of the Negro's "ancient bonds". Its main provision was a ban on POLL TAXES.

If voting changed anything, they'd make it illegal An ANARCHIST graffito from the 1979 UK election.

voucher scheme A key element of plans by the radical right (*see* RADICAL) to give citizens choice in their use of public service. It is most frequently advocated in the context of education, with parents allocated vouchers to be used on their children's education at the school of their choice. So far it has seldom been put into practice.

Vox populi, vox Dei The dictum of the 8th-century English educationist Alcuin that "the voice of the people is the voice of God". General William Tecumseh Sherman corrupted it to **Vox populi, vox humbug**. And Abraham LINCOLN earned the nickname **Fox Populi**. The phrase gave rise to **vox pop**, interviews conducted at random in the street to ascertain the public mood.

Vredeling directive In the European Community, measures for greater worker participation in industrial decision-making approved by the COMMISSION in 1980. They required companies to share basic information with their workers, and consultation on issues such as plant closures. Named after Henk Vredeling, the Dutch EC Social Affairs Commissioner who developed the proposals.

W

Wab or Hawold? (Rab or Harold?) The question put to each member of Anthony EDEN's Cabinet by Lord Salisbury, leader of the House of Lords, in the first week of 1957 to ascertain whether R. A. Butler (*see* RAB) or Harold Macmillan (*see* SUPERMAC) should succeed him as Prime Minister. Salisbury (*see* BOBBETTY) reported their almost unanimous preference for Macmillan to the Queen, who appointed him. *See also* MAGIC CIRCLE.

Wade-Davis Bill A measure for radical RECONSTRUCTION of the South after America's CIVIL WAR, passed by Congress on 4 July 1864 but pocket-VETOed by LINCOLN. The Bill, fiercely supported by Horace Greeley, would have required a majority of white male citizens in each Confederate state to take an oath of past as well as future loyalty to the Union, and barred former Confederate office-holders and military volunteers from voting. Promoted by Sen. Benjamin Wade and Rep. H. Winter Davis, its purpose was to prevent Lincoln "letting the South off too easily".

wage restraint A climate in which trade unions, at the urging of government, deliberately press for lower pay increases than they could secure by all-out COLLECTIVE BARGAINING and industrial ACTION. Union leaders are loth to embark on such a course, which is unpopular with the RANK AND FILE especially at a time of high INFLATION, but may agree to it as part of a SOCIAL CONTRACT, under which the Government takes parallel action to keep down price increases.

Wagner Act The Act, promoted by Sen. Robert F. Wagner and enacted in 1935 with the backing of FDR, that guaranteed US labour's right to organize and engage in COLLECTIVE BARGAINING following decades of "union-busting". Also known as the **Wagner-Connery Act,** it established the National Labour Relations Board to supervise bargaining and union elections. After its constitutionality was upheld by the Supreme Court in 1937, a number of states passed "Wagner Acts" of their own.

> The United Auto Workers and the CIO have paid cash on the barrel for every piece of legislation that we have gotten. The Wagner Act cost us many dollars in contributions to the Roosevelt administration with the explicit understanding of a quid pro quo.
>
> JOHN L. LEWIS (1880–1969).

wait. wait and see The remark which became ASQUITH's catch phrase. Originally said to Lord Helmsley on 3 March 1910, "We had better wait and see" became his habitual response to questioners, initially over whether hundreds of Liberal PEERS would have to be created to push Lloyd George's Budget through the House of Lords. Before long, Tory backbenchers would chant "wait and see" whenever Asquith answered questions in the Commons. His opponents turned the phrase against him over his alleged lack of urgency in prosecuting WORLD WAR I.

watchful waiting The phrase, first used by Andrew Jackson in 1836, harnessed by Woodrow WILSON in 1913 to describe his policy of non-recognition of General Huerta's Mexican government. The waiting period did not last long; the next year US troops occupied Vera Cruz.

walk. walk and chew gum at the same time LBJ's celebrated jibe at Gerald FORD's clumsiness in the days before circumstances catapulted him into the Presidency. The full phrase as published was "Jerry Ford is so dumb he can't walk and chew gum at the same time", but Johnson actually said "fart", not "walk". *See also* TOO MUCH FOOTBALL WITHOUT A HELMET.

walk in the woods The occasion in 1982 of a potential breakthrough in US–Soviet ARMS CONTROL talks, when their respective negotiators at Geneva, Paul Nitze and Yuli Kvitsinsky, broke away from formal talks to reach an understanding on limiting intermediate-range missiles in Europe. The understanding was sabotaged by the PENTAGON, enabling Kremlin hard-liners also to disown it.

walkabout An occasion when a politician stops his or her car and mingles with the crowd, without delivering a speech or making any meaningful remarks. A walkabout was originally an Australian term for when an Aborigine sets off to roam the country for months on end. First used by Queen Elizabeth

II, the walkabout has become a fixture in many politician's schedules. *See also* PHOTO-OPPORTUNITY.

walkout A common form of protest or gesture of disgust. Notably by the Soviet Union from the UNITED NATIONS just before the Korean War, by Eric Heffer from the 1985 Labour Party conference when Neil Kinnock attacked the MILITANT TENDENCY, and by Michael Heseltine (*see* TARZAN) resigning from Margaret Thatcher's Cabinet in mid-meeting in 1986 over WESTLAND.

Walker Report The report of the President's Commission on the Causes and Prevention of Violence, set up after the riots at the 1968 CHICAGO Democratic CONVENTION. The report blamed much of the violence on the provocative use of obscene language by the demonstrators, but termed the occasion "a police riot"; because Chairman Daniel Walker insisted on listing the words used by the rioters, the Government Printing Office refused to print The Report. *See also* DALEY MACHINE; YIPPIES.

Wallenberg hearing An international hearing convened in Stockholm in January 1980 to hear evidence suggesting that the Swedish banker and diplomat Raoul Wallenberg (1912–?) had not died in a Soviet prison in 1947 as claimed by Moscow but had remained alive in the GULAG. Wallenberg has earned the gratitude of humanity for his brazen success in snatching some 25,000 Hungarian Jews from imminent transportation to NAZI death camps by claiming they had Swedish citizenship. But when the Russians entered Budapest in 1945, Wallenberg was arrested, purportedly for espionage, and taken to Moscow. In 1991 the dying Soviet state handed Wallenberg's personal belongings to his family, but insisted he had died in 1947. Although reasonably firm evidence of sightings was reported well into the 1960s, the truth will probably never be known. Many countries have paid tribute to Wallenberg: in Israel he has a place at Yad Vashem, the memorial to the HOLOCAUST, as the most outstanding of the Righteous Gentiles; Budapest now boasts a fine memorial to him; and the United States in 1981, when there were hopes he might yet be alive, declared him an honorary citizen.

Walpole, Sir Robert, later Earl of Orford (1676–1745). Generally reckoned Britain's first PRIME MINISTER (Whig) and longest holder of the office (1721–42). Appointed First Lord of the TREASURY and CHANCELLOR OF THE EXCHEQUER 1715, he was from 1721 head of an inner circle of Ministers and thus effectively Prime Minister. He held office for so long by adroit use of PATRONAGE. Jonathan Swift declared:

> The whole system of his ministry was corruption, and he never gave bribe or pension without telling the receivers frankly what he expected of them, and threatening them to put an end to his bounty if they failed to comply in every circumstance.

But Walpole said in his own defence:

> I have lived long enough in the world to know that the safety of a Minister lies in his having the approbation of this House. Former Ministers neglected that and therefore they fell. I have always made it my first study to obtain it, and therefore I hope to stand.

The doctrine that "every man has his price" is attributed to him, but Walpole was actually speaking of his opponents when he said: "All those men have their price". Walpole was a country gentleman of his time. G. M. Trevelyan wrote: "Even as Prime Minister, he was said to open his gamekeeper's letters the first of the bunch." He was finally brought down by his handling of the Spanish-Austrian War of Succession, saying on his fall: "I have led a life of business for so long, I have lost my taste for reading. And now what shall I do?"

> The cur-dog of Britain, and spaniel of Spain.
>
> Dean SWIFT.

Walworth Road The headquarters in South London near the Elephant and Castle of Britain's LABOUR PARTY, which moved there from TRANSPORT HOUSE in 1981.

war. War aims The objectives of a state engaged in conflict, often published, sometimes not. WILSON'S FOURTEEN POINTS are a prime example.

War between the States A Southern term for America's CIVIL WAR.

War Book (1) A preparedness plan kept by the military, for activation if war becomes imminent. One has also been kept by the UK civil service continually since 1911, with wartime contingency plans for civilian life. (2) The file kept by the chairman of Britain's CONSERVATIVE PARTY for the conduct of a General Election campaign.

War Cabinet *See* CABINET.

war crimes Atrocities, generally against civilians and amounting at their worst to genocide, authorized during wartime by political leaders. The first prosecution of **war criminals** was at NUREMBERG in 1946 when 22 NAZI leaders were tried for torture, deportation, persecution, murder and mass extermination. Twelve were sentenced to death. In the US zone of Germany alone, 500,000 ex-Nazis were convicted of less serious offences. In Japan an international tribunal in Tokyo tried 25 civil and military leaders for planning an aggressive war and committing crimes against humanity; seven, including ex-Prime Minister Hideki Tojo, were hanged.

War Crimes Act The UK legislation passed in 1991, despite resistance from the House of Lords, for British residents to be tried for crimes allegedly committed in Nazi-occupied territory in continental Europe.

War games Theoretical exercises, often highly detailed, in which military planners test out possible scenarios for war.

The War Game A TV drama-documentary on the devastating effect of nuclear war, banned by the BBC in 1963 despite protests from CND.

War Hawks *See* HAWKS.

War is hell General William Tecumseh Sherman's celebrated observation, based on his personal experiences in the US CIVIL WAR. Speaking in Columbus, Ohio, in 1880, Sherman said:

> There is many a boy here today who looks on war as all glory, but, boys, war is hell.

As complications multiplied after World War II, President Truman said: "Sherman was wrong. Peace is hell."

War Is Peace. Freedom is Slavery. Ignorance is Strength The motto of the MINISTRY OF TRUTH in George Orwell's 1984.

War Measures Act Canada's 1914 wartime internal security legislation, first invoked in peacetime by Pierre TRUDEAU in 1970 to combat terrorism by Quebec SEPARATISTS. Trudeau justified the action by saying: "The Government is acting to make clear to kidnappers that in this country laws are made and changed by the elected representatives of all Canadians, not by a handful of self-styled dictators." But the NDP leader T. C. Douglas described it as "using a sledgehammer to crack a peanut".

War of Independence *See* AMERICAN REVOLUTION.

War of Jenkins' Ear The war between Britain and Spain which began in 1739 after the "war party" at Westminster had brought a Captain Jenkins to testify before the Commons that the ear he carried in a little box had been cut off by privateers protecting the Spanish Main. It is more than likely the ear had actually been cut off by the common hangman, but the event propelled a reluctant WALPOLE into declaring war. His action was greeted with public rejoicing, but Walpole observed:

> They now ring the bells, but they will soon wring their hands.

His words were prophetic; the war went badly for Britain and within three years Walpole was out of office.

War of Jennifer's Ear The most contentious episode of Britain's 1992 general election. Labour screened a broadcast based on seven-year-old Jennifer Bennett's lengthy wait for an NHS ear operation. The Conservatives branded it inaccurate, Jennifer's parents took different sides, Neil Kinnock's press secretary Julie Hall emotionally denied leaking details to the press, and Health Secretary William Waldegrave admitted the Conservative party had put the doctor in the case in touch with the *Daily Express* after another paper had got on to the story. The title echoed the War of Jenkins' Ear (*see above*).

war of the flea The title of Robert Taber's definitive book on GUERRILLA war. Taber wrote:

> The guerrilla fights the war of the flea, and his military enemy suffers the dog's advantages: too much to defend; too small, too ubiquitous, and agile an enemy to come to grips with.

war on poverty The theme of President Lyndon B. Johnson's (*see* LBJ) first State of the UNION message in January 1964, it provided close to $1 billion for a range of community-action projects for better health and housing and a Job Corps to train young people, under an office of Economic Opportunity. Johnson said:

> This administration today, here and now, declares unconditional war on poverty in America. I urge this Congress and all Americans to join with me in that effort.

Despite massive spending, poverty in America remained. And twenty years later Ronald Reagan declared:

> In the war on poverty, poverty won.

War Powers Act or **Resolution** The crucial measure, passed by Congress in 1973 over a presidential veto, which curbed the Executive's ability to commit US forces abroad in the wake or the VIETNAM WAR. Congressional approval is required for forces to be committed to a combat zone for more than 90 days. Sen. John Warner said that any attempt by Congress to invoke it would put US forces in "a byzantine thicket of quicksand".

War Room The two-storey building in Little Rock, Arkansas, from which the campaign team of Bill Clinton (*see* COMEBACK KID) fought and won the 1992 Presidential election.

war to end wars A popular contemporary term to justify World War I, or explain its horrors. The origin of the phrase was H. G. Wells's 1914 book *The War that will End War*. It was adapted as "the war to end war" by Woodrow WILSON, who said: "The war we have just been through, though it was shot through with terror, is not to be compared with the war we would have to face next time.". More cynically, Lloyd George (*see*

L.G.) observed: "This war, like the next war, is a war to end war."

Dirty War The campaign of terror against left-wing elements pursued by the Argentine military under the dictatorship of Generals Viola, Videla and Galtieri in the late 1970s and early 1980s. *See* DISAPPEARED; MONTONEROS.

He kept us out of War Woodrow WILSON's re-election slogan in 1916 – months before the US entered World War I.

I have told you once and I tell you again: your boys will not be sent into foreign wars Franklin D. Roosevelt's (*see* FDR) promise in his 1940 re-election campaign, overridden by PEARL HARBOR.

I want to stand by my country, but I cannot vote for war. I vote no The Montana Congresswoman Jeannette Rankin voting against declaring war on Germany in 1917. She was also to be the sole Congressional opponent of war in 1941 after PEARL HARBOR. *See also* STATUARY HALL.

In war, resolution. In defeat, defiance. In victory, magnanimity. In peace, goodwill A dictum attributed to CHURCHILL during World War II, but first said by his aide Sir Edward Marsh (1872–1953).

Just War The doctrine of St. Thomas Aquinas (*c.* 1225–74) setting out the circumstances in which war is permissible:

> In order for a war to be just, three things are necessary. First, the authority of the sovereign. . . . Secondly, a just cause. . . . Thirdly, a rightful intention.

limited war The notion that war can be levied against a particular enemy without the conflict expanding.

Make love, not war A slogan of the Hippie end of the Peace Movement from the 1960s.

> It didn't look to me as if they were capable of either.
> RONALD REAGAN.

moral equivalent of war *See* MORAL.

phoney war The period between the formal opening of World War II in September 1939 and Hitler's BLITZKRIEG through the Low Countries to France the following May. The phrase was coined by French prime minister Edouard Daladier in a speech to the National Assembly in December 1939: "It is a phoney war."

There ain't gonna be no war Anthony EDEN's comment on returning to London from the 1955 four-power east-west summit in Geneva. It came from the *c.*1910 musical *Pelissier's Follies*:

> There ain't going to be no war
> As long as we've a king like good King Edward.

There will be no war Woodrow WILSON's forecast in January 1917, three months before America finally entered World War I.

There will be no war this year, or next year either Lord Beaverbrook's morale-raising slogan on the masthead of his *Daily Express*, placed there in 1938 at the height of the SUDETEN CRISIS and quietly removed the following year after Hitler rolled up the rest of Czechoslovakia.

total war Goebbels's term for war fought with total devastation. The term became universal currency, but the doctrine predated the Nazis, Matthias Erzberger saying in 1914:

> If a way was found of entirely wiping out the whole of London it would be more humane to employ it than to allow the blood of a single German soldier to be shed on the battlefield.

trench warfare Originally the static but bloody conflict in World War I, later political debate between two sides sniping from entrenched positions, also industrial struggles of a similar nature.

warmonger A Cold War term used by STALINIST and subsequent Soviet leaders for Western leaders who armed against them.

ward The basic electoral unit, especially in local politics. In Britain, the area a district councillor represents.

ward heeler Pejorative in US politics for one of the cogs in the wheel of MACHINE POLITICS, who gives favours in return for loyalty at the polls (*See also* HAPPY WARRIOR).

Warm Springs The Georgia retreat where Franklin D. Roosevelt went for relaxation, and where he died on 12 April 1945 of a cerebral haemorrhage while recovering from the YALTA conference. FDR's former lover Lucy Mercer Rutherfurd was with him when he died – she left hurriedly before Eleanor Roosevelt arrived.

Warren. Warren Commission The seven-member Commission under US Chief Justice Earl Warren set up by President Johnson to investigate the circumstances of President KENNEDY's assassination, particularly claims that Lee Harvey Oswald had not been the sole assassin – or indeed the assassin at all. The commission took 26 volumes of testimony from over 500 people. In an 888-page report published in 1964, it concluded that Oswald had acted alone in shooting Kennedy, and that the night-club owner Jack Ruby had also acted on his own in shooting Oswald while the alleged assassin was in police custody. Yet the speculation has continued.

Warren court The liberal SUPREME COURT presided over from 1953 to 1969 by Earl Warren (1891–1974), former Democratic Governor of California. It opened the way for the promotion of CIVIL RIGHTS with the landmark BROWN decision in 1954 outlawing segregated public schools, and in 1964 struck down laws which rigged state legislatures in favour of rural voters. President Eisenhower described his appointment of Warren to head the court as "the biggest damfool mistake I ever made".

Warsaw. Warsaw Pact The treaty of friendship, co-operation and mutual assistance concluded in 1955 between the Soviet Union and its East European satellites – Albania (until 1968) Bulgaria, Czechoslovakia, East Germany, Hungary, Poland and Romania – as a counter to NATO which West Germany had just joined. The only European Communist country not to join was Yugoslavia. It gave the Soviet Union the right to station troops in signatory states, and the pretext to stamp out reform movements (Hungary 1956, Czechoslovakia 1968). The pact was scrapped in April 1991.

Warsaw uprising (1) The revolt in the Warsaw GHETTO on 19 April 1943 of its remaining Jews in a desperate attempt to halt their transportation to NAZI death camps. The 1500 Jewish guerrillas managed to kill several hundred Germans before resistance was ended on 16 May. (2) The attempt by the Polish underground to liberate Warsaw from the Germans as the RED ARMY approached from the East. The rising, on 1 August 1944 by the 50,000-strong Home Army and armed civilians, was not directed against the Russians – but the Soviet command, though within striking distance of the capital, called a halt while the NAZIS brutally suppressed the uprising. Stalin even vetoed the dropping of supplies by the Western allies until the rebels were certain of defeat. After a battle in which 15,000 Poles died, the last resisters surrendered on 27 September, after which the Germans killed 200,000 civilians in reprisal. Only when he was sure the non-Communist Home Army had been eliminated as a potential post-war rival did Stalin let the "liberation" of Warsaw proceed.

Washington, George (1732–99) Supreme commander (from 1775) and outstanding general of the American revolutionary army, and first President of the United States (1789–97). A Virginia gentleman and a senior officer in the colony's militia, he emerged as a natural leader as tension with Britain rose; when appointed commander-in-chief, he wrote:

> I am embarked on a wide ocean, boundless in its prospect and in which, perhaps, no safe harbour is to be found. I can answer for but three things: a firm belief in the justice of our cause, close attention in the prosecution of it, and the strictest integrity.

That reputation for integrity went back to his boyhood, when he allegedly told his father when asked if he had cut down a cherry tree: "I cannot tell a lie, Pa; you know I can't tell a lie. I did cut it with my hatchet." And as commander-in-chief he wrote:

> I beg leave to assure the Congress that as no pecuniary consideration could have tempted me to accept this arduous employment at the expense of my domestic ease and happiness I do not wish to make any profit from it.

Nevertheless he was to observe in old age:

> I long ago despaired of any other reward for my services than the satisfaction arising from a consciousness of doing my duty, and the esteem of my friends.

Throughout the revolutionary struggle, he maintained the spirits of his army and the movement it served. After the loss of Ticonderoga, he said: "Under a full persuasion of the justice of our cause, I cannot entertain an idea that it will finally sink, though it may remain for some time under a cloud." At times he professed to revel in the military life, saying: "I have heard the bullets whistle and, believe me, there is something charming in the sound." But he also declared:

> From the day I entered upon the command of the American armies, I date my fall, and the ruin of my reputation. £50,000 should not induce me to do again what I have done.

Although the office of President was created for him, Washington took it with reluctance, saying: "My movement to the chair of government will be accompanied by feelings not unlike those of a culprit who is going to the place of his execution". He seriously considered retirement after one term, and in 1796 was adamant that eight years as President was enough.

Washington had his sycophants, but he also had his critics, notably Thomas Paine, who wrote:

> As to you, sir, treacherous to private friendship (for so you have been to me, and that in the day of danger) and a hypocrite in public life, the world will be puzzled to decide whether you are an apostate or an impostor, whether you have abandoned good principles or whether you ever had any.

Sen. William Maclay considered him overbearing as President: "He wishes to tread on the necks of the Senate . . . to bear down our deliberations with his personal authority and presence." And Benjamin Bache declared: "If ever a nation was debauched by a man, the American nation has been debauched by Washington."

Washington made a great impression on most who met him. Lafayette exclaimed: "Never before had I beheld so superb a man." According to Abigail Adams, "he has a dignity which forbids familiarity, mixed with an easy affability which creates love and reverence". To JEFFERSON,

> his mind was slow in operation but sure in conclusion. On the whole his character was, in its mass, perfect, in nothing bad, in a few points indifferent; and it may truly be said that never did nature and fortune combine more perfectly to make a man great.

John ADAMS observed that "dignity with ease and complacency, the gentleman and the soldier, look agreeably blended in him. Modesty marks every line and feature of his face." But Adams did once remark: "He is too illiterate, unread, unlearned for his station and reputation". Gilbert Stuart noted those same characteristics: "All his features were indicative of the most ungovernable passions, and had he been born in the forests, it is my opinion that he would have been the fiercest man among the savage tribes." To Samuel Eliot Morison, Washington was "the last person you would ever suspect of having been a young man". And Nathaniel Hawthorne was to remark: "He had no nakedness, but was born with clothes on, and his hair powdered, and made a stately bow on his 1st appearance in the world."

On his death, Henry "Light Horse Harry" Lee set the tone with a eulogy describing Washington as **first in war, first in peace, and first in the hearts of his countrymen**. Byron hailed him as "next only to the divinity", writing:

> Washington
> Whose every battlefield is holy ground
> Which breathes of battles saved, not worlds undone.

To Gladstone, he was "the purest figure in history"; Thackeray wrote of "a life without a stain, a fame without a flaw"; and Thomas A. Bailey reckoned him "the only man in the history of the presidency bigger than the government itself". Daniel Webster orated that "the character of Washington is among the most cherished contemplations of my life. It is a fixed star in the firmament of great names, shining without twinkling or obscuration, with clear, steady, beneficent light." LINCOLN declared:

> Washington is the mightiest name on earth – long since mightiest in the cause of civil liberty, still mightiest in moral reformation. On that name no eulogy is expected. It cannot be. To add brightness to the sun or glory to the name of Washington is alike impossible. Let none attempt it. In solemn awe pronounce the name and in its naked deathless splendor leave it shining on.

But by the late 19th century Robert Ingersoll could write: "Washington is now only a steel engraving. About the real man who lived and loved and hated and schemed, we know but little."

Washington's farewell address The message to the American nation, largely drafted by HAMILTON, which the retiring President Washington published in the newspapers on 7 September 1796. He voiced satisfaction with his achievements on the home front, but regretted the onset of the party strife which was already shaping the divisions that led to CIVIL WAR. On foreign affairs, he did not warn against all "entangling alliances" (the phrase was Jefferson's). But he did say: "Taking care always to keep ourselves . . . on a respectable defensive posture, we may safely trust to temporary alliances for extraordinary emergencies."

Washington DC (DISTRICT OF COLUMBIA) America's federal capital, named after George Washington and established on a ten mile-square site taken from Virginia (later returned) and Maryland during his presidency. At the outset it barely possessed the basic amenities, leading Sen. Gouverneur Morris to complain: "[We need only] houses, cellars, kitchens, well informed men, amiable women, and other little trifles of this kind to make our city perfect." Habits were basic too, Charles Dickens naming Washington "the headquarters of tobacco-tinctured saliva". The climate did not help, President Buchanan declaring it "no place for a civilized man to spend the summer". Things were slow to improve, Horace Greeley branding it "not a place to live in. The rents are high, the food is bad, the dust is disgusting and the morals are deplorable." And President Garfield (*see* BOATMAN JIM) once exclaimed: "My God! What is there in this place that a man should ever want to get into it?" And as late as the 1960s, John F. KENNEDY could mock Washington as

> a city of Northern charm and Southern efficiency.

Washington has developed from what Henry Adams termed "a mere political camp" into the ultimate company town – and, through its urban problems, the murder capital of the United States. To many politicians it has held a special magic, President TAFT once exclaiming: "[This] is a Federal City, and it tingles down to the feet of any man, whether he comes from Washington state, or Los Angeles, or Texas, when he comes and walks these city streets." John Mason Brown drew a different moral: "The more I observed Washington, the more I understood how prophetic L'Enfant was when he laid it out as a city that goes round in circles". And as the modern Washington mushroomed, Ada Louise Huxtable branded it "an endless series of mock palaces clearly built for clerks". Washington has a large migrant political population. Eisenhower observed that "everyone has been too long away from home", and Sen. Claiborne Pell reckoned that "people only leave Washington by way of the box – ballot or coffin". Fanny Dixwell Holmes noted that "Washington is full of famous men and the women they married when they were young", while one commentator termed it "a city where half the people want to be discovered and the other half are afraid they'll be found out". To Elliott Richardson it was "a city of cocker spaniels – people who are more interested in being petted and admired, loved, than rendering the exercise of power". President Truman (*see* GIVE 'EM HELL HARRY) tartly observed: "If you want a friend in Washington, buy a dog." And Speaker Sam Rayburn reckoned it "a sour-bellied place".

Political Washington has been called "the hubbub of the Universe" and "the only place where sound travels faster than light". To Douglas Cater it was "a crazy quilt of people who have each other by the vulnerable parts". George E. Allen trustingly reckoned: "People who think the mighty in Washington can be persuaded, or corrupted, if you will, by anything less than votes just don't understand what it's all about and never will. They don't know what Washington juice is made of." Sen. Strom Thurmond reckoned that "the longer you stay, you realize that sometimes you can catch more flies with honey than with vinegar". Tim McNamar observed: "When you ask what time it is you get different answers from Democrats and Republicans; 435 answers from the House of Representatives; a 500-page report from some consultants on how to tell the time; no answer from your lawyer and a bill for $1000." And George Shultz admitted: "Nothing ever gets settled in this town. People never give up, including me." Washington's remoteness from mainstream America is legendary: Sen. Huey Long said: "The heart of America is felt less here than at any place I have ever been," and Jimmy CARTER found the capital "isolated from the mainstream of our nation's life".

Americans reckon a streak of lunacy runs through their capital and its proceedings. One wit branded it: "69.2 square miles surrounded by reality". Mark Twain termed it "a stud farm for every jackass in the country". Irwin S. Conn declared: "If I wanted to go crazy I would do it in Washington because it would not be noticed." Ronald Reagan reckoned that "common sense is about as common in Washington as a Fourth of July blizzard in Columbia, S. C.", and Anne Burford, head of the Environmental Protection Agency, deemed it "too small to be a State, but too large to be an asylum for the mentally deranged". Politicians know this, Norman Ornstein saying:

> If you are a member of Congress, the last thing you want is to be compared with all those creeps in Washington.

Washington has become a collective term for the US government, the administrative community, its lifestyle and state of mind. At the outset Jefferson wrote: "Were we directed from Washington when to sow and when to reap, we should soon want bread." And during his 1964 Presidential campaign, Sen. Barry Goldwater remarked: "I fear Washington and centralized government more than I do Moscow."

running against Washington Campaigning for office depicting oneself as an insider fighting the entire governmental system.

Washington conference The first Allied conference (codenamed *Arcadia*) between Franklin D. Roosevelt (FDR) and CHURCHILL, between 22 December 1941 and 12 January 1942. Hurriedly convened following PEARL HARBOR, the conference established long-term Allied strategy. Churchill secured a US commitment to the defeat of Germany in the Atlantic and European theatres before concentrating on Japan. A joint declaration, formally announcing an alliance to defeat the AXIS powers, was signed by 26 countries including China and the Soviet Union.

Washington naval treaty The 1922 agreement, masterminded by Secretary of State Charles Evans Hughes (1862–1948), which ended for a decade the naval race between the great powers, the US, Britain and Japan each agreeing to scrap large parts of their navies and respect each other's holdings in the Pacific. This was the only effective measure of disarmament achieved between the wars.

Washington State The most north-westerly state of America barring Alaska, acquired from Britain in 1846 and admitted as a state of the Union in 1889.

Mr. Smith goes to Washington Frank Capra's 1939 film, starring James Stewart as the idealistic young Wisconsin senator who sets out to cleanse the capital's Augean stables of corruption.

Treaty of Washington The 1871 agreement between the US and a UK/Canada delegation which settled the boundary between Vancouver Island and the US, admitted Canadian fish to America free of duty and gave America ten-year access to Canadian fisheries, and determined navigation rights on the Great Lakes and the St. Lawrence. It also refered the ALABAMA incident to an international tribunal.

WASPs White Anglo-Saxon Protestants. Derogatory term for America's traditionally dominant ethnic group, and especially the Northeastern upper class.

Wataugua Association America's first free civil government, set up in 1772 by settlers in the North Carolina and Tennessee mountains, between the Ohio and Tennessee rivers. As the settlers lived outside the colonies, Britain allowed them to band together; they secured the land in 1768 by agreement with the Indian "Six Nations", and drew up the "Articles of the Watauga Association" under which an elected 13-member assembly chose a ruling committee of five. *See also* FRANKLIN.

watching for googlies The cricketing analogy used by UK party managers for eternal vigilance against potentially damaging events, issues and remarks. It was coined by Angus (later Lord) Maude (1912–), the Minister in Margaret Thatcher's (*see* IRON LADY) original Cabinet responsible for presenting Government policy. A googly is an off-break with a leg-break action; the term originated in Australia in 1903–04 when the MCC tourist B. J. T. Bosanquet used the delivery to great effect.

water. like trying to nail a drop of water to the wall The verdict of Rep. George Danielson on the House Judiciary Committee's efforts to question former Attorney-General John Mitchell (*see* KATIE GRAHAM'S GOING TO GET . . .) on his involvement in Watergate, 10 July 1974. *Compare also* JFK's remarks on BUREAUCRACY.

Watergate The greatest peacetime crisis in America's political history, culminating in the resignation in disgrace of President Richard NIXON (*see* TRICKY DICK) on 8 August 1974. It took its name from the modernistic complex of apartments and offices in Washington beside the Potomac, where on 17 June 1972 a security guard named Frank Wills caught five men breaking into the headquarters of the Democratic NATIONAL COMMITTEE. With the Democrats facing heavy defeat in the coming election, Washington insiders felt the burglary was "like breaking into the Ford HQ to steal the plans for the Edsel". Partly as a result of investigative reporting by Carl Bernstein and Bob Woodward of the *Washington Post*, the five – and two accomplices – were found to have links with the White House. Gradually over the succeeding months a trail of "laundered" money was identified leading back from the five to Nixon's campaign committee (CREEP). Nixon denied any involvement, and the issue failed to take off during the 1972 Presidential campaign, largely because of fierce denunciations of the Press from Vice-President Spiro Agnew, who was soon afterwards disgraced over a completely separate matter. But after the election, first through ferocious sentencing of the five by Judge John (MAXIMUM JOHN) Sirica which led the burglars to talk, a chain of misdeed and corruption came to light involving almost all Nixon's closest associates except for Dr. Henry KISSINGER; by 1977, many would be in jail. Both Houses of CONGRESS began hearings which brought damaging evidence to light; Nixon alleged that "the fine hand of the Kennedys" was behind the Senate's 70–0 vote to investigate. When White House staff were subpoenaed to testify, Nixon told them:

> I don't give a shit what happens. I want you to stonewall . . . plead the FIFTH AMENDMENT, cover up, or anything else. If that will save it, save the plan.

But publicly he said: "I condemn any effort to cover up this case." He fought back by concentrating on "business as usual", saying: "Let others wallow in Watergate. We are going to do our job."

The case gained its critical mass in mid-1973. First, White House counsel John Dean, ignoring Nixon's advice, told the Senate's ERVIN COMMITTEE that former Attorney-General John Mitchell had consented to the burglary, that White House CHIEF OF STAFF H. R. Haldeman and domestic affairs adviser John Erlichman were aware of it – and that Nixon had approved the COVER-UP. Then in July White House aide Alexander Butterfield revealed that Nixon had kept tapes of all his conversations. Nixon at first resisted pressure to release the tapes, claiming EXECUTIVE PRIVILEGE. And when his own appointees demanded that he comply, he carried out the SATURDAY NIGHT MASSACRE to remove them. When the transcripts were finally released on 30 April 1974 with Nixon insisting: "The President has nothing to hide", they became a best-seller; the coarseness of Nixon's language and the depth of his involvement scandalized the nation. Vice-President FORD made a virtue of this, saying: "I cannot imagine any other country in the world where the opposition would seek – and the Chief Exceutive would allow – the dissemination of his most private and personal conversations with his staff – which, to be honest, do not exactly confer sainthood on anyone concerned." The tapes brought to the forefront the central question of Watergate, put by Nixon's ally Sen. Howard Baker:

> What did the President know and when did he know it?

In July 1974 the SUPREME COURT voted "eight-zip" that Nixon must hand over all tapes to the SPECIAL PROSECUTOR, and the House Judiciary Committee voted 27–11 to recommend Nixon's IMPEACHMENT. Nixon began to lose heart, telling his new Chief of Staff General Alexander Haig: "Well, there goes the Presidency." He also told Haig: "In your business you have a way of handling problems like this. Somebody leaves a pistol in the drawer. I don't have a pistol." With almost all his former supporters deserting him, an emotional Nixon admitted on 5 August that he had approved the cover-up and impeded FBI investigations; with impeachment now certain, he quit on 8 August to facilitate "the process of healing which is so desperately needed in America" and flew off to exile at SAN CLEMENTE; Gerald Ford was sworn in, PARDONing Nixon soon after. Ford said: "I assume the presidency under extraordinary circumstances. This is an hour of history that troubles our minds and hurts our hearts." And he concluded:

> Never again must America allow an arrogant, elite guard of political adolescents to bypass the regular party organization and dictate the terms of a national election.

Twenty-five of those "political adolescents", though not Nixon, ended in jail. *See also* DEEP THROAT; FROST INTERVIEWS; I AM NOT A CROOK; INOPERATIVE; KATIE GRAHAM'S GOING TO GET ...; MODIFIED, LIMITED HANGOUT; PLUMBERS; RATFUCKING; SMOKING GUN; WHITEWASH.

> Worse than a crime – it was a blunder. NIXON.

> I brought myself down. I gave them a sword and they stuck it in and they twisted it with relish. And I guess that if I had been in the same position, I'd have done the same thing. NIXON.

Watts The scene, from 11 to 16 August 1965, of the worst INNER-CITY riots in Los Angeles prior to the Rodney KING riot of 1992. Ten thousand black rioters burned and looted an area of 500 blocks, and 15,000 police and National Guardsmen were brought in to restore order. The riot was sparked on a hot, smoggy day when a police patrolman drew his gun on a young Black motorist; it left 34 people dead – 28 of them Black; over 3900 people were arrested and over 200 businesses destroyed. The *Los Angeles Times* angered city officials by blaming the riot on poor contact between them and the Black community, and demanding anti-poverty measures to combat 30% local unemployment.

waving the bloody shirt Rabble-rousing methods to perpetuate Northern hostility toward the South after America's CIVIL WAR. In March 1868 A. P. Huggins, a tax collector and superintendent who had come to Mississippi from Ohio, was wakened by Klansmen, stripped, given 75 lashes and ordered on pain of death to leave the state in ten days. Huggins reported the incident to the military, and an officer took his bloodstained nightshirt to Washington and gave it to the radical Massachusetts Congressman Ben Butler. When Butler proposed a Bill enabling President Johnson to use the army to enforce Federal laws in the South, he waved Huggins's gory shirt in the House Chamber. For the rest of the century Republican orators would "wave the bloody shirt" against the Democrats at election time. The term became used for any piece of political campaigning designed to reopen old enmities.

After Dr. Martin Luther KING was shot in April 1968, the Rev. Jesse Jackson actually put on the bloody shirt. Though a storey away from King when he was gunned down in a Memphis motel, the next day Jackson appeared before the cameras in a turtleneck covered with blood.

Ways and Means (1) In the US HOUSE OF REPRESENTATIVES, the powerful committee that writes tax legislation. Its 37 members handle every aspect of the raising of revenues – including taxes, tariffs and social security levies – and debt policy. (2) At Westminster the blanket term for the provision of public revenue; BUDGET proposals are set out in *Ways and Means Resolutions* on which the FINANCE BILL is based. The deputy Speaker of the Commons is officially known as the **Chairman of Ways and Means**; he or she presides over the Budget statement.

we. We are the masters now The assertion by Attorney-General Hartley (later Lord) Shawcross (1902–) which summed up for opposition Tories the quasi-revolutionary nature of the post-war Attlee government. Speaking in the Commons on 2 April 1946, Shawcross actually said:

> We are the masters at the moment, and not only at the moment, but for a very long time to come.

We got clobbered Press secretary Bill Hagerty's verdict on the violent reception accorded Vice-President and Mrs. Nixon when they arrived in Caracas, Venezuela, in May 1958. For 12 miles from the airport the crowd pelted their motorcade with garbage, spat and attacked the cars with baseball bats.

We grammar school boys must stick together The celebrated put-down administered by Leader of the House John Biffen (*see* BIFFO) to Dennis Skinner (*see* BEAST OF BOLSOVER) in 1987 when the Labour left-winger was in full flight condemning Tory-sponsored inequality.

We only have to be lucky once The IRA's chilling message to Margaret Thatcher after it had narrowly failed to assassinate her in the

BRIGHTON BOMBING of October 1984 (*see* a DAY I WAS MEANT NOT TO SEE).

We're just mild about Harry The slogan on many banners at the 1948 Democratic CONVENTION, which was lukewarm about nominating Harry S Truman for a full Presidential term; the party had tried and failed to attract Dwight D. Eisenhower. The words were a pun on the song title *I'm just wild about Harry*; Truman, of course, had the last laugh, coming from behind in his "GIVE 'EM HELL" campaign to defeat Thomas DEWEY.

We shall fight on the beaches, we shall fight on the landing grounds, we shall fight in the fields and in the streets, we shall fight in the hills, we shall never surrender CHURCHILL's speech in the House of Commons on 4 June 1940 after the successful evacuation of over 350,000 British and Allied troops from Dunkirk, but with the threat of German invasion looming. This section of the speech, also delivered on radio, began: "We shall go on to the end, we shall fight in France, we shall fight on the seas and oceans, we shall fight with growing confidence and growing strength in the air, we shall defend our island whatever the cost may be", and ended:

> And even if, which I do not for a moment believe, this island or a huge part of it were subjugated and starving, then our Empire beyond the seas, armed and guarded by the British Fleet, would carry on the struggle, until, in God's good time, the New World, with all its power and might, steps forth to the rescue and the liberation of the old.

We shall overcome The opening line of one of the anthems of America's CIVIL RIGHTS movement in the 1960s. The song, written by Zilphia Horton and added to by Pete Seeger and others, began:

> We shall overcome,
> We shall overcome,
> We shall overcome some day.
> And it's deep in my heart
> I do believe
> That we shall overcome some day.

> Revolutions are never waged singing "We Shall Overcome". Revolutions are based upon bloodshed.
>
> MALCOLM X, 1964.

We want eight and we won't wait The slogan taken up by advocates of a strong Royal Navy in 1909 in an effort to pressure Britain's Liberal government into boosting the building programme for Dreadnoughts (battle cruisers) to match Germany's buildup. The Admiralty proposed building six; Lloyd George and Churchill considered four enough. ASQUITH satisfied all parties with a compromise under which four ships were laid down immediately, with a further four as and when the need was proved; within a few months all eight were under construction.

We will bury you The alarming threat to the West, with its inference of nuclear war, delivered by the Soviet leader Nikita S. Khruschev (1894–1971) at a Polish embassy reception in Moscow on 26 November 1956. Three years later Khruschev explained in Washington that he had been referring to the inevitable triumph of the Communist economic system over capitalism.

Wealth of Nations, The One of the great works of political economics, published in 1776 by the Scottish economist Adam Smith (1723–90). It became one of the basics of liberal and free-market economics, and was one of the Bibles of THATCHERISM (*see* Adam SMITH INSTITUTE). Smith was robust in arguing the harmful effect of cartels, writing:

> People of the same trade seldom meet together but the conversation ends in a conspiracy against the public, or in some diversion to raise prices.

And this argument on taxation found powerful adherents in the 1980s:

> There is no art which one government sooner learns of another than that of draining money from the pockets of the people.

weasel words Words of convenient ambiguity, or consummate evasiveness. The phrase dates back to a story by Stewart Chaplin in the *Century Magazine* of 1900 in which this sentence occurs:

> Why, weasel words are words that suck the life out of the words next to them, just as a weasel sucks the egg and leaves the shell.

Theodore Roosevelt popularized the term when he said in 1916 of a speech by Woodrow Wilson:

> You can have universal training, or you can voluntary training, but when you use the word voluntary to qualify universal, you are using a weasel word; it has sucked all the meaning out of universal. The two words flatly contradict one another.

Prior to the 1992 General Election, John Major said of an evasion by Labour's employment spokesman Tony Blair over whether a minimum wage would push up unemployment: "It would make a weasel blush."

Weathermen Members of the **Weather Underground**, a US revolutionary terrorist group that operated during the VIETNAM WAR as the violent fringe of the NEW LEFT. The youthful militants were responsible for a series of bombings; three of them died when a townhouse bomb factory on New York City's West Eleventh Street exploded in 1970. Some of the group later turned to crime in protest against the capitalist system; three Weathermen, including their leader Kathy Boudin, were arrested in 1982 after two police officers and a security guard were killed in an attempted robbery of a Brinks armoured truck.

The Weathermen were not the conscience of their generation, but more like its id. TOM HAYDEN (1940–).

Webster-Ashburton treaty The agreement between Britain and America in 1842 which fixed the US–Canadian border around the state of Maine, giving more than half the land in dispute to America. It was negotiated by Secretary of State Daniel Webster (1782–1852) and Lord Ashburton, head of the Baring banking house and an ex-Tory MP, whose wife was American.

Most disgraceful and disadvantageous.
LORD PALMERSTON.

Wedgie The nickname of the UK Labour politician Anthony Wedgwood BENN, as he discarded the "Wedgwood" and his patrician origins to become plain Tony Benn. The transformation from technocrat to left-wing POPULIST took place in the 1970s, during which time Benn excised from his *Who's Who* entry the fact that he had been educated at the prestigious Westminster School.

Wedtech affair The scandal that resulted in Lyn Nofziger, President Reagan's former political director, being fined $30,000 and sentenced to 90 days in jail for violating Federal ethics laws. It stemmed from Nofziger's opening a lobbying firm in 1982, eight months after leaving the White House, with the military contractor Wedtech as a client. Nofziger solicited the help of deputy Attorney-General James Jenkins in securing Wedtech a $32 million Army contract. The corporation, which misrepresented itself as minority-owned and had been barred from competing because of poor performance, nevertheless won the contract. It hired Jenkins as a consultant and gave Nofziger's firm stock worth almost $1 million. The ensuing scandal resulted in four Wedtech executives pleading guilty to stealing $2 million from the corporation and bribing Federal, State and local officials, the conviction of two Maryland politicians for accepting bribes to obstruct a Congressional investigation and the indictment of a New York Congressman for racketeering.

week. weeks, rather than months Harold WILSON's over-optimistic forecast for the early collapse of Ian Smith's UDI regime in Rhodesia in the face of economic sanctions. It was made at the Commonwealth prime Ministers' meeting in Lagos on 12 January 1966; Rhodesia's RETURN TO LEGALITY took until 1980 to achieve, and Wilson came to be accused of complacency and glibness for his prediction. His actual words were:

The cumulative effects of the economic and financial sanctions might well bring the rebellion to an end within a matter of weeks rather than months.

a week is a long time in politics A comment made by Wilson to LOBBY correspondents on his election in October 1964, which has almost become his political epitaph. It was seized on by his detractors as representing a uniquely cynical approach, inferring that any action, no matter how unpopular, will be forgiven or forgotten by the voters. Wilson's intent was to stress that politics should be seen on a longer time-scale and not judged by day-to-day issues.

Weimar Republic The German federal republic established under the Constitution of 1919 after the forced ABDICATION of the Kaiser, which lasted until it was overthrown in 1933 by Hitler, the last Chancellor to be elected under it. It took its name from the Thuringian town of Weimar, otherwise known for its association with Goethe, where the constitution was adopted by a National Assembly.

Weinberger, Caspar *See* CAP THE KNIFE.

welcoming ceremony The ceremonial greeting staged on the SOUTH LAWN of the White House for foreign HEADS OF STATE and of government. The visitor with his or her spouse and principal aides is driven to the lawn, where a band and HONOR GUARD are on hand as the President greets the distinguished visitor. White House personnel, staff and families from the visitor's embassy and the media look on as President and guest stand on a ROSTRUM to exchange remarks.

welfare The American term for the culture of social security and anti-poverty schemes, and the payments received by the needy. MIDDLE AMERICA increasingly sees "welfare people" as INNER-CITY and usually Black one-parent families, and thus nothing to do with them or even with society (*see* ALIENATION; UNDERCLASS); welfare and foreign aid are the only fields of public spending where voters consistently demand cuts.

Hated by those who administer it; mistrusted by those who pay for it; and held in contempt by those who receive it.
PETER GOLDMARK (1937–), Johnson administration Budget Director.

Welfare State The system of comprehensive social security and services provision in Britain advocated by the BEVERIDGE REPORT and introduced by the post-war Labour government. Providing for sickness, unemployment, retirement, want and other needs, its cornerstones were the 1946 National

Insurance Act and the National Health Service (NHS). The British welfare state was much admired in Europe and beyond during the 1950s, but has since grown in cost rather than effectiveness. The left argues that it has been starved of funds and commitment, the right that it has spawned a DEPENDENCY CULTURE. The term itself even predates Beveridge, being credited to William Temple (1881–1944), Archbishop of Canterbury, who wrote in 1941:

> In place of the conception of the Power State, we are led to that of the Welfare State.

welfarism A mildly derogatory term for the social policies characteristic of a welfare state, and the attitudes that sustain them.

well, the The small space in the Chamber of the US HOUSE OF REPRESENTATIVES between the podium and the front row of seats, in which members mingle during and after a vote.

> Bills are won and lost in the well. If you see a guy who has voted for you in the well, he is going to switch.
> Rep. PHILIP BURTON (1926–83).

Wellington, Arthur Wellesley, 1st Duke of *See* IRON DUKE.

Welsh windbag A nickname for Neil KINNOCK, leader of Britain's LABOUR PARTY 1983–92, reflecting the over-lengthy and repetitive nature of some of his speeches, his prolixity when being interviewed and his protracted contributions in party committees. It did not reflect his parallel ability to electrify an audience with oratory comparable to that of Aneurin Bevan (*see* NYE).

Welsh wizard The popular nickname for the British Liberal Prime Minister David Lloyd George (*see* L. G.). It derived from his inspiring oratorical style, his ability to pull off political surprises – and in critics' eyes his deviousness.

> This siren, this goat-footed bard, this half-human visitor to our age from the hag-ridden and enchanted woods of Celtic antiquity. One catches in his company that flavour of final purposelessness, inner irresponsbility, existence outside or away from our Saxon good and evil, mixed with cunning, remorselessness, love of power. . . .
> JOHN MAYNARD KEYNES (1883–1946).

Weltanschauung (Ger. world view) The political outlook or IDEOLOGY of a person, movement or party. The word sets that ideology in the context of an overall perception of the world or society, and the working of political, social and economic systems.

Wenceslas Square The broad, sloping street in the heart of Prague where Czechs have customarily massed at times of crisis to demonstrate the strength of their feelings. In 1968 it was the scene of resistance to the Soviet tanks that moved in to crush the PRAGUE SPRING, and subsequently of the SELF-IMMOLATION of the student Jan Palach, whose memorial there became a shrine during the period of hard-line rule that followed. The almost continuous demonstrations which filled Wenceslas Square in late November 1989, and the readiness of the Czech and Slovak media to televise them, were a major factor in the final collapse of Communist rule; the most poignant moment was the heroes' reception accorded the DISSIDENT playwright Václav Havel and Alexander Dubček, exiled leader of the Prague Spring.

Wessel. Horst Wessel song The stirring official marching song of Germany's NAZI party, which came to send a chill through the hearts of Hitler's opponents and victims. It was written by Horst Wessel, a student and Nazi stormtrooper, and adopted by the movement as Wessel was elevated to the status of a virtual martyr by Dr. Josef Goebbels following his murder in a street brawl in 1930, supposedly by Communists. The tune was taken from an old fishermen's song; the lyrics incorporate many odious sentiments dear to the Nazis. The first verse translates as:

> Hold high the banner! Close the hard ranks serried!
> SA marches on with sturdy pride.
> Comrades, by Red Front and Reaction killed, are buried,
> But march with us in image at our side.

Wessi The nickname given at the time of German re-UNIFICATION in 1990 to inhabitants of the former West Germany. The eastern counterpart was OSSI.

West, the The collective term for the United States and its NATO allies during the COLD WAR, also used more generally to describe the advanced democracies of industrialized North America and Western Europe. Use of the term, and talk of "Western values", conveyed a sense of moral superiority.

West Bank The territory between the river Jordan and the eastern frontier of Israel. Formerly part of Palestine, it became part of Jordan after the ceasefire of 1949 but was occupied by Israel after the SIX DAY WAR of 1967. As the largest of the OCCUPIED TERRITORIES, with one million Arab inhabitants in towns, villages and refugee camps against some 50,000 Jews, it has been the focus of pressure for the creation of a Palestinian state. However successive LIKUD governments saw the West Bank, under the name JUDAEA AND SAMARIA, as part of Israel's Biblical birthright. Sixty per cent of the land is Jewish-owned, over 150 Jewish settlements have been built since 1967 and in recent years large numbers of Soviet Jews have been encouraged to settle there. Israeli military rule and the settlement policy have been a continuing source of tension, and are central to the Palestinian–Israeli conflict and to the INTIFADA. Enzo Scotti, Italian Foreign Minister for 25 days in July 1992, asked his officials if the West Bank was a publicly- or privately-owned US institution of credit.

West Front The elevation of the US CAPITOL atop JENKINS HILL, overlooking the MALL and facing the Lincoln Memorial and its Reflecting Pool. This is the aspect seen from the White House and the heart of the government district. Benjamin Latrobe's original design of 1810 was heavily modified between 1817 and 1829 by Charles Bulfinch. The crumbling sandstone of its central section was restored between 1983 and 1987; Congress rejected the option of expanding the building outward to a new frontage. The West Front witnessed its first Presidential INAUGURATION when Ronald Reagan was sworn in in 1981.

West Germany The everyday name for the German Federal Republic formed in 1948 from the zones of Germany under US, British and French occupation, plus West Berlin. A sovereign democracy, it soon became a member of NATO. The term became obsolete on 3 October 1990 when Germany was reunified.

West Lothian Question The question, asked repeatedly by Tam Dalyell, Labour MP for West Lothian, in 1977 in debates on the SCOTLAND BILL, which exposed a central flaw in proposals for DEVOLUTION. It revolved around whether, once a Scottish Parliament or Assembly had been set up, a full quota of Scottish representatives at Westminster could justifiably cast their votes on purely English matters. Faced with similar proposals in 1914, Arthur BALFOUR had asked:

> Are you going to leave the whole of these 72 Scottish members here to manage English education?

The persistence with which Dalyell (*see* CAMPAIGN GROUP) pursued the point 63 years later led to its being named after his constituency.

West Wing The wing of the White House which since 1902 has housed the offices of the President and his most valued staff; it replaced greenhouses built on the site of JEFFERSON's west pavilion. Bounded by the portico where visitors are greeted on one side and the ROSE GARDEN on the other, it includes the OVAL OFFICE, Cabinet Room, Roosevelt Room and Reception Room, and also houses the Press Room; the two-storey building is deceptively small as there is working space below ground. Though doubled in size in 1909, further enlarged in 1927 and 1934 and remodelled in 1969, it is still too small for all but the most essential functions of government; many aides have to make do with an office in the OLD EOB next door and consequently lack ACCESS to the President.

> People will kill to get an office in the West Wing.
> MIKE DEAVER.

Western White House The name given by Ronald Reagan's staff and the White House Press to the President's ranch home to the north-west of Santa Barbara, California, where he had lived before taking office and to which he retired in 1989.

Westland affair The explosive chain of events in December 1985 and January 1986 which brought Margaret Thatcher's government to its knees and triggered the resignations of two Cabinet Ministers. It stemmed from a move by the US helicopter company Sikorski to take a substantial stake in Westland, its smaller British counterpart. Leon Brittan, the Trade and Industry Secretary, backed Westland's directors in supporting the bid; Defence Secretary Michael Heseltine (*see* TARZAN) vehemently opposed it, championing a European consortium against a clear Cabinet majority. A bitter propaganda war was waged, with Ministers briefing against each other as their own meetings became more acrimonious. On 6 January a letter from the Solicitor-General accusing Heseltine of "material inaccuracies" was leaked to the press by Colette Bowe, head of information at the Department of Trade and Industry; Brittan had given his approval, and though a LEAK INQUIRY later fell just short of implicating Downing Street, hostility from the 1922 COMMITTEE forced his resignation on 24 January. By then Heseltine had already staged the most spectacular resignation in generations. Three days after the leak, he found himself faced in Cabinet with an ultimatum from Mrs. Thatcher and colleagues; he said: "I cannot accept that decision" and walked out – only returning after toppling Mrs. Thatcher almost five years later. When these events which cast great doubt on the government's integrity were debated in the Commons, Mrs Thatcher reputedly told a colleague: "This may be my last day as Prime Minister", but an unimpressive speech from Neil KINNOCK let Mrs. Thatcher off the hook. Yet Kinnock did utter the memorable phrase that Britain was experiencing "Government not only rotten to the core, but rotten from the core."

> Two men overboard and the captain confined to her cabin.
> JULIAN CRITCHLEY.

Westminster The location of Britain's HOUSES OF PARLIAMENT, and the overall term for the inward-looking and self-sustaining world that exists there (WHITEHALL is the comparable word for the world of government). Parliament is housed in the **Palace of Westminster**, the inconvenient Gothic spectacle designed by Sir Charles Barry (1795–1860) after the sprawling mediaeval palace on land reclaimed from the Thames had been razed to the ground in 1834. The building, which has slowly yielded up large under-used areas held back by officers under royal patronage, now accommodates some 3000 MPs, secretaries, research assistants, security, maintenance and catering staff, and a sizable press corps. Adolf Hitler, in *Mein Kampf*, described it as

> Barry's masterpiece, its thousand windows reflected in the waters of the River Thames.

When this phrase appeared (unattributed) in the Palace's post-war official guide, the young MP James Callaghan complained and a piece of paper was stuck over it.

Westminster Hall is the only part of the mediaeval palace to survive the fire. Built in 1099, the 238 ft. long, 67 ft. wide stone-built Hall with its fine wooden hammer-beam roof (dating from 1394) housed for centuries many activities of Parliament, plus the Law Courts until 1882 and even some shops. It was the scene of the trials of Guy Fawkes and King Charles I, the IMPEACHMENT of Warren Hastings and the LYING IN STATE in state of Gladstone, Churchill and a host of Kings and Queens. The Hall was nearly lost on 10 May 1941 when a dozen German bombs reduced the adjoining Commons chamber to rubble and severely damaged other parts of the Palace. The Conservative MP Colonel Walter Elliott broke down the Hall's oak door with an axe, shouting:

> Let the pseudo-Gothic go. We must save the Hall!

The historic roof and the Hall itself were saved – though Elliott could simply have opened the side door kept unlocked for emergencies.

Westminster system The system of Parliamentary democracy exported by Britain, in many cases only briefly, to its former overseas possessions. At its heart are a sovereign elected chamber in which a SPEAKER maintains good order, a government formed from the majority with a PRIME MINISTER responsible to the House, and a loyal OPPOSITION.

Statute of Westminster The legislation enacted by Britain's Parliament in 1931 which gave complete autonomy (barring a handful of residual powers mostly reserved to the PRIVY COUNCIL) to, within what became the British COMMONWEALTH, Australia, Canada, New Zealand, South Africa, Eire and Newfoundland. The Statute, which stemmed from pressure exerted by these states at Imperial Conferences in 1926 and 1930, recognized the right of each to control its own foreign as well as domestic affairs, to establish a diplomatic corps and be represented at the LEAGUE OF NATIONS.

Wet (1) An opponent of PROHIBITION in the United States; the Wets emerged as a force during the Coolidge administration as it became evident the "noble experiment" was having social effects at least as disastrous as those it was supposed to cure. (2) An opponent of the hard-line MONETARIST policies pursued by Margaret Thatcher, and a supporter of generous social provision by the State. The term was applied by Conservative right-wingers to the remaining supporters of Edward Heath, but above all to the initially large element in Mrs. Thatcher's Cabinet who opposed her policies but seldom united to check her.

> Wet is, I think, a schoolboy word to describe some wretched boy who doesn't dare do anything either athletic or naughty. The zenith of wetness is when somebody is described as "so wet you could shoot snipe off him".
> NICHOLAS RIDLEY.

slippery when wet The wording of one of America's most common highway signs, picked up by George BUSH to describe his Democratic rival Bill Clinton in his ACCEPTANCE SPEECH at the Republicans' Houston convention in August 1992.

wet concrete A serious hazard to CANVASSERS and others involved in doorstep electioneering, as stepping in it can bring instant unpopularity and loss of votes, not to mention the mess. The Leeds Labour MP Stan Cohen (1927–) once saw he had trodden a newly-concreted path to deliver a party leaflet – so he rescued it from the letter-box and put in a Conservative one instead. For another hazard of wet concrete, *see* SARAJEVO.

wetback An illegal Mexican immigrant to the United States, the word implying that he or she has had to swim the Rio Grande to evade border controls. The use of "wet" to describe livestock imported illegally from Mexico dates back to frontier times; it has applied to humans since visa requirements were imposed in 1924. The word has also been used to describe party activists from one state who travel to another to whip up support for their FAVOURITE SON; in 1983 Sen. Ernest F. Hollings of South Carolina had to apologize for claiming "wetbacks" from California had boosted that state's Sen. Alan Cranston at his expense in the IOWA CAUCUSES.

WEU Western European Union. The Paris-based grouping formed in 1955 to harmonize defence and security among its member states: France, Germany, Italy, the BENELUX countries, Portugal, Spain and Britain. Virtually dormant for 35 years, it was reactivated in 1990 to provide a European defence organization which in Britain's view would supplement NATO and in France's supersede it.

what. What is that man for? The unnerving question a little girl is supposed to have asked her mother on seeing Charles James Fox (1749–1806), the English liberal politician who was groomed for the Premiership but spent almost all his career in opposition (*see* MINISTRY OF ALL THE TALENTS). Many politicians in a different time and place would have found the question hard to answer if directed at them.

what people listening at home want to know is . . . The standard retort used by Tony BENN to divert a radio or television interview from the subject the interviewer wished to question him on to the issue he was anxious to discuss.

What's good for General Motors is good for the country A paraphrase of testimony given by Charles E. Wilson, president of General Motors, to the Senate Armed Services Committee in January 1953. Wilson had been nominated as President Eisenhower's Secretary of Defence, and did not wish to sell his GM stock as required by law. He told the committee:

> For many years I thought what was good for our country was good for General Motors, and *vice versa*.

What have you done for me lately? The punchline of a story told by the Kentucky Democrat Sen. Alben Barkley, later US Vice-President, during his 1938 re-election campaign. Barkley recalled meeting a CONSTITUENT for whom he had done favours as prosecuting attorney, county judge, congressman and senator, yet who was still thinking of voting for his opponent. Barkley reminded him how he had got an access road built to the man's farm, visited him in hospital in France when wounded in World War I, fixed him veteran's benefits and farm credit and got him a disaster loan when floods destroyed his home, and asked: "Surely you remember all these things I have done for you." "Yeah, I remember," said the farmer. "But what in hell have you done for me lately?"

when. When Adam delved and Eve span, who was then the gentleman? The slogan of the PEASANTS' REVOLT of 1381, taken from a sermon by John Ball, the priest who was among its leaders. He was executed after the collapse of the rebellion.

When in the course of human events . . . The opening words of the Preamble to the Declaration of INDEPENDENCE, written (and heavily revised) by Thomas JEFFERSON. The first sentence, containing four changes from Jefferson's draft, reads:

> When, in the course of human events, it becomes necessary for one people to dissolve the political bands which have connected them with another, and to assume, among the powers of the earth, the separate and equal station to which the laws of nature and of nature's God entitle them, a decent respect to the opinions of mankind requires that they should declare the causes which impel them to the separation.

When you have to kill a man it costs nothing to be polite Winston CHURCHILL's comment when insisting that the declaration of war against Japan on 8 December 1941 (*see* a DATE THAT WILL LIVE IN INFAMY) should follow the correct ceremonial wording.

where. Where's the beef? Walter Mondale's challenge to his fellow Democratic challenger Gary Hart at a debate in Atlanta in April 1984 which became a catch-phrase of that Presidential campaign. The words came from a little old lady in a TV commercial for Wendy's hamburgers; at the suggestion of his campaign manager Robert Beckel, Mondale (*see* NORWEGIAN WOOD) used them to disparage Hart's much-vaunted 'new ideas' and suggest there was nothing to them.

Where's the rest of me? The title of a 1965 autobiography by Ronald Reagan, taken from his own line in the film *King's Row* when the character he played had just had his leg amputated.

Where there is discord, may we bring harmony. Where there is error, may we bring truth. Where there is doubt, may we bring faith. Where there is despair, may we bring hope A variant of the prayer of St. Francis of Assisi, quoted by Margaret Thatcher on the steps of 10 Downing Street on 4 May 1979 after the first of her three election victories.

Where was George? The scornful question asked repeatedly by Sen. Edward KENNEDY about George BUSH's part in the Reagan administration at the 1988 Democratic Convention. The speech, reckoned to be one of Kennedy's finest, echoed criticism about Bush's alleged lack of achievement in a series of high offices levelled by Sen. Robert Dole in commercials during the Republican PRIMARIES.

whiff of grapeshot The use of troops to disperse demonstrators or rioters by firing either at or over them. The phrase was first used by Thomas Carlyle (1795–1881) in his *History of the French Revolution* to describe how Napoleon, as a young officer, quelled a minor riot in Paris.

Whigs (1) In Britain, the party born in the late 17th century to champion the Protestant succession, and which became broadly the predecessor of the LIBERAL PARTY. Its title was a nickname given by supporters of the Catholic James II to the Parliamentary faction led by Shaftesbury that between 1679 and 1682 tried to exclude him from the succession; it probably stems from an acronym of the Covenanters' motto "We hope in God." The Whigs became the dominant faction in English politics from 1685 as opposition to James grew; when he was ousted in the GLORIOUS REVOLUTION of 1688 they took control, the rival TORIES being tarred with their support for the exiled Catholic house of Stuart. The Whigs gradually shifted from being a party of patronage to one of enlightenment, social reform and curbs on the power of the throne. Their ascendancy reached its height under WALPOLE from 1721 to 1742, and though in opposition for most of the late 18th and early 19th century, they held power intermittently until the Liberal Party became established; most of the Whig aristocracy gradually shifted to the Conservatives.

> Nought's permanent among the human race
> Except the Whigs not getting into place.
>
> Lord BYRON (1788–1824), *Don Juan*.

> False, designing hypocrites, with liberty on their lips and tyranny in their hearts.
>
> WILLIAM COBBETT (1762–1835).

> An unnatural party standing between the people and the Tory aristocracy, chiefly for the pecuniary value of offices and the vanity of power. Their hearse is ordered.
>
> JOSEPH PARKES (1796–1865), 1836.

(2) In America, the original Whigs supported the American Revolution, blaming the ills of the colonies on George III; the TORIES had been loyal to the Crown, opposing independence. At the height of the revolutionary war the American General Nathaniel Greene wrote from South Carolina:

> The animosity between the Whigs and the Tories renders their situation truly deplorable. The Whigs seem determined to extirpate the Tories, and the Tories the Whigs. . . . If a stop cannot soon be put to these massacres, the country will be depopulated in a few months more.

The Whig Party grew out of the National Republican Party in the late 1830s, securing the election of the Harrison/Tyler ticket in 1840 and Taylor/Fillmore in 1848. It disintegrated over the issue of slavery in the early 1850s, most of its adherents joining the embryo REPUBLICAN PARTY; Abraham LINCOLN was originally a Whig.

Last of the Whigs The nickname of Millard Fillmore (1800–74), who became President of the United States on 9 July 1850 after the death of Zachary Taylor. Elected on the Whig ticket, he could see the party breaking up during his term; the Whig nominee General Winfield Scott was routed in 1852, and Fillmore ran as a KNOW-NOTHING candidate when he tried a comeback in 1856.

whine on harvest moon George BUSH's put-down of his Vice-Presidential opponent Rep. Geraldine Ferraro's electioneering style in the 1984 campaign. It was a play on the old song title *Shine on, Harvest Moon*. Bush's attitude to the debate was shown in his subsequent remark:

> We kicked a little ass last night.

whip (1) A parliamentary BUSINESS MANAGER responsible for maintaining discipline, ensuring the maximum turnout in any vote, reporting the mood of the party to its leadership and keeping an eye on members' personal problems. The word comes from "whipper-in", the huntsman who keeps the pack of dogs together. Whips operate in most legislatures, but the system is most highly developed in the UK HOUSE OF COMMONS where the two main parties operate a rigid disciplinary system under a **Chief Whip**. Sir Robert PEEL said that this post "combines all the qualities of a gentleman, but unfortunately no gentleman would ever accept it". The engine-room of the system is the **Whips' Office**, a traditionally all-male body through whose ranks many future Ministers pass. Chris Patten termed it "that amalgam of officers' mess and political cell"; Robert Atkins, another member of the Thatcher and Major governments, once declared:

> Parliament without a whips' office is like a city without sewerage.

(2) The summons to vote for one's party on a particular matter; the fiction of delicacy is maintained by requesting attendance rather than crudely demanding a vote, but the threat is implicit. At Westminster the number of times the request is underlined indicates the strength of the summons; a **three-line whip** means that attendance is obligatory.

(3) The Whip is also the sheet of paper sent weekly to its members by each party at Westminster outlining events they may wish to attend; there is also an all-party whip setting out a calendar of non-partisan occasions.

(4) The term "the whip" is also synonymous with membership of one's party. An MP who becomes disenchanted will, as a last resort short of joining another party, **resign the whip**, placing him- or herself outside their party's reach. A party which becomes correspondingly disenchanted with a legislator who will not toe the line may withdraw the whip; the member will sit as an independent alongside former colleagues, but will have to rely on

the goodwill of their local party or association to gain re-selection.

Whiskey Rebellion The revolt by western Pennsylvania farmers against George WASHINGTON's administration in 1794, in protest against the levying of Federal taxes on whiskey which they used as a means of exchange. Alexander HAMILTON, who had imposed the tax in 1791, persuaded Washington to call out 15,000 militiamen to put the rebellion down; the rebels stayed home and the reputation of Hamilton, who had accompanied the troops, suffered greatly.

Whiskey Ring A secret association of distillers and federal officials whose frauds on the government became a major scandal for the GRANT administration in 1875. It was headed by General John McDonald, supervisor of the Internal Revenue Bureau in St. Louis; his agents, in partnership with distillers, falsified production figures to lessen tax liability and used the proceeds to bribe other officials. The President knew McDonald well; when Treasury Secretary Benjamin Bristow began uncovering the scandal, Grant told him: "There is at least one honest man in St. Louis on whom we can rely – John McDonald." When Grant's private secretary General Orville Babcock was also implicated, the President belatedly ordered Bristow:

> Let no guilty man escape if it can be avoided. Be specially vigilant – or instruct those engaged in the prosecution of fraud to be – against all who insinuate that they have high influence to protect – or to protect them. No personal consideration should stand in the way of performing a high public duty.

McDonald was sent to jail and Babcock acquitted of corruption; the affair, together with the subsequent CRÉDIT MOBILIER scandal, tarnished Grant's reputation although there is no evidence he himself was involved.

whistle. whistleblower An official, or other well-placed person, who exposes GRAFT, malpractice or a COVER-UP to the media, often suffering dismissal without compensation. The word derives from the phrase to **blow the whistle on**, meaning to stop a corrupt practice in the same way a football referee blows his whistle to stop play after a foul. Washington's most celebrated whistleblower was A. Ernest Fitzgerald, fired from the PENTAGON in 1969 by President Nixon after telling Congress of cost overruns on the C-5A cargo plane. It took him 13 years to win reinstatement through the courts, but in 1984 the Air Force would not let him testify to Congress on his work in financial management, so a Senate subcommittee had to subpoena him. Fitzgerald told Senators that a "blue curtain" had been drawn round him, so he could not advise on current overcharging by contractors. Whitehall's best-known whistleblower, apart from deliberate violators of the OFFICIAL SECRETS ACT, was Leslie Chapman, a former Property Services Agency official who wrote a book entitled *Your Disobedient Servant*, and became an adviser to Margaret Thatcher.

whistle-stop tour A campaign swing in which a candidate travels on a train, making brief appearances at each town *en route*. Though tours of this kind had been a regular feature of US politics since at least the days of Theodore Roosevelt, the name only stuck when Harry S Truman took to the train in his 1948 UNDERDOG campaign against Thomas DEWEY. Presidential candidates no longer travel by train throughout, but still make occasional trips to provide PHOTO OPPORTUNITIES and a vote-winning sense of nostalgia. The phrase originates in railway practice, a whistle-stop being a town where trains only halt if signalled to do so.

White (1) A member of the Caucasian race.

> Whites must be made to realize that they are only human, not superior. Same with Blacks. They must be made to realise that they are also human, not inferior.
> STEVE BIKO (1946–77) (*see* BLACK CONSCIOUSNESS).

> Be nice to Whites. They need you to rediscover their humanity. Archbishop DESMOND TUTU (1931–).

(2) The Whites were the conservatives who sought to reverse the RUSSIAN REVOLUTION by defeating the BOLSHEVIKS; their White Army fought an ultimately unsuccessful CIVIL WAR against Trotsky's RED ARMY. The term **White Russian** came to apply to the aristocratic and middle-class *émigrés* who had fled from Russia to Paris and other centres as the Bolsheviks took control.

White Army The secret army of 30,000 men formed between the wars by small farmers in the Australian state of Victoria which backed up a campaign of militant agitation. Its title echoed that of the anti-Communist Russian Whites.

White Australia policy The policy embodied in the Australian Immigration Restriction Bill (1901) which barred immigrants from "non-White" countries, especially Japan and China. The fear of the economic and cultural impact of such immigration on Australia was a powerful impetus toward Federation in 1900; it echoed concern in America about the YELLOW PERIL which led to the US-Japanese GENTLEMAN'S AGREEMENT. In the first COMMONWEALTH Parliament of 1901, all parties agreed on the need to keep Australian society predominantly European and the Bill was introduced. It excluded Asians by the simple device of a dictation test in a European language, which all immigrants were required to pass. Determination to preserve Australia for Whites remained a feature of government policy even after the dictation test was abolished in 1958; only in the mid-1960s did the *Bulletin*, a national newspaper, drop the motto **Australia for the White Man** from its masthead and the measures against Asian immigration were officially relaxed.

> Two Wongs don't make a White.
> ARTHUR CALWELL, Labor Party leader 1960–67.

White Citizens' Councils The bodies which used intimidation to resist the CIVIL RIGHTS campaign in America's Deep South during the 1950s and 1960s. Known as "country club Klans", they aimed to unite middle-class professionals in maintaining SEGREGATION, to terrorize Blacks into letting slip their rights, and to hound out of public life White legislators who favoured change. The White Citizens' Council at LITTLE ROCK, Arkansas, took a particularly high profile in combating school desegregation.

White flight The process, most notable in America, of White middle-class and blue-collar voters moving out of the INNER CITIES into more prosperous, safer and less highly-taxed suburbs. Under way since at least the 1950s, it carries an inference of attempting to get away from increasing concentrations of Blacks and other ethnic groups perceived as hostile.

white heat of technology The most celebrated phrase coined by Harold WILSON during his 18 months as leader of Britain's LABOUR PARTY before taking power in October 1964. It was seen as committing Labour to creating a modern, technologically-based Britain in marked contrast to the GROUSE-MOOR IMAGE exuded by the Conservative government; Wilson also intended it as a signal that Labour was breaking with LUDDITE trade unionism. Addressing his party conference at Scarborough on 1 October 1963, Wilson said:

> We are redefining and we are restating our socialism in terms of the scientific revolution. . . . The Britain that is going to be forged in the white heat of this revolution will be no place for restrictive practices or outdated methods on both sides of industry.

White House (1) The official Washington residence of the President of the United States, and the heart of the US government. Designed by Dublin-born James Hoban, the grey sandstone "President's Palace" was built at 1600 Pennsylvania Avenue, a boggy site selected by George WASHINGTON. The cornerstone was laid at a Masonic ceremony on 13 October 1792, and its first rooms were just habitable for John and Abigail ADAMS in November 1800; water had to be brought from five blocks away and washing hung in the East Room, but Mrs. Adams said: "This home is built for ages to come." The British burned the house when they captured Washington on 24 August 1814. It took three years to rebuild and was now painted white, hence its title. Extended and modified countless times, it now has 132 rooms, including 34 bathrooms and 11 bedrooms; portable anti-aircraft missiles are rumoured to be deployed on the roof. Over the years the White House has aroused strong feelings among those required to live in it, Harry S Truman branding it "the finest prison in the world". John Quincy Adams's wife Louisa wrote:

> There is something in the great unsocial house which depresses my spirit beyond expression and makes it impossible for me to feel at home or to fancy that I have a home anywhere.

And Jacqueline Kennedy (*see* JACKIE O) complained:

> It looks like it's been furnished by discount stores. There is no trace of the past.

It was a deficiency she quickly managed to rectify, giving the Executive mansion a style it has retained over three decades.

The White House's claustrophobic nature has deterred many from seeking office, or from seeking to become a President's consort. General William Tecumseh Sherman declared:

> Having to choose between the White House and the penitentiary, I'd choose the penitentiary.

And the film actress Debra Winger, asked in 1992 if she would be FIRST LADY to Sen. Bob Kerrey (*see* COSMIC BOB) who was making a run for the Presidency, said:

> If I wanted to live in an aquarium, I'd buy an aquarium and live in it.

The White House, like 10 Downing Street, does have the advantage of being a home and office combined. Ronald Reagan said:

> When I was a very small boy in a small town in Illinois, we lived above the store where my father worked. I have something of the same arrangement here.

As well as denoting the building, the phrase "the White House" also covers the operations of government carried out there. Reagan's CABINET SECRETARY Al Kingon termed it "the most defensive operation in government. You're constantly under barrage." Alexander Haig, Nixon's CHIEF OF STAFF and Reagan's Secretary of State, considered that "there are three main levers of power in the White House: the flow of paper, the President's schedule and the press".

The President never really leaves the White House. He takes most of it with him.

HEDRICK SMITH, *The Power Game*.

(2) The headquarters in Moscow of the Parliament of the Russian republic, and the scene of the siege in 1991 after the KREMLIN COUP when Boris Yeltsin and his supporters defied Soviet tanks to remain at their posts until Mikhail Gorbachev was released from house arrest in the Crimea and flown back to Moscow.

White House Iceberg The nickname of **Benjamin Harrison** (1833–1901), 23rd President of the United States (Republican, 1889-93). A Civil War general and one-term Senator for Indiana, Harrison ousted President Cleveland (*see* BEAST OF BUFFALO) in 1888 despite polling fewer votes. There were also allegations of vote-buying; Pennsylvania's Boss Matt Quay said: "He will never know how close a number of men were compelled to approach the penitentiary to make him President." And Harrison lamented: "When I came into power, I found that the party managers had taken it all to themselves. I could not name my own Cabinet. They had sold every place to pay the election expenses." Theodore Roosevelt described Harrison as "a cold-blooded, narrow-minded, prejudiced, obstinate, timid old psalm-singing Indianapolis politician", and one anonymous Senator said of him: "It's like talking to a hitching post." When Cleveland had his revenge in 1892, Harrison said he felt "a good deal like the old camp horse that Dickens described: he is strapped up so he can't fall down".

coffee and Danish at the White House Washington code for breakfast meetings at which the President tries to sell his legislative agenda to Congressional leaders and others. The phrase originated during the Carter administration; to the uninitiated, "Danish" are Danish pastries. *Compare* BEER AND SANDWICHES AT NUMBER TEN.

White man's burden The late 19th-century IMPERIALIST view of the responsibility the colonial powers owed to the people of the territories they had taken over. The phrase was probably originated by Rudyard Kipling (1865–1936) who wrote:

Take up the White Man's Burden –
Send forth the best ye breed –
Go, bind your sons to exile
To serve your captives' need;
To wait in heavy harness
On fluttered folk and wild –
Your new-caught, sullen peoples,
Half-devil and half-child.

White Paper A document published by a government setting out the policy it has decided to follow on a particular matter, or giving authoritative information. In Britain publication of a White Paper generally amounts to a commitment to legislate; if there is any flexibility the paper is said to have **green edges**. In America a White Paper contains facts the administration wants to get across; one of the most celebrated was prepared for the Kennedy administration by Arthur Schlesinger to demonstrate prior to the Bay of PIGS that Fidel Castro had betrayed his own Cuban revolution by turning it over to the Communists. In the European Community, White Papers are produced by the COMMISSION to indicate the next step it believes should be taken to closer union or deepening that which already exists.

Whitehall The broad thoroughfare in London linking Trafalgar Square with Parliament Square (its final section is actually called Parliament Street). DOWNING STREET runs into it, and it is mainly lined by Government departments. The word "Whitehall" has become shorthand for the government bureaucracy, a collective term juxtaposed with WESTMINSTER which refers to the politicians. In the 1960s the veteran political journalist James Margach branded it "a conspiracy of secrecy".

the gentleman in Whitehall knows best The statement in 1947 by the junior Labour Minister Douglas Jay (later Lord Jay, 1907–) which summed up both the high-minded intentions of the 1945 ATTLEE government and what the Conservatives saw as a nightmare of BUREAUCRACY and centralized controls. In his book *The Socialist Case*, Jay wrote:

In the case of nutrition and health, just as in the case of education, the Gentleman in Whitehall really does know better what is good for people, than the people know themselves.

white supremacist A US term for the attitude of the (predominantly Democratic) political community that ran and represented the Deep South from the end of RECONSTRUCTION until the establishment of Black CIVIL RIGHTS from the early 1960s. The term is both a noun and an adjective.

whitewash An attempt to make a misdeed by those in office, or an ugly episode or policy, look harmless. In the early days of McCARTHYISM, Congressional Republicans claimed that the Truman administration's investigations of Federal employees' loyalty were only a whitewash. And in December 1973, as the WATERGATE scandal started to assume ominous proportions for Richard Nixon, the President promised the most thorough investigation, saying:

There can be no whitewash at the White House.

Whitlam, Gough (1916–) The LABOR Prime Minister of Australia (1972–75) controversially sacked by the GOVERNOR-GENERAL, Sir John Kerr. An intellectual but robust lawyer who entered the New South Wales Parliament in 1952 and in 1955 made his name with a bid to oust the party leadership; his colleague Fred Daly said: "Any one of us could have put up a solid fight, but Whitlam wanted three at a time." Elected to the House of Representatives in 1956, he became party leader in 1967. Labor lost the 1969 Federal elections, but in 1972 he led it back to power (*see* IT'S TIME!) after 12 years in the wilderness. A non-sectarian radical, his administration was progressive but not extreme, and he and his tall, literary wife Margaret occupied the LODGE with dignity. He saw himself as a reformer, saying: "From the time when John Curtin was Prime Minister in 1944 I was determined to do all I could to reform the Australian constitution." The political writer Patrick Weller called him "a brilliant parliamentarian, witty, articulate, capable of wounding with vicious shafts of ridicule", and if necessary he could act tough with his fractious party. In 1974 he told a CAUCUS meeting:

> I do not mind the Liberals, still less do I mind the Country Party, calling me a bastard. I am only doing my job if they do. But I hope you will not publicly call me a bastard, as some bastards in the caucus have.

Labor's grip on power weakened in the 1974 elections, and its supporters' high hopes were dashed as the economy deteriorated and a series of Ministers became involved in financial scandals. Those at the heart of the controversy objected to Whitlam's style, Federal Treasurer Dr. Jim Cairns asking: "Whose party is this, ours or his?" But Whitlam's speechwriter Graham Freudenberg wrote: "He could not accept that economic expertise was a necessary qualification for political leadership." With Parliament in deadlock over SUPPLY, Kerr abruptly called in Whitlam on 11 November 1975 and dismissed him (*see* KERR SACKING); Labor was outraged, but lost the subsequent general election. When the party finally returned to power under Robert Hawke (*see* SILVER BODGIE) in 1983, Whitlam was appointed ambassador to UNESCO, serving until 1986. Looking back on his career and its controversial climax, he said:

> My place in history will bring no discredit.

Whitley Council The negotiating body, comprising representatives of staff, management and the Department of Health, that determines pay and conditions for many workers in the UK's National Health Service (NHS). Doctors and nurses have their own pay review bodies.

who. Who am I? Why am I here? The revealingly frank question asked by Admiral James Stockdale, Ross PEROT's running-mate, when caught in crossfire between Dan QUAYLE and Sen. Albert Gore (*see* OZONE MAN) in the televised vice-presidential DEBATE at Atlanta on 13 October 1992.

who are we playing? The response reputedly given by the West German MEP Otto von Habsburg (1912–), grandson of the last Austro–Hungarian emperor and theoretical heir to the throne, when asked if he would be watching an Austria-Hungary football match.

who goes home? At Westminster, the traditional call from police officers in the LOBBIES of the HOUSE OF COMMONS when the House rises for the night.

who governs Britain? The theme of the UK general election of February 1974, and the unofficial slogan of Edward Heath's governing Conservatives. Heath (*see* GROCER) fought the election at the height of a miners' strike, with the country on a THREE-DAY WEEK; he aimed to win a new MANDATE by rallying the voters on the side of authority against the unions. The Tory MP Jock (later Lord) Bruce-Gardyne knew the strategy was doomed when he used the slogan at a public meeting and a constituent told him: "If you have to ask that question, you shouldn't be running the country." The election resulted in a HUNG PARLIAMENT, and Labour took power.

who is Mr. Round and why does he object? Winston CHURCHILL's baffled marginal note on receiving a proposal at the end of which an official had written "Round objects". The official, who regarded the proposal as idiotic, had wanted to write "Balls!" but did not feel he could use such language in a MINUTE to the Prime Minister.

who lost China? *See* CHINA LOBBY.

Who? Who? Ministry The derisive name given by its critics to the first Tory government formed by the Earl of Derby in 1852. It originated in the shouts of "Who? Who?" from the aged Duke of Wellington as the names of its members were read to him; they were little better known to the public, and the government did not survive an election five months later.

whose finger on the trigger? A paraphrase of the front-page headline carried by Britain's pro-Labour *Daily Mirror* the day before the October 1951 general election. In full it read: "Whose finger do you want on the trigger when the world's situation is so delicate?", the message being that with the COLD WAR and KOREAN WAR at their height, the cautious Clement ATTLEE would be safer for world peace than the Tories' war leader Winston CHURCHILL. The headline reflected a campaign Labour had been running since that May when Hugh Dalton had warned: "If we get Churchill and the Tory party back at the next election we shall be at war with Russia within twelve months." Churchill sued the *Mirror* for libel, and Labour lost the election.

why. Why England Slept The best-seller written by the young John F. KENNEDY, telling of Britain's complacency on the eve of WORLD WAR II. Based on his senior political science thesis at Harvard which won him a *magna cum laude*, it drew on insights and contacts he gained through his father's position as US ambassador in London.

Why not the best? The slogan of the outsider Jimmy CARTER's successful 1976 campaign for the Presidency, and of the book he wrote to accompany and explain his challenge.

Why, Sir? The words which, used as a SUPPLEMENTARY, can floor a Minister at QUESTION TIME in the House of Commons. They take effect when the Minister responding has been given a highly technical brief by his civil servants and has no personal knowledge of the subject. The most devastating instance was in the early 1980s when Peter (later Lord) Walker, then Minister of Agriculture, had the question sprung on him by the Labour MP Tam Dalyell.

Wild Thing A spoof of the number one hit rock single by the UK group *The Troggs*, recorded in America in 1967 by "Senator Bobby". A parody of efforts by politicians in general to be trendy as much as of RFK himself, it had the "Senator" delivering such lyrics as "wild thing . . . you move me" in a monotone, with voices off urging him to inject more feeling.

Wilkes. Wilkes and Liberty! The slogan with which the London mob embraced the radical and libertine John Wilkes (1727–97) after his imprisonment and exclusion from Parliament for publishing the NORTH BRITON and his *Essay on Woman*, which was peppered with four-letter words. Wilkes was a member of the Hell Fire Club, which staged exhausting and notorious orgies, until he entered politics; it took bribery to get elected, including paying a sea captain to deliver to Norway a boatload of voters shipped in by a rival candidate. But he became a popular hero for his opposition to Lord Bute and his advocacy of the rights of the people, and he was honoured in America for his sympathies with the colonists in their eventual move for independence. He overcame the political ESTABLISHMENT to become Sheriff of Middlesex and Lord MAYOR of London, and returned triumphantly to the Commons in 1774, but the mob deserted him when he spoke out against the GORDON RIOTS of 1780.

Williams v. Mississippi The US Supreme Court ruling in April 1898 which endorsed the suffrage clauses of the Southern states' new constitutions, under which the White supremacist BOURBONS had effectively disenfranchised almost all Black voters, and many poor Whites. The court held that they did not strictly discriminate between races, and were thus "within the field of permissive action under the limitations imposed by the Federal Constitution". The decision paved the way for further rulings upholding JIM CROW laws.

Willie The affectionate nickname for **William** (later Viscount) **Whitelaw** (1918–), the old-school Tory, bluff landowner and former Scots Guards officer who from 1979 until 1988 served Margaret Thatcher as a loyal, trusted and much-liked deputy. Elected to Parliament in 1955, he was a junior Minister under Macmillan and Douglas-Home, was Leader of the Commons, Northern Ireland Secretary (the first) and Employment Secretary under Heath, and showed his loyalty in 1975 by only standing for the Tory leadership once Margaret Thatcher had knocked Heath out of the running; had he challenged at the outset, he might have won. Mrs. Thatcher immediately appointed him her deputy, and in 1979 he kept that position when he became Home Secretary. At the Home Office Whitelaw had a bumpy ride, notably over the Brixton riots and the entry of an intruder into the Queen's bedroom. His imposition of the SHORT, SHARP SHOCK regime was not enough to head off demands from the Tory right for the return of hanging; Whitelaw was furious when Mrs. Thatcher applauded these critics during his 1981 party conference speech, telling her:

> I have been loyal to you through thick and thin, and I expect as much in return.

Whitelaw acted as Prime Minister in her absence, chairing key Cabinet committees and telling the Commons at the height of the RECESSION of the early 1980s that he did not understand her economic policies but was sure they were splendid. She put total confidence in his ability to detect political BANANA SKINS, and in 1983 sent him to the Lords as leader of the Upper House, with a hereditary Viscountcy. Whitelaw pushed through a mountain of legislation, but in 1987 suffered a stroke at the Parliamentary Christmas carol service and, though making a full recovery, decided to retire.

Slick Willie The nickname given to Bill Clinton (*see* COMEBACK KID) by George BUSH during America's 1992 Presidential campaign, which was designed to cast doubts on the Democratic nominee's trustworthiness. It entered the popular vocabulary, but did not prevent Clinton winning.

Wilmot proviso The proposal put to Congress in 1846 by Rep. David Wilmot of Pennsylvania, under which slavery would be forbidden in any territory annexed by America as a result of the MEXICAN WAR. The proviso was just 69 words long and had not even been written by the undistinguished Wilmot, but it threw Congress into turmoil for months as it raised an issue most legislators were anxious to evade. It passed the House but failed in the Senate, but the debate on it established Abraham LINCOLN as a formidable speaker.

Wilson, (James) **Harold** (1916–), later Lord Wilson of Rievaulx. The Yorkshire-born academic prodigy who led Britain's Labour Party from 1963 until 1976 and was Prime Minister 1964–70 and 1974–76, winning three of the four elections into which he led the party. Best known for his pipe and Gannex raincoat, his homespun accent and manner, mordant wit and a dominant speaking style, he held his party together and presided over a period of social and economic change which he was never quite able to control. He grew up near Huddersfield where "more than half the children in my class never had any boots or shoes to their feet. They wore clogs, because they lasted longer than shoes of comparable price." The Conservative MP Ivor Bulmer-Thomas commented: "If Harold Wilson ever went to school without boots, it was merely because he was too big for them." An Oxford University lecturer at 21 and a Whitehall economist under Churchill, he was elected to Parliament in the 1945 Labour LANDSLIDE and at 31 was President of the Board of Trade in ATTLEE's Cabinet; of one early visit to Moscow, when he took part in an impromptu cricket match, he recalled: "I must be the only Minister to have been dropped at silly mid on by a member of the NKVD." In 1951 Wilson resigned with Aneurin Bevan (*see* NYE) in protest at the imposition of NHS charges to help finance REARMAMENT, thus gaining credentials as a left-winger. Yet Wilson was not that close to Bevan, hence this reported exchange:

> *Bevan:* Where did you say you were born, boy?
> *Wilson:* Yorkshiremen are not born – they are forged.
> *Bevan:* I always knew there was something counterfeit about you.

Wilson showed flair in opposition, saying in 1957: "Every time that Mr. Macmillan comes back from abroad, Mr. Butler [*see* RAB] grips him firmly by the throat." And though never fully a Bevanite, he had the left's backing in a challenge to Hugh GAITSKELL's leadership in 1960. Three years later when Gaitskell died, he won the leadership over George BROWN and James Callaghan. Amid near-euphoria as he showed a new charisma in Parliamentary duels with Harold Macmillan, he united the party with talk of the WHITE HEAT OF TECHNOLOGY, and led Labour to a tight election victory in 1964. Adverse trade figures and a refusal to DEVALUE the pound boxed in the new government's hopes for economic expansion through a NATIONAL PLAN, and a 6-vote majority prevented it carrying out its full programme of NATIONALIZATION. In 1966 Wilson called a SNAP ELECTION, and Labour won a majority of almost 100. Again the party's hopes were frustrated, by further economic squalls leading to the 1966 JULY MEASURES and eventual devaluation in November 1967. However Wilson presided over a wide range of social reforms, and managed to keep British troops out of VIETNAM without wrecking Anglo–US relations, though left-wingers vilified him for subservience to Washington. Challenged by them at a party conference, he declared: "I am nobody's gigolo." Wilson described himself as a PRAGMATIST, stating: "I'm not a Kennedy. I'm a Johnson. I fly by the seat of my pants." David Frost put it another way, saying: "You knew where you were with Machiavelli." He held his party together despite frequent flare-ups with the colourful Brown, who eventually resigned from the Cabinet but stayed as deputy leader. But he was quick to detect "plots" against him by Cabinet colleagues, and eager to stamp out revolts below, reading the riot act to rebellious MPs in the DOG LICENCE SPEECH and telling party activists in 1968:

> I know what's going on. I am going on.

His kitchen CABINET, and particularly the influence of his political secretary Marcia Williams (*see* LADY FORKBENDER), attracted controversy, as did his relationship with the press which deteriorated sharply in the late 1960s. Being in Wilson's governments could be unnerving; Roy Jenkins wrote: "His style of leadership was so much more like that of the acrobat skilfully riding a bicycle on the tightrope than of the ringmaster imperiously cracking the whip that a fall seemed constantly possible." In the Spring of 1970, with the economy recovering under Jenkins, Wilson went to the country; halfway through the campaign Labour was 13% ahead, but unexpectedly lost to Edward Heath's Tories. Wilson was blamed for a vacuous campaign, but survived as leader though the party was moving uncomfortably to the left. Early in 1974, frustrated by a crippling miners' strike, Heath called an election on the theme of WHO GOVERNS BRITAIN?, and lost. Wilson returned as head of a minority government, and that October won a wafer-thin majority. For two years he presided over an economy dominated by inflation that peaked at 27%. His main achievement was the renegotiation of Britain's EC membership, reaffirmed in a REFERENDUM in 1975 that settled an issue on which the Labour Cabinet was firmly divided without weakening the government. In April 1976 Wilson suddenly resigned; conspiracy theorists believed some dark secret was about to emerge, but the truth was that after 13 years, Wilson had had enough. He had also detected the rise of the MILITANT TENDENCY and other hard LEFT groups, telling Labour's 1975 conference: "I have no wish to lead a party of political zombies." His retirement was followed by the storm over the highly controversial LAVENDER LIST of impresarios and property developers he nominated for honours. Wilson took a peerage in 1983, but his retirement was dogged by ill-health.

Wilson's common touch applied to the point of philistinism attracted ridicule; he once said: "If I had the choice between smoked salmon and tinned salmon, I'd have it tinned. With vinegar." His wife Mary, who preferred poetry to politics, confided: "If Harold has a fault it is that he will smother everything with HP sauce." Colleagues were wary of him from the start; Aneurin Bevan scorned him as "all bloody facts, no bloody vision", Hugh Dalton as "Nye's little dog". Nor was he widely trusted. One MP said: "You can always tell when he's lying. His lips move"; Iain Macleod declared: "Double-talk is his mother tongue", William F. Buckley Jr. called him "the world's most unbelievable politician", and Rebecca West wrote: "He always looks as if he were on the verge of being found out." He could be savage in his judgments, calling Robert Maxwell (prophetically) "the bouncing Czech" and saying of a political journalist: "She missed the last lobby briefing. At the vet's with hard pad, no doubt." He was devastating with HECKLERS, once telling an erratic leaflet thrower: "Your aim is as good as your material."

> A petit-bourgeois, he will remain so in spirit even if made a viscount. NEIL KINNOCK.

> He was essentially the weak leader of a broad party. To become a ruthless leader of a narrow party was not his style. ROY JENKINS.

> One of the world's most adroit politicians, but with perhaps a touch of paranoia about him.
> US Ambassador DAVID BRUCE.

Wilson's Fourteen Points The "only possible program" for a new world order after WORLD WAR I, put forward by President **Woodrow Wilson** (1856–1924) in an address to Congress on 8 January 1918. The "points" were drafted by the COLUMNIST Walter Lippmann after criticism from overseas of Wilson's long-winded speeches. The first point was "open covenants of peace, openly arrived at". Wilson also proposed freedom of the seas, FREE TRADE, DISARMAMENT, impartial settlement of colonial claims, SELF-DETERMINATION for the peoples of Europe and a LEAGUE OF NATIONS. Though welcomed by America's allies for their high moral tone as war aims, they ran into resistance at VERSAILLES once the war was over, and the League of Nations fell foul of ISOLATIONISTS in Congress, which kept America out. Wilson contributed to this by not including a leading Republican in the US delegation to the peace negotiations.

> Fourteen? The good Lord only has ten. CLEMENCEAU.

The Fourteen Points were the great hope of Wilson, America's 28th President. He was a Southern educationalist who entered politics with a burning moral commitment, was forced into WORLD WAR I against his beliefs, sought to dictate a moralistic peace settlement, and after a stroke in September 1919 governed through his second wife Edith. Wilson had been devoted to his first wife, who died in 1914, and was as close to his second whom he married the next year; Edith once confided: "When he proposed to me, I fell out of bed", and when the British ambassador Lord Grey repeated this the President refused to receive him for nine months.

A Virginia lawyer who became a "reformed character" as President of Princeton, Wilson became Democratic Governor of New Jersey in 1910 and in 1912 was elected President when the BULL MOOSE ticket of Theodore Roosevelt, who scorned him as a "Byzantine logothete", split the Republicans. Wilson, who termed himself a "progressive with the brakes on", once wrote:

> Why has Jesus Christ so far not succeeded in inducing the world to follow his teachings? I am proposing a practical scheme to carry out his aims.

He also said: "Sometimes people call me an idealist. Well, that is the only way I know I am an American." Wilson pushed himself relentlessly, saying: "It is only by working with an energy which is almost superhuman and looks to uninterested spectators like insanity that we can accomplish anything worth the achievement." He took office with high hopes for improving the American way of life – bringing in sheep to control the White House lawn – but confessed ominously: "It would be the irony of fate if my administration had chiefly to deal with foreign affairs." Indeed had world peace held, he would probably be best remembered as the President who VETOed PROHIBITION. When war broke out in Europe, he resolved to keep America clear, saying "there is such a thing as a man being too proud to fight". He won re-election as "Peace President", to the frustration of Lloyd George who said: "He has no international conscience. He thinks of nothing but the TICKET." But two months after his inauguration, U-boat atrocities and the ZIMMERMAN NOTE forced him into war. America's intervention ensured eventual defeat for Germany, and Wilson set about drafting a peace settlement that would free the peoples of Europe and prevent America ever again having to fight. George Slocombe wrote: "He was the Messiah of the new age, and his crucifixion was yet to come." He was foiled at Versailles, where Clemenceau asked: "How can I talk to a fellow who thinks himself the first man in two thousand years to know anything about peace on earth?", and on his return isolationists in Congress objected to the League. He embarked on a speaking tour to rally support; in Pueblo, Colorado, on 25 September 1919 he said:

> My clients are the children, my clients are the next generation. They do not know what promises and bonds I undertook when I ordered the armies of the United States to the soil of France, and I intend to redeem my pledges to the children; they shall not be sent on a similar errand.

That night he collapsed; back at the White House he suffered a stroke and the battle for the League was lost. From then on Edith Galt Wilson told subordinates what decisions the President had "taken" (*see* petticoat GOVERNMENT). His physician, Dr. Francis Dercum, told her: "For Mr. Wilson to resign would have a bad effect on the country, and a serious effect on our patient." When the isolationist Senator Albert Fall visited the recuperating Wilson and said: "Well, Mr. President, we have all been praying for you", Wilson asked him: "Which way, senator?"

> The greatest president of this century – and the best-educated. RICHARD NIXON.

> The President spent much of the evening entering Mrs. Galt. *Washington Post* misprint, 1915.

> The air currents of the world never ventilated his mind. WALTER HINES PAGE.

> There was something about the stiff white cuffs, the gleaming collar, the sparkling pince-nez, the beautifully pressed trousers, that he had dressed in a disinfected room with the assistance of a highly efficient valet, who had put on the clothes with pincers. He was like a dentist or a distinguished surgeon. BEVERLEY NICHOLS.

wimp. wimp factor One of the electoral minuses that George BUSH overcame to become President, based on his privileged background and a belief that, despite a courageous war record, he was not a man who enjoyed facing challenges or taking decisive steps. The term is associated with Bush, but had been used of previous candidates, including Walter Mondale (*see* NORWEGIAN WOOD).

Mush from the Wimp The headline anonymously inserted into the *Boston Globe* on 15 October 1980 over a report of President CARTER's anti-inflation programme. Earlier editions had borne the authorized headline: "All must share the burden."

wind. wind of change The phrase used dramatically by Harold Macmillan (*see* SUPERMAC) in a speech to the South African Parliament on 3 February 1960 to point up the inevitability of Black rule in Africa, and the futility of APARTHEID. He said:

> The most striking of all the impressions I have formed since I left London a month ago is the strength of this African national consciousness. . . . The wind of change is blowing throughout this continent, and, whether we like it or not, this growth of national consciousness is a political fact.

The phrase was not quite original; on 4 December 1934 Stanley BALDWIN told a meeting in London:

> There is a wind of nationalism and freedom blowing round the world, and blowing as strongly in Asia as elsewhere.

windbag Someone who talks at great length, without necessarily saying a great deal or knowing much. John F. KENNEDY kept his INAUGURAL address short because "I don't want people to think I am a windbag." Neil KINNOCK was known to his critics as the WELSH WINDBAG.

wind-up At WESTMINSTER, the final speeches from Government and Opposition in a major debate, leading up to a DIVISION at 10 p.m., and often accompanied by increasing noise and interruption.

window of opportunity A limited amount of time when it would be advantageous to take a particular action before unfavourable factors come into play. It is used particularly in UK politics when discussing the best moment for a Prime Minister to call an election.

Windsor The official name of the British ROYAL FAMILY adopted in 1917, in deference to anti-German sentiment, to replace the existing name of Saxe-Coburg-Gotha, derived from Queen Victoria's consort Prince Albert. It was changed in 1960 to Mountbatten-Windsor for the descendants of Queen Elizabeth II, other than those entitled to the style of Royal Highness or of Prince and Princess. After his ABDICATION on 11 December 1936, King Edward VIII was created Duke of Windsor. The name is taken from **Windsor Castle,** the mediaeval fortress 20 miles due west of London, which is one of the Queen's official homes and where the Prime Minister dines and stays early each Spring. Parts of the castle were severely damaged by fire in November 1992, after which a political storm broke out over the Government's announcement that it would foot the bill for repairs; John MAJOR dampened the controversy by disclosing that the Queen had agreed to pay income tax, from which the Sovereign had been exempt since 1937.

wine lake The vast surplus of virtually undrinkable red wine produced from Mediterranean vines as a result of high EC subsidies under the Common Agricultural Policy (CAP) and parallel restrictions on price-cutting to boost demand. *See also* MOUNTAIN.

Winnie The nickname by which Winston CHURCHILL was widely known during the latter part of his political career. During his final year as Prime Minister, one Fleet Street cartoonist depicted him as **Winnehaha** in a pastiche of **Hiawatha,** with Eisenhower in the name role.

Winston is Back The memorable signal telegraphed to all the ships of the Royal Navy by the Board of Admiralty on 3 September 1939, after Britain's declaration of war on Germany, when CHURCHILL was recalled from the political wilderness to be First Lord of the Admiralty in CHAMBERLAIN's Cabinet. Churchill had been a highly-popular First Lord 25 years before at the start of WORLD WAR I, until forced to resign by the Conservatives in May 1915 over the Dardenelles offensive which he had championed, but which had been shambolically executed.

winter. Winter of Discontent The period of bitter industrial strife in Britain early in 1979 which discredited the Labour government of James Callaghan (see SUNNY JIM) and probably guaranteed Margaret Thatcher's election victory the following May. After three years of government-imposed WAGE RESTRAINT, the frustration of PUBLIC SECTOR workers boiled over into strikes by dustmen, hospital porters, road-haulage and oil-tanker drivers and – most emotively – gravediggers in Liverpool who refused to bury the dead. The phrase, taken from the opening sentence of Shakespeare's *Richard III*:

> Now is the winter of our discontent
> Made glorious summer by this sun of York.

was used by Larry Lamb, editor of the *Sun*, to describe the industrial climate; it was taken up by the rest of the media – and in turn by the political community. *See also* CRISIS, WHAT CRISIS?

Winter War The Russo-Finnish War, fought between 30 November 1939 and 13 March 1940, which encouraged Hitler to believe the RED ARMY could be easily defeated. When Finland resisted Soviet overtures for a mutual defence pact to protect its Northwest flank, the Soviet Union launched an air attack on Helsinki and poured nearly a million troops into Finland. They were held at the **Mannerheim Line** across the Karelian isthmus by 300,000 more mobile and better organized Finns, most of them reservists, under the veteran Marshal Baron Carl Mannerheim. Britain and France prepared an expeditionary force to aid the Finns, but Norway and neutral Sweden refused it passage. By March a massive Soviet assault in the northwest, coupled with incessant attacks on the Mannerheim Line, forced a breakthrough and the Finns sued for peace. The war cost the Soviet Union 200,000 men, 700 planes and 1600 tanks, against Finnish losses of 25,000. The poor performance of the PURGED Red Army convinced Hitler that his war machine could defeat it; Britain and America also underestimated the fighting personnel of the Soviet force, which after the Winter War underwent a radical reorganization.

nuclear winter A period of darkness and cold weather after a thermonuclear war, threatening much of the surviving life on earth. The term was coined in 1983 by a group of US scientists who had studied the possible after-effects of large-scale nuclear war. They suggested that nuclear weapons on a global scale would cause uncontrolled firestorms; the smoke, particularly from plastics and other petroleum products in burning cities and factories, would eventually cover much of the Northern Hemisphere, blotting out the sun for several weeks. Low temperatures and lack of light would result in widespread loss of animal and plant life, and add to the human death-toll from nuclear blasts and radioactive fall-out. The theory is contentious, some scientists suggesting that the results would be less extreme – more of a nuclear autumn.

Wirtschaftswunder *See* ECONOMIC MIRACLE.

Wisconsin idea The revolution in state government brought about by Robert La Follette (*see* BATTLING BOB) after his inauguration as Republican Governor of Wisconsin in 1901. Intended as a PROGRESSIVE model for other states, it provided for tax reform, a State railroad commission, direct PRIMARIES and other measures to weaken political BOSSES.

witch-hunt A ruthless and over-zealous search within a nation, community or party for those lacking loyalty or total commitment, with those under suspicion facing ostracism or punishment unless they can prove their innocence. The term, originating in the hysteria against alleged witches in 17th-century New England, was invoked by liberals in America as McCARTHYISM reached its height, and by supporters of the MILITANT TENDENCY when the drive to purge them from Britain's Labour Party began in the mid-1980s.

withdraw (1) To leave the CHAMBER of a legislature, specifically when requested to do by the CHAIR as an alternative to being ordered to leave. (2) To pull out of an electoral contest. When Marilyn QUAYLE asked Louisiana Governor Edwin Edwards on 21 September 1992, in the middle of the BUSH/Quayle re-election campaign, if there was "anything we can do to help you all" after Hurricane Andrew, Edwards said: "You could withdraw from the race." (3) To retract a term deemed UNPARLIAMENTARY at the request of the Chair. In the House of Commons the Labour MP George Foulkes was once rebuked by the Speaker for calling a Tory member an "arrogant little shit". He replied:

> Which word do you want me to withdraw? "Arrogant", "little" or "shit"?

The word is often shouted by members who feel a remark is out of ORDER. When the Labour MP Willie Hamilton criticized Harold WILSON's U-TURNS on Europe as "the politics of *coitus interruptus*", several members were quick to shout: "Withdraw!"

wobbly. Wobblies The nickname of the International Workers of the World (IWW), a radical labour movement founded in Chicago on 7 July 1905 in response to the formation of the conservative AFL, which excluded unskilled and non-White workers. The firmly-socialist IWW was plagued from its inception by divisions betwen SYNDICALISTS such as the former miners' leader William D. (Big Bill) HAYWOOD, who wanted a campaign of strikes and sabotage, and those who favoured more conventional political methods. At the height of its popularity, 1912–17, the movement had over 100,000 members, mainly among migratory workers in western farms, lumber camps and mines. But violence by activists alienated popular support and allowed the Federal and state governments to arrest IWW members and, by the mid-1920s, hound the organization out of existence. The radical vision of the IWW lives on in popular folk songs, such as those of Joe Hill (*see* DON'T MOURN, ORGANIZE); the phrase "pie in the sky" derives from another song adapted for use by the movement. Immigrants who joined the IWW *c.* 1908 sang the more basic "Hallelujah, I'm a bum!"

Wobbly Thursday The day at the height of the 1987 UK election campaign, a fortnight before polling, when it looked for a moment as if Labour, who had started strongly (*see* KINNOCK - THE MOVIE) might overtake a Conservative party which had made a lacklustre and accident-prone start. There was a bad attack of jitters in Conservative CENTRAL OFFICE, after which a sense of proportion returned and the Tories, with Lord Young (*see* LORD SUIT) and his key aides drafted in to help chairman Norman Tebbit (*see* CHINGFORD SKINHEAD), cruised to a LANDSLIDE victory over a sputtering Labour Party.

> Wracked by an abscess on her tooth and suffering from an attack of nerves, Mrs. Thatcher blamed Central Office and Norman Tebbit. Voices were raised, but best faces put forward.
> JULIAN CRITCHLEY, *Heseltine.*

wog A highly-unpleasant term for a foreigner, specifically from the Middle East or the Indian subcontinent; even though it is a common British expression that ultra-nationalists believe **Wogs begin at Calais**. The word originated in the 1920s; it is believed to stand for "Westernized Oriental Gentleman". At the height of the SUEZ affair in 1956 the Conservative MP Julian Amery, warning of the danger from Egyptian air power, told the Commons: **"Wogs have Migs"**. (Migs, designed by *MI*koyan and *G*urevich, have been the main type of Soviet/Russian jet fighter for four decades.) Ironically it was an Egyptian, Boutros Boutros-Ghali, who responded in 1992 to UK press crtiticism of his performance as UNITED NATIONS General Secretary by saying: "Perhaps it's because I'm a wog."

Wolfenden report The report of the Home Office's Departmental Committee on Homosexual Offences and Prostitution, chaired by the academic Sir John (later Lord) Wolfenden, which in 1957 recommended the decriminalization of homosexual acts in Britain between consenting male adults; lesbianism had never been a criminal offence because Queen Victoria did not believe it possible. The immediate fruit of the committee's work was the Street Offences Act, which made soliciting for prostitution in a public place an offence and for a time drove prostitutes off the streets; it was ten years – Home Office officials had predicted 14 – before the law on homosexuality was liberalized. Wolfenden was invited to chair the committee in 1954 by the then Home Secretary Sir David MAXWELL-FYFE on a night sleeper from Liverpool to London. In his memoirs he wrote that as an expert on neither homosexuality nor prostitution he was baffled to be chosen, but

> if a government wants somebody to examine as objectively and dispassionately as possible some area which is likely to be controversial, it is not a bad thing to look to the universities to provide him.

womb to tomb One of the catchy phrases coined to describe Britain's comprehensive WELFARE STATE, established after World War II by ATTLEE's Labour government. From the CRADLE TO THE GRAVE is another.

women. women make policy as well as tea The slogan of women in Britain's LABOUR PARTY in the late 1980s; although women had always been prominent in party affairs, many had become irritated at the readiness of middle-aged male trade-union officials to get each other selected as Parliamentary candidates – while women were still expected to make the tea in COMMITTEE ROOMS when the election came round. Such attitudes were not confined to Britain; in 1976 the Louisiana politician Moon Landrieu told *Esquire* magazine of women's role in electioneering:

> Women do the lickin' and the stickin'.

women's issues are people's issues The response of the Colorado Congresswoman and Senator Pat Schroeder (1940–) to criticism that feminists were concentrating too much on "women's issues" such as abortion, child care and job opportunities.

Women's Lib The high-profile feminist movement aimed at freeing women from the domination of a male-ordered society, that emerged in the late 1960s. It grabbed the headlines through protests such as bra-burning, but helped pave the way for the spread of new social attitudes that eventually gave women a greater role in politics and a greater stake in the political agenda. The name caught on on both sides of the Atlantic (*see* NOW); in Britain it is linked to the formation of the Women's Liberation Workshop in London in 1969.

women's rights The umbrella term for the campaign to secure for women the same civil rights as men, including (but not confined to) the right to vote. Susan B. ANTHONY, in her book *The Revolution*, gave the rallying-call: "The True Republic: Men their rights and nothing more; Women their rights and nothing less." Such slogans and the response of many women to them horrified Queen Victoria, who wrote on 29 May 1870:

> The Queen is most anxious to enlist everyone who can speak or write to join in checking this mad, wicked folly of women's rights, with all its attendant horrors, on which her poor feeble sex is bent, forgetting every sense of womanly feeling and propriety. Lady Amberley ought to get a good whipping.

The struggle did not end with the winning of the vote, or even with EQUAL PAY. LADY BIRD Johnson would regularly ask her husband: "What did you do for women today?", and Gloria Steinem told fellow-feminists:

> We already know how to lose, thank you very much. Now we want to know how to win.

Margaret Thatcher enraged just such people in 1982 when she insisted, on the basis of her own experience, that

> The battle for women's rights has been largely won.

women's suffrage The securing of the VOTE for women on the same basis as for men, achieved throughout the United States with the ratification of the NINETEENTH AMENDMENT in February 1921 and in Britain in 1928 with the enfranchisement of women from 21 to 30 (*see* flapper VOTE). In America Wyoming granted women the vote as early as 1869 and by 1918 male voters in 15 states had given them equal suffrage; the rise of POPULISM and the campaigning of Susan B. ANTHONY and Carrie Catt played a crucial part, though the SENATE held out till the last moment. In Britain the serious campaign started later, with the SUFFRAGETTES both mobilizing and alienating public opinion from the turn of the century; the main obstacle, however, was ASQUITH, who held out against giving women the vote even though most of his Liberal Cabinet was in favour. Asquith's biographer Roy Jenkins wrote:

> There were only two effective obstacles to female enfranchisement before 1914. The first was the excesses of MILITANCY; and the second was the person of the Prime Minister in opposition to a majority of his own Cabinet.

Even more than in America, the role of women in Britain's war effort broke down resistance and women over 30 were granted the vote in 1918. That same year Countess Markievicz became the first woman elected to Parliament, but as a member of SINN FEIN she never took her seat; that distinction went soon after to the American-born Nancy, Lady Astor. The first woman elected to the US Congress was the Montana Republican Jeannette Rankin in 1916; she earned a place in history, and the STATUARY HALL, by voting against America's entry into both world wars.

> Serious and responsible women do not want to vote.
> GROVER CLEVELAND, 1905.

> The exclusion of women from the franchise is neither expedient, justifiable nor politically right.
> CAMPBELL-BANNERMAN.

> As women we realise that the condition of our sex is so deplorable that it is our duty even to break the law in order to call attention to the reasons why we do so.
> EMMELINE PANKHURST, speech in court, April 1913.

Women's Suffrage Amendment The contemporary name for the Nineteenth amendment (ANTHONY AMENDMENT) which gave all American women the vote. The deciding vote was cast in the Tennessee House of Representatives on 18 August 1920 by its youngest member, 24-year-old Harry Burns. His mother had written to him:

> Don't forget to be a good boy and help Mrs. Catt put "rat" in "RATIFICATION".

If you can't get a fighting man, get a fighting woman The slogan that Nancy, Lady Astor coined when Labour put up the PACIFIST W. T. Gay against her in an election at Devonport.

If you want anything said, ask a man. If you want anything done, ask a woman One of the most often-repeated dicta of Margaret Thatcher (*see* IRON LADY), when asked how she controlled the decision-making process as Britain's first woman prime minister.

Woolsack The cushion stuffed with COMMONWEALTH wool on which the LORD CHANCELLOR sits to chair the HOUSE OF LORDS. The use of the Woolsack instead of a chair dates back to the 14th century, when it was introduced to underline the importance of wool to the English economy. It has been said of several of the less impressive occupants that

> you couldn't tell where the Woolsack ended and the Lord Chancellor began.

Woolton. Woolton pie A pie making use of various leftovers and vegetables that was recommended to the British public during World War II as a means of making rationed food stretch as far as possible. It was one of the recipes publicized under the aegis of **Frederick Marquis**, First **Earl of Woolton** (1883–1964), who was Minister of Food 1940–43. Though not a politician by origin, Woolton showed his organizing genius after the war as a highly-successful chairman of the CONSERVATIVE PARTY 1946–55.

work. work ethic or **Protestant work ethic** The mind-set attributed specifically to northern Europeans (apart from the Irish) and their descendants in America who believe in hard work as the principal cause of self-respect and economic and social advancement. The term is, understandably, used most frequently by members of those groups and is regarded as a RACIST slur by those excluded from it.

work to rule A common form of industrial ACTION stopping short of an all-out STRIKE, in which workers carry out their tasks to the letter, thus taking an inordinate time over them and causing loss and disruption to their employers. The tactic was frequently adopted by UK PUBLIC SECTOR workers in the 1960s and 1970s, usually inconveniencing railway passengers, hospital patients and the like far more than the employing bureaucracies.

right to work *See* RIGHT.

Daily Worker *See* DAILY.

workers' bomb A term first used by STALINISTS to justify the Soviet nuclear arsenal, which became the cry taken up by some extreme leftist groups from the 1950s for the international working class movement to have the capacity to threaten monopoly capital with annihilation if it did not mend its ways. How such a bomb, if used, would leave workers unscathed was never actually explained.

workers' control The doctrine, central to TROTSKYISM and the CO-OPERATIVE movement, that the workers in an industry or other undertaking should also be in charge of it. Critics of Soviet Communism and MORRISONIAN NATIONALIZATION alike pointed out that each left the workers subordinate, as before, with BUREAUCRATS and even in some cases former bosses, replacing the previous capitalist owners.

Workers of the world, unite! You have nothing to lose but your chains The slogan of working-class SOLIDARITY based on the closing words of the COMMUNIST MANIFESTO. What Marx and Engels actually wrote in 1848 was:

> Let the ruling classes tremble at a communist revolution. The PROLETARIANS have nothing to lose but their chains. They have a world to win. Working men of all countries, unite!

Workers' Party The left-wing democratic party in both parts of Ireland that evolved from Official SINN FEIN in the 1980s, before transforming itself into the DEMOCRATIC LEFT in the early 1990s.

workers, peasants and intellectuals The three social classes identified by LENIN as critical for the success and continued forward thrust of the BOLSHEVIK revolution.

Workers' Revolutionary Party (WRP) A UK far-left fringe group containing more revolutionaries than workers, and best known for its active support of PALESTINIAN terrorist groups at the height of tension in the Middle East. Though it possessed some rank-and-file members, its best known activists were actors, notably Vanessa Redgrave and some other members of her family.

what about the workers? The archetypal left-wing HECKLER's comment at a Conservative meeting in Britain in the years after World War II – archetypal, at least, to those who seldom attended such a meeting. Real-life interruptions from the floor were generally more original and to the point.

workfare A system pioneered in several American states under which the receipt of social security payments by the unemployed is dependent on their taking work if offered it – generally on environmental schemes and public works. Successive UK governments resisted the idea, but in 1992 an experimental scheme was authorized in north Norfolk, home constituency of Ralph Howell, its strongest advocate in the Commons.

working class A collective term for those engaged on manual and industrial labour, used mainly by members of political parties and trade unions who see themselves as entitled to their support. The potential of a working-class movement was grasped to the full by the pioneers of Communism; Engels declared: "In England a real democratic party is impossible unless it be a working man's party", Marx that "the emancipation of the working classes must be achieved by the working classes themselves", and Lenin, a touch disillusioned, that "the history of all countries shows that the working class, exclusively by its own effort, is able to develop only trade union consciousness". The patrician Lord ROSEBERY was equally dubious about the working class's capacity for self-advancement:

> I believe that the labour of those who would ameliorate the conditions of the working class is slower and more imperceptible than that of the insect which raises the coral reef from the bed of the ocean.

> I never knew the working classes had such white skins.
> Lord CURZON, after a rare visit to an industrial city.

> The advantage of a working-class background is that I do not make the mistake of thinking every worker is a revolutionary.
> JANOS KADAR, last Communist ruler of Hungary.

working class movement An umbrella term for the left and the more politically-conscious trade unions, used more often by Communists than by Democratic Socialists.

the working class can kiss my arse The first line of one of the best-known skits on the RED FLAG and the entire concept of workers' solidarity. Intriguingly, it is as often sung by trade unionists in moments of levity as by anyone else. Of unknown authorship, it gained currency in Britain immediately before or after World War II:

> The working class can kiss my arse,
> I've got the foreman's job at last.
> And now that he is on the dole
> You can stuff the Red Flag up your hole.

The working men of Scotland have not a representative to urge their claims. It is in order to remedy this admitted grievance that I now claim your support The appeal of Keir Hardie (*see* QUEER HARDIE) to the voters of Mid-Lanark, when standing as the first-ever LABOUR candidate in 1888. Hardie soon became philosophical about how long the workers would elect their own, saying:

> It will take the working man 20 years to elect his equals to represent him. And then it will take another 20 years not to elect his equals.

working miners The pitmen who kept working during Britain's MINERS' STRIKE of 1984–85, insisting that they were not BLACKLEGS but were entitled to stay at work as their union's president, Arthur Scargill (*see* KING ARTHUR), had refused to call a national BALLOT.

an irreversible transfer of wealth and power to working people and their families The key phrase – for left-wingers – of the policy document approved by Britain's LABOUR PARTY in 1972–73, and which formed the heart of the party's February 1974 election MANIFESTO. The adoption of the document by the party CONFERENCE enabled Tony BENN and his supporters to make it the central theme of their policy campaigning well into the 1980s.

workshop of the world *See* WORLD.

world. World Bank The International Bank for Reconstruction and Development, established in accordance with the 1944 BRETTON WOODS agreements; the "twin" of the IMF. It began operations in 1947, providing economic aid to member countries. Initially the Bank provided finance for the reconstruction of war-torn Europe, but by 1949 its efforts were largely directed to funding aid projects in the developing countries. Most of its capital is provided by the developed countries, though the Bank also raises money on international capital markets. It operates strictly as a commercial entity, lending at commercial rates of interest to governments, or to private concerns with the government as guarantor, and only to countries capable of servicing and repaying debt. An affiliate agency, the **International Development Agency**, was established in 1960 to provide low-interest loans to the poorest countries.

world class shopper *See* IRON BUTTERFLY.

World Court The popular name – in so far as the public are aware of its existence – for the **International Court of Justice** in The Hague. The Court, which has borne this name since 1945 as an adjunct of the UNITED NATIONS, began its life as the International Court of Arbitration, founded as a result of conferences in 1899 and 1907 convened by the Scottish-born US steel magnate and philanthropist Andrew Carnegie. When the

LEAGUE OF NATIONS was formed, it became a World Court; the US Senate refused to ratify membership, even though an apparently sound formula was twice negotiated, but the Court did appoint two Americans as judges. It comprises 15 jurists elected for nine-year terms by the GENERAL ASSEMBLY and the SECURITY COUNCIL. Nations have made sparing use of the court, largely because they do not want the stigma of a ruling against them, but it has made a worthwhile contribution to a more ordered world.

World Peace Council An organization that flourished in the early years of the COLD WAR, which claimed to campaign for an end to war, but in fact championed the ends of international Communism while attracting support from the occasional gullible idealist.

world policeman The role which America has spent most of the 20th century trying to avoid, then has taken up at critical moments. President Benjamin Harrison (*see* WHITE HOUSE) declared in 1888: "We Americans have no commission from God to police the world", and Robert McNamara, Lyndon Johnson's Defence Secretary, said much the same 78 years later:

> Neither conscience nor security suggests that the United States is, or should or could be, the global gendarme.

world power An alternative term for GREAT POWER, emphasizing a global rather than a regional influence; in his GUILDHALL speech on 16 November 1964, Harold WILSON said of Britain:

> We are a world power, and a world influence, or we are nothing.

World Service The external broadcasting arm of the BBC which, since 1932, has built up a reputation for objective reporting of world events, free of influence by the UK government. This point was underlined in 1985 when staff at the World Service's Bush House headquarters in London struck in protest at the cancellation of the REAL LIVES television documentary at the request of Home Secretary Leon Brittan. The World Service, financed by a grant from the Foreign Office, broadcasts a radio service of news, current affairs, cultural items and entertainment, and an experimental but growing satellite television service; Bush House also transmits vernacular programmes in over 30 languages.

the world turned upside down The popular tune of the day reputedly played at YORKTOWN on 17 October 1781 by regimental bands as British troops stacked their arms following General Cornwallis's surrender which ended America's revolutionary war.

World War I The bloody conflict between 1914 and 1918 which engulfed the whole of Europe and eventually brought in the United States. It was started by the shooting of the Habsburg Archduke Franz Ferdinand in Sarajevo, after which Austria issued an ULTIMATUM to Serbia, causing Russia to mobilize. Russia's Foreign Minister Serge Witte asserted:

> The world is in flames today for a cause that interests Russia first and foremost; a cause that is essentially the cause of the Slavs, and which is of no concern to France or to England.

And ASQUITH's first reaction to the gathering storm was that "happily there seems no reason why we should be anything more than spectators". As the risk of British involvement grew, Queen Mary confided:

> To have to go to war on account of tiresome Serbia beggars belief.

However Germany mobilized and France responded, Germany moved against Belgium, and when Belgian NEUTRALITY was brushed aside, Britain entered the war on 4 August 1914. Lord Kitchener declared: "I do not believe any nation ever entered into a great controversy with a clearer conscience," and the Kaiser said much the same: "We draw the sword with a clean conscience and with clean hands." Sir Edward Grey (*see* "The lamps are going out all over EUROPE") declared that "if there is war, there will be Labour governments in every country – and quite right too!"

Millions died in sterile trench WARFARE on the western front, and the conflict spawned air warfare, nerve gas, submarines and tanks. In 1916 Asquith's still largely Liberal government became a casualty, with Lloyd George forming a more vigorous COALITION. Woodrow WILSON, who had done all he could to stay out of the war, relented in February 1917 after Germany's ZIMMERMAN NOTE seeking to entrap Mexico into an alliance with offers of US territory, and threats of unrestricted submarine warfare. Wilson told Congress:

> It is a fearful thing to lead this great peaceful people into war, into the most terrible and disastrous of all wars, civilization itself seeming to be in the balance. But the right is more precious than peace.

America's intervention ultimately broke the stalemate in the summer of 1918, and on 11 November, with Germany on the point of collapse but not defeated on the field, an ARMISTICE was called. By then the war had resulted in the RUSSIAN REVOLUTION, and the die was cast for the collapse of the Austro-Hungarian empire, the exile of the Kaiser and the instability in Germany that gave rise to Hitler. The Treaty of VERSAILLES both closed the book on 19th-century Europe and made World War II inevitable.

> We shall never sheathe the sword, which we have not lightly drawn, until Belgium receives in full measure all and more than all that she has sacrificed; until France is adequately secured against the menace of aggression; until the rights of the smaller nationalities of Europe are placed upon an unassailable foundation; and until the military domination of Prussia is wholly and finally destroyed. ASQUITH.

> The program of the world's peace is our program. WOODROW WILSON.

> A war of no tactics, no strategy, no mind. Just slaughter. PAUL FUSSELL.

> A war of plugging shellholes with live soldiers. SANCHE DE GRAMONT.

World War II The conflict which began with Germany's ANNEXATION of Poland in September 1939, and ended with Japan's surrender in August 1945. At the outset Britain and France were pitted against Germany, a strongly ISOLATIONIST America being determined not to be sucked into a European conflict as in 1917; Sen. Burton K. Wheeler echoed the public mood when he argued:

> By setting the United States on fire we will not help put out the fire in Europe.

The PHONEY WAR in Europe was followed by the BLITZKRIEG and CHURCHILL's emergence to lead Britain (*see* YOU HAVE SAT HERE LONG ENOUGH). Then came Hitler's invasion of Russia and PEARL HARBOR, and the great ATLANTIC ALLIANCE that has outlasted the war by 50 years was formed between Churchill and FDR. America, Britain and its Empire, the Soviet Union and the FREE FRENCH were now ranged against Germany, Japan and Italy. The main theatres of war were Western Europe and the Mediterranean, the German-Russian Eastern Front, and the Pacific. The turning points were the aerial Battle of Britain in 1940, the defeat of Germany's Afrika Korps in Egypt in 1942, the air-sea battle of Midway in 1942 and, above all, the Soviet victory after a bitter siege at Stalingrad early the following year. The war ended in the destruction of the Nazi state and the partition of Germany between Western democracy and Communism, Soviet HEGEMONY in Eastern Europe, the dropping of the atomic bomb at HIROSHIMA, the UNITED NATIONS, the COLD WAR and the rise of the SUPERPOWERS. *See also* DE GAULLE; STALIN; V; YALTA.

World War Three An apocalyptic term frequently used by politicians in the 1950s and 1960s for the nuclear conflict between East and West which was then widely feared and predicted. Also hyperbole for any violent argument that erupted during that period.

the world's best hope JEFFERSON's description of the young American republic during his INAUGURAL ADDRESS on 4 March 1801, much repeated since by others. He identified the strength of the new nation as its unified love of justice and of nationhood.

we have it in our power to begin the world all over again The closing words of Thomas Paine's COMMON SENSE, quoted by Ronald Reagan in his PRESIDENTIAL DEBATE with Walter Mondale on 7 October 1984. Paine had also said: "The world is my country, all mankind are my brethren and to do good is my religion."

workshop of the world A description of Victorian Britain taken from a speech by Disraeli in the House of Commons on 15 March 1838. It does not tell the whole story; what DIZZY presciently said was:

> The Continent will not suffer England to be the workshop of the world.

Would you buy a used car from this man? The most damaging remark ever made about Richard Nixon, eerily catching his ingratiating yet insecure manner and recalling his early nickname of TRICKY DICK. It was reputedly made by the comedian Mort Sahl (1927–), and stuck to Nixon like a second skin for most of the 1960s – and beyond.

Wounded Knee One of the most shameful episodes in America's treatment of its native population: the massacre by the US 7th Cavalry on 29 December 1890 at Wounded Knee Creek, South Dakota, of 350 half-starved survivors of the Sioux people (230 of them women and children) after a hidden rifle was discovered. The Sioux had been taken prisoner after they were interrupted at their Ghost Dance, which the Federal government had barred them from celebrating six years before. Fifty-one wounded Indians survived; 24 troopers died, mainly shot by their comrades. Some historians see in Wounded Knee the end of the frontier and the birth of IMPERIALISM, as from now on America had to expand outward. In February 1973 the trading post and church at Wounded Knee were occupied by members of the American Indian Movement to highlight continuing grievances.

wowser An Australian term for a puritanical person or killjoy, originally in the 1890s a fervent advocate of PROHIBITION. In 1983 Pierre TRUDEAU, on a visit to Australia, declared:

> You have wowserism – we have Toronto.

Woy A nickname for the UK and European statesman, biographer and *bon viveur* **Roy Jenkins** (1920–), later Lord Jenkins of Hillhead, playing on his inability to pronounce the letter R. A celebrated instance occurred in 1976 when he was leaving Westminster for Brussels, and taking his Parliamentary colleague David Marquand to join his CABINET. When he told a farewell meeting of Labour MPs: "I am leaving without bitterness or wancour", a voice at the back shouted: "I thought Marquand was going with you." The son of a Welsh miners' MP, Jenkins went from grammar school to Oxford and via the Army into banking and politics, becoming a Labour MP in 1948. In opposition he promoted the landmark Obscene Publications Act, and went on to be a reforming Home Secretary, holding the post twice: 1965–67 and 1974–76. He was also Minister of Aviation in Harold WILSON's first Labour government, CHANCELLOR from 1967 to 1970 (turning in a Budget surplus) and deputy Labour leader 1970–72, standing down because of his enthusiasm for joining the EUROPEAN COMMUNITY. From 1977 to 1981 he was PRESIDENT of the European Commission, where he was known, in a play on his name, as *Le Roi Jean Quinze*; the European Monetary System (EMS) was his principal achievement. Even before his return Jenkins was loth to rejoin a Labour Party that was heading leftwards, and after floating the idea of a new party in his EXPERIMENTAL AIRCRAFT speech in 1980 he joined the GANG OF FOUR to launch the SDP the following Spring. Jenkins had a misleadingly grand manner, once remarking of Speaker Bernard Weatherill: "Never cared much for the fellow. He made me a terrible suit once." This style, and his love of good wines, led to the new party being burdened with jokes about its fondness for claret. He became the SDP's first leader, fighting and nearly winning a by-election at Warrington before triumphing at Glasgow Hillhead in March 1982. In the 1983 election he was the ALLIANCE's PRIME MINISTER DESIGNATE until his role was reduced in the ETTRICK BRIDGE COUP. He resigned the leadership after that election, making way for David Owen, of whom Jenkins said: "I was more of a Garibaldi – he was more of a TITO." After losing his seat in 1987 he became the LIBERAL DEMOCRATS' leader in the House of Lords, and Chancellor of Oxford University.

> The only thing Roy ever fought for was a table for two at the Mirabelle. Former Labour colleague.

WPA Works Progress Administration. A NEW DEAL agency established by the Roosevelt administration in 1934 to provide employment for some of the many creative Americans unable to find work during the GREAT DEPRESSION. Five thousand artists worked on various projects, including the decoration of public buildings with enormous murals; writers produced histories of the States and playwrights took theatre to the most depressed parts of the Union. The artistic projects were closed down from 1939.

writ. writ of summons The documents sent at the direction of the LORD CHANCELLOR at the start of each new PARLIAMENT to all PEERS eligible to sit in the House of Lords; similar writs are sent to all those who succeed to hereditary peerages or are newly created during a Parliament.

moving the writ The procedure that has to be gone through in the House of Commons before a BY-ELECTION can be held; customarily the brief formality is undertaken by a WHIP from the party that previously held the vacant seat, which allows that party to determine the timing of the poll. Exceptionally, the SPEAKER may move the writ during a Parliamentary recess at the whips' request.

write. write-in The addition to the BALLOT by an individual voter of the name of a person not listed as a CANDIDATE. In US elections, especially PRIMARIES, it is not uncommon for a write-in campaign to be waged on behalf of an UNDECLARED CANDIDATE, with or without their permission; indeed there have been numerous occasions when a write-in candidate has won.

Written Answer At Westminster, the reply given by a Minister, and published in HANSARD, to a written QUESTION tabled a few days previously. MPs ask some 200 such questions a day; peers half a dozen.

Wurzel Gummidge The nickname accorded by PRIVATE EYE and television crews to **Michael Foot** (1913–), the left-wing firebrand who mellowed to become leader of Britain's LABOUR PARTY during its most troubled times, from 1980 to 1983, but who could not save it from electoral rout. It was an unflattering comparison with the scarecrow hero of a popular children's book and television series, a point hammered home in 1982 when opponents accused him of attending the CENOTAPH in a donkey-jacket. Chris Patten called him "a kind of walking obituary for the Labour Party"; the SKETCH WRITER Edward Pearce was kinder: "He makes up for not believing in God by looking rather like him". The son of the West County Liberal MP Isaac Foot and a campaigner who fought his first election in 1935 and was first elected in 1945, Foot was a fine writer (the biographer of Aneurin Bevan, whose seat he inherited after losing his own) and accomplished journalist, having briefly edited the *Evening Standard*. He was also the greatest Parliamentary orator of his age. Frank Johnson described him as "the only man who can get an audience to its feet by exclaiming: 'And!' " He complimented Iain Macleod on being "the most intelligent member of the stupid party", and described Sir Ian Gilmour as "a philosopher Tory – like military intelligence a contradiction in terms". And when a Conservative MP said of one of his Ministerial answers: "That's only words!", Foot replied: "What do you expect? Algebra?" He once made dozens of backbench Tories look foolish by telling them: "Hands up all those who believe in the Government's economic policies", then scorning those who had automatically obeyed him. Foot made his career on the BACK BENCHES as first a BEVANITE, then a UNILATERALIST and finally a pillar of the TRIBUNE GROUP until agreeing to join Harold WILSON's second government as Employment Secretary in 1974, becoming deputy party leader and Leader of the House in 1976. In November 1980 he unexpectedly defeated Denis Healey for the party leadership, the margin being just 10 votes. His leadership was marked by feuding between BENNITES and those party moderates who had not quit to join the SDP, with Foot himself caught in the crossfire. This feuding culminated in the chaotic 1983 election which brought Labour its worst defeat in half a century; Foot resigned at once, but stayed on in the Commons until 1992.

To an American it was incredible that this man who looked like an eccentric professor of ornithology could run for Prime Minister. NORMAN MAILER, 1983.

A good man fallen among politicians. *Daily Mirror*.

X

X The mark placed by a voter on a BALLOT paper to denote his or her choice of candidate in a FIRST PAST THE POST election.

X factor The magic factor that makes a candidate or party appeal to the voter; a play on X (*see above*), and on an intangible (mystery) ingredient.

X, Y and Z fever JEFFERSON's term for the clamour for America to go to war with France over the refusal in 1798 of Talleyrand, the French Foreign Minister, and the DIRECTORY to negotiate on calling off sea raiders and resuming commercial relations unless paid a $250,000 bribe. President John ADAMS reported the insult to Congress and the Senate printed the correspondence, referring to the offending Frenchmen only as X, Y and Z. *See* NO, NOT A SIXPENCE.

Malcolm X The assumed name of **Malcolm Little** (1925–65), a US Black militant leader and an influential figure in the campaign for racial equality. The son of a Baptist minister, he was converted to the faith of the BLACK MUSLIMS in prison in 1952. He changed his name to Malcolm X – he considered his surname a relic of slavery – and became actively involved in the sect on his release the following year. In 1963 he left the Black Muslims after a disagreement and founded the rival Organization of Afro-American Unity, which endorsed the use of violence in the pursuit of racial justice. He said at the time:

> The Negro revolution is controlled by foxy White liberals, by the Government itself. But the Black revolution is controlled only by God.

He subsequently converted to orthodox Islam, taking the name Malik El-Shabazz. The rivalry and hatred between the Black Muslims and Malcolm X's group culminated in his assassination at a rally in New York's Audubon Ballroom on 21 February 1965. Three Black Muslims were convicted of the killing, though some doubts remain as to the true culprits. A few weeks before, Malcolm X, hitherto a strict SEGREGATIONIST, had opened contacts with Dr. Martin Luther KING and others on creating a broader front for racial equality.

xenophobia Fear of foreigners verging on paranoia (Gr. *xenos*, foreigner; *phobos*, fear). Often harnessed by POPULISTs and by TOTALITARIAN regimes. Also a factor in RACISM, as recognized in the European Parliament's committee on racism and xenophobia. *See also* CHAUVINISM.

Y

yahoos Noisy, uncouth, ill-informed and vicious elements. The original Yahoos were found by Gulliver in Houyhnhnmland on his Travels. Gulliver's creator Jonathan Swift described them as brutes in human form with vicious propensities.

Yalta The conference in the Crimea from 4 to 11 February 1945 at which STALIN, Franklin D. Roosevelt (see FDR) and CHURCHILL met for the second and final time. To many in the West, Yalta became a symbol of betrayal of the countries left behind the IRON CURTAIN, with a dying FDR and a tired Churchill bullied by a militarily-strong Stalin into conceding a post-war Soviet takeover of Eastern Europe. This came about because Stalin promised to accept a broad-based democratic government in Poland, and free elections in other countries under RED ARMY occupation – then went back on his word. The leaders endorsed the ATLANTIC CHARTER, called the SAN FRANCISCO CONFERENCE to draw up the UNITED NATIONS charter, agreed to divide Germany into four post-war zones and established the post-war German–Polish border on the ODER-NEISSE LINE; Roosevelt also gained Stalin's commitment to enter the Japanese war three months after the end of the European conflict. FDR complained of the timetable, but Churchill told him:

> I do not see any other way of realising our hopes about world organisation in five or six days. Even the Almighty took seven.

Roosevelt returned home to hail the outcome as "the end of the system of unilateral action and exclusive alliances and spheres of influence and balance of power and all the other expedients which have been tried for centuries – and failed".

Yankee An American, specifically from New England or the Northern states, or on the UNION side in the CIVIL WAR. Often a term of abuse, first by LOYALISTS, then CONFEDERATES and more recently Latin American POPULISTS (*see* GRINGO). Devised in 1713 from an Indian corruption of the word "English" by Jonathan Hastings of Cambridge, New York, to describe anything of superior or American make or origin.

Yankee Doodle The nonsense rhyme concluding:

> Yankee Doodle went to town
> Riding on a pony.
> Stuck a feather in his cap
> And called it Macaroni.

It became a revolutionary air, being updated *c.* 1755 from a rhyme referring to Oliver Cromwell, by Dr. Richard Shuckburgh, a British Army surgeon in upper New York State. First played by the British as an insult to the colonials, it was turned against them by WASHINGTON's forces, most memorably at Saratoga.

Damned Yankee Originally used in the Revolutionary War against Northern "provincials" by "Yorkers" in General Schuyler's army, it became an abusive term for all Northeasterners, especially since the Civil War.

Yank Abbreviation of YANKEE. Originally used by US forces in World War I ("the Yanks are coming"), it was turned against them during and after World War II, especially in the UK.

Yanks go home A common slogan of post-war UK Communists and Peace activists. Anti-litter stickers were doctored to read:

> Keep Britain tidy – kick out the Yanks.

Yarralumla The official residence in Canberra of the GOVERNOR-GENERAL of Australia. It is notorious as the scene of the KERR SACKING in 1975. A decision to call a snap election is known as the **sprint for Yarralumla,** because of the need for the Prime Minister to secure a DISSOLUTION from the Governor-General.

year. years the locusts have eaten Stanley BALDWIN's term for the late 1920s and early 1930s when Britain's military capacity was eroded while Germany was rearming. It was taken from the Bible, *Joel* ii, 25 reading: "And I will restore to you the years that the locust hath eaten." In November 1936 Baldwin told the Commons:

> I want to say a word about the years the locusts have eaten . . . I put before the whole House my views with appalling frankness. . . . You will remember the election at Fulham in the autumn of 1933 when a seat . . . was lost by about 10,000 votes on no issue but the pacifist. . . . Supposing I had gone to the country and said that Germany was rearming and we must rearm. . . . I cannot think of anything that would have made the loss of the [1935] election from my point of view more certain.

The speech was turned against Baldwin as the world crisis deepened and war approached, G. M. Thomson writing that its echoes "pursued him to his dying day". More recently the term was used of the late 1960s, when Harold WILSON's Labour government experienced a chain of economic crises.

year zero The devastation inflicted on Cambodia by the KHMER ROUGE after their capture of power in 1975, eradicating all traces of civilization and killing an estimated 1.2 million people.

year zero jinx The tragic historical coincidence that only one US President elected since 1840 in a year ending in a zero has left the White House alive, the exception being Ronald Reagan (1980, *see* GREAT COMMUNICATOR). William Henry Harrison (1840) died of pneumonia a month after his inauguration; LINCOLN (1860) was assassinated, as were Garfield, (1880, *see* BOATMAN JIM) and McKINLEY (1900). HARDING (1920) died after a seizure three years later; Franklin D. Roosevelt (re-elected for a third term in 1940, *see* FDR) died in office in 1945; KENNEDY (1960) was assassinated.

yellow. Yellow Book The ambitious programme for conquering Britain's unemployment, in many ways a forerunner of the NEW DEAL, with which Lloyd George's LIBERALS (*see* L. G.) hoped to re-emerge as a serious force in the 1929 general election. They gained 19 seats, but with only 59 finished a poor third.

yellow peril A term used, especially in America and Australia, to dramatize the "threat" posed by potential immigration from China, Japan and the Far East. First coined in Germany in the 1890s (Ger. *die gelbe Gefahr*), the expression was taken up in 1905 by the Hearst newspaper chain in an emotive campaign against Asian immigrants. The ensuing controversy led San Francisco to SEGREGATE 100 Japanese children in a separate school, a decision Theodore Roosevelt denounced as "worse than criminal stupidity". But Roosevelt was obliged to negotiate the GENTLEMAN'S AGREEMENT with Japan to halt further immigration before public anxiety subsided.

yellow star The cloth badge which Jews were ordered to wear in NAZI Germany and the lands its armies occupied. It enabled them to be identified for victimization by ANTI-SEMITIC members of the public, and for brutality by Nazi thugs.

yes. Yes, Minister A highly popular BBC comedy programme throughout the 1980s which depicted Ministers as self-seeking and credulous, and totally under the control of suave Whitehall MANDARINS given to duplicity and double-speak. The programme, written by two former civil servants, Jonathan Lynn and Anthony Jay, was one of Mrs. Thatcher's favourites. It starred Paul Eddington as the bumbling Minister and eventual Prime Minister Jim Hacker, and Nigel Hawthorne as the Cabinet Secretary SIR HUMPHREY Appleby. The words "Yes, Minister" were normally uttered at the end of the programme by Sir Humphrey when he had manoeuvred Hacker into doing precisely the opposite of what he wanted, while letting Hacker believe he had scored a great personal success. The title probably originated from this passage in the CROSSMAN DIARIES:

> My Minister's room is like a padded cell, and in certain ways I am like a person who is suddenly certified a lunatic and put safely into this great, vast room, cut off from real life. Of course they don't behave quite like nurses, because the Civil Service is profoundly deferential. "Yes, Minister!", "No, Minister!", "If you wish it, Minister!"

won't take yes for an answer The rebuke administered to the Brezhnev regime by Sir Geoffrey HOWE during a visit to Moscow *c.* 1985. The accusation stemmed from the KREMLIN's refusal to accept an ARMS CONTROL package offered by the West, which was very similar to one they had previously been urging. The phrase was actually coined by Malcolm Rifkind, who was then Howe's Minister of State.

She didn't say yes; she didn't say no The old song which Harold Macmillan (*see* SUPERMAC) memorably quoted to the Conservative Party Conference at Llandudno in October 1962, scorning Labour's stance on his government's efforts to enter the EUROPEAN COMMUNITY. Macmillan said:

> What did the Socialists do? . . . They solemnly asked Parliament not to approve or disapprove, but to TAKE NOTE of our decision. Perhaps some of the older ones among you will remember that popular song:
>
> She didn't say yes, she didn't say no,
> She didn't say stay, she didn't say go.
> She wanted to climb, but dreaded to fall,
> She bided her time and clung to the wall.

The song was written by Jerome Kern and Otto Harbach for the 1931 musical *The Cat and the Fiddle*; Macmillan did not sing the words, but PRIVATE EYE came to his "assistance" by issuing the speech as a record with musical backing.

Yesterday's Men A BBC television documentary writing off Edward Heath's (*see* GROCER) Conservative SHADOW CABINET as "Yesterday's Men" which was shelved amid political controversy shortly before the 1970 election – which Heath won.

Yippie US slang for a politically-active hippie, from the initials of the Youth International Party, one of the noisiest and most anarchic (though outrageous rather than violent) elements of America's PROTEST MOVEMENT. Founded in 1968 by Jerry Rubin and Abbie Hoffman, it put up a pig as presidential candidate at the CHICAGO CONVENTION, but achieved little else apart from scandalizing MIDDLE AMERICA.

YMCA A progressive group of UK Tory MPs founded *c.* 1927 by Harold Macmillan, (*see* SUPERMAC), Robert (later Lord) Boothby, Oliver Stanley and John Loder. The name, copied from the Young Men's Christian Association, was bestowed upon the group by critics in the party.

Yom Kippur War The three-week Middle East war in October 1973 begun by Egypt and Syria with an attack on Israel, but ending in the rout of Arab forces and Israel's conquest of the Sinai peninsula. The attack was timed for Yom Kippur, the holiest day of the Jewish calendar, to heighten the element of surprise. Israel's Prime Minister Golda Meir knew the attack was coming, but held back from pre-emptive action against it because Israel would then have been branded the aggressor. The war was Egypt's final attempt to wipe out the Israeli state; five years later the CAMP DAVID AGREEMENT established an uneasy peace and returned Sinai to Egypt.

Yorkshire Rasputin, the Nickname for Sir **Bernard Ingham**, the bluff former journalist, ex-Labour candidate and senior civil servant who served as Margaret Thatcher's (see IRON LADY) press secretary from shortly after her election in 1979 until her overthrow eleven years later, in latter years as head of the Government Information service. It stems from his strong Yorkshire roots and the belief of the liberal media that he was able to manipulate both the press and the government itself on Mrs. Thatcher's behalf. *See also* MAD MONK.

Yorktown The battle on the Virginia coast which resulted in the final surrender on 19 October 1781 of Lord Cornwallis's forces, and thus the end of America's revolutionary war. Cornwallis had been waiting for the British fleet to assist him, but French ships kept them away and Yorktown fell after a siege of 24 days. Cornwallis reputedly surrendered to the tune "the WORLD TURNED UPSIDE DOWN"; General O'Hara, acting for him, wanted to turn over his sword to the French Count de Rochambeau who commanded three-quarters of the victorious force, but he insisted that the honour belonged to George WASHINGTON.

> Oh God! It is all over. Lord NORTH (1732–92).

you. you ain't seen nothing yet Ronald Reagan's view of the coming four years on his re-election in 1984. The words were originally uttered by Al Jolson at the start of the first talking picture, *The Jazz Singer*.

you can't hold a man down without staying down with him The judgment of the pioneer Black educationalist Booker T. Washington (1856–1915) on (specifically RACIST) oppression and what it does to the oppressor.

You have sat here long enough for any good you have been doing. Depart, I say, and let us have done with you. In the name of God, go Oliver Cromwell's dismissal of the RUMP Parliament on 20 April 1653. It was used against Neville CHAMBERLAIN's government with deadly effect from the Conservative benches by Leo Amery in the debate on 7 May 1940 which brought the fall of Chamberlain and CHURCHILL's appointment as Prime Minister. In America, it was later used by Sen. James McClure in frustration at slow Senate business.

You shall not press down upon the brow of labor this crown of thorns; you shall not crucify mankind upon a cross of gold The electrifying PERORATION of William Jenning's Bryan's ACCEPTANCE speech at the 1896 Democratic convention, denouncing President Cleveland's commitment to the GOLD STANDARD. Bryan (*see* BOY ORATOR) went on to fight a rousing POPULIST campaign, but was defeated by economic recovery.

> The importance of this speech, with its declaration of holy war against the rich and mighty, and its invocation of the sacred names of Jefferson and Jackson, was that, together with Bryan's subsequent campaign, it re-committed the Democratic Party to its original principles. HUGH BROGAN.

you're frit Margaret Thatcher's taunt to deputy Labour leader Denis Healey (*see* GROMYKO OF THE LABOUR PARTY) when he challenged her in the Commons to call an election in the spring of 1983; when she did call it, Labour were routed. In the dialect of Mrs. Thatcher's native Lincolnshire, "frit" means frightened. Her use of the word astonished those present, because of her success up to then in smothering her linguistic roots.

you've never had it so good The slogan, coined by the retiring President Truman (*see* GIVE 'EM HELL HARRY), to counter Republican assertions in the 1952 Presidential election that it was "time for a change". In Britain, the public mood which Harold Macmillan (*see* SUPERMAC) captured in 1959 to lead the Conservatives to re-election with a 100-plus Commons majority. On 20 July 1957, Macmillan had told a meeting in Bedford:

> Let's be frank about it; most of our people have never had it so good.

You were quite right; I forgot Goschen The gloomy reaction of Lord Randolph Churchill (1849–95) in December 1886 on realizing he had lost his power struggle with Lord Salisbury. Churchill had resigned as Chancellor in an effort to impose his terms on Salisbury, not realizing that the Prime Minister had been itching to be rid of him. Instead of surrendering to Churchill and inviting him back, Salisbury simply sent for the former Liberal Minister and financial expert George Goschen and made him Chancellor. Churchill never again held office, dying of syphilis nine years later.

your people The phrase used to a NAACP convention in Nashville on 11 July 1992 by H. Ross PEROT which highlighted doubts about his ability to carry the Black vote or stage a winning Presidential campaign. The words brought a chorus of boos, and a fulsome apology from the UNDECLARED Presidential candidate. The reaction may have contributed to Perot's decision a week later to quit the race – before re-entering it in October.

young. Young England An idealistic and patriotic, if ineffective, group of young Tory MPs active between 1837 and 1840, with Disraeli among its members. They tried to form an alliance between the aristocracy and the working class to achieve social reforms, and thus outflank the middle-class LIBERALISM promoted by the Tories' opponents. But they never progressed beyond effete Lakeland reading parties.

Young Fogeys In Britain, a group of middle-class young men who from the mid-1980s adopted a tweedy, middle-aged style of dress harking back to the turn of the century, and anachronistic right-wing opinions to match. The best-known were the writer A. N. Wilson and the journalists Charles Moore and Simon Heffer; their main outlets were the *Spectator* and the opinion pages of the *Sunday Telegraph*, whose Canadian proprietor, Conrad Black, felt a nostalgia for the England they seemed to invoke. Most Young Fogeys were ardent supporters of Margaret Thatcher (*see* IRON LADY) and especially her opinions on Europe, though they never displayed the ostentatious wealth of some of her acolytes. They mourned her overthrow and, through their opposition to the MAASTRICHT TREATY and their ambivalence toward him and his policies, were an irritant to John MAJOR.

Young Ireland An organization of young intellectuals under William Smith O'Brien (1803–64), who promoted violent opposition to British rule as the only means of ending deportations resulting from the IRISH POTATO FAMINE. Its members' outspokenness prompted the arrest in 1848 of Smith O'Brien and other leaders before any uprising had been organized.

Young Turks Young men in a political organization who see themselves having a future and who are impatient to take over leadership positions from an older generation they see as staid and tired. The term originates from the Turkish reforming party of that name which transformed the decadent Ottoman empire into a modern European state. Founded in Geneva in 1891, the Young Turks – young officers whose members included Kemal Ataturk – overthrew Sultan Abdul Hamid and replaced him with his reforming brother Mohammed V. The Young Turks remained a force in Turkish politics until the end of WORLD WAR I. The term has frequently been used of factions among Conservative MPs at Westminster and both parties in the US CONGRESS. In 1965 one such group of Republican Congressmen, demanding more energetic leadership, ousted Charles Halleck as House MINORITY LEADER and installed future President Gerald FORD.

Young Plan An agreement negotiated in The Hague during 1929–30 under which the Allied powers reduced the burden of REPARATIONS on Germany imposed by the Treaty of VERSAILLES. The plan, which came into operation on 17 May 1930, was named after Owen D. Young (1874–1962), a US banker and chairman of the Allied Committee, offering Germany greater relief than its predecessor the DAWES PLAN. It cut penalties by 75%, with the balance of 89 billion Reichsmarks to be paid in annuities into a Bank for International Settlements until 1988. Allied control of German finances was removed, German securities taken into Allied hands were returned, Germany was allowed responsibility for converting reparation payments into foreign currency, the Reparations Commission was abolished and the Allies gave up the right to impose sanctions if Germany defaulted. The plan was fiercely attacked by the NAZIs and German Conservatives, and payments were in any case suspended the following year when the GREAT DEPRESSION struck; Hitler formally repudiated reparations in 1935.

Yuppie factor From the 1980s, the electoral consequences of a previously run-down area being taken over by Yuppies: (Young Upwardly-mobile Professional Persons). In America this has tended to benefit the Republicans at the expense of the Democrats; in Britain the Conservatives at the expense of Labour. One instance was the Conservatives' capture of Battersea against the SWING in 1987 and its retention with a greatly increased majority in 1992.

Z

Zanu-PF Zimbabwe African National Union – Popular Front. The victorious party in the 1980 elections in former Southern Rhodesia which followed the end of UDI and the RETURN TO LEGALITY under temporary British colonial rule. Led by Robert Mugabe, the nominally-MARXIST party was based on the most effective GUERRILLA force against the regime of Ian Smith, who had already handed over as Prime Minister to the Black Bishop Abel Muzorewa.

Zapruder film The most important item of evidence on the assassination of President KENNEDY in DALLAS to those who disputed the conclusion of the WARREN COMMISSION that there had only been one gunman, Lee Harvey Oswald. Abraham Zapruder was the only cameraman whose film showed the President's car almost throughout the incident. In it, Kennedy's head jerked backwards as if he had been shot from the GRASSY KNOLL ahead of him, and not only by Oswald, behind and above the President in the TEXAS SCHOOL BOOK DEPOSITORY.

zero. zero based budgeting The budgeting practice pioneered by Jimmy CARTER as Governor of Georgia and as a Presidential candidate, under which every government programme has to be justified anew for each financial year. Its partial adoption did not prevent the budget deficit increasing.

zero deficit The aim set for budgeting by successive US Presidents, and since 1985 by Congress. *See* GRAMM-RUDMAN ACT.

zero option The proposal put forward by Ronald Reagan, and previously by some European SOCIAL DEMOCRATS, that the Soviet Union withdraw its SS20 missiles from Eastern Europe in return for non-deployment in the West of America's CRUISE and PERSHING II systems. The KREMLIN under Brezhnev and Andropov did not respond, and the US missiles were deployed. Both sides' systems were eventually scrapped under the INF TREATY.

zero sum game A political battle in which compromise is ruled out and both sides go for the jackpot, with wins cancelling out losses and no chips left on the table.

Zil The limousine specially built for the highest-ranking party officials in the final years of the Soviet Union and its Communist SATELLITES.

Zimmerman note A message from Alfred Zimmerman, German Under Foreign Secretary, to his ambassador in Mexico which finally provoked Woodrow WILSON into abandoning American neutrality and entering WORLD WAR I. Published by the Associated Press on 1 March 1917, it said that unrestricted submarine warfare was about to begin and that, while Germany wanted the US to stay neutral, it would offer Mexico an alliance and the incentive of recovering Texas, New Mexico and Arizona. Wilson was given the text by British Intelligence, but Zimmerman admitted its authenticity.

Zinoviev Letter A key factor in the defeat of RAMSAY MACDonald's first UK Labour government in the 1924 general election. The letter, purportedly to Britain's Communists from Grigoriy Zinoviev (1883–1936), president of the COMINTERN, incited them to violent revolution and enabled the Conservatives to scorn Labour's policy of better relations with Russia. Conservative CENTRAL OFFICE paid handsomely for the document, which was published on 25 October, four days before the election. Labour leaders believed it a forgery. Its authenticity was denied by the Soviet Union, and in 1966 the *Sunday Times* published a letter establishing that the letter was a forgery perpetrated by a group of White Russian *émigrés* (*see* WHITE), and suggesting that certain individuals at Central Office – though not the Tory party at large – knew it to be a fake.

Zionism The belief that the Jews should have a national home where they would be free from persecution, and that that home should be the Biblical land that is now Israel. Also the movement based on that belief, founded by Theodore Herzl in 1897 at the first World Zionist Congress in Basle. Zionism bore fruit in the BALFOUR DECLARATION which asserted the right to a Jewish national home, and in 1948 in the founding of the state of Israel.

Through subsequent Arab–Israeli conflict and Israel's settlement of the OCCUPIED TERRITORIES which hard-line Zionists term JUDAEA AND SAMARIA, Zionism has, to its critics, come to typify opposition to Palestinian rights; for a time, the UNITED NATIONS officially equated it with RACISM.

> Put three Zionists in a room and they will form four political parties.
>
> Prime Minister LEVI ESHKOL (1895–1967).

Zircon The codename for a satellite surveillance system developed by Britain's Ministry of Defence, a television programme about which created a political storm in 1987. The Director-General of the BBC, Alasdair Milne, barred transmission of a documentary revealing the existence of the project, to develop a satellite to "eavesdrop" on civilian and military communications. The *New Statesman* then printed an article describing Zircon, and a tape of the programme was shown to MPs by its originator, Duncan Campbell (*see* ABC TRIAL). The Speaker barred a repetition and a row over Parliamentary PRIVILEGE ensued. On 31 January the police Special Branch raided BBC studios in Glasgow, seizing tapes of the programme and the series of which it was part. In August *The Times* reported that Zircon – named after a gemstone with a very high refractive index – had been abandoned after £70 million had been spent on it because it would be obsolete by the time it entered service.

Zollverein (Ger. customs union) The FREE TRADE area between German states which operated before the unification of most of them in 1871 under the Prussian crown.

Zoo Plane The aircraft in which television technicians and non-regular members of the travelling media accompany a US Presidential candidate during the CAMPAIGN. The atmosphere is much more free-wheeling than on the plane occupied by the "serious" press. Reporters whom a candidate or his handlers cannot stand are also banished to the "zoo".

> The kinkier members of the press tended to gravitate on to the Zoo Plane. The atmosphere was much more comfortable. There were tremendous amounts of cocaine, for instance. HUNTER S. THOMPSON, 1972.

> A stewardess, finding out on the last day of the campaign that her paramour was married, sued him for "illegal acts committed over the state of Iowa".
>
> TIMOTHY CROUSE, *The Boys on the Bus* (1973).